KT-526-246

Data Communications, Computer Networks and Open Systems

Fourth Edition

Fred Halsall

Newbridge Professor of Communications Engineering

University of Wales, Swansea

PARK CAMPUS
LEARNING CENTRE
C&G C.H.E.P.O. Box 220
The Park
Cheltenham, GL50 2QF
Tel : (0242) 532721

Addison-Wesley Publishing Company

Harlow, England • Reading, Massachusetts • Menlo Park, California
New York • Don Mills, Ontario • Amsterdam • Bonn • Sydney • Singapore
Tokyo • Madrid • San Juan • Milan • Mexico City • Seoul • Taipei

© 1996 Addison-Wesley Publishers Ltd.
© 1996 Addison-Wesley Publishing Company Inc.

Addison Wesley Longman Limited
Edinburgh Gate
Harlow
Essex, CM20 2JE
United Kingdom

All rights reserved. No part of this publication may be reproduced, stored in a retrieval system, or transmitted in any form or by any means, electronic, mechanical, photocopying, recording or otherwise, without prior written permission of the publisher.

The programs in this book have been included for their instructional value. They have been tested with care but are not guaranteed for any particular purpose. The publisher does not offer any warranties or representations, nor does it accept any liabilities with respect to the programs.

Many of the designations used by manufacturers and sellers to distinguish their products are claimed as trademarks. Addison-Wesley has made every attempt to supply trademark information about manufacturers and their products mentioned in this book.

Cover designed by Op den Brouw, Design and Illustration, Reading
incorporating photograph © D. Redfearn/The Image Bank
and printed by The Riverside Printing Co. (Reading) Ltd.
Typeset by CRB Associates, Norwich.

Printed in the United States of America.

First edition published 1985. Reprinted 1986, 1987.
Second edition published 1988. Reprinted 1988, 1989.
Third edition published 1992. Reprinted 1992, 1993 (twice), 1994.
Fourth edition printed 1995. Reprinted 1996 (twice) and 1997.

ISBN 0-201-42293-X

British Library Cataloguing in Publication Data
A catalogue record for this book is available from the British Library.

Library of Congress Cataloging in Publication Data applied for.

3702315624

THE PARK
LEARNING CENTRE, CHELTENHAM

Data Communications, Computer Networks and Open Systems

Fourth Edition

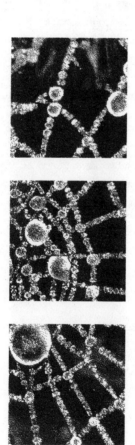

ELECTRONIC SYSTEMS ENGINEERING SERIES

Consulting editors   **E L Dagless**
University of Bristol

J O'Reilly
University College of Wales

OTHER TITLES IN THE SERIES

PREFACE

Objectives

Computers are now found in every walk of life: in the home, in the office, in banks, in schools and colleges, in industry, and so on. Although in some instances the computers carry out their intended function in a standalone mode, in others it is necessary to exchange information with other computers. This means that an essential consideration in the design of most forms of computing equipment installed today is the type of data communication facility that allows it to communicate with other computers. In many instances, not only do we need to know about the alternative types of data transmission circuits that may be used, but we also need to understand the interface requirements of the many different types of computer communication networks available. Data communications and the allied subject of computer networks have thus become essential topics in all modern courses on computer systems design.

In many applications of computer networks, providing a means for two systems to exchange information solves only part of the problem. For example, in an application, that involves a distributed community of heterogeneous (or dissimilar) computers exchanging files of information over a computer network, we must address such issues as the use of different operating (and hence file) systems and possibly different character sets and word sizes if the systems are to communicate in an unconstrained (open) way. It is thus essential when considering the applications of computer networks to gain an understanding of the various application-oriented communication protocols that have been defined to create communication environments in which computers from different manufacturers can exchange information in an open way. The three parts of this book – data communications, computer networks, and open systems – consider each of these issues.

Intended readership

This book has been written primarily as a course textbook for students studying the subjects of data communications, computer networks, and computer communication protocols. Typically, the students will be on electronic engineering, computer engineering, computer systems, or computer science courses. In addition, it is suitable for practicing engineers and computer professionals who wish or need to gain a working knowledge of these subjects.

Within most colleges and universities the subjects addressed are introduced at different points in a program. In some instances, one or more of the subjects are found in first-degree level courses while in others they are first introduced at a graduate level. For this reason, care has been taken not to assume too much background knowledge when introducing each subject except that which is found in all foundation courses taken by such students. Thus the only prerequisites are an understanding of basic logic circuits and computer architectures and a working knowledge of a high-level structured programming language.

The book does not attempt to cover the theory of digital communications in depth since this is primarily the domain of the electronics engineer. Rather, it starts by simply identifying the different types of transmission media that are used to transmit data and the essential theory that determines its maximum data transmission rate. This is followed by descriptions of the various functions associated with the interface units that are needed in each computer to achieve the reliable transfer of data between two computers over this basic data transmission facility. These include the different methods used to detect the presence of errors in the received data (messages) and the procedures followed to get the transmitting computer to send another copy of the data. These procedures are part of what is known as the data link protocol and there are a number of different protocols in use.

The foregoing relates to how data is transferred reliably between two computers that are connected directly by a physical data link. In order for data to be transferred to one of a number of different computers, a computer network must be used. Hence in the following chapters, firstly, the different types of computer network are described together with the operation of the interface circuits associated with each type of network and their related communication protocols. This is followed by a description of the additional protocols that enable two or more computers that are connected to a computer network to achieve a specific distributed application function.

In practice, beyond the basic data transmission level, the majority of communication protocols that are needed in each computer are implemented in software. When discussing the various protocols that are used, therefore, in addition to describing their operation in a qualitative way, a methodology that can be adopted for their implementation is also presented. Furthermore, it is equally important for the reader to gain an understanding of how a collection of such protocols cooperate and communicate one with another to achieve the overall communication function. This book addresses these issues in some detail.

Organization

The organization of the book closely follows the structure of the ISO reference model for open systems interconnection. Thus the first part – data communications – concentrates on the fundamental issues that need to be addressed to achieve the reliable transfer of data across a serial data link.

The second part – computer networks – builds on this and describes the operation of the different types of computer networks that are used to provide a switched communication facility over which a distributed set of computers can communicate one with another.

The third part – open systems – introduces and describes the operation of the additional protocols that enable a distributed set of application processes running in these computers to exchange data in an open way in order to carry out a range of distributed application functions, that is, irrespective of any differences that may exist between the character sets, word sizes, or the way local services are provided in each computer.

New in this edition

Since the last edition of this book was published, a number of important developments have taken place in the fields of data communications and, especially, computer networks. The primary aim of this edition, therefore, has been to incorporate these developments and to bring the material covered up to date. Also, the author has now given lecture courses on each of the three subject areas covered, at graduate and postgraduate level, and has given many in-house courses to practicing engineers and computer scientists. The experience gained from this has also been incorporated into the new edition.

In the field of data communications, a new generation of digital leased circuits has become available from the public carriers. These form part of the new synchronous optical transmission network (SONET) – also known as the synchronous digital hierarchy (SDH) – being installed by many public carriers and a description of these can be found in the chapter on data transmission. In addition, the essential theory associated with digital transmission has been included in this chapter in order for the reader to appreciate more fully the factors that limit the rate at which data can be transmitted through the different types of media.

In the field of computer networks, local area networks (LANs) which utilize either radio or light as the transmission medium are now being deployed. These are known as wireless LANs, and a full description of their operational characteristics has been introduced. Also, the continuing demand for higher transmission rates has resulted in the introduction of a number of high-speed LANs. These include, in addition to FDDI, two variants of the existing CSMA/ CD (Ethernet) LAN – 100 Base 4T and 100 Base X – and a new type of LAN known as 100 Base VG-AnyLAN.

Both wireless LANs and the various high-speed LANs offer similar services to the existing LAN types. However, in addition, a new generation of computer networks has been introduced which provide not only data services but also services that support the transfer of other media types such as sound and video. These networks are known as broadband multiservice networks and there is a new chapter devoted specifically to this type of network. These networks use a different operating mode from existing LANs, known as the asynchronous transfer mode

(ATM), and the networks described include ATM LANs and ATM metropolitan area networks (MANs). MANs are now being deployed by the public carriers for the interconnection of LANs over an area such as a town or city.

Intended usage

To the lecturer

The book is based on three separate lecture courses given by the author to electronic engineering, computer systems, and computer science students at both graduate and postgraduate levels, as well as to teams of practicing professionals involved in the implementation of data and computer communication systems. Care has been taken, therefore, to assume only a fundamental knowledge of each subject. This includes an understanding of basic logic circuits and computer architectures, and a working knowledge of a structured high-level programming language.

Users of the previous edition of the book have cited three main advantages compared with similar texts. Firstly, the protocols are presented in a form that enables students readily to see how they can be implemented in program code. Secondly, it explains how the various protocols that make up a complete protocol suite interact and communicate with one another to achieve a particular distributed information processing task. Thirdly, the extensive range of figures help to explain the many detailed issues considered and significantly reduce lecture preparation time. These three features have been retained in the new edition.

There is now sufficient material in the book to cover three complementary courses: one on data communications, one on computer networks, and one on open systems. Courses on data communications should be based on Part One of the book and the topic of forward error correction from Appendix A. Also, if the students have the necessary background, transmission control circuits from Appendix B.

The material in Part Two forms a comprehensive course on computer networks. However, if this is the only course being taught, then selected topics on transport protocols from Chapter 11 can also be included. The material in Part Three then forms the basis of a good course on the application-oriented protocols of open systems that includes both the TCP/IP and OSI suites. Again, if this is the only course being taught, selected topics on internetworking from Chapter 9 could also be included. Alternatively, the material from Parts One and Two can be combined to give a single longer course on data communications and computer networks or, the material from Parts Two and Three can be combined to give a single longer course on computer communications and open systems.

To the student

The book is suitable for self-study: worked examples are included in most chapters and the large number of figures help considerably to explain many of the topics covered. Also, to test understanding, there is a list of exercises at the end of each chapter.

To give some structure to the range of topics covered in each chapter, their order and interrelationships are summarized at the end of each chapter in a diagrammatic, flowchart-like style. These include not only the interrelationships of the topics covered within the chapter, but also how they relate to the material covered in other chapters.

Acknowledgments

I would like to take this opportunity to acknowledge the following for their detailed responses to a questionnaire relating to the previous edition which helped me to formulate the structure and content of the new edition: A. Houghton, Sheffield University, UK; G. Tagg, Oxford Brookes University, UK; A. Koelmans, Newcastle University, UK; L. MacKenzie, Glasgow University, UK; S. Benson, Staffordshire University, UK; R. Newman-Wolfe, University of Florida, USA; B. Veenendaal, Curtin University, USA; A. Ruighauer, University of Melbourne, USA; J. Silvester, University of Southern California, USA; A. Shaout, University of Michigan, USA; D. Jacobson, Iowa State University, USA; J. Jormakka, Helsinki University of Technology, Finland; T. Karvi, University of Helsinki, Finland; T. Bellika, Finnmark College, Finland; S. Knapskog, University of Trondheim, Norway; P. Vestøl, Agder College of Engineering, Norway; L. Christoff and T. Walasek, both of Uppsala University, Sweden. Especial mention is due to Dr S. Wilbur and her students (F. Ojuri, A. Killick, R. Payne, M. McDonald, T. Blomfield, A. Plewes, B. Robson) at Queen Mary and Westfield College. I would also like to thank the following for their helpful comments on much of the new material: Allan Fisher, Carnegie Mellon University, USA; Gong Su, Columbia University, USA; Andrew Scott, Lancaster University, UK; Jon Crowcroft, University College London, UK and Ian Whitworth, Cranfield University, UK.

Finally, I would like to take this opportunity to express my sincere thanks, firstly to Irene Dendle for her help with the preparation of the manuscript and making numerous corrections, alterations, and additions without a word of criticism; secondly, to my research assistants, for their help with obtaining numerous papers and documents relating to the new material; and finally, to my wife Rhiannon for her unwavering support, patience, and understanding while I was writing the book. It is to her that I dedicate the book.

Fred Halsall
September 1995

To my wife Rhiannon

CONTENTS

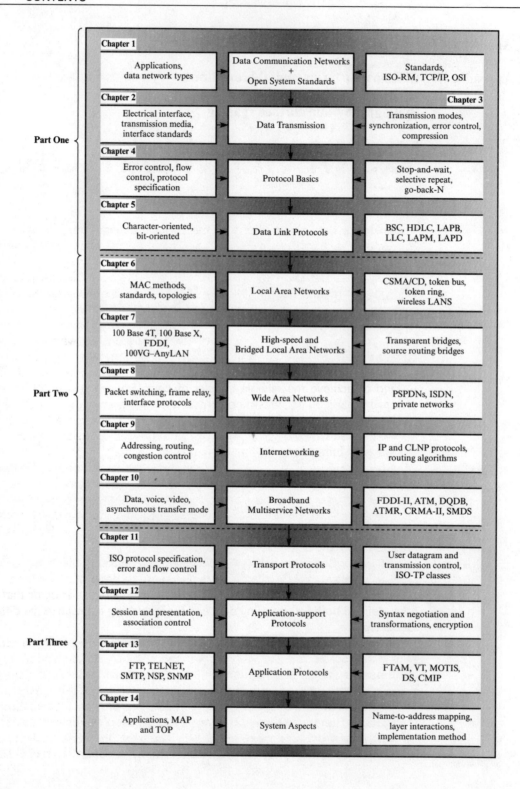

Part One

Chapter 1

Applications, data network types → Data Communication Networks + Open System Standards ← Standards, ISO-RM, TCP/IP, OSI

Chapter 2 / **Chapter 3**

Electrical interface, transmission media, interface standards → Data Transmission ← Transmission modes, synchronization, error control, compression

Chapter 4

Error control, flow control, protocol specification → Protocol Basics ← Stop-and-wait, selective repeat, go-back-N

Chapter 5

Character-oriented, bit-oriented → Data Link Protocols ← BSC, HDLC, LAPB, LLC, LAPM, LAPD

Part Two

Chapter 6

MAC methods, standards, topologies → Local Area Networks ← CSMA/CD, token bus, token ring, wireless LANS

Chapter 7

100 Base 4T, 100 Base X, FDDI, 100VG–AnyLAN → High-speed and Bridged Local Area Networks ← Transparent bridges, source routing bridges

Chapter 8

Packet switching, frame relay, interface protocols → Wide Area Networks ← PSPDNs, ISDN, private networks

Chapter 9

Addressing, routing, congestion control → Internetworking ← IP and CLNP protocols, routing algorithms

Chapter 10

Data, voice, video, asynchronous transfer mode → Broadband Multiservice Networks ← FDDI-II, ATM, DQDB, ATMR, CRMA-II, SMDS

Part Three

Chapter 11

ISO protocol specification, error and flow control → Transport Protocols ← User datagram and transmission control, ISO-TP classes

Chapter 12

Session and presentation, association control → Application-support Protocols ← Syntax negotiation and transformations, encryption

Chapter 13

FTP, TELNET, SMTP, NSP, SNMP → Application Protocols ← FTAM, VT, MOTIS, DS, CMIP

Chapter 14

Applications, MAP and TOP → System Aspects ← Name-to-address mapping, layer interactions, implementation method

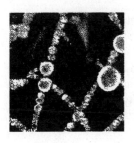

Part one
DATA
COMMUNICATIONS

The need for data communications has evolved almost from the earliest days of computing. However, although you are likely to be aware of the basic terminology and devices associated with computers themselves – bits and bytes, gates and highways, BASIC and Pascal, etc. – there is a fundamental set of techniques and terminology associated with data communications which is often less well understood. Before describing the different types of computer network we devote the first part of this book to a review of the fundamentals and terminology associated with data communications on which all forms of computer networks are based. In particular, we are concerned with the essential theory associated with digital transmission and the different techniques that are utilized to achieve the reliable transfer of data between two computers. The physical separation of the two computers may vary from a few tens of meters – for example, between two computers within an office or laboratory – to several hundreds of kilometers, for example, if the two computers are connected by a transmission path through a national telephone network.

Chapter 1 describes the historical evolution of distributed computing systems that has taken place as a result of advancing technology and identifies the different types of data communication networks that have evolved for use in such systems. Also, it identifies the intended application domain of each network type and the standards that have been defined for use with them. It thus lays the foundation for the remainder of the book.

Chapter 2 is concerned with the electrical characteristics of the different types of physical transmission medium used and the basic laws and theory that determine their use. It also outlines the various international standards that have been defined both for encoding data and for interfacing a device to the different media types.

As we shall see, data is normally transmitted between two devices bit serially in blocks comprising varying numbers of binary digits (bits). Chapter 3 describes the various techniques that enable the receiving device to determine, firstly, the start and end of each block being transmitted and, secondly, if any errors (bit corruptions) have occurred during transmission. It also discusses the subject of data compression and the different types of multiplexer equipment.

Chapter 4 presents the different techniques that are used, firstly, to overcome the effect of transmission errors and, secondly, to control the rate of flow of

1

data across a data link. Both these functions form part of the protocol associated with the data link. The chapter also describes how protocols are specified and a methodology for their implementation in program code.

Chapter 5 builds on the general principles introduced in Chapter 4 to describe the standard data link protocols that are in widespread use for controlling the exchange of data between a distributed community of computers.

1 DATA COMMUNICATION NETWORKS AND OPEN SYSTEM STANDARDS

Chapter objectives

When you have completed this chapter you should be able to:

- Identify the different applications of computer communication networks ☞ 3
- Appreciate the different types of data communication networks that are used in these applications ☞ 5
- Understand the concept of layering and structure of the ISO reference model for open systems interconnection ☞ 13
- Describe the functionality of each layer in the ISO reference model ☞ 16
- Know the protocols associated with the TCP/IP suite and how they relate to the ISO reference model ☞ 19
- Know some of the standard protocol suites that are based on the ISO protocols ☞ 20

Background

Computers are now used in every walk of life. In the home, for example, for games playing and word processing, in the office for word processing, spreadsheet and database management, in banks and other financial institutions for the maintenance of customer accounts, in travel agencies for airline and other reservations, in schools and colleges for computer-aided instruction, in universities and other research establishments for the analysis of scientific and other experimental data, in the process industry for the control of chemical and other plants, in manufacturing industries for the control of machine tools and robots, in department stores for point-of-sale accounting, and so on.

Although in many instances computers are used to perform their intended role in a stand-alone mode, in others there is a need to interwork and exchange data with other computers. In the home, for example, to transfer a file of data from one personal computer to another or to access information from a public database using the switched telephone network, in the office for the exchange of electronic mail either within the same establishment or between establishments, in financial institutions to carry out transfers of funds from one institution computer to another, in travel companies to access the reservation systems belonging to various airlines, in schools and colleges to share the use of an expensive peripheral such as a laser printer, in universities and other research establishments to access the results produced by a remote supercomputer, in the process industry to coordinate the control of the instrumentation equipment associated with a plant, in the manufacturing industry to control the transfer of parts and related data from one automated unit to another, in department stores for stock control and the automatic ordering of goods, and so on.

We are concerned specifically with the issues that must be considered when communicating data between two computers in such applications. This book provides not only an understanding of the different data and computer networks that are now available, but also details of the hardware and software that are required within each computer to interface with these facilities. In addition, it describes how application programs running in different computers with different word sizes and character sets cooperate to achieve a specific distributed application function. Figure 1.1 shows the three basic communication functions that must be considered.

The fundamental requirement in all applications that involve two or more computers is the provision of a suitable data communications facility. In practice, however, a wide range of different types of communications facility may be utilized, each intended for a specific application domain. For example, if the requirement is simply to transfer a file of data from one computer to another similar computer in the same room or office, then the communications facility will be much simpler than if data is to be transferred between different computers at different sites.

Figure 1.1
Computer communication schematic.

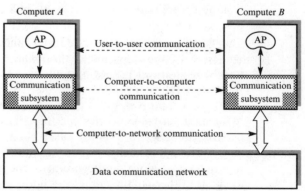

AP = Application process

Irrespective of the type of data communications facility being used, in most applications data is transmitted between computers in a **bit-serial mode**. Consequently, since data is transferred between subsystems within a computer in a **word-parallel mode**, it is necessary to perform a **parallel-to-serial conversion** operation at the computer interface prior to outputting data, and the reverse **serial-to-parallel conversion** on input. Also, the type of transmission mode and circuits that are required vary and depend on both the physical separation of the computers and the data transmission rate.

Once data is transmitted outside of a computer, there is a much increased probability that bit errors (corruptions) will occur. Therefore, in most applications it is necessary to incorporate not only a means to detect when bit (transmission) errors occur, but also a way to obtain another (hopefully correct) copy of the affected data. This is known as **error control** and is just one consideration when transmitting data between two computers. Other issues include regulating the rate at which data is transferred – known as **flow control** – and, if an intermediate data network is involved, establishing a communications path across the network.

In some instances, the application software can use this basic computer-to-computer communications facility directly, while in others additional functionality must be added. For example, in some applications the communicating computers may be of different types which means that their internal representation of characters and numerical values may be different. Hence a means of ensuring the transferred data is interpreted in the same way in each computer must be incorporated. Also, the computers may use different operating systems, for example, one may be a small single-user computer while another may be a large multi-user system. This means that the interface between user (application) programs – normally referred to as **application processes** or **APs** – and the underlying computer-to-computer communications services will also be different. All these points must be considered when communicating data between computers.

1.1 Data communication networks

As we have just said, the type of data communications facility used is a function of the nature of the application, the number of computers involved, and their physical separation. Typical data communication facilities are shown in Figures 1.2 through 1.6.

If only two computers are involved and both are in the same room or office, then the transmission facility can comprise just a simple point-to-point wire link, as shown in Figure 1.2(a). However, if they are located in different parts of a town or country, **public carrier** facilities must be used. Normally this involves the **public switched telephone network (PSTN)** which requires a device known as a **modem** for transmitting data. The general arrangement is as shown in Figure 1.2(b).

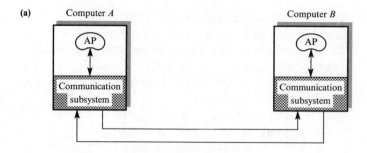

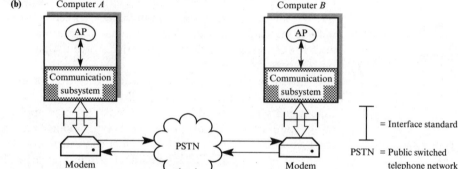

Figure 1.2
Simple computer-to-computer alternatives: (a) point-to-point wire link; (b) PSTN + modem link.

When more than two computers are involved in the application, a switched communication facility (network) is used to enable all the computers to communicate with one another at different times. If all the computers are distributed around a single office or building, it is possible to install your own network. Such a network is known as a **local area (data) network (LAN)**. A wide range of such LANs and allied equipment is available. Two LAN-based systems are shown in Figure 1.3.

When the computers are located in different establishments (sites), public carrier facilities must again be used. The resulting network is known as a **wide area network (WAN)**. The type of WAN used depends on the nature of the application. For example, if all the computers belong to the same enterprise and there is a requirement to transfer substantial amounts of data between sites, one approach is simply to lease transmission lines (circuits) from the public carriers and install a private switching system at each site to create what is known as an **enterprisewide private network**. Many large enterprises choose to do this; such networks normally incorporate both voice and data communications. The general scheme is shown in Figure 1.4.

Such solutions are viable only for large enterprises since there is sufficient intersite traffic to justify the cost of leasing lines and installing and running a

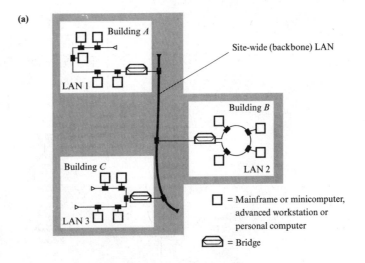

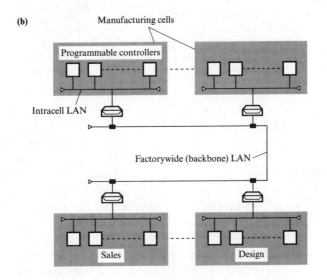

Figure 1.3
LAN-based distributed
systems: (a) technical
and office automation;
(b) manufacturing
automation.

private network. In most other cases, public carrier networks must be used. In addition to providing a public switched telephone service, most public carriers now provide a public switched data service. Indeed, such networks, like the PSTN, are now interconnected internationally and have been designed specifically for the transmission of data rather than voice. Consequently, for applications that involve computers distributed around a country or perhaps internationally, a **public switched data network (PSDN)** is normally used. Alternatively, many public carriers are now converting their existing PSTNs to enable data to be transmitted without modems. The resulting networks, which operate in an

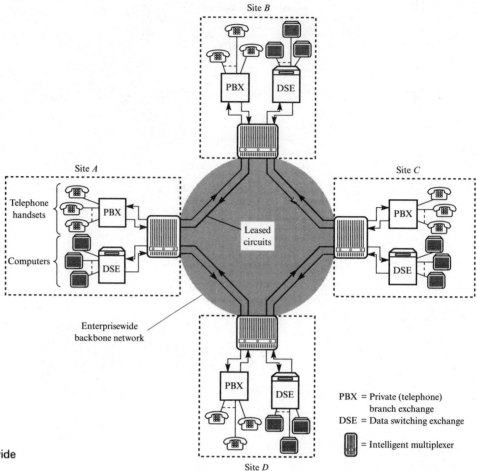

Figure 1.4
Typical enterprisewide
private network.

all-digital mode, are known as **integrated services digital networks (ISDNs)**. ISDNs may also be considered once they are in widespread use. The general schemes are shown Figure 1.5.

We have assumed in all these applications that all the computers are attached to the same LAN or WAN. In some applications, however, the data communications facility embraces multiple networks such as LAN–WAN–LAN. For example, a workstation (computer) attached to a LAN in one establishment may need to communicate with a computer that is attached to a LAN in a different establishment with the two LANs being interconnected by, say, a PSDN. This type of communications facility, which is known as an **internetwork** or **internet**, requires additional issues to be addressed both in relation to the network itself and when interfacing computers to such networks. An example of such a network is shown in Figure 1.6.

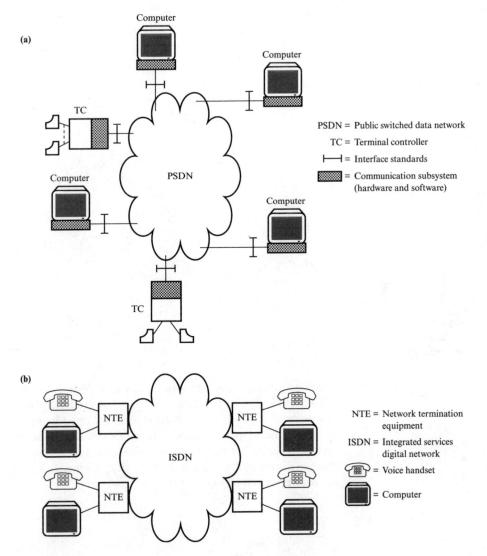

Figure 1.5
Public carrier data
networks: (a) PSDN;
(b) ISDN.

The networks we have discussed so far have been designed primarily for the transmission of data between workstations that support data-only services. More recently, workstations have evolved that support services that involve not only data but a range of other information types. These include workstations that support desktop video telephony, videoconferencing, and more general multimedia services. To support this richer set of services, a new generation of networks has been developed known as **broadband multiservice networks**, the term 'broadband' being used because of their high transmission bit rates.

Because of differences between data communications and speech and video communications, a new approach has been adopted for the transmission and

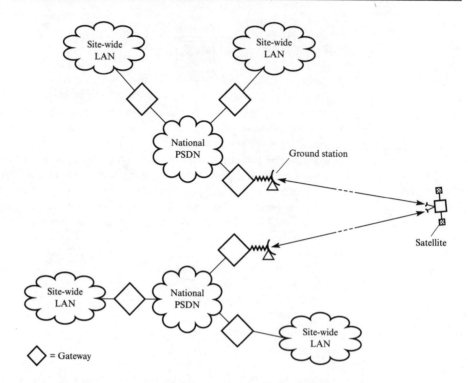

Figure 1.6
Worldwide
internetwork.

switching within these networks. This is known as **asynchronous transfer mode (ATM)**. ATM LANs are now available that are based on this operation mode. A new generation of ATM WAN has been developed to interconnect such LANs. In addition, a new type of network known as a **metropolitan area network (MAN)** has been introduced for the interconnection of ATM LANs – and data-only LANs – that are distributed around a town or city. A schematic diagram of a multiservice network is shown in Figure 1.7.

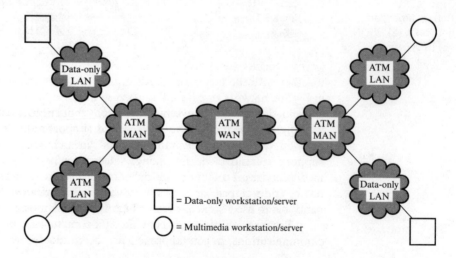

Figure 1.7
Broadband
multiservice networks.

1.2 Standards

Until recently, the standards used in the computer industry by the various international bodies were concerned primarily with either the internal operation of a computer or the connection of a local peripheral device. The result was that early hardware and software communications subsystems offered by manufacturers enabled only their own computers, and so-called **plug-compatible systems**, to exchange information. Such systems are known as **closed systems**, since computers from other manufacturers cannot exchange information unless they adhere to the (proprietary) standards of a particular manufacturer.

In contrast, the various international bodies concerned with public-carrier networks have for many years formulated internationally agreed standards for connecting devices to these networks. The **V-series recommendations**, for example, are concerned with the connection of equipment – normally referred to as **data terminal equipment (DTE)** – to a modem connected to the PSTN; the **X-series recommendations** for connecting a DTE to a public data network; and the **I-series recommendations** for connecting a DTE to the emerging ISDNs. The recommendations have resulted in compatibility between the equipment from different vendors, enabling a purchaser to select suitable equipment from a range of manufacturers.

Initially, the services provided by most public carriers were concerned primarily with data transmission, and hence the associated standards related only to the method of interfacing a device to these networks. More recently, the public carriers have started to provide more extensive distributed information services, such as the exchange of electronic messages **(Teletex)** and access to public databases **(Videotex)**. To cater for such services, the standards bodies associated with the telecommunications industry have formulated not only standards for interfacing to such networks, but also so-called higher-level standards concerned with the format (syntax) and control of the exchange of information (data) between systems. Consequently, the equipment from any manufacturer that adheres to these standards can be used interchangeably with equipment from any other manufacturer that complies with the standards. The resulting system is then known as an **open system** or, more completely, as an **open system interconnection environment (OSIE)**. A summary of the evolution of standards, together with the major standards organizations, is shown in diagrammatic form in Figure 1.8.

In the mid-1970s, as different types of distributed systems (based on both public and private data networks) started to proliferate, the potential advantages of open systems were acknowledged by the computer industry. As a result, a range of standards started to be introduced. The first was concerned with the overall structure of the complete communication subsystem within each computer. This was produced by the **International Standards Organization (ISO)** and is known as the **ISO Reference Model** for **Open Systems Interconnection (OSI)**.

The aim of the ISO reference model is to provide a framework for the coordination of standards development and to allow existing and evolving

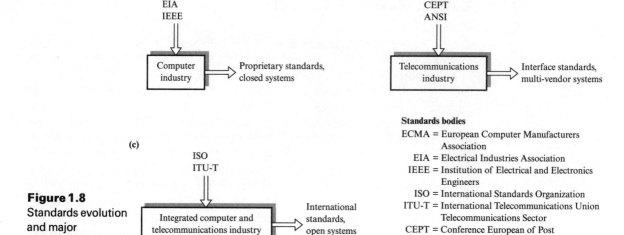

Figure 1.8
Standards evolution and major standardization organizations.

standards activities to be set within that framework. The aim is to allow an application process in any computer that supports a particular set of standards to communicate freely with an application process in any other computer that supports the same standards, irrespective of its origin of manufacture.

Examples of application processes that may wish to communicate in an open way are:

- A process (program) executing in a computer and accessing a remote file system

- A process acting as a central file service (server) to a distributed community of (client) processes

- A process in an office workstation (computer) accessing an electronic mail (e-mail) service

- A process acting as an electronic mail server to a distributed community of (client) processes

- A process in a supervisory computer controlling a distributed community of computer-based instruments or robot controllers associated with a process or automated manufacturing plant

- A process in an instrument or robot controller receiving commands and returning results to a supervisory system

- A process in a bank computer that initiates debit and credit operations on a remote system

OSI is concerned with the exchange of information between such processes. The aim is to enable application processes to cooperate in carrying out a particular (distributed) information processing task irrespective of the computers on which they are running.

1.3 ISO reference model

A communication subsystem is a complex piece of hardware and software. Early attempts at implementing the software for such subsystems were often based on a single, complex, unstructured program (normally written in assembly language) with many interacting components. The resulting software was difficult to test and often very difficult to modify.

To overcome this problem, the ISO has adopted a layered approach for the reference model. The complete communication subsystem is broken down into a number of layers, each of which performs a well-defined function. Conceptually, these layers can be considered as performing one of two generic functions: network-dependent functions and application-oriented functions. This gives rise to three distinct operational environments:

(1) The **network environment**, which is concerned with the protocols and standards relating to the different types of underlying data communication networks.

(2) The **OSI environment**, which embraces the network environment and adds additional application-oriented protocols and standards to allow end systems (computers) to communicate with one another in an open way.

(3) The **real systems environment**, which builds on the OSI environment and is concerned with a manufacturer's proprietary software and services, which have been developed to perform a particular distributed information processing task.

These environments are shown in diagrammatic form in Figure 1.9.

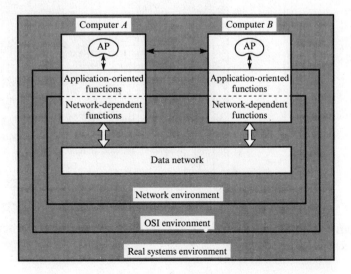

Figure 1.9
Operational
environments.

Both the network-dependent and application-oriented (network-independent) components of the OSI model are implemented as a number of layers. The boundaries between each layer and the functions performed by each layer have been selected on the basis of experience gained during earlier standardization activity.

Each layer performs a well-defined function in the context of the overall communication subsystem. The layer operates according to a defined **protocol** – set of rules – by exchanging messages, both user data and additional control information, with a corresponding **peer** (similar) layer in a remote system. Each layer has a well-defined interface with the layers immediately above and below. The implementation of a particular protocol layer is independent of all other layers.

The logical structure of the ISO reference model is made up of seven protocol layers, as shown in Figure 1.10. The three lowest layers (1–3) are network dependent and are concerned with the protocols associated with the data communication network being used to link the two communicating computers. The three upper layers (5–7) are application oriented and are concerned with the protocols that allow two end-user application processes to interact with each other, normally through a range of services offered by the local operating system. The intermediate transport layer (4) masks the upper application-oriented layers from the detailed operation of the lower network-dependent layers. Essentially, it builds on the services provided by the latter to provide the application-oriented layers with a network-independent message interchange service.

The function of each layer is specified formally as a protocol that defines the set of rules and conventions used by the layer to communicate with a similar peer

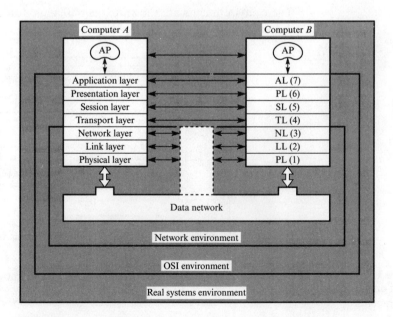

Figure 1.10
Overall structure of the ISO reference model.

layer in another (remote) system. Each layer provides a defined set of services to the layer immediately above. It also uses the services provided by the layer immediately below it to transport the message units associated with the protocol to the remote peer layer. For example, the transport layer provides a network-independent message transport service to the session layer above it and uses the service provided by the network layer below it to transfer the set of message units associated with the transport protocol to a peer transport layer in another system. Each layer communicates with a similar peer layer in a remote system according to a defined protocol. However, in practice, the resulting protocol message units of the layer are passed by means of the services provided by the next lower layer. The basic functions of each layer are summarized in Figure 1.11.

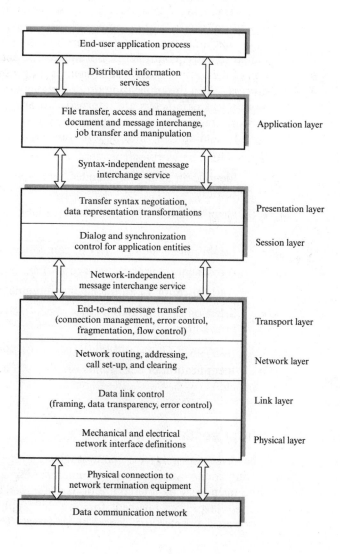

Figure 1.11
Protocol layer
summary.

1.3.1 The application-oriented layers

The application layer

The **application layer** provides the user interface – normally an application program/process – to a range of networkwide distributed information services. These include file transfer access and management, as well as general document and message interchange services such as electronic mail. A number of standard protocols are available for these and other types of service.

Access to application services is normally through a defined set of primitives, each with associated parameters, which are supported by the local operating system. The access primitives are the same as other operating system calls (as used for access to, say, a local file system) and result in an appropriate operating system procedure (process) being activated. These operating system procedures use the communication subsystem (software and hardware) as if it is a local device – similar to a disk controller, for example. The detailed operation and implementation of the communication subsystem is thus transparent to the (user) application process. When the application process making the call is rescheduled (run), one or more status parameters are returned indicating the success (or otherwise) of the network transaction that has been attempted.

In addition to information transfer, the application layer provides such services as:

- Identification of the intended communication partner(s) by name or by address
- Determination of the current availability of an intended communication partner
- Establishment of authority to communicate
- Agreement on privacy (encryption) mechanisms
- Authentication of an intended communication partner
- Selection of the dialog discipline, including the initiation and release procedures
- Agreement on responsibility for error recovery
- Identification of constraints on data syntax (character sets, data structures, etc.)

The presentation layer

The **presentation layer** is concerned with the representation (syntax) of data during transfer between two communicating application processes. To achieve true open systems interconnection, a number of common **abstract data syntax** forms have been defined for use by application processes together with associated **transfer** (or **concrete**) **syntaxes**. The presentation layer negotiates and selects the appropriate transfer syntax(es) to be used during a transaction so that the syntax (structure) of the messages being exchanged between two application entities is maintained. If this form of representation is different from the internal abstract form, the presentation protocol performs the necessary conversion.

Let's illustrate the services provided by the presentation layer by considering a telephone conversation between a French-speaking person and a Spanish-speaking person. Assume each uses an interpreter and that the only language understood by both interpreters is English. Each interpreter must translate from their local language to English, and vice versa. The two correspondents are analogous to two application processes with the two interpreters representing presentation layer entities. French and Spanish are the local syntaxes and English the transfer or concrete syntax. Note that there must be a universally understood language which must be defined to allow the agreed transfer language (syntax) to be negotiated. Also note that the interpreters do not necessarily understand the meaning (semantics) of the conversation.

Another function of the presentation layer is concerned with data security. In some applications, data sent by an application is first encrypted (enciphered) using a **key**, which is (hopefully) known only by the intended recipient presentation layer. The latter decrypts (deciphers) any received data using the corresponding key before passing it onto the intended recipient. Although this is not currently part of the standard, the subject of encryption is discussed in Section 12.4 in the context of the presentation layer.

The session layer

The **session layer** allows two application layer protocol entities to organize and synchronize their dialog and manage their data exchange. It is thus responsible for setting up (and clearing) a communication (dialog) channel between two communicating application layer protocol entities (presentation layer protocol entities in practice) for the duration of the complete network transaction. A number of optional services are provided, including the following:

- Interaction management   The data exchange associated with a dialog may be duplex – two-way simultaneous – or half-duplex – two-way alternate. In the latter case the session layer protocol provides facilities for controlling the exchange of data (dialog units) in a synchronized way.

- Synchronization   For lengthy network transactions, the user (through the services provided by the session layer) may choose periodically to establish synchronization points associated with the transfer. If a fault develops during a transaction, the dialog may be restarted at an agreed (earlier) synchronization point.

- Exception reporting   Non-recoverable exceptions arising during a transaction can be signaled to the application layer by the session layer.

The transport layer

The **transport layer** acts as the interface between the higher application-oriented layers and the underlying network-dependent protocol layers. It provides the session layer with a message transfer facility that is independent of the underlying network type. By providing the session layer with a defined set of message transfer facilities the transport layer hides the detailed operation of the underlying network from the session layer.

The transport layer offers a number of **classes of service** to compensate for the varying **quality of service (QOS)** provided by the network layers associated with the different types of network. There are five classes of service ranging from class 0, which provides only the basic functions needed for connection establishment and data transfer, to class 4, which provides full error control and flow control procedures.

As an example, class 0 may be selected for use with a PSDN while class 4 may be used with a PSTN. We shall expand upon this in Section 11.6 when the transport layer is discussed in detail.

1.3.2   The network-dependent layers

As the lowest three layers of the ISO reference model are network dependent, their detailed operation varies from one network type to another. In general, however, the **network layer** is responsible for establishing and clearing a networkwide connection between two transport layer protocol entities. It includes such functionality as network routing (addressing) and, in some instances, flow control across the computer-to-network interface. In the case of internetworking it provides various harmonizing functions between the interconnected networks.

The **link layer** builds on the physical connection provided by the particular network to provide the network layer with a reliable information transfer facility. It is responsible for functions such as error detection and, in the event of transmission errors, the retransmission of messages. Normally, two types of service are provided:

(1) **Connectionless**, which treats each information frame as a self-contained entity that is transferred using a best-try approach, that is, if errors are detected in a frame then the frame is simply discarded.

(2) **Connection oriented**, which endeavors to provide an error-free information transfer facility.

Finally, the **physical layer** is concerned with the physical and electrical interfaces between the user equipment and the network terminating equipment. It provides the link layer with a means of transmitting a serial bit stream between the two equipments.

1.4 Open system standards

The ISO reference model has been formulated simply as a template for the structure of a communication subsystem on which standards activities associated with each layer may be based. It is not intended that there should be a single standard protocol associated with each layer. Rather, a set of standards is associated with each layer, each offering different levels of functionality. For a specific OSI environment, such as that linking numerous computer-based systems in a fully-automated manufacturing plant, a selected set of standards is defined for use by all systems in that environment.

The three major international bodies actively producing standards for computer communications are the ISO, the American Institution of Electrical and Electronic Engineers (IEEE) and the International Telecommunications Union – Telecommunications Sector (ITU-T), formerly the International Telegraph and Telephone Consultative Committee (CCITT). Essentially, the ISO and IEEE produce standards for use by computer manufacturers while the ITU-T defines standards for connecting equipment to the different types of national and international public network. As the degree of overlap between the computer and telecommunications industries increases, however, there is an increasing level of cooperation and commonality between the standards produced by these organizations.

In addition, prior to and concurrently with ISO standards activity, the United States Department of Defense has funded research into computer communications and networking through its **Defense Advanced Research Projects Agency (DARPA)**. As part of this research, the computer networks associated with a large number of universities and other research establishments were linked to those of DARPA. The resulting internetwork, known as **ARPANET**, has now been extended to incorporate internets developed by other government agencies. The combined internets are now known simply as the **Internet**.

The protocol suite used with the Internet is known as **Transmission Control Protocol/Internet Protocol (TCP/IP)**. It includes both network-oriented protocols and application support protocols. Because TCP/IP is in widespread use with an existing internet, many of the TCP/IP protocols have been used as the basis for ISO standards. Moreover, since all the protocol specifications associated with TCP/IP are in the public domain – and hence no license fees are payable – they have been used extensively by commercial and public authorities for creating open system networking environments. In practice, therefore, there are two major open system (vendor-independent) standards: the TCP/IP suite and those based on the evolving ISO standards.

Figure 1.12 shows some of the standards associated with the TCP/IP suite. As we can see, because TCP/IP has developed concurrently with the ISO initiative, it does not contain specific protocols relating to all the ISO layers. Moreover, the specification methodology used for the TCP/IP suite differs from that used for the ISO standards. Nevertheless, most of the functionality associated with the ISO layers is embedded in the TCP/IP suite.

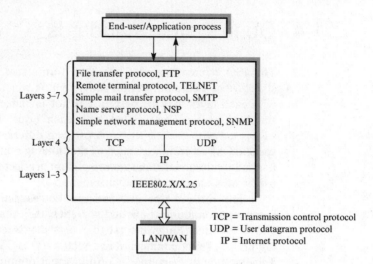

Figure 1.12
TCP/IP suite.

In the case of ISO/ITU-T standards, as Figure 1.13 shows, a range of standards is associated with each layer. Collectively they enable the administrative authority that is establishing the open system environment to select the most suitable set of standards for the application. The resulting protocol suite is known as the **open system interconnection profile**. A number of such profiles have now been defined, including the following: **TOP**, a protocol set for use in technical and

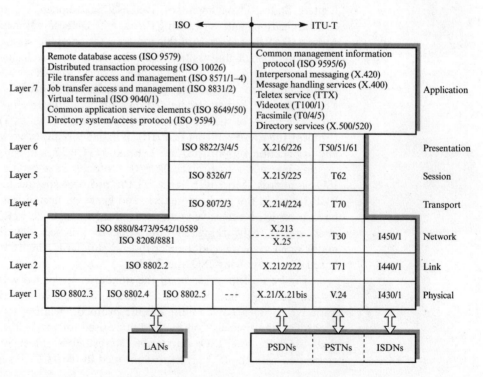

Figure 1.13
Standards summary.

office environments; **MAP**, for use in manufacturing automation; US and UK **GOSIP** for use in US and UK government projects, respectively; and a similar suite used in Europe known as the **CEN functional standards**. The last one has been defined by the Standards Promotion and Application Group **(SPAG)**, a group of 12 European companies.

As Figure 1.13 shows, the lowest three layers vary for different network types. The ITU-T has defined V-, X- and I-series standards for use with public carrier networks. The V-series is for use with the existing PSTN, the X-series for use with existing PSDNs and the I-series for use with the emerging ISDNs. X- and I-series are discussed in Chapter 8. Those produced by the ISO/IEEE for use with LANs are discussed in Chapters 6, 7, and 9.

Although different numbering systems are used by the ISO and ITU-T, the function and specification of the transport, session and presentation layers are almost identical. There is a range of application layer standards, some defined by the ISO for private networks and others by the ITU-T for public carrier services. The function and operation of the application-oriented (network-independent) protocol layers are described in Chapters 11, 12, 13, and 14.

Chapter summary

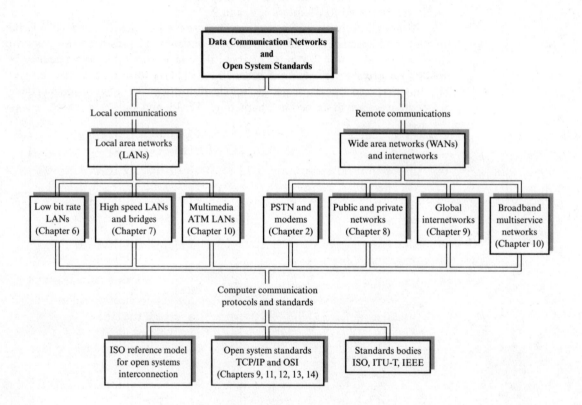

2

THE ELECTRICAL INTERFACE

Chapter objectives

When you have completed this chapter you should be able to:

Introduction

To transmit binary data over a transmission line, the binary digits making up each element to be transmitted must be converted into electrical signals. For example, we can transmit a binary 1 by applying a voltage signal (or level) of amplitude $+V$ volts to the sending end of a transmission line and a binary 0 by applying $-V$ volts. On receiving these signals, the receiving device interprets $+V$ volts as a binary 1 and $-V$ volts as a binary 0. In practice, transmitted electrical

23

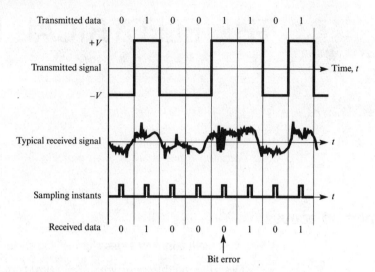

Figure 2.1
Effect of imperfect
transmission medium.

signals are **attenuated** (reduced) and **distorted** (misshapen) by the transmission medium, so that at some stage the receiver is unable to discriminate between the binary 1 and 0 signals, as shown in Figure 2.1. The extent of attenuation and distortion is strongly influenced by:

- The type of transmission medium

- The bit rate of the data being transmitted

- The distance between the two communicating devices

We shall discuss the various sources of impairment in Section 2.2.

As attenuation and distortion can be quantified for different types of transmission media and physical separations, international standards have been defined for the electrical interface between two items of data communications equipment. These standards define not only the electrical signal levels to be used but also the use and meaning of any additional control signals and conventions that are used at the physical interface. The two bodies that formulate standards for interconnecting data communications equipment are the **International Telecommunications Union – Telecommunications Sector (ITU-T)** – formerly the **International Telegraph and Telephone Consultative Committee (CCITT)** – in Europe and the **Electrical Industries Association (EIA)** in the United States. Although the standards defined by both bodies use slightly different terminology, the basic signals and their meanings are the same.

This chapter is divided into six sections: the first two describe the most widely used transmission media and the next two, the different forms of electrical signals; the fifth, the characteristics of public carrier circuits; and the sixth, some additional aspects of the more common physical layer interface standards. Although in most instances we shall consider the interface of a computer to the different data communication interfaces, it is normal to use the more general term data terminal equipment (DTE), rather than computer, since this implies any type of equipment.

2.1 Transmission media

The transmission of an electrical signal requires a transmission medium which normally takes the form of a **transmission line**. In some cases, this consists of a pair of conductors or wires. Common alternatives are a beam of light guided by a glass fiber and electromagnetic waves propagating through free space. The type of transmission medium is important, since it determines the maximum number of bits (**binary digits**) that can be transmitted per second or **bps**. We discuss the more common types of transmission media in the following subsections.

2.1.1 Two-wire open lines

A **two-wire open line** is the simplest transmission medium. Each wire is insulated from the other and both are open to free space. This type of line is adequate for connecting equipment that is up to 50 m apart using moderate bit rates (less than, say, 19.2 kbps). The signal, typically a voltage or current level relative to some ground reference, is applied to one wire while the ground reference is applied to the other.

Although a two-wire open line can be used to connect two computers (DTEs) directly, it is used mainly for connecting a DTE to local data circuit-terminating equipment (DCE) – for example a modem. Such connections usually utilize multiple lines, the most common arrangement being a separate insulated wire for each signal and a single wire for the common ground reference. The complete set of wires is then either enclosed in a single protected **multicore cable** or molded into a **flat ribbon cable** as shown in Figure 2.2(a).

With this type of line, you must take care to avoid cross-coupling of electrical signals between adjacent wires in the same cable. This is known as **crosstalk** and is caused by **capacitive coupling** between the two wires. In addition, the open structure makes it susceptible to the pick-up of spurious **noise signals** from other electrical signal sources caused by **electromagnetic radiation**. The main problem with such signals is that they may be picked up in just one wire – for example the signal wire – creating an additional difference signal between the two wires. Since the receiver normally operates using the difference signal between the two wires, this can give rise to an erroneous interpretation of the combined (signal plus noise) received signal. These factors all contribute to the limited lengths of line and bit rates that can be used reliably.

Figure 2.2
Copper wire
transmission media:
(a) two-wire open
lines.

(a)

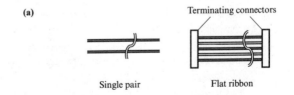

Single pair   Flat ribbon

2.1.2   Twisted-pair lines

We can achieve much better immunity to spurious noise signals by employing a **twisted-pair line** in which a pair of wires are twisted together. The proximity of the signal and ground reference wires means that any interference signal is picked up by both wires reducing its effect on the difference signal. Furthermore, if multiple twisted pairs are enclosed within the same cable, the twisting of each pair within the cable reduces crosstalk. A schematic of a twisted-pair line is shown in Figure 2.2(b).

Twisted-pair lines are suitable, with appropriate line driver and receiver circuits that exploit the potential advantages gained by using such a geometry, for bit rates in the order of 1 Mbps over short distances (less than 100 m) and lower bit rates over longer distances. More sophisticated driver and receiver circuits enable similar or even higher rates to be achieved over much longer distances. Such lines, known as **unshielded twisted pairs (UTPs)**, are used extensively in telephone networks and (with special integrated circuits) in many data communication applications. With **shielded twisted pairs (STPs)**, a protective screen or shield is used to reduce further the effects of interference signals (see Figure 2.2(c)).

2.1.3   Coaxial cable

The main limiting factors of a twisted-pair line are its capacity and a phenomenon known as the **skin effect**. As the bit rate (and hence frequency) of the transmitted

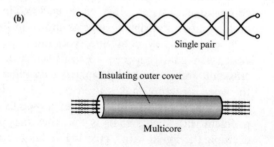

Single pair

Insulating outer cover

Multicore

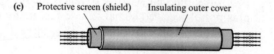

(c)   Protective screen (shield)   Insulating outer cover

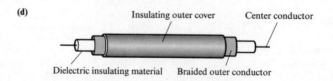

(d)   Insulating outer cover   Center conductor

Dielectric insulating material   Braided outer conductor

Figure 2.2 (cont.)
(b) Unshielded
twisted pair;
(c) shielded twisted
pair; (d) coaxial cable.

signal increases, the current flowing in the wires tends to flow only on the outer surface of the wire, thus using less of the available cross-section. This increases the electrical resistance of the wires for higher-frequency signals, leading to higher attenuation. In addition, at higher frequencies, more signal power is lost as a result of radiation effects. Hence, for applications that demand a bit rate higher than 1 Mbps, we must use either more sophisticated driver and receiver electronics or another type of transmission medium.

Coaxial cable minimizes both these effects. Figure 2.2(d) shows the signal and ground reference wires as a solid center conductor running concentrically (coaxially) inside a solid (or braided) outer circular conductor. Ideally the space between the two conductors should be filled with air, but in practice it is normally filled with a dielectric insulating material with a solid or honeycomb structure.

The center conductor is effectively shielded from external interference signals by the outer conductor. Also only minimal losses occur as a result of electromagnetic radiation and the skin effect because of the presence of the outer conductor. Coaxial cable can be used with a number of different signal types, but typically 10 Mbps over several hundred meters – or higher with modulation – is perfectly feasible. Also, as we shall see in Section 2.3.4, coaxial cable is applicable in both point-to-point and multipoint topologies.

2.1.4 Optical fiber

While the geometry of coaxial cable significantly reduces the various limiting effects, the maximum signal frequency, and hence the information rate that can be transmitted using a solid (normally copper) conductor, although very high, is limited. This is also the case for twisted-pair lines. **Optical fiber cable** differs from both these transmission media in that it carries the transmitted information in the form of a fluctuating beam of light in a glass fiber, rather than as an electrical signal on a wire. Light waves have a much wider bandwidth than electrical waves, enabling optical fiber cable to achieve transmission rates of hundreds of megabits per second. Light waves are also immune to electromagnetic interference and crosstalk. Optical fiber cable is also extremely useful for the transmission of lower bit rate signals in electrically noisy environments, in steel plants, for example, which employ much high-voltage and current-switching equipments. This cable is also being used increasingly where security is important, since it is difficult physically to tap.

An optical fiber cable consists of a single glass fiber for each signal to be transmitted, contained within the cable's protective coating which also shields the fiber from any external light sources. A diagram of such a cable is shown in Figure 2.3(a). The light signal is generated by an optical transmitter, which performs the conversion from normal electrical signals as used in a DTE. An optical receiver is used to perform the reverse function at the receiving end. Typically, the transmitter uses a **light-emitting diode (LED)** or **laser diode (LD)** to perform the conversion operation while the receiver uses a light-sensitive **photodiode** or **photo transistor**.

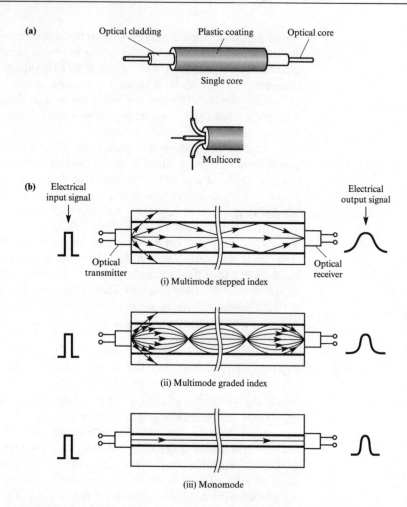

Figure 2.3
Optical fiber
principles: (a) cable
structure;
(b) transmission
modes.

The fiber itself consists of two parts: the glass core and a glass cladding with a lower refractive index. Light propagates along the optical fiber core in one of three ways depending on the type and width of core material used. These transmission modes are shown in Figure 2.3(b).

In a **multimode stepped index fiber** the cladding and core material each has a different but uniform refractive index. All the light emitted by the diode at an angle less than the critical angle is reflected at the cladding interface and propagates along the core by means of multiple (internal) reflections. Depending on the angle at which it is emitted by the diode, the light will take a variable amount of time to propagate along the cable. Therefore the received signal has a wider pulse width than the input signal with a corresponding decrease in the maximum permissible bit rate. This type of cable is used primarily for modest bit rates with relatively inexpensive LEDs compared to laser diodes.

Dispersion can be reduced by using a core material that has a variable (rather than constant) refractive index. As shown in Figure 2.3(b), in a

multimode graded index fiber light is refracted by an increasing amount as it moves away from the core. This has the effect of narrowing the pulse width of the received signal compared with stepped index fiber, allowing a corresponding increase in maximum bit rate.

Further improvements can be obtained by reducing the core diameter to that of a single wavelength (3–10 μm) so that all the emitted light propagates along a single (dispersionless) path. Consequently, the received signal is of a comparable width to the input signal. This **monomode fiber**, which is normally used with LDs, can operate at hundreds of megabits per second.

2.1.5   Satellites

All the transmission media we have discussed so far have used a physical line to carry the transmitted information. However, data can also be transmitted using electromagnetic (radio) waves through free space as in **satellite** systems. A collimated **microwave beam**, onto which the data is modulated, is transmitted to the satellite from the ground. This beam is received and retransmitted (relayed) to the predetermined destination(s) using an on-board circuit known as a **transponder**. A single satellite has many transponders, each covering a particular band of frequencies. A typical satellite channel has an extremely high bandwidth (500 MHz) and can provide many hundreds of high bit rate data links using a technique known as **multiplexing**. We shall describe this in Section 2.5.2 but, essentially, the total available capacity of the channel is divided into a number of subchannels, each of which can support a high bit rate link.

Satellites used for communication purposes are normally **geostationary**, which means that the satellite orbits the earth once every 24 hours in synchronism with the earth's rotation and hence appears stationary from the ground. The orbit of the satellite is chosen so that it provides a line-of-sight communication path to the transmitting station(s) and receiving station(s). The degree of the collimation of the microwave beam retransmitted by the satellite can be either coarse, so that the signal can be picked up over a wide geographical area, or finely focused, so that it can be picked up over only a limited area. In the second case the signal power is higher allowing smaller-diameter receivers called **antennas** or **dishes** (known as **very small aperture terminals** or **VSATs**) to be used. Satellites are widely used for data transmission applications ranging from interconnecting different national computer communication networks to providing high bit rate paths to link communication networks in different parts of the same country.

A typical satellite system is shown in Figure 2.4(a). Only a unidirectional transmission path is shown but a duplex path is used in most practical applications with the up and down channels associated with each ground station operating at different frequencies. Other common configurations involve a central hub ground station that communicates with a number of VSAT ground stations distributed around the country. Typically, a computer is connected to each VSAT and can communicate with a central computer connected to the hub, as shown in Figure 2.4(b). Normally, the central site broadcasts to all VSATs on

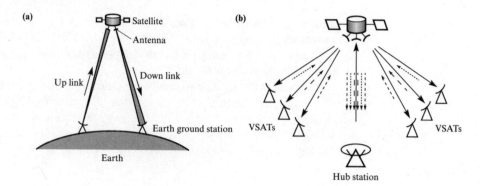

Figure 2.4
Satellite transmission:
(a) point-to-point;
(b) multipoint.

a single frequency, while in the reverse direction each VSAT transmits at a different frequency.

To communicate with a particular VSAT, the central site broadcasts the message with the identity of the intended VSAT at the head of the message. For applications that require VSAT-to-VSAT communication, all messages are first sent to the central site – via the satellite – which then broadcasts them to the intended recipients. With the next generation of higher-powered satellites it will be possible for the routing to be carried out on board the satellite without passing through a central site. Direct VSAT-to-VSAT communication is possible.

2.1.6   Terrestrial microwave

Terrestrial microwave links are widely used to provide communication links when it is impractical or too expensive to install physical transmission media, for example across a river or perhaps a swamp or desert. As the collimated microwave beam travels through the earth's atmosphere, it can be disturbed by such factors as manufactured structures and adverse weather conditions. With a satellite link, on the other hand, the beam travels mainly through free space and is therefore less prone to such effects. Nevertheless, line-of-sight microwave communication through the earth's atmosphere can be used reliably over distances in excess of 50 km.

2.1.7   Radio

Lower frequency **radio waves** are also used in place of fixed-wire links over more modest distances using ground-based transmitters and receivers. For example, to connect a large number of data gathering computers distributed throughout a rural area to a remote data logging/monitoring computer, or for connecting computers (or computer-based terminals) within a town or city to a local or remote computer.

It would be expensive to install fixed-wire cables for such applications. Radio is often used to provide a **cordless (wireless) link** between a fixed-wire termination point and the distributed computers. A radio transmitter (known as

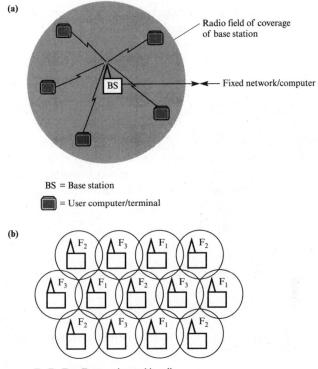

(a)

Radio field of coverage
of base station

BS

Fixed network/computer

BS = Base station

☐ = User computer/terminal

(b)

F_1, F_2, F_3 = Frequencies used in cell

Figure 2.5
Ground-based radio
transmission: (a) single
cell; (b) multiple cells.

the **base station**) is placed at the fixed-wire termination point, as shown in Figure 2.5(a), providing a cordless link between each computer and the central site.

Multiple base stations must be used for applications that require a wider coverage area or a higher density of users. The coverage area of each base station is restricted – by limiting its power output – so that it provides only sufficient channels to support the total load in that area. Wider coverage is achieved by arranging multiple base stations in a cell structure, as shown in Figure 2.5(b). In practice, the size of each cell varies and is determined by such factors as the terminal density and local terrain.

Each base station operates using a different band of frequencies from its neighbors. However, since the field of coverage of each base station is limited, it is possible to reuse its frequency band in other parts of the network. Base stations are connected to the fixed network as before. Normally, the usable data rate available to each of the computers within a cell is tens of kilobits per second.

A similar arrangement can be utilized within a building to provide cordless links to computer-based equipment within each office. In such cases one or more base stations are located on each floor of the building and connected to the fixed network. Each base station provides cordless links to the fixed network for all the computers in its field of coverage. This avoids rewiring whenever a new computer is installed or moved, but at the cost of providing a radio unit to convert the data into and from a radio signal. The usable data rate is often lower than with fixed wiring.

2.2 Attenuation and distortion sources

The various attenuation and distortion effects that can degrade a signal during transmission are shown in Figure 2.6. Any signal carried on a transmission medium is affected by attenuation, limited bandwidth, delay distortion, and noise. Although all are present and produce a combined effect, we shall consider each impairment separately.

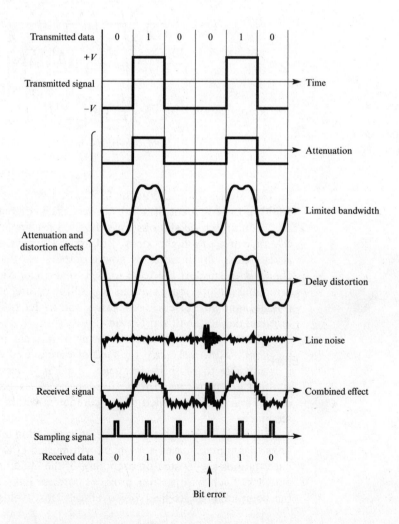

Figure 2.6
Sources of attenuation
and distortion.

2.2.1   Attenuation

As a signal propagates along a transmission medium (line) its amplitude decreases. This is known as **signal attenuation**. Normally, to allow for attenuation, a limit is set on the length of the cable that can be used to ensure that the receiver circuitry can reliably detect and interpret the received attenuated signal. If the cable is longer, one or more **amplifiers** – also known as **repeaters** – are inserted at intervals along the cable to restore the received signal to its original level.

Signal attenuation increases as a function of frequency. Hence, since a signal comprises a range of frequencies, the signal is also distorted. To overcome this problem, the amplifiers are designed to amplify different frequency signals by varying amounts. Alternatively, devices known as **equalizers** are used to equalize the attenuation across a defined band of frequencies.

We measure both attenuation and amplification – also known as **gain** – in **decibels (dB)**. If we denote transmitted signal power level by P_1 and the received power by P_2, then

$$\text{Attenuation} = 10 \, \log_{10} \frac{P_1}{P_2} \, \text{dB}$$

and

$$\text{Amplification} = 10 \, \log_{10} \frac{P_2}{P_1} \, \text{dB}$$

Since both P_1 and P_2 have the same unit of **watts**, then decibels are dimensionless and simply a measure of the relative magnitude of the two power levels. The use of logarithms means that the overall attenuation/amplification of a multisection transmission channel can be determined simply by summing together the attenuation/amplification of the individual sections.

Example 2.1

A transmission channel between two communicating DTEs is made up of three sections. The first introduces an attenuation of 16 dB, the second an amplification of 20 dB and the third an attenuation of 10 dB. Assuming a mean transmitted power level of 400 mW, determine the mean output power level of the channel.

Either:

For first section, $16 = 10 \, \log_{10} \dfrac{400}{P_2}$ Hence $P_2 = 10.0475 \, \text{mW}$

For second section, $20 = 10 \, \log_{10} \dfrac{P_2}{10.0475}$ Hence $P_2 = 1004.75 \, \text{mW}$

For third section, $10 = 10 \, \log_{10} \dfrac{1004.75}{P_2}$ Hence $P_2 = 100.475 \, \text{mW}$

That is, the mean output power level = 100.475 mW

or:

$$\text{Overall attenuation of channel} = (16 - 20) + 10 = 6\,\text{dB}$$

$$\text{Hence} \quad 6 = 10\,\log_{10}\frac{400}{P_2} \quad \text{and} \quad P_2 = 100.475\,\text{mW}$$

More generally, as will be expanded upon in Section 2.5.1, when we transmit binary information over a limited-bandwidth channel such as the PSTN, we can often use more than two signal levels. This means that each signal element can represent more than a single binary digit. In general, if the number of signal levels is M, the number of bits per signal element m, is given by:

$$m = \log_2 M$$

For example, if four signal levels are used to transmit a data bit stream, then each signal element can be used to transmit two binary digits.

The rate of change of the signal is known as the **signaling rate (R_s)**, and is measured in **baud**. It is related to the data bit rate, R, by the following expression:

$$R = R_s \log_2 M$$

2.2.2   Limited bandwidth

Any communications channel/transmission medium – twisted-pair wire, coaxial cable, radio, etc. – has a defined bandwidth associated with it which specifies the band of sinusoidal frequency components that will be transmitted by the channel unattenuated. Hence when transmitting data over a channel, we need to quantify the effect the bandwidth of the channel will have on the transmitted data signal.

We can use a mathematical technique known as **Fourier analysis** to show that any periodic signal – that is, a signal which repeats itself at equal time intervals (known as the period) – is made up of an infinite series of sinusoidal frequency components. The period of the signal determines the **fundamental frequency** component: the reciprocal of the period in seconds yields the frequency in **cycles per second (Hz)**. The other components have frequencies which are multiples of this and these are known as the **harmonics** of the fundamental. Mathematically we can express any periodic waveform as follows:

$$v(t) = a_0 + \sum_{n=1}^{\infty} a_n \cos n\omega_0 t + \sum_{n=1}^{\infty} b_n \sin n\omega_0 t$$

where:

$v(t)$ is the voltage signal representation as a function of time
ω_0 is the fundamental frequency component in radians per second
$T = 2\pi/\omega_0$ is the period of the waveform in seconds

The terms a_0, a_n and b_n are known as the **Fourier coefficients** and, for a particular waveform, we can derive them from the following set of integrals:

$$a_0 = \frac{1}{T} \int_0^T v(t)\mathrm{d}t$$

$$a_n = \frac{2}{T} \int_0^T v(t)\cos(n\omega_0 t)\mathrm{d}t$$

$$b_n = \frac{2}{T} \int_0^T v(t)\sin(n\omega_0 t)\mathrm{d}t$$

We can deduce from the first integral that a_0 is the mean of the signal over the period T and is known as the **DC component**.

In terms of data transmission, the signals of interest are binary sequences and, although in practice a transmitted binary message may be made up of randomly varying sequences, for analysis purposes we shall consider selected periodic sequences such as $101010\ldots$, $110110\ldots$, $11101110\ldots$, etc. In the first example, the sequence 10 repeats with a period of two bit-cell intervals; in the second example, the sequence 110 repeats with a period of three intervals, and so on. We can deduce from this that the sequence $101010\ldots$ has the shortest period and will yield the highest fundamental frequency component. This means that other sequences will yield frequencies less than this and hence, for analysis purposes, the sequence with the shortest period is often referred to as the **worst-case sequence**.

For transmission purposes there are two basic binary signal types: **unipolar** and **bipolar** (see Section 2.3). An example of each is shown in Figure 2.7(a). With a unipolar signal, the signal amplitude varies between a positive voltage – say $+V$ – and 0 volts. We call such signals **return-to-zero (RZ)** signals. With a bipolar signal, the signal amplitude varies between a positive and a negative voltage level – say $+V$ and $-V$. These signals are **non-return-to-zero (NRZ)** signals. A unipolar signal has a mean signal level of $V/2$ while a bipolar signal has a mean of zero. The amplitude variation of a unipolar signal is V while for a bipolar signal it is $2V$. These differences yield slightly different **Fourier series** which, for the two signal types, are as follows:

Unipolar $\quad v(t) = \dfrac{V}{2} + \dfrac{2V}{\pi}\left\{\cos\omega_0 t - \dfrac{1}{3}\cos 3\omega_0 t + \dfrac{1}{5}\cos 5\omega_0 t - \cdots\right\}$

Bipolar $\quad v(t) = \dfrac{4V}{\pi}\left\{\cos\omega_0 t - \dfrac{1}{3}\cos 3\omega_0 t + \dfrac{1}{5}\cos 5\omega_0 t - \cdots\right\}$

where:

$v(t)$ is the voltage signal representation as a function of time
ω_0 is the fundamental frequency component in radians per second
$f_0 = \omega_0/2\pi$ is the fundamental frequency in Hz
$T = 1/f_0$ is the period of the fundamental frequency in seconds

We can deduce from these expressions that any periodic binary sequence is made up of an infinite series of sinusoidal signals including the fundamental frequency component, f_0, a third harmonic component, $3f_0$, a fifth harmonic, $5f_0$, and so on. Note that for binary sequences only the odd harmonic components are present and that their amplitude diminishes with increasing frequency. To illustrate the effect of this, the fundamental together with the third and fifth harmonics of a bipolar signal are shown in diagrammatic form in Figure 2.7(b).

Since a communications channel has a limited bandwidth, as we can deduce from the foregoing, when a binary data signal is transmitted over a channel, only those frequency components that are within the channel bandwidth will be received. The effect of this on the example binary signal 101010... is shown in diagrammatic form in Figure 2.7(c). As we can see, the larger the channel bandwidth, the more higher-frequency components are received and hence the closer is the received signal to the original (transmitted) signal.

As the bandwidth of a channel is measured in hertz, normally, it is shown as a function of frequency as illustrated in Figure 2.7(d). In the figure, there are three alternative bandwidths: the first allows sinusoidal signals of frequencies up to f_0 to pass unattenuated, the second up to $3f_0$, and the third up to $5f_0$. In practice, however, when only a two-level (binary) signal is being transmitted, the receiver simply samples the received signal at the center of each bit-cell interval. This means that the receiver need only discriminate between the binary 1 and 0 levels at the sampling instant and the exact shape of the signal outside these instances is less important. As we discussed earlier, the sequence 101010... generates the highest-frequency components while a sequence of all 1s or all 0s is equivalent to a zero frequency of the appropriate amplitude. Hence a channel with a bandwidth from 0 Hz to a frequency (in Hz) equal to half the bit rate (in bps) – that is, a channel that passes only frequency components up to the fundamental frequency of the binary sequence 101010 – can often give a satisfactory performance.

Example 2.2

A binary signal of rate 500 bps is to be transmitted over a communications channel. Derive the minimum bandwidth required assuming (a) the fundamental frequency only, (b) the fundamental and third harmonic, and (c) the fundamental, third and fifth harmonics of the worst-case sequence are to be received.

The worst-case sequence 101010... at 500 bps has a fundamental frequency component of 250 Hz. Hence the third harmonic is 750 Hz and the fifth harmonic 1250 Hz. The bandwidth required in each case is as follows:

(a) 0–250 Hz;   (b) 0–750 Hz;   (c) 0–1250 Hz

As we shall see in Section 2.5, it is also possible to transmit more than one bit with each change in signal amplitude thereby increasing the data bit rate. Nevertheless, the bandwidth of the channel always limits the maximum data rate that can be obtained. A formula derived by **Nyquist** for determining the maximum

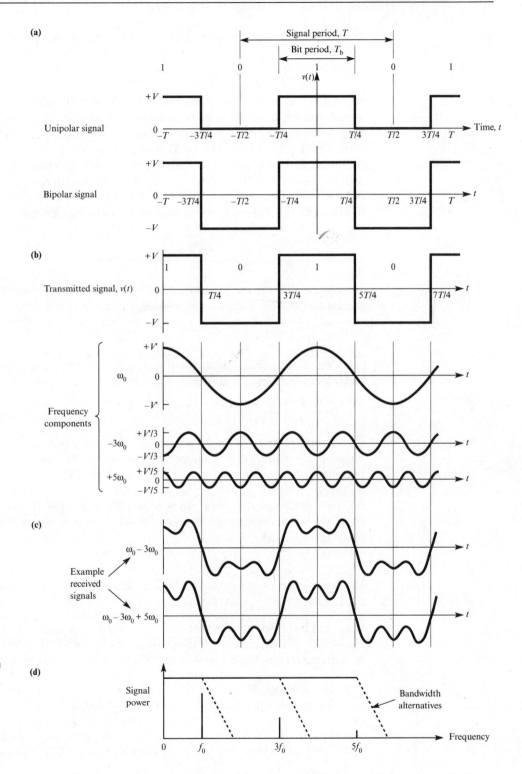

Figure 2.7
Effect of limited
bandwidth:
(a) alternative
binary signals;
(b) frequency
components of a
periodic binary
sequence;
(c) examples of
received signals;
(d) bandwidth
representations.

information transfer rate of a noiseless transmission channel, C, is given by the expression:

$$C = 2W \log_2 M$$

where W is the bandwidth of the channel in Hz and M is the number of levels per signaling element. In practice, as we shall see in Section 3.2.3, because with binary data extra bits are added for transmission control purposes, the useful data rate is often less than the actual bit rate. Therefore, when we transmit information over a communications channel three rates are involved – the signaling rate, the bit rate, and the data rate – all of which may be the same or different.

The duration of each bit (in seconds), T_b, is the reciprocal of the bit rate (in bits per second), R. Hence R is related to the signaling element time period, T_s, by the following expression:

$$R = \frac{\log_2 M}{T_s} = \frac{m}{T_s} \text{ bps}$$

Since T_b is the reciprocal of R, the effective time duration of each bit, T_b, is related to T_s by the following expression:

$$T_b = \frac{1}{R} = \frac{T_s}{m}$$

We can combine these two expressions to derive what is known as the **bandwidth efficiency** of a transmission channel, B. This is defined as:

$$B = \frac{R}{W} = \frac{m}{WT_s} = \frac{1}{WT_b} \text{ bps Hz}^{-1}$$

From this expression we can deduce that the higher the bit rate relative to the available bandwidth, the higher the bandwidth efficiency. Typical values of B range from 0.25 to 3.0 bps Hz^{-1}, the first corresponding to a low bit rate relative to the available bandwidth and the second a high bit rate that requires a relatively high signaling rate. In general, therefore, the higher the bandwidth efficiency the stricter are the design parameters of the associated equipment and hence the higher the cost.

Example 2.3

Data is to be transmitted over the PSTN using a transmission scheme with eight levels per signaling element. If the bandwidth of the PSTN is 3000 Hz, deduce the Nyquist maximum data transfer rate, C, and the modulation efficiency, B.

$$\begin{aligned} C &= 2W \log_2 M \\ &= 2 \times 3000 \times \log_2 8 \\ &= 2 \times 3000 \times 3 \\ &= 18\,000 \text{ bps} \end{aligned}$$

$$\begin{aligned} B &= \frac{1}{WT_b} \\ &= \frac{18\,000}{3000} = 6 \text{ bps Hz}^{-1} \end{aligned}$$

In practice both values will be less than these because of other effects such as noise.

2.2.3 Delay distortion

The rate of propagation of a sinusoidal signal along a transmission line varies with the frequency of the signal. Consequently, when we transmit a digital signal the various frequency components making up the signal arrive at the receiver with varying delays, resulting in **delay distortion** of the received signal. The amount of distortion increases as the bit rate of the transmitted data increases for the following reason: as the bit rate increases, so some of the frequency components associated with each bit transition are delayed and start to interfere with the frequency components associated with a later bit. Delay distortion is also known as **intersymbol interference**; its effect is to vary the bit transition instants of the received signal. Since the received signal is normally sampled at the nominal center of each bit cell, this can lead to incorrect interpretation of the received signal as the bit rate increases.

We can best observe the level of intersymbol interference associated with a transmission channel by means of an **eye diagram**, an example of which is shown in Figure 2.8. This diagram is obtained by displaying the signal received from the channel on an oscilloscope which is triggered by the transitions in the signal. Hence, assuming the received signal contains random binary 1 and 0 signal transitions, the oscilloscope will display all the possible signals superimposed on one another. Two examples are shown in the figure. In the absence of intersymbol interference the signal will be of the form shown as A, while with interference the signal will be of the form shown as B. We can deduce that the higher the level of interference, the smaller the central section – known as the **eye** – becomes.

2.2.4 Noise

In the absence of a signal, a transmission line or channel ideally has zero electrical signal present. In practice, however, there are random perturbations on the line even when no signal is being transmitted. This is known as the **line noise level**. In the limit, as a transmitted signal becomes attenuated, its amplitude is reduced to that of the line (background) noise. An important parameter associated with a transmission medium, therefore, is the ratio of the average power in a received signal, S, to the power in the noise level, N. The ratio S/N is known as the **signal-to-noise ratio (SNR)** and normally is expressed in decibels, that is:

$$\text{SNR} = 10 \log_{10}\left(\frac{S}{N}\right) \text{dB}$$

Clearly, a high SNR ratio means a high power signal relative to the prevailing noise level, resulting in a good-quality signal. Conversely, a low SNR

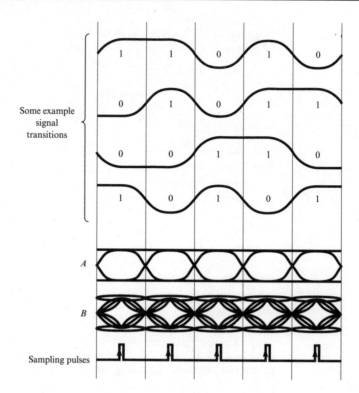

Figure 2.8
Examples of (binary) eye diagrams resulting from intersymbol interference: *A*, ideal; *B*, typical.

ratio means a low-quality signal. The theoretical maximum information (data) rate of a transmission channel is related to the SNR ratio and we can determine this rate using a formula attributed to Shannon and Hartley. This is known as the **Shannon–Hartley law**, which states:

$$C = W \log_2\left(1 + \frac{S}{N}\right) \text{ bps}$$

where C is the information (data) rate in bps, W is the bandwidth of the line/channel in Hz, S is the average signal power in watts and N is the random noise power in watts.

Example 2.4

■ ■ ■ ■ ■ ■ ■ ■ ■ ■

Assuming that a PSTN has a bandwidth of 3000 Hz and a typical signal-to-noise power ratio of 20 dB, determine the maximum theoretical information (data) rate that can be achieved.

$$\text{SNR} = 10 \log_{10}\left(\frac{S}{N}\right)$$

Therefore:

$$20 = 10 \log_{10}\left(\frac{S}{N}\right)$$

Hence:

$$\frac{S}{N} = 100$$

Now:

$$C = W \log_2\left(1 + \frac{S}{N}\right)$$

Therefore:

$$C = 3000 \times \log_2(1 + 1000)$$
$$= 19\,963 \text{ bps}$$

We identified one source of noise, crosstalk, in Section 2.1 when we discussed open-wire and twisted-pair transmission lines. Crosstalk is caused by unwanted electrical coupling between adjacent lines. This coupling results in a signal that is being transmitted in one line being picked up by adjacent lines as a small but finite (noise) signal. An example of crosstalk is when you hear another call in the background when you use the telephone; even though you are not talking, a signal is still present on the line.

There are several types of crosstalk but in most cases the most limiting impairment is **near-end crosstalk** or **NEXT**. This is also known as **self-crosstalk** since it is caused by the strong signal output by a transmitter circuit being coupled (and hence interfering) with the much weaker signal at the input to the local receiver circuit. As we noted in Section 2.2.1, the received signal is normally significantly attenuated and distorted and hence the amplitude of the coupled signal from the transmit section can be comparable with the received signal.

Special integrated circuits known as **adaptive NEXT cancelers** are now used to overcome this type of impairment. A typical arrangement is shown in Figure 2.9. The canceler circuit adaptively forms an attenuated replica of the crosstalk signal that is coupled into the receive line from the local transmitter and this is subtracted from the received signal. Such circuits are now used in many applications involving UTP cable, for example, to transmit data at high bit rates.

Another related form of noise pick-up is **impulse noise**. This, as its name implies, is caused by impulses of electrical energy associated with external activity or equipment being picked up by a signal line. Examples are a lightning discharge or, in the case of a telephone network, electrical impulses associated with the switching circuits used in old telephone exchanges. Normally, the latter example takes the form of loud clicks on the line and, although unimportant during a telephone conversation, such sources can be particularly troublesome

(a)

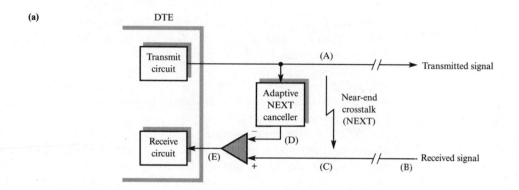

(b)

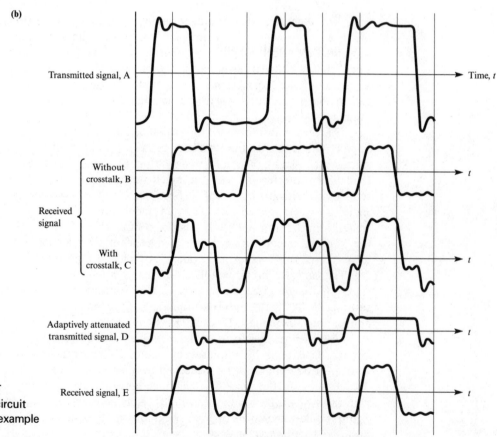

Figure 2.9
Adaptive NEXT
cancelers: (a) circuit
schematic; (b) example
waveforms.

when transmitting data. An impulse (click) of, say, one-half of a second might corrupt 1200 bits of data at a transmission rate of 2400 bps. Fortunately, these sources of noise are relatively infrequent.

Both crosstalk and impulse noise are caused by electrical activity that is external to the transmission line. In contrast, a third type of noise, known as **thermal noise**, is present in all electronic devices and transmission media irrespective of any external effects. It is caused by the thermal agitation of electrons associated with each atom in the device or transmission line material. At all temperatures above absolute zero, all transmission media experience thermal noise. It is made up of random frequency components (across the complete frequency spectrum) of continuously varying amplitude. It is also known, therefore, as **white noise**.

We should stress that the Shannon–Hartley law gives the theoretical maximum information rate. When considering the effect of noise in practice, it is important to determine the minimum signal level that must be used, relative to the noise level, to achieve a specific minimum **bit error rate ratio**, that is, over a defined period, an acceptably low probability that a single bit will be misinterpreted by the receiver. For example, a bit error rate probability of 10^{-4} means that, on average, 1 bit in every 10^4 received will be misinterpreted. The energy measured in joules ($=$ watts $\times$ seconds) per bit in a signal, E_b, is given by the following formula:

$$E_b = ST_b \text{ watt-second}$$

where S is the signal power in watts and T_b is the time period for 1 bit in seconds. Now the data transmission rate R equals $1/T_b$ and hence:

$$E_b = \frac{S}{R}$$

The level of (thermal) noise in a bandwidth of 1 Hz in any transmission line is given by the formula:

$$N_0 = kT \text{ watts Hz}^{-1}$$

where N_0 is the noise power density in watts Hz^{-1}, k is Boltzmann's constant (1.3803×10^{-23} joule K^{-1}) and T is the temperature in kelvin (K).

To quantify the effect of noise, the energy per bit E_b is expressed as a ratio of the noise energy per Hz N_0:

$$\frac{E_b}{N_0} = \frac{S/R}{N_0} = \frac{S/R}{kT}$$

or, in decibels:

$$\frac{E_b}{N_0}(\text{dB}) = 10 \log_{10}\left(\frac{S}{R}\right) - 10 \log_{10}(kT)$$

We can readily deduce that the signal power level S required to achieve an acceptable E_b/N_0 ratio – and hence minimum bit error rate – increases with the temperature T and bit rate R.

The expression for E_b/N_0 can also be expressed in terms of the channel bandwidth, W. Since N_0 is the noise power density in watts Hz^{-1}, for a channel of bandwidth W Hz the noise power in a received signal, N, is given by:

$$N = WN_0$$

Hence

$$\frac{E_b}{N_0} = \frac{S}{N}\frac{W}{R}$$

or, in decibels:

$$\frac{E_b}{N_0}\,(\text{dB}) = 10\,\log_{10}\left(\frac{S}{N}\right) + 10\,\log_{10} W - 10\,\log_{10} R$$

As we shall see in Section 2.5, when we transmit data over the PSTN we must first convert the digital data into an analog form using a technique known as **modulation**. Similarly, at the destination, we recover the digital data using the reverse process known as **demodulation**. In practice, there is a range of different modulation/demodulation schemes in use and the value of E_b/N_0 required to achieve a particular bit error rate varies for each different scheme. For example, to achieve a bit error rate of 10^{-6} using either amplitude-shift keying or frequency-shift keying (see Section 2.5.1) requires an E_b/N_0 of 13 dB, while with phase-shift keying an E_b/N_0 of 10 dB is required. Therefore, for a channel of a given bandwidth, to achieve the same data rate the minimum received signal-to-noise power ratio varies for the different modulation schemes.

Example 2.5

Data is to be transmitted over the PSTN which has a bandwidth of 3000 Hz. If the mean signal-to-noise power ratio at the receiver is to be 12 dB, determine the maximum data rate that can be obtained assuming an E_b/N_0 of (a) 13 dB and (b) 10 dB. Determine the bandwidth efficiency in each case.

$$10\,\log_{10} R = \frac{S}{N}\,(\text{dB}) + 10\,\log_{10} W - \frac{E_b}{N_0}\,(\text{dB})$$

Bandwidth efficiency, $B = R/W$

(a) $10\,\log_{10} R = 12 + 10\,\log_{10} 3000 - 13 = 33.77$

Hence:

$R = 2382.32\,\text{bps}$ and $B = 0.79$

(b) $10\,\log_{10} R = 12 + 34.77 - 10 = 36.77$

Hence:

$R = 4753.35\,\text{bps}$ and $B = 1.58$

2.3 Signal types

When two items of equipment (DTEs) are close to one another and we use only modest bit rates, we can transmit data using two-wire open lines and simple interface circuits. These change the signal levels used within the equipment to a level compatible with the interconnecting cable. However, as the physical separation between the DTEs and the bit rate increase, we must employ more sophisticated circuits and techniques. Moreover, if the DTEs are in different parts of the country (or world) and no public data communication facilities are available, the only cost-effective approach is to use lines provided by the authorities responsible for the provision of telephony and other telecommunication services. The latter are known as PTTs. When we use this type of communication medium, we normally have to convert the electrical signals output by the source DTE into a form analogous to the signals used to convey spoken messages. Similarly, on reception we must convert these signals back into a form suitable for use by the destination DTE. The equipment used to perform these functions is known as a **modem**. Some of the different signal types used by modems and other forms of transmission lines are discussed in the following sections.

2.3.1 V.28

To enable manufacturers of different types of equipment to use the transmission facilities of the switched telephone network, a range of modems is available. As will be expanded upon in Section 2.5.1, these operate at different rates and use various types of modulation methods. There are many manufacturers of modems. To ensure two modems from different manufacturers can communicate with one another, the precise operation of each modem type has been standardized. A standard interface has been defined for use with all of the modem types which specifies both the number and function of the electrical signals, the physical size of the plug and socket, and the pin configurations within them. This is known either as the **EIA-232D interface** (defined by the EIA) or the **V.24 interface** (defined by the ITU-T), the EIA-232D interface being the latest version of the earlier RS-232A, B and C standards, the first of which originated in the late 1950s.

Normally a modem is located within a short distance of the DTE and, since the bandwidth of an analog telephone circuit is relatively low (in the order of 3000 Hz), the maximum bit rate used is also low. Hence since the introduction of the modem, the same interface has been adopted as the standard for connecting any character-oriented peripheral device – for example a terminal or a printer – to a computer, thus allowing peripherals from different manufacturers to be connected to the same computer.

Because of the short distances (less than a few centimeters) between neighboring integrated circuits within a DTE, the signal levels used to represent binary data are often quite small. For example, a common logic family used in digital equipment is **transistor–transistor logic (TTL)**. This uses a voltage signal of between 2.0 V and 5.0 V to represent a binary 1 and a voltage of between 0.2 V and 0.8 V to represent a binary 0. Voltages between these two signal levels can yield an indeterminate state and, in the worst case, if the voltage level is near one of the limits, even modest signal attenuation or electrical interference can lead to misinterpretation. Consequently, the voltage levels used when connecting two items of equipment are normally greater than those used to connect integrated circuits within the equipment.

The electrical signal levels defined for use with the EIA-232D/V.24 interface are defined in recommendation V.28. The signals used in both standards are shown in Figure 2.10 together with the appropriate interface circuits. The voltage signals used on the lines are symmetric with respect to the ground reference signal and are at least 3 V: $+3$ V for a binary 0 and -3 V for a binary 1. In practice, the actual voltage levels used are determined by the supply voltages applied to the interface circuits, ±12 V or even ±15 V not being uncommon. The transmit circuits convert the low-level signal voltages used within the equipment to the higher voltage levels used on the transmission lines. Similarly, the receive circuits perform the reverse function. Interface circuits, known as **line drivers** and **line receivers** perform the necessary voltage conversion functions.

The relatively large voltage levels used with these interfaces mean that the effects of signal attenuation and noise are much less significant than at, say, TTL levels. The EIA-232D/V.24 interface normally uses a flat ribbon or multicore cable with a single ground reference wire for connecting the equipment. Noise picked up in a signal wire can therefore be troublesome. To reduce crosstalk, a **capacitor** is commonly connected across the output of the transmitter circuit. This rounds off the transition edges of the transmitted signals, which in turn removes some of the troublesome higher-frequency components in the signal. As the line length or signal bit rate increases, the attenuation of the line reduces the received signal levels to the point at which even low-amplitude external noise signals produce erroneous operation. The EIA-232D and V.24 standards specify maximum physical separations of less than 15 m and bit rates lower than 20 kbps, although larger values are often used when connecting a peripheral to a computer.

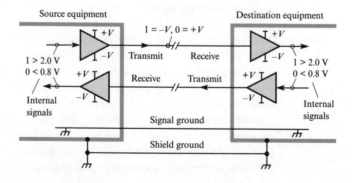

Figure 2.10
V.28 signal levels – single ended/ unbalanced.

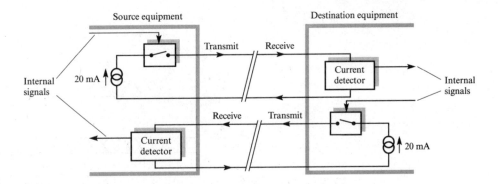

Figure 2.11
20 mA current loop.

2.3.2   20 mA current loop

An alternative to the EIA-232D/V.28 standard is the 20 mA current loop. This, as the name implies, utilizes a current signal, rather than a voltage. Although it does not extend the available bit rate, it substantially increases the potential physical separation between two communicating devices. The basic approach is shown in Figure 2.11.

Essentially, the state of a switch (relay or other similar device) is controlled by the bit stream to be transmitted: the switch is closed for a binary 1, thus passing a current (pulse) of 20 mA, and opened for a binary 0, thus stopping the current flow. At the receiver, the flow of the current is detected by a matching current-sensitive circuit and the transmitted binary signal is reproduced.

The noise immunity of a current loop interface is much better than a basic voltage-driven interface since, as can be seen from Figure 2.11, it uses a pair of wires for each signal. This means that any external noise signals are normally picked up in both wires – often referred to as **common-mode noise** or **pick-up** – which has a minimal effect on the basic current-sensitive receiver circuit. Consequently, 20 mA current loop interfaces are particularly suitable for driving long lines (up to 1 km), but at modest bit rates because of the limited operational rate of the switches and current-sensitive circuits. It is for this reason that some manufacturers often provide two separate interfaces with a piece of equipment, one producing voltage output signals and the other 20 mA current signals. The user can then decide which interface to use depending on the physical separation between the equipment.

2.3.3 · RS-422A/V.11

If we increase both the physical separation and the bit rate, then we should use the alternative RS-422A/V.11 signal definition. This is based on the use of a twisted-pair cable and a pair of **differential** (also referred to as **balanced** or **double-ended**) **transmitter and receiver circuits**. A typical circuit arrangement is shown in Figure 2.12(a).

A differential transmitter produces twin signals of equal and opposite polarity for every binary 1 or 0 signal to be transmitted. As the differential

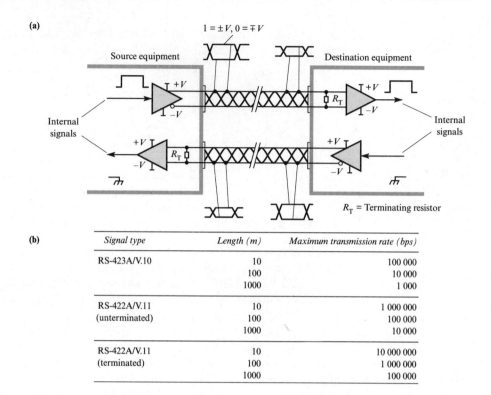

Figure 2.12
Differential signals:
(a) EIA-422A/V.11
signal levels;
(b) maximum
transmission rates/
distance.

(b)

Signal type	Length (m)	Maximum transmission rate (bps)
RS-423A/V.10	10	100 000
	100	10 000
	1000	1 000
RS-422A/V.11 (unterminated)	10	1 000 000
	100	100 000
	1000	10 000
RS-422A/V.11 (terminated)	10	10 000 000
	100	1 000 000
	1000	100 000

receiver is sensitive only to the difference between the two signals on its two inputs, noise picked up by both wires will not affect receiver operation. Differential receivers, therefore, are said to have good **common-mode rejection** properties. A derivative of the RS-422A, the RS-423A/V.10, can be used to accept single-ended (**unbalanced**) voltages output by an EIA-232D interface with a differential receiver. The RS-422A is suitable for use with twisted-pair cable for physical separations of between 10 m at 10 Mbps and 1000 m at 100 kbps.

An important parameter of any transmission line is its **characteristic impedance (Z_0)** because a receiver absorbs all of the received signal only if the line is terminated by a resistor equal to Z_0. If this is not the case, **signal reflections** occur which further distort the received signal. Lines are therefore normally terminated by a resistor equal to Z_0, with values from 50 to 200 Ω being common. A summary of the alternative cable lengths and transmission rates with both signal types is given in Figure 2.12(b).

2.3.4   Coaxial cable signals

In contrast to the low bandwidth available with a connection through an analog-switched telephone network, the usable bandwidth with a coaxial cable can be as much as 350 MHz (or higher). We can utilize potentially high bandwidth in one of two ways:

(1)   **Baseband mode**, in which all the available bandwidth is used to derive a single high bit rate (10 Mbps or higher) transmission path (channel).

(2)   **Broadband mode**, in which the available bandwidth is divided to derive a number of lower bandwidth subchannels (and hence transmission paths) on one cable.

Baseband mode

In baseband mode, normally the cable is driven from a single-ended voltage source. Because of the geometry of coaxial cable, however, the effect of external interference is very low. A number of matching transmit and receive interface circuits are available for use with coaxial cable. A typical connection is shown in Figure 2.13(a), which also shows the effect of terminating a line with the correct terminating resistance, Z_0. Such arrangements are suitable for transmitting data at up to 10 Mbps over a distance of several hundred meters.

In some applications, the cable is used exclusively for the transmission of data between two systems – that is, **point-to-point** – while in others the normally high bit rate transmission channel is time-shared by a number of systems – referred to as **multipoint** or **multidrop** configuration. Both arrangements are shown in Figure 2.13(b).

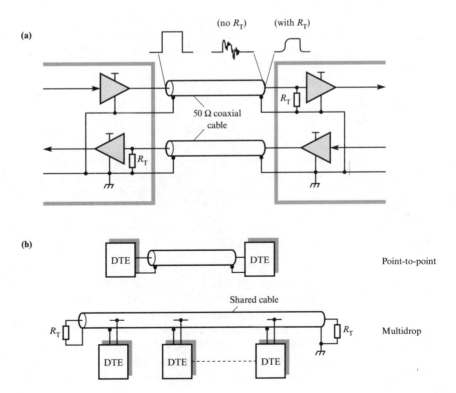

Figure 2.13
Baseband principles:
(a) coaxial cable
signals; (b) connection
methods.

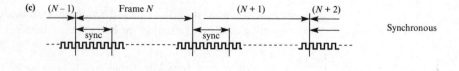

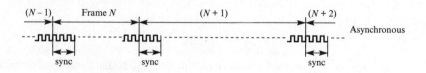

Figure 2.13 (cont.)
(c) TDM methods.

Time-division multiplexing (TDM) is used to share the available capacity of a baseband transmission channel. Two types of TDM are used:

(1)   Synchronous (or fixed cycle)   Each user has access to the channel at precisely defined (synchronized) time intervals.

(2)   Asynchronous (or on demand)   Each user has random access to the channel and, on acquiring access, is the sole user of the channel for the duration of the transmission.

These two forms of TDM are shown diagrammatically in Figure 2.13(c).

As we discuss in Chapter 3, data is normally transmitted between two systems (DTEs) in the form of **frames** – blocks of characters or bytes – and, with synchronous TDM, each frame is of a fixed length. To ensure that all systems connected to the (shared) cable transmit data at their allotted time, a special bit pattern, known as the **synchronizing** (or simply **sync**) **pattern** is transmitted at the beginning of each frame. From this, each system can determine both the start of each frame and the position of the frame (frame number) in a complete cycle of frames. With asynchronous TDM, in addition to being able to detect the start of each new frame (with a sync pattern), a mechanism is employed to ensure that each system can gain access to the channel in a fair way, since each system has random access to the channel. As will be described in Chapter 6, asynchronous TDM is used in certain types of **local area data network**.

Broadband mode

Using the broadband mode, multiple (independent and concurrent) transmission channels are derived from a single distribution (coaxial) cable using a technique known as **frequency-division multiplexing (FDM)**. FDM requires a device known as a **radio frequency (RF) modem** – similar in principle to the (audio frequency) modems used with the PSTN – between each connected device and the cable. We use the term 'radio frequency' because the frequencies used for each channel are in the radio frequency spectrum. The selected (carrier) frequency for the transmit (forward) direction is modulated with the data to be transmitted and the selected frequency for the receive (reverse) direction is demodulated to derive the received data.

The bandwidth required for each channel is determined by the desired data (bit) rate and the modulation method. Typically the bandwidth efficiency of RF modems is between 0.25 and 1.0 bits per Hz. Thus, a 9600 bps channel may require a bandwidth of about 20 kHz and a 10 Mbps channel around 18 MHz.

The principles of broadband working and the subunits within an RF modem are summarized in Figure 2.14. Normally, modulation (and demodulation) within a modem is carried out in two phases. Firstly, a selected frequency signal is modulated, using phase- or frequency-shift keying, by the data to be transmitted. Then, the modulated signal is mixed (multiplied) with a second frequency so that the frequency-translated signal is in the assigned frequency band. The filters shown in Figure 2.14 allow only the signals associated with the assigned frequency band to be transmitted (on output) or processed (on input).

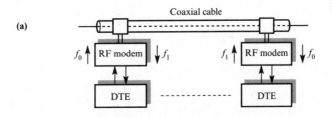

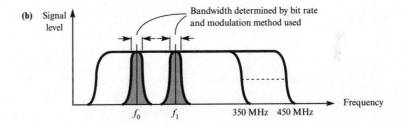

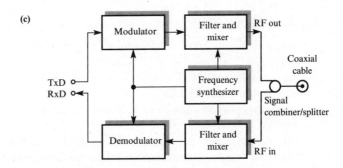

Figure 2.14
Broadband principles:
(a) cable schematic;
(b) bandwidth; (c) RF
modem schematic.

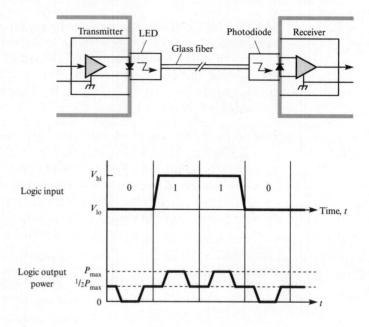

Figure 2.15
Optical fiber signals.

2.3.5 Optical fiber signals

There are a variety of forms of optical signal encoding. One, based on a bipolar encoding scheme, is shown in Figure 2.15. This type of encoding produces a three-level optical output which makes it suitable for operating the cable from DC (zero frequency equivalent to a continuous string of binary 0s or 1s) up to 50 Mbps. The three optical power output levels are zero, half-maximum power and maximum power. The transmit module performs the conversion from the internal binary voltage levels to the three-level optical signal that is applied to the fiber using special connectors and a high-speed LED. Other signal encoding schemes used with optical fiber are given in Section 3.3.1.

At the receiver, the fiber is terminated with a special connector to a high-speed photodiode housed within a special receiver module. This contains the control electronics needed to convert the electrical signal output by the photo-diode, which is proportional to the light level, into the internal voltage levels corresponding to binary 1s and 0s.

Currently, optical fiber is used mainly in a point-to-point mode but, as with baseband coaxial cable, the transmission capacity available may be utilized either for a single high bit rate channel or, with (normally synchronous) TDM, to derive multiple lower bit rate channels on a single link.

2.3.6 Satellite and radio

In Section 2.1 we indicated that transmission channels in satellite and other radio-based systems are obtained by frequency division multiplexing. In addition, the available (baseband) capacity of each channel is normally further subdivided using synchronous time-division multiplexing techniques.

A number of different **access control methods** are used to control access to the available capacity including:

- **Random access** All stations compete for a transmission channel in a random (uncontrolled) way.

- **Fixed assignment** Both the channel frequency and the channel time slot are preassigned to each ground or cordless station.

- **Demand assignment** When a station wishes to transmit data, it first requests channel capacity from a central site which assigns the required capacity (time slots) to the requesting station.

Random access is the oldest type of access control method and was first used to control access to a single (shared) satellite channel. It works only in those applications in which firstly, the total offered load is only a small fraction of the available channel capacity and secondly, all transmissions are randomly distributed. The technique is known as **Aloha** since it was first used by the University of Hawaii to link a community of computers distributed around several islands to a central computer located on the island of Oahu. The two versions of the scheme are shown in Figure 2.16(a).

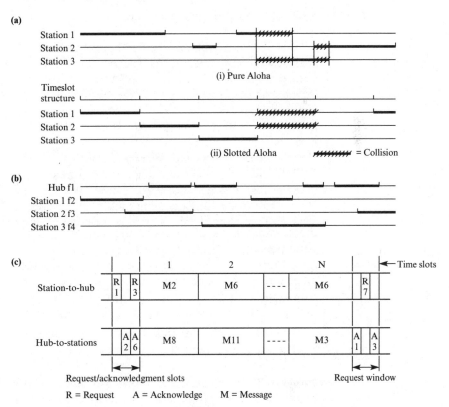

Figure 2.16
Satellite and radio access control methods: (a) Aloha; (b) preassigned FDMA; (c) demand-assigned TDMA.

With pure Aloha, when a station has a message (data) to transmit, it simply transmits (broadcasts) it. If a second station starts to transmit while the first station is transmitting its message, both transmissions are corrupted and a **collision** occurs. Thus the scheme only works satisfactorily if the probability of two transmissions overlapping is small. Assuming randomly generated messages, the mean achievable throughput with this scheme is less than 20% of the available capacity. This can be improved by establishing a synchronous time slot structure and constraining all transmissions to be carried out in these time slots. This scheme is known as **slotted Aloha** and, because a transmission can corrupt another transmission only in the same time slot, utilizations in excess of 30% are possible.

With fixed assignment, both the channel frequency and/or channel time slot are preassigned to each station in advance. In general, the preassignment of frequency channels is easier than time slot assignment. For example, in satellite applications based on a central hub, a fixed frequency channel is normally preassigned to each VSAT and the central site then broadcasts on another preassigned frequency channel. Generally, since there is only a single hub-to-VSAT channel, the frequency band (and hence bit rate) of this is wider than those used for VSAT-to-hub transmissions. Typical bit rates are 64 kbps for each VSAT-to-hub channel and up to 2 Mbps for the hub-to-VSAT broadcast channel. This type of access control scheme, known as **preassigned frequency-division multiple access** or **preassigned FDMA**, is shown in Figure 2.16(b).

We can achieve much better channel utilization by using a demand assignment access control method. This scheme provides a number of time slots – known as **request time slots** – in which a VSAT or cordless station can make a request to the hub or base station site for the use of one or more message time slots. If free capacity is available, the central site assigns specific message time slots for that transmission and informs the requesting station in a corresponding **acknowledge time slot**. Figure 2.16(c) illustrates this scheme which is known as **demand-assigned time-division multiple access (TDMA)**.

As we can see from Figure 2.16(c), a request slot is much shorter than normal message slots. A request message includes the identity of the requesting station and, assuming multiple time slots per message, the number of message time slots required. The corresponding request acknowledge message then indicates which message time slots should be used. All transmissions from the central site are made directly with the identity of the intended recipient station at the head of the message. To decrease the probability of a collision occurring in request slots, a station randomly selects a slot to use. If a collision does occur (indicated by no response) then the station tries again in the next **request window**.

Finally, we should stress before leaving the subject of radio that the BER of a radio link (channel) is, in general, much higher than for a fixed-wire link. Consequently, as we shall see in Chapter 3, small message blocks are normally used and more sophisticated error detection and correction methods employed.

2.4 Signal propagation delay

There is always a short but finite time delay for a signal (electrical, optical or radio) to propagate (travel) from one end of a transmission medium to the other. This is known as the **transmission propagation delay**, T_p, of the medium. At best, signals propagate (radiate) through free space at the speed of light (3×10^8 ms^{-1}). The speed of propagation for twisted-pair wire or coaxial cable is a fraction of this figure. Typically, it is in the region of 2×10^8 ms^{-1}, that is, a signal will take 0.5×10^{-8} s to travel 1 m through the medium. Although this may seem insignificant, in some situations the resulting delay is important.

In Chapter 3, we show that data is normally transmitted in blocks (also known as frames) of bits. On receipt of a block, an acknowledgment of correct (or otherwise) receipt is returned to the sender. An important parameter of a data link, therefore, is the **round-trip delay** associated with the link, that is, the time delay between the first bit of a block being transmitted by the sender and the last bit of its associated acknowledgment being received. Clearly, this is a function not only of the time taken to transmit the frame at the link bit rate – known as the transmission delay, T_x – but also of the propagation delay of the link, T_p. The relative weighting of the two times varies for different types of data link and hence the two times are often expressed as a ratio a such that:

$$a = \frac{T_p}{T_x}$$

where:

$$T_p = \frac{\text{physical separation } S \text{ in meters}}{\text{velocity of propagation } V \text{ in meters per second}}$$

and:

$$T_x = \frac{\text{number of bits to be transmitted } N}{\text{link bit rate } R \text{ in bits per second}}$$

Example 2.6

A 1000-bit block of data is to be transmitted between two DTEs. Determine the ratio of the propagation delay to the transmission delay, a, for the following types of data link.

(a)   100 m of twisted-pair wire and a transmission rate of 10 kbps.

(b)   10 km of coaxial cable and a transmission rate of 1 Mbps.

(c)   50 000 km of free space (satellite link) and a transmission rate of 10 Mbps.

   Assume that the velocity of propagation of an electrical signal within each type of cable is 2×10^8 ms^{-1} and that through free space is 3×10^8 ms^{-1}.

(a) $T_p = \dfrac{S}{V} = \dfrac{100}{2 \times 10^8} = 5 \times 10^{-7}$ s

$T_x = \dfrac{N}{R} = \dfrac{1000}{10 \times 10^3} = 0.1$ s

$a = \dfrac{T_p}{T_x} = \dfrac{5 \times 10^{-7}}{0.1} = 5 \times 10^{-6}$

(b) $T_p = \dfrac{S}{V} = \dfrac{10 \times 10^3}{2 \times 10^8} = 5 \times 10^{-5}$ s

$T_x = \dfrac{N}{R} = \dfrac{1000}{1 \times 10^6} = 1 \times 10^{-3}$ s

$a = \dfrac{T_p}{T_x} = \dfrac{5 \times 10^{-5}}{1 \times 10^{-3}} = 5 \times 10^{-2}$

(c) $T_p = \dfrac{S}{V} = \dfrac{5 \times 10^7}{3 \times 10^8} = 1.67 \times 10^{-1}$ s

$T_x = \dfrac{N}{R} = \dfrac{1000}{10 \times 10^6} = 1 \times 10^{-4}$ s

$a = \dfrac{T_p}{T_x} = \dfrac{1.67 \times 10^{-1}}{1 \times 10^{-4}} = 1.67 \times 10^3$

We can conclude from Example 2.6 that:

- If a is less than 1, then the round-trip delay is determined primarily by the transmission delay.
- If a is equal to 1, then both delays have equal effect.
- If a is greater than 1, then the propagation delay dominates.

Furthermore, in case (c) it is interesting to note that, providing blocks are transmitted contiguously, there will be:

$$10 \times 10^6 \times 1.67 \times 10^{-1} = 1.67 \times 10^6 \text{ bits}$$

in transit between the two DTEs at any one time, that is, the sending DTE will have transmitted 1.67×10^6 bits before the first bit arrives at the receiving DTE. We shall discuss these implications in Chapter 3.

2.5 Public carrier circuits

When we wish to transmit data between two DTEs in the same building or establishment, we (relatively) simply instal a cable. Typically, this cable may be unshielded or shielded twisted pair, coaxial or optical fiber. In some instances, radio may be used. When we wish to transmit data between two DTEs in different establishments, however, we can achieve this only by using microwave or satellite links, or lines from one of the public carrier telephone companies. The last solution is widely used; both switched circuits and leased (dedicated) circuits are possible.

We can set up switched circuits using the analog PSTN or an ISDN, depending on availability. Although the analog PSTN was designed specifically for voice communications, it is also possible to transmit data using a modem. In the case of an ISDN, we can set up calls and transmit data directly. Also much higher bit rates are possible.

With leased circuits, although in some circumstances we must still use leased PSTN lines – and hence modems – in most cases leased circuits are now all-digital for reasons that we shall see in Section 2.5.2. Since public carrier circuits are used extensively in many data communication applications, this section describes the characteristics of such circuits in terms of their usage.

2.5.1 Analog PSTN circuits

When we wish to transmit data using existing analog PSTN transmission lines, we must convert the electrical signals output by the source DTE into a form that is acceptable to the PSTN. The latter was designed for speech communications which are assumed to be made up of a mix of (audio) frequencies in the range 400–3400 Hz, as shown in Figure 2.17.

The range of signal frequencies the PSTN passes – its bandwidth – is from 400 to 3400 Hz or simply 3000 Hz. This means that a telephone line will not pass the low-frequency signals that could occur if, for example, the data stream to be transmitted is made up of a continuous string of binary 1s or 0s. For this reason, it is not possible simply to apply two voltage levels to the telephone line, since zero output will be obtained for both levels if the binary data stream is all 1s or all 0s. Instead, we must convert the binary data into a form compatible with a speech signal at the sending end of the line and reconvert this signal back into its binary form at the receiver. The circuit that performs the first operation is

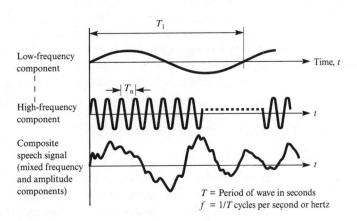

Figure 2.17
Speech waveform
frequency
components.

known as a **modulator**, and the circuit performing the reverse function a **demodulator**. Since each end of a data link normally both sends and receives data, the combined device is known as a modem.

Using modems, data can be transmitted through the PSTN either by dialing and thereby setting up a switched path through the network, as with a normal telephone call, or by leasing a **dedicated** (or **leased**) **line** from the PTT. Since leased lines bypass the normal switching equipment (exchange) in the network and are set up on a permanent or long-term basis, they are economically justifiable only for applications having a high utilization factor. An added advantage of a leased line is that its operating characteristics can be more accurately quantified than for a short-term switched circuit, making it feasible to use higher signaling (bit) rates. We shall now consider a number of alternative modulation methods.

Modulation

We employ three basic types of modulation for the conversion of a binary signal into a form suitable for transmission over the PSTN: amplitude, frequency and phase. Since binary data is to be transmitted, only two signal levels are required. The signal switches (shifts) between these two levels as the binary data signal alternates (keys) between a binary 1 and 0. The three basic modulation types are known as **amplitude-shift keying (ASK)**, **frequency-shift keying (FSK)** and **phase-shift keying (PSK)**, respectively. We shall discuss the general principle of each scheme separately.

Amplitude-shift keying.   The principle of operation of ASK is shown in Figure 2.18(a). A waveform set is given in Figure 2.18(b). Essentially, the amplitude of a single-frequency **audio tone** is switched between two levels at a rate determined by the bit rate of the transmitted binary data signal. The single-frequency audio tone is known as the **carrier frequency** since, as we shall see, the binary data signal is effectively carried by the carrier signal during its transmission through the channel. The carrier is selected to be within the band of frequencies – the bandwidth – available with the PSTN. The amount of bandwidth required to transmit the binary data signal is then determined by the signal's bit rate: the higher the bit rate, the larger the required bandwidth. In practice, the different modulation methods require different amounts of bandwidth to transmit a binary signal and hence it is necessary to quantify the level of bandwidth required with each method.

Mathematically, the modulation operation – ASK, FSK or PSK – is equivalent to multiplying the carrier signal by the binary data signal. Since the carrier is a single-frequency audio tone, assuming a unity-amplitude signal, we can represent it by the following expression:

$$v_c(t) = \cos \omega_c t$$

where ω_c is the carrier frequency in radians per second. Also, as we discussed in Section 2.2, we can represent a unipolar periodic data signal, $v_d(t)$, with unity amplitude and fundamental frequency ω_0, by the Fourier series:

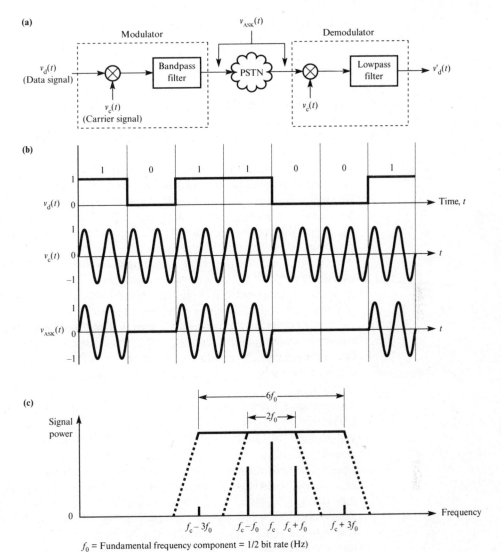

Figure 2.18
Amplitude-shift
keying: (a) circuit
schematic;
(b) waveform set;
(c) bandwidth
alternatives.

f_0 = Fundamental frequency component = 1/2 bit rate (Hz)

$$v_d(t) = \frac{1}{2} + \frac{2}{\pi}\left\{\cos\omega_0 t - \frac{1}{3}\cos 3\omega_0 t + \frac{1}{5}\cos 5\omega_0 t - \cdots\right\}$$

Hence ASK can be represented mathematically by the following expression:

$$v_{ASK}(t) = v_c(t) \cdot v_d(t)$$

that is:

$$v_{ASK}(t) = \frac{1}{2}\cos\omega_c t + \frac{2}{\pi}\left\{\cos\omega_c t \cdot \cos\omega_0 t - \frac{1}{3}\cos\omega_c t \cdot \cos 3\omega_0 t + \cdots\right\}$$

However:

$$2 \cos A \cos B = \cos(A - B) + \cos(A + B)$$

Hence:

$$v_{ASK}(t) = \frac{1}{2} \cos \omega_c t + \frac{1}{\pi} \{ \cos(\omega_c - \omega_0)t + \cos(\omega_c + \omega_0)t$$
$$- \frac{1}{3} \cos(\omega_c - 3\omega_0)t - \frac{1}{3} \cos(\omega_c + 3\omega_0)t + \cdots \}$$

We can therefore deduce that an ASK signal is equivalent to the original data signal translated up in frequency by the carrier signal, ω_c, but with two frequency components for the fundamental – $(\omega_c - \omega_0)$ and $(\omega_c + \omega_0)$ – and two for the harmonics – $(\omega_c - 3\omega_0)$ and $(\omega_c + 3\omega_0)$. All are equally spaced either side of the carrier and are known as **sidebands**. The bandwidth of an ASK signal, therefore, is as shown in Figure 2.18(c).

From our discussion on bandwidth, recall that the higher the bandwidth, the closer the received signal is to that transmitted. In general, however, satisfactory operation can be obtained if the bandwidth of the channel is sufficient to pass the fundamental frequency component of the sequence 101010 . . . since the bandwidth required for all other sequences is less than this. This sequence has a fundamental frequency component, f_0 (in Hz), which is equal to half the bit rate (in bps). Hence, the minimum bandwidth required for ASK is equal to the bit rate in Hz ($2f_0$) or, to receive the third harmonic components, three times the bit rate in Hz ($6f_0$).

From Figure 2.18(c) we can deduce that with ASK the carrier signal is present in the received signal even though it does not have an information signal – $f_0, 3f_0$, etc. – within it. From the discussion on the Nyquist formula in Section 2.2, you may recall that, for a binary signal, the maximum data rate achievable from a channel is twice the bandwidth. Alternatively, assuming a bandwidth of $2f_0$, the Nyquist rate is twice that just computed. The reason for this is that both primary sidebands are being used in the determination of the minimum required bandwidth. As we can see from Figure 2.18(c), either of the sidebands contains the required signal, f_0. To use the bandwidth more efficiently, therefore, we can use the **bandpass filter** shown in the circuit schematic to limit the band of frequencies passed to $f_c + (f_c + f_0)$ thereby removing the lower sideband, $(f_c - f_0)$. This reduces the bandwidth required to f_0 and hence yields the Nyquist rate. However, this will halve the power in the primary sideband signal relative to the carrier signal, as we can see from Figure 2.18(c). The power reduction, in turn, reduces the signal-to-noise ratio and hence results in an increase in the bit error rate ratio.

To recover the transmitted data signal from the received signal, we pass the latter through a **demodulator circuit**. In this, the received signal is again multiplied by the same carrier signal. This produces two versions of the received signal: one centered around a frequency of $2f_c$ ($f_c + f_c$) and the other centered around zero frequency ($f_c - f_c$). Both versions contain the required information in the sidebands, but we can select the latter by passing the signal through a

lowpass filter. This filter is designed to pass only the frequencies 0 through f_0 or, if the third harmonic is to be received, 0 through $3f_0$. The output from the lowpass filter, therefore, is the bandwidth-limited version of the transmitted data signal.

Although ASK is relatively simple to implement, it was not used in the earlier-generation low bit rate modems. At that time, all of the long-haul transmission and switching systems used in the PSTN were analog, that is, all source voice – and modulated data – signals were transmitted and switched in their original analog form throughout. This often resulted in varying levels of signal attenuation caused, for example, by varying propagation conditions over different routes through the network, and hence schemes based on amplitude variations were not used. More recently, however, all transmission and switching within the network has been carried out digitally. This means, therefore, that the source signal is transmitted in its analog form only over the circuit connecting the customer premises equipment to its local network point of attachment, for example a local exchange. At that point the signal is converted into its digital form and from there it retains its original characteristics. This has resulted in a significant improvement in the electrical characteristics of circuits that are set up through the PSTN, with the effect that ASK is now used in conjunction with phase-shift keying in the more recent higher bit rate modem designs.

Example 2.7

Assuming ASK modulation is to be used, estimate the bandwidth required of a channel to transmit at the following bit rates assuming (a) the fundamental frequency component of the sequence 101010... is to be received and (b) the fundamental plus third harmonics: 300 bps, 1200 bps, and 4800 bps.

Comment on your results in relation to the PSTN.

Bit rate	300 bps	1200 bps	4800 bps
Fundamental frequency component	150 Hz	600 Hz	2400 Hz
Third harmonic component	450 Hz	1800 Hz	7200 Hz
Bandwidth with fundamental only	300 Hz	1200 Hz	4800 Hz
Bandwidth with fundamental and third harmonic	900 Hz	3600 Hz	14400 Hz

Recall that the usable bandwidth of the PSTN is 3000 Hz. Hence only the 300 bps rate can be obtained with the third harmonic. A rate of 1200 bps can be achieved but only with the fundamental frequency component. A bit rate of 4800 bps cannot be transmitted using ASK only.

Frequency-shift keying.   FSK is the modulation method that was used in all early low bit rate modems. Its principle of operation is shown in Figure 2.19(a). To avoid the reliance on variations in amplitude, with FSK we use two fixed-amplitude carrier signals, one for a binary 0 and the other for a binary 1.

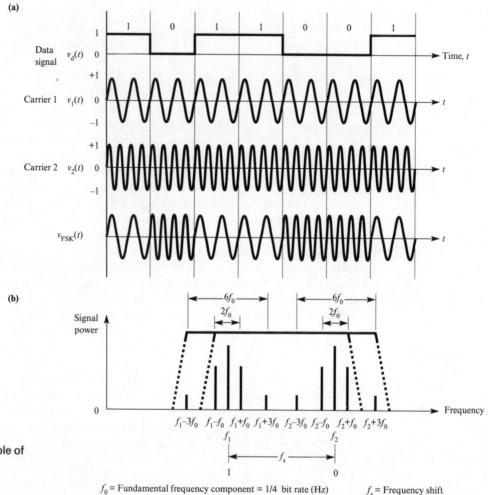

Figure 2.19
Frequency shift
keying: (a) principle of
operation;
(b) bandwidth
alternatives.

f_0 = Fundamental frequency component = 1/4 bit rate (Hz) f_s = Frequency shift

The difference between the two carriers is known as the **frequency shift** and, as
shown in Figure 2.19, the modulation operation is equivalent to summing
together the outputs of two separate ASK modulators: one performed on
one carrier using the original data signal and the other performed on the second
carrier using the complement of the data signal. Mathematically, we can derive
the bandwidth required for FSK using the following expression:

$$V_{FSK}(t) = \cos \omega_1 t \cdot v_d(t) + \cos \omega_2 t \cdot v_d'(t)$$

where ω_1 and ω_2 are the two carrier signals and $v_d'(t)$ is the complement of the
original data signal, $v_d(t)$. Mathematically, $v_d'(t) = 1 - v_d(t)$ hence if we assume
periodic data signals with a fundamental frequency ω_0:

$$v_{FSK}(t) = \cos \omega_1 t \left\{ \frac{1}{2} + \frac{2}{\pi} \left(\cos \omega_0 t - \frac{1}{3} \cos 3\omega_0 t + \cdots \right) \right\}$$
$$+ \cos \omega_2 t \left\{ \frac{1}{2} - \frac{2}{\pi} \left(\cos \omega_0 t - \frac{1}{3} \cos 3\omega_0 t + \cdots \right) \right\}$$

that is:

$$v_{FSK}(t) = \frac{1}{2} \cos \omega_1 t + \frac{1}{\pi} \left\{ \cos(\omega_1 - \omega_0)t + \cos(\omega_1 + \omega_0)t \right.$$
$$- \frac{1}{3} \cos(\omega_1 - 3\omega_0)t - \frac{1}{3} \cos(\omega_1 + 3\omega_0)t + \cdots \right\}$$
$$+ \frac{1}{2} \cos \omega_2 t + \frac{1}{\pi} \left\{ \cos(\omega_2 - \omega_0)t + \cos(\omega_2 + \omega_0)t \right.$$
$$- \frac{1}{3} \cos(\omega_2 - 3\omega_0)t - \frac{1}{3} \cos(\omega_2 + 3\omega_0)t + \cdots \right\}$$

We can deduce that the bandwidth required for FSK is simply the sum of two separate ASK-modulated carriers of frequencies ω_1 and ω_2. The bandwidth requirements of an FSK signal, therefore, are as shown in Figure 2.19(b).

As we indicated in Section 2.2.2, the highest frequency signals are generated for the binary sequence 101010.... With FSK, since the binary 1 and 0 signals each modulate a separate carrier, the minimum bandwidth required for each carrier is half the bit rate, that is, the highest fundamental frequency component for each carrier, f_0, is one half that for ASK. Hence, if we assume that just the (highest) fundamental frequency component is to be received, the total bandwidth required with FSK is $4f_0$ plus the frequency shift, f_s. However, since f_0 is half that for ASK, the total bandwidth required is the same as that for ASK plus the frequency shift. Similarly, if the third harmonic pair is to be received, a bandwidth of $6f_0$ plus the frequency shift is required.

For example, if the maximum bit rate is 600 bps, the maximum bit rate per carrier is 300 bps, which has a maximum fundamental frequency component of 150 Hz. The frequency spectrum, therefore, will contain primary sidebands spaced at 150 Hz on each side of both carriers. Hence if we select a frequency shift between the two carriers of, say, 400 Hz, then this will provide 100 Hz between the primary sidebands of both carriers. This means the total bandwidth required is in the order of 900 Hz. Clearly, since the bandwidth of a connection through the analog PSTN is 3000 Hz, then it is possible to derive two such channels – one for each direction of transmission – from a single PSTN connection.

As an example, Figure 2.20 illustrates the frequency assignments that are used for two types of FSK modem to provide a full-duplex (two-way simultaneous) 300 bps link between two DTEs. One set of frequency assignments is defined by the EIA for the Bell 103 modem and the other by the ITU-T for the **V.21 modem**. Note that in such modems the fundamental frequency component associated with each carrier is 75 Hz. Hence the frequency shift of 200 Hz allows 50 Hz between the two primary sidebands.

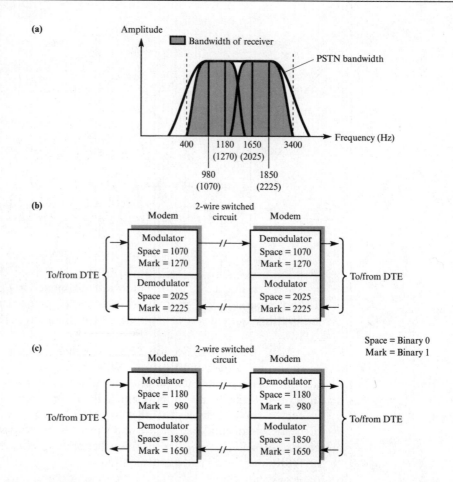

Figure 2.20
300 bps full-duplex
modem: (a) frequency
spectrum;
(b) EIA frequency
assignments;
(c) ITU-T frequency
assignments (V.21).

Phase-shift keying. In PSK the frequency and amplitude of the carrier signal are kept constant while the carrier is shifted in phase as each bit in the data stream is transmitted. The principle of operation of the scheme is shown in Figure 2.21(a). As we can see, two types of PSK are used. The first uses two fixed carrier signals to represent a binary 0 and 1 with a 180° phase difference between them. Since one signal is simply the inverse of the other, it is known as **phase-coherent PSK**. The disadvantage of this scheme is that a reference carrier signal is required at the receiver against which the phase of the received signal is compared. In practice, this requires more complex demodulation circuitry than the alternative **differential PSK**. With this scheme, phase shifts occur at each bit transition irrespective of whether a string of binary 1 or 0 signals is being transmitted; a phase shift of 90° relative to the current signal indicates a binary 0 is the next bit while a phase shift of 270° indicates a binary 1. As a result, the demodulation circuitry need determine only the magnitude of each phase shift rather than its absolute value.

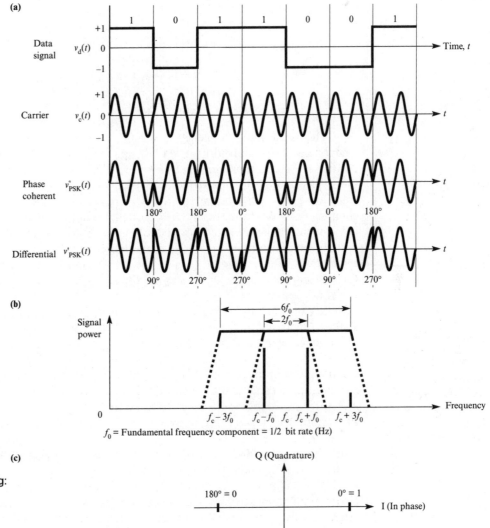

Figure 2.21
Phase-shift keying:
(a) principle of
operation;
(b) bandwidth
alternatives;
(c) phase diagram.

Mathematically, we can determine the bandwidth requirements of PSK by representing the binary data signal in its bipolar form since the negative signal level used with bipolar then results in a 180° phase change in the carrier. As we indicated in Section 2.2, a bipolar periodic data signal of unity amplitude and fundamental frequency ω_0 is represented by the Fourier series:

$$v_d(t) = \frac{4}{\pi} \left\{ \cos \omega_0 t - \frac{1}{3} \cos 3\omega_0 t + \frac{1}{5} \cos 5\omega_0 t - \cdots \right\}$$

Hence:

$$v_{PSK} = \frac{4}{\pi} \left\{ \cos\omega_c t \cdot \cos\omega_0 t - \frac{1}{3}\cos\omega_c t \cdot \cos 3\omega_0 t + \cdots \right\}$$

$$= \frac{2}{\pi} \left\{ \cos(\omega_c - \omega_0)t + \cos(\omega_c + \omega_0)t \right.$$

$$\left. - \frac{1}{3}\cos(\omega_c - 3\omega_0)t - \frac{1}{3}\cos(\omega_c + 3\omega_0)t + \cdots \right\}$$

This is the same frequency spectrum as for ASK except there is no carrier component. The bandwidth of a PSK signal, therefore, is as shown in Figure 2.21(b). Hence if we assume that only the fundamental frequency component of the sequence 101010... is to be received, the minimum bandwidth required is equal to $2f_0$ which is equal to the bit rate in Hz. The absence of a carrier component, however, means there is more power in the sidebands – containing the data – which makes PSK more resilient to noise than ASK or FSK. Also, by band-limiting the transmitted signal to f_c through $f_c + f_0$, that is, a bandwidth of f_0, then the Nyquist rate is achieved. Again, this is the same as ASK except in this case there is no carrier signal and hence all the received power is in the information-carrying signal, $f_c + f_0$.

Since with PSK a single-frequency carrier is used but with different phase shifts to represent each binary digit, we often represent PSK in the form of a **phase diagram** as shown in Figure 2.21(c). A phase diagram represents the sinusoidal carrier as a single line – known as a **vector** – whose length is equal to the amplitude of the signal. This line rotates about the axis counter-clockwise at a constant speed equal to the angular frequency, ω. A binary 1 is then represented as a vector in phase with the carrier while a binary 0 is a vector 180° out of phase with the carrier. The two axes are known as the I (in-phase) and Q (quadrature) axes.

Multilevel modulation methods. As we mentioned at the beginning of Section 2.5, all-digital transmission and switching has now been introduced within the PSTN. As a result, to achieve bit rates in excess of those available with the basic modulation schemes, more sophisticated modulation methods are used which involve either multiple signal levels or a mix of the basic schemes, particularly amplitude and phase.

In all the examples we have discussed so far, the bit rate was the same as the signaling rate, that is, the number of times the signal level changes per second. However, we can utilize more than two different values, four or eight being common. This means that each signal element may then represent two bits (four values) or three bits (eight values) of binary information. The bit rate is then two or three times the signaling (baud) rate. An example is a PSK modem in which four different phase changes (0°, 90°, 180°, 270°) are employed instead of just two. This enables each phase change to convey two bits. This is shown in two different forms in Figure 2.22. Because we use four phases, this is known as **quadrature phase shift keying (QPSK)** or **4-PSK**.

Higher bit rates are achieved using 8 and even 16 phase changes. In practice, however, there is a limit to how many different phases can be used, as the reducing

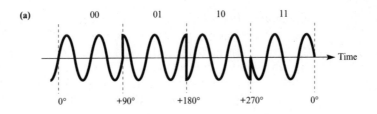

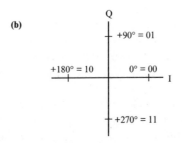

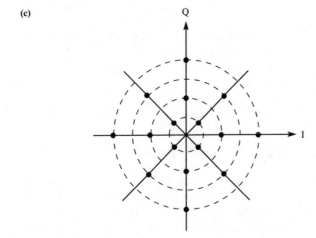

Figure 2.22
Alternative modulation
techniques: (a) 4-PSK
phase–time waveform;
(b) 4-PSK phase
diagram; (c) 16-QAM
phase diagram.

phase differences make the scheme progressively more prone to noise and phase impairments introduced during transmission. Hence to increase the bit rate further, it is more common to introduce amplitude as well as phase variations of each vector. This type of modulation is then known as **quadrature amplitude modulation (QAM)**. An example is shown in the phase diagram in Figure 2.22(c). This has 16 levels per signal element – and hence 4-bit symbols – and is known as 16-QAM. The phase diagram is also known as a 16-point **constellation**.

As we have just indicated, the robustness of all of the modulation schemes to errors is determined by the proximity of adjacent points in the constellation. Hence with this scheme, as we can see from Figure 2.22, 8 phases are used but the amplitude levels associated with adjacent phases are different. Collectively, this makes the discrimination operation at the receiver less prone to errors but is achieved at the expense of adding redundancy since not all of the four amplitude levels are used for each phase. As with all the modulation schemes, prior to modulation the bit stream is first passed through a **scrambler** circuit which converts the stream into a pseudorandom sequence. This has the effect of reducing the probability that consecutive bits in the sequence are in adjacent bit positions. At the receiver, after the demodulation process, the bit stream is passed through a matching **descrambler** circuit which restores the bits in the stream to the original sequence. This type of modulation is used in **V.29 modems** – used mainly for facsimile transmission – and achieves a bit rate of up to 9600 bps.

Another way of using redundancy is to use all 32 amplitude–phase alternatives, but the resulting 5-bit **symbols** then contain only 4 data bits. The fifth bit is used for error correction purposes and is generated using a **convolutional encoder**. The principle of operation of the latter is described in Appendix A. Essentially, however, each set of 4 bits in the source data stream is converted into 5 bits in such a way that, at the receiver, the *most likely* 4 data bits can be determined even in the presence of bit errors in the received sequence. Since convolutional encoders utilize a trellis diagram (see Appendix A) to identify each possible 5-bit symbol, the scheme is also known as **trellis-coded modulation (TCM)**. This approach is used in the V.32 modem to achieve a bit rate of 9600 bps and in the V.32bis modem to achieve a rate of up to 14 400 bps. Rates of 19 200, 24 000 and 28 800 bps are now available under the banner of **V.34/V-Fast modems**. A summary of the different modem types is given at the end of the chapter.

2.5.2 Digital leased circuits

Digital leased circuits are used not only to provide a direct connection between two DTEs but also as the basis of most private data (and voice) networks. We shall discuss these networks later in Chapter 8. Normally, leased circuits are used when a single organization or enterprise has a very high level of intersite traffic.

All the information relating to calls – voice and data – associated with most public carrier networks is now transmitted between the switching exchanges within the network in digital form. Moreover, the digital mode of working is steadily being extended to many customer premises. The resulting network is known as an **integrated services digital network (ISDN)** since the user can readily transmit data (with voice) without the use of modems. We shall discuss the transmission of data using an ISDN in Chapter 8. One result of the use of digital transmission is that it is now possible to lease from many public carrier operators all-digital circuits operating at rates from tens of kilobits per second to hundreds of megabits per second.

Such circuits are derived from – and hence must coexist with – those being used for normal interexchange traffic. When using such circuits, therefore, we must know how they are organized in terms of usable capacity.

Voice digitization

Digital circuits have evolved from our need to transmit voice in digital form. As Section 2.5 showed, voice transmissions are limited to a maximum bandwidth of less than 4 kHz. To convert such signals into digital form, the **Nyquist sampling theorem** states that their amplitude must be sampled at a minimum rate of greater than twice the highest frequency component. Hence to convert a 4 kHz voice signal into digital form, it must be sampled at a rate of 8000 times per second. The general arrangement is shown in Figure 2.23(a). Part (b) illustrates more detailed aspects.

Part (b) shows a single (analog) frequency signal, although a typical voice signal comprises a mix of frequencies. As we can see, the sampled signal is first converted into a pulse stream, the amplitude of each pulse being equal to the amplitude of the original analog signal at the sampling instant. The resulting signal is thus known as a **pulse amplitude modulated (PAM)** signal.

The PAM signal is still analog since its amplitude can vary over the full amplitude range. It is converted into an all-digital form by **quantizing** each pulse into its equivalent binary form. Eight binary digits (bits) are used to quantize each PAM signal which includes one bit to indicate the sign of the signal – positive or negative. This means 256 distinct levels are used – from eight 0 bits to eight 1 bits. The resulting digital signal is known as a **pulse code modulated (PCM) signal** and has a bit rate of 64 kbps – 8000 samples per second each of 8 bits – and is the minimum unit of transmission capacity available with a digital leased circuit.

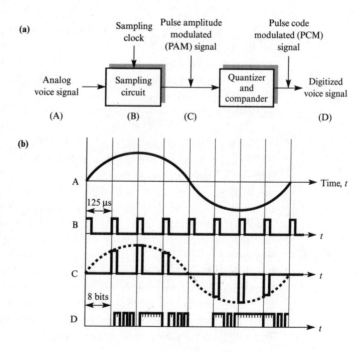

Figure 2.23
Digitization principles:
(a) coder schematic;
(b) coder signals.

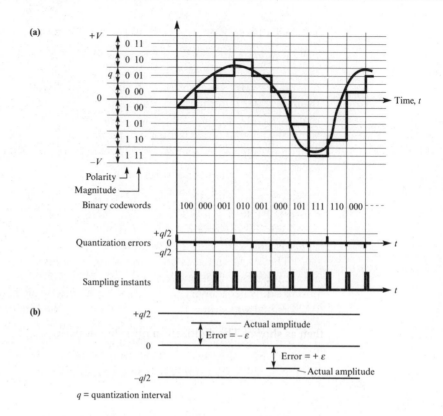

Figure 2.24
Quantization
procedure:
(a) source of errors;
(b) quantization noise
range.

To represent the amplitude of the analog samples precisely would require an infinite number of binary digits. Hence the use of just 8 bits means that each sample can be represented only by a corresponding number of discrete levels. The difference between adjacent levels – known as the **quantization interval**, q – determines the accuracy of the quantization process. We can see this by considering the quantization example shown in Figure 2.24(a).

In this example, we use three binary digits to represent each sample, including a polarity (sign) bit, which results in eight quantization intervals. Normally, a binary 0 indicates a positive value and a 1 a negative value. The magnitude bits are determined by the particular quantization interval the analog input signal is in at the time of each sample.

Figure 2.24(a) shows that a signal anywhere within a quantization interval is represented by the same binary codeword. Each codeword corresponds to a nominal input voltage which is at the center of the corresponding quantization interval and the actual input voltage may differ from this by up to plus or minus $q/2$. The difference between the actual signal amplitude and the corresponding sample amplitude is known as the **quantization error** and its signed values are shown expanded in Figure 2.24(b). For a speech signal the values of quantization error vary randomly from sample to sample and are known also as **quantization noise**.

As we have just indicated, with linear (equal) quantization intervals, small amplitude signals will experience larger quantization noise than large amplitude signals. The ear, however, is more sensitive to noise on quiet – low amplitude – speech signals than on louder signals. To alleviate this effect, in practical PCM systems the quantization intervals are made non-linear (unequal) by varying the range of the input signal amplitude associated with each quantization interval, that is, as the amplitude of the input signal increases, the corresponding codewords represent a larger signal range. The principle of the scheme is shown in Figure 2.25(a).

The figure shows that prior to the input signal being sampled and converted into a digital form, it is passed through a circuit known as a **compressor**. Similarly, at the destination, the reverse operation is performed on the output of the **digital-to-analog converter (DAC)** by a circuit known as an **expander**. The combined operation is thus known as **companding**. The input/output relationship of both circuits is shown in Figure 2.25(b) and (c); part (b) is known as the **compression characteristic** and part (c) the **expansion characteristic**.

To illustrate the principle, we show only 5-bit codewords. These are made up of a polarity bit, a 2-bit segment code and a 2-bit quantization code. The resulting segmentation and quantization codes over the complete input signal range are then as shown. The digitization operation is performed in two stages as we can see in Figure 2.25. In the compressor stage the input signal is first compressed by an amount determined by the segment in which the input signal falls. The resulting compressed (analog) signal is then passed to the **analog-to-digital converter (ADC)**

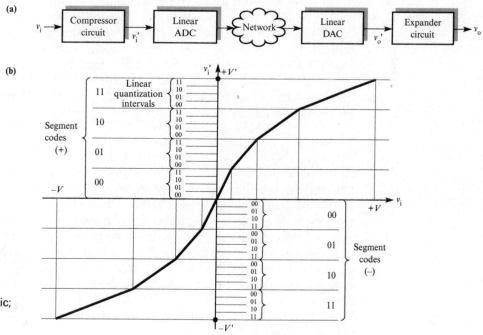

Figure 2.25
Companding
principles:
(a) circuit schematic;
(b) compression
schematic.

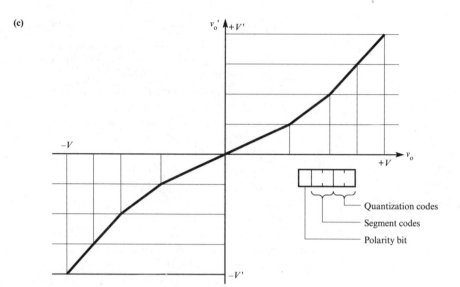

Figure 2.25 (cont.)
(c) Expansion
characteristic.

which, in turn, performs a linear quantization operation on the compressed signal.

Similarly, at the destination, each received codeword is converted back into its original analog form using a two-stage process. Each codeword is first fed into a linear DAC and the (analog) output of this is then passed to the expander circuit which performs the reverse operation of the compressor circuit.

In practice, although early PCM codecs (coder/decoder circuits) operated in this way, most codecs now perform the compression and expansion operations digitally. There are two different compression characteristics in use: μ-law (used in North America and Japan) and A-law which is the ITU-T recommended characteristic. Conversion is needed when using leased and switched circuits that span continents which use different standards. Fortunately this is necessary only for voice communications and not for data.

Multiplexing

Circuits that link exchanges carry multiple calls concurrently in a digital form by using time-division multiplexing (TDM). Recall that with TDM, digital signals from multiple sources are each assigned a specific time slot in a higher bit rate aggregate link. Since each analog signal is sampled 8000 times per second, this produces an 8-bit sample once every 125 microseconds. The aggregate link bit rate, therefore, is a function of the number of voice channels it carries. In North America and Japan, 24 voice channels are grouped together, whereas 30 channels are used in countries that comply with the ITU-T recommendations. This yields aggregate bit rates of 1.544 Mbps and 2.048 Mbps respectively. The general scheme is shown in Figure 2.26(a).

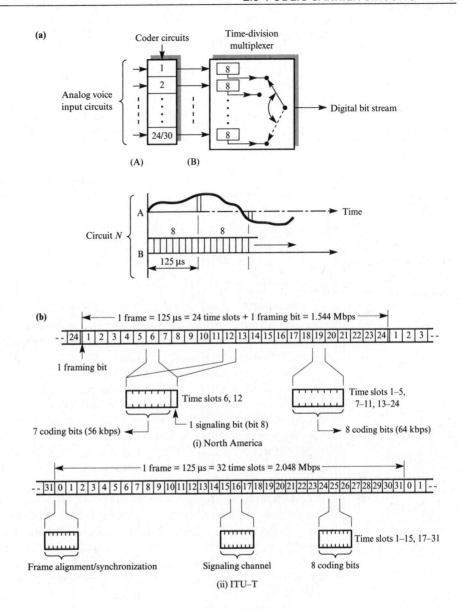

Figure 2.26
Multiplexing
hierarchy: (a) TDM
schematic; (b) framing
structures.

We must also include additional bits (or channels) for other purposes
(Figure 2.26(b)), such as bits to indicate the start of each frame – frame
synchronization – and bits for call setup (signaling). Frame synchronization in
the North American system uses a single bit at the start of each frame which
toggles (alternates) between 1 and 0 for consecutive frames. Signaling information
is carried in the first bit of time slots 6 and 12 leaving just 7 user bits in these slots.
Thus the aggregate bit rate is $(24 \times 8 + 1)$ bits/125 μs = 1.544 Mbps. Such circuits
are known as **DS1** or **T1 links**.

Table 2.1   Multiplexing hierarchies used in North America and ITU-T digital transmission systems.

	Circuit	*Bit rate (Mbps)*	*Voice/data channels*
North America	DS1	1.544	24
	DS1C	3.152	48
	DS2	6.312	96
	DS3	44.736	672
	DS4E	139.264	1920
	DS4	274.176	4032
ITU-T	E1	2.048	30
	E2	8.448	120
	E3	34.368	480
	E4	139.264	1920
	E5	565.148	7680

In the ITU-T recommended system, time slot 0 (zero) is used for frame synchronization – also known as **frame alignment** since it allows the receiver to interpret the time slots in each frame on aligned boundaries. Signaling information is carried in time slot 16 yielding an aggregate bit rate of 32×8 bits/$125\,\mu s$ = 2.048 Mbps. Such circuits are referred to as **E1 links**. In both T1 and E1 systems, the lower bit rates are known as **fractional T1/E1**.

We can achieve higher aggregate link bit rates by multiplexing together several such groups. Table 2.1 shows the range of bit rates for the two systems, together with their names. The higher bit rate links require additional bits for framing and control. For example, $4 \times 2.048 = 8.192$ and hence 0.256 Mbps is used for control functions. The various bit rates are often abbreviated to 1.5, 3, 6, 44, 274, and 2, 8, 34, 140, 565, respectively.

Although the generation of the higher-order multiplexed circuits is relatively straightforward, a number of complications arise when providing customers with leased circuits that are derived from high-order multiplexed circuits. Most early digital transmission systems were introduced in an incremental way as earlier analog systems were upgraded. The effect of this was that each TDM stream was derived using a separate timing source. Hence when combining two or more lower-order multiplex streams of this type, steps have to be taken to compensate for the slight differences in timing of each stream that arise owing to small differences in their clock signals. To overcome such differences, we use an output (multiplexed) bit rate that is slightly higher than the sum of the combined input rates. Any bits that are then unused are filled with what are known as **justification bits**. This type of higher-order multiplexing is known as **plesiochronous** – meaning nearly synchronous – **multiplexing** or sometimes **asynchronous multiplexing**. The resulting higher-order multiplexing rates are known as the **plesiochronous digital hierarchy (PDH)**.

Although the use of justification bits at each level in the hierarchy does not in itself pose a problem, their presence means that we cannot identify precisely the start of a lower-level multiplex bit stream within a higher-order stream. The effect of this is best seen by considering a typical operational requirement. Assume three switching centers/exchanges located in different towns/cities are interconnected by 140 Mbps (PDH) trunk circuits as shown in Figure 2.27(a). A business customer, with sites located somewhere between them, makes a request to link the sites together with, say, 2 Mbps leased circuits to create a private network. This is shown in schematic form in Figure 2.27(b). Because it is not possible to identify a lower bit rate channel from the higher-order bit stream, the operator must fully demultiplex the 140 Mbps stream down to the 2 Mbps level before this can be allocated to the customer. This stream must then be remultiplexed back into the 140 Mbps stream for onward transmission. This type of demultiplexing/multiplexing operation is performed by a device known as a **drop-and-insert** or **add-drop multiplexer (ADM)** and, as we can see from Figure 2.27(c), the equipment required to meet this relatively simple request is very complicated.

Although it is not shown in the figure, at each switching office/exchange the allocated 2 Mbps leased circuit must be similarly identified and the switch bypassed in order to form a direct link between the customer sites. Therefore, when leased circuits are provided for customers in this way, careful records must be kept of the circuits and equipment being used for each customer so that, if a

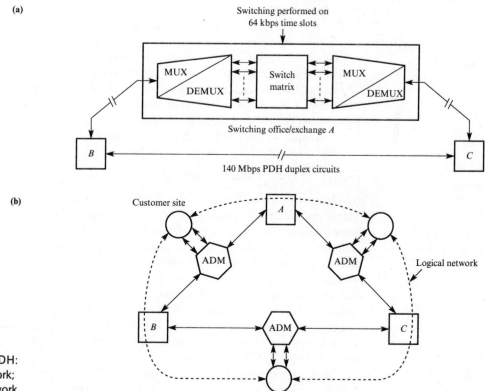

Figure 2.27
Private network
provision in the PDH:
(a) existing network;
(b) modified network.

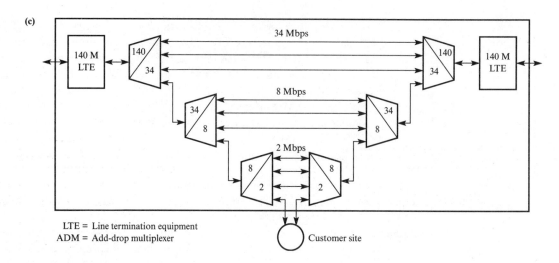

LTE = Line termination equipment
ADM = Add-drop multiplexer   Customer site

Figure 2.27 (cont.)
(c) ADM principle.

fault is reported, appropriate remedial action can be taken. In practice, the provision of only basic performance monitoring within the frame formats of the PDH means that it is normally the customer who has to alert the provider of the occurrence of faults.

As we shall see in Chapter 10, the demand for high bit rate leased circuits is expanding rapidly as new high bit rate networks are introduced. Also, the operators themselves are having to provide a more flexible transmission network as new services are introduced that require transmission facilities between many diverse locations. To meet these needs a completely new type of transmission system is being introduced that overcomes all of the limitations of the PDH just identified. This is known as the **synchronous digital hierarchy (SDH)** and, since most leased circuits that require higher-order multiplex rates are now derived from SDH circuits, we shall now look briefly at SDH.

Synchronous digital hierarchy

SDH was developed initially by Bellcore in the United States under the title of **synchronous optical network (SONET)**. All equipment is synchronized to a single master clock. The basic transmission rate defined in the SDH is 155.52 Mbps – abbreviated to 155 Mbps – and is known as a **synchronous transport module level 1** signal or simply **STM-1**. Higher rates of **STM-4** (622 Mbps) and **STM-16** (2.4 Gbps) are also defined. In the SONET hierarchy the term **synchronous transport signal (STS)** or sometimes **optical signal (OC)** is used to define the equivalent of an STM signal. In SONET the lower rate of 51.84 Mbps forms the first level signal – STS-1/OC-1. An STM-1 signal is produced by multiplexing three such signals together and hence is equivalent to an STS-3/OC-3 signal.

As with the PDH, the STM-1 signal is comprised of a repetitive set of frames which repeat with a period of 125 microseconds. The information content of each frame can be used to carry multiple 1.5/2/6/34/45 or 140 Mbps PDH streams.

SONET	SDH	Bit rate (Mbps)
STS-1/OC-1		51.84
STS-3/OC-3	STM-1	155.52
STS-9/OC-9		466.56
STS-12/OC-12	STM-4	622.08
STS-18/OC-18		933.12
STS-24/OC-24		1244.16
STS-36/OC-36		1866.24
STS-48/OC-48	STM-16	2488.32

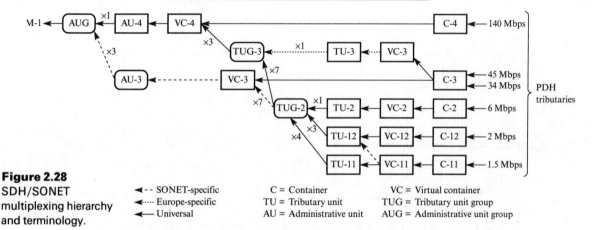

Figure 2.28
SDH/SONET
multiplexing hierarchy
and terminology.

◄- - SONET-specific   C = Container   VC = Virtual container
◄···· Europe-specific   TU = Tributary unit   TUG = Tributary unit group
◄── Universal   AU = Administrative unit   AUG = Administrative unit group

Each of these streams is carried in a different **container** which also contains additional stuffing bits to allow for variations in actual rate. To this is added some control information known as the **path overhead** which allows such things as the BER of the associated container to be monitored on an end-to-end basis by network management. The container and its path overhead collectively form a **virtual container (VC)** and an STM-1 frame can contain multiple VCs either of the same type or of different types. Some example multiplexing alternatives are shown in Figure 2.28. Note that the first digit of the lowest level container – and hence VC – is a 1 and the second digit indicates whether it contains a 1.5 Mbps PDH signal (1) or 2 Mbps (2).

The higher-order transmission rates are produced by multiplexing multiple STM-1 (STS-3/OC-3) signals together. For example, an STM-16 (STS-48/OC-48) signal is produced by multiplexing either 16 STM-1 (STS-3/OC-3) signals or 4 STM-4 (STS-12/OC-12) signals. To provide the necessary flexibility for each higher-order signal, in addition to the overheads at the head of each lower-level STM frame, a pointer is used to indicate the lower-level STM frame's position within the higher-order frame.

We can best describe the structure of an SDH/SONET frame in relation to a complete synchronous transmission system since each frame contains management information relating to each constituent part. These parts include **sections**, **lines** and **paths** and their interrelationships are shown Figure 2.29(a).

A section is a single length of transmission cable. Both ends of the cable are terminated with a **section termination equipment (STE)**. An example of an STE is a repeater which regenerates the optical/electrical signals being transmitted on this section of cable. A line extends across multiple cable sections and is terminated by a **line termination equipment (LTE)**. Examples of LTEs are multiplexers and switching nodes. A path is an end-to-end transmission path through the complete transmission system. Each end of the path is terminated by a **path termination equipment (PTE)**.

The structure of an STM-1 (STS-3/OC-3) frame is shown in Figure 2.29(b). Each frame comprises 2430 bytes/octets and repeats every 125 microseconds producing a bit rate of 155.52 Mbps. A frame comprises nine 270-byte **segments** each of which has a 9-byte header associated with it and a 261-byte **payload**. The header bytes are known as **overheads**. Normally, the segments making up a frame are shown with the segments one on top of the other since specific bytes in each header relate to one another.

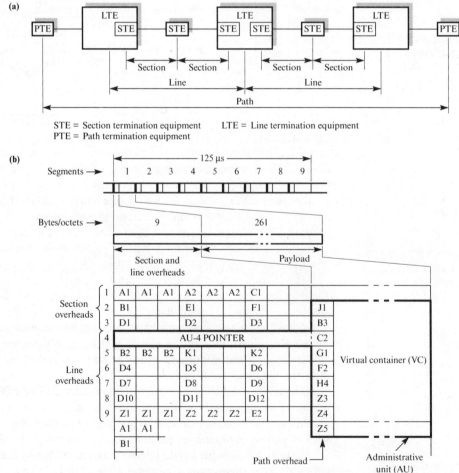

Figure 2.29
SDH detail:
(a) managed entities;
(b) frame format.

(c)

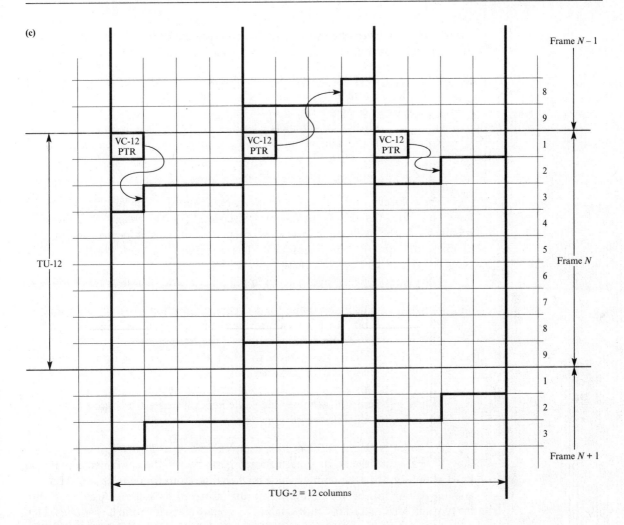

Figure 2.29 (cont.)
(c) Example VC mapping.

The **section overhead** bytes relate to the management of a specific section. As we can see in Figure 2.29, some bytes are replicated for error protection purposes. The use of each byte is as follows:

A1–A2   Always the first bytes transmitted; used for framing.

B1   An 8-bit parity check used to monitor bit errors on the section.

C1   Identifies a specific STM-1 frame in a higher-order (STM-n) frame.

D1–D3   Form a data communication channel for network management messages relating to the section.

E1   Used for orderwire channels which are voice channels used by maintenance personnel.

F1   User channels, available for the management of customer premises equipment.

The **line overhead** bytes relate to the management of a complete line. The use of each byte is as follows:

B2	An 8-bit parity check used to monitor bit errors on the line.
D4–D12	Form a data communication channel for network management messages relating to the line.
E2	Orderwire channels relating to the complete line.
K1–K2	Form a signaling channel for automatic protection switching of the complete line.
Z1–Z2	Reserved for national use.

The columns in the payload field can be assigned in various ways to carry lower bit rate signals. To transport lower-level PDH streams – known as **tributaries** – the payload capacity in each container is allocated in integral numbers of columns. Each container has a column of path overhead bytes assigned to it and collectively these form the VC.

The identity of each byte is given in Figure 2.29 and their uses are as follows:

J1	This byte verifies the VC path connection.
B3	8-bit parity for monitoring the bit error rate of the path.
C2	Indicates the composition of the VC payload.
G1	Used by the receiver to return the status of the received signal back to the transmitter.
F2	Provides a user data communication channel.
H4	Indicates whether the payload is part of a multiframe.
Z3–Z5	Available for national use.

A pointer is placed at the head of each VC and is used to indicate the start of the VC relative to the start of each frame. Note that if the container contains a PDH tributary, then the pointer value may change from frame to frame owing to possible timing differences. Different combinations of VCs can be used to fill up the payload area of a frame with smaller VCs being carried within larger ones. The VC and its pointer are known as a **tributary unit (TU)** if the VC carries a lower-order tributary or a **tributary group (TUG)** if it carries a number of lower-order tributaries. The largest VC in an STM-1 frame is known as an **administrative unit (AU)** and, as can be seen in Figure 2.29(b), the pointer to the start of this is written into the first octet position of the line overhead.

The example given in Figure 2.29(c) shows how three VC-12s can be carried within a TUG-2 frame. Each VC-12 comprises 4 columns of the STM-1 payload area and hence the TUG-2 comprises 12 columns. The VC-12 and its pointer form a TU-12. The pointer always occupies the first byte position but, if the timing of the VC-12 contents relative to the STM-1 frame varies, then the position of the VC-12 is allowed to slip to accommodate this with the value in the pointer changing so that it always points to the first byte in the VC. A VC-12 will accommodate $4 \times 9 = 36$ bytes. Hence, since a VC-12 comprises 33 bytes – 32 bytes for the E1 frame plus 1 byte for the pointer – the remaining bytes are filled with what is referred to as **fixed stuff**.

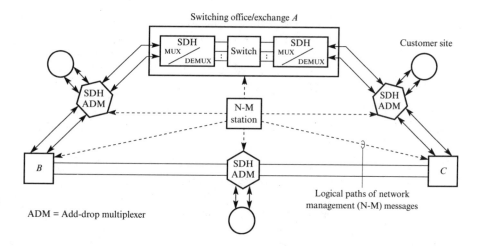

Figure 2.30
Service provision with
SDH using network
management.

ADM = Add-drop multiplexer

In order to carry other signals which do not have a container defined to accept them, two or more TUs can be combined using a technique known as **concatenation**. For example, five TU-2s can be concatenated to carry a single 32 Mbps signal. Four such signals can then be carried in a VC-4 instead of three if a standard C-3 container has been used. This technique is used also for the transport of ATM traffic. The latter are known as **cells** and we shall describe their use in Chapter 10.

All SDH equipment has software associated with it known as a **network management (NM) agent** and the communication channels in the overhead bytes are used by this to report any malfunctions of sections, lines, or paths to a central network management station. They are also used for the latter to download commands to change the allocation of the payload field associated with each STM-1 frame. For example, SDH ADMs can be configured – and reconfigured – remotely to provide any desired bandwidth mix without the need for demultiplexing. The general principle is shown in Figure 2.30. Redundant (standby) links are used between each pair of SDH multiplexers and these can be brought into service using commands received from a remote network management station. More details about the operation and protocols associated with network management are given in Chapter 13.

2.6 Physical layer interface standards

In the preceding sections we have been concerned with some of the alternative transmission media and the associated electrical signals that may be used to transmit a binary data stream between two DTEs. However, it is important to note that the various standards introduced define not only the form of the electrical signals to be used, but also a complete range of additional signals that control the order and timing of data transfer across the appropriate interfaces.

Collectively, these signals are said to form the **physical layer interface standard**. Although it is not practicable to describe here the complete range of signal definitions presented in the various standards documents, we shall discuss some of the additional control signals used with the various interface standards introduced previously.

2.6.1   EIA-232D

As we saw in Section 2.3.1, the EIA-232D/V.24 standards were originally defined as a standard interface for connecting a DTE to a PTT-supplied (or approved) modem. More generally, the modem is referred to as a **data circuit-terminating equipment (DCE)**. A schematic diagram indicating the position of the interface standard with respect to the two communicating DTEs is shown in Figure 2.31(a). The connector used between a DTE and a modem is a 25-pin connector of the type shown in Figure 2.31(b). It is defined in standard ISO 2110 and is known as a **DB25 connector**. Also shown is the total set of signals associated with the interface together with their names and pin assignments.

The transmit data (TxD) and receive data (RxD) lines are lines used by the DTE to transmit and receive data respectively. The other lines collectively perform the timing and control functions associated with the setting-up and clearing of a switched connection through the PSTN and with performing selected test operations. The second (secondary) set of lines allows two data transfers to take place simultaneously over the one interface. All the lines use the V.28 electrical signals described in Section 2.3.1.

The timing control signals are concerned with the transmission (TxClk) and reception (RxClk) of the data on the corresponding data line. As we shall see in Chapter 3, data is transmitted using either an asynchronous or a synchronous transmission mode. In the asynchronous mode, the transmit and receive clocks are both generated by an independent clock source and fed directly to the corresponding pins of the DTE. In this mode, only the transmit and receive data lines are connected to the modem. In the synchronous mode, however, data is transmitted and received in synchronism with the corresponding clock signal and these are normally generated by the modem. The latter is then known as a **synchronous modem** and, when the signal (baud) rate is less than the data bit rate – that is, multiple signal levels are being used – then the transmit and receive clocks generated by the modem operate at the appropriate fraction of the line-signaling rate.

We can best see the function and sequence of the various call-control lines by considering the setting-up and clearing of a call. Figure 2.32 shows how a connection (call) is first set up, some data is exchanged between the two DTEs in a half-duplex (two-way alternate) mode and the call is then cleared. We assume that the calling DTE is a user at a terminal/personal computer and its modem has automatic calling facilities. The called DTE is also a computer and its modem has automatic answering facilities. Such facilities are defined in recommendation V.25. When a DTE is ready to make or receive data transfer requests, it

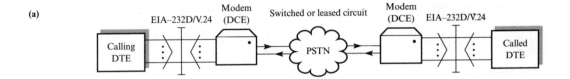

(a)

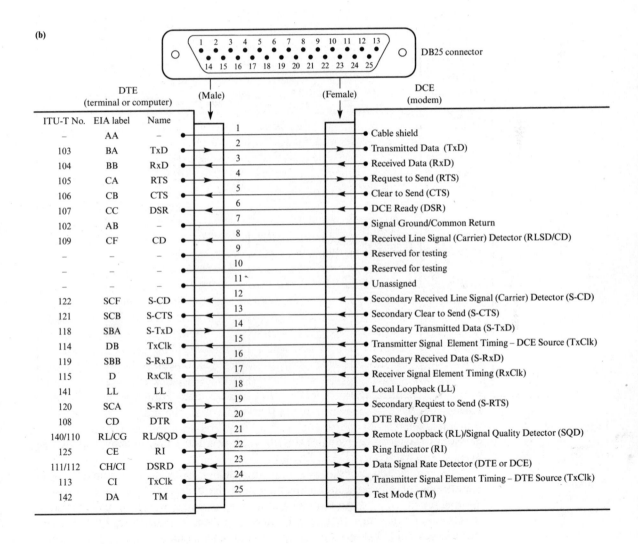

Figure 2.31 EIA-232D/V.24 standard interface: (a) interface function; (b) socket, pin and signal definitions.

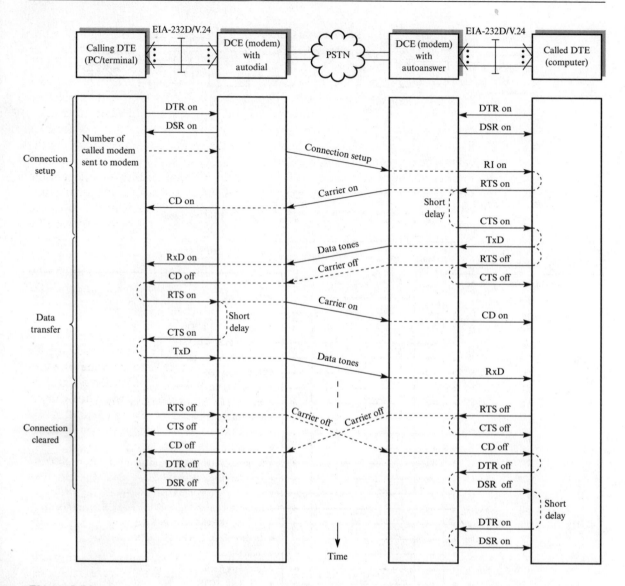

Figure 2.32
EIA-232D/V.24 connection setup, two-way alternate data transfer, and connection clearing sequences.

sets the data terminal ready (DTR) line on and the local modem responds by setting the DCE ready (DSR) line on.

A connection is established by the calling DTE sending the telephone number of the modem (line) associated with the called DTE. On receipt of the ringing tone from its local switching office/telephone exchange, the called modem sets the ring indicator (RI) line to on and the called DTE responds by setting the request-to-send (RTS) line on. In response, the called modem sends a carrier signal – the data tone for a binary 1 – to the calling modem to indicate that the call has been accepted by the called DTE and, after a short delay to allow the calling modem to prepare to receive data, the called modem sets the clear-to-send (CTS) line on to inform the called DTE that it can start sending data. On detecting the carrier signal, the calling modem sets the carrier detect (CD) line on. The connection is now established and the data transfer phase can begin.

Typically, the called DTE (computer) starts by sending a short invitation-to-send message over the set-up connection. When this has been sent, it prepares to receive the response from the calling DTE by setting the RTS line off and, on detecting this, the called modem stops sending the carrier signal and sets the CTS line off. At the calling side, the removal of the carrier signal is detected by the calling modem and, in response, it sets the CD line off. In order to send its response message, the calling DTE (PC) sets the RTS line on and, on receipt of the CTS signal from the modem, starts to send the message. This procedure then repeats as messages are exchanged between the two DTEs. Finally, after the complete transaction has taken place, the call is cleared. This is accomplished by both DTEs setting their RTS line off which, in turn, causes the two modems to switch their carriers off. This is detected by both modems and they set their CD line off. Both DTEs then set their DTR line off and their modems respond by setting the DSR line off thereby clearing the call. Typically, the called DTE (computer) then prepares to receive a new call by resetting its DTR line on after a short delay.

We have described the use of a half-duplex switched connection to illustrate the meaning and use of some of the control lines available with the standard. In practice, however, the time taken to change from the receive to the transmit mode in the half-duplex mode – known as the **turnaround time** – is not insignificant. It is preferable to operate in the **duplex mode** whenever possible, even when half-duplex working is required. In the duplex mode, both RTS lines are permanently left on and both modems maintain the CTS line on and keep sending a carrier signal to the remote modem.

When two DTEs are communicating and a fault develops, it is often difficult to ascertain the cause of the fault – the local modem, the remote modem, the communications line, or the remote DTE. To help to identify the cause of faults, the interface contains three control lines: the local and remote loopback (LL and RL) and the test mode (TM). Their function is shown in Figure 2.33: in (a) a local loopback test is used while in (b) a remote loopback is used.

The DCE (modem) always sets its DSR line on when it is ready to transmit or receive data. To perform a test on its local modem, the DTE sets the LL line on and, in response, the modem internally connects the output from the modulator circuit back to the input of the demodulator circuit. It then sets the TM line on and, when the DTE detects this, it transmits a known test (data) pattern on its TxD line and simultaneously reads the data from its RxD line. If the received data is the same as the test data, then the DTE assumes the local modem is working satisfactorily. If it is not – or no signal is present at all – then the local modem is assumed faulty.

If the local modem is deemed to be working correctly, then the DTE proceeds to test the remote modem by this time setting the RL control line on. On detecting the RL line going on, the local modem sends a predefined command to the remote modem which, in turn, performs a remote loopback as shown. The

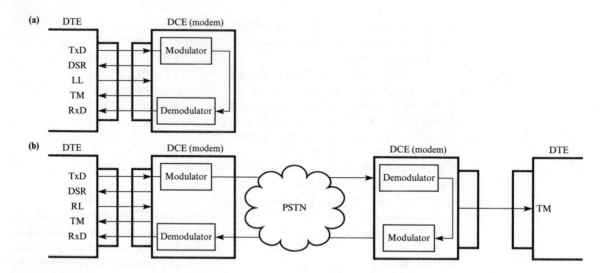

Figure 2.33
Loopback tests:
(a) local; (b) remote.

remote modem then sets its TM line on to inform the remote DTE it is involved in a test – and hence cannot transmit data – and returns an acknowledgment command back to the modem originating the test. The modem, on receipt of this, sets its TM line on and, on detecting this, the local DTE starts to transmit the test data pattern. Again, if this data is received correctly, then both modems are assumed to be working correctly and the fault lies with the remote DTE. Alternatively, if the received data is badly corrupted then the remote modem is assumed to be faulty or, if no signal is received at all, then the PSTN line is assumed faulty.

The null modem

With the signal assignments shown in Figure 2.34 the terminal and computer both receive and transmit data on the same lines, since the modem provides the same function for both devices. However, since its original definitions, the EIA-232D/V.24 standard has been adopted as a standard interface for connecting character-oriented peripherals (terminals, printers, etc.) to a computer. For this type of use, it is necessary to decide which of the two devices – peripheral or computer – is going to emulate the modem, since clearly both devices cannot transmit and receive data on the same lines. The same applies when linking the serial ports associated with two computers.

There are three possible options:

(1)   The terminal emulates the modem and the appropriate line definitions are used accordingly.

(2)   The computer emulates the modem.

(3)   Both the terminal and computer remain unchanged and the interconnecting wiring is modified.

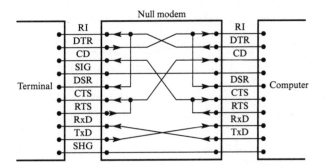

Figure 2.34
Null modem
connections.

The disadvantage of the first two is that neither the terminal nor the computer can be used directly with a modem. Nevertheless, a common approach is for the computer EIA-232D port to be wired to emulate a modem, enabling an unmodified terminal to be connected directly to it. The third alternative is also widely used, but requires a **null modem** (or **switch box**) to be inserted between the terminal and computer to modify the interconnecting lines, as shown in Figure 2.34.

As we can see, in addition to reversing the transmit and receive data lines, some of the control lines are reversed. For example, since a computer and terminal normally operate in duplex mode, the RTS and CTS lines are connected together at each end and this signal is then connected to the CD input line of the other device. Similarly, the DSR and RI lines are connected together at each end and these signals are cross-connected to the DTR inputs. The signal and shield ground lines are connected directly.

When the two devices communicate via a synchronous data link, the transmit clock from each device is normally cross-connected and is used as the receive clock by the other device. In some instances, neither device contains a clock source and the clock for both devices is generated within the null modem which is then known as a **modem eliminator**.

2.6.2 EIA-530

The EIA-530 interface has the same set of signals as the EIA-232D interface. The difference is that the EIA-530 interface uses RS-422A/V.11 differential (balanced) electrical signals to achieve both longer cable lengths and higher bit rates. This means that a 37-pin connector is required with an additional 9-pin connector if the secondary set of signal lines is also to be used.

2.6.3 V.35

The V.35 interface was originally defined to interface a DTE to a wideband (analog) synchronous modem operating in the range 48–168 kbps. The interface uses a similar set of signal lines to the EIA-232D interface except no secondary channel lines or test lines are supported. The electrical signals are a mixture of unbalanced (V.28) and balanced (RS-422A/V.11); the unbalanced lines are used for the control signals and the balanced lines for the data and associated timing/clock lines. The mixture of signal types means that the maximum cable length is the same as that with EIA-232D/V.24. In some applications, however, only the transmit and receive data lines (with clocks) are used. Since all these lines use differential/balanced signals, then longer cable lengths can be used. The full V.35 interface uses a 34-pin connector, but for those applications that use only the data and associated clock signals a smaller connector is normally used.

2.6.4   X.21

The X.21 interface has been defined for interfacing a DTE to the DCE of a public data network. Examples of public data networks are described in Chapter 8 and include X.25 packet-switching networks and circuit-switched data networks. The X.21 interface is also used as the termination interface for digital leased circuits of $n \times 64$ kbps. The connector and associated signal lines are shown in Figure 2.35.

All the signal lines use balanced (RS-442A/V.11) drivers and receivers. It is a synchronous interface and, in addition to the transmit (T) and receive (R) data lines/pairs has a signal element timing (clock) line, S, and a byte timing line, B. As we shall see in Chapter 8, the control (C) and indication (I) lines are used in conjunction with the transmit and receive lines for setting up a connection through an all-digital circuit-switched data network.

A variation of X.21, known as X.21bis, is also sometimes used to interface a DTE that is designed for use with an (analog) synchronous modem to a public data network. The normal control lines associated with the V.24/V.35 interfaces are used.

2.6.5   ISDN interface

The ISDN is the all-digital replacement of the (analog) interface to the PSTN. As Section 2.5.2 explained, a digitized voice circuit operates at 64 kbps (duplex) and, as we shall see in Chapter 8, a single basic-rate ISDN termination provides two such circuits together with an additional 16 kbps (duplex) circuit for call setup and clearing purposes. Although three separate circuits are present, these are

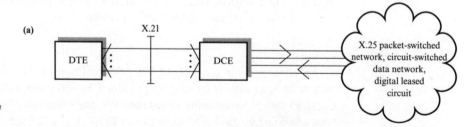

Figure 2.35
X.21 standard
interface: (a) interface
function.

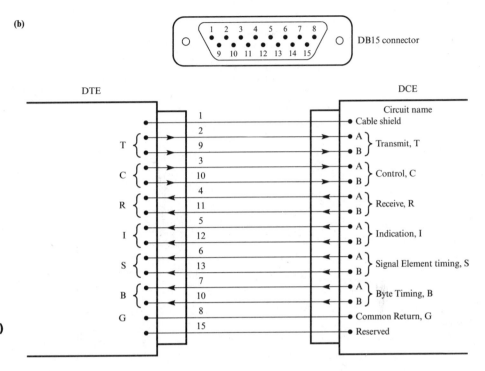

Figure 2.35 (cont.)
(b) Socket, pin, and
signal definitions.

multiplexed together for transmission purposes to and from the nearest switching office/exchange onto a single pair of wires. The **network termination (NT)** equipment separates the forward and return paths – each comprising the three identified circuits – onto two separate wire pairs. Power is also provided by the NT for the user terminal equipment if this is required. The set of forward and return paths is known as the **S-interface** and an 8-pin connector – defined in standard ISO 8877 and known as a **RJ45** – is used to connect the terminal equipment to the NT. This interface is shown in Figure 2.36.

The primary power source from the NT to the terminal equipment is derived from the transmit and receive pairs. An optional second power source is also available via pins 7 and 8. In order to connect lower bit rate equipment – designed for use with the analog PSTN – to the higher bit rate S-interface, a device known as a **terminal adapter (TA)** is used. As we shall see in Chapter 8, the TA performs what is known as a **rate adaption function**. This function is defined in the V-series standards V.110 and V.120.

2.6.6 Standards summary

The various standards discussed here are only part of the full range of standards that have been defined by ITU-T for use with public telephone networks (PSTNs) Collectively, they are known as the V-series standards. Some of them are summarized in Figure 2.37(a).

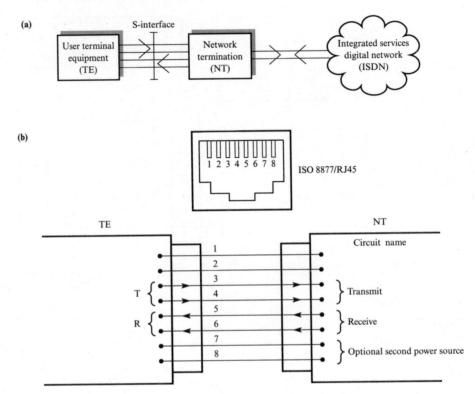

Figure 2.36
ISDN S-interface:
(a) interface function;
(b) socket, pin, and
signal definitions.

As the figure shows, the two physical interface standards are V.24 (EIA-232D) and V.35 (EIA-430). The former is intended for use with normal (and hence low bit rate) telephone circuits and the latter with wider bandwidth (**wideband**) circuits. These wideband circuits are normally leased from the PTT authority. Because they bypass the normal switching circuits, they provide a direct point-to-point circuit (link) between two sites. Typically, such circuits can operate at data rates of from 48 to 168 kbps. As we shall see in Section 3.3, a synchronous mode of transmission must be used on these circuits because of their relatively high data rates.

The various standards listed in Figure 2.37(a) are rigidly defined and include a precise definition of both the type of modulation scheme that must be used and the number and use of the additional interface control lines. In this way, a user buying a modem that adheres to, say, the V.21 standard, can readily use it with a V.21-compatible modem from a different manufacturer.

Some modems are designed to be used with 2-wire switched connections, while others can be used with both 2-wire switched circuits (connections) and 4-wire leased circuits. The two different circuit arrangements are shown in Figure 2.37(b).

With 4-wire leased (permanent) circuits, a pair of circuits is set up through the PSTN and leased to the user. One pair is used for transmission and the other for reception thus providing a duplex capability. Such circuits are used for

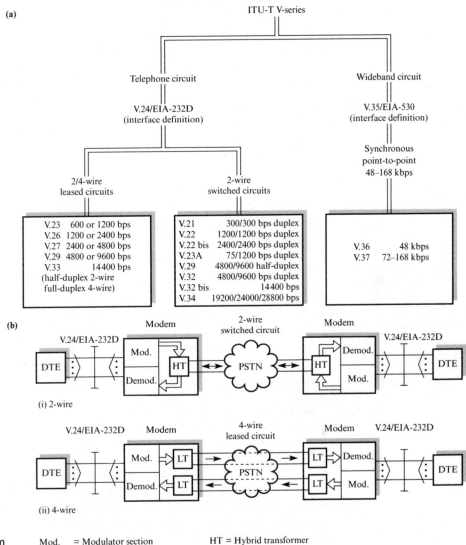

Figure 2.37
Modem summary:
(a) ITU-T V-series
standards; (b) modem
alternatives.

Mod.   = Modulator section   HT = Hybrid transformer
Demod. = Demodulator section   LT = Line transformer

permanent connections between two DTEs. Because of their high running cost, the circuits are used for applications involving high user-traffic densities.

For applications that either require a switched connection or do not have sufficient traffic to justify a permanent circuit, a normal switched connection must be used. Such connections use only a single pair of lines (2-wire); duplex (two-way) operation is achieved by a device known as a 4-wire to 2-wire **hybrid transformer**. This has two sets of windings which are terminated and interconnected such that the modulated (analog) signal output from the modulator section of the modem is coupled only to the 2-wire line. Similarly, the signal received from the 2-wire line is coupled only to the input of the demodulator section.

Because of imperfections in hybrid transformers, a fraction of the signal output from the modulator section – known as the **echo signal** – is received at the input to the local demodulator section. Therefore, only half-duplex (two-way alternate) working is normally used with this type of circuit. Using more sophisticated modulation techniques and additional circuits known as **echo cancelers**, it is now possible to have duplex (two-way simultaneous) operation over 2-wire switched circuits at high bit rates (9600 bps). This approach is used in V.32/V.33 modems, which also include error correction facilities built into the modem. We shall discuss this feature further in Section 5.3.4.

Exercises

2.1 Give a brief description of the application and limitations of the following types of transmission media:
(a) Two-wire open lines
(b) Twisted-pair lines
(c) Coaxial cable
(d) Optical fiber
(e) Microwaves

2.2 With the aid of sketches, explain the differences between the following transmission modes used with optical fiber:
(a) Multimode stepped index
(b) Multimode graded index
(c) Monomode

2.3 The maximum distance between two terrestrial microwave dishes, d, is given by the expression:
$$d = 7.14\sqrt{Kh}$$
where h is the height of the dishes above ground and K is a factor that allows for the curvature of the earth. Assuming $K = 4/3$, determine d for selected values of h.

2.4 With reference to Figure 2.5(b), determine the frequency assignments for a cellular system assuming a 7-cell repeat pattern. Explain the advantages of this over the 3-cell repeat pattern shown in the figure.

2.5 With the aid of sketches, explain the effect on a transmitted binary signal of the following:
(a) Attenuation
(b) Limited bandwidth
(c) Delay distortion
(d) Line and system noise

2.6 Use the integrals listed in Section 2.2 to derive the Fourier series for a periodic binary signal assuming (a) unipolar and (b) bipolar encoding.

2.7 Explain why the binary sequence 101010... is referred to as the worst-case sequence when deriving the minimum bandwidth requirements of a channel.

2.8 Derive the minimum channel bandwidth required to transmit at the following bit rates assuming (i) the fundamental frequency only and (ii) the fundamental and third harmonic of the worst-case signal are to be received:
(a) 500 bps
(b) 2000 bps
(c) 1 Mbps

2.9 A modem to be used with the PSTN uses QPSK modulation with four levels (phases) per signaling element. Assuming a noiseless channel and a bandwidth of 3000 Hz, deduce:
(a) The Nyquist maximum information transfer rate in bps
(b) The bandwidth efficiency of the modulation scheme

2.10 Starting with the Fourier series expression for a unipolar binary signal as derived in Exercise 2.6, derive an expression for the output produced by the following digital modulators:
(a) ASK
(b) FSK
For each scheme, show in diagrammatic form the channel bandwidth required assuming only the fundamental and third harmonic of the worst-case periodic signal are to be received.

2.11 Assuming FSK modulation is to be used, estimate the minimum bandwidth required of a communications channel to transmit data at the following rates assuming (i) the fundamental of the worst-case signal is to be received, (ii) the fundamental plus third harmonic:
(a) 300 bps
(b) 1200 bps
(c) 4800 bps
Compare your results with those derived in the text for ASK modulation.

2.12 Starting with the Fourier series expression for a bipolar signal derived in Section 2.5, derive an expression for the output produced by a binary (two-level) PSK modulator.

Use your expression to show how the minimum bandwidth required of a communications channel can be estimated.

2.13 Explain the term 'NEXT canceler' and how such circuits can improve the data transmission rate of a line.

2.14 Describe the principle of operation of the following satellite/radio access control methods:
(a) Aloha
(b) Preassigned FDMA
(c) Demand-assigned TDMA

2.15 Explain the terms 'signal propagation delay' and 'transmission delay'. Assuming the velocity of propagation of an electrical signal is equal to the speed of light, determine the ratio of the signal propagation delay to the transmission delay, a, for the following types of data link and 1000 bits of data:
(a) 100 m of UTP wire and a transmission rate of 1 Mbps
(b) 2.5 km of coaxial cable and a transmission rate of 10 Mbps
(c) A satellite link and a transmission rate of 512 kbps

2.16 Make a sketch showing the interface circuits and the associated signal levels used to transmit binary data between two DTEs using the following signal types and transmission media:
(a) V.28 and open lines
(b) 20 mA current loop and open lines
(c) RS-422 and twisted-pair

(d) Coaxial cable
(e) Optical fiber
Outline the properties of each signal type.

2.17 (a) Why must a modem be used to transmit binary data through a PSTN? Use sketches and additional text to describe the following modulation methods:
(i) Amplitude shift keying (ASK)
(ii) Frequency shift keying (FSK)
(iii) Phase-coherent PSK
(iv) Differential PSK
(b) Discuss the factors that influence the choice of carrier frequency and the bandwidth used by the demodulator section of a modem.

2.18 Deduce the maximum theoretical information rates associated with the following transmission channels:
(a) Telex (international message switching) network with a bandwidth of 500 Hz and a signal-to-noise ratio of 5 dB
(b) Switched telephone network with a bandwidth of 3100 Hz and a signal-to-noise ratio of 20 dB

2.19 Data is to be transmitted using a modem at 9600 bps. Determine the minimum bandwidth of the system with the following modulation methods:
(a) FSK
(b) 16-QAM

2.20 Data is to be transmitted through a PSTN at 4800 bps with a minimum bit error rate of 10^{-6} using a PSK modem. If the E_b/N_0 ratio needed to achieve this error rate is 10 dB with PSK modulation, deduce the minimum received signal level that is required assuming a temperature of 20°C.

2.21 List the main signals used with the EIA-232D/V.24 standard interface and state their functions. Derive a time sequence diagram to show the use of each line. Use as an example a user at a terminal establishing a half-duplex connection through a PSTN to carry out a transaction involving the exchange of data between the terminal and a remote computer.

2.22 (a) What is the function of a null modem? Show the internal connections used within a null modem and explain the significance of each connection.

(b) List the main signals used with the EIA-530/V.35 standard interface and state their functions.

2.23 With aid of sketches, explain the meaning of the following terms relating to the digitization of an analog voice signal:

(a) Sampling and PAM signals

(b) Quantization

(c) Companding

2.24 Explain the digital hierarchy used in North America and the ITU-T recommendation relating to leased digital circuits.

Use sketches of the frame structure used in each of these schemes to show how the basic multiplexing groups are derived and hence derive the usable data rate with each circuit.

Chapter summary

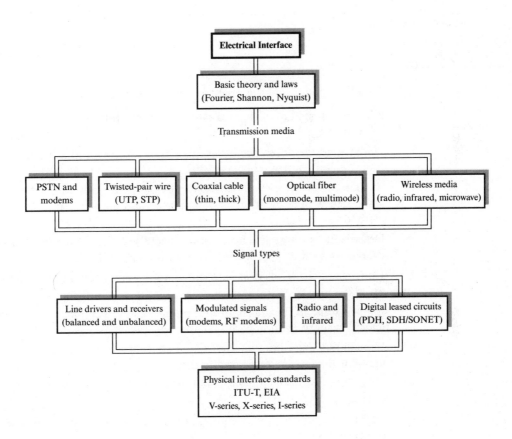

3 DATA TRANSMISSION

Chapter objectives

When you have completed this chapter you should be able to:

- Know the structure of the two most common information interchange codes ☞ 98, 99

- Understand the difference between an asynchronous and a synchronous transmission control scheme ☞ 102

- Explain the bit (clock) and character (byte) synchronization methods associated with asynchronous transmission and the different encoding methods used ☞ 107

- Describe how frame synchronization is achieved with asynchronous and character-oriented synchronous transmission ☞ 110, 121

- Understand the terms data transparency, and character and bit stuffing ☞ 111, 124

- Explain some of the alternative techniques that are employed to obtain bit (clock) synchronization with synchronous transmission ☞ 112

- Explain the operation and application areas of some of the alternative methods that can be employed to detect transmission (bit) errors ☞ 125

- Describe some of the most widely used methods for the compression of data ☞ 137

- Explain the principle of operation of the different types of multiplexer equipment ☞ 157

Introduction

Data communication is concerned with the exchange of digitally encoded information between two DTEs. The physical separation of the two pieces of equipment may vary from a few tens of meters – for example, between two personal computers – to several hundreds of kilometers – if, for example, the two devices are connected using a public carrier network.

96

Within the data communication community, we normally reserve the term 'data' for describing a set or block of one or more digitally encoded alphabetic and numeric characters being exchanged between two devices. Typically, this data represents a string of numbers or the contents of a computer file containing a stored document. When using a data communication facility to transfer this type of data, the two communicating parties (DTEs) must also exchange control messages in addition to data messages, for example, to overcome the effect of transmission errors within the communication facility. To discriminate between the two types of message, therefore, we use the more general term **information** to describe the actual user data being exchanged across the data communication facility.

In any digital system, the loss or corruption of a single bit (binary digit) of information can be critical. We must therefore ensure that when we design a data communication facility we take adequate precautions to detect and, if necessary, correct any possible loss or corruption of information during transmission. Data communication is concerned, therefore, not only with the way data is transmitted over the physical transmission medium, but also with the techniques that may be adopted to detect and, if necessary, correct transmission errors. It is also concerned with the control of the data transfer rate, the format of the data being transferred, and related issues.

In both this chapter and the next we are concerned with the fundamental concepts associated with data communication and, in particular, with the techniques that are used to achieve the reliable (error free and no losses or duplicates) transfer of information across a **bit-serial transmission medium** connecting two DTEs. As we saw in Chapter 2, the transmission medium may be a physical circuit – twisted pair, coaxial cable or optical fiber – or a radio-based channel. In many instances, therefore, we use the more general term **data link** to describe the link connecting two DTEs. In this chapter we deal with the basic techniques and circuits used for the transmission of data between two DTEs, while in Chapter 4 we describe the basic techniques employed for the control of data transfer between the two communicating parties. We must stress that, irrespective of the type of error-detection (and correction) scheme adopted, it is impossible to detect all possible combinations of transmission errors with 100% certainty. In practice, therefore, the aim of the various error-detection and correction techniques is to make the probability that undetected errors are present in a received message acceptably low.

3.1 Data transmission basics

When we enter data into a computer via a keyboard, each selected keyed element – an alphabetic or numeric character, for example – is **encoded** by the electronics within the keyboard into an equivalent binary-coded pattern using one of the standard coding schemes that are used for the interchange of information. In order to represent all the characters on a keyboard with a unique pattern, 7 or 8 bits are utilized. The use of 7 bits means that 128 different elements can be represented, while 8 bits can represent 256 elements. A similar procedure is followed on output except in this case the printer will **decode** each received binary-coded pattern to print the corresponding character. We refer to the coded bit patterns for each character as **codewords**.

The two most widely used codes that have been adopted for this function are the **Extended Binary Coded Decimal Interchange Code (EBCDIC)** and the **American Standards Committee for Information Interchange (ASCII)**. EBCDIC is an 8-bit code that is used with most equipment manufactured by IBM. As such it is a **proprietary code** but, owing to the widespread use of IBM equipment in the computer industry, it is frequently used. The codeword definitions used with EBCDIC are shown in Figure 3.1(a).

The ASCII code is the same as that defined by the ITU-T – known as **International Alphabet Number 5 (IA5)** – and also that used by the International Organization for Standardization known as ISO 645. Each is a 7-bit code; the codeword definitions used are shown in Figure 3.1(b).

Both coding schemes cater for all the normal alphabetic, numeric and punctuation characters – collectively referred to as **printable characters** – plus a range of additional **control characters** – also known as **non-printable characters**. Examples of nonprintable characters include:

Figure 3.1
Standard interchange codes: (a) EBCDIC.

- Format control characters – BS (backspace), LF (line feed), CR (carriage return), SP (space), DEL (delete), ESC (escape), and FF (form feed);

(a)

Bit positions	4	0	0	0	0	0	0	0	0	1	1	1	1	1	1	1	1
	3	0	0	0	0	1	1	1	1	0	0	0	0	1	1	1	1
	2	0	0	1	1	0	0	1	1	0	0	1	1	0	0	1	1
	1	0	1	0	1	0	1	0	1	0	1	0	1	0	1	0	1
8	7	6	5																
0 0 0 0		NUL	SOH	STX	ETX	PF	HT	LC	DEL			SMM	VT	FF	CR	SO	SI
0 0 0 1		DLE	DC1	DC2	DC3	RES	NL	BS	IL	CAN	EM	CC		IFS	IGS	IRS	IUS
0 0 1 0		DS	SOS	FS		BYP	LF	EOB	PRE			SM			ENQ	ACK	BEL
0 0 1 1				SYN		PN	RS	UC	EOT			`		DC$_4$	NAK		SUB
0 1 0 0		SP										¢	.	<	(	+	|
0 1 0 1		&										!	$	*	)	;	¬
0 1 1 0		–	/									'	%	-	>	?
0 1 1 1												:	#	@	,	=	"
1 0 0 0			a	b	c	d	e	f	g	h	i						
1 0 0 1			j	k	l	m	n	o	p	q	r						
1 0 1 0				s	t	u	v	w	x	y	z						
1 0 1 1																	
1 1 0 0			A	B	C	D	E	F	G	H	I						
1 1 0 1			J	K	L	M	N	O	P	Q	R						
1 1 1 0				S	T	U	V	W	X	Y	Z						
1 1 1 1		0	1	2	3	4	5	6	7	8	9						□

(b)

	Bit positions										
		7	0	0	0	0	1	1	1	1
		6	0	0	1	1	0	0	1	1
		5	0	1	0	1	0	1	0	1
4	3	2	1								
0	0	0	0	NUL	DLE	SP	0	@	P	\	p
0	0	0	1	SOH	DC1	!	1	A	Q	a	q
0	0	1	0	STX	DC2	"	2	B	R	b	r
0	0	1	1	ETX	DC3	#	3	C	S	c	s
0	1	0	0	EOT	DC4	$	4	D	T	d	t
0	1	0	1	ENQ	NAK	%	5	E	U	e	u
0	1	1	0	ACK	SYN	&	6	F	V	f	v
0	1	1	1	BEL	ETB	'	7	G	W	g	w
1	0	0	0	BS	CAN	(	8	H	X	h	x
1	0	0	1	HT	EM	)	9	I	Y	i	y
1	0	1	0	LF	SUB	*	:	J	Z	j	z
1	0	1	1	VT	ESC	+	;	K	[	k	{
1	1	0	0	FF	FS	,	<	L	\	l		
1	1	0	1	CR	GS	–	=	M	]	m	}
1	1	1	0	SO	RS	.	>	N	^	n	~
1	1	1	1	SI	US	/	?	O	_	o	DEL

Figure 3.1 (cont.)
(b) ASCII/IA5.

- Information separators – FS (file separator) and RS (record separator);
- Transmission control characters – SOH (start-of-heading), STX (start-of-text), ETX (end-of-text), ACK (acknowledge), NAK (negative acknowledge), and SYN (synchronous idle).

The use of some of these will be described in Section 3.2.3.

Although such codes are used for input and output, once numerical data has been input into the computer, it is normally converted and stored in an equivalent, fixed-length binary form, typically of 8, 16, or 32 bits. We call an 8-bit binary pattern a **byte** and longer patterns **words**. Because of the range of bits used to represent each word, it is usual when communicating data between two DTEs to use multiple, fixed-length elements each of 8 bits. Thus in some instances the 8 bits being transmitted across a data link may represent a binary-encoded printable character (7 bits plus an additional bit for error-detection purposes) while in others it may represent an 8-bit component of a larger value. In the latter case, we refer to the element as a byte or, for communication purposes, as an **octet**.

3.1.1 Bit-serial transmission

Within a piece of equipment, the distances and hence lengths of wire used to connect each subunit are short. Thus it is normal practice to transfer data between subunits using a separate wire to carry each bit of the data. This means that there are multiple wires connecting each subunit and data is said to be exchanged using a **parallel transfer mode**. This mode of operation results in minimal delays in transferring each word.

When transferring information between two physically separate pieces of equipment, especially if the separation is more than a few meters, for reasons of cost it is more usual to use a single pair of lines. Each octet making up the data is transmitted a single bit at a time using a fixed time interval for each bit. This mode of operation is known as **bit-serial transmission**.

The two alternative modes of operation are shown in Figure 3.2. We normally represent a bit within a piece of digital electronic equipment as a specific voltage level relative to a reference level. In Figure 3.2, a high signal relative to the reference indicates the transmission of a binary 1 while a low signal level, equal to the reference, represents a binary 0. In contrast, as we described in Chapter 2, with serial transmission the high- and low-level signals are normally positive and negative voltages relative to the reference.

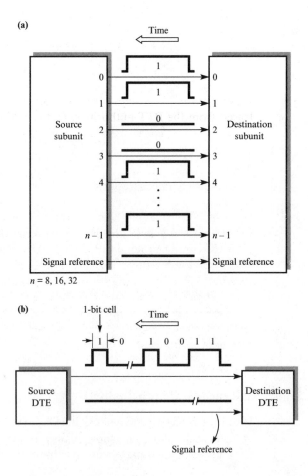

Figure 3.2
Transmission modes:
(a) parallel; (b) serial.

3.1.2 Communication modes

When a person is giving a lecture or speech, information is primarily conveyed in one direction. During a conversation between two people, however, spoken messages (information) are usually exchanged in both directions. These messages are normally exchanged alternately but can, of course, be exchanged simultaneously! Similarly, when data is transmitted between two pieces of equipment, three analogous modes of operation can be used:

(1) **Simplex**   This is used when data is to be transmitted in one direction only, for example, in a data logging system in which a monitoring device returns a reading at regular intervals to the data gathering facility.

(2) **Half-duplex**   This is used when the two interconnected devices wish to exchange information (data) alternately, for example, if one of the devices returns some data only in response to a request from the other. Clearly, the two devices must be able to switch between send and receive modes after each transmission.

(3) **Duplex**   This is also referred to as full-duplex and is used when data is to be exchanged between the two connected devices in both directions simultaneously, for example, if for throughput reasons data can flow in each direction independently.

The alternative communication modes are important since in many distributed systems the circuits (lines) used to provide the communication facilities are often leased from the PTT authorities, and it is less expensive to lease a single circuit, rather than two circuits, if only simplex operation is required, for example.

3.1.3 Transmission modes

As we mentioned at the beginning of Section 3.1, data is normally transmitted between two DTEs in multiples of a fixed-length unit, typically of 8 bits. In some instances, for example, if a computer is transferring a data file comprising, say, a source program, the data will be made up of a block of 8-bit binary-encoded characters. In others, for example, if the file comprises the object (compiled) code of the program, then the data will be made up of a block of 8-bit bytes.

Since each character or byte is transmitted bit serially, the receiving DTE receives one of two signal levels which vary according to the bit pattern (and hence character string) making up the message. For the receiving device to decode and interpret this bit pattern correctly, it must be able to determine the following:

(1) The start of each bit cell period (in order to sample the incoming signal in the middle of the bit cell)

(2) The start and end of each element (character or byte)

(3) The start and end of each complete message block (the message block is also known as a **frame**)

These three tasks are known as **bit** or **clock synchronization**, **character** or **byte synchronization**, and **block** or **frame synchronization**, respectively.

In general, we can accomplish synchronization in one of two ways, the method being determined by whether the transmitter and receiver clocks are independent (asynchronous) or synchronized (synchronous). With **asynchronous transmission**, each character (byte) is treated independently for clock (bit) and character (byte) synchronization purposes and the receiver resynchronizes at the start of each character received. With **synchronous transmission**, the complete frame (block) of characters is transmitted as a contiguous string of bits and the receiver endeavors to keep in synchronism with the incoming bit stream for the duration of the complete frame (block).

Asynchronous transmission

We use this method of transmission primarily when the data to be transmitted is generated at random intervals, for example, by a user at a keyboard communicating with a computer. Clearly, with this type of communication, the user keys in each character at an indeterminate rate, with possibly long random time intervals between each successive typed character. This means that the signal on the transmission line will be in the idle (known as **marking**) state for long time intervals between characters. With this type of communication, therefore, the receiver must be able to resynchronize at the start of each new character received. To accomplish this, each transmitted character or byte is encapsulated between an additional **start bit** and one or more **stop bits**, as shown in Figure 3.3.

Although it is used mainly for the transmission of characters between a keyboard (or more generally a terminal) and a computer, asynchronous transmission can also be used for the transmission of blocks of characters (or bytes) between two computers. In this case, the start bit of each subsequent character immediately follows the stop bit(s) of the previous character since the characters in a block are transmitted one after the other with no delay between them.

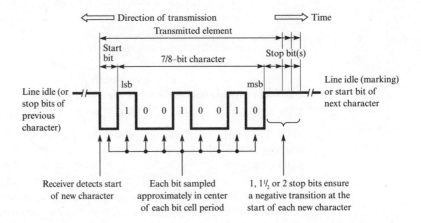

Figure 3.3
Asynchronous
transmission basics.

As Figure 3.3 shows, the polarity of the start and stop bits is different. This difference ensures that there is always a minimum of one transition $(1 \rightarrow 0 \rightarrow 1)$ between each successive character, irrespective of the bit sequences in the characters being transmitted. The first $1 \rightarrow 0$ transition after an idle period is then used by the receiving device to determine the start of each new character. In addition, by utilizing a clock whose frequency is N times higher than the transmitted bit rate frequency ($N = 16$ is typical), the receiving device can determine (to a good approximation) the state of each transmitted bit in the character by sampling the received signal approximately at the center of each bit cell period. This is shown in Figure 3.3; we shall discuss this further in Section 3.2.

We can deduce that to transmit each item of user data, 10 (one start bit and one stop bit) or possibly 11 (one start bit and two stop bits) bits are utilized. Assuming a single start bit and two stop bits per 8-bit element and a data transmission rate of, say, 1200 bps, the data rate is 1200/11 or about 110 bytes per second. The useful data rate is, in fact, less than this for reasons that will be described in Section 3.2.3.

When defining the transmission rate of a line, the term **baud** is often used by communication engineers. When correctly used, however, this term indicates the number of line signal transitions per second. Thus, if each transmitted signal can be in one of two states, the terms baud and bits per second (bps) are equivalent. However, as we described in Chapter 2, in some instances the line signal can take on more than two states, and hence each transmitted cell can be used to convey more than a single bit of information. To avoid confusion, therefore, we use the term **signaling rate** to define the number of line signal transitions per second (in baud) while the data or information transfer rate represents the number of data bits per second (bps). For example, a signaling rate of 300 baud with 4 bits per signaling element would yield a data rate of 1200 bps. The most common signaling rates in use on asynchronous lines are 110, 300, 1200, 4800, 9600, and 19 200 bps, although higher rates are also used over short distances.

Finally, when blocks of characters (or bytes) are being transmitted, each block is encapsulated between a pair of reserved (transmission control) characters to achieve block (frame) synchronization. This ensures that the receiver, on receipt of the opening character (byte) after an idle period, can determine that a new frame is being transmitted, similarly, on receipt of the closing character (byte), that the end of the frame has been reached.

Synchronous transmission

As we have just indicated, we normally use asynchronous transmission either when the rate at which characters are generated is indeterminate, or for the transmission of blocks of characters at relatively low data rates. In asynchronous transmission, both the use of additional bits per character for character synchronization and the relatively coarse bit synchronization method are acceptable. For the transmission of large blocks of data at higher bit rates, however, we use the synchronous transmission alternative.

With synchronous transmission, the complete block or frame of data is transmitted as a contiguous bit stream with no delay between each 8-bit element. To enable the receiving device to achieve the various levels of synchronization:

(1) The transmitted bit stream is suitably encoded so that the receiver can be kept in bit synchronism.

(2) All frames are preceded by one or more reserved bytes or characters to ensure the receiver reliably interprets the received bit stream on the correct character or byte boundaries (character or byte synchronization).

(3) The contents of each frame are encapsulated between a pair of reserved characters or bytes for frame synchronization.

In the case of synchronous transmission, during the period between the transmission of successive frames, either synchronous idle characters (or bytes) are continuously transmitted to allow the receiver to retain bit and byte synchronism, or each frame is preceded by two or more special synchronizing bytes or characters to allow the receiver to regain synchronism. This is shown in Figure 3.4.

We shall describe the alternative bit-encoding methods that are used to achieve bit synchronization in Section 3.3.1. As with asynchronous transmission, we must ensure that the start-of-frame and end-of-frame characters (bytes) are unique, that is, they are not present in the contents of the frame being transmitted. Clearly, if the frame contains, say, the contents of a binary code file, this cannot be guaranteed and hence we have to take additional steps to allow for this possibility. We shall discuss these aspects in more detail in Sections 3.2.3, 3.3.2 and 3.3.3.

Example 3.1

Deduce the number of additional bits required to transmit a message comprising one hundred 8-bit characters over a data link using each of the following transmission control schemes:

(a) Asynchronous with one start bit and two stop bits per character and a single start-of-frame and end-of-frame character per message

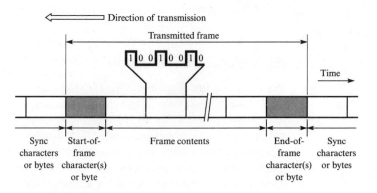

Figure 3.4
Synchronous
transmission basics.

(b)   Synchronous with two synchronization characters and a single start-of-frame and end-of-frame character per message

(a)   Number of bits per character = 1 + 2 = 3. Therefore $(3 \times 100) + 2 \times (3 + 8) =$ 322 additional bits are required.

(b)   With synchronous transmission, the number of additional bits is simply the two synchronization characters and one start-of-frame and one end-of-frame character, that is, $4 \times 8 = 32$ bits.

■ ■

3.1.4   Error control

During the transmission of a serial bit stream between two DTEs, it is very common – especially when the physical separation is large and, say, the PSTN is being used – for the transmitted information to become corrupted, that is, the signal level corresponding to a binary 0 is modified and, in the limit, is interpreted by the receiver as the level for a binary 1, and vice versa. When data is being transmitted between two devices, therefore, we normally provide a means for detecting possible transmission errors and, should errors arise, a means for correcting them.

We can use a number of alternative schemes, but the one we select is normally determined by the transmission method. When we use asynchronous transmission, for example, since each character is treated as a separate entity, we normally embed an additional binary digit (bit) within each transmitted character. This additional digit is known as a **parity bit**; we shall describe its function in Section 3.4.1.

In contrast, when we use synchronous transmission, we usually determine possible transmission errors on the complete frame, as the basic unit of transmission is a frame. Moreover, since the contents of a frame may be large, the probability of more than one bit being corrupted increases. A more sophisticated error check sequence must be used. Again, this may take a number of different forms but, in general, the transmitting device computes a sequence of error check digits, based on the contents of the frame being transmitted, and appends these to the tail of the frame either after the character or before the byte signaling the end of the frame.

During transmission of the frame, the receiver can recompute a new set of error check digits based on the received contents and, on receipt of the end-of-frame characters or byte, can compare this with the transmitted check digits. If these are not equal, a transmission error is assumed.

Both schemes allow the receiver to detect the occurrence of transmission errors only. Consequently, we need a scheme to enable the receiver to obtain another copy of the original transmission when errors are detected. A number of schemes are possible. For example, consider the case of a terminal and a computer transmitting data using asynchronous transmission. As the user keys in each character, the encoded character is normally transmitted to the computer as already outlined. The character corresponding to the received bit stream is then 'echoed' back by the computer and displayed on the screen of the user terminal. If the displayed character is different from the selected keyed character, the user may send a special (delete) character to inform the computer to ignore the last (erroneous) character received. This is referred to as **error control**. A way of performing the same function when blocks of characters are being transmitted must be employed. We discuss some of the more common error control methods in Chapter 4.

3.1.5 Flow control

If the amount of data to be transmitted between two devices is small, it is possible for the sending device to transmit all the data immediately because the receiving device will have sufficient resources (storage space) to hold the data. In many data communication situations, however, this is not the case. Thus we often have to adopt a method to control the flow of data transfer to ensure that the receiver does not lose any of the transmitted data because the receiving device has insufficient storage. This is particularly important when the two devices are communicating through an intermediate data communication network, as very often the network will buffer only a limited amount of data. If the two devices operate at different data rates, we often have to control the mean output rate of the faster device to prevent the communication network from becoming congested. The control of the flow of information between two DTEs is known as **flow control**. We shall introduce some of the alternative methods used in Chapter 4.

3.1.6 Data link protocols

Error and flow control are two essential components of the more general topic of data link control protocols. Essentially, a protocol is a set of conventions or rules that must be adhered to by both communicating parties to ensure that information being exchanged across a serial data link is received and interpreted correctly. In addition to error and flow control, a data link protocol also defines such things as:

- The format of the data being exchanged, that is, the number of bits per element and the type of encoding scheme being used

- The type and order of messages that are to be exchanged in order to achieve reliable (error free and no duplicates) information transfer between the two communicating parties.

For example, it is normal before transferring any data from one DTE to another to set up a connection between them to ensure that the receiving DTE is free and ready to receive the data. This is often accomplished by the sending device transmitting a specific control message – a call or connect request, for example – and the receiver returning a defined response message – a call connected or reject, for example. We shall discuss a number of different data link control protocols in Chapter 5.

3.2 Asynchronous transmission

As we discussed in Section 3.1, data is normally transmitted between two DTEs bit serially in multiple 8-bit elements (characters or bytes) using either asynchronous or synchronous transmission. Within the DTEs, however, each element is normally stored, processed and transferred in a parallel form. Consequently, the transmission control circuits within each DTE, which form the interface between the device and the serial data link, must perform the following functions:

- Parallel-to-serial conversion of each character or byte in preparation for its transmission on the data link

- Serial-to-parallel conversion of each received character or byte in preparation for its storage and processing in the device

- A means for the receiver to achieve bit, character, and frame synchronization

- The generation of suitable error check digits for error detection and the detection of such errors at the receiver should they occur

Parallel-to-serial conversion is performed by a **parallel-in, serial-out (PISO) shift register**. This shift register, as its name implies, allows a complete character or byte to be loaded in parallel and then shifted out bit serially. Similarly, serial-to-parallel conversion is performed by a **serial-in, parallel-out (SIPO) shift register** which executes the reverse function.

To achieve bit and character synchronization, we must set the receiving transmission control circuit (which is normally programmable) to operate with the same characteristics as the transmitter in terms of the number of bits per character and the bit rate being used.

3.2.1 Bit synchronization

In asynchronous transmission, the receiver clock (which is used to shift the incoming signal into the SIPO shift register) runs asynchronously with respect to the incoming signal. In order for the reception process to work reliably, we must devise a scheme whereby the local (asynchronous) receiver clock samples (and hence shifts into the SIPO shift register) the incoming signal as near to the center of the bit cell as possible.

To achieve this, a local receiver clock of N times the transmitted bit rate ($N = 16$ is common) is used and each new bit is shifted into the SIPO shift register after N cycles of this clock. The first $1 \rightarrow 0$ transition associated with the start bit of each character is used to start the counting process. Each bit (including the start bit) is sampled at (approximately) the center of each bit cell. After the first transition is detected, the signal (the start bit) is sampled after $N/2$ clock cycles and then subsequently after N clock cycles for each bit in the character. The general scheme is shown in Figure 3.5(a), the timing principles in part (b), and three examples of different clock rate ratios in part (c).

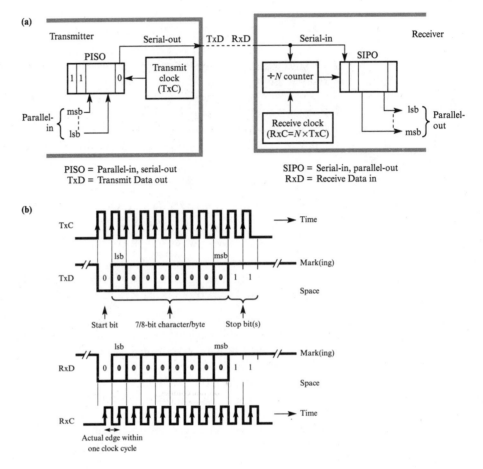

Figure 3.5
Asynchronous
transmission:
(a) principle of
operation;
(b) timing principles.

Remembering that the receiver clock (RxC) is running asynchronously with respect to the incoming signal (RxD), the relative positions of the two signals can be anywhere within a single cycle of the receiver clock. Those shown in Figure 3.5(c) are just arbitrary positions. Nevertheless, we can deduce from these examples that the higher the clock rate ratio, the nearer the sampling instant will be to the nominal bit cell center. Because of this mode of operation, the maximum bit rate normally used with asynchronous transmission is 19.2 kbps.

Example 3.2

■ ■ ■ ■ ■ ■ ■ ■ ■ ■ ■

A block of data is to be transmitted across a serial data link. If a clock of 19.2 kHz is available at the receiver, deduce the suitable clock rate ratios and estimate the worst-case deviations from the nominal bit cell centers, expressed as a percentage of a bit period, for each of the following data transmission rates:

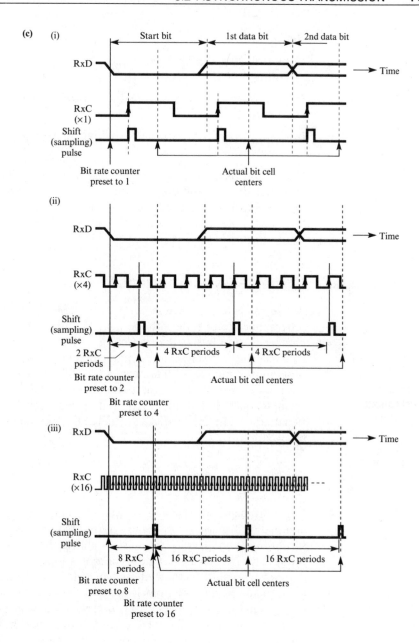

Figure 3.5 (cont.)
(c) Examples of
different clock rates.

(a)   1200 bps

(b)   2400 bps

(c)   9600 bps

It can readily be deduced from Figure 3.5(c) that the worst-case deviation from the nominal bit cell centers is approximately one cycle of the receiver clock.

Hence:

(a)   At 1200 bps, the maximum RxC ratio can be × 16. The maximum deviation is thus 6.25%.

(b)   At 2400 bps, the maximum RxC ratio can be × 8. The maximum deviation is thus 12.5%.

(c)   At 9600 bps, the maximum RxC ratio can be × 2. The maximum deviation is thus 50%.

Clearly, the last case is unacceptable. With a low-quality line, especially one with excessive delay distortion, even the second may be unreliable. It is for this reason that a × 16 clock rate ratio is used whenever possible.

3.2.2   Character synchronization

As we indicated in Section 3.1.3, the receiving transmission control circuit is programmed to operate with the same number of bits per character and the same number of stop bits as the transmitter. After the start bit has been detected and received, the receiver achieves character synchronization simply by counting the programmed number of bits. It then transfers the received character (byte) into a local **buffer register** and signals to the controlling device (a microprocessor, for example) that a new character (byte) has been received. It then awaits the next line signal transition that indicates a new start bit (and hence character) is being received.

3.2.3   Frame synchronization

When messages comprising blocks of characters – normally referred to as **information frames** – are being transmitted, in addition to bit and character synchronization, the receiver must be able to determine the start and end of each frame. This is known as frame synchronization.

The simplest method of transmitting blocks of printable characters is to encapsulate the complete block between two special (nonprintable) transmission control characters: STX (start-of-text) which indicates the start of a new frame after an idle period, and ETX (end-of-text) which indicates the end of the frame. As the frame contents consist only of printable characters, the receiver can interpret the receipt of an STX character as signaling the start of a new frame and an ETX character as signaling the end of the frame. This is shown in Figure 3.6(a).

Although the scheme shown is satisfactory for the transmission of blocks of printable characters, when transmitting blocks of data that comprise pure binary data (for example, the contents of a file containing a compiled program), the use of a single ETX character to indicate the end of a frame is not sufficient. In the case

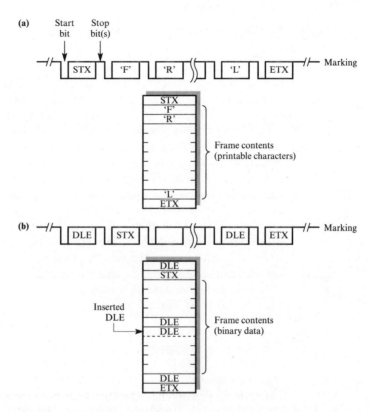

Figure 3.6
Frame
synchronization:
(a) printable
characters;
(b) binary data.

of binary data one of the bytes might be the same as an ETX character, which would cause the receiver to terminate the reception process abnormally.

To overcome this problem, when transmitting binary data the two transmission control characters STX and ETX are each preceded by a third transmission control character known as **data link escape (DLE)**. The modified format of a frame is then as shown in Figure 3.6(b).

Remember that the transmitter knows the number of bytes in each frame to be transmitted. After transmitting the start-of-frame sequence (DLE–STX), the transmitter inspects each byte in the frame prior to transmission to determine if it is the same as the DLE character pattern. If it is, irrespective of the next byte, a second DLE character (byte) is transmitted before the next byte. This procedure is repeated until the appropriate number of bytes in the frame have been transmitted. The transmitter then signals the end of the frame by transmitting the unique DLE–ETX sequence.

This procedure is known as **character** or **byte stuffing**. On receipt of each byte after the DLE–STX start-of-frame sequence, the receiver determines whether it is a DLE character (byte). If it is, the receiver then processes the next byte to determine whether that is another DLE or an ETX. If it is a DLE, the receiver discards it and awaits the next byte. If it is an ETX, this can reliably be taken as being the end of the frame.

3.3 Synchronous transmission

The use of an additional start bit and one or more stop bits per character or byte means that asynchronous transmission is relatively inefficient in its use of transmission capacity, especially when transmitting messages that comprise large blocks of characters. Also, the bit (clock) synchronization method used with asynchronous transmission becomes less reliable as the bit rate increases. This results, firstly, from the fact that the detection of the first start bit transition is only approximate and, secondly, although the receiver clock operates at N times the nominal transmit clock rate, because of tolerances there are small differences between the two which can cause the sampling instant to drift during the reception of a character or byte. We normally use synchronous transmission to overcome these problems. As with asynchronous transmission, however, we must adopt a suitable method to enable the receiver to achieve bit (clock), character (byte) and frame (block) synchronization. In practice, there are two synchronous transmission control schemes: character-oriented and bit-oriented. We shall discuss each separately but, since they both use the same bit synchronization methods, we shall discuss these methods first.

3.3.1 Bit synchronization

Although we often use the presence of a start bit and stop bit(s) with each character to discriminate between asynchronous and synchronous transmission, the fundamental difference between the two methods is that with asynchronous transmission the receiver clock runs asynchronously (unsynchronized) with respect to the incoming (received) signal, whereas with synchronous transmission the receiver clock operates in synchronism with the received signal.

As we have just indicated, start and stop bits are not used with synchronous transmission. Instead each frame is transmitted as a contiguous stream of binary digits. The receiver then obtains (and maintains) bit synchronization in one of two ways. Either the clock (timing) information is embedded into the transmitted signal and subsequently extracted by the receiver, or the receiver has a local clock (as with asynchronous transmission) but this time it is kept in synchronism with the received signal by a device known as a **digital phase-lock-loop (DPLL)**. As we shall see, the DPLL exploits the $1 \rightarrow 0$ or $0 \rightarrow 1$ bit transitions in the received signal to maintain bit (clock) synchronism over an acceptably long period. Hybrid schemes that exploit both methods are also used. The principles of operation of these schemes are shown in Figure 3.7.

Clock encoding and extraction

Three alternative methods of embedding timing (clock) information into a transmitted bit stream are shown in Figure 3.8. In part (a), the bit stream to be transmitted is encoded so that a binary 1 is represented by a positive pulse and binary 0 by a negative pulse. This is known as **bipolar encoding**. Each bit cell in the

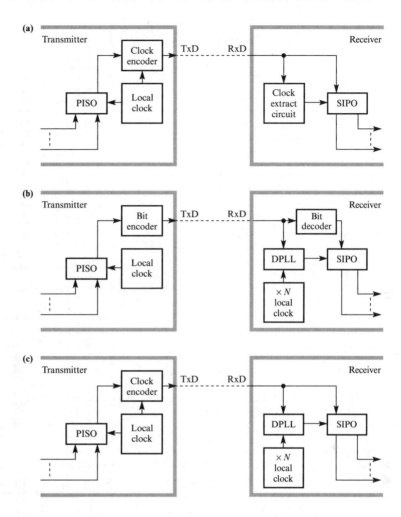

Figure 3.7
Synchronous
transmission clock
synchronization
alternatives: (a) clock
encoding; (b) DPLL;
(c) hybrid.

bipolar encoded signal contains clocking information. A simple electronic circuit
enables the clock signal to be extracted from the received bipolar signal. Since the
encoded signal returns to the zero level after each encoded bit (positive or
negative), we refer to this type of signal as a **return-to-zero (RZ) signal**.

Three distinct amplitude levels ($+$, 0, $-$) are utilized with bipolar encoding.
In contrast, the scheme shown in Figure 3.8(b) requires only two levels. The
resulting signal is known as a **non-return-to-zero (NRZ) signal** and the encoding
scheme **phase** or **Manchester encoding**. With this scheme a binary 1 is encoded as
a low–high signal and a binary 0 as a high–low signal. However, there is always a
transition ($1 \rightarrow 0$ or $0 \rightarrow 1$) at the center of each bit cell. This transition is used by
the clock extraction circuit to produce a clock pulse in the center of the second half
of the bit cell. At this point, the received (encoded) signal is either high (for binary
1) or low (for binary 0) and hence the correct signal will be shifted into the SIPO
shift register.

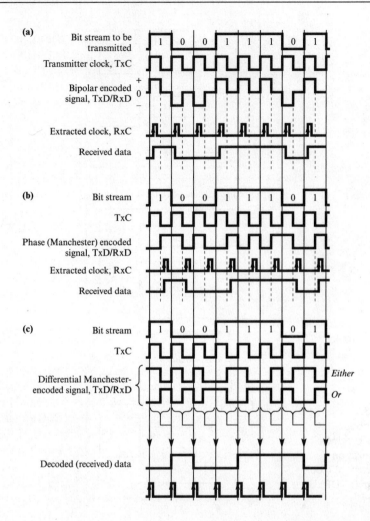

(a)
Bit stream to be transmitted
Transmitter clock, TxC
Bipolar encoded signal, TxD/RxD
Extracted clock, RxC
Received data

(b)
Bit stream
TxC
Phase (Manchester) encoded signal, TxD/RxD
Extracted clock, RxC
Received data

(c)
Bit stream
TxC
Differential Manchester-encoded signal, TxD/RxD
Decoded (received) data

Figure 3.8
Clock encoding methods: (a) bipolar; (b) Manchester; (c) differential Manchester.

The scheme shown in Figure 3.8(c) is known as **differential Manchester encoding**. This differs from Manchester encoding in that although there is still a transition at the center of each bit cell, a transition at the start of the bit cell occurs only if the next bit to be encoded is a 0. This has the effect that the encoded output signal may take on one of two forms depending on the assumed start level (high or low). As we can see, however, one is simply an inverted version of the other. This can be a useful feature with, say, point-to-point twisted-pair links since, if we are using differential drivers and receivers, it does not matter which way round the two terminating wires at the receiver are connected. With a nondifferential encoding scheme, the output will be inverted giving incorrect operation. The clock is generated at the end of each bit cell and the transitions in the bit cell determine whether the received bit is a 0 or 1.

The two Manchester encoding schemes are **balanced codes** which means there is no mean (DC) value associated with them. This is so since a string of binary 1s (or 0s) will always have transitions associated with them rather than a constant (DC) level. This is also an important feature since it means that the received signal can then be **AC coupled** to the receiver electronics using, for example, a **transformer**. The receiver electronics can then operate using its own power supply since this is effectively isolated from the power supply of the transmitter.

Digital phase-lock-loop

An alternative approach to encoding the clock in the transmitted bit stream is to utilize a stable clock source at the receiver which is kept in time synchronism with the incoming bit stream. However, as there are no start and stop bits with a synchronous transmission scheme, we must encode the information in such a way that there are always sufficient bit transitions ($1 \rightarrow 0$ or $0 \rightarrow 1$) in the transmitted waveform to enable the receiver clock to be resynchronized at frequent intervals. One approach is to pass the data to be transmitted through a **scrambler** which randomizes the transmitted bit stream, removing contiguous strings of 1s or 0s. Alternatively, the data may be encoded in such a way that suitable transitions will always be present.

The bit pattern to be transmitted is first differentially encoded as shown in Figure 3.9(a). We refer to the resulting encoded signal as a **non-return-to-zero-inverted (NRZI)** waveform. With NRZI encoding the signal level (1 or 0) does not change for the transmission of a binary 1, whereas a binary 0 causes a change. This means that there will always be bit transitions in the incoming signal of an NRZI waveform, providing there are no contiguous streams of binary 1s. On the surface, this may seem no different from the normal NRZ waveform but, as we shall describe in Section 3.3.3, if a bit-oriented scheme with zero bit insertion is used, an active line will always have a binary 0 in the transmitted bit stream at least every five bit cells. Consequently, the resulting waveform will contain a guaranteed number of transitions, since long strings of 0s cause a transition every bit cell. This enables the receiver to adjust its clock so that it is in synchronism with the incoming bit stream.

The circuit used to maintain bit synchronism is known as a digital phase-lock-loop (DPLL). A crystal-controlled oscillator (clock source), which can hold its frequency sufficiently constant to require only very small adjustments at irregular intervals, is connected to the DPLL. Typically, the frequency of the clock is 32 times the bit rate used on the data link and is used by the DPLL to derive the timing interval between successive samples of the received bit stream.

Assuming the incoming bit stream and the local clock are in synchronism, the state (1 or 0) of the incoming signal on the line will be sampled (and hence clocked into the SIPO shift register) at the center of each bit cell with exactly 32 clock periods between each sample. This is shown in Figure 3.9(c).

Now assume that the incoming bit stream and local clock drift out of synchronism because of small variations in the latter. The sampling instant is adjusted in discrete increments as shown in Figure 3.9(d). If there are no

(a)

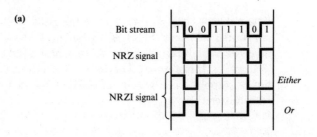

(b)

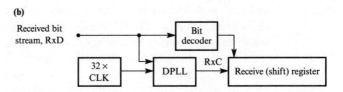

(c)

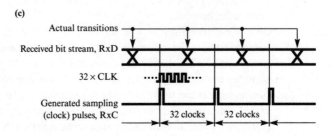

(d)

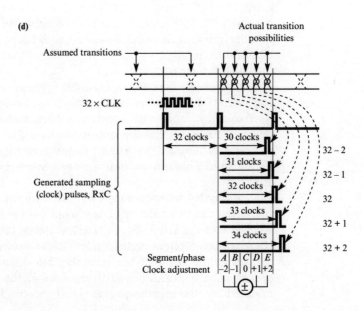

Figure 3.9
DPLL operation:
(a) bit encoding;
(b) circuit schematic;
(c) in phase; (d) clock
adjustment rules.

transitions on the line, the DPLL simply generates a sampling pulse every 32 clock periods after the previous one. Whenever a transition ($1 \rightarrow 0$ or $0 \rightarrow 1$) is detected, however, the time interval between the previously generated sampling pulse and the next is determined according to the position of the transition relative to where the DPLL thought it should occur. To achieve this, each bit period is divided into five segments, shown as A, B, C, D, and E in Figure 3.9(d). For example, a transition occurring during segment A indicates that the last sampling pulse was too close to the next transition and hence late. The time period to the next pulse is therefore shortened to 30 clock periods. Similarly, a transition occurring in segment E indicates that the previous sampling pulse was too early relative to the transition. The time period to the next pulse is therefore lengthened to 34 clock periods. Transitions in segments B and D are clearly nearer to the assumed transition and hence the relative adjustments are less (-1 and $+1$, respectively). Finally, a transition in segment C is deemed to be close enough to the assumed transition to warrant no adjustment.

In this way, successive adjustments keep the generated sampling pulses close to the center of each bit cell. In practice, the widths of each segment (in terms of clock periods) are not equal. The outer segments (A and E), being further away from the nominal center, are made longer than the three inner segments. For the circuit shown, a typical division might be $A = E = 10$, $B = D = 4$, and $C = 4$. We can readily deduce that in the worst case the DPLL requires 10 bit transitions to converge to the nominal bit center of a waveform: 5 bit periods of coarse adjustments (± 2) and 5 bit periods of fine adjustments (± 1). Hence when using a DPLL, it is usual before transmitting the first frame on a line, or following an idle period between frames, to transmit a number of characters/bytes to provide a minimum of 10 bit transitions. Two characters/bytes each composed of all 0s, for example, provide 16 transitions with NRZI encoding. This ensures that the DPLL generates sampling pulses at the nominal center of each bit cell by the time the opening character or byte of a frame is received. We must stress, however, that once in synchronism (lock) only minor adjustments can normally take place during the reception of a frame.

We can deduce from Figure 3.9 that with NRZI encoding the maximum rate at which the encoded signal changes polarity is one half that of bipolar and Manchester encoding. If the bit period is T, with NRZI encoding the maximum rate is $1/T$, whereas with bipolar or Manchester encoding it is $2/T$. The maximum rate is known as the modulation rate. As we described in Section 2.2, the highest fundamental frequency component of each scheme is $1/T$ and $2/T$, respectively. This means that, for the same data rate, bipolar and Manchester encoding require twice the transmission bandwidth of an NRZI encoded signal, that is, the higher the modulation rate, the wider is the required bandwidth.

The effect of this is that Manchester and differential Manchester encoding are both used extensively in applications such as LANs while schemes like NRZI are used primarily in WANs. LANs operate in a single office or building and hence use relatively short cable runs. This means that even though they operate at high bit rates – for example 10 Mbps and higher – the attenuation and bandwidth of the transmission medium are not generally a problem.

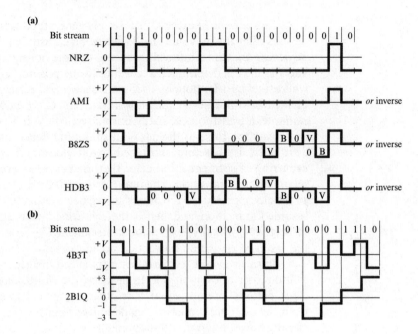

Figure 3.10
Some alternative coding schemes used with WANs: (a) binary codes; (b) multilevel codes.

In contrast, in WANs twisted-pair cable is often used with relatively high bit rates and over distances of several kilometers. Hence encoding schemes such as NRZI are often used with each bit occupying a full-width pulse. Some additional examples of the encoding schemes used in WANs are shown in Figure 3.10. The three examples in Figure 3.10(a) are all differentially encoded signals and use multiple levels per cell period. The use of differential encoding means that the signals shown may all be inverted if a different polarity start point is chosen. The use of multiple levels with alternative transitions means that any errors that result in a violation of the alternative transitions can be identified.

The three codes in Figure 3.10(a) use a three-level code ($+V$, 0, $-V$) to represent the bit stream. With **alternate mark inversion (AMI)**, signal transitions are triggered by a binary 1 (mark) in the input bit stream. The disadvantage of this basic scheme is that a long string of binary 0s will have no associated signal transitions. Consequently, the DPLL associated with the circuit may lose bit synchronization whenever a string of 0s is present.

To overcome this limitation, a number of derivatives of this basic scheme are also used. For example, a modified version is used in which signal transitions are triggered by a binary 0 rather than a binary 1. As we shall discuss in Section 3.3.3, with a bit-oriented scheme a binary 0 is inserted automatically into the transmitted bit stream whenever a string of five binary 1s is to be sent. This means that a signal transition is present at least every five-bit cells which, at bit rates up to several hundred kilobits per second, is sufficient for a DPLL to maintain clock synchronization. Such a scheme is used, for example, in the customer premises network associated with the European integrated services digital network (ISDN).

A second derivative of the basic AMI encoding scheme known as **bipolar with eight zeros substitution (B8ZS)** is also used. B8ZS is basically the same as AMI except that if a string of eight zeros is detected then these are encoded as 000VB0VB prior to transmission where B represents a normal (opposite polarity) transition and V a violation (same polarity). The maximum number of zero bits that can be obtained is seven. This scheme is widely used in the North American digital transmission network.

A third scheme that is used in the digital transmission network outside North America is known as **high density bipolar 3 (HDB3)**. This operates by replacing any string of four zeros by three zeros followed by a violation that is of the same polarity as the previous transition. Thus in the example the first string of four zeros is replaced by 000V. With this basic rule, however, the presence of a long string of zeros leads to a mean DC level being introduced into the signal as each set of four zeros is encoded in the same way. To avoid this with a long string of zeros the encoding of each successive four zeros is changed to B00V, producing a signal of alternating polarity. It can be deduced that with HDB3 the maximum number of zeros without a transition is three. We refer to HDB3 and the previous two schemes as the **modulation format**.

The two coding schemes shown in Figure 3.10(b) are used on the access circuits to an ISDN. As we shall see in Chapter 8, these operate at bit rates of 160 kbps over twisted-pair wire and span distances up to several kilometers. Both codes are examples of **baud rate reduction codes** which means that more than one bit is represented in a single pulse (time cell). The major advantage is that crosstalk is reduced owing to the smaller signal amplitude variations between adjacent pulses.

Both codes are classified as **mBnL codes** which means that a sequence of m input bits is represented by n pulses each of L levels where $n < m$ and $L > 2$. Thus with the **4B3T code** – also known as **modified monitoring state 43** or **MMS 43** – the T indicates three (ternary) levels, represented by the symbols $+$, $-$, 0. Hence four input bits are represented by three pulses each of three levels. The baud rate is thus 3/4 giving a **baud rate reduction** of 1/4.

The three symbol codes transmitted for each 4-bit input sequence are selected from one of the four columns in Table 3.1. Normally, transformers are used in wide area network applications in order to isolate the transmit and receive sections of a line from one another. This means that there is no path for direct current (DC). Hence it is necessary to ensure the mean (DC) level of the transmitted signal is zero, otherwise the zero signal at the receiver will vary. This phenomenon is known as **DC wander** and its effect is for the receiver to incorrectly interpret the received signal.

By inspection of the codes in the different columns, we can see that the combined weight of each codeword – and hence mean level – varies. In column 1, for example, the codeword $0 - +$ has a weight of zero while the code $+ + -$ has a weight of $+1$. Clearly, if a string of codewords all of weight $+1$ was transmitted directly, then the mean signal level at the receiver would move away from zero. To overcome this effect the codes used for each binary sequence vary from one column to another in such a way that the mean signal level always tends to zero.

Table 3.1   4B3T encoding patterns.

| Binary sequence | 1 | | 2 | | 3 | | 4 | |
	Code	Next col.	Code	Next col.	Code	Next col.	Code	Next col.
0001	0 − +	1	0 − +	2	0 − +	3	0 − +	4
0111	− 0 +	1	− 0 +	2	− 0 +	3	− 0 +	4
0100	− + 0	1	− + 0	2	− + 0	3	− + 0	4
0010	+ − 0	1	+ − 0	2	+ − 0	3	+ − 0	4
1011	+ 0 −	1	+ 0 −	2	+ 0 −	3	+ 0 −	4
1110	0 + −	1	0 + −	2	0 + −	3	0 + −	4
1001	+ − +	2	+ − +	3	+ − +	4	− − −	1
0011	0 0 +	2	0 0 +	3	0 0 +	4	− − 0	2
1101	0 + 0	2	0 + 0	3	0 + 0	4	− 0 −	2
1000	+ 0 0	2	+ 0 0	3	+ 0 0	4	0 − −	2
0110	− + +	2	− + +	3	− − +	2	− − +	3
1010	+ + −	2	+ + −	3	+ − −	2	+ − −	3
1111	+ + 0	3	0 0 −	1	0 0 −	2	0 0 −	3
0000	+ 0 +	3	0 − 0	1	0 − 0	2	0 − 0	3
0101	0 + +	3	− 0 0	1	− 0 0	2	− 0 0	3
1100	+ + +	4	− + −	1	− + −	2	− + −	3

(*Note*: the symbol 000 is decoded into the binary sequence 0000.)

Associated with each code in a column is a number (1–4) that indicates the next column from which the following code should be chosen. In Figure 3.10(b), the first 4-bit sequence 1011 is chosen from column 1 (+ 0 −) and the next column is 1. The next sequence 1001 is thus chosen from column 1 (+ − +) and the next column is 2, and so on. It can be deduced from the table that there are 27 different codewords. Since there are only 16 possible input sequences (4 bits), the code contains redundancy which can be exploited for error control. Also, the contents of the table are chosen such that with a random input sequence the mean bandwidth required is lower than when coding is not used.

The second code in Figure 3.10(b) is known as **2B1Q**, the Q indicating four (quaternary) level pulses – known as **quats**. Each 2-bit input sequence is transmitted in one 4-level pulse. As we can see in Figure 3.10(b), the four levels are represented by the symbols $+3$, $+1$, -1, -3 to indicate symmetry about zero and equal spacing between states. The first bit in each pair of binary digits determines the sign ($1 = +$, $0 = -$) and the second bit the magnitude ($1 = 1$, $0 = 3$). There is no redundancy with this code but the baud (signaling) rate is $1/2$ compared with $3/4$ with 4B3T.

Hybrid schemes

As the bit rate increases, so it becomes increasingly difficult to obtain and maintain clock (bit) synchronization. Although Manchester and DPLL schemes

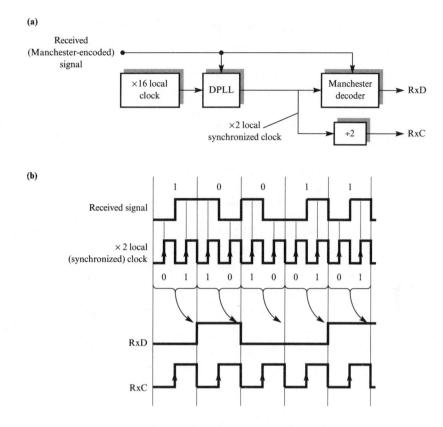

Figure 3.11
Bit synchronization
using Manchester
encoding and a DPLL:
(a) circuit schematic;
(b) waveform set.

are both widely used, there are additional hybrid schemes. A typical scheme is shown in Figure 3.11(a). It uses a combination of Manchester encoding and a DPLL.

The DPLL keeps the local clock in synchronism with the incoming received signal. Manchester encoding, however, means that there is at least one signal transition every bit cell rather than, say, one per five bits with an NRZI signal. The local clock thus keeps in synchronism more reliably and, as we can deduce from the waveform set shown in Figure 3.11(b), the availability of a local (× 2) clock in synchronism with the incoming signal provides a reliable means of decoding the received (Manchester-encoded) signal. The price to pay is the increased bandwidth required for Manchester encoding compared with NRZI.

3.3.2 Character-oriented synchronous transmission

As we indicated at the beginning of Section 3.3, there are two types of synchronous transmission control scheme: character-oriented and bit-oriented. Both use the same bit synchronization methods. The major difference between the two schemes is the method used to achieve character and frame synchronization.

Character-oriented transmission is used primarily for the transmission of blocks of characters, such as files of ASCII characters. Since there are no start or stop bits with synchronous transmission, an alternative way of achieving character synchronization must be found. To achieve this the transmitter adds two or more transmission control characters, known as **synchronous idle** or **SYN** characters, before each block of characters. These control characters have two functions. Firstly, they allow the receiver to obtain (or maintain) bit synchronization. Secondly, once this has been done, they allow the receiver to start to interpret the received bit stream on the correct character boundaries – **character synchronization**. The general scheme is shown in Figure 3.12.

Part (a) shows that frame synchronization (with character-oriented synchronous transmission) is achieved in just the same way as for asynchronous transmission by encapsulating the block of characters – the frame contents – between an STX–ETX pair of transmission control characters. The SYN control characters used to enable the receiver to achieve character synchronization precede the STX start-of-frame character. Once the receiver has obtained bit synchronization it enters what is known as the **hunt mode**. This is shown in Figure 3.12(b).

When the receiver enters the hunt mode, it starts to interpret the received bit stream in a window of eight bits as each new bit is received. In this way, as each bit is received, it checks whether the last eight bits were equal to the known SYN

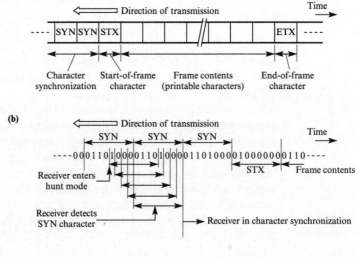

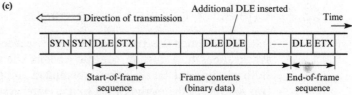

Figure 3.12
Character-oriented transmission: (a) frame format; (b) character synchronization; (c) data transparency (character stuffing).

character. If they are not, it receives the next bit and repeats the check. If they are, then this indicates it has found the correct character boundary and hence the following characters are then read after each subsequent eight bits have been received.

Once in character synchronization (and hence reading each character on the correct bit boundary), the receiver starts to process each subsequently received character in search of the STX character indicating the start of the frame. On receipt of the STX character, the receiver proceeds to receive the frame contents and terminates this process when it detects the ETX character. On a point-to-point link, the transmitter normally then reverts to sending SYN characters to allow the receiver to maintain synchronism. Alternatively, the above procedure must be repeated each time a new frame is transmitted.

Finally, as we can see in Figure 3.12(c), when binary data is being transmitted, data transparency is achieved in the same way as described previously by preceding the STX and ETX characters by a DLE (data link escape) character and inserting (stuffing) an additional DLE character whenever it detects a DLE in the frame contents. In this case, therefore, the SYN characters precede the first DLE character.

3.3.3   Bit-oriented synchronous transmission

The need for a pair of characters at the start and end of each frame for frame synchronization, coupled with the additional DLE characters to achieve data transparency, means that a character-oriented transmission control scheme is relatively inefficient for the transmission of binary data. Moreover, the format of the transmission control characters varies for different character sets, so the scheme can be used only with a single type of character set, even though the frame contents may be pure binary data. To overcome these problems, a more universal scheme known as **bit-oriented transmission** is now the preferred control scheme as it can be used for the transmission of frames comprising either printable characters or binary data. The three main bit-oriented schemes are shown in Figure 3.13. They differ mainly in the way the start and end of each frame is signaled.

The scheme shown in Figure 3.13(a) is used primarily on point-to-point links. The start and end of a frame are both signaled by the same unique 8-bit pattern 01111110, known as the **flag byte** or **flag pattern**. We use the term 'bit-oriented' because the received bit stream is searched by the receiver on a bit-by-bit basis for both the start-of-frame flag and, during reception of the frame contents, for the end-of-frame flag. Thus in principle the frame contents need not necessarily comprise multiples of 8 bits.

To enable the receiver to obtain and maintain bit synchronism, the transmitter sends a string of **idle bytes** (each comprising 01111111) preceding the start-of-frame flag. Recall that with NRZI encoding the 0 in the idle byte enables the DPLL at the receiver to obtain and maintain clock synchronization. On receipt of the opening flag, the received frame contents are read and

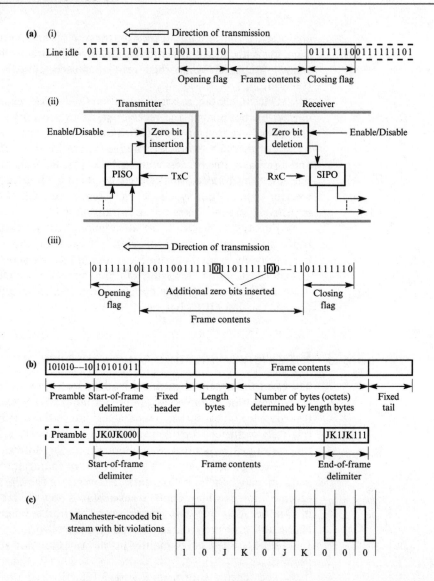

Figure 3.13
Bit-oriented
transmission frame
synchronization
methods: (a) flags;
(b) start-of-frame
delimiter and length
indication; (c) bit-
encoding violations.

interpreted on 8-bit (byte) boundaries until the closing flag is detected. The reception process is then terminated.

To achieve data transparency with this scheme, we must ensure that the flag pattern is not present in the frame contents. We do this by using a technique known as **zero bit insertion** or **bit stuffing**. The circuit that performs this function is located at the output of the PISO register, as shown in Figure 3.13(a). It is enabled by the transmitter only during transmission of the frame contents. When enabled, the circuit detects whenever it has transmitted a sequence of five contiguous binary 1 digits, then automatically inserts an additional binary 0 digit. In this way, the flag pattern 01111110 can never be present in the frame contents between the opening and closing flags.

A similar circuit at the receiver located prior to the input of the SIPO shift receiver performs the reverse function. Whenever a zero is detected after five contiguous 1 digits, the circuit automatically removes (deletes) it from the frame contents. Normally the frame also contains additional error detection digits preceding the closing flag which are subjected to the same bit stuffing operation as the frame contents. An example stuffed bit pattern is shown in Figure 3.13(a)(iii).

The scheme shown in Figure 3.13(b) is used with some LANs. In such networks, as will be explained in Chapter 6, the transmission medium is a broadcast medium and is shared by all the attached DTEs (stations). When a station wants to send a frame, it simply transmits it on the medium with the address (identity) of the intended recipient station at the head of the frame.

To enable all the other stations to obtain bit (clock) synchronization, the sending station precedes the frame contents with a bit pattern, known as the **preamble**, which comprises a string of 10 (binary) bit-pairs. Once in bit synchronism, the receiver searches the received bit stream on a bit-by-bit basis until it detects the known start of frame byte – 10101011 – the **start-of-frame delimiter**. A fixed header then follows, which includes the address of the intended recipient. The header is followed by two **length bytes** which indicate the number of bytes in the contents field. Thus with this scheme the receiver simply counts the appropriate number of bytes (octets) to determine the end of each frame.

The scheme shown in Figure 3.13(c) is also used with LANs. The start and end of a frame are both signaled by the use of nonstandard bit encoding patterns known as **bit-encoding violations**. For example, if Manchester encoding is being used, instead of a signal transition occurring in the center of the bit cell, the signal level remains either at the same level as the previous bit for the complete bit period (J) or at the opposite level (K).

Again, to detect the start and end of each frame, the receiver searches the received bit stream on a bit-by-bit basis, first for the start-of-frame delimiter – JK0JK000 – and then for the end-of-frame delimiter – JK1JK111. Since the J and K symbols are nonstandard bit encodings, the frame contents will not contain such symbols and data transparency is achieved.

We shall discuss each of the schemes in more detail when the different network types and protocols are introduced in Chapters 5 and 6.

3.4 Error detection methods

As we indicated in Chapter 2, when data is being transmitted between two DTEs it is very common, especially if the transmission lines are in an electrically noisy environment such as the PSTN, for the electrical signals representing the transmitted bit stream to be changed by electromagnetic interference induced in the lines by neighboring electrical devices. This means that signals representing a binary 1 are interpreted by the receiver as a binary 0 signal and vice versa. To ensure that information received by a destination DTE has a high probability of being the same as that transmitted by the sending DTE, there must be some way for the receiver to deduce, to a high probability, when received information contains errors. Furthermore, if errors are detected, a mechanism is needed to obtain a copy of the (hopefully) correct information.

There are two approaches for achieving this:

(1)   **Forward error control**, in which each transmitted character or frame contains additional (redundant) information so that the receiver can not only detect when errors are present but also determine where in the received bit stream the errors are. The correct data is then obtained by inverting these bits.

(2)   **Feedback (backward) error control**, in which each character or frame includes only sufficient additional information to enable the receiver to detect when errors are present but not their location. A retransmission control scheme is used to request that another, hopefully correct, copy of the information be sent.

In practice, the number of additional bits required to achieve reliable forward error control increases rapidly as the number of information bits increases. Hence, feedback error control is the predominant method used in the types of data communication and networking systems discussed in this book. A brief introduction to the subject of forward error control is given in Appendix A.

Feedback error control can be divided into two parts:

(1)   the techniques that are used to achieve reliable error detection, and

(2)   the control algorithms that are available to perform the associated retransmission control schemes.

In this section we are concerned with the most common error-detection techniques currently in use. We shall discuss some of the alternative retransmission control algorithms in Chapter 4.

The two factors that determine the type of error detection scheme used are the **bit error rate (BER)** of the line or circuit and the type of errors, that is, whether the errors occur as random single-bit errors or as groups of contiguous strings of bit errors. The latter are referred to as **burst errors**. The BER is the probability P of a single bit being corrupted in a defined time interval. Thus a BER of 10^{-3} means that, on average, 1 bit in 10^3 will be corrupted during a defined time period.

If we are transmitting single characters using asynchronous transmission (say 8 bits per character plus 1 start and 1 stop bit), the probability of a character being corrupted is $1 - (1 - P)^{10}$ which is approximately 10^{-2}. Alternatively, if we are transmitting blocks of characters using synchronous transmission (say 125 characters per block, each of 8 bits), then the probability of a block (frame) containing an error is approximately 1. This means that on average every block will contain an error and must be retransmitted. Clearly, this length of frame is too long for this type of line and must be reduced to obtain an acceptable throughput.

The type of errors present is important since, as we shall see, the different types of error detection scheme detect different types of error. Also, the number of bits used in some schemes determines the burst lengths that are detected. The three most widely used schemes are parity, block sum check and cyclic redundancy check. We shall consider each separately.

3.4.1 Parity

The most common method used for detecting bit errors with asynchronous and character-oriented synchronous transmission is the **parity bit method**. With this scheme the transmitter adds an additional bit – the parity bit – to each transmitted character prior to transmission. The parity bit used is a function of the bits that make up the character being transmitted. On receipt of each character, the receiver then performs the same function on the received character and compares the result with the received parity bit. If they are equal, no error is assumed, but if they are different, then a transmission error is assumed.

To compute the parity bit for a character, the number of 1 bits in the code for the character are added together (modulo 2) and the parity bit is then chosen so that the total number of 1 bits (including the parity bit itself) is either even – **even parity** – or odd – **odd parity**. The principles of the scheme are shown in Figure 3.14.

The two examples in Figure 3.14(d) show that the parity bit method detects only single (or an odd number of) bit errors and that two (or an even number of) bit errors go undetected.

The circuitry used to compute the parity bit for each character comprises a set of **exclusive-OR (XOR) gates** connected as shown in Figure 3.14(c). The XOR gate is also known as a **modulo-2 adder** since, as shown by the **truth table** in Figure 3.14(b), the output of the exclusive-OR operation between two binary digits is the same as the addition of the two digits without a carry bit. The least significant pair of bits are first XORed together and the output of this gate is then XORed with the next (more significant) bit, and so on. The output of the final gate is the required parity bit which is loaded into the transmit PISO register prior to transmission of the character. Similarly, on receipt, the recomputed parity bit is compared with the received parity bit. If it is different, this indicates that a transmission error has been detected.

The term used in coding theory to describe the combined message unit, comprising the useful data bits and the additional error detection bits, is **codeword**. The minimum number of bit positions in which two valid codewords differ is known as the **Hamming distance** of the code. As an example, consider a coding scheme that has seven data bits and a single parity bit per codeword. If we assume even parity is being used, consecutive codewords in this scheme will be:

0000000 0
0000001 1
0000010 1
0000011 0

We can deduce from this list that such a scheme has a Hamming distance of 2 since each valid codeword differs in at least two bit positions. This means that

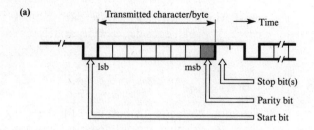

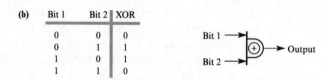

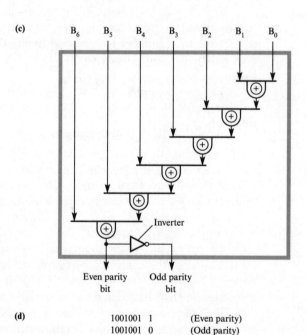

Figure 3.14
Parity bit method:
(a) position in
character; (b) XOR
gate truth table and
symbol; (c) parity bit
generation circuit;
(d) two examples.

(d)   1001001 1   (Even parity)
1001001 0   (Odd parity)

the scheme does not detect 2-bit errors since the resulting (corrupted) bit pattern will be a different but valid codeword. It does, however, detect all single-bit errors since, if a single bit in a codeword is corrupted, an invalid codeword will result.

3.4.2 Block sum check

When blocks of characters are being transmitted, there is an increased probability that a character (and hence the block) will contain a bit error. The probability of a block containing an error is known as the **block error rate**. When blocks of

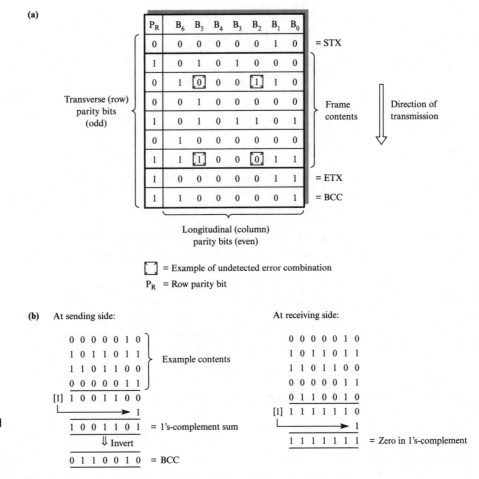

Figure 3.15
Block sum check example: (a) row and column parity bits; (b) 1's complement sum.

(a)

P_R	B_6	B_5	B_4	B_3	B_2	B_1	B_0	
0	0	0	0	0	0	1	0	= STX
1	0	1	0	1	0	0	0	
0	1	[0]	0	0	[1]	1	0	
0	0	1	0	0	0	0	0	
1	0	1	0	1	1	0	1	
0	1	0	0	0	0	0	0	
1	1	[1]	0	0	[0]	1	1	
1	0	0	0	0	0	1	1	= ETX
1	1	0	0	0	0	0	1	= BCC

Transverse (row) parity bits (odd)

Frame contents

Direction of transmission

Longitudinal (column) parity bits (even)

☐ = Example of undetected error combination
P_R = Row parity bit

(b)   At sending side: At receiving side:

```
    0 0 0 0 0 1 0 ⎫                    0 0 0 0 0 1 0
    1 0 1 1 0 1 1 ⎪ Example contents   1 0 1 1 0 1 1
    1 1 0 1 1 0 0 ⎬                    1 1 0 1 1 0 0
    0 0 0 0 0 1 1 ⎭                    0 0 0 0 0 1 1
[1] 1 0 0 1 1 0 0                      0 1 1 0 0 1 0
    └──────────→ 1                 [1] 1 1 1 1 1 1 0
    1 0 0 1 1 0 1  = 1's-complement sum    └──────────→ 1
       ⇓ Invert                         1 1 1 1 1 1 1  = Zero in 1's-complement
    0 1 1 0 0 1 0  = BCC
```

characters (frames) are being transmitted, we can achieve an extension to the error-detecting capabilities obtained from a single parity bit per character (byte) by using an additional set of parity bits computed from the complete block of characters (bytes) in the frame. With this method, each character (byte) in the frame is assigned a parity bit as before (**transverse** or **row parity**). In addition, an extra bit is computed for each bit position (**longitudinal** or **column parity**) in the complete frame. The resulting set of parity bits for each column is referred to as the **block (sum) check character** since each bit making up the character is the modulo-2 sum of all the bits in the corresponding column. The example in Figure 3.15 uses odd parity for the row parity bits and even parity for the column parity bits, and assumes that the frame contains printable characters.

We can deduce from this example that although two bit errors in a character will escape the row parity check, they will be detected by the corresponding column parity check. This is true, of course, only if no two bit errors occur in the same column at the same time. Clearly, the probability of this occurring is much less than the probability of two bit errors in a single character occurring. The use of a block sum check significantly improves the error-detection properties of the scheme.

A variation of the scheme is to use the 1's-complement sum as the basis of the block sum check instead of the modulo-2 sum. The principle of the scheme is shown in Figure 3.15(b).

In this scheme, the characters (or bytes) in the block to be transmitted are treated as unsigned binary numbers. These are first added together using 1's-complement arithmetic. All the bits in the resulting sum are then inverted and this is used as the block check character (BCC). At the receiver, the 1's-complement sum of all the characters in the block – including the block check character – is computed and, if no errors are present, the result should be zero. Remember that with 1's-complement arithmetic, end-around-carry is used, that is, any carry out from the most significant bit position is added to the existing binary sum. Also, zero in 1's-complement arithmetic is represented by either all binary 0s or all binary 1s.

We can deduce from Figure 3.15(b) that the error-detection properties of this scheme are better than the modulo-2 sum method. As we shall see in Chapters 9 and 11, since the 1's-complement sum is readily computed, it is used as the error-detection method in a number of applications which require the error-detection operation to be performed in software only.

3.4.3 Cyclic redundancy check

The previous two schemes are best suited to applications in which random single-bit errors are present. When bursts of errors are present, however, we must use a more rigorous method. An error burst begins and ends with an erroneous bit, although the bits in between may or may not be corrupted. Thus, an error burst is defined as the number of bits between two successive erroneous bits including the incorrect two bits. Furthermore, when determining the length of an error burst, the last erroneous bit in a burst and the first erroneous bit in the following burst must be separated by B or more correct bits, where B is the length of the error burst. An example of two different error burst lengths is shown in Figure 3.16. Notice that the first and third bit errors could not be used to define a single 11-bit error burst since an error occurs within the next 11 bits.

Parity, or its derivative block sum check, does not provide a reliable detection scheme against error bursts. In such cases, the most common alternative is based on the use of **polynomial codes**. Polynomial codes are used with frame (or block) transmission schemes. A single set of check digits is generated (computed) for each frame transmitted, based on the contents of the frame, and is appended by the transmitter to the tail of the frame. The receiver then performs a similar computation on the complete frame and check digits. If no errors have been induced, a known result should always be obtained; if a different answer is found, this indicates an error.

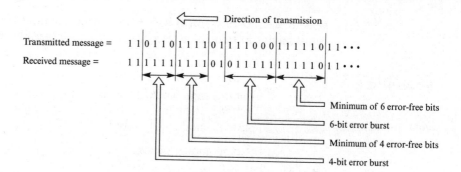

Figure 3.16
Error burst examples.

The number of check digits per frame is selected to suit the type of transmission errors anticipated, although 16 and 32 bits are the most common. The computed check digits are referred to as the **frame check sequence (FCS)** or the **cyclic redundancy check (CRC)** digits.

The underlying mathematical theory of polynomial codes is beyond the scope of this book but, essentially, the method exploits the following property of binary numbers if modulo-2 arithmetic is used. Let:

$M(x)$ be a k-bit number (the message to be transmitted)
$G(x)$ be an $(n + 1)$-bit number (the divisor or generator)
$R(x)$ be an n-bit number such that $k > n$ (the remainder)

Then if:

$$\frac{M(x) \times 2^n}{G(x)} = Q(x) + \frac{R(x)}{G(x)}, \text{ where } Q(x) \text{ is the quotient,}$$

$$\frac{M(x) \times 2^n + R(x)}{G(x)} = Q(x), \text{ assuming modulo-2 arithmetic.}$$

We can readily confirm this result by substituting the expression for $M(x) \times 2^n/G(x)$ into the second equation, giving:

$$\frac{M(x) \times 2^n + R(x)}{G(x)} = Q(x) + \frac{R(x)}{G(x)} + \frac{R(x)}{G(x)}$$

which is equal to $Q(x)$ since any number added to itself modulo 2 will result in zero, that is, the remainder is zero.

To exploit this, the complete frame contents, $M(x)$, together with an appended set of zeros equal in number to the number of FCS digits to be generated (which is equivalent to multiplying the message by 2^n, where n is the number of FCS digits) are divided modulo 2 by a second binary number, $G(x)$, the **generator polynomial**, containing one more digit than the FCS. The division operation is equivalent to performing the exclusive-OR operation bit by bit in parallel as each bit in the frame is processed. The remainder $R(x)$ is then the FCS which is transmitted at the tail of the information digits. Similarly, on receipt, the received bit stream including the FCS digits is again divided by the same generator polynomial – that is, $(M(x) \times 2^n + R(x))/G(x)$ – and, if no errors are present, the remainder is all zeros. If an error is present, however, the remainder is nonzero.

Example 3.3

A series of 8-bit message blocks (frames) is to be transmitted across a data link using a CRC for error detection. A generator polynomial of 11001 is to be used. Use an example to illustrate the following:

(a)   The FCS generation process

(b)   The FCS checking process

Generation of the FCS for the message 11100110 is shown in Figure 3.17. Firstly, four zeros are appended to the message, which is equivalent to multiplying

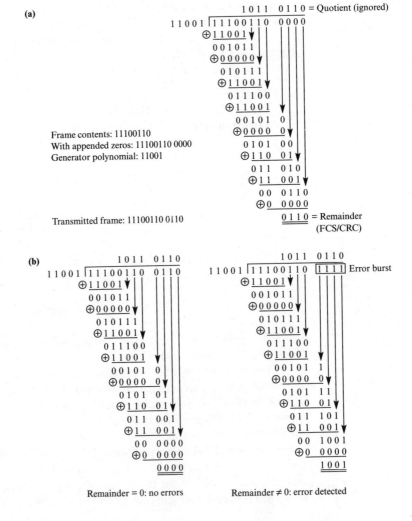

Figure 3.17
CRC example.

the message by 2^4, since the FCS will be four bits. This is then divided (modulo 2) by the generator polynomial (binary number). The modulo-2 division operation is equivalent to performing the exclusive-OR operation bit by bit in parallel as each bit in the dividend is processed. Also, with modulo-2 arithmetic, we can perform a division into each partial remainder, providing the two numbers are of the same length, that is, the most significant bits are both 1s. We do not consider the relative magnitude of both numbers. The resulting 4-bit remainder (0110) is the FCS, which is then appended at the tail of the original message when it is transmitted. The quotient is not used.

At the receiver, the complete received bit sequence is divided by the same generator polynomial as used at the transmitter. Two examples are shown in Figure 3.17(b). In the first, no errors are assumed to be present, so that the remainder is zero – the quotient is again not used. In the second, however, an error burst of four bits at the tail of the transmitted bit sequence is assumed. Consequently, the resulting remainder is nonzero, indicating that a transmission error has occurred.

■ ■

The choice of generator polynomial is important since it determines the types of error that are detected. Assume the transmitted frame, $T(x)$, is:

110101100110

and the error pattern, $E(x)$, is:

00000000 1001

that is, a 1 in a bit position indicates an error. Hence, with modulo-2 arithmetic:

Received frame $= T(x) + E(x)$

Now:

$$\frac{T(x) + E(x)}{G(x)} = \frac{T(x)}{G(x)} + \frac{E(x)}{G(x)}$$

but $T(x)/G(x)$ produces no remainder. Hence an error is detected only if $E(x)/G(x)$ produces a remainder.

For example, all $G(x)$ have at least three terms (1 bits) and $E(x)/G(x)$ will yield a remainder for all single-bit and all double-bit errors with modulo-2 arithmetic and hence be detected. Conversely, an error burst of the same length as $G(x)$ may be a multiple of $G(x)$ and hence yield no remainder and go undetected.

In summary, a generator polynomial of R bits will detect:

• All single-bit errors

• All double-bit errors

- All odd number of bit errors

- All error bursts $< R$

- Most error bursts $\geqslant R$

The standard way of representing a generator polynomial is to show those positions that are binary 1 as powers of X. Examples of CRCs used in practice are thus:

$$CRC - 16 \quad = X^{16} + X^{15} + X^2 + 1$$
$$CRC - CCITT = X^{16} + X^{12} + X^5 + 1$$
$$CRC - 32 \quad = X^{32} + X^{26} + X^{23} + X^{16} + X^{12} + X^{11} + X^{10} + X^8 + X^7$$
$$+ X^5 + X^4 + X^{22} + X + 1$$

Hence CRC-16 is equivalent in binary form to:

1 1000 0000 0000 0101

With such a generator polynomial, 16 zeros would be appended to the frame contents before generation of the FCS. The latter would then be the 16-bit remainder. CRC-16 will detect all error bursts of less than 16 bits and most error bursts greater than or equal to 16 bits. CRC-16 and CRC-CCITT are both used extensively with WANs, while CRC-32 is used in most LANs.

Although the requirement to perform multiple (modulo-2) divisions may appear to be relatively complicated, in practice it can be done quite readily in either hardware or software. To illustrate this, a hardware implementation of the scheme used in Figure 3.17 is given in Figure 3.18(a).

In this example, since we are to generate four FCS digits, we need only a 4-bit shift register to represent bits x^3, x^2, x^1, and x^0 in the generator polynomial. We often refer to these as the **active bits** of the generator. With this generator polynomial, digits x^3 and x^0 are binary 1 while digits x^2 and x^1 are binary 0. The new states of shift register elements x^1 and x^2 simply take on the states of x^0 and x^1 directly; the new states of elements x^0 and x^3 are determined by the state of the feedback path XORed with the preceding digit.

The circuit operates as follows. The FCS shift register is cleared and the first 8-bit byte in the frame is parallel-loaded into the PISO transmit shift register. This is then shifted out to the transmission line, most significant bit first, at a rate determined by the transmitter clock TxC. In time synchronism with this, the same bit stream is XORed with x^3 and passed via the feedback path to the selected inputs of the FCS shift register. As each subsequent 8-bit byte is loaded into the transmit shift register and bit-serially transmitted to line, the procedure repeats. Finally, after the last byte in the frame has been output, the transmit shift register is loaded with zeros and the feedback control signal changes from 1 to 0 so that the current contents of the FCS shift register – the computed remainder – follow the frame contents onto the transmission line.

(a)

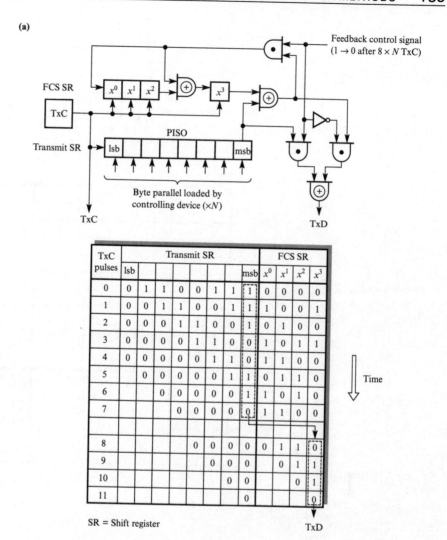

TxC pulses	Transmit SR								FCS SR			
	lsb							msb	x^0	x^1	x^2	x^3
0	0	1	1	0	0	1	1	1	0	0	0	0
1	0	0	1	1	0	0	1	1	1	0	0	1
2	0	0	0	1	1	0	0	1	0	1	0	0
3	0	0	0	0	1	1	0	0	1	0	1	1
4	0	0	0	0	0	1	1	0	1	1	0	0
5		0	0	0	0	0	1	1	0	1	1	0
6			0	0	0	0	0	1	1	0	1	0
7				0	0	0	0	0	1	1	0	0
8					0	0	0	0	0	1	1	0
9						0	0	0		0	1	1
10							0	0			0	1
11								0				0

Time

SR = Shift register

Figure 3.18
CRC hardware schematic: (a) generation.

In Figure 3.18(a) the contents of the transmit and FCS shift registers assume just a single-byte frame ($N = 1$), and hence correspond to the earlier example in Figure 3.17. In Figure 3.18 the contents of both the transmit and FCS shift registers are shown after each shift (transmit clock) pulse. The transmitted bit stream is as shown in the hashed boxes.

The corresponding receiver hardware is similar to that used at the transmitter, as shown in Figure 3.18(b). The received data (RxD) is sampled (shifted) into the SIPO receive shift register in the center (or later with Manchester encoding) of the bit cell. Also, as before, in time synchronization with this the bit stream is XORed with x^3 and fed into the FCS shift register. As each 8-bit byte is

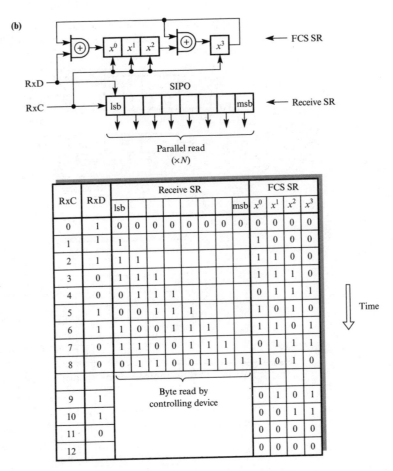

RxC	RxD	Receive SR lsb							msb	FCS SR x^0	x^1	x^2	x^3
0	1	0	0	0	0	0	0	0	0	0	0	0	0
1	1	1								1	0	0	0
2	1	1	1							1	1	0	0
3	0	1	1	1						1	1	1	0
4	0	0	1	1	1					0	1	1	1
5	1	0	0	1	1	1				1	0	1	0
6	1	1	0	0	1	1	1			1	1	0	1
7	0	1	1	0	0	1	1	1		0	1	1	1
8	0	0	1	1	0	0	1	1	1	1	0	1	0
9	1									0	1	0	1
10	1									0	0	1	1
11	0									0	0	0	0
12										0	0	0	0

Byte read by controlling device

Time

Remainder = 0

Figure 3.18 (cont.)
(b) Checking.

received, it is read by the controlling device. Again, the contents shown are for a frame comprising just a single byte of data.

The hardware in Figure 3.18 is normally incorporated into the transmission control circuits associated with bit-oriented transmission. In some instances, however, a CRC is used in preference to a block sum check with character-oriented transmission. In such cases, the CRC must normally be generated in software by the controlling device rather than in hardware. This is relatively straightforward as we can see from the pseudocode in Figure 3.19.

The code assumes an 8-bit generator polynomial (divisor) and that the preformatted frame – STX, ETX, etc. – is stored in an array. The same code can be used for CRC generation and checking; for generation the array will contain a byte/character comprising all zeros at its tail.

{ Assume a preformatted frame to be transmitted (including a zero byte at its tail) or a received frame is stored in a byte array buff[1.. count]. Also that the 8 active bits of a 9-bit divisor are stored in the most-significant 8 bits of a 16-bit integer CRCDIV. The following function will compute and return the 8-bit CRC }

```
function  CRC : byte;
var       i, j : integer;
          data : integer

begin     data := buff[1] shl 8;
          for j := 2 to count do
              begin
                  data := data + buff [j];
                  for i := 1 to 8 do
                      if ((data and $8000) = $8000) then
                      begin data := data shl1;
                            data := data xor CRCDIV; end
                      else   data := data shl 1;
          end;

          CRC := data shr 8;
end;
```

Figure 3.19
Pseudocode for 8-bit
computation/
checking.

3.5 Data compression

We have assumed until now that the contents of transmitted frames (blocks) are comprised of the original (source) data in the form of strings of fixed-length characters or bytes. Although this is the case in many data communication applications, there are others in which the source data is *compressed* prior to transmission. This is mainly done in applications involving public transmission facilities, such as the PSTN, in which charges are based on time (duration) and distance. Hence, for a particular call, if the time to transmit each block of data can be reduced, it will automatically reduce the call cost.

For example, assume we are transmitting data at, say, 4800 bps over the PSTN and the time needed to transmit the data associated with the call is 20 minutes. Clearly, if by using data compression we can halve the amount of data to be transmitted, we can obtain a 50% saving in transmission costs. This is the same as saying we can achieve the same performance with, say, a 4800 bps modem with compression as with a 9600 bps modem without compression.

In practice, we can employ a range of compression algorithms, each suited to a particular type of data. Some modems – often referred to as **intelligent modems** – now offer an **adaptive compression** feature which selects a compression algorithm to suit the type of data being transmitted. We shall describe some of the more common types of data compression algorithm in this section.

3.5.1 Packed decimal

When frames comprising just numeric characters are being transmitted, we can obtain significant savings by reducing the number of bits per character from seven to four by using simple binary-coded-decimal (BCD) encoding instead of ASCII. We can deduce from the table of ASCII codes in Figure 3.1(b) that the 10 numeric digits (0–9) all have 011 in their three high-order bit positions. Normally, the three bits (011) are needed to discriminate between numeric and alphabetic (and

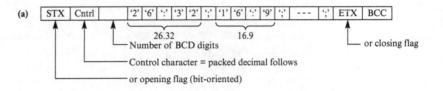

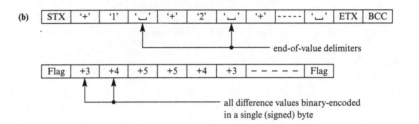

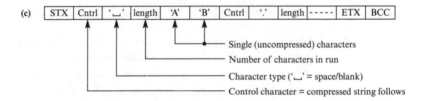

Figure 3.20
Examples of
compression
algorithms:
(a) packed decimal;
(b) relative encoding;
(c) character
suppression.

other) characters in the codeset. If the data comprises only numeric digits, however, these three bits are redundant and need not be transmitted, as Figure 3.20(a) shows.

As we can see, if character-oriented transmission is being used, it is not possible simply to insert the compressed binary-coded digits between the STX and ETX control characters since the digit pair 0, 3 would be interpreted as an ETX. Hence at the start of the data a (known) control character code is used to indicate that packed decimal follows. A second character (byte) then follows that indicates the number of digits in the run. Two characters in the same column – for example, ':' and ';' – are often used as a decimal point and space, respectively.

3.5.2 Relative encoding

An alternative to packed decimal when transmitting numeric data that has only small differences between successive values is to send only the difference in magnitude between each value together with a known reference value. This is known as **relative encoding** and it can be particularly effective in data logging applications.

For example, if we are remotely monitoring the water level of a river, we normally read the level at set time intervals and store (log) these readings prior to transmission. When we have obtained a preset number of readings, we transmit them to the central monitoring site using, for example, the PSTN and an **autodial modem**. To minimize the time needed to transmit the readings, instead of sending the absolute water level values, we send just the difference values. An example frame content with this scheme is shown in Figure 3.20(b). As can be seen, the savings obtained are a function of the format used for representing the difference values. In general, binary values with a bit-oriented protocol produce the largest saving.

3.5.3   Character suppression

A variation of the relative encoding scheme that we can use in a more general way to compress other character types is shown in Figure 3.20(c). Normally, when frames comprising printable characters are being transmitted, there are often sequences in the frame when the same character repeats, for example the space character. The control device at the transmitter scans the frame contents prior to transmission and, if a contiguous string of three or more characters is located, replaces these with the three-character sequence shown in the figure.

The sequence comprises a (known) control character indicating that a compressed string follows, the character type, and a count of the number of characters in the string. Normally, the count is in binary form, but since it is preceded by a known control character the receiver can discriminate between a count value of 3 and the ETX control character. Any character can be compressed in this scheme. The receiver, on detecting the compression control character, simply reads the following character type and count values and inserts the appropriate number of these characters into the received frame at this point. This scheme is an example of a more general encoding technique known as run-length encoding.

3.5.4   Huffman coding

Huffman coding exploits the property that not all symbols in a transmitted frame occur with the same frequency, for example, in a frame comprising strings of characters, certain characters occur more often than others. Instead of using a fixed number of bits per character, we use a different encoding scheme in which the most common characters are encoded using fewer bits than less frequent characters. It is thus a form of **statistical encoding**. Because of the variable number of bits per character, we must use bit-oriented transmission.

Firstly, the character string to be transmitted is analyzed and the character types and their relative frequency determined. The coding operation then involves creating an unbalanced tree with some branches (and hence codewords, in practice) shorter than others. The degree of imbalance is a function of the relative frequency of occurrence of the characters; the larger the spread, the more unbalanced is the tree. The resulting tree is known as the **Huffman code tree**.

A Huffman (code) tree is a **binary tree** with branches assigned the value 0 or 1. The base of the tree, normally the geometric top, in practice, is known as the **root node**, and the point at which a branch divides as a **branch node**. The termination point of a branch is known as a **leaf node** to which the symbols being encoded are assigned. An example of a Huffman tree is shown in Figure 3.21(a). This corresponds to the string of characters AAAABBCD.

As each branch divides, a binary value of 0 or 1 is assigned to each new branch: a binary 0 for the left branch and a binary 1 for the right branch. The codewords used for each character (shown in the leaf nodes) are determined by tracing the path *from* the root node out to each leaf and forming a string of the binary values associated with each branch traced. We can deduce from the codes that it would take

$$4 \times 1 + 2 \times 2 + 1 \times 3 + 1 \times 3 = 14 \text{ bits}$$

to transmit the complete string AAAABBCD.

We derive the average number of bits per codeword by summing together the number of bits in each codeword multiplied by its probability of occurrence. That is:

$$1 \times 0.5 + 2 \times 0.25 + 3 \times 0.125 + 3 \times 0.125 = 1.75 \text{ bits per codeword}$$

The theoretical minimum average number of bits per codeword to transfer the message string is known as the **entropy**, **H**, of the message. We can calculate H using a formula derived by Shannon which states:

$$H = -\sum_{i=1}^{n} P_i \log_2 P_i \text{ bits per codeword}$$

where n is the number of characters in the message and P_i is the probability of character (i) occurring in the message. Hence for the message AAAABBCD, the minimum average number of bits per codeword is given by:

$$H = -(0.5 \log_2 0.5 + 0.25 \log_2 0.25 + 0.125 \log_2 0.125 + 0.125 \log_2 0.125)$$
$$= 1.75 \text{ bits per codeword}$$

In this case, this is the same result as achieved using the Huffman coding.

Using 7-bit ASCII codewords would require $8 \times 7 = 56$ bits to transmit the complete message string which is significantly more than the 14 bits required with Huffman coding.

In practice, this is not a fair comparison since, with Huffman coding, the receiver must know the reduced character set being transmitted and the corresponding codewords, that is, their frequency of occurrence or Huffman tree. A better comparison is to consider the number of bits required with normal binary coding: four characters (A–D) require two bits for each character, so a total of 16 bits are required to transmit the 8 characters. Clearly, the savings are nominal. In general, Huffman coding is most efficient when the frequency distribution of the characters being transmitted is wide and long character strings are involved. Conversely, it is not suitable for the transmission of binary-coded computer data since the 8-bit bytes generally occur with about the same frequency.

To illustrate how the Huffman tree in Figure 3.21(a) is determined, we must add information concerning the frequency of occurrence of each character as

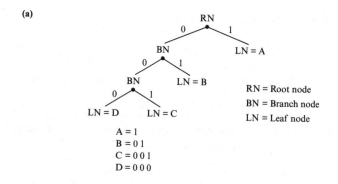

(a)

RN = Root node
BN = Branch node
LN = Leaf node

A = 1
B = 0 1
C = 0 0 1
D = 0 0 0

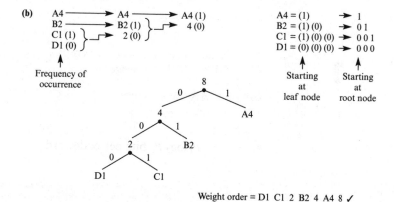

Figure 3.21
Huffman code tree construction: (a) final tree with codes; (b) tree derivation.

listed in Figure 3.21(b). The characters are listed in a column in decreasing (weight) order. We derive the tree as follows.

The first two leaf nodes at the base of the list – C1 and D1 – are assigned to the (1) and (0) branches respectively of a branch node. The two leaf nodes are then replaced by a branch node whose weight is the sum of these two weights – 2. A new column is formed containing the new node, combined with the remaining nodes from the first column, again arranged in their correct weight order. This procedure is repeated until only two nodes remain.

To derive the resulting codewords for each character, we start with the character in the first column and then proceed to list the branch numbers – 0 or 1 – as they are encountered. Thus for character A the first (and only) branch number is (1) in the last column while for C the first is (1) then (0) at branch node 2 and finally (0) at branch node 4. However, the codewords start at the root and not the leaf node hence the actual codewords are the reverse of these numbers. The Huffman tree can then be readily constructed from the set of codewords.

We check that this is the optimum tree – and hence set of codewords – by listing the resulting weights of all the leaf and branch nodes in the tree starting with the smallest weight and proceeding from left to right and from bottom to top. The codewords are optimum if the resulting list increments in weight order.

Example 3.4

A series of messages is to be transferred between two computers over the PSTN. The messages comprise just the characters A through H. Analysis has shown that the relative frequency of occurrence of each character is as follows:

A and B = 0.25,   C and D = 0.14,   E, F, G, and H = 0.055

(a) Use Shannon's formula to derive the minimum average number of bits per character.

(b) Use Huffman coding to derive a codeword set and prove this is the minimum set by constructing the corresponding Huffman code tree.

(c) Derive the average number of bits per character for your codeword set and compare this with:

   (i)   Shannon's value
   (ii) Fixed-length binary codewords
   (iii) 7-bit ASCII codewords

(a) Shannon's formula states:

$$\text{Entropy, } H = -\sum_{i=1}^{8} P_i \log_2 P_i \text{ bits per codeword}$$

Therefore:

$$H = -(2(0.25 \log_2 0.25) + 2(0.14 \log_2 0.14) + 4(0.055 \log_2 0.055))$$
$$= 1 + 0.794 + 0.921 = 2.715 \text{ bits per codeword}$$

(b) The derivation of the codeword set using Huffman coding is shown in Figure 3.22(a). The characters are first listed in weight order and the two characters at the bottom of the list are assigned to the (1) and (0) branches. Note that in this case, however, when the two nodes are combined, the weight of the resulting branch node (0.11) is greater than the weight of the two characters E and F (0.055). Hence the branch node is inserted into the second list higher than both of these. The same procedure then repeats until there are only two entries in the list remaining.

   The Huffman code tree corresponding to the derived set of codewords is given in Figure 3.22(b), and, as we can see, this is the optimum tree since all leaf and branch nodes increment in numerical order.

(c) Average number of bits per codeword using Huffman coding is:

$$2(2 \times 0.25) + 2(3 \times 0.14) + 4(4 \times 0.055) = 2.72 \text{ bits per codeword}$$
that is, 99.8% of Shannon's value.

Using fixed-length binary codewords:

A–H have 8 characters and hence 3 bits per codeword
that is, 90.7% of Huffman value.

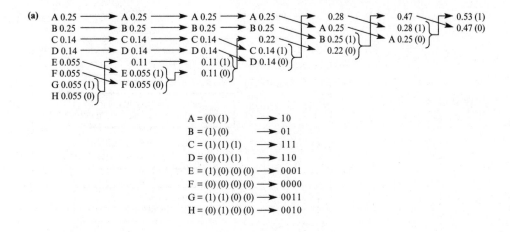

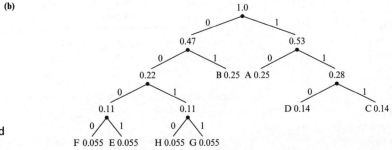

Figure 3.22
Huffman coding example: (a) codeword generation; (b) Huffman code tree.

Using 7-bit ASCII codewords:

7 bits per codeword
that is, 38.86% of Huffman value.

Since each character in its encoded form has a variable number of bits, the received bit stream must be interpreted (decoded) in a bit-oriented way rather than on fixed 8-bit boundaries. Because of the order in which bits are assigned during the encoding procedure, however, Huffman codewords have the unique property that a shorter codeword will never form the start of a longer codeword. If, say, 011 is a valid codeword, then there cannot be any longer codewords starting with this pattern. We can confirm this by considering the codes derived in the earlier examples in Figures 3.21 and 3.22.

This property, known as the **prefix property**, means that the received bit stream can be decoded simply by carrying out a recursive search bit by bit until each valid codeword is found. A flowchart of a suitable decoding algorithm is

(a)

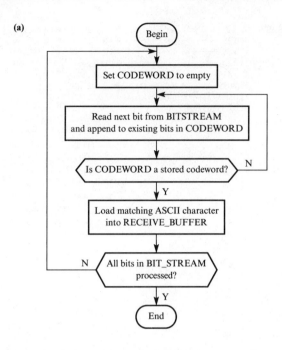

Figure 3.23
Decoding of a
received bit string
assuming codewords
derived in Figure 3.21:
(a) decoding algorithm;
(b) example.

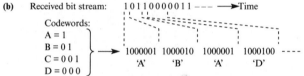

given in Figure 3.23(a). The algorithm assumes a table of codewords is available at the receiver and this also holds the corresponding ASCII codeword. The received bit stream is held in the variable BITSTREAM and the variable CODEWORD is used to hold the bits in each codeword while it is being constructed. As we can deduce from the flowchart, once a codeword is identified the corresponding ASCII codeword is written into the variable RECEIVE_BUFFER. The procedure repeats until all the bits in the received string have been processed. An example of a decoded string corresponding to the codeword set derived in Figure 3.21 is given in Figure 3.23(b).

As the Huffman code tree (and hence codewords) varies for different sets of characters being transmitted, for the receiver to perform the decoding operation it must know the codewords relating to the data being transmitted. This can be done in two ways. Either the codewords relating to the next set of data are sent before the data is transmitted, or the receiver knows in advance what codewords are being used.

The first approach leads to a form of adaptive compression since the codewords can be changed to suit the type of data being transmitted. The disadvantage is the overhead of having to send the new set of codewords (and corresponding characters) whenever a new type of data is to be sent. An alternative is for the receiver to have one or more different sets of codewords and for the sender to indicate to the receiver (through an agreed message) which codeword set to use for the next set of data.

For example, since a common requirement is to send text files generated by a word processor (and hence containing normal textual information), detailed statistical analyses have been carried out into the frequency of occurrence of the characters in the English alphabet in normal written text. This information has been used to construct the Huffman code tree for the alphabet. If this type of data is being sent, the transmitter and receiver automatically use this set of codewords. Other common data sets have been analyzed in a similar way; consult the bibliography at the end of the book for further examples.

3.5.5 Dynamic Huffman coding

The basic Huffman coding method requires both the transmitter and the receiver to know the table of codewords relating to the data being transmitted. An alternative method allows the transmitter (encoder) and receiver (decoder) to build the Huffman tree – and hence codeword table – dynamically as the characters are transmitted/received. This is known as **dynamic Huffman coding**.

With this method, if the character to be transmitted is currently present in the tree its codeword is determined and sent in the normal way. If the character is not present – that is, it is its first occurrence – the character is transmitted in its uncompressed form. The encoder updates its Huffman tree either by incrementing the frequency of occurrence of the transmitted character or by introducing the new character into the tree.

Each transmitted codeword is encoded in such a way that the receiver, in addition to being able to determine the character that is received, can also carry out the same modifications to its own copy of the tree so that it can interpret the next codeword received according to the new updated tree structure.

To describe the details of the method, assume that the data (file) to be transmitted starts with the following character string:

This is simple . . .

The steps taken by the transmitter are shown in Figure 3.24(a–g).

Both transmitter and receiver start with a tree that comprises the root node and a single **empty leaf node** – a leaf node with a zero frequency of occurrence – assigned to its 0-branch. There is always just one such node in the tree and its position – and codeword – varies as the tree is being constructed. It is represented in Figure 3.24 as e0.

The encoder then starts by reading the first character – T – and assigning this to the 1-branch of the root. Since this is the first occurrence of this character, it is shown as T1 and it is transmitted in its uncompressed – say, ASCII – form. Since the decoder's tree is also empty, it interprets the received bit string as an

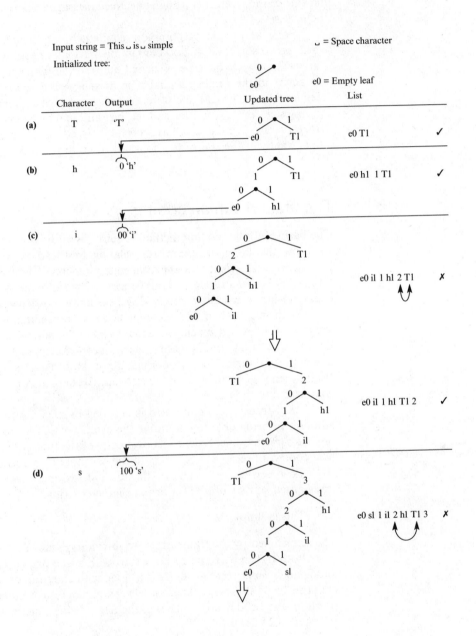

Figure 3.24
Dynamic Huffman
coding example.

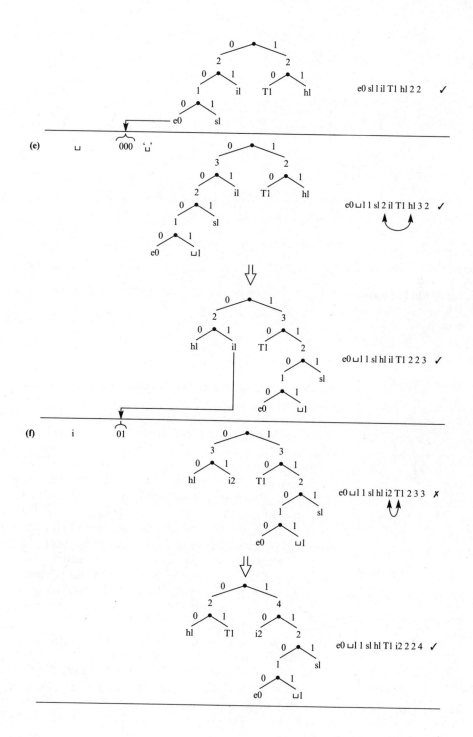

Figure 3.24 (cont.)
Dynamic Huffman
coding example.

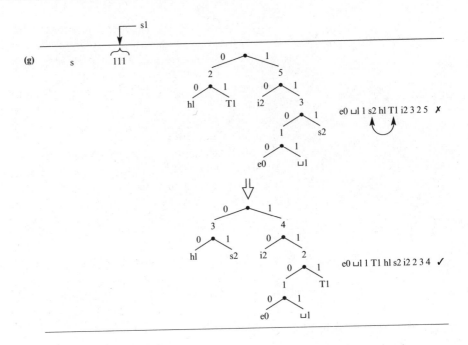

Figure 3.24 (cont.)
Dynamic Huffman
coding example.

uncompressed character and proceeds to assign the character to its tree in the same way (Figure 3.24(a)).

For each subsequent character, the encoder first checks whether the character is already present in the tree. If it is, then the encoder sends the codeword for the character in the normal way, the codeword being determined by the position of the character in the tree. If it is not present, then the encoder sends the current codeword for the empty leaf – again determined by its position in the tree – followed by the uncompressed codeword for the character. Since the decoder has the same tree as the encoder, it can readily deduce from the received bit string whether it is the codeword of a (compressed) character or that of the empty leaf followed by the character in its uncompressed form.

The encoder and decoder proceed to update their copy of the tree based on the last character that has been transmitted/received. If it is a new character, the existing empty leaf node in the tree is replaced with a new branch node, the empty leaf being assigned to the 0-branch and the character to the 1-branch (Figure 3.24(b)).

If the character is already present in the tree, then the frequency of occurrence of the leaf node is incremented by unity. On doing this, the position of the leaf node may not now be in the optimum position in the tree. Hence, each time the tree is updated – either by adding a new character or by incrementing the frequency of occurrence of an existing character – both the encoder and decoder check, and if necessary modify, the current position of all the characters in the tree.

To ensure that both the encoder and decoder do this in a consistent way, they first list the weights of the leaf and branch nodes in the updated tree from left to right and from bottom to top starting at the empty leaf. If they are all in weight order, all is well and the tree is left unchanged. If there is a node out of order, the structure of the tree is modified by exchanging the position of this node with the other node in the tree – together with its branch and leaf nodes – to produce an incremented weight order. The first occurrence is in Figure 3.24(c) and other examples are in parts (d)–(g).

The steps followed when a character to be transmitted has previously been sent are shown in Figure 3.24(f). At this point, the character to be transmitted is 'i' and when the encoder searches the tree, it determines that 'i' is already present and transmits its existing codeword – 01. The encoder then increments the character's weight – frequency of occurrence – by unity to i2 and updates the position of the modified node as before. Another example is shown in Figure 3.24(g) when the character 's' is to be transmitted.

We can deduce from this example that the savings in transmission bandwidth start only when characters begin to repeat themselves. In practice, the savings with text files can be significant, and dynamic Huffman coding is now used in many data communication applications, such as the data compression algorithm that is used in V.32 modems.

3.5.6 Facsimile compression

Although we can obtain compression ratios of up to 2 : 1 with character files using Huffman coding, the most pronounced savings are realized for the transmission of the digitized images produced by the scanners associated with **facsimile (fax) machines**. As Figure 3.25 shows, these scan a page with a vertical resolution of 3.85 or 7.7 lines per millimeter – approximately 100 or 200 lines per inch. Each scan line is digitized at the rate of 8.05 **picture element** or **pels** per millimeter – a 0 for white and a 1 for black. Thus a typical scanned page produces about two million binary

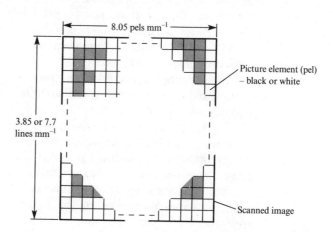

Figure 3.25
Facsimile scanned
image schematic.

digits. To transmit this in its uncompressed form at, say, 4800 bps, would require in excess of 6 minutes.

In practice, in most documents, many scanned lines comprise only long strings of white pels while others comprise a mix of long strings of white and long strings of black pels. Since facsimile machines are normally used with public carrier networks, ITU-T has produced standards relating to them. These are T2 (Group 1), T3 (Group 2), T4 (Group 3), and T6 (Group 4). The first two are earlier standards and are now rarely used. The last two, however, both operate digitally; Group 3 with modulation for use with an analog PSTN, and Group 4 all-digital for use with digital networks such as the ISDN. Both use data compression, and compression ratios in excess of 10 : 1 are common with most document pages. The time taken to transmit a page is reduced to less than a minute with Group 3 machines and, because of the added benefit of a higher transmission rate (64 kbps), to less than a few seconds with a Group 4 machine.

As part of the standardization process, extensive analyses of typical scanned document pages were made. Tables of codewords were produced based on the relative frequency of occurrence of the number of contiguous white and black pels found in a scanned line. The resulting codewords are fixed and grouped into two separate tables: the **termination-codes table** and the **make-up codes table**. The codewords in each table are shown in Figure 3.26.

Codewords in the termination-codes table are for white or black run lengths of from 0 to 63 pels in steps of 1 pel; the make-up codes table contains codewords for white or black run lengths that are multiples of 64 pels. A technique known as **overscanning** is used which means that all lines start with a minimum of one white pel. In this way, the receiver knows the first codeword always relates to white pels and then alternates between black and white. Since the scheme uses two sets of codewords (termination and make-up) they are known as **modified Huffman codes**. As an example, a run length of 12 white pels is coded directly as 001000. Similarly, a run length of 12 black pels is coded directly as 0000111. A run length of 140 black pels, however, is encoded as 000011001000 + 0000111; that is, 128 + 12 pels. Run lengths exceeding 2560 pels are encoded using more than one make-up code plus one termination code.

There is no error-correction protocol with Group 3. From the list of codewords, we can deduce that if one or more bits are corrupted by transmission errors, the receiver will start to interpret subsequent codewords on the wrong bit boundaries. The receiver thus becomes unsynchronized and cannot decode the received bit string. To enable the receiver to regain synchronism, each scanned line is terminated with a known **end-of-line (EOL) code**. In this way, if the receiver fails to decode a valid codeword after the maximum number of bits in a codeword have been scanned (parsed), it starts to search for the EOL pattern. Also, if it fails to decode an EOL after a preset number of lines, it aborts the reception process and informs the sending machine. A single EOL precedes the codewords for each scanned page and a string of six consecutive EOLs indicate the end of a page.

Because each scanned line is encoded independently, the T4 coding scheme is known as a **one-dimensional coding** scheme and, as we can conclude, it works satisfactorily providing the scanned image contains significant areas of white or

White run length	Code-word	Black run length	Code-word
0	00110101	0	0000110111
1	000111	1	010
2	0111	2	11
3	1000	3	10
4	1011	4	011
5	1100	5	0011
6	1110	6	0010
7	1111	7	00011
8	10011	8	000101
9	10100	9	000100
10	00111	10	0000100
11	01000	11	0000101
12	001000	12	0000111
13	000011	13	00000100
14	110100	14	00000111
15	110101	15	000011000
16	101010	16	0000010111
17	101011	17	0000011000
18	0100111	18	0000001000
19	0001100	19	00001100111
20	0001000	20	00001101000
21	0010111	21	00001101100
22	0000011	22	00000110111
23	0000100	23	00000101000
24	0101000	24	00000010111
25	0101011	25	00000011000
26	0010011	26	000011001010
27	0100100	27	000011001011
28	0011000	28	000011001100
29	00000010	29	000011001101
30	00000011	30	000001101000
31	00011010	31	000001101001
32	00011011	32	000001101010
33	0010010	33	000001101011
34	00010011	34	000011010010
35	00010100	35	000011010011
36	00010101	36	000011010100
37	00010110	37	000011010101
38	00010111	38	000011010110
39	00101000	39	000011010111
40	00101001	40	000001101100
41	00101011	41	000001101101
42	00101011	42	000011011010
43	00101100	43	000011011011
44	00101101	44	000001010100
45	00000100	45	000001010101
46	00000101	46	000001010110
47	00001010	47	000001010111
48	00001011	48	000001100100
49	01010010	49	000001100101
50	01010011	50	000001010010
51	01010100	51	000001010011
52	01010101	52	000000100100
53	00100100	53	000000110111
54	00100101	54	000000111000
55	01011000	55	000000100111

(a)

White run length	Code-word	Black run length	Code-word
56	01011001	56	000000101000
57	01011010	57	000001011000
58	01011011	58	000001011001
59	01001010	59	000000101011
60	01001011	60	000000101100
61	00110010	61	000001011010
62	00110011	62	000001100110
63	00110100	63	000001100111

(a) cont.

White run length	Code-word	Black run length	Code-word
64	11011	64	0000001111
128	10010	128	000011001000
192	010111	192	000011001001
256	0110111	256	000001011011
320	00110110	320	000000110011
384	00110111	384	000000110100
448	01100100	448	000000110101
512	01100101	512	000001101100
576	01101000	576	000001101101
640	01100111	640	000000101010
704	011001100	704	0000001001011
768	011001101	768	0000001001100
832	011010010	832	0000001001101
896	011010011	896	0000001110010
960	011010100	960	0000001110011
1024	011010101	1024	0000001110100
1088	011010110	1088	0000001110101
1152	011010111	1152	0000001110110
1216	011011000	1216	0000001110111
1280	011011001	1280	0000001010010
1344	011011010	1344	0000001010011
1408	011011011	1408	0000001010100
1472	010011000	1472	0000001010101
1536	010011001	1536	0000001011010
1600	010011010	1600	0000001011011
1664	011000	1664	0000001100100
1728	010011011	1728	0000001100101
1792	00000001000	1792	00000001000
1856	00000001100	1856	00000001100
1920	00000001101	1920	00000001101
1984	000000010010	1984	000000010010
2048	000000010011	2048	000000010011
2112	000000010100	2112	000000010100
2176	000000010101	2176	000000010101
2240	000000010110	2240	000000010110
2304	000000010111	2304	000000010111
2368	000000011100	2368	000000011100
2432	000000011101	2432	000000011101
2496	000000011110	2496	000000011110
2560	000000011111	2560	000000011111
EOL	0000000001	EOL	0000000001

(b)

Figure 3.26
ITU-T Group 3 and 4 facsimile conversion codes: (a) termination codes; (b) make-up codes.

black pels, for example where documents comprise letters and line drawings. Documents containing photographic images, however, are not satisfactory as the different shades of black and white are represented by varying densities of black and white pels. This, in turn, results in a large number of very short black or white run lengths which, with the T4 coding scheme, can lead to a negative compression ratio, that is, more bits are needed to send the scanned document in its compressed form than are needed in its uncompressed form.

For this reason the alternative T6 coding scheme has been defined. It is an optional feature in Group 3 facsimile machines but is compulsory in Group 4 machines. When supported in Group 3 machines, the EOL code at the end of each (compressed) line has an additional tag bit added. If this is a binary 1 then the next line has been encoded using the T4 coding scheme, if it is a 0 then the T6 coding scheme has been used. The latter is known as **modified–modified READ (MMR) coding**. It is also known as **two-dimensional** or **2D coding** since it identifies black and white run lengths by comparing adjacent scan lines. READ stands for **relative element address designate**, and it is 'modified' since it is a modified version of an earlier (modified) coding scheme.

MMR coding exploits the fact that most scanned lines differ from the previous line by only a few pels. For example, if a line contains a black run then the next line will normally contain the same run plus or minus three pels. With MMR coding the run lengths associated with a line are identified by comparing the line contents, known as the **coding line (CL)**, relative to the immediately preceding line, known as the **reference line (RL)**. We always assume the first reference line to be an (imaginary) all-white line and the first line proper is encoded relative to this. Next the encoded line becomes the reference line for the following line and so on. To ensure that the complete page is scanned, the scanner head always starts to the left of the page, so each line always starts with an imaginary white pel.

We identify the run lengths associated with a coding line as one of three possibilities or modes relative to the reference line. Examples of the three modes are shown in Figure 3.27. The three modes are identified by the position of the next run length in the reference line ($b_1 b_2$) relative to the start and end of the next pair of run lengths in the coding line ($a_0 a_1$ and $a_1 a_2$). Note that each of these can be black or white. The three possibilities are:

(1) **Pass mode** This is the case when the run length in the reference line ($b_1 b_2$) is to the left of the next run length in the coding line ($a_1 a_2$), that is, b_2 is to the left of a_1. An example is given in Figure 3.27(a); for this mode, the run length $b_1 b_2$ is coded using the codewords given in Figure 3.26. Note that if the next pel on the coding line, a_1, is directly below b_2 then this is not pass mode.

(2) **Vertical mode** This is the case when the run length in the reference line ($b_1 b_2$) overlaps the next run length in the coding line ($a_1 a_2$) by a maximum of plus or minus 3 pels. Two examples are given in Figure 3.27(b); for this mode, just the difference run length $a_1 b_1$ is coded. Most codewords are in this category.

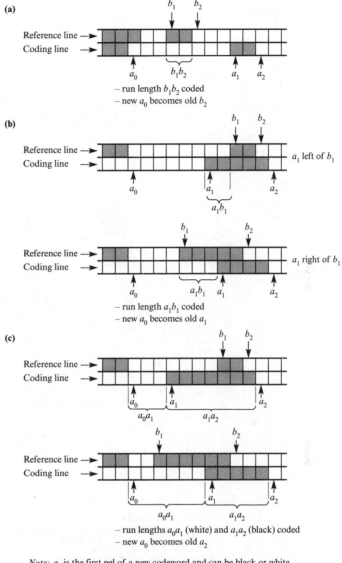

Figure 3.27
Some example run
length possibilities:
(a) pass mode;
(b) vertical mode;
(c) horizontal mode.

(3) **Horizontal mode** This is the case when the run length in the reference line
($b_1 b_2$) overlaps the run length ($a_1 a_2$) by more than plus or minus 3 pels. Two
examples are given in Figure 3.27(c); for this mode, the two run lengths $a_0 a_1$
and $a_1 a_2$ are coded using the codewords in Figure 3.26.

A flowchart of the coding procedure is shown in Figure 3.28. Note that the
first a_0 is set to an imaginary white pel *before* the first pel of the line and hence

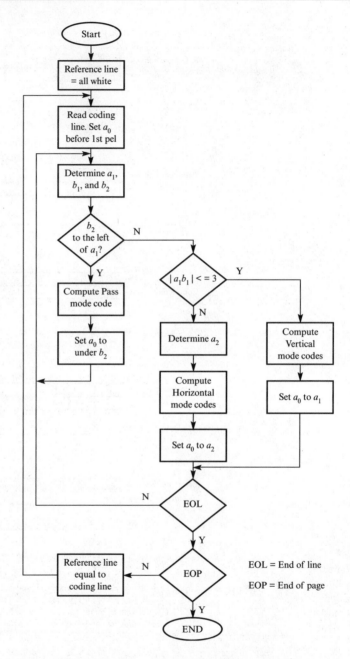

Figure 3.28
Modified–modified
READ coding
procedure.

the first a_0a_1 run length will be $a_0a_1 - 1$. If during the coding of a line a_1, a_2, b_1, or b_2 are not detected, then they are set on an imaginary pel positioned immediately after the last pel on the respective line.

Once the first/next position of a_0 has been determined, the positions of a_1, a_2, b_1, and b_2 for the next codeword are located. The mode is then determined by computing the position of b_2 relative to a_1. If it is to the left, this indicates pass

Table 3.2 Two-dimensional code table contents.

Mode	Run length to be encoded	Abbreviation	Codeword
Pass	$b_1 b_2$	P	$0001 + b_1 b_2$
Horizontal	$a_0 a_1, a_1 a_2$	H	$001 + a_0 a_1 + a_1 a_2$
Vertical	$a_1 b_1 = 0$	V(0)	1
	$a_1 b_1 = -1$	$V_R(1)$	011
	$a_1 b_1 = -2$	$V_R(2)$	000011
	$a_1 b_1 = -3$	$V_R(3)$	0000011
	$a_1 b_1 = +1$	$V_L(1)$	010
	$a_1 b_1 = +2$	$V_L(2)$	000010
	$a_1 b_1 = +3$	$V_L(3)$	0000010
Extension			0000001000

mode. If it is not to the left, then the magnitude of $a_1 b_1$ is used to determine if the mode is vertical or horizontal. The codeword for the identified mode is then computed and the start of the next codeword position, a_0, updated to the appropriate position. This procedure repeats until the end of the line is reached. This is an imaginary pel positioned immediately after the last pel of the line and is assumed to have a different color from the last pel. The current coding line then becomes the new reference line and the next scanned line the new coding line.

Since the coded run lengths relate to one of the three modes, additional codewords are used either to indicate to which mode the following codeword(s) relate – pass or horizontal – or to specify the length of the codeword directly – vertical. The additional codewords are given in a third table known as the **two-dimensional code table**, as shown in Table 3.2. The final entry in the table, known as the **extension mode**, is a unique codeword that aborts the encoding operation prematurely before the end of the page. This is provided to allow a portion of a page to be sent in its uncompressed form or possibly with a different coding scheme.

3.6 Transmission control circuits

Most major semiconductor manufacturers offer a range of integrated circuits (ICs) to perform all the functions discussed in this chapter. In the case of asynchronous transmission, there are ICs that perform the clock (bit) and character synchronization functions and generate and check the parity bit per character. Similarly, in the case of synchronous transmission, there are ICs to perform the character synchronization and parity generation and checking functions in relation to character-oriented transmission. Others are available for the zero bit insertion and deletion and CRC generation and checking functions with bit-oriented transmission. Normally, the clock encoding and decoding functions are carried out by separate ICs, especially at high bit rates. Again, a range of ICs is available.

Most transmission control circuits are **programmable** which means that the user can define the precise mode of operation of the device – asynchronous/

synchronous, character-oriented/bit-oriented, parity/CRC, etc. – by writing defined bit patterns into selected internal registers. We also referred to these circuits as **universal communication interface circuits**. Normally, a single circuit provides one, two or even four separate (full-duplex) transmission line interface circuits.

The device controlling the operation of the circuit – a microprocessor, for example – first programs the desired operating mode by writing a defined byte (bit pattern) into the **mode register**. The device is then made ready to transmit and/or receive characters/bytes by writing a second byte into a **command register**. The transmit and receive channels are always **double-buffered** which means that the controlling device has a full character (or byte) time to process each character (byte) prior to transmission or after reception, rather than a single bit time.

The names and functions of the most common devices are as follows:

- *Universal asynchronous receiver transmitter (UART)*
  - Start and stop bit insertion and deletion
  - Bit (clock) synchronization
  - Character synchronization
  - Parity bit generation and checking per character (BCC computed by controlling device)

- *Universal synchronous receiver transmitter (USRT)*
  - Low bit rate DPLL clock synchronization
  - Character synchronization
  - Synchronous idle character generation
  - Parity generation and checking per character (BCC computed by controlling device)

- *Universal synchronous/asynchronous receiver transmitter (USART)*
  - Can be programmed to operate as either a UART or a USRT
  - Has all the programmable features of both devices

- *Bit-oriented protocol circuits (BOPs)*
  - Opening and closing flag insertion and deletion
  - Zero bit insertion and deletion
  - CRC generation and checking
  - Idle pattern generation

- *Universal communications control circuits*
  - Can be programmed to operate either as a UART, a USRT, or a BOP
  - Has all the programmable features of each circuit

3.7 Communications control devices

In many data communication applications, a common requirement is to have a distributed community of terminals – personal computers, for example – that all require to access a central computing facility. This facility could operate a central

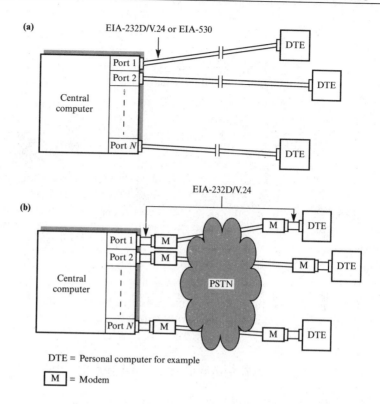

Figure 3.29
Simple terminal
networks: (a) locally
distributed;
(b) remotely
distributed.

electronic mail service for an enterprise, or house a central database to which the distributed community of terminals requires access.

If all the terminals are situated in different locations, the only solution is to provide a separate communications line for each terminal, as shown in Figure 3.29. In part (a) we assume that the terminals are distributed around a single establishment, whereas in part (b) we assume that they are each located in different establishments. In the latter case, it is likely that modems will be required operating over switched connections or leased lines, depending on the amount of data to be transferred and the frequency of calls. In the case of switched connections, the terminals will normally have autodial facilities associated with the communications interface.

For applications in which a number of terminals are located together, we can use a device known as a **multiplexer (MUX)** to minimize the number of transmission lines required. Such devices are used with a single transmission line that operates at a higher bit rate than the individual user terminal rates. As Figure 3.30 shows, we normally use a similar multiplexer at each end of the link. In this way the presence of the multiplexers is transparent to both the terminals and the central computer.

There are two types of multiplexer: **time-division multiplexers** and **statistical multiplexers**. A time-division multiplexer assigns each terminal a dedicated

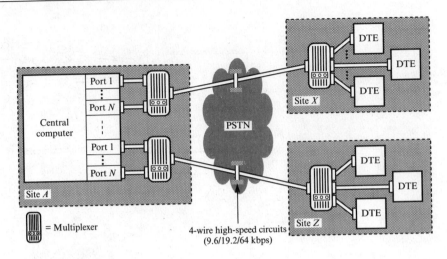

Figure 3.30
Multiplexer-based
network schematic.

portion of the transmission capacity of the shared line. A statistical multiplexer allocates transmission capacity on an on-demand or statistical basis.

3.7.1   Time-division multiplexer

A typical time-division multiplexer application is shown in Figure 3.31(a). The terminals located in each establishment associated with an enterprise all require access to the central computer. We assume that each site has a large number of terminals that generate sufficient intersite traffic to justify high bit rate leased circuits being used to link the various sites to the central site. Typically, these are 64 kbps or higher, depending on the number of terminals.

Figure 3.31(b) shows the internal architecture of each MUX. Typically, each terminal operates in an asynchronous transmission mode and is connected to a UART. The controlling microprocessor within the MUX controls the transfer of characters between the UARTs and the high-speed link interface circuit. As the latter normally operates in a character-oriented synchronous transmission mode it will comprise a USRT.

To ensure that the presence of the MUXs is transparent to the terminals/ computer, the transmission capacity associated with the high bit rate circuit is divided in such a way that the UARTs in the terminal and computer ports can operate at their programmed rate. This is achieved by a technique known as **rate adaption** which involves breaking the available link capacity into a number of frames as shown in Figure 3.31(c).

Each frame comprises N bytes such that the bit rate associated with a single byte position in each frame forms a suitable basic multiplexing rate. The bit rates associated with each terminal are then derived by using multiple bytes per frame. However, not all the bits in each byte are used for user data. The first bit in each byte is used for framing; a fixed repetitive bit pattern is sent in this bit position of

(a)

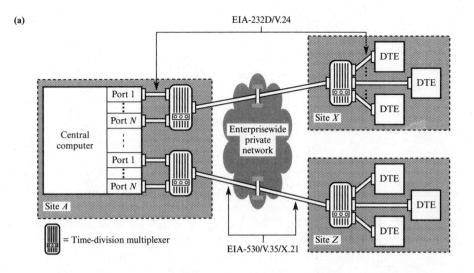

(b)

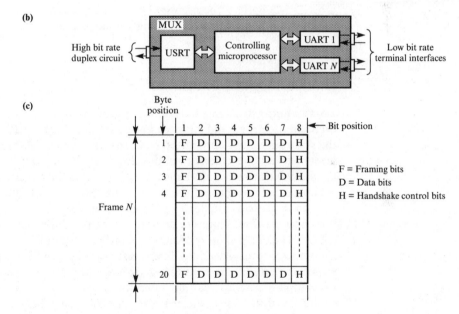

Figure 3.31
Time-division
multiplexer principles:
(a) application;
(b) MUX schematic;
(c) rate adaption.

all bytes in a frame so that the receiver can determine the start and end of each frame. Also, the eighth bit is used to transmit the state of the handshake control bits – DSR/DTR and RTS/CTS, for example – associated with the V.24/EIA-232D interface control lines of each UART.

As an example, assume the bit rate of the high-speed circuit is 64 kbps and that a frame length of 20 bytes is being used. The user data rate associated with the six D bits in each byte is then 2400 bps. Thus the high-speed circuit can be used to support one of:

    20   2400 bps terminals
    10   4800 bps terminals
     5   9600 bps terminals
     1   48 kbps terminal

Alternatively, a suitable mix of these can be supported, for example:

    8   2400 bps terminals
    4   4800 bps terminals
    1   9600 bps terminal

To perform the multiplexing operation, the microprocessor uses two 2-byte buffers for each UART – one pair for transmission and the other for reception. For transmission, each byte received from a UART – a 7-bit character plus a parity bit, for example – is simply stored in a repetitive way in the 2-byte (circular) buffer. Concurrently, the microprocessor reads the current contents of each 2-byte buffer in 6-bit segments in synchronism with the high-speed link bit rate. The reverse procedure is used for reception from the high-speed link using the other 2-byte buffer. The handshake control bits are then set in an agreed way to reflect the state of the corresponding lines associated with the respective interface.

3.7.2   Statistical multiplexer

Each terminal in a time-division multiplexer is allocated a fixed character slot in each frame. If the terminal or computer has no character ready to transmit when the controlling microprocessor polls the associated UART, the microprocessor must insert a NUL character in this slot, thus leading to inefficiencies in the use of the available transmission bandwidth. If the data link is a private line, this is not necessarily important, but if PTT lines are used, it can be costly. A more efficient method is to use a statistical multiplexer (stat MUX).

Statistical multiplexers operate on the principle that the mean data rate of characters entered at a terminal keyboard is often much lower than the available transmission capacity of the line – certainly the case with a human user. If the mean user data rate is used rather than the transmission line rate, the bit rate of the common data link can be much lower, with the effect that transmission line costs are substantially reduced. For example, suppose a remote location has 8 terminals that need to be connected to a single remote central computer over a PTT line, which has a maximum bit rate of, say, 4800 bps. Using a basic MUX and a single line, the nominal operating rate of each terminal has to be less than 600 bps – say 300 bps. The effect of this limit is that the response time of the computer to each character keyed in at the terminal is relatively slow or, if a block of characters is being transmitted to the terminal, the delay will be noticeable. Alternatively, if the mean data rate of the terminal is, say, 300 bps, then with a stat MUX the data can be transmitted by a terminal at the maximum available bit rate of 4800 bps. Thus, the average response time to each keyed character is much improved.

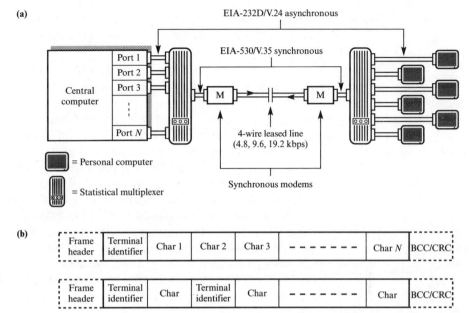

(a)

(b)

Figure 3.32
Statistical multiplexer principles: (a) network schematic; (b) framing alternatives.

To implement this scheme, the controlling microprocessor within the stat MUX must not only perform the normal polling function associated with the terminal UARTs, but also provide and manage a limited amount of buffer storage facilities to allow for possible transient overload conditions on the common data link when a number of terminals are active simultaneously. Because characters are being transmitted on the common data link on a statistical rather than a preallocated basis, each character or group of characters transmitted must also carry identification information.

Another function of the microprocessor in a stat MUX is related to error control. With a normal MUX, simple echo checking is often a perfectly acceptable mode of working, since each terminal and computer port is allocated a fixed character slot in each frame on the duplex link. However, because of the statistical mode of working of a stat MUX, we more commonly perform error control on a block of characters on the shared data link. A typical arrangement is shown in Figure 3.32(a).

To reduce the overheads associated with each transmitted character, we usually group a number of characters together for transmission on the shared data link. We can do this in a number of ways, two examples of which are shown in Figure 3.32(b). In one, the controlling microprocessor waits until it has a number of characters from a single terminal – a string of characters making up a single line, for example – and then transmits them as a complete block with a single terminal (channel) identifier at the head. In the other, each block contains a mix of characters from all currently active terminals each with a separate terminal identifier. As we can see, the assembled characters collectively occupy the information field (I-field) of each block or frame transmitted on the shared data link. The communication protocol used on the link is normally a character-oriented or a bit-oriented synchronous protocol, details of which we give in Chapter 4.

3.7.3 Block-mode devices

More sophisticated terminals, bank data entry terminals, and department store point-of-sale terminals normally operate in a block mode rather than a character mode. In block mode, as each character is keyed in it is echoed to the display screen directly by the terminal's local processor. The data is then passed to the central computing complex where it is processed when a complete block of data (a message) has been assembled. Such terminals normally support a more sophisticated block-oriented communication protocol to control the transfer of messages. Also, because the acceptable response time to each transmitted message can be much slower than that expected with an interactive character-mode network, equipment aimed at reducing the communication line costs at the expense of the response time is often used in block-mode terminal networks.

Multidrop lines

A common method of reducing transmission line costs in block-mode terminal networks is to employ **multidrop** (also known as **multipoint**) **lines**. A schematic of a network that uses multidrop lines is shown in Figure 3.33(a). Instead of connecting each terminal directly to the central computer by a separate line, a number of terminals share the line. In this way, we greatly reduce the number of lines (and hence modems or line drivers, depending on the geographical scope of the network). However, with only one line for each community of terminals, only one message block can be sent at a time, either by a terminal or by the central computer. All transmissions on each line are therefore controlled by the central computer using an arbitration procedure known as **poll–select**.

Poll–Select

To ensure that only one message is transmitted at any instant on each shared communication line, the central computer, or its agent, either **polls** or **selects** each terminal connected to the line in a particular sequence. As each terminal connected to the shared line is allocated a unique identifier, the central computer communicates with a terminal by sending it messages with the identity of the terminal at the head. Messages can be of two types: control or data.

Periodically the central computer sends each terminal, in turn, a poll control message, which effectively invites the polled terminal to send a message if it has one waiting. If it has, it responds with a data message, otherwise it responds with a nothing-to-send control message. Similarly, whenever the central computer wishes to send a message to a terminal, it sends a select control message addressed to the particular terminal. Assuming the selected terminal is able to receive a message, it responds by returning a ready-to-receive control message. The central computer

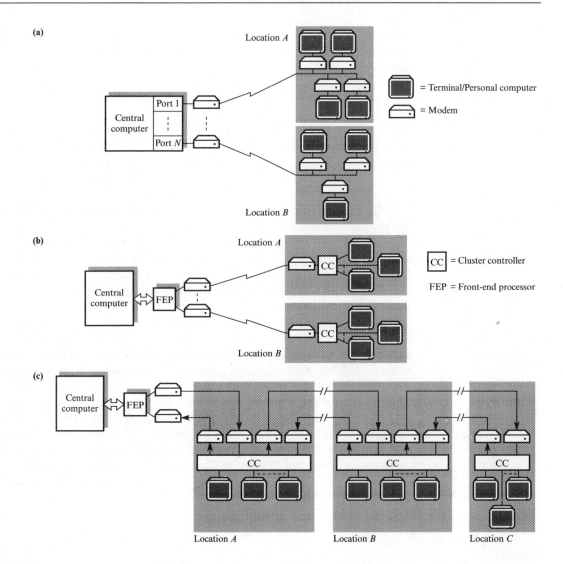

Figure 3.33
Polling network alternatives:
(a) multidrop;
(b) cluster controllers;
(c) hub polling.

then sends the data message. Finally, the terminal acknowledges correct receipt of the data message and the central computer continues by either polling or selecting another terminal. This type of polling, known as **roll-call polling**, results in quite long response times for larger networks since each terminal in the network must be polled or selected before it can send or receive a message. The communication overheads imposed on the central computer can be very high.

To overcome these problems, a more common type of multidrop network uses a **cluster controller** to reduce the response time of the network and a **front-end processor (FEP)** to reduce the communication overheads on the central computer. An example of such a network is shown in Figure 3.33(b). Each cluster controller acts as an agent for the central computer by polling and selecting the terminals connected to it, thereby managing all message transfers to and from the terminals. The central computer, or the FEP, in practice, needs only to poll or select each controller.

An FEP is typically a small computer that is closely coupled to the central computer. The FEP is programmed to handle all the polling and selection procedures, allowing the central computer to devote its time to the main task of application processing. The advantage of an FEP is that the central computer need be involved only when a data message has been received or is to be sent. Furthermore, since all the communication overheads associated with each message transfer are handled by the FEP, the central computer need only initiate the transfer of each message to and from the FEP.

If terminal clusters are widely separated, an alternative mechanism known as **hub polling** is sometimes cost justified. Hub polling is shown in Figure 3.33(c). In this configuration each cluster controller is connected to its nearest neighbor rather than to the central computer. As before, the central computer manages all transfers to and from the cluster controllers. The central computer selects and sends a data message to any of the controllers at any time by means of the top line shown in Figure 3.32(c).

To receive messages from the controllers, the central computer sends a poll control message to the furthest controller which responds by sending either a data message or a nothing-to-send control message on the bottom (return) line to its nearest neighbor controller. On receipt of this message, the next controller interprets this as a poll message and, if it has a message waiting, responds by adding its own data message to the tail of the received message from its upstream neighbor. The composite message is then forwarded to its downstream neighbor, again on the return line. This procedure continues down the chain, each controller adding its own response message as it relays the message toward the central computer. Finally, on receipt of the composite response message, the FEP disassembles the message and passes on any valid data messages contained within it to the central computer for further processing.

Exercises

3.1   (a)   Explain the difference between asynchronous and synchronous transmission.

(b)   Assuming asynchronous transmission, one start bit, two stop bits, one parity bit, and two bits per signaling element, derive the useful information transfer rate in bps for each of the following signaling (baud) rates:
(i)   300
(ii)   600
(iii) 1200
(iv)   4800

3.2   With the aid of a diagram, explain the clock (bit) and character synchronization methods used with an asynchronous transmission control scheme. Use a receiver clock rate ratio of $\times 1$ and $\times 4$ of the transmitter clock.

3.3   With the aid of diagrams, explain how clock synchronization can be achieved using:
(a)   Bipolar encoding
(b)   Phase (Manchester) encoding
(c)   Differential Manchester encoding

3.4 Use example waveform sets to illustrate the main features associated with the following encoding schemes:
  (a) AMI
  (b) B8ZS
  (c) HDB3
  (d) 2B1Q
  Comment on the relative advantages of each scheme.

3.5 Derive the signaling rate in baud for each of the encoding schemes in Exercise 3.4 assuming a bit rate of 64 kbps.

3.6 (a) Explain under what circumstances data encoding and a DPLL circuit may be used to achieve clock synchronization. Also, with the aid of a diagram, explain the operation of the DPLL circuit.
  (b) Assuming the receiver is initially out of synchronism, derive the minimum number of bit transitions required for a DPLL circuit to converge to the nominal bit center of a transmitted waveform. How may this be achieved in practice?

3.7 Assuming a synchronous transmission control scheme, explain how character and frame synchronization are achieved:
  (a) With character-oriented transmission
  (b) With bit-oriented transmission

3.8 Explain what is meant by the term data transparency and how it may be achieved using:
  (a) Character stuffing
  (b) Zero bit insertion

3.9 Explain the operation of the parity bit method of error detection and how it can be extended to cover blocks of characters.
  Draw a circuit to compute the parity bit for a character and explain the difference between the terms odd and even parity.

3.10 With the aid of examples, define the following terms:
  (a) Single-bit error
  (b) Double-bit error
  (c) Error burst
  Produce a sketch showing the contents of a frame to illustrate the type of transmission errors that are not detected by a block sum check.

3.11 (a) Explain the principle of operation of a CRC error detection method. By means of an example, show how:
    (i) The error detection bits are generated
    (ii) The received frame is checked for transmission errors
  Use the generator polynomial
  $$x^4 + x^3 + 1$$
  (b) Use an example to show how an error pattern equal to the generator polynomial used in (a) will not be detected. List other error patterns that would not be detected with this polynomial.

3.12 In an engine management system, the sixteen binary messages 0000 through 1111 are to be transmitted over a data link. Each message is to be protected by a 3-bit CRC generated using the polynominal:
  $$x^3 + x^2 + 1$$
  (a) Derive the 3 check bits for each of the three messages:

  0000   0001   0010

  (b) State the meaning of the term 'Hamming distance' and derive this for your code.
  (c) Show how a single-bit error and a double-bit error in a transmitted codeword are detected at the receiver assuming the transmitted message is 1111.
  (d) Give an example of an invalid received codeword that will not be detected.

3.13 (a) Produce sketches of circuits to generate and check the CRC of a transmitted frame using the following generator polynomial:
  $$x^4 + x^3 + 1$$
  Show the contents of the transmit and FCS shift registers as the data is being transmitted to and received from the line.
  (b) Develop an algorithm in pseudocode to show how the generation and check functions can be carried out in software.

3.14 Use examples to explain the operation of the following data compression algorithms:
  (a) Packed decimal
  (b) Relative encoding
  (c) Character suppression

3.15 With the aid of an example, illustrate the rules that are used to construct the Huffman code tree for a transmitted character set.

3.16 Messages comprising seven different characters, A through G, are to be transmitted over a data link. Analysis has shown that the relative frequency of occurrence of each character is:

A   0.10, B   0.25, C   0.05, D   0.32,
E   0.01, F   0.07, G   0.2

(a) Derive the entropy of the messages.
(b) Use static Huffman coding to derive a suitable set of codewords.
(c) Derive the average number of bits per codeword for your codeword set to transmit a message and compare this with both fixed-length binary and ASCII codewords.

3.17 (a) State the prefix property of Huffman codes and hence show that your codeword set derived in Exercise 3.16 satisfies this.
(b) Derive a flowchart for an algorithm to decode a received bit string encoded using your codeword set.
(c) Give an example of the decoding operation assuming the received bit string comprises a mix of the seven characters.

3.18 The following character string is to be transmitted using Huffman coding:

ABACADABACADABACABAB

(a) Derive the Huffman code tree.
(b) Determine the savings in transmission bandwidth over normal ASCII and binary coding.

3.19 With reference to the example shown in Figure 3.24 relating to dynamic Huffman coding:
(a) Write down the actual transmitted bit pattern corresponding to the character string:

'This is'

assuming ASCII coding is being used.
(b) Deduce the extensions to the existing Huffman tree if the next word transmitted is 'the'.

3.20 Given a scanned line from a Group 3 fax machine stored in a binary array, deduce an algorithm to:
(a) Determine the transmitted codewords.
(b) Decode the received string of codewords.
Use the Huffman tables in Figure 3.26 as a guide.

3.21 With the aid of example pel patterns, explain the meaning of the terms:
(a) Pass mode
(b) Vertical mode
(c) Horizontal mode
as used with Group 4 fax machines.
      Use your examples to deduce an algorithm to perform the encoding operation.

3.22 Explain the difference between a time-division multiplexer and a statistical multiplexer.
      Produce a sketch showing the internal architecture of a time-division multiplexer and explain its operation. Describe the organization of the shared data link and how the controlling device determines the destination of each received character.

3.23 Make a sketch of a terminal network that uses a statistical multiplexer. Describe the organization of the shared data link with such a device and how the controlling device determines the destination of each character.

3.24 Make a sketch of a typical block-mode terminal network that uses multidrop lines and a poll-select control protocol. Explain the operation of the network and describe how the computer sends and receives messages to and from each terminal.

3.25 (a) Explain the function of
        (i)   A cluster controller
        (ii) A front-end processor.
(b) Distinguish between roll-call polling and hub polling. Make a sketch of each polling method and explain its operation.

Chapter summary

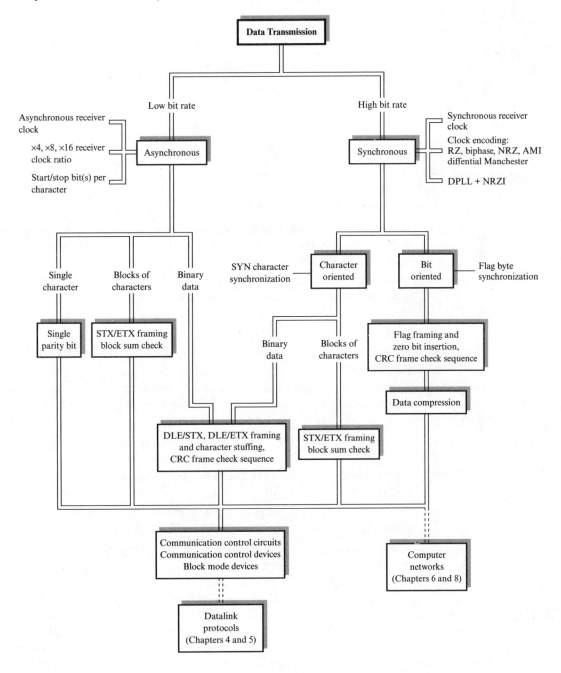

PROTOCOL BASICS

Chapter objectives

When you have completed this chapter you should be able to:

Introduction

Chapter 3 described the circuits and techniques that can be employed to transmit a frame of information between two DTEs across a point-to-point data link. In addition, it described the various error-detection schemes which allow the receiving DTE to determine, to a known probability, the presence of any errors in the transmitted bit stream. Alternatively, if forward error correction is used, the receiver can deduce from the received bit stream, again to a known probability, the information being transmitted even when errors are present.

However, in general, the techniques described provide only the basic mechanism for transmitting information and for the receiver to detect the presence of any transmission errors. When a transmission error is detected, even if it is only a single (unknown) bit, then the complete data block must be discarded. This type of scheme is thus known as **best-try transmission** or, for reasons we shall discuss in Section 4.4, **connectionless mode transmission**.

In addition to this mode of operation, an alternative operating mode known as **reliable transmission** or **connection-oriented transmission** is also used in many applications. With this mode, in addition to detecting when errors are present, a defined set of rules or control procedures must be adopted by both communicating parties to ensure the reliable (that is, to a high probability, free of errors and duplicates and in the correct sequence) transfer of messages. To accomplish this, the controlling device at the destination informs the source that an error has been detected and that another copy of the affected frame should be sent. The combined error detection/correction cycle is known as **error control**. In addition, there are often other control mechanisms that must be observed by the two communicating parties. Collectively these constitute the **data link (control) protocol** for the link. We shall consider some of the basic components of a data link protocol in this chapter; in Chapter 5 we shall give the descriptions of practical realizations of the basic protocols introduced.

4.1   Error control

When we enter data into a computer by means of a keyboard, as we press each key the resulting codeword is normally transmitted to the computer bit-serially using a UART and asynchronous transmission. The program in the computer controlling the input process then reads and stores the received character and initiates its output to the display screen. If the displayed character is different from what was entered or intended, then we simply enter a suitable control character – a delete or backspace, for example. When the control is received, the control program discards the previously entered character and removes it from the screen. In this way we are performing a form of **manual error control**.

A similar procedure is used when a terminal is connected to a remote computer via, say, the analog PSTN and a modem. Instead of each entered character being displayed directly on the terminal display, it is first transmitted to the remote computer. The latter reads and stores the character and retransmits it back to the terminal which displays it. If this is different from what was keyed in or intended, the user can again initiate the transmission of a suitable delete character. This mode of error control is known as **echo checking**.

In contrast, when a computer is transferring blocks of characters (frames) across a serial data link to another computer, the program in the receiving computer controlling the reception process must perform the error control procedure automatically without any intervention from the user. Typically, the receiving computer checks the received frame for possible transmission errors and then returns a short control message (frame) either to acknowledge its correct receipt or to request that another copy of the frame is sent. This type of error control is known as **automatic repeat request (ARQ)**.

There are two basic types of ARQ: **idle RQ**, which is used with character-oriented (or byte-oriented) data transmission schemes, and **continuous RQ**, which employs either a **selective repeat** or a **go-back-N retransmission strategy**. Continuous RQ is used primarily with bit-oriented transmission schemes. Although idle RQ is being replaced in many applications by the more efficient continuous RQ scheme, there are still many data link protocols in use based on idle RQ. More importantly, however, since it is the simplest type of error control scheme, it forms an ideal vehicle for explaining many of the more general issues relating to data link (control) protocols. We shall discuss both idle RQ and continuous RQ schemes.

4.2 Idle RQ

The idle RQ error control scheme has been defined to enable blocks (frames) of printable and formatting control characters to be reliably transferred – that is, to a high probability, without error or replication and in the same sequence as they were submitted – over a serial data link between a source DTE and a destination DTE. To discriminate between the sender (source) and receiver (destination) of data frames – more generally referred to as **information frames** or **I-frames** – the terms **primary (P)** and **secondary (S)** are normally used, respectively. Thus the idle RQ error control scheme is concerned with the reliable transfer of I-frames between a primary and a secondary across a serial data link.

The idle RQ protocol operates in a half-duplex mode since the primary, after sending an I-frame, must wait until it receives an indication from the secondary as to whether the frame was correctly received or not. The primary then either sends the next frame, if the previous frame was correctly received, or retransmits a copy of the previous frame if it was not.

There are two ways of implementing this scheme. In **implicit retransmission** S acknowledges only correctly received frames and P interprets the absence of an acknowledgment as an indication that the previous frame was corrupted. Alternatively, when S detects that a frame has been corrupted, it returns a **negative acknowledgment** to request that another copy of the frame is transmitted – **explicit request**.

Some example frame sequences with the implicit retransmission control scheme are shown in Figure 4.1(a). The following points should be noted when interpreting the frame sequences:

- P can have only one I-frame outstanding (awaiting an **acknowledgment frame** or **ACK-frame**) at a time.
- On receipt of an error-free I-frame, S returns an ACK-frame to P.

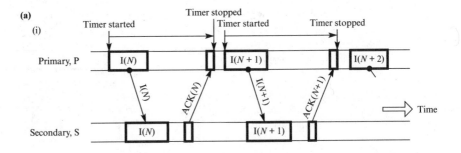

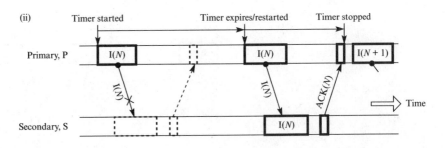

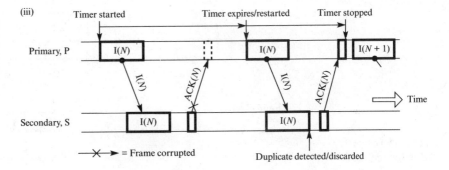

Figure 4.1
Idle RQ operation:
(a) implicit
retransmission.

- On receipt of an error-free ACK frame, P can transmit another I-frame – part (i).

- When P initiates the transmission of an I-frame it starts a timer.

- If S receives an I-frame or P receives an ACK-frame containing transmission errors, the frame is discarded.

- If P does not receive an ACK-frame within a predefined time interval (the **timeout interval**), then P retransmits the waiting I-frame – part (ii).

- If an ACK-frame is corrupted, then S receives another copy of the frame and hence this is rejected by S – part (iii).

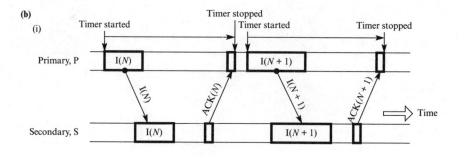

(b)

(i)

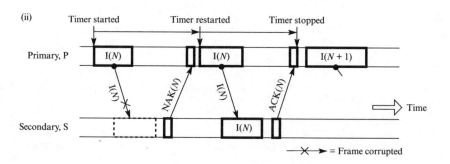

(ii)

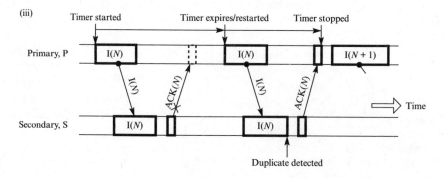

(iii)

Figure 4.1 (cont.)
(b) Explicit request.

As we can see in part (i), after initiating the transmission of a frame, P must wait a minimum time before transmitting the next frame. The wait time is equal to the time the I-frame takes to be received and processed by S plus the time for the ACK-frame to be transmitted and processed. In the worst case, P must wait a time equal to the timeout interval, which must exceed the minimum time by a suitable margin, to avoid an ACK-frame being received after another copy of the previous frame has been retransmitted.

The relative magnitude of each component making up the minimum time varies for different types of data link. It is determined by such factors as the physical separation of the two communicating systems (P and S) and the data transmission rate of the link. In general, however, a significant improvement in the utilization of the available link capacity can be obtained if S informs P immediately whenever it receives a corrupted I-frame, by returning a **negative acknowledgment frame** or **NAK-frame**. Some example frame sequence diagrams with this scheme are shown in Figure 4.1(b).

The following points should be noted when interpreting the frame sequences:

- As with the implicit acknowledgment scheme, on receipt of an error-free I-frame, S returns an ACK-frame to P.

- On receipt of an error-free ACK-frame, P stops the timer and can then initiate the transmission of another I-frame – part (i).

- If S receives an I-frame containing transmission errors, the frame is discarded and it returns a NAK-frame – part (ii).

- If P does not receive an ACK-frame (or NAK-frame) within the timeout interval, P retransmits the waiting I-frame – part (iii).

Since with the idle RQ scheme the primary must wait for an acknowledgment after sending a frame, the scheme is also known as **send-and-wait** or **stop-and-wait**. As we can see from Figure 4.1, the scheme ensures that S receives at least one copy of each frame transmitted by P. With both schemes, however, it is possible for S to receive two (or more) copies of a particular I-frame. These copies are known as **duplicates**. In order for S to discriminate between the next valid I-frame (as it expects) and a duplicate, each frame transmitted contains a unique identifier known as the **sequence number** (N, $N + 1$, etc.) as shown in Figure 4.1. S must therefore retain a record of the sequence number contained within the last I-frame it correctly received. If S receives another copy of this frame, then the copy is discarded. To enable P to resynchronize, S returns an ACK-frame for each correctly received frame with the related I-frame identifier within it.

We can observe the improvement in link utilization by using an explicit request scheme by considering the frame sequences in part (ii) of each scheme. With implicit retransmission, the time before the next I-frame can be transmitted is the timeout interval, whereas the time is much shorter with a NAK-frame. The relative improvement in link utilization is determined ultimately by the bit error rate (BER) of the link and hence the number of frames that are corrupted and need to be retransmitted. However, most data communication applications for which the idle RQ protocol is suitable use the explicit request scheme with NAK-frames.

The sequence number carried in each I-frame is known as the **send sequence number** or **N(S)**, and the sequence number in each ACK and NAK frame as the **receive sequence number** or **N(R)**. As Chapter 3 described, the ASCII (and EBCDIC) character sets contain a number of control characters (for example, STX, ETX), some of which are used for transmission control. Three other transmission control characters are needed to implement the basic idle RQ error control procedure: SOH (start-of-header), NAK, and ACK. Their use is shown in Figure 4.2.

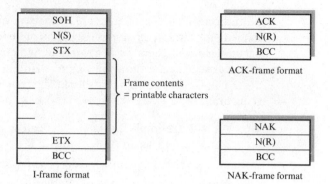

Figure 4.2
Idle RQ frame (PDU) formats.

Each I-frame must contain a sequence number at the head of the frame and, as we can see, this precedes the STX character. The SOH character is inserted at the head of the complete block so that a unique character always signals the start of a new frame.

The ACK and NAK control characters used for acknowledgment purposes are followed by the receive sequence number. Again, to enhance the error-detection probability, the complete NAK- or ACK-frame contains a block sum check character. Collectively, the three frames – I-frame, ACK-frame, and NAK-frame – are known as the **protocol data units (PDUs)** of the idle RQ protocol, and P and S as the primary and secondary **protocol entities**.

4.2.1 Layered architecture

The frame sequence diagrams shown in Figure 4.1 illustrate the essential features of the operation of the idle RQ protocol. Before we proceed with more details relating to the protocol, however, we introduce the concept of **layering**. This involves decoupling the combined application and communication tasks to create two well-defined subtasks or **layers** with a formal interface between them.

To illustrate this, consider an **application process (AP)** running in one computer transferring a file of data to another similar AP (program) running in a second computer across a serial data link using an idle RQ error control protocol. As we have described, the idle RQ protocol will endeavor to send a series of blocks of information – printable characters or bytes – across the data link in a reliable way. Also, depending on the BER of the link, a maximum block size will be specified that ensures, to a high probability, that a good percentage of I-frames transmitted will be free of errors.

The idle RQ **protocol layer** in the source computer thus offers a defined **service** to the user AP layer above it, which is to transfer a series of blocks of information each of a defined maximum length, to a similar (peer) AP in the destination computer. The two peer idle RQ protocol entities are concerned with the various issues discussed earlier relating to error detection: the generation and return of acknowledgment frames, timeouts, and the delivery of blocks of information in the same sequence as they were submitted.

In contrast, the two peer APs are concerned only with the procedure to transfer the file of data using the service provided by the communications (idle RQ) layer, such as the name of the file, its length, the segmentation of the file contents into smaller blocks prior to submitting them to the communications layer, and the reassembly of the blocks into a complete file on receipt. Thus for each application, the sequence of message blocks expected, their syntax and structure must be defined. This implies an AP-to-AP protocol with its own set of (AP-to-AP) PDUs. The two AP protocol entities then use the services of the lower communications layer to transfer their own PDUs. To the communications layer, however, these are all simply blocks of information which are transferred in the same way.

Normally, the service provided by a communications layer is expressed in the form of a **service primitive** with the data to be transferred – normally referred to as **user data** – as a **parameter**. Since the service is associated with the link layer (L) and for the transfer of data (blocks of information), the user service primitive at the sending interface is expressed as L_DATA.request and that at the interface with the recipient AP as L_DATA.indication. This is shown in Figure 4.3(a).

In many instances, since the users of a layer are concerned with the service provided rather than how the service is implemented, when we define the services associated with a (protocol) layer we normally represent them in the form shown in Figure 4.3(b). This is known as a (service) **time sequence diagram**. To decouple the two layers in a clean way, we introduce a **queue** between them, as shown in Figure 4.3(c). This is simply a data structure that implements a **first-in, first-out (FIFO)** queuing discipline. Elements are added to the **tail** of the queue and are removed from the **head**.

Normally, the user service primitive(s) associated with a layer is (are) passed between layers using a data structure known as an **event control block (ECB)**. Generally this is a record or structure with the primitive type in the first field and a character or byte array containing the user data in a second field. Whenever the source AP – or higher protocol layer – wishes to send a message block, it first obtains a free ECB, writes the segment of user data in a character or byte array, sets the primitive type field to L_DATA.request and inserts the ECB at the tail of the link layer (LS_user) input queue ready for reading by the idle RQ primary.

When the idle RQ protocol entity software is next run, it detects the presence of an entry (ECB) in the link layer (LS_user) input queue, reads the entry from the head of the queue, and proceeds to create an I-frame with the message block – the contents of the character/byte array – as the frame contents and the appropriate header and trailer characters. It then initiates the transmission of the frame to the secondary protocol entity. Assuming the received frame is error free, the secondary protocol entity strips off the header and trailer characters, and passes the frame contents – the message block – up to the destination AP in an ECB using the link layer (LS_provider) output queue with the primitive type set to L_DATA.indication. It then creates and returns an ACK-frame to P.

When the destination AP is next run, it detects and reads the ECB from the LS_provider queue and proceeds to process the contents of the message block according to the defined AP-to-AP protocol. Typically, if this is the first message

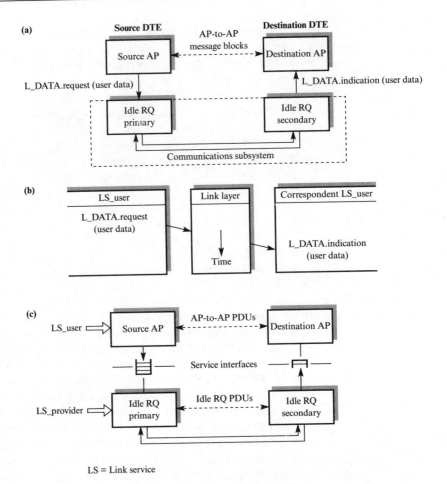

Figure 4.3
Layered architecture:
(a) service primitives;
(b) time sequence
diagram; (c) service
interfaces.

block containing, say, the file name, it will involve creating a file with this name and opening it ready for subsequent write/append file operations.

At the sending side, assuming the ACK-frame is received free of errors, P frees the memory buffer holding the acknowledged I-frame and checks the LS_user input queue for another waiting ECB. If there is one, the procedure is repeated until all the file segments have been transferred. Normally the source AP sends an end-of-transfer message block to inform the destination AP that the complete file contents have been transferred.

We can conclude that the adoption of a layered architecture means that each layer performs its own well-defined function in the context of the overall communications task (file transfer, for example). Also, that the lower (data link control) layer offers a defined service to the layer above it and operates according to a defined protocol. As we shall see in Part three, a layered architecture means that more sophisticated communication subsystems can be implemented simply by adding layers between the application layer and the lower link layer, each new layer concerned with a complementary function.

4.2.2   Protocol specification

Although the three frame sequence diagrams shown in each part of Figure 4.1, coupled with the descriptive text, are probably sufficient to illustrate the operation of an idle RQ protocol, with more sophisticated protocols it is often not practicable to describe fully the operation of the protocol using just this method. Indeed, as we shall see in this and later chapters, defining the operation of a protocol while allowing for all the possible events and error conditions that can arise is very complex. In general, therefore, we specify protocols using one of a number of more precise methods and formalisms. We normally use frame sequence diagrams of the type shown in Figure 4.1 simply to illustrate selected aspects of a protocol, rather than as a means of specifying the protocol.

The three most common methods for specifying a communication protocol are **state transition diagrams**, **extended event–state tables**, and high-level **structured programs**. In many instances, we define a protocol as a combination of these coupled with time sequence diagrams to illustrate the user service primitives associated with the protocol.

Irrespective of the specification method, we model a protocol as a **finite state machine** or **automaton**. This means that the protocol – or, more accurately, the protocol entity – can be in just one of a finite number of defined **states** at any instant. For example, it might be idle waiting for a message to send, or waiting to receive an acknowledgment. Transitions between states take place as a result of an **incoming event**, for example, a message becomes ready to send, or an ACK-frame is received. As a result of an incoming event, an associated **outgoing event** is normally generated, for example, on receipt of a message, send the created I-frame on the link, or on receipt of a NAK-frame, retransmit the waiting I-frame.

Obviously, some incoming events may lead to a number of possible outgoing events. The particular outgoing event selected is determined by the computed state of one or more **predicates** (boolean variables). As an example, predicate P1 may be true if the N(R) in a received ACK-frame is the same as the N(S) in the I-frame waiting to be acknowledged. Hence, if P1 is true, then free the memory buffer in which the I-frame is being held; if it is false, initiate retransmission of the frame.

Finally, an incoming event, in addition to generating an outgoing event (and possibly a change of state), may also have one or more associated **local** or **specific actions**. Examples include *start a timer* and *increment the send sequence variable*.

We shall now expand upon all of these aspects of the specification of a protocol by considering the specification of the error control procedure associated with the idle RQ protocol.

4.2.3   Idle RQ specification

All finite state machines – and hence protocol entities – operate in an **atomic** way. This means that once an incoming event has started to be processed, all processing functions associated with the event, including the generation of any outgoing event(s), local (specific) actions, and a possible change in state, are all carried out

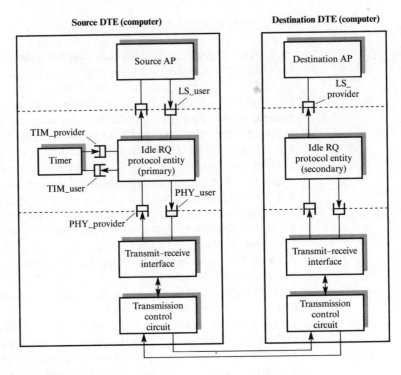

Source DTE (computer)   Destination DTE (computer)

Figure 4.4
Communications
subsystem architecture
and protocol entity
interfaces.

TIM = Timer
PHY = Physical

in their entirety (that is, in an indivisible way) before another incoming event is
accepted.

To ensure this happens, the various incoming (and outgoing) event
interfaces are decoupled from the protocol entity itself by means of queues as
shown in Figure 4.4. There is an additional pair of queues between the protocol
entity and the transmit–receive procedure that controls the particular transmission
control circuit being used. Similarly, there is a pair of queues between the protocol
entity and the timer procedure. Normally, the latter is run at regular (tick)
intervals by means of an **interrupt** and, if a timer is currently running, its current
value is decremented by the tick value. If the value goes to zero, a **timer expired**
message is returned to the protocol entity via the appropriate queue.

The role of the transmit–receive procedure is simply to transmit a
preformatted frame passed to it or to receive a frame from the link and queue
the frame for processing by the protocol entity. This procedure may also be run as
a result of an interrupt, but this time from the transmission control circuit. Finally,
although in principle only a single input and output queue is necessary to interface
the primary and secondary to their respective APs, in practice a pair of queues is
necessary at each interface in order to handle the duplex flows of primitives.

To simplify the specification procedure, we give each of the various incoming
events, outgoing events, predicates, specific actions, and states associated with

each protocol entity an abbreviated name. Prior to specifying the protocol, the various abbreviated names are normally listed; all subsequent references are made using these names. For the error control component of the idle RQ protocol, the list of abbreviated names for the primary and secondary are as shown in Figure 4.5(a) and (b), respectively.

Since each protocol entity is essentially a sequential system, we must retain information that may vary as different incoming events are received. This information is held in a number of **state variables**. Examples, for the primary, are the send sequence variable V(S) – Vs in the specification – which holds the sequence number to be allocated to the next I-frame to be transmitted, the PresentState variable which holds the present state of the protocol entity, RetxCount which is used to limit the number of retransmissions of a frame, and ErrorCount which is a count of the number of erroneous frames received. Typically, if either RetxCount or ErrorCount reaches its maximum limit then the frame is discarded, an error message is sent to the AP layer above and the protocol (entity) reinitializes.

Just two state variables are needed for the secondary: the receive sequence variable V(R) – Vr in the specification – which holds the sequence number of the

(a)   **Incoming events**

Name	Interface	Meaning
LDATAreq	LS_user	L_DATA.request service primitive received
ACKRCVD	PHY_provider	ACK-frame received from S
TEXP	TIM_provider	Wait-ACK timer expires
NAKRCVD	PHY_provider	NAK-frame received from S

States

Name	Meaning
IDLE	Idle, no message transfer in progress
WTACK	Waiting an acknowledgment

Outgoing events

Name	Interface	Meaning
TxFrame	PHY_user	Format and transmit an I-frame
RetxFrame	PHY_user	Retransmit I-frame waiting acknowledgment
LERRORind	LS_provider	Error message: frame discarded for reason specified

Predicates

Name	Meaning
P0	N(S) in waiting I-frame = N(R) in ACK-frame
P1	Block sum check (BSC) in ACK/NAK-frame correct

Specific actions

[1] = Start_timer using TIM_user queue
[2] = Increment Vs
[3] = Stop_timer using TIM_user queue
[4] = Increment RetxCount
[5] = Increment ErrorCount
[6] = Reset RetxCount to zero

State variables

Vs	= Send sequence variable
PresentState	= Present state of protocol entity
ErrorCount	= Number of erroneous frames received
RetxCount	= Number of retransmissions for this frame

Figure 4.5
Abbreviated names used in idle RQ specifications:
(a) primary.

(b)   **Incoming events**

Name	Interface	Meaning
IRCVD	PHY_provider	I-frame received from P

States

Name	Meaning
WTIFM	Waiting a new I-frame from P

Outgoing events

Name	Interface	Meaning
LDATAind	LS_provider	Pass contents of received I-frame to user AP with an L_DATA.indication primitive
TxACK(X)	PHY_user	Format and transmit an ACK-frame with N(R) = X
TxNAK(X)	PHY_user	Format and transmit a NAK-frame with N(R) = X
LERRORind	LS_provider	Issue error message for reason specified

Predicates

Name	Meaning
P0	N(S) in I-frame = Vr
P1	Block sum check (BSC) in I-frame correct
P2	N(S) in I-frame = Vr – 1

Figure 4.5 (cont.)
(b) Secondary.

Specific actions	State variables		
[1] = Increment Vr	Vr	=	Receive sequence variable
[2] = Increment ErrorCount	ErrorCount	=	Number of erroneous frames received

last correctly received I-frame, and ErrorCount which keeps a record of the number of erroneous frames received. Again, if ErrorCount reaches its defined maximum limit an error message is sent to the AP layer above.

The formal specification of both the primary and secondary (protocol entities) are shown in Figures 4.6 and 4.7, respectively, in state transition diagram form and extended event–state table form.

Using the state transition diagram method, the possible states of the protocol entity are shown in ovals with the particular states written within them. **Directional arrows** (also known as **arcs**) indicate the possible transitions between the states, with the incoming event causing the transition and any resulting outgoing event and specific actions, written alongside. If, for example, an L_DATA.request (LDATAreq) is received from the LS_user interface, then the frame is formatted and output to the PHY_user interface (TxFrame), a timer is started for the frame [1], the send sequence variable incremented [2], and the WTACK state entered. Similarly, if an ACK-frame is received with an N(R) equal to the N(S) in the waiting frame and the block sum check is correct, then the timer is stopped [3] and the retransmission count reset to zero [6], and the IDLE state entered. The other transitions can be interpreted in a similar way.

Although state transition diagrams are useful for showing the correct operation of a protocol, because of space limitations it is not always practicable to show all possible incoming event possibilities including error conditions. Hence

(a)

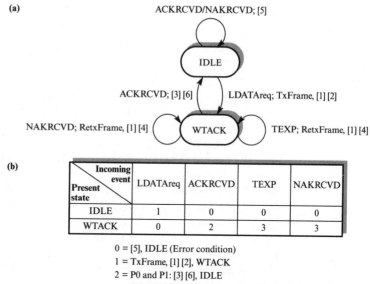

(b)

Present state \ Incoming event	LDATAreq	ACKRCVD	TEXP	NAKRCVD
IDLE	1	0	0	0
WTACK	0	2	3	3

0 = [5], IDLE (Error condition)
1 = TxFrame, [1] [2], WTACK
2 = P0 and P1: [3] [6], IDLE
     P0 and NOT P1: RetxFrame, [1] [4], WTACK
     NOT P0 and NOT P1: [5], IDLE
3 = RetxFrame, [1] [4], WTACK

Figure 4.6
Idle RQ specification – primary: (a) state transition diagram; (b) extended event–state table.

most state transition diagrams are incomplete specifications. Moreover, with all but the simplest of protocols, we need many such diagrams to define even the correct operation of a protocol. It is for these reasons that we use the event–state table and the structured program code methods.

Using the extended event–state table method, as in Figures 4.6 and 4.7, we can show all the possible incoming events and protocol (present) states in the form of a table. For each state, the table entry defines the outgoing event, any specific action(s), and the new state for all possible incoming events, also, if predicates are involved, the alternative set of action(s). Clearly, the extended event–state table is a far more rigorous method since it allows for all possible incoming-event, present-state combinations. A basic event–state table has only one possible action and next state for each incoming-event, present-state combination. It is the presence of

(a)

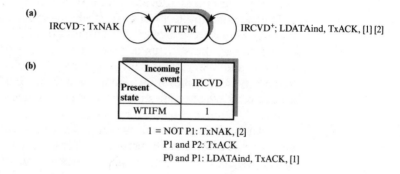

(b)

Present state \ Incoming event	IRCVD
WTIFM	1

1 = NOT P1: TxNAK, [2]
     P1 and P2: TxACK
     P0 and P1: LDATAind, TxACK, [1]

Figure 4.7
Idle RQ specification – secondary: (a) state transition diagram; (b) extended event–state table.

predicates – and hence possible alternative actions/next states – that gives rise to the use of the term 'extended' event–state table.

When we are interpreting the actions to be followed if predicates are involved, we must note that these are shown in order. Hence the action to be followed if the primary is in the WTACK state and an ACK-frame is received (ACKRCVD), is first to determine if P0 and P1 are both true. If they are, then carry out specific action [3] and [6] and enter the IDLE state. Else, determine if {P0 and NOTP1} is true and so on. If neither condition is true then an error is suspected and the actions are as shown.

A feature of the extended event–state table is that it lends itself more readily to implementation in program code than a state transition diagram. We can see this by considering an example: implementation of the idle RQ primary and secondary. Their outline structures are shown in Figure 4.8(a) and (b), respectively. They are written in a high-level pseudocode for readability and each is shown as a separate program. In practice, they may be procedures but this will not affect their basic operation.

When each program is first run, the Initialize procedure is invoked. This performs such functions as initializing all state variables to their initial values and the contents of the EventStateTable array to those in the extended event–state table. The program then enters an infinite loop waiting for an incoming event to arrive at one of its input queues.

The incoming event which causes the program to run is first assigned to EventType. The current contents of PresentState and EventType are then used as indices to the EventStateTable array to determine the integer – 0, 1, 2, or 3 – that defines the processing actions associated with that event. For example, if the accessed integer is 2, this results in the predicate functions P0 and P1 being invoked and, depending on their computed state (true or false), the invocation of the appropriate outgoing event procedure, coupled with any specific action procedure(s) as defined in the specification, for example, starting or resetting the timer, and updating PresentState.

We have simplified the pseudocode to highlight the structure of each program and hence the implementation methodology. No code is shown for the various outgoing event procedures nor for the predicate functions. In practice, these must be implemented in an unambiguous way using the necessary steps listed in the specification.

Although many protocols are specified in the form of an extended event–state table, some protocols are specified in a structured program code form. This type of specification is similar to the pseudocode implementations shown in Figure 4.8. However, the structured code used is more formal since all the variables required and the various outgoing event and specific action procedures and functions are all shown in detail. Hence the implementation of a protocol specification which is in structured code is much simplified and less prone to errors.

An outline structure of the error control procedure of the idle RQ primary using the structured code method is shown for comparison purposes in Figure 4.8(c). The approach is known as the **extended state transitional model (Estelle)**. As

(a)
```
program   IdleRQ_Primary;
const     MaxErrCount;
          MaxRetxCount;
type      Events = (LDATAreq, ACKRCVD, TEXP, NAKRCVD);
          States  = (IDLE, WTACK);
var       EventStateTable = array [Events, States] of 0..3;
          PresentState : States;
          Vs, ErrorCount, RetxCount : integer;
          EventType : Events;
procedure Initialize;          } Initializes state variables and contents of EventStateTable
procedure TxFrame;             ⎫
procedure RetxFrame;           ⎬ Outgoing event procedures
procedure LERRORind;           ⎭
procedure Start_timer;         ⎫ Specific action procedures
procedure Stop_timer;          ⎭
function  P0 : boolean;        ⎫ Predicate functions
function  P1 : boolean;        ⎭

begin     Initialize;
          repeat Wait receipt of an incoming event
                  EventType := type of event
                  case EventStateTable [EventType, PresentState] of
                      0 : begin ErrorCount := ErrorCount + 1; PresentState = IDLE;
                                if(ErrorCount = MaxErrCount) then ERRORind end;
                      1 : begin TxFrame; Start_timer; Vs := Vs + 1; PresentState := WTACK end;
                      2 : begin if(P0 and P1) then begin Stop_timer; RetxCount := 0; PresentState := IDLE end;
                                else if (P0 and NOTP1) then begin RetxFrame; Start_timer;
                                                                  RetxCount := RetxCount + 1;
                                                                  PresentState := WTACK end;
                                else if (NOTP0 and NOTP1) then begin PresentState := IDLE; ErrorCount := ErrorCount + 1 end;
                                                                  if (ErrorCount = MaxErrorCount) then begin LERRORind; Initialize; end;
                          end;
                      3 : begin RetxFrame; Start_timer; RetxCount := RetxCount + 1; PresentState := WTACK;
                                if (RetxCount = MaxRetxCount) then begin LERRORind; Initialize; end;
                          end;
                  until Forever;
end.
```

(b)
```
program   IdleRQ_Secondary;
const.    MaxErrorCount;
type      Events = IRCVD;
          States = WTIFM;
var       EventStateTable = array [Events, States] of 1;
          EventType : Events;
          PresentState : States;
          Vr, X, ErrorCount : integer;
procedure Initialize;          } Initializes state variables and contents of EventStateTable
procedure LDATAind(X);         ⎫
procedure TxACK(X);            ⎬ Outgoing event procedures
procedure TxNAK(X);            ⎪
procedure LERRORind;           ⎭
function  P0 : boolean;        ⎫
function  P1 : boolean;        ⎬ Predicate functions
function  P2 : boolean;        ⎭

begin     Initialize;
          repeat Wait receipt of incoming event; EventType := type of event;
                  case EventStateTable[EventType, PresentState] of
                      1 : X := N(S) from I-frame;
                          if (NOTP1) then TxNAK(X);
                          else if(P1 and P2) then TxACK(X);
                          else if(P0 and P1) then begin LDATAind; TxACK(X); Vr := Vr + 1; end;
                          else begin ErrorCount := ErrorCount + 1; if (ErrorCount = MaxErrorCount) then
                                  begin LERRORind; Initialize; end;
                              end;
                  until Forever;
end.
```

Figure 4.8   Idle RQ specification: (a) pseudocode for primary; (b) pseudocode for secondary.

(c)   – Type and constant definitions
       – Interface definitions {interface queue names and ECB record structure definitions}
       – Formal finite state machine definition.

       module
          – states
          – incoming events
          – outgoing event procedures
          – specific action procedures
          – predicate functions
      trans (* begin state transition definitions *)
        from IDLE *to* IDLE
        when PHY_provider.ACKRCVD
          begin
          end;
        from IDLE *to* IDLE
        when TIM_provider.TEXP
          begin
          end;
           ·
           ·
        from WTACK *to* IDLE
        provided P0 *and* P1
        when PHY_provider.ACKRCVD
          begin
          end;
           ·
           ·
           ·
    end.

Figure 4.8 (cont.)
(c) Outline of the
structure of the
primary in Estelle.

we can see, this is similar in structure to the specifications in parts (a) and (b) except that the actual protocol entity is defined in the form of a **module** and all the possible transitions are defined separately in a more formal way. In practice only a small number of specifications are in this form; the majority are in extended event–state table form. By applying the outlined implementation methodology, we can produce similar structured program code.

4.2.4   Link utilization

Before considering the error control procedures associated with the two types of continuous RQ protocol, we shall first quantify the efficiency of utilization of the available link capacity with the idle RQ protocol. The efficiency of utilization U is a ratio of two times, each measured from the point in time the transmitter starts to send a frame. It is defined as:

$$U = \frac{T_{ix}}{T_t}$$

where T_{ix} is the time for transmitter to transmit a frame and T_t equals T_{ix} plus any time the transmitter spends waiting for an acknowledgment.

To quantify the link utilization with idle RQ, a frame sequence diagram with the various component times identified is given in Figure 4.9. In practice, in most cases for which the idle RQ protocol is adequate, the time to process an I-frame T_{ip} and its associated ACK-frame T_{ap} are both short compared with their

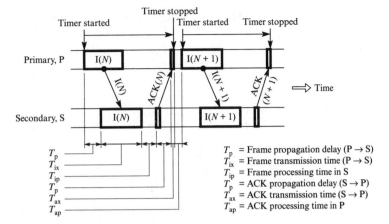

Figure 4.9
Idle RQ link utilization
schematic.

transmission times T_{ix} and T_{ax}. Also, since an ACK-frame is much shorter than an I-frame, T_{ax} is negligible compared with T_{ix}. Hence the minimum total time before the next frame can be transmitted is often approximated to $T_{ix} + 2T_p$. An approximate expression for U is thus:

$$U = \frac{T_{ix}}{T_{ix} + 2T_p}$$

or:

$$U = \frac{1}{1 + 2T_p/T_{ix}}$$

As we described in Section 2.4, the ratio T_p/T_{ix} is often given the symbol a and hence:

$$U = \frac{1}{1 + 2a}$$

In Example 2.6 we saw that, a can range from a small fraction for low bit rate links of modest length to a large integer value for long links and high bit rates. For these two extremes, U varies between near unity (100%) and a small fraction.

Example 4.1

A series of 1000-bit frames is to be transmitted using an idle RQ protocol. Determine the link utilization for the following types of data link assuming a data transmission rate of (i) 1 kbps and (ii) 1 Mbps. The velocity of propagation of the link is 2×10^8 ms^{-1} and the bit error rate is negligible.

(a) A twisted pair cable 1 km in length
(b) A leased line 200 km in length
(c) A satellite link of 50 000 km

The time taken to transmit a frame T_{ix} is given by:

$$T_{ix} = \frac{\text{Number of bits in frame, } N}{\text{Bit rate in bps}}$$

Bit rate R in bps

At 1 kbps:

$$T_{ix} = \frac{1000}{10^3} = 1 \text{ s}$$

At 1 Mbps:

$$T_{ix} = \frac{1000}{10^6} = 10^{-3} \text{ s}$$

$$T_p = \frac{S}{V} \quad \text{and} \quad U = \frac{1}{1 + \dfrac{2T_p}{T_{ix}}} = \frac{1}{1 + 2a}$$

(a) $T_p = \dfrac{10^3}{2 \times 10^8} = 5 \times 10^{-6} \text{ s}$

  (i) $a = \dfrac{5 \times 10^{-6}}{1} = 5 \times 10^{-6}$ and hence $(1 + 2a) \simeq 1$ and $U = 1$

  (ii) $a = \dfrac{5 \times 10^{-6}}{10^{-3}} = 5 \times 10^{-3}$ and hence $(1 + 2a) \simeq 1$ and $U = 1$

(b) $T_p = \dfrac{200 \times 10^3}{2 \times 10^8} = 1 \times 10^{-3} \text{ s}$

  (i) $a = \dfrac{1 \times 10^{-3}}{1} = 1 \times 10^{-3}$ and hence $(1 + 2a) \simeq 1$ and $U = 1$

  (ii) $a = \dfrac{1 \times 10^{-3}}{10^{-3}} = 1$ and hence $(1 + 2a) > 1$ and $U = \dfrac{1}{1 + 2} = 0.33$

(c) $T_p = \dfrac{50 \times 10^6}{2 \times 10^8} = 0.25 \text{ s}$

  (i) $a = \dfrac{0.25}{1} = 0.25$ and hence $(1 + 2a) > 1$ and $U = \dfrac{1}{1 + 0.5} = 0.67$

  (ii) $a = \dfrac{0.25}{10^{-3}} = 250$ and hence $(1 + 2a) > 1$ and $U = \dfrac{1}{1 + 500} = 0.002$

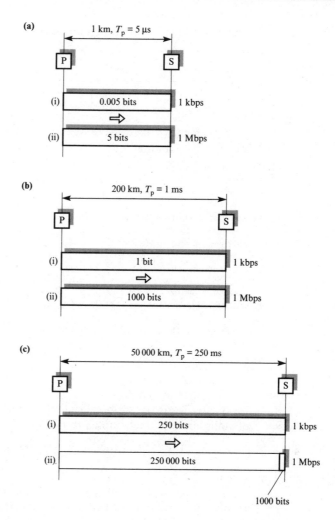

Figure 4.10
Effect of propagation
delay as a function of
data transmission rate;
parts correspond to
Example 4.1.

The results are summarized in Figure 4.10 from which we can make some interesting observations. Firstly, for relatively short links for which a is less than 1, the link utilization is (to a good approximation) 100% and is independent of the data rate. This means that an idle RQ protocol is perfectly adequate for short links and modest data rates. Examples are networks based on modems and the analog PSTN. Secondly, for longer terrestrial links, the link utilization is high for low data rates (and hence low values of a) but falls off significantly as the data rate (and hence a) increases. Thirdly, the link utilization is poor for satellite links, even at low data rates. We can conclude that an idle RQ protocol is unsuitable for such applications and also for those that involve high bit rate terrestrial links, such as LANs (see Chapter 6) and most public carrier WANs (see Chapter 8).

In the link utilization calculations in Example 4.1 we assumed no transmission errors, although in practice, the links have a nonzero BER. Hence, to transmit a frame successfully, an average N_r transmission attempts will be required. We can modify the expression for link utilization, therefore, to give:

$$U = \frac{T_{ix}}{N_r T_{ix} + 2N_r T_p} = \frac{1}{N_r \left(1 + \dfrac{2T_p}{T_{ix}}\right)}$$

We can derive the value of N_r from a knowledge of the BER, P, of the link. If P is the probability that a bit will be corrupted then, if we assume random errors, the probability that a frame of length N_i bits is received without errors is given by:

$$P_f = 1 - (1 - P)^{N_i}$$

Hence the probability that a frame is received with errors is given by:

$$P_f = 1 - (1 - P)^{N_i}$$
$$\simeq N_i P \text{ if } N_i P \ll 1$$

For example, a BER of 10^{-4} means that, on average, 1 bit in 10^4 will be corrupted. Hence for, say, 1000-bit frames:

$$P_f = 1 - (1 - 10^{-4})^{1000} = 0.095$$

or

$$P_f = 10^3 \times 10^{-4} = 0.1$$

Now, if P_f is the probability that a frame is corrupted, then $(1 - P_f)$ is the probability that an uncorrupted frame will be received. Hence:

$$N_r = \frac{1}{1 - P_f}$$

For example, if $P_f = 0.5$, $N_r = 2$, that is, if on average 50% of the frames are corrupted, then each frame will have to be transmitted twice. This is so since 50% of the retransmitted frames will also be corrupted, assuming ACK-frames are not corrupted. Because of their short length relative to I-frames, this is a reasonable assumption. In practice, therefore, all the link efficiency values must be divided by N_r. That is:

$$U = \frac{1 - P_f}{1 + 2a}$$

The major advantage of the idle RQ scheme is that it requires a minimum of buffer storage for its implementation, since both P and S need contain sufficient storage for only one frame. In addition, S must retain only a record of the identifier of the last correctly received frame to enable it to detect duplicates. In general, the various retransmission schemes trade buffer storage requirements for transmission efficiency. Because of its low storage requirements, however, idle RQ is used extensively in applications that involve a relatively simple device (such as a terminal or personal computer) at one end of the link.

4.3 Continuous RQ

With a continuous RQ error control scheme, link utilization is much improved at the expense of increased buffer storage requirements. As we shall see, a duplex link is required for its implementation. An example illustrating the transmission of a sequence of I-frames and their returned ACK-frames is shown in Figure 4.11.

Note the following points when interpreting the operation of the scheme:

- P sends I-frames continuously without waiting for an ACK-frame to be returned.

- Since more than one I-frame is waiting acknowledgment, P retains a copy of each I-frame transmitted in a **retransmission list** that operates on a FIFO queue discipline.

- S returns an ACK-frame for each correctly received I-frame.

- Each I-frame contains a unique identifier which is returned in the corresponding ACK-frame.

- On receipt of an ACK-frame, the corresponding I-frame is removed from the retransmission list by P.

- Frames received free of errors are placed in the **link receive list** to await processing.

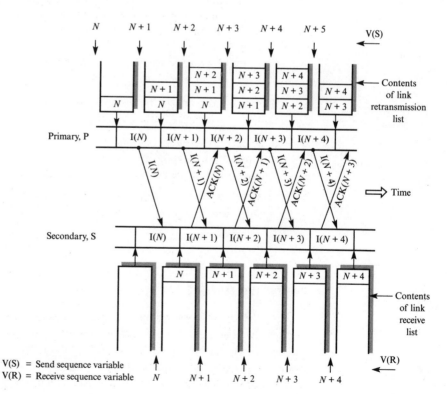

Figure 4.11
Continuous RQ frame
sequence.

V(S) = Send sequence variable
V(R) = Receive sequence variable

- On receipt of the next in-sequence I-frame expected, S delivers the information content within the frame to the upper (LS_user) layer immediately it has processed the frame.

- In the event of frames being received out of sequence – see Section 4.3.1 – S retains these in the link receive list until the next in-sequence frame is received.

As we described in Section 4.2.1, the interface between the higher-layer software and the communication protocol software normally takes the form of two FIFO queues. We must stress, however, that there is no relationship between these and the link retransmission list (at P) and the link receive list (at S). These two lists are for internal use by the communications layer to ensure the reliable transfer of message blocks between the two higher-layer entities.

To implement the scheme, P must retain a send sequence variable V(S), which indicates the send sequence number N(S) to be allocated to the next I-frame to be transmitted. Also, S must maintain a receive sequence variable V(R), which indicates the next in-sequence I-frame it is awaiting.

We can conclude from Figure 4.11 that, in the absence of transmission errors, the link utilization of a continuous RQ scheme (to a reasonable approximation) is always 100% providing the sending of I-frames by P is unrestricted. As we shall see in Section 4.3.3, however, this is not necessarily the case, as normally there is a limit set on the number of I-frames that P can send before the corresponding ACK-frame is received. We shall therefore delay further discussion of the link utilization with a continuous RQ scheme until Section 4.3.6.

Figure 4.11 assumed that no transmission errors occur. When an error does occur, one of two retransmission strategies may be followed:

- S detects and requests the retransmission of just those frames in the sequence that are corrupted – selective repeat.

- S detects the receipt of an out-of-sequence I-frame and requests P to retransmit all outstanding unacknowledged I-frames from the last correctly received, and hence acknowledged, I-frame – go-back-N.

Note that with all continuous RQ schemes, corrupted frames are discarded and retransmission requests are triggered only after the next error-free frame is received.

4.3.1 Selective repeat

As with the idle RQ error control scheme, selective repeat can be implemented in one of two ways; either S acknowledges correctly received frames and P determines from the sequence of ACK-frames received that a frame has been lost – implicit retransmission – or S returns a specific negative acknowledgment for a frame that is missing from the sequence – explicit request. In both schemes, in the event of frames being received out of sequence, S retains these in the link receive list until the next in-sequence frame is received.

Two frame sequence diagrams illustrating aspects of the first scheme are shown in Figure 4.12. Part (a) assumes all ACK-frames are received correctly, while part (b) illustrates the effect of a corrupted ACK-frame. To follow the sequence in Figure 4.12(a), note the following:

- Assume I-frame $N + 1$ is corrupted.

- S returns an ACK-frame for each correctly received I-frame as before.

- S returns an ACK-frame for I-frames N, $N + 2$, $N + 3$, ...

- On receipt of the ACK for I-frame $N + 2$, P detects that frame $N + 1$ has not been acknowledged.

- To allow for the possibility of more than one I-frame being corrupted, on detecting an unacknowledged frame P enters the **retransmission state**.

- When in this state, the transmission of new frames is suspended until all unacknowledged frames have been retransmitted.

- P removes I-frame $N + 2$ from the retransmission list and retransmits I-frame $N + 1$ before transmitting frame $N + 5$.

- On receipt of I-frame $N + 1$, the contents of the queued frames in the link receive list are delivered by S to the LS_user in the correct sequence.

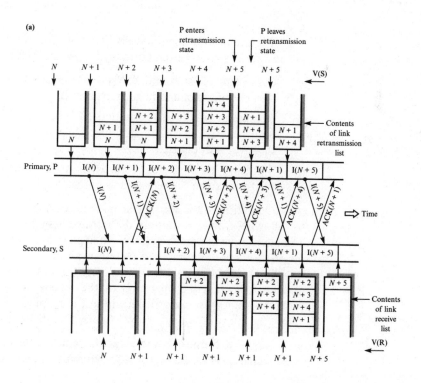

Figure 4.12
Selective repeat –
implicit retransmission:
(a) corrupted I-frame.

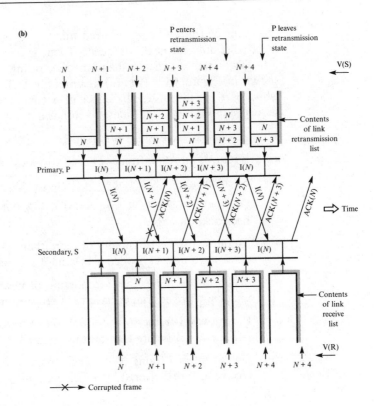

Figure 4.12 (cont.)
(b) Corrupted
ACK-frame.

The frame sequence shown in Figure 4.12(b) relates to the situation in which all the I-frames are received correctly but ACK-frame N is corrupted. Note that:

- On receipt of ACK-frame $N + 1$, P detects that I-frame N is still awaiting acknowledgment and hence retransmits it.

- On receipt of the retransmitted I-frame N, S determines from its receive sequence variable that this has already been received correctly and is therefore a duplicate.

- S discards the frame but returns an ACK-frame for it to ensure P removes the frame from the retransmission list.

Operation of the above scheme relies on the receipt of ACK-frames relating to following frames to initiate the retransmission of an earlier corrupted frame. The alternative approach is to use an explicit negative acknowledgment frame to request for a specific frame to be retransmitted. The negative acknowledgment is known as **selective reject**. Figure 4.13 shows two example frame sequence diagrams showing the operation of the scheme. Again the sequence shown in part (a) assumes no acknowledgments are corrupted, while the sequence in part (b) shows the effect of a lost acknowledgment. Note that:

- An ACK-frame acknowledges all frames in the retransmission list up to and including the I-frame with the sequence number the ACK contains.

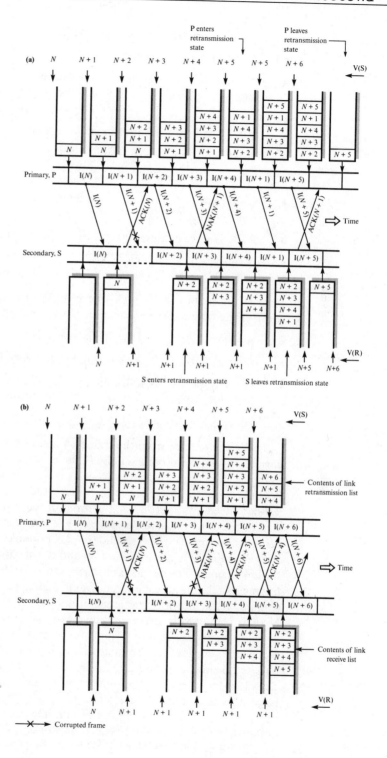

Figure 4.13
Selective repeat –
explicit request:
(a) correct operation;
(b) effect of no
retransmission state.

- Assume I-frame $N + 1$ is corrupted.

- S returns an ACK-frame for I-frame N.

- When S receives I-frame $N + 2$ it detects I-frame $N + 1$ is missing and hence returns a NAK-frame containing the identifier of the missing I-frame $N + 1$.

- On receipt of NAK $N + 1$, P interprets this as S is still awaiting I-frame $N + 1$ and hence retransmits it.

- When S returns a NAK-frame it enters the retransmission state.

- When in the retransmission state, the return of ACK-frames is suspended.

- On receipt of I-frame $N + 1$, S leaves the retransmission state and resumes returning ACK-frames.

- ACK $N + 4$ acknowledges all frames up to and including frame $N + 4$.

- A timer is used with each NAK-frame to ensure that if it is corrupted (and hence frame $N + 1$ is not received), it is retransmitted.

To understand why only one NAK-frame can be outstanding at a time, consider the frame sequence diagram shown in Figure 4.13(b). Note that:

- Assume I-frame $N + 1$ is again corrupted.

- S returns NAK $N + 1$ as before but this time it is corrupted.

- On receipt of ACK-frame $N + 3$, this would acknowledge all frames including I-frame $N + 1$ and hence this frame will not be retransmitted.

- I-frame $N + 1$ would be lost.

We can deduce from the frame sequences shown that although S receives a correct copy of each frame sent by P, the order of reception is not maintained. For example, S receives I-frames $N + 2$, $N + 3$, and $N + 4$ before frame $N + 1$. Selective repeat is used primarily when either the frames being transmitted are self-contained entities (that is, the order of reception is not important), or all the frames relate to the same message (or larger frame) and messages (frames) are being reassembled by the secondary. An example of the latter is when we use a high BER link (such as a radio link) and the maximum frame size associated with the link is small. The normal approach is to use selective repeat for the small frame fragments relating to each larger frame and to reassemble the smaller fragments (frames) back into a single larger frame before the frame is delivered. A single NAK is then used to request retransmission of any lost fragments.

In many applications, however, frames must be delivered in the same sequence as they were submitted. Hence frames received out of sequence must be buffered (held) by S until the missing frame(s) is (are) received. Since the frames can often be large, and the number of frame buffers required can also become large, this makes the buffer storage capacity required in the communications subsystem unacceptably high. For this reason most applications of the type outlined, as well as most terrestrial networks, use the go-back-N retransmission control scheme.

4.3.2 Go-back-N

With go-back-N, as the name implies, when the secondary detects an out-of-sequence frame, it informs the primary to start to retransmit frames from a specified frame number. It does this by returning a special negative acknowledgment frame known as a **reject**. Two frame sequences illustrating the operation of go-back-N are shown in Figure 4.14. When interpreting the sequence in Figure 4.14 note that:

- Assume I-frame $N + 1$ is corrupted.

- S receives I-frame $N + 2$ out of sequence.

- On receipt of I-frame $N + 2$, S returns NAK $N + 1$ informing P to go back and start to retransmit from I-frame $N + 1$.

- On receipt of NAK $N + 1$, P enters the retransmission state.

- When in this state, it suspends sending new frames and commences to retransmit the frames waiting acknowledgment in the retransmission list.

- S discards frames until it receives I-frame $N + 1$.

- On receipt of I-frame $N + 1$, S resumes accepting frames and returning acknowledgments.

- A timeout is applied to NAK frames by S and a second NAK is returned if the correct in-sequence I-frame is not received in the timeout interval.

Again, we have assumed in Figure 4.14(a) that an I-frame was corrupted and that the acknowledgment frames were received correctly. The effect of a corrupted acknowledgment on the frame transmission sequence is shown in Figure 4.14(b). Note that:

- S receives each transmitted I-frame correctly;

- Assume ACK-frames N and $N + 1$ are both corrupted;

- On receipt of ACK-frame $N + 2$, P detects that there are two outstanding I-frames in the retransmission list (N and $N + 1$);

- Since it is an ACK-frame rather than a NAK-frame, P assumes that the two ACK-frames for I-frames N and $N + 1$ have both been corrupted and hence accepts ACK-frame $N + 2$ also as an acknowledgment for the outstanding frames.

Figure 4.14(b) shows that with a go-back-N strategy, the correct frame sequence is maintained, thus minimizing the buffer storage required for its implementation. However, since some correctly received frames must be retransmitted, it is less efficient in its use of the available transmission capacity than a selective retransmission scheme. There is thus the trade-off between buffer storage requirements and link utilization.

Finally, we assumed in Figures 4.11–4.13 relating to continuous RQ that the loss of an I-frame was detected only after the next I-frame had been correctly received. This requires a continuous stream of I-frames being ready to send,

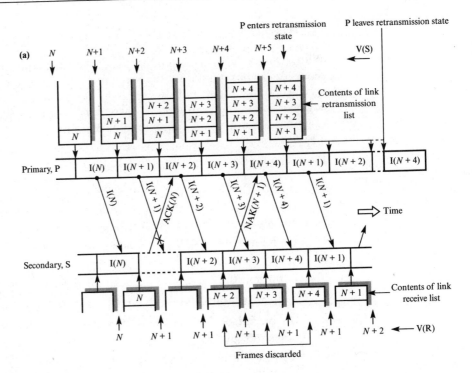

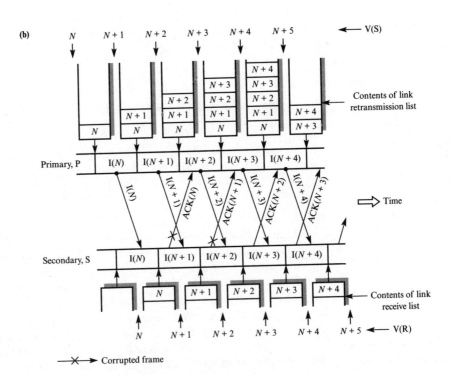

Figure 4.14
Go-back-N
retransmission
strategy: (a) corrupted
I-frame; (b) corrupted
ACK-frame.

otherwise unacceptably long delays are experienced while S waits for the next I-frame to be transmitted.

To allow for this, P normally employs an additional timeout mechanism similar to the one outlined for the idle RQ control scheme. A number of schemes are possible, but the one selected in the earlier protocol definitions assumes a separate timer is started each time an I-frame is transmitted by P, and is stopped (reset) when an acknowledgment indicating its correct receipt is received. If an acknowledgment for a frame is not received before its timeout interval expires, the frame is retransmitted. This is shown in Figure 4.15.

The timeout interval selected must be greater than the worst-case propagation delay between transmitting a frame and receiving the associated acknowledgment. Also, with a timeout mechanism it is possible for S to receive duplicate copies of a frame even if it is correctly received by S since the resulting acknowledgment frame may be corrupted on its return to P. In the absence of an acknowledgment, P assumes that the initial frame has been corrupted and erroneously retransmits another copy.

With a go-back-N control scheme, this does not create a problem since the $N(S)$ in the duplicate frame(s) will not be equal to the current $V(R)$ held by S and will be discarded automatically. With a selective retransmission scheme, however, the possibility of one or more duplicate frames being sent by P is allowed for if S retains an ordered list (the receive list) of the last N correctly received I-frames. In this way, S can check if a received frame is a duplicate of an already correctly

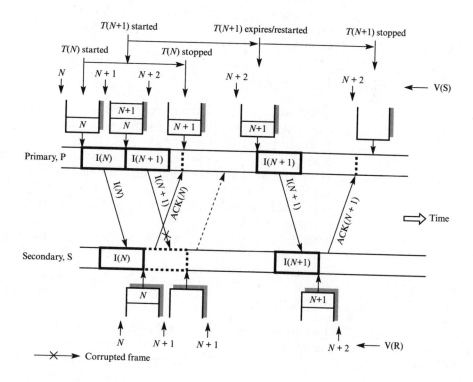

Figure 4.15
Timeout mechanism.

received (and therefore acknowledged) frame or a new frame. As we shall see in Section 4.3.4, the number of frames to be retained, N, is influenced by the flow control algorithm.

For clarity, we have assumed that information frames flow in one direction and that the return path is used simply for acknowledgment. Normally, however, most communication links that use continuous RQ are duplex links and carry information frames in both directions. To accommodate this, each side of these links contains both a primary and a secondary: the first controlling the sequence of I-frames transmitted and the second controlling the sequence of I-frames received. Thus, each side of the link contains both a V(S), which is controlled by the primary, and a V(R), which is controlled by the secondary. Although separate ACK- and NAK-frames are utilized, since there is the possibility of an I-frame awaiting transmission in the reverse direction when an ACK or NAK is to be returned, some protocols utilize the I-frames flowing in the return direction to carry acknowledgment information about the transmission of I-frames in the forward direction, as a way of improving link utilization. Each I-frame transmitted then contains both an N(S), indicating the send sequence number, and an N(R), containing acknowledgment information for the reverse direction. This scheme is referred to as **piggyback acknowledgment**. A protocol that uses this technique is the high-level data link control (HDLC) protocol (see Chapter 5).

Finally, although all the ACK- and NAK-frames we have discussed carried an N(R) that is the same as the N(S) to which they relate, in practice the V(R) at the secondary is incremented immediately the I-frame is received and before the acknowledgment is generated. This means that with most practical protocol implementations ACK N acknowledges frame $N - 1$. Again HDLC uses this technique.

4.3.3   Flow control

Error control is only one component of a data link protocol. Another important and related component is **flow control**. As the name implies, it is concerned with controlling the rate of transmission of characters or frames on a link so that the receiver always has sufficient buffer storage resources to accept them prior to processing. With a character-oriented terminal-to-computer link, for example, if the remote computer is servicing many terminals, it may become temporarily overloaded and be unable to process all the characters sent to it at the available transmission rates. Similarly, with a frame-oriented selective retransmission scheme, the receiver may run out of buffer storage capacity if it is trying to buffer an indeterminate number of frames. We shall consider the two most common flow control schemes.

X-ON/X-OFF

From Section 4.1 we can deduce that echo checking, in addition to performing (manual) error control, implicitly performs flow control since, if the remote computer runs out of buffer storage, it will cease echoing characters back to the terminal screen. Hence the user will automatically stop keying-in further characters. Normally, however, the lack of echoed characters from the computer is caused when the computer becomes temporarily overloaded. In this case, if the user does not cease transmitting new characters, the computer incurs further and unnecessary processing overheads by simply reading each character and then discarding it.

Consequently an additional automatic flow control facility is often invoked to ensure that a terminal does not send any further characters until an overload condition has been cleared. To do this the computer returns a special control character **X-OFF** to the controlling device within the terminal, instructing it to cease transmission. On receipt of the X-OFF character, the terminal either ignores any further characters entered at the keyboard or buffers them in a local buffer until the overload has been cleared. In this way, the computer does not incur any unnecessary processing overheads. Then, when the overload condition decays and the computer is able to accept further characters, it returns a companion control character **X-ON** to inform the terminal control device that it may restart sending characters. This mechanism is also used when a computer is sending characters to a printer or other terminal that cannot sustain the same rate of output as the computer. In such cases, it is the controlling device within the printer (or terminal) that controls the flow of characters.

The RTS/CTS handshake control lines we discussed in Section 2.6.1 associated with the EIA-232D/V.24 interface can be used to perform a similar function. To discriminate between the two methods, therefore, the latter is referred to as **out-of-band flow control** while X-ON/X-OFF is an example of **in-band flow control**.

Sliding window

To control the flow of frames across a data link, an alternative mechanism known as a **sliding window** is used. Recall that an idle RQ error control scheme, although inefficient in its use of transmission bandwidth, requires a minimum of buffer storage capacity since, after a frame is transmitted by P, it must wait until an acknowledgment is returned by S before transmitting the next frame. The flow of I-frames across the link is therefore automatically tightly controlled.

With a continuous RQ error control scheme, however, P may send I-frames continuously before receiving any acknowledgments. With this type of scheme it is possible for the destination to run out of available buffer storage if, for example, it is unable to pass on the frames at the rate they are received. It is usual to introduce an additional regulating action into such schemes. The approach is similar to the idle RQ control scheme in that it essentially sets a limit on the number of I-frames that P may send before receiving an acknowledgment. P monitors the number of outstanding (unacknowledged) I-frames currently held in the retransmission list. If the destination side of the link is unable to pass on the frames sent to it, S stops returning acknowledgment frames, the retransmission list at P builds up and this in turn can be interpreted as a signal for P to stop transmitting further frames until acknowledgments start to flow again.

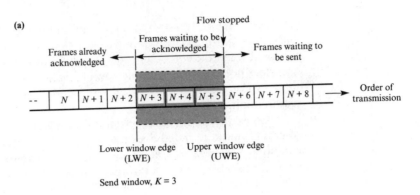

Figure 4.16
Flow control principle: (a) sliding window example; (b) send and receive window limits.

(b)

Protocol	Send window	Receive window
Idle RQ	1	1
Selective repeat	K	K
Go-back-N	K	1

To implement this scheme, a maximum limit is set on the number of I-frames that can be awaiting acknowledgment and hence are outstanding in the retransmission list. This limit is the **send window**, K for the link. If this is set to 1, the transmission control scheme reverts to idle RQ with a consequent drop in transmission efficiency. The limit is normally selected so that, providing the destination is able to pass on or absorb all frames it receives, the send window does not impair the flow of I-frames across the link. Factors such as the maximum frame size, available buffer storage, link propagation delay, and transmission bit rate must all be considered when selecting the send window.

Operation of the scheme is shown in Figure 4.16. As each I-frame is transmitted, the **upper window edge (UWE)** is incremented by unity. Similarly, as each I-frame is acknowledged, the **lower window edge (LWE)** is incremented by unity. The acceptance of any new frames (message blocks), and hence the flow of I-frames, is stopped if the difference between UWE and LWE becomes equal to the send window K. Assuming error-free transmission, K is a fixed window that moves (slides) over the complete set of frames being transmitted. The technique is thus known as 'sliding window'.

The maximum number of frame buffers required at S is known as the **receive window**. We can deduce from the earlier frame sequence diagrams that with the idle RQ and go-back-N schemes only one buffer is required. With selective repeat, however, K frames are required to ensure frames are delivered to the LS_user in sequence.

4.3.4　Sequence numbers

Until now, we have assumed that the sequence number inserted into each frame by P is simply the previous sequence number plus one and that the range of numbers available is infinite. Defining a maximum limit on the number of I-frames being transferred across a link not only limits the size of the link retransmission and receive lists, but also makes it possible to limit the range of sequence numbers required to identify each transmitted frame uniquely. The number of identifiers is a function of both the retransmission control scheme and the size of the send and receive windows.

For example, with an idle RQ control scheme, the send and receive windows are both 1 and hence only two identifiers are required to allow S to determine whether a particular I-frame received is a new frame or a duplicate. Typically, the two identifiers are 0 and 1; the send sequence variable is incremented modulo 2 by P.

With a go-back-N control scheme and a send window of K, the number of identifiers must be at least $K + 1$. We can see this by considering the example shown in Figure 4.17(a). Note that:

- The send window used in the example is 3.

- P sends its full window of three I-frames.

- The three I-frames are correctly received by S.

- The three ACK-frames returned by S are all corrupted.

- P times-out each I-frame and retransmits them.

- S discards each duplicate I-frame and returns a NAK-frame indicating I(3) is the next frame expected.

- Since the sequence number in the NAK is equal to V(S), P takes this as an acknowledgment for the three waiting frames, thereby reopening the window.

If only three identifiers are used – that is, the same number as the send window – S will not be able to determine whether I-frame I(0) is a new frame or a duplicate, since 0 will be the next in-sequence identifier. With four identifiers (the send window + 1), S knows that the next in-sequence I-frame has an identifier of 3, whereas the retransmitted (duplicate) frame has an identifier of 0. It therefore correctly discards the latter.

With a selective repeat scheme and a send and receive window of K, the number can be deduced of identifiers must not be less than $2K$. Again, we can deduce this by considering the case when P sends a full window of K frames and all subsequent acknowledgments are corrupted. S must be able to determine if any of the next K frames are new frames. The only way of ensuring that S can deduce this is to assign a completely new set of K identifiers to the next window of I-frames transmitted, which requires at least $2K$ identifiers. The limits for each scheme are shown in Figure 4.17(b).

In practice, since the identifier of a frame is in binary form, a set number of binary digits must be reserved for its use. For example, with a send window of, say, 7 and a go-back-N control scheme, three binary digits are required for the send and receive sequence numbers yielding eight possible identifiers: 0 through 7.

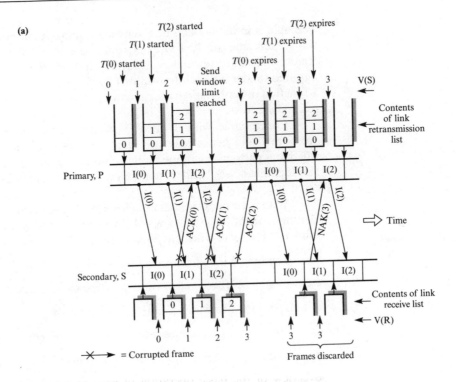

(a)

(b)

Protocol	Maximum number of frame identifiers
Idle RQ	2
Selective repeat	2K
Go-back-N	K + 1

(c)

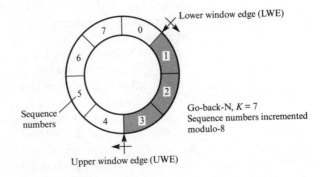

Figure 4.17
Sequence numbers:
(a) maximum range
example; (b) maximum
number for each
protocol; (c) example
assuming eight
sequence numbers.

The send and receive sequence variables are then incremented modulo-8 by P and S, respectively. This is shown in Figure 4.17(c).

4.3.5 Protocol specification

The frame sequence diagrams in Figures 4.11–4.18 and accompanying text provide a qualitative description of the error control and flow control components of the continuous RQ protocol. We can now derive a more formal specification based on the methodology we described in Section 4.2.2. To simplify the description, we shall consider only a unidirectional flow of I-frames – from the source DTE to the destination DTE. In most applications, however, a two-way flow is needed and both sides require a primary and a secondary.

First we can identify the various interfaces associated with each protocol entity in Figure 4.18. A go-back-N error control strategy, together with a window flow control mechanism, are used as the basis of the two specifications shown in Figures 4.19 and 4.20. The primary is specified in Figure 4.19 and the secondary in Figure 4.20.

In both specifications, the abbreviated names to be used are defined in part (a) of the figures. The specifications of each protocol – primary and secondary – using the three methods are then presented in parts (b), (c), and (d). As we can see from each specification, although the state transition diagrams give a good overview of the basic operation of each protocol, all possible aspects of their operation cannot be illustrated using this method.

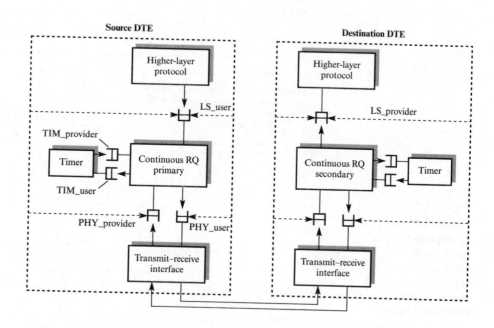

Figure 4.18
Continuous RQ
protocol layer
interfaces.

The extended event–state tables allow more detail to be included since predicates can be embedded into the specification. The specification of each protocol in structured (pseudo) code can then be carried out in a systematic way. The resulting pseudocode specifications are given in part (d) of Figures 4.19 and 4.20. In subsequent chapters we shall derive the extended event–state tables for the various protocols discussed, or the essential features of them. You can apply the same methodology to derive the corresponding structured code.

(a)   **Incoming events**

Name	Interface	Meaning
LDATAreq	LS_user	L_DATA.request service primitive received
ACKRCVD	PHY_provider	ACK-frame received from S
TEXP	TIM_provider	Wait ACK timer for frame expires
NAKRCVD	PHY_provider	NAK-frame received from S

States

Name	Meaning
DATA	Data transfer

Outgoing events

Name	Interface	Meaning
TxFrame(X)	PHY_user	Format a frame with N(S) = X and transfer to tail of PHY_user queue
RetxFrame(X)	PHY_user	Transfer frame(X) to tail of PHY_user queue

Predicates

Name	Meaning
P0	Send window open

Specific actions

[1] = Start_timer (X) using TIM_user queue
[2] = Stop_timer (X) using TIM_user queue
[3] = Increment Va
[4] = Decrement Va
[5] = Increment Vs
[6] = Get frame from head of retransmission list
[7] = Put frame at tail of retransmission list

State variables

Vs = Send sequence variable
PresentState = Present state of protocol entity
Va = Number of unacknowledged frames in retransmission list

Figure 4.19
Continuous RQ (go-back-N) specification: (a) abbreviated names; (b) state transition diagram.

(b)

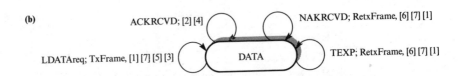

ACKRCVD; [2] [4]   NAKRCVD; RetxFrame, [6] [7] [1]

LDATAreq; TxFrame, [1] [7] [5] [3]   DATA   TEXP; RetxFrame, [6] [7] [1]

(c)

Present state \ Incoming event	LDATAreq	ACKRCVD	TEXP	NAKRCVD
DATA	1	2	3	4

1 = P0: TxFrame, [1] [7] [5] [3]
2 = [2] [4]
3 = RetxFrame, [6] [7] [1]
4 = RetxFrame, [6] [7] [1]

(d)
```
program    Continuous RQ_Primary;
const      K; { Send Window Limit }
type       Events = (LDATAreq, ACKRCVD, TEXP, NAKRCVD);
           States = DATA;
var        EventStateTable = array[Events, States] of 1..4;
           EventType : Events;
           PresentState : States;
           Vs = 0..K;
           Va = 0..K – 1;
           RetxList; { FIFO queue holding I-frame buffer pointers awaiting
                         acknowledgment }
procedure  Initialize; { Initializes contents of EventStateTable and state variables }
procedure  TxFrame (X : integer);      ⎫
procedure  RetxFrame (X : integer);    ⎬ Outgoing event procedures
procedure  Start_timer (X : integer);  ⎫
procedure  Stop_timer (X : integer);   ⎬ Specific action procedures
procedure  Get_frame;                  ⎪
procedure  Put_frame;                  ⎭
function   P0 : boolean;               } Predicate function

begin      Initialize;
           repeat Wait for an incoming event;
                  EventType := type of incoming event;
                  case EventStateTable[EventType, PresentState] of
                      1 : begin if P0 then begin TxFrame(Vs); Start_timer(Vs); Put_frame;
                                               Vs := Vs + 1; Va := Va + 1;
                                          if Va = K then P0 := false end;
                          end;
                      2 : repeat; X := N(R) from frame; Stop_timer(X);
                                  Va := Va – 1; P0 := true;
                          until   X = N(R) in ACK-frame;
                      3 : begin   Get_frame; X := N(S) from frame; RetxFrame(X);
                                  Start_timer(X); Put_frame; end;
                      4 : repeat Get_frame; X := N(S) from frame; RetxFrame(X);
                                  Start_timer(X); Put_frame;
                          until   X = N(R) in NAK-frame;
           until Forever;
end.
```

Figure 4.19 (cont.)   (c) Extended event–state table; (d) structured pseudocode.

(a)   **Incoming events**

Name	Interface	Meaning
IRCVD	PHY_provider	I-frame received from P

States

Name	Meaning
DATA	Waiting for next I-frame with N(S) = Vr
NAK_SENT	Waiting for missing I-frame with N(S) = Vr

Outgoing events

Name	Interface	Meaning
LDATAind(X)	LS_provider	Pass contents of I-frame with N(S) = X to layer above
TxACK(X)	PHY_user	Format and transmit an ACK-frame with N(R) = X
TxNAK(X)	PHY_user	Format and transmit a NAK-frame with N(R) = X
LERRORind	LS_provider	Issue an error message

Predicates

Name	Meaning
P0	N(S) in I-frame received = Vr

Specific actions

[1] = Start_timer
[2] = Stop_timer
[3] = Increment Vr
[4] = Increment RetxCount
[5] = Increment ErrorCount
[6] = Discard frame

State variables

Vr = Receive sequence variable
RetxCount = Number of NAK-frames retransmitted
ErrorCount = Number of error conditions
PresentState = Present state of protocol entity

(b)

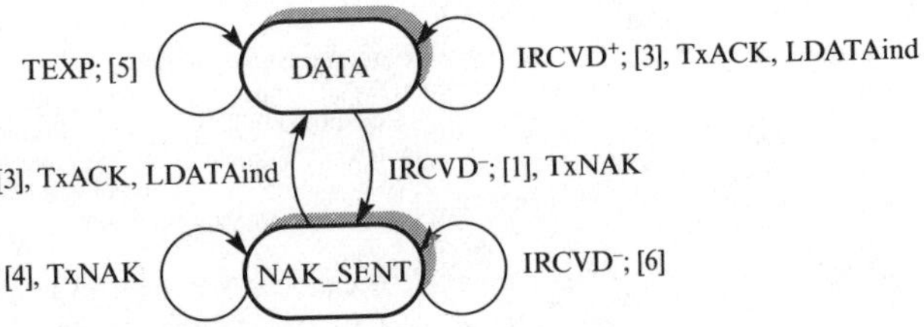

(c)

Present state \ Incoming event	IRCVD	TEXP
DATA	1	0
NAK_SENT	2	3

0 = [5]
1 = P0: TxACK, LDATAind, [3]
    NOT P0: TxNAK, [1], NAK_SENT
2 = P0: TxACK, LDATAind, [2] [3], DATA
    NOT P0: [6]
3 = TxNAK, [1] [4]

Figure 4.20
Continuous RQ (go-back-N) specification
– secondary:
(a) abbreviated names; (b) state transition diagram;
(c) extended event–state table.

```
(d)     program   Continuous RQ_Secondary;
        const     MaxRetxCount;
                  MaxErrorCount;
        type      Events = (IRCVD, TEXP);
                  States = (DATA, NAK_SENT);
        var       EventStateTable = array [Events, States] of 0..3;
                  EventType : Events;
                  PresentState : States;
                  Vr, RetxCount, ErrorCount : integer;
        procedure Initialize; { Initializes contents of EventStateTable and state variables }
        procedure LDATAind(X);  ⎫
        procedure TxACK(X);     ⎬ Outgoing event procedures
        procedure TxNAK(X);     ⎪
        procedure LERRORind;    ⎭
        procedure Start_timer;  ⎫
        procedure Stop_timer;   ⎬ Specific action procedures
        procedure DiscardFrame; ⎭
        function  P0 : boolean;  } Boolean function

        begin     Initialize;
                  repeat Wait for an incoming event; EventType = type of event;
                      case EventStateTable[EventType, PresentState] of
                          0 : begin ErrorCount := ErrorCount – 1; if (ErrorCount = MaxErrorCount) then
                                      begin LERRORind; Initialize; end;
                              end;
                          1 : X := N(S) from I-frame received;
                              begin if P0 then begin TxACK(X); LDATAind(X); Vr := Vr + 1; end;
                                      else begin TxNAK(X); Start_timer; PresentState := NAK_SENT; end;
                              end;
                          2 : X := N(S) from I-frame received;
                              begin if P0 then begin TxACK(X); LDATAind(X); Vr := Vr + 1; Stop_timer; end;
                                      else DiscardFrame;
                              end;
                          3 : begin TxNAK(Vr); Start_timer; RetxCount := RetxCount + 1;
                                      if (RetxCount = MaxRetxCount) then begin LERRORind; Initialize; end;
                              end;
                      until Forever;
        end.
```

Figure 4.20 (cont.)
(d) Structured
pseudocode.

4.3.6   Link utilization

During the discussion of the idle RQ protocol in Section 4.2.4, we saw that to a good approximation the link utilization U is a function of the time T_{ix} to transmit an I-frame and the propagation delay of the link T_p. However, for links with T_p greater than T_{ix}, the link utilization is also influenced by the send window, K.

Recall that the example in Figure 4.10 showed that with a typical satellite link, T_p, is often much greater than T_{ix}. In this example, T_{ix} was 1 ms and T_p about 250 ms for a 1 Mbps channel and 1000-bit frames. Theoretically, therefore, it is possible for 250 such frames to be in transit between P and S at any one time. To achieve a link efficiency of 100%, we require a send window in excess of 500, since an ACK-frame for the first frame in the sequence will not be received until 500 ms ($2T_p$) later.

In general, the link utilization U for a send window K is given by:

$$U = 1$$

if K is greater than or equal to $1 + 2a$ and:

$$U = \frac{KT_{ix}}{T_{ix} + 2T_p} = \frac{K}{1 + \dfrac{2T_p}{T_{ix}}} = \frac{K}{1 + 2a}$$

if K is less than $1 + 2a$.

We can see this by considering when $T_p = T_{ix}$. In this case, the last bit of a frame sent by P is not received until $2T_p$ (and hence $2T_{ix}$) later. The associated ACK-frame takes a further T_p (and hence T_{ix}) to be received by P. If $K = 1$ (idle RQ), then $U = 1/3$. To raise this to 100% (K greater than $1 + 2a$), K must be in excess of 3, that is, three or more frames must be sent by P before an ACK is received.

Example 4.2

A series of 1000-bit frames is to be transmitted using a continuous RQ protocol. Determine the link efficiency for the following types of data link if the velocity of propagation is 2×10^8 ms^{-1} and the bit error rates of the links are all negligibly low:

(a)   A 1 km link of 1 Mbps and a send window $K = 2$

(b)   A 10 km link of 200 Mbps and a send window $K = 7$

(c)   A 50 000 km satellite link of 2 Mbps and a send window $K = 127$

$$T_p = \frac{S}{V} \qquad T_{ix} = \frac{N_i}{R} \qquad a = \frac{T_p}{T_{ix}} \qquad N_i = \text{Number of information bits}$$

(a) $T_p = \dfrac{10^3}{2 \times 10^8} = 5 \times 10^{-6}$ s

$T_{ix} = \dfrac{1000}{1 \times 10^6} = 10^{-3}$ s

Hence:

$$a = \frac{5 \times 10^{-6}}{1 \times 10^{-3}} = 5 \times 10^{-3}$$

Now $K = 2$ is greater than $1 + 2a$ and hence $U = 1$.

(b) $T_p = \dfrac{10 \times 10^3}{2 \times 10^8} = 5 \times 10^{-5}$ s

$T_{ix} = \dfrac{1000}{200 \times 10^6} = 5 \times 10^{-6}$ s

Hence:

$$a = \frac{5 \times 10^{-5}}{5 \times 10^{-6}} = 10$$

Now $K = 7$ is less than $1 + 2a$ and hence:

$$U = \frac{K}{1 + 2a} = \frac{7}{1 + 20} = 0.33$$

(c) $T_p = \dfrac{50 \times 10^6}{2 \times 10^8} = 0.25 \text{ s}$

$T_{ix} = \dfrac{1000}{2 \times 10^6} = 5 \times 10^{-4} \text{ s}$

Hence:

$$a = \frac{0.25}{5 \times 10^{-4}} = 500$$

Now $K = 127$ is less than $1 + 2a$ and hence:

$$U = \frac{K}{1 + 2a} = \frac{127}{1 + 1000} = 0.127$$

We can deduce from these results that the choice of K has a strong impact on the link utilization in certain cases. As we can see, even with a K of 127, the link utilization of a satellite link is still very low. For this reason a large K (and hence sequence number range) is utilized. This also applies to terrestrial links operating at high bit rates as we shall see in Chapter 5.

In the results we calculated in Example 4.2 we assumed no transmission errors. Any errors further reduce the link utilization since some frames must be retransmitted. However, the effect differs slightly for the two retransmission schemes. For example, with a selective repeat scheme, U is reduced simply by the number of attempts to transmit each frame N_r since only the corrupted frame is retransmitted. If P_f is the frame error rate of the link then, assuming random errors:

$$N_r = \frac{1}{1 - P_f}$$

The modified value of U is thus:

$$U = \frac{K}{N_r(1 + 2a)} = \frac{K(1 - P_f)}{1 + 2a}$$

for K less than $1 + 2a$. For values of K greater than or equal to $1 + 2a$, we find U simply by substituting $K = 1 + 2a$ in this expression, since $1 + 2a$ is the maximum number of frames that can be transmitted before receiving an acknowledgment in time $T_{ix} + 2T_p$. Hence:

$$U = \frac{(1 + 2a)(1 - P_f)}{1 + 2a} = 1 - P_f$$

for K greater than or equal to $1 + 2a$.

With a go-back-N scheme, the link utilization is reduced further since, if a frame is corrupted, more than one frame must be retransmitted. Again, the number of additional frames to be transmitted is determined by the magnitude of K relative to $1 + 2a$.

For K less than $1 + 2a$, the number of times $(K - 1)$ frames must be retransmitted is simply $P_f(K - 1)$. For each occurrence, a further $1 + 2a$ delay will occur. The modified expression is thus:

$$U = \frac{K(1 - P_f)}{(1 + 2a) + (1 + 2a)P_f(K - 1)} = \frac{K(1 - P_f)}{(1 + 2a)(1 + P_f(K - 1))}$$

for K less than $1 + 2a$, and:

$$U = \frac{(1 + 2a)(1 - P_f)}{(1 + 2a)(1 + P_f(K - 1))} = \frac{1 - P_f}{1 + P_f(K - 1)}$$

for K greater than or equal to $1 + 2a$.

Note that these formulae are only approximations and will give meaningful results only if the earlier approximations hold. Nevertheless, they give a good guide both to the level of performance that can be expected and the relative performance of each method.

Example 4.3

A series of 1000-bit frames is to be transmitted across a data link 100 km in length at 20 Mbps. If the link has a velocity of propagation of 2×10^8 ms^{-1} and a BER of 4×10^{-5}, determine the link utilization using the following link protocols:

(a)   Idle RQ

(b)   Selective repeat and a send window of 10

(c)   Go-back-N and a send window of 10

$$T_p = \frac{S}{V} = \frac{100 \times 10^3}{2 \times 10^8} = 5 \times 10^{-4} \text{ s}$$

$$T_{ix} = \frac{N_i}{R} = \frac{1000}{20 \times 10^6} = 5 \times 10^{-5} \text{ s}$$

$$a = \frac{T_p}{T_{ix}} = \frac{5 \times 10^{-4}}{5 \times 10^{-5}} = 10$$

Hence:

$$1 + 2a = 21$$

Now:

$$P_f \simeq N_i P = 1000 \times 4 \times 10^{-5} = 4 \times 10^{-2}$$

Hence:

$$1 - P_f = 96 \times 10^{-2}$$

(a) $U = \dfrac{(1 - P_f)}{1 + 2a} = \dfrac{96 \times 10^{-2}}{21} = 0.046$

(b)   For K less than $1 + 2a$

$$U = \frac{K(1 - P_f)}{1 + 2a} = \frac{10 \times 96 \times 10^{-2}}{21} = 0.46$$

(c)   For K less than $1 + 2a$

$$U = \frac{K(1 - P_f)}{(1 + 2a)(1 + P_f(K - 1))} = 0.336$$

4.4 Link management

Error and flow control are both concerned with the correct transfer (in sequence and without error or duplication) of frames across an imperfect communication line. For the schemes we have outlined to function correctly, we have assumed that both communicating parties have been initialized so that they are ready to exchange information. For example, both sides of the link must start with the same send and receive sequence variables before any information frames are transmitted. In general, this is known as the initialization or **link set-up** phase. Normally after all data has been exchanged across a link, there is a **link disconnection phase**. Since the link set-up and disconnection phases are not concerned with the actual transfer of user data, they are collectively referred to as **link management**.

For a link between a terminal and a computer with a relatively short separation (up to, say, 20 m), management functions can be achieved by exchanging signals on additional handshake (control) lines associated with the physical interface. This is known as a **handshake procedure**. A user wishing to open a dialog with the computer first switches the terminal on. This results in one of the control lines becoming set (active), indicating to the computer that the terminal is ready to send characters – data terminal ready. The terminal must then wait until the computer responds by setting a corresponding response control line to indicate that it is ready to receive characters. The exchange of characters can then commence.

When both communicating devices are computers and they are transferring frames across a data link, the link is established (set up) when the link-level protocol within each computer exchanges an agreed set of **control** or **supervisory frames**. In our terminal-to-computer example, the link was established when the user switched on the terminal. However, in the case of a computer-to-computer link, the setting up of a link is normally initiated when higher-layer software (an application program, for example) in one of the computers signals to the communication software that it wishes to open a dialog with a remote computer. Typically, this might be the execution of a send or transfer request statement (primitive) in the application program which, in turn, invokes the communication software. In practice, as we shall see in Part three, the communication software is normally made up of a number of separate protocol layers, each responsible for a specific function in the overall communication task. Before any data is sent, each layer is first initialized. As an example, the initialization primitives associated with the data link layer are shown in Figure 4.21(a).

As we can see, prior to sending any data – using the L_DATA.request service – the LS_user (layer) first sends an **L_CONNECT.request** service primitive to the link layer. Unlike the L_DATA service, this is known as a **confirmed service** since, when the source link protocol entity has established a link (logical connection) with the destination (link) protocol entity, it returns an **L_CONNECT.confirm** primitive to the source LS_user. Note, however, that this confirms that a logical link has been set up with the destination link protocol

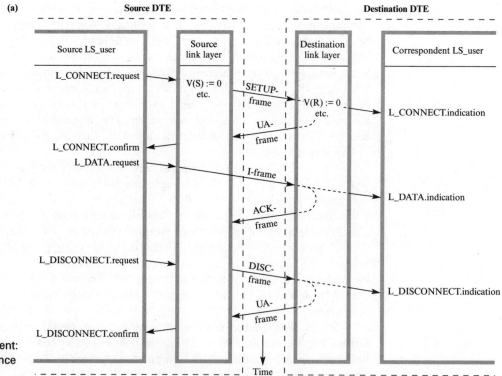

Figure 4.21
Link management:
(a) time sequence
diagram.

(b)

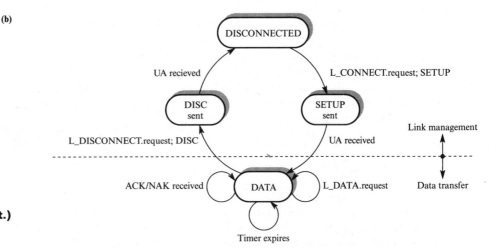

Figure 4.21 (cont.)
(b) State transition
diagram.

entity only and not with the destination LS_user. As we shall see in Part three, the latter is normally the case for all higher protocol layers.

On receipt of an L_CONNECT.request primitive, using an ECB (see Section 4.2.1), the link protocol entity at the source initializes all state variables and then creates a **link SETUP** frame (PDU). This is sent to the correspondent (peer) link protocol entity in the destination DTE using the selected transmission mode. On receipt of the SETUP frame, the destination DTE initializes its own state variables and proceeds by sending an **L_CONNECT.indication** primitive to the correspondent LS_user and an acknowledgment frame back to the source.

Since this acknowledgment does not relate to an I-frame, it does not contain a sequence number. It is known, therefore, as an **unnumbered acknowledgment** or **UA-frame**. On receipt of this UA-frame, the source protocol entity issues the L_CONNECT.confirm primitive to the LS_user and the link is now ready for the transfer of data using the L_DATA service. Finally, after all data has been transferred, the set-up link is released using the L_DISCONNECT service, which is also a confirmed service. The corresponding frame, known as a **disconnect** or **DISC frame**, is acknowledged using a UA-frame. This mode of operation is also known as a connection-oriented mode.

Clearly, adding the link management function affects the idle RQ and continuous RQ protocol specifications discussed earlier. To illustrate this, the modifications to the state transition diagram for the primary are shown in Figure 4.21(b).

As we can see, three new states are needed; the incoming events that cause the transitions between these new states and the data transfer state are shown in the figure. A similar extension to the state transition diagram for the secondary can readily be developed. Moreover, the structure of both the extended event–state table and the corresponding pseudocode is such that the same additions can readily be incorporated into these without any major changes to their structure.

Exercises

4.1   Assume a terminal is connected to a computer. Explain the two techniques that are used to achieve error control and flow control. Clearly outline the effect of each mechanism on the user of the terminal.

4.2   Explain the meaning of the following terms relating to a data link control protocol:
(a) Connectionless
(b) Connection-oriented

4.3   With the aid of frame sequence diagrams and assuming an idle RQ error control procedure, describe the difference between an implicit and an explicit retransmission control scheme.

4.4   With the aid of frame sequence diagrams and assuming an idle RQ error control procedure with explicit retransmission, describe the following:
(a) The factors influencing the minimum time delay between the transmission of two consecutive information frames
(b) How the loss of a corrupted information frame is overcome
(c) How the loss of a corrupted acknowledgment frame is overcome

4.5   Explain the meaning of the following terms relating to a protocol:
(a) Protocol layer
(b) User services
(c) Time sequence diagram
(d) Interlayer queue

4.6   Explain the meaning of the following terms relating to a protocol specification:
(a) Finite state machine or automaton
(b) Protocol state
(c) Incoming event
(d) Outgoing event
(e) Predicate
(f) Local or specific action

4.7   Use the frame sequence diagrams derived for Exercise 4.4 to define the operation of the primary and secondary sides of a link that is operating with an idle RQ error control scheme using:

(a) A state transmission diagram
(b) An extended event–state table
(c) Structured program code written in a pseudo high-level language

4.8   A series of information frames with a mean length of 100 bits is to be transmitted across the following data links using an idle RQ protocol. If the velocity of propagation of the links is 2×10^8 ms^{-1}, determine the link efficiency (utilization) for each type of link.
(a) A 10 km link with a BER of 10^{-4} and a data transmission rate of 9600 bps
(b) A 500 m link with a BER of 10^{-6} and a data transmission rate of 10 Mbps

4.9   With the aid of frame sequence diagrams, describe the difference between an idle RQ and a continuous RQ error control procedure. For clarity, assume that no frames are corrupted during transmission.

4.10 With the aid of frame sequence diagrams and assuming a selective repeat error control scheme, describe how the following are overcome using both implicit and explicit retransmission:
(a) A corrupted information frame
(b) A corrupted ACK/NAK-frame

4.11 Use the frame sequence diagrams derived for Exercise 4.10 to define the operation of the primary and secondary sides of a link that is operating with a continuous RQ and selective repeat error control scheme using:
(a) A state transition diagram
(b) An event–state table
(c) Structured program code written in pseudo high-level code
Deduce the factors that influence the maximum size of the link receive list with a selective repeat retransmission strategy.

4.12 With the aid of frame sequence diagrams and assuming a go-back-N error control scheme, describe how the following are overcome:
(a) A corrupted I-frame
(b) A corrupted ACK-frame
(c) A corrupted NAK-frame

Include in these diagrams the contents of the link retransmission and link receive lists in addition to the state of the send and receive sequence variables as each frame is transmitted and received.

4.13 Using a continuous RQ error control scheme as an example, describe how the operation of the primary and secondary side of a link may be defined in the form of a finite-state machine and:
(a) A state transition diagram
(b) A state transition table
(c) A high-level language program segment written in pseudocode

4.14 What is the function of a timeout mechanism? Use frame sequence diagrams to illustrate how a timeout interval may be used to overcome the effect of a corrupted information frame assuming:
(a) Idle RQ
(b) Selective repeat
(c) Go-back-N
Deduce the factors that determine the duration of the timeout interval to be used with each scheme and how duplicates are detected.

4.15 Discriminate between the send window and receive window for a link and how they are related with:
(a) A selective repeat retransmission scheme
(b) A go-back-N control scheme

4.16 With the aid of frame sequence diagrams, illustrate the effect of a send window flow control limit being reached. Assume a send window of 2 and a go-back-N error control procedure.

4.17 Assuming a send window of K, deduce the minimum range of sequence numbers (frame identifiers) required with each of the following error control schemes:
(a) Idle RQ
(b) Selective repeat
(c) Go-back-N
Clearly identify the condition when the maximum number of identifiers is in use.

4.18 A series of information frames with a mean length of 1000 bits is to be transmitted across a data link 4000 km long at a data rate of 2 Mbps. If the link has a velocity of propagation of 2×10^8 ms^{-1} and a BER of 10^{-4}, determine the link efficiency using the following link protocols:
(a) Idle RQ
(b) Selective retransmission and a send window of 7
(c) Go-back-N and a send window of 127
Indicate the effect of bit errors on each of the results obtained.

4.19 Explain what is meant by the term 'link management'. Use an example set of user primitives and a time sequence diagram to show how a logical communication path is established (set-up) between two systems and subsequently cleared (disconnected).

4.20 Assuming the user primitives used in Exercise 4.19 and an idle RQ error and flow control scheme, derive:
(a) A state transition diagram
(b) An extended event–state table
for the protocol. Outline how the protocol can be defined in a pseudo high-level code form.

Chapter summary

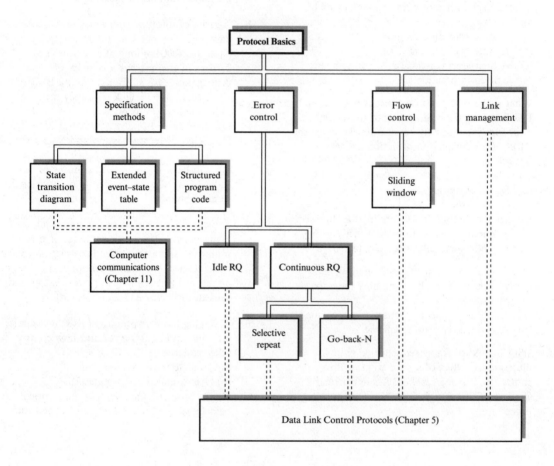

DATA LINK CONTROL PROTOCOLS

Chapter objectives

When you have completed this chapter you should be able to:

- Know the different types of character-oriented and bit-oriented data link control protocols that are in use and the application domains of each protocol type ☞ 217, 219

- Understand the application and operation of the simplex, character-oriented protocol Kermit ☞ 222

- Describe the character-oriented binary synchronous control protocol as used in poll–select, multipoint networks ☞ 226

- Explain the operation of a duplex character-oriented protocol ☞ 235

- Understand the frame formats and frame types used in the high-level data link control (HDLC) protocol and explain selected aspects of its operation ☞ 237, 242

- Explain the operation and application domains of the various derivatives of HDLC including LAPB, LAPM, LAPD, and LLC ☞ 250, 253, 255, 258

- Know the differences between a single link and a multilink control procedure ☞ 252

Introduction

The data link control layer – often abbreviated simply to data link layer – is concerned with the transfer of data over a serial data link. The link can be either a point-to-point physical circuit (twisted-pair wire, coaxial cable or optical fiber), or a radio-based channel such as a satellite link, or a physical or logical link through a switched network. The transmission mode may be either asynchronous or synchronous and based on either a character-oriented or a bit-oriented transmission control protocol. The data link layer is thus fundamental to the operation of all data communication applications.

In simple point-to-point applications, the data link layer normally serves the application layer directly. In more sophisticated applications, such as those utilizing switched networks, it provides a defined service to a set of (higher) protocol layers. Depending on the application, the user service provided by the data link layer may be either a simple **best-try (connectionless) service** or a **reliable (connection-oriented) service**. The two types of service are shown in the time sequence diagram of Figure 5.1.

The connectionless (best-try) service means that although error check bits are used to detect errors, any frames that are found to contain transmission errors are simply discarded by the link layer protocol entity. It is also referred to as an **unacknowledged service** and retransmission becomes a function of a higher protocol layer. For example, this is done in applications based on switched networks in which the BER of the transmission lines is very low and hence the probability of retransmissions is relatively small, such as LANs and ISDNs.

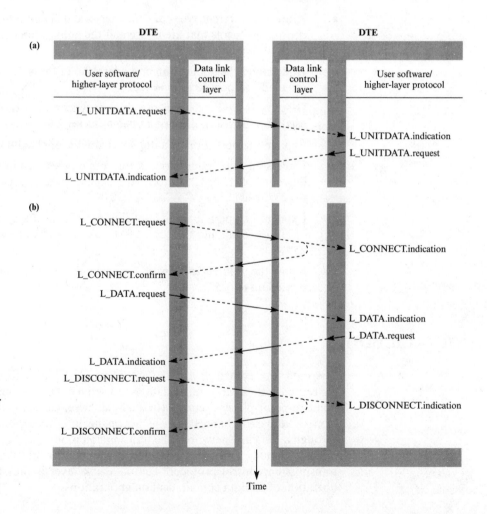

Figure 5.1
Data link control layer – user service primitives:
(a) connectionless (best-try);
(b) connection-oriented (reliable).

The user service primitives associated with the connection-oriented mode are the same as those discussed in Chapter 4. Recall that with this type of service the data link protocol employs error and flow control procedures to provide a reliable service. Therefore there is a high probability that the data will be error free without duplicates and that messages (data blocks) will be delivered in the same sequence as they were submitted. To achieve this, prior to sending any data (information frames), a logical connection between the two data link protocol entities is established using the L_CONNECT service. All data is transferred using a suitable retransmission and flow control protocol. When all data (information) has been exchanged, the logical connection is cleared using the L_DISCONNECT service.

Because of the range of applications of the data link layer, we shall first look at some of the different application environments to which they relate. We shall consider the detailed operation of the different protocols in Sections 5.1 and 5.2.

5.1 Application environments

Some application environments are shown in Figure 5.2. As we can see, in some instances the data link protocols are located in the two communicating DTEs – computers, for example – and the protocol is said to operate on an **end-to-end basis**. In others, it operates over the local link connecting, for example, the DTE to a network. The protocol is then said to have only **local significance**.

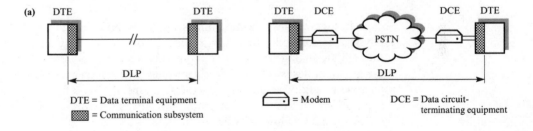

Figure 5.2
Data link protocol application environments:
(a) point-to-point;
(b) multipoint (multidrop).

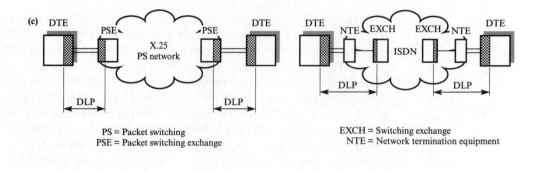

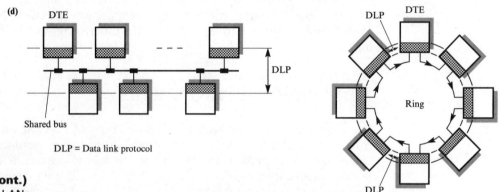

Figure 5.2 (cont.)
(c) WANs; (d) LANs.

In Figure 5.2(a), the data link is a point-to-point circuit which can be a direct physical connection (twisted-pair wire, coaxial cable or fiber), a circuit set up through the analog switched telephone network using modems, a circuit through a private multiplexer network, or a radio-based link such as a satellite or terrestrial microwave link. The data link operates on an end-to-end basis and, in many such applications, serves the application directly. Therefore a reliable connection-oriented service is normally used.

The type of data link protocol used is a function of the physical separation of the two communicating DTEs and the bit rate of the link. For lower bit rate links such as those used with modems, a character-oriented idle RQ (stop and wait) protocol is often used. Examples of such protocols are **Kermit** and **X-modem**. Both are simple file transfer protocols that are used extensively for PC-to-PC communications. They are very similar to the basic idle RQ protocol described in Chapter 4.

For higher bit rate links, and especially those involving long physical separations such as radio-based satellite links or circuits through private multiplexer networks, the alternative (and more efficient) continuous RQ protocol known as **high-level data link control (HDLC)** is used. This is a bit-oriented protocol suitable for many different operational modes.

The application architecture shown in Figure 5.2(b) is known as a **multipoint** or **multidrop topology**. As we can see, a single transmission line – known as a **bus** or **data highway** – is used to connect all the computers together. Therefore we must ensure that all transmissions are carried out in a controlled way and no two transmissions occur simultaneously. Such architectures are normally used in applications that involve a single **master (supervisory) computer** communicating with a distributed community of **slave computers**. Examples are a **back-of-store computer** controlling a distributed set of point-of-sale terminals (computers) in a department store or a supervisory computer in a process plant controlling a distributed community of intelligent (computer-based) instruments. All transmissions are between the master and a selected slave computer, so the master controls the order of all transmissions.

In order to control access to the shared transmission medium equitably, a connection-oriented data link protocol is used. Earlier protocols for use with such architectures were based on a development of the character-oriented idle RQ protocol known as **binary synchronous control (BSC)** or **bisync**. More recent implementations are based on one of the alternative operating modes of the bit-oriented HDLC protocol known as **normal response mode (NRM)**. Both bisync and NRM operate in a **poll–select mode**; when the master wishes to receive data from a slave it sends the slave a **poll message**, and if it wants to send data to the slave, it sends a **select message**.

The two architectures shown in Figure 5.2(c) both relate to applications involving switched WANs. In the first example, the link protocol has only local significance and operates between the DTE and the local data circuit-terminating equipment (DCE), as in an **X.25 packet-switching network**. The X.25 protocol set used with such networks applies only to the local link between the DTE and DCE. The data link protocol with X.25 is also based on HDLC and is known as **link access procedure, balanced (LAPB)**.

The second arrangement is used with circuit-switched data networks such as an ISDN. Once a circuit (connection) has been set up through the network it provides the equivalent of a point-to-point link – known as a virtual circuit – for the data transfer phase. The protocol can be either connection-oriented (reliable) or connectionless (best-try) – known as **frame switching** and **frame relay**, respectively. In addition, the call setup procedure associated with ISDN is carried out using a separate link known as the **signaling** or **D channel**. This uses a link protocol which is a variation of HDLC known as **link access procedure D channel (LAPD)**.

Finally, the two configurations shown in Figure 5.2(d) relate to applications involving LANs. A feature of such networks is the use of relatively short, low bit error rate links that operate at high bit rates ($\sim 10\,\text{Mbps}$). The overall result is that errors are relatively infrequent and the end-to-end frame transfer time is very fast. Such networks normally operate in a connectionless, best-try mode. In this mode, all retransmission and flow control functions are left to a higher protocol layer in the two end systems (DTEs). The link protocol used with LANs is a subclass of HDLC known as **logical link control (LLC)**.

In summary, there is a range of data link protocols, each of which is intended for use in a particular application environment.

5.2   Character-oriented protocols

Character-oriented protocols are in use in both point-to-point and multipoint applications. They are characterized by the selected transmission control characters used to perform the various transmission control functions associated with link management, start-of-frame and end-of-frame delimiting, error control, and data transparency.

In our discussion of character-oriented protocols in Chapter 4, we considered a point-to-point data link and a simplex (unidirectional) flow of information frames to introduce the various aspects of link protocols. However, in most practical applications we must extend the concepts introduced to allow for data (information) to be transferred in both directions. Also, if more than two communicating parties are involved in a multipoint configuration, we need a method for controlling access to the shared transmission medium. We shall discuss all of these issues as we discuss the different protocols.

5.2.1   Simplex protocols

This class of protocol is the simplest since it allows just a simplex – one direction only – transfer of data from one computer (DTE) to another over a point-to-point data link. It is used with the topologies shown in Figure 5.2(a). A typical application is the transfer of data files from one computer to another. One of the most widely used protocols for this function is Kermit.

Kermit is used extensively for the transfer of the contents of a specified file or group of files from one computer – for example, a personal computer – to another over a point-to-point data link. The link can be either a circuit set up through the switched telephone network using modems or a pair of twisted-pair lines with appropriate line drivers and receivers. Normally synchronous transmission is used. Kermit is a practical example of the idle RQ (stop and wait) protocol we described in Chapter 4.

A number of versions of Kermit allow it to transfer files either between two personal (single-user) computers or between a personal computer and a file server or mainframe computer. The basic file transfer mechanism associated with each version is the same. The main differences are associated with how the user of the source computer gains access – through the Kermit program – to the Kermit program in the destination machine at start-up. We shall consider the version used for the transfer of files between two single-user computers.

A simple set of commands is available to the two users after the Kermit programs have been run in both systems. These are shown in the time sequence diagram of Figure 5.3.

If modems are being used then one modem must be set into the **originate mode** and the other the **answer mode**. Of course both modems must be set to operate at the same baud rate. Each user runs the Kermit program and then enters the CONNECT command, resulting in a physical link being set up between the two systems. The user in the system that wants to receive a file (or files) then enters

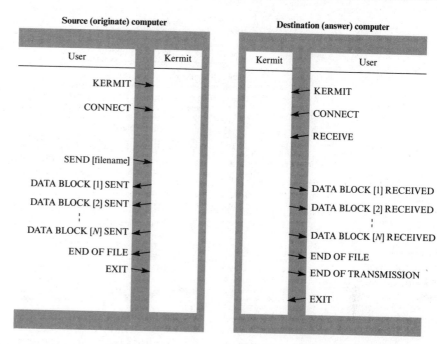

Figure 5.3
Kermit user
commands.

the RECEIVE command and the user in the sending system enters the SEND command followed by the file name. Kermit in the sending system then transfers the file(s) in its (their) entirety. As each file segment is transferred, a message is output on both user screens. After all file segments have been transferred, both users exit Kermit and return to the local operating system by giving an EXIT command. To transfer files in the opposite direction, the order of the commands is reversed.

We can see that Kermit is not simply a data link protocol since it performs a number of additional functions such as file reading/writing and file segmentation and reassembly. It also has frame types associated with each of these functions as we can see from the standard frame format shown in Figure 5.4(a).

There are two main differences between the frame format used with Kermit and those we discussed in Chapter 4. Firstly, a length character is used to specify the length of each frame instead of an ETX transmission control character and, secondly, information (data) and ACK- and NAK-frames all have the same basic format. Also, an additional (redundant) control character – carriage return (CR) – is used at the end of each frame. The use of a length character has the added benefit that the frame (and hence file) contents can be either text characters or binary bytes since the receiver simply receives and appends the appropriate number of characters or bytes (as specified in the frame header) as the file is being reassembled. Normally the user in the receiving computer either knows the file type or can deduce it from the name.

The contents of a text file are sent as a sequence of 80 character blocks each terminated by a pair of carriage-return/line-feed characters. However, binary files

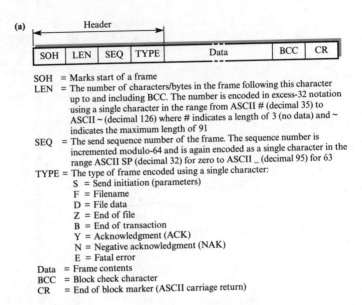

Figure 5.4
Kermit operation:
(a) frame format and
types.

SOH = Marks start of a frame
LEN = The number of characters/bytes in the frame following this character
up to and including BCC. The number is encoded in excess-32 notation
using a single character in the range from ASCII # (decimal 35) to
ASCII ~ (decimal 126) where # indicates a length of 3 (no data) and ~
indicates the maximum length of 91
SEQ = The send sequence number of the frame. The sequence number is
incremented modulo-64 and is again encoded as a single character in the
range ASCII SP (decimal 32) for zero to ASCII _ (decimal 95) for 63
TYPE = The type of frame encoded using a single character:
    S = Send initiation (parameters)
    F = Filename
    D = File data
    Z = End of file
    B = End of transaction
    Y = Acknowledgment (ACK)
    N = Negative acknowledgment (NAK)
    E = Fatal error
Data = Frame contents
BCC = Block check character
CR = End of block marker (ASCII carriage return)

are sent simply as a string of 8-bit bytes. Any format control characters in the file contents – text or binary – are encoded prior to transmission to ensure that they do not affect the state of the communication equipment during transfer. This is a feature of the flow control operation of some modems. Each control character detected is converted into a two-character printable character sequence consisting of a control prefix character – ASCII # – followed by the ASCII printable character that is in the same row of the ASCII table and either column 4 or 5 corresponding to columns 0 or 1, respectively. Thus Ctrl-A becomes #A, CR becomes #M and FS becomes #\. Any # characters are preceded by an additional #.

The sequence of frames exchanged by the Kermit protocol entities to transfer a file is shown in Figure 5.4(b). The first information frame sent prior to initiating the transfer of a file is a send-invitation (S) frame. It includes a list of parameters associated with the protocol, such as the maximum frame length and the timeout interval to be used for retransmission. The receiver returns an acknowledgment (Y) frame with the agreed transmission control parameters.

The sender then proceeds to transfer the file contents. Firstly, a file header (F) frame containing the file name is sent, followed by a sequence of data (D) frames containing the frame contents. After the last data frame in the file has been sent, the receiver is informed by sending an end-of-file (Z) frame. Other files can then be sent in the same way. Finally, when all file transfers have been carried out, the source sends an end-of-transaction (B) frame.

Kermit is an idle RQ protocol. Hence, after sending each information (I) frame, the source waits until it receives either a positive acknowledgment (Y) frame – block sum check correct – or a negative acknowledgment (N) frame – BCC incorrect. Also, to allow for the possibility of either of these two frames being corrupted, a timer is started each time a new frame is sent. The send

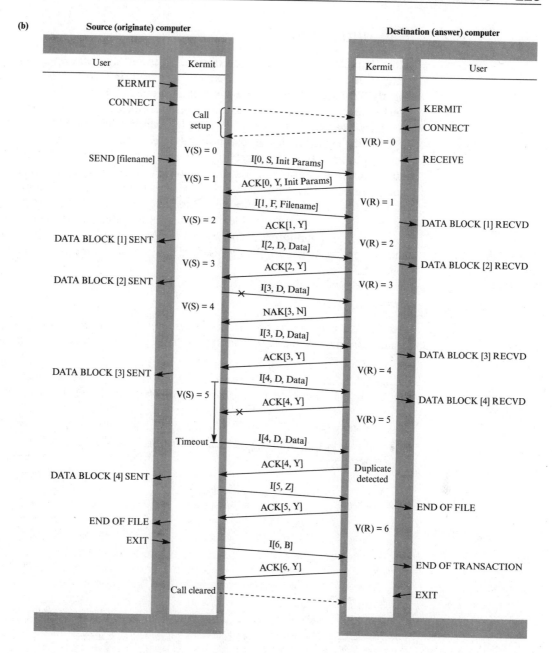

Figure 5.4 (cont.)
(b) Frame sequences.

sequence number in each I-frame increments modulo 64 and the receive sequence number in each ACK (Y) and NAK (N) frame carries the same sequence number as the I-frame being positively, or negatively, acknowledged.

The features we have described are the minimum features associated with Kermit. Refer to the bibliography relating to this chapter for books containing a more detailed coverage.

5.2.2   Half-duplex protocols

Most character-oriented protocols operate in the half-duplex, stop-and-wait mode. Large computer manufacturers frequently have their own versions which differ slightly. Probably the best known is that developed by IBM and known as binary synchronous control, often shortened to bisync or BSC. As it is the basis of the ISO character-oriented protocol known as **basic mode**, we shall use BSC as an example.

As the name implies, BSC is normally used with a synchronous transmission control scheme. It is a connection-oriented protocol and is used primarily in multipoint (multidrop) applications in which there is a single master station (computer) which controls all message transfers to and from a community of slave stations. The slave stations are connected to the master by either a **multipoint network** if all the stations are located in different establishments and modems are being used, or a **multidrop bus network** if all the stations are at the same site and line drivers/receivers are being used. The two configurations are shown in Figure 5.5.

Frame formats

Recall that to perform the various functions associated with link management, control frames are needed in addition to normal information (data carrying)

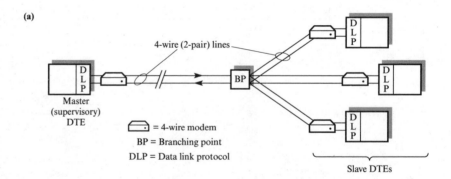

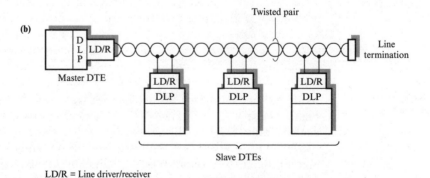

Figure 5.5
Character-oriented
bus networks:
(a) multipoint;
(b) multidrop.

Table 5.1   Transmission control characters used with BSC.

Character	Function
SOH (TC1)	Start of header: used to indicate the start of the header (if one is present) of an information frame (block)
STX (TC2)	Start of text: used both to terminate a header (if one is present) and to signal the start of a text string
ETX (TC3)	End of text: used to signal the end of a text string
EOT (TC4)	End of transmission: used to indicate the end of the transmission of one or more text (information) blocks and to terminate (clear) the connection
ENQ (TC5)	Enquiry: used as a request for a response from a remote station – the response may include the identity and/or status of the station
ACK (TC6)	Acknowledge: positive acknowledgment transmitted by a receiver in response to a message from the sender
DLE (TC7)	Data link escape: used to change the meaning of other selected transmission control characters
NAK (TC8)	Negative acknowledge: negative response transmitted by a receiver to a message from the sender
SYN (TC9)	Synchronous idle: used to provide the means for a receiver to achieve or retain (idle condition) character synchronization with a synchronous transmission control scheme
ETB (TC10)	End of transmission block: used to indicate the end of a block of data when a message is divided into a number of such blocks (frames)

frames (blocks). Also, that with character-oriented synchronous transmission the receiver must be able to achieve both character (byte) and frame synchronization.

With BSC, these functions are carried out using selected EBCDIC (or ASCII/IA5 with basic mode) transmission control characters. We described the role of some of these characters in Chapter 4. A more complete list, together with their functions, is given in Table 5.1.

The different types of information frame – known as data blocks in BSC – are shown in Figure 5.6(a). BSC uses character-oriented synchronous transmission and hence all data (and control) blocks transmitted are preceded by at least two SYN characters to allow the receiver to achieve character synchronization. Short user messages (less than the defined maximum length) are transmitted in a single data block while longer messages are transmitted in multiple blocks. The header field, when present, is for general use and normally defines how the data field is to be interpreted. In addition, with basic mode a single block sum check is used after the end-of-block delimiter (ETX or ETB) which is a longitudinal (column) parity check (see Section 3.4.2). This starts the check with the STX character and ends with the particular end-of-block delimiter character being used. As parity has only limited error-detection capabilities, BSC often uses a two-character (byte) CRC computed using CRC-16 instead of a single BCC. Both schemes set a limit on the number of characters allowed in each transmitted data block. This limit is determined by the BER of the link being used, the maximum block size being

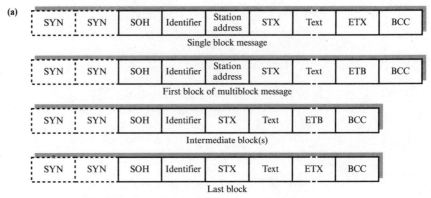

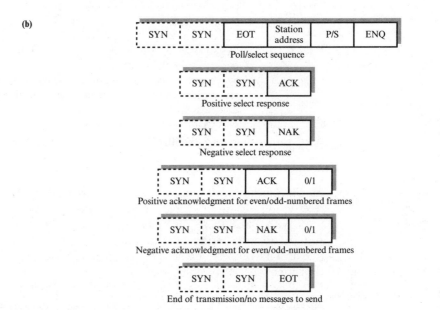

Figure 5.6
BSC block/frame
formats: (a) data;
(b) supervisory.

chosen to ensure that most blocks are received error free. Longer messages are transmitted as a sequence of shorter data blocks of a fixed size, each terminated with an ETB control character. The last data block of such a sequence terminates with an ETX control character.

The different control frames associated with the BSC protocol are shown in Figure 5.6(b). The ACK and NAK control characters have two functions:

- As an acknowledgment: one or other is returned in response to a previously transmitted data block and hence contains an identifier (sequence number).

- As a response to a select control message: an ACK indicates that the selected station is able to receive a data block whereas a NAK indicates that it is not.

The ENQ control character is used in both poll and select control frames. The address of the polled or selected slave station is followed by either a P (for poll) or an S (for select) character, which is in turn followed by the ENQ character.

Finally, the EOT control character has two functions:

- To signal the end of a complete message exchange sequence and clear the logical link between the two communicating parties

- To provide a means of resetting the link to the idle state

Data transparency

We described the use of the DLE character to achieve data transparency when transmitting pure binary data rather than character strings in Section 3.2.3. Essentially, the various framing character sequences shown in Figure 5.6 are modified to be DLE/STX, DLE/ETX, etc. Also, whenever the transmitter detects a binary pattern corresponding to a DLE character in the text, it adds (inserts) an extra DLE. The receiver performs a similar check. Whenever the receiver detects two consecutive DLEs, it removes the inserted DLE before passing the data on for further processing. A further difference when operating in the transparent mode is error control. Instead of a simple 8-bit longitudinal parity check per block, we use a more sophisticated polynomial code with each block terminated by a 16-bit CRC rather than an 8-bit BCC.

Protocol operation

As we described earlier, the master computer (station) is responsible for scheduling all transmissions on each shared data link. The poll control message is used to request a specific slave computer to send any waiting data message it may have; the select control message is used to ask the selected slave whether it is ready to receive a data message.

Figure 5.7(a) shows a typical poll and select sequence. A typical sequence of frames exchanged on a multidrop line is shown in Figure 5.7(b) and (c). Part (b) shows both a successful and an unsuccessful sequence associated with a select operation while part (c) shows two sequences associated with a poll operation.

To select a particular slave station, the master station sends an ENQ select control message with the address of the slave station preceding the ENQ character. Assuming the selected station is ready to receive a message, it responds with an ACK control message. The master station then sends the message either as a single data block (as shown in Figure 5.7) or as a sequence of data blocks with the last block terminating with an ETX character. As each data block is received and stored, the slave station recomputes the parity check sequence and, assuming there are no transmission errors, responds with an ACK control message for each block. Finally, after the complete message has been sent, the master station sends an EOT control message, which terminates the message transfer and clears the logical connection.

(a)

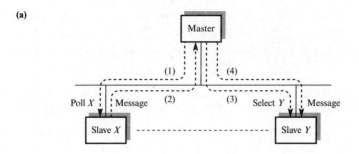

(b)

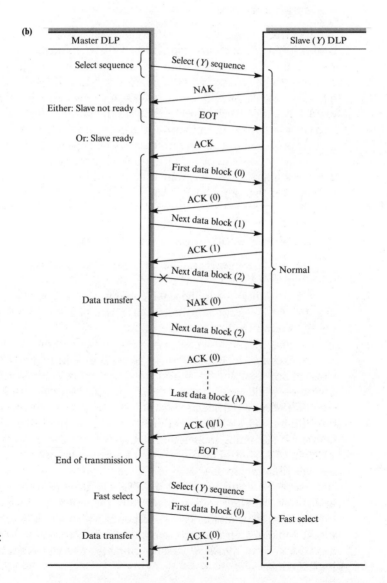

Figure 5.7
BSC frame sequences:
(a) poll-select
schematic; (b) select.

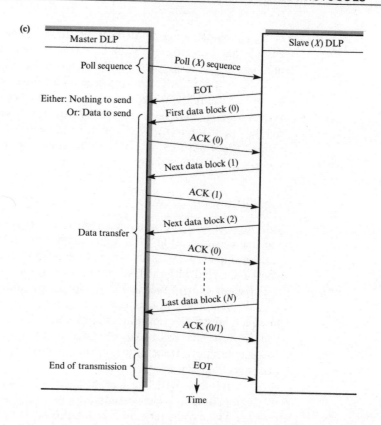

(c)

Master DLP

Slave (X) DLP

Poll sequence { Poll (X) sequence

EOT

Either: Nothing to send
Or: Data to send

First data block (0)

ACK (0)

Next data block (1)

ACK (1)

Next data block (2)

Data transfer {

ACK (0)

Last data block (N)

ACK (0/1)

End of transmission { EOT

Time

Figure 5.7 (cont.)
(c) Poll.

In some situations, when selecting a station it is not always necessary to wait for an acknowledgment to the ENQ control message before sending a message. For example, if a station has been selected previously and the logical connection has not been closed. In such cases the master station sends the message immediately after the select control message, without waiting for an ACK (or NAK) response. This is known as a **fast select sequence**.

During the polling phase, the master station first sends an ENQ poll control message with the address of the polled slave station preceding the ENQ character. Then, assuming the polled station has a message awaiting transmission, it responds by sending the message. On receipt of the data block, the master station recomputes the parity check sequence and, assuming no transmission errors, acknowledges its correct receipt. Finally, after the complete message has been transferred and acknowledged, the logical connection is cleared with an EOT control message.

Figure 5.7 illustrates that BSC is an idle RQ protocol because, after sending each data block, the transmitter waits for either an ACK or a NAK control message before sending the next block and, in the latter case, retransmits the corrupted block. The use of an additional NAK control message ensures that a corrupted data block will be retransmitted on receipt of the NAK message rather than after the timeout interval. As we discussed in Section 4.2, if the transmitted block is completely corrupted, an additional timeout mechanism is required to ensure that the affected block is retransmitted. The identifier (send sequence number) is then used to enable the receiver to detect duplicates.

Note that in BSC the send sequence number simply increments up (modulo an agreed number), whereas the receive sequence number in ACK- and NAK-frames simply increments modulo 2 (0 or 1). As a result, a receive sequence number of 0 refers to even-numbered frames while 1 refers to odd-numbered frames. Since only a single duplicate frame is possible, this is sufficient to enable the receiver to detect them.

User interface

It is important to discriminate between the services provided by the link layer and the detailed operation of the link layer protocol entity. To illustrate this, the relationship between the user services and the various message blocks (control and data) associated with the BSC protocol are shown in Figure 5.8. As we can see, the initial select control message is acknowledged and this is used as a confirmation that the remote station is ready to accept a message. With the poll sequence, however, an ACK is not returned in response to the initial poll message and so the confirm primitive has to be generated by the local protocol entity after the poll message has been transmitted. A similar procedure is also followed with the link disconnection procedure.

In common with the Kermit protocol, BSC performs a segmentation and reassembly function. Hence, on receipt of an L_DATA.request primitive (with the message as a parameter), the sending protocol entity segments the message into a sequence of data blocks for transmission. Similarly, the receiving entity reassembles the blocks into a complete message before passing it to the user using an L_DATA.indication primitive.

Because BSC is effectively a half-duplex protocol, BSC cannot exploit full-duplex transmission even if it is supported by the physical link. Nevertheless, as it needs minimal buffer storage facilities, it is still widely used for networks of the type considered. However, in recent years there has been a shift toward the more flexible and potentially more efficient bit-oriented protocols. This is certainly the case for computer networks which require transparent working.

Protocol performance

We discussed the basic link efficiency (utilization) achieved with the idle RQ protocol was discussed in Section 4.2.4. However, the major use of BSC is in applications where there is a single master (primary) station which sends and receives messages to and from multiple slave (secondary) stations. An important additional performance parameter with such configurations is the average time taken to poll or select all the slave stations on a link.

In practice, because of the low link utilization of idle RQ relative to continuous RQ, idle RQ protocols are used primarily with multidrop links operating at data rates of up to, say, 64 kbps. In such links, the time taken to

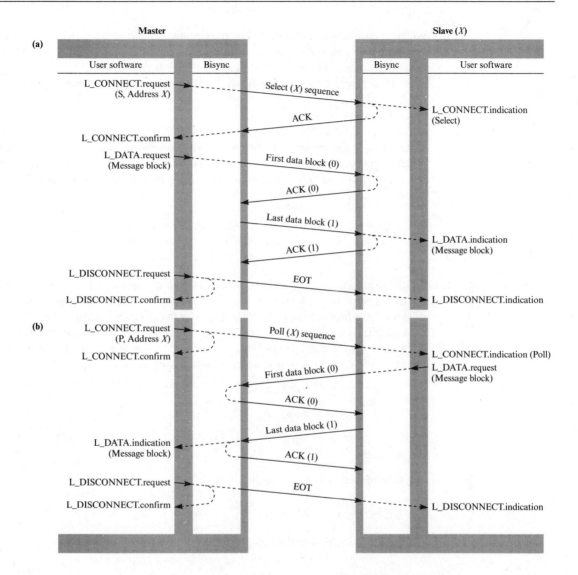

Figure 5.8
User/link layer
interactions: (a) select;
(b) poll.

transmit a message is the dominant time in a poll or select sequence. For example, if an average message is 1000 bits and the data rate is 10 kbps, the time required to transmit a message is 0.1 s. In contrast, the control messages associated with a poll (or select) sequence are short (say 30 bits), so the time to transmit these messages is also short (0.003 s at 10 kbps). Even allowing a small additional time of, say, 0.001 s to process these messages, the total time for each poll (or select) sequence (0.004 s) is still small compared with the message transmission time.

In the absence of any messages to send, the minimum time required to poll all secondaries is N times the time taken to poll a single secondary, where N is the number of secondaries on the link. As messages become ready to transmit, the average time to poll all secondaries increases and depends on the average rate at which messages are generated. The maximum poll time occurs when the average rate at which messages are generated approaches the link bit rate since, beyond this rate, the link becomes overloaded and delays progressively increase.

In general, the average time to poll each secondary can be expressed as:

$$T_{avr} = \frac{T_{min}}{1 - M_r T_{ix}}$$

where T_{min} is the minimum time to poll all secondaries, M_r is the average rate at which messages are generated, and T_{ix} is the time to transmit an average-sized message. If M_r is low compared with T_{ix}, then T_{avr} is approximately T_{min}; however, as M_r increases, so does T_{avr}.

Example 5.1

A BSC protocol is to be used to control the flow of messages between a computer (master station) and 10 block-mode terminals (secondaries) over a multipoint data link. The link data rate, R, is 10 kbps and the average length of a message, N_i, is 1000 bits. If a poll message and its associated ACK is 30 bits and the total time to process these messages is 1 ms, determine the average time each terminal will be polled if the average rate at which messages are generated is:

(a)   One message per minute

(b)   Six messages per second

The bit error rate and signal propagation delay times of the link can be assumed to be negligible.

The time to transmit an average message, T_{ix}, is:

$$\frac{N_i}{R} = \frac{1000}{10^4} = 100 \, ms$$

The time to transmit a poll and its ACK is:

$$\frac{30}{10^4} = 3 \, ms$$

The time to poll a single secondary is:

$$3 + 1 = 4 \, ms$$

The minimum time to poll all secondaries is:

$$T_{min} = 10 \times 4 = 40 \, ms$$

Now:

$$T_{avr} = \frac{T_{min}}{1 - M_r T_{ix}}$$

(a) M_r = one message per minute = $\dfrac{10^{-3}}{60}$ messages ms^{-1}. Hence:

$$T_{avr} = \frac{40}{1 - \dfrac{10^{-3}}{60} \times 100} = 40 \text{ ms}$$

(b) M_r = six messages per second = 6×10^{-3} messages ms^{-1}. Hence:

$$T_{avr} = \frac{40}{1 - 6 \times 10^{-3} \times 100} = \frac{40}{0.4} = 100 \text{ ms}$$

5.2.3 Duplex protocols

A few character-oriented protocols operate in a (full) duplex mode. As an example, we shall consider the data link protocol used in the early ARPANET network to control the flow of information frames across the links connecting the internal network switching nodes – known as **interface message processors (IMPs)**. The protocol operates over the point-to-point duplex links that connect two switching nodes.

The protocol supports the transmission of information frames in both directions simultaneously – duplex – and utilizes a continuous RQ transmission control scheme for both directions. The protocol operates with an effective send window of either 8 for terrestrial links or 16 for satellite links. To ensure a continuous flow of frames, 8 (or 16 for satellite) separate stop-and-wait information flows can be in progress at any instant.

To achieve this, the single physical link is operated as 8 (or 16) separate **logical links**, the flow of frames over each link being controlled by its own stop-and-wait protocol machine. The send sequence number in the header of each frame transmitted on the physical link is a concatenation of two fields: a single-bit sequence number – 0 or 1 – which is the normal send sequence number associated with the idle RQ (send and wait) protocol, and a **logical channel number (LCN)** which indicates the logical channel to which the frame relates.

In common with most duplex schemes, character-oriented and bit-oriented, acknowledgment information relating to the flow of information frames flowing in one direction is piggybacked in the header of information frames flowing in the reverse direction. Thus a single type of frame is used and the various fields in its header relate to a specific function. The general frame format and the fields in the header that are associated with the data link protocol are shown in Figure 5.9, together with the general operation of the protocol.

To support a duplex flow of frames, the forward and reverse physical links both support 8 (or 16) logical links. Thus, for each logical channel, the data link protocol at each side of the link maintains separate send and receive sequence variables. The send sequence variable – 0 or 1 – is the send sequence number that will be assigned to the next new frame to be transmitted on the forward channel, while the receive sequence variable is the sequence number of the next information

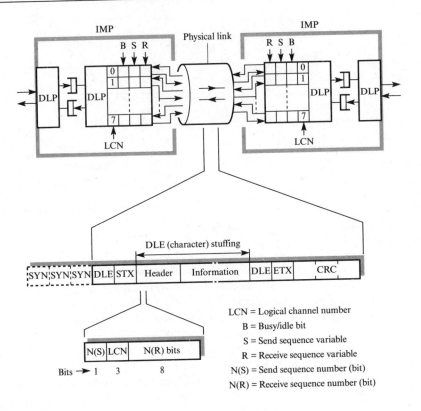

Figure 5.9
ARPANET IMP-to-
IMP data link protocol
detail.

frame expected to be received on the reverse channel. In addition, to ensure each forward channel operates in a stop-and-wait mode, each side also has a busy/idle bit associated with each channel that indicates whether the channel is busy, that is, an acknowledgment is still outstanding on this channel.

Within the ARPANET network, each frame is treated as a separate entity, that is, the frames relating to the same (user) message are treated independently. On receipt of a frame to be forwarded, the sending data link protocol simply scans the busy/idle bit associated with each logical channel to determine whether a channel is free and, if so, inserts the appropriate send sequence number – 0 or 1 – and logical channel number in the frame header, starts a timer for the frame and initiates its transmission. If a channel is not free, the frame is left in the input queue to wait for a free channel.

The protocol uses a 24-bit (3 byte) CRC for error detection. Error correction uses an acknowledgment byte in the header of each frame. The eight bits are a concatenation of the eight receive sequence numbers relating to the flow of frames in the eight logical channels of the reverse path. On receipt of a frame, the data link protocol reads the acknowledgment byte and, for all active channels, interprets the corresponding bit according to the idle RQ protocol described in Section 4.2. In this way, acknowledgment information relating to all channels is received every time a new frame is received. This has the same effect as utilizing a send window of 8 (or 16) for the link. Also, it means that an implicit acknowledgment scheme – ACK only – can be used.

In conclusion, although many character-oriented protocols are still widely used, the availability of inexpensive integrated circuits that support the more efficient bit-oriented protocols means that all new (and many current) protocols are of the bit-oriented type.

5.3 Bit-oriented protocols

All new data link protocols are bit-oriented protocols. Recall that such protocols use defined bit patterns rather than transmission control characters to signal the start and end of a frame. The receiver searches the received bit stream on a bit-by-bit basis for the known start-of-frame and end-of-frame bit pattern. Three methods of signaling the start and end of a frame – known as **frame delimiting** – were shown in Figure 3.13. These were:

- Unique start-of-frame and end-of-frame bit patterns, known as flags (01111110), together with zero bit insertion

- A unique start-of-frame bit pattern, known as the start delimiter (10101011), and a length (byte) count in the header at the start of the frame

- Unique start-of-frame and end-of-frame delimiters that include bit **encoding violations**

In general, the first is used with the high-level data link control (HDLC) protocol while the other two are used with the logical link control (LLC) protocol. In practice, all the bit-oriented protocols, are derivatives of the HDLC protocol, therefore we shall describe this first.

5.3.1 High-level data link control

The HDLC protocol is an international standard that has been defined by ISO for use on both point-to-point and multipoint (multidrop) data links. It supports full-duplex, transparent-mode operation and is now extensively used in both multipoint and computer networks. Although the acronym HDLC is now widely accepted, a number of large manufacturers and other standards bodies still use their own acronyms. These include IBM's **SDLC** (synchronous data link control), which was the forerunner of HDLC, and **ADCCP** (advanced data communications control procedure), which is used by the American National Standards Institute (ANSI).

Because HDLC has been defined as a general-purpose data link control protocol, we can use it in a number of different network configurations, as shown in Figure 5.10. In HDLC, the frames sent by the primary station to the secondary station are known as **commands** and those from the secondary to the primary as **responses**. The two configurations shown in parts (a) and (b) have a single primary

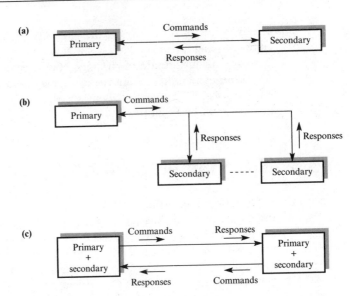

Figure 5.10
Alternative HDLC network configuration: (a) point-to-point with single primary and secondary; (b) multipoint with single primary and multiple secondary; (c) point-to-point with two primaries and two secondaries.

station and are known as **unbalanced configurations** while that in part (c) has two primary stations and is known as a **balanced configuration**. In the balanced configuration, since each station has both a primary and a secondary, they are also known as **combined stations**.

HDLC has three operational modes:

(1)   **Normal response mode (NRM)**   This is used in unbalanced configurations. In this mode, slave stations (or secondaries) can transmit only when specifically instructed by the master (primary) station. The link may be point-to-point or multipoint. In the latter case only one primary station is allowed.

(2)   **Asynchronous response mode (ARM)**   This is also used in unbalanced configurations. It allows a secondary to initiate a transmission without receiving permission from the primary. This is normally used with point-to-point configurations and duplex links and allows the secondary to send frames asynchronously with respect to the primary.

(3)   **Asynchronous balanced mode (ABM)**   This is used mainly on duplex point-to-point links for computer-to-computer communication and for connections between, say, a computer and a PSDN. In this mode, each station has an equal status and performs both primary and secondary functions. It is the mode used in the protocol set known as X.25, which is discussed in Section 8.2.

Frame formats

Unlike BSC, in HDLC both data and control messages are carried in a standard format frame. This format is shown in Figure 5.11 together with the different

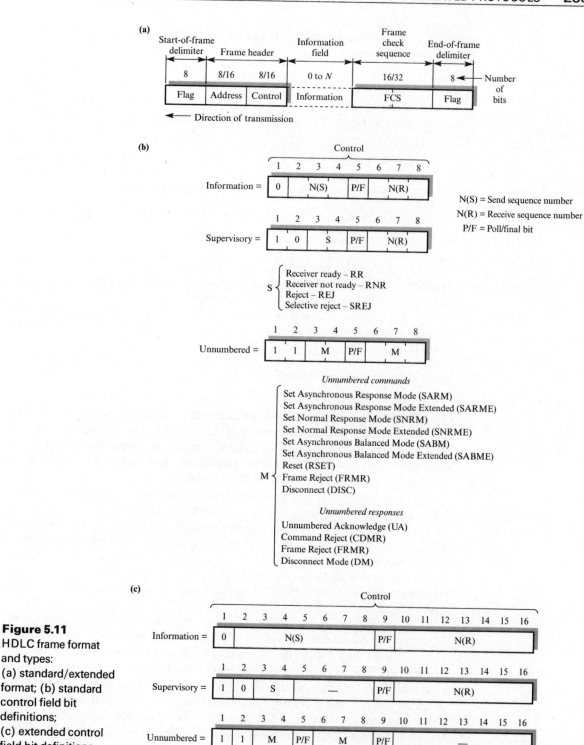

Figure 5.11
HDLC frame format
and types:
(a) standard/extended
format; (b) standard
control field bit
definitions;
(c) extended control
field bit definitions.

frame types that are defined in the control field of the frame header. Three classes of frame are used in HDLC:

(1) **Unnumbered frames**   These are used for such functions as link setup and disconnection. The name derives from the fact that they do not contain any acknowledgment information, which is contained in sequence numbers.

(2) **Information frames**   These carry the actual information or data and are normally referred to simply as I-frames. I-frames can be used to piggyback acknowledgment information relating to the flow of I-frames in the reverse direction when the link is being operated in ABM or ARM.

(3) **Supervisory frames**   These are used for error and flow control and hence contain send and receive sequence numbers.

The use of the flag field as a start-of-frame and end-of-frame delimiter, together with zero bit insertion and deletion to achieve data transparency, was described in Chapter 3 and is not repeated here.

The frame check sequence (FCS) is a 16-bit CRC for the complete frame contents enclosed between the two flag delimiters. The generator polynomial used with HDLC is normally CRC-CCITT:

$$x^{16} + x^{12} + x^5 + 1$$

The FCS is generated by the procedure described in Section 3.4.3 enhanced by procedures to make the check more robust. An example is adding sixteen 1s to the tail of the dividend prior to division (instead of zeros) and inverting the remainder. This has the effect that the remainder computed by the receiver is not all zeros but a special bit pattern – 0001 1101 0000 1111.

The contents of the address field depend on the mode of operation. In NRM, for example on a multidrop line, every secondary station is assigned a unique address. Whenever the primary station communicates with a secondary, the address field contains the address of the secondary. Certain addresses known as **group addresses** can be assigned to more than one secondary station. All frames transmitted with a group address are received by all stations in that group. Also, a **broadcast address** can be used to transmit a frame to all secondary stations on the link.

When a secondary station returns a response message (frame) to the primary, the address field always contains the unique address of that secondary. In the case of large networks containing a large number of secondaries, the address field may be extended beyond eight bits. The least significant bit (lsb) of each 8-bit field is then used to indicate whether there is another octet to follow (lsb = 0) or whether it is the last or only octet (lsb = 1). Note that the address field is not used in this way in ABM because only direct point-to-point links are involved. Instead, it is used to indicate the direction of commands and their associated responses.

The various control field bit definitions are shown in Figure 5.11(b). The S-field in supervisory frames and the M-field in unnumbered frames are used to define the specific frame type. The send and receive sequence numbers – N(S) and N(R) – are used in conjunction with the error and flow control procedures.

The **P/F bit** is known as the **poll/final bit**. A frame of any type is called a **command frame** if it is sent by the primary station and a **response frame** if it is sent by a secondary station. The P/F bit is called the poll bit when used in a command frame and, if set, indicates that the receiver must acknowledge this frame. The receiver acknowledges this frame by returning an appropriate response frame with the P/F bit set; it is then known as the final bit.

The use of 3 bits for each of N(S) and N(R) means that sequence numbers can range from 0 through 7. This, in turn, means that a maximum send window of 7 can be selected. Although this is large enough for many applications, those involving very long links (satellite links, for example) or very high bit rates, require a larger send window if a high link utilization is to be achieved. The **extended format** uses 7 bits (0 through 127), thereby increasing the maximum send window to 127.

The address field identifies the secondary station that sent the frame, and is not needed with point-to-point links. However, with multipoint links, the address field can be either eight bits – normal mode – or multiples of eight bits – extended mode. In the latter case, bit 1 of the least significant address octet(s) is (are) set to 0 and bit 1 is set to 1 in the last octet. The remaining bits form the address. In both modes, an address of all 1s is used as an all-stations broadcast address.

Frame types

Before we describe the operation of the HDLC protocol, it is perhaps helpful to list some of the frame types and to outline their function. Three classes of frame are used. Some of the different types of frame in each class are listed in Figure 5.11(b).

Unnumbered frames are used for link management. For example, SNRM- and SABM-frames are used both to set up a logical link between the primary and a secondary station and to inform the secondary station of the mode of operation to be used. A logical link is subsequently cleared by the primary station sending a DISC-frame. The UA-frame is used as an acknowledgment to the other frames in this class.

Although there are four types of supervisory frame, only RR and RNR are used in both NRM and ABM. These frames are used both to indicate the willingness or otherwise of a secondary station to receive an I-frame(s) from the primary station, and for acknowledgment purposes. REJ- and SREJ-frames are used only in ABM which permits simultaneous two-way communication across a point-to-point link. The two frames are used to indicate to the other station that a sequence error has occurred, that is, an I-frame containing an out-of-sequence N(S) has been received. The SREJ-frame is used with a selective repeat transmission procedure, whereas the REJ-frame is used with a go-back-N procedure.

Protocol operation

This section highlights some of the more important features of the HDLC protocol, rather than giving a full description of its operation. The two basic functions are link management and data transfer (including error and flow control).

Link management.   Before any information (data) may be transmitted, either between the primary and a secondary station on a multidrop link or between two stations connected by a point-to-point link, a logical connection between the two communicating parties must be established. This is accomplished by the exchange of two unnumbered frames, as shown in Figure 5.12.

In a multidrop link (Figure 5.12(a)), an SNRM-frame is first sent by the primary station with the poll bit set to 1 and the address of the appropriate secondary in the address field. The secondary responds with a UA-frame with the final bit set and its own address in the address field. As we can see, the setup procedure has the effect of initializing the sequence variables held by each station. These variables are used in the error and flow control procedures. Finally, after all

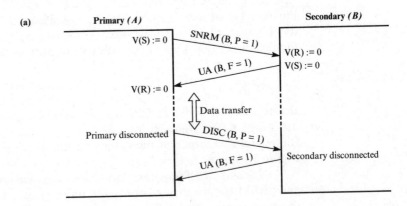

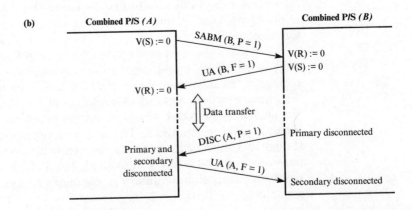

Figure 5.12
Link management
procedure: (a) normal
response mode –
multidrop link;
(b) asynchronous
balanced mode –
point-to-point link.

data has been transferred, the link is cleared when the primary sends a DISC-frame and the secondary responds with a UA-frame.

The procedure followed to set up a point-to-point link is the same as that used for a multidrop link. However, in the example shown in Figure 5.12(b) ABM has been selected and hence an SABM-frame is sent first. In this mode, both sides of the link may initiate the transfer of I-frames independently, so each station is often referred to as a combined station, since it must act as both a primary and a secondary. Either station may initiate the setting-up or clearing of the link in this mode. In Figure 5.12(b), station A initiates link setup while station B initiates the clearing of the (logical) connection. A single exchange of frames sets up the link in both directions. As we can see, the address field is used to indicate the direction of the command frame (SABM/DISC) and its associated response.

If the receiver wishes to refuse a setup command in either mode, a disconnected mode (DM) frame is returned in response to the initial mode setting frame (SNRM or SABM). The DM-frame indicates the responding station is logically disconnected.

Data transfer.   In NRM, all data (I-frames) is transferred under the control of the primary station. The unnumbered poll (UP) frame with the P bit set to 1 is normally used by the primary to poll a secondary. If the secondary has no data to transmit, it returns an RR-frame with the F bit set. If data is waiting, it transmits the data, typically as a sequence of I-frames, with the F bit set to 1 in the last frame of the sequence.

The two most important aspects of the data transfer phase are error control and flow control. Error control uses a continuous RQ procedure with either a selective repeat or a go-back-N retransmission strategy, while flow control is based on a window mechanism. We described the basic operation of both these procedures in Chapter 4, therefore we shall give only typical frame sequences here to illustrate the use of the different frame types.

Figure 5.13(a) illustrates the basic acknowledgment and retransmission procedure; this example uses only RR-frames and assumes a go-back-N strategy. Only a unidirectional flow of I-frames is shown in the figure, so all acknowledgment information must be returned using specific acknowledgment supervisory frames. As we can see, each side of the link maintains both a send and a receive sequence variable. V(S) indicates the next send sequence number N(S) which is allocated to an I-frame transmitted by that station, and V(R) the send sequence number of the next in-sequence I-frame expected by that station.

Each RR (positive acknowledgment) supervisory frame contains a receive sequence number N(R) which acknowledges correct receipt of all previously transmitted I-frames up to and including that with an N(S) equal to $[N(R) - 1]$. Similarly, Figure 5.13(b) shows that each REJ (negative acknowledgment) supervisory frame contains an N(R) which indicates that an out-of-sequence I-frame has been received and the sender must start to retransmit from the I-frame with N(S) equal to N(R).

(a)

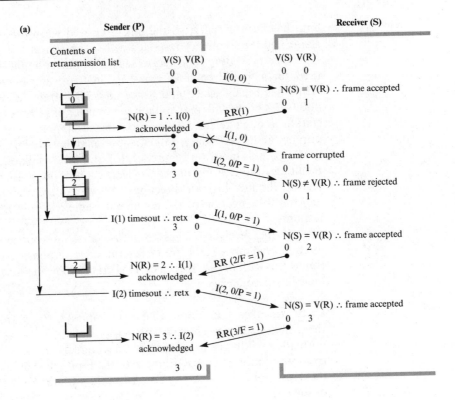

(b)

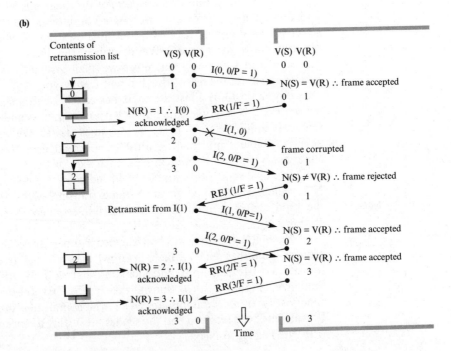

Figure 5.13
Use of
acknowledgment
frames: (a) positive
acknowledgment
(RR) only;
(b) negative
acknowledgment
(REJ).

Figure 5.13(a) shows that any I-frames received out of sequence are simply discarded. Hence on receipt of frame I(2, 0/P = 1) – the P bit set because the previous frame has not been acknowledged – the frame is discarded and no action is taken by the receiver. In the absence of acknowledgments, the timer associated with frames I(1) and I(2) expires and both frames are retransmitted. The example assumes each frame is received correctly and is acknowledged using an RR-frame.

In Figure 5.13(b), negative acknowledgment (REJ) frames are used. When the receiver detects that frame I(2, 0/P = 1) – that is, the last frame in the sequence with P = 1 – is out of sequence, it returns an REJ-frame with the F bit set. The sender then retransmits frames I(1, 0) and I(2, 0) with the P bit again set to 1 in frame I(2, 0). The receiver acknowledges correct receipt of each frame with the F bit set to 1 in the last RR-frame. If selective retransmission is being used, then frame I(2, 0/P = 1) will be accepted and an SREJ-frame returned to request that frame I(1, 0) is retransmitted.

The frame sequence in Figure 5.13 is typical of information transfer over a multidrop link operating in NRM. However, for a point-to-point link in ABM, a duplex flow of I-frames is possible. As in NRM, acknowledgment information relating to the flow of I-frames in one direction can be piggybacked in I-frames flowing in the reverse direction. An example is given in Figure 5.14. For clarity, no transmission errors are shown.

As each I-frame is received, its N(S) and N(R) are both read. N(S) is first compared with the receiver's V(R). If they are equal, the frame is in the correct sequence and is accepted; if they are not equal, the frame is discarded and an REJ- or SREJ-frame returned. N(R) is examined and used to acknowledge any outstanding frames in the retransmission list. Finally, as no further I-frames are awaiting transmission, an RR-frame is used to acknowledge the outstanding unacknowledged frames in each retransmission list.

Flow control is particularly important when two-way simultaneous working is used and the link is being operated in ABM. With NRM, if the primary experiences transient overload conditions, it can simply suspend polling, thereby allowing the overload to subside. However, when both sides of the link are operating independently, we must use an alternative mechanism. The flow control procedure used in HDLC is based on a sliding window mechanism similar to that already discussed in Section 4.3.3.

As we have seen in the examples shown in Figures 5.13 and 5.14, the send and receive sequence numbers are incremented modulo 8 so the maximum send window K that can be used is 7. Thus a maximum of 7 I-frames can be awaiting acknowledgment in the retransmission list at any time. Each side of the link maintains a separate variable known as the retransmission count (RetxCount) which is initialized to zero when the logical link is set up. It is incremented each time an I-frame is transmitted, and hence each time a frame is placed in the retransmission list, and is decremented whenever a positive acknowledgment is received, and hence each time a frame is removed from the retransmission list. The primary stops sending I-frames when the retransmission count reaches K and does not resume until a positive acknowledgment is received either as a separate RR

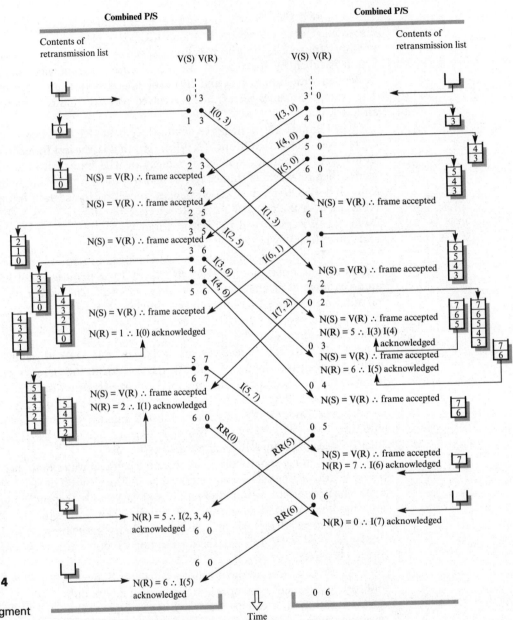

Figure 5.14
Piggyback
acknowledgment
procedure.

supervisory frame or piggybacked in an I-frame flowing in the reverse direction. We can conclude that transmission of I-frames is stopped when:

$$V(S) = \text{last } N(R) \text{ received} + K$$

Note that the window mechanism controls the flow of I-frames in only one direction and that supervisory and unnumbered frames are not affected by the

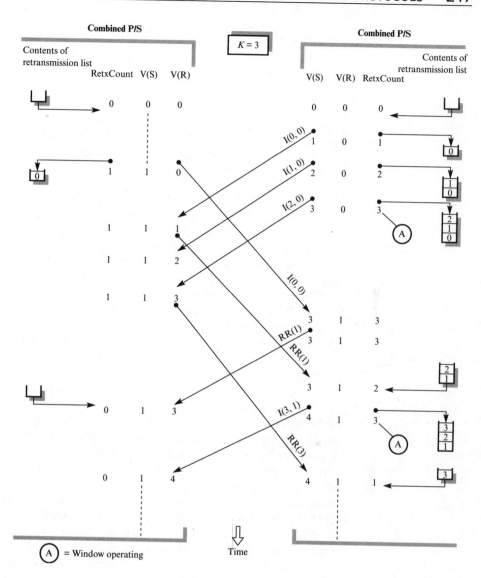

Figure 5.15
Window flow control procedure.

mechanism. Hence, these frames can still be transmitted when the window is operating. An example is shown in Figure 5.15; for clarity, only the flow of I-frames in one direction is affected.

The use of a window mechanism means that the sequence numbers in all incoming frames must lie within certain boundaries. On receipt of each frame the secondary must check to establish that this is the case and, if not, take corrective action. Therefore each received N(S) and N(R) must satisfy the following conditions:

(1)   V(R) is less than or equal to N(S) which is less than V(R) + K.

(2)   V(S) is greater than N(R) which is greater than or equal to V(S) – RetxCount.

If N(S) equals V(R), then all is well and the frame is accepted. If N(S) is not equal to V(R) but is still within the range, then a frame has simply been corrupted and an REJ (go-back-N) or an SREJ (selective repeat) frame is returned, indicating to the primary that a sequence error has occurred and from which frame to start retransmission. This was illustrated in Figure 5.13.

If N(S) or N(R) is outside the range, then the sequence numbers at both ends of the link have become unsynchronized and the link must be reinitialized (set up). This is accomplished when the secondary, on detecting an out-of-range sequence number, discards the received frame and returns a **frame reject (FRMR)** – ABM – or a **command reject (CMDR)** – NRM – frame to the primary. The primary discards all waiting frames and proceeds to set up the link again by sending an SABM/SNRM and waiting for a UA response. On receipt of this response, both sides of the link reset their sequence and window variables enabling the flow of I-frames to be resumed. In fact, this is only one reason why a link may be reset; another is the receipt of an unnumbered frame, such as a UA, during the data transfer phase which indicates that the primary and secondary have become unsynchronized.

The flow control procedure just outlined is controlled by the primary side of the link controlling the flow of I-frames according to the send window. In addition, it may be necessary for the secondary to stop the flow of I-frames as a result of some event occurring at its side of the link. For example, with a go-back-N retransmission strategy the receive window is 1 and it is reasonably straightforward to ensure that there are sufficient memory buffers available at the receiver. However, if selective retransmission is used, it is possible for the secondary to run out of free buffers to store any new frames. Hence, when the secondary approaches a point at which all its buffers are likely to become full, it returns an RNR supervisory frame to the primary to instruct it to stop sending I-frames. Acknowledgment frames are not affected, of course. When the number of full buffers drops below another preset limit, the secondary returns an RR-frame to the primary with an N(R) indicating from which frame to restart transmission.

User interface

We can now establish the relationship between the link layer user services shown earlier in Figure 5.1 and the various protocol message units associated with HDLC. These are shown in Figure 5.16.

On receipt of the initial L_CONNECT.request from the user, the link layer protocol entity in the calling system first sends an SNRM/SABM supervisory frame to the link layer protocol entity in the called system. On receipt of this

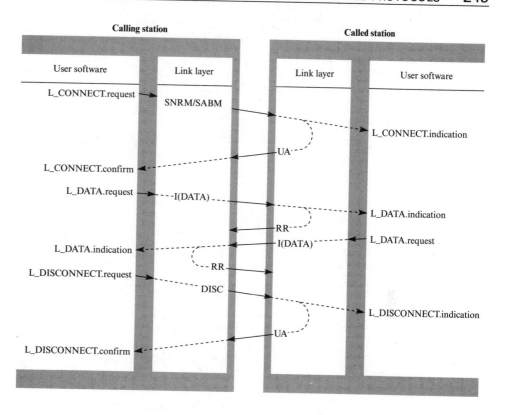

Figure 5.16
User/link layer
interaction.

frame, the link layer protocol creates and passes an L_CONNECT.indication primitive to the called user. In addition, it creates a UA-frame and returns this to the calling side. When the calling side receives the UA-frame it creates an L_CONNECT.confirm primitive and passes it to the user so that the transfer of user data can commence using the L_DATA service. Finally, after all data (information) has been exchanged, the link is disconnected using the DISC and UA supervisory frames.

A summary of the various service primitives and frame types (protocol data units) associated with HDLC is given in Figure 5.17(a). In practice, there are more unnumbered frames associated with HDLC than shown in the figure but, as mentioned earlier, the aim is simply to highlight selected aspects of HDLC operation. To reinforce understanding further, a (simplified) state transition diagram for HDLC is given in Figure 5.17(b). The first entry alongside each arc is the incoming event causing the transition (if any); the second entry is the resulting action. Note that a state transition diagram shows only the correct operation of the protocol entity; normally it is accompanied by a more complete definition in the form of an event–state table and/or pseudocode.

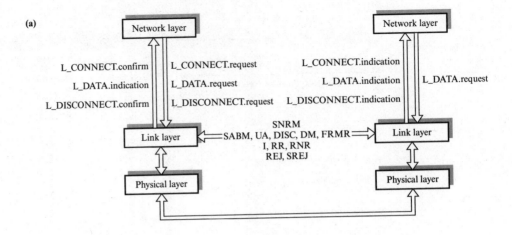

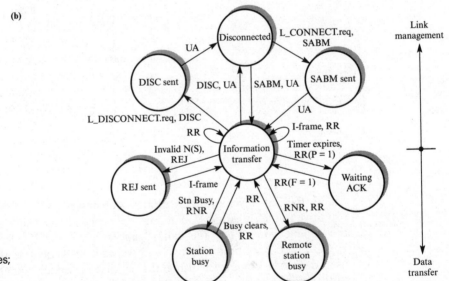

Figure 5.17
LAPB summary:
(a) service primitives;
(b) state transition
diagram (ABM).

5.3.2 Link access procedure version B

Link access procedure version B (LAPB) is a subset of HDLC that is used to control the transfer of I-frames across a point-to-point duplex data link that connects a computer to a public (or private) packet-switching network. Such networks are normally referred to as X.25 networks; we shall discuss them in more detail in Section 8.2. LAPB is in fact an extended version of an earlier subset known simply as **link access procedure version A (LAPA)**.

Table 5.2

Type	LAP Commands	LAP Responses	LAPB Commands	LAPB Responses
Supervisory	RR	RR	RR	RR
		RNR	RNR	RNR
		REJ	REJ	REJ
Unnumbered	SARM	UA	SABM	UA
	DISC	CMDR	DISC	DM
				FRMR
Information	I		I	

The applicability of LAPB was shown in Figure 5.2(c). The computer is the DTE and the packet switching exchange is the data circuit-terminating equipment (DCE). LAPB is used to control the transfer of information frames across the local DTE–DCE interface and is said to have local significance.

LAPB uses asynchronous balanced mode with the DTE and DCE as combined stations and all I-frames treated as command frames. The earlier LAP protocol used an asynchronous response mode and did not use REJ- or RNR-frames as command frames. A summary of the frames used with LAP and LAPB is given in Table 5.2. The RR- and REJ-frames are used for error control and RNR for flow control. These frames do not support selective repeat (SREJ). The example frame sequences shown in the earlier figures relating to the operation of HDLC apply directly to LAPB. As we have indicated, the sending of an information (command) frame with the P bit set results in the receiving station returning a supervisory frame with the F bit set. Either station can set up the link. To discriminate between the two stations, the DTE and DCE addresses used are as shown in Table 5.3. If a DTE that is not logically operational receives a setup request frame (SABM/SABME), it must reply with a DM frame.

A summary of the use of the P/F bit with LAPB is given in Table 5.4.

Recall that in the normal SABM mode a single octet is used for the control field. The send and receive sequence numbers are each 3 bits – 8 sequence numbers – allowing a maximum send window of 7. If the extended mode (SABME) is selected, two octets are used for the control field. The send and receive sequence numbers are thus extended to 7 bits – 128 sequence numbers – which in turn allows

Table 5.3

Direction	Addresses Commands	Addresses Responses
DTE → DCE	01 Hex (B)	03 Hex (A)
DCE → DTE	03 Hex (A)	01 Hex (B)

Table 5.4

Command frame sent with P = 1	Response frame returned with F = 1
SABM/SABME	UA/DM
I-frame	RR, REJ, RNR, FRMR
RR, REJ, RNR	RR, REJ, RNR, FRMR
DISC	UA/DM

for a much larger window. This is used, for example, with very long links and/or high bit rate links.

Integrated circuits are now available that implement LAPB in firmware-preprogrammed memory. These are often referred to as X.25 circuits although they implement only the LAPB protocol rather than the full X.25 protocol set. The availability of these circuits has significantly increased the use of LAPB for many additional computer-to-computer communication applications.

5.3.3 Multilink procedure

We have described the use of HDLC for controlling the transfer of information frames across a single duplex link. HDLC is thus known as a **single link procedure (SLP)**. However, in some instances the throughput (or reliability) available with just a single link is not sufficient to meet the requirements of the application, so we must use multiple (physical) links. To allow for this, an extension to LAPB, known as **multilink procedure (MLP)**, has been defined.

Figure 5.18(a) shows that the transfer of frames across each physical link is controlled by a separate single link procedure in the way just described. The single MLP operates above the set of link procedures and simply treats them as a pool of links available to transfer user information. This means that the user software is unaware of multiple physical links being used and is presented with a single (logical) link interface as before.

As indicated, the MLP simply treats the set of single link procedures as a pool of links over which to transfer user frames. It operates with its own set of sequence numbers and error and flow control procedures which are independent of those being used by each SLP. Hence if an SLP becomes unoperational, then the MLP will initiate the retransmission of frames in the normal way but using the reduced set of links (SLPs) available.

To implement this scheme, the MLP adds an additional control field to the head of each frame it receives for transmission prior to passing the frame to an SLP. This is known as the **multilink control (MLC)** field and is effectively transparent to an SLP. The SLP treats the combined MLC and frame contents as the information field and proceeds to add its own address (A) and control (C)

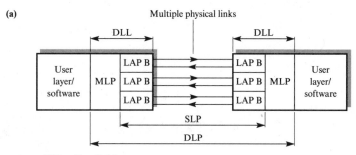

(a)

Multiple physical links

DLL = Data link layer

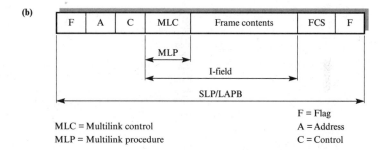

(b)

MLC = Multilink control
MLP = Multilink procedure

F = Flag
A = Address
C = Control

Figure 5.18
Multilink procedure:
(a) position in relation
to data link layer;
(b) frame format.

field as shown in Figure 5.18(b). The error and flow control mechanisms associated with MLP are essentially the same as those used with LAPB.

The MLC field comprises two octets and contains a 12-bit sequence number. This provides 4096 (0 through 4095) sequence numbers and hence a maximum window size of 4095, allowing a significant number of links to be used, each possibly operating at a high data rate. An example is when two X.25 packet-switching networks are being connected together. We shall expand upon this in Chapter 8.

5.3.4 Link access procedure for modems

Link access procedure for modems (LAPM) is the protocol used in error correction modems, such as the V.32 modem. These modems accept asynchronous (start–stop) data from the DTE but transmit the data in frames using bit-oriented synchronous transmission and an HDLC-based error correcting protocol. The applicability of LAPM is shown in Figure 5.19(a).

Each modem comprises two functional units: a **user (DTE) interface part (UIP)** and an **error correcting part (ECP)**. The LAPM protocol is associated with the latter while the UIP is concerned with the transfer of single characters/bytes across the local V.24 interface and with the interpretation of any flow control signals across this interface.

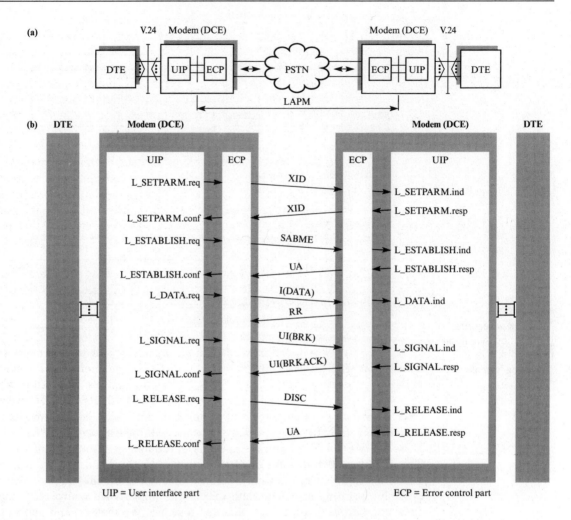

Figure 5.19
LAPM: (a) operational scope; (b) user service primitives and corresponding frame types.

The UIP communicates with the ECP using a defined set of service primitives, as shown in the time sequence diagram in Figure 5.19(b). The different HDLC frame types used by the LAPM protocol machine to implement the various services are also shown.

Before establishing a (logical) link, the originating and responding ECPs must agree on the operational parameters to be used with the protocol. These parameters include the maximum number of octets in I-frames, the acknowledgment timer setting, the maximum number of retransmission attempts, and the window size. Default values are associated with each of these, but if they are not used, the originating UIP must issue an L_SETPARM.request primitive with the desired operational parameter values. The values are negotiated when the two ECPs exchange two special unnumbered frames – known as **exchange identification (XID)** – one as a command and the other as a response.

Once the operational parameters have been agreed, a link can then be set up when the UIP issues an L_ESTABLISH.request primitive. This, in turn, results in an SABM (normal) or SABME (extended) supervisory frame being sent by the ECP. The receiving ECP then issues an L_ESTABLISH.indication primitive to its local UIP and, on receipt of the response primitive, the receiving ECP returns a UA-frame. On receipt of this frame, the originating ECP issues a confirm primitive and the (logical) link is now set up. Data transfer can then be initiated using the L_DATA service.

Typically, the UIP first assembles a block of data, comprising characters or bytes received over the V.24 interface, then passes the complete block to the ECP using an L_DATA.request primitive. The ECP packs the data into the information field of an I-frame as a string of octets and transfers this using the normal error correcting procedure of the HDLC protocol. The receiving ECP then passes the (possibly error corrected) block of data to its local UIP which transfers it a character (byte) at a time across the local V.24 interface.

If a flow control (break) condition is detected during the data transfer phase – for example, an X-OFF character is received or the DTR line becomes inactive – then the UIP stops outputting data to the local DTE and immediately issues an L_SIGNAL.request primitive to its local ECP. The local ECP then informs the distant ECP to (temporarily) stop sending any more data by sending a BRK (break) message in a special information frame known as an **unnumbered information (UI) frame**. This, as the name implies, does not contain sequence numbers since it bypasses any error/flow control mechanisms. The receiving ECP then issues an L_SIGNAL.indication primitive to its local UIP and acknowledges receipt of the break message by returning a BRKACK message in another UI-frame. The UIP then initiates the same flow control signal across its own V.24 interface.

Finally, after all data has been transferred, the link is cleared when the originating UIP issues an L_RELEASE.request primitive. Again this is a confirmed service and the associated LAPM frames are DISC and UA.

5.3.5 Link access procedure D-channel

Link access procedure D-channel (LAPD) is the HDLC subset for use with the ISDN. It has been defined to control the flow of I-frames associated with the signaling (call setup) channel. The latter is known as the **D-channel**. LAPD is also used in a slightly extended form to control the flow of I-frames over a user channel associated with a service known as **frame relay**. We shall defer further details relating to ISDN until Chapter 8 when we shall discuss WANs. In this section we shall simply discuss the basic operation of LAPD and how it relates to HDLC.

Two types of service have been defined for use with LAPD. A time sequence diagram showing the two sets of service primitives is shown in Figure 5.20. As we can see, both an unacknowledged (best-try) and an acknowledged (connection-oriented) service are supported. The ISDN, like the analog PSTN it is replacing, is

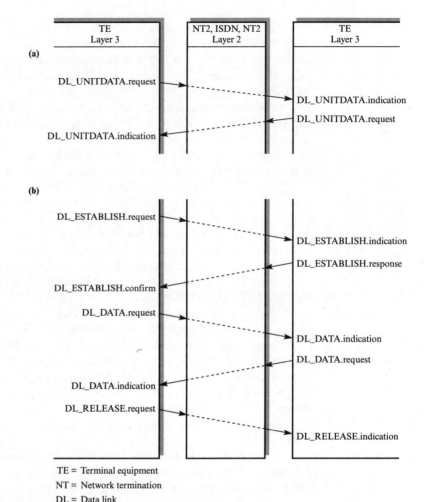

Figure 5.20
LAPD user services
primitives:
(a) connectionless;
(b) connection-
oriented.

TE = Terminal equipment
NT = Network termination
DL = Data link

basically a circuit-switched network which means that a circuit must be established before any user information is transferred. This is done using a separate signaling channel – the D-channel – which has its own protocol set of which LAPD is a constituent part.

The connection-oriented service is used to transfer call setup messages between an item of user equipment – a telephone or a DTE – and the local exchange. The associated protocol incorporates error control. The connectionless service is used for the transfer of management-related messages and the associated protocol uses a best-try, unacknowledged approach.

As we shall see in Chapter 8, up to eight different items of terminal equipment – telephones, DTEs or combinations of the two – can share a basic access circuit (and hence D-channel) between a customer's premises and the local ISDN exchange. However, all (higher layer) call setup messages are sent to a specific terminal equipment using the LAPD address field. This is similar in

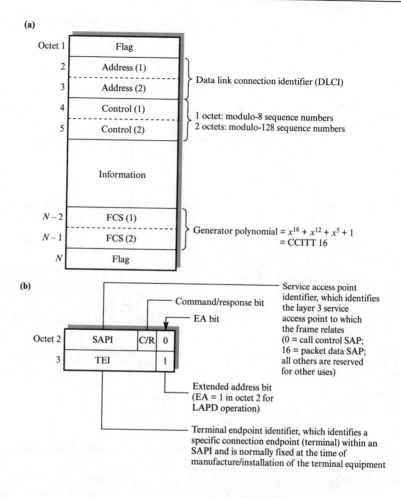

Figure 5.21
LAPD: (a) frame format; (b) address field usage.

principle to the addressing mechanism used in the NRM mode, except that with LAPD there is no master and the physical bus structure to which the terminal equipments are attached allows each terminal to access the bus in a fair way. The general structure of each LAPD frame is shown in Figure 5.21.

Two octets are used for the address field. These consist of two subaddresses: a **service access point identifier (SAPI)** and a **terminal endpoint identifier (TEI)**. Essentially, the SAPI identifies the class of service to which the terminal relates – voice, data, voice and data – and the TEI then uniquely identifies the terminal within that class. There is also a broadcast address – all binary 1s – that allows a message to be sent to all terminals in a class. This can be used, for example, to allow all telephones to receive an incoming call setup request message.

The various control field formats – octets 4 and 5 – associated with LAPD are summarized in Figure 5.22, which also shows which frames can be sent as command frames and which as response frames.

In LAPD, as with LAPM, the additional unnumbered frame known as **unnumbered information (UI)** is used. LAPD uses this with the connectionless

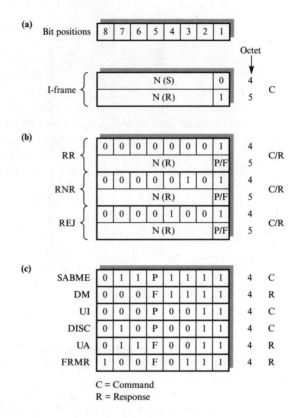

Figure 5.22
LAPD control field bit
definitions:
(a) information;
(b) supervisory;
(c) unnumbered.

service. Since there is no error control associated with this service (best-try), all information is sent with a single control field with neither N(S) nor N(R). Such frames do have an FCS field; should this fail, the frame is simply discarded. Normally with this service the higher (user) layer must then detect the discarded frame – for example, by the lack of a suitable response (also in a UI-frame) – and make another attempt. As we shall see in Section 5.3.6, this procedure is also used in LANs.

The LAPD service definition and protocol specification are specified in ITU-T recommendations I.440 and I.441, respectively. These are the same as recommendations Q.920 and Q.921.

5.3.6   Logical link control

Logical link control (LLC) is the HDLC derivative used with LANs. LANs are discussed in detail in Chapter 6 but the general arrangement of the two basic types of LAN topology – bus and ring – together with the scope of the DLP – LLC – was shown earlier in Figure 5.2.

Both topologies utilize a shared transmission medium – the bus or ring – which is used to carry all frame transmissions. As with a multipoint network, we need a way of controlling the order in which frames are transmitted. Unlike multipoint networks, there is no single master computer, so a distributed algorithm ensures that the medium is used in a fair way by all the connected DTEs – workstations, servers, etc. With LANs, the data link layer is comprised of two sublayers, the **medium access control (MAC) sublayer**, which implements the distributed access control algorithm, and the LLC sublayer. The detailed operation of the different MAC sublayers are described in Chapter 6 when LANs are discussed; this section concentrates on the operation of the LLC sublayer. Note that with a LAN, since there are no switching exchanges within the network itself, the LLC (DLP) layer operates on a peer basis, that is, between the LLC sublayer in the two communicating DTEs.

User services

Two types of user service are provided by the LLC layer: an **unacknowledged connectionless service** and a set of connection-oriented services. The unacknowledged connectionless service allows the user to initiate the transfer of service data units with a minimum of protocol overheads. Typically, this service is used when functions such as error recovery and sequencing are being provided in a higher protocol layer and need not be replicated in the LLC layer. Alternatively, the connection-oriented services allow the user to establish a link-level logical connection before initiating the transfer of any service data units and, if required, to implement error recovery and sequencing of the flow of these units across an established connection.

In certain real-time LAN applications, such as in the process control industry for interconnecting computer-based instrumentation equipment distributed around a chemical plant, the time overhead of setting up a logical connection prior to sending data is often unacceptable. Nevertheless, some acknowledgment of correct receipt of a transmitted item of data is often needed, so the basic unacknowledged connectionless service is not acceptable. An additional service, known as the **acknowledged connectionless service**, caters for this type of requirement. Similarly, a service known as the **obtain reply service** allows an item of data to be requested from a remote user without a connection first being established.

The various primitives associated with the two sets of services are shown in the time sequence diagram of Figure 5.23. Each of the primitives illustrated has parameters associated with it. These include a specification of the source (local) and destination (remote) addresses. The source and destination addresses, which are present in all primitives, specify at a minimum the physical addresses to be used on the network medium. However, normally both addresses are a concatenation of the addresses used on the physical medium and the local service access point identifier (LLC-SAP). We shall consider LLC-SAP further in Chapter 6.

With the unacknowledged connectionless service, when the LLC protocol entity receives a data transfer request primitive (L_DATA.request), it makes a best attempt to send the accompanying data using the MAC sublayer. There is no confirmation that the transfer has been successful or unsuccessful. However,

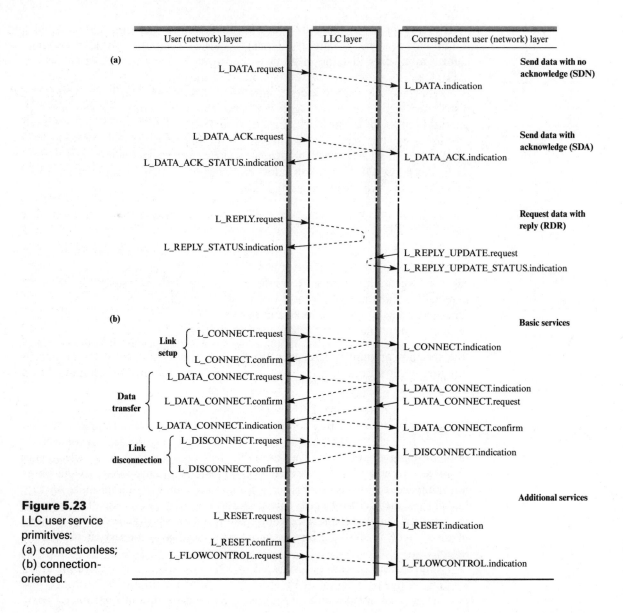

Figure 5.23
LLC user service
primitives:
(a) connectionless;
(b) connection-
oriented.

with the acknowledged connectionless service, the user is notified of the success or failure of the passing of the L_DATA_ACKNOWLEDGE.indication to the remote user by means of the L_DATA_ACKNOWLEDGE_STATUS.indication primitive.

The various primitives associated with the obtain reply service allow a user:

- To request the contents of a message buffer maintained by a remote LLC entity – L_REPLY.request/indication

- To update the contents of a message buffer that is maintained by its local LLC entity – L_REPLY_UPDATE.request and L_REPLY_UPDATE_STATUS.indication

With the connection-oriented service, a logical connection must be established using the L_CONNECT primitives prior to any data transfer. Similarly, after all data transfers have taken place, the connection must be cleared using the L_DISCONNECT primitive. During the data transfer phase, the receipt of each error-free data unit is acknowledged by the remote LLC entity which is converted by the local entity into an L_DATA_CONNECT.confirm primitive and passed to the user.

The RESET and FLOWCONTROL service primitives allow the user to control the flow of service data units across an established connection. The RESET service has an abortive action as it results in any unacknowledged data being discarded. Therefore, it is used only if the network layer protocol entity loses track of the sequence of data units being transferred.

The two flow control primitives have only local significance: the L_FLOWCONTROL.request primitive specifies the amount of data the user is prepared to accept from its local LLC protocol entity and the L_FLOWCONTROL.indication primitive the amount of data the LLC protocol entity is prepared to accept from the user, both related to a specific connection. If the specified amount is zero, then the flow of data is stopped; if the amount is infinite, no flow control is to be applied on the connection. The amount of data allowed is dynamically updated by each request.

Protocol operation

The format of each LLC frame is shown in Figure 5.24(a). The source and destination address fields both refer to the LLC service access point only; they do not contain the addresses to be used on the network medium. There is no FCS field. Essentially, the complete LLC frame is passed to the MAC sublayer in the form of a primitive which includes the frame and the address to be used on the network medium as parameters. The MAC sublayer handles the network addressing and error-detection functions. Therefore, in the context of the ISO reference model, the link layer is equivalent to a combination of the LLC and a portion of the MAC sublayers.

The control field in each frame is a single octet. It defines the type of the frame and, where appropriate, the send and receive sequence numbers for error and sequence control. The use of the various bits in this field is shown in more detail in Figure 5.24(b).

The LLC protocol entity supports two types of operation: type 1 to support the unacknowledged connectionless service and type 2 to support the connection-oriented service. Type 2 is in practice very similar to the HDLC protocol except that the framing and error-detection functions are provided by the MAC sublayer.

The data link control functions for type 2 operation are shown in Figure 5.24(c). The major difference between the LLC protocol and HDLC is the

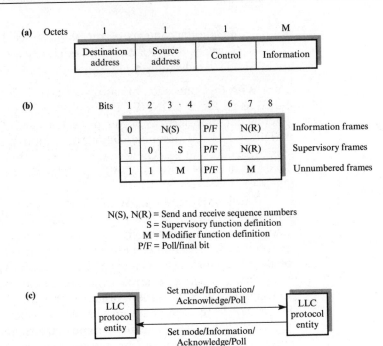

Figure 5.24
Aspects of LLC protocol: (a) frame format; (b) control field bit definitions; (c) data link control function (type 2).

provision of the unacknowledged connectionless (type 1) service. The set of commands and responses supported in type 1 is listed in Table 5.5.

The UI command frame is used to send a block of data (information) to one or more LLCs. Since there is no acknowledgment or sequence control associated with type 1 operation, the UI-frame contains neither an N(S) nor an N(R) field. Also, there is no response to a UI.

The XID and TEST command frames are optional. However, if they are sent, the receiving LLC(s) is (are) obliged to respond. The uses of these commands include the following:

- The XID command with a group address determines the current membership of the group. Each member of the group responds to the command by returning an XID response frame addressed specifically to the originating LLC entity.

- An LLC entity may use an XID command with a broadcast (global) destination address to announce its presence on the network medium.

Table 5.5

Commands	Responses
UI	–
XID	XID
TEST	TEST

- The TEST command provides a loopback test facility on each LLC-to-LLC transmission path.

MAC services

Irrespective of the mode of operation of the underlying MAC sublayer, a standard set of user services is defined for use by the LLC layer to transfer LLC frames to a corresponding LLC layer. The user service primitives supported are the following:

- MA_UNITDATA.request
- MA_UNITDATA.indication
- MA_UNITDATA.confirmation

A time sequence diagram illustrating their use is shown in Figure 5.25. For some LANs, the confirm primitive indicates that the request has been successfully (or not) transmitted – part (a) – while for others it indicates that the request has been successfully delivered (or not) _ part (b).

Each service primitive has associated parameters. Included in the MA_UNITDATA.request primitive are the required destination address (this may be an individual, group, or broadcast address), a service data unit (containing the LLC frame), and the required class of service associated with the frame. The last one is used with some types of LAN when a prioritized medium access control protocol is being used.

The MA_UNITDATA.confirm primitive includes a parameter that specifies the success or failure of the associated MA_UNITDATA.request primitive. However, as we can see from Figure 5.25, the confirm primitive is not generated as a result of a response from the remote LLC layer but rather by the local MAC entity. If the parameter is successful, this simply indicates that the MAC protocol entity (layer) was successful in transmitting the service data unit on to the network medium; if unsuccessful, the parameter indicates why the transmission attempt failed. We shall discuss this and other MAC-related topics further in Chapter 6.

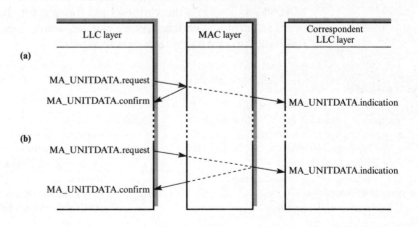

Figure 5.25
MAC sublayer user service primitives:
(a) local confirm;
(b) remote confirm.

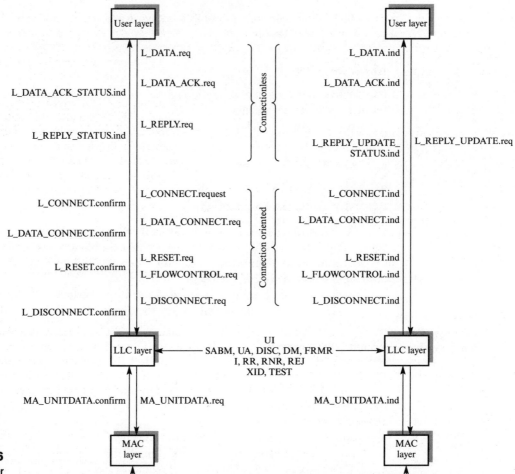

Figure 5.26
LLC sublayer
summary.

Figure 5.26 summarizes the various services associated with the LLC and MAC layers and lists the various LLC frame types that are exchanged between two LLC protocol entities. As we can see, apart from the UI, XID, and TEST these are the same as those used with HDLC.

Exercises

5.1 Explain the meaning of the following terms relating to data link protocols:
(a) Character-oriented
(b) Bit-oriented
(c) Framing and data transparency
(d) Poll–select
(e) Primary and secondary

5.2 Produce a sketch of a time sequence diagram showing the user service primitives associated with the data link control layer assuming the following operational modes:
(a) Connectionless (best-try)
(b) Connection-oriented (reliable)

5.3 With the aid of sketches, identify the scope of operation of the data link protocol in the following application environments:
(a) Point-to-point
(b) Multipoint (multidrop)
(c) WANs
(d) LANs

5.4 Explain the operation of the Kermit protocol used for the transfer of files of data from one computer to another. Include in your description:
(a) The user commands
(b) The frame format and frame types used
(c) Example frame sequences, including retransmissions

5.5 List the 10 transmission control characters from the ASCII character set and explain their function in character-oriented protocols.

5.6 Produce sketches of the various data and supervisory frames (blocks) used with the binary synchronous control (BSC) protocol showing clearly the position of the various transmission control characters.

5.7 Discriminate between the terms 'poll', 'select', and 'fast-select' in relation to the BSC protocol.
    Produce sketches of typical data and supervisory frame (block) sequences to illustrate these three operational modes of BSC.

5.8 Produce a sketch of the frame format used and explain how a continuous duplex flow of I-frames is maintained with the ARPANET data link protocol.
    Identify the state variables that are required at each side of the data link to implement the combined error control scheme.

5.9 With the aid of sketches, identify the direction of commands and responses associated with the high-level data link control (HDLC) protocol for the following network configurations:
(a) Point-to-point with a single primary and secondary
(b) Point-to-point with combined stations
(c) Multipoint with a single primary

5.10 Produce a sketch of the basic and extended frame formats associated with the HDLC protocol. Show clearly the structure of the control field in each case and explain the meaning and use of each subfield.

5.11 Assuming an HDLC protocol, distinguish between the NRM and ABM modes of working. Sketch typical frame sequences to show how a link is first set up (established) and then cleared (disconnected) for each mode. Clearly show the different frame types used and the use of the address and poll/final bit in each frame.

5.12 Define the supervisory frames used for acknowledgment purposes in the HDLC protocol. Assuming a unidirectional flow of I-frames, sketch a typical frame sequence to illustrate the acknowledgment procedure used in the HDLC protocol. Include in the diagram the contents of the link retransmission list and the state of the send and receive sequence variables as each frame is transmitted and received. Also show the send and receive sequence numbers contained within each frame and the state of the poll/final bit, where appropriate.

5.13 Explain the meaning of the term 'piggyback acknowledgment'. Sketch a typical frame sequence to illustrate how piggyback acknowledgments are used in the HDLC protocol. Clearly show the send and receive sequence numbers contained within each frame transmitted and the contents of the retransmission lists and send and receive variables at each side of the link.

5.14 Outline the operation of a window flow control mechanism. Assuming a send window of K and a send window variable V(W), deduce the range within which the send and receive sequence numbers contained within each received frame should be, assuming both sides of the link are in synchronism.
    Assuming a send window of 3 and a unidirectional flow of I-frames, sketch a frame sequence to illustrate the operation of the window flow control mechanism used with the HDLC protocol.

5.15 Explain the meaning of the term 'multilink procedure' in relation to data link protocols.

Use a diagram to illustrate its relationship to a single link procedure and show how the frame format is extended to include additional sequence numbers.

5.16 Produce a time sequence diagram to show the user service primitives associated with the LAPD protocol with the following information transfer:

(a) Unacknowledged (best-try)

(b) Acknowledged

Sketch the frame format associated with LAPD and clearly explain the structure and use of the address field octets.

5.17 With the aid of a time sequence diagram, list the user service primitives associated with the LLC protocol with the following operation:

(a) Connectionless

(b) Connection-oriented

In relation to the above, discriminate between the terms:

(a) Send data with no acknowledge

(b) Send data with acknowledge

(c) Request data with reply

5.18 Use a time sequence diagram to show the user service primitives associated with the medium access control (MAC) sublayer used in the data link layer of LANs.

Hence show how the supervisory and information frames associated with the above LLC sublayer user services are transferred using the various MAC user primitives.

Chapter summary

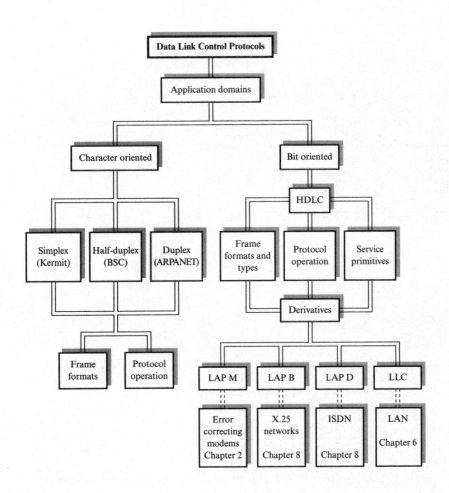

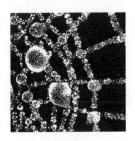

Part two
COMPUTER NETWORKS

In Part Two we are concerned with the mode of operation of the different types of computer network that are used to interconnect a distributed community of computers and their various interface standards and protocols. When the computers are distributed over a localized area – such as a building or campus – the network used is known as a local area network (LAN), when the computers are distributed over a wider geographical area – such as a country – the network is known as a wide area network (WAN), when the complete network comprises an interconnected set of local and wide area networks, it is known as an internetwork.

Chapter 6 describes the operation and interface protocols associated with the different types of wired LAN that are now international standards. Also, the operational characteristics of wireless LANs, that is, networks that use either radio or light (infrared) as the transmission medium.

In Chapter 7, we describe the operation of high-speed LANs. We also discuss the operation and protocols associated with the bridge, the two types of which are used to extend the capacity and field of coverage of LANs.

Chapter 8 describes the operation and interface protocols associated with the two types of WANs: public data networks and private networks. The former are installed and managed by the public carriers while the latter are installed, managed, and run by large national and multinational companies.

Chapter 9 discusses the issues that must be addressed and the additional protocols that are needed when the network comprises an interconnected set of networks such as a mix of LANs and WANs, that is an internetwork.The issues include addressing and routing.

Chapter 10 is concerned with broadband multiservice networks. These provide not only data services but also services which support the transfer of other media types such as sound and video.

6 LOCAL AREA NETWORKS

Chapter objectives

When you have completed this chapter you should be able to:

- Describe the different topologies and transmission media commonly used in wired local area networks ☞ 273
- Know the difference between baseband and broadband working ☞ 275
- Describe the alternative medium access control methods used in local area networks ☞ 280
- Describe the major components and mode of operation of a CSMA/CD bus network ☞ 285
- Describe the major components and mode of operation of a token ring network ☞ 292
- Describe selected aspects of the operation of a token bus network ☞ 307
- Describe the technological issues associated with wireless LANs ☞ 317
- Understand the operational characteristics of wireless LANs ☞ 325, 334
- Appreciate the function of the various network-dependent protocols used with local area networks and be able to describe the services and operation of the logical link control and network protocol layers ☞ 342, 344, 346

Introduction

Local area data networks, which we normally refer to simply as **local area networks** or **LANs**, are used to interconnect distributed communities of computer-based DTEs located within a single building or localized group of buildings. For example, we may use a LAN to interconnect workstations distributed around offices within a single building or a group of buildings such as a university campus, to interconnect computer-based equipment distributed around a factory or hospital complex. However, since all the equipment is located within a single establishment, LANs are normally installed and maintained by the organization. Hence they are also referred to as **private data networks**.

The main difference between a communication path established using a LAN and a connection made through a public data network is that a LAN normally offers much higher data transmission rates because of the relatively short physical separations involved. In the context of the ISO reference model for OSI, this difference manifests itself only at the lower network-dependent layers. In many instances the higher protocol layers in the reference model are the same for both types of network. This chapter is primarily a description of the different types of LAN and the function and operation of the associated network-dependent protocol layers.

There are two quite different types of LAN: **wired LANs** and **wireless LANs**. As the names imply, wired LANs utilize (fixed) wiring – such as twisted-pair or coaxial cable – as the transmission medium while wireless LANs utilize radio or light waves. As we shall see, the selection and technology issues associated with both types are quite different and therefore we shall consider each type separately.

6.1   Wired LANs

Before we describe the structure and operation of the different types of wired LAN, let us first identify some of the selection issues that must be considered. A summary of some of these issues is given in Figure 6.1. Note that this is only a summary; there are also many possible links between the tips of the branches in the figure. We shall consider each of the issues identified in some detail.

6.1.1   Topology

Most WANs, such as the PSTN, use a **mesh** (sometimes referred to as a **network**) **topology**. However, with LANs the limited physical separation of the subscriber DTEs allows us to use simpler topologies. The four topologies in common use are star, bus, ring, and hub, as shown in Figure 6.2.

Perhaps the best example of a LAN based on a **star topology** is the digital **private automatic branch exchange (PABX)**. A connection established through a traditional analog PABX is in many ways similar to a connection made through an analog PSTN in that all paths through the network are designed to carry limited-bandwidth analog speech. Therefore, to use them to carry data, we require modems, as we discussed in Chapter 2. However, most modern PABXs use digital-switching techniques within the exchange and are therefore also referred to as **private digital exchanges (PDXs)**. Moreover, the availability of inexpensive integrated circuits to perform the necessary analog-to-digital and digital-to-analog conversion functions means that it is rapidly becoming common practice to extend the digital mode of working right back to the subscriber outlets. This means that a switched 64 kbps path, which is the digitizing rate normally used for digital voice, is available at each subscriber outlet, which can therefore be used for both voice and data.

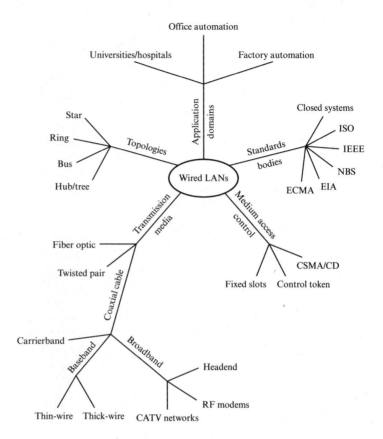

Figure 6.1
LAN selection issues.

However, the main use of a **PDX** is likely to be to provide a switched communication path between a local community of integrated voice and data terminals (workstations) for the exchange of electronic mail, electronic documents, etc., in addition to normal voice communications. Furthermore, digital techniques within the PDX enable it to provide such services as **voice store-and-forward** (that is, a subscriber may leave (store) a voice message for another subscriber for later retrieval (forwarding)) and teleconferencing (multiple subscribers taking part in a single call).

The preferred topologies for LANs designed to function as data communication subnetworks for the interconnection of local computer-based equipment are bus (linear) and ring. In practice, bus networks are normally extended into an interconnected set of buses and thus more closely resemble an **uprooted tree**. Typically, with a **bus topology** the single network cable is routed through those locations (for example, offices) that have a DTE to be connected to the network, and a physical connection (tap) is made to the cable to allow the user DTE to access the network services supported. Appropriate medium access control (MAC) circuitry and algorithms are then used to share the available transmission bandwidth among the attached community of DTEs.

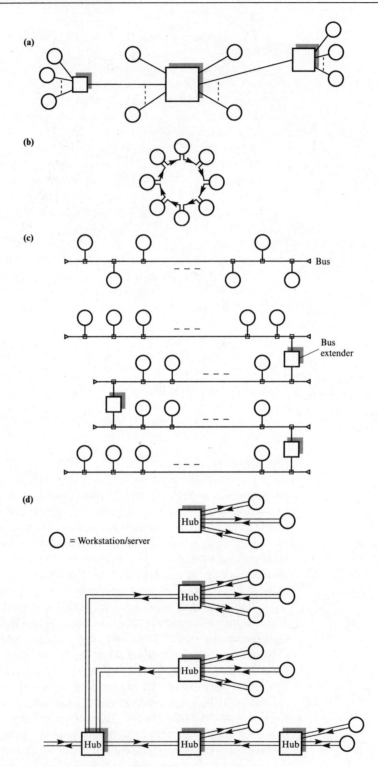

Figure 6.2
LAN topologies:
(a) star; (b) ring;
(c) bus; (d) hub/tree.

With a **ring topology**, the network cable passes from one DTE to another until the DTEs are interconnected in the form of a loop or ring. A feature of a ring topology is a direct point-to-point link between each neighboring DTE which is unidirectional in operation. Appropriate MAC algorithms then ensure the use of the ring is shared between the community of users.

The data transmission rates used with both ring and bus topologies (typically from 1 to 10 Mbps) mean that they are best suited for interconnecting local communities of computer-based equipment, such as workstations in an office environment or intelligent controllers around a process plant.

A variation of the bus and ring, known as a **hub topology**, is shown in Figure 6.2(d). Although such networks have the appearance of a star topology, the hub is simply the bus or ring wiring collapsed into a central unit. The wires used to connect each DTE to the bus or ring are then extended out from the hub. Therefore, unlike a PDX, the hub does not perform any switching function but simply consists of a set of repeaters that retransmit all the signals received from DTEs to all other DTEs in the same way as the bus or ring network. As we can see, hubs can also be connected in a hierarchical way to form a **tree topology**. The combined topology again functions as a single ring or bus network or an interconnected set of such networks. We shall discuss practical examples in Section 6.2.

6.1.2   Transmission media

Twisted pair, coaxial cable (coax), and optical fiber are the three main types of transmission medium used for LANs.

Twisted pair – both unshielded and shielded – is used primarily in star and hub networks. Because it is less rigid than coaxial cable or fiber, twisted pair is most readily installed. Also, since wiring ducts suitable for twisted-pair cable are already in place at most office desks for telephony, it is less costly to install additional twisted pairs for data purposes than it is to install new cable ducts for coax or fiber. The general scheme is shown in Figure 6.3(a).

As Chapter 2 showed, there is a maximum limit on the length of twisted-pair cable depending on the bit rate being used. Typically the limit is 100 m at 1 Mbps or, with the aid of additional circuits to remove crosstalk, 100 m at 10 Mbps. A typical arrangement is to use twisted pair between each DTE and the nearest wiring closet on a floor and then coaxial cable to link the floor wiring closets to the main building hub. For an installation involving multiple buildings, fiber is normally used to link each building hub to a main central hub. The latter normally works at a higher bit rate and is logically configured as a ring network. This type of arrangement is often referred to as **structured wiring**.

Coaxial cable is also widely used for LANs, primarily with bus networks, operating with either baseband or broadband transmission. We discussed the basic operation of these in Chapter 2. Two types of cable are used with baseband: **thin wire** and **thick wire**. The terms refer to the cable diameter: thin wire of 0.25 inch diameter and thick wire of 0.5 inch diameter. Normally, both operate at

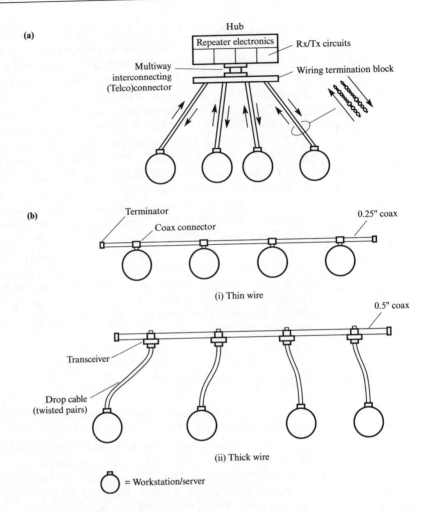

Figure 6.3
Transmission media:
(a) twisted pair;
(b) baseband coaxial
cable.

the same bit rate – 10 Mbps – but thin-wire cable results in greater signal attenuation; the maximum length of thin-wire cable between repeaters is 200 m compared with 500 m with thick wire. Recall that a repeater is used to regenerate a received signal to its original form. The two operating modes thick- and thin-wire cables are known as **10 Base 2** – 10 Mbps, baseband, 200 m maximum length – and **10 Base 5**, respectively.

Thin-wire coax is often used to interconnect workstations in the same office or laboratory. The physical connector to the coaxial cable attaches directly to the interface card in the workstation. The cable bus takes the form of a daisy chain as it passes from one DTE to the next.

In contrast, thick coax, because of its more rigid structure, is normally installed away from the workstations, for example along a corridor. Additional wiring – known as a **drop cable** – and transmit and receive electronics – known as a **transceiver** – must be used between the main coaxial cable tapping (connection) point – known as the **attachment unit interface (AUI)** – and the point of attachment to each workstation. This arrangement is more expensive and is, therefore, used primarily when the workstations are each located in different offices or for interconnecting thin-wire segments. Both are illustrated in Figure 6.3(b).

As we described in Chapter 2, with broadband transmission, instead of transmitting information on to the cable in the form of, say, two voltage levels corresponding to the bit stream being transmitted (baseband), the total available bandwidth (frequency range) of the cable is divided into a number of smaller subfrequency bands or channels. Each subfrequency band is used, with the aid of a pair of special modems, to provide a separate data communication channel. This style of working is known as frequency-division multiplexing and, since the frequencies used are in the radio frequency band, the modems are rf modems. This principle, known as broadband working, is also widely used in the **community antenna television (CATV)** industry to multiplex a number of TV channels onto a single coaxial cable.

A typical CATV system is shown in Figure 6.4(a). Each TV channel is allocated a particular frequency band, typically of 6 MHz bandwidth. Each received video signal (from the various antennas or aerials) is used to modulate a **carrier frequency** in the selected frequency band. The modulated carrier signals are transmitted over the cable network and are available at each subscriber outlet. The subscriber selects a particular TV channel by tuning to the appropriate frequency band.

In a similar way, we can derive a range of data transmission channels from a single cable by allocating each channel a portion of the total bandwidth, the bandwidth for each channel being determined by the required data rate. However, for data communication a two-way (duplex) capability is normally required. We can do this in two ways:

(1) **Single-cable system**   The transmit and receive paths are assigned two different frequency bands on the same cable.

(2) **Dual-cable system**   Two separate cables are used, one for the transmit path and the other for the receive path.

Figure 6.4
Broadband coaxial cable systems:
(a) basic CATV system components.

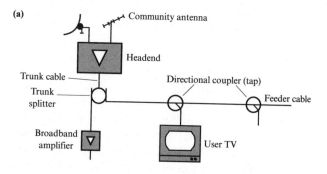

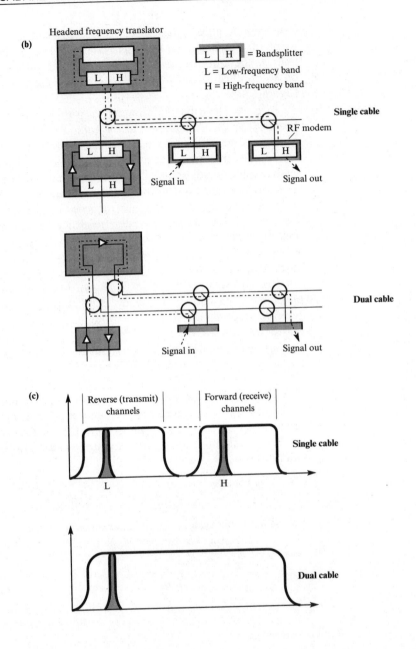

Figure 6.4 (cont.)
(b) Data network
alternatives;
(c) frequency usage.

A schematic of each type of system is shown in Figure 6.4(b). The main difference between them is that a dual-cable system requires twice the amount of cable and cable taps to install. With this system the total cable bandwidth (typically 5 through 450 MHz) is available in each direction. Moreover, the **headend (HE)** equipment is simply an amplifier, whereas with a single-cable system a device known as a **frequency translator** is required to translate the incoming frequency signals associated with the various receive paths into the corresponding outgoing frequencies used for the transmit paths.

A sinusoidal signal in the selected frequency band in the reverse direction (that is, to the headend) is first modulated by the data to be transmitted using an rf modem. This signal is fed onto the cable using a special **directional coupler** or **tap** which is designed so that most of the transmitted signal flows in the reverse direction to the cable headend. A frequency translator is then used to convert (translate) the signals received on the different receive frequency bands to a corresponding set of forward frequency bands. The received modulated signal is thus frequency-translated by the HE, and the rf modem associated with the receiving DTE is tuned to receive the matching frequency-translated signal frequency band. The transmitted data is demodulated from the received signal by the receiving modem and passed on to the attached DTE.

We can deduce that a single pair of frequencies provides just a simplex (unidirectional) data path between the two DTEs. Consequently, two separate pairs of frequencies must be used to support duplex communication. Nevertheless, a 9.6 kbps simplex data channel requires only in the order of 20 kHz of the total available bandwidth, so a pair of 6 MHz subfrequency bands can be used to provide 300 such channels or 150 duplex channels. Higher data rate channels require progressively more of the available bandwidth, for example, two 6 MHz bands for a 5 Mbps full-duplex channel or three 6 MHz bands for a 10 Mbps full-duplex channel.

The price we pay for deriving this multiplicity of different data channels from a single cable is the relatively high cost of each pair of rf modems. However, a broadband coaxial cable can be used over longer distances than a baseband cable. Therefore, the primary use of broadband coaxial cable tends to be as a flexible transmission medium for use in manufacturing industry or in establishments comprising multiple buildings, especially when the buildings are quite widely separated (up to tens of kilometers). When used in this way, other services, such as closed-circuit television and voice, can readily be integrated onto the cable being used for data. Hence broadband is a viable alternative to baseband for networks providing a range of services.

Optical fiber (see Chapter 2) is made of glass or plastic and can operate at data rates well in excess of those possible with twisted-pair or coaxial cable. Since data is transmitted via a beam of light, the signal is not affected by electromagnetic interference. Optical fiber is thus best suited to applications that demand either a very high data rate or high levels of immunity to electromagnetic interference, such as industrial plants containing large electrical equipment. Also, since the fibers do not emit electromagnetic radiation, which could be picked up by an eavesdropper, they are suited to applications that demand high levels of security.

Because data is transmitted using a beam of light, special electrical-to-optical and optical-to-electrical transmitter and receiver electronics are used. Also, the physical connectors used with optical fiber are more expensive than those used with twisted-pair or coaxial cable, and it is also more difficult to make physical taps to a fiber cable. For these reasons, we use optical fiber either in hub configurations or in high-speed ring and other networks that employ point-to-point transmission paths. Two examples of the latter are the fiber distributed data interface (FDDI) and the distributed-queue, dual-bus (DQDB) networks described in Chapter 7.

6.1.3   Medium access control methods

When a communication path is established between two DTEs through a star network, the central controlling element (for example, a PDX) ensures that the transmission path between the two DTEs is reserved for the duration of the call. However, with both the ring and bus topologies there is only a single logical transmission path linking all the DTEs. Consequently, a discipline must be imposed on all the DTEs connected to the network to ensure that the transmission medium is accessed and used in a fair way. The two techniques that have been adopted for use in the various standards documents are **carrier-sense multiple-access with collision detection (CSMA/CD)**, for bus network topologies, and **control token**, for either bus or ring networks. An access method based on a **slotted ring** is also widely used with ring networks.

CSMA/CD

The CSMA/CD method is used solely with bus networks. With this network topology, all DTEs are connected directly to the same cable, which is used for transmitting all data between any pair of DTEs. The cable is said to operate in a **multiple access (MA) mode**. To transmit data the sending DTE first encapsulates the data in a frame with the required destination DTE address at the head of the frame. The frame is then transmitted (or **broadcast**) on the cable. All DTEs connected to the cable detect whenever a frame is being transmitted. When the required destination DTE detects that the frame currently being transmitted has its own address at the head of the frame, it continues reading the data contained within the frame and responds according to the defined link protocol. The source DTE address is included as part of the frame header so that the receiving DTE can direct its response to the originating DTE.

   With this style of operation, two DTEs can attempt to transmit a frame over the cable at the same time, causing the data from both sources to be corrupted. To reduce this possibility, before transmitting a frame the source DTE first listens – electronically – to the cable to detect whether a frame is currently being transmitted. If a **carrier** signal is **sensed (CS)**, the DTE defers its transmission until the passing frame has been transmitted, and only then does it attempt to send the frame. Even so, two DTEs wishing to transmit a frame may simultaneously determine that there is no activity (transmission) on the bus, and both start to transmit their frames simultaneously. A collision is then said to occur since the contents of both frames will collide and be corrupted. This is shown in diagrammatic form in Figure 6.5.

   A DTE simultaneously monitors the data signal on the cable when transmitting the contents of a frame on the cable. If the transmitted and

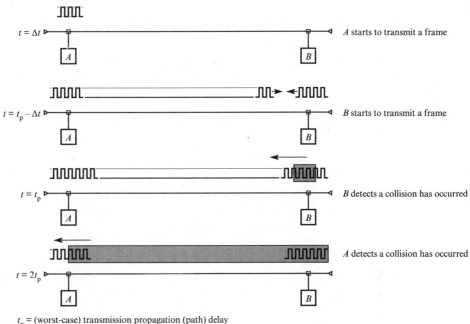

Figure 6.5
CSMA/CD collision
schematic.

t_p = (worst-case) transmission propagation (path) delay

monitored signals are different, a collision is assumed to have occurred – **collision detected (CD)**. To ensure that the other DTE(s) involved in the collision is (are) aware that a collision has occurred, the first DTE reinforces the collision by continuing to send a random bit pattern for a short period. This is known as the **jam sequence**. The two (or more) DTEs involved then wait for a further short random time interval before trying to retransmit the affected frames. We can conclude that access to a CSMA/CD bus is probabilistic and depends on the network (cable) loading. Note that since the bit rate used on the cable is very high (up to 10 Mbps), the network loading tends to be low. Also, since the transmission of a frame is initiated only if the cable is inactive, the probability of a collision occurring is in practice also low.

Control token

Another way of controlling access to a shared transmission medium is by a control (permission) token. This token is passed from one DTE to another according to a defined set of rules understood and adhered to by all DTEs connected to the medium. A DTE may transmit a frame only when it is in possession of the token and, after it has transmitted the frame, it passes the token on to allow another DTE to access the transmission medium. The sequence of operation is as follows:

- A logical ring is first established which links all the DTEs connected to the physical medium, and a single control token is created.

- The token is passed from DTE to DTE around the logical ring until it is received by a DTE waiting to send a frame(s).

- The waiting DTE then sends the waiting frame(s) using the physical medium, after which it passes the control token to the next DTE in the logical ring.

Monitoring functions within the active DTEs connected to the physical medium provide a basis for initialization and recovery both of the connection of the logical ring and from loss of the token. Although the monitoring functions are normally replicated among all the DTEs on the medium, only one DTE at a time carries the responsibility for recovery and reinitialization.

The physical medium need not be a ring topology; a token can also be used to control access to a bus network. The establishment of a logical ring on the two types of network is shown in Figure 6.6.

With a physical ring (Figure 6.6(a)), the logical structure of the token-passing ring is the same as the structure of the physical ring, with the order of token passing being the same as the physical ordering of the connected DTEs. However, with a bus network (Figure 6.6(b)) the ordering of the logical ring need not be the same as the physical ordering of the DTEs on the cable. Moreover, with a token access method on a bus network, all DTEs need not be (logically) connected into the logical ring. For example, DTE *H* is not part of the logical ring shown in Figure 6.6(b). This means that DTE *H* can operate only in a receive mode, since it will never own the control token. Another feature of the token

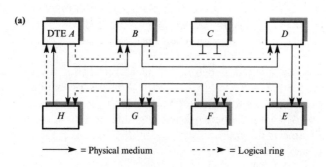

(a)

DTE *C* assumed switched off
and hence in bypass mode

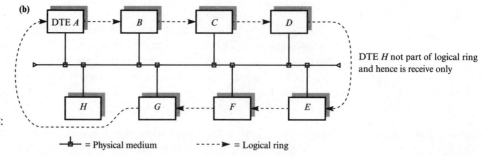

(b)

DTE *H* not part of logical ring
and hence is receive only

Figure 6.6
Control token MAC:
(a) token ring;
(b) token bus.

access method is that a priority can be associated with the token, thereby allowing higher priority frames to be transmitted first. We shall expand upon other aspects of the token access method in Sections 6.2.2 and 6.2.3.

Slotted ring

Slotted rings are used primarily for controlling access to a ring network. The ring is first initialized to contain a fixed number of bits by a special node in the ring known as a **monitor**. This stream of bits continuously circulates around the ring from one DTE to another. Then, as each bit is received by a DTE, the DTE interface examines (reads) the bit and passes (repeats) it to the next DTE in the ring, and so on. The monitor ensures that there is always a constant number of bits circulating in the ring, irrespective of the number of DTEs making up the ring. The complete ring is arranged to contain a fixed number of **slots**, each made up of a set number of bits and capable of carrying a single, fixed-size frame of information. The format of a frame slot is shown in Figure 6.7(a).

Initially, all the slots are marked empty when the monitor sets the full/empty bit at the head of each slot to the empty state. When a DTE wishes to transmit a frame, it waits until an empty slot is detected. The DTE then marks the slot as full

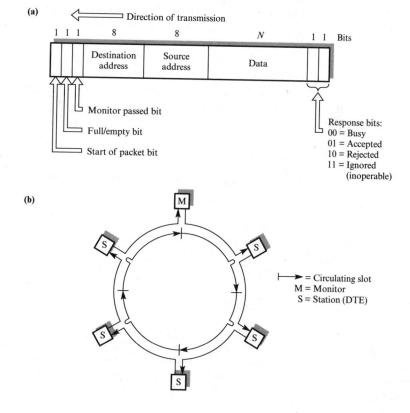

Figure 6.7
Slotted ring principles: (a) bit definitions of each slot; (b) outline topology.

and proceeds to insert the frame contents into the slot with both the required destination DTE address and the source DTE address at the head of the frame and both the response bits at the tail of the frame are set to 1. The slot containing this frame then circulates around the physical ring from one DTE to another. Each DTE in the ring examines the destination address at the head of any slot marked full and, if it detects its own address and assuming it is willing to accept the frame, reads the frame contents from the slot while at the same time repeating the unmodified frame contents around the ring. After reading the frame contents, the destination DTE modifies the pair of response bits at the tail of the slot to indicate that it has read the frame contents or, alternatively, if the addressed DTE is either busy or inoperable, the response bits are marked accordingly or left unchanged (inoperable).

The source DTE, after initiating the transmission of a frame, waits until the frame has circulated the ring by counting the (fixed number) of slots that are repeated at the ring interface. On receipt of the first bit of the slot used to transmit the frame, it marks the slot as empty once again and waits to read the response bits from the tail of the slot to determine what action to take next.

The monitor-passed bit is used by the monitor to detect whether a DTE fails to release a slot after it has transmitted a frame. This bit is reset by the source DTE as it transmits a frame on to the ring. The monitor subsequently sets the bit in each full slot as it is repeated at its ring interface. If the monitor detects that the monitor-passed bit is set when it repeats a full slot, it assumes that the source DTE has failed to mark the slot as empty and hence resets the full/empty bit at the head of the slot.

Note that with a slotted ring medium access method each DTE can have only a single frame in transit on the ring at a time. Also, it must release the slot used for transmitting a frame before trying to send another frame. In this way, access to the ring is fair and shared among the various interconnected DTEs. The main disadvantages of a slotted ring are as follows:

(1)   A special (and hence vulnerable) monitor node is required to maintain the basic ring structure.

(2)   The transmission of each complete link-level frame normally requires multiple slots.

Of course, with a token ring once a DTE receives the control token it may transmit a complete frame containing multiple bytes of information as a single unit.

6.1.4   Standards

As LANs evolved in the late 1970s and early 1980s, a wide range of different network types were proposed and implemented. However, because of small differences between them, such networks could be used to interconnect only computers or workstations provided by the supplier of the LAN. Such networks are known as **closed systems**.

To alleviate this situation, some major initiatives were launched by various national standards bodies with the aim of formulating an agreed set of standards for LANs. The major contributor to this activity was the IEEE which formulated the IEEE 802 series of standards, which have now been adopted by the ISO as international standards. As we have seen, there is not just a single type of wired LAN. Rather, there is a range of different types, each with its own topology, MAC method, and intended application domain. We shall now look at some of the different types of wired LAN in the standards documents; the protocols associated with them are presented in Section 6.5.

6.2 Wired LAN types

The two dominant types of wired LAN that have been developed for inter-connecting local communities of computer-based equipment are bus and ring. Currently, there are numerous varieties of both types, although many do not adhere to the international standards for LANs. The three types in the standards documents are CSMA/CD bus, token ring, and token bus. The descriptions that follow will be restricted to these three types.

6.2.1 CSMA/CD bus

CSMA/CD bus networks are used extensively in technical and office environments. For historical reasons, a CSMA/CD bus network is also known as **Ethernet**. Normally, it is implemented either as a 10 Mbps baseband coaxial cable network, or as a 10 Mbps twisted-pair cable network, although other cable media are supported in the standards documents. These include:

10 Base 2	Thin-wire (0.25 inch diameter) coaxial cable with a maximum segment length of 200 m
10 Base 5	Thick-wire (0.5 inch diameter) coaxial cable with a maximum segment length of 500 m
10 Base T	Hub (star) topology with twisted-pair drop cables
10 Base F	Hub (star) topology with optical fiber drop cables

Although different media are used, they all operate using the same MAC method. With thin- and thick-wire coax, the major difference is the location of the transceiver electronics. In the case of thick wire this is located with the cable tap, which is thus known as an **integrated tap and transceiver unit**. With thin wire the cable connects directly to the interface board in the DTE and hence the transceiver is located on the latter. Thin-wire coax networks are also known as **cheapernets** since they are less costly to install than thick-wire networks.

The various components associated with a thick-wire configuration are shown in Figure 6.8. A **tap** is used to make a nonintrusive – that is, the cable does not need to be cut – physical connection to the cable. This comprises a screw mechanism that pierces the outer protective shield of the cable and makes contact

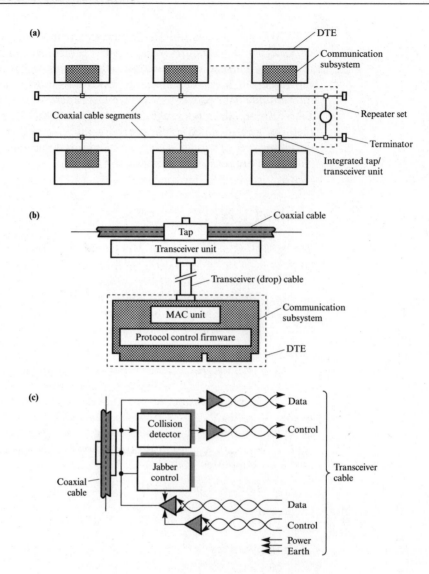

Figure 6.8
Thick-wire CSMA/CD
bus network
components:
(a) cable layout;
(b) DTE interface;
(c) transceiver
schematic.

with the center conductor. The outer part of the screw also makes contact with the
outer screen of the cable thus completing the electrical connection.

The transceiver contains the necessary electronics to do the following:

- Send and receive data to and from the cable

- Detect collisions on the cable medium

- Provide electrical isolation between the coaxial cable and cable interface
  electronics

- Protect the cable from any malfunctions in either the transceiver or the
  attached DTE

The last function is often referred to as **jabber control** since without the appropriate protection electronics, if a fault develops a faulty transceiver (or DTE) may continuously transmit random data (jabber) onto the cable medium and hence inhibit or corrupt all other transmissions. The jabber control isolates the transmit data path from the cable if certain defined time limits are violated. For example, all frames transmitted on the cable have a defined maximum length. If this is exceeded, the jabber control inhibits further output data from reaching the cable.

The transceiver unit is connected to its host DTE by a shielded cable containing five sets of twisted-pair wires: one for carrying power to the transceiver from the DTE, two for data (one send and one receive), and two for control purposes (one to allow the transceiver to signal a collision to the DTE and the other for the DTE to initiate the isolation of the transmit data path from the cable). The four signal pairs are differentially driven, which means that the host DTE may be up to 50 m from the transceiver and hence from the cable tapping point.

With twisted-pair cable and a hub configuration, as with thin-wire coax, the collision detection function is located on the interface board within the DTE. The function of the hub is purely to receive and retransmit (repeat) electrical signals reliably. A hub configuration and the repeater electronics function are shown in Figure 6.9.

As we can see, there are two twisted-pair (or optical fiber) wires connecting each DTE to the hub – a transmit pair and a receive pair. To enable the collision detection electronics to function at the DTE, the repeater electronics within the hub retransmit the signal received on an input pair on all the other output pairs. The major task of the repeater electronics is to ensure that the (strong) retransmitted signal being output on the outgoing pairs does not interfere with the received signal on the input pair which is relatively weak as a result of attenuation. This effect is known as near-end crosstalk (NEXT). Special integrated circuits known as **adaptive crosstalk cancellation circuits** are needed to ensure reliable operation at 10 Mbps with 100 m wire lengths.

Irrespective of the transmission media being used, the communications controller card within each DTE comprises the following:

- A medium access control (MAC) unit, which is responsible for such functions as the encapsulation and de-encapsulation of frames for transmission and reception on the cable, error detection, and implementation of the MAC algorithm.

- A **dual-port random access memory (RAM)** that allows the MAC unit to receive and transmit frames at the high link bit rate and the (host) computer to read/write the information content of frames.

The complete communication subsystem is normally self-contained on a single printed circuit card that slots into the host system bus and associated low-level routines provide a defined set of frame transmission and reception

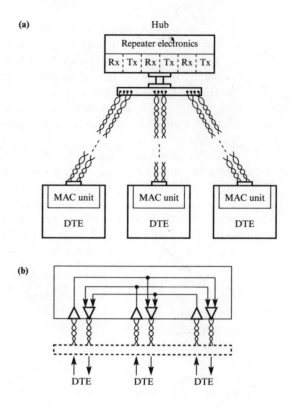

Figure 6.9
Hub configuration
principles:
(a) topology;
(b) repeater
schematic.

services to the host software. Most commercial cards provide multiple connectors to support the different types of transmission medium.

Frame format and operational parameters

The format of a frame and the operational parameters of a typical CSMA/CD bus network are shown in Figure 6.10. We shall describe the meaning and use of the various parameters as the operation of the MAC unit is presented.

Each frame transmitted on the cable has eight fields. All the fields are of fixed length except the data and associated padding fields.

The **preamble field** is sent at the head of all frames. Its function is to allow the receiving electronics in each MAC unit reliably to achieve bit synchronization before the actual frame contents are received. The preamble pattern is a sequence of seven octets, each equal to the binary pattern 10101010. All frames are transmitted on the cable using Manchester encoding. As we saw in Chapter 3, the preamble results in a periodic waveform being received by the receiver electronics in each DTE. The start-of-frame delimiter (SFD) is the single octet 10101011 which immediately follows the preamble and signals the start of a valid frame to the receiver.

(a)

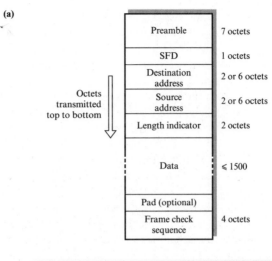

Octets
transmitted
top to bottom

(b)

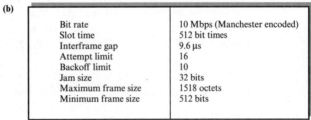

Bit rate	10 Mbps (Manchester encoded)
Slot time	512 bit times
Interframe gap	9.6 μs
Attempt limit	16
Backoff limit	10
Jam size	32 bits
Maximum frame size	1518 octets
Minimum frame size	512 bits

Figure 6.10
CSMA/CD bus
network
characteristics:
(a) frame format;
(b) operational
parameters.

The **destination** and **source network addresses** specify the identity of both the intended destination DTE(s) and the originating DTE, respectively. Each address field can be either 16 or 48 bits, but for any particular LAN installation the size must be the same for all DTEs. The first bit in the destination address field specifies whether the address is an **individual address** or a **group address**. If an individual address is specified, the transmitted frame is intended for a single destination DTE. If a group address is specified, the frame is intended either for a logically related group of DTEs (group address) or for all other DTEs connected to the network (**broadcast** or **global address**). In the latter case, the address field is set to all binary 1s.

The **length indicator** is a two-octet field which indicates the number of octets in the data field. If this value is less than the minimum number required for a valid frame (minimum frame size), a sequence of octets is added, known as **padding**. Finally, the FCS field contains a four-octet (32-bit) CRC value that is used for error detection.

Frame transmission

When a frame is to be transmitted, the frame contents are first encapsulated by the MAC unit into the format shown in Figure 6.10(a). To avoid contention with other transmissions on the medium, the MAC section of the MAC unit first monitors the carrier sense signal and, if necessary, defers to any passing frame. After a short additional delay (known as the **interframe gap**) to allow the passing frame to be received and processed by the addressed DTE(s), transmission of the frame is initiated.

As the bit stream is transmitted, the transceiver simultaneously monitors the received signal to detect whether a collision has occurred. Assuming a collision has not been detected, the complete frame is transmitted and, after the FCS field has been sent, the MAC unit awaits the arrival of a new frame, either from the cable or from the controlling microprocessor. If a collision is detected, the transceiver immediately turns on the collision detect signal. This, in turn, is detected by the MAC unit which enforces the collision by transmitting the jam sequence to ensure that the collision is detected by all other DTEs involved in the collision. After the jam sequence has been sent, the MAC unit terminates the transmission of the frame and schedules a retransmission attempt after a short randomly selected time interval.

In the event of a collision, retransmission of the frame is attempted up to a defined maximum number of tries known as the **attempt limit**. Since repeated collisions indicate a busy medium, the MAC unit tries to adjust to the medium load by progressively increasing the time delay between repeated retransmission attempts. The scheduling of retransmissions is controlled by a process called **truncated binary exponential backoff** which works as follows. When transmission of the jam sequence is complete, and assuming the attempt limit has not been reached, the MAC unit delays (backs off) a random integral number of slot times before attempting to retransmit the affected frame. As Figure 6.5 showed, a given DTE can experience a collision during the initial part of its transmission, the **collision window**, which is effectively twice the time interval for the first bit of the preamble to propagate to all parts of the cable medium (network). The slot time is thus the worst-case time delay a DTE must wait before it can reliably know a collision has occurred. It is defined as:

$$\text{Slot time} = 2 \times (\text{transmission path delay}) + \text{safety margin}$$

where **transmission path delay** is the worst-case signal propagation delay going from any transmitter to any receiver on the cable network. This includes any delays experienced in repeaters. The slot time is double this delay (to allow for the corrupted signal to propagate back to the transmitting DTE) plus a safety margin. The slot time used is made equal to this figure rounded up to be a multiple number of octets at the bit rate used. For example, for a 10 Mbps baseband coaxial cable network with a maximum of 2.5 km between any transmitter and any receiver, the slot time is equal to 512 bit times or 64 octets. The number of slot times before the Nth retransmission attempt is then chosen as a uniformly distributed random integer R in the range $0 \leqslant R < 2^K$, where $K = \min(N, \text{backoff limit})$. A flowchart summarizing the frame transmission sequence is shown in Figure 6.11(a).

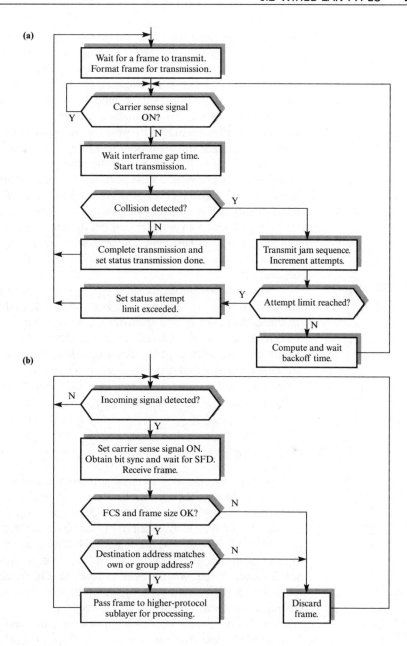

Figure 6.11
CSMA/CD MAC
sublayer operation:
(a) transmit;
(b) receive.

Frame reception

Figure 6.11(b) summarizes the frame reception process. At each active DTE connected to the cable, the MAC unit first detects the presence of an incoming signal from the transceiver and switches on the carrier sense signal to inhibit any new transmissions from this DTE. The incoming preamble is used to achieve bit synchronization and then the Manchester-encoded data stream is translated back into normal binary form. The incoming bit stream is then processed.

First, the remaining preamble bits are discarded together with the start-of-frame delimiter, when it is detected. The destination address field is processed to determine whether the frame should be received by this DTE. If so, the frame contents comprising the destination and source addresses and the data field are loaded into a frame buffer to await further processing. The received FCS field is then compared with that computed by the MAC unit during reception of the frame and, if they are equal, the start address of the buffer containing the received frame is passed to the next higher protocol layer, in the form of a service primitive, for further processing. Other validation checks are also made on the frame before initiating further processing. These include checks to ensure that the frame contains an integral number of octets and that it is neither too short nor too long. If any of these checks fail, the frame is discarded and an error status is sent to the higher sublayer. We shall look at the higher sublayer in more detail in Section 6.5.

Initially, the transmitted bit stream resulting from a collision is received by each active DTE in the same way as a valid frame. After the colliding DTEs have detected the collision and transmitted the jam sequence, they cease transmission. Fragments of frames received in this way violate the minimum frame size limit and hence are discarded by the receiving DTEs. Also, the adoption of a **maximum frame size** means that the length of the frame buffers used for transmission and reception can be quantified. The FCS field is a 32-bit sequence generated using CRC-32 which, as we saw in Chapter 3, has a generator polynomial of degree 32.

6.2.2   Token ring

Token ring networks are also used primarily in technical and office environments. Their principle of operation is illustrated in Figure 6.12. Whenever a DTE (station) wishes to send a frame, it first waits for the token. On receipt of the token, it initiates transmission of the frame, which includes the address of the intended recipient at its head. The frame is repeated (that is, each bit is received and then retransmitted) by all DTEs in the ring until it circulates back to the initiating DTE, where it is removed. In addition to repeating the frame, the intended recipient retains a copy of the frame and indicates that it has done this by setting the **response bits** at the tail of the frame.

A DTE releases the token in one of two ways depending on the bit rate (speed) of the ring. With slower rings (4 Mbps), the token is released only after the response bits have been received. With higher speed rings (16 Mbps), it is released after transmitting the last bit of a frame. This is known as **early (token) release**.

A typical token ring network is shown in Figure 6.13(a) and the various components needed to connect a DTE to the cable medium are illustrated in parts (b) and (c). The (trunk) cable medium is typically a screened twisted-pair which, since each segment around the ring forms a point-to-point link, is differentially driven at a bit rate of between 4 and 16 Mbps.

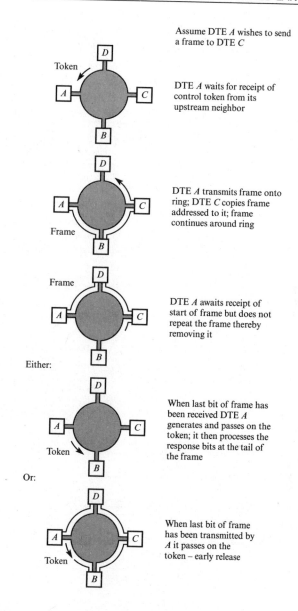

Figure 6.12
Token ring network:
principle of operation.

As Figure 6.13(b) shows, a DTE can be connected directly to the ring or through a **concentrator** (see Figure 6.13(a)). This device connects directly to the main trunk cable and provides direct drop connections to a number of DTEs. A concentrator is often used to simplify the wiring within a building. Typically, it is located at the point where the trunk cable enters (and leaves) an office. Direct drop connections are used to connect each DTE in the office to the concentrator. It is also known as a **wiring concentrator**; a typical installation may use many such devices.

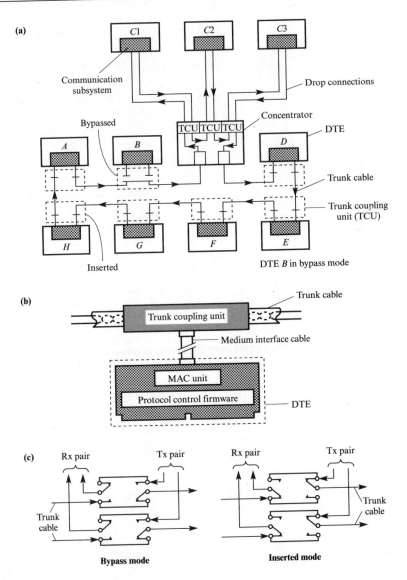

Figure 6.13
Token ring network components: (a) ring configuration; (b) DTE interface; (c) TCU schematic.

Ring interface

The **trunk coupling unit (TCU)** forms the physical interface with the cable medium. It contains a set of relays and additional electronics to drive and receive signals to and from the cable. The relays are so arranged that whenever the DTE is switched off, the TCU is in the **bypass state** and a continuous transmission path through the TCU is maintained. The insertion of a DTE into the ring is controlled by the MAC unit on the communication controller card within the DTE. The MAC unit initiates the insertion of the DTE by activating both pairs of relays in the TCU. As we can see in Figure 6.13(c), when inserted, this arrangement causes all received signals to be routed through the MAC unit. The receive/transmit electronics in the MAC unit then either simply read and relay (repeat) the received signal to the transmit side, if this DTE is not the originator of the frame, or remove the received signal from the ring, if it initiated the transmission.

The use of two pairs of relays connected in this way means that the MAC unit can detect certain open-circuit and short-circuit faults in either the transmit or the receive pair of signal wires. Also, in the bypass state the MAC unit can conduct self-test functions, since any data output on the transmit pair is looped back on the receive pair. The DTE is connected to the TCU by a shielded cable containing two twisted-pair wires: one for transmission and the other for reception.

The MAC unit is responsible for such functions as frame encapsulation and de-encapsulation, FCS generation and error detection, and the implementation of the MAC algorithm. Also, it supplies the ring master clock which is used for data encoding and decoding when the DTE is the active ring monitor (see 'ring management' p. 304). Each circulating bit stream is differentially Manchester encoded by the active ring monitor and all other DTEs on the ring then frequency and phase lock to this bit stream using a DPLL circuit. In addition, when the DTE is the active ring monitor, it ensures the ring has a **minimum latency time**. This is the time, measured in bit times at the ring data transmission rate, taken for a signal to propagate once around the ring. The ring latency time includes the signal propagation delay through the ring transmission medium together with the sum of the propagation delays through each MAC unit. For the control token to circulate continuously around the ring when none of the DTEs requires to use the ring (that is, all DTEs are simply in the repeat mode), the ring must have a minimum latency time of at least the number of bits in the token sequence to ensure that the token is not corrupted.

The token is 24 bits long, so when a DTE is the active ring monitor, its MAC unit provides a fixed 24-bit buffer, which effectively becomes part of the ring to ensure its correct operation under all conditions. Although the mean data signaling rate around the ring is controlled by a single master clock in the active monitor, the use of a separate DPLL circuit in each MAC unit means that the actual signaling rate may vary slightly around the ring. The worst-case variation is when the maximum number of DTEs (250) are all active, which is equivalent to plus or minus three bits. Unless the latency of the ring remains constant, however, bits will be corrupted as the latency decreases, or additional bits will be added as the latency increases. To maintain a constant ring latency, an additional **elastic (variable) buffer** with a length of 6 bits is added to the fixed 24-bit buffer. The resulting 30-bit buffer is initialized to 27 bits. If the received signal at the master MAC unit is faster than the master oscillator, the buffer is expanded by a single bit. Alternatively, if the received signal is slower, the buffer is reduced by a single bit. In this way the ring always comprises sufficient bits to allow the token to circulate continuously around the ring in the quiescent (idle) state.

Frame formats

Two basic formats are used in token rings: one for the control token and the other for normal frames. The control token is the means by which the right to transmit (as opposed to the normal process of repeating) is passed from one DTE to another, whereas a normal frame is used by a DTE to send either data or MAC information around the ring. The format of the two types of frame is given in Figure 6.14 together with the bit sequence used for each field.

The start delimiter (SD) and end delimiter (ED) fields are special bit sequences used to achieve data transparency. They exploit the symbol encoding method used on the cable medium: all information bits transmitted on the medium are Manchester encoded, except for selected bits in the SD and ED fields. In contrast, the J and K symbols depart from the normal encoding rules, being used instead to represent constant levels for the complete bit cell period. The J symbol has the same polarity as the preceding symbol, whereas a K symbol has the opposite polarity to the preceding symbol. In this way the receiver can reliably detect the start and end of each transmitted token or frame irrespective of its contents or length. Note, however, that only the first six symbols (JK1JK1 in Figure 6.14(c)) are used to indicate a valid end of frame. The other two bits, I and E, have other functions:

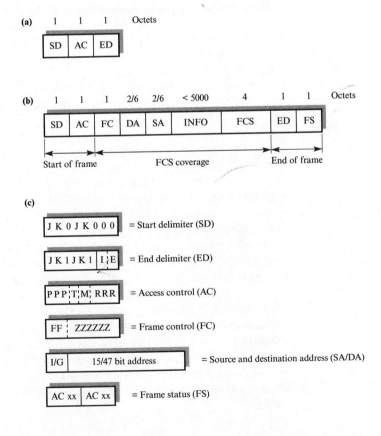

Figure 6.14
Token ring network
frame formats and
field descriptions:
(a) token format;
(b) frame format;
(c) field descriptions.

- In a token, both the I and E bits are 0.

- In a normal frame, the I bit is used to indicate whether the frame is the first (or an intermediate) frame in a sequence (I = 1) or the last (or only) frame (I = 0).

- The E bit is used for error detection. It is set to 0 by the originating DTE but, if any DTE detects an error while receiving or repeating the frame (for example, FCS error), it sets the E bit to 1 to signal to the originating DTE that an error has been detected.

The access control (AC) field comprises the priority bits, the token and monitor bits, and the reservation bits. As its name implies, the AC field is used to control access to the ring. When it is part of the token, the priority bits (P) indicate the priority of the token and hence which frames a DTE may transmit on receipt of the token. The token bit (T) discriminates between a token and an ordinary frame (0 indicates a token, 1 a frame). The monitor bit (M) is used by the active monitor to prevent a frame from circulating around the ring continuously. Finally, the reservation bits (R) allow DTEs holding high-priority frames to request (in either repeated frames or tokens) that the next token to be issued is of the requisite priority.

The frame control (FC) field defines the type of the frame (MAC or information) and certain control functions. If the frame type bits (F) indicate a MAC frame, all DTEs on the ring interpret and, if necessary, act on the control bits (Z). If it is an I-frame, the control bits are interpreted only by the DTEs identified in the destination address field.

The source address (SA) and destination address (DA) fields can be either 16 bits or 48 bits long, but for any specific LAN they are the same for all DTEs. The DA field identifies the DTE(s) for which the frame is intended. The first bit of the field indicates whether the address is an individual address (0) or a group address (1); individual addresses identify a specific DTE on the ring while group addresses are used to send a frame to multiple destination DTEs. The SA is always an individual address and identifies the DTE originating the frame. In addition, a DA consisting of all 1s is a broadcast address denoting that the frame is intended for all DTEs on the ring.

The information (INFO) field is used to carry either user data or additional control information when included in a MAC frame. Although no maximum length is specified for the information field, it is limited in practice by the maximum time for which a DTE is allowed to transmit a frame when holding the control token. A typical maximum length is 5000 octets.

The frame check sequence (FCS) field is a 32-bit CRC. Finally, the frame status (FS) field is made up of two fields: the address-recognized bits (A) and the frame-copied bits (C). Both the A and C bits are set to 0 by the DTE originating the frame. If the frame is recognized by one or more DTEs on the ring, the DTE(s) sets the A bits to 1. Also, if it copies the frame, it sets the C bits to 1. In this way, the originating DTE can determine whether the addressed DTE(s) is non-existent or switched off, is active but did not copy the frame, or is active and copied the frame.

Frame transmission

On receipt of a service request to transmit a data message (which includes the priority of the data as a parameter), the data is first encapsulated by the MAC unit into the standard format shown in Figure 6.14. The MAC unit awaits the reception of a token with a priority less than or equal to the priority of the assembled frame. Clearly, in a system that employs multiple priorities, a procedure must be followed to ensure that all DTEs have an opportunity to transmit frames in the correct order of priority. This procedure works as follows.

After formatting a frame and prior to receiving an appropriate token (that is, one with a priority less than or equal to the priority of the waiting frame), each time a frame or a token with a higher priority is repeated at the ring interface, the MAC unit reads the value of the reservation bits contained within the AC field. If these are equal to or higher than the priority of the waiting frame, the reservation bits are simply repeated unchanged. If it is lower, the MAC unit replaces the current value with the priority of the waiting frame. Then, assuming there are no other higher priority frames awaiting transmission on the ring, the token is passed on by the current owner (user) with this priority. On receipt of the token, the waiting MAC unit detects that the priority of the token is equal to the priority of the frame it has waiting to be transmitted. It therefore accepts the token by changing the token bit in the AC field to 1, prior to repeating this bit, which effectively converts the token to a start-of-frame sequence for a normal frame. The MAC unit then stops repeating the incoming signal and follows the converted start-of-frame sequence with the preformatted frame contents. While the frame contents are being transmitted, the FCS is computed and subsequently appended after the frame contents, before transmitting the end-of-frame sequence.

Once transmission of the waiting frame(s) has been started, the MAC unit stops repeating, thus removing the transmitted frame(s) after it has circulated the ring. In addition, the MAC unit notes the state of the A and C bits in the FS field at the tail of the frame(s) to determine whether the frame(s) has (have) been copied or ignored. It then generates a new token and forwards this on the ring to allow another waiting DTE to gain access to the ring. More than one frame may be sent providing, firstly, that the priority of the other waiting frame(s) is greater than or equal to the priority of the token and, secondly, that the total time taken to transmit the other frame(s) is within a defined limit known as the token holding time. The default setting for the latter is 10 ms. Flowcharts showing the frame transmission and reception operation are given in Figure 6.15.

Frame reception

In addition to repeating the incoming signal (bit) stream, the MAC unit within each active DTE on the ring detects the start of each frame by recognizing the special start-of-frame bit sequence. It then determines whether the frame should

(a)

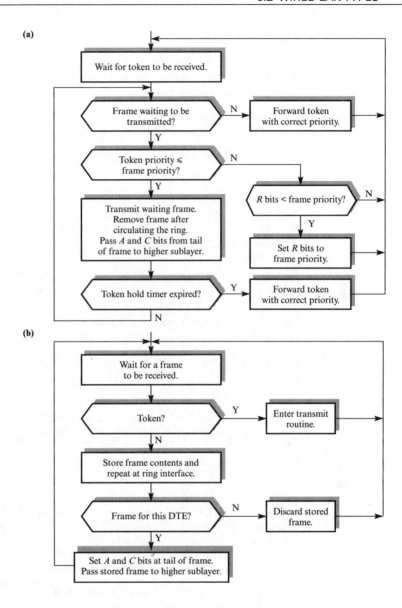

(b)

Figure 6.15
Token ring MAC
sublayer operation:
(a) transmit;
(b) receive.

simply be repeated or copied. If the F bits indicate that it is a MAC frame (see 'Ring management' on p. 304), the frame is copied and the C bits are interpreted and, if necessary, acted upon. However, if the frame is a normal data-carrying frame and the DA matches either the DTE's individual address or relevant group address, the frame contents are copied into a frame buffer and passed on for further processing. In either case, the A and C bits in the frame status field at the tail of the frame are set accordingly prior to being repeated. A flowchart showing the reception operation is given in Figure 6.15(b).

Priority operation

The priority assigned to a token by a MAC unit after it has completed transmitting any waiting frame(s) is determined by a mechanism that endeavors to ensure both of the following:

(1)   Frames with a higher priority than the current ring service priority are always transmitted on the ring first.

(2)   All DTEs holding frames with the same priority have equal access rights to the ring.

This is accomplished by using both the P and the R bits in the AC field of each frame coupled with a mechanism that ensures that a DTE that raises the service priority level of the ring returns the ring to its original level after the higher priority frames have been transmitted.

To implement this scheme, each MAC unit maintains two sets of values. The first set comprises three variables Pm, Pr and Rr. Pm specifies the highest priority value contained within any of the frames currently awaiting transmission at the DTE. Pr and Rr are known as **priority registers** and contain, respectively, the priority and reservation values held within the AC field of the most recently repeated token or frame. The second set of values comprises two stacks known as the Sr and Sx stacks which are used as follows.

All frames transmitted by a DTE, on receiving a usable token, are assigned a priority value in the AC field equal to the present ring service priority Pr, and a reservation value of zero. After all waiting frames at or greater than the current ring priority have been transmitted, or until the transmission of another frame cannot be completed before the token holding time expires, the MAC unit generates a new token with:

(1)   P = Pr   and   R = the greater of Rr and Pm

if the DTE does not have any more waiting frames with a priority (as contained in register Pm) equal to or greater than the current ring service priority (as contained in register Pr), or does not have a reservation request (as contained in register Rr) greater than the current priority.

(2)   P = the greater of Rr and Pm and R = 0

if the DTE has another waiting frame(s) with a priority (as contained in Pm) greater than the current priority Pr, or if the current contents of Rr are greater than the current priority.

Since in the latter case the DTE effectively raises the service priority level of the ring, it becomes what is known as a **stacking station** (DTE) and, as such, stores the value of the old ring service priority (Pr) on stack Sr and the new ring service priority (P) on stack Sx. These values are saved, as it is the responsibility of the DTE that becomes the stacking station to lower the ring service priority level when there are no frames ready to transmit, at any point on the ring, with a priority equal to or greater than the P stacked on Sx. Also, a stack is used rather than a single register because a stacking station may need to raise the service

(a)

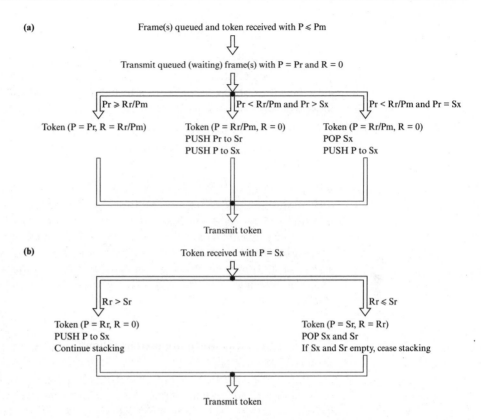

Frame(s) queued and token received with $P \leqslant Pm$

⇩

Transmit queued (waiting) frame(s) with $P = Pr$ and $R = 0$

⇩

| $Pr \geqslant Rr/Pm$ | $Pr < Rr/Pm$ and $Pr > Sx$ | $Pr < Rr/Pm$ and $Pr = Sx$ |

Token ($P = Pr$, $R = Rr/Pm$)

Token ($P = Rr/Pm$, $R = 0$)
PUSH Pr to Sr
PUSH P to Sx

Token ($P = Rr/Pm$, $R = 0$)
POP Sx
PUSH P to Sx

⇩

Transmit token

(b)

Token received with $P = Sx$

⇩

| $Rr > Sr$ | $Rr \leqslant Sr$ |

Token ($P = Rr$, $R = 0$)
PUSH P to Sx
Continue stacking

Token ($P = Sr$, $R = Rr$)
POP Sx and Sr
If Sx and Sr empty, cease stacking

⇩

Transmit token

Figure 6.16
Token generation and stack modifications: (a) token generation [*Note:* Sx = 0 if stack empty]; (b) stack modification.

priority of the ring more than once before the service priority is returned to a lower priority level. The different values assigned to the P and R bits of the token and the actions performed on the two stacks are summarized in Figure 6.16(a).

Having become a stacking station, the MAC unit claims every token that it receives with a priority equal to that stacked on Sx. The MAC unit examines the value in the R bits of the AC field to determine if the service priority of the ring should be raised, maintained, or lowered. The new token is then transmitted with:

(1) $P = Rr$ and $R = 0$

if the value contained in the R bits (the current contents of register Rr) is greater than Sr. The new ring service priority (P) is stacked (PUSHed) onto Sx and the DTE continues its role as a stacking station.

(2) $P = Sr$ and $R = Rr$ (unchanged)

if the value contained in the R bits is less than or equal to Sr. Both values currently on the top of stacks Sx and Sr are POPped from the stack and, if both stacks are then empty, the DTE discontinues its role as a stacking station. These two operations are summarized in Figure 6.16(b).

Example 6.1

A token ring network has been configured to operate with four priority classes: 0, 2, 4, and 8, with 8 the highest priority. After a period of inactivity when no transmissions occur on successive rotations of the token, four stations generate frames to send as follows:

Station1	1 frame of priority 2
Station7	1 frame of priority 2
Station15	1 frame of priority 4
Station17	1 frame of priority 4

Assuming the order of stations on the ring is in increasing numerical order and that Station1 receives the token first with a zero priority and reservation field, derive and show in table form the transmissions made by each station for the next eight rotations of the token. Include in your table the values in the priority and reservation fields both as each new token is generated and as each frame circulates around the ring. Also include the actions taken by the stacking station.

The transmissions made by each station for the next eight rotations of the token are shown in Table 6.1.

On the first rotation of the token, Station1 seizes the token and initiates the transmission of its waiting frame. Also on this rotation the reservation field in the frame is raised first by Station7 to 2 and then by Station15 to 4.

On the second rotation, Station1 reads the reservation field from the frame and determines it must release the token with a priority of 4. Since it is raising the ring priority, it must become a stacking station. The token then rotates and is seized by Station15. Also on this rotation Station17 raises the reservation field from 0 to 4.

On the third rotation, Station15 releases the token with a priority and reservation field of 4. Station17 therefore seizes the token and initiates the transmission of its waiting frame.

On the fourth rotation, Station7 updates the reservation field from 0 to 2 and this causes the token to be released by Station17 with the same priority but a reservation value of 2.

On the fifth rotation, since Station1 is a stacking station, it detects Rr is greater than Sr and hence lowers the priority of the token/ring from 4 to 2 and saves the lower priority on the stack. Station7 is therefore able to transmit its waiting frame.

On the sixth rotation, Station7 releases the token with the same priority since no reservations have been made.

On the seventh rotation, Station1 detects the reservation field in the token is less than the priority field and hence reduces the priority to 0 and thereby ceases to be a stacking station. The token has thus returned to its initial state and continues rotating until further frames are generated.

Table 6.1 Token ring priority mechanism example.

Rotation	Station1 Pm = 2 F/T (P,R)	Station7 Pm = 2 F/T (P,R)	Station15 Pm = 4 F/T (P,R)	Station17 Pm = 4 F/T (P,R)
0	T(0,0) ⟶	T(0,0) ⟶	T(0,0) ⟶	T(0,0) ⟶
1	⟶ T(0,0) Pr = 0, Rr = 0, Pm = 2 Pm > Pr F(0,0) P = Pr = 0; Rr = 0	F(0,0) Pr = 0, Rr = 0, Pm = 2 Pm > Rr F(0,2) P = Pr = 0; R = Pm = 2	F(0,2) Pr = 0, Rr = 2, Pm = 4 Pm > Pr F(0,4) P = Pr = 0; R = Pm = 4	F(0,4) Pr = 0, Rr = 4, Pm = 4 Pm = Rr F(0,4) ⟶ P = Pr = 0; R = Rr = 4
2	F(0,4) Pr = 0, Rr = 4 Rr > Pr T(4,0) P = Rr = 4; R = 0 - - - - - - - - - - - - - - - - Stacking Sr = 0, Sx = 4	T(4,0) Pr = 4, Rr = 0, Pm = 2 Pr > Pm > Rr T(4,2) P = Pr; R = Pm = 2	T(4,2) Pr = 4, Rr = 2, Pm = 4 Pm = Pr F(4,0) P = Pr = 4; R = 0	F(4,0) Pr = 4, Rr = 0, Pm = 4 Pm > Rr F(4,4) ⟶ P = Pr; R = Pm = 4
3	F(4,4) no frame to transmit F(4,4) - - - - - - - - - - - - - - - - Sr = 0, Sx = 4	F(4,4) Pr = 4, Rr = 4, Pm = 2 Pm < Rr F(4,4) P = Pr; R = Rr	F(4,4) Pr = 4, Rr = 4 Rr = Pr T(4,4) P = Pr = 4; R = Rr = 4	T(4,4) Pr = 4, Rr = 4, Pm = 4 Pm = Pr F(4,0) ⟶ P = Pr; R = 0
4	F(4,0) no frame to transmit F(4,0) - - - - - - - - - - - - - - - - Sr = 0, Sx = 4	F(4,0) Pr = 4, Rr = 0, Pm = 2 Pm > Rr F(4,2) P = Pr; R = Pm	F(4,2) no frame to transmit F(4,2)	F(4,2) Pr = 4, Rr = 2 Rr < Pr T(4,2) ⟶ P = Pr; R = Rr
5	T(4,2) Pr = 4, Rr = 2, Sr = 0, Sx = 4 Pr = Sx, Rr > Sr T(2,0) P = Pr = 2; R = 0 - - - - - - - - - - - - - - - - Sr = 0, Sx = 2	T(2,0) Pr = 2, Rr = 0, Pm = 2 Pm = Pr F(2,0) P = Pr; R = Rr	F(2,0) no frame to transmit F(2,0)	F(2,0) no frame to transmit F(2,0) ⟶
6	F(2,0) no frame to transmit F(2,0) - - - - - - - - - - - - - - - - Sr = 0, Sx = 2	F(2,0) Pr = 2, Rr = 0 Rr < Pr T(2,0) P = Pr; R = Rr	T(2,0) no frame to transmit T(2,0)	T(2,0) no frame to transmit T(2,0) ⟶
7	T(2,0) Pr = 2, Rr = 0, Sr = 0, Sx = 2 Pr = Sx, Rr ⩽ Sr T(0,0) P = Sr; R = Rr - - - - - - - - - - - - - - - - Cease stacking	T(0,0) no frame to transmit T(0,0)	T(0,0) no frame to transmit T(0,0)	T(0,0) no frame to transmit T(0,0) ⟶
8	⟶ T(0,0) ⟶	T(0,0) ⟶	T(0,0) ⟶	T(0,0)

Ring management

We have been primarily concerned with the transmission of frames and tokens during normal operation of the ring. However, the ring must be set up before normal operation can take place. If a DTE wishes to join an already operational ring, that DTE must first go through an initialization procedure to ensure that it does not interfere with the correct functioning of the established ring. In addition, during normal operation it is necessary for each active DTE on the ring to monitor continuously its correct operation and, if a fault develops, to take corrective action to try to re-establish a correctly functioning ring. Collectively, these functions are known as **ring management**. A list of the various MAC frame types associated with these functions is given in Figure 6.17.

Initialization.   When a DTE wishes to become part of the ring after being either switched on or reset, it enters an initialization sequence to ensure that no other DTEs in the ring are using the same address and to inform its immediate downstream neighbor that it has (re)entered the ring.

The initialization procedure starts with the transmission of a duplicate address test (DAT) MAC frame by the DTE with the A bits in the FS field set to 0. On receipt of a DAT frame, each active DTE in the ring inspects the DA field and, if it determines that the DA field is the same as its own address, sets the A bits to 1. Hence, if the DAT frame returns to its originator with the A bits set to 1, the originator informs the network management sublayer and returns to the bypass state. The network management sublayer (as we shall see in Section 14.4.3) then determines whether it should try again to become part of the ring. Alternatively, if the A bits are still set to 0 when the DAT frame returns to its originator, the DTE continues the initialization sequence by transmitting a standby monitor present (SMP) MAC frame.

A DTE that receives an SMP frame with the A and C bits set to 0 regards the frame as having originated from its immediate upstream neighbor and hence records the SA as the upstream neighbor's address (UNA). The UNA is required for fault detection and monitoring functions. The initialization phase is then complete.

Figure 6.17
Token ring management of MAC frame types.

Frame type	Function
Duplicate address test (DAT)	Used during the intialization procedure to enable a station to determine that no other stations in the ring are using its own address
Standby monitor present (SMP)	Used in the initialization procedure to enable a station to determine the address of its upstream neighbor (successor) in the ring
Active monitor present (AMP)	These types of frames are transmitted at regular intervals by the currently active monitor and each station monitors their passage
Claim token (CT)	Used in the procedure to determine a new active monitor if the current one fails
Purge (PRG)	Used by a new active monitor to initialize all stations into the idle state
Beacon (BCN)	Used in the beaconing procedure

Standby monitor.   Upon completion of the initialization sequence, the DTE can start to transmit and receive normal frames and tokens. In addition, the DTE enters the standby monitor state to monitor continuously the correct operation of the ring. It does this by monitoring the passage of tokens and special active monitor present (AMP) MAC frames, which are periodically transmitted by the currently active monitor, as they are repeated at the ring interface. If tokens or AMP frames are not detected periodically, the standby monitor times out (it maintains two timers for this function) and enters the claim token state.

In the claim token state, the DTE continuously transmits claim token (CT) MAC frames and inspects the SA in any CT frames it receives. Each CT frame transmitted contains, in addition to the SA of the originating DTE, the latter's stored UNA. If a CT frame is received with an SA that matches its own address and a UNA that matches its own stored UNA, this means that the CT frame has successfully circulated around the ring. Consequently the DTE becomes the new active ring monitor. Alternatively, if a CT frame is received with an SA greater than its own address, this means that another DTE has made an earlier bid to become the new monitor. In this case the DTE effectively relinquishes its bid by returning to the standby monitor state.

Active monitor.   If the DTE is successful in its bid to become the new active monitor, it first inserts its latency buffer into the ring and enables its own clock. (Note that there is only one active monitor in the ring at any time.) It then initiates the transmission of a purge (PRG) MAC frame to ensure that there are no other tokens or frames on the ring before it initiates the transmission of a new token. When the DTE receives a PRG frame containing an SA equal to its own address, this indicates that the ring has been successfully purged. The DTE initiates the neighbor notification process by broadcasting an AMP MAC frame. After a short delay, this is followed by the transmission of a new control token.

The DTE immediately downstream of the active monitor detects that the A bits in the AMP frame are 0 and hence reads the UNA from within the frame and updates its existing UNA variable. It sets the A and C bits to 1 and repeats the frame. Subsequent DTEs around the ring detect that the A bits are nonzero and just record the passage of the AMP frame by resetting the AMP timer.

In addition, the DTE immediately downstream from the active monitor, after repeating the AMP frame, continues the neighbor notification process by broadcasting a similar SMP frame. In turn the next DTE downstream detects that the A bits are set to 0 in this frame, updates its UNA variable, sets the A and C bits to 1, and repeats the frame. It continues the process by broadcasting a new SMP frame with the A bits again set to 0. This procedure is carried out by each DTE around the ring and is subsequently reinitiated by the active monitor which transmits a new AMP frame at regular intervals. In this way, each active DTE in the ring can detect such failures as a DTE jabbering (for example, continuously sending tokens): the absence of AMP frames flowing around the ring means that the AMP timer in all the other DTEs will expire, thus initiating the transmission of CT frames followed, if the fault is still present, by all DTEs entering a failure diagnostic procedure known as beaconing.

Beaconing. If a serious failure such as a broken cable arises in the ring, a procedure known as **beaconing** informs each DTE on the ring that the token-passing protocol has been suspended (until the affected failure domain has been located and repaired). The failure domain consists of the following:

- The DTE that reports the failure, which is referred to as the **beaconing station**

- The DTE upstream of the beaconing station

- The ring medium between them

Figure 6.18
Ring fault detection
and isolation:
(a) failure detection;
(b) redundant ring
configuration;
(c) segment isolation;
(d) DTE (station)
isolation.

As an example, Figure 6.18(a) illustrates a failure domain assuming a break has occurred in the ring medium between DTEs *F* and *G*. In this example, *G* is the beaconing station and *F* its upstream neighbor. Normally, the beaconing state is entered if the timers associated with the AMP or token-passing procedures expire. When in this state, beacon (BCN) supervisory frames are continuously transmitted until either a beacon frame is received or a timer expires. If the latter occurs, the network management sublayer is notified and transmissions cease. Alternatively, if a beacon frame is received by a DTE with an SA equal to its own address, the failure is assumed to have cleared and the DTE enters the claim token state or, if a beacon frame is received with an SA different from the DTE address, the DTE enters the standby monitor state.

If the network comprises just a single ring, in the event of a failure the faulty segment must be repaired before network transmissions can be resumed. An optional feature with the token ring is to utilize a second, redundant ring

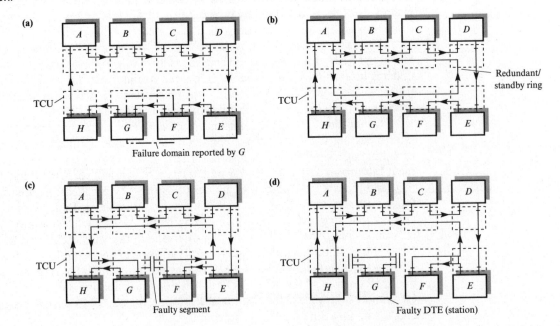

transmitting in the opposite direction to the first ring. This network configuration is shown in Figure 6.18(b).

In such networks the TCU not only supports the functions outlined earlier, but also can be used to bypass a faulty ring segment or DTE. As an example, Figure 6.18(c) shows how the faulty ring segment (failure domain) illustrated in Figure 6.18(a) is bypassed. Essentially, once the failure domain has been located and reported, the relays in the TCU of *F* and *G* are activated to (hopefully) re-establish a continuous ring. If isolating the suspected faulty segment does not remove the fault, the next step is to initiate the isolation of DTE *G* completely, as shown in Figure 6.18(d). Note from these figures that the redundant ring does not have a direct path to the MAC unit and simply provides a means of bypassing a section of the ring. The order of the DTEs on a re-established ring is the same as that in the original ring.

We can see that the MAC procedures used with a token ring network are quite complicated, certainly compared with a CSMA/CD bus, for example. Remember, however, that most of the procedures are implemented in special controller integrated circuits within the MAC unit, so their operation is transparent to the user. Moreover, many of these ring management procedures are invoked only when faults develop and so the overheads associated with them are, on the whole, modest.

6.2.3   Token bus

The third type of LAN supported in the standards documents is the **token bus** network. Because of the deterministic nature of a token MAC method and the ability to prioritize the transmission of frames, token bus networks are used in the manufacturing industry (for factory automation) and other related domains, such as the process control industry. Under normal (error-free) conditions, the operation of this type of network is similar to that of the token ring network. However, because of differences in the two medium access methods (broadcast for bus, sequential for ring), the procedures used for handling management of the logical ring, such as initialization and lost token, are inevitably different. To avoid repetition, we shall concentrate mainly on the management procedures associated with token bus networks.

Various aspects of the operation and components associated with token bus networks are shown in Figure 6.19. Token bus networks normally use coaxial cable as the transmission medium and operate in either a broadband mode or a modified baseband mode known as **carrierband**. The modulation and interface control circuitry, as illustrated in Figure 6.19(a), performs the following functions:

- Transmit data encoding (modulation)

- Receive data decoding (demodulation)

- Clock generation

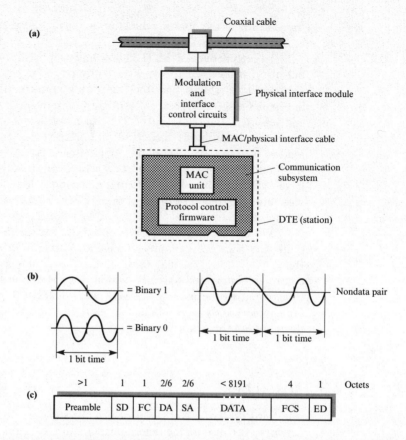

Figure 6.19
Token bus network principles: (a) DTE interface schematic; (b) carrierband encoding; (c) frame format.

There is a standard interface between the physical interface module (PIM) and the attached DTE. In some cases, the PIM is integrated onto the communication board in the DTE.

The principle of operation of the carrierband mode is shown in Figure 6.19(b). Although the carrierband mode is the same as baseband in that each transmission occupies the complete cable bandwidth, in carrierband mode all data is first modulated before transmission using phase-coherent FSK. As we can see, a binary 1 is transmitted as a single cycle of a sinusoidal signal of frequency equal to the bit rate, normally between 1 and 5 Mbps, while a binary 0 is transmitted as two cycles of a signal of twice the bit rate frequency. Notice also that there is no change of phase at the bit cell boundaries, hence the term 'phase coherent'.

Recall from Chapter 2 that any extraneous noise signals picked up in the cable consist of an infinite number of frequency components. A basic baseband signal (waveform) is also made up of a possibly infinite number of frequency components. In contrast, a carrierband waveform has only two frequency components. Therefore it is possible to use a filter at the receiver which passes only these two frequencies, effectively blocking most of the noise signal and significantly improving the noise immunity of the system. This cannot be done with baseband since the filter would also affect the data signal.

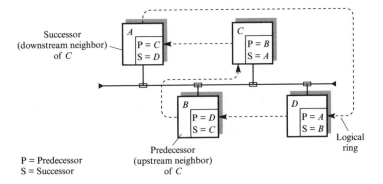

Figure 6.20
Token bus network
principle of operation.

P = Predecessor
S = Successor

Successor
(downstream neighbor)
of C

Predecessor
(upstream neighbor)
of C

Logical
ring

The frame format used with token bus networks is shown in Figure 6.19(c). It is almost identical to that used with a token ring network. However, the J and K nondata bits, which are used in the SD and ED fields of a token ring to achieve data transparency, are replaced in carrierband mode by pairs of special nondata symbols.

Basic operation

Figure 6.20 illustrates the basic operation of a token bus network. There is a single control token and only the possessor of the token can transmit a frame. All DTEs that can initiate the transmission of a frame are linked in the form of a **logical ring**. The token is passed physically using the bus around the logical ring. Thus, on receipt of the token from its *predecessor* (upstream neighbor) on the ring, a DTE may transmit any waiting frames up to a defined maximum. It then passes the token on to its known *successor* (downstream neighbor) on the ring.

Before we describe the various ring management procedures, let us restate two basic properties of bus networks. Firstly, with a bus network all DTEs are connected directly to the transmission medium. Hence, when a DTE transmits (broadcasts) a frame on the medium, it is received (or heard) by all active DTEs in the network. Secondly, there is a maximum time a DTE need wait for a response to a transmitted frame before it can assume that either the transmitted frame is corrupted or the specified destination DTE is inoperable. This time is known as the slot time (not the same as that used with a CSMA/CD bus) and can be defined as follows:

Slot time $= 2 \times$ (transmission path delay) $+$ processing delay

where transmission path delay is the worst-case transmission propagation delay going from any transmitter to any receiver in the network, and processing delay is the maximum time for the MAC unit within a DTE to process a received frame and generate an appropriate response. A safety margin is then added and the slot time value is expressed in bit times rounded up to a multiple number of octets.

Under normal operation, the token is passed from one DTE in the logical ring to another using a short token frame. Therefore each DTE need only know

Frame type	Function
Claim token	Used during the initialization sequence of the (logical) ring
Solicit successor	Used during both the recovery procedure when a station leaves the ring and the procedure that allows a station to (re)enter the ring
Who follows me	Used during the procedure that enables a station to determine the address of the station that is its successor in the ring
Resolve contention	Used during the procedure that allows a new station to enter the ring
Set successor	Allows a new station entering the ring to inform its new predecessor that it has joined the ring
Token	The control token frame

Figure 6.21
Token bus ring management of MAC frame types.

the address of the next (downstream neighbor or successor) DTE in the logical ring. If a DTE fails to accept the token, the sending DTE uses a series of recovery procedures to find a new successor; these procedures get progressively more drastic if the DTE fails to evoke a response from a neighboring DTE. Other procedures are concerned with the initialization of the ring and maintaining the correct operation of the ring as DTEs enter and leave the ring. Although it is possible to prioritize the token, as with a token ring, we shall consider only a single priority ring initially. The MAC frame types used with the various ring management procedures, together with a brief explanation of their use, are shown in Figure 6.21. We shall give more detailed explanations as the various procedures are discussed.

Token passing

On receipt of a valid token frame, a DTE may transmit any frames it has waiting. It then passes the token to its known successor. After sending the token, the DTE listens to any subsequent activity on the bus to make sure that its successor is active and has received the token. If it hears a valid frame being transmitted, it assumes that all is well and that its successor received the token correctly. If it does not hear a valid frame being transmitted after the slot time interval, it must take corrective action.

If, after sending the token, the DTE hears a noise burst or frame with an incorrect FCS, it continues to listen for up to four more slot times. If nothing more is heard, the DTE assumes that the token itself has become corrupted during transmission and it repeats the token transmission. Alternatively, if a valid frame is heard during the delay of four slot times, the DTE again assumes that its successor has the token. If a second noise burst is heard during this interval, the DTE treats this as a valid frame being transmitted by its successor and assumes that the token has been passed.

If, after repeating the token-passing operation and the monitoring procedures, the successor does not respond to the second token frame, the DTE assumes that its successor has failed and hence proceeds to establish a new successor. The sender first broadcasts a **who-follows-me frame** with its current successor's address in the data field of the frame. On receipt of this type of frame, each DTE compares the address in the data field of the frame with its own predecessor address, that is, the address of the DTE that normally sends it the token. The DTE whose predecessor is the same as the successor contained within the frame responds by sending its own address in a **set-successor frame**. The DTE holding the token has thus established a new successor and in so doing has bridged around the failed DTE.

If the sending DTE does not receive a response to a who-follows-me frame, it repeats the frame a second time. If there is still no response, it takes more drastic action by sending a **solicit-successor frame** with its own address in the DA field. This asks any DTE in the network to respond to it. If any operational DTEs hear the frame, they respond and the logical ring is re-established using a procedure known as **response window**. Alternatively, if no response is received, the DTE assumes that a catastrophe has occurred, for example, all other DTEs have failed, the medium has broken, or the DTE's own receiver section has failed (and hence cannot hear the response(s) from other DTEs to its own requests). Under these conditions, the DTE becomes silent but continues to listen for another DTE's transmissions.

Response window

This procedure is followed at random time intervals to allow new DTEs to enter an operational logical ring. The response window is the interval for which a DTE needs to wait for a response after transmitting a frame, and is thus the same as the network slot time. Each **solicit-successor frame** transmitted by a DTE specifies an SA and a DA; the frame is responded to by a DTE that wishes to enter the ring and has an address between the two addresses specified. Each DTE sends a solicit-successor frame at random intervals whenever it is the owner of the token.

When a DTE sends a solicit-successor frame, it is said to have opened a response window since, after sending this type of frame, the sending DTE waits for a response within the response window period. If a DTE with an address within the range specified in the solicit-successor frame is waiting to enter the ring, it responds by sending a request to the sender of the frame to become its new successor in the logical ring. If the sender hears the response, called a set-successor frame, it allows the new DTE to enter the ring by making it its new successor and, in turn, passes it the token. Clearly, the specified address range may contain multiple DTEs all waiting to enter the ring in which case the response frames returned by each DTE will be corrupted. Should this happen, the soliciting DTE must try to identify a single responder by entering an arbitration procedure which works as follows.

Having ascertained that more than one DTE in the specified address range is waiting to enter the ring, the soliciting DTE starts to sequence through them by sending a **resolve-contention frame**. This procedure continues until the DTE receives a positive reply. Any DTEs that responded to the earlier solicit-successor frame but which did not subsequently receive the token, each choose a value in the range 0 to 3 and listen for any further activity on the bus for this number of slot times. If a DTE hears a transmission during its selected time, it delays its request and waits for another opportunity to become part of the ring, that is, when the next response window is opened. Alternatively, if it does not hear a transmission during its selected time, it continues to wait for the possible receipt of a resolve-contention frame. In this way, the worst-case delay the soliciting DTE need spend resolving the contention is limited.

Initialization

The initialization procedure is built on top of the response window procedure. Each DTE in the network monitors all transmissions on the bus and, whenever it hears a transmission, resets a timer, known as the **inactivity timer**, to a preset value. If a DTE loses the token during normal operation, this inactivity timer expires and the DTE enters the initialization phase, at which point it sends a **claim-token frame**. As before, a number of DTEs may try to send a claim-token frame simultaneously, so the following procedure ensures that only a single token is generated.

Each potential initializer sends a claim-token frame with an information field length that is an integer number of slot times. The integer is either 0, 2, 4, or 6, the choice being based on the first two bits in the DTE's network address. After sending its claim-token frame, the DTE waits a further slot time before listening to the transmission medium. If it hears a transmission, it knows that another DTE(s) has (have) sent a longer claim-token frame and so that DTE simply eliminates itself from trying to become the first owner of the token. If a transmission is not heard, the DTE repeats the above process using the next two bits from its address field. Again, if no transmission is detected, it uses the next pair of bits and so on until it has used all address bits. If the medium is still quiet, the DTE has successfully become the first owner of the token. The unique owner of the token continues the initialization process by using the response window procedure to allow the other waiting DTEs to enter the logical ring.

Although a DTE may remove itself from the logical ring at any time simply by not responding when the token is passed to it, a cleaner method is for the DTE to wait until it receives the token and then send a set-successor frame to its predecessor with the address of its own successor in the information field. The DTE then sends the token to its own successor, as usual, in the knowledge that it is no longer part of the (logical) ring.

Priority operation

As with a token ring network, a priority mechanism can be implemented with a token bus network. However, the access method used with a token bus distinguishes only four priority levels, called **access classes**, named 0, 2, 4, and 6, with 6 being the highest priority. As we said earlier, token bus networks are used primarily in application domains such as manufacturing automation and process control. Typical usages of the four access classes are as follows:

- Class 6: urgent messages such as those relating to critical alarm conditions and associated control functions

- Class 4: messages relating to normal control actions and ring management functions

- Class 2: messages relating to routine data gathering for data logging

- Class 0: messages relating to program downloading and general file transfers, that is, long low-priority messages

Each DTE has two timers which control the transmission of frames: the **token hold timer (THT)** and the **high-priority token hold timer (HP-THT)**. The latter controls the transmission of high-priority frames to ensure that the available ring capacity (bandwidth) is shared between all DTEs. Thus when a DTE receives the token, it first sends any high-priority frames it has waiting up to a maximum determined by the HP-THT. Assuming the DTE is using the priority mechanism and providing the THT has not expired, the DTE begins to transmit any waiting lower priority frames using the following control algorithm.

Each DTE in the logical ring keeps a timer which indicates the time that has expired since it last received the token. This is held in a variable known as the **token rotation time (TRT)**. When the DTE next receives the token, it first transfers the current value in the TRT into the THT and resets the contents of the TRT to zero. It then transmits any waiting high-priority frames, increasing the TRT at the same time, and computes the difference between a fixed time known as the **target token rotation time (TTRT)** and its current THT. If the difference is positive, the DTE can send any waiting lower-priority frames until the TTRT is reached; if the difference is zero or negative, the DTE cannot send any lower-priority frames on this pass of the token. Each DTE using the priority mechanism can transmit any waiting frames working from a higher to a lower access class until the TTRT is reached.

To illustrate the operation of this mechanism, consider the example shown in Figure 6.22. For clarity, the example assumes only two access classes. Also, we assume all frames transmitted are of a fixed length so the various times are directly proportional to the number of frames. The example assumes DTEs 9 and 1 send only high-priority frames each time they receive the token whereas DTEs 7 and 5 send lower-priority frames whenever possible. Note that the logical ring is built so that the physical DTE addresses are in descending numerical order. The TTRT for the lower-priority frames is fixed at a value equivalent to 8 frames. The values in the left-hand column under each DTE labelled 'TRT' are the token rotation times measured by that DTE for the previous rotation of the token. The values in the right-hand column labelled 'XMIT' are the number of frames transmitted by the DTE each time it receives the token. Each row represents one rotation of the token.

We assume that all transmissions begin after a period of inactivity and hence after the token has been rotating as rapidly as possible. Therefore the TRT in DTE 9 is shown as zero to begin with. This assumes that the token-passing and propagation delays are negligible compared with the time taken to transmit a

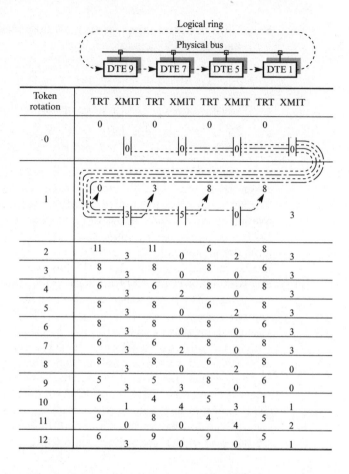

Figure 6.22
Prioritized ring example.

Token rotation	TRT	XMIT	TRT	XMIT	TRT	XMIT	TRT	XMIT
2	11	3	11	0	6	2	8	3
3	8	3	8	0	8	0	6	3
4	6	3	6	2	8	0	8	3
5	8	3	8	0	6	2	8	3
6	8	3	8	0	8	0	6	3
7	6	3	6	2	8	0	8	3
8	8	3	8	0	6	2	8	0
9	5	3	5	3	8	0	6	0
10	6	1	4	4	5	3	1	1
11	9	0	8	0	4	4	5	2
12	6	3	9	0	9	0	5	1

normal frame. We also assume that the high-priority token-hold time is such that a DTE can send up to three high-priority frames on receipt of the token.

During the first rotation of the token, DTE 9 receives the token and sends its maximum of three high-priority frames before passing the token. When DTE 7 receives the token from DTE 9 its TRT will have incremented to 3, since three frames have been transmitted since it last received the token. This means that DTE 7 can transmit five (TTRT − TRT) lower-priority frames before passing the token. On receipt of the token, the TRT held by DTE 5 will now be 8, as a total of eight frames have been transmitted since it last received the token. It cannot, therefore, transmit any lower-priority frames on this pass of the token. DTE 1 then transmits three high-priority frames unconstrained by its computed TRT.

During the second rotation of the token, both DTE 9 and DTE 1 send three high-priority frames unaffected by their computed TRT, but this time DTE 7 is blocked from transmitting any lower-priority frames (since its computed TRT exceeds 8 on receipt of the token) and DTE 5 is able to transmit two lower-priority frames (TTRT − TRT = 2).

During the third rotation of the token, DTE 9 and DTE 1 each again send three high-priority frames but this time both DTE 7 and DTE 5 are blocked from sending any lower-priority frames, since both their computed TRTs have reached the TTRT limit (8).

During the fourth rotation of the token, a situation similar to that in the second rotation prevails, but notice this time that the computed TRTs are such that DTE 7 has an opportunity to send two lower-priority frames instead of DTE 5, which this time cannot send any frames. Similarly, during the fifth rotation of the token, DTE 5 can transmit two lower-priority frames while DTE 7 is inhibited from sending any lower-priority frames. The cycle then repeats itself. We can readily deduce that, over any three rotations, DTEs 9 and 1 use 18/22nds (82%) of the available capacity and DTEs 7 and 5 share the remaining 4/22nds (18%) equally.

During the eighth rotation of the token, we assume that DTE 1 temporarily runs out of high-priority frames to transmit and hence DTEs 7 and 5 are able to transmit more of their waiting lower-priority frames. Similarly, during the tenth rotation, DTE 9 runs out of high-priority frames, and so on.

Although this is a simple example, it nevertheless shows how the priority mechanism allows high-priority frames to be transmitted relatively unconstrained and lower-priority frames to be transmitted in a fair manner whenever spare capacity is available.

6.3 Performance

To illustrate the relative performance of the three medium access methods discussed, the author has carried out a set of simulations, the results of which are presented in Figure 6.23.

In the simulations all LAN segments are of the same length – 2.5 km – and operate at the same bit rate – 10 Mbps. One hundred DTEs/stations are attached in each case.

The graphs show the mean time a frame takes to be transferred across the LAN as a function of the offered load. The load is expressed as a fraction of the available bit rate and is referred to as the **normalized throughput**. In Figure 6.23(a) all frames to be transmitted are 512 bits in length and those in part (b) are 12 000 bits. In the case of the smaller frame size, only a single frame is transmitted on receipt of the token. In practice, a number of such frames may be transmitted but, since this is a function of the priority of the frames, only a single frame is considered.

In addition there will, of course, be a mix of short and long frames and hence the mean transfer times will be between those shown on each set of graphs.

Frames are randomly generated at each station and the **transfer time** is defined as the time from the generation of a frame – and hence when it arrives at

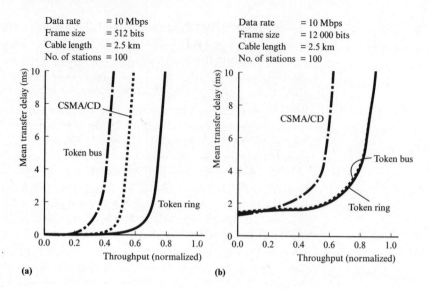

Figure 6.23
LAN performance
comparisons: (a) 512-
bit frames; (b) 12 000-
bit frames.

that MAC sublayer input queue – to the time it is successfully received at the destination. Thus it includes the time the frame is waiting in the MAC sublayer input queue, the delay associated with the particular MAC method, and the time to transmit the frame.

As we can see from the graphs, the mean throughput is higher with the larger frame size with each type of LAN. This is because the overheads associated with each frame relative to the frame contents are less with the larger frame size. Notice also, however, that with a token ring LAN, the throughput is less sensitive to the smaller frame size than the token bus LAN. This is because the size of the token is only 24 bits with a token ring, compared with 152 bits with a token bus. Also, the processing overheads associated with a token bus are higher than with a token ring.

With each set of graphs note that since the throughput is normalized, to achieve a particular throughput a larger number of frames will be generated with a smaller frame size. Hence with the CSMA/CD access method, the probability of a collision at a particular throughput level is higher with the smaller frame size. In addition, with the smaller frame size the overheads associated with the medium access method increase significantly in terms of the fraction of the time that is lost for collisions and the associated recovery procedure.

In conclusion, the differences in throughput are significant only for offered loads in excess of, say, half the total throughput capacity. For offered loads less than this, the mean transit time of all three LANs is similar. In practice, with all but the more advanced applications of the type that we shall identify in Chapter 7, most LANs operate with only modest offered loads relative to their maximum capacity. In cases where the load is significant, however, the token access method is superior.

6.4 Wireless LANs

The LAN types we have discussed so far in this chapter all use either twisted-pair wire or coaxial cable as the physical transmission medium. A major cost associated with such LANs is that of installing the physical wire cables. Moreover, if the layout of the interconnected computers changes, then a cost similar to the initial installation cost can be incurred as the wiring plan is changed. This is one of the reasons why wireless LANs, that is, LANs which do not utilize physical wires as the transmission medium, have evolved.

A second reason is the advent of handheld terminals and portable computers. Advancing technology means that such devices are rapidly becoming comparable in power to many static computers. Although the primary reason for using these devices is portability, they often have to communicate with other computers. These may be other portable computers or, more likely, computers (servers) that are attached to a wired LAN. Examples are a handheld terminal in a retail store communicating with a back-of-store computer to update stock records or, in a hospital, a nurse with a portable computer accessing a patient record in a database held in a mainframe computer.

A schematic diagram of the two applications of wireless LANs is given in Figure 6.24(a). As we can see, in the first application, to access a server computer that is attached to a wired LAN, an intermediate device known as a **portable access unit (PAU)** is used. Typically, the range of coverage of the PAU is between 50 and 100 m and in a large installation there are many such units distributed around a

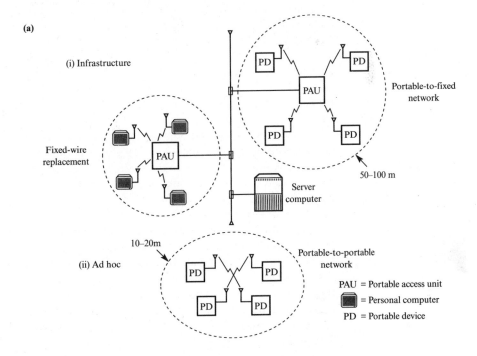

Figure 6.24
Wireless LANs:
(a) application
topologies.

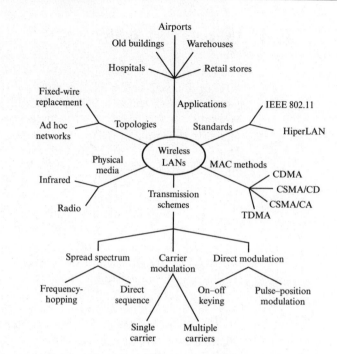

Figure 6.24 (cont.)
(b) Technology
issues.

site. Collectively, these provide access to the site LAN – and hence server computers – by a handheld terminal, a portable computer, or a static computer, each of which may be located anywhere around the site. This type of application is known as an **infrastructure wireless LAN**.

In the second application, a set of portable computers may wish to communicate one with another to form a self-contained LAN. For example, this may be in a conference room during a meeting, or at an airport. Since such networks are created on demand, they are often referred to as **ad hoc wireless LANs**. As with wired LANs, there are a number of points that must be considered when describing the operation of wireless LANs and these are summarized in Figure 6.24(b). In practice, there are many cross-linkages between the issues identified but for description purposes each will be considered independently.

6.4.1   Wireless media

The two types of media used for wireless LANs are radio-frequency waves and infrared optical signals. We shall discuss the characteristics of each separately although, as we shall see, similar techniques are used with both types.

Radio

Radio-frequency waves are used extensively for many applications. These include radio and television broadcasting, and cellular telephony networks. Since radio waves can readily propagate through objects such as walls and doors, tight controls are applied to the use of the radio spectrum. The wide range of applications also means that radio bandwidth is scarce. For a particular application, a specific frequency band must be officially allocated. Historically this has been done on a national basis but, increasingly, international agreements are being signed that set aside selected frequency bands for those applications that have international relevance.

The requirements to confine radio emissions to a specific frequency band and for the related receivers to select only those signals within this band mean that, in general, the circuitry associated with radio-based systems is more sophisticated than that used in infrared optical systems. Nevertheless, the widespread use of radio – particularly in high-volume consumer products – means that sophisticated radio system designs can be implemented at reasonable costs.

Path loss. All radio receivers are designed to operate to a specified signal-to-noise ratio or SNR, that is, the ratio of the power of the received signal to the power of the receiver noise signal must not fall below the specified value. In general, the complexity (and hence cost) of the receiver increases as the SNR decreases. The falling cost of portable computers, however, means that the acceptable cost of the radio network interface unit must be comparable with the cost of portable computers. This means, therefore, that the SNR of the radio receiver must be set at as high a level as possible.

In practice, the SNR is dependent on a number of interrelated parameters and each of these must be considered in relation to the design of the radio receiver. As we described in Section 2.2, the receiver noise figure is a function of both the ambient temperature – which gives rise to thermal noise – and the bandwidth of the received signal; the larger the bandwidth or temperature, the larger the noise figure. Hence for a specific application, the receiver noise figure is essentially fixed.

The signal power at the receiver is a function not only of the power of the transmitted signal but also of the distance between the transmitter and receiver. In free space, the power of a radio signal decays inversely with the square of the distance from the source. In addition, in an indoor environment, the decay is increased further, firstly because of the presence of objects such as furniture and people and secondly, because of destructive interference of the transmitted signal caused by the reflected signals from these objects. These combine to produce what is known as the **path loss** of the radio channel.

Therefore in order for the radio receiver to operate with an acceptable SNR, it must operate with as high a transmitter power level as possible and/or with a limited range of coverage. In practice, with portable computers, the power of the transmitted signal is limited by the power consumption of the radio network interface unit which leads to an increase in the load on the computer's battery. It is for these reasons that the range of coverage of an ad hoc LAN is normally shorter than that of an infrastructure LAN.

Adjacent channel interference. Since radio propagates through most objects with only modest attenuation, it is possible to get interference from other transmitters that are operating in the same frequency band and are located either in adjacent rooms within the same building or in other buildings. With ad hoc LANs, therefore, since multiple such LANs may be set up in adjacent rooms/areas, techniques must be adopted that allow several users of the same frequency band to coexist.

In an infrastructure wireless LAN, since the topology is known and the total area of coverage of the wireless network is much larger – effectively that of the existing wired LAN – the available bandwidth can be divided into a number of sub-bands so that the area of coverage of adjacent sub-bands utilize a different frequency. The general scheme is shown in Figure 6.25(a). The scheme shown is known as a **three-cell repeat pattern** although larger patterns are possible. The amount of bandwidth available within each cell is chosen to provide an acceptable level of service for the predicted number of active users within that area. This leads to better utilization of the available bandwidth and, by ensuring adjacent cells all use a different frequency, the level of **adjacent channel interference** is much reduced.

Multipath.   Radio signals, like optical signals, are affected by **multipath**, that is, at any point in time the receiver receives multiple signals originating from the same transmitter, each of which has followed a different path between the transmitter and receiver. This is known as **multipath dispersion** or **delay spread** and causes the signals relating to a previous bit/symbol to interfere with the signals relating to the next bit/symbol. This is known as **intersymbol interference (ISI)** and is shown in Figure 6.25(b). Clearly, the higher the bit rate – and hence the shorter each bit cell period – the larger the level of intersymbol interference.

In addition, an impairment known as **frequency-selective fading** is caused by the variation in path lengths of the different received signals. This gives rise to relative phase shifts between them which, at radio frequencies, can cause the various reflected signals to significantly attenuate the direct path signal and, in the limit, to cancel each other out. This is known as **Rayleigh fading** and is shown in Figure 6.25(c). In practice, the amplitude of the reflected wave is a fraction of the direct wave, the amount of attenuation being determined by the reflecting material. One solution to this problem is to exploit the fact that the wavelength associated with radio frequency signals is very short – a fraction of a meter – and hence is sensitive to small variations in the location of the antenna. To overcome this effect two antennas are often used with a physical separation between them of one-quarter wavelength. The signals received from both antennas are combined to form the composite received signal. This technique is known as **space diversity**.

An alternative solution is to use a technique known as **equalization**. Delayed and attenuated images of the direct signal – equivalent to the multipath reflected signals – are subtracted from the actual received signal. Since the reflected signals will vary for different locations of the transmitter and receiver, the process has to be adaptive. The circuit used is known, therefore, as an **adaptive equalizer**. Clearly, the use of such circuits adds cost to the receiver implementation.

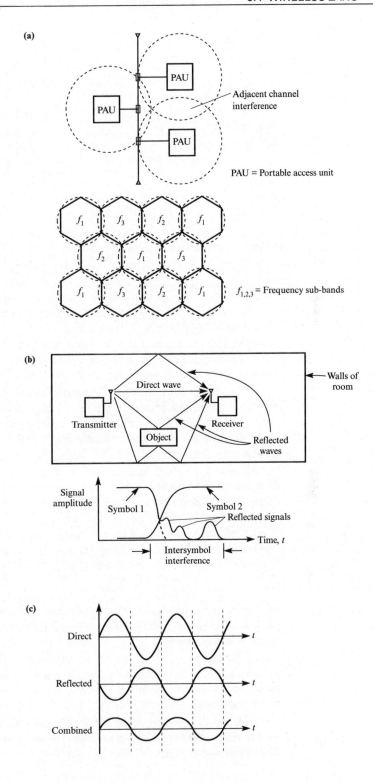

Figure 6.25
Radio impairments:
(a) adjacent channel
interference and
example frequency
allocation strategy;
(b) intersymbol
interference;
(c) Rayleigh fading.

Infrared

Infrared emitters and detectors have been used for many years in various applications. These include optical fiber transmission systems and various remote control applications such as those used with television sets, CD players, and VCRs. Infrared emissions are at frequencies that are very much higher than radio frequency waves – greater than 10^{14} Hz – and normally devices are classified by the wavelength of the infrared signal transmitted and detected rather than its frequency. The wavelength is measured in nanometers (nm) – 1 nm $= 10^{-9}$ m – and is the distance travelled by light in the time of a single cycle of the signal. That is:

$$\text{Wavelength, } \lambda = \frac{c}{f}$$

where c is the speed of light $(3 \times 10^8 \, \text{ms}^{-1})$ and f is the signal frequency in Hz.

Two widely used infrared devices have wavelengths of 800 nm and 1300 nm respectively.

An advantage of infrared over radio is the lack of regulations relating to its use. Also, infrared has a similar wavelength to visible light and hence exhibits similar behavior: for example, it is reflected from shiny surfaces, and it will pass through glass but not through walls or other opaque objects. Hence infrared emissions are limited to a single room which, in wireless LAN applications, reduces the level of adjacent channel interference.

Another point that must be considered when using infrared as the physical medium is the interference caused by background (ambient) light. Sunlight and light produced by filament and fluorescent light sources all contain significant levels of infrared. This is received by the detector together with the infrared from the emitter. This means that the noise power can be high, which leads to a requirement for a high signal power to obtain an acceptable signal-to-noise ratio. In practice, the path loss with infrared can be high. Also, infrared emitters have a relatively low electrical-to-optical power conversion efficiency. Collectively, these can lead to a high power demand on a battery source. To reduce the level of noise, it is common practice to pass the composite received signal through an **optical bandpass filter** which attenuates those infrared signals that are outside of the frequency band of the transmitted signal.

Devices.   For wireless LAN applications, the operational mode is to modulate the intensity of the infrared output of the emitter using an electrically modulated signal. The variations in intensity of the infrared signal are received by the detector which directly converts this into an equivalent electrical signal. This mode of operation is known as **intensity modulation with direct detection (IMDD)** and, as we shall see in Section 6.4.2, various modulation methods are used including baseband modulation.

There are two kinds of infrared emitters: **laser diodes** and **light-emitting diodes**. Laser diodes are used extensively in optical fiber transmission systems. They produce a coherent source of light, that is, a very narrow band of frequencies (typically between 1 and 5 nm), and when the light is confined in a small area high power densities are obtained. In wireless LAN applications, since the light is not constrained to propagate in the confines of an optical fiber, the laser light source must be diffused otherwise severe eye damage can result. In contrast, light emitting diodes (**LEDs**) produce a light source comprising a band of frequencies – typically between 25 and 100 mm – and, with the low power outputs used, are quite safe. The modulation bandwidth available with LEDs limits at about 20 MHz which imposes a limit on the maximum bit rate that can be used to less than 10 Mbps. Because of their low cost, we normally use LEDs for bit rates up to this level.

For bit rates greater than 10 Mbps we must use laser diodes. The modulation bandwidth available with laser diodes is several hundreds of MHz. The wide band of frequencies – spectral width – associated with LEDs means that, at the receiver, an optical filter with a wide passband must be used to detect all the transmitted signal. However, this increases the receiver noise signal which, at high bit rates, makes the receiver design more difficult.

Topologies.   Infrared links can be used in one of two modes: point-to-point and diffuse. In the point-to-point mode the emitter is pointed directly at the detector – a photodiode in practice – and hence much lower power emitters and less sensitive detectors can be used. This mode of operation is best suited to providing a wireless link between two pieces of equipment, for example, to enable a portable computer to download files to another computer.

For wireless LAN applications, a one-to-many (broadcast) mode of operation is required. To achieve this, the output of the infrared source is optically diffused so that the light is spread over a wide angular area. This is the **diffused mode**: there are three alternative operating modes, as shown in Figure 6.26. In the basic mode – part (a) – there is a wide-angle optical emitter and detector associated with each computer. The infrared signal output by any emitter is received by all detectors after multiple reflections within the room. The effect of this operating mode is that multiple copies of the same source signal arrive at each detector within varying time intervals of each other determined by the physical path followed by each signal. As indicated earlier, this is multipath dispersion and its effect is delay spread since the pulses representing the individual bits within the transmitted bit stream spread or widen. As with radio waves, the amplitude of the various reflected signals vary relative to the most direct signal as a function of the path they have followed and the attenuation they have incurred. In a typical room/office, meaningful signals can be received with delay spreads as high as 100 nanoseconds. This mode of operation is satisfactory only at bit rates up to 1 Mbps, since at higher rates ISI effects increase considerably.

With infrared (and radio), in addition to equalization, we can reduce the effects of delay spread by using multiple directional emitters and detectors – **directional antennas** with radio – as shown in Figure 6.26(b). With this approach, all emitters and detectors are oriented to point in the general direction of a fixed

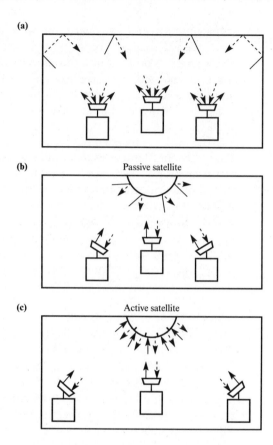

Figure 6.26
Infrared operational
modes: (a) point-to-
point; (b) passive
satellite; (c) active
satellite.

reflecting dome on the ceiling known as a satellite. To maximize the received signal power and minimize reflections, the source signal is optically focused to form a relatively narrow beam. The shape of the satellite reflecting dome is chosen to ensure all transmitted signals are received by all detectors. To reduce the effects of multipath, the aperture of the detectors is made small so that they receive only the direct signal from the satellite.

The satellite in the scheme just described acts only as a light reflector. Therefore to obtain an acceptable signal power level at the detector, the emitted signal power must be relatively high. With portable devices that derive their power from batteries, this is a disadvantage and hence a further refinement of the basic scheme is to utilize an **active satellite** as shown in Figure 6.26(c). With this scheme, an array of detectors – photodiodes – are distributed around the dome together with a set of infrared emitters. All signals received by one or more sets of detectors are then repeated by the emitters. This means that the power of the signal emitted by each portable device can be much lower since it need only be sufficient to form a direct path to the satellite.

6.4.2 Transmission schemes

The different propagation characteristics of infrared and radio give rise to different transmission schemes. We shall discuss the schemes used with each media type separately.

Radio

There are four transmission schemes used with radio wireless LANs: **direct sequence spread spectrum**, **frequency-hopping spread spectrum**, **single-carrier modulation**, and **multi-subcarrier modulation**.

Direct sequence spread spectrum. Compared with most other applications of the radio spectrum, wireless LANs are relatively new. Although there is free radio spectrum available, in general this is at relatively high frequencies in the tens of gigahertz range. At such frequencies the components required are new and their cost is relatively high. This is a distinct disadvantage for wireless LAN applications since the cost of comparable network interface cards for the fixed-wiring LAN types are now very low. Moreover, as the cost of portable computers has fallen, so the acceptable cost of a wireless LAN interface has fallen also. For these reasons the first radio-based wireless LAN standard uses an existing frequency band for which components are readily available. This is one of the frequency bands set aside for general industrial, scientific, and medical (ISM) applications and known as the **ISM bands**. Examples of existing applications of these bands include high-power radio frequency heating equipment and microwave ovens. Amateur radio operators are authorized to use these bands also, often at high transmission power levels. In order to coexist with such applications, it is essential that the transmission scheme selected has a high level of co-channel interference rejection. For wireless LAN applications, this is achieved using a technique known as **spread spectrum**. There are two forms of spread spectrum, direct-sequence and frequency-hopping. We shall discuss the former in the remainder of this section and the latter in the next section.

The principle of operation of direct sequence spread spectrum is shown in schematic form in Figure 6.27. The source data to be transmitted is first exclusive-ORed with a **pseudorandom binary sequence**, that is, the bits making up the sequence are random but the same sequence is made much larger than the source data rate. Hence when the exclusive-ORed signal is modulated and transmitted, it occupies – and is said of be spread over – a proportionately wider frequency band than the original source data bandwidth, which makes the signal appear as (pseudo) noise to other users of the same frequency band.

All the members of the same wireless LAN know the pseudorandom binary sequence being used. All data frames being transmitted are preceded by a preamble sequence followed by a start-of-frame delimiter. Hence after demodulating the transmitted signal, all receivers first search for the known preamble sequence – normally a string of all binary 1s – and, once the sequence has been found, the receivers start to interpret the received bit stream on the correct source

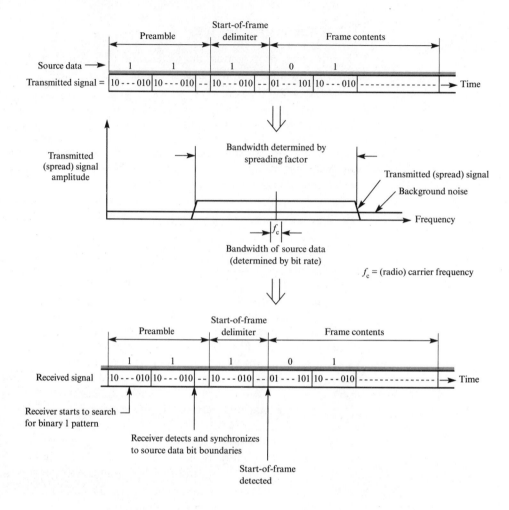

Figure 6.27
Direct sequence
spread spectrum
principle of
operation.

data bit boundaries. They then wait for the start-of-frame delimiter to be received and then proceed to receive the frame contents. The intended recipient(s) is (are) determined by the destination address at the head of the frame in the normal way.

Clearly, since all the stations belonging to the same wireless LAN occupy the same allocated frequency band and use the same pseudorandom binary sequence, their transmissions will interfere with one another. Hence an appropriate MAC method must be used to ensure only one transmission takes place at a time.

In practice, the generation of a pseudorandom binary sequence is relatively straightforward since it can be produced digitally using only a number of shift registers and a number of exclusive-OR gates connected in a feedback loop. The principle is shown in Figure 6.28(a). In this example a single 3-bit shift register and a single exclusive-OR gate are used and this produces the 7 pseudorandom 3-bit codes – also known as (shift register) states – before it repeats. Note that the 000 state is not present since the shift register contents would then remain unchanged

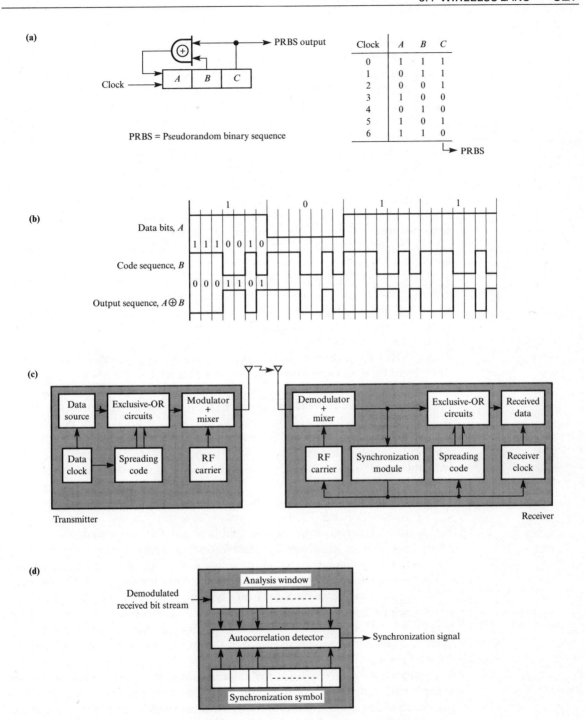

Figure 6.28 Direct sequence spectrum principles: (a) pseudorandom sequence generator; (b) spread sequence generation; (c) transmitter and receiver schematic; (d) synchronization module schematic.

after each successive clock pulse. In general, there are a maximum of $2^n - 1$ states for an n-bit shift register and, if the feedback combination produces all $2^n - 1$ states, it is known as a **maximal-length shift register**. The output from the most significant element of the shift register is used as the pseudorandom binary sequence which, in this case, is equal to the 7-bit binary pattern 1110010.

The pseudorandom sequence is used by performing an exclusive-OR operation between the sequence and each data bit to be transmitted. As an example, if we assume the 7-bit pseudorandom pattern derived in Figure 6.28(a), then part (b) illustrates the transmitted bit pattern corresponding to a set of four data bits. Note that for each data bit 7 bits are transmitted. Also, that for any data bit position, the transmitted bit sequence for a binary 0 is simply the inverse of that for a binary 1. The pseudorandom binary sequence is also known as the **spreading sequence**, each bit in the sequence as a **chip**, the resulting transmission bit rate as the **chipping rate**, and the number of bits in the sequence as the **spreading factor**.

The spreading factor determines the performance of a spread spectrum system. Normally, it is expressed in decibels (dB) and is then known as the **processing gain**, that is, the processing gain is the logarithm of the spreading factor. For example, a spread spectrum system with a spreading factor of 10:1 has a processing gain of 10 dB, 100:1 20 dB, and so on. In terms of the signal-to-noise ratio (SNR) – also expressed in dB – the processing gain effectively subtracts from this. Hence for a non spread spectrum system that requires an SNR of, say, 10 dB – that is, the signal power must be 10 times the noise power for satisfactory operation – then with spread spectrum and a processing gain of 10 dB, the system will operate satisfactorily even when the signal power is equal to the noise power.

A schematic diagram of a simple direct sequence radio transmitter and receiver is shown in Figure 6.28(c). After each data bit has been exclusive-ORed with the pseudorandom sequence, the resulting high bit rate binary signal is transmitted by modulating a carrier signal. The frequency of the resulting signal is then increased – using a **mixer circuit** – so that the transmitted signal is in the defined frequency band. Typical modulation schemes used are binary phase shift keying (BPSK) and quadrature phase shift keying (QPSK), the principles of which we described earlier in Section 2.5.1 when modems were described.

We can therefore deduce that the receiver must operate in synchronism with the received signal so that the results of performing the exclusive-OR operation are interpreted on the correct data bit (symbol) boundaries. To achieve this, a known binary pattern is transmitted at the beginning of each frame – the preamble – and the receiver uses this to achieve both clock (bit) and symbol synchronization. A schematic diagram of the synchronization module is shown in Figure 6.28(d).

Clock synchronization (at the chipping rate) is achieved using one of the standard methods described in Section 3.3.1. To achieve symbol synchronization (at the data rate), each transmitted frame is preceded by a preamble that comprises a string of binary 1 symbols (data bits). As the spread preamble is received, it is passed through an n-bit shift register – where n is the number of bits in the spreading sequence – and compared on a chip-by-chip basis with the known sequence corresponding to a 1 data bit. If the two bits in a particular chip position are the same, then an agreement (A) is said to occur, while if they are different, a disagreement (D) occurs. A measure of the difference between the two symbols is then computed by subtracting the number of Ds from the number of As and this is known as the **autocorrelation function**. Clearly, when the known symbol is located then the autocorrelation function will be a maximum positive value equal to the number of chips in the spreading sequence. The receiver is then in symbol synchronization. The reliability of the synchronization process is determined by the autocorrelation between the chosen spreading sequence and shifted versions of it. This becomes increasingly important when chip errors are present in the received (demodulated) spread sequence because of, for example, excessive noise. This is best illustrated by Example 6.2.

Example 6.2

A typical spreading sequence used in direct sequence spread spectrum systems is the 11-bit binary-sequence 10110111000. It is an example of a **Barker sequence**. Determine and plot the autocorrelation for this sequence for ±10 bits (chips) either side of it.

The solution is summarized in Figure 6.29. In part (a) the received bit (chip) sequence is shown with the analysis window coinciding with the spreading

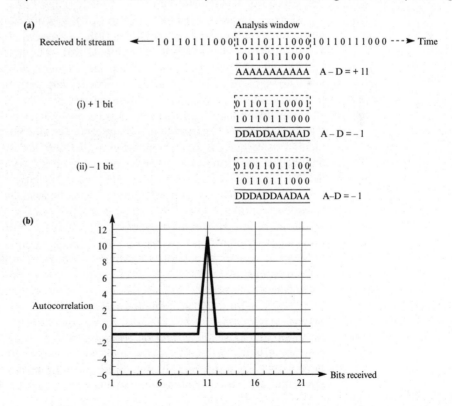

Figure 6.29
Synchronization example:
(a) autocorrelation example;
(b) autocorrelation graph.

sequence – synchronization symbol – together with an additional sequence either side of it. Clearly, in this position, all bit positions will be in agreement and the autocorrelation equal to +11. The two other examples correspond to the situation plus or minus 1 bit of the spreading sequence and, as we can be see, this yields an autocorrelation of −1. In fact, with this psuedorandom sequence all bit positions either side of it yield an autocorrelation of −1. The autocorrelation plot is thus as shown in Figure 6.29(b) and, as we can see, the signal output by the synchronization module will be positive only when the synchronization symbol is received.

■ ■

Frequency-hopping spread spectrum. The principle of operation of frequency-hopping spread spectrum is shown in Figure 6.30(a). The allocated frequency band is divided into a number of lower-frequency sub-bands known as **channels**. Each channel is of equal bandwidth and is determined by the data bit rate and the modulation method used. A transmitter then uses each channel for a short period of time before moving/hopping to a different channel. When a channel is being used, a carrier frequency at the center of the channel is modulated with the bit(s) being transmitted at that time. The pattern of usage of the channel is pseudorandom and is known as the **hopping sequence**, the time spent on each channel as the **chip period**, and the hopping rate as the **chipping rate**.

There are two modes of operation of frequency-hopping which are determined by the ratio of the chipping rate to the source data rate. These are shown in Figure 6.30(b) and (c). When the chipping rate is higher than the data rate the operational mode is known as **fast frequency-hopping**, while if the chipping rate is lower than the data rate it is **slow frequency-hopping**. In both cases, a carrier frequency is used in the center of each channel.

An advantage of frequency-hopping over direct sequence is its ability to avoid using selected (narrowband) channels within the overall allocated frequency band. This can be particularly useful with the ISM bands because of the possible presence of one or more high-power narrowband interference sources within the field of coverage of the LAN. As we discussed earlier, although with direct sequence the interference signal is spread over the assigned frequency band, with high-power sources this can still result in a significant level of interference which, in the limit, can render particular bands unusable. However, with frequency-hopping, if an interference source that operates at a specific frequency is known to be present, then it is possible to eliminate the use of that frequency from the hopping sequence.

This technique is particularly useful with slow frequency-hopping since, with fast frequency-hopping, multiple frequency hops per data bit are used and hence only a single chip will be affected. A majority decision can then be used to determine the most likely data bit transmitted, 0 or 1. However, fast frequency-hopping systems are more costly than slow frequency-hopping systems. Also, since both transmitter and receiver must be in synchronism – that is, must hop together – slow frequency-hopping systems are easier to synchronize. Therefore

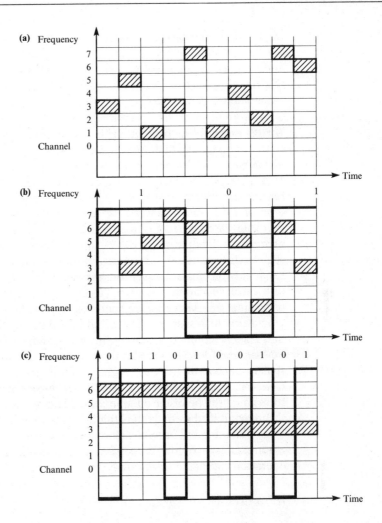

Figure 6.30
Frequency-hopping
spread spectrum:
(a) principle of
operation; (b) fast
frequency-hopping;
(c) slow frequency-
hopping.

slow frequency-hopping systems provide a lower cost alternative for wireless LANs.

Single-carrier modulation.   With this approach a single-frequency carrier signal – located in the center of the allocated frequency band – is modulated with the data to be transmitted using an appropriate modulation circuit. In principle, it is simply an extension of the modulation schemes described in Section 2.5.1 for transmitting data over an analog switched telephone network, except for wireless LANs the required bit rate – and hence bandwidth – is much larger.

Recall that there are many different modulation schemes involving amplitude, frequency, and phase or combinations of them. However, the high bandwidth required with wireless LANs mitigates against modulation schemes which involve amplitude variations since power amplifiers that are linear over wide bandwidths both are costly and consume significant power. Normally modulation schemes based on phase variations of a single, constant-amplitude carrier are used, such as quadrature phase shift keying or variations of this. In addition, as we indicated earlier, for bit rates in excess of 1–2 Mbps, multipath dispersion gives rise to high levels of ISI and hence sophisticated equalization circuits must also be used.

Multi-subcarrier modulation.   The principle of operation of this approach is first to divide the high bit rate binary signal to be transmitted into a number of lower bit rate streams. Each lower bit rate stream is then used to modulate a separate subcarrier – from the allocated frequency band – as with a single-carrier scheme. However, in this case, because of the relatively low bit rate per carrier, the level of ISI is much reduced, which removes the need for equalizers. Although frequency-selective fading may still occur, it is likely that only one (or a small number) of the subcarriers will be affected. Forward error correction techniques – such as convolutional codes described in Appendix A – can be used to improve the residual BER of the channel. In practice, the subcarriers used are integer multiples of the first subcarrier – f_1, $2f_1$, $3f_1$, etc. – and hence the scheme is known also as **orthogonal frequency division multiplexing (OFDM)**.

Prior to transmission, the individual modulated subcarriers are combined into a single composite signal using a mathematical technique known as the **fast Fourier transform (FFT)**. This produces a time-domain output signal which has a similar bandwidth to that required for a single-carrier scheme. In this case, however, at the receiver, the signal is reconverted back into its multi-subcarrier form using the inverse FFT operation. The demodulated low bit rate streams are then recombined to form the high bit rate binary output stream.

The trade-off between the two modulation schemes is the cost – and power requirements – of the processing power required to perform the equalization operation compared to that required to perform the FFT operations.

Infrared

There are a number of ways used to transmit data using an infrared signal, including direct modulation and carrier modulation.

Direct modulation.   Unlike radio, which must operate in a specific frequency band, infrared is naturally constrained to a single room, therefore it is possible to modulate the infrared source signal directly, a binary 1 turning the emitter on and a binary 0 turning it off. This type of modulation is known as **on–off keying (OOK)** and is widely used in optical fiber transmission systems. It is the simplest type of modulation and requires relatively straightforward electronics for its implementation. A schematic of the scheme is shown in Figure 6.31(a).

As with baseband transmission over fixed-wire links, for the receiver to achieve clock/bit synchronization, the source bit stream must be encoded at the transmitter prior to modulation using one of the standard clock encoding methods described in Section 3.3.1. Typically, this is either Manchester encoding or NRZI with zero bit insertion and a DPLL.

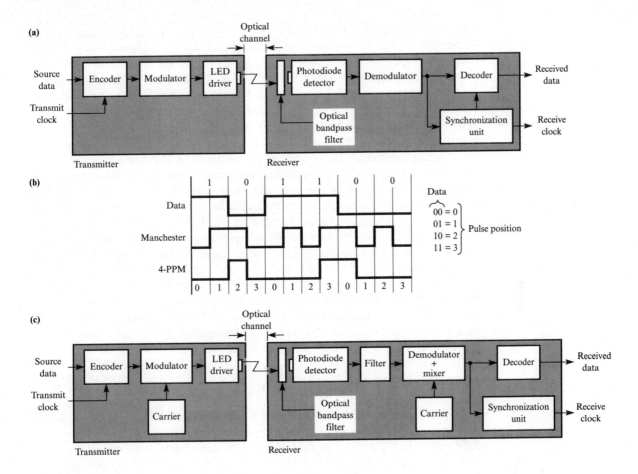

Figure 6.31
Infrared coding and modulation schemes: (a) direct modulation schematic; (b) pulse-position modulation; (c) carrier modulation schematic.

In addition, a technique known as **pulse-position modulation (PPM)** is used in optical systems to reduce the optical power requirements of the LED infrared source. The principle of operation of PPM is shown in Figure 6.31(b). With this scheme the bit stream to be transmitted is first divided into sets of n-bit symbols. For each symbol, a single pulse is sent in one of the 2^n time slot positions. In the example, $n = 2$ and hence a single pulse is sent in one of the 4 possible time slots. Systems with 4 bits per symbol – and hence 16 pulse positions – are also used in high bit rate systems operating at 1–2 Mbps. This is the maximum symbol size that can be used with currently available devices. In addition, at higher bit rates equalization circuitry is normally required to reduce the effects of multipath dispersion.

As Section 6.4.1 indicated, an optical filter is used to reduce the interference caused by sunlight and artificial light. The effect of any remaining interference is to raise the off signal level of the photodiode and, in the limit, to cause the detector circuitry to misinterpret the received signal. This is another contributing factor that limits the bit rate that can be achieved with OOK to about 2 Mbps.

Carrier modulation. To achieve higher bit rates, we need to use carrier modulation techniques similar to those in radio systems. A schematic is shown in Figure 6.31(c). Example modulation methods include FSK and PSK, the principles of which were described in Section 2.5.1. Since with such schemes the binary data is transmitted using a modulated – in frequency or phase – carrier signal, at the receiver it is possible to pass the signal output from the infrared detector through an additional electronic filter prior to demodulation. As indicated in Section 2.5.1, such filters pass only a limited band of frequencies – that contain the source data – around the carrier. The effect of this is further to filter out any remaining interference signals thereby giving improved performance over a direct modulation system. Bit rates from 2–4 Mbps are readily achievable.

At higher bit rates, ISI caused by multipath becomes the limiting factor and hence techniques to overcome this must be employed. One approach is to use multi-subcarrier modulation. With this scheme the available bandwidth is divided into a number of sub-bands and each is used to transmit a portion of the bit stream. For example, if two sub-bands are used then each will transmit alternate bits in the bit stream. This means that each sub-band need only transmit at half the bit rate with the consequent increase in each bit cell period to twice the original period. This makes the signal less susceptible to ISI and bit rates of 10 Mbps can be obtained. Clearly this increase in signal period is obtained with added complexity in the transmitter and receiver electronics.

6.4.3 Medium access control methods

Both radio and infrared operate using a broadcast medium, that is, all transmissions are received by all receivers within the field of coverage of the transmitter. As a result, in the same way that we need to use a MAC method with shared-medium wired LANs – CSMA/CD, control token, etc. – to ensure only one transmitter is using the medium, so a MAC method is also needed with wireless LANs. The main schemes used are CDMA, CSMA/CD, CSMA/CA, TDMA, and FDMA.

CDMA

Code-division multiple access (CDMA) is used specifically with spread spectrum radio systems. As described in Section 6.4.2, both direct sequence and frequency-hopping use a unique pseudorandom spreading/hopping sequence as the basis of their operating modes. In such systems, therefore, a different pseudorandom sequence can be allocated to each node and the complete set of sequences may be known by all nodes. To communicate with another node, the transmitter simply selects and uses the pseudorandom sequence of the intended recipient. In this way, multiple communications between different pairs of nodes can take place concurrently.

In practice, as Figure 6.32 shows, this is possible only with frequency-hopping systems since, with direct sequence, a phenomenon known as the **near–far effect** can occur. This is experienced when a second transmitter – for

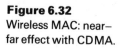

Figure 6.32
Wireless MAC: near–
far effect with CDMA.

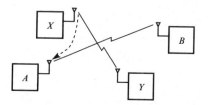

example node X in the figure – is operating that is physically nearer to the intended receiver – node A – than the other communicating partner – node B. Although the transmissions from node X are suppressed by the despreading process in node A, because of its closer proximity, the (spread) interference signal may have more power than the required signal from node B which, in turn, causes the receiver in node A to miss the transmission. This is also known as the **hidden terminal effect**.

In contrast, with frequency-hopping, since the two transmitters are constantly changing frequency channels, the probability of both operating in the same channel at the same time is very low. This can be reduced even further by careful planning of the hopping sequences. The disadvantage of both schemes, however, is the need for all nodes to know the pseudorandom sequence of all other nodes which, in a wireless LAN, is difficult to administer.

CSMA/CD

Section 6.1.3 described how CSMA/CD – carrier-sense multiple-access with collision detection – is used widely in wired LANs as a MAC method. In wireless LANs, CSMA also allows a waiting node to defer to another node that may already be using the broadcast – radio or infrared – medium. With radio and infrared, however, it is not possible to transmit and receive simultaneously and hence collision detection in its basic form cannot be used. However, a variation of the collision detection function has been proposed for use with wireless LANs known as **collision detection (comb)**.

With this scheme, when a node has a frame to transmit, it first generates a short pseudorandom binary sequence – known as the comb – and appends this to the front of the preamble of the frame. The node then goes through the carrier sense operation in the normal way and, assuming the medium is quiet, it proceeds to transmit the comb sequence. For a binary 1 in the sequence, the node transmits a signal for a short time interval but for a binary 0 in the sequence, the node switches to the receive mode. If a node detects the transmission of a signal during the time it is in the receive mode, then it drops out of contention for the channel and defers until the other transmitting node(s) has (have) transmitted the frame. The principle of operation of the scheme is shown in Figure 6.33.

In this example, three nodes – A, B, and C – are in contention for the channel and the pseudorandom codes generated by each are as shown. Since the first bit in the sequence is a binary 1 for all nodes, no node is listening and hence the transmission goes undetected. During the second comb interval, nodes A and C are still transmitting but node B is in the receive mode and hence will detect a

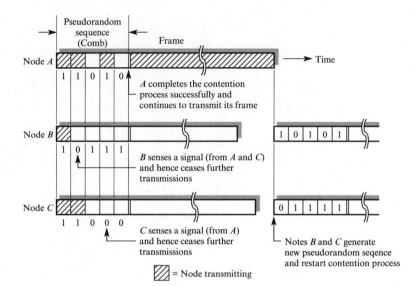

Figure 6.33
Wireless MAC:
CSMA/CD comb.

signal and drop out of contention for the channel at this point. During the third interval, since node *B* is now inactive and both node *A* and node *C* are in the receive mode, neither *A* nor *C* will detect a signal. During the fourth interval, node *A* is transmitting and node *C* is in the receive mode and hence node *C* will detect a signal and drop out of contention. Node *A* is then left and, after completing the remainder of the contention process successfully, proceeds to transmit its waiting frame.

The efficiency of the scheme is determined by the number of bits in the pseudorandom sequence – and hence comb – since if two nodes generate the same sequence, then a collision may occur. In practice, the number of nodes in contention at any time is likely to be low and hence the comb length can be relatively short. Also, since there is a maximum limit on the rate at which a radio (or infrared) transceiver can switch between the transmit and receive modes – typically one microsecond – a shorter comb length reduces the duration of the contention resolution (collision detection) period.

CSMA/CA

Another adaptation of CSMA/CD known as **CSMA with collision avoidance (CSMA/CA)** is also used. Its principle of operation is shown in Figure 6.34.

As we can see, instead of initiating the transmission of a frame immediately the medium becomes quiet, the node first waits a further short random time interval, and only if the medium is still quiet after this interval does it start to transmit. In this way, if other nodes are also waiting then the node that computes the shortest time will gain access first and the remaining nodes will defer to this. Again, the efficiency of the scheme is a function of the number of time increments

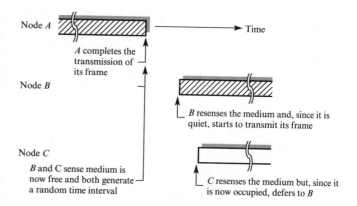

Figure 6.34
Wireless MAC:
CSMA/CA protocol.

– and hence bits in the pseudorandom sequence – in the maximum collision avoidance time period.

Another issue that must be addressed when using radio (and infrared) arises because there is no guarantee that an intended communications partner (node) is in radio contact with the source node. Hence although the CSMA/CA – or CSMA/CD – algorithm ensures a node gains access to the medium, the intended recipient(s) of the frame may never receive it because it is out of radio contact. Therefore, an additional handshake procedure over and above the basic MAC method is incorporated into the MAC protocol. Since it is intended that this should be used with the different types of MAC method, it is known as the **distributed foundation wireless MAC (DFW MAC) protocol**. The four-way handshake procedure used is shown in Figure 6.35. It is intended for use in both infrastructure and ad hoc applications.

Whenever a portable unit needs to send a frame, it first sends a short **request-to-send (RTS)** control message/frame – to either its PAU or another portable unit – using one of the MAC methods just described – CSMA/CD or CSMA/CA. The RTS control message contains the MAC address of both the source and destination units and, on receipt of this, providing the intended destination receives the request and is ready to receive a frame, it broadcasts a **clear-to-send (CTS)** reply message/frame with the same pair of addresses – but with their order reversed – within it. Alternatively, if the destination is not prepared to receive a frame, it returns a **receiver-busy (RxBUSY)** reply. If the reply is positive, then the requesting unit transmits the waiting frame (**DATA**) and, if this is received correctly, the destination returns a positive **acknowledgment (ACK)** message. However, if the frame is corrupted, then a **negative acknowledgment (NAK)** message is returned and the source tries to send it again. This procedure will repeat up to a defined number of retries. Remember that all of the control messages identified are sent using the particular MAC method adopted.

The state transition diagram relating to the protocol is also shown in Figure 6.35. Recall from Section 4.2.2 that in addition to defining the operation of the protocol under error-free conditions, its operation must also be defined when

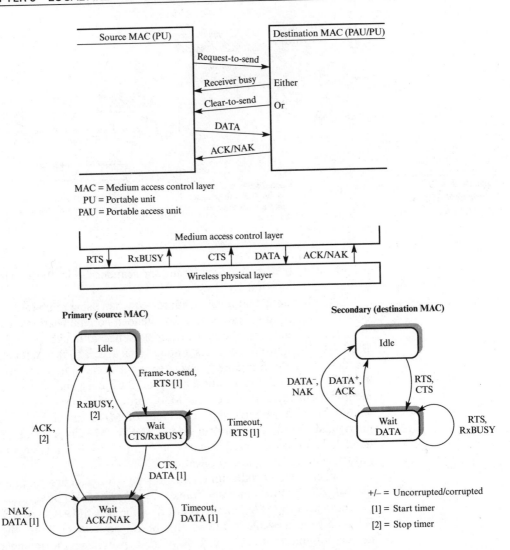

Figure 6.35
Wireless MAC: 4-way
handshake procedure
in DFW MAC
protocol.

corrupted frames/control messages occur. The figure shows that in the event of the latter, a timer is used to initiate the retransmission of the corrupted frame/ message. Normally, a defined retry limit will be used in each case.

TDMA

The principle of operation of time-division multiple access (TDMA) in the context of wireless LANs is shown in Figure 6.36. With this method, each transmitter (node) has a specific time interval/slot and, once the time slot of a transmitter is reached, it transmits at the full bandwidth for the (fixed) duration of the time slot. Normally, the duration of each time slot is short and is chosen so that the probability of transmission errors occurring within it is low. The frame/cycle

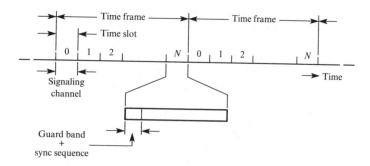

Figure 6.36
Wireless MAC: TDMA.

period is determined by the time duration of each slot and the number of transmissions/slots supported.

Normally, TDMA is used when there is a single (base) station through which all transmissions occur. For example, in a fixed-wire replacement application the PAU – see Figure 6.24 – acts as the base station and it is this that establishes the slot/timing structure. Each portable computer/terminal within the field of coverage of the base station is allocated a specific time slot or, more usually, a separate (signaling) time slot is provided to enable each portable device to make a request to the base station for a (free) time slot whenever it has a frame to transmit. Transmissions from the base station to the portables take place either in a broadcast mode using a specific time slot – with the address of the intended recipient at the head of the transmitted frame – or in a specific time slot set up using the signaling channel. This mode of operation is also known as **slotted Aloha with demand assignment**. Alternatively, the use of each time slot can be controlled by a separate signaling subslot within it.

As Figure 6.36 shows, there is a **guard band** and a **sync sequence** at the start of each time slot. The guard band allows for the different propagation delays between the distributed set of portables and the base station, while the synchronization interval allows the receiver – portable or base station – to tune into the transmitter prior to receiving the slot contents.

FDMA

The principle of operation of frequency-division multiple access (FDMA) is shown in Figure 6.37. FDMA is used mainly in radio systems and, like TDMA,

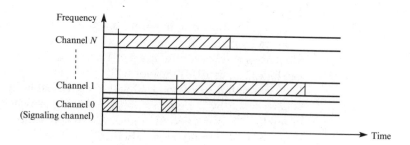

Figure 6.37
Wireless MAC: FDMA.

requires a base station to control its operation. Using FDMA the total allocated frequency bandwidth is divided into a number of frequency sub-bands or channels similar in principle to frequency-hopping spread spectrum. With FDMA, however, once assigned, a particular frequency channel is used for the total duration of a frame transmission. Normally, the frequency channels are assigned on demand using a separate signaling channel.

In general, the base station in a FDMA system is more complex than that used with a TDMA system and hence the latter is more widely used. Hybrid schemes are also used which utilize FDMA to derive multiple frequency channels each of which is then used with TDMA.

Additional functionality

As we shall see in Section 6.5 when LAN protocols are described, although there are different MAC protocols in use – both for wired LANs and wireless LANs – the MAC layer offers a standard set of service primitives to the layer above it. In the case of wireless LANs, this means that the MAC layer, in addition to performing the MAC function, performs some further functions. These include fragmentation, flow control, and multiple rate handling.

Fragmentation is necessary because of the significantly higher BER with radio and infrared. The large frame sizes used with the different wired LAN types is possible because of the very low BER of the transmission media used – coaxial cable, etc. – values in the range 10^{-9} to 10^{-11} being typical. In contrast, multipath and other interference effects with radio and infrared can increase this considerably, values in the range 10^{-3} to 10^{-5} being typical. This means that a smaller frame size must be used when transmitting over these media types. If the MAC layer is to provide a similar service to that provided with wired LANs, the MAC layer must fragment each submitted frame into multiple smaller subframes for transmission over the wireless medium. Similarly, on receipt of each fragment, it must reassemble them back into the original frame prior to its delivery.

It is possible to incorporate an error control scheme into the DFW MAC protocol. If there is no error control performed by the MAC layer, however, then any reassembled frames with errors are simply discarded. Nevertheless, it is necessary for the MAC layer to perform a flow control function. As each fragment is passed to the physical layer, the MAC layer must wait until this has been transmitted before submitting the next fragment. Normally, the flow of frames between the two layers is controlled by the control lines shown earlier in Figure 6.35.

The multiple rate handling function is necessary because often the physical layer can operate at a number of alternative rates. For example, with direct sequence spread spectrum rates of 1 and 2 Mbps are used while with infrared this can be 1, 2, 4, or 10 Mbps. Normally, the operational rate is specified by the MAC layer in a parameter associated with the physical layer service primitives. The rate is determined by the quality of service being provided by the physical layer, for example, if a high ratio of frames is corrupted then a lower bit rate is selected, while if no corruptions are obtained the rate may be increased. The receiving physical layer must of course operate at the same rate – and modulation method – as the transmitting layer and hence this must be agreed by both communicating parties if this is to be changed. Typically, this is accomplished by the exchange of additional control parameters in the request-to-send and clear-to-send frames. This exchange is done at the lowest rate and only if the receiver returns a positive response does the transmitter move up to a higher rate. Normally the current operating rate with different destinations is held in a look-up table to avoid renegotiation of the rate prior to each transmission.

6.4.4 Standards

There is a range of wireless LAN products currently available. However, all of these have been developed by a single company and they differ significantly one from another. The need for international standards is now acknowledged and currently two standards for wireless LAN products are under development. In the United States, the standard is being developed under the banner of the IEEE and is known as **IEEE 802.11**. In Europe, the standard is being developed by the European Telecommunications Standards Institute (ETSI) and is known as **HiperLAN**. Both standards utilize many of the features described in the previous sections.

As with wired LANs, there is not just a single standard. For example, IEEE 802.11 allows for a range of different physical layer standards based on the two media types. These include the following:

1 and 2 Mbps using frequency-hopping spread spectrum radio
1 and 2 Mbps using direct sequence spread spectrum radio
1 and 2 Mbps using direct-modulated infrared
4 Mbps using carrier-modulated infrared
10 Mbps using multi-subcarrier-modulated infrared

The HiperLAN standard is intended for use in both infrastructure and ad hoc applications. Some of the operational parameters are still being finalized but the current specification is as follows:

User bit rate 10–20 Mbps
Operation range 50 m
Radio medium
Single-carrier modulation using a modified version of quadrature phase-shift keying – known as **offset QPSK** – and an equalizer
CSMA/CD or CSMA/CA MAC method

To cater for the different modulation and media types, the physical layer comprises two sublayers: the **physical layer convergence (PLC) sublayer** and the **physical medium dependent (PMD) sublayer**. The PMD sublayer is different for the different modulation and media types and the services it provides are determined by these. The PLC sublayer carries out the convergence functions needed to map the standard services offered at the physical layer interface to those provided by the particular PMD sublayer being used.

6.5 Protocols

The various protocol standards for LANs, which deal with the physical and link layers in the context of the ISO reference model, are those defined in IEEE 802. This standard defines a family of protocols, each relating to a particular type of MAC method. The various IEEE standards and their relationship to the ISO reference model are shown in Figure 6.38.

The three MAC standards together with their associated physical media specifications are contained in the following IEEE standards documents:

- IEEE 802.3: CSMA/CD bus
- IEEE 802.4: Token bus
- IEEE 802.5: Token ring
- IEEE 802.11: Wireless

The relevant ISO standards are the same except an additional 8 is used: ISO 8802.3, etc.

The descriptions presented so far have been concerned with the MAC and physical layers of these four standards. Although each is different in its internal operation, they all present a standard set of services to the logical link control (LLC) layer, which is intended to be used in conjunction with any of the underlying MAC standards. In general, as mentioned in Section 6.2, the various MAC and physical layers are normally implemented in firmware in special-purpose integrated circuits. In this section, therefore, we shall concentrate only on the LLC and network layers and simply define the interface between the LLC and MAC layers. Note that with a LAN the network, LLC, and MAC layers are peer (end-to-end) protocols, since there are no intermediate switching nodes within the network itself similar, for example, to a packet-switching exchange in a public data network (see Section 8.1).

As we can see in Figure 6.38, in the context of the ISO reference model the MAC and LLC layers collectively perform the functions of the ISO data link

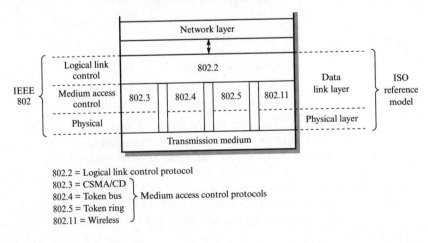

802.2 = Logical link control protocol
802.3 = CSMA/CD
802.4 = Token bus   } Medium access control protocols
802.5 = Token ring
802.11 = Wireless

Figure 6.38
IEEE 802 protocol set.

(control) layer. In this context, the MAC and LLC layers are referred to as sublayers rather than layers. Recall from Chapter 5 that the functions of the data link layer are framing (signaling the start and end of each frame) and error detection. Also, for a reliable (connection-oriented) service, error control, flow control, and link management. Thus the MAC sublayer performs the framing and error detection components – together with the MAC operation – while the LLC sublayer performs the remaining functions.

6.5.1   MAC sublayer services

Irrespective of the mode of operation of the underlying MAC sublayer – CSMA/CD, token ring, token bus, wireless – a standard set of user services is defined for use by the LLC sublayer to transfer LLC PDUs to a correspondent layer. The user service primitives supported are:

- MA_UNITDATA.request
- MA_UNITDATA.indication
- MA_UNITDATA.confirm

A time sequence diagram illustrating their use is shown in Figure 6.39. For a CSMA/CD LAN, the confirm primitive indicates that the request has been successfully (or not) transmitted while for a token LAN it indicates that the request has been successfully (or not) delivered.

Each service primitive has associated parameters. Included in the MA_UNITDATA.request primitive are the required destination address (this may be an individual, group, or broadcast address), a service data unit (containing the data to be transferred – that is, the LLC PDU), and the required class of

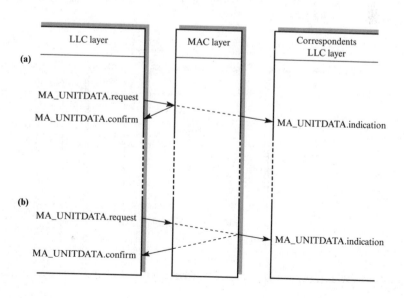

Figure 6.39
MAC user service primitives: (a) CSMA/CD; (b) token ring/bus.

service associated with the PDU. The last is used with token ring and token bus networks, for example, when a prioritized MAC protocol is being used.

The MA_UNITDATA.confirm primitive includes a parameter that specifies the success or failure of the associated MA_UNITDATA.request primitive. However, Figure 6.39 shows the confirm primitive is not generated as a result of a response from the remote LLC sublayer but rather by the local MAC entity. If the parameter indicates success, this simply shows that the MAC protocol entity (layer) was successful in transmitting the service data unit onto the network medium. If unsuccessful, the parameter indicates why the transmission attempt failed. As an example, if the network is a CSMA/CD bus, 'excessive collisions' may be a typical failure parameter.

6.5.2 LLC sublayer

The user services and operation of the LLC sublayer were discussed in Chapter 5 when data link control protocols were described. Recall that the LLC protocol is based on the high-level data link control (HDLC) protocol, and that two types of user service and associated protocol are supported: connectionless and connection-oriented. However, in almost all LAN installations, and especially in the technical and office environment, only a **send-data-with-no-acknowledge (SDN)** connectionless protocol is used. The only user service primitive is thus the L_DATA.request and, because this is a best-try protocol, all data is transferred using the unnumbered information (UI) frame. The interactions between the LLC and MAC sublayers are as shown in Figure 6.40.

The L_DATA.request primitive has associated parameters. These are a specification of the source (local) and destination (remote) addresses and the user data (service data unit). The latter is the **network-layer protocol data unit (NPDU)**. The source and destination addresses are each a concatenation of the MAC

Figure 6.40
LLC/MAC sublayer
interactions.

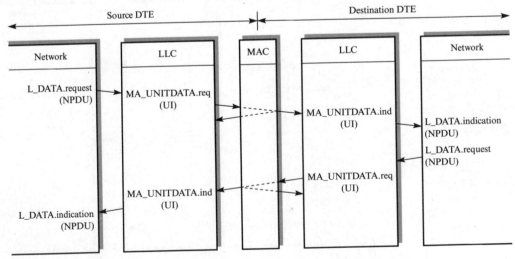

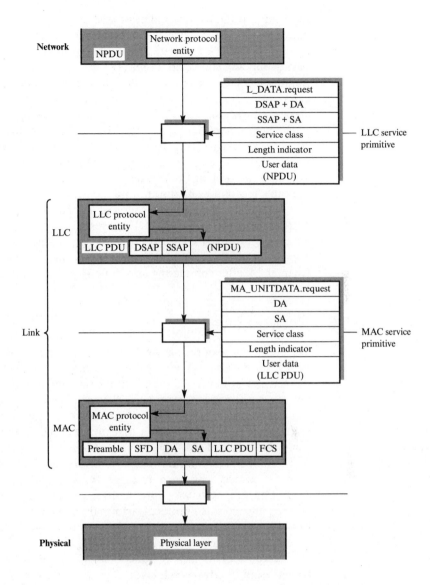

Figure 6.41
Interlayer primitives
and parameters.

sublayer address of the DTE and an additional **service access point (SAP)** interlayer address – the **LLC SAP**. This is used for interlayer routing purposes within the DTE, as we shall see in Section 8.2.3.

A more detailed illustration of the interactions between the LLC and MAC sublayers is shown in Figure 6.41. The LLC sublayer reads the destination and source LLC service access point addresses (DSAP and SSAP) from the two address parameters associated with the L_DATA.request service primitive and inserts these at the head of an LLC PDU. It then adds the network layer protocol data unit (NPDU) to this and passes the resulting LLC PDU to the MAC sublayer as the user data parameter of an MA_UNITDATA.request MAC primitive. Other parameters associated with this primitive include the MAC sublayer destination and source addresses (DA and SA), the desired service class, and the number of octets (length indicator) in the user data field. Typically, the service class is used by the MAC sublayer protocol entity to determine the priority to be associated with the frame if a token network is being used.

On receipt of the request, the MAC protocol entity creates a frame ready for transmission on the link. In the case of a CSMA/CD bus network, it creates a frame containing the preamble and SFD fields, the DA and SA fields, an I-field, and the appropriate FCS field. The complete frame is transmitted bit serially onto the cable medium using the appropriate MAC method.

A similar procedure is followed in the destination DTE except that the corresponding fields in each PDU are read and interpreted by each layer. The user data field in each PDU is then passed up to the next layer together with the appropriate address parameters. We shall discuss layer interactions further in Chapter 14, after considering application-oriented protocols.

6.5.3   Network layer

The primary role of the network layer is to route the messages associated with the higher protocol layers above it – in the context of the ISO reference model – across the network(s) that links the distributed community of DTEs. As with the data link layer, the network layer can operate either in a connectionless mode or in a connection-oriented mode. In the case of LANs, messages (frames) are addressed and routed between the DTEs that are attached to the same LAN using their **point-of-attachment** (MAC sublayer) **addresses**. Moreover, since LANs use high bit rate transmission media that have a very low BER, the DTE-to-DTE **transit delay** associated with each message transfer and the probability of message corruption are both very low. Consequently, a connectionless network layer service and associated protocol is normally used when all the DTEs are connected to a single LAN. Any error and flow control that is needed is then left to the transport layer protocol above it.

Because of its lack of functionality in LANs, the network layer is often known as an **inactive** or **null layer**. The user service primitives associated with the network service and their parameters are shown in Figure 6.42.

The basic message transfer service is N_UNITDATA – request and indication – which is a best-try service. The DA and SA parameters associated with this are concatenations of the MAC sublayer point-of-attachment address of the DTE (source or destination) and the LLC SAP interlayer address extension. A **network service access point (NSAP)** interlayer address extension is also used. Its role is the same as the LLC SAP and it allows messages to be routed through the various protocol layers to different APs (programs) within the same DTE. An example is a network server DTE that supports multiple applications such as electronic mail and file transfer.

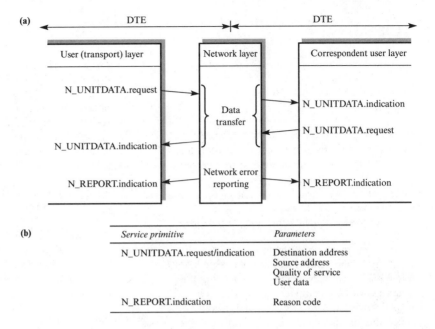

Figure 6.42
Network layer
services: (a) time
sequence diagram;
(b) service parameters.

In general, the **quality of service (QOS)** parameter includes fields to allow the transit delay, message priority, and other network parameters to be specified. In the case of a single LAN, just the priority field has any significance. Finally, the user data parameter points to the message data to be transmitted.

The N_REPORT.indication primitive is used by the network provider – LLC and MAC sublayers – to report any error conditions that may occur relating to the transfer request. In the case of LANs, an example is excessive collisions if a CSMA/CD LAN is being used.

We can therefore conclude that the protocol associated with the network layer is minimal. It involves creating an NPDU from the parameters associated with the incoming N_UNITDATA.request primitive and passing this to the LLC sublayer in the user data parameter of an L_DATA.request. Similarly, on receipt of an NPDU from the LLC sublayer – in the user data parameter associated with an L_DATA.indication – the protocol takes the source and destination network addresses from the NPDU and passes these, together with the remaining user data, to the user (transport) layer using an N_UNITDATA.indication primitive.

In conclusion, note that if the network comprises a number of interconnected networks rather than a single LAN, then the network layer protocol is far more complex. The total network is then known as an internetwork or internet and the individual networks as subnetworks or subnets. We shall consider the network layer further in Chapter 9 when internetworking is discussed.

Exercises

6.1 List the four main types of network topology currently in widespread use for LANs and, with the aid of sketches, explain their operation.

6.2 Use a sketch and associated text to describe how a set of DTEs is interconnected to form a CSMA/CD LAN using the following types of transmission media:
(a) Twisted pair
(b) Thin-wire coaxial cable
(c) Thick-wire coaxial cable and drop cables

6.3 Explain the meaning of the term 'broadband working' in the context of a coaxial cable LAN. Sketch a typical broadband LAN showing the main networking components required and explain their function. Describe the overall operation of such a network and how multiple data transmission services are derived from a single cable.

6.4 Describe the principle of operation of the following MAC methods as used in LANs:
(a) CSMA/CD
(b) Control token
(c) Slotted ring

6.5 Explain the meaning of the following terms associated with a CSMA/CD bus network:
(a) Slot time
(b) Jam sequence
(c) Truncated binary exponential backoff

6.6 Describe the principle of operation of the control token MAC method and, with the aid of diagrams, explain how it may be used with both a bus and a ring network topology. Clearly identify the various control fields associated with each topology.

6.7 Define the structure and contents of a typical frame as used in a slotted ring. Describe the meaning of each field within a frame and the operation of the associated ring protocol. Clearly explain how access to the ring is shared between the stations (DTEs) making up the ring.

6.8 Produce a sketch showing the components necessary to attach a DTE (station) to a thick-wire CSMA/CD bus network. Give an outline of the function of each component in the context of the overall operation of such a network. Define the structure and contents of each frame transmitted and the meaning of each field.

6.9 With the aid of a sketch, explain how a collision can occur with the CSMA/CD MAC method.
Explain the meaning of the terms 'interframe gap' and 'jam sequence' and hence, with the aid of flowcharts, describe the principle of operation of the transmit and receive sections of the MAC sublayer.

6.10 Explain the operation of the CSMA/CD MAC method in relation to a hub wiring configuration.

6.11 Produce a schematic diagram showing the components necessary to attach a DTE (station) to a token ring network and give an outline of the function of each component. Include sufficient detail to show how a DTE, once attached to the network, may operate in either inserted or bypassed mode. Show also the location and function of a wiring concentrator.

6.12 With the aid of a series of sketches, explain the principle of operation of the token MAC method in relation to a token ring network.
Clearly identify the two alternative token release methods that are used.

6.13 Describe the structure and contents of a token and an information frame as used in a token ring LAN. Explain the meaning of each field within the two frame types and, with the aid of flowcharts, describe the principle of operation of the transmit and receive sections of the MAC sublayer.

6.14 Explain the fault detection method that is used with token ring LANs. Explain also how the reliability of the LAN can be enhanced by the introduction of a redundant ring.

6.15 Explain what is understood by the following terms as used in a token ring network:
(a) Minimum latency time
(b) Token-holding time
(c) Differential Manchester encoding

6.16 Describe the operation of the priority control scheme used with token ring networks to control the order of transmission of frames of varying priority onto the ring. Include in this description the function of:
(a) The priority and reservation bits contained within each frame
(b) The priority registers and stacks held in each station
(c) A stacking station

6.17 State the aims of the following ring management procedures used with a token ring network and explain their operation:
(a) Initialization
(b) Standby monitor
(c) Active monitor
(d) Beaconing

6.18 Assume four stations – A, B, C, and D – are interconnected in a token ring network. After a period of inactivity, stations A and B each have a frame of priority 2 to send and stations C and D each have a frame of priority 4 (highest priority) to send.

Assuming station A has just captured the token and starts to transmit its waiting frame, trace the state of the priority and reservations fields during the next six rotations of frames/tokens around the ring. State also the actions taken by the stacking station.

6.19 Discuss the influence of the following on the design of a radio receiver to be used with a wireless LAN: signal-to-noise ratio, thermal noise, signal bandwidth, range of coverage, transmitter power level.

6.20 Discuss the following in relation to the radio environment and wireless LANs: adjacent channel interference and how it can be reduced, multipath and its effects, equalization, directional antennas.

6.21 Derive the frequency of an infrared emission that has a wavelength of (a) 800 nm and (b) 1300 nm.

6.22 Discuss the following relating to infrared systems:
(a) Why adjacent channel interference is lower than with radio
(b) The need for optical filters
(c) The effect of the modulation bandwidth of the infrared source on the maximum bit rate that can be obtained

6.23 With the aid of sketches, explain the principle of operation of the following operational modes of infrared LANs and how the effects of multipath dispersion can be reduced:
(a) Point-to-point
(b) Passive satellite
(c) Active satellite

6.24 Explain the principle of operation of a direct sequence spread spectrum wireless LAN and why such an application can coexist with other users of the same frequency band. Explain also why a MAC protocol is required by all nodes within the wireless LAN.

6.25 A pseudorandom binary sequence generator is comprised of a 4-bit shift register, ABCD, and a single exclusive-OR gate. If the A input is the exclusive-OR of the C and D outputs and the initial contents are 1111, derive the shift register states and hence output sequence. Is it maximal length?

6.26 Define the following terms relating to a direct sequence spread spectrum system: spreading sequence, chip, chipping rate, spreading factor, processing gain.

6.27 With the aid of a sketch, explain how symbol synchronization is achieved in a direct sequence spread spectrum system. For example purposes use the sequence 0101001100000. Derive the autocorrelation for this sequence.

6.28 With the aid of sketches, explain the principle of operation of both fast and slow frequency-hopping spread spectrum systems. Clearly identify the information that is being transmitted on each carrier when it is active with each scheme and how the receiver determines the transmitted bit sequence.

6.29 Discuss the advantages of frequency-hopping over direct sequence in the presence of strong narrowband interference signals within the operational frequency band.

6.30 Discuss the advantages and disadvantages of a single-carrier modulation scheme compared with a multi-subcarrier scheme for use in high bit rate wireless LANs.

6.31 Discriminate between direct modulation and carrier modulation in relation to an infrared transmission system.

6.32 With the aid of a waveform set, show how a binary sequence is modulated using a 16-PPM scheme.

6.33 With the aid of a sketch, explain the principle of operation of the CSMA/CD (comb) MAC method used in wireless LANs. Identify the factors that determine the efficiency of the scheme.

6.34 With the aid of a sketch, explain the principle of operation of the CSMA/CA MAC method used in wireless LANs. Identify the factors that determine the efficiency of the scheme.

6.35 State why an additional procedure is required with wireless LANs (in addition to the basic MAC method) to ensure a transmission over a wireless medium is successful. Hence explain the principle of operation of the four-way handshake procedure used in the distributed foundation MAC protocol.

6.36 Define the meaning of the term 'slot time' as used with a token bus network and explain the token-passing procedure used with such networks during both normal and abnormal operation. Include in these descriptions references to the following:
(a) To bridge around a faulty DTE
(b) To allow new DTEs to enter an operational logical ring

(c) To create a new token when a ring is first established

6.37 Explain the function of the following variables held by each DTE to control the order of transmission of frames that have varying priority on a token bus network:
(a) High-priority token-hold time
(b) Token rotation timer
(c) Target token rotation time
Produce a sketch, with an accompanying description of an example, to illustrate how the token rotation timer varies as frames are transmitted and the token rotates around the ring. Assume just two priority levels and deduce, from the example, the percentage of the available transmission capacity at each level.

6.38 (a) Outline the function of the LLC and MAC protocol layers as defined in the IEEE 802 standards documents and indicate their relationship with the lower protocol layers in the ISO reference model. Define a typical set of user service primitives for both the LLC and MAC layers and produce a time sequence diagram to illustrate how each LLC primitive is implemented using the defined MAC services.
(b) Explain the interlayer interactions that occur when an L_DATA.request service primitive is received by the LLC layer. Clearly identify the parameters associated with each primitive.

6.39 Explain the function of a connectionless network layer. Use a time sequence diagram to show the service primitives provided with the layer and also the parameters associated with each primitive.

6.40 Given the graphs of Figure 6.23(a) and (b), explain the relative performance of a CSMA/CD, token bus, and token ring LAN.

Chapter summary

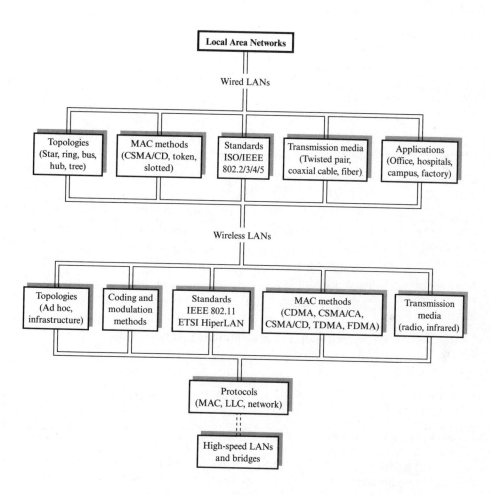

7 HIGH-SPEED AND BRIDGED LOCAL AREA NETWORKS

Chapter objectives

When you have completed this chapter you should be able to:

- Describe the operation of an Ethernet switching LAN and the two high-speed Ethernet derivatives ☞ 355, 357
- Describe the operation of the new IEEE 802.12 standard and the FDDI high-speed LAN ☞ 366, 376
- Understand the function and basic architecture of a bridge ☞ 390
- Know the advantages of a bridge relative to a repeater ☞ 391
- Describe the operation of a transparent bridged LAN and the spanning tree algorithm associated with it ☞ 393, 397
- Describe the operation of a source routing bridged LAN and the route finding procedure associated with it ☞ 409, 410
- Appreciate the differences and advantages and disadvantages of spanning tree and source routing bridged LANs ☞ 414

Introduction

The rapid establishment of standards relating to local area networks (LANs), coupled with the development by the major semiconductor manufacturers of inexpensive chipsets for interfacing computers to them, means that LANs form the basis of almost all commercial, research, and university data communication networks.

As the application of LANs has grown, so the demands on them in terms of data throughput and reliability have also grown. For example, an early application of LANs was to enable a distributed community of personal workstations (such as PCs) to access an electronic mail server or, say, a laser printer. Such applications involve a relatively small number of transactions, so the resulting demand on the transmission bandwidth of the LAN is only modest. More recently, however, there has been an increase in applications that demand significantly higher bandwidth. For example, the introduction of local communities of diskless workstations that share a common (networked) file system. This means that all file accesses by each of the workstations are via the network thus considerably increasing the demands on network bandwidth. Also, sophisticated applications involving the transmission of documents incorporating high-resolution images are becoming more common, again considerably increasing the demands on the capacity of the LAN.

To meet these requirements, a number of higher-speed LAN types have been developed. These include a number of variations of the basic CSMA/CD (Ethernet) LAN. This is by far the most widely installed type of LAN. The aim of the manufacturers has been to obtain higher performance with minimum changes to existing software and cable installations. One variation of the basic LAN is known as **Ethernet switching** and the other **Fast Ethernet**. A third development is the IEEE 802.12 standard. Like Fast Ethernet, it has been developed to use existing installed cable. However, IEEE 802.12 uses a different MAC protocol.

Most early LAN installations comprised just a single LAN segment to which the distributed community of workstations and associated peripheral servers were attached. However, as Chapter 6 indicated, the number of stations (DTEs) that can be attached to a single LAN segment and its physical length are limited. Hence, as the acceptance and applications of LANs have become more widespread, LAN installations comprising multiple linked segments have evolved. This trend has steadily continued and today most large LAN installations are of this type. A small, but typical, establishmentwide LAN showing some of the different interconnection devices and topologies is shown in Figure 7.1.

As we saw in Chapter 6, the basic means of interconnecting LAN segments is to use physical layer repeaters. However, with repeaters the frame transmissions originating from each station propagate (and hence load) the complete network, even though many of these frames may be intended for a station on the same segment as the originating station. This means that the more advanced applications of the type just outlined often result in a substantial load on the total network bandwidth, even though only a small percentage of the traffic on each segment is intended for systems attached to other segments. To overcome this problem, devices known as **bridges** have been introduced as an alternative means of interconnecting LAN segments. A basic bridge interconnects just two segments, but more sophisticated bridges – known as **multiport bridges** – can be used for the interconnection of a larger number of segments. Normally, the segments have only a relatively small physical separation between them, so multiport bridges are used mainly in a single office complex.

An alternative way of using bridges is to create what is known as a backbone subnetwork. Normally no end systems (workstations, servers, etc.) are connected to a backbone and they are used solely for intersegment traffic. For interconnecting only a small number of segments in a single building, backbones

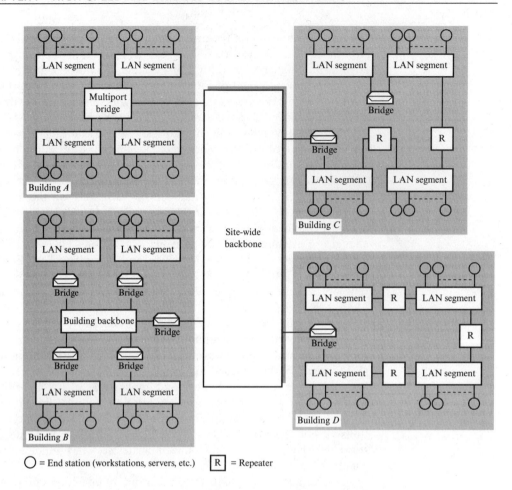

○ = End station (workstations, servers, etc.)   [R] = Repeater

Figure 7.1
Typical
establishmentwide
LAN.

of the same type as the interconnected segments (CSMA/CD, token bus, or token ring) are used. They are known as **building backbones**.

As the number of interconnected segments increases, there comes a point at which the transmission bandwidth required by the backbone to meet the intersegment traffic starts to exceed that available with the basic LAN types. To overcome this problem, backbones based on newer high-speed LAN types are used. An example is the **fiber distributed data interface (FDDI)** LAN. This is an optical fiber-based ring network that supports a bit rate of 100 Mbps. It can be used for the interconnection of segments that are spread over a wider geographical area than a single building, such as a university campus or manufacturing plant. The resulting network is then known as an **establishment** or **site backbone**. This chapter includes descriptions of each of these high-speed LAN types and also two types of bridge that are now international standards.

7.1 Ethernet switching

The most widely installed type of LAN is that based on the CSMA/CD access protocol. This is defined in IEEE 802.3/ISO 8802.3 and, for historical reasons, it is known as Ethernet. Early installations used thick-wire coaxial cable or, in laboratories and other similar locations, thin-wire coaxial cable. More recent installations use twisted-pair wiring with hubs. As Figure 6.9 showed, this is based on a star topology, with the hub located in a wiring closet for example. The DTEs/ stations within its field of coverage are connected to it via voice-grade twisted-pair cables.

As we can see, there is a separate transmit and receive pair of wires and the repeater electronics within the hub repeats – retransmits – the signal received on any of its input pairs onto all the output pairs. This emulates the broadcast mode of transmission used with coaxial cable and allows collisions to be detected by each attached DTE in the normal way. Clearly, only one transmission can be in progress at any time.

By increasing the complexity of the repeater electronics, the hub can operate in a nonbroadcast mode. Since the hub repeats each frame, it can learn the MAC address of the DTE that is attached to each of its ports by reading the *source* address from the header of each frame it repeats. In this way the hub can build a (routing) table that contains the MAC address of the DTE that is attached to each of its ports. Once this has been done – following the first transmission from each attached DTE – the repeater, on reception of the *destination* MAC address at the head of each received frame, can then repeat the frame only to the port(s) to which it is addressed, or, if the frame is not for any of its own DTEs, onto the link to the next hub. This is the principle of Ethernet switching.

The potential advantage of doing this is that, providing transmissions are between different DTEs, more than one frame transfer through the hub can take place concurrently. However, this requires the hub backplane to be able to repeat more than one frame in parallel. In practice, this can be done in a number of ways but the simplest approach is to provide a separate (serial) backplane bus line for each DTE. On receipt of each frame, the frame is relayed onto the required output port via the port's own backplane bus line. A schematic diagram showing this approach is given in Figure 7.2(a).

Each port input line is terminated with a first-in first-out (FIFO) buffer and the contents of all incoming frames are relayed through this. In the learning mode, after the source address at the head of a frame has been received into the FIFO buffer, the control processor reads this and makes an entry in its routing table of the port number and corresponding DTE address. The control processor then initiates the relaying of the whole frame – via the FIFO buffer – on all backplane bus lines.

Once the control processor has learnt the MAC address at each port, on receipt of all subsequent frames it simply reads the destination MAC address from the head of each frame, consults its routing table to determine the corresponding destination port number, and initiates the transfer of the frame to this using the

(a)

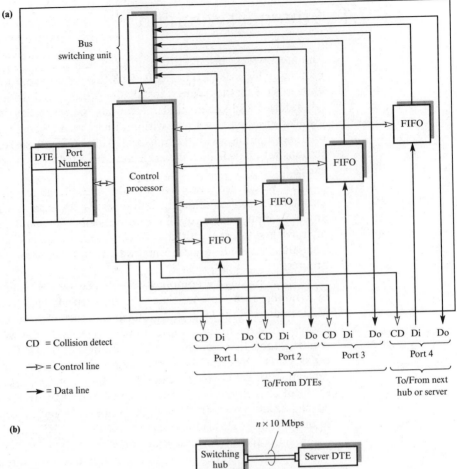

CD = Collision detect

——▷ = Control line

——▶ = Data line

Port 1   Port 2   Port 3   Port 4

To/From DTEs   To/From next hub or server

(b)

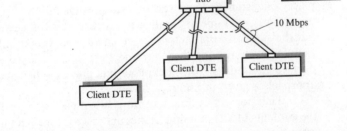

Figure 7.2
Ethernet switching:
(a) switching hub
schematic;
(b) switching hub
derivative.

corresponding backplane bus line. For group or broadcast addresses, a copy of the frame is forwarded on multiple lines. Similarly, in a multihub network, if the destination MAC address is not for one of its own ports/DTEs, then the frame is forwarded via the port connecting it to the next hub.

The final point to consider is collision detection. With this scheme, the only possibility of a collision is when a received frame requires a destination port that is already receiving a frame from another port. To allow for this an additional line – pair of wires – must be used to signal back to the transmitting DTE that a collision has occurred. In practice, this is readily achieved since unshielded twisted-pair voice-grade cable normally has four pairs per attached DTE.

We can therefore conclude that even though more than one transmission can take place in parallel, each transmission takes place at only 10 Mbps. Also, in many workgroup situations, a single server DTE is shared by multiple (client) DTEs and hence most transmissions involve the server. Clearly, since only one transmission involving the server can be in place at a time, the performance gains obtained will be limited.

To overcome this limitation, a derivative of the basic switching hub has evolved which provides a port which operates at a higher rate than the other ports. Typically, this is used to connect two hubs together or to connect a server to the hub as shown in Figure 7.2(b). With this arrangement, the speed-changing operation is carried out by providing more memory and operating the input and output ports of the FIFO buffer at different rates. On input of a frame from a client DTE, the frame is stored in its entirety before outputting it at the higher rate to the server port. Similarly, in the reverse direction, the server FIFO can buffer several frames, each of which is then output at the lower rate. This means that the server can support multiple concurrent transactions each operating at 10 Mbps. Similarly, when the high-speed port is used to connect two hubs together, multiple frame transfers can occur concurrently.

7.2 Fast Ethernet

The aim of Fast Ethernet is to obtain an order of magnitude increase in speed over 10 Base T Ethernet – IEEE 802.3 – while at the same time retaining the same wiring systems, MAC method, and frame formats.

The IEEE 802.3 specification allows for a total cable length – with repeaters – of 2.5 km. The worst-case signal propagation delay is the time for a signal to propagate twice this length. The standard allows a worst-case signal propagation delay – including repeater delay – of 50 μs which is equivalent to 500 bits at 10 Mbps. A safety margin is added to give a minimum frame size of 512 bits. Clearly, if this maximum length is reduced, then the CSMA/CD access method can be used with higher bit rates. This is the basis of the Fast Ethernet standard.

In practice, the vast majority of 10 Base T installations use less than 100 m of cable to connect each DTE to the hub. This means that the maximum distance between any two DTEs is 200 m and hence the worst-case path length for collision detection purposes is 400 m. Clearly, a higher bit rate can be used while still retaining the same CSMA/CD MAC method and minimum frame size of 512 bits. In the standard, the data bit rate is set at 100 Mbps and hence the standard is also known as **100 Base T**.

The major problem with Fast Ethernet is how to achieve a data transfer rate of 100 Mbps over 100 m of unshielded twisted-pair (UTP) cable. In practice, there are two standards, one that is intended for use with voice-grade category 3 cable and the other with either higher-quality category 5 cable, shielded twisted-pair

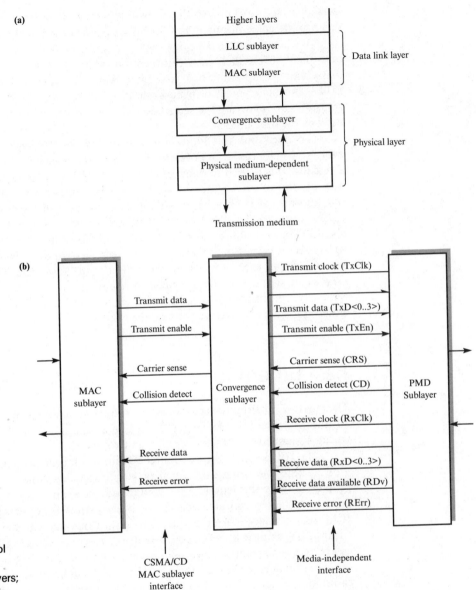

Figure 7.3
100 Base T protocol
architecture:
(a) protocol sublayers;
(b) interface signals.

(STP) cable, or optical fiber. The first standard is known as **100 Base 4T** and the second **100 Base X**. A schematic diagram showing the protocol architecture of both standards is given in Figure 7.3(a).

As we can see, the convergence sublayer (CS) provides the interface between the CSMA/CD MAC sublayer and the underlying physical medium-dependent (PMD) sublayer. The role of the CS is to make the use of the higher bit rate and different media types transparent to the MAC sublayer. To facilitate the use of different media types, a **media-independent interface (MII)** has been defined for use between the convergence and PMD sublayers. The set of signals associated with this interface is shown in Figure 7.3(b).

At a data transmission rate of 100 Mbps, it is not feasible to use clock encoding – for example Manchester – because the high resulting clock rate would violate the limit set for use over UTP cable. Instead, bit encoding schemes are used. The schemes ensure that each encoded symbol has sufficient transitions within it to enable the receiver to maintain clock synchronization.

The encoding schemes in both standards use one or more groups of four data bits to yield each encoded symbol. Hence, all data transfers over the MII are in 4-bit nibbles. The other control lines are concerned with the reliable transfer of these nibbles over the interface. Therefore, the major functions of the CS are to convert the transmit and receive serial data streams at the MAC sublayer interface into and from 4-bit nibbles for transfer across the MII, and to relay the carrier sense and collision detect signals generated by the PMD sublayer to the MAC sublayer. The two standards use different PMD sublayers to achieve a data transmission rate of 100 Mbps. We shall consider both standards in more detail.

7.2.1 100 Base 4T

Category 3 UTP cable contains four separate twisted-pair wires. To reduce the bit rate used on each wire, with 100 Base 4T all four wire pairs are used to achieve the required data transmission rate of 100 Mbps in each direction. This is the origin of the '4T' in the name.

With the CSMA/CD access control method, in the absence of contention for the medium, all transmissions are half-duplex, that is, either DTE-to-hub or hub-to-DTE. In a 10 Base T installation, just two of the four wire pairs are used for data transfers, one in each direction. Collisions are detected when the transmitting DTE (or hub) detects a signal on the receive pair while it is transmitting on the transmit pair. Since the collision detect function must also be performed in 100 Base T, the same two pairs are used for this function. The remaining two pairs are operated in a bidirectional mode as shown in Figure 7.4(a).

The figure shows that data transfers in each direction utilize three pairs – pairs 1, 3, and 4 for transmissions between a DTE and the hub and pairs 2, 3, and 4 for transmissions between the hub and a DTE. Transmissions on pairs 1 and 2 are used for collision detection and carrier sense purposes as with 10 Base T. This means that the bit rate on each pair of wires need only be 33.33 Mbps.

Line code

If we use Manchester encoding, a bit rate of 33.33 Mbps requires a clock rate of 33.33 MHz which exceeds the 30 MHz limit set for use with such cables. To reduce the clock rate a 3-level **(ternary) code** is used instead of straight (2-level) binary coding. The code used is known as **8B6T** which means that, prior to transmission, each set of 8 binary bits is first converted into 6 ternary (3-level) symbols. From

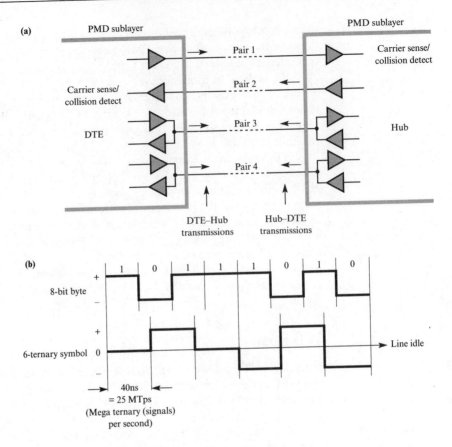

Figure 7.4
100 Base T: (a) use of wire pairs; (b) 8B6T encoding.

the example shown in Figure 7.4(b) we can deduce that this yields a symbol signaling rate of:

$$\frac{100 \times 6/8}{3} = 25\,\text{MHz}$$

which is well within the set limit.

The three signal levels used are $+V, 0, -V$ which are represented simply as $+, 0, -$. The codewords are selected such that the line is d.c. balanced, that is, the mean line signal is zero. This maximizes the receiver's discrimination of the three signal levels since these are then always relative to a constant 0 (DC) level. To achieve this, we exploit the inherent redundancy present in the use of 6 ternary symbols. The 6 ternary symbols mean that there are 729 (3^6) possible codewords. Since only 256 codewords are required to represent the complete set of 8-bit byte combinations, the codes used are selected, firstly, to achieve DC balance and secondly, to ensure all codewords have at least two signal transitions within them. This is done so that the receiver maintains clock synchronization.

To satisfy the first condition, we choose only those codewords with a combined weight of 0 or +1; 267 codes meet this condition. To satisfy the second condition, we eliminate those codes with fewer than two transitions – 5 codes – and also those starting or ending with four consecutive zeros – 6 codes. This leaves the required 256 codewords that are listed in Table 7.1.

DC balance

As we have just indicated, all the codewords selected have a combined weight of either 0 or +1. For example, the codeword +−−+00 has a combined weight of 0 while the codeword 0+++−− has a weight of +1. Clearly, if a string of codewords each of weight +1 is transmitted, then the mean signal level at the

Table 7.1 8B6T codeword set.

Data byte	Codeword	Data byte	Codeword	Data byte	Codeword	Data byte	Codeword
00	− + 0 0 − +	20	− + + − 0 0	40	− 0 0 + 0 +	60	0 + + 0 − 0
01	0 − + − + 0	21	+ 0 0 + − −	41	0 − 0 0 + +	61	+ 0 + − 0 0
02	0 − + 0 − +	22	− + 0 − + +	42	0 − 0 + 0 +	62	+ 0 + 0 − 0
03	0 − + + 0 −	23	+ − 0 − + +	43	0 − 0 + + 0	63	+ 0 + 0 0 −
04	− + 0 + 0 −	24	+ − 0 + 0 0	44	− 0 0 + + 0	64	0 + + 0 0 −
05	+ 0 − − + 0	25	− + 0 + 0 0	45	0 0 − 0 + +	65	+ + 0 − 0 0
06	+ 0 − 0 − +	26	+ 0 0 − 0 0	46	0 0 − + 0 +	66	+ + 0 0 − 0
07	+ 0 − + 0 −	27	− + + + − −	47	0 0 − + + 0	67	+ + 0 0 0 −
08	− + 0 0 + −	28	0 + + − 0 −	48	0 0 + 0 0 0	68	0 + + − + −
09	0 − + + − 0	29	+ 0 + 0 − −	49	+ + − 0 0 0	69	+ 0 + + − −
0A	0 − + 0 + −	2A	+ 0 + − 0 −	4A	+ − + 0 0 0	6A	+ 0 + − + −
0B	0 − + − 0 +	2B	+ 0 + − − 0	4B	− + + 0 0 0	6B	+ 0 + − − +
0C	− + 0 − 0 +	2C	0 + + − − 0	4C	0 + − 0 0 0	6C	0 + + − − +
0D	+ 0 − + − 0	2D	+ + 0 0 − −	4D	+ 0 − 0 0 0	6D	+ + 0 + − −
0E	+ 0 − 0 + −	2E	+ + 0 − 0 −	4E	0 − + 0 0 0	6E	+ + 0 − + −
0F	+ 0 − − 0 +	2F	+ + 0 − − 0	4F	− 0 + 0 0 0	6F	+ + 0 − − +
10	0 − − + 0 +	30	+ − 0 0 − +	50	+ − − + 0 +	70	0 0 0 + + −
11	− 0 − 0 + +	31	0 + − − + 0	51	− + − 0 + +	71	0 0 0 + − +
12	− 0 − + 0 +	32	0 + − 0 − +	52	− + − + 0 +	72	0 0 0 − + +
13	− 0 − + + 0	33	0 + − + 0 −	53	− + − + + 0	73	0 0 0 + 0 0
14	0 − − + + 0	34	+ − 0 + 0 −	54	+ − − + + 0	74	0 0 0 + 0 −
15	− − 0 0 + +	35	− 0 + − + 0	55	− − + 0 + +	75	0 0 0 + − 0
16	− − 0 + 0 +	36	− 0 + 0 − +	56	− − + + 0 +	76	0 0 0 − 0 +
17	− − 0 + + 0	37	− 0 + + 0 −	57	− − + + + 0	77	0 0 0 − + 0
18	− + 0 − + 0	38	+ − 0 0 + −	58	− − 0 + + +	78	+ + + − − 0
19	+ − 0 − + 0	39	0 + − + − 0	59	− 0 − + + +	79	+ + + − 0 −
1A	− + + − + 0	3A	0 + − 0 + −	5A	0 − − + + +	7A	+ + + 0 − −
1B	+ 0 0 − + 0	3B	0 + − − 0 +	5B	0 − − 0 + +	7B	0 + + 0 − −
1C	+ 0 0 + − 0	3C	+ − 0 − 0 +	5C	+ − − 0 + +	7C	− 0 0 − + +
1D	− + + + − 0	3D	− 0 + + − 0	5D	− 0 0 0 + +	7D	− 0 0 + 0 0
1E	+ − 0 + − 0	3E	− 0 + 0 + −	5E	0 + + + − −	7E	+ − − − + +
1F	− + 0 + − 0	3F	− 0 + − 0 +	5F	0 + + − 0 0	7F	+ − − + 0 0

Table 7.1 (cont.) 8B6T codeword set.

Data byte	Codeword	Data byte	Codeword	Data byte	Codeword	Data byte	Codeword
80	− 0 0 + − +	A0	− + + 0 − 0	C0	− + 0 + − +	E0	− + + 0 − +
81	0 − 0 − + +	A1	+ − + − 0 0	C1	0 − + − + +	E1	+ − + − + 0
82	0 − 0 + − +	A2	+ − + 0 − 0	C2	0 − + + − +	E2	+ − + 0 − +
83	0 − 0 + + −	A3	+ − + 0 0 −	C3	0 − + + + −	E3	+ − + + 0 −
84	− 0 0 + + −	A4	− + + 0 0 −	C4	− + 0 + + −	E4	− + + + 0 −
85	0 0 − − + +	A5	+ + − − 0 0	C5	+ 0 − − + +	E5	+ + − − + 0
86	0 0 − + − +	A6	+ + − 0 − 0	C6	+ 0 − + − +	E6	+ + − 0 − +
87	0 0 − + + −	A7	+ + − 0 0 −	C7	+ 0 − + + −	E7	+ + − + 0 −
88	− 0 0 0 + 0	A8	− + + − + −	C8	− + 0 0 + 0	E8	− + + 0 + −
89	0 − 0 + 0 0	A9	+ − + + − −	C9	0 − + + 0 0	E9	+ − + + − 0
8A	0 − 0 0 + 0	AA	+ − + − + −	CA	0 − + 0 + 0	EA	+ − + 0 + −
8B	0 − 0 0 0 +	AB	+ − + − − +	CB	0 − + 0 0 +	EB	+ − + − 0 +
8C	− 0 0 0 0 +	AC	− + + − − +	CC	− + 0 0 0 +	EC	− + + − 0 +
8D	0 0 − + 0 0	AD	+ + − + − −	CD	+ 0 − + 0 0	ED	+ + − + − 0
8E	0 0 − 0 + 0	AE	+ + − − + −	CE	+ 0 − 0 + 0	EE	+ + − 0 + −
8F	0 0 − 0 0 +	AF	+ + − − − +	CF	+ 0 − 0 0 +	EF	+ + − − 0 +
90	+ − − + − +	B0	+ 0 0 0 − 0	D0	+ − 0 + − +	F0	+ 0 0 0 − +
91	− + − − + +	B1	0 + 0 − 0 0	D1	0 + − − + +	F1	0 + 0 − 0 +
92	− + − + − +	B2	0 + 0 0 − 0	D2	0 + − + − +	F2	0 + 0 0 − +
93	− + − + + −	B3	0 + 0 0 0 −	D3	0 + − + + −	F3	0 + 0 + 0 −
94	+ − − + + −	B4	+ 0 0 0 0 −	D4	+ − 0 + + −	F4	+ 0 0 + 0 −
95	− − + − + +	B5	0 0 + − 0 0	D5	− 0 + − + +	F5	0 0 + − + 0
96	− − + + − +	B6	0 0 + 0 − 0	D6	− 0 + + − +	F6	0 0 + 0 − +
97	− − + + + −	B7	0 0 + 0 0 −	D7	− 0 + + + −	F7	0 0 + + 0 −
98	+ − − 0 + 0	B8	+ 0 0 − + 0	D8	+ − 0 0 + 0	F8	+ 0 0 0 + −
99	− + − + 0 0	B9	0 + 0 + − −	D9	0 + − + 0 0	F9	0 + 0 + − 0
9A	− + − 0 + 0	BA	0 + 0 − + −	DA	0 + − 0 + 0	FA	0 + 0 0 + −
9B	− + − 0 0 +	BB	0 + 0 − − +	DB	0 + − 0 0 +	FB	0 + 0 − 0 +
9C	+ − − 0 0 +	BC	+ 0 0 − − +	DC	+ − 0 0 0 +	FC	+ 0 0 − 0 +
9D	− − + + 0 0	BD	0 0 + + − −	DD	− 0 + + 0 0	FD	0 0 + + − 0
9E	− − + 0 + 0	BE	0 0 + − + −	DE	− 0 + 0 + 0	FE	0 0 + 0 + −
9F	− − + 0 0 +	BF	0 0 + − − +	DF	− 0 + 0 0 +	FF	0 0 + − 0 +

receiver will move away rapidly from the zero level, causing the signal to be misinterpreted. This is known as **DC wander** and is caused by the use of transformers at each end of the line. The presence of transformers means there is no path for direct current (DC).

To overcome this, whenever a string of codewords with a weight of +1 is to be sent, the symbols in alternate codewords are inverted prior to transmission. For example, if a string comprising the codeword 0+++−− is to be sent, then the actual codewords transmitted will be 0+++−−, 0−−−++, 0+++−−, 0−−−++, etc., yielding a mean signal level of 0. At the receiver, the same rules are applied and the alternate codewords will be reinverted into their original form

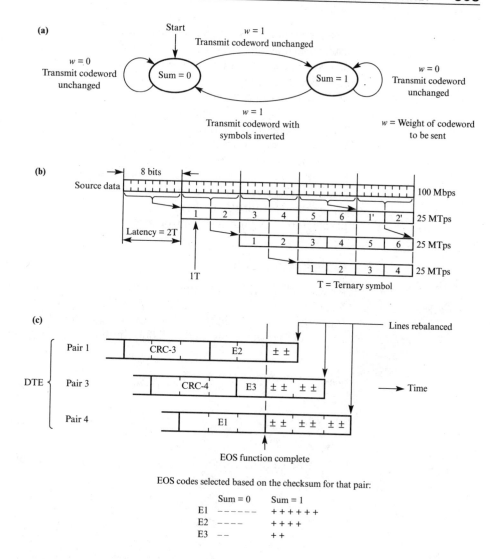

Figure 7.5
100 Base T
transmission detail:
(a) DC balance
transmission rules;
(b) 8B6T encoding
sequence; (c) end of
stream encoding.

prior to decoding. The procedure used for transmission is shown in the state transition diagram in Figure 7.5(a).

To reduce the latency during the decoding process, 6 ternary symbols corresponding to each encoded byte are transmitted on the appropriate three wire pairs in the sequence shown in Figure 7.5(b). This means that the sequence of symbols received on each pair can be decoded independently. Also, the frame can be processed immediately after the last symbol is received.

End-of-frame sequence

The transmission procedure adopted enables further error checking to be added to the basic CRC. We can deduce from the state transition diagram in Figure 7.5(a) that the running sum of the weights is always either 0 or +1. At the end of each frame transmission – that is, after the four CRC bytes have been transmitted – one of two different **end-of-stream (EOS)** codes is transmitted on each of the three pairs. The code selected effectively forms a checksum for that pair. The principle of the scheme is shown in Figure 7.5(c).

In this figure, we assume the last of the four CRC bytes (CRC-4) is on pair 3. The next codeword transmitted on pair 4 is determined by whether the running sum of the weights on that pair – referred to as the checksum – is 0 or +1. The EOS function is complete at the end of this codeword and the length of the other two EOS codes are reduced by two or one times the latency, that is, 4T or 2T. This means the receiver can detect reliably the end of a frame since all signals should cease within a short time of one another. This allows for very small variations in propagation delay on each pair of wires.

Collision detection

An example DTE hub transmission without contention is shown in Figure 7.6(a). Recall that a DTE detects a collision by detecting a signal on pair 2 while it is transmitting and, similarly, the hub detects a collision by the presence of a signal on pair 1. However, as Figure 7.6(a) shows, the strong (unattenuated) signals

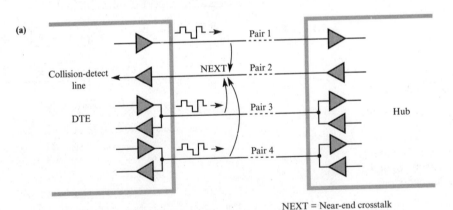

NEXT = Near-end crosstalk

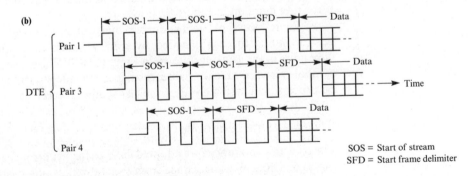

Figure 7.6
Start-of-frame detail:
(a) effect of NEXT;
(b) preamble
sequence.

SOS = Start of stream
SFD = Start frame delimiter

transmitted on pairs 1, 3, and 4 from the DTE side each induce a signal into the collision detect – pair 2 – wire. This is **near-end crosstalk (NEXT)** and, in the limit, is interpreted by the DTE as a (collision) signal being received from the hub. The same applies for transmissions in the reverse direction from hub to DTE.

To minimize NEXT the preamble at the start of each frame is encoded as a string of 2-level (as opposed to 3-level) symbols, that is, only positive and negative signal levels are present in each encoded symbol. This increases the signal-level amplitude variations which, in turn, helps the DTE/hub to discriminate between an induced NEXT signal and the preamble of a colliding frame.

The preamble pattern on each pair is known as the **start of stream (SOS)** and is made up to two 2-level codewords, SOS-1 and SFD. The complete pattern transmitted on each of the three pairs is shown in Figure 7.6(b) and, as we can see, the SFD codeword on each pair is staggered by sending only a single SOS-1 on pair 4. This means that the first byte of the frame is transmitted on pair 4, the next on pair 1, the next on pair 3, and so on. An acceptable start of frame requires all three SFD codes to be detected, and the staggering of them means that it takes at least four symbol errors to cause an undetectable start-of-frame error.

On detecting a collision, a DTE transmits the jam sequence and then stops transmitting. At this point, the DTE must be able to determine when the other DTE(s) involved in the collision cease transmitting in order to start the retry process. In practice, this is relatively easy since, in the nontransmitting (idle) state with 8B6T encoding, a zero signal level is present on the three data wires. This means that there is no induced NEXT signal in the collision detect wire which, in turn, enables the completion of the jam sequence from the hub side to be readily determined. Also, to improve the utilization of the cable, the interframe gap time is reduced from $9.6 \mu s$ to $960 ns$.

7.2.2   100 Base X

As the beginning of this section indicated, 100 Base X was designed for use with the higher quality category 5 cable now being used in most new installations. In addition, it is intended for use with STP and optical fiber cables. This use of various types of transmission media is the origin of the 'X' in the name.

Each type of transmission medium requires a different PMD sublayer. The first to be developed is that for multimode optical fiber cable as used in FDDI networks. The FDDI LAN, as indicated at the beginning of this chapter, is intended primarily as a backbone subnetwork since, unlike 100 Base T, it can span a distance up to 100 km. Transmissions over a FDDI network use a bit encoding scheme known as **4B5B** (sometimes written as 4B/5B) and this has been adopted also for use with 100 Base X.

Using 4B5B, each group of 4 data bits is encoded into a 5-bit (binary) symbol. The choice of symbols is such that there is a guaranteed signal transition at least every two bits which enables clock synchronization to be maintained. In addition, the use of 5 bits to represent the sixteen 4-bit data groups means that there are a further sixteen unused combinations of the 5 bits. A selection of these is used for various link control functions. In the case of 100 Base X, two of these symbols – J and K – indicate the start of a (MAC) frame and two others – T and R – signal the end of a frame. The frame contents, including the preamble and FCS, are encoded using the 5-bit symbols corresponding to each 4-bit nibble making up the frame. In this way, the J–K and T–R symbol pairs are unique and transparent to the frame contents.

The cable comprises two fibers, one of which is used for transmissions between the DTE and hub and the other for transmissions between the hub and DTE. As with 100 Base T, collisions are detected if a (colliding) signal is present on the receive fiber during the period the DTE is transmitting. Further details of the 4B5B coding scheme are given in Section 7.4 together with the bit patterns of the set of 5-bit symbols.

7.3 IEEE 802.12

Like the 100 Base T (Fast Ethernet) standard, IEEE 802.12 was developed as a high-speed follow-on to the IEEE 802.3 10 Base T standard. As we saw in Section 7.2, the major goal in the design of the 100 Base T standard was the retention of the CSMA/CD protocol. In contrast, the IEEE 802.12 standard provides only the same MAC service interface and uses a quite different MAC protocol. This has been done firstly, to enable large (cascaded) networks to be built without bridges, secondly, to enable the length of the submitted (MAC) service data unit to be variable to help interworking with all the existing LAN types, and thirdly, to support additional nondata traffic with real-time requirements.

As we have seen, the majority of existing 10 Base T wiring installations use a star topology with 4-pair voice-grade (VG), category 3, UTP cable. One of the aims has been to design the system so that this installed base can be used without rewiring. The IEEE 802.12 standard is also known as 100 (Base) VG-AnyLAN where 'VG' implies voice-grade cable and 'AnyLAN' indicates it can be configured to interwork with any of the existing LAN types. However, in addition to category 3 cable, it can be used with category 4 or 5 UTP cable and also 2-pair STP or 2-pair optical fiber.

7.3.1 Topologies

The MAC protocol has been designed to operate with a range of different network topologies as shown in Figure 7.7. The simplest topology is known as a **single-level network** and is shown in part (a).

As we can see, it is a simple star topology with a device known as a **repeater** – of different functionality to an IEEE 802.3 repeater – at the hub with the various end stations/DTEs connected to its set of **downlink ports**. The DTEs can be personal computers, workstations, servers, etc. In keeping with the goal of using installed wiring, the maximum length of cable between the repeater and any DTE

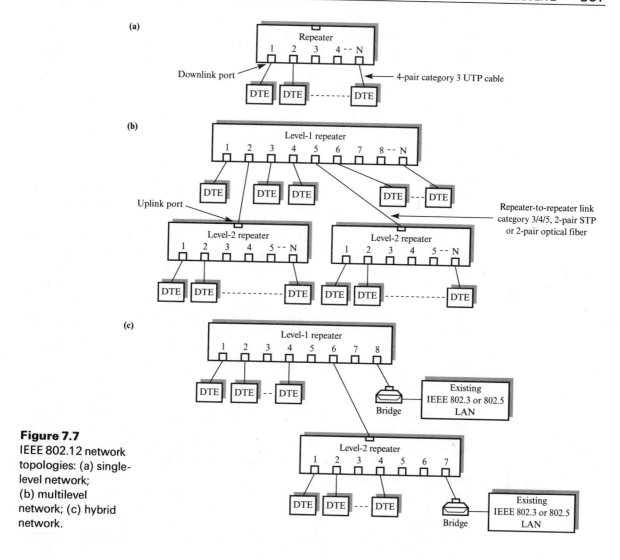

Figure 7.7
IEEE 802.12 network
topologies: (a) single-
level network;
(b) multilevel
network; (c) hybrid
network.

is 100 m with category 3 cable and proportionately more with the other cable types.

To build a network with larger coverage/number of ports, we can cascade a number of such configurations together in a hierarchical way as shown in Figure 7.7(b). The resulting topology is then known as a multilevel network with the highest-level repeater having overall control. When part of a larger network, each lower-level repeater has an **uplink port** associated with it. This, in turn, is connected to one of the downlink ports of the next higher-level repeater in the hierarchy. We can cascade repeaters in this way to cover distances up to 2.5 km before bridges are required. A bridge, as we shall see in Section 7.5, effectively terminates the LANs on each of its ports.

It is also possible to interwork with the other existing LAN types as shown in Figure 7.7(c). In this case, however, we must use bridges and they must support the new MAC protocol at the port at which they are connected to the IEEE 802.12 network. To facilitate interworking in this way, the IEEE 802.12 frame format can be either the IEEE 802.3 or 802.5 format. However, for any particular network only one format can be used.

7.3.2   MAC protocol

The MAC protocol is based on a polling principle. The repeater, in addition to relaying all frame transmissions between its attached DTEs/repeaters, also controls the order of all transmissions from them. This is accomplished using a set of control messages – signals – which are exchanged between the repeater and each attached DTE/repeater. Prior to sending a frame a DTE must wait until it has been granted permission by the repeater to which it is attached. When a DTE has a frame to send, it first sets a Request control signal on the repeater link. This also indicates whether the request is normal priority or high priority. Typically, normal priority is used for data frames and high priority for delay-sensitive information.

Only one frame transmission can be in progress across the total network at a time and, after the completion of each transmission, a repeater polls/examines all of its ports to determine if there are any outstanding requests. The order of transmission is controlled using a **round-robin scheduling algorithm**, that is, all transmissions take place in a strict numerical (port) order. Since there are two different priority classes, the repeater must retain a record of the port (DTE) allowed to transmit next for each priority class. The two port numbers are known as the **normal next-port pointer (NNPP)** and the **high-priority next-port pointer (HPNPP)** respectively. All high-priority requests are serviced first followed by the normal-priority requests, both starting with the current stored port number in the NPP for its class. This scheduling algorithm is known as **demand priority scheduling**.

In addition, to ensure waiting normal-priority requests/frames are not delayed excessively during periods when many high-priority requests are generated, a timer is kept for each outstanding normal-priority request and, if a request is not serviced within its timeout interval – from 200 to 300 ms – then the request is serviced as if it is a high-priority request.

The procedure followed by the repeater to relay a frame in a single-level network is shown in Figure 7.8. At the time of the first poll, the repeater determines that the DTE with a request pending can transmit next and hence returns a Clear control signal back to the waiting DTE – which acts as an acknowledgment – and, at the same time, alerts all the other DTEs connected to its ports to prepare for the possible arrival of a frame by sending to them an Incoming control signal. In response, each DTE returns a Clear control signal which, in turn, is interpreted by the repeater that it is ready to receive a frame.

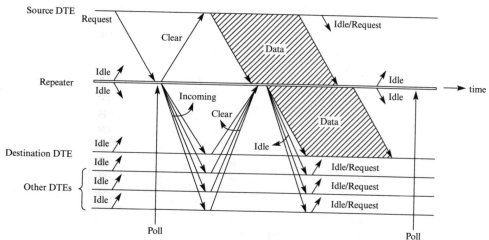

Figure 7.8
Timing diagram illustrating the sequence of control signals exchanged to transfer a data frame in a single-level IEEE 802.12 network.

On receipt of the Clear signal, the selected DTE begins to transmit its waiting frame. The repeater starts to receive this and temporarily stores it in a FIFO buffer – also known as an **elasticity buffer** – until it has received the destination address field at the head of the frame. It then uses this to determine the required output port(s) – from a stored look-up table that it maintains – and, while the remainder of the frame is being received, it relays the complete frame contents to the required destination port(s)/DTE(s) via the FIFO buffer and sends Idle signals to all the other DTEs. On detecting the end of the frame, the repeater then carries out another poll sequence. We can deduce that, unlike CSMA/CD, only the addressed DTE(s) receives a copy of the frame thereby improving the intrinsic security of the system. In order for the repeater to learn the MAC address of the DTE connected to each port, the DTE sends a short message containing its MAC address when it is first powered up.

Example 7.1

To illustrate the operation of the demand priority control algorithm, an example sequence of requests and related transmissions are shown in Figure 7.9. The sequence assumes the network is initially idle with both NPPs at 1. The requests from each DTE occur in the time order shown, normal requests are shown as N and high priority requests as H. Explain how the order of transmissions is derived.

(i)   The normal request on port 3 is detected on the first poll cycle and this is transmitted first and the NNPP advanced to 4.

(ii)   During the period this is being transmitted, a number of normal- and high-priority requests are set and these are detected by the repeater on the next poll after the first transmission ends. As Figure 7.9 shows, although the high-priority request on port 5 was set before that on port 2, the repeater selects port 2 first as this is nearer to the current HPNPP (1). The latter is then incremented to 3.

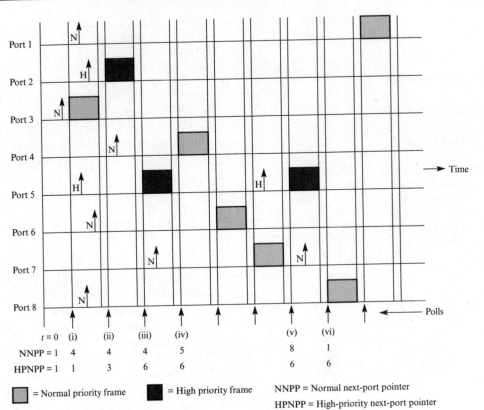

Figure 7.9
Example frame
transmission
sequence for a
single-level network.

(iii) After the frame at port 2 has been transmitted, the high-priority frame at port 5 is transmitted, advancing the HPNPP to 6.

(iv) At the next poll, the repeater detects outstanding normal requests on ports 1, 4, 6, 7, and 8. Since its current NNPP is 4, the repeater selects port 4 for the next transmission followed by ports 6 and 7 for the next two transmissions with the NNPP now set at 8.

(v) During the transmission of the frame from port 7, a new high-priority request is made on port 5. Hence after completing the relaying of the frame from port 7, the repeater detects this from its poll and proceeds to initiate the transmission of the high-priority frame at port 5 with the HPNPP left at 6.

(vi) During this transmission new normal requests are received on ports 7, 4, and 3. Hence the next poll detects outstanding normal requests on ports 1, 3, 4, 7, and 8. Since the NPP is currently 8, the frame from port 8 is transmitted next, followed by that on port 1, and so on.

(vii) Note that for clarity each request is shown only once but, in practice, a request will be made during each frame transmission until it has been serviced.

In a cascaded network, the highest-level repeater – known also as the **root repeater** – has primary control over all frame transmissions over the complete network. To explain the polling procedure, consider the 2-level network shown in Figure 7.10(a).

Each lower-level repeater polls its own ports in the normal way and, if requests are present, it sets either a normal or a high-priority request – determined by the requests present – on its uplink port. This procedure is followed by each lower-level repeater and hence the presence of any requests on repeater ports lower down the hierarchy will result in one or more requests on the corresponding ports of the root repeater.

Each higher-level repeater has a stored record of the type of device – DTE or repeater – that is connected to each of its downlink ports. The root repeater starts the pool sequence and, if the next port request to be serviced is from a DTE, it is handled in a similar way to that for a single-level network. Firstly, all repeaters – and through these their DTEs – and the other DTEs that are attached to the root are alerted of a possible incoming frame. The root then decodes the destination address at the head of the frame as this is received and, if it is for one of its local DTEs, relays the frame to the particular DTE. In addition, the root relays a copy of the frame on all ports that have a repeater connected to them. The same procedure is followed by all the other repeaters in the hierarchy which enables them to detect the end of each frame transmission. At this time, they each start a new poll sequence.

Alternatively, if the next request to be serviced by the root is from a repeater port, the request acknowledgment is passed to it in the normal way but the lower-level repeater then keeps the selection authority for a complete round-robin cycle of its ports. Therefore the network operates logically as though it is a single-level network with, for the example network shown in Figure 7.10, the ports ordered as shown. In a similar way, any transmissions that occur through a lower-level repeater are relayed on all repeater ports and so propagate throughout the whole network.

(a)

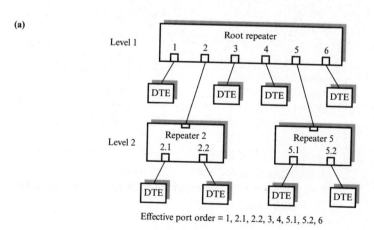

Figure 7.10
Two-level IEEE
802.12 network
example: (a) effective
port order.

Effective port order = 1, 2.1, 2.2, 3, 4, 5.1, 5.2, 6

(b)

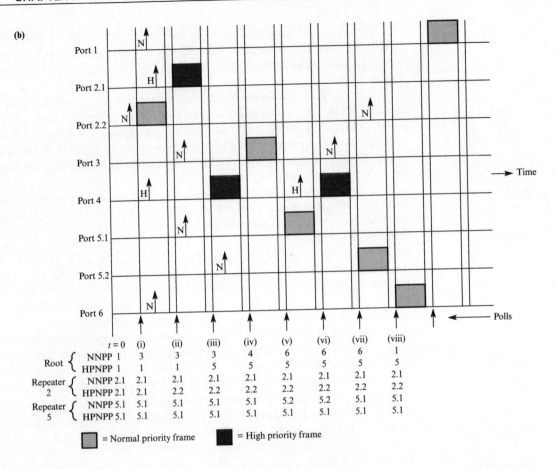

$t = 0$		(i)	(ii)	(iii)	(iv)	(v)	(vi)	(vii)	(viii)
Root {	NNPP 1	3	3	3	4	6	6	6	1
	HPNPP 1	1	1	5	5	5	5	5	5
Repeater {	NNPP 2.1	2.1	2.1	2.1	2.1	2.1	2.1	2.1	2.1
2	HPNPP 2.1	2.1	2.2	2.2	2.2	2.2	2.2	2.2	2.2
Repeater {	NNPP 5.1	5.1	5.1	5.1	5.1	5.2	5.2	5.1	5.1
5	HPNPP 5.1	5.1	5.1	5.1	5.1	5.1	5.1	5.1	5.1

▢ = Normal priority frame   ■ = High priority frame

Figure 7.10 (cont.)
(b) Example frame transmission sequence.

In order to ensure that high-priority requests from any port (DTE) in the network are serviced before normal-priority requests, an additional mechanism is required. If the root repeater detects a high-priority request on one of its ports during the period a lower-level repeater has control and is transmitting a normal-priority frame, on detecting the end of the frame, the root suspends further transmissions from the lower-level repeater – in its current round-robin cycle – by sending a Pre-empt control signal on all of its repeater ports. This causes the lower-level repeater currently in control to suspend servicing any further requests and return control to the root. The root then initiates the transmission of the high-priority frame in the normal way before returning control back to the lower-level repeater to complete its suspended round-robin cycle.

Example 7.2
■ ■ ■ ■ ■ ■ ■ ■ ■ ■

To illustrate the operation of the demand priority algorithm in a multilevel network, an example sequence of requests and related transmissions for the 2-level network shown in Figure 7.10(a) is given in part (b). The sequence assumes the network is initially idle with all NPPs at 1. Explain how the order of trans-missions is derived.

(i)   The normal-priority request at port 2.2 results in repeater 2 setting a normal-priority request on its uplink to port 2 of the root repeater. During its next poll, the root detects this and returns an acknowledgment to repeater 2 via port 2 and updates its NNPP to 3. On receipt of the acknowledgment, repeater 2 initiates a poll sequence of its ports and detects the normal-priority request pending on port 2.2. The DTE connected to this port then starts to transmit its waiting frame. Repeater 2 relays this onto the port 2 uplink to the root and then proceeds to read the destination address from the head of the frame to determine if it is addressed to a DTE connected to one of its other downlink ports. On receipt of the frame, the root relays it on to repeater 5 so both can detect the end of the frame.

(ii)   On detecting the end of the frame, repeater 2 continues with its round-robin poll of both classes and detects that a high-priority request is now pending on port 2.1. It therefore initiates the transmission of this next and updates its own HPNPP. There being no further outstanding requests on its ports, repeater 2 returns control to the root.

(iii) During this time, a number of other requests have been made on other repeater ports that result in normal-priority requests being present on root ports 1, 3, 5, and 6 and a high-priority request on port 4. The transmission of the latter is initiated first and the HPNPP is incremented to 5.

(iv)   During the transmission of this, a further normal-priority request has been made but, since root port 5 already has a normal-priority request pending, this will have no effect. The root NNPP is currently 3 and hence the trans-mission from the DTE connected to port 3 is initiated first and the NNPP is incremented is to 4.

(v)   On the next poll, the root detects the request on port 5 and hence issues an acknowledgment to the repeater that is connected to it and increments its NNPP to 6. On receipt of the acknowledgment repeater 5 initiates its own round-robin poll sequence of its ports and as a result initiates the trans-mission of the frame on port 5.1, incrementing its NNPP to 5.2.

(vi)   During this time a high-priority request is detected at port 4 and hence the root interrupts repeater 5 and initiates this transmission before returning control to repeater 5.

(vii) On receipt of an acknowledgment, repeater 5 continues its round-robin and initiates the transmission of the frame from port 5.2 before returning control to the root.

(viii) The next poll by the root detects outstanding normal-priority requests on ports 1, 2, 3, and 6. Hence since its NNPP is currently 6, the transmission of the frame from this port is initiated first and its NNPP is updated to 1. The procedure continues.

7.3.3 Physical layer

As Section 7.3 mentioned, the MAC protocol does not use collision detection and hence all four pairs within the cable may be used to transmit each MAC data frame, each operating at 25 Mbps. In practice, this is increased to 30 Mbps by the encoding scheme used but this is still within the defined limits. A schematic diagram of the main units making up the physical layer is shown in Figure 7.11.

The encoding scheme used is known as **5B6B** since each set of 5 data bits – known as a **quintet** – in the source data stream is translated into a 6-bit symbol – known as a **sextet** – each of which has the same number of binary 1 and 0 bits within it. This ensures clock/bit synchronization can be maintained. Additionally, to help to balance the number of 1s and 0s in the transmitted bit stream – to remove any DC offset – prior to performing the encoding operation, each of the four source data streams is scrambled, that is, randomized in a pseudorandom way so that it can be descrambled by the receiver.

Since the incoming data stream is transmitted on four wire pairs in parallel, the order of transmission of each quintet is selected so that they can be readily recombined into the original stream by the receiver. The order used – excluding the scrambling process – is shown in Figure 7.11(b). The contents of the MAC frame are first segmented into quintets. After encoding, these are transmitted on the four wire pairs in a round-robin fashion. As we can see, after encoding the quintets – these would be scrambled in practice – the resulting sextets have an equal number of 1s and 0s thereby removing any DC offset. This is necessary when transmitting via transformers to avoid DC wander.

The various control signals associated with the MAC protocol are formed from combinations of two fixed-frequency tones, one low and the other high. Since these are exchanged prior to any data transmissions, they are transmitted on the same set of four wire pairs as the data. However, in the case of the control signals, two pairs are used for one direction – DTE-to-repeater, for example – and the other two pairs in the reverse direction. The meaning of each pair of tones is dependent on whether it is transmitted or received and a selection of these was shown earlier in Figure 7.8.

7.3.4 Performance

If we assume a single-level network and just normal-priority requests, the maximum delay between a DTE making a request to send a frame at a repeater port and the frame being received by the destination DTE is equal to the time to transmit a maximum length frame from one DTE to another multiplied by the number of active ports on the repeater. With IEEE 802.3 (Ethernet) frames and a 32-port repeater, in the standard this is quoted to be in the order of 3.84 ms. This is the worst-case delay of course. With a modestly loaded network and a mix of frame sizes, the actual delay is significantly less than this. Also, all DTEs are guaranteed to get an equal share of the available bandwidth.

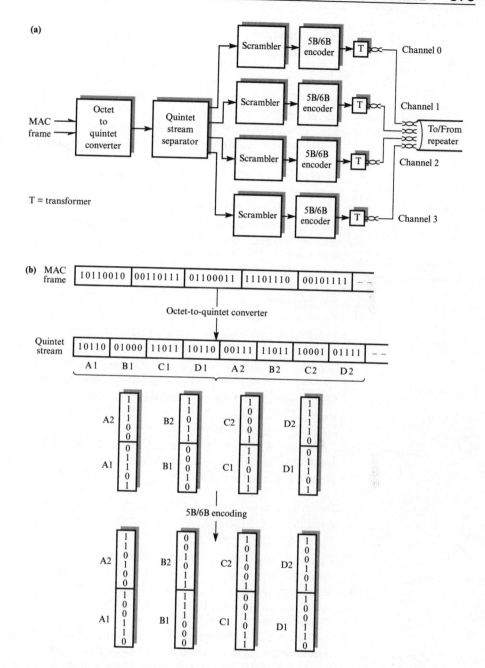

Figure 7.11
IEEE 802.12 physical layer principles: (a) main units; (b) example encodings.

Although this delay satisfies most real-time requirements, for large networks with many attached DTEs, the resulting delay will increase and, for some applications, become unacceptable. With such applications, we must adopt the dual-priority protocol. With this, the worst-case delay for high-priority frames can be quantified in the same way as that for normal-priority frames in a single-priority network. In addition, because of the presence of low-priority frames, we must introduce a mechanism for allocating the use of the available high-priority bandwidth.

To set bounds on the maximum delay experienced by any DTE in the network, we define a **target transmission time (TTT)**. Firstly, we determine the throughput that is achievable with the particular network configuration being used within this time, and then we divide this throughput between those DTEs that require to send time-critical traffic. The traffic is then transmitted using high-priority requests and the protocol ensures that this is divided equally between all the DTEs sending such traffic. In the limit, of course, the aggregate bit rate of such traffic cannot exceed 100 Mbps for the total network. For large networks with many workstations transmitting time-critical traffic, this is the limiting factor. Chapter 10 describes alternative network architectures that have been designed to meet such requirements.

7.4 FDDI

The FDDI LAN standard was developed by the American National Standards Institute (ANSI). It is now an international standard and is defined in ISO 9314. It is based on a ring topology and operates at a data rate of 100 Mbps. Like the token ring, it uses dual counter-rotating rings to enhance reliability. Multimode fiber connects each station together and the total ring can be up to 100 km in length. Up to 500 stations (DTEs) can be connected in the ring and hence it forms an ideal backbone network. The MAC method is based on a control token and, in addition to normal data traffic, optionally the ring can also support delay-sensitive traffic that requires a guaranteed maximum access delay, for example, digitized speech. Let us now consider the standard in more detail.

7.4.1 Network configuration

FDDI uses two counter-rotating rings to enhance reliability: the **primary ring** and the **secondary ring**. As we saw in Figure 6.18, the secondary ring can be used either as an additional transmission path or purely as a back-up in the event of a break occurring in the primary ring. A typical network configuration is shown in Figure 7.12.

As we can see, there are two types of station (DTE): a **dual attach station (DAS)** which is connected to both rings and a **single attach station (SAS)** which is attached only to the primary ring. In practice, most user stations are attached to the ring via **wiring concentrators** since then only a single pair of fibers is needed and the connection cost is lower.

If the LAN is being used as a backbone, then most attached stations are bridges. The protocol used to reconfigure the LAN into a single ring in the event of a ring failure was described in Section 6.2.2.

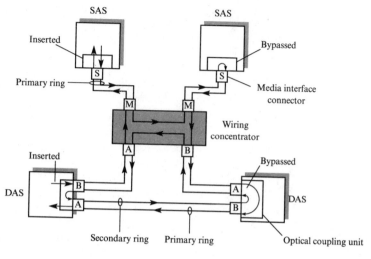

Figure 7.12
FDDI networking
components.

SAS = Single attach station   S = Slave key
M = Master key   DAS = Dual attach station

The basic fiber cable is **dual core** with **polarized duplex** (two-position) connectors at each end. This means that each end of the cable has a different physical key so that it can be connected into a matching socket only. This prevents the transmit and receive fibers from becoming inadvertently interchanged and bringing down the total network. As a further precaution, we use different connectors to connect each station type – SAS and DAS. In common with the basic token ring, we use special coupling units to isolate (bypass) a station when its power is lost. With FDDI, these are either active or passive fiber devices.

Although the topology is logically a ring, physically it is normally implemented in the form of a hub/tree structure. An example is shown in Figure 7.13(a). To ensure that changes to the wiring are carried out in a controlled way, a combination of **patch panels** and wiring concentrators are used. Typically these are located in the wiring closet (room) associated with either a floor (if a local FDDI ring is being used) or a building (if the ring is a backbone). In the latter case, the patch panels are interconnected as shown in Figure 7.13(b) to create a tree structure with the root located in, say, the computer center. Drop cables are used to connect each station – workstations or bridges – to the ring.

Each patch panel has a number of possible attachment points associated with it. In the absence of a connection at a particular point, the ring is maintained using short **patch cables**, each with the same type of connector. Adding a new station or concentrator simply involves removing a patch cable and replacing it with a corresponding drop cable. This approach is known as structured wiring (see Section 6.1.2).

(a)

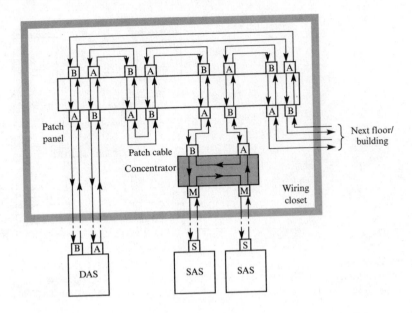

(b)

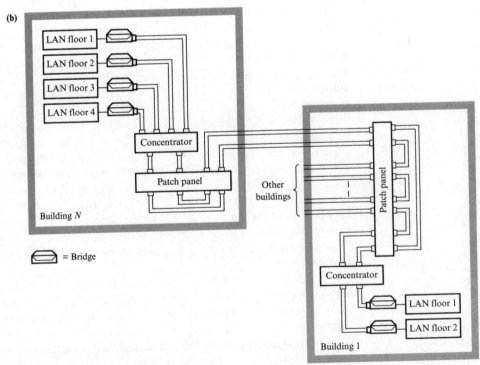

Figure 7.13
FDDI wiring
schematic:
(a) building;
(b) establishment.

7.4.2 Physical interface

The physical interface to the fiber cable is shown in Figure 7.14. In a basic token ring network, at any instant, there is a single active ring monitor which, among other things, supplies the master clock for the ring. Each circulating bit stream is encoded by the active ring monitor using differential Manchester encoding. All the other DTEs (stations) in the ring then frequency and phase lock to the clock extracted from this bit stream. However, such an approach is not suitable at the data rates of an FDDI ring since this would require a rate of 200 Mbaud. Instead, each ring interface has its own local clock. Outgoing data is transmitted using this clock while incoming data is received using a clock that is frequency and phase locked to the transitions in the incoming bit stream. As we shall see, all data is encoded prior to transmission so that there is a guaranteed transition in the bit stream at least every two bit cell periods, ensuring that each received bit is sampled (clocked) very near to the nominal bit cell center.

All data to be transmitted is first encoded, prior to transmission, using a **4 of 5 group code**. This means that for each 4 bits of data to be transmitted, a corresponding 5-bit codeword or symbol is generated by an encoder known as a **4B5B encoder**. The 5-bit symbols corresponding to each of the sixteen possible 4-bit data groups are shown in Figure 7.15(a). As we can see, there is a maximum of two consecutive zero bits in each symbol. The symbols are then shifted out through a further NRZI encoder which produces a signal transition whenever a 1 bit is being transmitted and no transition when a 0 bit is transmitted. In this way, there is a guaranteed signal transition at least every two bits.

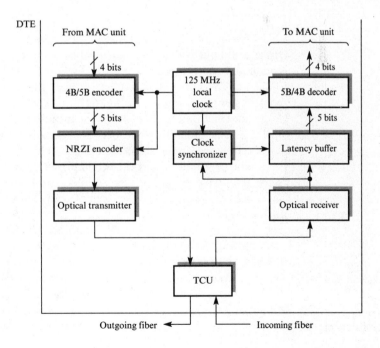

Figure 7.14
FDDI physical
interface schematic.

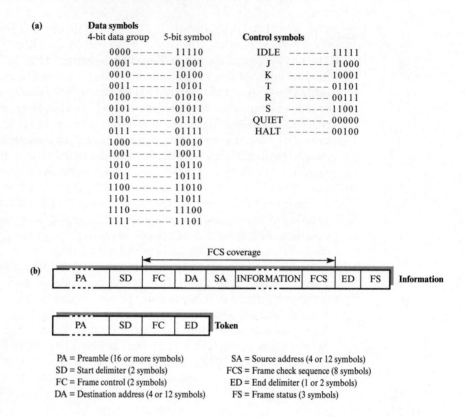

Figure 7.15
FDDI line coding and
framing detail:
(a) 4B5B codes;
(b) frame formats.

The use of 5 bits to represent each of the sixteen 4-bit data groups means that there are a further sixteen unused combinations of the 5 bits. Some of these combinations (symbols) are used for other (link) control functions, such as indicating the start and end of each transmitted frame or token. A list of the link control symbols is shown in Figure 7.15(a), while part (b) shows the format used for frames and tokens. In general, the meaning and use of each field is the same as with the basic token ring but, because symbols are used rather than bits, there are some differences in the structure of each field.

The preamble (PA) field is comprised of 16 or more IDLE symbols which, since they each consist of five 1 bits, cause the line signal to change at the maximum frequency. The line signal transitions are used for establishing (and maintaining) clock synchronization at the receiver. The start delimiter (SD) field consists of two control symbols (J and K) which enable the receiver to interpret the following frame contents on the correct symbol boundaries. The FC, DA, and SA fields have the same meaning as before, but the (decoded) information field in the data frames can be up to 4500 octets with FDDI. The end delimiter (ED) field contains one or two control symbols (T). Finally, the frame status (FS) field, although it has a similar function to the FS field in the basic ring, consists of three symbols that are combinations of the two control symbols R and S.

The local clock used in the physical interface is 125 MHz which, because of 4B5B encoding, yields a data rate of 100 Mbps. Since all transmissions are encoded into 5-bit symbols, each 5-bit symbol must first be buffered at the receiver before it can be decoded. However, the use of two symbols (J and K) for the SD field to establish correct symbol boundaries means that a 10-bit buffer is used at the receiver. This is known as the **latency** (or elastic) **buffer** since it introduces 10 bits of delay – latency – into the ring. At 125 Mbps, this is equivalent to a delay of $0.08\ \mu s$ but, allowing for additional gate and register transfer delays, this is normally rounded up to $1\ \mu s$ per ring interface.

Example 7.3

Assuming a signal propagation delay in the fiber of $5\ \mu s$ per 1 km, derive the latency of the following FDDI ring configurations in both time and bits assuming a usable bit rate of 100 Mbps.

(a)   2 km ring with 20 stations

(b)   20 km ring with 200 stations

(c)   100 km ring with 500 stations

Ring latency, $T_l =$ Signal propagation delay, $T_p + N \times$ station latency, T_s

where N is the number of stations.

(a) $T_l = 2 \times 5 + 20 \times 1$
$= 30\ \mu s$ or 3000 bits

(b) $T_l = 20 \times 5 + 200 \times 1$
$= 300\ \mu s$ or 30 000 bits

(c) $T_l = 100 \times 5 + 500 \times 1$
$= 1000\ \mu s$ or 100 000 bits

Note that the above values assume that the primary ring only is in use. If a fault occurred, the three signal propagation delay values would each be doubled. Also, for dual attach stations, the station latency would be doubled.

7.4.3   Frame transmission and reception

The short latency time (and hence number of bits in circulation) of the basic token ring means that a station (DTE), after initiating the transmission of an information frame, can wait until the FS field at the tail of the frame has been received before transmitting a new token without any noticeable loss in ring utilization. However, from Example 7.3 we can deduce that with an FDDI ring the loss in ring utilization will be significant if this mode of operation is adopted. With an FDDI ring, therefore, the early token release method is utilized, that is, a new token is transmitted immediately after the station has transmitted the FS symbol at the tail of a frame. The station then follows the token with IDLE symbols until it receives the SD symbols indicating the start of a new frame or token. The basic scheme is shown in diagrammatic form in Figure 7.16.

As we can see, as with the basic token ring, the source station removes a frame after it has circulated the ring. However, because of the long latency of an FDDI ring more than one frame may be circulating around the ring at one time. Although not shown in Figure 7.16, the ring interface must repeat the SD, FC and DA fields (symbols) of any received frames before it can determine if its own address is in the SA field. This can result in one or more frame fragments – comprising SD, FC, and DA fields – circulating around the ring. This means that a station, on receipt of the token, starts to transmit a waiting frame and concurrently receives and discards any frame fragments that may be circulating around the ring.

7.4.4   Timed token rotation protocol

Unlike the transmission control method used with the basic token ring which is based on the use of the priority and reservation bits in the access control field of token and information frames, an FDDI ring uses the same principle as that used with a token bus network. Recall that this is based on a timed token rotation protocol that is controlled by a preset parameter known as the target token rotation time (TTRT).

For each rotation of the token, each station computes the time that has expired since it last received the token. This is known as the token rotation time (TRT) and includes the time taken by a station to transmit any waiting frames plus the time taken by all other stations in the ring to transmit any waiting frames for this rotation of the token. Clearly, if the ring is lightly loaded, then the TRT is short but, as the loading of the ring increases, so the TRT measured by each station increases also. The TRT is thus a measure of the total ring loading.

The timed token rotation protocol ensures access to the ring is shared fairly between all stations by allowing a station to send any waiting frames only if its measured TRT is less than the preset TTRT for the ring. Hence, when a station has frames waiting to send, on receipt of the token it computes the difference between the TTRT and its current TRT. This is known as the token hold timer (THT) since it determines for how long the station may transmit waiting frames before releasing the token. If the THT is positive, then the station can transmit for up to this interval. If it is negative, then the station must forego transmitting any waiting frames for this rotation of the token. A positive THT is thus known as an **early token** while a negative THT is known as a **late token**. An example was given in Section 6.2.3 that showed how the TTRT controlled access to a token bus network with mixed priority traffic. In an FDDI network, however, the TTRT is used to control access to the ring for data frames that all have the same priority.

Assume station *A* has a frame waiting to send to station *C* and station *B* has a frame waiting to send to station *D*

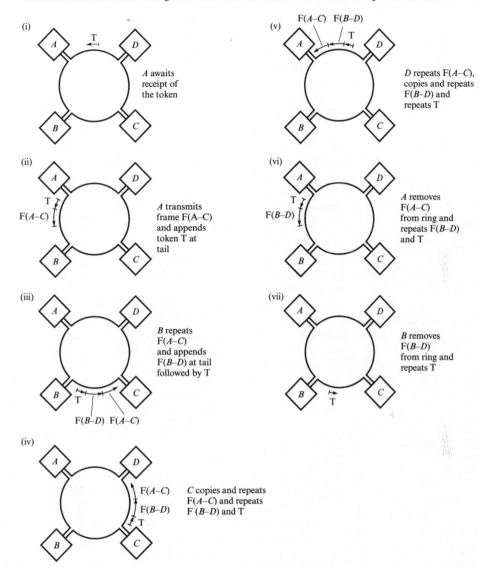

(i) *A* awaits receipt of the token

(ii) *A* transmits frame F(A–C) and appends token T at tail

(iii) *B* repeats F(A–C) and appends F(B–D) at tail followed by T

(iv) *C* copies and repeats F(A–C) and repeats F(B–D) and T

(v) *D* repeats F(A–C), copies and repeats F(B–D) and repeats T

(vi) *A* removes F(A–C) from ring and repeats F(B–D) and T

(vii) *B* removes F(B–D) from ring and repeats T

Figure 7.16
FDDI transmission example.

Example 7.4

The timed token rotation protocol is to be used to control access to a four-station FDDI ring network. All frames to be transmitted are of the same length and the TTRT to be used is equivalent to the transmission of four frames plus any ring latency. After an idle period when no frames are ready to send, all four stations receive four frames to send. Assuming the time for the token to rotate around the ring in the idle state is equal to the time to transmit the token, T_t, plus the ring latency, T_l, derive and show in table form the number of frames each station can transmit for the next four rotations of the token.

The number of frames that each station can transmit on the first four rotations of the token are shown in diagrammatic form in Figure 7.17. They are derived as follows.

After the idle period, the TRT of all stations will be $T_t + T_l$ since no frames have been transmitted. Once frames become ready to send, on receipt of the token station 1 computes a THT of 4 and hence transmits (XMIT) four waiting frames before passing on the token. However, since station 1 has sent four frames, none of the other stations are able to send any frames for this rotation of the token. This is so since their TRT is now greater than four in each case and hence their corresponding computed THT is negative.

On the second rotation of the token, the TRT of station 1 has incremented to 4 plus the ring latency, hence it is not able to send any waiting frames. This means that the TRT of station 2 is less than the TTRT and hence it can send four waiting frames. Again this will block stations 3 and 4 from sending any waiting frames on this rotation of the token.

On the third rotation of the token, the THT of stations 1 and 2 are both 4 plus the ring latency and hence neither can send frames. The TRT of station 3, however, is this time less than the TTRT and hence it can transmit four waiting frames. Again station 4 is blocked.

Token rotation	Station 1		Station 2		Station 3		Station 4	
	TRT	XMIT	TRT	XMIT	TRT	XMIT	TRT	XMIT
0	$T_t + T_l$	0	$T_t + T_l$	0	$T_t + T_l$	0	$T_t + T_l$	0
1	$T_t + T_l$	4	$4 + T_t + T_l$	0	$4 + T_t + T_l$	0	$4 + T_t + T_l$	0
2	$4 + T_t + T_l$	0	$T_t + T_l$	4	$4 + T_t + T_l$	0	$4 + T_t + T_l$	0
3	$4 + T_t + T_l$	0	$4 + T_t + T_l$	0	$T_t + T_l$	4	$4 + T_t + T_l$	0
4	$4 + T_t + T_l$	0	$4 + T_t + T_l$	0	$4 + T_t + T_l$	0	$T_t + T_l$	4

Figure 7.17
FDDI timed token rotation protocol example.

TRT = Token rotation time
XMIT = Number of frames transmitted on this rotation of the token
TTRT = Target token rotation time

T_t = Time to transmit the token
T_l = Ring latency
TTRT = $4 + T_t + T_l$

Finally, on the fourth rotation of the token, stations 1, 2, and 3 are all blocked and station 4 can transmit four frames. This simple example shows that the available transmission capacity is shared in an equitable way between all four stations.

7.4.5 Performance

There are two important performance measures associated with shared-medium networks: the **maximum obtainable throughput** and the **maximum access delay**. Both are strongly influenced by the MAC algorithm used to share the available transmission capacity between the attached stations. As we have just seen, in the case of an FDDI ring this is based on the use of a control token and the timed token rotation protocol. The important parameter associated with the protocol is the TTRT and, since this must be preset to the same value in all stations, it is important to quantify its effect on both the obtainable throughput and the access delay.

Although the nominal throughput of an FDDI ring is 100 Mbps, because of the ring latency and access control mechanism, the maximum obtainable throughput is less than this. Maximum obtained throughput (and access delay) implies that there are always frames waiting to be sent on receipt of the token at each ring interface. Under such conditions, we can compute the obtainable maximum throughput by considering the operating scenario in Example 7.4. In this, on receipt of the token, the first station transmits a set of frames up to the point when the TTRT expires before passing on the token. All the other stations in the ring are blocked from transmitting any frames during this rotation of the token. It is not until the token is passed to the next station in the ring on the following rotation that the second transmission burst of frames occurs.

Therefore, the transmission time lost during successive rotations of the token is made up of two parts: the time lost while the set of frames transmitted by the first station rotates around the ring – the ring latency – and the time taken for the token to be passed to the next station on the ring. We can express the maximum utilization of the nominal ring capacity, $U_{\max}$, as follows:

$$U_{\max} = \frac{\text{TTRT} - T_1}{(\text{TTRT} - T_1) + T_1 + T_t + (T_1/n)} = \frac{n(\text{TTRT} - T_1)}{n(\text{TTRT} - T_1) + (n+1)T_1 + T_t}$$

where TTRT is the target token rotation time, T_1 is the ring latency, T_t is the time to transmit the token, and n is the number of stations in the ring.

In practice, the TTRT is very much greater than T_t. Hence the maximum utilization can be approximated to:

$$U_{\max} = \frac{n(\text{TTRT} - T_1)}{n\,\text{TTRT} + T_1}$$

We can conclude that, to achieve a high level of ring utilization, we must select a TTRT which is significantly greater than the total ring latency. In addition, the selected TTRT must allow at least one frame of the maximum size to be present on the ring. The maximum size frame is 4500 bytes which requires 0.36 ms to transmit at 100 Mbps. The maximum ring latency was derived in Example 7.3 and, allowing for the secondary ring to be in use and the 500 stations to be all dual attach stations, this is approximately 2 ms. Therefore the minimum TTRT allowable is 2.36 ms which, allowing for a safety margin, is set to 4 ms in the standard.

The access delay is defined as the time delay between the arrival of a frame at the ring interface of the source station and its delivery by the ring interface at the destination station. Thus access delay includes any time spent waiting in the ring interface queue at the source until a usable token – that is, an early token – arrives. It is meaningful only if the offered load is less than the maximum obtainable throughput of the ring, otherwise the interface queues continuously build up and the access delay gets progressively larger.

Provided the offered load is less than the maximum obtainable throughput, the maximum (worst case) access delay can also be deduced from Example 7.4. Assume that all stations simultaneously receive a set of frames at their ring interface queues such that they will each utilize the full TTRT quota for each rotation of the token. Assuming that station 1 is the first station able to transmit frames, the maximum access delay will be experienced by the last station on the ring – that is, station 4 – since this will receive a usable token only at the start of the fourth rotation of the token. Also, if the four frames in its ring interface queue are all addressed to station 3, then a further delay equal to the ring latency will be experienced while they are all transmitted around the ring to this station. The general expression used to compute the maximum access delay of an FDDI ring, A_{max}, is given by:

$$A_{max} = (n-1)(TTRT - T_1) + nT_1 + T_1$$
$$= (n-1)TTRT + 2T_1$$

where A_{max} is the worst-case time to receive a usable token and the other terms have the same meaning as before.

Clearly, since the ring latency is fixed for a particular ring configuration, the larger the ring TTRT, the larger the maximum access delay. As Example 7.5 shows, for all but the largest networks, the maximum obtainable throughput of an FDDI ring can be obtained with a TTRT equal to the minimum value of 4 ms. Hence although in the standard the maximum TTRT can be as high as 165 ms, it is quite common to operate the ring with a TTRT significantly less than this.

Example 7.5

Derive the maximum obtainable throughput and the maximum access delay for the following three ring configurations. Assume a TTRT of 4 ms has been chosen for each configuration.

(a)   2 km ring with 20 stations

(b)   20 km ring with 200 stations

(c)   100 km ring with 500 stations

The three ring configurations are the same as those used in Example 7.3 and hence the same computed ring latency times will be used here. Now:

$$\text{Maximum available throughput, } U_{max} = \frac{n(\text{TTRT} - T_\text{l})}{n(\text{TTRT}) + T_\text{l}}$$

$$\text{Maximum access delay, } A_{max} = (n-1)\text{TTRT} + 2T_\text{l}$$

(a)   From Example 7.3, $T_\text{l} = 0.03$ ms. Hence:

$$U_{max} = \frac{20(4 - 0.03)}{20 \times 4 + 0.03} = 0.99$$

and

$$A_{max} = 19 \times 4 + 0.06 = 76.06 \text{ ms}$$

(b)   From Example 7.3, $T_\text{l} = 0.3$ ms. Hence:

$$U_{max} = \frac{200(4 - 0.3)}{200 \times 4 + 0.3} = 0.92$$

and

$$A_{max} = 199 \times 4 + 0.6 = 796.06 \text{ ms}$$

(c)   From Example 7.3, $T_\text{l} = 1$ ms. Hence:

$$U_{max} = \frac{500(4 - 1)}{500 \times 4 + 1} = 0.75$$

and

$$A_{max} = 499 \times 4 + 2 = 1.998 \text{ s}$$

7.4.6 Synchronous data

The timed token rotation protocol ensures that stations gain access to the shared transmission medium of the ring in a fair way for the transmission of data frames of equal priority. In this context equal priority implies frames of data that are generated by text-only workstations and relate, typically, to file transfers, electronic mail, and other similar transactions. Since such frames are generated at random time intervals, they are known as **asynchronous data** frames.

In addition to asynchronous data, the standard includes an optional service that is intended for the transfer of **synchronous data**, that is, data that is delay sensitive and hence must be transferred within a guaranteed maximum time interval. An example is a set of frames each containing a block of successive samples of speech. As Chapter 2 explained, digitized speech samples are generated at regular (125 µs) time intervals and hence it is essential that such frames are transferred within a guaranteed maximum time interval to avoid variations in the time successive speech samples arrive at the receiver.

To cater for synchronous data, those stations that support such traffic are allocated a fixed portion of the ring bandwidth that may be used each time the token is received. This is known as the **synchronous allocation time (SAT)** and defines the maximum length of time for which a station can transmit synchronous data each time it receives the token. Synchronous data is not controlled by the timed token rotation protocol; instead, the allocation of ring bandwidth to individual stations for synchronous data is controlled by a separate ring management station. The general scheme is shown in Figure 7.18(a).

All requests for synchronous bandwidth are expressed as a proportion of the ring TTRT. These requests are sent to the network management station and, provided there is free synchronous bandwidth available, the stations are each allocated their requested amount. Not all stations need to provide a synchronous data service and not all portions of synchronous bandwidth need to be the same. To implement the scheme, each station must be able to communicate with the network management station. This is achieved by each station having its own ring management – known as **station management (SMT)** – agent that communicates with the ring management station, via the ring in the normal way, using a defined protocol. The general scheme is shown in Figure 7.18(b).

In addition to its use for negotiating synchronous data allocation, the same SMT configuration is used to negotiate the ring TTRT. Recall that the ring TTRT can have a minimum value of 4 ms and a maximum value of 165 ms. The actual value is decided by the ring management station. If a station requires a higher value than 4 ms – the default value – then it can make a bid to the ring management station for the ring TTRT to be set to this higher value. If this is agreed, then the higher value is downloaded to each station, again using the same ring management protocol. We shall discuss SMT protocols further in Chapter 13.

In order to ensure that the token is received by each station offering the synchronous data service within a guaranteed maximum time interval, the network management station keeps a record of the synchronous allocation time that has been granted to each station. The aggregate of this is not allowed to be greater than the negotiated TTRT that is being used by stations to control the transmission of asynchronous data frames. Recall from Section 7.4.5 that the TTRT defines the maximum time that the token will take to circulate around the ring when transmitting asynchronous data. Hence since the total bandwidth allocated for synchronous data is made equal to the TTRT, the maximum time interval that will expire before a station receives the token will be twice the TTRT.

When a station is supporting both synchronous and asynchronous data, on receipt of the token the station first transmits any waiting synchronous data up to its synchronous data allocation time limit. During this time, its TRT is suspended. Then, assuming the station has asynchronous data waiting to send, it subtracts its current TRT from the TTRT in the normal way. The result – positive or negative –

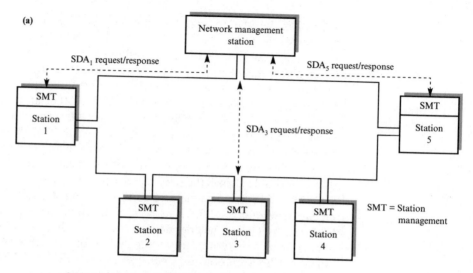

(a)

Stations 1, 3, 5 support asynchronous and synchronous data
Stations 2 and 4 support asynchronous data only

SDA_n = Synchronous data allocation time for station n

Also $\sum_{i=1}^{n} SDA_i$ = Ring target token rotation time, TTRT

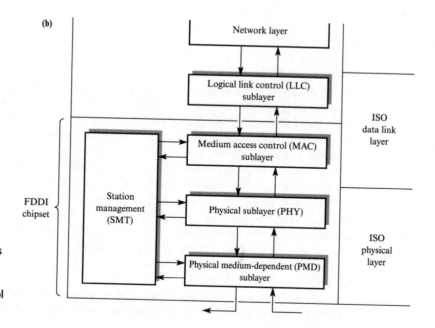

(b)

Figure 7.18
FDDI synchronous
data negotiation:
(a) schematic;
(b) station protocol
architecture.

determines whether it can transmit any waiting asynchronous data on this rotation of the token.

Note that the foregoing procedure defines the *maximum* time that may expire before the token is received by a station. If the asynchronous data traffic on the ring is light, then the token will be received in approximately half this time. Moreover, if the actual amount of synchronous data transmitted during a rotation of the token is less than the maximum allocated, then the maximum time will be reduced still further by this amount. This means that the actual time intervals between successive token rotations will vary from a possibly small value up to the defined maximum value. For time-critical (synchronous) data this does not present a problem since the main requirement for this is the worst-case maximum time. For data that is generated (and hence must be delivered and output) at regular time intervals, this can be problematic. This type of data is known as **isochronous data** and includes digitized voice and digitized video. A feature of such data is its sensitivity not only to delay but also to **delay variation** or **jitter**. The inherent delay variation just described restricts the use of FDDI for this type of traffic. Therefore a derivative of FDDI known as **FDDI-II** has been developed. We shall describe this in Chapter 10 when we consider mixed media – also known as multimedia – networks and, as we shall see, FDDI-II supports both asynchronous and isochronous data.

A second derivative of FDDI – known as **copper distributed data interface (CDDI)** – has also been developed. This operates in a similar way to FDDI except, as the name implies, it uses copper wire as the transmission medium. The maximum physical separation of the interconnected stations is much reduced. It is intended for use in LANs that span much shorter distances such as a single office or building.

7.5 Bridges

Before we describe the operation of a bridge, let us review the basic operation of a repeater. Repeaters are used to ensure that the electrical signals transmitted by the drive electronics within each DTE (station) propagate throughout the network. In the context of the ISO reference model, they operate purely at the physical layer, as shown in Figure 7.19(a).

For any type of LAN segment, a defined maximum limit is set on both the physical length of the segment and on the number of (end) stations that may be attached to it. When interconnecting segments, a repeater is used to limit the electrical drive requirements of the output circuits associated with the physical interface to that of a single segment. In this way, the presence of multiple segments (and hence repeaters) in a transmission path is transparent to the source station. The repeater simply regenerates all signals received on one segment and forwards (repeats) them onto the next segment.

We may conclude that there is no *intelligence* (a microprocessor, for example) associated with a repeater. Hence if just repeaters are used for interconnection

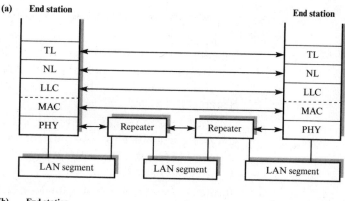

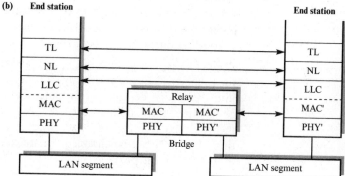

Figure 7.19
LAN interconnection
schematic:
(a) repeaters;
(b) bridges.

purposes, all frame transmissions from any station connected to a segment will propagate throughout the network. This means that, in terms of bandwidth, the network behaves like a single segment. Thus as the demands on each LAN segment (in terms of transmission bandwidth) increase, so the loading of the total LAN increases with a corresponding deterioration in overall network response time.

Bridge functions

The function of a bridge is similar to a repeater in that it is used for interconnecting LAN segments. However, when bridges are used, all frames received from a segment are buffered (stored) and error checked before they are repeated (forwarded). Moreover, only frames that are free of errors and are addressed to stations on a different segment from the one on which they were received are forwarded. Consequently, all transmissions between stations connected to the same LAN segment are not forwarded and hence do not load the rest of the network. A bridge thus operates at the MAC sublayer in the context of the ISO reference model. This is shown in Figure 7.19(b). The resulting LAN is then referred to as a **bridged LAN**.

Buffering frames has advantages and disadvantages relative to a repeater. In general, the advantages far outweigh the disadvantages but it is perhaps helpful to list both.

The advantages of a bridge are as follows:

- Removal of any physical constraints associated with the interconnection function means that both the total number of attached stations and the number of segments making up the LAN can be readily increased. This is particularly important when building large LANs distributed over wide geographical areas.

- The buffering of frames received on a segment before forwarding them on another means that the two interconnected segments can operate with a different MAC protocol. Thus it is easier to create a LAN that is a mix of the different basic LAN types.

- Bridges perform their relaying function based solely on the MAC subaddress in a frame with the effect they are transparent to the protocols being used at higher layers in the protocol stack. This means they can be used with LANs supporting different protocol stacks.

- Bridges allow a large network to be managed more readily and effectively via the LAN itself. For example, by incorporating management-related software into the bridge design, performance data relating to a LAN segment can be readily logged and later accessed. Also, access control mechanisms can be incorporated to improve network security, and the operational configuration of a LAN can be changed dynamically by controlling the status of the individual bridge ports.

- Partitioning a LAN into smaller segments improves the overall reliability, availability, and serviceability of the total network.

The disadvantages of bridges are as follows:

- Since a bridge receives and buffers all frames in their entirety before performing the relaying (forwarding) function, it introduces an additional store-and-forward delay compared with a repeater.

- There is no provision for flow control at the MAC sublayer and hence bridges may overload during periods of high traffic, that is, a bridge may need to store more frames (prior to forwarding them on each link) than it has free buffer storage.

- Bridging of segments operating with different MAC protocols means that the contents of frames must be modified prior to forwarding because of the different frame formats. A new frame check sequence must be generated by each bridge with the effect that any errors introduced while frames are being relayed across a bridge will go undetected.

As we have indicated, bridges are now widely used because the advantages far outweigh the disadvantages. The two most widely adopted types of bridge are **transparent** (also known as spanning tree) **bridges** and **source routing bridges**, the main difference between them being the routing algorithm.

With transparent bridges, the bridges themselves make all routing decisions while with source routing bridges, the end stations perform the major route-finding function. There is now an international standard relating to transparent bridges – IEEE 802.1 (D) – and source routing forms a part of the IEEE 802.5 – token ring – standard for interconnecting token ring segments.

We shall describe each separately, but note that the descriptions are intended only as technical overviews. Moreover the standards are still evolving, so if you require more details you should refer to the relevant standards directly.

7.6   Transparent bridges

With a transparent bridge, as with a repeater, the presence of one (or more) bridges in a route between two communicating stations is transparent to the two stations. All routing decisions are made exclusively by the bridge(s). Moreover, a transparent bridge automatically initializes and configures itself (in terms of its routing information) in a dynamic way after it has been put into service. A schematic of a bridge is shown in Figure 7.20(a) and a simple bridged LAN in part (b).

A LAN segment is physically connected to a bridge through a **bridge port**. A basic bridge has just two ports whereas a **multiport bridge** has a number of connected ports (and hence segments). In practice, each bridge port comprises the MAC integrated circuit chipset associated with the particular type of LAN segment – CSMA/CD, token ring, token bus – together with some associated port management software. The software is responsible for initializing the chipset at start-up – the chipsets are all programmable devices – and for buffer management. Normally, the available memory is logically divided into a number of fixed-size units known as buffers. Buffer management involves passing a free buffer (pointer) to the chipset ready for frame reception and also passing frame buffers (pointers) to the chipset for onward transmission (forwarding).

Every bridge operates in the **promiscuous mode** which means it receives and buffers all frames received on each of its ports. When a frame has been received at a port and put into the assigned buffer by the MAC chipset, the port management software prepares the chipset for a new frame and then passes the pointer of the memory buffer containing the received frame to the **bridge protocol entity** for processing. Since two (or more) frames may arrive concurrently at the ports and two or more frames may need to be forwarded from the same output port, the passing of memory pointers between the port management software and the bridge protocol entity software is carried out via a set of queues.

As we shall see in Section 7.6.1, each port may be in a number of alternative states and processing of received frames is carried out according to a defined protocol. The function of the bridge protocol entity software is to implement the particular bridge protocol being used.

Frame forwarding (filtering)

A bridge maintains a **forwarding database** (also known as a **routing directory**) that indicates, for each port, the outgoing port (if any) to be used for forwarding each

(a) Bridge

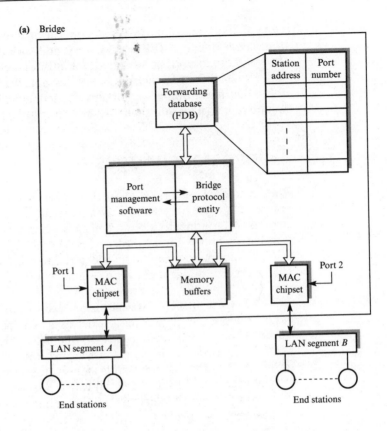

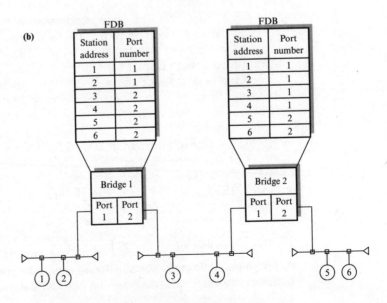

Figure 7.20
Bridge schematic:
(a) architecture;
(b) application
example.

frame received at that port. If a frame is received at a port that is addressed to a station on the segment (and hence port) on which it was received, that frame is discarded; otherwise it is forwarded via the port specified in the forwarding database. The normal routing decision involves a simple look-up operation: the destination address in each received frame is first read and then used to access the corresponding port number from the forwarding database. If this is the same as the port on which it was received, the frame is discarded, else it is queued for forward transmission on the segment associated with the accessed port. This process is also known as **frame filtering**.

Bridge learning

A major problem with transparent bridges is the creation of the forwarding database. One approach is for the contents of the forwarding database to be created in advance and held in a fixed memory, such as programmable read-only memory (PROM). The disadvantage is that the contents of the forwarding database in all bridges have to be changed whenever the network topology is changed – a new segment added, for example – or when a user changed the point of attachment (and hence segment) of his or her station. To avoid this, in most bridged LANs the contents of the forwarding database are not statically set up but rather are dynamically created and maintained during normal operation of the bridge. This is accomplished using a combination of a learning process and a dialog with other bridges to ascertain the topology of the overall installed LAN. An overview of the learning process is as follows.

When a bridge first comes into service, its forwarding database is initialized to empty. Whenever a frame is received, the *source address* within it is read and the incoming port number on which the frame was received is entered into the forwarding database. In addition, since the forwarding port is not known at this time, a copy of the frame is forwarded on all the other output ports of the bridge. As these frames propagate through the network, this procedure is repeated by each bridge. Firstly, the incoming port number is entered in the forwarding database against the source (station) address and a copy of the frame is forwarded on all the other output ports of the bridge. This action is often referred to as **flooding** since it ensures that a copy of each frame transmitted is received on all segments in the total LAN. During the learning phase this procedure is repeated for each frame received by the bridge. In this way, all bridges in the LAN rapidly build up the contents of their forwarding databases.

This procedure works satisfactorily as long as stations are not allowed to migrate around the network (change their point of attachment) and the overall LAN topology is a simple tree structure (that is, there are no duplicate paths (routes) between any two segments). Such a tree structure is known as a **spanning tree**. Since in many networks, especially large networks, both these possibilities may occur, the basic learning operation is refined as follows.

The MAC address associated with a station is fixed at the time of its manufacture. If a user changes the point of attachment to the network of his or her workstation, the contents of the forwarding database in each bridge must be periodically updated to reflect such changes. To accomplish this, an **inactivity timer** is associated with each entry in the database. Whenever a frame is received from a station, the corresponding timer for that entry is reset. If no frames are received from a station within the predefined time interval, the timer expires and the entry is removed. Whenever a frame is received from a station for which the entry has been removed, the learning procedure is again followed to update the entry in each bridge with the (possibly new) port number. In this way the forwarding database in a bridge is continuously updated to reflect the current LAN topology and the addresses of the stations that are currently attached to the segments it interconnects. The inactivity timer also limits the size of the database since it contains only those stations that are currently active. This is important since the size of the database influences the speed of the forwarding operation.

The learning process works only if the total bridged LAN has a simple (spanning) tree topology. This means that there is only a single path between any two segments in the network. However, this condition may not always be met since additional bridges may be used to link two segments, for example, to improve reliability or perhaps by mistake when a LAN is being updated.

Multiple paths between two segments cannot exist with the basic learning algorithm we have outlined since the flooding operation during the learning phase would cause entries in the forwarding database to be continuously overwritten. We can see this by considering the simple LAN topology shown in Figure 7.21. Clearly, if station 10 transmits a frame on segment 1 during the learning phase, then bridges B1 and B2 will both create an entry in their forwarding database and forward a copy of the frame onto segment 2. Each of these frames will in turn be received by the other bridge, an entry will be made (in port 2) and a copy of the frame output at port 1. In turn, each of these will be received by the other bridge,

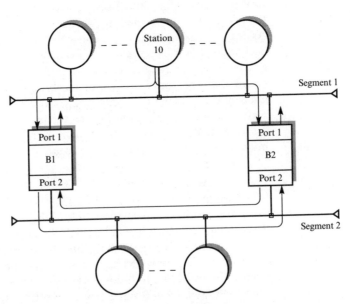

Figure 7.21
Effect of dual paths on
learning algorithm.

resulting in their corresponding entry for port 1 being updated. The frame will thus continuously circulate in a loop with the entries for each port being continuously updated.

Consequently, for topologies which offer multiple paths between stations, we need an additional algorithm to select just a single bridge for forwarding frames between any two segments. The resulting logical or **active topology** behaves as a single spanning tree and the algorithm is known as the **spanning tree algorithm**. Note that although the algorithm selects only a single bridge for connecting two segments – making redundant any alternative bridges that may have been introduced to improve reliability, for example – it is run at regular intervals and will dynamically select a set of bridges from those currently operational.

7.6.1   Spanning tree algorithm

With the spanning tree algorithm, all the bridges regularly exchange special frames (messages), known as **bridge protocol data units (BPDUs)**. Each bridge has a priority value and a unique identifier. For the total bridged LAN, a single bridge is dynamically chosen by the spanning tree algorithm to be the **root bridge**. This is the bridge with the highest priority and the smallest identifier. It is determined/confirmed at regular intervals.

After the root bridge has been established, the cost of the path from the root bridge to all other bridge ports is determined. This is known as the **root path cost** and is the least cost path followed by a frame send from the root bridge to the port under consideration. Each bridge then determines which of its ports forms the least path cost to the root. This is known as the **root port** since subsequently it receives all BPDUs sent by the root on this port.

The path cost associated with a port is determined by the bit rate – known as the **designated cost** – of the segment to which it is attached. The higher the bit rate, the smaller the designated cost. If there are, say, two alternative paths from the root, one comprising two 10 Mbps CSMA/CD segments and the other two 2 Mbps segments, then the path with the two higher bit rate segments will have the lower path cost. In the event of the path cost of two ports within the same bridge being equal, the port identifiers are used as tie-breakers.

Once the root port for each bridge has been determined, a single bridge (port) is selected for forwarding frames onto each segment. This is known as the **designated bridge**. Its selection is based on the least path cost to the root bridge from the segment under consideration. If two bridge ports connected to a segment have the same path cost, the bridge with the smaller identifier is chosen. The bridge port connecting the segment to its designated bridge is known as the **designated port**. In the case of the root bridge, this is always the designated bridge for all the segments to which it is connected. Hence all its ports are designated ports.

When establishing the designated bridge port to be used with a segment, note that once a bridge port has been selected as a root port, it will not take part in the arbitration procedure to become a designated port. The choice of designated port is thus between the nonroot ports connected to the segment under consideration.

The exchange of the configuration BPDUs between the two (or more) bridges involved will allow the two (or more) bridges to make a joint decision as to the port to be selected.

After the root bridge and the root and designated ports of all other bridges have been established, the state of the bridge ports can be set either to **forwarding** or to **blocking**. Initially, since all ports of the root bridge are designated ports, they are set to the forwarding state. For all the other bridges, only the root and designated ports are set to the forwarding state; the others are set to the blocking state. This establishes an active topology equivalent to a spanning tree.

Topology initialization

All the bridges in a LAN have a unique MAC group address which is used for sending all BPDUs between bridges. BPDUs received by a bridge are not directly forwarded; the information they contain can be used by the bridge protocol entity to create the BPDU(s) which it subsequently forwards on its other port(s).

When a bridge is first brought into service, it assumes it is the root bridge. A bridge that believes it is the root (all initially) initiates the transmission of a **configuration BPDU** on all of its ports (and hence the segments connected to it) at regular time intervals known as the **hello time**.

Each configuration BPDU contains a number of fields including:

- The identifier of the bridge which the bridge transmitting the BPDU believes to be the root (itself initially)

- The path cost to the root from the bridge port on which the BPDU was received (zero initially)

- The identifier of the bridge transmitting the BPDU

- The identifier of the bridge port from which the BPDU was transmitted

On receipt of a configuration BPDU, each bridge connected to the segment on which it was transmitted can determine, by comparing the root identifier contained within it with its own identifier, firstly, whether the bridge has a higher priority or, if the priorities are equal, whether its own identifier is less than the identifier from the received frame. If this is the case, it will carry on assuming it is the root and simply discard the received frame.

Alternatively, if the root identifier from the received BPDU indicates that it is not the root, the bridge proceeds by adding the path cost associated with the port on which the BPDU was received to that already within the frame. A bridge knows the designated cost of the segments connected to its ports as a result of earlier network management messages sent to it. It creates a new configuration BPDU containing this information, together with its own identifiers (bridge and port), and forwards a copy on all its other ports. This procedure is repeated by all bridges in the LAN. In this way the configuration BPDUs flood away from the root to the extremities of the network.

As the configuration BPDUs span out from the root, the path cost associated with each port of all the other bridges is computed. Thus, in addition to a single root being established, all the other bridges will have determined the path cost associated with each of their ports. They can thus select their root ports and, since at any point in the hierarchy two (or more) bridges connected to the same segment will exchange configuration BPDUs, they can determine from the aggregate root path costs in the BPDU(s) each receives which is to be the designated bridge for that segment. The bridge identifier is again used as a tie-breaker in the event of equal path costs. The designated port is then selected.

We can make the following basic observations:

- A bridge receives BPDUs on its root port and transmits them on its designated port(s).
- All root and designated ports are in the forwarding state.
- A bridge that has a root port connected to a segment cannot be the designated bridge for that segment.
- There can be only one designated port on each segment.

Topology change

As we mentioned earlier, redundant bridges are often introduced to improve the overall reliability of a LAN. Hence, since the procedure we have just described will set some (or all) of the ports associated with such bridges into the blocking state, a procedure must be incorporated into the algorithm to allow the state of bridges and their associated ports to be dynamically changed in the event of bridge or port failure. This is known as the **topology change procedure**.

Once a single root bridge and associated active topology have been established, only the root bridge transmits configuration BPDUs. These are sent out at regular intervals on each of its ports every time the hello timer expires. Such BPDUs propagate throughout the network. Consequently, as each bridge updates the information contained within the BPDUs, the status of each bridge and its associated ports will be confirmed at regular intervals.

To enable other bridges to detect when a failure occurs, a **message age timer** is kept by each bridge for all of its ports. Under error free conditions, this is reset every time a configuration BPDU is received. If a designated bridge or active bridge port fails, the configuration BPDUs stop being forwarded through this bridge or port. The effect is that the message age timer expires in bridges that are downstream from the failed bridge or port.

The expiry of a message age timer associated with a port causes the bridge protocol entity to invoke a **become designated port procedure**. This is invoked by all affected bridges. After it has been carried out, one or more new designated bridges and/or ports are established. If the current root bridge failed, a new root bridge is elected.

In addition, whenever the state of a port is changed from the blocking to the forwarding state, a **topology change notification BPDU** is sent out from the upgraded port in the direction of the root bridge. All designated bridges between it and the root bridge note the change and relay it on toward the root bridge via their root ports. In this way, all bridges affected by the failure are made aware of the topology change. To ensure such BPDUs reach the root reliably, an acknowl-edgment BPDU and a timer are associated with the sending procedure used to relay them.

After the topology has changed, the end stations connected to each LAN segment can be reached by a different port from that currently in the forwarding database of each bridge. Since the timer used by a bridge to timeout entries in its database (that is, the entries relating to end stations that have not transmitted any frames since the timer was started) is relatively long, the next set of configuration BPDUs transmitted by the root after receipt of a topology change notification BPDU have a field (bit) within them to notify bridges to shorten this time. The existing entries in each database thus timeout and new entries are established when each station next sends a frame.

Port status

To ensure that no transient loops are created during the period when the active topology is being established, a bridge port is not allowed to go directly from the blocking to the forwarding state. Instead, two intermediate states are defined known as the **listening state** and the **learning state**. A fifth state, the **disabled state**, is also defined to allow a network manager, through special management PBDUs sent via the network, to block specific bridge ports permanently.

While in the various states, normal BPDUs and information frames may or may not be forwarded. Frames that are forwarded when in each state are as follows:

- In the disabled state, only management BPDUs are received and processed.

- In the blocked state, only configuration and management BPDUs are received and processed.

- In the listening state, all BPDUs are received and processed.

- In the learning state, all BPDUs are received and processed; information frames are submitted to the learning process but not forwarded.

- In the forwarding state, all BPDUs are received and processed; all information frames are received, processed, and forwarded.

State transitions

Transitions between port states are effected by the bridge protocol entity and take place as a result of either the reception BPDUs relating to a port or the expiry timers associated with the bridge protocol. The possible transitions – (1) to (5) – are shown in the state transition diagram of Figure 7.22.

Normally, all bridge ports enter the disabled state when the bridge is first switched on. The transition to the blocking state occurs as a result of the reception of a specific network management BPDU from a network manager station via the network (1). Similarly, the network manager can disable a specific bridge port at any time by sending a management BPDU via the network (2).

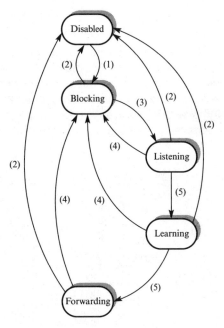

(1) Port enabled by receipt of a management BPDU
(2) Port disabled either by receipt of a managment BPDU or failure
(3) Port selected as a root or designated port
(4) Port ceases to be a root or designated port
(5) Forwarding timer expires

Figure 7.22
Port states and
transition possibilities.

Once a bridge receives an initialization command from the network manager, it sets all its ports into the blocking state and starts to send out configuration BPDUs. The bridge then takes part in the topology initialization procedure mentioned earlier. During this procedure it will start to establish its ports as either root or designated ports. We can conclude that the state of ports may change during this procedure. For example, bridges lower down in the tree structure (that is, away from the root bridge) may start to assume some of their ports are designated or root ports as a result of local BPDU exchanges. But, as BPDUs start to filter down from the true root, their states may well change. Thus instead of the root and designated ports being transferred directly from the blocking to the forwarding state, they go through the intermediate listening and learning states, each for a fixed time period.

When a bridge determines that one of its ports is a root or a designated port, it is transferred from the blocking to the listening state (3) and a **forwarding timer** is started. If a port is still a root or designated port when this timer expires, it will be transferred to the learning state (5). The forwarding timer is then restarted and the same procedure repeated when it expires. This time, however, ports that are still root or designated ports are now set into the forwarding state (5). If a port ceases to be a root or designated port during this period, it is returned to the blocking state directly (4).

Example 7.6

To illustrate how the various elements of the spanning tree algorithm work, consider the bridged LAN shown in Figure 7.23(a). The unique identifier of each bridge is shown inside the box representing the bridge together with the port numbers in the inner boxes connecting the bridge to each segment. Typically, the additional bridges on each segment are added to improve reliability in the event of a bridge failure. Also, assume that the LAN is just being brought into service.

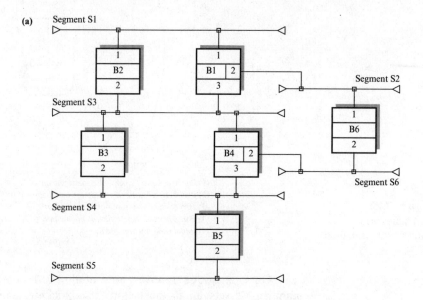

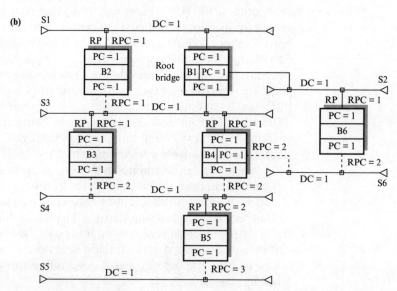

Figure 7.23
Active topology derivation examples:
(a) LAN topology;
(b) root port selection.

Determine the active (spanning tree) topology for the following cases:

(a) All bridges have equal priority and all segments have the same designated cost (bit rate) associated with them.

(b) As for (a) except bridge B1 fails.

(c) All bridges are in service but segments S1, S2, S4, and S5 have three times the designated cost of segments S3 and S6; that is, segments S3 and S6 have the higher bit rates.

(d) The segments have the same designated cost as in (c) but the priority of bridge B5 is set (by network management) to be higher than the other bridges.

(a) (i) First the exchange of configuration BPDUs will establish bridge B1 as the root bridge since this has the lowest identifier.

(ii) After the exchange of configuration BPDUs, the root path cost (RPC) of each port will have been computed. These are shown in part (b) of Figure 7.23.

(iii) The root port (RP) for each bridge is then chosen as the port with the lowest RPC. For example, in the case of bridge B3, port 1 has an RPC of 1 and port 2 an RPC of 2, so port 1 is chosen. In the case of B2, both ports have the same RPC and hence port 1 is chosen since this has the smaller identifier. The selected RPs are also shown in the figure.

(iv) B1 is the root bridge so all its ports have a designated port cost (DPC) of 0. Hence they are the designated ports for segments S1, S2, and S3.

(v) For S4, port 1 of B5 is an RP and hence is not involved in selecting the designated port. The two other ports connected to S4 both have a DPC of 1. Hence port 2 of B3 is selected as the designated port because of its lower identifier.

(vi) For S5, the only port connected to it is port 2 of B5 and hence this is selected.

(vii) Finally, for S6 both ports have a DPC of 1, so port 2 of B4 is selected rather than port 2 of B6.

The DPCs are shown in Figure 7.23(c) and the resulting active topology is thus as shown in part (d).

(b) (i) First the BPDUs exchanged as part of the topology change procedure establish B2 as the new root bridge since this now has the lowest identifier.

(ii) The new RPCs for each port are then computed and the RP for each of the bridges established.

(iii) Since B2 is now the root bridge, its ports are the designated ports for S1 and S3.

(iv) For S2, the only port connected to it is port 1 of B6 and hence this is selected.

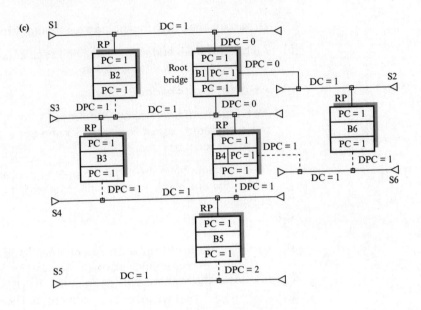

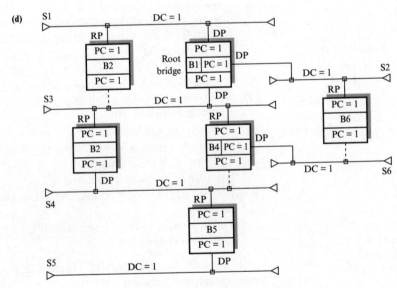

Figure 7.23 (cont.)
(c) Designated port
selection; (d) active
topology example.

(v)   For S4, the two ports in contention again have equal DPCs and hence port 2 of B3 is selected.

(vi) For S5, port 2 of B5 is selected.

(vii) Finally, for S6 both ports connected to it have equal DPCs and hence port 2 of B4 is selected.

The modified active topology is as shown in Figure 7.23(e).

(c)   (i)   The root bridge is again B1 as this has the lowest identifier.

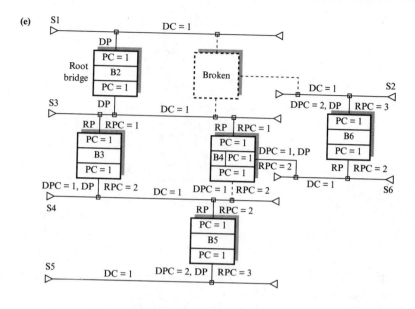

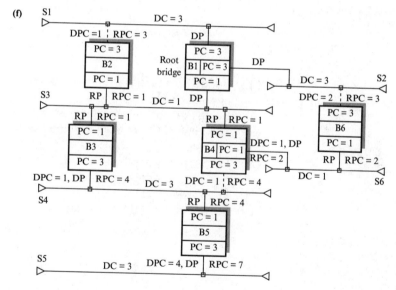

Figure 7.23 (cont.)
(e)–(f) Active
topology examples.

(ii)   The RPCs and RPs are as shown; note that port 2 of B6 is now the RP since it now has a lower RPC than port 1.

(iii) B1 is the root bridge and hence its ports are the designated ports for S1, S2, and S3.

(iv)   For S4, port 2 of B3 is again selected.

(v)   For S5, port 2 of B5 is again selected.

(vi)   For S6, port 2 of B4 is again selected.

The new active topology is thus as shown in Figure 7.23(f).

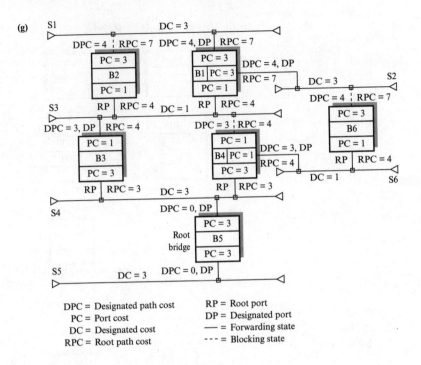

Figure 7.23 (cont.)
(g) Active topology
example.

(d)   (i)   Bridge B5 now has the highest priority and is therefore selected as the new root bridge.

(ii)   Being the root bridge its ports are the designated ports for S4 and S5.

(iii) The new RPCs for each port are as shown and hence the RPs are as indicated.

(iv) For S1, port 1 of B1 is selected.

(v)   For S2, port 2 of B1 is selected.

(vi) For S3, port 1 of B3 is selected.

(vii) For S6, port 2 of B1 is selected.

The active topology is thus as shown in Figure 7.23(g).

7.6.2 Topology tuning

We can deduce from Example 7.6 that if all the bridges in a LAN have the same priority, it is unlikely that the spanning tree algorithm will produce the optimum active topology in terms of its use of the available bandwidth. This can be an important factor in large networks since it then becomes important to maximize the use of any higher bit rate segments that are available.

The inclusion of the priority field in each bridge identifier helps to achieve this goal. Although the unique identifier field of a bridge is fixed at the time of manufacture, the priority field can be set dynamically from a network manager station via the network. Bridges that can respond to network management commands are known as **managed bridges**. By selectively setting the priority of bridges, a network manager is able to optimize or tune the performance of the overall network.

Typically, we construct a computer model of the physical topology to observe the performance of the overall LAN with different active topologies and traffic distributions, thereby identifying potential bottlenecks. Careful selection of the priority of selected bridges enables the performance of the active topology to be optimized.

7.6.3 Remote bridges

Many large corporations have establishments (and hence LANs) distributed around a country or over many countries. In addition to being able to exchange information between stations connected to the same LAN within a single establishment, many large corporations require to exchange information between stations connected to LANs in different establishments. Clearly, a facility is needed to interconnect these LANs.

A number of alternatives are possible. One solution is to use a public (or private) packet-switching network for the inter-LAN communication functions. A limited number of permanent virtual circuits may be used or, alternatively, switched connections may be established dynamically. However, both these solutions need full network layer addresses for the routing function, making it necessary to use a **router** to connect each LAN to the packet-switching network. We shall discuss this type of solution more fully in Chapter 9 when internetworking is discussed.

An alternative, and simpler, solution is to interconnect the LANs with dedicated leased (private) lines. Although this approach sacrifices some of the advantages gained by using routers, it often provides a faster relaying service.

As Chapter 2 indicated, leased lines are hired from a public or private telephone company to create a network of direct (point-to-point) links between, in this instance, the distributed set of LANs. Normally, no routing is involved across the resulting WAN. The 48-bit MAC addresses at the head of each frame can be used instead. The MAC addresses used in LANs are normally unique across the total network (that is, across all the LANs). Hence the MAC addresses and bridges can be used to provide the routing function. Such bridges are normally connected directly to the establishmentwide backbone subnetwork on one port and to the leased line(s) on the other. A similar bridge is used at the other end of the leased line. To discriminate between these and the bridges used for the interconnection of LAN segments, they are known as **remote bridges**. An example network based on remote bridges is shown in Figure 7.24.

Many large corporations use leased lines in this way to interconnect the (private) telephone exchanges in each establishment, thereby creating an enterprisewide private telephone network. The leased lines used for data

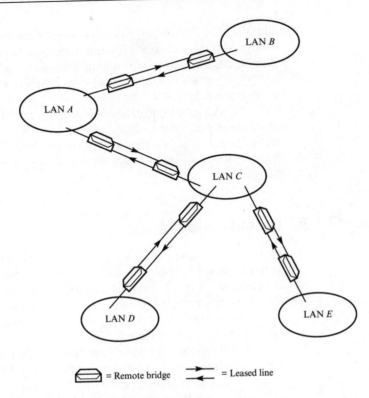

Figure 7.24
LAN interconnection
through remote
bridges.

⬡ = Remote bridge   ⇄ = Leased line

communication are normally integrated with those used for telephony. The bit rate of the leased lines range from multiples of 56 kbps (64 kbps in Europe) to multiples of 1.54 Mbps (2.048 Mbps in Europe). The possibly long distances spanned by such lines means that we must consider the propagation delay of the lines when determining their transmission delay.

In general, the reliability of a leased line is significantly less than that of a LAN segment, so it is normal to have back-up paths (lines) in the event of failures. Although in principle the spanning tree algorithm can be implemented in remote bridges (thus extending the coverage of the spanning tree algorithm across the entire network), in practice this is not always done.

As we saw in Example 7.6, with the spanning tree algorithm some of the ports associated with selected bridges (for example, those introduced to enhance reliability) are set to the blocking state to ensure an active spanning tree topology. With leased lines, this means that an available line may not be used since the bridge port to which it is connected is in the blocking state. Unlike the transmission media used with LANs, leased lines are expensive, so it is important to maximize their usage.

In many instances the leased lines are part of a much larger, enterprisewide, voice and data network. Normally, such networks have an integral network management facility, one of its main tasks being to reallocate the available bandwidth to the various voice and data services in the event of failure of a leased line.

A common solution is for the network manager (via the network) to assign dynamically an alternative line (channel) for use in the event of a line failure. The remote bridges are not involved in the spanning tree algorithm, but simply perform the basic learning and forwarding (filtering) operations. Although this leads to a slight degradation in performance during the reconfiguration period, it often leads to a more efficient usage of the available transmission capacity.

7.7 Source routing bridges

Although we can use **source routing bridges** with any type of LAN segment, we use them primarily for the interconnection of token ring LAN segments. A typical network based on source routing bridges is shown in Figure 7.25(a).

The major difference between a LAN based on source routing bridges and one based on spanning tree bridges is that with the latter the bridges collectively perform the routing operation in a way that is transparent to the end stations.

(a)

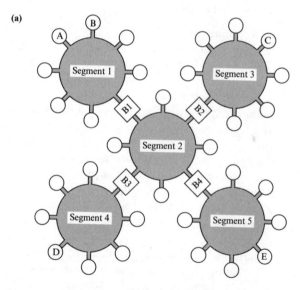

(b)   Routing table held by A: Destination B = Segment 1 (same segment)

C = Segment 1, B1, Segment 2, B2, Segment 3
|
|
E = Segment 1, B1, Segment 2, B4, Segment 5

Routing table held by B: Destination A = Segment 1 (same segment)
|
|
D = Segment 1, B1, Segment 2, B3, Segment 4

Routing table held by E: Destination A = Segment 5, B4, Segment 2, B1, Segment 1
|
|
C = Segment 5, B4, Segment 2, B2, Segment 3

Figure 7.25
An example source routing bridged LAN:
(a) topology;
(b) routing table entries.

Conversely, with source routing, the end stations perform the routing function. With source routing, a station ascertains the route to be followed by a frame to each destination before any frames are transmitted. This information is inserted at the head of the frame and is used by each bridge to determine whether a received frame is to be forwarded on another segment or not. The routing information comprises a sequence of segment–bridge, segment–bridge identifiers. Routing tables for selected stations in the example network are shown in Figure 7.25(b).

On receipt of each frame, a bridge needs only to search the routing field at the head of the frame for its own identifier. Only if it is present and followed by the identifier of a segment connected to one of its output ports does it forward the frame on the specified LAN segment. Otherwise it is not forwarded. In either event, the frame is repeated at the ring interface by the bridge and, if forwarded, the address-recognized (A) and frame-copied (C) bits in the frame status (FS) field at the tail of the frame are set to indicate to the source station (bridge) that it has been received (forwarded) by the destination station (bridge).

7.7.1 Routing algorithm

The routing information field contained within each frame immediately follows the source address field at the head of the normal (IEEE 802.5) information frame. The modified format is thus as shown in Figure 7.26(a).

Since a routing information field is not always required, for example, if the source and destination stations are on the same segment, the first bit of the *source address* – the individual/group (I/G) address bit – is used to indicate whether routing information is present in the frame (a logical 1) or not (0). This can be done since the source address in a frame must always be an individual address, so the I/G bit is not needed for this purpose.

If routing information is present, its format is as shown in Figure 7.26(b). The routing information field consists of a **routing control field** and one or more route designator fields. The routing control field itself comprises three subfields: frame type, maximum frame size, and routing field length. In addition to normal information frames, two other frame types are associated with the routing algorithm. The **frame type** indicates the type of the frame.

Source routing bridges can be used for the interconnection of different types of LAN segments in addition to token rings. Since there is a different maximum frame size associated with each segment type, the **maximum frame size** field determines the largest frame size that can be used when transmitting a frame between any two stations connected to the LAN.

Prior to transmitting a route finding frame, a station sets the maximum frame size field to the (known) largest frame size that can be used in the total LAN. Before a bridge forwards the frame onto a segment, the bridge checks this field with the (known) maximum frame size of the new segment. If the latter is smaller, the bridge reduces the frame size field to the lower value. In this way, the source station, on receipt of the corresponding route reply frame, can use this information when preparing frames for transmission to that destination.

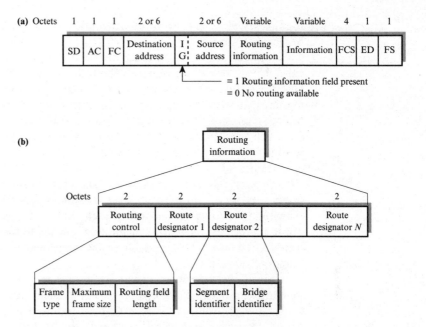

Figure 7.26
Token ring frame
format: (a) position of
routing information
field; (b) structure of
routing information
field.

Since the number of segments (and bridges) traversed by a frame when going from a source to a destination may vary, the **routing field length** indicates the number of **route designators** present in the rest of the routing information field. Each route designator is comprised of a pair of segment and bridge identifiers.

The two additional frame types associated with the route finding algorithm are the **single-route broadcast frame** and the **all-routes broadcast frame**. To find a route, a station first creates and transmits a single-route broadcast frame with a zero routing field length and the maximum frame size set to the known largest value for the total LAN. As with spanning tree bridges, source routing bridges operate in the promiscuous mode and hence receive and buffer all frames at each of their ports. On receipt of a single-route broadcast frame, a bridge simply broadcasts a copy of the frame on each of the segments connected to its other ports. Since this procedure is repeated by each bridge in the LAN, a copy of the frame propagates throughout the LAN and is thus received by the intended destination station irrespective of the segment on which it is attached.

As indicated in Figure 7.21, if there are redundant bridges (and hence loops) in the LAN topology, multiple copies of the frame will propagate around the LAN. To prevent this, before any route finding frames are sent, the bridge ports are configured to give a spanning tree active topology. On the surface, this may appear to be the same procedure used with transparent bridges. With source routing bridges, however, the resulting spanning tree active topology is used only for routing the initial single-route broadcast frames. This ensures that only a single copy of the frame propagates through the network. The spanning tree active topology is not used for routing either normal information frames or the all-routes broadcast frame.

On receipt of a single-route broadcast frame, the destination station returns an all-routes broadcast frame to the originating station. Unlike the single-route broadcast, this frame is not constrained to follow the spanning tree active topology at each intermediate bridge. Instead, on receipt of such frames, the bridge simply adds a new route designator field (comprising the segment identifier on which the frame was received and its own bridge identifier), increments the routing field length, and then broadcasts a copy of the frame on each of its other port segments.

In this way, one or more copies of the frame will be received by the originating source station via all the possible routes between the two stations. By examining the route designators in their routing control fields, the source station can select the best route for transmitting a frame to that destination. This route is then entered into its routing table and is subsequently used when transmitting any frames to that station.

Since the all-routes broadcast frame is not constrained to follow the spanning tree active topology, on receipt of such frames additional steps must be taken by each bridge to ensure that no frames are simply circulating in loops. Before transmitting a copy of the all-routes broadcast frame on an output segment, each bridge first searches the existing routing information in the frame to determine if the segment identifiers associated with the incoming and outgoing ports are already present together with its own bridge identifier. If they are, a copy of the frame has already been along the route, so this copy of the frame is not transmitted on the segment.

Note that it is not necessary to perform the route finding operation for each frame transmitted. Once a route to an intended destination has been determined and entered (cached) into the routing table of a station, this will be used for the transmission of all subsequent frames to that destination. Moreover, since most stations transmit the majority of their frames to a limited number of destinations, the number of route-finding frames is relatively small compared with normal information frames for modest sized LANs.

Example 7.7

Assume the bridged LAN shown in Figure 7.27(a) is to operate using source routing. Also assume that all bridges have equal priority and all rings have the same designated cost (bit rate). Derive the following when station A wishes to send a frame to station B:

(a) The active spanning tree for the LAN

(b) All the paths followed by the single-root broadcast frame(s)

(c) All the paths followed by the all-routes broadcast frame(s)

(d) The route (path) selected by A

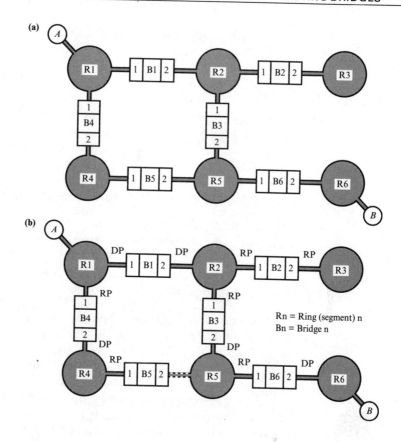

Figure 7.27
Source routing
example: (a) topology;
(b) spanning tree.

(a) (i)   Bridge B1 has the lowest identifier and is selected as the route.
     (ii)   The root ports for each bridge are then derived as shown.
     (iii) The designated ports for each segment can now be derived and these
            are as shown.
     (iv)   The active topology is as shown in Figure 7.27(b).

(b) Paths of single-route broadcast frames:

$$R1 \longrightarrow B1 \longrightarrow R2 \longrightarrow B2 \longrightarrow R3$$
$$\longrightarrow B3 \longrightarrow R5 \longrightarrow B6 \longrightarrow R6$$
$$\longrightarrow B4 \longrightarrow R4 \longrightarrow B5$$

(c) Paths of all-routes broadcast frames:

$$R6 \longrightarrow B6 \longrightarrow R5 \longrightarrow B3 \longrightarrow R2 \longrightarrow B2 \longrightarrow R3$$
$$\longrightarrow B1 \longrightarrow R1$$
$$\longrightarrow B4 \longrightarrow R4 \longrightarrow B5 \longrightarrow R5 \longrightarrow B3$$

(d)   Since each ring has the same bit rate, the route (path) selected is either:

$$R1 \longrightarrow B1 \longrightarrow R2 \longrightarrow B3 \longrightarrow R5 \longrightarrow B6 \longrightarrow R6$$

or:

$$R1 \longrightarrow B4 \longrightarrow R4 \longrightarrow B5 \longrightarrow R5 \longrightarrow B6 \longrightarrow R6$$

7.7.2   Comparison with transparent bridges

Each of the two bridging schemes – source routing and transparent – has advantages and disadvantages relative to the other. The following sections compare the two schemes based on different criteria.

Routing philosophy

In a LAN based on transparent bridges, the routing of a frame is transparent to the end stations. The latter simply add the MAC address of the destination station to the head of each frame and the bridges then collectively route the frames through the network to their intended destinations. Thus it is the bridges that cooperate to perform the route finding operation.

With a LAN based on source routing bridges, the route to be followed by a frame is inserted at the head of the frame by the source station before transmission. Thus the route to be followed by a frame is determined by the end stations and not by the bridges. A source routing bridge simply forwards each frame from one segment to another based on the routing information in the head of the frame.

Quality of routes

In the case of transparent bridges, the spanning tree algorithm ensures there are no loops in the active topology and the resulting tree is used as the basis for routing all frames through the network. Although the assignment of bridge priorities and designated costs to segments helps, it is unlikely that the resulting spanning tree topology will yield optimum routes between all stations. The spanning tree algorithm will inevitably block some segments that ideally should be used when routing frames between two stations.

With source routing bridges, the all-routes broadcast frames identify all the possible routes between a source and a destination station. Hence the source can select the optimum route to be followed for each destination. Note, however, that this is only true providing the choice of route is based not only on the number of segments (and hence bridges) in the route (the **hop count**) but also on the designated cost (bit rate) of each segment. Moreover, with uneven traffic distributions, this may still not give the optimum route. An alternative is simply to select the route from the first all-routes broadcast frame received since this is likely to have experienced the minimum delay.

Use of available bandwidth

To ensure a spanning tree active topology, transparent bridges block selected ports. Hence the attached segments are not used for forwarding frames from this bridge, and the full available bandwidth provided by all segments in the LAN is not always used.

With source routing bridges, all available segments are used during the route finding process so, in theory, the total available bandwidth is used. Again, however, this is the case only if the routes selected by source stations use a strategy that ensures an even loading of all the network segments. In practice, it is unlikely that this will always be the case.

Route forwarding overheads

With a transparent bridge, the processing of each received frame takes longer than with a source routing bridge. This is because a transparent bridge must maintain an entry in its forwarding database for every station in the network that is active and uses routes that pass through that bridge. Thus in large LANs, the forwarding database can have many entries in it, so the time taken to process each frame (that is, to determine the bridge port relating to the destination station of a received frame) can be significant.

To minimize the number of entries in the database, an **inactivity timer** is used for each entry. If a frame is not received from a station while the timer is running, then the entry is said to be **aged** and is removed. Clearly, if an entry is removed, when a source station next sends a new frame to the aged entry, the received frame must be broadcast on each of its outport ports that are in the forwarding state. To minimize the number of such broadcasts, the duration of the inactivity time is normally selected such that the forwarding database may still contain a significant number of entries at any point in time.

In contrast, with a source routing bridge, the processing overhead per frame required by the routing function is small since it need search only the routing field at the head of the frame for its own identifier.

The processing overhead is not normally significant with lower bit rate LAN segments (less than, say, 16 Mbps). However, with higher bit rate LAN types like FDDI, which operate at rates in excess of 100 Mbps, it becomes essential to minimize the processing overhead per frame if the use of the available transmission bandwidth is to be maximized.

Route finding efficiency

With transparent bridges, once an active spanning tree topology has been established, a bridge rapidly builds up entries in its forwarding database as stations start to transmit frames. Entries in the database must be aged to ensure that it contains entries only for stations that regularly transmit frames to stations that have a route through the bridge. The result is that a copy of any new frames that arrive from a station that no longer has an active entry in the database must be broadcast by the bridge on each of its other ports. Because of the active spanning tree topology, the resulting number of frames is limited to one frame per branch of the tree leading from this bridge node.

In contrast, with source routing bridges, although the initial single-route broadcast frames are constrained to follow a spanning tree, the subsequent all-routes broadcast frames originating from the destination are not. This means that there may be considerable overhead (in terms of their use of transmission bandwidth and bridge processing) associated with these frames, particularly in the case of large LANs comprising many segments and replicated bridges.

Reliability

With a transparent bridged LAN, the bridges periodically check for bridge or link failures. This is triggered by the root node, which transmits configuration BPDUs at regular time intervals (determined by the hello timer setting). If a failure does occur, the topology change component of the spanning tree algorithm establishes a new active topology to be used by the remaining bridges.

With source routing bridges, the source stations must detect when a failure has occurred since they hold the routing information. When a network failure does occur, the routing information held by each station may be incorrect with the effect that wrongly addressed frames (frames with no available route) will be transmitted. Moreover, the absence of a response frame often triggers a timer, normally in the transport layer of the protocol stack, that results in another copy of the frame being transmitted by the source station. Assuming the fault is still present, this will unnecessarily load the network. Thus source stations must take corrective action (update their routing tables to reflect the unavailability of a station or a new route) as soon as possible after a fault occurs.

One approach is for each station to have a timer – similar to the inactivity timer used by bridges – associated with each entry in its routing table. If a timer expires – that is, a frame is not sent to that destination station during the period the associated timer is running – a new route will be established before sending any new frames to that station. Clearly, the shorter this time, the less likely it is that frames with incorrect routing information will be generated. Hence a timer setting comparable to that used for the inactivity timer in the bridges is used. Since the processing of each timer must be carried out by every station and not just by bridges, the effect on the network load is significantly greater.

An alternative approach exploits the topology change procedure associated with the spanning tree algorithm. Since the spanning tree algorithm is needed for routing single-route broadcast frames, it also utilizes the associated topology change procedure. Recall that associated with this procedure, the root node transmits a topology change notification BPDU whenever a change is triggered by a link or bridge failure. The BPDU is used by each bridge to timeout the entries in its forwarding database so that they will be updated to reflect the new topology. In principle, on receipt of such a BPDU, a bridge can send a corresponding frame to each of the stations on its segments informing them that a topology change has occurred. This eliminates the need for stations to maintain timers for the entries in their routing tables, thereby significantly reducing the effect on the network load.

7.7.3 Internetworking with different LAN types

As Section 7.3.1 indicated, because of their store-and-forward mode of operation, bridges can be used to interconnect LAN segments that operate with a different MAC method. In practice, this is not straightforward for a number of reasons.

Frame format

Because of the different transmission modes used with the three basic LAN types – broadcast with 802.3 and 802.4 and point-to-point with 802.5 – and their different MAC methods – CSMA/CD with 802.3 and token with 802.4 and 802.5 – they all have different frame formats, as shown in Figure 7.28. For instance, the use of the broadcast mode by 802.3 and 802.4 means that they use a preamble at the start of each frame to allow a receiving station to acquire clock (bit) synchronization prior to receiving the start of the frame contents. This is not necessary with a token ring, since the local clocks in all stations are kept in synchronization by the continuously circulating bit stream.

Similarly, the use of a token for MAC means that 802.4 and 802.5 have a frame control field preceding the address fields as well as an end delimiter after the FCS. An 802.3 LAN does not use these fields, although it does use a length byte and possibly some additional padding bytes with small frames. To confuse things

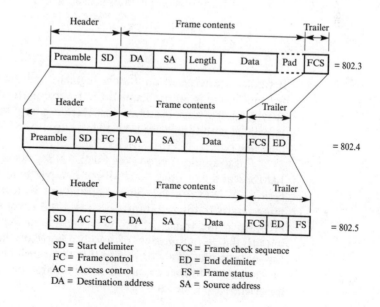

Figure 7.28
Comparison of LAN
frame formats.

SD = Start delimiter   FCS = Frame check sequence
FC = Frame control   ED = End delimiter
AC = Access control   FS = Frame status
DA = Destination address   SA = Source address

further, a token ring also uses an additional access control field at the start of the frame to manage the priority and reservation features.

Collectively, these features mean that when a frame passes from one type of LAN segment to another it must be reformatted prior to being forwarded on the new LAN type. In general, this is not a real problem since most of the fields identified are automatically added (and deleted) by the different MAC integrated circuit chipsets at the LAN interfaces before the actual frame contents are transmitted (and stored). However, this is not true of the length and pad fields used with 802.3 LANs, since these are treated as part of the frame contents by the MAC chipsets. This means that for 802.3 LANs, the total frame contents must be reformatted in software by the bridge before the frame is forwarded.

Frame reformatting increases the processing overheads (and hence delay) within the bridge. In addition, and more importantly, a new FCS field must therefore be used when the frame is being forwarded. Again, this can readily be done since it is computed and added by the MAC chipset. A potential source of errors with bridged LANs is caused when additional bit errors are introduced into frames while they are being stored and retrieved from memory within each bridge. Clearly such errors go undetected by the new FCS.

A common solution to this problem when all the LAN segments are of the same type is to use the same FCS field from source to destination. This is not possible if a frame is reformatted by a bridge, in which case any bit errors introduced (during processing and storage) go undetected. These are then carried forward as residual errors. To minimize this possibility, error correcting memory is often used.

Bit rate

A range of transmission bit rates is used with LANs. These include the following:

802.3	1, 2, 10 Mbps
802.4	1, 5, 10 Mbps
802.5	1, 4, 16 Mbps

If frames are received on a slow segment and are to be forwarded on a faster segment, there is no problem. If the reverse is true, and especially if the LAN is heavily loaded, a problem can arise if frames have to be queued at the output port associated with the slower LAN. This is true even if the two LAN segments are of the same type.

For example, if two token bus LAN segments are bridged, one operating at 10 Mbps and the other at 1 Mbps, a rapid build-up of frames occurs during periods of heavy traffic. Since the amount of memory available is limited, the bridge starts to discard frames because insufficient storage is available. Although in practice the transport protocol entities in the source stations affected will initiate the retransmission of another copy of these frames, the long timeout associated with this action means that the transit delay of frames will be increased considerably. Moreover, there is no guarantee that the new copies will not experience a similar fate.

Frame size

The three LAN types each use a different maximum frame size: 802.3 uses 1518 bytes, 802.4 uses 8191 bytes, and that used with 802.5 is determined by the size of the ring. A serious problem can arise if a frame is first transmitted on, say, an 802.4 (token bus) segment but is to be subsequently forwarded on an 802.3 segment. Assuming maximum frame sizes are being used, the only way this can be overcome is for the bridge at the interface with the 802.3 segment to divide the larger frame into smaller subunits, each with the same destination and source addresses, prior to transmission.

Although this can be done, so-called **segmentation** is not part of the 802.1(d) standard and so bridges do not normally offer this function. Moreover, it adds overheads within the bridge. Thus, if standard bridges are used to perform the interconnection function, the only solution is for each source station to know the range of maximum frame sizes used in the total bridged LAN and to select the minimum size. Clearly, this solution destroys the transparency feature of 802.1 bridged LANs and hence bridges with an additional segmentation capability are often used.

An alternative solution is to use a device known as a **bridge-router** or **brouter** instead of a conventional (transparent or source routing) bridge to perform the interconnection function between segments of different types. As we shall see in Chapter 9, routers perform their relaying function at the network layer rather than at the MAC sublayer. Moreover, they have been designed from the outset to perform a range of harmonizing functions (including segmentation) for going from one network type to another. Thus a brouter can perform its relay function either as a conventional bridge or as a router and is often used for interconnecting different segment types.

Exercises

7.1 With the aid of a sketch, describe the principle of operation of the following:
(a) A passive repeater hub
(b) An active switching hub

7.2 Produce a schematic diagram of a switching hub. Explain its operation including the role of the FIFO buffers and routing table. Why is a separate collision detect line required for each DTE?

7.3 In relation to a 100 Base 4T LAN, with the aid of sketches, explain how half-duplex communication is obtained using 4-pair UTP cable. Include in your description:
(a) How the carrier sense and collision detect functions are performed

(b) The principle of operation of the 8B6T symbol encoding scheme and how the symbols are transmitted over the cable
(c) How the effects of NEXT are minimized in relation to collision detection

7.4 Produce a sketch of a single-level 100VG AnyLAN (IEEE 802.12) network. A single source DTE makes a request to send a frame over this network. Use a sketch to show the signals that are generated by the hub repeater (and all the other DTEs that are attached to the hub) as a result of the request. Also show the signals that are generated during and after frame transmission.

7.5   Using the example given in Figure 7.9 relating to a single-level 8-port IEEE 802.12 demand priority transmission cycle, determine the NNPP and HPNPP values for the missing fifth and sixth poll cycles.

7.6   For the IEEE 802.12 two-level network given in Figure 7.10(a), derive the frame transmission sequence corresponding to the following requests. Assume all requests occur at the same instant of time after an idle period when both NPPs are 1:

> port 1 = H, ports 2.1/2.2 = N,
> ports 3/4 = H, ports 5.1/5.2 = N,
> port 6 = H

7.7   With the aid of sketches, describe how data is transmitted over a 100VG AnyLAN network cable. Include in your explanation the operation of any encoding scheme that is used.

7.8   With the aid of a diagram, describe the meaning of the following components relating to an FDDI network:
(a) Primary and secondary ring
(b) Single attach and dual attach station
(c) Optical coupling unit
(d) Wiring concentrator
(e) Polarized duplex connectors

7.9   Produce a sketch of a wiring plan for an establishment based on a site-wide FDDI backbone network. Assume there are three buildings and that each building patch panel has four ports. Produce a sketch of a single building wiring plan assuming there is a wiring concentrator on each of three floors with two single attach stations per concentrator.

7.10   State why 4B/5B encoding is used in FDDI networks rather than differential Manchester encoding.
Produce a sketch of the physical interface with a single fiber and explain the meaning of the following terms: latency buffer, 4B/5B encoder/decoder, and clock synchronizer.

7.11   A 100 Mbps FDDI ring network can be up to 100 km in length with up to 500 attached stations. Making reasonable assumptions, determine the ring latency expressed in bits.

7.12   Derive expressions for the utilization, U, and worst-case access delay, A_{max}, of an FDDI ring network in terms of the ring latency, T_l, and target token rotation timer setting, TTRT. Hence derive U and A_{max} for the following ring configurations. Assume a TTRT of 4 ms and a signal propagation velocity of $2 \times 10^8\,ms^{-1}$:
(a) A 2 km ring with 20 stations
(b) A 100 km ring with 500 stations

7.13   Explain the meaning of the following terms relating to bridged LANs:
(a) Bridge
(b) Multiport bridge
(c) Building backbone
(d) Establishment backbone

7.14   List and discuss the advantages and disadvantages of bridges relative to a repeater.

7.15   Produce a sketch of a typical bridge architecture and, with the aid of an example, describe its principle of operation. Include in your description the following terms: promiscuous mode, forwarding database, bridge learning, and spanning tree.

7.16   In relation to the spanning tree algorithm, explain the meaning of the following terms:
(a) Root bridge
(b) Root port
(c) Designated port
(d) Configuration BPDU
(e) Topology change BPDU

7.17   Produce a sketch of a state transition diagram showing the port states and transition possibilities of a bridge and explain the outgoing events and actions relating to each transition.

7.18   For the example bridged LAN shown in Figure 7.23(a), determine the active (spanning tree) topology for the following cases:
(a) All segments have the same designated cost but bridge B6 has a higher priority than the other bridges.
(b) As for (a) except bridge B4 fails.
(c) All bridges are in service but segments S3 and S4 have one half the path cost of the other segments.

7.19 With the aid of sketches, explain the meaning of the following terms:
(a) Topology tuning
(b) Remote bridges

7.20 Produce a sketch of an example bridged LAN based on source routing and, with the help of some example routing table entries, explain how frames are routed across the LAN from one station to another. Include in your description the structure of the routing control information carried in each frame.

7.21 In relation to the routing algorithm used with a source routing bridged LAN, explain the meaning of the following terms:
(a) Single-route broadcast frame
(b) All-routes broadcast frame

7.22 Assuming the bridged LAN shown in Figure 7.27(a) but with an additional bridge used to link ring segments R3 and R6, derive the following when station A wishes to send a frame to station B:
(a) The active spanning tree for the LAN

(b) All the paths followed by the single-route broadcast frame(s)
(c) All the routes followed by the all-routes broadcast frame(s)
(d) The route (path) selected by A

7.23 Repeat Exercise 7.22 assuming that ring R5 operates at twice the bit rate of the other rings, that is, its path cost is one half of that of the other rings.

7.24 Compare the operation of a transparent bridged LAN and a source routing bridged LAN in relation to the following:
(a) Routing philosophy
(b) Quality of routes
(c) Use of bandwidth
(d) Routing overheads
(e) Route finding efficiency
(f) Reliability

7.25 With the aid of a sketch showing the format of the different basic LAN types, discuss the issues involved in producing a bridged LAN comprising the different LAN segment types.

Chapter summary

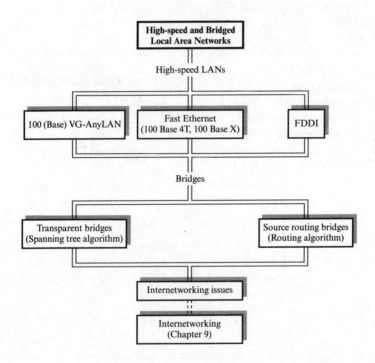

8 WIDE AREA NETWORKS

Chapter objectives

When you have completed this chapter you should be able to:

- Describe the different types of public data network ☞ 424

- Understand the difference between a circuit switched and a packet switched network and the relative advantages and disadvantages of each type ☞ 425

- Describe the structure of the X.25 protocol as used in packed switched networks and the operation of the packet (network) layer in the context of the ISO reference model ☞ 429, 432

- Describe the function of a packet assembly and disassembly device and the various protocols associated with its use and operation ☞ 448

- Explain how a call is established and cleared using the X.21 protocol and a circuit switched data network ☞ 458

- Understand the aims of an ISDN and its various user interfaces and protocols ☞ 461, 462, 466

- Describe the operation of frame relay networks and inverse multiplexers ☞ 470, 475

- Understand the main features of a private integrated voice and data network ☞ 477

Introduction

In Chapters 2 and 5, we considered the use of the PSTN for the transmission of data. Indeed, prior to the advent of public data networks, this was the only method available for transmitting data between user equipment located at different establishments. As we saw, a switched connection made through the PSTN currently supports only a modest user data rate, typically less than 9600 bps. Furthermore, as telephone calls are charged on a time and distance basis, a typical transaction can be very expensive owing to the often long distances and times, especially when a human user is involved.

For these reasons many large organizations have established their own national and international private data networks. Typically, these use dedicated lines leased from the telephone authorities to interconnect a number of privately owned switching nodes or multiplexers of the type we describe at the end of this chapter. Although networks of this type offer the user security, flexibility, and ultimate control, they also involve high investment in purchasing or leasing the equipment. Therefore, such networks are generally owned and managed by large organizations, such as the major clearing banks, who can both afford the initial capital outlay and also generate sufficient traffic to justify this level of investment. These networks are known as private **enterprisewide networks**.

When many private data networks were introduced, the PTT authorities would lease lines to an organization to enable it to build its own private data network, but would not supply lines to allow such networks to be connected together. The demand and subsequent establishment of public data networks stemmed from the ever-increasing demands from users of private networks for facilities to enable them to communicate with each other.

The generic name given to networks that link DTEs (or indeed establishmentwide LANs) that are physically located in different establishments is **wide area network (WAN)**. WANs include both public data networks and enterprisewide private data networks. In this chapter we discuss the operation and protocols associated with such networks.

8.1   Characteristics of public data networks

Most WAN standards have been developed for use by the PTT and public-carrier data networks. A **public data network (PDN)** is a network established and operated by a national network administration authority specifically for the transmission of data. A primary requirement for a PDN is that it should facilitate the interworking of equipment from different manufacturers, which in turn requires agreed standards for access to and use of these networks. After much discussion and experimentation at national and later at international level, a set of internationally agreed standards have been accepted by ITU-T for use with a range of PDNs. These X-series and I-series recommendations include standards for user data signaling rates and user interfaces with such networks.

There are two main types of PDN – **packet switched (PSPDNs)** and **circuit switched (CSPDNs)** – each with its own standards. Since the PSTN is still widely used for data transmission, standards have also been established for interfacing to this type of network. In general, the standards for each of these networks refer to the lowest three layers of the ISO reference model and the functions of each of these layers is shown in Figure 8.1. Remember that the characteristics of the network-dependent layers in the ISO reference model are made transparent to the higher protocol layers by the *transport layer*, which offers the higher layers a

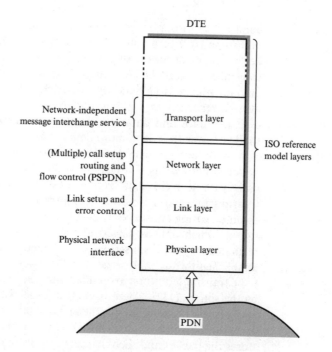

DTE

Network-independent
message interchange service } Transport layer

(Multiple) call setup
routing and
flow control (PSPDN) } Network layer

Link setup and
error control } Link layer

Physical network
interface } Physical layer

ISO reference
model layers

PDN

Figure 8.1
Network-dependent
protocol layers in
PDNs.

network-independent message transport service. We are concerned with the different types of PDN and the various interface protocols that have been defined for use with each type.

8.1.1 Circuit and packet switching

Before we describe the various interface standards associated with PDNs, let us outline the differences between the two types of switching used in these networks. Each connection through a circuit switched network results in a physical communication channel being set up through the network from the calling to the called subscriber equipment. This connection is used exclusively by the two subscribers for the duration of the call. An example of a circuit switched network is the PSTN; indeed, all connections established through the PSTN are of the circuit switched type.

In the context of data transmission, a feature of a circuit switched connection is that it effectively provides a fixed data rate channel at which both subscribers must operate. Also, before any data can be transmitted over such a connection, a connection must be set up or established through the network. Currently, the time required to set up a call through the PSTN can be relatively long (tens of seconds), owing to the type of equipment used in each exchange. Normally, therefore, when transmitting data, a connection is established and kept open for the duration of the transaction. However, the widespread introduction of new computer-controlled switching exchanges, coupled with the adoption of digital transmission throughout the network, means that the setup time of a connection through the PSTN is rapidly becoming much shorter (tens of milliseconds). Furthermore, the extension of digital transmission to the subscriber's equipment means that a high bit rate (typically 64 kbps or higher) switched transmission path will be available at each subscriber outlet. This path can then be used for transmitting data without using modems. The resulting digital PSTN can also be regarded as a public CSDN or, since such networks can support both digitized voice and data, as an integrated services digital network (ISDN). We shall consider ISDNs in more detail in Section 8.4.

Although the connection setup time associated with an all-digital circuit switched network is relatively fast, the resulting connection still provides only a path with a fixed data rate which must be used by both subscribers for transmission and reception. In contrast, with a packet switched network, two communicating subscribers (DTEs) can operate at different data rates, since the rate at which data is passed at the two interfaces to the network is separately regulated by each subscriber's equipment. Also, no physical connections are established through the network with a packet switched network. Instead, all data to be transmitted is first assembled into one or more message units, called **packets**, by the source DTE. These packets include both the source and destination DTE network addresses. They are then passed bit serially by the source DTE to its local **packet switching exchange (PSE)**. On receipt of each packet, the exchange first stores the packet and then inspects the destination address it contains. Each PSE contains a **routing directory** specifying the outgoing link(s) (transmission path(s)) to be used for each network address. The PSE forwards the packet on the appropriate link at the maximum available bit rate. This mode of working is often referred to as **packet store-and-forward**.

Similarly, as each packet is received (and stored) at each intermediate PSE along the route, it is forwarded on the appropriate link interspersed with other packets being forwarded on that link. At the destination PSE, determined by the destination address within the packet, the packet is finally passed to the destination DTE, as shown in Figure 8.2.

As we can see, each overall transaction occupies only a (random) portion of the available bandwidth on each link, since packets from different sources are interspersed with packets from other sources on the various network links. In the limit, the available bandwidth will vary from zero when the user is not transmitting any data to the full bandwidth if it is transmitting packets continuously.

A number of packets may arrive simultaneously at a PSE on different incoming links and each may require forwarding on the same outgoing link. If a number of particularly long packets are waiting to be transmitted on the same link, other packets may experience unpredictably long delays. To prevent this and to ensure that the network has a reliably fast transit time, a maximum length is allowed for each packet. Therefore, when a packet switched network is being used, a message submitted to the transport layer within the DTE may first have to be divided by the source transport protocol entity into a number of smaller packet units before transmission. These smaller units are reassembled into a single message by the correspondent transport protocol entity at the destination DTE.

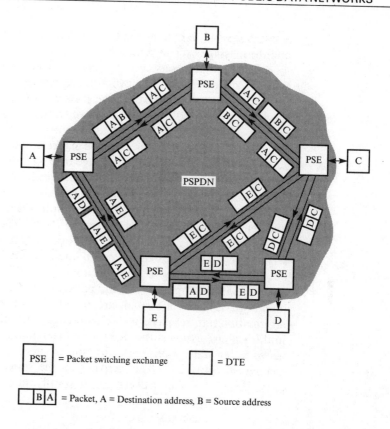

Figure 8.2
Packet switching
schematic.

This is transparent to the transport layer user who is offered a network-independent message transport.

Another difference between a CSPDN and a PSPDN is that with a CSPDN, the network does not apply any error or flow control on the transmitted data, so this must be performed by the user. With a PSPDN, however, sophisticated error and flow control procedures are applied on each link by the network PSEs. Consequently, the class of service provided by a PSPDN is normally much higher than that provided by a CSPDN.

Circuit and packet switching offer the user two different types of service. Even with the advent of all-digital networks, both types of service will still be supported and it will then be up to the user to select a particular service.

8.1.2 Datagrams and virtual circuits

With a PSPDN, two types of service are normally supported: **datagram** and **virtual call (circuit)**. We can explain the difference between the two types of service using an analogy of exchanging messages by letter and by a telephone call. In the first case, the letter containing the message is treated as a self-contained entity by the postal authorities and its delivery is independent of any other letters. In the case of a telephone call, a communication path is first established through the network and the message exchange then takes place.

The datagram service is analogous to sending a message by a letter, since each packet entering the network is treated as a self-contained entity with no relationship to other packets. The packet is simply received and forwarded in the way just outlined. Consequently, we normally use the datagram service for the transfer of short, single-packet messages.

If a message contains multiple packets, we select the virtual call service. This is analogous to sending a message by a telephone call, since when we use this service, before any information (data packets) associated with a call is sent, the source DTE sends a special **call request** packet to its local PSE containing, in addition to the required physical destination DTE network address, a reference number called the **virtual circuit identifier (VCI)**. This is noted by the PSE and the packet is forwarded through the network as before. At the destination PSE, a second VCI is assigned to the call request packet before it is forwarded on the outgoing link to the required destination DTE. Then, assuming the call is accepted, an appropriate response packet is returned to the calling DTE. At this point, we say that a virtual circuit (VC) exists between the two DTEs. The information transfer phase is then entered and all subsequent data packets relating to this call are assigned the same reference numbers on each interface link to the network. In this way, both the source and destination DTEs can readily distinguish between packets arriving on the same link but relating to different calls. The relationship between a virtual call and a VC is shown in Figure 8.3.

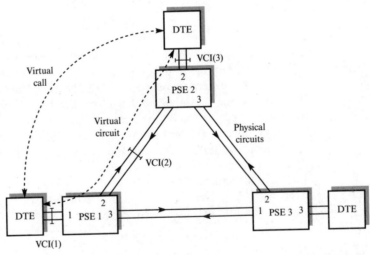

Virtual circuit = VCI(1) + VCI(2) + VCI(3)

VCI = Virtual circuit identifier
PSE = Packet switching exchange

Figure 8.3
Virtual call/virtual circuit relationship and packet routing principles.

	In	Out
PSE 1 routing table	VCI(1)/Link (1) →	VCI(2)/Link (2)
	VCI(2)/Link (2) →	VCI(1)/Link (1)
PSE 2 routing table	VCI(2)/Link (1) →	VCI(3)/Link (2)
	VCI(3)/Link (2) →	VCI(2)/Link (1)

Note that although a VC might appear to the user to be similar to a connection established through a circuit switched network, as the name implies, it is purely a logical connection. Moreover, since the PSPDN provides error and flow control procedures at the packet level in addition to those used at the link level, the **class of service** supported by a VC is very high. This means that there is a very high probability of all the packets relating to a particular call being delivered free of errors and in the correct sequence without duplicates.

Normally, a virtual circuit is cleared and the appropriate VCIs are released after all data relating to a call has been exchanged. However, the virtual circuit may be left permanently established, so that a user who frequently requires to communicate with another user does not have to set up a new VC for each call. This is known as a **permanent virtual circuit (PVC)**. Although the user must pay for this facility, the cost of each call is based only on the quantity of data transferred. As we mentioned, with a circuit switched network, charges are normally made on a distance and call duration basis.

8.2 Packet switched data networks

The internationally agreed network access protocol defined to interface a DTE to a PSPDN is X.25. In fact, X.25 is a set of protocols; the various protocol layers are shown in Figure 8.4. As we can see, the three protocols making up X.25 have only

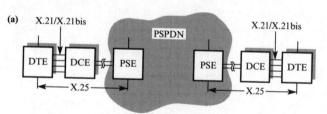

PSPDN = Packet switched public data network

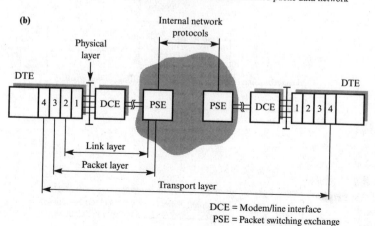

DCE = Modem/line interface
PSE = Packet switching exchange

Figure 8.4
X.25 network access protocol:
(a) applicability;
(b) protocol components.

local significance in contrast to the transport layer which operates on an **end-to-end** basis.

At the lowest layer, the X.21 interface standard is used to define the physical interface between the DTE and the PTT-supplied local DCE. The link layer protocol used with X.25 is a version of the HDLC protocol known as LAPB and its function is to provide the packet layer with an error-free packet transport facility over the physical link between the DTE and its local PSE. Finally, the packet layer is concerned with the reliable transfer of transport layer messages – known as **transport protocol data units (TPDUs)** – and with the multiplexing of one or more virtual calls – network service access points (NSAPs) – on the single physical link controlled by the link layer. The message units and interactions between the various layers are shown in Figure 8.5. We shall consider each layer separately.

8.2.1   Physical layer

The physical interface between the DTE and the local PTT-supplied DCE is defined in ITU-T recommendation X.21. The DCE plays an analogous role to a synchronous modem since its function is to provide a full-duplex, bit-serial, synchronous transmission path between the DTE and the local PSE. It can operate at data rates from 600 bps to 64 kbps. As we shall see in Section 8.3, X.21 is in fact the same interface as that used with an all-digital circuit switched network. Note also that a second standard known as X.21bis has been defined for

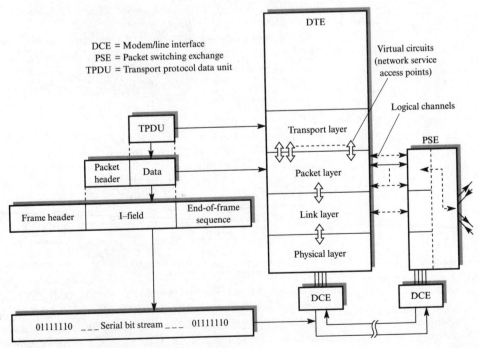

Figure 8.5
X.25 message units and layer interactions.

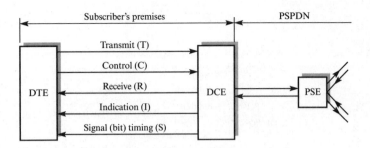

Figure 8.6
X.21 physical layer
interface circuits.

use with existing (analog) networks. An X.21bis is a subset of EIA-232D/V.24, therefore existing user equipment can be readily interfaced using this standard. The various interchange circuits associated with X.21 and X.21bis are defined in recommendation X.24 and are shown in Figure 8.6. We shall discuss the use of each line in more detail in Section 8.3.

8.2.2 Link layer

The aim of the link layer, which we often refer to as level 2 because of its position in the ISO reference model, is to provide the packet layer with a reliable (error free and no duplicates) packet transport facility across the physical link between the DTE and the local PSE. The link layer has no knowledge of the logical channel to which a packet may belong – this is known only by the packet layer. Therefore, the error and flow control procedures used by the link layer apply to all packets irrespective of the virtual circuits to which they belong.

The frame structure and error and flow control procedures used by the link layer are based on the HDLC protocol. We described the basic operation of HDLC in Chapter 5. HDLC uses the ABM of operation, which is also referred to as LAPB in the ITU-T X.25 standards documents. This stands for 'link access procedure' balanced B since it superseded the earlier version A link access procedure.

In the context of the ISO reference model, the services provided by the link layer to the network (packet) layer above it, together with a list of the PDUs associated with the operation of the link layer protocol entity, are summarized in Figure 8.7(a). The service primitives are shown in the order in which they can be issued with the initiating and corresponding reply primitives on the same line. Remember that either of the packet layers can initiate the three service requests shown.

Using ABM, both the DTE and PSE operate asynchronously, and hence both can initiate the transmission of commands and responses at any time. Also, since the protocol controls only the flow of I-frames across a point-to-point link – that is, across the link between the DTE and its local PSE – the address field in each frame is not used to convey networkwide address information; this is carried in the I-field since network addressing is handled by the packet layer. Instead, the address field contains either the DTE or DCE (PSE) address: if the frame is a

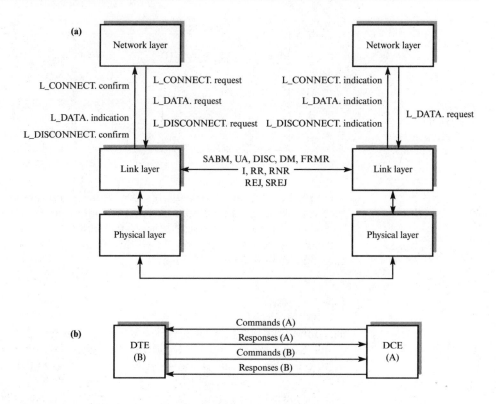

Figure 8.7
Link layer:
(a) summary;
(b) address usage.

command frame, the address specifies the recipient's address; if the frame is a response frame, the address specifies the sender's address. This is shown in Figure 8.7(b).

8.2.3 Packet (network) layer

In the context of the ISO reference model, the packet layer is the same as the network layer. Also, because of its position in the reference model, we often refer to the packet layer simply as level 3. The transport layer uses the services provided by the packet layer to enable it to exchange TPDUs with one or more remote transport layers.

User services

The user services provided by the network (packet) layer are listed in Figure 8.8(a) and their order of usage is shown in the time sequence diagram of Figure 8.8(b). As we can see, a further service primitive (N_EXPEDITED_DATA) is provided in addition to the normal data transfer service primitive (N_DATA). This is an optional service that allows the user to send a single data packet over a connection (logical channel) even though the normal flow of data packets may be stopped by flow control constraints. Another optional service

(N_DATA_ACKNOWLEDGE) allows the user specifically to acknowledge receipt of a previously transmitted packet of user data sent using the N_DATA service. Finally, the N_RESET service allows two users to resynchronize should the flow of packets over a logical channel become out of synchronism while the DISCONNECT service clears the virtual circuit.

All of the primitives have parameters associated with them as listed in Figure 8.8(a). For example, the parameters associated with the N_CONNECT primitives include the **called (destination) NSAP** and **calling (source) NSAP**. The **network service access point (NSAP)** is a concatenation of the physical point-of-attachment address and the internal (interlayer) logical channel (virtual circuit) identifier known as an **address extension**.

The quality of service (QOS) parameter comprises two lists of parameters: the desired and the minimum acceptable parameters expected from the network for the connection being set up. These include (packet) transit delay, residual error probability, priority (if applicable), cost (charge for the call), and specified (rather than arbitrary) route. Finally, the two selection parameters allow the two correspondent network service users – transport protocol entities – to negotiate the inclusion of the two optional services which may be used during the subsequent data transfer phase.

As we can see from Figure 8.5, the transport layer may have a number of network connections (calls) set up at one time, each call associated with a single NSAP. The packet layer thus performs a multiplexing function. All connections – VCs and PVCs – are multiplexed onto a single data link controlled by the link layer. The flow of packets over each virtual circuit is then separately controlled by the packet layer protocol.

(a)

Primitive	Parameters
N_CONNECT.request	Called NSAP, Calling NSAP, QOS, Receipt confirmation selection, Expedited data selection, NS_user data
.indication	Called NSAP, Calling NSAP, QOS, Receipt confirmation selection, Expedited data selection, NS_user data
.response	Responding (called) NSAP, QOS, Receipt confirmation selection, Expedited data selection, NS_user data
.confirm	Responding (called) NSAP, QOS, Receipt confirmation selection, Expedited data selection, NS_user data
N_DATA.request	NS_user data
.indication	NS_user data
N_DATA_ACKNOWLEDGE.request	–
.indication	–
N_EXPEDITED_DATA.request	NS_user data
.indication	NS_user data
N_RESET.request	Originator, Reason
.indication	Originator, Reason
.response	–
.confirm	–
N_DISCONNECT.request	Originator, Reason, NS_user data, Responding address
.indication	Originator, Reason, NS_user data, Responding address

NSAP = Network service access point (address); QOS = Quality of service

Figure 8.8
Network layer services: (a) primitives and their parameters.

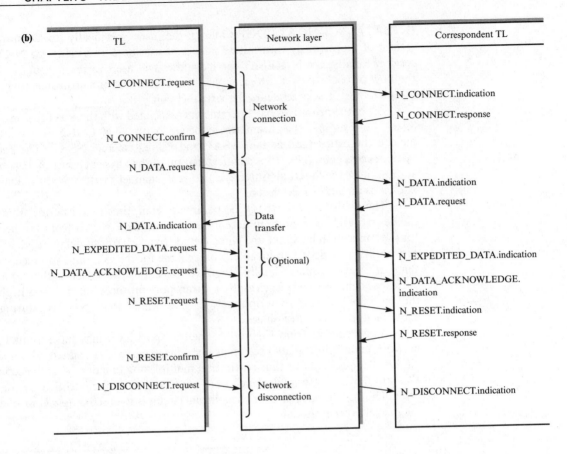

Figure 8.8 (cont.)
(b) Sequence of usage.

NSAP address structure

Most countries have one or more public-carrier PSDNs which are now inter-connected globally to form an international PSPDN. Hence the NSAP address associated with each DTE must be a globally unique network address. Normally, since the total network consists of a number of countrywide PSPDNs, each country network is known as a **subnetwork** or **subnet** in the context of the total network. The structure of the NSAP addresses used in the international PSPDN is defined in ITU-T recommendation X.121. In practice, the addresses associated with all the international networks controlled by ISO and ITU-T have a standard format as shown in Figure 8.9.

The addresses are hierarchical and comprised of two parts: the **initial domain part (IDP)** and the **domain specific part (DSP)**. Both parts are defined in the form of either packed BCD digits or pure binary; the total NSAP length can be up to 40 decimal digits or 20 binary bytes. The actual length of the addresses used normally precedes the address field so that the recipient DTE can interpret the various fields on their correct byte boundaries.

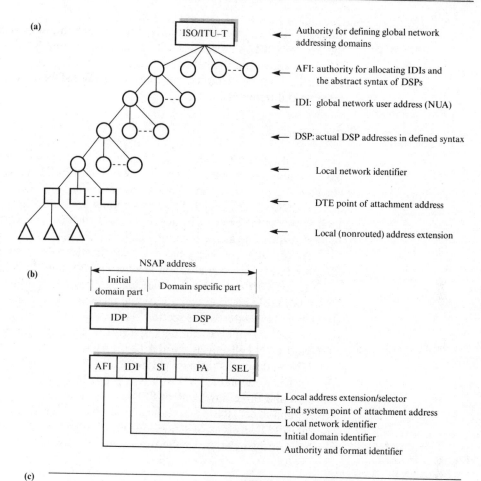

(a)

Authority for defining global network addressing domains

AFI: authority for allocating IDIs and the abstract syntax of DSPs

IDI: global network user address (NUA)

DSP: actual DSP addresses in defined syntax

Local network identifier

DTE point of attachment address

Local (nonrouted) address extension

(b)

NSAP address

Initial domain part | Domain specific part

IDP | DSP

AFI | IDI | SI | PA | SEL

Local address extension/selector
End system point of attachment address
Local network identifier
Initial domain identifier
Authority and format identifier

(c)

	AFI value		IDI length (decimal digits)	DSP length (decimal digits)
	Decimal	Binary		
International PSPDN – X.121	36	37	14	24
International Telex – F.69	40	41	8	30
International PSTN – E.163	42	43	12	26
International ISDN – E.164	44	45	15	23
ISO-assigned country codes – ISO DCC	38	39	3	35
Local (private)	48	49	Null	38

Figure 8.9
NSAP address:
(a) hierarchical
structure; (b) contents;
(c) examples.

The IDP is made up of two subfields: the **authority and format identifier (AFI)** and the **initial domain identifier (IDI)**. The AFI specifies the authority responsible for allocating IDIs, the format of IDIs, and the abstract syntax of the DSP. The IDI specifies the global network address of the customer DTE. The DSP then, if present, allows a further set of addresses to be defined for use at the customer site. In the case of the international PSPDN, the IDI is a 14 decimal-digit hierarchical address which comprises a 3-digit country code and a 1-digit network code plus an area code and a local number. Normally, the DSP is also hierarchical and comprises a **subnet identifier (SI)** and a local point of attachment field. Finally, the **selector (SEL)** subfield has only local meaning and is not used for routing the frame/packet within the network. For example, with an X.25 network it contains the virtual circuit identifier, whereas with an ISDN it identifies one of eight possible end terminals.

Packet types

The packet types associated with the packet layer protocol (PLP) are known as **packet protocol data units (PPDUs)**. The different PPDU types and their usage are shown in Figure 8.10(a) and their structure in part (b). The pairs of PPDU types across the two interfaces – DTE–DCE and DCE–DTE – have different names but their syntax is the same at both interfaces. Thus the syntax (structure) of the call request is the same as the incoming call and so on.

All PPDUs (packets) have a fixed header comprising the **group format identifier (GFI)**, the **logical group number (LGN)**, and the **logical channel number (LCN)**. The GFI is a 4-bit field consisting of a data qualifier (Q bit), a delivery confirmation (D bit) and two additional **modulo bits**. We shall consider the use of the Q and D bits later in this section. The modulo bits indicate the modulo (range) of the (packet) sequence numbers used for flow control purposes – 8 or 128. The LGN and LCN collectively form a 12-bit VCI.

The next octet is the **packet type** field. All control PPDUs have a 1 bit in the lsb position while data PPDUs have a 0 bit. It is thus known as the **control bit**. The data and three flow control PPDUs – receive ready (RR), receive not ready (RNR), and reject (REJ) – each have a receive sequence number in the type field. The data PPDU also has a send sequence number and a single **more-data (M) bit**. We shall consider the use of the three flow PPDUs and the M bit in Figure 8.12.

(a)

Packet (PPDU) types		
DTE → DCE	*DCE → DTE*	*Protocol usage*
Call request	Incoming call	Call setup
Call accepted	Call confirmation	
Clear request	Clear indication	Call clearing
DTE clear confirmation	DCE clear confirmation	
DTE data	DCE data	Data transfer
Interrupt request	Interrupt confirmation	
DTE receiver ready	DCE receiver ready	
DTE receiver not ready	DCE receiver not ready	
DTE reject		Flow control
Reset request	Reset indication	
DTE reset confirmation	DCE reset confirmation	
Restart request	Restart indication	Resynchronize
DTE restart confirmation	DCE restart confirmation	
Diagnostic	Diagnostic	Network error reporting

Figure 8.10
PPDU types:
(a) usage.

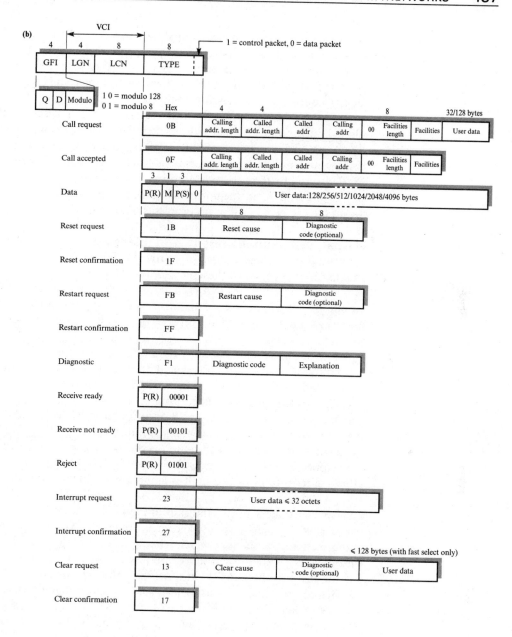

Figure 8.10 (cont.)
(b) Format.

GFI = Group format identifier   Q = Qualifier bit
LCN = Logical channel number   D = Delivery confirmation bit
P(R) = Packet receive sequence number   P(S) = Packet send sequence number
VCI = Virtual circuit identifier

The maximum amount of user data present in a data PPDU is 128 octets although some public carriers use longer lengths of up to 4096 octets. The interrupt request PPDU allows the network service user – **NS_user** – to send up to 32 octets of control data outside the normal flow control mechanism. Such PPDUs are acknowledged with an interrupt confirmation.

The **facilities** field in the call request and call accepted PPDUs enable selected operational parameters to be negotiated when a call is being set up. These parameters include the use of fast select, extended sequence numbers, alternative window and packet sizes, reverse charging, and others. Finally, the **diagnostic** PPDU is used by the network to inform a user DTE of any error conditions that may be detected. These include invalid send and receive sequence numbers, invalid packet type received, call setup problems, and others.

Virtual call establishment and clearing. A time sequence diagram illustrating the various phases of a virtual call is shown in Figure 8.11. A VC is established (set up) when the user issues an N_CONNECT.request primitive at a user service access point (SAP). The parameters associated with this primitive include the NSAP address of the called DTE and a limited amount of user data. As we can see, two alternative procedures may be adopted to set up the network connection.

In the first (**normal**) an X.25 VC is established on receipt of the N_CONNECT.request primitive and the network connect request (N_CR) is then passed over this circuit using an X.25 data packet.

The overheads associated with this method are high and hence the alternative (**fast select**) mode has been introduced by some carriers. In this case, the network connect request is mapped directly onto an X.25 call request packet, significantly reducing the call setup overheads. The reset and disconnect services are mapped in a similar way, as shown in Figure 8.11(a)(i). A second application of fast select is to provide a limited **datagram service**; this is shown in part (ii).

Although a connection-oriented service is suitable for applications that involve the transfer of a significant amount of data, many applications involve just a single request/response message exchange. An example is a credit card authorization transaction which simply involves the transfer of the credit card number followed by a short response message. It is unnecessary to set up a VC for this type of transfer; in a network that supports fast select, the type of transfer can be carried out using a single message exchange, as shown.

With fast select both the call request and call accepted packets and the clear request and clear accepted packets include a user data field of up to 128 bytes. On receipt of the user data from the incoming N_CONNECT.indication, the destination simply responds with an N_DISCONNECT.request with the response message in the NS_user data parameter. The NS_user data is then transported back to the sender in a clear request/confirm packet that, at the same time, clears the VC.

A time sequence diagram illustrating the use of the VCIs – logical channels – is shown in Figure 8.11(b), assuming the fast select facility. On receipt of the N_CONNECT.request primitive, the source protocol entity first selects the next

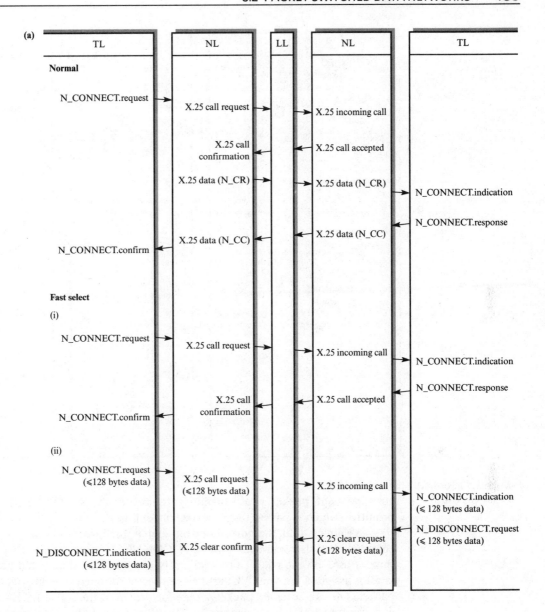

Figure 8.11
Network (packet) services: (a) mapping alternatives.

free VCI and creates a call request packet (PPDU) containing the calling and called DTE addresses and the selected VCI. The packet is then passed to the link layer for forwarding to its local PSE.

On receipt of the packet, the local PSE notes the VCI selected and forwards the packet, according to the internal protocol of the network, to the appropriate destination PSE. The PSE selects the next free VCI for use on the link to the called DTE, writes this into the packet and changes the packet type into an incoming call packet. This is forwarded to the called DTE where its contents are used by the

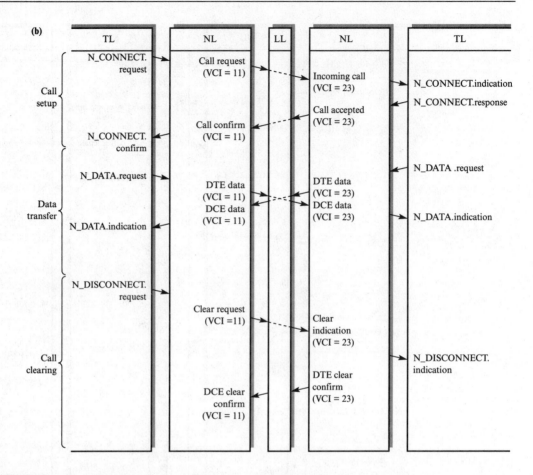

Figure 8.11 (cont.)
(b) example use of VCIs.

correspondent packet protocol entity to create an N_CONNECT.indication primitive, which is passed to the correspondent user.

Assuming that the correspondent user is prepared to accept the call, the correspondent user responds with an N_CONNECT.response primitive which, in turn, is used by the packet protocol entity to create a call accepted packet. The latter is assigned the same VCI as the one used in the corresponding incoming call packet. The call accepted packet is then forwarded to the called DTE's local PSE and the reserved logical channel on this link enters the data transfer phase. Similarly, the source PSE, on receipt of the call accepted packet, inserts the previously reserved VCI for use on this part of the circuit into the packet and sets this logical channel into the data transfer state. It converts the packet into a call connected packet and forwards it to the calling DTE. Finally, on receipt of the packet, the calling packet protocol entity issues an N_CONNECT.confirmation primitive to the user and enters the data transfer state.

If the correspondent user does not wish, or is not able, to accept an incoming call, it responds to the N_CONNECT.indication primitive with an N_DISCONNECT.request primitive. Thus the called packet protocol entity returns a clear request packet to its local PSE, which first releases the previously reserved VCI and then returns a clear confirmation packet to the called DTE. It then sends a clear request packet to the source PSE which, in turn, passes the packet to the packet protocol entity in the calling DTE as a clear indication packet. The DTE first releases the reserved VCI and then passes an N_DISCONNECT.indication primitive to the user. The DTE then returns a clear confirmation packet to its local PSE to complete the clearance of the VC. Similarly, either the user or the correspondent user can initiate the clearing of a call at any time by issuing an N_DISCONNECT.request primitive at the corresponding user interface.

Data transfer.   After a virtual call (network logical connection) has been established, both the user and correspondent user may initiate the transfer of data independently of one another by issuing an N_DATA.request primitive at its network interface with the data to be transferred as a parameter. As we have mentioned, the maximum length of each data packet in a public-carrier packet switched network is limited, typically to 128 octets of data, to ensure a reliably fast response time. If a user wishes to transfer a message containing more than this number of octets, the message is first divided into an appropriate number of data packets and each packet is sent separately. So that the recipient user knows when each message is complete, each data packet sent through the network contains a single bit in its header known as the **more-data** or **M bit**, which is set whenever further data packets are required to complete a user-level (that is, transport layer) message.

Although the transport layer normally initiates the transfer of its own protocol control messages (TPDUs) to one or more peer transport layers using an N_DATA.request primitive with the TPDU as a data parameter, the X.25 packet layer also allows the user to specify whether the associated parameter contains user-level control or data information. The information type is embedded into the resulting data packet by the packet layer, which sets a special bit in the packet header known as the **qualifier** or **Q bit**. On receipt of each data packet by the destination packet layer, this information is passed with the associated data to the correspondent user.

Although the three protocol layers associated with the X.25 protocol set normally have only local significance, acknowledgment information at the packet level can be given end-to-end significance using a special bit in each packet header known as the **delivery confirmation** or **D bit**. The D bit in the header of a data packet is set to 1 if the source DTE requires an end-to-end confirmation (acknowledgment) of correct receipt by the remote peer packet layer. As we shall see in Section 8.3, this information is carried in the header of a packet flowing in the reverse direction.

Flow control.   All packet layer packets are transferred from a DTE to its local PSE using the services provided by the link layer. The use of the HDLC protocol at the link layer means that the basic packet transport facility supported is relatively reliable. Thus, the emphasis at the packet layer is on flow control rather than on error control. The flow control algorithm is based on a sliding window mechanism similar to that introduced in Chapter 4. The flow of packets is controlled separately for each logical channel and for each direction of a call, that is, the flow of data packets relating to each call from DTE to PSE is controlled separately from the flow of packets from PSE to DTE.

To implement the window mechanism, all data packets contain a **send sequence number P(S)**, and a **receive sequence number P(R)**. The P(R) contained in each data packet relates to the flow of data packets in the reverse direction. Alternatively, if no data packets are awaiting transmission in the reverse direction, the P(R) may be sent by the receiver in a special **receiver ready (RR)** supervisory packet.

The first data packet in each direction (DTE to PSE and PSE to DTE) of a logical channel is given a P(S) of 0; each subsequent packet in the same direction carries the previous P(S) incremented by 1. The number of packets relating to the same call that may be sent in each direction before a response is received is limited by the agreed window size K for the channel which, for reasons described in Chapter 4, has a maximum value of 7 if eight unique sequence numbers are being used. Thus, once the sender has initiated the transfer of a number of data packets up to the window size, it must cease transmitting further packets until it receives either a data packet or an RR supervisory packet containing a P(R) that indicates the willingness of the receiver to accept further packets on this channel.

To implement this scheme, the DTE and PSE each maintain three variables for each active logical channel (and hence VC):

- V(S) The **send sequence variable** indicates the P(S) that will be assigned to the next data packet *sent* on this logical channel.

- V(R) The **receive sequence variable** indicates the P(S) of the next in-sequence data packet that is expected to be *received* on this logical channel.

- V(A) The **acknowledgment variable** is used to determine when the flow of data packets should be stopped.

All three variables are set to 0 when the VC is first set up or subsequently reset (see 'Error recovery', p. 444). As each data packet is prepared for sending, it is assigned a send sequence number P(S) equal to the current V(S), which is then incremented modulo 8 or 128 as defined in the GFI field. Similarly, on receipt of each data packet or RR flow control packet by the destination packet layer, the receive sequence number, P(R), contained within it is used to update V(A). The sender can continue sending data packets until either the window size is reached (that is, until the incremented V(A) reaches K) or a data or a RR packet is received containing a P(R) that advances the current V(A). Further data packets may then be sent until the window limit is again reached. A typical packet sequence illustrating this procedure for a window size of 3 is given in Figure 8.12(a). For clarity, a single logical channel is assumed and only a unidirectional flow of data packets is shown.

The use of a window mechanism to control the flow of data packets means that the maximum number of packet buffers required to handle each call is readily

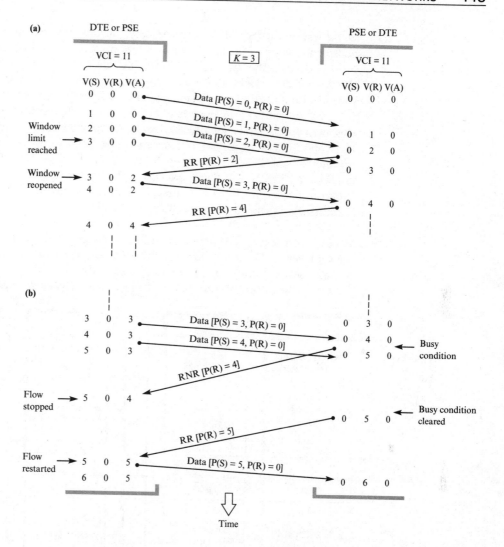

Figure 8.12
Flow control
examples:
(a) window
operation; (b) RNR
operation.

determined. In practice, the total number of buffers provided to cater for all the calls that may be currently active is often less than the maximum number required. Therefore, a facility is provided in the protocol to allow the DTE (or PSE) temporarily to suspend the flow of data packets associated with a specific call (virtual circuit) by having the receiver return a **receiver not ready (RNR)** packet for this logical channel, instead of an RR packet. Each RNR packet contains a P(R) that defines the new V(A) for this channel. However, on receipt of an RNR, the sender must cease transmission of further packets until the receiver is ready to continue receiving data packets on this channel. The receiver indicates this by returning an RR packet. A typical packet sequence illustrating the use of the RNR packet is shown in Figure 8.12(b). We can deduce from the figure that the RNR packet cannot stop the flow of packets immediately, since some packets may be in transit on the link. However, any packets received in this way must be accepted because of the lack of any error control associated with the packet layer.

Although the two mechanisms just described are provided to control the flow of data packets over each logical channel, provision is also made in the protocol for a DTE to send a single high-priority data packet (interrupt packet) to a correspondent DTE independently of the normal flow control procedures. Since this interrupt packet is not affected by the normal flow control mechanisms, it may be received out of sequence from other data packets over this circuit. On receipt of an interrupt packet, the receiving DTE (packet layer) must return an interrupt confirm packet, since there can be only one outstanding unacknowledged interrupt packet per VC at any time. This allows a further such packet to be sent if necessary, as shown in Figure 8.13(a).

Error recovery. The main error recovery mechanisms associated with the packet layer are the reset and restart procedures. The reset procedure is used only during the data transfer phase and affects just a single virtual call (circuit). However, the restart procedure affects all virtual calls currently in progress.

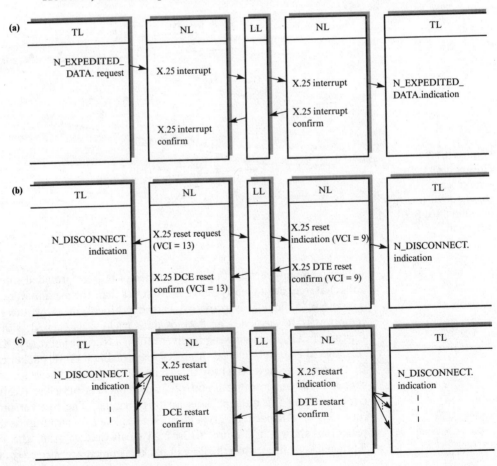

Figure 8.13
Additional services:
(a) expedited data; (b) reset;
(c) restart.

A reset request packet is sent by either DTE if it receives a data packet that is outside the current window limit. This indicates that the two DTEs have become unsynchronized and hence the flow of data packets must be restarted. A typical packet sequence associated with the reset procedure is shown in Figure 8.13(b). Any data packets associated with the affected VC are discarded by the packet layer and the user is informed that the network connection has been cleared. The reason for the clearing is passed as a parameter and it is then up to the user (the transport layer, in practice) to recover from any possible loss of data.

The restart procedure is used simultaneously to clear all VCs currently in progress at a DTE. The procedure is used when the DTE and PSE become unsynchronized at a level that affects all currently active calls; for example, if an incoming call with an LCN that is currently in use is received from the PSE. A typical packet sequence associated with the restart procedure and the effect on a number of active VCs is shown in Figure 8.13(c). The figure shows the possible effect only at a single correspondent packet layer, but clearly a number of other DTEs may be affected in a similar way.

Packet layer summary

Figure 8.14 summarizes the overall operation of the packet layer. We have used the same form of presentation as for the link layer. We can clearly identify three aspects of the operation of the layer:

- The services it offers to the transport layer above it

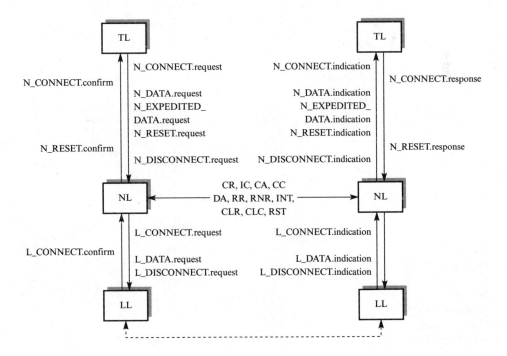

Figure 8.14
X.25 packet layer summary.

- The PDUs exchanged between two correspondent network (packet) layer protocol entities
- The link layer services it uses to transport these PDUs

Protocol specification

We shall now consider the call establishment phase of the packet layer protocol to give an insight into its specification. The time sequence diagram for this phase was shown in Figure 8.11. For clarity, we have assumed that the fast select facility is being used and that a data link has already been set up.

In keeping with the style of presentation we used in Chapter 4, Figure 8.15 lists all the incoming events, states, outgoing events, predicates, and specific actions related to the call establishment phase of the protocol. To aid understanding, a state transition diagram of the call establishment phase is shown in Figure 8.16(a). Note that the incoming event and associated outgoing event are shown alongside each transition arc. Figure 8.16(b) gives a more formal definition of the protocol in the form of an event–state table.

Note that these definitions are not intended to be complete but rather serve as an introduction to understanding the formal specification of the X.25 packet layer protocol.

(a)

Name	Interface	Meaning
NCONreq	NS_user	N_CONNECT.request received
NCONresp	NS_user	N_CONNECT.response received
CALLconn	Link layer	Call connected packet received
INCcall	Link layer	Incoming call packet received
TCALLconn	Timer	Call connected timer expires

(b)

Name	Meaning
IDLE	No connection established
WFCC	Waiting for a call connected packet
WFNCR	Waiting for an N_CONNECT.response from NS_user
WFCLCF	Waiting for a clear confirm packet
DATA	Connection established and ready for data transfers

(c)

Name	Interface	Meaning
NCONind	NS_user	Send N_CONNECT.indication
NCONconf	NS_user	Send N_CONNECT.confirm
NDISind	NS_user	Send N_DISCONNECT.indication
CALLreq	Link layer	Send call request packet
CALLacc	Link layer	Send call accepted packet
CLRreq	Link layer	Send clear request packet

Figure 8.15
Abbreviated names for call establishment phase of network (packet) layer:
(a) incoming events;
(b) states;
(c) outgoing events.

(d)

Name	Meaning
P0	N_CONNECT.request from NS_user unacceptable
P1	N_CONNECT.response from NS_user unacceptable
!	
!	
!	

(e)

Name	Meaning
[1]	Start TCALLconn timer
[2]	Stop TCALLconn timer
!	
!	

Figure 8.15 (cont.)
(d) Predicates;
(e) specific actions.

(a)

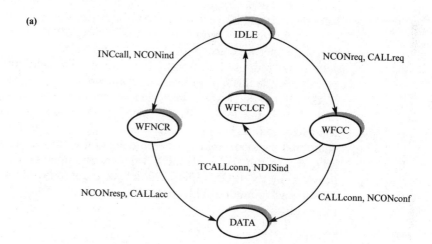

(b)

Event \ State	IDLE	WFCC	WFNCR	WFCLCF	DATA	---
NCONreq	1	0	0	0	0	
NCONresp	0	0	3	0	0	
CALLconn	0	2	0	0	0	
INCcall	4	0	0	0	0	
TCALLconn	0	5	0	0	0	
!						

0 = NDISind, CLRreq, WFCLCF   (Error condition)

1 = P0: NDISind, IDLE;
    NOT P0: CALLreq, [1], WFCC

2 = NCONconf, [2], DATA

3 = NOT P1: CALLacc, DATA

4 = NCONind, WFNCR

5 = NDISind, CLRreq, WFCLCF

Figure 8.16
Protocol specification
for call establishment:
(a) state transition
diagram; (b) event–
state table.

8.2.4 Terminal access

In the preceding sections relating to the X.25 network access protocol we have assumed that the DTE to be connected to the network has sufficient intelligence (or processing capability) to implement the various protocol layers just described. In general, this assumption is valid, certainly if the DTE is a computer. However, in some instances the DTE may neither operate in a packet mode nor have sufficient processing capability to implement a protocol like X.25. To interface this type of DTE to the network we must provide an additional piece of equipment which implements the various protocol layers on behalf of the DTE and provides a much simpler user-level interface to the DTE. An example of a DTE in this category is a simple asynchronous character-mode terminal like a personal computer or VDU. This normally has only a limited level of intelligence with a simple EIA-232D/V.24 physical interface.

To meet this type of requirement, the user may choose to provide the additional equipment to perform the necessary assembly of character strings from the terminal into network packets and vice versa. Alternatively, because this is not an uncommon requirement, the various PSPDN authorities offer users an alternative network access protocol, known as X.28, which is intended for use with asynchronous character-mode terminals. The additional equipment necessary to provide this type of interface is known as a **packet assembler–disassembler (PAD)**. Since the PAD is provided by the PSPDN authority, it is normally located with the local PSE. A single PAD is used to support a number of character-mode DTEs. The functions and location of a PAD, together with the additional protocols that have been defined for use with it, are shown in Figure 8.17. As we can see, protocol X.3 defines the operation and facilities that are provided by the PAD, while X.29 defines the interface between the PAD and a remote packet-mode DTE. We shall now consider selected aspects of this mode of working.

PAD and X.3

Essentially, the function of a PAD is to assemble the individual characters entered by a user at a character-mode asynchronous terminal into meaningful packets that are suitable for transmission through an X.25 PSPDN. Similarly, on receipt of such packets, the PAD disassembles them and passes their individual characters to the terminal a single character at a time. Thus the PAD must perform all the X.25 protocol functions on behalf of the terminal (such as call establishment, flow control) and in general make the packet mode of working of the network transparent to the user.

The functions and facilities of a PAD are defined in recommendation X.3. In addition to the basic functions just outlined, each terminal connected to a PAD has a number of associated parameters, because character-mode terminals vary widely in their operation and characteristics. These parameters are normally set by commands entered at the terminal or, alternatively, from the remote packet-mode DTE being accessed, and relate to such features as the following:

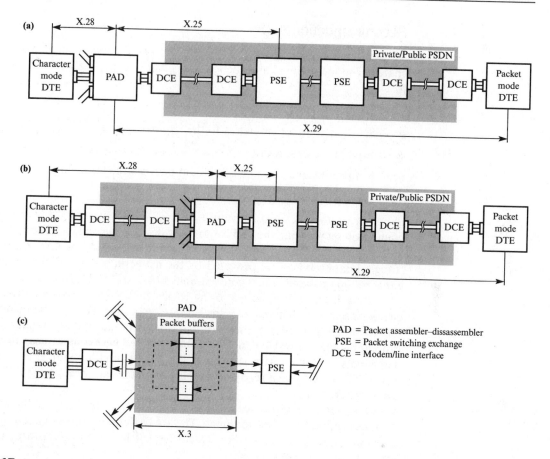

Figure 8.17
PAD location and its protocols: (a) with character-mode DTE; (b) with PSE; (c) internal schematic.

- Whether local **echo checking** is required

- Selection of **packet terminating (data forwarding)** characters which allow the user of the terminal to signal to the PAD that the transmission of a (partly complete) packet should be initiated

- Specification of alternative control characters for such functions as line feed and carriage return

To facilitate the use of the PAD, all the parameters associated with a terminal have a **default value**. Only parameters that differ from the default values need be changed. The initial parameter settings are determined by the **standard profile** selected for the terminal. A number of alternative standard profiles have been defined for the more popular types of terminal. Both the standard profile and any changes are normally selected and entered when a communication link between the terminal and the PAD is first established. The procedure is defined in recommendation X.28.

Recommendation X.28

This recommendation specifies the protocol to be used between an asynchronous character-mode terminal and the PAD. It contains the procedures to be followed to:

- Access the PAD
- Set the terminal parameters to the required values
- Establish a virtual call to a destination packet-mode DTE
- Control the exchange of user's data between the terminal and the PAD
- Clear an established call

Access to the PAD may take several forms. It may be via a switched connection set up using the PSTN or it may be over a leased line. If the PSTN uses analog transmission, modems must be used at each end of the link. Alternatively, if digital data services are provided by the network, a direct digital path can be either set up or leased, and a conventional EIA-232D/V.24 interface may be used.

Once it has gained access to the PAD, the terminal sends a service request character sequence. This enables the PAD to determine the data rate being used by the terminal and allows the terminal to select an initial standard profile. Procedures are defined by the standard to allow the terminal user to read the parameters associated with the profile and, if required, to change them to other values. The PAD is then ready to establish a virtual call through the PSPDN to a remote packet-mode DTE.

To establish a virtual call, the user first indicates to the PAD the address of the required packet-mode terminal. The PAD follows the virtual call establishment procedure outlined earlier. Once the call has been established, the PAD enters the data transfer phase.

In the data transfer phase, the PAD performs the necessary packet assembly and disassembly functions. During the assembly process, the PAD initiates the transfer of a packet either when the user enters an agreed packet termination control character or after an agreed timeout period. Finally, after all information has been exchanged, the user may request the PAD to initiate the clearing of the call.

Recommendation X.29

This recommendation specifies the interaction between the PAD and the remote packet-mode DTE. The basic procedures associated with X.29 for call establishment and data transfer are essentially the same as those used in X.25. However, additional procedures are defined in the recommendation which reflect the presence of the PAD between the terminal and remote packet-mode DTE. For example, during the call establishment phase, the PAD uses the first four octets of the optional user data field in a call request packet as a so-called **protocol identifier** field. This allows different types of calling subscriber (terminal) to be identified so that the called packet-mode DTE can utilize alternative protocols if necessary.

Similarly, in the reverse direction, in the data transfer phase the packet-mode DTE is able to communicate with the PAD directly using the Q bit in the header of each data packet. When the Q bit is set, the remaining information in the packet is intended for use by the PAD and should not be disassembled and passed to the user terminal. This procedure allows, for example, the remote packet-mode DTE to read and, if necessary, set the current values of the parameters associated with the calling terminal.

8.2.5 Interconnection of X.25 networks

As has been described, X.25 is the protocol set used for interfacing a DTE to the DCE associated with a PSDN. It is a connection-oriented protocol which means that a VC is established between the two communicating DTEs prior to transmission of any data. Associated with this VC are two logical channel identifiers: one for use over the link connecting the calling DTE to its local DCE/PSE and the other for use over the called DCE–DTE link. These identifiers are used to relate the subsequent data packets associated with the call to that VC.

Although it is not part of the X.25 standard, when a VC is being set up, it must also be established across the network to enable the data packets associated with each call to be routed by the packet-switching exchanges within the network. We shall discuss some of the routing algorithms that are used with WANs in Chapter 9. However, irrespective of the routing algorithm used to compute routes, each exchange contains a number of routing tables to route packets: a **network routing table**, which indicates the outgoing link from this exchange to use for each destination DTE in the network, and an additional set of **link routing tables**, one per link.

On receipt of a call request packet, each exchange involved in a route first uses the destination DTE address within the packet to determine from the network routing table which outgoing link to use to forward the packet. It then obtains the next free VCI to be used on this link – from a list of free VCIs – and makes an entry in the two link routing tables. An example is shown in Figure 8.18.

We have assumed that the call request packet arrived on link 1 with a VCI of 10 and a destination DTE address of 25. The exchange first determines from the network routing table that the required outgoing link is 2. Assuming the next free VCI on link 2 is 15, the exchange makes an entry first in link 1 routing table at location (VCI) 10 of the corresponding outgoing link number (link-out) and VCI (VCI-out) and then in link 2 routing table at location 15 of link 1 and VCI 10. It then initiates the forwarding of the call request packet on link 2 with a VCI of 15 in its header.

This procedure is repeated at each exchange until the call request packet reaches the exchange to which the destination DTE is attached. The subsequent call accepted and related data packets are forwarded along this established route (VC) as each exchange simply reads, from the incoming link routing table, the outgoing link number and VCI, writes these into the packet header and initiates the forwarding of the packet on the outgoing link.

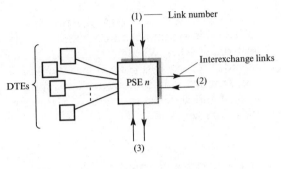

PSE n Network routing table

Dest.DTE	Link-out
¦	¦
25	2
¦	¦

Note: DTEs connected to this PSE have zero entries

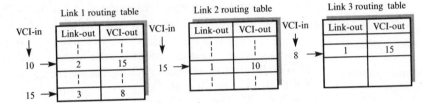

Link 1 routing table

VCI-in	Link-out	VCI-out
	¦	¦
10 →	2	15
	¦	¦
15 →	3	8

Link 2 routing table

VCI-in	Link-out	VCI-out
	¦	¦
15 →	1	10
	¦	¦

Link 3 routing table

VCI-in	Link-out	VCI-out
8 →	1	15

Figure 8.18
Intranetwork routing example.

We can conclude that if the total network comprises multiple interconnected networks and the two DTEs are connected to different networks, then a separate VC must be set up across each intermediate subnetwork. Moreover, to relate packets to a particular call, a VC must also be set up across the links that interconnect these networks. Thus with a large network that comprises multiple subnetworks, the VC set up between two DTEs comprises a number of separate VCs (and hence logical channel identifiers), each of use over a particular link. This is shown in Figure 8.19. For clarity, just a single VC is shown for each subnetwork.

Typically, the individual networks shown in the figure are public-carrier data networks, so many thousands of DTEs may be connected to each network. The interconnecting links between networks are normally multiple 64 or 56 kbps lines or channels. The equipment used to interconnect each network is a special DCE known as a **signaling terminal exchange (STE)**; the **X.75** protocol is used to establish and release VCs across these links. This protocol is also often used for setting up and releasing VCs across a single network, although this is not specified by ITU-T. Figure 8.19 shows the VCs associated with a single call between two DTEs.

The presence of multiple VCs associated with a call is transparent to the two communicating DTEs; each DTE knows only the identity of the VC associated with the local link to its DCE/PSE. Flow and error control for all data packets carried over these links is performed in the normal way. The controlling devices associated with each of the other VCs (DCE–STE, STE–STE, etc.) operate in the

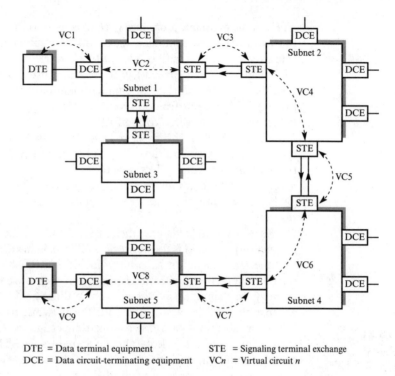

Figure 8.19
VC structure across a network that comprises multiple subnetworks.

DTE = Data terminal equipment   STE = Signaling terminal exchange
DCE = Data circuit-terminating equipment   VC*n* = Virtual circuit *n*

same way and impose their own flow and error control procedures over these circuits. Because the STE between each pair of networks consists of two halves, each associated with its own network, an STE is also referred to as a **half gateway**.

Recommendation X.75

The applicability of X.75 is shown in Figure 8.20. As with X.25, three protocols are associated with the X.75 standard: the packet layer protocol (PLP), the data link protocol (DLP), and the physical layer protocol (PHY). Normally, to enhance reliability and throughput, we use multiple links to interconnect two

Figure 8.20
Applicability of the X.75 protocol.

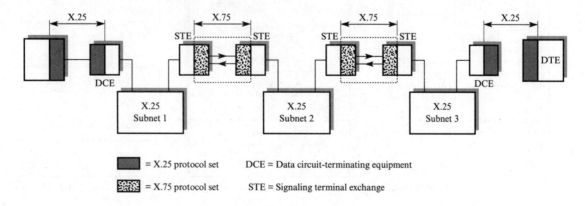

= X.25 protocol set   DCE = Data circuit-terminating equipment

= X.75 protocol set   STE = Signaling terminal exchange

STEs so the **multilink procedure (MLP)** is used as the DLP. Recall from Chapter 5 that with MLP the combined set of links (or subchannels relating to a higher bit rate circuit) is treated as a single entity when transmitting frames across such links. Thus when a frame (packet) is to be transmitted, any available link is selected regardless of the VC (logical channel identifier) within it. The multilink control (MLC) field in each frame is used by the recipient MLP to resequence frames before they are delivered to the PLP.

The X.75 PLP is simpler than the X.25 PLP in that it requires fewer packet types for its implementation. This is because in X.75 communication is between two directly connected STEs, whereas with X.25 two intermediate DCEs are also involved in the communications path between two DTEs. The reduced set of packet types and their general format are shown in Figure 8.21(a) and (b), respectively.

The various fields and their usage are virtually the same as for X.25. The main additional field is the **network utilities field** in each call request packet. Recall that the same packet in X.25 has a facilities field which is used to request certain operational facilities with this connection, such as selection of the retransmission strategy. In a similar way, the network utilities field allows one STE to indicate to another the utilities associated with the network to which it is attached. These include window and packet size indication, estimated transit delay, and its support (or otherwise) of fast select. This field enables an STE to determine whether the specified minimum facilities required for the connection can be met.

Elements of the operation of the PLP are outlined in Figure 8.22; part (a) shows the various protocols, while part (b) shows the end-to-end packet sequence used to set up a VC, then to transfer a single packet of data, and finally to clear the

Figure 8.21
X.75 packets:
(a) packet types and
their usage; (b) packet
formats (i) call
request, (ii) control,
(iii) data.

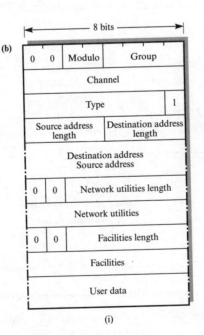

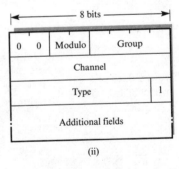

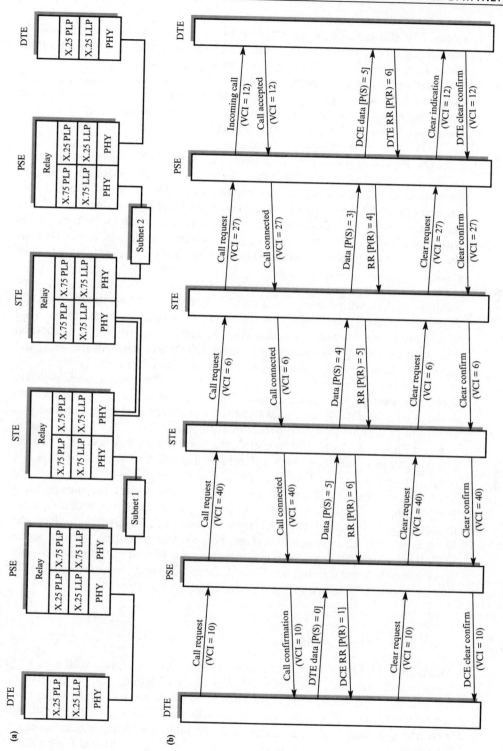

Figure 8.22 End-to-end packet flow: (a) protocol stacks; (b) packet sequence diagram.

circuit. For convenience, we assume that the X.75 protocol is used for transfers across each subnet as well as across the STE–STE links. The relay function within each STE is used to perform any packet format conversions.

Each STE has a specific X.121 address. Since this is hierarchical, on receipt of a packet the receiving STE (and each intermediate packet switching exchange within the network) can use the highest-order part of the destination address to determine the route to be followed either to the next STE or to the destination DCE/DTE.

On receipt of a call request packet, the source PSE determines from the (DTE) destination address within it that it is for a different network. The PSE uses its routing table to determine the outgoing link to be used to forward the packet to the appropriate STE. On receipt of the packet, the relay layer within the STE first makes a record of the VCI associated with this call and then reformats the packet with a new VCI and the appropriate network utilities parameters. It then initiates the transfer of the packet across the STE–STE link using the appropriate protocol stack.

The relay layer within the receiving STE makes a record of the network utilities and VCI within the packet, enters a new VCI, and again uses the DTE destination address contained within the packet to forward the packet through the second subnetwork to the destination PSE. The relay layer within the destination PSE reformats the packet into an incoming call packet, changes the VCI, and forwards the packet to the destination DTE using the X.25 PLP.

A similar procedure is used with call accepted/call connected packets except that in this case the utilities associated with the second network are made known to the other STE. Finally, data packets can be transferred over the established VCs on receipt of the call connected packet by the source DTE.

As Figures 8.12 and 8.13 indicated, the normal X.25 flow and error control procedures are applied over each VC in turn. Thus if the flow is stopped at any point in a network, this will be reflected back to the neighboring network VC and so on back to the source DTE. This type of flow control is known as **back pressure**.

Figure 8.22(b) shows a single data packet being transferred with a separate (nonpiggybacked) acknowledgment being used on each VC. Alternatively, if the D bit is set in a data packet then it remains set throughout its transfer across the total network. The resulting acknowledgment is treated in the same way and hence has end-to-end significance. Finally, the call clearing procedure is similar to that used with X.25 except that it is extended across the complete network.

8.2.6   X.25 PLP over LANs

Although the DTEs (stations) connected to many LANs operate with a best-try connectionless network layer protocol, they can also operate with an X.25 PLP, for example, when the DTEs (stations) connected to the LAN require to communicate with a remote system through an X.25-based WAN. All the networks are then of the same type and the internetworking issues are much simplified. A simple interconnected network of this type is shown in Figure 8.23.

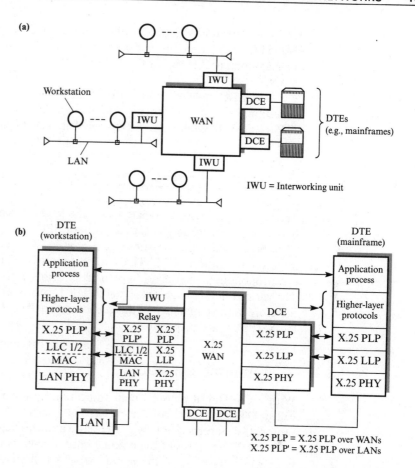

Figure 8.23
X.25 PLP over LANs:
(a) example
application;
(b) possible protocol
hierarchy.

In this example, we assume that the total network comprises a distributed community of LANs each connected to an X.25-based WAN. The aim is for all stations connected to each LAN either to communicate with another station on the same LAN directly or to access, say, a mainframe computer connected to the X.25 WAN.

To meet such a requirement, a special node on each LAN acts as the interface point to the X.25 WAN. Because of its role, it is known (in ITU-T terminology) as an **interworking unit (IWU)**. It has a known X.25 WAN address. If the X.25 PLP in a station determines that the required destination network address is different from its own, then it sends the call request packet to the IWU using the latter's (known) MAC address. The relay function in the IWU then sends a separate call request packet across the X.25 WAN in the normal way.

Two problems with this type of interworking are the selection of VC (logical channel) identifiers and the disparity in frame (packet) sizes. Clearly, the IWU associated with each LAN essentially has a number of independent DTEs connected to it each of which can initiate the sending of a call request packet. To overcome the (high) probability of a collision in the selection of VCIs, one (or more) identifiers is (are) assigned to each DTE in advance; this is known by the DTE. In the case of different packet sizes, the normal approach is to adopt the maximum packet size of the X.25 WAN for all communications involving the WAN.

The LLC sublayer can be either LLC1 or LLC2, both of which we described in Section 5.3.6. Since this type of network is commonly used, the use of the X.25 PLP over a LAN is now an international standard defined in ISO 8881.

8.3 Circuit switched data networks

The various protocols associated with the lowest three network-dependent layers in the ISO reference model for use with a CSPDN are as shown in Figure 8.24(a). The operational characteristics of the physical interface to a CSPDN are defined in recommendation X.21. The aim is to provide the user with a full-duplex synchronous data transmission path which is available for the duration of the call. The various interchange circuits associated with X.21 were shown in Figure 8.6, therefore in the remainder of this section we shall concentrate on the operation of the X.21 interface protocol.

8.3.1 X.21 interface protocol

With a CSPDN, a physical communication path exists between the calling and called DTEs once a call has been established. Therefore, the X.21 interface protocol is concerned only with the setup and clearing operations associated with each call. The control of the ensuing data transfer is the responsibility of the link layer which, because of the operation of a CSPDN, operates on an end-to-end basis. This is shown in Figure 8.24(b).

A typical interchange sequence to set up a call, exchange data, and then clear the call using the various interchange circuits associated with X.21 is

Figure 8.24
CSPDNs: (a) network-dependent protocols; (b) applicability.

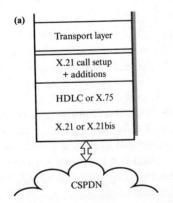

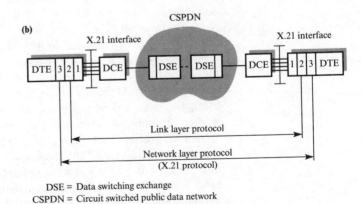

DSE = Data switching exchange
CSPDN = Circuit switched public data network

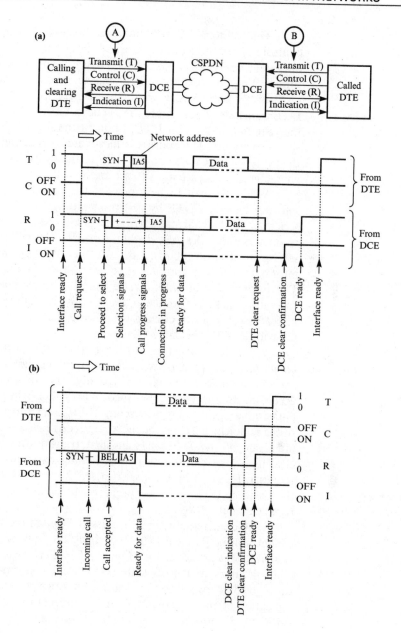

Figure 8.25

Successful call and clear interchange sequences: (a) calling DTE–DCE interface (A); (b) called DTE–DCE interface (B).

shown in Figure 8.25. Part (a) shows the interchange sequence across the calling DTE–DCE interface and (b) shows the interchange sequence across the called DTE–DCE interface. Initially, the transmit (T) circuits from both the calling and called DTEs are set at logical 1, indicating that they are both ready either to initiate or to receive a call. Similarly, the receive (R) circuits from each DCE are also at logical 1, indicating their availability.

The calling DTE first indicates that it wishes to make a call by setting its control (C) circuit to the on state and simultaneously setting its transmit circuit to logical 0 (Figure 8.25a). When the DCE is ready to accept the call, it responds by transmitting two (or more) SYN characters on the receive circuit followed by a series of ' + ' IA5 (ASCII) characters. On receipt of the ' + ' characters, the calling DTE transmits two (or more) SYN characters followed by the network address of the required destination DTE, again in the form of IA5 characters each with a single parity bit. The address is terminated by a single ' + ' character. The DTE then enters a wait state and the DCE responds by transmitting idle (call progress) characters while it attempts to set up the call.

When the call request reaches the required destination DCE, the latter informs the called DTE by first transmitting two SYN characters followed by a series of BEL characters (Figure 8.25b). SYN and BEL are two control characters from the ASCII character set. The called DTE accepts the call by setting its control circuit to on and the DCE, in turn, passes other call setup information in the form of a series of IA5 characters on the receive circuit. This information includes reverse charging and similar information. Finally, the call setup phase is completed when both the calling and called DCEs set their indication (I) control circuits to indicate that a circuit has been set up and the network is ready for data.

After the connection has been established, a data transparent, full-duplex communication path is available to both the calling and called DTEs for the transfer of link layer data. (Typically, this involves the exchange of frames according to the HDLC protocol.) Each DTE initiates the transmission of a data frame on its transmit circuit. This is sent through the network and passed to the recipient DTE on the incoming receive circuit from its local DCE. Finally, after one of the DTEs has finished transmitting all its data, it initiates the clearing of the call (circuit) by switching its control circuit to off (DTE clear request) (Figure 8.25a). As we can see, however, since the circuit is full-duplex, the clearing DTE must be prepared to accept further data on the incoming receive circuit.

The clear request signal is passed through the network to the remote DCE which informs its local DTE by setting the indication control circuit to the off state (DCE clear indication) (Figure 8.25b). The local DTE responds by setting its control circuit to the off state (DTE clear confirmation). The signal is passed through the network to the clearing DCE which informs the DTE by setting its indication circuit to off (DCE clear confirmation) (Figure 8.25a). Finally, both sides of the connection return to the interface ready state.

8.3.2 X.21 bis

The X.21 interface protocol is intended for use with an all-digital CSPDN. However, before such networks become widely available, and to ease the transition from existing EIA-232D/V.24-based equipment to the newer equipment needed with X.21, an alternative interface protocol has been defined, known as X.21bis, the 'bis' indicating that it is the alternative protocol. We discussed the use of this interface in Chapter 2 with a synchronous modem – that is, one that supplies a bit-timing clock signal – since it must perform digital-to-analog conversion for transmitting data through the network and analog-to-digital conversion on receipt of data from the network.

8.3.3 Link and network layers

As Figure 8.24 indicated, in a CSPDN both the link layer and network layer protocols are end-to-end protocols. However, with an all-digital network, the link layer protocol can be the same as that used in X.25 since a full-duplex circuit is set up, that is, HDLC with LAPB. With older analog access circuits and networks, only a two-wire, half-duplex circuit is set up so recommendation X.75 must be used. The link setup procedure with X.75 is a derivative of LAPB known as LAPX. This again is intended for the setup of a logical data link over a half-duplex physical circuit.

If no flow control functions are supported, the CSPDN network layer (level 3) can be relatively simple, since, after setting up the connection, each network data transfer service primitive issued by the transport layer can be mapped directly into a similar request to the intermediate link layer. The transport layer then performs its own flow control functions. Alternatively, to ease interworking with other types of network, we can have a network layer similar to that used with X.25. If this is the case, the various VCIs we have discussed would have an end-to-end significance rather than local significance, as with an X.25 PSPDN. Also, in a CSPDN each call would, of course, be a separate circuit.

8.4 Integrated services digital networks

The PTT authorities in most countries are rapidly upgrading their existing PSTNs to all-digital operation. When this changeover is complete, a high bit rate, all-digital interface will be available at each subscriber outlet. Also, since the new networks employ all-digital transmission and switching, a very fast connection (call) setup time is provided for local, national, and international calls. The new subscriber interface will have sufficient capacity to handle not only voice communications but also data communications directly, the two services operating concurrently if desired. These new networks are referred to as **integrated services digital networks (ISDNs)**.

Because of the far-reaching consequences of such networks ITU-T has already defined a set of standards for interfacing equipment; these standards are referred to as the I-series recommendations. In the remainder of this chapter we give an overview of the different types of user interface proposed for ISDNs and of some of the I-series recommendations.

8.4.1   User interfaces

A limited set of standard, multipurpose user (subscriber) interfaces proposed for ISDNs is summarized in Figure 8.26. As we can see, the basic service offered is for voice communications, as is the case for existing telephone networks. Note, however, that since the subscriber outlet is digital, voice traffic has to be digitized in the subscriber (telephone) handset prior to transmission and converted back to analog form on reception. As a bit rate of 64 kbps is required to transmit digitized voice, the user interface offers multiples of this basic rate.

In the second example in Figure 8.26(a), the same outlet (but with a different user terminal, of course) provides a circuit switched connection for data communications. The basic data rate is 64 kbps, and, because digital transmission and switching are used, a very fast call setup time is available. Also, as in the third example, the user may use the outlet as an integrated voice and data facility, both operating concurrently.

The fourth example shows that, with an appropriate terminal, the basic outlet may also provide access to a packet switching service. This, as we shall see, may be at 64 kbps or, optionally, at a lower bit rate of 16 kbps.

These four types of user service use the ISDN simply to provide a switched transmission path and are referred to as **bearer services**. However, it is intended that PTT authorities will provide additional, more sophisticated equipment to allow the ISDN to be used as fast **Teletex, facsimile,** or **Videotex** networks. These are referred to as **teleservices** and are illustrated in Figure 8.26(b). A Teletex network provides a general-purpose facility for exchanging messages (comprising

Figure 8.26
ISDN user services:
(a) bearer services;
(b) teleservices.

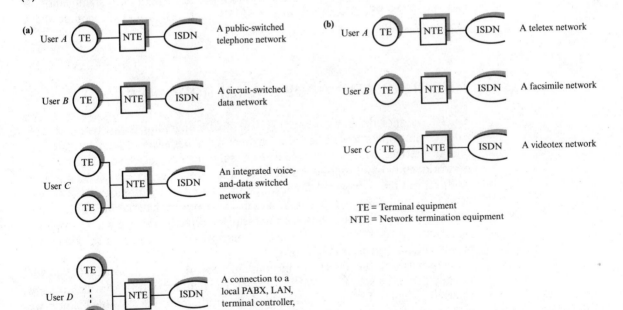

alphanumeric and graphical characters) between similar terminals. A facsimile network is a general-purpose facility for transmitting scanned images of documents electronically between similar terminals. And a Videotex network is a general-purpose facility for gaining access to a remote database storing various types of information such as stocks and share prices.

8.4.2 Network access points

To allow for this wide range of uses, the **network termination equipment (NTE)** provided by the PTT authorities has a number of associated alternative access points. These are shown in Figure 8.27.

By the time ISDN networks became fully operational, many users had invested heavily in equipment that conformed to existing standards, such as the V- and X-series. To cater for this, the NTE associated with ISDNs support not only the newer generation of equipment but also existing equipment and interfaces, by providing a range of **terminal adapters** to perform the necessary mapping function.

The alternative access points (R, S, and T) in Figure 8.27 clearly imply a varying level of intelligence in the NTE. In relation to the ISO reference model, these access points require a varying number of protocol layers. Figure 8.28 summarizes the layers required to support each service. As we can see, these range from layer 1, which supports a basic transmission service, layers 1–3, which

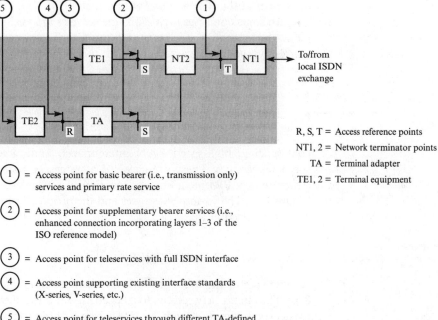

<figcaption>

1 = Access point for basic bearer (i.e., transmission only) services and primary rate service

2 = Access point for supplementary bearer services (i.e., enhanced connection incorporating layers 1–3 of the ISO reference model)

3 = Access point for teleservices with full ISDN interface

4 = Access point supporting existing interface standards (X-series, V-series, etc.)

5 = Access point for teleservices through different TA-defined interfaces

R, S, T = Access reference points
NT1, 2 = Network terminator points
TA = Terminal adapter
TE1, 2 = Terminal equipment

</figcaption>

Figure 8.27
ISDN customer access points.

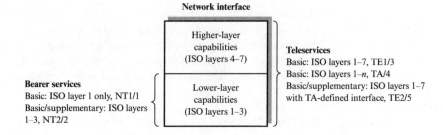

Figure 8.28
Customer access
summary.

support such services as a switched voice and/or data terminal, to layers 1–7,
which support various teleservices.

8.4.3   Channel types

The **basic rate interface (BRI)** to an ISDN provides two 64 kbps channels, known
as **B channels**, and an additional 16 kbps channel, known as the **D channel**. The
basic use of the D channel is for signaling; the NTE uses it to inform the local
ISDN exchange of the address of the destination NTE. The separate channel for
signaling results in a significantly faster call setup time. In addition, because new
calls are set up relatively infrequently, it is proposed in the I-series standards that
the D channel should also be available to the subscriber when signaling is not in
progress. For example, it is proposed that the D channel should be used for packet
switching albeit with a reduced packet size. The total available bit rate to the
subscriber at the BRI is thus 144 kbps $(2B + D)$.

In some countries higher bit rate services are available on request. These are
all available through a **primary rate interface (PRI)** and are known as **H channels**.
Currently, the bit rate associated with these channels includes the following:

- H0   384 kbps
- H11   1536 kbps
- H12   1920 kbps

Uses of these channels include video telephone (view phone), video
conferencing, high-speed LAN interconnect, and switched channels for high-
speed teleservices. These are accessed at reference point 1, the T interface. The
structure of a PRI including the location of the signaling channel was shown in
Figure 2.25. The various interfaces and the proposed range of alternative bit rates
are summarized in Figure 8.29.

8.4.4   User–Network interface

A schematic of the user–network physical (layer 1) interface is shown in Figure
8.30. The circuit between the local exchange and the customer premises is a single
twisted-pair wire. For the basic rate access service this must support duplex (2-way
simultaneous) transmission for the $2B + D$ channels. As Chapter 2 described, the

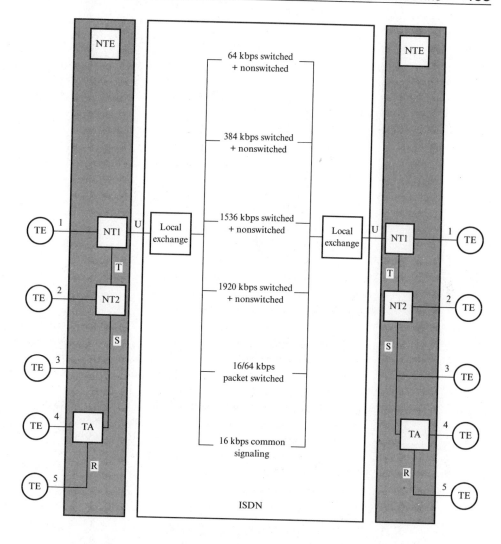

Figure 8.29
User–network
interface summary.

transmission line code used on this circuit is 2B1Q; a hybrid transformer is used for duplex transmission. In principle, the transformer should allow only the received signal to be passed to the receiver section but, owing to imperfections, a portion of the (much stronger) transmitted signal also feeds back to the receiver section. To overcome this, an **adaptive hybrid** or **echo canceler** is used to cancel the (known) transmitted signal from the composite received signal. For the echo canceler to operate correctly, there must be no correlation between the transmitted and received signals. To avoid correlation, two **scrambler circuits** are used, one for transmit and one for receive, to randomize the bit sequence in a pseudorandom (and hence repeatable) way.

In some countries the equipment that performs the network termination function (NT1) technically belongs to the customer. However, in others it belongs to the network provider and the user interface thus starts at the customer side of

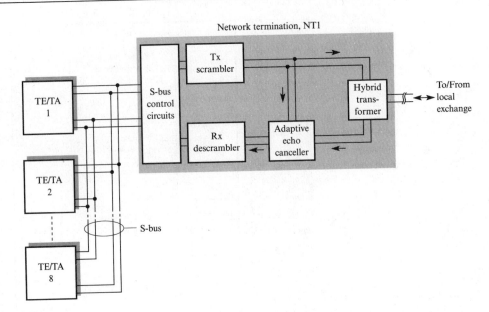

Figure 8.30
User–network
physical interface
schematic.

the NT equipment. This is a 4-wire (2-pair) interface with one pair for transmit and the other for receive. Each pair of wires carries the 2B + D bit stream using a standard frame structure to allow the bit periods associated with each B and D channel to be identified.

Since the customer side of the NT is the S interface, the 4-wire circuit is known as the S bus. It allows up to eight independent terminal equipments or terminal adapters to be connected to it. A contention control scheme is incorporated to allow the various items of equipment to time-share the use of the two B and one D channel in a fair way. Consequently, the NT equipment is a relatively sophisticated box owing to its rich functionality.

8.4.5   User interface protocols

A key feature of the ISDN is the logical separation of the signaling channel from the normal voice and/or data channels. The signaling channel, because it is used for call setup, is said to be part of the control or **C plane**, while the user channels are said to belong to the user or **U plane**. As we have indicated, the ISDN supports both circuit switched and packet switched services. Two new frame-level services, one known as **frame relay** and the other as **frame switching**, are also supported. The different service types are shown in Figure 8.31.

Irrespective of the type of service, a circuit/virtual path must first be set up through the network before any user data is transferred. With a switched connection this is done at the time of the call, although **semipermanent connections** (similar to leased circuits) can also be provided. To set up a circuit or virtual path, signaling messages are exchanged over the D channel between a TE/TA and its local exchange using a 3-layer protocol stack. Within the network itself, a

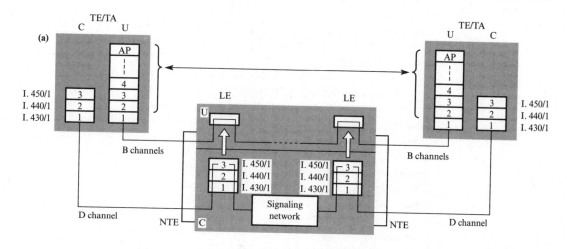

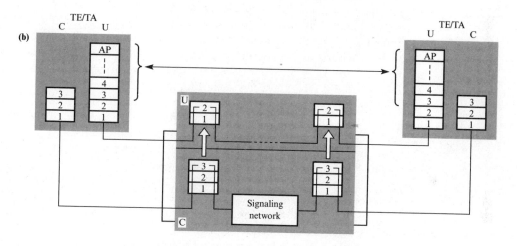

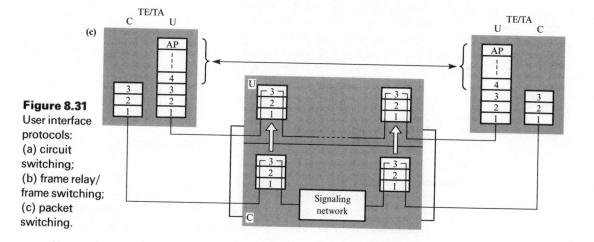

Figure 8.31
User interface
protocols:
(a) circuit
switching;
(b) frame relay/
frame switching;
(c) packet
switching.

separate **signaling network** which involves a full 7-layer protocol stack is used to set up the necessary circuits or virtual paths through the network. This is known as **common channel signaling system number 7 (CCSS-7)**. The separate signaling network allows the network operator to provide a wide range of advanced services more readily since a path is simply set up to the required service on demand.

For a circuit switched service, a circuit is set up in the same way as with the PSTN, as shown in Figure 8.31(a). The setup circuit provides a transparent 64 kbps transmission path.

For the two frame-based services, a VC – known as a **virtual path** – is set up in an analogous way to a VC through a PSPDN. Additional routing information is retained at each intermediate exchange that allows the subsequent frames of user data to be routed (relayed) across the setup virtual path, as shown in Figure 8.31(b). With frame relay, a simple best-try service is supported. With frame switching, on the other hand, error and flow control are performed on each frame. In comparison with packet switching, the routing of frames is much simpler and can be carried out at much higher bit rates. A user may have a number of virtual paths to different destinations set up at the same time and the network will route frames to their intended destination using addressing information contained within each frame. Semipermanent virtual paths can also be requested.

The packet switched service uses a full 3-layer user stack similar to that used in an X.25 PSPDN, as we can see in Figure 8.31(c). In practice, since PSPDNs are now widely available, an alternative arrangement to that shown has also been proposed in the I-series standards which provides interworking between an ISDN and a PSPDN. This is defined in ITU-T recommendations **X.31** and **I.462**. With this scheme, a basic circuit switched connection is set up through the ISDN – as in Figure 8.31(a) – to a gateway associated with the PSPDN. This gateway operates in a similar way to an STE; the ISDN simply provides a transparent 64 kbps switched or semipermanent circuit between the packet-mode terminal equipment and the PSPDN gateway. The user protocol stack uses the X.25 PLP at layer 3 and the link layer protocol defined in I.420.

The I-series standards proposed that the D channel is used in a similar way. In this case, however, X.25 packets will be routed across the ISDN to the gateway using the signaling network rather than over a B channel circuit. Although this will avoid setting up a circuit, the use of the D channel limits the packet size to 260 octets compared with 1024 octets for the other service. The 16 kbps rate of the D channel is also lower.

8.4.6 Signaling protocols

The three protocols associated with the signaling (D) channel are identified in Figure 8.31(a). The two layer 1 protocols I.430/1 collectively define the physical interface from the user TE to the local exchange. Recall that the protocols include, in addition to the definition of the proposed interface arrangement, the mechanisms to be used for bit, octet, and frame synchronization, as well as power feeding, which enables (telephone) calls to be made in the event of a local power failure.

The conversion from 4-wire to 2-wire and different transmission formats and the presence of other TEs on the bus are thus transparent to the layer 2 (and 3) protocol which sees just a duplex transmission path for 2B + D channels.

The layer 2 protocol is defined in I.440/1 which is the same as Q.920/1. Known as LAPD, this procedure is used to transfer the level 3 call setup messages. Chapter 5 described the basic operation of LAPD, hence we shall consider only its relationship with respect to the signaling procedure.

Recall from the earlier discussion of the physical interface that since up to eight different items of equipment may be sharing the user and signaling channels, we must incorporate a way of identifying specific items of equipment. This is achieved using the address field in the header of each layer 2 (LAPD) frame. The address contains two subaddresses (identifiers): the **service access point identifier (SAPI)** and a **terminal endpoint identifier (TEI)**. The SAPI allows different terminals to belong to a different **service class** (voice or data, for example), while the TEI identifies a specific terminal associated with that class. A **broadcast address** also allows the exchange to send a frame to multiple terminals, so that for example, an incoming voice (telephone) call can be received by all voice TEs.

Note, however, that this address has only local significance on the user access line and plays no part in the routing of signaling messages within the network signaling system. As Figure 8.9 showed, the final part of the address has only local significance and this is passed transparently by the network signaling system. Hence, with ISDN addresses, a typical scheme is to use part of this address to identify the specific TE/TA required. If the user data is also being carried on the D channel (packet switching), then the remainder can be used for interlayer address selectors (SAPs). Alternatively, if the user data is to be carried on a B channel then the address selectors will not be required. In the latter case, the SAPs used will be a function of the application protocol that is associated with the U plane.

The layer 3 protocol is defined in I.450/1, which is the same as Q.931. This protocol is concerned with the sequence of messages (packets) that are exchanged over the D channel to set up a call. An abbreviated list of the message types used is as follows:

- Call establishment: ALERTing
                         CONNECT
                         CONnect ACKnowledge
                         SETUP
                         Others

- Information transfer: USER INFOrmation
                         Others

- Call clearing: DISConnect
                         RELEASE
                         RELease COMPlete
                         Others

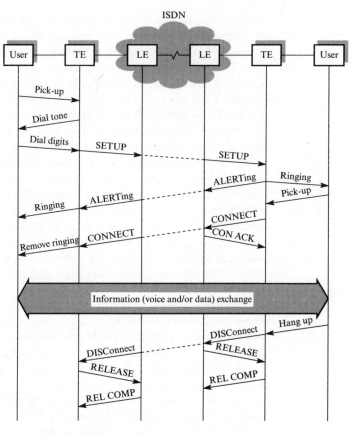

Figure 8.32
Example message
sequence – circuit
switched call.

TE = Terminal equipment   LE = Local exchange

Some of these messages have local significance (TE/NT) while others have end-to-end significance (TE/TE). However, all the messages are transferred within layer 1 I-frames. An example illustrating the use of these messages is shown in Figure 8.32; it assumes a circuit switched call which may be used for voice and/or data over the B channel(s).

8.4.7   Frame relay service

As Section 8.4.5 indicated, there are two new frame-mode services associated with the ISDN: frame relay and frame switching. The same signaling procedures are used for both services. The major difference is that the network performs error and flow control procedures only with frame switching. The procedures associated with the frame services are defined in ITU-T recommendation I.122/Q.922. In practice, frame relay is by far the dominant service, owing to its minimal overheads, therefore we shall discuss it in more detail.

Recall that with X.25, the multiplexing of multiple VCs (calls) is handled by the packet layer, while the link (frame) layer is concerned only with error control of the resulting frames over the local DTE–DCE link. Therefore, the combined link/PLP is relatively complex, and the corresponding packet throughput of each network exchange is limited by the high processing overheads per packet.

In contrast, with frame relay, multiplexing and routing are performed at the link (frame) layer. Moreover, the routing of frames is very straightforward so the combined link bit rates can be much higher than with packet switching. Therefore, although it is defined for use with ISDNs, frame relay is also finding widespread use in private networks.

Frame relay allows multiple calls to different destinations to be in progress concurrently. Hence, when each call (virtual path) is first set up – using the D channel in response to an L_CONNECT.request service primitive – it is allocated a unique connection identifier known as the **data link connection identifier (DLCI)**. All subsequent data transfer requests relating to this call include the allocated DLCI as a parameter. The DLCI is embedded into the header of the resulting frames and is used to route (relay) the frames to their intended destination. In the case of semipermanent virtual paths, the DLCIs are allocated at registration time.

The format of each frame transmitted on the user B channel is shown in Figure 8.33(a). It comprises a 2-byte (extended) address header with no control field owing to the lack of any error control. In addition to the DLCI, the header contains the **forward explicit congestion notification (FECN) bit**, the **backward explicit congestion notification (BECN) bit** and the **discard eligibility (DE) bit**. These are used for controlling congestion within the network.

The DLCI, like the VCI in packet switched networks, has only local significance on a specific network link and therefore changes as a frame traverses the links associated with a virtual path. When the virtual path is being set up, on receipt of a call request packet – on the D channel – each exchange along the path (route) determines the outgoing link to be used for the required (ISDN) destination address, obtains a free DLCI for the link, and then makes an entry in that links routing table of the incoming link/DLCI and the corresponding outgoing link/DLCI, as shown in Figure 8.33(b). Again, for semipermanent virtual paths, entries are made at subscription time.

When a frame is received during the subsequent data transfer – frame relay – phase, the frame handler within each exchange simply reads the DLCI from within the frame and combines this with the incoming link number to determine the corresponding outgoing link and DLCI. The new DLCI is written into the frame header and the frame is queued for forwarding on the appropriate link. The order of relayed frames is thus preserved and their routing is very fast.

Since multiple calls can be in progress concurrently over each link within the network and frames relating to each call are generated at random intervals, during periods of heavy traffic an outgoing link may become temporarily overloaded resulting in its queue starting to build up. This is known as **congestion**: the

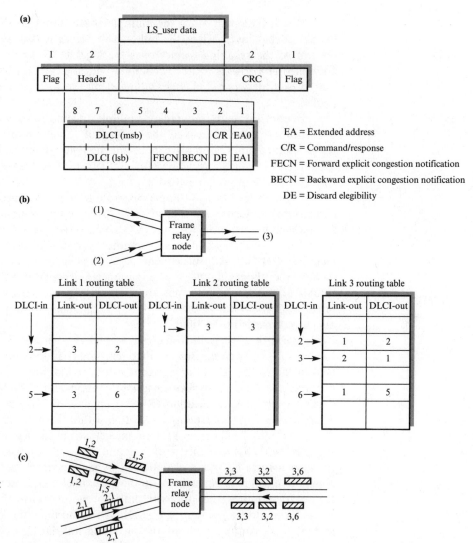

Figure 8.33
Frame relay principles:
(a) frame format;
(b) frame routing;
(c) frame relay
schematic.

additional congestion control bits in each frame can be used to alleviate this
condition.

Whenever the frame handler relays a frame to a link output queue, it checks
the size of the queue. If this exceeds a defined limit, the frame handler signals this
condition to the two end users involved in the call. This is done in the forward
direction by setting the CF bit in the frame header. In the backward direction, it is
done by setting the CB bit in the header of all frames which are received on this
link. If the condition persists, the frame handler also returns a special frame
known as a **consolidated link layer management (CLLM)** frame to all user devices
that have routes (paths) involving the affected link. Such frames are simply relayed
by each intermediate exchange in the normal way.

When the frame handler in an end-user device receives an indication of network congestion, it temporarily reduces its frame forwarding rate until there are no further indications of congestion. If the overload increases, however, the exchange must start to discard frames. In an attempt to achieve fairness, the DE bit in the frame header is used since this is set by the frame handler in each user system whenever a user exceeds its negotiated throughput rate.

To minimize the possibility of wrongly delivered frames, the CRC in each frame trailer is used to detect bit errors in the frame header (and information) fields. Then, if an error is detected, the frame is discarded. With the frame relay service, error recovery is left to the higher protocol layers in the end-user devices.

Although the frame relay service was defined in relation to the ISDN, many public operators have set up networks to offer just the frame relay service. A schematic diagram of a typical public frame relay network is shown in Figure 8.34(a). Normally, the frame relay service is used by large corporate customers to interconnect the LANs at the different sites to create an enterprisewide data network. The customer first informs the service provider of the sites that need to be interconnected. The provider then creates a set of permanent virtual connections that interconnect all the sites by setting up appropriate routing table entries in each frame relay switching node. The provider then informs the network manager at each site of the DLCI value that should be put into the header of a frame to reach each of the other sites.

All frames are multiplexed together onto the link connecting the **customer interface equipment (CIE)** to its nearest switching node. Logically, this appears to the customer equipment like a set of point-to-point connections between itself and all the other sites, each identified by the corresponding DLCI. The CIE can be

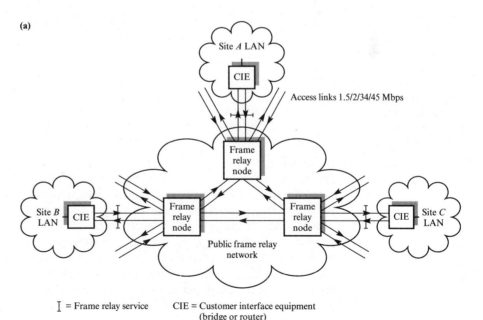

(a)

Figure 8.34
Public frame relay networks: (a) network schematic.

I = Frame relay service   CIE = Customer interface equipment
                                          (bridge or router)

(b)

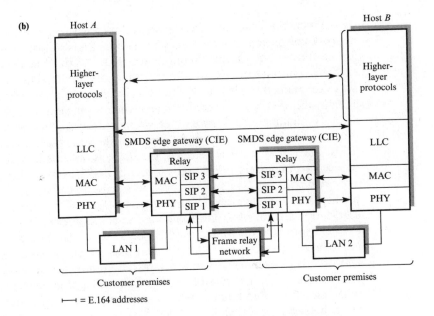

(c)

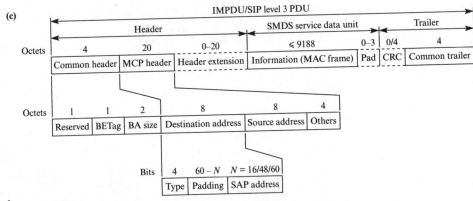

Figure 8.34 (cont.)
(b) SMDS protocol architecture; (c) initial MAC PDU format.

IMPDU = Initial MAC PDU   MCP = MAC convergence protocol
SIP = SMDS interface protocol   SAP = Service access point
BETag = Begin–end tag   BA = Buffer allocation

either a bridge or a router. Assuming it is a bridge, although it has just two physical ports, logically it operates as a multiport bridge with each DLCI being equivalent to a different port. The DLCI value assigned to reach each of the other sites is loaded into the bridge by network management. Whenever the bridge receives a frame that needs to be forwarded to a different site (port), the bridge encapsulates the frame in a frame-relay frame with the corresponding DLCI in its header. The switching nodes in the frame relay network route this to its intended destination over the related permanent virtual connection.

In a public network the connectionless data service offered to users is known as the **switched multimegabit data service (SMDS)** – also known as the

connectionless broadband data service (CBDS) in Europe – and the CIE as an **SMDS edge gateway**. Assuming remote bridges are being used for the gateways, a typical internetworking protocol architecture is shown in Figure 8.34(b).

The protocol layers associated with the SMDS are known as the **SMDS interface protocols (SIP)** levels 1, 2, and 3. Since the different LAN types use different header formats and maximum frame sizes, the size of an SMDS service data unit can be up to 9188 octets to accommodate the largest LAN frame. Also, because of the different address formats used, prior to the transmission of a MAC frame, the level 3 SIP first encapsulates the frame between a standard header and trailer. To simplify the buffering operation at the destination, if necessary, it adds additional padding octets at the tail of the submitted frame so that its length is a multiple of 4 octets. The resulting message unit – referred to as a packet – is known as an **initial MAC protocol data unit (IMPDU)** and its format is shown in Figure 8.34(c).

As we can see, the header comprises two or possibly three fields. The common header contains an 8-bit sequence number – known as the begin–end tag and used to enable the level 3 SIP to detect missing frames – and a specification of the amount of buffer memory required to store the complete IMPDU. The MAC convergence protocol (MCP) header contains a number of subfields relating to the protocol. These include the addresses of the source and destination gateways which, in a public network, are 60-bit E.164 addresses as defined for use with the ISDN. However, to cater for other address types, these are both 64-bit address fields with the four most significant bits used to identify the address types in the remaining 60 bits – for example, 16/48-bit MAC addresses. Other subfields include the number of PAD octets present and an indication of whether a CRC is present or not. The header extension has been included to allow additional subfields to be added in the future. As just indicated, the trailer may include an optional 32-bit CRC which, if present, is used for error detection on the complete IMPDU. The common trailer contains the same information as the common header. The resulting IMPDU is encapsulated into a frame-relay frame by the SIP level 2 (frame relay) protocol layer. The level 1 SIP performs a physical layer convergence function and is responsible for the transmission of the resulting frame over the access link.

8.4.8   Inverse multiplexing

The various higher bit rate services we identified in Section 8.4.3 – H0/H11/H12 (384/1536/1920 kbps) – are all provided by means of a PRI circuit. Like the BRI, the PRI uses a separate (out-of-band) signaling channel to set up the call and, as part of the call setup phase, the required bandwidth – 384/1536/1920 – is provided. In addition, a new service known as **ISDN multirate** is available from some carriers that allows the user to request the bandwidth of a call to be any multiple of 64 kbps. The service is also known, therefore, as **switched** $N \times$ **64 kbps** where N can be up to either 24 or 30 depending on the carrier.

In addition, the user can derive a similar set of services from a PRI using equipment – known as an **inverse multiplexer** – located at the customer premises.

Multiplexing was first introduced in Section 2.5.2 as a means of transmitting multiple low bit rate – 64 kbps – digitized voice signals over a single high bit rate circuit. In contrast, inverse multiplexing is used to derive a single high bit rate channel using multiple lower bit rate circuits. For example, an inverse multiplexer can be used to derive a single 384 kbps channel from six independent 64 kbps circuits. A schematic diagram showing the principle of operation of an inverse multiplexer is given in Figure 8.35(a).

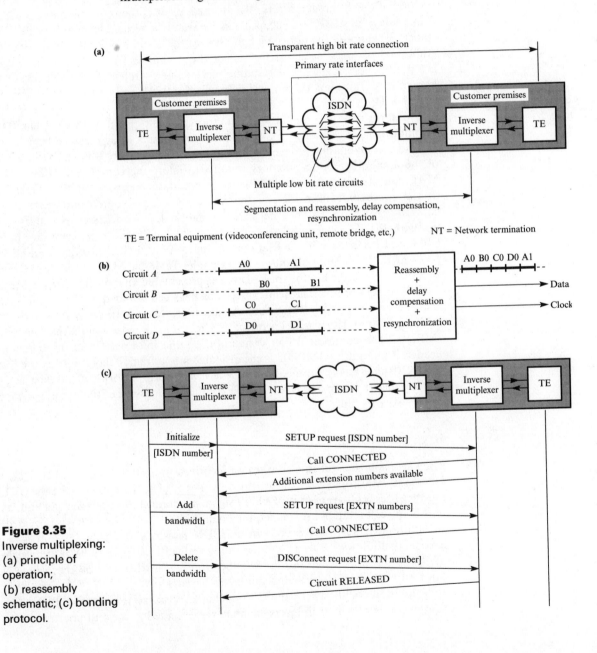

Figure 8.35
Inverse multiplexing:
(a) principle of
operation;
(b) reassembly
schematic; (c) bonding
protocol.

At the transmitting side, the inverse multiplexer first sets up the appropriate number of 64 kbps circuits to the required destination. It then proceeds to segment the high bit rate digital stream output by the user equipment – for example a video conferencing unit – ready for transmission over the multiple low bit rate circuits. At the receiving side, once the multiple circuits have been set up, the inverse multiplexer accepts the bit streams received from these circuits and reassembles them back into a single high bit rate channel for onward transmission to the receiving terminal equipment.

Therefore, the function of the inverse multiplexers, in addition to call setup, is to make the segmentation and reassembly operations transparent to the user equipment. In practice, because each channel is set up independently, they all may traverse the ISDN trunk network across different routes/paths. This results in small time differences in the signals received from each circuit. To compensate for this, the inverse multiplexer at the receiving side must perform delay compensation and resynchronization of the reassembled bit stream. The general scheme is shown in Figure 8.35(b).

To obtain a similar service to that provided by switched $N \times 64$, inverse multiplexers are available for the user terminal equipment to set up and clear 64 kbps on demand. The technique is known as **bonding** and the general scheme is shown in Figure 8.35(c).

In response to a user request, the inverse multiplexer at the calling side requests a single 64 kbps circuit to be set up to the remote site. Once this is in place, the inverse multiplexer at the called side sends back a list of available local (extension) numbers. The calling multiplexer sets up the required number of additional circuits – one at a time – and the two user equipments can then exchange data. During the call, a user terminal equipment can request that the aggregated bandwidth available is either increased or decreased by setting up or clearing circuits dynamically. For example, if the terminal equipments are remote bridges – being used for LAN interconnection – then the aggregate bandwidth can be regulated to match the data traffic being exchanged at any point in time. An international standard has now been defined by the ITU-T, **recommendation H.221**, which is concerned with the operation of this type of equipment.

8.5 Private networks

As we indicated in the introduction to this chapter, as an alternative to using PTT or public-carrier networks many large corporations install (and manage) their own enterprisewide private integrated voice and data networks.

Telephone (voice) calls made through a PSTN or public ISDN are charged on a time and distance basis. If the networks are used for the transmission of data – using a modem with the PSTN – calls are charged on the same basis. Similarly, calls made using a public data network are normally charged either on the same basis or on the basis of the quantity of data transferred.

In most establishments (companies, universities, hospitals, etc.) the majority of communications (voice and data) are local to the establishment with only a small percentage of the calls outside. To avoid public network charges, all establishments install their own private automatic branch exchange (PABX) for telephony and a (private) local area network (LAN) for data communication.

For an enterprise operating on a single site (establishment), all external calls must be made using a PTT or public-carrier network. However, for an enterprise operating at multiple sites, an alternative is to extend the private facilities associated with each site to embrace all sites, since again there is often a significant proportion of intersite calls. In practice, the choice is based on a number of factors, the major one being the level of intersite traffic. This is because the creation of an enterprisewide private network normally involves the leasing of transmission circuits from the PTTs or public carriers. Leases are charged for on a daily rather than on a per call basis.

For many small to medium-sized enterprises the number of intersite calls does not justify linking the sites with leased lines. Instead external calls are made using public-carrier networks, certainly for voice. For data, if an (analog) PSTN is to be used, an additional factor is the relatively long call setup time with a switched call. Also, the level of security with public facilities is often cited as a factor for the choice of private networks or public networks.

For many large enterprises, however, the level of intersite traffic – both voice and data – can be considerable. Consequently, many install and manage their own private integrated voice and data networks. An added benefit is that more sophisticated services can be more readily offered and, since the network is private – apart from the transmission lines, of course – more secure. Such networks are known simply as **private networks** or **enterprisewide networks**. If they span multiple countries, they are known as **global networks**.

8.5.1   Architecture

A schematic of a typical private network configuration is shown in Figure 8.36(a). Generally a private network consists of a linked set of **intelligent multiplexers (IMUX)** – one per site – interconnected by leased lines which form an **enterprisewide backbone** transmission network. Typically, the network uses high-speed digital leased lines of the type described in Section 2.5.2. These operate at multiples of 64 kbps; 1.544 Mbps (DS1/T1) and 2.048 Mbps (E1) are common.

Each IMUX has a range of voice and data interfaces to meet the requirements at that site. In the case of voice, these can involve direct links to telephone handsets or, more usually, a high bit rate link to a PABX. As we indicated in Chapter 3, normally 64 kbps is used for each voice circuit but some multiplexer manufacturers incorporate sophisticated compression algorithms to provide good-quality voice communication using 32, 16, or even 8 kbps. This means that two, four, or eight voice circuits can be multiplexed onto a single 64 kbps time slot giving a substantial saving in the number of circuits required between sites. This technique is known as **subrate multiplexing**.

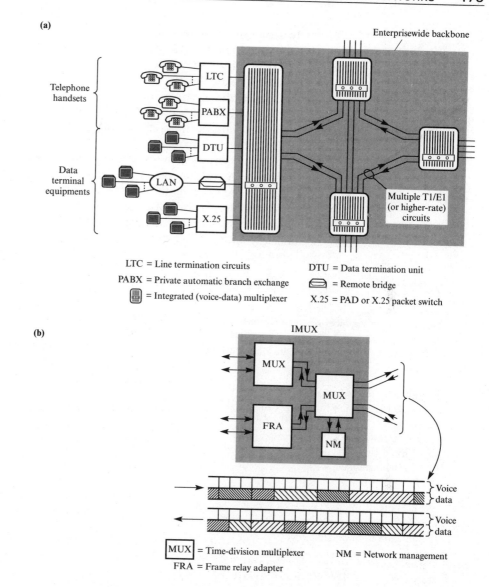

Figure 8.36
Private WAN:
(a) network
schematic; (b) node
schematic.

As Section 3.7.1 described, a similar technique is used for connecting asynchronous or synchronous terminals, such as PCs. In this case a 64 kbps channel can be used to support multiple terminals. Examples include 20×2.4 kbps and 5×9.6 kbps. The technique is known as **rate adaption**. Such links are often used to connect a distributed community of data terminals to a central computer holding, for example, an enterprisewide electronic mail server or database.

The increasing use of LANs in many establishments means that it is now common practice to provide a means of linking them. As Chapter 7 described, this is normally done using **remote bridges**. Private X.25 packet switching exchanges are also sometimes incorporated. Alternatively, as we can see in Figure 8.36(c), private **frame relay adapters (FRAs)** are now being incorporated to achieve added levels of (statistical) multiplexing. Since in private networks circuits are normally set up throughout the network on a semipermanent basis using network management, each FRA needs only to 'packetize' data. This is done only when data is to be transmitted, thus eliminating the need to allocate permanent channels.

Although many private networks are run and managed by the enterprises to which they belong, a number of PTTs and public-carrier operators are now cooperating to provide a facility that enables an equivalent private network to be set up within the public network. Known as **virtual private networks (VPNs)**, they offer similar services to a private network but are managed and operated by the PTT or public carrier.

Exercises

8.1   Describe the differences between a circuit switched data network and a packet switched data network. Clearly identify the effects on the users of these networks.

8.2   Explain what is understood by the following terms used in relation to packet switched data networks:
(a) Datagram
(b) Virtual call (circuit)
(c) Logical channel

8.3   Use sketches to illustrate the applicability and components of the X.25 network access protocol and write explanatory notes describing the function of each component.

8.4   Define the set of user service primitives associated with the packet (network) layer of the X.25 protocol. Explain the use of the following additional facilities:
(a) More-data
(b) Qualifier
(c) Delivery confirmation

8.5   Tabulate the main PDUs (packet types) used by the packet layer of protocol X.25 to perform the following operations:
(a) Establish a virtual call (circuit)
(b) Exchange a message unit over this circuit
(c) Clear the call

Sketch a time sequence diagram to illustrate the sequence in which the PDUs are exchanged to implement these operations.

8.6   Explain the structure and meaning of the various fields that make up an X.121 address as used at the interface to an X.25 PSPDN.

8.7   Explain the meaning of the term 'fast select' in relation to the X.25 packet layer protocol.
With the aid of a time sequence diagram, describe how a datagram service is obtained with the fast select facility.

8.8   (a) Describe the flow control method used by the packet layer protocol of X.25 and list the packet layer PDUs (packet types) that are used to implement it.
(b) Sketch diagrams to illustrate how the flow of data packets relating to a single logical channel is controlled by:
(i)   The window mechanism
(ii) The use of additional supervisory packets
Include in the diagrams the state of the send and receive variables (V(S) and V(R)) and the acknowledgment variable (V(A)) at both sides of the logical channel as each data packet is transmitted.

8.9   Discriminate between the reset and restart error recovery procedures used in the packet layer of X.25 and explain their operation.

8.10   (a) Describe the function of a PAD as used in X.25-based networks and identify on a diagram the various protocols that have been defined for use with it.

(b) Outline the essential features of the following protocols used with PADs:
  (i)   X.3
  (ii) X.28
  (iii) X.29

8.11   Describe how a packet switching exchange in an X.25 network routes packets. Include in your description the structure and use of the network and link routing tables.

8.12   Explain the role of a signaling terminal exchange – half gateway – for the interconnection of X.25 networks.

8.13   Use a sketch of an X.25-based internetwork to identify the applicability of the X.75 protocol.

Explain the use of the following fields in an X.75 PPDU:
  (a) Network utilities
  (b) D bit

8.14   (a) Outline the function of the three lowest network-dependent protocol layers used with a circuit switched data network.

(b) Sketch a diagram showing the various interchange circuits associated with X.21 and outline their functions.

(c) With the aid of a time sequence diagram, describe the operation of the X.21 interface protocol. Clearly show the transitions on each interchange circuit at both the calling DTE–DCE interface and the called DTE–DCE interface. Identify on this diagram the call setup, data transfer, and call clearing phases.

8.15   (a) Explain the meaning of the term 'ISDN'.

(b) Give examples of the following user services related to an ISDN:
  (i)   Bearer services
  (ii) Teleservices

8.16   Produce a sketch and associated descriptions of an ISDN NTE and indicate on the sketch the following customer access points:
  (a) Basic bearer services
  (b) Supplementary bearer services
  (c) Teleservices
  (d) Existing X-series services

8.17   Produce a sketch showing the outline structure of the NTE associated with the customer interface to an ISDN and explain the main features associated with it.

8.18   Explain the meaning of the terms 'control (C) plane' and 'user (U) plane' in relation to the customer access to an ISDN network.

Use sketches to identify the role of the C and U planes for the following cell types:
  (a) Circuit switched
  (b) Frame relay
  (c) Packet switched

8.19   Use the setting up of an ISDN circuit switched call to explain the function of the various signaling protocols that operate over the D channel.

8.20   Explain the principle of operation of frame relay and how it differs from X.25 packet switching. Include in your description how frames are routed.

Chapter summary

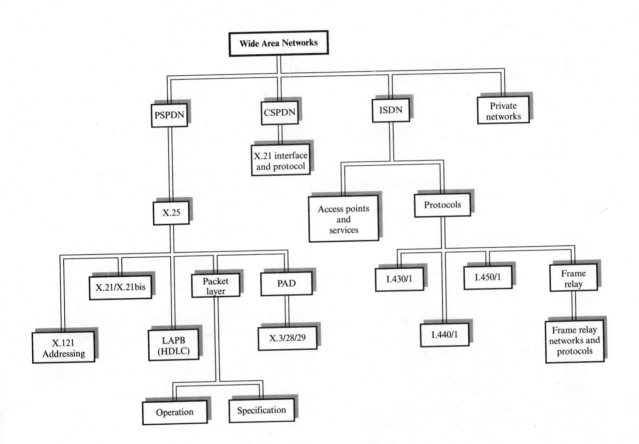

9 INTERNETWORKING

Chapter objectives

When you have completed this chapter you should be able to:

Introduction

In the earlier chapters on LANs and WANs we assumed that stations/DTEs – normally referred to as **end systems (ESs)** or **hosts** – were all attached to the one network type, that is, all the systems were attached either to a single LAN (or bridged LAN) or to a single WAN. We made this assumption to defer discussion of the additional problems that must be considered when two systems communicate through networks consisting of two or more different network types.

In addition to open system networking environments comprising just a single type of network (LAN or WAN), there are networking environments that comprise an interconnected set of networks. An example is a distributed community of LANs, each located in a different university and interconnected through a countrywide WAN, that has been established to allow ESs attached to different LANs to exchange electronic mail or computer files. Another is an interconnected set of WANs that enables programs in a distributed community of bank computers to carry out funds transfers and other transactions. There are many such applications.

When two or more networks are involved in an application, we normally refer to the mode of working between systems as **internetworking**. We used the term **internetwork** (or **internet**) to refer to the composite network (for example, LAN/WAN/LAN) being used. Each constituent network (LAN or WAN) of the internetwork is a **subnetwork** (or **subnet**).

The device that interconnects the two networks is known in ISO terminology either as an **intermediate system (IS)** or an **interworking unit (IWU)**. Alternatively, since one of the major functions performed by an IS is that of routing, it is sometimes referred to as a **router** or, since it provides the link between two networks, as a **gateway**. A **protocol converter** is an IS that links two networks which operate with completely different protocol stacks, for example, an ISO stack and a proprietary stack relating to a specific manufacturer. As we shall see, a router performs its routing (and other) functions at the network layer. In an open system environment, the upper layer protocols – transport through application – are the same in all ESs. The difference between a router and a protocol converter is shown in Figure 9.1

In Figure 9.1(a) we assume that each network is of a different type and hence that the router has a different set of network protocols associated with each network port. Packets (NPDUs) received from one network are thus processed and passed up through the set of protocols relating to that network then, after the relaying function, down through the different set of protocols relating to the other network.

In contrast, as we can see in Figure 9.1(b), a protocol converter performs its relaying function above the application layer. This is because, in addition to difference in the network protocols for the two network types, the higher network-independent protocol layers are also different. Moreover, the network protocols used in different proprietary protocol stacks are different. This means that a protocol converter must also be used for the interconnection of two proprietary systems that are connected to the same network. This requirement highlights the advantages to be gained by moving toward an open systems approach: firstly, systems connected to the same network can communicate directly, and secondly, although a router may be required to perform the relaying functions if two different networks are involved, the higher-layer protocols are the same in all systems.

9.1   Internetwork architectures

Before we discuss the issues to be addressed with internetworking, let us first consider some typical internetwork architectures. Some example architectures are shown in Figure 9.2.

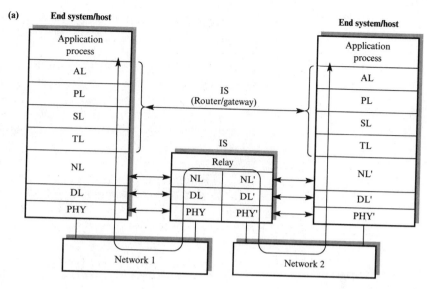

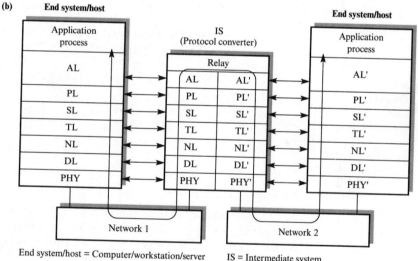

Figure 9.1
Example ISs:
(a) router/gateway;
(b) protocol converter.

End system/host = Computer/workstation/server   IS = Intermediate system

Part (a) shows two examples of single network types. The first is a site-wide LAN which, typically, as we discussed in Chapter 7, comprises a set of LANs, one per office or building, interconnected by a backbone network. The devices connecting each LAN to the backbone are either bridges, if all the LANs are the same type, or routers, if they are different.

The second example is a single WAN, such as an X.25 network. In this case, as we discussed in Chapter 8, each packet switching exchange (DCE/PSE) services its own set of DTEs, either directly or through a PAD, and the PSEs are interconnected by a mesh topology switching network.

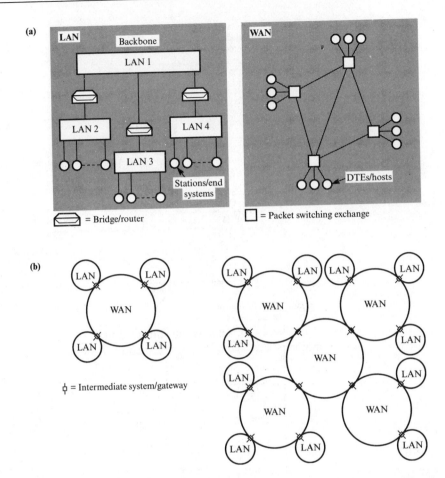

Figure 9.2
Internetwork
architectures:
(a) single LAN and
WAN;
(b) interconnected
LAN/WAN examples.

Irrespective of the type of network – LAN or WAN – from the point of view of internetworking, we consider each as a single network with its own internal routing protocols. Two internetworks are shown in Figure 9.2(b); each consists of a linked set of such networks. In this chapter we are concerned with the additional problems in creating networking environments of the types shown and, in particular, those comprising multiple network types. We are also concerned with the alternative solutions and associated network protocols.

9.2 Internetworking issues

From the point of view of an internet user, a transport protocol entity in practice, the internet should provide a defined network service at the user network service access point (NSAP) address which enables it to communicate with similar users in remote systems. The possible presence of multiple networks (and possibly network

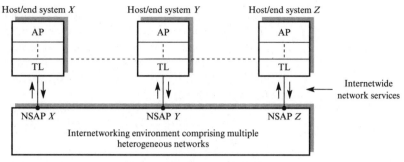

Figure 9.3
Internet network
service schematic.

NSAP X = Network service access point associated with end system X

⇄ = Network service primitives

AP = Application process

TL = Transport layer

types) should be transparent to the users who simply view the internet as providing a defined network service as though it were a single LAN or WAN. This is shown in Figure 9.3(a).

Before we discuss the solutions used to achieve this goal, let us first list the major points that we must consider:

● Network service

● Addressing

● Routing

● Quality of service

● Maximum packet size

● Flow and congestion control

● Error reporting

Network service

Recall that within a LAN, MAC sublayer addresses are used to identify ESs (stations/DTEs) and, with transparent bridges, to route frames between systems. Moreover, because of the short transit delays and low bit error rate of LANs, a simple (best-try) connectionless network protocol is normally used. This means that many LAN-based networks have a **connectionless network service (CLNS)** associated with them.

In contrast to LANs, link layer addresses in most WANs have only local significance; network layer addresses are used to identify ESs and to route packets across the network. Also, because of the relatively long transit delays and inferior bit error rate of WANs, a more sophisticated connection-oriented protocol is normally used. This means that most WANs have a **connection-oriented network service (CONS)** associated with them.

Since NS_users may be connected to different networks in an internet, one of the first decisions we must make is the type of network service (CL or CO) to be used at the internet interface in each ES. Moreover, in internetworks that consist of multiple subnet types, we must consider how the selected service is married or **harmonized** with the varying services associated with the different networks that make up the internet.

Addressing

Recall that the NSAP address used to identify an NS_user in an ES is a unique network-wide address which allows that user to be uniquely identified within the total network. Thus within a single LAN or WAN, only NSAP addresses must be unique within that limited, single-network addressing domain. Since within a single network the point of attachment (PA) address of an ES is unique within that network, the NSAP address of an NS_user is made up of the PA address of the system concatenated with the LSAP (link) and NSAP (network) interlayer address selectors within the system.

For an internet comprising multiple networks each of a different type – for example, LANs and X.25 WANs – the format (structure) and syntax of the PA addresses of ESs (and hence ISs) will differ from one network to another. As many such networks are already in existence and have addresses assigned to them, the **network point of attachment (NPA)** address of each system cannot be used as the basis of the NS_user NSAP address in the combined internet. Instead, when creating an **open system internetworking environment (OSIE)**, a completely different set of NSAP addresses must be used to identify each NS_user uniquely. These addresses are independent of the NPA addresses of the systems in which the NS_users (transport entities) reside. The relationship between NSAP and NPA addresses is shown in Figure 9.4.

We can conclude from the figure that two completely different addresses are associated with each ES connected to an internet: the NPA and the NSAP. The NPA address enables a system to send and receive NPDUs over its local network and hence only has meaning within that network. However, its NSAP address is an internetwide identifier which uniquely identifies NS_users within the total OSIE. Also, since an IS is attached to more than one network, it will have an associated NPA address for each network to which it is attached.

Routing

A service request primitive received at an NSAP in an ES has only a specification of the required destination NSAP. For a single network, the PA subaddress within the NSAP is sufficient to route the resulting NPDU to the required destination. For example, if the network is a LAN, the NPDU is broadcast within a frame with the required destination MAC address at its head. Alternatively, if the network is an X.25 packet switching network, then the NPDU is transferred to the X.25 PLP within its local DCE/PSE. From there

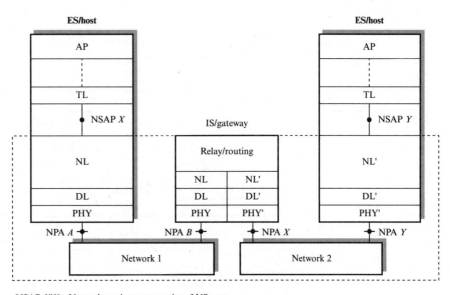

Figure 9.4
Relationship between
NSAP and NPA
addresses.

NSAP X/Y = Network services access point of NS_user
NPA = Network point of attachment address
(e.g., NPA A/B = LAN MAC addresses; NPA X/Y = X.25 WAN X.121 addresses)

the destination NSAP is used directly to route it through the network to the destination DCE (and hence DTE).

For internetworks comprising multiple networks interconnected by ISs, the destination NSAP address does not necessarily refer to an ES attached to the same network as the originating ES. Rather, it may refer to an ES attached to any of the other networks in the internet. Clearly, the routing of NPDUs is more difficult with internets.

To identify the routing requirements, consider the hypothetical internet shown in Figure 9.5. Firstly, remember that since the NPA address of a system and the NS_user NSAP address are different, we cannot use the destination NSAP address directly to route an NPDU to its destination. Also, the NPA addresses of an IS each have a similar format to that of any other ES on each of the interconnected networks. We can assume, therefore, that an ES can send an NPDU directly to an IS on the same network providing it knows the latter's NPA address. In addition, since an IS has an NPA address for each network to which it is attached, it can send an NPDU to another IS that is attached to that same network as long as it knows the NPA address of the other IS.

Assuming these basic capabilities, consider the sending of an NPDU from ES 1.1 on network 1 to ES 4.1 on network 4. A number of alternative routes are possible but perhaps the most obvious (assuming all networks have the same operational parameters) is:

$$ES\ 1.1 \rightarrow IS\ 1 \rightarrow IS\ 2 \rightarrow ES\ 4.1$$

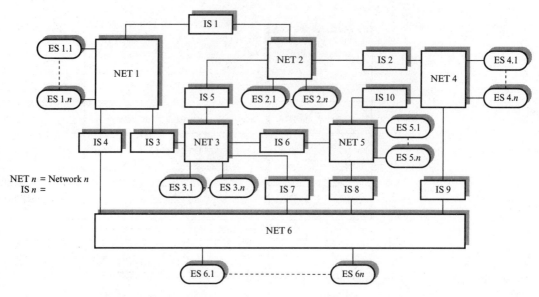

Figure 9.5
Hypothetical internet.

NET *n* = Network *n*
IS *n* = Intermediate system/gateway *n*
ES *n* = End system/host *n*

Others include:

$$ES\ 1.1 \rightarrow IS\ 3 \rightarrow IS\ 6 \rightarrow IS\ 10 \rightarrow ES\ 4.1$$

$$ES\ 1.1 \rightarrow IS\ 4 \rightarrow IS\ 9 \rightarrow ES\ 4.1$$

$$ES\ 1.1 \rightarrow IS\ 4 \rightarrow IS\ 7 \rightarrow IS\ 6 \rightarrow IS\ 8 \rightarrow IS\ 9 \rightarrow ES\ 4.1$$

Although we can deduce this simply by looking at the internet topology, we must answer a number of questions in practice. These include the following:

- How does an ES determine the NPA address(es) of the IS(s) attached to its network?

- How does an IS determine the NPA addresses of ESs attached to its networks?

- How does an ES select a specific IS when sending an NPDU?

- How does an IS determine the NPA addresses of other ISs that are attached to the same network?

- How does an IS select a specific IS to route an NPDU to a given destination ES?

Quality of service

A quality of service (QOS) parameter is associated with each service request primitive received at an NSAP. In practice this is a set of parameters that collectively specify the performance of the network service that the NS_user expects from the NS_provider in relation to this request. In addition, QOS is also used to specify the optional services to be used with this request.

QOS parameters include the following: the transit delay expected of the network (NS_provider) to deliver an NSDU to the specified destination; the level of protection required from unauthorized monitoring or modification of the NSDU; cost limits associated with this request; expected residual error probability; and the relative priority associated with the NSDU.

With a CONS, a peer-to-peer negotiation takes place between the two NS_users when a call is being established. The originating NS_user specifies the QOS parameters expected and the responder, if necessary, modifies selected parameters. In contrast, with a CLNS, since no virtual call is established, the NS_user initiating a request must know about the QOS expected from the NS_provider.

Thus when internetworking between different network types, since the QOS may vary from one network to another, the network entity in each ES must be able to build up a knowledge of the expected internetwide QOS when going to any specified destination NSAP.

Maximum packet size

The maximum packet size in different networks varies and is determined by the following factors:

- *Bit error rate*   The higher the bit error rate of the network links, the smaller the maximum packet size must be to ensure a significant number of packets are received error free with a high probability.

- *Transit delay*   The longer the maximum packet size, the longer other packets must wait at each link before being forwarded, with a consequential increase in the packet transit delay.

- *Buffer storage requirements*   The smaller the maximum packet size, the smaller the size of memory buffers required for storage.

- *Processing overheads*   The smaller the maximum packet size, the larger the number of packets required to send each message (NSDU), with a consequential increase in processing overheads per message.

Typical maximum packet sizes vary from 128 bytes for some public-carrier networks to 8000 bytes (and higher) for some LANs.

With a single network, the maximum packet size is normally known and so the transport layer protocol entity can itself divide – **segment** or **fragment** – larger messages into smaller units for transfer across the network. However, with internets comprising networks with varying maximum packet sizes, either the minimum packet size must be known and used, or the network layer in each ES and IS must perform the necessary segmentation (fragmentation) and reassembly operations. The first alternative results in some networks being used inefficiently, while the second requires an additional function to be performed by the network layer.

Flow and congestion control

Flow control is implemented to control the flow of packets relating to a single call in order to overcome the difference between the rate at which a source system sends packets and the rate at which a destination can accept packets. If the destination can accept packets faster than the source can send them, clearly there is no problem. However, if the reverse is true a harmonization (flow control) function must be provided.

Congestion control is concerned with a similar function within the network itself. If the composite rate at which packets enter the network exceeds the rate at which packets leave, then the network becomes congested. Similarly, at a more local level, if packets arrive at a network node – for example, an IS – faster than they can be processed and forwarded, then the node becomes congested thus affecting the flow of packets relating to all calls through that node.

With a connection-oriented network such as X.25, flow control is performed on a VC basis across the local DTE–DCE and DCE–DTE interfaces. A send window is defined and when this number of packets have been sent (typically two), the sender must wait until an acknowledgment relating to either of them is received. Since this function is being performed at the periphery of the network on a per call basis, in addition to regulating the flow of packets into the network, it helps to control congestion. However, it does not prevent congestion completely.

In contrast, with a connectionless network no flow control is applied to the packets associated with a call within the network. Instead it is left to the transport protocol entity within each ES to perform flow control on an end-to-end basis. If congestion occurs within the network, flow control information is delayed and the source transport protocol entities stop sending new data into the network. Again, although sending new data helps to relieve network congestion, as with a connection-oriented network, it does not always avoid it. Therefore, with both schemes we must incorporate a congestion control algorithm within the network. Moreover, for internets comprising multiple network types, the congestion control algorithm must harmonize between the different network algorithms.

Error reporting

The way in which errors are reported varies from one network type to another. Consequently, we must establish a means of error reporting across multiple networks.

All these problems must be addressed by any internetworking solution.

9.3   Network layer structure

The role of the network layer in each ES is to provide an end-to-end, internetwide network service to its local NS_user(s). This can be either a CONS or a CLNS. In both cases the NS_users should be unaware of the presence of multiple, possibly different, network types. Hence the routing and all other functions relating to the

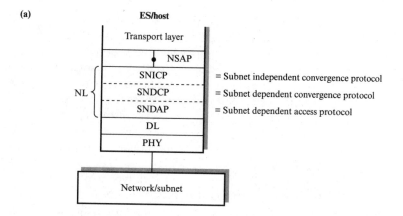

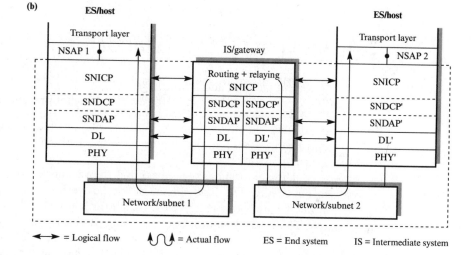

Figure 9.6
Network layer
structure: (a) sublayer
protocols; (b) IS
structure.

relaying of NSDUs must be carried out in a transparent way by the network layer
entities in each of the end and intermediate systems.

To achieve this goal, in the context of the ISO reference model the network
layer in each ES and IS consists not just of a single protocol but rather of three
(sublayer) protocols, each performing a complementary role in providing the
network layer service. In ISO terminology, each network that makes up an
internet is known as a subnet and hence the three protocols are known as follows:

● Subnetwork independent convergence protocol (SNICP)

● Subnetwork dependent convergence protocol (SNDCP)

● Subnetwork dependent access protocol (SNDAP)

The relative position of the three protocols in an ES is given in Figure 9.6(a); part
(b) shows the protocols in relation to an IS.

The SNICP supports the network service provided to NS_users at the interface with the internet. Its role is to carry out the various harmonizing (convergence) functions which may be necessary to route and relay user data (transport protocol data units) across the internet. Its operation is independent of the characteristics of the specific subnets (networks) used in the internet and it assumes a standard network service from them.

The SNDAP is the access protocol associated with a specific subnet (network) in the internet. Examples are the X.25 packet layer protocol for an X.25 network and the connectionless network protocol that is often used for LANs. Because the service and operational characteristics associated with the SNDAPs differ from one network type to another, an intermediate sublayer must be provided between the SNICP and the SNDAP. This is the role of the SNDCP. Clearly, the detailed mapping operation that it performs will vary for different subnet/network types.

9.4 Internet protocol standards

As we discussed in Chapter 8, multiple X.25 WANs can be interconnected by X.75-based gateways. The introduction of a standard specifying the operation of the X.25 packet layer protocol for use with LANs means that one approach to internetworking is to adopt X.25 as an internetwide protocol. The latter can be operated in either a connection-oriented mode or in a pseudoconnectionless mode by using fast select.

This solution has the appeal that the various internetworking functions are much reduced. The disadvantage is that the overheads associated with X.25 packet switching are high and hence the packet throughput of these networks is relatively low. This is also true with fast select, since the same VC/error control functions are still used. Moreover, the much improved bit error rate performance of the next generation of WANs, such as ISDN, means that frame relay and cell (fast packet) switching will be the preferred operational modes rather than conventional packet switching.

The solution adopted by ISO is based on a connectionless internet service and an associated connectionless SNICP. The SNICP is defined in ISO 8475. It is based on the internet protocol that has been developed as part of research into internetworking funded by the **US Defense Advanced Research Projects Agency (DARPA)**. The early DARPA internet – **ARPANET** – was used to interconnect the computer networks associated with a small number of research and university sites with those of DARPA. When it came into being in the early 1970s, ARPANET involved just a small number of networks and associated host computers. Since that time, the internet has grown steadily. Instead of just a small number of mainframe computers at each site, there are now large numbers of workstations. Moreover, the introduction of LANs means that there are now several thousand networks/subnets. ARPANET is now linked to other internets. The combined internet, which is jointly funded by a number of agencies, is thus known simply as the **Internet**.

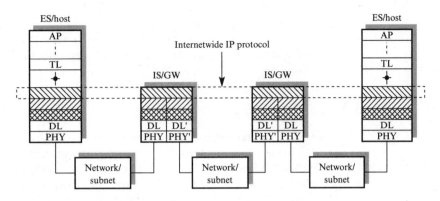

Figure 9.7
Internetwide IP
schematic.

The internet protocol is only one protocol associated with the complete protocol suite (stack) used with the Internet. The complete suite, known as **TCP/IP**, includes transport and application protocols which are now used as the basis of many other commercial and research networks. All the TCP/IP specifications are publicly available, as a result of which the Internet is by far the largest currently operational internet based on open standards. The two protocols we shall discuss in this chapter are the internet protocol associated with the Internet – known as the **Internet IP** or simply **IP** – and the ISO Internet Protocol known as **ISO-IP** or **ISO CLNP**, which is intended for use with OSI stacks. The general approach of both standards is illustrated in Figure 9.7.

IP is an internetwide protocol that enables two transport protocol entities resident in different ESs/hosts to exchange message units (NSDUs) in a transparent way. This means that the presence of multiple, possibly different, networks/subnets and ISs/gateways is completely transparent to both communicating transport entities. As the IP is a connectionless protocol, message units are transferred using an unacknowledged best-try approach.

Although the operational features associated with ISO CLNP are based on experience gained from the evolution and use of IP, there are differences both in terms of terminology and operational detail. Hence we shall discuss each protocol separately.

9.5 Internet IP

TCP/IP is now widely used in many commercial and research internets in addition to the Internet. Nevertheless, almost all the protocols associated with the TCP/IP have been researched and developed as part of the Internet. Indeed, new protocols are introduced relatively frequently as research associated with the combined

Internet continues. However, there is a core set of protocols that forms an integral part of all TCP/IP implementations. Other optional protocols are intended for open systems of varying size and complexity. We shall consider only the core protocols.

9.5.1 Address structure

Recall that there are two network addresses associated with a host/ES attached to an internet. In ISO terminology, these are the network service access point (NSAP) address and the subnet point of attachment (SNPA) address. With TCP/IP, these are the IP address and the network point of attachment (NPA) address, respectively. The NPA address is different for each network/subnet type, whereas the IP address is a unique internetwide identifier. The structure of an IP address is shown in Figure 9.8. In order to give the authority establishing the internet some flexibility in assigning addresses, the address structure shown in part (a) has been adopted.

To ensure that all hosts have a unique identifier, a 32-bit integer is used for each IP address. Then three different address formats are defined to allow for the

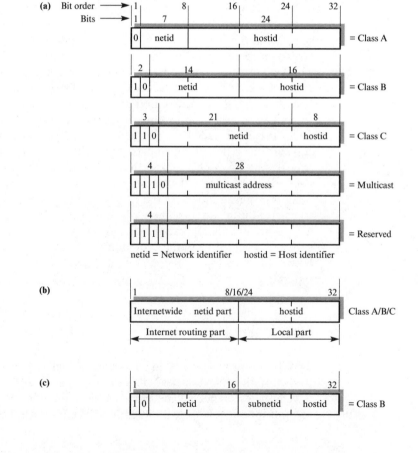

Figure 9.8
IP address formats:
(a) frame; (b) subnet addressing;
(c) modified class B address.

different sizes of network to which a host may be attached. Each format is known by an **address class**; a single internet may use addresses from all classes. The three primary classes are A, B, and C; each is intended for use with a different size of network. The class to which an address belongs can be determined from the position of the first zero bit in the first four bits. The remaining bits specify two subfields – a **network identifier (netid)** and a **host identifier (hostid)**. The subfield boundaries are located on byte boundaries to simplify decoding.

Class A addresses have 7 bits for the netid and 24 bits for the hostid; class B addresses have 14 bits for the netid and 16 bits for the hostid; and class C addresses have 21 bits for the netid and 8 bits for the hostid. Class A addresses are intended for use with networks that have a large number of attached hosts (up to 2^{24}) while class C addresses allow for a large number of networks each with a small number of attached hosts (up to 256). An example of a class A network is ARPANET; an example of a class C network is a single site-wide LAN.

An address with a hostid of zero is used to refer to the network in the netid field rather than to a host. Similarly, an address with a hostid of all 1s refers to all hosts attached to the network in the netid field or, if the latter is all 1s also, then to all hosts in the internet. Such addresses are used for broadcast purposes.

To make it easier to communicate IP addresses, the 32 bits are broken into four bytes. These are converted into their equivalent decimal form with a dot (period) between each. This is known as **dotted decimal**. Example addresses are as follows:

$$00001010\ 00000000\ 00000000\ 00000000 = 10.0.0.0. = \text{class A}$$
$$= \text{netid } 10\ (\text{ARPANET})$$

$$10000000\ 00000011\ 00000010\ 00000011 = 128.3.2.3 = \text{class B}$$
$$= \text{netid } 128.3,\ \text{hostid } 2.3$$

$$11000000\ 00000000\ 00000001\ 11111111 = 192.0.1.255 = \text{class C}$$
$$= \text{all hosts broadcast on netid}$$
$$192.0.1$$

Class D addresses are reserved for **multicasting**. In a LAN, a frame may be sent to an individual, broadcast, or **group address**. The last one allows a group of hosts – for example, workstations – that are cooperating in some way, to arrange for network transmissions to be sent to all members of the group. This is often referred to as **computer-supported cooperative working (CSCW)**; class D addresses allow this mode of working to be extended across an internet.

Although this basic structure is adequate for most addressing purposes, the introduction of multiple LANs at each site can mean unacceptably high overheads in terms of routing. As Chapter 7 described, MAC bridges are normally used to interconnect LANs of the same type. This solution is attractive for routing purposes, since the combined LAN then behaves like a single network. When interconnecting dissimilar LAN types, the differences in frame format and, more importantly, frame length, mean that routers are normally used since the fragmentation and reassembly of packets/frames is a function of the network layer rather than the MAC sublayer. However, the use of routers means that each

LAN must have its own netid. In the case of large sites, there may be a significant number of such LANs.

This means that with the basic addressing scheme, all the routers relating to a site need to take part in the overall internet routing function. The efficiency of any routing scheme is strongly influenced by the number of routing nodes that make up the internet. The concept of subnets has been introduced to decouple the routers – and hence routing – associated with a single site from the overall internet routing function. Essentially, instead of each LAN associated with a site having its own netid, only the site is allocated an internet netid. The identity of each LAN then forms part of the hostid field. This refined address format is shown in Figure 9.8(b).

The same address classes and associated structure are used, but the netid now relates to a complete site rather than to a single network. Hence, since only a single gateway attached to a local site network performs internetwide routing, the netid is considered as the **internet part**. For a single netid with a number of associated subnetworks the hostid part consists of two subfields: a **subnetid part** and a **local hostid part**. Because these have only local significance, they are known collectively as the **local part**.

Because of the possibly wide range of subnets associated with different site networks, no attempt has been made to define rigid subaddress boundaries for the local address part. Instead, an **address mask** is used to define the subaddress boundaries for a particular network (and hence netid). The address mask is kept by the internet gateway and the routers at the site. It consists of binary 1s in those bit positions that contain a network address – including the netid and subnetid – and binary 0s in positions that contain the hostid. Hence an address mask of

11111111 11111111 11111111 00000000

means that the first three bytes (octets) contain a network/subnet identifier and the fourth octet contains the host identifier.

For example, if the address is a class B address – a zero bit in the second bit position – this is readily interpreted as: the first two octets are the internetwide netid, the next octet the subnetid, and the last octet the hostid on this subnet. Such an address is shown in Figure 9.8(c).

Dotted decimal is normally used to define address masks, in which case the above mask is written:

255.255.255.0

Byte boundaries are normally chosen to simplify address decoding. Hence with this mask, and assuming the netid was, say, 128.10, then all the hosts attached to this network would have this same internet routing part. The presence of a possibly large number of subnets and associated routers is thus transparent to the internet gateways for routing purposes.

To ensure IP addresses are unique, they must be assigned by the central authority that is setting up the open system environment. For a small internet, this is relatively straightforward. However, in the case of large internets, such as the

Internet, this is normally done at two levels. Firstly, a central authority is set up to allocate netids and multicast addresses. Secondly, an authority associated with each network assigns hostids on that network. The central authority for the Internet is known as the **Network Information Center (NIC)**.

9.5.2 Datagrams

Before we consider the various functions and protocols associated with the IP, let us describe the format of an IP data unit. This is known as a **datagram**. The format and contents of a datagram are shown in Figure 9.9.

The **version** field contains the version of the IP used to create the datagram and ensures that all other systems – gateways and hosts – that process the datagram during its transit across the internet interpret the various fields correctly. The current version number is 4 and is referred to as **IP version 4**, or, simply, **IPv4**.

The header can be of variable length. The **header length** specifies the actual length of the datagram in multiples of 32-bit words. The minimum length – without options – is 5. If the datagram contains options, these must be in multiples of 32 bits. Any unused bytes must be filled with **padding** bytes.

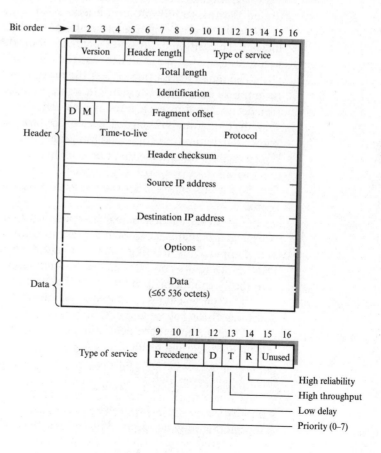

Figure 9.9
Internet datagram
format and contents.

The **type of service** plays the same role as the QOS parameter used in ISO networks. It allows an application process to specify the preferred attributes associated with the route and is, therefore, used by each gateway during route selection. For example, if a reliable delivery service is preferred to a best-try transfer, then given a choice the gateway should choose a connection-oriented network rather than a connectionless network. The **total length** defines the total length of the datagram including the header and user data parts. The maximum length is 65 536 bytes.

As we shall explain in Section 9.5.4, user messages may be transferred across the internet in multiple datagrams, with the **identification** field being used to allow a destination host to relate different datagrams to the same user message.

The next three bits are known as **flag bits** of which two are currently used. The first, known as the **don't fragment** or **D bit**, is again intended for use by intermediate gateways. A set D bit indicates that a network should be chosen that can handle the datagram as a single entity rather than as multiple smaller datagrams – known as **fragments**. Hence if the destination host is connected to that network (or subnet) it will receive the user data in a single datagram or not at all. The transit delay of the user data can therefore be more accurately quantified.

The second flag bit, known as the **more fragments** or **M bit**, is also used during the reassembly procedure associated with user data transfers involving multiple datagrams. The **fragment offset** is also used by the same procedure to indicate the position of the (data) contents of the datagram in relation to the initial user data message. We shall describe the reassembly procedure in Section 9.5.4.

The **time-to-live** value defines the maximum time for which a datagram can be in transit across the internet. The value, in seconds, is set by the source IP. It is then decremented by each gateway by a defined amount. Should the value become zero, the datagram is discarded. This procedure allows the destination IP to wait a known maximum time for a datagram fragment during the reassembly procedure. It also enables datagrams that are looping to be discarded.

More than one protocol is associated with the TCP/IP suite. The **protocol** field is used to enable the destination IP to pass the datagram to the required protocol.

The **header checksum**, which applies just to the header part of the datagram, is a safeguard against corrupted datagrams being routed to incorrect destinations. It is computed by treating each 16-bit field as an integer and adding them all together using 1's-complement (end-around-carry) arithmetic. The checksum is then the 1's-complement (inverse) of the sum.

The **source address** and **destination address** are the internetwide IP (NSAP) addresses of the source and destination hosts.

Finally, the **options** field is used in selected datagrams to carry additional information relating to the following:

- *Security* The data field may be encrypted for example, or be made accessible only to a specified user group.

- *Source routing* If known, the actual route to be followed through the internet may be specified in this field as a list of gateway addresses.

- *Route recording* This field is used by each gateway visited during the passage of a datagram through the internet to record its address. The resulting list can be used, for example, in the source routing field of subsequent datagrams.

- *Stream identification* This enables a source to indicate the type of data being carried in the datagram if this is not computer data, for example, samples of speech.

- *Timestamp* If present, this is used by each gateway along the path followed by the datagram to record the time it processed the datagram.

9.5.3 Protocol functions

The IP provides a number of core functions and associated procedures to carry out the various harmonizing functions that are necessary when interworking across dissimilar networks. These include the following:

- *Fragmentation and reassembly* This concerns the transfer of user messages across networks/subnets which support smaller packet sizes than the user data.

- *Routing* To perform the routing function, the IP in each source host must know the location of the internet gateway or local router that is attached to the same network or subnet. Also, the IP in each gateway must know the route to be followed to reach other networks or subnets.

- *Error reporting* When routing or reassembling datagrams within a host or gateway, the IP may discard some datagrams. This function is concerned with reporting such occurrences back to the IP in the source host and with a number of other reporting functions.

We shall discuss each of these functions separately.

9.5.4 Fragmentation and reassembly

The size of the user data – normally referred to as an NSDU – associated with an NS_user request can be up to 64K or 65 536 octets (bytes). The maximum packet sizes associated with different types of network are much less than this, ranging from 128 octets for some X.25 packet switching networks to over 8000 octets for some LANs. The fragmentation and reassembly functions associated with the IP fragment the NSDU associated with an NS_user request into smaller fragments – segments in ISO terminology – so that they can be transferred across a particular network in appropriately sized datagrams. On receipt of the fragments of data relating to the same NSDU contained in each IP datagram, the IP reassembles the NSDU before passing it on to the destination NS_user.

One of two approaches may be adopted since the maximum packet size may vary from one network to another. Either the fragmentation and reassembly functions can be performed on a per network basis – **intranet fragmentation** – or on an end-to-end (internetwide) basis – **internet fragmentation**. The two approaches are shown in Figure 9.10(a) and (b), respectively.

In general, the IP in a host knows only the maximum packet size associated with its local network. Similarly, the IP in each gateway knows only the maximum packet sizes associated with the two networks to which it is connected. With intranet segmentation, the IP in the source host first fragments the NS_user data – the NSDU – into a number of individually addressed datagrams as dictated by the network to which it is attached. It initiates the sending of these either to the

Figure 9.10
Fragmentation
alternatives:
(a) intranet;
(b) internet.

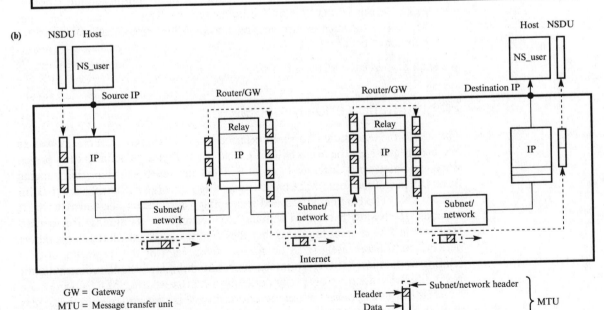

GW = Gateway
MTU = Message transfer unit
NSDU = Network service data unit

Header →
Data →

Subnet/network header
Subnet/network trailer
} MTU

destination host or to the first IS (gateway) in the route using the SNDCP, which obtains the NPA address of the host or gateway.

We shall discuss the way in which it obtains the NPA address in Section 9.5.5. On receipt of each datagram, the IP in the host or gateway reassembles the NSDU. Next it refragments the reassembled NSDU into a possibly different set of individually addressed datagrams as dictated by the maximum packet size of the second network.

This procedure is repeated by each gateway until the datagram reaches the IP in the destination host, where the NSDU is again reassembled and passed to the destination NS_user.

With internet fragmentation, the IP in the source host carries out the same fragmentation procedure as before and sends the resulting datagrams to the IP in the first gateway. However, this time the IP does not reassemble the NSDU. Instead it either modifies the appropriate fields and sends the received datagrams directly onto the second network (if the latter can support this size of datagram), or refragments the datagram into smaller fragments (datagrams). In Figure 9.10, we assume that the maximum packet size associated with the second network/ subnet is smaller than that used by the first. Consequently, the IP will segment each datagram it receives into a number of smaller datagrams, each with the same source and destination addresses.

This procedure is repeated at the next gateway. However, since in Figure 9.10 the last network/subnet can support a larger packet size than the datagrams it receives, the received datagrams are transmitted directly with only selected modifications to some header fields. As before, the IP in the destination host reassembles the user data from each datagram it receives and passes the resulting NSDU to the destination NS_user.

We can deduce, especially from the packet flows associated with the third network in Figure 9.10, that intranet fragmentation allows the maximum packet size of each network to be used, since the individual fragments are reassembled by each gateway in the route. With internet fragmentation this is not necessarily the case, but it has the advantage that the reassembly processing is not needed at each gateway.

The IP does in fact use internet fragmentation. This may at first appear surprising but it is used because of the problem of lost datagrams. Some networks operate with a best-try connectionless protocol with the possibility that one or more datagrams relating to a single NSDU may be corrupted while being transmitted. As we have seen, with intranet fragmentation the receiving IP in each gateway reassembles the complete NSDU before relaying it to the next network. If any fragments are missing (for example, a datagram is discarded because it has been corrupted), the receiving IP must decide at what point to abort the reassembly function.

To determine this the IP in the source host defines a maximum time limit that a gateway may wait for any datagrams relating to an NSDU during each reassembly operation. Known as the time-to-live, this limit is carried in the header of all datagrams relating to the NSDU. It is set by the IP in the source host and is then decremented by each IP that processes the datagram. If a datagram is fragmented, the current value is copied into the header of the new datagrams. If it reaches zero at any point during the reassembly processing in a gateway (or host), the reassembly function is aborted and all fragments relating to that NSDU are discarded.

The time-to-live field in each datagram is in multiples of 1 second, so the amount it is decremented by each IP varies depending on the (known) mean transit delay of the associated network. In the case of internet fragmentation, the IP in each gateway still decrements the time-to-live lifetime field in each datagram it receives and discards any datagrams for which the value reaches zero. The IP in the destination host aborts its reassembly operation in the same way. In both cases, if fragments are missing and the reassembly operation is aborted, a **time exceeded** error message is generated and returned to the IP in the source host.

Example 9.1

An NSDU of 1000 octets is to be transmitted over a network which supports a maximum NS_user data size of 256 octets. Assuming the header in each IP datagram requires 20 octets, derive the number of datagrams (fragments) required and the contents of the following fields in each datagram header:

- Identification
- Total length
- Fragment offset
- More fragments flag

Maximum usable data per datagram = 256 − 20 = 236 octets
Use, say, 29 × 8 = 232 octets
Hence five datagrams are required, four with 232 octets of user data and one with 72 octets
The fields are as follows:

Identification	20 (say)	20	20	20	20
Total length	252		252	252	252	92
Fragment offset	0		29	58	87	116
More fragments flag	1		1	1	1	0

9.5.5 Routing

As each network (or subnet) in an internet may use different types of point of attachment addresses, a system – host or gateway – attached to a network can send a datagram directly to another system only if it is attached to the same network. To route datagrams across multiple networks, the IP in each internetwork gateway must know either the point of attachment address of the destination host – if it is attached to a network to which the gateway is attached – or the next gateway along the route to the required destination network, if it is not. Again, the next gateway must be attached to a network to which the gateway is attached. The major problem with routing is how the hosts and gateways within the internet obtain and maintain their routing information.

Two basic approaches are used for routing within an internet: centralized and distributed. With a **centralized routing** scheme, the routing information associated with each gateway is downloaded from a central site using the network and special network management messages. The network management system endeavors to maintain their contents up to date as networks and hosts are added or removed and faults are diagnosed and repaired. In general, for all but the smallest internets, this is a viable solution only as long as each individual network has its own network management system which incorporates sophisticated configuration and fault management procedures.

With a **distributed routing** scheme, all the hosts and gateways cooperate in a distributed way to ensure that the routing information held by each system – hosts and gateways – is up to date and consistent. Routing information is retained by each system in the form of a **routing table** which contains the NPA address to be used to forward each datagram. The Internet uses such a scheme.

The routing procedure associated with the IP first reads the destination IP (NSAP) address from within a datagram and then uses this to find the corresponding point of attachment address – of a host or a gateway – from the routing table. In addition, a set of routing protocols is used to create and maintain the contents of each routing table in a distributed way. The general scheme used within a host IP is shown in Figure 9.11.

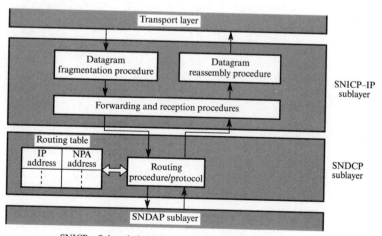

Figure 9.11
General routing
scheme within a host.

SNICP = Subnet independent convergence protocol
SNDCP = Subnet dependent convergence protocol
SNDAP = Subnet dependent access protocol
NPA = (Sub)net point of attachment (address)

Autonomous systems

Before we discuss the various routing protocols relating to the Internet, let us look at its architecture and the associated terminology. To reflect the fact that the Internet is made up of a number of separately managed and run internets, each internet is treated as an **autonomous system** with its own internal routing algorithms and management authority. The combined Internet is considered as a **core backbone network** to which a number of autonomous systems are attached. The general architecture is shown in Figure 9.12 together with some (very much simplified) autonomous system topologies.

To discriminate between the gateways used within an autonomous system and those used to connect an autonomous system to the core network, we use the terms **interior gateway** and **exterior gateway**, respectively. The corresponding routing protocols are the **interior gateway protocol (IGP)** and the **exterior gateway protocol (EGP)**. Since the Internet consists of an interconnected set of internets, each of which has evolved over a relatively long period of time, each autonomous system has its own IGP. However, the Internet EGP is, as indeed it must be, an internetwide standard.

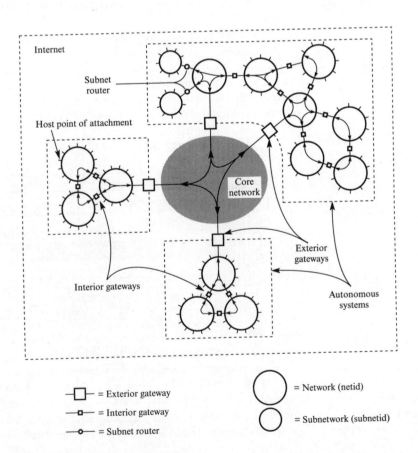

Figure 9.12
General internet architecture and terminology.

Although each autonomous system within the Internet comprises a large number of networks/subnets, in a more general application an autonomous system might consist of just one network managed and run by a single corporation. Others might consist of a set of subnets connected to a site-wide backbone network with a single exterior gateway. An example is a site with multiple LANs interconnected by routers. To simplify the discussion, we shall consider only autonomous systems that consist of multiple networks since the presence of subnets just adds another level of routing between an interior gateway and the hosts.

If every gateway and host system in an internet contained a separate entry in its routing table for all other systems, the size of the routing tables and the amount of processing and transmission capacity needed to maintain the tables would be excessive and, for the Internet, unmanageable. Instead, the total routing information is organized hierarchically as follows:

- Hosts maintain sufficient routing information to forward datagrams to other hosts or an interior gateway(s) that is (are) attached to the same network.

- Interior gateways maintain sufficient routing information to forward datagrams to hosts or other interior gateways within the same autonomous system.

- Exterior gateways maintain sufficient routing information to forward datagrams either to an interior gateway, if the datagram is for the same autonomous system, or to another exterior gateway, if it is not.

A number of routing protocols have been developed to implement this scheme. These include an intranet protocol known as the **address resolution protocol (ARP)**, a number of interior gateway protocols (IGPs), and an exterior gateway protocol (EGP). The scope of each protocol and the associated routing tables are shown in Figure 9.13. We shall discuss each separately.

Address resolution protocol

To enable an interior gateway to forward any datagrams it receives for hosts that are attached to one of its local networks, it must keep a record of the hostid and corresponding NPA address – known as an **address pair** – for all the hosts attached to each of these networks. To obtain this information, each host simply informs the local gateway of its existence by sending it its IP/NPA address pair. Typically, this is stored at the host in permanent storage (such as the hard disk) and is then broadcast. With nonbroadcast networks, the address pair of its local gateway(s) is (are) also stored and used directly. As a result, each interior gateway builds up a **local routing table** with the IP/NPA address pairs of all hosts that are attached to each of the networks to which the interior gateway is itself attached.

When a host wishes to send a datagram to another host on the same network, the IP simply sends the datagram to its local gateway for forwarding. Although this must be done for datagrams addressed to hosts on other networks, for hosts attached to the same network it can lead to excessively high overheads,

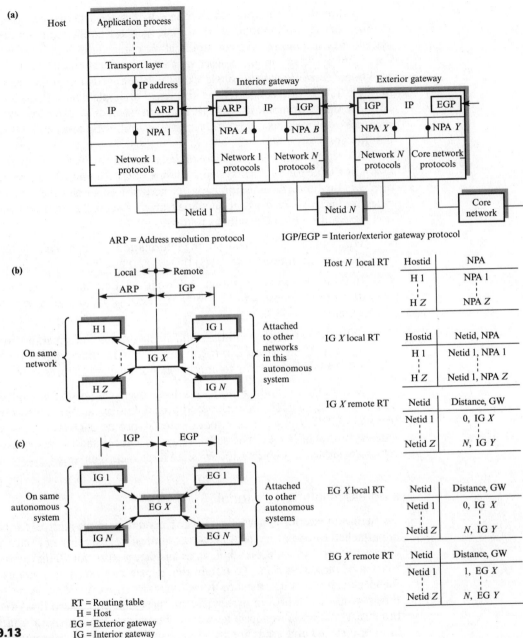

Figure 9.13
Routing protocols:
(a) general
architecture; (b) ARP/
IGP scope and routing
tables; (c) IGP/EGP
scope and routing
protocols.

especially if a large number of hosts are attached to the network. To overcome this, the IP in each host endeavors to obtain the hostid/NPA address pair of all hosts on the same network with which it communicates. This enables a host to send a datagram to hosts on the same network directly without involving the gateway.

The protocol that performs this function is the address resolution protocol (ARP). ARP forms an integral part of the IP in each host; there is a peer ARP in each interior gateway, as shown in Figure 9.13(a).

Whenever the fragmentation procedure associated with the IP creates a datagram for forwarding, it first passes the address pointer of the memory buffer in which the datagram is stored to the ARP. The ARP maintains a local routing table which contains the hostid/NPA address pairs of all the hosts connected to this network with which the host communicates. If the destination IP address in the datagram is present in the table, then the ARP simply passes the datagram address pointer with the corresponding NPA address to the SNDAP protocol, with the netid field of the IP address set to zero to indicate this network. The SNDAP then initiates the sending of the datagram either by broadcast or directly.

If the NPA address is not present, the ARP endeavors to find it by creating and sending an **ARP request message** and waiting for a reply. The request message contains both its own IP/NPA address pair and the required (target) IP address. Again, this can either be broadcast – in which case it is received by the ARP in all hosts – or sent directly to the ARP in the gateway using the gateway's (known) NPA address. In the second case, the ARP in the gateway simply relays the message to the required host using its own local routing table and the required destination IP address in the request message.

The ARP in the required destination host recognizes its own IP address in the request message and proceeds to process it. It first checks to see whether the source hostid/NPA address pair is within its own routing table; if not, it enters them. It then responds by returning an **ARP reply message** containing its own NPA address to the ARP in the requesting host, using the latter's NPA address from the request message. On receipt of the reply message, the ARP in the source host first makes an entry of the requested hostid/NPA pair in its own routing table and then passes the waiting datagram address pointer to the SNDAP protocol together with the corresponding NPA address which indicates where it should be sent. The hostid/NPA pair is recorded by the destination since it is highly probable that the destination host will require it later when the higher-layer protocol responds to the datagram.

As we indicated earlier, the IP/NPA address pair of a host is normally held in permanent storage and read by the computer operating system at startup. With diskless hosts, this is not possible, so an associated protocol known as the **reverse address resolution protocol (RARP)** is used. The server associated with each set of diskless hosts has a copy of the IP/NPA address pair of all the hosts it serves. When a diskless host first comes into service, it broadcasts an RARP request message to the server containing its own physical hardware network address, that is, its NPA. On receipt of such messages, the RARP in the server responds with a reply message containing both the IP address of the requester and its own IP/NPA address pair. In practice, the format of the request and reply messages associated with ARP and RARP are the same, as shown in Figure 9.14.

The **operation** field specifies the particular message type: ARP request/reply, RARP request/reply. When making an ARP request, the sender writes its own **hardware address (HA)** and IP address in the appropriate fields together with the

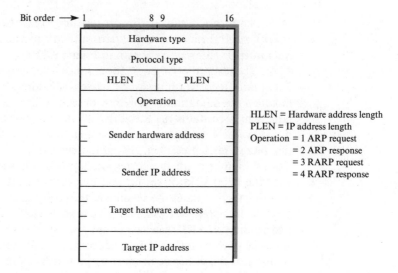

Figure 9.14
ARP and RARP
message formats.

destination IP address in the **target IP** field. In the case of a RARP, the sender simply includes its own HA address. To ensure that the HA address is interpreted correctly, the **hardware type** field identifies the type of LAN, for example, CSMA/CD is 1. The **protocol type** field indicates the type of protocol being used: ARP, RARP, and others to be defined in subsequent sections.

Interior gateway protocol

As we indicated earlier, the interior gateway routing protocol can vary from one autonomous system to another. The most widely used protocol is the **IP routing information protocol (RIP)**. It is a **distributed routing protocol** which is based on a technique known as the **distance vector algorithm (DVA)**. A more recently introduced protocol is based on two algorithms known as the **link state (LS)** and **shortest-path-first algorithms (SPF)**. The **link state open shortest-path-first (link state OSPF)** protocol has been adopted as the international standard for use with the ISO CLNP. Since the DVA is specific to the TCP/IP we shall discuss it here. We shall discuss the link state OSPF in Section 9.8.3 in the context of the ISO CLNP.

The term *distance* is used as a **routing metric** between two gateways. For example, if the metric is *hops*, then this is the number of intermediate networks between two gateways. If the metric is *delay*, then this is the mean transit delay between the two gateways, and so on. Whichever metric is used, the DVA uses a distributed algorithm to enable each interior gateway in an autonomous system to build up a table containing the distance between itself and all the other networks in that system.

Initially, each gateway knows only the netid of each network to which it is attached as well as the IP/NPA address pair of each gateway attached to these networks. Typically this information is entered by management when the gateway is initialized; the netid in the **remote routing table** and the IP/NPA address pairs in the **adjacency table** for the gateway. The format of the remote routing table associated with an interior gateway was shown in Figure 9.13(b). If the metric is hops, the remote routing table contains simply the netid of each of its local networks, a distance of zero, and its own IP address as the gateway from which the distance applies. Similarly, if the metric is delay, this is determined by a gateway which sends a message (datagram) to each of the gateways attached to its own networks and measures the time delay before it receives the responses. The distance is then set to, say, half of these values.

Periodically, each gateway sends the current contents of its (remote) routing table to each of its neighbors. Based on the contents of its neighbors' tables which it receives, it updates, or adds to, the contents of its own routing table. The receiving gateway simply adds the known distances to each of its immediate neighbors to the distances contained in the received tables. Since this procedure repeats, after each iteration the routing table starts to build up as new distances are reported. If a reported distance to a network is less than a current entry, the entry is updated. After a number of iterations, each gateway has an entry for each of the networks in the autonomous system. The time taken to achieve this is a function of the size of the system and the frequency with which routing information is exchanged. The time for routing information to propagate throughout the system is known as the **route propagation delay**.

For example, consider the simple network shown in Figure 9.15(a) and assume the metric is hops. The way in which the routing tables build up is shown in part (b). The initial contents of each gateway simply contain the netid of its local networks. For this network, the contents of each routing table are complete after just two exchanges of routing tables. The final routing table for each gateway contains the distances to each network in the system and the immediate neighbor gateway to be used to reach it. Thus from gateway 1, the distance to netid 6 is two hops – that is, two intermediate networks – via gateway 2. At gateway 2, netid 6 is a distance of one hop via gateway 3 to which netid 6 is attached.

We can readily deduce that a metric of hops can lead to the selection of inferior routes. For example, if the delay metric associated with each network is the same as its netid, it would be quicker to go from gateway 4 to netid 6 via gateways 1, 2, and 3 in three hops rather than 5 and 6 with two hops. The delay metric often gives a better performance. A protocol that uses delay is **HELLO**. As its name implies, the delay is determined by periodically sending **hello messages** to each of its neighbors and timing their responses.

To ensure that table entries reflect the current topology of the network when faults develop, each entry has an associated timer. If the entry is not confirmed within a defined time, then it is timed-out. This means that each gateway transmits its complete routing table at regular intervals, typically 30 seconds. For a small network this is not necessarily a problem, but for large networks the overheads associated with the distance vector algorithm can be very high. Also, gateways may have dissimilar routes to the same destination since entries are made in the order in which they are received and equal distance routes are discarded. As a result, datagrams between certain routes may loop rather than going directly to

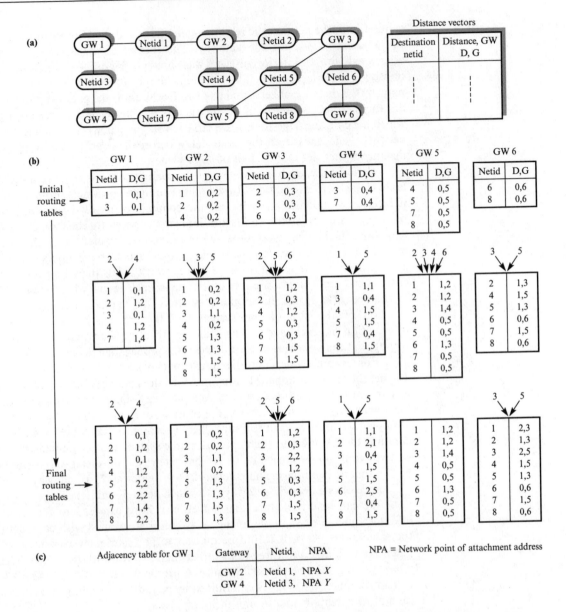

Figure 9.15
Distance vector
algorithm example:
(a) topology;
(b) buildup of routing
tables assuming hop-
count metric;
(c) reachability table
for gateway.

the desired gateway. Also, only a single route is held in the routing tables so
alternative routes are not used. For these reasons OSPF is becoming the preferred
IGP for large internets.

Exterior gateway protocol

The management authority associated with each autonomous system nominates
one or more gateways to function as exterior gateways for that system. Within
the autonomous system, these communicate with the other interior gateways

using the IGP for that system. Each exterior gateway, through its local routing table, knows about the netids within that system and their distances from that gateway. The contents of the routing table are built up in the way we have just described.

When each exterior gateway is first initialized, it is given the unique identity of the autonomous system to which it is attached. It also receives the contents of a routing table, known as the **reachability table**, which enables it to communicate with all the other exterior gateways via the core network. The EGP then causes each exterior gateway to make contact with selected exterior gateways, as required, and to exchange routing information with them. This routing information consists of the list of netids within the corresponding autonomous system together with their distances and routes from the reporting exterior gateway. This information is used by a sending gateway to select the best exterior gateway for forwarding datagrams to a particular autonomous system.

The three main functions associated with the EGP are as follows:

- Neighbor acquisition

- Neighbor reachability

- Routing update

Each function operates using a request–response message exchange. The messages associated with each function are shown in Table 9.1.

Since each autonomous system is managed and run by a different authority, before any routing information is exchanged two exterior gateways attached to

Table 9.1   EGP message types and their meaning.

Function	EGP message	Meaning
Neighbor acquisition	Acquisition request	Requests a gateway to become a neighbor
	Acquisition confirm	Gateway agrees to become a neighbor
	Acquisition refuse	Gateway refuses
	Cease request	Requests termination of a neighbor relationship
	Cease confirm	Confirms breakup of relationship
Neighbor reachability	Hello	Requests neighbor to confirm a previously established relationship
	I-heard-you	Confirms relationship
Routing update	Poll request	Requests network reachability update
	Routing update	Network reachability information
Error response	Error	Response to any incorrect request message

different systems must first agree to exchange such information. This is the role of the **neighbor acquisition and termination** procedure. When two gateways agree to such an exchange, they are said to have become **neighbors**. When a gateway first wants to exchange routing information, it sends an **acquisition request** message to the EGP in the appropriate gateway which then returns either an **acquisition confirm** message or, if it does not want to accept the request, an **acquisition refuse** message which includes a reason code.

Once a neighbor relationship has been established between two gateways – and hence autonomous systems – they periodically confirm their relationship. This is done either by exchanging specific messages – **hello** and **I-heard-you** – or by embedding confirmation information into the header of normal routing information messages.

The actual exchange of routing information is carried out by one of the gateways, which sends a **poll request** message to the other gateway asking it for the list of networks (netids) that are reachable via that gateway and their distances from it. The response is a **routing update** message which contains the requested information. Finally, if any request message is incorrect, an **error message** is returned as a response with an appropriate reason code.

As with the other IP protocols, all the messages (PDUs) associated with the EGP are carried in the user data field of an IP datagram. All EGP messages have the same fixed header; the format is shown in Figure 9.16.

The **version** field defines the version number of the EGP. The **type** and **code** fields collectively define the type of message while the **status** field contains message-dependent status information. The **checksum**, which is used as a safeguard against the processing of erroneous messages, is the same as that used with IP. The **autonomous system number** is the assigned number of the autonomous system to which the sending gateway is attached; the **sequence number** is used to synchronize responses to their corresponding request message.

Neighbor reachability messages contain only a header with a type field of 5, a code of 0 = hello, and a 1 = I-heard-you.

Neighbor acquisition messages have a type field of 3; the code number defines the specific message type. The **hello interval** specifies the frequency with which hello messages should be sent; the **poll interval** performs the same function for poll messages.

A poll message has a type field of 2. The code field is used to piggyback the neighbor reachability information: a code of 0 = hello and a code of 1 = I-heard-you. The **source network IP address** in both the poll and the routing update response messages indicates the network linking the two exterior gateways. This allows the core network itself to consist of multiple networks.

The routing update message contains the list of networks (netids) that are reachable via each gateway within the autonomous system arranged in distance order from the responding exterior gateway. As indicated, this enables the requesting gateway to select the best exterior gateway through which to send a datagram for forwarding within an autonomous system. Notice that to conserve space, each netid address is sent in three bytes (24 bits) only with the most significant 8-bit hostid field missing. The latter is redundant for all class types.

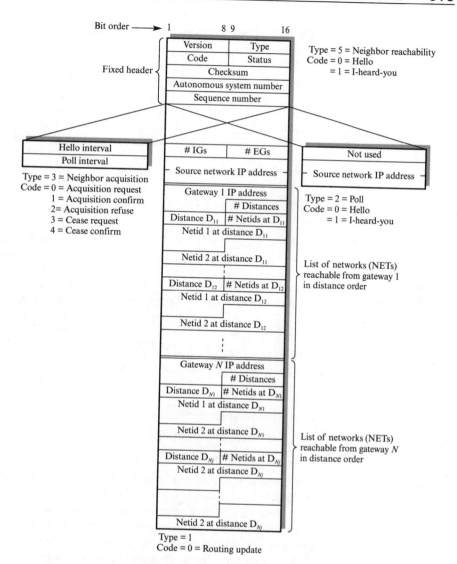

Figure 9.16
EGP message formats.

9.5.6 Internet control message protocol

The **internet control message protocol (ICMP)** forms an integral part of all IP implementations. It is used by both hosts and gateways for a variety of functions, and especially by network management. The main functions associated with the ICMP are as follows:

- Error reporting

- Reachability testing

- Congestion control

Table 9.2   ICMP message types and their use.

Function	ICMP message(s)	Use
Error reporting	Destination unreachable	A datagram has been discarded due to the reason specified in the message
	Time exceeded	Time-to-live parameter in a datagram expired and hence discarded
	Parameter error	A parameter in the header of a datagram is unrecognizable
Reachability testing	Echo request/ reply	Checks the reachability of a specified host or gateway
Congestion control	Source quench	Requests a host to reduce the rate at which datagrams are sent
Route exchange	Redirect	Used by a gateway to inform a host attached to one of its networks to use an alternative gateway on the same network for forwarding datagrams to a specific destination
Performance measuring	Timestamp request/reply	Determines the transit delay between two hosts
Submit addressing	Address mask request/reply	Used by a host to determine the address mask associated with a subnet

ICMP = Internet control message protocol

- Route-change notification
- Performance measuring
- Subnet addressing

The message types associated with each of these functions are shown in Table 9.2. Each is transmitted in a standard IP datagram.

Since the IP is a best-try (unacknowledged) protocol, datagrams may be discarded while they are in transit across the internet. Of course, transmission errors are one cause, but datagrams can be discarded by a host or gateway for a variety of reasons. In the absence of any error reporting functions, a host does not know whether the repeated failure to send a datagram to a given destination is the result of a poor transmission line (or other fault within a network) or simply the destination host being switched off. The various messages associated with the **error reporting** function are used for this purpose.

If a datagram is corrupted by transmission errors, it is simply discarded. If a datagram is discarded for any other reason, the ICMP in the host or gateway that discards the datagram generates a **destination unreachable** error report message and returns it to the ICMP in the source host with a reason code. Reasons include the following:

- Destination network unreachable
- Destination host unreachable

- Specified protocol not present at destination

- Fragmentation needed but don't fragment (DF) flag set in datagram header

- Communication with the destination network not allowed for administrative reasons

- Communication with the destination host not allowed for administrative reasons

Other error report messages include **time exceeded**, which indicates that the time-to-live parameter in a discarded datagram has expired, and **parameter error**, which indicates that a parameter in the header of the discarded datagram was not recognized.

If a network manager receives reports from a user that a specified destination is not responding, the reason must be determined using the **reachability testing** function. Typically, on receipt of such a report, the network manager initiates the sending of an **echo request** message to the suspect host to determine whether it is switched on and responding to requests. On receipt of an echo request message, the ICMP in the destination simply changes this to an **echo reply** message which it returns to the source. A similar test can be performed on selected gateways if necessary.

If a datagram is discarded because no free memory buffers are available as a result of a temporary overload condition, a **source quench** message is returned to the ICMP in the source host. Such messages can be generated either by a host or by a gateway. They request the source host to reduce the rate at which it sends datagrams. When a host receives such a message, it reduces the sending rate by an agreed amount. A new source quench message is generated each time a datagram is discarded so that the source host incrementally reduces the sending rate. Such messages help to alleviate congestion control within the internet. Congestion is discussed further in the context of the ISO CLNP in Section 9.7.3.

When a network has multiple gateways attached to it, a gateway may receive datagrams from a host even though it determines from its routing table that they would be better sent via a different gateway attached to the same network. To inform the source host of this, the ICMP in the gateway returns a **redirect** message to the ICMP in the source indicating which is the better gateway to the specified destination. The ICMP in the source then makes an entry in its routing table for this destination.

An important operational parameter for an internet is the mean transit delay of datagrams. This is a measure of the time a datagram takes to traverse the internet from a specified source to a specified destination. To ascertain this time, a host or a network manager can send a **timestamp request** message to a specific destination. Each message contains the following three time-related parameters (known as **timestamps**):

- The time the datagram was sent by the source

- The time the datagram was received by the destination

- The time the datagram was returned by the destination

On receipt of a timestamp request message, the ICMP in the destination simply fills in the appropriate timestamp fields and returns the datagram to the source. On receipt of the reply, the source can quantify the current round-trip delay to that destination and from this determine the datagram transit delay.

Finally, when subnet addressing is being used, the **address mask request** and corresponding reply messages are used by a host to ascertain the address mask associated with a local subnet. This is needed by a host to determine, for example, whether a specified destination is attached to the same subnet. The address mask is held by the local router associated with the subnet. The ICMP in a host can obtain the address mask sending a request message and reading the mask from the reply.

9.6 IPv6

The rapid expansion in the number of interconnected networks making up the Internet means that the 32-bit addresses currently used with IPv4 will need to be extended in the not too distant future if the current rate of growth continues. In anticipation of this, the **Internet Engineering Task Force (IETF)** has embarked upon the specification of a successor to the current IPv4 protocol. It is known as **IP next generation (IPng)** or, more correctly, **IP version 6 (IPv6)**.

A second motivator for moving to a new protocol is the increasing size of the routing tables that are required within each exterior gateway as the number of networks increase. As we explained in Section 9.5, each exterior gateway must know the address of the next gateway that should be used to reach any network in the Internet. Clearly, as the number of networks increases, so the size of the routing table in each exterior gateway also increases. It is intended that IPv6 should reduce the size of the routing table that is required within such gateways. Other motivators include better support for multicasting and improved levels of network security. Since the new protocol is currently under development, the aim here is simply to present an overview of its main features.

9.6.1 Datagram structure

To speed up the processing of the IP datagram header, the header of the IPv6 has been divided into two parts: a **basic header** and one or more optional **extension headers**. The format of the basic header is shown in Figure 9.17 and, as we can see, it contains fewer fields than the IPv4 datagram header. This means that the processing of many datagrams is much faster since only those datagrams containing an extension header have additional fields.

The **version number** has the same position and function as the earlier versions. It is assigned version number 6. In this way, the recipient of a datagram can readily determine the version number of the IP to which it relates and hence process the remaining bits according to the particular format. This will enable the new protocol to coexist with the existing IPv4 protocol during any transitional phase.

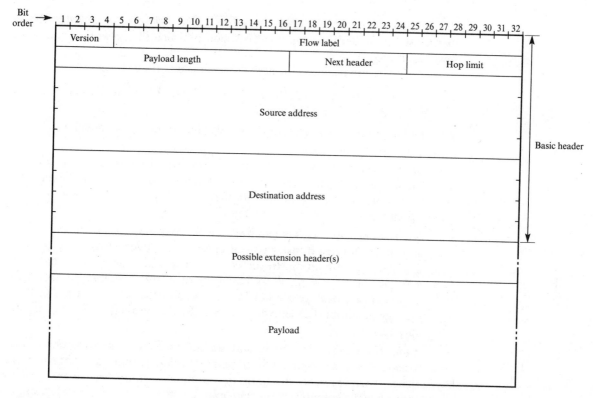

Figure 9.17
IPv6 datagram format and header fields.

The **flow label** has been introduced to enable a source to indicate the type of information in the data – known as **payload** – field. For example, this may be speech samples or perhaps a video frame, both of which should be given priority over normal computer data by intermediate gateways during the transfer of the datagram across the Internet.

The **payload length** indicates the number of octets in the payload field following the header. The default maximum length is 64K octets as before, but larger values can be used by setting this field to zero and including an extension field with the actual value within it.

Additional (header) information is carried in separate extension headers. These immediately follow the destination address field and currently a small number of such headers has been defined. Each is identified by means of a different value in the **next header** field.

The **hop limit** is used to prevent a datagram continuously circulating in a loop. The value in this field is decremented by one by each gateway visited and, if it falls to zero before reaching its intended destination, then the datagram is discarded.

The **source address** and **destination address** are both 128-bit hierarchical addresses. This significantly increases the number of addresses available. To reduce the size of the routing tables held by the exterior gateways connected to the backbone core network, a new higher-order address – that is, in addition to the netid and subnetid – has been introduced. This is known as a **cluster address** and is used to identify the topological region in which the network – and hence host – is located.

The extension headers currently defined include the following:

- *Hop-by-hop header*   Used to carry information that must be examined by all gateways visited along a route.

- *End-to-end header*   Used to carry information that is examined only by the intended destination.

- *Routing header*   This is present when source routing is being used. It contains a list of the addresses of the gateways that are along the intended route. The destination address in the basic header is then changed as the datagram is routed from one gateway to the next.

- *Fragment header*   This is required only if the course data is larger than the maximum message transfer unit of any of the networks along the route to the intended destination. In such cases, the course fragments the data into multiple datagrams prior to initiating their transmission. In this way, intermediate gateways are not involved in fragmentation and the fields in the fragmentation header are used only by the destination for reassembly purposes.

- *Authentication header*   As we shall see in Chapter 12, authentication is used to ensure a source cannot later repudiate that it sent some information. Hence, when present, the fields in the authentication header are used to authenticate the source of the datagram.

- *Privacy header*   This is present when the data to be transferred is to be made secure during its passage across the internet. The data is first encrypted by the source and is then sent in the data portion of this header.

9.6.2 Multicast support

In addition to defining a new generation of IP, an experimental overlay back-bone network is being introduced that supports multicasting more efficiently. The network is known as the **multicast backbone (m-bone)**. Recall that multicasting involves sending a copy of all the datagrams generated by each member (host) in a multicast group to all the other members of the group. With the current backbone network, the multiple copies of datagrams from each host result in a significant level of traffic flooding the network. As we shall see in Chapter 10, when datagrams containing different media from computer data are being transmitted – for example, audio samples and video frames – the number of datagrams per multicast session increases significantly.

To reduce this load, a single copy of all multicast datagrams is first sent to a new type of switching node known as a **multicast router (m-router)**. There is one such router at each interface to the backbone and these are interconnected by high bandwidth links to form the multicast backbone network. To minimize the transmission bandwidth used per multicast session, when a multicast group is set up, a **routing tree** is established between each m-router involved and all the other m-routers in the group. Then, when routing a multicast datagram, multiple copies are generated by an m-router only if it is a branch node in a particular tree.

9.7 The ISO Internet Protocol

The ISO approach to internetworking is based on an internetwide, connectionless, subnetwork-independent convergence protocol known as the **ISO Internet Protocol (ISO-IP)** or **ISO CLNP**. It is defined in ISO 8473 and has many of the features of the IP protocol we described in Section 9.5, on which it is based.

In addition to the full internetworking protocol, there are two subsets: the **inactive network layer protocol** and the **nonsegmenting protocol**. The former is the connectionless network protocol often used with LANs and is intended for applications involving a single network. Thus the source and destination ESs (stations) are both connected to the same network so none of the harmonizing functions identified earlier are required.

The nonsegmenting protocol (nonfragmenting in IP terminology) is intended for use in internets that consist of subnets – networks in IP terminology – which have maximum packet sizes all less than or equal to that required to transfer the NS_user data (NSDU) in a single internet protocol data unit. The segmentation function associated with the protocol is not required in this case.

9.7.1 User services

The user service primitives associated with the protocol and their parameters are shown in Figure 9.18. They are the same as those used with the inactive network layer protocol – shown in Section 6.5.3 – except that the QOS and service characteristics relate to the complete internet rather than to a single network. Normally, the N_FACILITY service is used by an NS_user to determine the QOS and service characteristics to be expected from the internet when communicating with the specified destination NSAP address. This information is used by the source NS_user when specifying the QOS associated with each N_UNITDATA.request primitive.

The source and destination addresses are the internetwide NSAP addresses of the two communicating NS_users. Their format is shown in Figure 9.19 and is the same as that defined in Chapter 8 by ISO and ITU-T for use with public-carrier WANs and other networks. Recall that NSAP addresses are hierarchical and are 20 octets in length (40 BCD digits). The AFI specifies the authority responsible for allocating IDIs, the format of IDIs, and the abstract syntax of the DSP. The IDI specifies the particular network addressing scheme to which the DSP addresses relate. The DSP is itself hierarchical and comprises: an optional

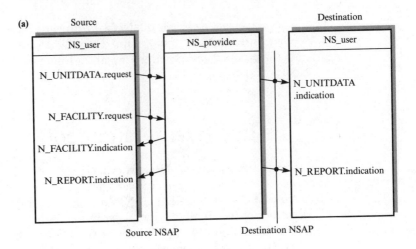

Figure 9.18
Internet service
primitives:
(a) sequence;
(b) parameters.

Primitive	Parameters
N_UNITDATA.request .indication	Destination address (NSAP) Source address (NSAP) QOS/service characteristics User data (NSDU)
N_FACILITY.request .indication	Destination address (NSAP) QOS/service characteristics
N_REPORT.indication	Destination address (NSAP) QOS/service characteristics Reason code

QOS = Quality of service

address domain part, an area part, a subnet identifier part, and a system identifier
(ID) part. The length (number of digits) used for each part may differ from one
open system environment to another. However, once defined for an environment,
all systems (ES and IS) have the same NSAP format. The final SEL octet at the
end of each NSAP is used at the NS_user interface to allow multiple (up to 256)
transport entities within a single ES to be identified, for example, in ESs that
support multiple application layer entities.

As we shall see in Section 9.8.3, with large internets a single addressing
domain may be divided into a number of areas. Typically, the least significant two
octets of the **high-order domain specific part (HODSP)** are used to identify each
area/subnet within a domain. The remainder of the HODSP field is set to all zeros.
Alternatively, if there is a real need to interconnect domains – analogous to
autonomous systems within the Internet – the remainder of the HODSP field is
used for interdomain routing. In small open system environments an area may
relate to a single site, in which case each area address will identify, say, a single
site-wide LAN. However, with larger environments, the area address may itself be

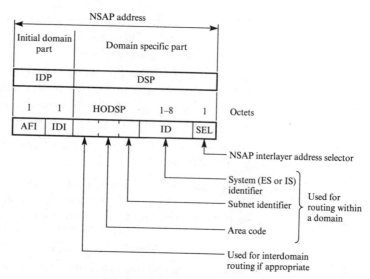

Figure 9.19
ISO CLNP NSAP
address structure.

HODSP = High order domain specific part

hierarchical to allow an area to contain multiple sites. In both cases, the ID field uniquely identifies an NS_user within that area/subnet hierarchy.

The user data parameter is an (NS_user) transport protocol data unit which can be up to 64 512 octets in length. Since the protocol provides only a best-try connectionless service, the NS_user (the transport protocol entity) normally performs additional end-to-end error control and is therefore unlikely to use such a large user data length because of the possibly long transit delays associated with retransmitted NSDUs. The transit delay is related to the QOS expected of the internet and can be used by the transport entity when selecting the length of the user data field to be adopted.

The QOS parameter is in fact a list of parameters that collectively express the service performance of the internet in relation to the specified destination (NSAP) address. The list includes the following:

- *Transit delay*   The mean time to transmit an NSDU successfully across the internet from the source NSAP to the specified destination NSAP. This is used by the local source transport protocol entity to determine the timeout interval for its retransmission protocol.

- *Cost determinants*   This optional field consists of a set of costs and options that allow an NS_user to influence the choice of route selected by the ISs for this NSDU.

- *Residual error probability*   This defines the number of lost, duplicated, or incorrectly delivered NSDUs as a percentage of the total number of NSDUs transmitted. This information influences the choice of maximum user data field selected by the source transport entity.

- *Priority* This optional parameter allows the NS_user to specify the relative priority of an NSDU in relation to others it transmits. For example, it might be used to send expedited data.

- *Source routing* This optional parameter consists of a set of subparameters that allow an NS_user to specify the route through the internet – a sequential list of ISs, in practice – to be followed by this NSDU. Normally, this is not known in a large internet and so the parameter is not present.

The list of internet characteristics associated with the N_FACILITY service include the following:

- *Congestion control* This specifies whether flow control will be exercised by the internet (NS_provider) at the NS_user interface. With a connectionless service, the local ISO CLNP returns an N_REPORT.indication primitive in response to an N_UNITDATA.request with the reason code set to NS_provider congestion.

- *Sequence preservation probability* This is the result of a measurement made by the local ISO CLNP indicating the ratio of sequence-preserved transmissions to total transmissions and is again used by the local transport entity in relation to its error and flow control functions.

- *Maximum NSDU lifetime* This indicates the maximum time the internet is allowed to take to deliver the NSDU before discarding it. This allows the transport protocol entity to quantify the maximum time it must wait for receipt of acknowledgment information before retransmitting an NSDU.

9.7.2 Used service

As indicated in Section 9.7.1, the internet protocol (SNICP) offers the same set of user service primitives to all NS_users irrespective of the service offered by the underlying subnet to which the ES is attached. In an internet comprising multiple subnet (network) types, these subnets can be connection-oriented or connectionless. Since the ISO CLNP is subnet independent, a choice must be made as to the service provided by each subnet. With the ISO CLNP, we assume that all subnets provide a connectionless service. Because this is the same as that offered at its own NS_user interface, the prefix SN instead of N is used to indicate the service assumed from each constituent subnet to transfer its protocol data units. Clearly, in some ESs a connectionless service is the same service as that provided by the underlying subnet, while in others it is different. To allow for this difference, the SNDCP is used to perform any necessary mapping operations. Two examples are given in Figure 9.20.

In part (a), we assume that the ES is attached to an X.25 packet switching subnet, so the actual subnet service is connection oriented. The interactions shown relate to those that occur at the source DTE–DCE interface. However, in part (b) we assume that the ES is attached to a LAN which provides a connectionless service. Typically, the interactions shown take place between the ISO CLNP in the ES and the ISO CLNP in an IS attached to the same LAN.

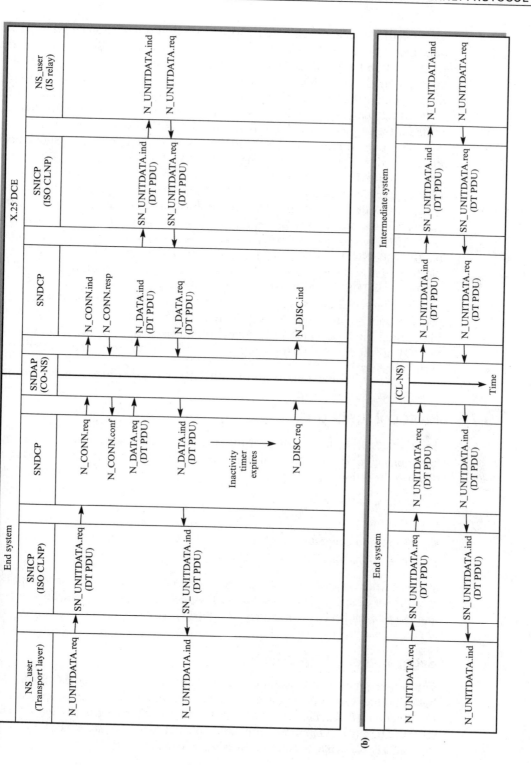

Figure 9.20   SNDCP function: (a) COSNDAP; (b) CLSNDAP.

On receipt of an N_UNITDATA.request primitive, the ISO CLNP creates a **data protocol data unit (data PDU)** using the parameters associated with the primitive. It initiates the sending of the PDU (to a peer IP) via the SNDCP using an SN_UNITDATA.request primitive with the PDU as the user data parameter. Since in Figure 9.20(a) the subnet is connection oriented, the SNDCP must set up a virtual call (circuit) using the N_CONNECT service before sending the PDU. It waits for the N_CONNECT.confirm primitive and then sends the PDU using an N_DATA.request primitive with the PDU as the user data parameter. Subsequent PDUs can then be sent directly using the N_DATA service.

Since the IP provides a connectionless user service, the question arises as to what triggers the clearing of this VC. In the absence of a specific disconnection request from the IP (SNICP), the SNDCP must itself initiate the clearing of the virtual call. To do this, the SNDCP has a timer – the **inactivity timer** – which is restarted every time a primitive is received relating to this virtual call from either the IP or the SNDAP (X.25 PLP). If the timer expires, the SNDCP assumes that the dialog associated with the call is finished and initiates the clearing of the call by issuing an N_DISCONNECT.request primitive.

In Figure 9.20(b), since the subnet is connectionless, the SNDCP needs to perform only a simple one-to-one mapping. It thus initiates the sending of the PDU using an N_UNITDATA.request primitive directly to the SNDAP with the PDU as the user data parameter. Transfers in the reverse direction are treated in the same way.

9.7.3 Protocol functions

The ISO CLNP includes a number of separate functions to carry out the various harmonizing operations identified in Section 9.2. These include functions to perform the following:

- Segmentation and reassembly
- Routing
- Flow and congestion control
- Error reporting

Various fields in each data PDU relate to each of the above functions. The structure of each data PDU is shown in Figure 9.21; we shall discuss the meaning and use of each field as the various functions are discussed.

Segmentation and reassembly

The segmentation and reassembly functions associated with the ISO CLNP are basically the same as the fragmentation and reassembly functions associated with the Internet IP. In fact the ISO CLNP supports both intranet and internet segmentation (fragmentation), although the latter is the default. When a PDU (or an NSDU) is segmented into a number of smaller PDUs – datagrams in IP

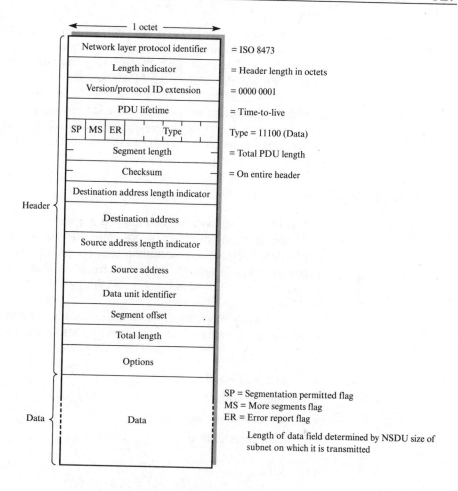

← 1 octet →

Network layer protocol identifier	= ISO 8473
Length indicator	= Header length in octets
Version/protocol ID extension	= 0000 0001
PDU lifetime	= Time-to-live
SP | MS | ER | Type	Type = 11100 (Data)
Segment length	= Total PDU length
Checksum	= On entire header
Destination address length indicator	
Destination address	
Source address length indicator	
Source address	
Data unit identifier	
Segment offset	
Total length	
Options	

SP = Segmentation permitted flag
MS = More segments flag
ER = Error report flag

Data

Length of data field determined by NSDU size of subnet on which it is transmitted

Figure 9.21
ISO CLNP – data PDU
structure.

terminology – the smaller PDUs are known as **derived PDUs** while the former is known as the **initial PDU**. Also, with the ISO CLNP the time-to-live field is known as the **PDU lifetime** and is in multiples of 500 milliseconds.

The fields in each data PDU (datagram) relating to the segmentation and reassembly functions are as follows:

- *Segment length* The number of octets (bytes) in the PDU including both header and data

- *Segment offset* The offset from the start of the first octet in the initial NSDU that the data in the segment begins

- *More segments flag* Set to 1 if this is not the last PDU relating to the initial PDU from which it was derived

- *Total length* Specifies the entire length of the initial NSDU

Derived PDUs are related to their initial NSDU by the source and destination NSAP addresses and an additional unique **data unit identifier (DUI)** that is assigned by the IP in the source ES when it is created. It is the same as the identification field in an IP datagram. A **segmentation permitted flag** is used to indicate to the IP in each IS whether or not further segmentation is permitted. This is used during the routing of PDUs since, if segmentation is not permitted (flag = 0), a route (subnet) must be selected that can support the current size of the PDU. In the event of a suitable route not being available, the PDU is discarded and an error report is generated with the reason code set to destination unreachable. Example 9.2 illustrates the use of each field.

Example 9.2

Assume two NS_users are communicating over the internet shown in Figure 9.10 and that the NSDU to be transferred is 1024 octets in length. Also, the SNDAPs associated with the three subnets are all connectionless with a maximum user data length of 512 octets for SN 1, 128 octets for SN 2, and 256 octets for SN 3. The header associated with each data PDU is fixed and is equal to 24 octets.

Assuming internet segmentation, derive the contents of the following fields in the header of each PDU as it is transferred across the three subnets:

- Total length
- Segment length
- Segment offset
- More segment flag
- Data unit identifier

(a)   *SN 1*
The user data field of SN 1 = 512 octets
Header = 24 octets and hence actual data = 488 octets
Therefore, there are three initial PDUs for SN 1: the first two with 488 data octets and the third with 48 octets of data.
The contents of the various fields for each PDU are thus:

Total length	1024	1024	1024
Segment length	512	512	72
Segment offset	0	488	976
More segments flag	1	1	0
Data unit identifier, say,	20	20	20

(b)   *SN 2*
The user data field of SN 2 = 128 octets
Header = 24 octets and hence actual data = 104 octets
Hence the first two initial PDUs from SN 1 each require five derived PDUs for SN 2. The third can be transmitted without change.
The contents of the various fields in each derived PDU are thus:

Total length:
   1024 1024 1024 1024 1024 | 1024 1024 1024 1024 1024 | 1024
Segment length:
   128   128   128   128   96 | 128   128   128   128   96 | 72
Segment offset:
     0   104   208   312   416 | 488   592   696   800   904 | 976
DUI:
    20   20   20   20   20 | 20   20   20   20   20 | 20

(c)   *SN 3*

The data field with SN 3 = 256 octets and hence, with internet segmentation, all the incoming PDUs are transmitted without change over SN 3.

At the receiving IP in the destination ES:

(i)   From the total length it can proceed to reassemble a 1024-octet NSDU.

(ii)   The DUI with the source and destination addresses is used to relate all derived PDUs to the initial NSDU.

(iii)   The segment offset relative to the NSDU total length can be used to reassemble all the segments in the correct sequence.

- -

Routing

Again, the basic routing operation associated with the ISO CLNP is similar to that used with the IP except that we use different terminology. To enable each ES and IS to build up the local routing information associated with a single subnet (network), a protocol known as the **end system-to-intermediate system (ES-to-IS)** is used. This is defined in ISO 9542 and performs a similar function to the ARP used with the IP. The protocol used for routing between ISs (gateways) is known as the **intermediate system-to-intermediate system (IS-to-IS)** protocol. It is defined in ISO 10589 and performs a similar function to the IGPs used with the IP. The ISO protocol which performs a similar function to the EGP used with the IP is defined in ISO 10747.

Since routing is the major function associated with an SNICP and the terminology used with the ISO CLNP is different, we shall describe the two routing protocols associated with the ISO CLNP in some detail. Two routing protocols and their associated routing information databases are shown in Figure 9.22(a) and (b).

As the ES-to-IS and IS-to-IS routing protocols are both part of the SNICP sublayer, their PDUs are exchanged between systems using the same SNDCP/SNDAP sublayers as are used by the ISO CLNP. The routing database in each ES – known as the **ES routing information base (ES-RIB)** – is maintained solely by the ES-to-IS protocol, whereas that in each IS – known as the **IS routing information base (IS-RIB)** – is maintained jointly by the ES-to-IS and IS-to-IS protocols.

Section 9.8 gives a more detailed description of both protocols. Basically, the PDUs relating to each protocol, containing the routing information, are created

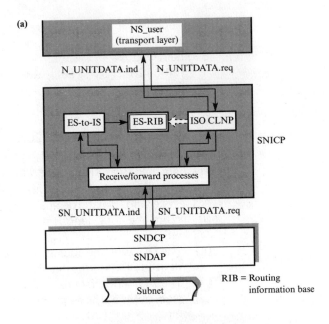

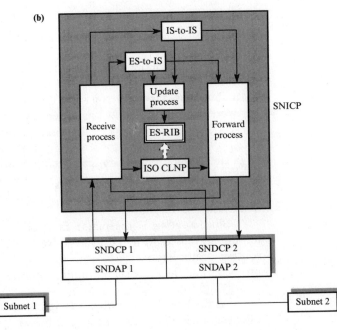

Figure 9.22
SNICP outline
structure: (a) ES;
(b) IS.

and exchanged periodically. Hence the information contained within each routing database is continuously being updated. At any point in time, the current contents of the two databases are used to route the data PDUs.

The scope of each protocol in relation to an example internet is shown in Figure 9.23(a); example entries in the two RIBs for this internet are shown in parts

(b) and (c). As we can see, each RIB comprises a number of tables. For ease of identification, the SNPA addresses show only the identity of the particular subnet to which they relate. In practice, they may be ISO 8802 MAC addresses, ITU-T X.121 addresses or even privately assigned addresses.

Remember that the NSAP address is hierarchical and comprises an internetwide subnet (plus area) identifier and a system identifier (ID) which uniquely identifies the NS_user/IS within the total internet. Also, that each IS has multiple SNPA addresses, one for each subnet to which it is attached, but a single ID. The latter is known as its **network entity title (NET)** in ISO terminology.

Initially, the ESs attached to a subnet do not know the SNPA addresses of their local ISs, that is, the ISs attached to the same subnet. Similarly, ISs do not

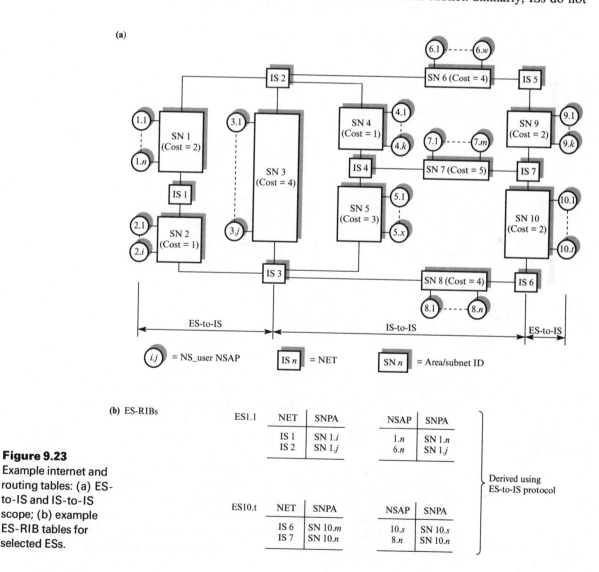

Figure 9.23
Example internet and routing tables: (a) ES-to-IS and IS-to-IS scope; (b) example ES-RIB tables for selected ESs.

(b) ES-RIBs

ES1.1

NET	SNPA	NSAP	SNPA
IS 1	SN 1.i	1.n	SN 1.n
IS 2	SN 1.j	6.n	SN 1.j

ES10.t

NET	SNPA	NSAP	SNPA
IS 6	SN 10.m	10.s	SN 10.s
IS 7	SN 10.n	8.n	SN 10.n

Derived using ES-to-IS protocol

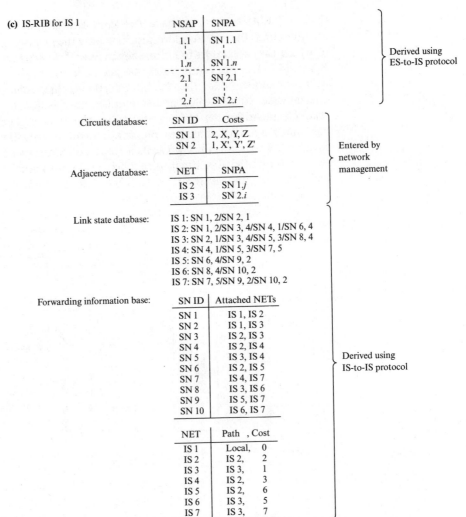

(c) IS-RIB for IS 1

NSAP	SNPA
1.1	SN 1.1
1.n	SN 1.n
2.1	SN 2.1
2.i	SN 2.i

Derived using ES-to-IS protocol

Circuits database:

SN ID	Costs
SN 1	2, X, Y, Z
SN 2	1, X', Y', Z'

Entered by network management

Adjacency database:

NET	SNPA
IS 2	SN 1.j
IS 3	SN 2.i

Link state database:

IS 1: SN 1, 2/SN 2, 1
IS 2: SN 1, 2/SN 3, 4/SN 4, 1/SN 6, 4
IS 3: SN 2, 1/SN 3, 4/SN 5, 3/SN 8, 4
IS 4: SN 4, 1/SN 5, 3/SN 7, 5
IS 5: SN 6, 4/SN 9, 2
IS 6: SN 8, 4/SN 10, 2
IS 7: SN 7, 5/SN 9, 2/SN 10, 2

Forwarding information base:

SN ID	Attached NETs
SN 1	IS 1, IS 2
SN 2	IS 1, IS 3
SN 3	IS 2, IS 3
SN 4	IS 2, IS 4
SN 5	IS 3, IS 4
SN 6	IS 2, IS 5
SN 7	IS 4, IS 7
SN 8	IS 3, IS 6
SN 9	IS 5, IS 7
SN 10	IS 6, IS 7

NET	Path , Cost
IS 1	Local, 0
IS 2	IS 2, 2
IS 3	IS 3, 1
IS 4	IS 2, 3
IS 5	IS 2, 6
IS 6	IS 3, 5
IS 7	IS 3, 7

Derived using IS-to-IS protocol

Figure 9.23 (cont.)
(c) Example IS-RIB tables for IS 1.

know the SNPA addresses of the ESs that are attached to its subnets. Thus, as part of the ES-to-IS protocol, each ES broadcasts its identity – NSAP/SNPA – over its local subnet, and each IS broadcasts its identity – NET/SNPA – over each of the subnets to which it is attached. Normally, ESs record only the NET/SNPA pairs of its local ISs while ISs record the NSAP/SNPA pairs of all the ESs attached to their subnets.

Hence the minimum routing information in each ES comprises a list of NET/SNPA pairs, one for each IS connected to the same subnet as the ES. These are shown in Figure 9.22(c) and are used by an ES to forward each PDU to an appropriate IS attached to the same subnet that will relay it to the necessary destination. On receipt of a PDU, the IS either forwards it to the destination ES directly if it is attached to one of its local subnets or to a **neighbor IS** if the PDU is to be routed to a remote subnet. Two ISs are said to be neighbors if they are both attached to the same subnet.

The list of subnets that are attached to an IS, together with their path costs, are entered by network management and kept in a table known as the **circuits database**. Another table known as the **adjacency database** is used to hold the NETs of the neighbors of an IS together with their SNPA addresses.

Concurrently with PDUs being exchanged as part of the ES-to-IS protocol, neighbor ISs exchange routing information with one another as part of the IS-to-IS protocol. This is contained within IS-to-IS PDUs known as **link state PDUs**. Each PDU contains a list of the subnets (links) that are currently attached (and hence are reachable) via the IS that sends the PDU, together with their corresponding path cost values (one for each metric being used). Thus, on receipt of a link state PDU, the IS-to-IS protocol first initiates entry/confirmation of the NET of the sending IS in its adjacency database and recording of the information contained within the PDU – using the **update process** – in another table known as the **link state database**. It then forwards a copy of the PDU to each of its neighbors except for the one that sent the PDU. In this way, all the ISs in the internet build up the same connectivity matrix (graph) of the internet with the ISs as nodes, the current direct links (subnets) that exist between them, and the costs associated with each link.

A new set of link state PDUs is initiated at regular intervals. After each new set has been received, each IS performs an algorithm, known as the **shortest-path first (SPF)**, on the updated connectivity matrix. Section 9.8.2 describes the actual operation of the SPF. Basically, it computes the shortest path between a specified source IS and all the other ISs – and hence subnets – in the internet. The output of the SPF is entered into one of two tables that are collectively known as the **forwarding information base (FIB)**. The other table is derived directly from the link state database and contains the list of ISs (NETs) that are attached to each subnet in the internet.

After both procedures have been carried out, the internet is ready to route data PDUs between any pair of NS_users (ESs). The ISO CLNP in the source ES simply sends each data PDU to one of its local ISs using the latter's SNPA address obtained from its RIB. The ISO CLNP in the receiving IS first determines the subnet identifier from the destination NSAP address in the PDU and then consults its FIB to determine to where it should be forwarded. If it is for an ES attached to one of its own subnets, the ISO CLNP sends it directly to that ES. If it is for an ES attached to a remote subnet, however, then it sends it to the neighbor IS (adjacency) which is on the shortest path to its intended destination. For example, for the internet in Figure 9.23(a), if the destination ES is attached to subnet 5 then it can be reached via either IS 3 or IS 4. The path costs to reach each of these from IS 1 are one and three units, respectively, hence IS 3 is chosen.

In addition, after forwarding the PDU, if it is addressed to an ES that is attached to the same subnet as the source ES, as part of the ES-to-IS protocol, the IS sends another PDU to the source ES containing the NSAP/SNPA pair of the destination ES. This informs the source ES of the SNPA of the destination ES just requested. The source ES can then (optionally) make an entry in its RIB to enable it to send future PDUs directly to the destination ES.

In the same way, the IS may inform the ES if a better IS connected to the same subnet – that is, one with a more direct path – should be used for routing PDUs to the destination NSAP contained within the earlier PDU. Thus the NSAP entries shown in the ES-RIBs in Figure 9.23(b) are intended to be arbitrary ESs that the NS_user in the ES has called.

We can see from this discussion that for large internets comprising many hundreds of subnets, each with a large number of attached ESs, the FIB in each IS will be very large. It is for this reason that large addressing domains are divided into a number of **areas**. Also, although only a single FIB is shown in Figure 9.23 for each IS, in practice there may be a number of FIBs, one for each routing metric. Again, we shall look at this in more detail in Section 9.8.

The interactions between the various sublayers during the forwarding process are shown in Figure 9.24. On receipt of an NS_user request, the IP in the source ES first creates a data PDU (DT PDU) using the parameters associated with the request. It then consults its RIB and initiates the sending of the PDU using the subnet request service with the SNPA address of the IS obtained from the RIB as the destination address parameter and the created PDU as user data. In Figure 9.24, we assume that both subnets are connectionless. Hence, on receipt of the network request, each SNDAP in turn creates a new NPDU with the DT PDU in the data field and the IS SNPA from the RIB in the destination address field. The SNDAP then forwards this in the normal way.

A similar procedure is followed in the IS. The PDU is first passed up through the sublayers of the subnet as user data to the IP. The IP consults the FIB – using the destination NSAP address from the PDU – to determine the SNPA address either of the ES, if it is attached to a local subnet, or of the IS attached to an adjacent subnet, if it is for a remote subnet. Assuming no segmentation is necessary, the PDU is then forwarded unchanged on the adjacent subnet using the SNDCP service with the address of the next IS obtained from the FIB as a parameter.

We have assumed that, for PDUs addressed to remote subnets, the RIB in each ES contained only the SNPA address of the first (local) IS involved in the route. However, in some instances the RIB may contain not just a single entry but rather the complete (or partial) list of IS identifiers (NETs) involved in a route. This information is obtained by the IP in a source ES by selecting the **record route** parameter in the PDU options field. When this is set, the IP in each IS that processes the PDU, in addition to routing the PDU, records the NET of the IS in the options field. In this way the route followed by the PDU is built up as it traverses the internet. This information can be stored in the RIB at the destination ES and subsequently used for forwarding PDUs in the reverse direction. A similar procedure is followed in the reverse direction. Thus, after the first exchange of PDUs, a route between the two ESs is known.

When using this feature, the IP in the ES receiving requests for an ES whose route is known, simply loads the complete list of IS identifiers into the options field and selects the **source routing** parameter code. Associated with this field is an offset

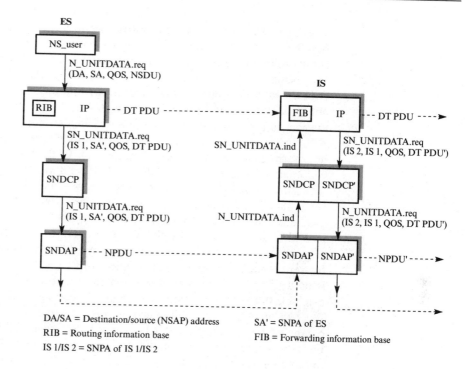

Figure 9.24
Sublayer interactions.

DA/SA = Destination/source (NSAP) address
RIB = Routing information base
IS 1/IS 2 = SNPA of IS 1/IS 2

SA' = SNPA of ES
FIB = Forwarding information base

which is incremented as the PDU is forwarded from one IS to the next. On receipt of a PDU for which the source routing parameter is selected, the IP simply accesses the identity of the next IS in the list, increments the offset, and then initiates the forwarding of the PDU to that IS.

The IS-to-IS protocol, as we shall see in Section 9.8.3, tries to maintain up-to-date entries in all routing tables so that they reflect current traffic distributions and IS failures. As a result, in the event of an IS failure, all recorded routes involving that IS will be only partially valid. If this is the case, then only the partial list will be loaded and the **partial source routing** parameter selected. After reaching the last entry in the list, the remaining part of the route is derived dynamically from the entries in the FIBs of the ISs involved.

In addition to being used for routing, the record route option can be used for network management functions. By analyzing routes followed by PDUs, a knowledge of the behavior of the internet can be obtained and potential problems/bottlenecks identified. Indeed, this is the principal function of the record route option as the normal dynamic routing method, in general, yields the optimum route to be followed by each PDU.

Flow and congestion control

Since the ISO CLNP is a connectionless protocol, flow control is not applied on a per call basis within the internet. It is left to the transport protocol entities in each ES to control the flow of data relating to each call on an end-to-end basis. As we shall see in Chapter 11, the flow control algorithm used with a connection-oriented (reliable) transport protocol is based on a modified sliding-window mechanism similar to that used with the X.25 packet layer protocol described in Chapter 8. As congestion within the internet starts to build up, the flow control information relating to calls that pass through the congested region(s) are delayed and consequently the transport entities slow down the entry of new NSDUs. The internet introduces an additional form of **implicit flow control** on affected calls. Although this helps to alleviate congestion within the internet, it does not necessarily stop new calls from being set up. In the limit, if the number of calls continues to build up, then the flow of PDUs relating to all calls will be affected.

As Section 9.2 indicated, congestion arises when the number of NSDUs (and hence data PDUs) entering the internet starts to approach the total resources available within the internet to handle them. Or, at a more local level, an individual IS becomes congested if the number of PDUs entering the IS starts to approach its total available resources. Since all subnets operate in a store-and-forward mode, the resources include the processing capacity within each IS which is used to process received PDUs and the number of memory buffers that are available to store PDUs waiting to be forwarded on a particular outgoing link.

Normally, ISs are designed to process received PDUs faster than the combined maximum rate at which they can arrive. Thus only a single input buffer is required for each input link. However, since two or more PDUs received on different input links may need to be forwarded on the same output link after processing, a separate (output) queue is needed for each output link. As the internet load increases and the rate of arrival of PDUs increases, so the size of the output queues will build up and increasing delays will be experienced in each IS. This signals the start of congestion and, in the limit, if all the buffers become full, the available resources are exceeded. The IS is said to be overloaded and delays experienced by PDUs will increase rapidly. The effect of congestion on the performance of an internet (or an IS) is shown in Figure 9.25.

Part (a) shows that although in the ideal case the maximum mean throughput rate of PDUs is maintained when overload occurs, without a congestion control algorithm this does not necessarily happen in practice. This is so because the segmentation and reassembly function carried out within the internet can cause a phenomenon known as **deadlock**. A congestion control scheme must be incorporated in each IS to avoid deadlock. However, as such schemes are not perfect, the actual throughput is less than that in the ideal case. The difference between the two is a measure of the efficiency of the congestion control scheme. The effect of congestion and overload on the mean transit delay experienced by PDUs is shown in Figure 9.25(b). This is directly related to the mean throughput graph.

The feature incorporated into the protocol to help control congestion on an internetwide basis is for the IP in the source ES to monitor the performance of the internet and, if congestion is suspected, to start to reject new N_UNITDATA.requests. This is done by the IP in the source ES returning an N_REPORT.indication to the source NS_user with the reason code set to internet congestion. The IP in ESs monitor the performance of the internet by

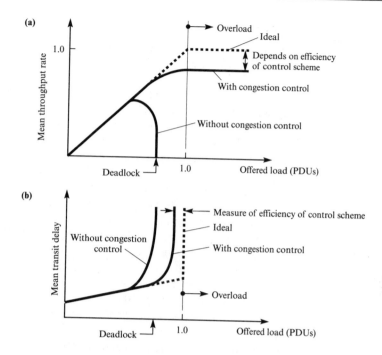

Figure 9.25
Effect of congestion
on: (a) throughput;
(b) transit delay.

maintaining counts of selected parameters in internet-generated **error report PDUs**. If the number of such PDUs received with internet congestion as the reason code is above a defined threshold, the IP starts to reject new requests. This is similar to using flow control at the DTE–DCE interface in an X.25 packet switching network.

Another feature in the protocol that helps to alleviate (rather than control) congestion on an internetwide basis is the inclusion of the PDU lifetime field in each initial and derived PDU. As indicated in Section 9.5.4, this is first set by the IP in the source ES and then decremented by each IP that processes the PDU. If it reaches zero at any point during its transit across the internet, it is discarded. Hence, in the event of one or more ISs becoming congested, the PDU lifetime associated with affected PDUs will expire on processing and these PDUs will be discarded. This means that as long as the timeout interval used by transport entities in ESs exceeds twice the PDU lifetime value – to allow related acknowledgment information to be returned – unnecessary duplicate copies of NSDUs should not be sent. The inclusion of the PDU lifetime field thus provides a form of **implicit congestion control** by preventing multiple copies of PDUs from being sent by ESs into the internet.

Although such schemes endeavor to control congestion on an internetwide basis, uneven traffic distributions mean that they do not necessarily stop individual ISs from becoming overloaded. Additional procedures must be incorporated into the basic operation of each IS to minimize this possibility.

Before we describe the types of congestion that can occur within an IS, let us consider the distribution and use of the memory buffers associated with the

SNICP sublayer. A typical layout is shown in Figure 9.26(a). In this example we assume that 12 buffers are available and that intranet segmentation is being used. Thus all (derived) PDUs received must be reassembled before they can be processed.

At any point in time, the 12 buffers are distributed between input buffers (one per subnet), reassembly buffers, and output queues. In practice, once a PDU has been received and stored in a (memory) buffer, all references to the PDU are made relative to the start address of the buffer, which is known as the **buffer pointer**. When buffers (PDUs) are being transferred from one place to another, it is the buffer pointers that are transferred and not the buffer contents.

On receipt of a (derived) PDU in an input buffer (from the SNDCP), the receive process transfers it to the appropriate reassembly buffer, obtains a new buffer from the free buffer pool, and transfers the new buffer to the input buffer ready for receipt of the next PDU. If the received PDU completes an initial PDU, this is transferred by the receive process to the ISO CLNP for processing.

In Figure 9.26, we assume that the packet sizes associated with the three subnets are the same. Thus the ISO CLNP simply changes the appropriate fields in each derived PDU and passes these to the forward process for forwarding. The forward process reads the destination NSAP address from each PDU, consults the FIB for the output link (subnet) to be used, and transfers the buffer to the tail of the appropriate output queue. The SNDCP associated with this output queue initiates the sending of the PDU and the freed buffer is returned to the free buffer pool by the forward process.

We can deduce the most basic cause of congestion by considering the buffer distribution shown in Figure 9.26(b). We assume that the three subnet inputs are operating near their maximum capacity and that all received PDUs from these links, after reassembly, require to be forwarded on the same output link. If the three links operate at the same rate, the output queue associated with link (subnet) 1 will start to build up, thereby increasing the transit delays experienced by PDUs using that link. If this condition continues, in the limit all the buffers will become full and queued for output link 1. Any new PDUs will then be discarded as there are no free buffers to store them, even though they may require a different output link.

Note that increasing the number of buffers does not necessarily ease the problem since this may simply allow a single output queue to become even longer. Therefore, the increased delays experienced by PDUs waiting to be forwarded in those queues are likely to cause the timers being used by the transport protocol entities in ESs to expire. These will start to retransmit the affected NSDUs – and hence PDUs – which, in turn, will simply increase the load on the affected links.

We can observe a more subtle type of congestion by considering the buffer distribution shown in Figure 9.26(c). We assume that intranet segmentation is being used and hence all received (derived) PDUs must be reassembled before being forwarded. If we assume that 12 memory buffers are available and that each initial PDU comprises 3 derived PDUs, then none of the 6 initial PDUs being reassembled is complete and can be forwarded. However, the absence of any further memory buffers means that no new PDUs can be received to complete

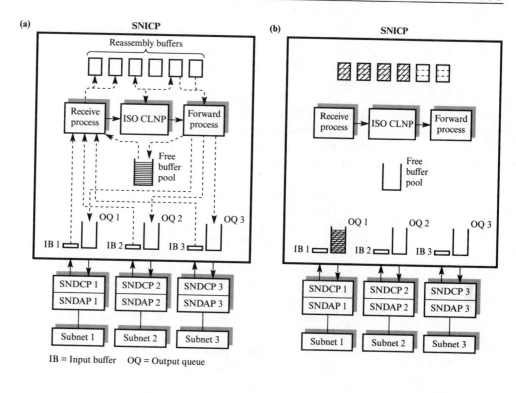

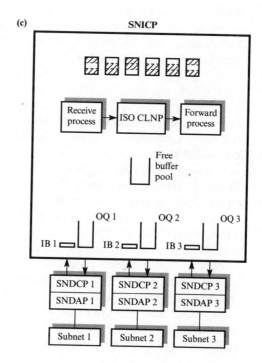

Figure 9.26
Congestion
possibilities: (a) buffer
usage; (b) direct
store-and-forward
deadlock;
(c) reassembly
deadlock.

any of them. Deadlock is said to have occurred since the flow of all PDUs through the IS will come to a halt. This type of congestion is known as **reassembly deadlock** or **reassembly lockup**. A similar condition can arise at an ES with internet segmentation.

Congestion of the type shown in Figure 9.26(b) can be controlled by limiting the number of PDUs that are allowed to be queued for a single output link. Allowing all the buffers to be queued for a single link causes PDUs using that link to experience unacceptable delays and affects the flow of PDUs on all other links since no free buffers are available to receive them. To avoid this happening, a limit is set on the number of buffers that can be queued on each output link. Normally, the limit is set so that a free buffer is always available for each input link in addition to a minimum number of buffers available for each of the other output links. Firstly, this ensures a flow of PDUs on all links in the presence of congestion. Secondly, it sets a maximum limit on the delays experienced within each IS. The latter can be particularly helpful when determining the value to be assigned to the PDU lifetime value carried in each PDU. This is important with large internets comprising many subnets.

In practice, determining the optimum number of buffers to be queued for a single output link – as a percentage of the total number of buffers available – is a complex problem and depends on the number of output links and the routing scheme being used. Also, the optimum value is not static since it varies with the loading of the IS, thus implying some form of dynamic allocation.

Although many schemes have been researched, the scheme that has been shown to give a good (not optimum) level of performance in a large internet – ARPANET – is based on an empirical formula that defines the maximum number of buffers per link as a function of the number of links and the number of free buffers being used. The **square root limiter** is the scheme that is currently proposed for use with the ISO CLNP. The formula is as follows:

$$U_{\mathrm{d}} = \frac{N_{\mathrm{b}}}{\sqrt{N_{\mathrm{c}}}}$$

where U_{d} is the maximum buffer limit in a link output queue; N_{b} is the number of free buffers available (excluding input buffers); and N_{c} is the number of (active) output links.

In addition, a minimum number of buffers is dedicated to each output link to ensure that flow is not stopped on these links when one (or more) other links are overloaded. An example is shown in Figure 9.27(a).

We assume that internet segmentation is being used so no reassembly of PDUs is required, and that the three subnets all use the same maximum packet size. We also assume that there are 12 free buffers available plus an additional 3 buffers for use with the input links. The maximum number of entries in each output queue is thus $6(12/\sqrt{3})$. Hence sufficient buffers are available to ensure that there is a single buffer for each input link and a minimum of two buffers for each output link. Thus if a new PDU is received for forwarding on link 3, it is discarded and the freed buffer is returned to the buffer pool. However, if a new PDU is received for forwarding on either link 1 or link 2, then it can be forwarded

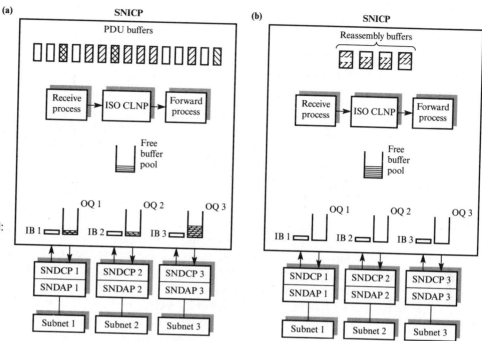

Figure 9.27
Congestion control:
(a) square root
limiting (internet
segmentation);
(b) reassembly
deadlock control
(intranet
segmentation).

as it is unaffected by the overload on link 3. Similarly, if the situation arises in which, say, OQ 2 and OQ 3 contain four and six entries, respectively, and a PDU is to be forwarded on either of these links, then it is discarded to ensure that at least two buffers are available for OQ 1.

If intranet segmentation is being used, the allocation of buffers for reassembly purposes must be controlled to prevent reassembly deadlock. One scheme is to set a limit on the number of initial PDUs that can be in the process of reassembly at any point in time and, when this limit is reached, to discard any derived PDUs that are received relating to new PDUs. In this way, since the maximum size of PDUs being used with each subnet connected to the IS is known, the IS can ensure that it always has enough free buffers available to complete the reassembly processing.

An example is shown in Figure 9.27(b). Again, we assume intranet segmentation and that each initial PDU comprises three derived PDUs. By setting a limit of 4 initial PDUs being reassembled at any point in time, no reassembly deadlock will occur with 12 buffers with 3 additional buffers for the input buffers.

Note that these congestion control schemes are not part of the protocol as such, but rather are examples of **buffer management**. There is a number of variations of these basic schemes. However, the aim is to ensure that a flow of PDUs is maintained even in the presence of temporary overload conditions.

In conclusion, discarding PDUs is not an ideal solution since it inevitably leads to an increase in the transit delay associated with the internet. However, it is necessary if we are to control congestion and deadlock. The subject of congestion control in large internets, together with the allied subject of routing, are still active areas of research.

Error reporting

As Figure 9.21 showed, each data PDU contains an error report (ER) flag in its header. This flag enables the IP in a source ES to request that it is informed if another IP, either in an IS or in the destination ES, discards the PDU during its transit across the internet. Then, if the flag is set and the PDU is discarded by an IS, the IP in the IS generates an **error report PDU** with a reason code indicating why the PDU was discarded, the identity of the PDU, and where in the internet the error was detected. The IP in the IS then replaces the destination (NSAP) address with the source address from the data PDU and initiates the return of the PDU to the source IP in the normal way.

The IP in each ES is able to build up knowledge of the performance of the internet by maintaining counts of the various reason codes during a particular monitoring period. The use of a flag means that such PDUs are generated only when an ES wishes to update its knowledge of the internet performance.

A PDU may be discarded for a number of reasons, including the following:

- IS congestion
- PDU lifetime expired
- Destination address unreachable

By maintaining counts of the error report PDUs received with either a reason code of IS congestion or PDU lifetime expired, the IP in a source ES can detect the onset of congestion and, if necessary, start to reject new NS_user service requests. Similarly, counts of the reason codes PDU lifetime expired and destination address unreachable can help to determine the efficiency of the routing protocol being used.

Finally, the checksum field in the header of each data (and error report) PDU is included to minimize the probability of processing a PDU with erroneous fields. The checksum is normally software generated and comprises two octets. The algorithm used is the same as that for transport protocol data units; we shall describe these in Chapter 11. The checksum is verified each time fields in the PDU are processed and before processing takes place. If the fields in the PDU are changed by the processing, then a new checksum for the PDU is computed. If a checksum error is detected with the ER flag set, an error report PDU is generated with a reason code set to checksum error.

9.8 ISO routing protocols

An outline structure of the SNICP sublayer showing the two ISO routing protocols in each ES and IS and their relationship with the ISO CLNP was shown in Figure 9.22. The routing information contained within the ES-RIB in each ES and the IS-RIB in each IS is created from the routing information exchanged as part of the ES-to-IS and IS-to-IS protocols. The PDUs relating to both protocols are periodically created and exchanged. Consequently, the information contained within each database is continuously being updated and thus reflects the current active topology of the internet. However, at any instant, the current contents of the two databases are used to route a data PDU to the next IS involved in the route to the destination NSAP address contained within it. As we discussed the routing procedure in Section 9.7.3, here we shall concern ourselves only with how this information is built up using the two routing protocols.

9.8.1 ES-to-IS protocol

Recall that a PDU relating to the ISO CLNP cannot be routed directly by inspecting the destination NSAP address contained within it. Normally, all routing information is held at ISs. To send a PDU, a source ES must first send it to one of the ISs attached to the same subnet. To do this, all the ESs on each subnet must know the SNPA addresses of their local ISs. Also, for an IS to be able to route PDUs received from other subnets, it must know the NSAP/SNPA address pairs of all the ESs attached to its local subnets. This is the basic role of the ES-to-IS protocol.

The ES-to-IS protocol in each ES and IS broadcasts its identity over its local subnet(s). It is intended for use with broadcast subnetworks such as LANs since the overheads of a system broadcasting to all other systems are low. To carry out the same function with a general (mesh) topology subnet involves prohibitively high overheads, especially if a large number of ESs are involved. With such subnets, the equivalent routing information must be loaded into each system (ES and IS) by other means, such as by network management.

There are three PDU types associated with the ES-to-IS protocol, namely:

- *End system hello (ESH)*   This is used by an ES to inform all ISs on the subnet of the NS_user NSAP(s) in that ES.

- *Intermediate system hello (ISH)*   This is used by an IS to inform all ESs on each of its subnets of its NET.

- *Redirect (RD)*   This is used by an IS to inform an ES of the SNPA address on its own subnet of either the destination NSAP just requested or the NET of another (better) IS to route PDUs to that NSAP.

Each of the PDUs comprises a common header part, an address part, and an options part. The general structure of each PDU type is shown in Figure 9.28. All the fields in the header part have the same meaning as those used with ISO CLNP data (and error) PDUs except that the **holding time** field replaces the segment length. Since no data is associated with these PDUs, the segment length is not required. The holding time is used to specify the maximum time for which the receiving protocol entity should retain the address (routing) information contained within the PDU. To ensure that address information relating to each ES

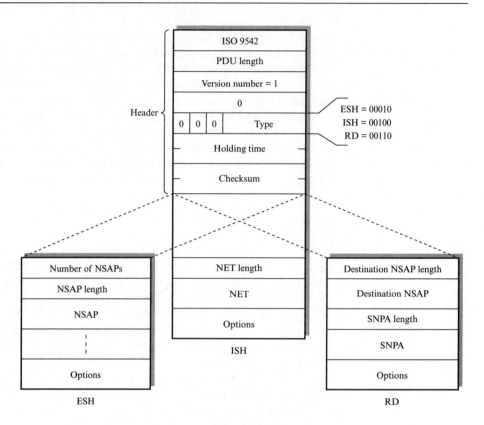

Figure 9.28
ES-to-IS PDU
structure.

and IS is kept up to date, new information is exchanged at regular intervals by each system. Thus the holding time essentially ages the current address information and, if an ES is switched off, its routing entry will automatically be removed from the RIB in each IS until it is switched on again and makes a new network request.

The address part of each PDU contains the NSAP/NET, and/or SNPA addresses, depending on the particular PDU type. Finally, the contents of the options part are similar to those used with the ISO CLNP.

Two broadcast (group) addresses are associated with the protocol for broadcasting PDUs: the **All ES** and the **All IS**. For an ES to inform its local ISs of its presence on the subnet (and its SNPA address), it creates an ESH PDU containing the NSAP address(s) currently present in this ES and issues an SN_UNITDATA.request primitive to its SNDCP with the PDU as user data and the All IS as the destination address.

The broadcast address used on a particular subnet to reach all ISs may vary for different subnets, with any translation being carried out by the SNDCP. When the local SNDAP broadcasts the PDU, it includes the SNPA of the ES as the source address in the particular subnet NPDU. On receipt of the NPDU, the peer SNDAP in the IS passes the SNPA up as a parameter (with the ESH PDU) to the

ES-to-IS protocol. The latter then makes an entry – NSAP/SNPA – in its RIB which is retained until the specified holding time expires.

Similarly, in order for the ESs attached to a subnet to learn the SNPA addresses of their local ISs, each IS broadcasts an ISH PDU at regular intervals with its NET in the address field. The corresponding SNPA is again received as a parameter with the PDU by all active ESs. The ES-to-IS protocol in the latter then makes an entry – NET/SNPA – in their RIBs.

Finally, the RD PDU is used by an IS to inform an ES attached to one of its local subnets of the SNPA address either of another local NS_user NSAP or of a better IS which can be used to reach the destination NSAP specified in an earlier data PDU. Recall that this information – NSAP/SNPA – may be (optionally) retained in its RIB to speed up the routing process.

9.8.2 Routing algorithm

Before we discuss the operation of the IS-to-IS protocol, let us describe the routing algorithm – known as the **shortest-path first algorithm** – used by ISs to route PDUs across the internet. There are a number of such algorithms but the one used by ISO is the **Dijkstra algorithm**. This is already used in a number of large networks, including ARPANET.

Since all routing is carried out by ISs, for routing purposes an internet is considered simply as a distributed community of ISs that are interconnected by (logical) links. In practice, the links may be a path through a LAN or WAN or a direct point-to-point link. Associated with each link are a number of routing metrics each of which has a cost value associated with it. These are:

- *Capacity* A measure of the throughput of the circuit in bits per second, a higher value indicating a lower capacity. This is the default metric that is used in practice.

- *Delay* This relates to the mean transit delay associated with a link (subnet) and thus includes the queuing delays in bridges and exchanges. Again, a higher value indicates a longer transit delay.

- *Expense* A measure of the monetary cost of using a link, a high value indicating a larger monetary cost. Clearly, if a private subnet can be used, then this is preferable to using, say, a link through a switched public-carrier subnet.

- *Error* A measure of the mean residual error probability associated with the circuit, higher values indicating a larger probability of undetected errors.

Recall that all the above relate to parameters of the QOS which is therefore used when selecting the routing metric.

The term 'path cost' is used to indicate the aggregate total cost of the links used in a particular path (route) through the internet between any pair of ESs. The path cost associated with a route may thus differ from one metric to another.

The term 'shortest-path cost' therefore refers to a path (route) using a single routing metric.

We can best describe the shortest-path first algorithm by considering a specific internet, such as the one shown in Figure 9.23 which was used to describe the ISO CLNP routing procedure. A simplified representation of this is shown in Figure 9.29(a).

The links between each IS are shown as point-to-point circuits each with an associated cost value which may vary for different metrics. For each metric, the task is to find the path (route) through the internet from a signal source IS to each of the other ISs in the internet that has the minimum aggregate cost associated with it. The various steps in the algorithm are shown in parts (b) through (h) of Figure 9.29. We assume that IS 1 is the source.

Associated with each of the other ISs is a measure (shown in parentheses) of the aggregate distance from that IS back to the source IS via the IS indicated. Thus an entry of (2, IS 4) means that the cost of the path back to IS 1 is 2 units via IS 4. Initially, the path costs to all ISs not directly connected to the source are unknown and are therefore marked with an infinite path cost figure, that is, the largest possible cost. Also, until a cost value is known to be the minimum cost, it is **tentative** and the IS box is shown unshaded. When the shortest-path cost from an IS to the source is known, it is **permanent** and the IS box is shaded.

Initially, since IS 1 is the source it is shown shaded. The path costs to the two directly-connected (neighbor) ISs – IS 2 and IS 3 – are shown equal to their respective link path costs. Thus IS 2 has an entry (2, IS 1), indicating the cost is 2 units to get back to IS 1 directly, while IS 3 has an entry of (1, IS 1). All the other costs remain at their maximum value. The IS with the minimum cost value is chosen from *all* the ISs that are still tentative. Clearly, the minimum cost value is for IS 3 with a cost of 1. This is now marked as permanent and the new set of aggregate path cost values from IS 3 is computed. These are shown in part (c).

For example, the entry for IS 4 of (4, IS 3) indicates that the aggregate path cost back to the source via IS 3 is 4 units – 3 to get back to IS 3 and a further 1 to return to IS 1. In the case of IS 2, since the path cost via IS 3 would be 5 units – 4 plus 1 – the existing smaller tentative value is left unchanged. The IS with the minimum cost value is again chosen from all those that remain tentative; this is IS 2 with a cost value of 2. This is marked permanent and the new path costs computed from this IS, as shown in part (d).

As we can see, the new path cost for IS 4 via IS 2 is only 3 units, so the existing entry is replaced by (3, IS 2). Once all the other distances have been computed, the minimum is again chosen – IS 4 – and the procedure is repeated. The remaining steps are thus as shown in parts (e) through (h).

Finally, with the minimum path cost value from IS 1 to all other ISs determined, that is, they are all now permanent, the shortest (minimum) path cost routes from IS 1 to each of the other ISs can be determined. These are shown in part (i). Thus to get to, say, IS 5 from IS 1, the route is IS 1 → IS 2 → IS 5.

Now consider the same procedure applied first with IS 2 as the source and then with IS 3. The final path cost values associated with each IS together with

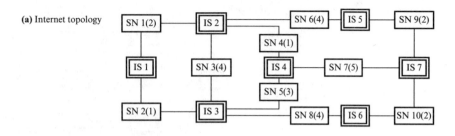

(a) Internet topology

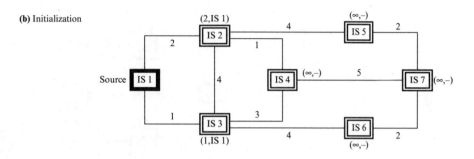

(b) Initialization

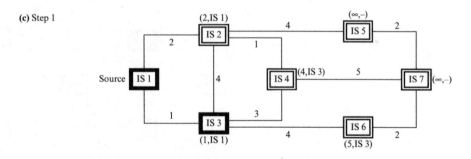

(c) Step 1

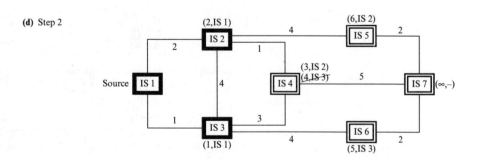

(d) Step 2

Figure 9.29
Shortest path cost
route calculations.

(e) Step 3

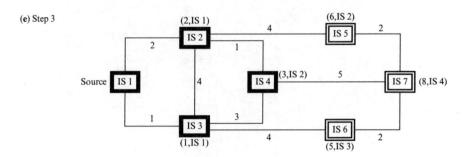

(f) Step 4

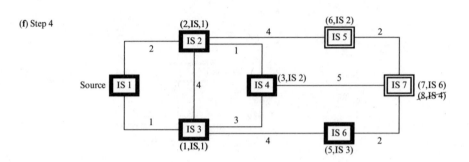

(g) Step 5

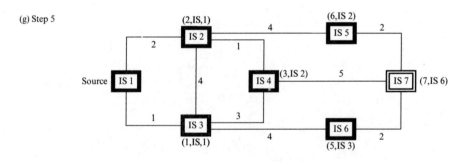

(h) Final path costs from IS 1

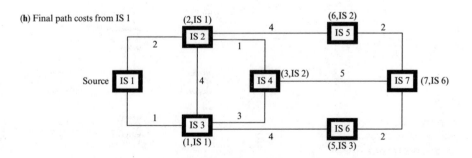

Figure 9.29 (cont.)
Shortest path cost
route calculations.

(i) Shortest path cost routes from IS 1

IS 1━━━▶Source (Cost = 0)
IS 1━━━▶IS 2 (Cost = 2)
IS 1━━━▶IS 3 (Cost = 1)
IS 1━━━▶IS 2━━━▶IS 4 (Cost = 3)
IS 1━━━▶IS 2━━━▶IS 5 (Cost = 6)
IS 1━━━▶IS 3━━━▶IS 6 (Cost = 5)
IS 1━━━▶IS 3━━━▶IS 6━━━▶IS 7 (Cost = 7)

(j) Path cost calculations from IS 2

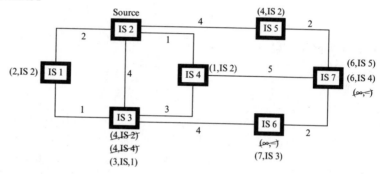

(k) Shortest path cost routes from IS 2

IS 2━━━▶IS 1(Cost = 2)
IS 2━━━▶Source (Cost = 0)
IS 2━━━▶IS 1━━━▶IS 3(Cost = 3)
IS 2━━━▶IS 4(Cost = 1)
IS 2━━━▶IS 5(Cost = 4)
IS 2━━━▶IS 1━━━▶IS 3━━━▶IS 6(Cost = 7)
IS 2━━┳━▶IS 4━━━▶IS 7(Cost = 6)
      ┗━▶IS 5━━━▶IS 7(Cost = 6)

(l) Path cost calculations from IS 3

Figure 9.29 (cont.)
Shortest path cost
route calculations.

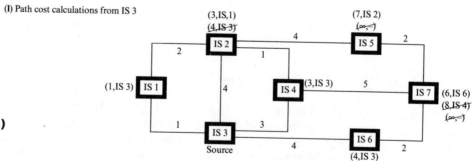

(m) Shortest path cost routes from IS 3

IS 3 ────► IS 1 (Cost = 1)
IS 3 ────► IS 1 ────► IS 2 (Cost = 3)
IS 3 ────► Source (Cost = 0)
IS 3 ────► IS 4 (Cost = 3)
IS 3 ────► IS 1 ────► IS 2 ────► IS 5 (Cost = 7)
IS 3 ────► IS 6 (Cost = 4)
IS 3 ────► IS 6 ────► IS 7 (Cost = 6)

(n) Routing table examples

IS 1:

Destination	Path	Cost
IS 1	–	–
IS 2	IS 2	2
IS 3	IS 3	1
IS 4	IS 2	3
IS 5	IS 2	6
IS 6	IS 3	5
IS 7	IS 3	7

IS 2:

Destination	Path	Cost
IS 1	IS 1	2
IS 2	–	–
IS 3	IS 1	3
IS 4	IS 4	1
IS 5	IS 5	4
IS 6	IS 1	7
IS 7	IS 4/IS 5	6

IS 3:

Destination	Path	Cost
IS 1	IS 1	1
IS 2	IS 1	3
IS 3	–	–
IS 4	IS 4	3
IS 5	IS 1	7
IS 6	IS 6	4
IS 7	IS 6	6

Figure 9.29 (cont.)
Shortest path cost
route calculations.

their corresponding shortest path cost routes are shown in parts (j) through (m). We can make some observations about the algorithm:

- If two ISs have the same computed path cost, then an arbitrary selection can be made as to which is made permanent.

- If a new computed path cost for a tentative IS via a different route (IS) is the same as that already shown, both can be retained since load sharing then becomes possible.

- If an IS is on the shortest path cost route from IS 1 to another destination IS, then it is also the shortest path from that IS to the same destination. For example, the shortest route from IS 1 to IS 7 is IS 1 → IS 3 → IS 6 → IS 7 and the route from IS 3 is IS 3 → IS 6 → IS 7.

- The computed shortest path cost routes are reversible, for example, IS 2 → IS 1 → IS 3 and IS 3 → IS 1 → IS 2.

The combined effect of this is that if each IS computes its own set of shortest paths from itself to all other ISs, then the paths computed for each IS will coincide. This means that an IS may retain only routing information to allow it to route a PDU to the first (neighbor) IS on the route, that is, routing can be carried out on a **hop-by-hop** basis. The routing tables for IS 1, IS 2, and IS 3 are thus as shown in Figure 9.29(n).

9.8.3 IS-to-IS protocol

The aim of the IS-to-IS protocol is to determine the contents of the RIB in each IS, that is, the neighbor ISs (adjacencies) to be used when routing ISO CLNP data PDUs. However, before the route finding algorithm can be started, each IS must first establish the NET/SNPA pair of each of its neighbors.

With broadcast subnets, each IS broadcasts an **IS-to-IS (II) PDU** on each of its subnets using the All IS destination address. This contains the NET of the source IS within it and each receiving SNDAP passes the corresponding SNPA address (on this subnet) up to the IS-to-IS protocol as a parameter using the intermediate SNDCP. For nonbroadcast subnets, the IS-to-IS PDU must again be entered by network management. In either event, this information is stored in a separate database known as the **adjacency database**. Once this has been carried out, the IS-to-IS protocol can take part in the shortest-path cost derivation procedure.

Recall that the identities of the subnets that are attached to an IS, together with their cost metrics, are entered into a table (known as the circuit database) by network management. Therefore, at regular intervals each IS (in practice, the IS-to-IS protocol) sends to each of its neighbors a **link state (LS) PDU** containing the NET of the IS, and a list of the identifiers of the subnets to which the IS is attached together with the cost values (one for each metric) associated with each subnet. In this way, an IS receives an LS PDU from each of its neighbors informing it of the subnets (links) that are attached to it and their cost values. This information is stored in the **link state database** by the update process in the SNICP.

When it has done this, the update process in each IS sends a copy of the LS PDU to each of its neighbors (except the one that sent the PDU). As a result, each IS receives a further set of LS PDUs which have effectively originated from its neighbors' neighbors. This procedure continues. Therefore, over a period of time each IS receives a complete set of LS PDUs containing the identities of the subnets – and their path cost values (one for each metric) – which are attached to all other ISs in the internet. This type of routing procedure is known as **flooding**.

Whenever a new set of LS PDUs is entered into the link state database, **decision process** is run. Its role is firstly to perform the SPF algorithm on the link state database, and secondly to determine, from all the entries in the various databases, which neighbor IS should be used to reach each of the other ISs based on their corresponding path cost values. This is done for each routing metric in turn. A separate forwarding information base is created for each metric.

To illustrate this procedure, consider its application to the example subnet shown in Figure 9.29. This is repeated in Figure 9.30(a), again using a single routing metric for illustrative purposes. The initialized adjacency and circuit databases are shown in part (b) and the first set of LS PDUs that are received by each IS is shown in part (c). For example, IS 1 receives two LS PDUs, one from IS 2 and the other from IS 3. Similarly, IS 2 receives four LS PDUs, one each from IS 1, 3, 4, and 5.

As we just described, on receipt of each of these PDUs, each IS generates another set of LS PDUs, and passes them on to each of its neighbors. This procedure then repeats. The first, second, and third sets of LS PDUs that are received by IS 1 are as shown in Figure 9.30(d).

Finally, part (e) shows the output of the decision process for IS 1. This RIB is computed by the decision process performing the SPF algorithm on the contents of the link state database to determine the shortest (minimum) path cost to each destination IS. As we can see, the contents of the RIB are the same as those shown

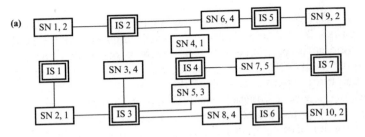

(a)

(b) Adjacency database for IS 1:

NET	SNPA
IS 2	SN 1,j
IS 3	SN 2.i

Circuit database for IS 1:

SN ID	Costs
SN 1	2, X, Y, Z
SN 2	1, X', Y', Z'

(c)

IS 1

from IS 2(1) − IS 2 : SN 1, 2/SN 3, 4/SN 4, 1/SN 6, 4
IS 3(1) − IS 3 : SN 2, 1/SN 3, 4/SN 5, 3/SN 8, 4

IS 2

from IS 1(1) − IS 1 : SN 1, 2/SN 2, 1
IS 3(1) − IS 3 : SN 2, 1/SN 3, 4/SN 5, 3/SN 8, 4
IS 4(1) − IS 4 : SN 4, 1/SN 5, 3/SN 7, 5
IS 5(1) − IS 5 : SN 6, 4/SN 9, 2

IS 7

from IS 4(1) − IS 4 : SN 4, 1/SN 5, 3/SN 7, 5
IS 5(1) − IS 5 : SN 6, 4/SN 9, 2
IS 6(1) − IS 6 : SN 8, 4/SN 10, 2

(d)

Circuit database: IS 1 : SN 1, 2/SN 2, 1

IS 1

Set (1) { IS 2(1) − IS 2 : SN 1, 2/SN 3, 4/SN 4, 1/SN 6, 4
IS 3(1) − IS 3 : SN 2, 1/SN 3, 4/SN 5, 3/SN 8, 4 ⇒

Set (2) { IS 2(2) − IS 3 : SN 2, 1/SN 3, 4/SN 5, 3/SN 8, 4
IS 4 : SN 4, 1/SN 5, 3/SN 7, 5
IS 5 : SN 6, 4/SN 9, 2
IS 3(2) − IS 2 : SN 1, 2/SN 3, 4/SN 4, 1/SN 6, 4
IS 4 : SN 4, 1/SN 5, 3/SN 7, 5
IS 6 : SN 8, 4/SN 10, 2   ⇒

Set (3) { IS 2(3) − IS 3 : SN 2, 1/SN 3, 4/SN 5, 3/SN 8, 4
IS 4 : SN 4, 1/SN 5, 3/SN 7, 5
IS 5 : SN 6, 4/SN 9, 2
IS 6 : SN 8, 4/SN 10, 2
IS 7 : SN 7, 5/SN 9, 2/SN 10, 2
IS 3(3) − IS 2 : SN 1, 2/SN 3, 4/SN 4, 1/SN 6, 4
IS 4 : SN 4, 1/SN 5, 3/SN 7, 5
IS 5 : SN 6, 4/SN 9, 2
IS 6 : SN 8, 4/SN 10, 2
IS 7 : SN 7, 5/SN 9, 2/SN 10, 2   ⇒

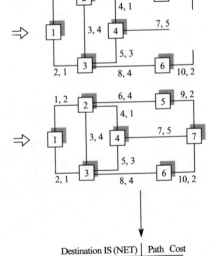

(e)

SN ID	Attached ISs
SN 1	IS 1/IS 2
SN 2	IS 1/IS 3
SN 3	IS 2/IS 3
SN 4	IS 2/IS 4
SN 5	IS 3/IS 4
SN 6	IS 2/IS 5
SN 7	IS 4/IS 7
SN 8	IS 3/IS 6
SN 9	IS 5/IS 7
SN 10	IS 6/IS 7

Destination IS (NET)	Path	Cost
IS 1	Local	0
IS 2	IS 2	2
IS 3	IS 3	1
IS 4	IS 2	3
IS 5	IS 2	6
IS 6	IS 3	5
IS 7	IS 3	7

Figure 9.30
Routing information base derivation example: (a) internet topology; (b) initialized adjacency and circuit databases; (c) link state database examples after first set of LS PDUs; (d) link state database development for IS 1; (e) final RIB for IS 1.

in Figure 9.29(n). We can also readily deduce how an IS performs the redirect function. For example, if an ES attached to, say, SN 2 sends a PDU to IS 1 addressed to an ES on SN 5, then IS 1 can readily deduce that the shortest route is via IS 3 which is in fact one of its adjacencies on SN 2 and hence should be used in preference to itself.

In our discussion, we have assumed that the transmission of LS PDUs is reliable and that none are lost as a result of transmission errors. To allow for the possibility that errors will occur each LS PDU contains a sequence number. This is retained with the PDU when it is placed in the link state and forwarding databases. At regular intervals, ISs exchange other PDUs known as **sequence number PDUs** which contain the sequence numbers of the LS PDUs in the RIB of the transmitting IS. This information is used to ensure the RIBs in all ISs are consistent.

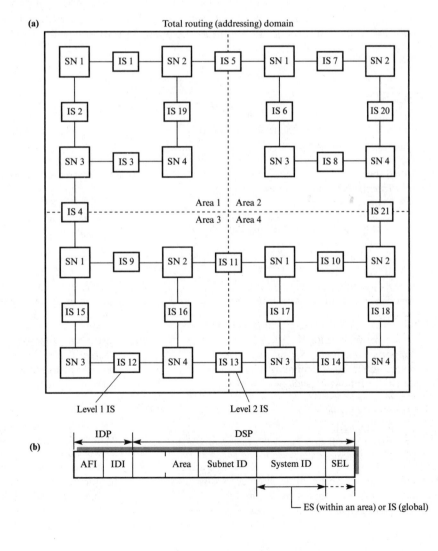

Figure 9.31
Hierarchical routing:
(a) example topology;
(b) address structure.

With very large internets the number of entries in each database can become unacceptably large. To overcome this, the protocol allows **hierarchical routing**. Using this technique, the total routing (addressing) domain is divided into a number of areas, each containing a number of subnets and first level (level 1) ISs. If a required destination ES is attached to a subnet in this area (determined by the area address in the high-order part of the DSP address), it is routed directly using the procedure we have described.

Alternatively, if the required destination is in a different area, the PDU is first sent to a second, higher-level (level 2) IS. This IS routes the PDU using other level 2 ISs until it reaches a (level 2) IS attached to the required destination area. From there it is routed within the area using level 1 ISs. In this case, each database is much smaller and hence the routing overheads are significantly reduced. Figure 9.31 illustrates this general approach.

Finally, be aware that the IS-to-IS protocol is complex, especially when hierarchical routing is included. This chapter has provided only an overview of the protocol. For a more detailed description, refer to the ISO 10589 document directly.

Exercises

9.1 Explain the meaning of the following terms relating to internetworking:
(a) Internet
(b) Subnet
(c) Intermediate system/gateway/router
(d) Protocol converter

9.2 With the aid of sketches, describe the structure of the following:
(a) IP addresses
(b) IP datagrams
Clearly identify each field and explain its function in the context of the IP protocol.

9.3 An NSDU of 2000 octets is to be transmitted over a network, using the IP protocol, that supports a maximum NS_user data size of 512 octets. Assuming a minimum IP header size, derive the following fields in each of the datagram headers:
(a) Identification
(b) Total length
(c) Fragment offset
(d) More fragments flag

9.4 (a) Produce a sketch of an internet to illustrate the role of a subnet router, interior gateway, and exterior gateway.

(b) In relation to the internet produced for part (a), identify the scope of the following routing protocols and produce example entries in the routing tables associated with each protocol:
(i) ARP
(ii) IGP
(iii) EGP

9.5 With the aid of an example internet, explain the operation of the distance vector algorithm. Use your internet to show how the routing tables in each gateway are derived assuming a routing metric of hop count.

9.6 List the message types associated with the internet control message protocol (ICMP) and hence explain the various functions associated with the protocol.

9.7 The length of the data field associated with a user request is 1200 octets. Assuming the data is to be sent to a host that is attached to the same network and the maximum NS_user data size associated with the network is 512 octets, derive the number of IP datagrams that are required to send the data if the header associated with each datagram is 20 octets.

Determine the contents of the following fields in each datagram header:
(a) Identification
(b) Total length
(c) Fragment offset
(d) More fragments flag

9.8 List and discuss the reasons for the specification of the IPv6 protocol. Also, describe the feature in the new protocol that overcomes each of the identified limitations of IPv4.

9.9 Explain the meaning of the following terms in relation to the ISO CLNP:
(a) NS_user
(b) NS_provider
(c) NSAP
(d) CONS and CLNS

9.10 With the aid of sketches, describe the structure of an ISO internet NSAP address and the relationship between an NSAP address and an SNPA address.

9.11 List the names of the three sublayers that make up the network layer and describe their function in both an ES and an IS.

9.12 Assuming an ISO CLNP based internet, produce a time sequence diagram showing the service primitives that are exchanged between the three network sublayers, to transfer an NSDU between two NS_users in both directions assuming:
(a) A connection-oriented subnet
(b) A connectionless subnet

9.13 Produce a sketch of the structure of an ISO CLNP data PDU and explain the meaning of each field.

9.14 Discriminate between the terms intranet segmentation and internet segmentation in relation to the ISO CLNP.
   Assuming the internet shown in Figure 9.10, produce a sketch showing the segmentation and reassembly operations at each ES and IS if the NSDU = 512 octets, the three subnets are all connectionless and operate with maximum user data lengths of 128 octets, 256 octets, and 512 octets, and intranet segmentation is being used.

9.15 In relation to Exercise 9.14, if now internet segmentation is used, derive the content of the following fields in the header of each PDU as it is transferred across the three subnets:
(a) Total length
(b) Segment length
(c) Segment offset
(d) More segment flag

9.16 Assuming ISO internetworking, produce a sketch showing the outline structure of the SNICP sublayer in both an ES and an IS. Include in your sketch the ISO CLNP and the two routing protocols ES-to-IS and IS-to-IS.
   Write an outline description of the operation of each system and the interactions between each protocol.

9.17 Assuming the internet structure and the table contents shown in Figure 9.23, describe the routing of an ISO CLNP data PDU from NSAP 1.1 to
(a) NSAP 1.10
(b) NSAP 3.5
(c) NSAP 10.3

9.18 With the aid of a sketch, explain the meaning of the terms 'overload', 'congestion control', and 'congestion control efficiency' in relation to an IS in an internet.

9.19 Describe the operation of the two functions in the ISO CLNP that are provided to help avoid congestion in the internet.
   Assuming the memory buffer structure shown in Figure 9.26(a), derive an example worst-case buffer distribution assuming square root limiting, 15 free buffers available, and internet segmentation.

9.20 Using the sketch in Figure 9.26(c), explain the meaning of the term 'reassembly deadlock' assuming intranet segmentation is being used.

9.21 Assume for a different routing metric the path cost values of the 10 subnets shown in Figure 9.29 are 1, 2, 3, 2, 2, 3, 4, 1, 2, and 2 units, respectively. Use Dijkstra's algorithm to derive the shortest path cost routes from IS 1 to each of the 6 other ISs.

9.22   Describe the routing of an ISO CLNP data PDU, using the forwarding information base tables shown in Figure 9.30(e), between NSAP 1.1 and the following NSAPs:
(a) 1.5
(b) 3.4
(c) 9.3

9.23   Assuming an ES attached to SN 1 sends a PDU to IS 2 addressed to an NSAP on SN 2, describe the steps taken by IS 2 to route the PDU and the subsequent redirect operation. Explain clearly how IS 2 can determine the redirection that is possible.

9.24   Assuming the internet shown in Figure 9.30(a) and the path cost values in Exercise 9.21, derive the first set of link state PDUs received by each IS.

Chapter summary

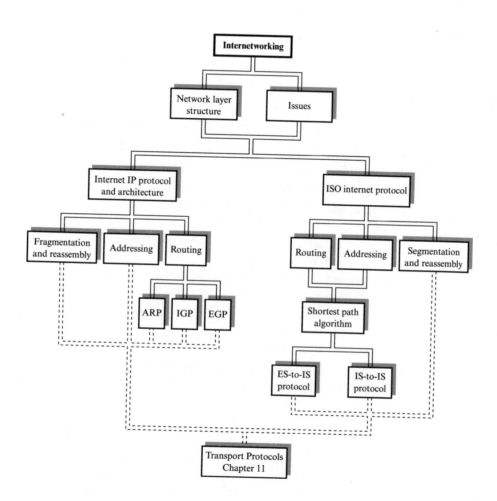

10 BROADBAND MULTISERVICE NETWORKS

Chapter objectives

When you have completed this chapter you should be able to:

Introduction

All the networks described in the previous chapters were designed primarily to support data-only services. Typically, these services involve the exchange of frames of data that comprise either strings of characters from a particular character set – ASCII, EBCDIC, etc. – or strings of binary bytes – for example, the output of a compiled program. More recently, workstations (and the networks that are used to interconnect them) have evolved that support services that involve not only data but also a range of other information types. For example, workstations that incorporate a video camera, a microphone, and speakers that enable two communicating parties to hold a telephone conversation – **telephony** – or to open a window on their display and show on it the talking picture of the other party –

558

videophony. Additionally, the two communicating parties can discuss the contents of a report or document, for example, that is displayed in another window.

In addition, such workstations can often support the display of documents that are themselves made up of multiple media types, that is, **multimedia documents**. Typically, these comprise multiple windows containing, in addition to textual information, high-resolution images or perhaps moving images (video) with sound. There is now a range of teaching and other information packages that contain suites of such documents that can be interactively accessed by a user. These packages can be stored either locally within the workstation – for example, on a CD ROM – or in a server connected to the network. Example applications include **computer aided learning (CAL)** and various **computer-supported cooperative working (CSCW) activities**. In general, because of the range of services such workstations offer, they are known as **multiservice workstations**, and the networks used to interconnect them as **broadband multiservice networks**, the term 'broadband' indicating their use of very high bit rate transmission circuits. A schematic diagram showing a selection of the applications of such networks is given in Figure 10.1(a), and an example videophone transaction involving two multiservice workstations is shown in Figure 10.1(b).

(a)

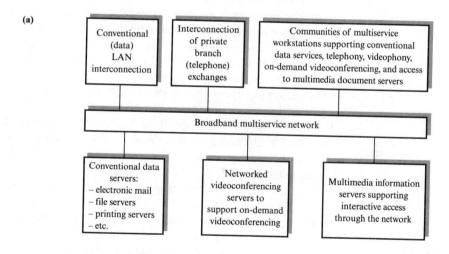

(b)

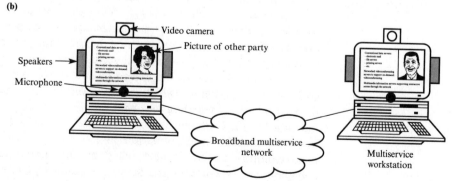

Figure 10.1
Broadband
multiservice networks:
(a) selected
application examples;
(b) example
videophone
transaction involving
two multiservice
workstations.

10.1   Networking requirements

Multiservice networks have to be far more flexible than the data-only network types described in the previous chapters. In data-only networks, a typical transaction may involve the transfer of, say, 10 kilobytes of data. At 10 Mbps this would take just 8 ms to transfer, while at 100 Mbps, 0.8 ms. Clearly, a number of such transactions can readily time-share the same transmission medium and still obtain a satisfactory service.

In contrast, transactions that involve the transfer of audio and video information require **constant bit rate** transmission capacity – and hence reserved bandwidth – possibly for the total duration of the transaction. For example, if a multimedia document includes a window containing 5 s of video with sound, then this requires a significant portion of the full 10 Mbps of a conventional LAN continuously for the entire 5 s interval. Clearly, for those applications such as videophony and **videoconferencing** in which a video camera is involved, the demands on the network are more severe since a similar bandwidth is required for the duration of the entire session/call.

To reduce the network bandwidth required to support these additional media types, normally **compression** is applied to the source information prior to its transmission. An associated decompression algorithm is applied to the received information prior to its output. As we saw in Section 3.5, the algorithms used for data (text) compression must be **lossless**, that is, no information is lost following the compression and subsequent decompression operations. However, with the compression algorithms associated with speech, image, and video, the main aim is to minimize the amount of information that needs to be transmitted while retaining only the **intelligibility** of the source information. In general, all the compression algorithms that are used with these media types do not yield an exact replica of the source information after decompression but rather a version of it which, hopefully, is of an acceptable quality to the recipient. They are known, therefore, as **lossy compression algorithms**. Over the past few years there have been significant advances made in the field of compression and, indeed, research in this area is still continuing. To help to quantify the communication requirements of such networks, both the uncompressed and typical compressed bandwidths associated with various media types are given in Table 10.1. Clearly, transactions involving more than one media type require proportionately more bandwidth.

We derived the uncompressed bandwidth associated with conventional (narrowband) telephony in Section 2.5.2. Recall that the digitization process uses a sampling rate of 8000 samples per second and each sample is quantized into an 8-bit value to yield an uncompressed bit rate of 64 kbps. In general, applications such as teleconferencing – which involve several users – require a wider bandwidth than conventional telephony – owing to a higher sampling rate – to allow each individual in the conference to be more readily identified.

The amount of information in its uncompressed form associated with high-resolution images is determined by the spatial resolution of the image and the range of colors – and hence the number of bits – associated with each

Table 10.1 Bandwidth requirements of different media types.

Media	Transaction type	Format	Sampling dimensions pixel, line, frame/s	Uncompressed bit rate	Compressed maximum bit rate
Speech and music	Telephony		8 ksps ×8 bit/sample	64 kbps	8–32 kbps
	Telecon-ferencing		16 ksps ×8 bit/sample	128 kbps	48–64 kbps
	CD-audio		44.1 ksps × 16 bit/sample	705.6 kbps	128 kbps
Image	Normal resolution image	SVGA	640 pixel × 480 line ×8 bit/pixel	2.458 Mbits	24 k–245 kbits
		JPEG	720 pixel × 576 line ×16 bit/pixel	6.636 Mbits	104 k–830 kbits
	Very high resolution image		1280 pixel × 1024 line × 24 bit/pixel	31.46 Mbits	300 k–3 Mbits
Business video	Videophone	QCIF (H.261)	176 pixel × 144 line ×12 bit × 30 frame/s*	9.115 Mbps	$p \times 64$ kbps (p = 1, 2)
		MPEG-4 (H.320)	176 pixel × 144 line ×12 bit × 10 frame/s	3.04 Mbps	64 kbps
	Video conferencing	CIF (H.261)	352 pixel × 288 line ×12 bit × 30 frame/s*	36.45 Mbps	$m \times 384$ kbps (m = 1, 2, ... 5)
		MPEG-1 (PAL)	352 pixel × 288 line ×12 bit × 25 frame/s	30.4 Mbps	1.15 M–3 Mbps
		MPEG-1 (NTSC)	352 pixel × 240 line ×12 bit × 30 frame/s	30.4 Mbps	1.15 M–3 Mbps
Entertainment video	VCR	CIF (MPEG-2)	352 pixel × 240 line ×12 bit × 30 frame/s	30.4 Mbps	4 Mbps
	Broadcast television	MPEG-2 (PAL)	720 pixel × 576 line ×12 bit × 25 frame/s	124.4 Mbps	15 Mbps
		MPEG-2 (NTSC)	720 pixel × 480 line ×12 bit × 30 frame/s	124.3 Mbps	15 Mbps
	High quality television	HDTV	1920 pixel × 1080 line ×16 bit × 30 frame/s	994.3 Mbps	135 Mbps
		MPEG-3	1920 pixel × 1080 line ×12 bit × 30 frame/s	745.8 Mbps	20 M–40 Mbps

* Frame rate can be 30, 15, 10, 7.5 frame/s.

CIF = Common intermediate format   QCIF = Quarter common intermediate format

MPEG = Moving pictures expert group   JPEG = Joint photographic experts group

picture element (pixel). The two entries shown in the table relate first to a spatial resolution of 480 lines each of 640 pixels with 8 bits per pixel for color, while the second relates to a very high resolution image with a spatial resolution of 1024 lines of 1280 pixels each of 24 bits. As we can see, even with compression, the amount of bandwidth can be high and hence a high bandwidth link is required if such images are to be transmitted in an acceptable time interval.

The requirements for applications involving video depend not only on the spatial resolution of each frame (image) but also on the frame refresh rate. To avoid flicker effects, with broadcast video a refresh rate of at least 25 frames per second is used. For videophony, normally there is very little movement from one frame to the next and, what movement there is, is localized to a small part of the overall picture. Hence lower refresh rates and higher levels of compression can be used. The combined effect is that both the uncompressed and compressed bandwidths associated with videophony and videoconferencing are significantly less than those required for broadcast television.

We can deduce from Table 10.1 that although compression reduces the amount of bandwidth required, it is still substantial and especially for video. Moreover, because of the constant bit rate requirement of much of this information, networks of the type described in the previous chapters are, in general, inadequate to support applications that involve multiple media types. Therefore, a range of new networks have been developed which can support, in addition to conventional data communications, communications involving a range of media types. We shall consider the operation of these networks in this chapter.

10.2   FDDI-II

As we saw in Chapter 7 when we discussed the operation of FDDI, although it has an optional feature to support the transmission of delay-sensitive (synchronous) data, the variation in delay that can be obtained with the token access control method makes such a service unsuitable for the transfer of some types of constant bit rate data. Recall that the latter is known as isochronous data since it is generated at regular time intervals and hence must be delivered at the same constant rate.

To support isochronous data, a variant of FDDI known as **FDDI-II** has been developed. In its **basic mode**, FDDI-II behaves in the same way as FDDI, that is, all transmissions are controlled by a control token and the available ring bandwidth (capacity) is then time-shared between the attached stations using the timed token rotation protocol (see Chapter 7). However, with FDDI-II, providing all stations in the ring have been upgraded to support this – that is, they have the alternative chipset – then they may switch from basic mode to an alternative mode known as the **hybrid mode**. In this mode, instead of using the full 100 Mbps ring bandwidth entirely for the transmission of conventional data – often referred to as asynchronous data – the bandwidth is divided up into a number of smaller units –

known as **channels** – using **time-division multiplexing**. Each of the resulting channels may be used for either asynchronous data or isochronous data.

The establishment of multiple channels is carried out by a selected station known as the **cycle master** which also controls the utilization of the channels. This is carried out in response to request messages for isochronous services received from stations using the station management subsystem. The cycle master informs all stations of each new allocation of isochronous channels and only the remaining bandwidth is utilized for asynchronous data transmission. Let us consider this in more detail.

10.2.1   Cycle structure

The cycle master generates a repetitive string of cycles every 125 μs which, as may be recalled from Section 2.5.2, is the basic sampling interval used for digitizing an analog speech signal. At 100 Mbps, this results in a cycle length of 12 500 bits. For all of the stations in the ring to synchronize to the start of each cycle, a clock synchronization pattern of 20 bits is included at the head of each cycle followed by a unique start-of-cycle framing pattern of 8 bits. The contiguous string of cycles circulates around the ring from station to station in the normal way. Since the ring latency is always greater than 125 μs, the ring will contain a number of cycles at any instant with the actual ring latency controlled by the cycle master as an integer multiple of the cycle time. The general scheme is shown in diagrammatic form in Figure 10.2(a); part (b) shows how each cycle is subdivided into multiple channels.

As indicated, at the start of each cycle is a clock synchronization pattern of 20 bits which is known as the **preamble** or sometimes the **interframe gap**. The same line code symbols that are used with FDDI are utilized and the preamble is made up of five IDLE symbols which, for transmission purposes, are encoded into five 5-bit symbols by the 4B/5B encoder. The remaining 12 480 bits in each cycle are interpreted as a string of 1560 octets (bytes). Following the preamble is a 12-octet field known as the **cycle header**, the first octet of which is used as a **start-of-cycle delimiter**. The remaining octets in the header define how the channels making up the cycle body (payload) are currently being used. The octets in the cycle body are multiplexed together to form a single 12-octet field, known as the **dedicated packet group**, plus sixteen 96-octet fields each known as a **wideband channel (WBC)**.

As Figure 10.2 shows, the 1548 octets in the cycle body are made up of twelve 129-octet groups. The first octet in each group forms part of the dedicated packet group (DPG0–11). The remaining 128 octets are then further subdivided into sixteen 8-octet subgroups, one for each wideband channel. As we shall see in Section 10.2.3, this affords great flexibility in the use of each channel.

The 12 octets that make up the cycle header are interpreted as twenty-four 4-bit symbols which, as indicated earlier, are encoded into 5-bit symbols prior to transmission by the 4B/5B encoder. The fields in the cycle header are as follows (further details of their usage are given in the following sections):

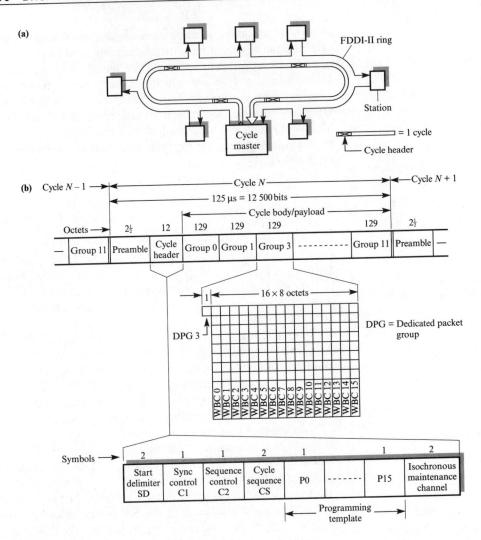

Figure 10.2
FDDI-II: (a) cycle schematic; (b) cycle format.

- **Start delimiter** This two-symbol field immediately follows the preamble and is used to indicate the start of a new cycle. It is made up of a J–K symbol pair.

- **Synchronization control (C1)** A single symbol that indicates whether all stations in the ring have achieved synchronization. It is set to the symbol R by any station that has not yet synchronized and is set to the symbol S by the cycle master when it detects all stations have become synchronized.

- **Sequence control (C2)** Again, a single symbol which can be either the S or the R symbol. During the initialization process when the ring is being set into the hybrid mode, stations bid to become the cycle master. During this process each station writes the symbol R into the sequence control field. Once the bidding process is over and a cycle master has been appointed, the cycle sequence (number) in the cycle header should increment by unity for each successive cycle received. The cycle master writes the symbol S into the sequence control field as it issues each new cycle but if a station detects an invalid sequence number then it resets the field to the symbol R.

- **Cycle sequence (CS)** A two-symbol field that is interpreted as an 8-bit binary number. It can thus range from 0 to 255. During the initialization process it contains the preassigned number – known as the **monitor value** – of the station that is bidding to become the cycle master. This can range from 0 to 63 and the station with the highest value wins. During normal operation the value indicates the cycle sequence number. Successive cycles are assigned incremental values and these can range from 64 to 255.

- **Programming template** This consists of 16 symbols – one for each wideband channel – each of which can be either the S or the R symbol. An R symbol indicates that the corresponding channel is being used for asynchronous data while an S symbol indicates it is being used for isochronous data. The complete programming template is assigned by the cycle master in response to requests from stations for isochronous bandwidth.

- **Isochronous maintenance channel** A two-symbol field that has been reserved for maintenance functions; its use has yet to be defined.

10.2.2 Initialization process

During the initialization process each station can bid to become the cycle master. All stations in the ring first initialize into the basic mode then each station starts its bid by issuing a new cycle with an R symbol in both the C1 and C2 fields of the cycle header and its preassigned monitor value in the CS field.

If a station receives a cycle with a monitor value greater than its own, then it stops generating new cycles and instead starts to repeat the cycles that it receives. Eventually, the station with the highest monitor value will be left generating new cycles with the remaining stations simply repeating these. This is detected by the issuing station as it starts to receive cycles with its own monitor value and it then assumes the role of cycle master. At this point it starts to issue cycles with the S symbol in both the C1 and C2 fields and to increment sequence numbers in the range 64–255 in the CS field. It increments the value in the CS field by unity as each new cycle is issued and, when this reaches 255, it restarts at 64.

10.2.3 Bandwidth allocation

Each of the 16 wideband channels provides a transmission bandwidth of 6.144 Mbps which, because of the multiplexing method described earlier, can be used in a variety of ways. The actual usage is determined by how the bytes that

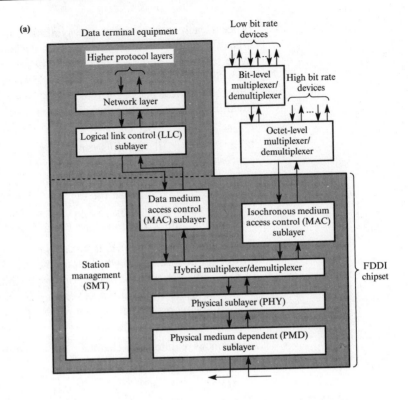

(a)

Figure 10.3
FDDI-II: (a) protocol
architecture;
(b) example WBC
utilization.

(b)

Bits/cycle	Composite subchannel rate (kbps)	Example usage
1/2/4	8/16/32	Compressed voice or data
8	64	Uncompressed voice channel
16	128	Videophone
48	384	Videoconferencing
192	1536	Telephone (PBX) interconnection
256	2048	
768	6144	Broadcast video

make up each 128-octet group are multiplexed together. Lower bit rate services can also be offered by multiplexing at the bit level. A schematic diagram of the station protocol architecture showing how this is achieved is given in Figure 10.3(a); part (b) gives some examples of how a single wideband channel can be used. Any wideband channels not used for isochronous data are added to the dedicated packet group to form a single higher bit rate channel for the transmission of asynchronous data. As indicated, the basic packet group is made up of a single octet from each of the twelve 129-octet groups in each cycle. This is equivalent to a bit rate of 768 kbps which can be increased progressively in 6.144 Mbps steps.

Example 10.1

An FDDI-II network is to be used as the backbone communications network to link together five financial institutions all closely located in a city. At each institution site is a private branch (telephone) exchange (PBX), a video-conferencing suite, and a local area network (LAN). At the peak (busy) period there can be up to 46 simultaneous voice calls in place from each site. Also, provision must be made to provide a permanent videoconferencing link between all sites. Assume each voice call requires a 64 kbps duplex link and a further 64 kbps duplex link is required for signaling (call setup) purposes by each PBX for each set of 23 voice calls. Also, the videoconferencing link requires 384 kbps between each site. Derive the bandwidth required to support the voice and video-conferencing traffic and hence the amount of residual bandwidth available for LAN interconnection.

Voice   A duplex channel must be set up between the PBX at each site and the PBXs at each of the other sites. Also, we must assume that, in the worst case, all calls originating at a site may go to another single site. Hence each of these channels must be capable of supporting 2×24 (23 voice + 1 signaling) subchannels, each of 64 kbps.

All FDDI-II isochronous channels are unidirectional (simplex) and hence two are required to set up a duplex channel. The number of simplex channels required to establish a duplex channel between all five PBXs is given by $5 \times (5 - 1)$:

$$
\begin{aligned}
1 &\rightarrow 2, 3, 4, 5 \\
2 &\rightarrow 1, 3, 4, 5 \\
3 &\rightarrow 1, 2, 4, 5 \\
4 &\rightarrow 1, 2, 3, 5 \\
5 &\rightarrow 1, 2, 3, 4
\end{aligned}
$$

that is, the number of simplex channels required is 20. Since each of these must support 2×24 subchannels each of 64 kbps, the total bandwidth required for the voice traffic is given by:

$$20 \times 2 \times 24 \times 64 = 61\,440 \text{ kbps}$$

that is, 10 wideband channels.

Videoconferencing   A videoconferencing link requires the video source from each site to be sent to each of the other sites. As for voice, this requires 20 simplex channels. Since each of these is to be 384 kbps, the total bandwidth required for the videoconferencing traffic is given by:

$$20 \times 384 = 7680 \text{ kbps}$$

that is, 2 wideband channels.

LAN interconnection   At each site there will be a single point of attachment to the intersite backbone. For example, a bridge if all the sites have the same type of LAN. Hence for data, just a unidirectional (simplex) link is required between each site to form the backbone ring.

Since the voice and videoconferencing traffic requires 12 wideband channels, the remaining 4 wideband channels can be used for asynchronous data (LAN interconnection). The basic provision for data (dedicated packet group) is 768 kbps. Hence the total available bandwidth is given by:

$$0.768 + 4 \times 6.144 = 25.344 \text{ Mbps}$$

10.3   Cell-based networks

As Section 10.2 described, one approach to providing transmission and switching support for multimedia services is first to separate the different media sources and then to provide support for each independently. An alternative approach is to adopt a transmission and switching system that is independent of the source media but has the necessary flexibility to support any type of media. This is the basis of cell-based transmission and switching networks.

Historically, constant bit rate traffic such as digitized voice has been transmitted and switched using preassigned time slots. In contrast, data is normally transmitted and switched in the form of variable length frames which are multiplexed together on a statistical basis. In networks that must support both media types a hybrid scheme has been adopted. All source media is first broken down into a stream of fixed-sized units known as **cells**. The cell streams relating to the different media types are multiplexed together for transmission purposes on a statistical basis while the adoption of a standard sized cell for all media means that the switching of the cell streams can be performed at very high rates. The resulting networks are known as **cell-based networks** or, because the cells relating to the different media are statistically multiplexed together for transmission – and hence have random time intervals between them – **asynchronous transfer mode (ATM) networks**.

The next decision to be made was the size of a cell. Small cells have advantages for constant bit rate traffic since only a short delay is experienced as successive bytes relating to the same call are assembled and disassembled into and from cells at the periphery of the network. Conversely, since each cell must contain additional information for routing purposes, small cells have the disadvantage that the overheads associated with each cell are disproportionately high. A compromise was reached by the various international standards bodies and a cell size of 53 octets/bytes was chosen. This comprises a 48-octet information (payload) field with a 5-octet header containing routing and other fields. The adoption of a 5-octet header is possible firstly, because no error control is performed on cells – and hence no sequence numbers are required for retransmission purposes – and secondly, because networkwide addresses are not carried in each cell. Note that the adoption of cell-based transmission and switching within the network is transparent to the applications associated with the workstations and other devices connected to them. Cells are used simply to provide a more uniform transmission and switching system for multimedia traffic and all conversions of the source media to and from cells are performed at the network interface. A number of alternative network types have been developed that are cell-based and we shall discuss a selection of these in the following sections. As we shall see, all utilize the asynchronous transfer mode of transmission.

10.4 ATM LANs

A schematic diagram showing a selection of the applications associated with next-generation, multimedia networks was shown in Figure 10.1. We saw that such networks must provide both a switched communication path between distributed communities of next-generation multiservice workstations and workstation access to a range of networked servers supporting, in addition to data-only services, a variety of newer services. Therefore, the communication requirements of the network involve data, images, voice, and video, possibly all integrated together in some instances. Clearly, since many network transactions (calls) involve voice and video information, its time-sensitive nature means that, for each call, a path must be provided through the network that has a guaranteed transfer delay time associated with it.

Therefore, the bandwidth requirements of a multiservice workstation are significantly higher than those required for a data-only workstation. Hence, in a network for the interconnection of multiservice workstations, shared-medium topologies of the type used for data are inappropriate since the cost of providing a very high performance interface in each workstation is too high. To meet this type of requirement, **ATM LANs** utilize a mesh topology comprising a number of interconnected switching exchanges similar in principle to that used in existing telephone networks. A schematic diagram of a typical establishmentwide ATM LAN is shown in Figure 10.4.

As we shall see in Section 10.4.2, an **ATM switch** has a defined number of ports and its function is to provide a high bit rate switched communications path between ports. The cost of a switch is a function of the number of ports that it supports. If all the workstations are connected directly to the switch then as the deployment of multiservice workstations increases, switches with a very large number of ports are required. However, not all workstations require network services at the same time. To minimize the number of ports, groups of workstations – for example, in a building – are connected to the switch through a **remote concentrator unit (RCU)**. There is no switching function in the RCU and its role is simply to multiplex/demultiplex the cell streams from/to those workstations that are involved in a network transaction onto/from the link connecting the concentrator to a switch port. In this way, providing the interconnecting link has sufficient capacity to support the anticipated number of

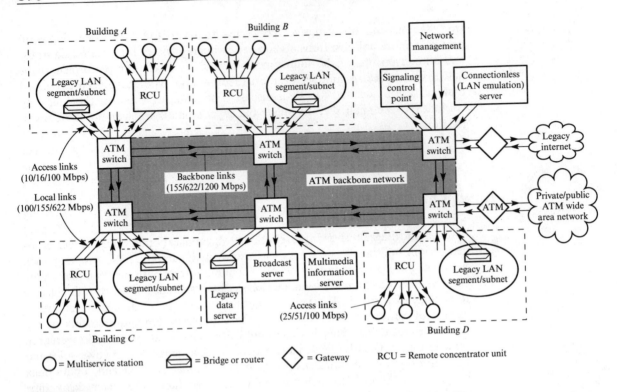

Figure 10.4
ATM LAN schematic.

concurrent transactions, the number of switch ports required is reduced considerably.

Prior to sending any information relating to a call, a communications path through the network is first established. All the cells relating to the call are constrained to follow this same path and are delivered in the same order as they were submitted. Recall that the conversion of all information into streams of fixed-sized cells has the advantage that the cells relating to the different media types can be switched in a uniform way and independent of the type of media to which they relate. In addition, the use of cells has advantages in terms of the utilization of transmission bandwidth.

As we discussed in Section 10.1, to reduce the amount of bandwidth required for image and video, the source information is first compressed prior to transmission. This is particularly advantageous for video since in its uncompressed form each video frame contains a fixed amount of information which is generated at a constant rate determined by the frame refresh rate – for example, 25 or 30 frames per second. However, with compression only the changes that occur between successive frames are transmitted, with the effect that the amount of information transmitted per frame varies considerably from a small number of cells if few changes occur to a large number of cells when complete frame (scene) changes occur. This variation in cell rate is exploited when reserving transmission capacity for calls; instead of reserving capacity at the maximum rate, it is reserved at the mean rate. To ensure sufficient capacity is available for each call, the cell streams relating to different calls are multiplexed together on a statistical basis. The connections/paths through the network are known as **virtual connections (VCs)**, the term 'virtual' indicating the connection is a logical rather than a physical one.

The networking services supported by a multiservice workstation include telephony, videophony, conventional data networking, and access to a range of related servers. These include, in addition to those present with existing data networks – electronic mail, printing services, etc. – a broadcast server, a database server supporting multimedia information packages, and so on. For example, the **broadcast server** enables a user at a multiservice workstation to set up on demand a videoconferencing session between three or more similar workstations by sending the video output from all the workstations involved directly to the server in real time. The server relays the appropriate video pictures (with sound) to the other workstations as the conference proceeds. Similarly, the server holding multimedia information packages enables a user at a workstation to access a particular package and then interactively work through it.

Of course, multiservice workstations are being introduced in an incremental way and currently a majority of LAN installations are still of the data-only type. Within the context of ATM LANs, these are often referred to as **legacy LANs**. The major bottleneck associated with such networks is access to servers, since these require significant bandwidth to support multiple concurrent transactions. Hence in addition to providing direct access to the newer multimedia servers, the backbone switches also provide connections both to the existing data-only LANs in each building – through bridges or routers – and to the servers associated with them. Typically, these are all interconnected by a set of point-to-point VCs. In the context of existing LANs, the interconnected set of backbone switches can be viewed as providing the same function as a high-speed backbone subnetwork.

All communications across an ATM network are carried out over previously established VCs. These can be set up either on demand by a user or semipermanently by network management. With **on-demand connections**, the user device, before sending any information cells, sends a request for a **switched virtual connection (SVC)** to be set up (between itself and the required destination) to a central control unit known as the **signaling control point (SCP)**. This is responsible for the overall management of both the transmission bandwidth and the setting up and clearing of switched connections through the network. On receipt of the request – known as a **signaling message** – the SCP first determines the availability of both the required destination and the transmission bandwidth appropriate to the call across the network. All the workstations are connected to the SCP – normally a powerful workstation – by a separate VC and, assuming the required destination and network resources are available, the SCP sets up routing information in the switch network to link the two user devices (VCs) involved in the call. It then informs the originator that it can commence sending information cells. All the signaling messages associated with the setting up and clearing of calls/connections are transferred across the network to and from the SCP in the form of cells over a separate set of VCs that are permanently set up for this function. The latter are known as **signaling virtual channel connections (SVCCs)**.

To access networked servers such as electronic mail and multimedia information servers, as we shall see in Part 3, we use a protocol stack such as TCP/IP. Recall from Chapter 9 that the IP provides a connectionless best-try service. Hence because the ATM network is connection oriented, before any datagrams can be transferred a VC must be in place between each workstation and the set of servers. In practice, the number of servers may be large and this requirement can be met by setting up **permanent VCs (PVCs)** between all workstations and servers and a central data forwarding point known as the **connectionless server (CLS)** or, because it provides a similar service to that provided by a legacy (broadcast) LAN, the **LAN emulation server (LES)**. We shall discuss the operation of this and the SCP in more detail in Section 10.4.6.

The permanent virtual connections associated with the various services are all set up under the overall control of the **network management station**. A reserved VC is permanently in place between the network management station and the control processor in each backbone ATM switch and RCU. Also between all multiservice workstations and servers and their network point of attachments. These are used by the network manager to set up the VCs associated with the various services. The network manager uses these connections to download routing information for entry into the routing tables held by these devices. We shall look at the setting up of such connections in Section 10.4.1.

As with existing data-only networks, users of multiservice workstations, as well as needing to communicate with other users at the same site, also want to communicate with users connected to an ATM LAN at a different site. Hence an ATM LAN has **gateways** to existing (legacy) internets and also to newer private/public wide area ATM networks. To meet these needs, new generations of private networks based on the ATM are being introduced. Also, the public carriers are introducing a new generation of public network that is based on the same technology. This is comprised of ATM MANs which, in the future, will be connected to ATM WANs. The resulting network is known as the **broadband integrated services digital network (BISDN)**.

10.4.1   Cell format and switching principles

All the cells relating to a call follow the same previously established VC through the network. During the setup procedure, a separate identifier known as the **protocol connection identifier (PCI)** is assigned to the connection on each link through the network. This is used both to identify and route the cells belonging to the same call/connection on each link within the network and also to identify the different cell streams relating to each call at the periphery of the network. However, the assigned identifier has only local significance to a link and changes from one link to the next as the cells relating to a call/connection pass through each switch. This means that the routing information carried in each cell header can be relatively small. The principle of the routing scheme is shown in Figure 10.5(a).

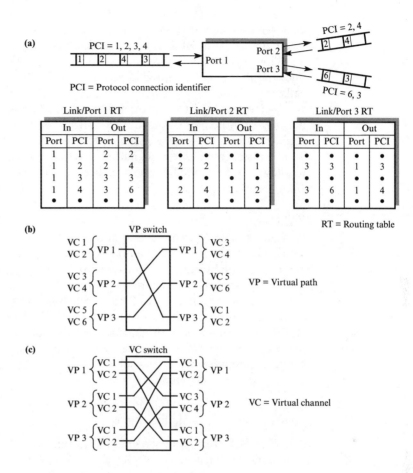

Figure 10.5
Cell switching
principles: (a) routing
schematic; (b) VP
routing; (c) VC
routing.

Associated with each incoming link/port is a routing table that contains, for each incoming PCI, the corresponding outgoing link/port and the new PCI to be used. The routing of cells in both directions along a route is thus very fast as it involves a simple look-up operation. As a result, cells from each link can be switched independently and at very high rates. This allows parallel switch architectures to be used and high-speed transmission links in the gigabit range, each operating at its maximum rate.

In practice, the PCI is made up of two subfields: a **virtual path identifier (VPI)** and a **virtual channel identifier (VCI)**. Routing can be performed using either one or a combination of the two. Two examples are shown in Figure 10.5. In part (b), switching is performed on virtual paths and the VCIs within each virtual path remain unchanged. In part (c), switching is performed on the virtual channels within each virtual path independently and the virtual paths simply terminate at each switch port.

An example of the use of virtual path switching is when multiple calls originating at the same network entry point are all intended for the same destination exit point. Each individual call is assigned a separate VCI and the calls are multiplexed together at the source interface onto a single virtual path. The multiplexed set of calls are then switched using the VPI field only and hence all follow the same path through the network. In this way, the set of VCIs remains unchanged and is used at the destination to identify (demultiplex) the individual calls.

An example of the use of virtual channel switching is when each call at the network entry point is intended for a different destination. In this case, each call is again assigned a different VCI but switching also is performed using the VCI field. The VPI field then has local significance to each link only and is used, for example, to allow calls to be multiplexed together for transmission purposes.

Example 10.2

A segment of an ATM network is shown in Figure 10.6(a). The numbers alongside each RCU/switch are the port identifiers. Assume that semipermanent VCs are to be set up by network management between stations *A*, *B*, *C*, and *D*, firstly, to the SCP for on-demand calls – for both signaling and information transfer – and secondly, to the CLS/LES for the cell streams relating to connectionless calls. Also, assume that a separate VC is required to connect the server to the CLS/LES. Derive typical routing table entries for RCU 1 and RCU 2 and SW 1 and SW 2 to provide these connections assuming VP-only switching is used within the network switches and, within the RCUs, the VPI/VCI field is used to identify specific calls/stations.

A suitable set of routing table entries is given in Figure 10.6(b). Note the following points when interpreting the entries:

● The SCP, CLS, and server are all connected to their switches by separate transmission links.

● For on-demand calls, two separate VCs are shown: one between each workstation and the SCP for the signaling messages associated with a call – the signaling channel (SC) – and the other for the cell streams associated with the call – the call channel (CC). Since the latter are to be semipermanent, these are shown set up between each workstation and SW 2. Alternatively, these could be set up on-demand by the SCP between each pair of workstations involved in a call.

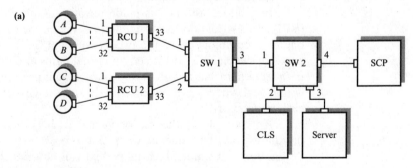

(a)

Figure 10.6
Routing example:
(a) network segment.

(b)

RCU 1:

	In Port	VPI	VCI	Out Port	VPI	VCI		In Port	VPI	VCI	Out Port	VPI	VCI
SC	1	0	1	33	1	1		33	1	1	1	0	1
CC	1	0	2	33	2	1		33	2	1	1	0	2
CLS	1	0	3	33	3	1		33	3	1	1	0	3

	In Port	VPI	VCI	Out Port	VPI	VCI		In Port	VPI	VCI	Out Port	VPI	VCI
SC	32	0	1	33	1	32		33	1	32	32	0	1
CC	32	0	2	33	2	32		33	2	32	32	0	2
CLS	32	0	3	33	3	32		33	3	32	32	0	3

RCU 2:

	In Port	VPI	VCI	Out Port	VPI	VCI		In Port	VPI	VCI	Out Port	VPI	VCI
SC	1	0	1	33	1	1		33	1	1	1	0	1
CC	1	0	2	33	2	1		33	2	1	1	0	2
CLS	1	0	3	33	3	1		33	3	1	1	0	3

	In Port	VPI	VCI	Out Port	VPI	VCI		In Port	VPI	VCI	Out Port	VPI	VCI
SC	32	0	1	33	1	32		33	1	32	32	0	1
CC	32	0	2	33	2	32		33	2	32	32	0	2
CLS	32	0	3	33	3	32		33	3	32	32	0	3

SW 1:

	In Port	VPI	VCI	Out Port	VPI	VCI		In Port	VPI	VCI	Out Port	VPI	VCI
SC	1	1	X	3	1	X		3	1	X	1	1	X
CC	1	2	X	3	2	X		3	2	X	1	2	X
CLS	1	3	X	3	3	X		3	3	X	1	3	X
SC	2	1	X	3	4	X		3	4	X	2	1	X
CC	2	2	X	3	5	X		3	5	X	2	2	X
CLS	2	3	X	3	6	X		3	6	X	2	3	X

X = 1–32

SW 2:

	In Port	VPI	VCI	Out Port	VPI	VCI		In Port	VPI	VCI	Out Port	VPI	VCI
SC	1	1	X	4	1	X		4	1	X	1	1	X
CC	1	2	X	1	Y	X		1	Y	X	1	2	X
CLS	1	3	X	2	3	X		2	3	X	1	3	X
SC	1	4	X	4	4	X		4	4	X	1	4	X
CC	1	5	X	1	Y	X		1	Y	X	1	5	X
CLS	1	6	X	2	6	X		2	6	X	1	6	X
CLS'	2	10	Z	3	10	Z		3	10	Z	2	10	Z

X = 1–32
Y = 2/5
Z = 1–64

CLS:

In VPI	VCI	Out VPI	VCI		In VPI	VCI	Out VPI	VCI
3	X	10	Y		10	Y	3	X
6	X	10	Y		10	Y	6	X

X = 1–32
Y = 2/5

Figure 10.6 (cont.)
(b) Example routing entries.

SCP: Calls in progress

Signaling channel		Call channels						Call type details
		In			Out			
VPI	VCI	Port	VPI	VCI	Port	VPI	VCI	
1	X	1	2	X	1	Y	X	–
4	X	1	5	X	1	Y	X	–

Figure 10.6 (cont.)
(b) (cont.) Example routing entries.

SC = Signaling channel   CC = Call channel
CLS = Workstation/CLS channel   CLS' = CLS/server channel

- For connectionless traffic, a separate VC is required between each workstation and the CLS and also between the CLS and the server.

- The SCP, CLS, and server all use the combined VPI/VCI in the cell header to identify the cells relating to specific calls/server transactions.

- On the workstation side of each RCU, the port number identifies each workstation and the VCI identifies specific VCs.

- On the network side of each RCU, the VCI field identifies the port number – and hence workstation – within each virtual path. Also, in this example, only three virtual paths are required per RCU rather than per workstation. This allows the approach to be scaled to large installations.

- Within the network, all switching is carried out using VPIs only.

- To set up an on-demand call, the SCP creates entries in the routing table of SW 2 to link the port/VPI/VCI of the calling party to that of the called party.

- For connectionless traffic, when relaying the cell streams received from each workstation to the server, the CLS assigns a new VPI/VCI. Also, in order to relay the cell streams in the reverse direction, it maintains a table that maps the incoming VPI/VCI from the workstations to those used for communicating with the server.

- When responding to a request, the server uses the same VPI/VCI values for the cells making up the response as were used in the request.

The format of each cell is shown in Figure 10.7 and, as can be seen, the header is made up of six fields. Their function is as follows:

- **Generic flow control (GFC)**   Present only in cells transferred over the user–network interface (UNI) and included to enable a local switch/RCU to regulate – flow control – the entry of cells by a user into the network. Within the network, cells transferred over the interexchange links – known as the network–network interface (NNI) – this field is not present and the four bits are part of the VPI field.

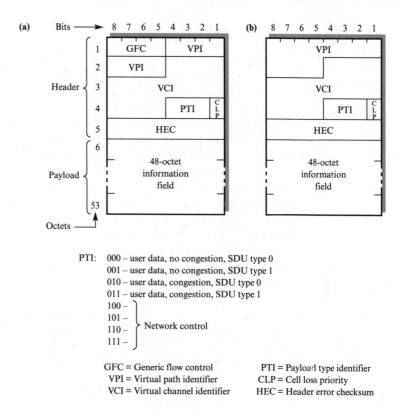

Figure 10.7
ATM cell formats:
(a) user–network
segment; (b) within
network, network–
network interface.

- **Virtual path identifier (VPI)**   This is 8 bits at the UNI and, as just indicated, 12 bits at the NNI. As described previously, it is used for identification/ routing purposes within the network.

- **Virtual channel identifier (VCI)**   A 16-bit field used for identification/ routing purposes within the network.

- **Payload type indicator (PTI)**   Indicates the type of information carried in the cell; the different types are shown Figure 10.7. All cells containing user data have a zero in the most significant bit. The next bit indicates whether the cell has experienced excessive delay/congestion or not, and the third bit the service data unit (SDU) type – 0 or 1. We shall discuss its use in Section 10.4.4 in relation to the AAL 5 service. The four remaining cell types are used for network control purposes.

- **Cell loss priority (CLP)**   Within the network, the statistical multiplexing of cells on each link may result occasionally in cells having to be discarded during heavy load conditions. This field has been included to enable the user to specify a preference as to which cells should be discarded; CLP = 0 high priority, CLP = 1 low priority and hence discard first.

- **Header error checksum (HEC)**   Generated by the physical layer and is an 8-bit CRC on the first 4 octets of the header.

10.4.2 Switch architectures

The general structure of an ATM switch is shown in Figure 10.8(a). Each input link is terminated by an **input controller (IC)** which performs the routing of cells arriving at each link (port) to their required output link. This involves a simple look-up and mapping operation of the VPI/VCI in the header of the incoming cell into the corresponding output VPI/VCI. Normally, the output port number obtained from the routing table is used to determine the path to be followed through the switching fabric to the required output controller.

Because there is no reservation of slots on the output links, cells may arrive simultaneously at two (or more) input ports that require the same output port/link. This is handled in one of two ways: either the input controllers contain a set of cell buffers that hold the additional cell(s) or the buffering is provided in the **output controllers**. In both cases the buffers are organized in the form of a FIFO queue to ensure the cells from each input controller are output in the same order as they arrived. The output controllers simply forward received cells at the appropriate link bit (and hence cell) rate.

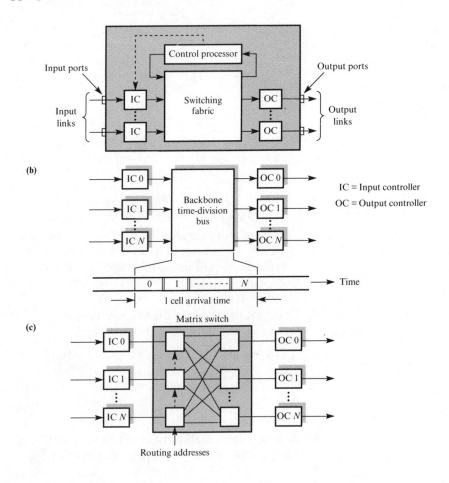

Figure 10.8
ATM switch architectures:
(a) general structure;
(b) time-division bus schematic; (c) fully connected matrix switch.

The main role of the **control processor** is to download routing information into the routing tables in each input controller. Normally, the routing information is received through the network either from the network management or from the signaling control point processors. In both cases, semipermanent VCs are used and, on arrival at the switch, the related cells are routed through the switching fabric directly from the input controller that receives the cells to the control processor. In addition, the control processor may generate network management messages itself – fault reports, performance statistics, etc. – and these also are routed through the switching fabric to the required output controller for onward transmission to the network management processor.

A number of alternative switching fabrics are used in ATM switches. These can be classified as either time division or space division. Normally, all the input controllers are synchronized so that each set of incoming cells from all controllers is presented to the switching fabric in synchronism. The switching fabric also operates synchronously which means that the cells from each input controller are transferred to their required output controller in a single cell time.

A schematic diagram of a **time-division switch** is shown in Figure 10.8(b). In such switches we use a time-division backplane bus that is capable of transferring N cells – where N is the number of input ports – in a single cell arrival time. Each input controller is assigned its own cell (slot) time to transfer a cell over the backplane bus. The input controller appends the required output port number to the head of the cell and this is used by the set of output controllers to determine which output controller should read and buffer the cell. If more than one cell is received by an output controller in a single cell arrival time then these are queued in the controller. Also, for one-to-many communications (multicast), more than one output controller may be specified to receive the cell. Typically, this type of switching fabric is used in switch designs which have a relatively small number of ports, the number being limited by the speed of operation of the backplane bus and also the output controllers; for example, a 2.5 Gbps bus can support 16×155 Mbps or 4×622 Mbps duplex links/ports.

In a **space-division switch** the switch fabric is comprised of a matrix of interconnected **switching elements** that collectively provide a number of alternative paths through the switch. An example is shown in Figure 10.8(c). This is known as a **fully connected switch matrix** since a path is provided from all input ports/controllers to all output ports/controllers. In the example shown, each input switching element is capable of passing a copy of each received cell to any of the output switching elements. The latter then receive the cells offered and pass them on to the output controller(s) for transmission. Although queuing is necessary in the input or output controllers, normally the aim is to avoid additional queuing within the switching fabric itself. To avoid internal queuing with this type of switch the cell transfer operation must be performed N times faster than the cell arrival rate, where N is the number of input ports. First the cell from the first input switching element is transferred, then the cell from the second element, and so on. Providing this can be done, then no additional buffering is required within the switching matrix and the switch is said to be internally **nonblocking**.

We can deduce from Figure 10.8 that in a fully connected switch the number of interconnection paths required through the switch – and hence output/input circuits associated with each switching element – grows as a function of N^2 and the speed of operation of the output switching element by N. In practice, this limits the maximum size of such switches and, therefore, most practical matrix switch designs use multiple switching stages, each made up of a number of smaller switching elements interconnected in a regular matrix. This also simplifies considerably the implementation of the switching fabric in integrated circuit form.

A switching fabric that comprises multiple switching stages is the **delta switch matrix**, an example of which is shown in Figure 10.9. As we can see, these switches are made up from an interconnected set of identical switching elements. In this example, a 2×2 switching element is used although larger sizes are also used. In general, the number of switching elements per stage, X, is determined from the expression $X = M/N$ where M is the total number of input lines and N is the number of inputs per switching element. Also, the number of stages required, Y, is determined from the expression $N^Y = M$. In the example, $N = 2$ and $M = 8$ and hence 3 stages are required each comprising 4 switching elements.

The internal interconnections between switching elements are such that there is a path through the switch from any input to any output. Associated with each switching element is a routing control bit known as the **routing tag**. If the tag bit is a binary 0, then a cell arriving on either input is routed to the upper output, while if the tag is a binary 1, then it is routed to the lower output. As we can deduce from Figure 10.9, the same set of three routing tag bits will route a cell through the matrix from any input port to the same output port. Such networks are said to be **self-routing**.

With this type of switch, to route cells through the switch matrix each input controller simply reads the required output port number/address from its routing table and appends this to the head of the cell. The switching element at each stage along the path through the matrix then uses its own bit from the routing tag –

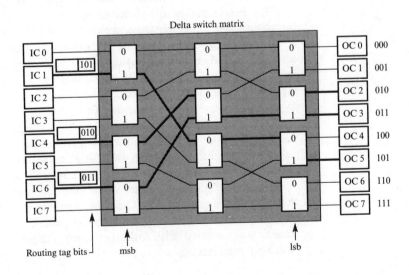

Figure 10.9
Delta switch matrix example.

most significant bit first – to perform its routing operation. In this way, routing is very fast and each cell arrives at its intended destination port regardless of the switch port on which it arrived.

The disadvantage of this type of switching fabric is **blocking**. Three example paths through the switch are shown as bold lines in Figure 10.9 and, as we can see, although the cell addressed to port 5 (101) has an unimpeded path through the matrix, those addressed to ports 2 (010) and 3 (011) both arrive at the second switching element simultaneously. Both require the same output line and blocking is said to occur. In practice, the performance of this type of matrix degrades rapidly for large numbers of ports.

There are a number of ways of overcoming blocking. One approach is for the switching element to discard one of the two cells. In support of this, note that not all ports will enter a cell into the matrix during each cell arrival time since only in the heaviest load conditions do cells arrive contiguously at all inputs. This means that under normal loads, several ports will receive idle/empty cells which do not need routing and hence in practice the probability of blocking is small. Nevertheless, in general, discarding cells in this way leads to an unacceptably high cell loss rate.

A second approach is to perform the switching operation several times faster than the cell arrival rate, for example by allowing each cell into the matrix after the preceding cell leaves the first stage switching element. There is a limit to the speed of operation of the switching elements and their interconnecting links and hence for larger switching fabrics this becomes impractical on its own. A third approach is to introduce buffering into each switching element but this has the disadvantage of introducing additional delay to the switching operation. In practice, a combination of all three approaches is used in practical switch designs.

An example of a switching fabric that avoids internal blocking is shown in Figure 10.10. It is known as the **Batcher–Banyan switch**. With a delta switch, blocking occurs when either different inputs all require a path through the switch to the same output, or the paths through the switch between different input and output ports involve a common output line from a switching element. In the Batcher–Banyan switch, blocking is avoided firstly by ensuring that no two cells entering the switching matrix require the same output port and, secondly, within the switching matrix itself, by ensuring that there are no common interconnecting links within the paths through the switch.

To satisfy the first condition, the buffering of cells is performed in the input controllers instead of the output controllers. Then, if two (or more) cells arrive simultaneously at different input ports that require the same output port, just one cell is selected for transfer across the switching fabric and the other is queued in the input controller until the next cell transfer time. To satisfy the second condition, as Figure 10.10 shows, the (Banyan) switching matrix is preceded by a **(Batcher) sorting matrix** and the two are interconnected using what is known as a **shuffle exchange**. The combined effect is that all cells arriving at the switching matrix are ordered such that they each follow a unique path through the switching matrix and hence, providing independent routing paths are available

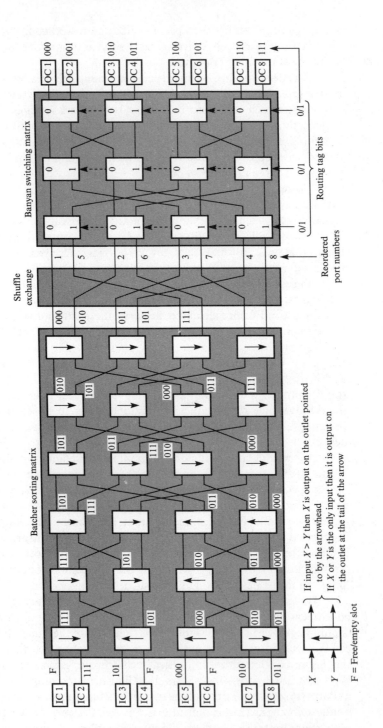

Figure 10.10 Batcher–Banyan switch matrix.

within each switching element, the cells from all input ports can be switched simultaneously. The size of a Batcher sorting network grows by $N(\log N^2)$ and can be considerable for large switches.

Another approach used in practical switch designs to reduce the blocking probability is a switching fabric that has multiple paths between each pair of input and output ports. For example, with the simple delta switch, this can be achieved by replicating the total switch matrix an appropriate number of times. Each input controller uses a different matrix to transfer each cell. Alternatively, the basic Banyan switching matrix can be extended by adding extra switching stages. In both cases, the number of additional stages can be selected so that the blocking – and hence cell loss – probability is at an acceptable level.

Another issue which has an impact on switch design is multicasting. Recall from Section 9.5.1 that this requires all the cells from each workstation in a (multicast) group to be sent to all the other workstations in the group. In practice, the most efficient way of achieving this is to use the switches to route copies of cells to multiple destinations. Although this can be done readily with both the time-division and fully connected switch designs, with matrix switches, because of their self-routing property, additional switching stages are needed if multicasting is to be supported. Further details relating to both these issues can be found in the bibliography.

10.4.3   Protocol architecture

As Figure 10.11 shows, the ATM protocol architecture supports three separate application functions (planes). These are the control (C) plane, the user (U) plane and the management (M) plane. The protocols associated with the **C-plane** are concerned with signaling, that is, the setting up and clearing of on-demand VCs. Typically, these are set up and cleared using a signaling protocol set in the station communicating with a similar protocol set in the network signaling control point. The protocols in the **U-plane** depend on the application and, in general, communicate on a user-to-user (peer) basis with a similar protocol set in the destination station. The protocols in the **M-plane** are concerned with the management of the station; examples include reporting any error conditions that may arise during normal operation to the network management station and receiving notifications of the virtual path/channel identifiers that have been allocated for PVCs. These three application functions use the services provided by the three lower ATM protocol layers for the transfer of the associated messages over the cell-based ATM switching network.

The ATM network supports a range of different services. The use of cell switching and transmission within the network is transparent to the upper application protocols which view the ATM network simply as a flexible facility for the transfer of information relating to any media type. To achieve this transparency, the highest of the three ATM layers is known as the **ATM adaptation layer (AAL)**. As the name implies, it performs an adaptation (convergence) function between the class of service provided to the user layer

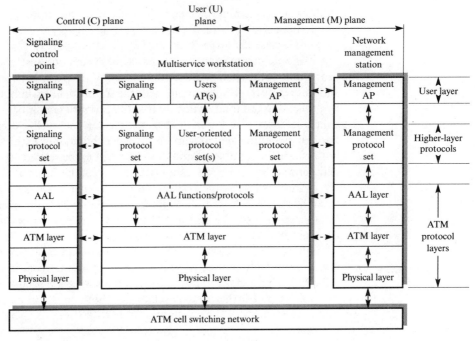

Figure 10.11
ATM protocol
architecture.

AP = Application process   ATM = Asynchronous transfer mode
AAL = ATM adaptation layer

above – for example, the transfer of a data frame between two legacy LANs – and
the cell-based service provided by the underlying ATM layer.

To support the various information sources, the AAL provides a range of
alternative service types known as **service classes**. Associated with each service
class is a different adaptation function/protocol which converts the source
information into streams of 48-octet segments. It passes these to the **ATM
layer** for transfer across the network. The ATM layer is concerned with adding
the correct cell header information to each segment and multiplexing the cells
relating to different connections into a single stream of cells for transmission
over the network. It is also concerned with the demultiplexing of received cell
streams and relaying their contents to the appropriate AAL protocol at the
destination.

The **physical layer** can take on a number of different forms and depends on
the type of transmission circuits being used. The upper part of the physical layer is
known as the **transmission-convergence sublayer** and is concerned with such
functions as the generation of the header check sequence in the cell header and
the delineation of the cell boundaries. The lower part takes on different forms
and is known as the **medium-dependent sublayer**. It is concerned with such
functions as line coding and bit/clock synchronization. We shall discuss the
operation of the AAL and ATM layer in more detail.

10.4.4 ATM adaptation layer

The AAL provides a range of alternative service types/classes for the transport of the byte streams/message units generated by the various higher protocol layers associated with the U-, C-, and M-planes. It converts the submitted information into streams of 48-octet segments and transports these in the payload field of multiple ATM cells. Similarly, on receipt of the stream of cells relating to the same call, it converts the 48-octet information field contained within each cell into the required form for delivery to the particular higher protocol layer.

The service types are classified according to three criteria: the existence of a time relationship between the source and destination users (for example, voice), the bit rate associated with the transfer (constant or variable), and the connection mode (connection oriented or connectionless). Currently, five service types have been defined. They are referred to as AAL 1–5 and their interrelationship, based on these criteria, is illustrated in Figure 10.12(a).

Both AAL 1 (Class A) and AAL 2 (Class B) are connection oriented and there is a timing relationship between the source and destination users. The difference between the two is that AAL 1 provides a **constant bit rate (CBR) service** while AAL 2 provides a **variable bit rate (VBR) service**. An example use of AAL 1 is for the transfer of the constant bit rate byte stream associated with a voice call, for example, 1 byte per $125\,\mu s$. AAL 1 is also known as **circuit (switched) emulation**. An example use of AAL 2 is for the transmission of the variable bit rate stream associated with compressed video. Although video produces frames at

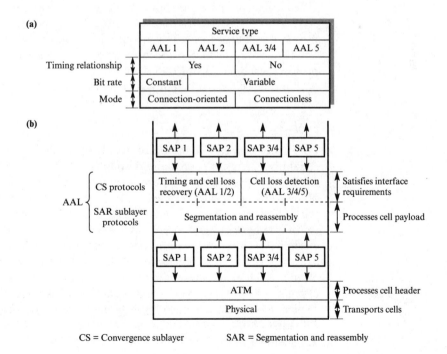

Figure 10.12
ATM adaptation layer:
(a) service class relationship;
(b) sublayer protocols and their functions.

a constant rate, a video codec will produce frames containing a variable amount of compressed data.

There is no timing relationship between source and destination with either AAL 3/4 (Class C/D) or AAL 5. Initially, AAL 3 was defined to provide a connection-oriented, VBR data service. Later, this service type was dropped and it is now merged with AAL 4. Both AAL 3/4 and AAL 5 provide a similar connectionless VBR service. An example use is for the transfer of data frames between two legacy LANs – through a remote bridge or a router – or for the transfer of frames containing multimedia information between a multiservice workstation and a server. It is also used for the transfer of the message units associated with the signaling and management protocol sets in such workstations. In all of these cases, as we shall see in Section 10.4.6, although the service offered is connectionless, the resulting cell streams produced by the AAL are transferred over previously established PVCs, for example, to the signaling control point or network management station.

In order to implement this range of services, the AAL is comprised of two sublayers as shown in Figure 10.12(b). The **convergence sublayer (CS)** performs a convergence function between the service offered at the layer interface and that provided by the underlying ATM layer. The **segmentation and reassembly (SAR)** sublayer performs the necessary segmentation of the source information ready for transfer in the 48-octet payload field of a cell and also, the corresponding reassembly function at the destination prior to the delivery of the source information.

Since the submitted information differs for each service type, there is a different convergence function – and hence CS protocol – associated with each service type. Associated with each protocol is a **service access point (SAP)** which is used to direct all information submitted for transfer – the service data unit (SDU) – to the appropriate CS protocol. Similarly, there are four different types of SAR protocol, each with its own PDU structure. Each utilizes the 48-octet information field in each cell in a different way. Let us consider the operation of each protocol.

AAL 1

For this type of service the CS protocol endeavors to maintain a constant bit rate stream between the source and destination SAPs. The bit rate can range from a few kilobits per second – for example, for a single compressed voice call – to tens of megabits per second – for example, for a single uncompressed video. However, the agreed rate must be maintained, even when occasional cell losses or cell transfer time variations occur. Cell losses are overcome in an agreed way, for example, by inserting dummy bits/bytes into the delivered stream. Cell transfer delay variations are compensated for by buffering segments at the destination: the output of the bits/bytes relating to a call is started only after a predefined number of segments have been received, this number being determined by the user bit rate. Typical figures are 2 segments at kilobit rates and 100 segments at megabit rates. The use of buffering at the destination also provides a crude way of overcoming any small variations between the input rate at the source interface and the output

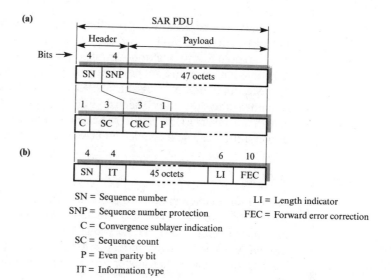

Figure 10.13
SAR protocol data
unit types: (a) AAL 1;
(b) AAL 2.

SN = Sequence number
SNP = Sequence number protection
C = Convergence sublayer indication
SC = Sequence count
P = Even parity bit
IT = Information type

LI = Length indicator
FEC = Forward error correction

rate at the destination, for example, if each is based on a separate clock. The preferred solution is for both the input and output clocks to be provided by the network.

The format of each PDU associated with the SAR protocol is shown in Figure 10.13(a). To detect segment losses, the first octet contains a 4-bit sequence number and an associated 4-bit protection field which is used to protect the sequence number against single bit errors. The sequence number is itself made up of a 3-bit sequence count field – for the detection of lost cells – and a single convergence sublayer indication bit. The latter can be used for the transfer of timing and/or other information relating to the payload field. The sequence number protection field comprises a 3-bit CRC, generated by the polynomial $x^3 + x + 1$, and an even parity bit. The latter is used to detect errors in the CRC.

AAL 2

With this type of service, although there is a timing relationship between the source and destination SAPs – determined by the frame rate, for example, for compressed video – the amount of information associated with each compressed frame may vary from one frame to the next. The CS protocol at the source receives bursts of information at the frame rate with each burst containing a variable amount of information. Hence the peer CS protocol at the destination must endeavor to output the received information in this same way even when occasional cell losses or cell transfer time variations occur. With AAL 2, the time variations are overcome using similar techniques to those described for AAL 1.

The format of each PDU associated with the corresponding SAR protocol is shown in Figure 10.13(b). As with AAL 1, the sequence number is present to detect (and recover from) lost cells and to carry timing information. The information type field indicates either the position of the segment in relation to a submitted message unit – for example, a compressed frame – or whether the segment contains timing or other information. The three segment types relating to positional information are beginning of message (BOM), continuation of message (COM), and end of message (EOM). Also, because of the variable size of submitted message units, the last (EOM) segment may not be full and hence the length indicator (LI) at the tail indicates the number of useful bytes in the segment. Finally, the FEC field enables bit errors to be detected and a selection corrected.

AAL 3/4

AAL 3 was defined initially to provide a connection-oriented data transfer service. Later, this type of service was dropped and combined with AAL 4. AAL 3/4 provides a connectionless data transfer service for the transfer of variable length frames up to 65 535 bytes in length. Error detection and other fields are added to each frame prior to its transfer and the resulting frame is padded so that it is an integral multiple of 32 bits.

The operation of AAL 3/4 is best described by considering the format of the PDUs associated with both the CS and SAR protocols. The format of the additional fields added by the CS protocol to each submitted user SDU – at the corresponding SAP – is shown in Figure 10.14(a). The figure also shows how the resulting CS PDU is segmented by the SAR protocol into multiple 48-octet SAR PDUs.

The header and trailer fields added to the submitted SDU by the CS protocol at the source are used by the peer CS protocol at the destination to detect any missing or malformed SDUs. The PDU-type field is a legacy of the earlier AAL 3 which required multiple types of PDU. It is set to zero with AAL 3/4. The begin–end (BE) tag is a modulo-256 sequence number and is repeated in the trailer for added resilience. It enables SDUs to be delivered at the user interface in the same sequence as they were submitted although, again, this facility is not normally used with a connectionless service. The buffer allocation (BA) field is inserted in the header by the source to help the CS protocol at the destination to allocate an appropriate amount of (buffer) memory for the complete SDU. At the trailer, the pad field is used to make the total number of octets in the complete CS PDU an integral multiple of 4 octets. Similarly, the alignment (AL) field is a single (dummy) octet to make the trailer 4 octets also. Collectively this leads to easier memory management at the destination. The length field indicates the total length of the complete PDU and this is used by the receiving protocol to detect any malformed SDUs.

On receipt of each CS PDU, the SAR protocol segments this into multiple 48-octet segments – SAR PDUs – as shown in Figure 10.14. In the header, the segment type (ST) indicates whether the segment is the first, continuation, last, or only segment resulting from the segmentation of the CS PDU. The sequence number (SN) is used to detect missing segments. In practice, a device like a network server may have a number of frames – and hence CS PDUs – being received concurrently from multiple sources. Hence for the receiving SAR

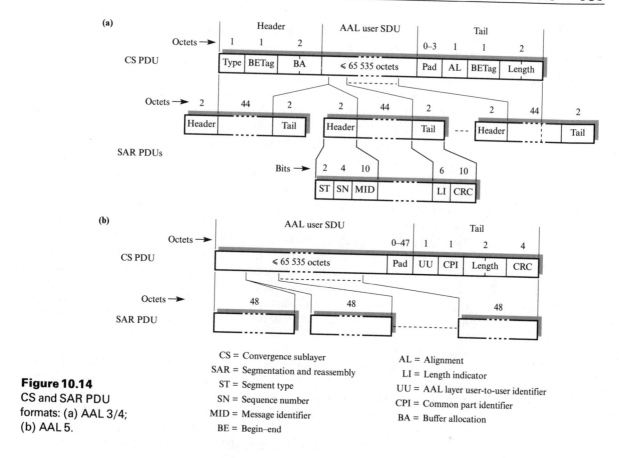

Figure 10.14
CS and SAR PDU
formats: (a) AAL 3/4;
(b) AAL 5.

CS = Convergence sublayer
SAR = Segmentation and reassembly
ST = Segment type
SN = Sequence number
MID = Message identifier
BE = Begin–end

AL = Alignment
LI = Length indicator
UU = AAL layer user-to-user identifier
CPI = Common part identifier
BA = Buffer allocation

protocol to relate each incoming segment to the correct PDU, the source SAR protocol adds the same multiplexing identifier (MID) field to the head of each segment relating to the same CS PDU. At the tail, the length indicator (LI) indicates the number of useful octets in the segment since the CS PDU is not necessarily an integral number of 44-octet segments. Clearly, this field has meaning either in the last segment relating to a multisegment CS PDU or, if it is the only segment. The CRC is used to detect possible transmission errors introduced during the transfer of segments.

AAL 5

Because of the origin of AAL 3/4, the CS PDU contains a number of fields in the header which were included primarily to support a connection-oriented service. The MID field at the head of each SAR PDU – which is present to enable the destination to relate segments to a specific frame – also performs a similar function to the protocol connection identifier – VPI/VCI – present in the header of each ATM cell. As a result, the alternative AAL 5 service class has been defined. This provides a similar service to AAL 3/4 but with a reduced number of control fields in both the CS and SAR PDUs. It is known as the **simple and efficient adaptation layer (SEAL)**. As with AAL 3/4, its operation is best described by considering the format of the PDUs associated with both the CS and SAR protocols. These are shown in Figure 10.14(b).

As we can see, with AAL 5 there is no header associated with the constructed CS PDU. Also, the pad field in the trailer is longer (0–47 octets) so that the length of each CS PDU can be an integral number of complete 48-octet segments. This has the advantage that the fields at the tail of the CS PDU are always the last eight octets of the last segment, which leads to faster processing at the destination. The AAL user-to-user identifier (UU) enables the two correspondent user layers to relate the AAL SDU to a particular SAP. The use of the CPI field has yet to be defined. It is included to support future functions and currently to make the tail an even number of octets. The length field indicates the number of octets in the user data field and is an integer value in the range 0 to 65 535. The CRC field detects the presence of any transmission errors in the reassembled CS PDU. If errors are detected, then the user layer above is informed when the SDU contained within the PDU is delivered. In this way, it is left to the user layer to decide what action to take: in some instances this will be to discard the SDU – for example, if it contains normal data – while in others, it will be to accept it and take appropriate recovery steps – for example, if the SDU contents relate to a video or voice portion of a multimedia document.

As we can see, there is no head or tail associated with the SAR PDU. Each comprises the full 48 octets and the SAR protocol is said to be null. The lack of an MID field at the head of each segment means that the segments relating to the same CS PDU are identified using the field in the header of the ATM cell that is used to transport the segment. With AAL 5, the SDU type bit in user data cells – also known as **ATM-layer user-to-user (AUU) cells** – is used to indicate whether the cell contents form the beginning or continuation of the CS PDU (binary 0) or the end (binary 1). Although this means the operation of the AAL is now linked with that of the ATM layer, it is done to improve the efficiency of the segmentation process. AAL 5 is used also as the AAL in the C-plane for the segmentation and reassembly of the messages associated with the signaling protocol. It is then known as the **signaling AAL (SAAL)**.

10.4.5   ATM layer

The ATM layer performs all the functions relating to the routing and multiplexing of cells over VCs, which may be semipermanent or set up on demand. Its main function is to assign a header to the segment streams generated by the AAL relating to a particular call. Similarly, on receipt of cell streams, its function is to remove the header from each cell and pass the cell contents – segments – to the appropriate AAL protocol.

To perform these functions, the ATM layer maintains a table which contains a list of VCIs. Normally, in ATM LANs all switching is carried out using VPIs only and the VCI field in the cell header is used to multiplex/demultiplex the cells relating to specific calls/transactions which are transported over the same path. In the case of semipermanent VCs, the VPIs are downloaded by network management – via the network management protocol stack – and in the case of on-demand VCs, the VPIs are obtained using the appropriate signaling protocol set. In both cases the cell streams relating to the management/signaling protocol messages are transferred over permanently assigned VCs.

10.4.6   Call processing

As we saw in Figure 10.4 and its associated text, there are two types of traffic associated with an ATM LAN: that relating to the message flows exchanged between the distributed community of multiservice workstations and their associated servers, and that relating to the message flows exchanged between the bridges/routers that form the interface with the various legacy LAN segments/subnets and their associated servers. Also, in the case of multiservice workstations, there are two types of call: one connection oriented and the other connectionless. The first relates to network services such as telephony and videophony, while the second relates to more conventional data services similar to those used with legacy LANs. We shall consider the three types separately.

Connection-oriented calls

Services such as telephony and videophony require a separate VC to be set up between any pair of workstations for the duration of the call. The standards relating to this type of service are based on those used to set up calls in the ISDN since, in principle, the operation of setting up and clearing calls is the same as that used to perform the same function within the ISDN. All the (signaling) messages relating to the setting up and clearing of calls are carried over a separate channel – the signaling virtual channel connection (SVCC) – which is independent of that used for carrying the message flows associated with the call. When the network is first configured or a new outlet added, a semipermanent VC is set up by network management between each network outlet and the central signaling control point. This is analogous to installing a physical wire connection between each telephone outlet and a local (telephone) PBX.

When an SVCC is set up by network management, an entry is also made in the routing table of the SCP. This comprises the ATM network address of the workstation together with the allocated routing address, that is, the VPI/VCI addresses used in the header of cells that are received/output by the SCP from/to this workstation. The network address of each workstation is analogous to that of a telephone outlet and hence is a hierarchical address that uniquely identifies the workstation in the context of the total network. As Section 8.2.3 showed, these have a standard format and, in ATM LANs, are 20-byte NSAP addresses.

To initiate the setting up of a call, the user of the workstation follows a dialog which involves specifying the address of the required recipient of the call and also the call type – telephone, videophone, etc. This, in turn, results in the exchange of signaling messages using the signaling protocol set in the workstation and a similar protocol set in the SCP computer. The protocol architecture to support this was shown earlier in Figure 10.11 and the signaling protocol is defined in **recommendation Q.2931**. This is based on the ISDN user–network signaling protocol described earlier in Section 8.4.6. On receipt of the call request, the SCP communicates with the user of the called workstation – using the signaling protocol set – to ascertain whether the user is prepared to receive a call. If the response is positive, this is communicated back to the SCP which proceeds to set up a (duplex) VC across the network by adding entries into each switch routing table that links the port/VPI/VCI of the calling workstation with that of the called workstation. The SCP then informs the calling workstation that a VC has been set up and the call commences. In a similar way, either user can invoke the clearing of the connection at any time by initiating the sending of appropriate disconnection messages over the separate signaling channel.

To set up a call involving multiple workstations – for example, for a teleconferencing or videoconferencing session – all the workstations must be fully interconnected. For small numbers of workstations this can be done by the SCP directly using a similar procedure to that used for a two-party call. Since in some instances the number of workstations involved may be large, an alternative approach is to route all the information flows relating to such calls via a central routing point known as the broadcast server.

Using this approach, to set up a conferencing session the initiator of the session communicates with the SCP as before – using the signaling channel – but this time indicates a conferencing call – and its type – and the addresses of the workstations involved. The SCP, in turn, communicates with the user of each of these workstations – using their signaling channels and associated protocol set – to ascertain their availability and willingness to participate in a conferencing session. On receipt of their responses, the SCP initiates the setting up of a switched VC between each workstation that returns a positive response and the broadcast server. It then informs, firstly, the broadcast server of the type of call and the set of switched VCs involved, and secondly, the users of the workstations that the session can commence. The session proceeds with the broadcast server relaying the information flows received from each workstation out to all the other workstations. These playout the received information under the control of the user of the workstation, for example, by using a separate window for each member of a videoconferencing session.

Connectionless calls

As we saw at the beginning of Section 10.4, multiservice workstations are being introduced in an incremental way as existing data-only workstations are replaced by those offering a wider range of services. A major issue when considering connectionless working is interworking, not only between ATM (cell-based) workstations, but also between such workstations and existing data-only workstations.

As we saw in Chapter 7, most large legacy LANs are comprised of a number of LAN segments of the same type interconnected by bridges. Alternatively, if the segments are of different types, as we saw in Chapter 9, the segments are interconnected by routers. Recall that when using bridges all routing is carried out at the MAC sublayer and, when using routers, routing is carried out at the IP layer – CLNP layer in an OSI stack. Both the MAC and IP layers provide a best-try connectionless service for the transfer of preconfigured frames or datagrams, respectively. To support interworking between an ATM workstation and a workstation that is connected to a legacy LAN, two alternatives must be supported: one for use with a bridged LAN and the other for use with a router-based LAN. With the first, the interface between the ATM LAN and the legacy LAN is a bridge and with the second the interface is a router. Two different protocol architectures are used, each of which provides seamless interworking in the appropriate environment. We shall consider each separately.

LAN emulation.   The method used when bridges form the interface to the legacy LAN has been developed by a group of companies that are all involved in the manufacture of LAN networking equipment. The group is known as the **ATM Forum**. A schematic diagram showing the various networking components used with this method are shown in Figure 10.15(a).

The aim of the various networking components is to emulate the broadcast mode of operation of a legacy LAN over a connection-oriented ATM LAN. The term used to describe this method is known as **LAN emulation (LE)**. The three components used are an **LE configuration server (LECS)**, an **LE server (LES)**, and a **broadcast and unknown address server (BUS)**. Although each is shown as a separate entity in Figure 10.15, for a small LAN, they may all be implemented in a single computer. In this case, the messages/frames relating to each component are identified by the type of virtual channel connection (VCC) on which they arrive.

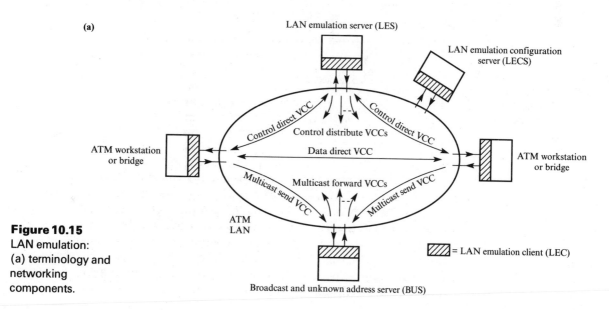

(a)

Figure 10.15
LAN emulation:
(a) terminology and networking components.

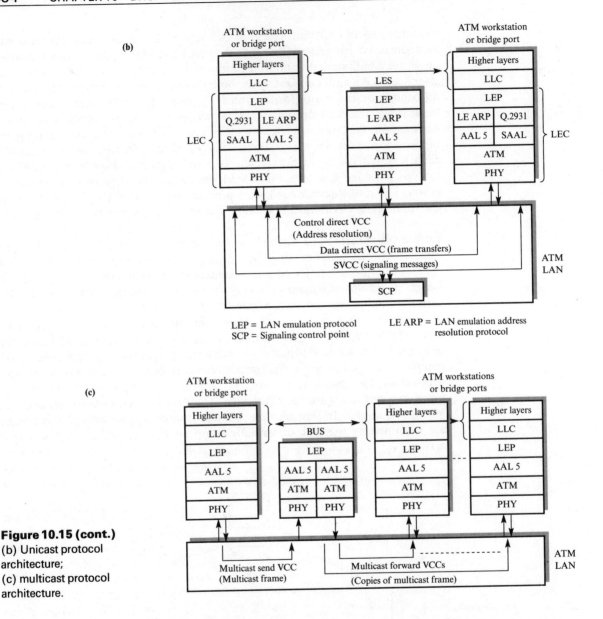

Figure 10.15 (cont.)
(b) Unicast protocol
architecture;
(c) multicast protocol
architecture.

In a large installation there may be multiple emulated LANs each of which has its own LES and BUS. The LECS is used by all stations that are connected to the total ATM LAN to determine the ATM addresses of the LES and BUS. There is a reserved VCC to connect all stations to the LECS for this purpose. The LES provides an address resolution service to convert from conventional 48-bit MAC addresses into 20-byte ATM addresses. The BUS is responsible, firstly, for supporting multicasting/broadcasting, and secondly, for relaying frames to stations whose MAC address is unknown by the LES.

All stations connected to the ATM LAN – ATM workstations, bridges, etc. – have an **LE client (LEC)** subsystem associated with them. This comprises hardware and software that provides a similar service to the MAC chipset (and associated software) in a workstation that is connected to a legacy LAN. When a station is powered up, it goes through an initialization procedure at the end of which it has initialized certain operational parameters and its own set of addresses – as described below, a station has more than one address. As we can see in Figure 10.15(a), a separate pair of VCCs is used to connect each LEC to the LECS, the LES, and the BUS. Once initialized, the LEC first obtains the pair of VCCs of the LES and BUS from the LECS and then proceeds to register itself with both the LES and BUS. At the end of the initialization phase, both the LES and BUS have the set of addresses of all active stations that are connected to the ATM LAN. In the case of a bridge, the LEC can either register the MAC addresses of all stations that are connected to its legacy LAN port or, more usually, just the address set of the port through which it is connected to the ATM LAN. In the first case the bridge operates in the **nonproxy mode** and in the second, the **proxy mode**.

We can see in Figure 10.15(b) that the protocol stack within each LEC contains a **LAN emulation protocol (LEP)** layer – immediately below the LLC sublayer – which communicates with a similar layer in the LES. In order to make the underlying network transparent to the LLC sublayer, the service provided by the LEP layer is a connectionless service similar to that offered by the MAC sublayer. The two user service primitives are LE_UNITDATA.request and LE_UNITDATA.indication.

To emulate a broadcast LAN, both primitives have a source and destination MAC address as parameters. This means that each workstation and bridge connected to the ATM LAN, in addition to a 20-byte ATM address, has a 48-bit MAC address associated with it. It also has a 2-byte **LEC identifier (LECID)** which is used to identify uniquely the ATM workstation or bridge port among those currently attached to the LES. We shall look at the function of the LECID later.

The VCC that (logically) connects an LEC to the LES is known as the **control direct VCC**. On receipt of an LE service request primitive, the LEP in the source LEC reads the source and destination MAC addresses and passes these to the **LE address resolution protocol (LE ARP)**. The latter forms an address resolution request message – containing the two MAC addresses and the ATM address of the LEC – and sends this to the LE ARP in the LES over the control direct VCC. Assuming the LE ARP in the LES knows the ATM address of the destination LEC, it returns this in a reply message to the requesting LE ARP – the latter then initiates the setting up of a **data direct VCC** between itself and the LE ARP in the destination LEC. This is done using either the SCP and the signaling protocol set described earlier for connection-oriented calls or, with some ATM switch architectures, directly by the two LE ARPs involved. The connection is cleared by the LE ARP when no further frames are received for the same destination LEC within a defined timeout interval.

If the LE ARP in the LES does not have the ATM address of the destination LEC – for example, if the destination MAC address relates to a station connected to the legacy LAN port of a bridge – the LES sends a copy of the LE ARP request message to all registered LECs using the set of **control distribute VCCs**. The LE ARP which has knowledge of the destination MAC address then replies with the corresponding ATM address – or its own ATM address if it is a bridge – using the control direct VCC. The LE ARP in the LES then relays the reply to the source LE ARP, again using the corresponding control direct VCC. Once the source LE ARP has obtained the ATM address of the destination, it sets up a data direct VCC as before.

The flow of data frames, each of which has the source and destination MAC addresses at its head, can then start. Since bridges are involved, these can be either 802.3 or 802.5 frames with the frame type defined in the header of the frame. No FCS field is required since, in an ATM LAN, this is performed by the AAL 5 sublayer. Because of the use of the intermediate address resolution phase, the LE connectionless service is said to be provided *indirectly*.

The foregoing relates to unicasting, that is, there is a single destination station for each submitted MAC frame. To implement multicasting, a copy of the created MAC frame must be forwarded to all stations that belong to the same multicast group. Clearly, using the method just described, a multiplicity of switched VCs would be required between each member of the group and all other members. To avoid this requirement, the BUS is used and the associated protocol architecture is as shown in Figure 10.15(c).

An additional pair of VCCs is used between the LEC in each station and the LEC in the BUS. In the station-to-BUS direction, the VCC is known as the **multicast send VCC** and in the reverse direction, the **multicast forward VCC**. On receipt of a service primitive with a multicast destination address, the LEP creates a frame as before but with its own 2-byte LECID at the head. It sends this directly to the LEP in the BUS over the multicast send VCC. On receipt of the frame, the LEP broadcasts a copy of the frame to all stations using the set of multicast forward VCCs. The LEP in each station first determines from the LECID at the head of the frame whether it originated the frame. If it did, then the LEP simply discards the frame. This is known as **echo suppression**. If the LECID does not match that of the station, the receiving LEP determines from the multicast address at the head of the frame whether this station is part of the multicast group. If it is, the frame is passed up to the LLC layer, if not, the frame is discarded.

The unknown address service associated with the BUS enables an LEP to send a limited number of frames to their intended destination during the period a data direct VCC is being set up. The procedure followed is the same as that for a multicast frame and, since multiple copies of each frame are sent – each over a separate multicast forward VCC – a limit is set on the number of such frames the LEP can send. Any further frames received must then be retained – cached – until the data direct VCC is in place.

Classical IP over ATM. The method used when routers form the interface to the legacy LAN has been developed by the **Internet Engineering Task Force (IETF)**. The basic method is known as **classical IP over ATM**.

Recall from Chapter 9 that, using the IP (or CLNP), before a workstation can exchange datagrams with another workstation, it must first know the IP/NPA (CLNP/SNPA) address pair of its local router (intermediate system). Also, the local router must know the address pair of all the workstations that are connected to the LAN segments to which is attached. These are acquired using the ARP (IP) – or ES-to-IS (CLNP) – protocol and exploiting the broadcast nature of legacy LANs. Once these have been acquired, all datagrams are exchanged between two stations via the router/IS and it is this that relays the datagrams to their intended destination using the NPA address – for example, MAC address – corresponding to the IP destination address in the datagram header.

To emulate the same operation with a nonbroadcast ATM LAN, a permanent VCC is set up between all stations and router ports that are connected to the ATM LAN and a central node known as the **connectionless server (CLS)**. The CLS provides a dual function of address resolution and a datagram relaying service. Since with this method all datagrams are relayed directly by the CLS, the connectionless service is said to be provided *directly*. A schematic diagram of the protocol architecture used with a CLS is shown in Figure 10.16.

The ARP in each station/router port first registers its own address pair – IP and ATM addresses – with the ARP in the CLS using the corresponding permanent VCC. In a similar way, the ARP in the CLS can acquire the address pair of a station or router port that is connected to it by a VCC. In this way, the ARP in the CLS builds up a routing table containing the address pair of all stations and router ports that are connected to it. Whenever a station IP has a datagram to send, it simply sends the datagram to the IP layer in the CLS over the VCC that connects the station to the CLS. On receipt of the datagram, the IP in the CLS first reads the destination IP address from the head of the datagram and uses this to obtain the corresponding ATM address of the destination from its routing table. The IP then forwards the datagram to the destination over the corresponding VCC.

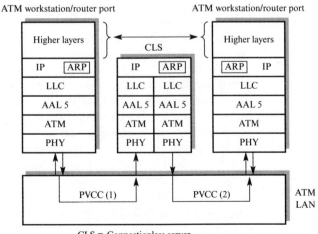

Figure 10.16
Protocol architecture to support classical IP over an ATM LAN.

CLS = Connectionless server
PVCC = Permanent virtual channel connection

Multicasting with a CLS is carried out in a similar way to that described with an LES except that with a CLS a separate broadcast server is not required. Instead, on receipt of a datagram with a multicast address, the IP layer in the CLS simply sends a copy of the datagram to all other stations using their corresponding VCC. Each recipient IP then determines from the multicast address at the head of the datagram whether it is a member of the multicast group. If it is, the datagram is passed to the higher protocol layers, if not, the datagram is discarded.

When a CLS is being used, there are two alternative relaying modes. With the first, the complete datagram is reassembled by the AAL before it is processed by the IP layer. Clearly, this introduces delays and requires significant buffer storage for its implementation. In order to reduce these overheads, we may use a second mode of working known as **streaming** or **pipelining**. In practice, the destination address required for routing is carried in the first ATM segment/cell and hence in this mode, the first (beginning of message) segment is passed directly to the IP layer for processing as soon as it is received by the AAL protocol. The new VC is then determined and this and the remaining segments making up the datagram are relayed directly without reassembly. The AAL with this method is AAL 3/4 since the MID field in the header of each cell is required for identification purposes during the reassembly process.

Wide area networking

The two connectionless architectures we discussed in the last section are both intended for use within a single ATM LAN. However, for communications between such LANs over an intermediate WAN, a different protocol architecture has been defined. Since this relates to a (public) WAN, the protocol architecture has been defined by the ITU-T.

As we shall see in Section 10.5, the first generation of ATM WANs is comprised of an interconnected set of ATM-based **metropolitan area networks (MANs)**. A schematic diagram showing a typical arrangement for interconnecting two ATM LANs over such a network, together with the associated protocol architecture, is given in Figure 10.17(a). In this example, we assume that the connectionless service is provided at the IP layer although it could equally be provided at the MAC layer.

As we can see, an ATM gateway is located at each customer site, one port of which is connected to the site ATM LAN and the other port to an ATM MAN. Typically, there are a number of gateways (sites) connected to the MAN in a particular area and this provides a local gathering and distribution function. A **MAN switching system (MSS)** is also connected to each MAN and the set of MSSs are interconnected to form a countrywide switched service. The service provided to users within a gateway is a switched multimegabit data service (SMDS) – similar to that described in Section 8.4.7 for frame relay networks – and the gateway is known as an **SMDS edge gateway**.

We shall discuss the role of the various protocols associated with SMDS – known as the connectionless broadband data service (CBDS) by the ITU-T – in Section 10.5.7. Essentially, on receipt of a datagram with a destination address

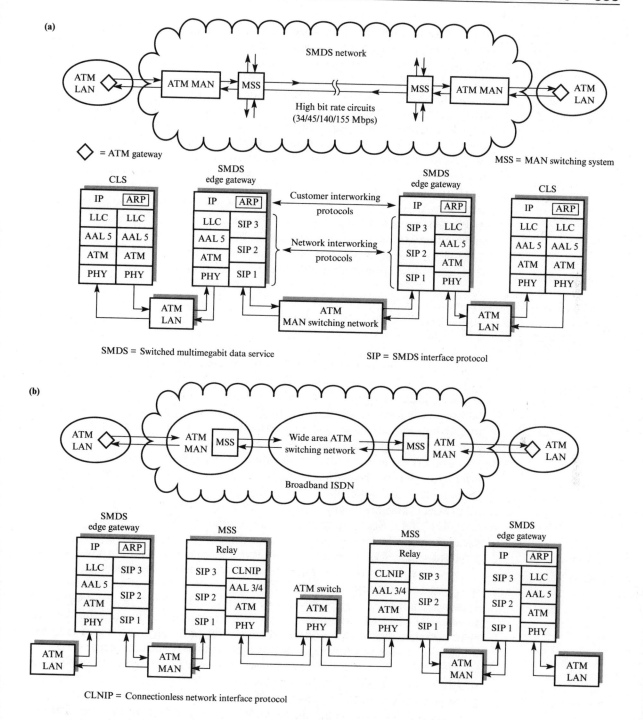

Figure 10.17   Connectionless working over wide area ATM networks: (a) ATM MAN switching network; (b) broadband ISDN.

that indicates a different site network address (netid), the CLS within the ATM LAN relays the datagram to the ATM LAN port of the SMDS edge gateway. The datagram – or MAC frame if LAN emulation is being used – is first encapsulated into a standardized frame format by the SIP level 3 protocol and then relayed across the SMDS network to the appropriate destination gateway. From there it is relayed first to the site CLS and from there to the destination station.

In a longer time frame, the MSSs within the ATM WAN are themselves interconnected by an ATM switching network. The total network is known as the broadband ISDN (BISDN). A schematic diagram of this type of structure, together with the protocol architecture associated with it, is shown in Figure 10.17(b). As we can see, this is similar to part (a) except in this case an intermediate ATM switching network is present. The **connectionless network interface protocol (CLNIP)** provides a similar service to the SIP level 3 protocol and the format of each CLNIP PDU is similar to that given later in Figure 10.27. The main difference is that there is no common header or trailer with the CLNIP PDU since this is provided by the AAL in an ATM network.

10.5   DQDB

Distributed queue dual bus (DQDB) is a cell-based broadcast network that has been developed primarily as a high-speed LAN interconnection facility. In addition, it can support limited isochronous (constant bit rate) communication services. The LANs may be physically distributed over a single site or, more usually, over multiple sites. Such networks are known as metropolitan area networks (MANs). The connection point to networks distributed over multiple sites is either a remote bridge or a router. Since workstations are not connected directly to the network, normally MANs utilize a high bit rate shared transmission medium such as 34/45/140/155 Mbps public carrier circuits. DQDB is now an international standard and is defined in **IEEE 802.6 (ISO 8802.6)**.

The DQDB standard relates to a single subnetwork in the context of a larger network; typically, the larger network comprises a number of interconnected DQDB subnetworks. Each subnetwork is made up of **dual contradirectional buses** – that is, two unidirectional buses running in opposite directions – to which a distributed community of **access nodes** – also known as **customer network interface units** – are attached. The buses may be in an **open bus topology** or a **looped bus topology**, in which case the two ends are separate but physically colocated. As we shall see later, this can be used to provide better fault tolerance. Three example applications are shown in Figure 10.18: part (a) shows a single subnetwork MAN; part (b) a typical split-site private network; and part (c) a large wide area public network comprising multiple interconnected MANs.

As part (a) shows, a single DQDB MAN subnetwork can cover an area in excess of 50 km (30 miles). In this example, the access nodes will be located at the telephony switching offices in that area. The use of 34/45/140/155 Mbps circuits provide **seamless interconnection** for many LANs distributed around the city, that

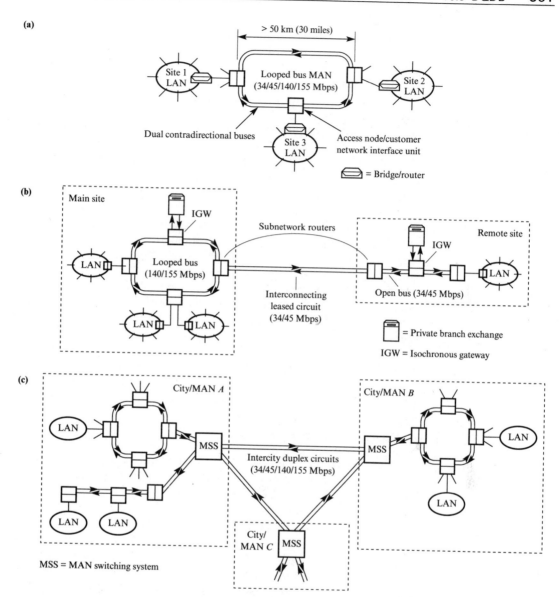

Figure 10.18
DQDB/MAN network
architectures:
(a) single schematic
MAN; (b) dual-site
private network;
(c) wide area multiple
MAN network.

is, two users at different sites communicating with one another will be unaware of the fact that an intermediate network is involved.

Part (b) illustrates the use of two DQDB subnetworks in a private network application. In this instance, all the networking equipment located at both sites is privately owned and run and the high bit rate circuit interconnecting both sites leased from a public carrier. One site is assumed to have a looped bus topology and the other an open bus. This example also shows how a DQDB network can be used for the interconnection of two private telephone exchanges (PBXs) which requires a constant bit rate channel.

Part (c) illustrates how several multisubnetwork MANs can be interconnected to form a larger network that spans several cities. As we can see, in this case each DQDB subnetwork in a city is connected to a MAN switching system (MSS). The MSS, on receipt of each LAN frame, either relays it directly to the required subnetwork if it is connected to it or, otherwise, it forwards the frame to the required MSS over the appropriate intercity duplex circuit. Such a network provides a switched multimegabit data service (SMDS) similar to that provided by a frame relay network.

Normally, a LAN is connected to its nearest access node by either a remote bridge or a router. All frames are transported across each DQDB subnetwork in the form of fixed-sized units known as segments. At the interface to each subnetwork, the frames are first fragmented into segments and then reassembled back into their original form at the destination. Because the format of LAN frames differs from one type of LAN to another, prior to the transfer of a frame, a standard header and trailer are added to it. With public networks, the header contains two new source and destination addresses which are the networkwide addresses of the corresponding customer access/interface units. As we shall see in Section 10.5.7, these are hierarchical addresses which identify the MSS, the subnetwork, and the customer access unit. All segments are transferred over each subnetwork using both buses which, because these pass data in opposite directions, ensures that a copy of each segment transmitted is received by all nodes on the subnetwork. Between subnetworks, routing is carried out on reassembled frames using the networkwide destination address at the head of each frame.

10.5.1   Subnetwork architectures

A schematic diagram of an open dual-bus subnetwork is shown in Figure 10.19(a). At the head of each bus is a **slot generator** which generates a contiguous stream of **slots** each capable of transferring a standard 53-octet cell. Access nodes are attached to both buses through read and write connections, with the read operation performed ahead of the write operation. The physical layer in each access node reads the contents of each slot without modifying its contents, and only if new data is to be sent by an access node does it overwrite the existing contents. We can conclude, therefore, that an access node only copies (reads) data from a bus, it does not remove it. Also, it changes the contents of a slot only when it is permitted to do so by the access protocol. Therefore, failure of the access unit within a node does not have any affect on the contents of the slots that pass by on the two buses provided the failure does not cause the node continuously to write.

A looped bus architecture is shown in Figure 10.19(b) and, as we can see, in this configuration both slot generators are colocated. Alternatively, the same slot generator can be used for both buses. In both cases, the two buses are still independent and are not connected together as in a ring network. Also, in addition to generating slots, the **head of bus** is responsible for passing management information to the access nodes. Typically, this management information is generated by a separate network management station and relates to either the

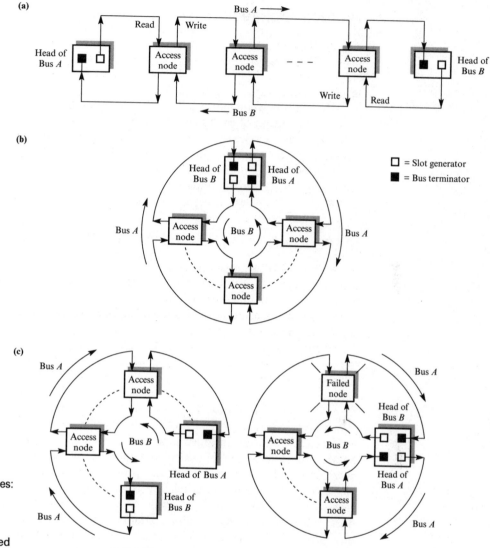

Figure 10.19
DQDB architectures:
(a) open bus;
(b) looped bus;
(c) example
reconfigured looped
bus networks.

allocation of isochronous bandwidth or the operational integrity of the sub-network.

With a looped bus topology reconfiguration can be supported in the event of a link or a node failure by replicating the head of bus functions so that more than one node can assume the role of head of bus. Two examples of reconfigured loops are shown in Figure 10.19(c); the first illustrates the reconfigured loop after a link failure and the second the reconfigured loop after the failure of an access node. The reconfiguration operation is carried out under the control of a remote network management station.

10.5.2 Protocol architecture

A schematic diagram identifying the components of the protocol architecture defined in IEEE 802.6 is shown in Figure 10.20(a). As with the other IEEE 802 standards, this defines the operation of the MAC sublayer – known as the DQDB layer in the standard – and the physical layer.

In addition to the normal connectionless (best try) data service provided for the interconnection of the basic LAN types, the DQDB MAC sublayer provides two additional services: a connection-oriented (reliable) data service and an isochronous service. Typically, the latter is used for the interconnection of two private (telephone) branch exchanges. For such applications, the multiplexed voice samples within the duplex link connecting the exchanges to their access nodes must be transferred across the bus at the same rate as the access link.

MAC sublayer

As Figure 10.20 shows, the MAC sublayer comprises four main functions: convergence, bus arbitration, common, and layer management. As we indicated earlier, all information is transferred across the dual buses in the form of fixed-sized segments. The convergence functions are required to convert all incoming source information into segments before its transfer and back into its original form before its delivery. For example, the MAC convergence function fragments the data frames submitted by a bridge or router into multiple segments ready for their transfer and, on receipt, reassembles them back into frames prior to their delivery.

There are two alternative control modes for gaining access to the slots on the two buses: **queued arbitrated (QA)** and **prearbitrated (PA)**. When isochronous services are supported, in order to provide a constant bit rate service, the required number of slots are preallocated and marked by the head-of-bus node. The prearbitrated function in each node providing the service is responsible for identifying the reserved slots relating to it – from an identifier at the head of each slot – and then either initiating the transmission of the isochronous data within these or receiving the data contained within them. All the remaining bus slots are used for the transfer of LAN data frames. Access to these slots is controlled by a distributed queuing algorithm in the queued arbitrated function block.

We can see from Figure 10.20 that the common function block forms the interface between the physical layer and the two bus arbitration function blocks. The physical layer interface takes the form of single octet transfers – read and write – to and from both buses. The main role of the common function block is to relay octets between the physical layer and the appropriate bus arbitration function. This involves detecting the start and end of each slot and examining selected octets within the slot/cell header according to its defined format. We shall consider this in more detail in Section 10.5.6. In addition, since more than one node can act as the head of bus (to enhance reliability) the nodes which can perform this function take part in the reconfiguration operation of the bus/loop

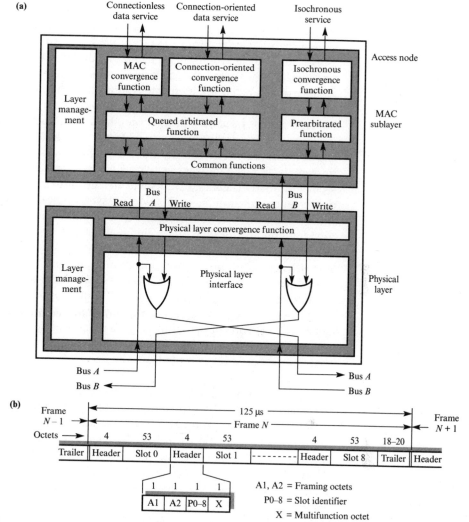

Figure 10.20
DQDB protocol
architecture: (a) layer
functions; (b) example
physical layer
convergence function.

when faults are detected. Also, when selected as the head of bus, the node generates contiguous streams of slots. Both these operations form part of the common functions.

Physical layer

The physical layer provides a standard interface to the MAC sublayer. However, as Figure 10.18 showed, the physical layer can be implemented using a range of different transmission media. For example, with public networks this can be 34, 45, 140, or 155 Mbps. As we saw in Chapter 2, such circuits utilize different framing formats and so a **physical layer conversion function** which establishes a contiguous sequence of slots over the selected physical transmission medium must be provided. An example of how this is achieved is shown in Figure 10.20(b).

The example relates to the use of a 34.368 Mbps E3 digital circuit. As the numbering indicates, this is at the third level in the (plesiochronous) ITU-T multiplexing hierarchy and is used to transmit four 8.448 Mbps streams. A number of bits/octets are used for framing and other purposes and hence a lower bit rate is available for the transmission of DQDB slots. When using such circuits for each bus, the head of bus establishes the frame structure shown in Figure 10.20 using the available transmission bandwidth. This has a duration of 125 μs which ensures that the frame can be used to support various constant bit rate voice services as well as data transfer. As we can see, preceding each 53-octet slot is a 4-octet header. The first two octets of the header enable the physical layer convergence function in each node to synchronize to the start of each new frame. The third octet identifies the slots within each frame. The fourth octet is used for a number of functions including the transfer of management information from the head of bus to the two layer management entities in the attached nodes. The physical layer convergence function reads and interprets the octets in the header field but passes only the 53-octet cell in each slot to the MAC sublayer. Because of the fixed 125 μs interval, each frame does not contain an exact multiple of 57 octets. The unused octets in this field arise due to the plesiochronous (nearly synchronous) mode of operation of such circuits as described in Chapter 2. With higher bit rate circuits, the 125 μs interval is maintained and hence each frame contains proportionately more (DQDB) slots.

Finally, as with all the protocol layers, the layer management entities associated with the physical layer and MAC sublayer are provided for a remote management entity to control and monitor the operation of both these layers. For the MAC sublayer this involves receiving and acting upon information relating to the slots, for example, the list of identifiers that are carried at the head of each prearbitrated slot and the message identifiers that are at the head of queued arbitrated slots, the use of which we shall describe in Section 10.5.6. It also involves the setting of operational parameters such as timers and the activation of the configuration control procedure. All information relating to such operations is carried in the header that precedes each slot.

10.5.3 Queued arbitrated access protocol

Access to the slots that are available for the transfer of asynchronous data is based on a distributed queuing algorithm. This is known as **queued packet distributed switch (QPSX)** and the principles of the method are shown in Figure 10.21.

As part (a) shows, each slot contains two bits at its head that are used in the distributed queuing algorithm: the **busy** or **B-bit** and the **request** or **R-bit**. Also, as part (b) shows, access to the slots on each bus is controlled by a separate **request counter**. Requests for slots on one bus are made using the R-bit in slots on the other bus. Then, for each counter, whenever a slot passes with the R-bit set,

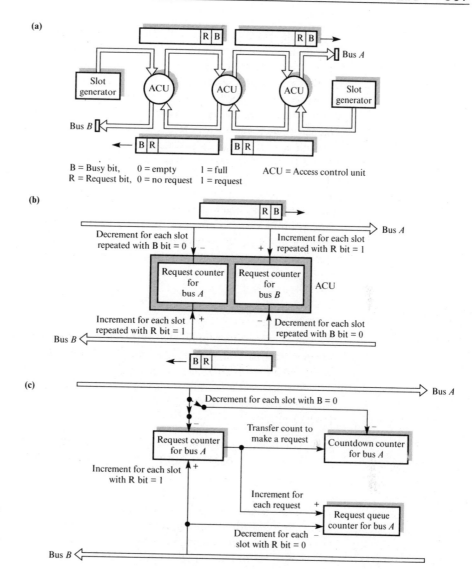

Figure 10.21
DQDB access control principles: (a) request/busy bits; (b) request counters; (c) queuing mechanism.

the contents of the corresponding counter are incremented by one. Similarly, whenever an empty slot is repeated at the interface of the opposite bus, the counter is decremented by one. At any point in time, the request counter for the corresponding bus contains the number of outstanding requests for slots on that bus from the access nodes that are downstream of the access node. Note that each bus operates independently of the other.

Figure 10.21(c) shows that, to transmit a cell (containing a segment of data), the sending access node transfers the current contents of the request counter for the required bus to a second counter known as the **countdown counter**. The node then resets the contents of the request counter to zero and sets the R-bit in the first slot received on the opposite bus with the R-bit reset. This has the effect of placing the segment into the distributed queue for the bus.

While a segment is queued for a bus, any slots that are repeated with their R-bit set cause the corresponding request counter to be incremented as before. However, slots which are repeated at the opposite bus interface with their B-bit reset, cause only the countdown counter for that bus to be decremented. The queued segment is transmitted on the bus when the corresponding countdown counter is zero and an empty slot is received.

In practice, since both buses operate independently, it is possible for a string of slots to be received all with their R-bits set. This means that it may not be possible to set the R-bit in a slot – in response to a new request – until more than one segment has been queued and transmitted on the opposite bus. To allow for this, a third counter known as the (local) **request queue counter** keeps a record of outstanding requests. Whenever a new request is made, the counter is incremented and, all the time the counter contents are greater than zero, whenever a slot is received with its R-bit reset, the R-bit is set and the counter is decremented.

Example 10.3

Derive a flowchart showing the steps taken by the queued arbitrated function to effect the transmission of a set of queued segments produced by the MAC convergence function on a single bus of a dual-bus DQDB subnetwork.

A flowchart showing the steps to control the transmission of segments on bus *A* is given in Figure 10.22. Consider the following points when interpreting the flowchart:

- On receipt of a full slot on either bus, the queued arbitrated function simply passes the contents of the slot payload directly to the MAC convergence function. This function determines whether the segment is intended for this node.

- Only a single segment can be queued for transmission by the queued arbitrated function at one time. Hence only after this function has transmitted a segment does it return to the output queue of the MAC convergence function to determine whether another segment is awaiting transmission.

10.5.4 Bandwidth balancing

Following the introduction of the draft standard of DQDB, detailed performance analyzes of the queued arbitrated protocol demonstrated that, under heavy load conditions, the nodes nearest to the head of each bus start to obtain preferential access to both buses relative to the nodes nearer the center of the bus. We can best understand the reason for the unfairness by remembering that the node at the head of each bus has first call on the use of the request bit in the slots that pass on one of

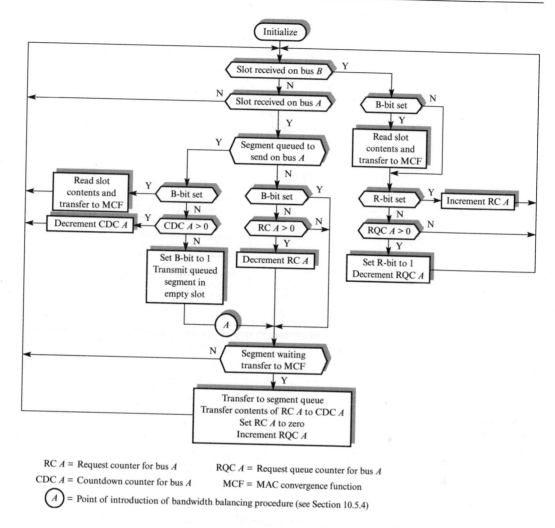

RC A = Request counter for bus A RQC A = Request queue counter for bus A

CDC A = Countdown counter for bus A MCF = MAC convergence function

$\textcircled{A}$ = Point of introduction of bandwidth balancing procedure (see Section 10.5.4)

Figure 10.22

Flowchart of algorithm
used to control the
transmission of
segments on bus A of
a dual bus DQDB
subnetwork.

the buses. Also, although the same node is the last to make requests on the other
bus, the related empty slots pass this node first. Under heavy load conditions when
the demand for slots starts to exceed supply, this has the effect shown in graphical
form in Figure 10.23(a). The access delay variation relates to a heavily loaded
subnetwork and is the same for both buses. As we can see, the unfairness increases
as the network size increases and/or the bit rate increases.

To overcome this effect, a modification to the basic access control algorithm
known as the **bandwidth balancing mechanism** has been introduced. To implement
the scheme, a fourth counter known as the **bandwidth balancing (BWB) counter** is
introduced for each bus. Whenever a segment is transmitted on a bus, the BWB
counter for that bus is incremented. Then, whenever the counter reaches a preset
limit, the node allows an additional free slot to pass by on this bus by incrementing
the corresponding request counter. The BWB counter is then reset to zero and the

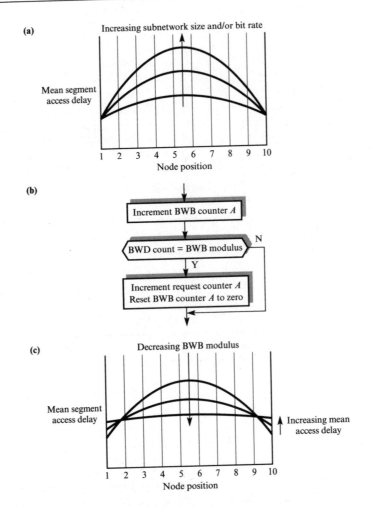

Figure 10.23
Bandwidth balancing:
(a) unfairness effect;
(b) remedial actions;
(c) effect on mean
access delay.

process repeats. The preset limit is known as the **bandwidth balancing modulus**. This operation means that each node, after transmitting a block of segments equal to the BWB modulus, must allow an additional slot to pass by on the related bus. This can be used by the first node lower down the bus which has a queued segment to transmit and a zero countdown counter. The additional processing steps required are shown in Figure 10.23(b) and these are introduced at point A in the flowchart shown in Figure 10.22.

The bandwidth balancing mechanism obtains the necessary effect by reducing the utilization of each bus; the smaller the BWB modulus, the larger the bandwidth loss. This is shown in graphical form in Figure 10.23(c), which illustrates the impact of reducing the modulus for a single network type – size and bit rate. As we can see, as the modulus decreases, the unfairness decreases, but at the expense of an increase in mean access delay. In practice, a compromise is made and a value of 8 is normally used. In the worst case, this results in a loss of utilization of $1/(8 + 1)$ or 11.1%.

10.5.5 Prioritized distributed queuing

Although not always implemented, the basic queued arbitrated access control scheme just described can be extended to support the transmission of prioritized cells/segments. There can be three priority classes and each has a separate set of counters – request counter, countdown counter and request-queue counter – for each bus. The three priority classes are 0, 1, and 2, with 2 having the highest priority. Cells/segments relating to data-only LANs are always allocated class 0, and class 2 is reserved for the transfer of cells relating to network management messages. Class 1 is intended for the transfer of cells containing information that is sensitive to delay or delay variation. Note that bandwidth balancing is not used in this mode.

An example application that may use class 1 cells is the transfer of compressed video information. Although the information is generated at a constant rate – determined by the video frame refresh rate – the amount of information associated with each compressed frame varies and depends on the level of movement that has taken place relative to the previous frame. We can deduce that if the isochronous service is used then the (preallocated) bandwidth needs to be that required to transfer a completely new frame at the refresh rate. However, by using the queued arbitrated access method, the amount of information transferred can vary from one frame to the next. By assigning a higher priority to such segments, the priority control method endeavors to ensure that these are transferred before slots containing data-only LAN traffic.

The general arrangement for controlling access to bus A is shown in Figure 10.24. For clarity only the request and countdown counters are shown. A similar arrangement is used for access to bus B. As we can see, there is a separate R-bit for each priority class at the head of each slot/cell. These are shown as R0, R1, and R2, where R2 is the highest priority. Assume initially there are no segments waiting transmission on bus A from this node – part (a). The operation is as follows:

- When an empty slot $(B = 0)$ is repeated at the interface with bus A, the access control unit for this bus decrements all three request counters by one.

- When a slot is repeated at the interface with bus B – with a priority of 1 for example – the access unit for bus B increments only request counters 1 and 0 – RC 1 and RC 0 – and leaves the higher-priority counter – RC 2 – unchanged. This means that lower-priority requests do not delay the transmission of higher-priority segments.

Now assume that a segment becomes ready to transmit on bus A of priority 1 – part (b). The steps are as follows:

- The current contents of RC 1 are transferred to CDC 1 (and RC 1 is reset to zero) when a slot is repeated at the interface to bus B with the corresponding request bit reset to zero.

- When an empty slot is repeated at the interface with bus A, request counters RC 0 and RC 2 and countdown counter CDC 1 are decremented.

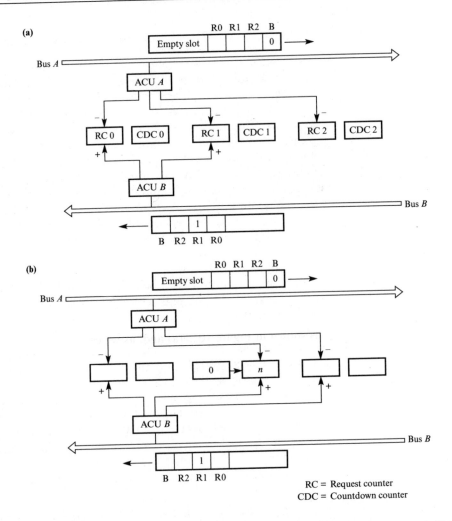

Figure 10.24
Priority access control
schematic: (a) no
segments waiting;
(b) segments queued
at priority 1.

- If a slot with an R-bit of, say, priority 2, passes then request counters RC 0 and 2 and countdown counter CDC 1 are incremented.

- The segment is transmitted when CDC 1 becomes zero and an empty slot is received.

Therefore, incrementing the lower-priority countdown counter when a request for a higher-priority slot is received effectively delays the transmission of the lower-priority segment. This means that segments with a higher priority are always transmitted ahead of lower-priority segments.

10.5.6 Slot and segment formats

As indicated in Section 10.5.2, the 53-octet slot/cell on each bus comprises a 5-octet header and a 48-octet payload (contents) field. The structure of the header

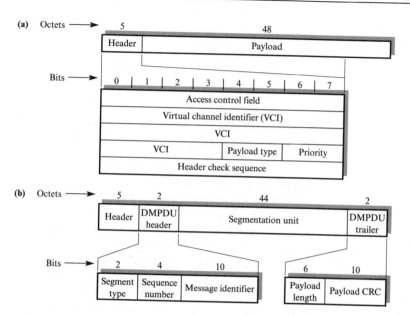

Figure 10.25
Slot and segment formats: (a) slot header; (b) connectionless data segment format.

is shown in Figure 10.25(a) and, as we can see, is similar to that used with ATM networks.

The **access control field** contains, in addition to the busy bit and three request bits, a **slot type** bit which indicates whether the slot is to be used for queued arbitrated or prearbitrated (isochronous) data. For slots containing either connection-oriented or isochronous data, the 20-bit **virtual channel identifier (VCI)** identifies the logical connection to which the cell contents relate. For LAN (also known as connectionless) data, the VCI is set to all 1s. The **payload type** indicates the type of data being carried. It is 00 for all user data – both queued arbitrated and prearbitrated – and the other bit combinations are reserved for use in the future for management information. The **priority** has a default value of 00 and, for the moment, no other values have been defined. Finally, the **header check sequence** is an 8-bit CRC for error-detection purposes.

To transfer connectionless data across the subnetwork – for example, a MAC frame between two remote bridges – the submitted frame is first divided (segmented) into multiple segments by the MAC convergence protocol in the source access control unit. On receipt, the same protocol at the destination reassembles the received segments back into the original frame. For connection-oriented and isochronous data, the VCI in the cell header is used by the destination to identify those cells which are intended for it. However, for connectionless data, an additional 2-octet header at the start of the 48-octet payload field is used instead. In addition, as Figure 10.25(b) shows, a 2-octet trailer is added at the end of the payload field.

Since segments containing connectionless data are part of a larger (MAC) data frame, they are called **derived MAC protocol data units (DMPDUs)**. The segments relating to a frame – referred to as a message in the standard – are transferred in one of four segment types:

- **Single segment message (SSM)** If the frame/message can be carried in a single segment.

- **Beginning of message (BOM)** Indicates this is the first segment of a multiple segment frame/message.

- **Continuation of message (COM)** Indicates the contents are between the start and end of a multiple segment frame/message.

- **End of message (EOM)** Indicates the last segment.

The **sequence number** and **message identifier** are used together to enable the destination to reassemble the segments relating to a multiple segment message back into its original form.

The sequence number is used to detect any missing segments. It is set to zero in the first segment (BOM) and increments for each successive continuation segment (COM) and last segment (EOM). If a missing segment is detected, the remaining segments of the frame/message are discarded.

All segments relating to the same frame are allocated the same message identifier (MID) by the source access unit. This enables the remaining access units on the bus to identify the segments that relate to the same frame. To ensure these are unique, each access unit is allocated a separate block of identifiers when it is initialized. Clearly, a message identifier is not required in single segment messages and hence it is set to zero.

The trailer comprises two fields: the **payload length** and the **payload CRC**. As we shall see in Section 10.5.7, all submitted frames are padded out to be a multiple of 4 octets. This means that a segment may contain from 4 to 44 octets in multiples of 4 octets. Clearly, not all submitted frames will comprise multiples of 44 octets and hence the payload length indicates the actual number of octets in a single segment message or end of message segment. The payload CRC is a 10-bit CRC and is used to detect transmission errors in the entire 48-octet segment.

10.5.7 SMDS

In a public network the connectionless data service offered by the MAC convergence function is known as the switched multimegabit data service (SMDS). In such networks, the various sublayer functions/protocols shown in Figure 10.20 are known as the SMDS interface protocols (SIPs): the MAC convergence protocol is known as SIP level 3; the queued arbitrated protocol SIP level 2; and the physical convergence protocol SIP level 1. A typical interconnection schematic and associated internetworking protocol architecture are shown in Figure 10.26. In part (a) the two LANs are interconnected through MAC bridges while in part (b) IP routers are used.

Recall from earlier chapters that the different types of LAN utilize different header formats, address types, and maximum frame sizes. To accommodate all types of MAC frame, the size of the **SMDS service data unit** can be up to 9188 octets. Also, because of the different addressing formats, prior to segmenting a submitted frame (SDU), the level 3 SIP first encapsulates the frame between a

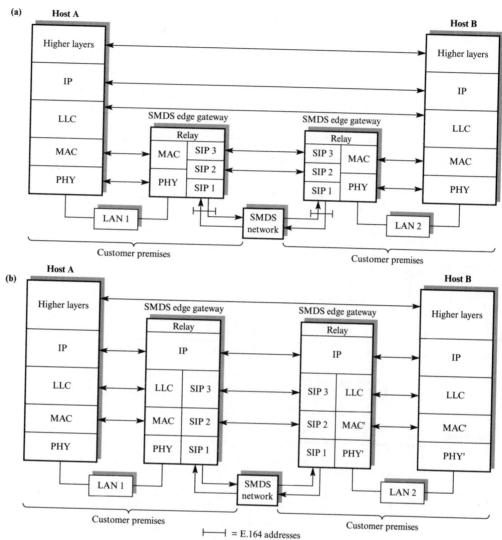

Figure 10.26
SMDS
internetworking
protocol architectures:
(a) bridges;
(b) routers.

standard header and trailer. In addition, to simplify the buffering operation at the destinations, if necessary, it adds additional padding octets at the tail of the submitted frame so that its length is a multiple of 4 octets. The resulting message unit – referred to as a packet – is known as an initial MAC PDU (IMPDU) – or SIP level 3 PDU – and its format is shown in Figure 10.27(a).

Thus the SMDS network provides a connectionless service that is transparent to the customer's internetworking method. To achieve this, on receipt of a frame the access gateway – known as an SMDS edge gateway – simply broadcasts the frame over its local DQDB subnetwork using the queued arbitrated access control protocol. In this way, a copy of all submitted frames is received by all the other gateways – access nodes – attached to the same subnetwork and, through

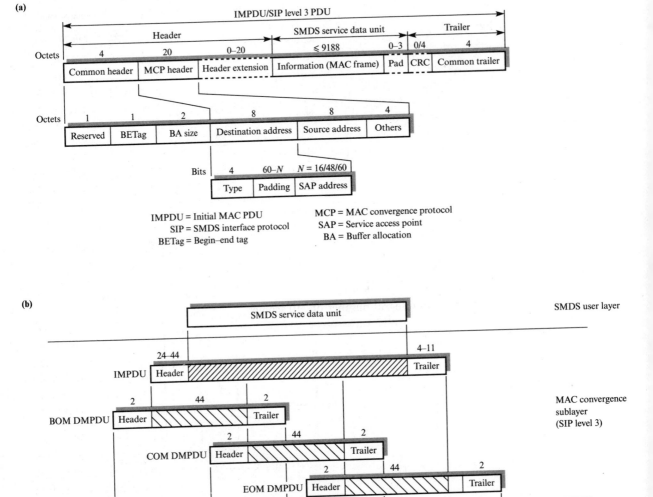

Figure 10.27 Frame transmission overheads: (a) initial MAC PDU format; (b) frame segmentation schematic.

them, by all the other bridges/routers. A decision is made by the latter whether to forward the frame on its LAN or simply to discard it.

As we can see, the header comprises two or possibly three fields. The common header contains an 8-bit sequence number – known as the **begin-end tag** and used to enable the level 3 SIP to detect missing frames – and a specification of the amount of buffer memory required to store the complete IMPDU. The MAC convergence protocol (MCP) header contains a number of subfields relating to the protocol. These include the addresses of the source and destination gateways which, in a public network, are 60-bit E.164 addresses as defined for use with the ISDN. However, to cater for other address types these are both 64-bit address fields with the most significant 4 bits identifying the address types used in the remaining 60 bits – for example, 16/48-bit MAC addresses. Other subfields include the number of Pad octets present and an indication of whether a CRC is present or not. The header extension has been included to allow additional subfields to be added in the future.

The trailer may include an optional 32-bit CRC which is used for error detection on the complete IMPDU. The common trailer contains the same information as the common header. Hence if the maximum header extension and CRC fields are present and the information field is the maximum 9188 octets, there is an integral number of 210 segments after segmentation.

As Figure 10.18(c) showed, larger SMDS public networks comprise multiple DQDB subnetworks interconnected through a set of intermediate MAN switching systems (MSSs). For the MSSs to perform their routing/switching function, the E.164 addresses in the header of each IMPDU are networkwide addresses which identify the MSS and subnetwork to which each access gateway is attached. In addition, group addressing is supported and, when the access node receives an IMPDU with a preassigned group address in its destination address field, a copy of the IMPDU is sent to all members of the group.

The steps taken to transfer a submitted MAC frame across the SMDS network, together with the overheads associated with each sublayer function, are summarized in Figure 10.27(b). The submitted SMDS service data unit is first encapsulated by the MAC convergence protocol to form an IMPDU. It then segments this into a number of DMPDUs, each with the corresponding header and trailer. The resulting 48-octet segments are passed to the queued arbitrated function which adds the appropriate 5-octet header to them. Finally, these are passed to the common function which initiates their transmission via the physical layer convergence sublayer. We can best quantify the overheads associated with each of these functions using Example 10.4.

Example 10.4

A 510-octet MAC frame is to be transferred across a DQDB subnetwork. Stating clearly any assumptions you make, derive the number of queued arbitrated slots that are required to carry out the transfer and hence the total number of overhead octets involved.

With reference to Figure 10.27(b):

- MAC convergence protocol:
  - Adds 2 octets to make the frame 512 octets which is an integral multiple of 4 octets.
  - Assuming a header extension and CRC are not used, a 24-octet header and a 4-octet trailer are added to create a $(512 + 24 + 4)$ 540-octet IMPDU.
  - Total overheads $= 2 + 24 + 4 = 30$ octets.
  - After segmentation, the IMPDU requires 13 DMPDUs: 12 containing a full complement of 44 octets and one with 12 octets.
  - Total overheads are 4 for each of the 13 DMPDUs $(= 52)$ plus 32 for the part-full EOM DMPDU.
- Queued arbitrated (QA) sublayer:
  - A further 5 octets are added to each 48-octet DMPDU to create 13 QA slots.
  - Total overheads $= 5 \times 13 = 65$ octets.
- Physical layer:
  - A further 4-octet header is added to each QA slot.
  - Total overheads $= 4 \times 13 = 52$ octets.
- In summary:
  - QA slots required $= 13$.
  - Total overheads $= 30 + 52 + 32 + 65 + 52 = 231$ octets.

10.6 ATMR

The **asynchronous transfer mode ring (ATMR)** is a new ISO standard that is being developed for use in similar application areas to DQDB. It is based on a high-speed shared medium but, instead of dual buses, it uses **dual contradirectional slotted rings**. Typically, the physical medium is made up of high bit rate – 155/622 Mbps – public carrier circuits. The standard cell size of 53 octets/bytes is used and the cell format is the same as was shown in Figure 10.25(a). The major difference between ATMR and DQDB is the MAC method that is used to gain access to the shared transmission medium. In the following descriptions, we shall concentrate on this aspect of the standard only.

The general scheme is shown in Figure 10.28. As we can see, the two rings are contradirectional and, as with an FDDI ring, one ring is active and the other is on standby. The rings interconnect a number of **access nodes** which provide interfaces to LANs – for LAN interconnection – and also direct cell-based services. The access control field (ACF) in the cell header contains three

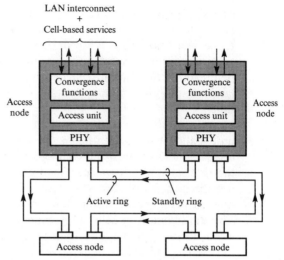

Figure 10.28
ATMR configuration
schematic.

PHY = Physical layer convergence function

subfields: a monitor bit, a reset bit, and the busy address. When the ring is first initialized, a bidding process similar to that used in token ring networks elects a master node. Once elected, its function is firstly, to inform all the other nodes which of the two rings is active, secondly, to provide clock (bit) timing for the ring and to establish the slot structure and thirdly, to remove cells from the ring that have not been removed by their intended recipient. The last function is achieved by the **monitor bit** in each cell header. The master sets this in each full slot that it repeats at its ring interface and, if a full slot is received with this bit set, then the access unit sets the cell contents to zero.

10.6.1   Access control protocol

Within each access node is an **access unit** which performs both the physical layer convergence function and the access control function. Access to the active ring is controlled by a combination of a window mechanism and a global reset procedure. The window mechanism limits the number of cells a node can transmit at one time and the global reset reinitializes the window in all access units to a predefined value.

When an access unit has cells queued for transmission, it sends these in empty slots received at the ring interface with the address of the destination in the VCI field of the cell header. In an ATMR network, the VCI field is known as the **ring virtual channel identifier (RVCI)**. The RVCI field in the header of all cells received at the ring interface of each node is checked and, if the cell is addressed to this node, the cell contents are copied and passed to the appropriate convergence sublayer. The RVCI field is then set to zero – which indicates an empty cell – and the cell is relayed to the next node in the ring. If a match is not found, then the cell is relayed unchanged. This mechanism, known as **destination release**, allows slots to be used more than once during a single rotation around the ring. This is particularly important for rings with large physical separations between access nodes and/or high bit rate transmission media since in such cases the **ring latency** is large, that is, the ring may contain a large number of slots in circulation at any time.

Transmissions on the ring occur in cycles and, during each cycle, each access unit is allocated a fixed **window size** which indicates the number of cells that the access unit can transmit in this cycle before issuing or receiving a **reset cell** at the ring interface. A **window counter** is maintained by each access unit. This is initialized to the window size each time the ring is reset and is decremented each time the access unit transmits a cell from its transmission queue in an empty slot. The transmission of cells stops either when the window count reaches zero or when no more cells are waiting in its transmission queue. This mechanism is followed by all access units in the ring and hence eventually all units become inactive and the flow of cells around the ring ceases.

To reinitiate the transmission of cells, all the time an access unit is active – that is, it has a window count greater than zero *and* one or more cells waiting in its transmission queue – it overwrites its own address in the **busy address** field in the header of all cells repeated at the ring interface. In this way, if an active access unit receives a cell with its own address in the busy address field, it concludes that all the other access units are now inactive. After completing sending any remaining queued cells – assuming the window count is still greater than zero – it sets the reset bit in the header of the next cell repeated at the ring interface – creating a reset cell – and reinitializes its wait counter to the window size value. The reset cell circulates around the ring in the normal way and causes all the other access units to reinitialize their window counters. The reset bit is cleared by the same access unit that set the bit after the cell has circulated around the ring. Once reinitialized, any access units that now have cells queued for transmission revert to the active state and restart sending cells.

Example 10.5

An ATMR ring is comprised of four nodes and operates with a window size of 4. Assume access unit 1 receives 6 cells in its transmission queue to send to node 3 and access unit 2 receives 6 cells to send to node 4. The ring has a latency of 8 cells. Assuming access unit 2 starts to transmit cells two cell times after access unit 1, produce a sequence of figures that illustrate the transfer of both sets of cells across the ring.

Figure 10.29 and its explanatory notes illustrate the transfer. Note how access unit 2 is able to send its second set of two cells first as it was the last active node.

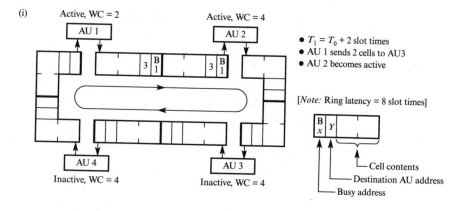

(i)

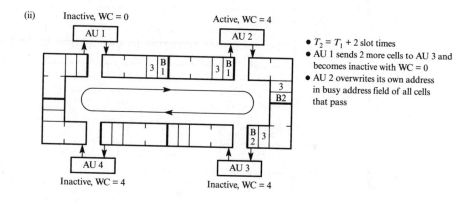

(ii)

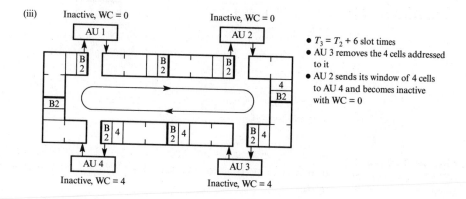

Figure 10.29
ATMR access control
example.

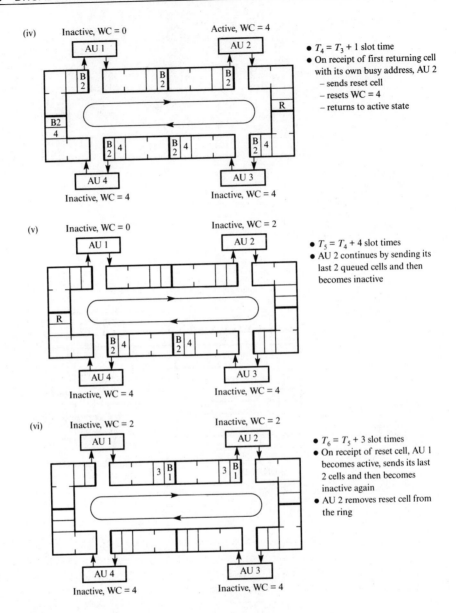

(iv)

- $T_4 = T_3 + 1$ slot time
- On receipt of first returning cell with its own busy address, AU 2
  - sends reset cell
  - resets WC = 4
  - returns to active state

(v)

- $T_5 = T_4 + 4$ slot times
- AU 2 continues by sending its last 2 queued cells and then becomes inactive

(vi)

- $T_6 = T_5 + 3$ slot times
- On receipt of reset cell, AU 1 becomes active, sends its last 2 cells and then becomes inactive again
- AU 2 removes reset cell from the ring

Figure 10.29 (cont.)
ATMR access control
example.

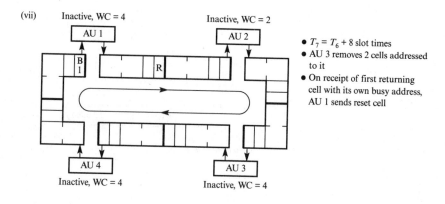

(vii)

- $T_7 = T_6 + 8$ slot times
- AU 3 removes 2 cells addressed to it
- On receipt of first returning cell with its own busy address, AU 1 sends reset cell

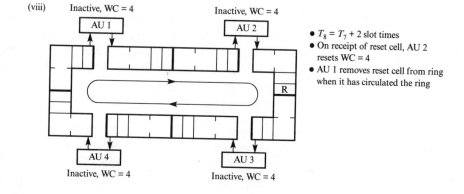

(viii)

- $T_8 = T_7 + 2$ slot times
- On receipt of reset cell, AU 2 resets WC = 4
- AU 1 removes reset cell from ring when it has circulated the ring

Figure 10.29 (cont.)
ATMR access control
example.

10.6.2　Multipriority protocol

From Section 10.6.1 we can deduce that the adoption of a defined window size per node means that, with a defined number of nodes, the worst-case time delay for an access unit before it is able to transmit waiting cells is bounded. This **reset period** is the feature that enables the ring to be used to transfer time-sensitive information. The maximum reset period is determined by the sum of the window size allocated to all nodes plus the overhead to perform the ring reset operation. The reset time is determined primarily by the ring latency. Although the worst-case time delay is bounded, the actual time will vary – up to this maximum value – with the current loading of the ring. Therefore, to transfer isochronous traffic that is sensitive to delay variations less than this, the basic window and reset mechanisms just described can be extended to two priority classes. In this mode of operation the access units operate in one of two states known as **transmission levels**. The possible transitions between the two states and the events that cause each transition are shown in Figure 10.30.

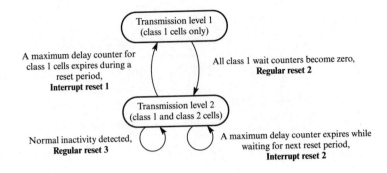

Figure 10.30
Multipriority state
transition diagram.

As we can see, transitions between the two states occur when one of four different types of reset cell is issued. The two priority classes are known as class 1 and class 2, class 1 being the highest priority. The cells relating to each priority class are held by each access unit in separate queues and a separate window size and window counter is used for each class. The normal (basic) state is transmission level 2 and in this state all access units can transmit cells belonging to both high and low priority classes. When all access units become inactive, an access unit detects this in the normal way and issues a reset cell known as a **regular reset 3**.

In the basic state, class 1 cells may experience excessive delays for one of two reasons:

(1)   An access unit cannot send all its queued class 1 cells in the current reset period, for example, because of other access units sending class 2 cells.

(2)   An access unit still has more class 1 cells queued after its class 1 window counter expires during a particular reset period.

To overcome these possibilities, there are two additional resets – known as interrupt resets 1 and 2. Both resets are triggered by a timer running in each access unit that is set to expire before the maximum cell delay associated with its queued class 1 cells is reached. For case (1), if its timer expires during a reset period, it issues an **interrupt reset 1** which, as we can see in Figure 10.30, causes all access units to transfer to transmission level 1. In this state, only class 1 cells can be sent and hence only window counter 1 is decremented. Inactivity is detected in the normal way and the access unit that transmits its queued class 1 cells last issues a reset known as **regular reset 2**. This causes all access units to revert to transmission level 2 and to initialize their wait counters for both classes.

For case (2), if an access unit still has class 1 cells queued while waiting for the next reset period and the timer expires, the access unit issues an **interrupt reset 2**. This causes all access units to reinitialize their class 1 window counters but this time they stay in the same state. This enables the access unit initiating the reset to send its delayed cells, and those access units that have already sent their class 2 cells in the current cycle to miss sending any in the next cycle thereby reducing the access delay for class 1 cells.

10.7 CRMA-II

The **cyclic reservation multiple access (CRMA)** protocol is a MAC protocol developed for use in similar application environments to DQDB and ATMR. It is intended to support both frame-based LAN traffic and cell-based traffic. The access protocol has been defined for use with a single-ring topology but it can also be used with both dual-ring and dual-bus topologies. The protocol provides fair access to multiple concurrent users and the fairness is maintained with rings operating at gigabit rates. CRMA-II is a development of an earlier version of the protocol. The general system configuration is shown in Figure 10.31(a).

As with DQDB and ATMR, access to the ring is through a distributed set of access nodes. The access protocol is based on a cyclic reservation control scheme which ensures fairness and a worst-case access delay for all nodes. The scheme is managed by a single **scheduler node**. In practice, the scheduling function is present in all nodes but is enabled in only one node at any time. The active scheduler is selected using a distributed bidding algorithm and, in a dual-ring system, a different node may be the active scheduler for each ring.

With both DQDB and ATMR the cells queued for transmission at a node are sent independently, that is, each cell competes for access to a slot on the bus or ring independently. However, with CRMA a block of queued cells – relating to a LAN frame for example – can be sent in contiguous slots once an empty slot is received. To achieve this, internal buffering within the node is used to delay a corresponding block of incoming slots while those queued are transmitted. This technique is known as **buffer insertion** – since the set of slot buffers is effectively inserted into the ring – and the FIFO queue used to hold the delayed slots is known as the insertion buffer.

The format of each slot is shown in Figure 10.31(b). All slots start with a defined sync pattern known as the **start delimiter**. This is followed by a 2-byte **slot control** field which comprises a number of subfields, the function of which we shall identify in the following descriptions. Associated with the source and destination node addresses is a flag bit in the slot control field which indicates whether the slot contents are to be deleted by the destination node or by the source node after the slot has circulated around the ring. Recall from Section 10.6 that for large rings destination release of slots can increase the potential network throughput beyond the transmission rate of the ring.

The payload field can be up to 60 bytes in length and is terminated by an **end delimiter**. This is followed by a duplicate copy of the slot control field which is included for error-detection purposes. However, when transmitting frames of data in contiguous slots, each slot contains a start delimiter but only the last slot contains an end delimiter. Also, only the first slot contains a specification of the destination and source node addresses. A subfield in the slot control field indicates whether the slot contents are the first, middle, last, or only slot relating to the multislot frame. Therefore, the amount of data in such slots varies from 56 bytes in the first slot to 60 bytes in subsequent slots. For cell-based services, just 53 bytes of the payload field are used.

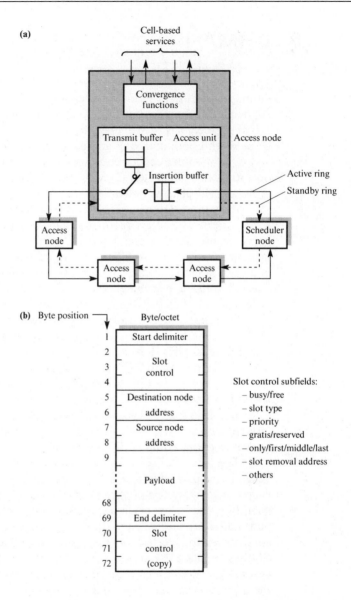

Figure 10.31
CRMA-II: (a) system configuration; (b) slot format.

10.7.1   Frame transmission

The slot control field contains a single bit – known as the **busy/free** bit – which indicates whether the slot is busy (full) or free (empty). A node can transmit queued segments/cells only in free slots. In addition, a second bit – known as the **gratis/reserved** bit – indicates whether the slot can be used by any node (gratis) or only by a node that has received a positive confirmation to an earlier reservation request made to the scheduler node. On receipt of a reservation request, this node marks a corresponding number of free slots as reserved as they are repeated at its ring interface. Once used and subsequently freed, the same slots are returned to the gratis state. The commands relating to the slot reservation procedure are separate entities with the type of command embedded between a start and end delimiter pair.

Whenever a node has a set of frame segments queued in its transmit buffer, it awaits the arrival of a free slot at the ring interface. It then transmits the first segment in this slot and immediately follows this with the remaining segments in contiguous slots. While transmitting these, the node queues any busy slots received from its predecessor in the ring in the insertion buffer. Similarly, on receipt of a busy slot at its ring interface, the node first examines the destination address at the head of the slot and, if a match is found, then the slot contents are copied. The slot is then either set to free or, if slots are queued to be sent, the contents of the received slot are replaced by those in the slot that is at the head of either the insertion buffer or the transmit buffer.

10.7.2 Access control mechanism

There are two separate mechanisms for accessing slots: immediate access using gratis slots and reservation access using previously reserved slots. The **immediate access mechanism** is used during light traffic conditions and is controlled solely by the busy/free bit in the slot control field. The reservation access mechanism is used during heavy traffic conditions. A simple example is shown in Figure 10.32.

The reservation mechanism operates in cycles under control of the current active scheduler node. The latter starts each cycle by issuing a **reserve command** which is comprised of only a start and end delimiter pair back to back. On receipt of this, each node either relays this unchanged or inserts two parameters between the start and end delimiter pair during the relaying operation. This procedure is repeated by each node as the reserve command circulates around the ring back to the scheduler. The two parameters are the combined number of slots the node currently has queued in its transmit and insertion buffers – x for node 1 and y for node 2 – and the number of slots transmitted from its transmit buffer since it last received a reserve command – X for node 1 and Y for node 2. If a node has no slots queued in either buffer and has not transmitted any slots in the last cycle, it makes no entry when repeating the reserve command.

When the reserve command returns to the scheduler node, the scheduler uses the parameter pairs within it to determine the number of (free) reserved slots to generate, by adding the two parameters from each node together and computing a value known as the **fairness threshold**, T. The algorithm endeavors to ensure that access to the ring by all nodes is fair while at the same time minimizing the occasions when a node must defer from the use of free slots. The simplest algorithm is to sum all the parameters together – $X + Y + x + y$ – and to find their mean. This is then assigned to the threshold value. The scheduler node notifies all the other nodes of this value by inserting it in a **confirm command** which circulates around the ring. Immediately after sending the confirm command, the scheduler

(a)

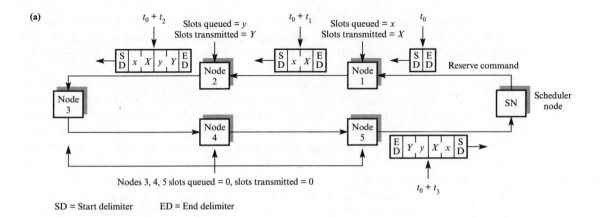

$t_0 + t_2$

Slots queued = y
Slots transmitted = Y

$t_0 + t_1$

Slots queued = x
Slots transmitted = X

t_0

Reserve command

Scheduler node

Nodes 3, 4, 5 slots queued = 0, slots transmitted = 0

$t_0 + t_3$

SD = Start delimiter   ED = End delimiter

(b)

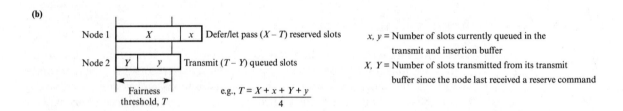

Node 1 | X | x | Defer/let pass $(X - T)$ reserved slots

Node 2 | Y | y | Transmit $(T - Y)$ queued slots

Fairness threshold, T

e.g., $T = \dfrac{X + x + Y + y}{4}$

x, y = Number of slots currently queued in the transmit and insertion buffer

X, Y = Number of slots transmitted from its transmit buffer since the node last received a reserve command

(c)

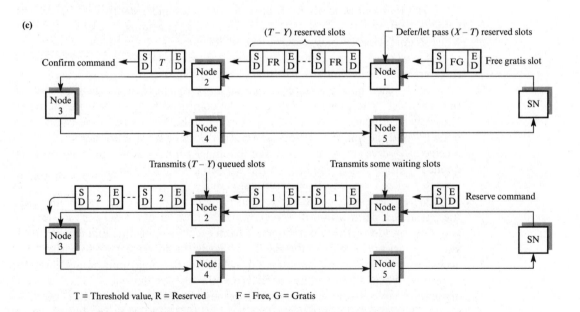

$(T - Y)$ reserved slots

Defer/let pass $(X - T)$ reserved slots

Confirm command

Free gratis slot

Transmits $(T - Y)$ queued slots

Transmits some waiting slots

Reserve command

T = Threshold value, R = Reserved   F = Free, G = Gratis

Figure 10.32 CRMA-II reservation mechanism: (a) reservation cycle; (b) fairness threshold and node transmission computations; (c) confirmation cycle.

computes the sum of confirmations allocated to all nodes and marks this number of gratis slots as reserved.

On receipt of the confirm command, each node determines the number of reserved slots that it can use by computing the difference between the returned threshold value and the number of slots it transmitted in the last cycle, that is, $(T - X)$ for node 1 and $(T - Y)$ for node 2. If the result is positive, then the node can transmit in that number of free reserved slots in this cycle, for example $(T - Y)$. If it is negative, then the node has already exceeded its fair share of the ring bandwidth and hence must defer from the use of that number of gratis slots before trying to transmit any waiting slots, for example $(X - T)$. The same procedure is repeated each cycle.

While the scheduler node is performing each reservation cycle, the nodes continue to transmit slots using any free gratis slots that pass. The reservation procedure ensures that those nodes that are able to transmit more waiting frames/cells during this period are allowed to access fewer slots during the next cycle. Also, to minimize the reservation access delay, reservation request commands bypass any slots that may be queued in the insertion buffer during their passage through each node. Example 10.6 illustrates selected aspects of the access control method.

Example 10.6

A high bit rate CRMA-II ring is being used to transmit LAN frames between a set of access nodes. Assuming all frames are comprised of four segments, show in diagrammatic form the use of the insertion buffer and the order of transmission of the segments on the ring from a single node for each of the following ring conditions and access control modes:

(a)   Light traffic conditions and immediate access using free gratis slots

(b)   Heavy traffic conditions and reservation access using free reserved slots

(c)   Heavy traffic conditions and deferred access using free gratis slots

(a)   A sequence of slot transmissions when using immediate access is shown in Figure 10.33(a). The following points should be noted when interpreting the figure:

- Before the frame segments arrive for transmission, the insertion buffer is empty and free gratis slots are being repeated at the ring interface.
- After the node has transmitted two slots, the slots relating to a different frame are received followed by a period of inactivity.
- Once the node has started to transmit its queued segments, it transmits these in their entirety irrespective of what is received.
- Only when free gratis slots are received does the insertion buffer empty.

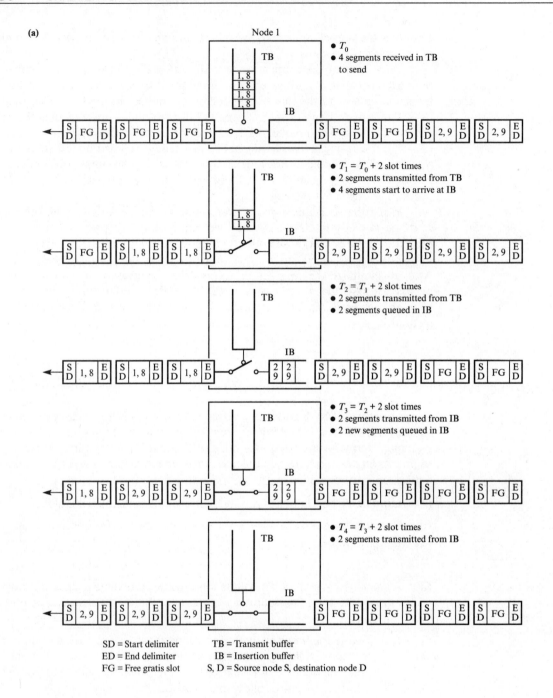

Figure 10.33 (a) Example frame transmission under light traffic conditions and immediate access using free gratis slots.

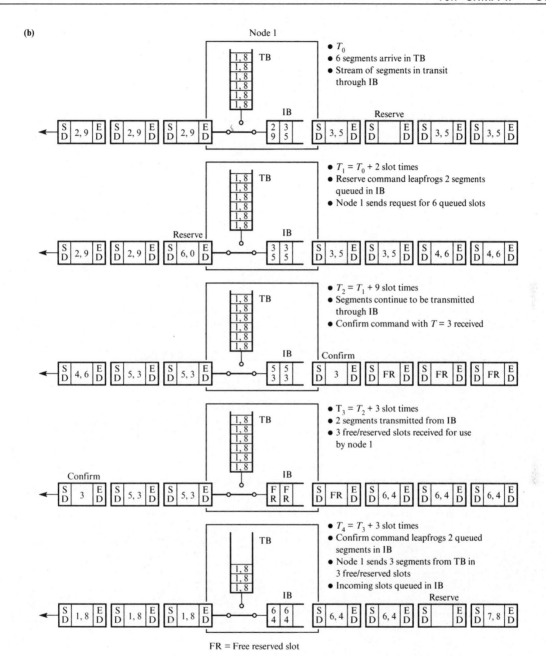

Figure 10.33 (cont.)   (b) Example frame transmission under heavy traffic conditions and reservation access using free reserved slots.

(c)

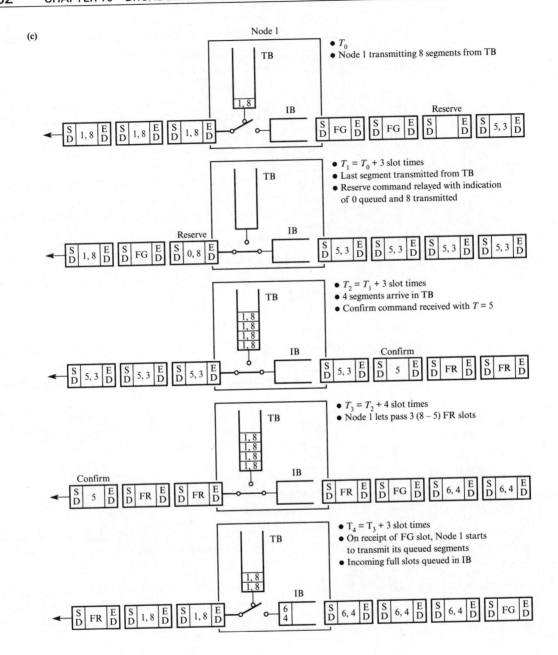

Figure 10.33 (cont.)   (c) Example frame transmission under medium traffic conditions and deferred access using free gratis slots.

(b)   A sequence of slot transmissions when using reservation access is shown in Figure 10.33(b). The following points should be noted:

- The insertion buffer is assumed to contain two queued slots from an earlier transmission sequence.
- The four segments in the transmit buffer are held up by a string of passing slots/frames with a reserve command inserted between the first two frames.
- The reserve command bypasses the two slots queued in the insertion buffer.
- The contents of the reserve command from this node indicate six slots queued and zero slots transmitted in this cycle.
- The node must wait until it receives the confirm command before it can transmit any segments.
- The threshold value returned is 3 which enables the node to empty its insertion buffer and to transmit its waiting frame.

(c)   A sequence of slot transmissions when using deferred access is shown in Figure 10.33(c). The following points should be noted:

- The node has just completed transmitting two queued 4-segment frames before it receives the reserve command.
- The node indicates in the reserve command that it has zero slots queued and it has transmitted eight slots in this cycle.
- A second 4-segment frame is received for transmission but this time the ring is now busy.
- The confirm command contains a threshold value of only 5 hence the node computes that it must defer (let pass) three free gratis slots before it can start to transmit its queued segments.

Exercises

10.1   Using the compressed bandwidth values for each of the different media types listed in Table 10.1, estimate the transmission bandwidth that is required for each of the applications identified in Figure 10.1.

10.2   With the aid of sketches, explain:
(a)   The principle of operation of an FDDI-II ring
(b)   How the link transmission bandwidth is partitioned to provide multiple services
(c)   The protocol architecture used in an attached station
(d)   Examples of the utilization of a single wideband channel to meet various voice and video services.

10.3   Explain the principle of operation of cell-based networks and the reason why a cell size of 53 bytes has been chosen.

10.4   Deduce the outline structure of the cell streams – in terms of the number of cells and the time intervals between then – relating to the following call types:
(a)   Telephony
(b)   Videophony
(c)   Electronic mail (data)

10.5   Sketch typical DQDB-based network architectures to meet the following application requirements:
(a)   A single subnetwork MAN

(b)   A dual-site private network

(c)   A wide-area multiple MAN network

In relation to these, explain the role of a customer interface unit, and isochronous gateway, and a subnetwork router.

10.6   With the aid of sketches, discriminate between an open-bus and a looped-bus DQDB topology. Explain the principle of operation of each type.

10.7   With the aid of sketches, describe how a DQDB looped-bus subnetwork can continue working in the presence of (a) a communications link failure and (b) a node failure.

10.8   In the context of a DQDB subnetwork:

(a)   Define the meaning of the terms 'slot', 'cell', and 'segment'.

(b)   Explain the function of the slot, cell, and segment headers.

10.9   Use a sketch to identify the major function blocks that make up the MAC and physical layers of the DQDB protocol architecture and explain their role in providing connectionless, connection-oriented, and isochronous services. Assume the physical links used are E3 digital circuits.

10.10   With the aid of sketches, explain the principle of operation of the queued arbitrated access protocol used with DQDB subnetworks. Include in your description:

(a)   The role of the busy and request bits in the header of each slot

(b)   The function of the request, countdown, and request-queue counters

(c)   A flowchart of the algorithm for accessing one bus only

10.11   Explain why bandwidth balancing is used with the DQDB queued arbitrated access protocol. Describe the algorithm used to implement bandwidth balancing and identify where it is performed in relation to the flowchart derived in Exercise 10.10.

10.12   With the aid of a sketch, explain the principle of operation of the distributed priority queuing mechanism used with DQDB subnetworks. Include the role of the counters used and the effect on their contents of the request and busy bits when:

(a)   No segments are queued for transmission

(b)   A segment is queued at a specified priority level

10.13   Use a sketch to show the fields that make up the 5-octet header of a DQDB slot and explain their function.

10.14   Assuming a frame of data is to be transmitted over a DQDB subnetwork and the frame requires multiple slots, produce a sketch showing the format of the payload field of each slot and explain the function of each field.

Describe the steps followed by the receiver when reassembling the frame.

10.15   Define the service offered by an SMDS network.

Assuming an SMDS network is being used, produce a sketch showing the protocol architecture used in each SMDS edge gateway when (a) bridges and (b) routers are being used at each customer site.

10.16   Explain the function of the SIP level 3 (MAC convergence) protocol used in the edge gateway associated with an SMDS network.

Define the format of the source and destination addresses used in the header of an IMPDU and why the size of an SMDS service data unit can be up to 9188 octets.

10.17   A 1000-byte MAC frame is to be transferred across a DQDB SMDS network. Using the transmission overheads identified in Figure 10.27, derive the number of queued arbitrated slots that are required to carry out the transfer of the frame and hence the total number of overhead octets used. State any assumptions you make.

10.18   The access control protocol associated with an ATMR network uses a combination of a window limit and a global reset procedure. Explain in outline how this works.

10.19   Using a similar set of figures to Figure 10.29, assume a window count of 2 and only AU 1 is active. Show how AU 1 sends 4 cells to AU 3. Include how the ring is reset.

10.20   Define the meaning of the term 'reset period' in relation to an ATMR network.

10.21 With the aid of a state transition diagram, explain the principle of operation of the multipriority protocol used in ATMR networks. Include in your description the conditions that cause the state transitions and the function of the various counters involved.

10.22 The access control field in the slot header of a CRMA-II network has a busy/free bit and a gratis/reserved bit. Explain how these are used together with register insertion to send a frame over the network.

10.23 With the aid of a sketch, describe how stations make bids for ring capacity to the scheduler node in a CRMA-II network. Also describe how the nodes subsequently determine how many free reserved slots they can use for a particular scheduling cycle.

10.24 Assuming just free gratis slots are to be used, use a set of figures similar to those in Figure 10.33 to show how a node interrupts the flow of incoming slots to transmit a waiting frame comprising four slots.

Using the same set of figures, show how the reservation/command operation works when the network is heavily loaded.

10.25 With the aid of a sketch and example routing table entries, explain how cells are routed through an ATM switch. Explain why the header of each cell can be relatively short.

10.26 With the aid of sketches, explain the difference between VP routing and VC routing. Give an example of each routing type.

10.27 Based on the ATM LAN architecture shown in Figure 10.4, produce a sketch of a small ATM LAN that supports the same set of services as that shown but is comprised of just two RCUs and a single ATM switch.

10.28 Using the single-switch ATM LAN topology derived in Exercise 10.27, determine suitable routing table entries – for the two RCUs and the switch – for the following call types assuming the two communicating multiservice workstations are connected to different RCUs:
(a) A videophone call
(b) Access to a cell-based networked server

10.29 With the aid of a sketch, explain the principle of operation of an ATM switch. Include in your explanation the role of the input and output controllers, the switching matrix, and the switch control processor. Also explain why cell buffers are required in the input and output controllers.

10.30 Explain the principle of operation of the following ATM switch matrix types:
(a) Time-division bus
(b) Fully-connected
Assuming they are to operate in a nonblocking mode, estimate the maximum number of I/O ports associated with each matrix type and what determines this.

10.31 Explain why large switching fabrics are comprised of multiple switching stages each made up of a number of smaller switching elements interconnected in a regular matrix.

10.32 In the context of a multistage delta switching matrix comprised of a number of switching elements, if M is the number of input ports and N is the number of inputs per switching element, derive expressions for the number of switching elements per stage, X, and the number of stages, Y.

10.33 Produce a sketch of an 8-port delta switching matrix that is comprised of a matrix of 2×2 switching elements.

Explain how a cell is routed through the matrix and how blocking can occur.

10.34 An example of a switching matrix that avoids blocking is the Batcher–Banyan matrix. Explain the principle of operation of such switches and how blocking is avoided.

10.35 Using the Batcher–Banyan switch matrix shown in Figure 10.10, identify the paths through the matrix followed by the following set of cells. Assume they arrive simultaneously at the 8 input ports and the routing tags given start at port 1:

111, 100, 011, 000, 101, 001, 110, 010

Assume now that the routing tag of the cell arriving at port 4 is 111 instead of 000. Determine the effect of this and how it is overcome in practice.

10.36 Use a sketch to illustrate the protocol architecture used in a multiservice workstation that is connected to an ATM LAN. Include in your sketch the protocol layers associated with the U-, C-, and M-planes.

Explain the function of each protocol layer and give an example of the application of the protocol set associated with each plane.

10.37 Summarize the functionality of the four classes of ATM adaptation layer (AAL) in the form of a sketch. Hence explain the function of the two AAL sublayer protocols associated with each service class.

10.38 Show how the 48-octet information field of an ATM cell is used by the segmentation and reassembly (SAR) protocol sublayer for both AAL 1 and AAL 2. Explain the function of each field in both cases.

10.39 Explain the difference between the AAL 3/4 and AAL 5 layers and why the latter was developed.

Using the PDU formats for the convergence sublayer (CS) and the segmentation and reassembly (SAR) sublayer shown in Figure 10.14, derive the number of protocol overhead octets/bytes required to send an AAL service data unit of 1024 bytes using (a) AAL 3/4 and (b) AAL 5.

10.40 Explain the role of the broadcast server in relation to the ATM LAN shown in Figure 10.4.

Outline the steps followed by the user of a multiservice workstation connected to an RCU to set up a videophone call through the signaling control point (SCP). Describe also how this procedure is extended to set up a desktop videoconferencing session using the broadcast server.

10.41 With the aid of the connectionless protocol architectures shown in Figures 10.15 and 10.16, outline the steps followed to enable:
(a) A cell-based client to access a cell-based server.
(b) A workstation connected to a legacy LAN to access a server that is connected to a different legacy LAN (of the same type) both of which are connected to an ATM backbone by bridges.
(c) A workstation that is connected to a legacy LAN to access a server that is connected directly to the ATM backbone. Assume the legacy LAN is connected to the backbone by a router.

Chapter summary

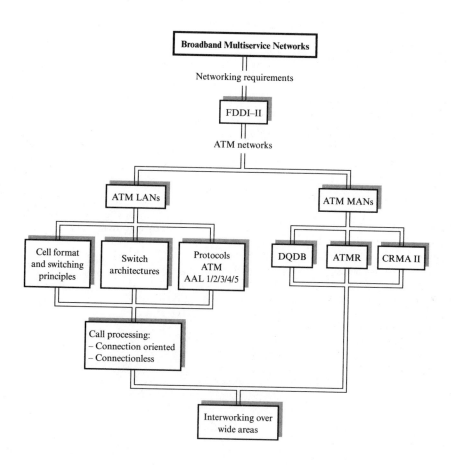

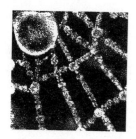

Part three
OPEN SYSTEMS

In this part of the book we describe the function and operation of the additional protocols that enable a set of application programs – running in computers from different manufacturers and interconnected by different types of computer network – to communicate with one another to perform specific distributed application functions. The protocols are known as application-oriented protocols and the resulting communication environment is known as an open system interconnection environment. Two sets of protocols are available: TCP/IP and OSI, both of which we shall discuss.

Chapter 11 presents an overview of the function of the application-oriented protocols associated with both the TCP/IP and the OSI suites. It also gives a detailed description of the two protocols that convert the variable service provided by the different network types into a network-independent message transport service.

Chapter 12 introduces and describes the protocols in the OSI suite that provide general, application-support services. These include the protocols needed to establish a session connection, to provide syntax conversions if the representation of data in the two communicating computers is different, and other support services.

Chapter 13 discusses the functionality and operation of the more specific application protocols in both protocol suites. These include protocols to support the transfer of electronic mail and files between dissimilar mail or file systems.

The additional system aspects that we must address to achieve open system interconnection are discussed in Chapter 14. These include name-to-address mapping, known as directory services, and how the protocols in a complete protocol suite cooperate and exchange information with a similar protocol suite.

Chapter objectives

When you have completed this chapter you should be able to:

- Know the various transport protocols associated with the TCP/IP suite and the OSI suite ☞ 643, 645

- Know the interlayer address selectors associated with the TCP/IP suite ☞ 644

- Understand the role of the UDP and describe the format and meaning of each field in the header of a UDP datagram ☞ 645

- Understand the role of the TCP and the service primitives associated with the reliable stream service ☞ 646

- Explain the format of the PDU (segment) associated with the TCP and the meaning of each field in its header ☞ 650

- Describe the connection establishment, data transfer, and connection termination phases of the TCP ☞ 651, 652, 654

- Understand the terminology used in the ISO standards documents to describe the services provided by a protocol layer and the operation and specification of a protocol entity ☞ 657, 664, 668

- Describe the services and operation of the ISO connectionless and connection-oriented transport protocols ☞ 671, 674

- Understand the formal specification of the ISO transport protocol and a methodology for its implementation in structured program code ☞ 683, 686

Introduction

The position of the transport layer in the context of both a TCP/IP suite and an OSI suite is shown in Figure 11.1.

With the TCP/IP suite, irrespective of whether the underlying data communications network is a single network – LAN or WAN – or an internetwork, the internet protocol (IP) is always present in the network layer. Thus there is a

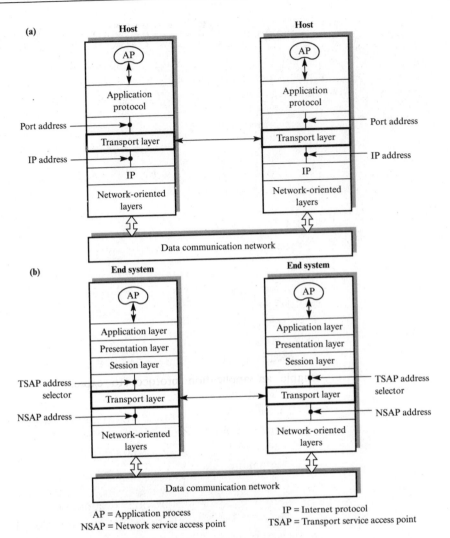

Figure 11.1
Position of transport layer: (a) in a TCP/IP suite; (b) in an OSI protocol suite.

close coupling between the protocols in the transport layer and the IP. Also, all the protocol data units (PDUs) associated with the transport layer protocols are transferred across the underlying network in IP datagrams.

In contrast, with an OSI suite, the network-oriented protocols normally reflect the type of underlying network being used. This means that the network layer interface may be connection oriented, if the underlying network is based on X.25, or connectionless, if the underlying network utilizes the ISO CLNP. Moreover, with the TCP/IP suite, the transport layer serves the application protocols directly, whereas with the OSI suite it serves the application protocols through the intermediate session and presentation layers.

Despite these differences, both transport layers perform a similar set of functions. Thus there is a best-try (connectionless) protocol associated with both suites as well as a reliable (connection-oriented) protocol. Clearly, not all applications require a reliable service. For example, if files of data containing digitized images are being transferred, occasional errors are relatively less important than speed of transfer. A similar requirement applies to digitized voice messages. Note, however, that although the bit error rate probability may be low with networks such as LANs, it is nonzero and hence we should use the connectionless transport protocol only for applications in which occasional errors are acceptable. For all other applications, we should use the connection-oriented protocol.

We shall describe the two transport protocols associated with both protocol suites, starting with the two protocols associated with TCP/IP.

11.1 User datagram protocol

The transport layer in TCP/IP always operates with the IP. Recall that this protocol provides a best-try (connectionless) service for the transfer of individually addressed message units known as datagrams.

This mode of operation minimizes the overheads associated with each message transfer since no network connection is established prior to a message (datagram) being sent. Also, the IP does not perform any error control. To enable an application protocol to exploit this property, TCP/IP provides a connectionless transport protocol known as the **user datagram protocol (UDP)**.

The TCP/IP that provides a user application process with a reliable service is known as the **transmission control protocol (TCP)**. The position of the two protocols, UDP and TCP in relation to the other protocols, together with the PDUs associated with each protocol and the interlayer address selectors are shown in Figure 11.2. In this section we shall describe UDP; we shall consider TCP in Section 11.2.

Figure 11.2 shows the outline structure of an information frame that is transmitted/received by a host. At the network interface it comprises the LAN/WAN frame header, the information (user data) field, and an associated trailer (end-of-frame marker plus CRC). Recall from Section 9.5.1 that the IP address – comprising the netid and hostid addresses – is used to route datagrams to a specific host. Also, the protocol field in the datagram header indicates the attached protocol within that host to which the user data part of the datagram should be sent. This may be a protocol associated with IP – for example, ICMP – or one of the two transport protocols, UDP or TCP.

As we can see from Figure 11.2, UDP and TCP can both serve multiple applications. Hence for the UDP (or TCP) to relay the user data part of their respective PDUs to the appropriate application protocol, we must incorporate an additional address field in the header of each PDU. In an OSI suite this is the role of the interlayer **transport service access point (TSAP)** (or **address selector**), while in TCP/IP it is known as the **(protocol) port address**.

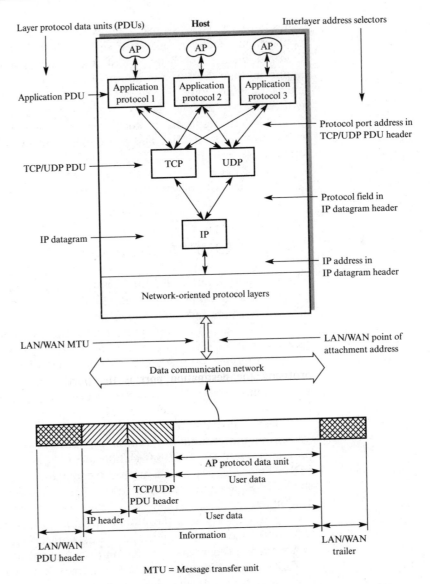

Figure 11.2
TCP/IP with associated PDUs and interlayer address selectors.

With TCP/IP, the composite address of an application protocol is the internetwide IP address of the host plus the additional protocol port address. In dotted notation, an example address of an application protocol is:

128.3.2.3, 53

The first part is the IP address – netid = 128.3 and hostid = 2.3 – and the second part the port address (53). In ISO terminology, the composite address is known as the **fully qualified address**. It comprises the internetwide NSAP address plus the interlayer address selectors between the transport layer and each of the higher protocol layers.

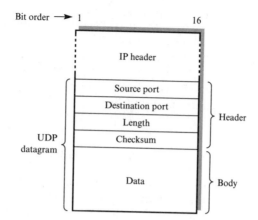

Bit order ⟶ 1   16

IP header

Source port
Destination port
Length
Checksum

UDP
datagram

Data

Header

Body

Figure 11.3
UDP datagram header
format.

As we indicated earlier, as UDP is a connectionless protocol only a single PDU – also known as a datagram – associated with the protocol is transmitted in the user data field of an IP datagram. To distinguish between an IP datagram and the datagram in the user data field associated with UDP, we call the latter a **user datagram**. The format of the header part of a user datagram – the UDP PDU – is shown in Figure 11.3.

The **source port** is the port address of the source (sending) application protocol; the **destination port** is the port address of the intended recipient application protocol. Both are 16-bit integers. The source port is optional in a UDP datagram and is included only if a reply is expected. If a reply is not required, the source port is set to zero.

The **length** field is a count of the total number of octets in the complete (UDP) datagram, including the header. The checksum in the IP header applies only to the fields in the IP header and not to the user data field. Hence the **checksum** field in the UDP header relates to the complete UDP datagram. In view of the various applications for the UDP, the checksum is also optional; if not used, the checksum is set to zero. Note that with 1's-complement number representation, zero can be all 0s or all 1s. Hence if a checksum is being used and the computed sum is zero, then we use all 1s.

Therefore, before an application protocol can send a user datagram to another application protocol in a remote host, it is necessary for the application protocol to know the IP and port addresses of the destination process. This is a function of the application, not of the UDP (or TCP), as we shall see in Section 11.4.2.

11.2 Transmission control protocol

The UDP is used either when error correction is not needed or for a single short request/response message exchange between two application protocols. However, in most open distributed applications we require a reliable (connection-oriented) message transport service. An example is the transfer of the contents of a file containing a customer's bank record. Clearly, in such applications, even the corruption of a single binary bit is all important.

In the TCP/IP suite, the connection-oriented transport protocol is the **transmission control protocol (TCP)** and the service it offers to users – through application protocols – is known as the **reliable stream transport service**.

11.2.1   The reliable stream service

The reliable stream service is similar to the user services associated with the class 4 transport protocol in the OSI suite (see Section 11.6). Service primitives are provided so that an application protocol – through the presentation and session layers in the case of an ISO suite – can establish a logical connection with a similar (peer) application protocol in a remote host, exchange messages over this connection in a duplex (two-way simultaneous) way, and clear the connection. TCP endeavors to transfer the data associated with these exchanges in a reliable way, that is, error free with no losses or duplicates and in the same order as it was submitted.

The term 'stream' is used with TCP since it treats all the user data associated with a connection – for example, a sequence of request/response messages – as two separate data streams, one in each direction, each comprising a string (stream) of octets/bytes. To achieve a reliable service, the TCP transmits all data in units known as **segments**. Normally the TCP decides when a new segment is transmitted. At the destination side, the receiving TCP buffers the data received in a segment in a memory buffer associated with the application and delivers it when the buffer is full. Thus a segment may consist of multiple user messages if short message units are being exchanged, or part of a single large message if, say, the contents of a large file are being transferred. The maximum length of each segment is a function of the TCP which simply endeavors to ensure that the total submitted octet stream associated with each direction is delivered to the other side in a reliable way.

In addition, to allow a user to force a message unit to be transferred and delivered immediately – for example, a short request message for some data – the user can indicate in a parameter associated with the data transfer request primitive that data should be sent (and delivered) directly. Also, a user can indicate that the data to be transferred is **urgent** which means that it should be sent outside of the flow control mechanism used by the TCP for normal data. This provides a similar function to the expedited data service associated with an OSI suite.

A list of the user service primitives associated with TCP, together with their parameters, is given in Table 11.1. The majority of open distributed applications are based on the **client–server model**. We can best understand this by considering an application program (process) accessing and using a remote file system (application process). The file system is thus the server, since it responds only to requests for file services, and the user application program is the client, since it always initiates requests. Note also that a single server process must normally be

Table 11.1 TCP user service primitives and their parameters.

Primitive	Type	Client/ server	Parameters
UNSPECIFIED_PASSIVE_OPEN	Request	S	Source port, *timeout, timeout-action, precedence, security range*
FULL_PASSIVE_OPEN	Request	S	Source port, destination port, destination address, *timeout, timeout-action, precedence, security range*
ACTIVE_OPEN	Request	C	Source port, destination port, destination address, *timeout, timeout-action, precedence, security range*
ACTIVE_OPEN_WITH_DATA	Request	C	Source port, destination port, destination address, data, data length, push flag, urgent flag, *timeout, timeout-action, precedence, security range*
OPEN_ID	Local response	C	Local connection name, source port, destination port, destination address
OPEN_SUCCESS	Confirm	C	Local connection name
OPEN_FAILURE	Confirm	C	Local connection name
SEND	Request	C/S	Local connection name, data, data length, push flag, urgent flag, *timeout, timeout-action*
DELIVER	Indication	C/S	Local connection name, data, data length, urgent flag
ALLOCATE	Request	C/S	Local connection name, data length
CLOSE	Request	C/S	Local connection name
CLOSING	Indication	C/S	Local connection name
TERMINATE	Confirm	C/S	Local connection name, reason code
ABORT	Request	C/S	Local connection name
STATUS	Request	C/S	Local connection name
STATUS_RESPONSE	Local response	C/S	Local connection name, source port, source address, destination port, destination address, connection state, receive window, send windows, waiting ack, waiting receipt, urgent, precedence, security, timeout
ERROR	Indicator	C/S	Local connection name, reason code

able to support access requests from a distributed community of clients concurrently. Many of the user service primitives reflect this mode of interaction. Those that relate to each type of user – client/server – are indicated in Table 11.1.

The **destination address parameter** is the IP address of the destination host and the **source** and **destination ports** are the interlayer port addresses associated with the source and destination protocols, respectively.

The **timeout** parameter allows a user application protocol to specify a maximum time interval that the source TCP should wait for an acknowledgment relating to a segment that it sends. Recall that since IP provides a best-try service a segment may be discarded during transfer. Therefore, the timeout value is normally set to be greater than twice the time-to-live value carried in each IP datagram. The **timeout-action** parameter specifies the action to be taken if a timeout occurs. Normally this is to close the connection.

The **precedence** parameter is a collection of parameters that allow a user to specify the contents of the service type field in the IP datagram header that is used to transport the TCP segment. The contents of this field were identified in Figure 9.9 when we discussed the IP. Recall that it performs the same function as the QOS parameter associated with the corresponding ISO primitives. Note that this parameter is used by the IP and not the TCP. It is an example of a **pass-through parameter**, that is, it is simply passed down from one protocol layer to another without modification.

The **security range** parameter allows a server application protocol to specify a level of security that should be applied to potential users. The **push flag** and **urgent flag** enable a user to indicate to the TCP how it should treat the data in the **data** parameter: push, transmit immediately, and urgent outside the normal flow. Finally, the **local connection name** is allocated by the local TCP entity when a connection is first established. Although the port address enables the TCP to relate a received segment to a particular application protocol, in the case of a server, multiple transactions – and hence logical connections – may be in progress concurrently. The **local connection name** allows the TCP to relate primitives to the same connection. The connection endpoint identifier parameter in an OSI suite performs the same function. Most of the parameters associated with the STATUS primitive relate to the TCP entity and hence will be identified later (Section 11.2.2).

Many of the parameters are concerned with the (relatively) low-level operation of the transport protocols TCP and IP. Since, in many cases the same parameter values are used with different primitives, the parameters shown in italics have default values. If a value is not explicitly stated, we shall assume the default values. To illustrate the interrelationship of the various primitives, they are shown in the form of a time sequence diagram in Figure 11.4.

The UNSPECIFIED_PASSIVE_OPEN and FULL_PASSIVE_OPEN primitives are used by a server to indicate its readiness to accept a connection(s) request. The term 'passive' is used to indicate that it is ready to receive a connection request rather than (actively) initiate the setting up of a connection. 'Unspecified open' indicates that it is prepared to accept a request from any process that meets the specified security level (if present). 'Full open' also includes a destination port and IP address parameter which indicates a specific application protocol/process from which the server is awaiting a request. Normally, a server is opened when first run and remains open until the machine on which it is running is switched off.

At the client side, a user – through the application protocol – can initiate the establishment of a connection in two ways. Firstly, the client protocol can simply issue an ACTIVE_OPEN request specifying the port and IP addresses of the destination. The local TCP responds by returning an OPEN_ID which informs the application protocol of the identifier – connection name – it has assigned to this connection (request). It then initiates the setting up of a connection. If successful, both users can start to exchange data messages using the SEND and DELIVER primitives.

Secondly, the client can issue an ACTIVE_OPEN_WITH_DATA request primitive which, as the name implies, contains a user data message in a parameter. The local TCP responds as before by returning a connection name. However, it then initiates the setting up of a connection concurrently with transferring the

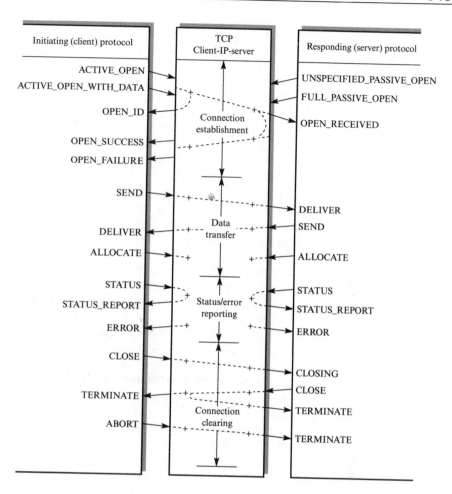

Figure 11.4
TCP user services:
time sequence
diagram.

submitted data message. This mode is useful for a single short (reliable) request/response message exchange since the overheads associated with the call are reduced.

As Figure 11.4 shows, data is transferred in each direction using the SEND/DELIVER primitives together with the push and urgent flags as required. The ALLOCATE primitive is used by a user to increase the amount of message buffer storage for this connection at the local side. Also, while in the data transfer phase, the user can request the status of the connection using the STATUS primitive. The local TCP responds using the STATUS_RESPONSE primitive. Should an error condition arise – for example, the two TCP protocol entities become unsynchronized – the user is informed by the ERROR primitive.

Finally, the connection can also be cleared in two ways. Since the flow of message data in each direction is controlled separately, the connection is usually cleared in each direction separately. This is known as **graceful disconnection** and requires both users to issue a separate CLEAR request primitive after all data has been submitted to the local TCP. The alternative mode is for a user to issue an ABORT primitive which results in both sides discarding any outstanding data and terminating the connection.

11.2.2   Protocol operation

The TCP incorporates many of the features of the HDLC protocol we discussed in Chapter 5. It supports duplex message transfers and incorporates a go-back-N error control procedure with a type of sliding window flow control mechanism.

All the PDUs that the TCP uses to set up a connection, transfer data, and clear a connection have a standard format and are known as segments. All segments are transferred between two TCP entities in the user data field of IP datagrams. Their format is shown in Figure 11.5(a).

As with a UDP datagram, the first two fields in the header are the **source port** and **destination port** addresses. They have the same meaning as in a UDP datagram except that with TCP the two addresses indicate the end points of the logical connection between the two application protocols.

The **sequence number** has the same role as the send sequence number in the HDLC protocol, and the **acknowledgment number** the same role as the receive sequence number. The former thus relates to the flow of data in the direction of the sending TCP entity and the latter to the flow in the reverse direction. However, with TCP, although data is submitted for delivery in blocks, the flow of data in each direction is treated simply as a stream of octets for error and flow control purposes. Thus the sequence and acknowledgment numbers relate to the position of an octet in the complete message stream rather than to the position of a message block in the sequence. The sequence number indicates the position of the first octet in the data field of the segment relative to the start of the complete message, while the acknowledgment number indicates the octet in the data stream flowing in the reverse direction that the sending TCP expects to receive next.

The presence of an options field in the segment header means that the header can (in theory) be of variable length. The **header length** indicates the number of 32-bit words in the header. The **reserved** field, as its name implies, is reserved for future use.

All segments (and hence PDU types) have the same header format and the validity of selected fields in the segment header is indicated by the setting of bits in the 6-bit **code** field; if a bit is set ($=1$), the corresponding field is valid. Note that multiple bits can be set in a single segment. The bits have the meaning shown in Figure 11.5(b).

The **window** field relates to the sliding window flow control scheme. It indicates the number of data octets relative to the octet number in the acknowledgment field that the source is prepared to accept. It is determined by the amount of buffer storage the source has available for this connection.

As with a UDP datagram, the checksum relates to the complete segment, header plus contents. The checksum is the complement of the sum of all the 16-bit words in the segment added together using 1's-complement arithmetic.

(a)

Bit order ⟶ 1 2 3 4 5 6 7 8 9 10 11 12 13 14 15 16

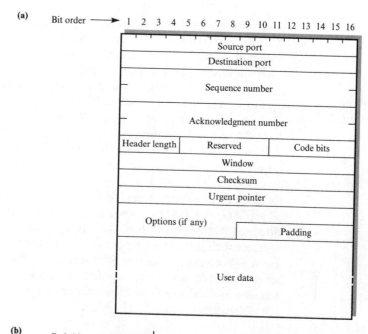

Figure 11.5
TCP: (a) segment
(PDU) format;
(b) code bit
definitions.

(b) Code bits:

Bit position	Name – function
11	URG – urgent pointer field valid
12	ACK – acknowledgment field valid
13	PSH – deliver data on receipt of this segment
14	RST – reset the sequence/acknowledgment numbers
15	SEQ – sequence number valid
16	FIN – end of byte stream from sender

When the URG flag is set in the code field, the **urgent pointer** indicates the amount of urgent (expedited) data in the segment. Normally this is delivered by the receiving TCP entity immediately it is received.

The default maximum number of octets in the data field of a segment is 536. This has been chosen on the assumption that WANs are present in the route since, in general, they have an inferior bit error rate probability. When the two communicating application protocols are running in hosts that are both attached to a network that has a low bit error rate – for example, a LAN – a larger segment size can be used. Hence the **options** field is used to enable the sending TCP entity to indicate to the receiver the maximum number of octets in the user data field of a segment it is prepared to receive.

Connection establishment

Although in a client–server interaction the client always initiates the setting up of a connection, in more general applications not based on the client–server model both parties may try to set up a connection at the same time. To allow for this, a connection is established using a three-way message (segment) exchange known as a **three-way handshake** procedure. Also, as Section 11.2.2 described, the flow of data in each direction of a connection is controlled independently. To avoid any ambiguity with the initial sequence number settings at both sides of a connection, each side informs the other of the initial sequence number it proposes to use. These are in turn acknowledged as part of the handshake procedure. Two example segment exchanges are shown in Figure 11.6.

A connection is set up by the initiating side which sends a segment with the SEQ flag set and the proposed initial sequence number in the sequence number field (seq = X). On receipt of this, the responding side first makes a note of the sequence number setting for the incoming direction. It then returns a segment with both the SEQ and ACK flags set with the sequence number field set to its own assigned value for the reverse direction (seq = Y) and an acknowledgment field of $X+1$ (Ack = $X+1$) to acknowledge it has noted the initial value for its incoming direction. On receipt of this, the initiating side makes a note of Y and returns a segment with just the ACK flag set and an acknowledgment field of $Y+1$. In the event of both sides sending a SEQ segment at the same time – part (b) – each side simply returns an ACK segment acknowledging the appropriate sequence number. Both sides of the connection are now set up and can start to send data independently.

Figure 11.6
TCP connection
establishment:
(a) client–server;
(b) collision
possibility.

Data transfer

As we indicated earlier, the error and flow control procedures associated with the data transfer phase are based on a go-back-N error control strategy and a sliding

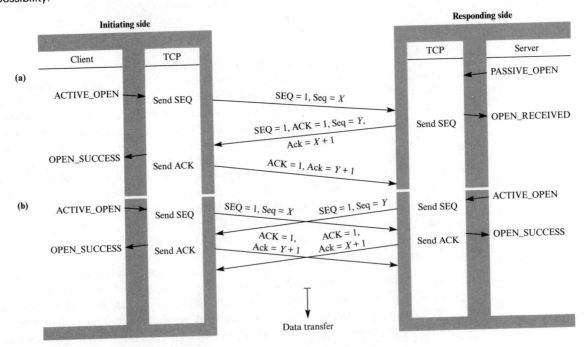

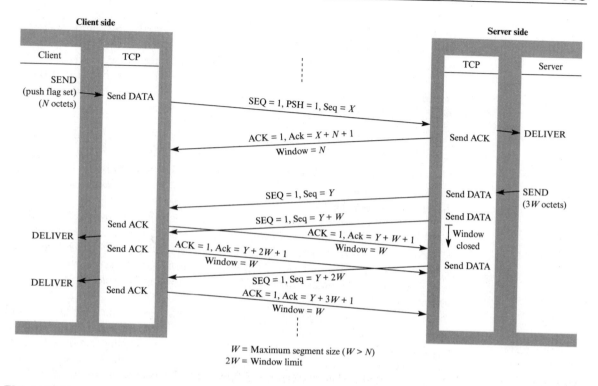

W = Maximum segment size ($W > N$)
$2W$ = Window limit

Figure 11.7
TCP data transfer
example.

window flow control mechanism. Since we discussed these in some detail in Chapter 4, and again in Chapter 5 when the HDLC protocol was described, we shall not discuss them here. However, to illustrate the use of the push flag, consider the example of a typical segment exchange relating to a client–server request/response message exchange shown in Figure 11.7.

We assume that the client issues a short request message of N octets and, to force delivery, sets the push flag parameter. The sending TCP sends this directly in a segment with the SEQ and PSH flags set and a sequence number set to its current value – assumed to be X. On receipt of the segment, the receiving side detects the PSH flag is set and hence delivers this directly and returns a segment with the ACK flag set and an acknowledgment number of $X + N + 1$ – indicating the next octet it expects to receive – and a window value of N to return the window to its original setting.

The server returns a response message which we assume to be three times the maximum segment size W. The local TCP must therefore send the message in three segments. To illustrate the window mechanism, we assume that the send window is equal to $2W$, that is, sufficient for two maximum segments to be sent. After sending two segments, the server must wait until it receives an acknowledgment with a further credit allocation in its window field.

On receipt of each segment, the client TCP returns a segment with the ACK flag set; on receipt of the second segment, it delivers the current contents of its buffer – containing the two segments – to the client AP. At the server, on receipt of the first ACK segment, the server TCP increments its credit value and proceeds to send the third segment. In Figure 11.7 we assume that this third segment is delivered to the client application directly by the recipient TCP.

Although not shown, if a segment is received with an incorrect sequence or acknowledgment field, then a segment is returned with the RST and SEQ/ACK flags set and the expected value(s) in the appropriate field(s).

Connection termination

The actions of each TCP entity in response to the two alternative connection termination methods are shown in Figure 11.8. The first relates to a graceful disconnection and the second to the abort sequence.

In part (a), we assume that the client protocol has finished sending all its data and simply wants to terminate the connection. Hence, on receipt of the CLOSE primitive, the client sends a segment with the FIN flag set. On receipt of this segment, the server issues a CLOSING primitive to the server protocol and returns an ACK segment to the client acknowledging receipt of the FIN segment.

We assume that the server protocol has also finished submitting data and hence issues a CLOSE primitive in response to the CLOSING primitive. However, in the example we assume that the server TCP still has outstanding data to send, which it sends in a segment together with the SEQ and FIN flags set. On receipt of this segment, the client TCP issues a TERMINATE primitive and returns an ACK for the data just received. When it receives the ACK, the server TCP issues its own TERMINATE to the server protocol. Alternatively, if an ACK is not received

Figure 11.8
TCP connection termination:
(a) normal; (b) abort.

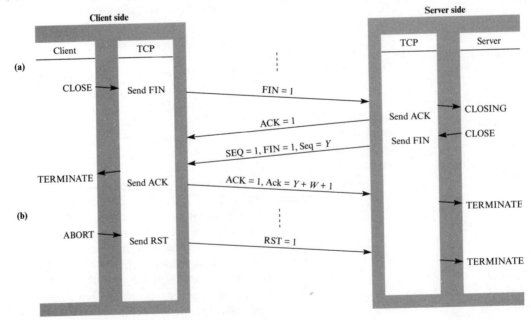

within a time of twice the time-to-live period, it assumes the ACK has been corrupted and issues a TERMINATE to the server.

With the abort sequence, the client side immediately terminates both sides of the connection and sends a segment with the RST flag set. On receipt of this segment, the server terminates both sides of the connection abruptly and issues a TERMINATE primitive with a reason code set to connection aborted.

To reinforce our understanding of the connection establishment and termination phases of two TCP protocol entities, one a server and the other a client, consider the state transition diagram of each as shown in Figure 11.9.

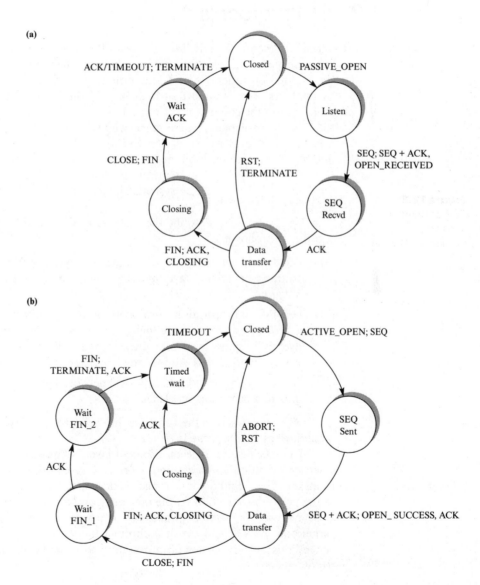

Figure 11.9
TCP state transition diagram: (a) server; (b) client.

Recall from Chapter 4 that the various states associated with each automaton (finite state machine) are shown in circles with directional lines (known as arcs) indicating the transitions between states. Alongside each arc is the incoming event that initiates the transition – a service primitive or the arrival of a TCP segment (PDU) – followed by the resulting outgoing event(s). You should be able to relate the various transitions at each side to the segment exchanges associated with the connection establishment and termination phases shown in Figures 11.6 and 11.8.

11.3 OSI protocols

When we describe the operation of any of the protocols in the OSI suite, we must, from the outset, be able to discriminate between the services provided by the layer, the internal operation (that is, the protocol) of the layer, and the services used by the layer. This is important because only then can we define the function of each layer in the context of the other layers. The isolation of each layer also has the effect that a person (programmer) who is implementing a single protocol layer needs to know only which services the layer is to provide to the layer above, the internal protocol of the layer, and the services that are provided by the layer below to transfer the appropriate items of information associated with the protocol to the similar layer in a remote system. The implementer does not need any further knowledge of the other layers.

For example, to describe the function of the transport layer, we need only consider the following:

(1)   The defined set of services the transport layer provides to the session layer (to transport session layer message units to a peer session layer in a remote system).

(2)   The internal operation (protocol) of the transport layer (for example, establishing and managing logical connections with a similar peer transport layer in a remote system, and the error and flow control of transport layer message units across established connections).

(3)   The services provided by the (lower) network layer to transfer these message units to a peer transport layer.

When we describe the functions of each protocol layer, we shall consider these three aspects separately.

The specification of each protocol layer comprises two sets of documents: a **service definition document** and a **protocol specification document**. The service definition document contains a specification of the services provided by the layer to the layer above it, that is, the **user services**. Normally, these take the form of a defined set of **service primitives** each with an associated set of **service parameters**. As we shall see, it is through the service parameters that the layer above initiates the transfer of information to a similar **correspondent layer** in a remote system.

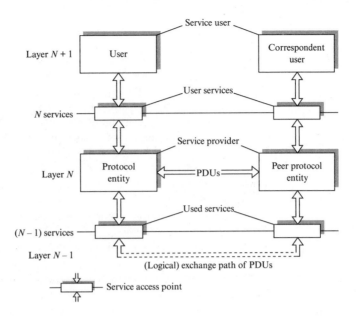

Figure 11.10
Protocol layer model.

The protocol specification document contains the following:

(1) A precise definition of the protocol data units (PDUs) used by the protocol entity of that layer to communicate with a similar (peer) protocol entity in a remote system.

(2) A specification of the services used by the layer (that is, the services provided by the layer immediately below it) to transfer each PDU type.

(3) A precise definition of the operation of the protocol entity presented in one of the formal specification methods.

Some of the terms just introduced are summarized in Figure 11.10.

11.4 Service definition

In any networking system we must discriminate between the *identity* of a user application process and the *location* in the network where the process currently resides. The identity of a user application process is normally in the form of a symbolic *name* or *title* while the location in the network is in the form of an *address*. This is similar to names and addresses we use when we send a letter via the postal system: we use a name to identify the recipient of the letter, and the address indicates where the recipient is currently resident. Because a number of application processes may be resident in the same computer, the address must contain not only the physical address of the computer within the network, but also addressing information for use within the computer itself. This is analogous to, say, the floor and room numbers within an apartment block.

11.4.1 Names

As symbolic names are used for identification purposes at the user level, the names utilized for each user application process (AP) must be unique within a specific OSI environment. Normally, the actual physical location of other APs in the network is not known by an AP and so an AP communicates with another AP simply by specifying the name or title of the intended correspondent. To ensure that names are unique within a particular (OSI) environment, we must provide some means of managing the allocation of names to APs (user processes and service provider processes). The system that provides this function is known as a **name server**. It is normally maintained by the authority administering the environment.

For a relatively small environment comprising, say, a distributed community of computer-based systems connected to a single LAN, a single name server is usually sufficient for the complete system. However, for larger environments comprising perhaps several thousand systems interconnected by a number of LANs and WANs, a single name server often becomes unmanageable. In this case, a separate name server is used for each subnetwork. To ensure that each name is unique within the complete environment, the name associated with a user on one subnetwork is prefaced by the identity of the subnetwork within the complete OSI environment.

11.4.2 Addresses

Although names are used at the user level, addresses are used within the OSI environment itself to ascertain, firstly, the physical location of the computer within the network in which the required AP currently resides and, secondly, the identity of the application layer protocol entity to which the AP is currently said to be attached. It is the responsibility of the OSI environment to relate the required correspondent symbolic name specified by a user AP to a specific networkwide address. The list of relationships or mappings between symbolic names and addresses is contained in a **system directory**. In principle, the actual physical location of an AP may vary simply by changing its entry in the system directory.

The addresses used in the OSI environment comprise a concatenation of a number of subaddresses known as **service access points (SAPs)** or, because of their function, **interlayer address selectors**. They are used at the interface between each protocol layer in the system to which the AP is currently attached. Thus, the address of an AP is made up as follows:

$$\text{AP address} = \text{PSAP} + \text{SSAP} + \text{TSAP} + \text{NSAP}$$

where PSAP is the service access point subaddress between the application layer protocol entity (to which the AP is attached) and the presentation layer, SSAP is the service access point subaddress between the presentation layer and the session layer, and so on. The NSAP contains the networkwide address of the system in which the AP is resident. The P/SSAP and TSAP addresses are used within the

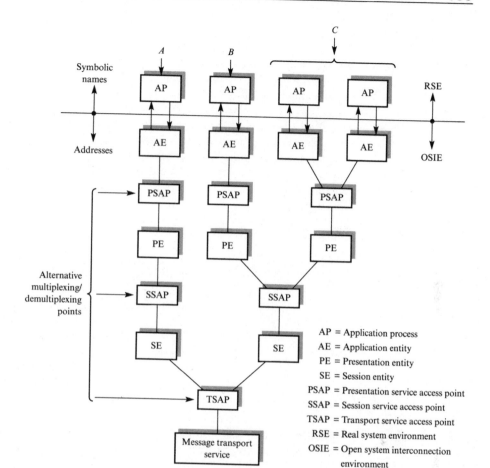

Figure 11.11
Some alternative uses
of the PSAP/SSAP
address selectors.

system to determine the specific application layer protocol entity to which the user AP is currently attached. This is shown in Figure 11.11.

An AP address is known either as a **presentation address** or, because of its structure, as a **fully qualified address**. As we can see, the PSAP and SSAP selectors can be used in a number of ways. In *A* the PSAP and SSAP are not used for multiplexing/demultiplexing purposes; it is the TSAP address selector that selects a specific application entity/process within the system. This is similar to the scheme used in a TCP/IP suite. However, in *B* and *C* a further level of selection is provided by the PSAP and SSAP.

In *B* a further level of selection is provided by the SSAP address selector thus allowing multiple application/presentation entities to use the same session connection. Alternatively, in *C* the PSAP allows multiple application entities/ processes to use the same presentation connection. We shall look at the topic of addresses in more detail in Chapters 13 and 14.

If multiple transactions involving the same application entity are in progress concurrently – for example, multiple transactions involving an AP acting as a server such as a file server – it is an implementation-dependent (local) matter for each protocol layer within that system to know the identity of the particular transaction to which messages relate. That is, it is not part of the SAP address structure. To allow for this, a **connection (endpoint) identifier** or **instance number** is associated with the appropriate PDUs exchanged. We shall consider this further when we discuss the transport layer in Section 11.6.

Finally, although in Figure 11.11 the AP is shown separate from the AE, this is simply to identify the dividing line between the OSI environment and the real system environment. In practice, as we shall see in Chapter 13, the application entity(s) involved in an application is (are) closely bound to the application processes. For this reason an AE is said to be **attached** to an AP.

11.4.3 Service primitives

The user services provided by a layer are specified by a set of service primitives. The services associated with a layer can be of two types: confirmed or unconfirmed. Figure 11.12 illustrates the difference between the two types.

Normally, a transfer starts when the user of the layer passes a **request primitive** across the layer interface. This results in an associated PDU being generated by the local protocol entity within the layer and this is passed, using the services provided by the underlying layer, to a correspondent (peer) protocol entity in a remote system. On receipt of the PDU, the peer protocol entity in the remote system creates an associated **indication primitive** and passes this up to the correspondent user. In the case of an unconfirmed service this completes the transfer, but with a confirmed service the correspondent user then issues a **response primitive**. Again, this results in an associated PDU being generated by the local protocol entity which is then sent back to the originating protocol entity, using the services provided by the underlying layer. On receipt of this PDU, the originating protocol entity creates a **confirm primitive** and passes it up to the user to complete the transfer.

There is a logical relationship between the various service primitives and these relationships are related in time. The interrelationship between the service primitives within a layer are often illustrated in the form of a **time sequence diagram**. As an example, Figure 11.12(b) shows the interrelationship of the four primitives just described. Clearly, a time sequence diagram is only an abstract way of representing the logical relationships between the service primitives of a layer and does not indicate how the specified services are implemented by the layer.

Normally, the type of primitive and the identity of the layer providing the service are included with the primitive name. Thus:

- T_CONNECT.request is a request primitive, issued by the transport service user (TS_user), that is, the session layer, to set up a (logical) transport connection with a remote TS_user (session layer).

- S_DATA.indication is an indication primitive issued by a peer (correspondent) session layer to the presentation layer above it and is concerned with the transfer of data received from a remote presentation layer.

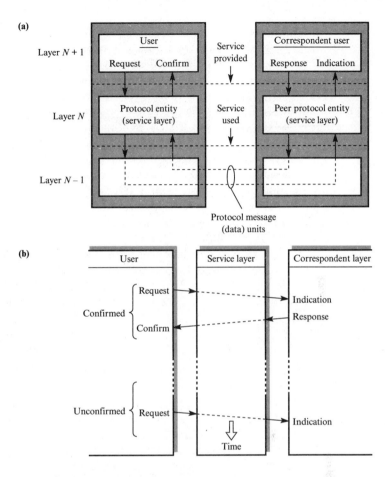

Figure 11.12
Service primitives:
(a) space
representation;
(b) time sequence
representation.

11.4.4 Service parameters and layer interactions

Associated with each service primitive is a defined set of parameters. As we shall see, it is through these parameters that adjacent layers within the same system can pass information and also how two correspondent user layers in different systems can exchange PDUs. For example, the parameters associated with the previous service primitives may include the following:

T_CONNECT.request (called address, calling address, ..., user data)
S_DATA.indication (connection identifier, user data)

In the first example, the called address and calling address parameters are concatenations of the relevant SAP subaddresses associated with the particular logical connection being established. Normally, the user data field parameter is an address pointer to a memory buffer. This contains the PDU generated by the protocol entity in the user layer above, which is to be passed to the correspondent protocol entity in the user layer in the remote system. Thus, although we use the term 'user data', this does not necessarily imply data as generated by a user application process. Rather, it means that it is data with meaning only to the user layer above and, as we shall see, it may contain protocol control information being exchanged between two correspondent user layers.

The user data parameter associated with a service primitive is known as a **service data unit (SDU)** by the recipient layer. Since this contains a PDU relating to the layer above, an $(N + 1)$ PDU is the same as an (N) SDU. Typically, on receipt of a service primitive, the protocol entity of the layer reads selected parameters associated with the primitive and combines them with additional **protocol control information (PCI)** to form a PDU for that layer. The resulting PDU is passed to the layer below in the user data field of a suitable primitive with additional parameters as appropriate, as shown in Figure 11.13(a).

We can conclude from this discussion that the user data field (parameter) associated with the service primitive at each layer interface grows as it passes down through the layers, with each layer adding its own PCI. Also, once the link layer protocol entity has added its own PCI, it is this that is encoded and transmitted to the remote system. Conversely, at the remote system, the user data field reduces at each layer interface as it passes up through the layers and the protocol entity in each layer reads and interprets the PCI relating to it. This is shown in Figure 11.13(b); we shall consider this in Chapter 14 after we have discussed the detailed operation of each layer.

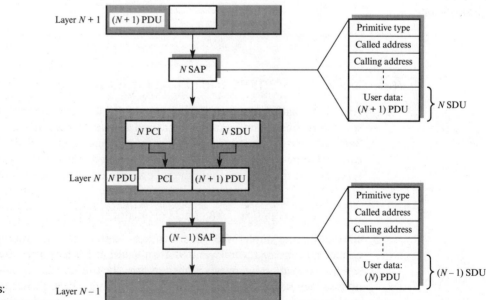

Figure 11.13
Layer interactions:
(a) single layer.

(b)

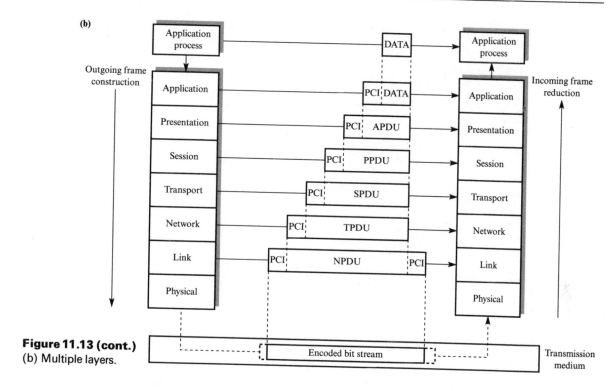

Figure 11.13 (cont.)
(b) Multiple layers.

11.4.5 Sequencing of primitives

Each layer has an associated range of primitives to provide such services as connection establishment and data transfer. On receipt of a service primitive at the interface of a layer, it is necessary for the layer protocol entity to determine whether the primitive is in the correct sequence. For example, it is not normally possible for the user layer to issue a data transfer request primitive before a connection has been established. Therefore, within the standards documents the acceptable sequence of service primitives associated with a layer is illustrated in the form of either a state transition diagram or a **sequence table**. An example of each is shown in Figure 11.14.

In the figure, the user services supported are intended to allow a user first to establish a logical connection with a remote (correspondent) user, then to transfer data across this connection, and finally to disconnect (clear) the connection. For clarity, only the connect and data transfer primitives are included. Normally, the state transition diagram is used simply to show the correct sequence of primitives that are allowed at the user interface. The sequence table, in contrast, is a more precise definition as it shows all possible sequences, both valid and invalid. Therefore, the sequence table is used for implementation purposes to ascertain whether a received primitive is in the

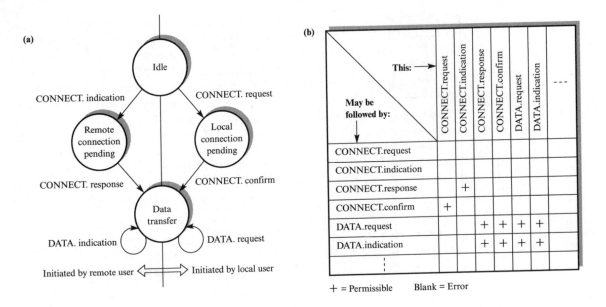

Figure 11.14
Service primitives:
(a) state transition
diagram; (b) sequence
table.

permitted sequence. Normally, receipt of an out-of-sequence primitive is a protocol violation and results in the clearing (disconnection) of the associated connection.

11.5 Protocol specification

The protocol specification document for a layer comprises the following:

- A qualitative description of the types of PDU associated with the protocol entity and their purpose, together with a description of the fields present in each PDU and their use.

- A description of the procedures followed during the various phases of operation of the protocol entity and the services it uses to transfer each PDU type.

- A formal definition of the structure of each PDU type.

- A precise definition of the operation of the protocol entity in one of the formal specification methods.

11.5.1 PDU definition

Two peer protocol entities communicate with each other by exchanging PDUs. Typically, a PDU contains user data and a PCI generated by the layer (protocol entity) itself. Since the parameters associated with a service primitive have only local significance (meaning), they are normally defined in terms of abstract data types, such as *INTEGER, BOOLEAN*. In contrast, PDUs generated by a protocol entity are passed *between* systems. To avoid ambiguity, these must be defined in a precise way so that they have a common meaning in both systems.

To achieve this, the PDUs associated with a protocol entity are defined in the standards documents in a precise way using either a specific bit string form or an abstract data type form (known as Abstract Syntax Notation Number One or ASN.1) coupled with an associated set of **encoding rules**. An example of a PDU defined in each form is given in Figure 11.15. Part (a) shows a PDU used by a transport layer protocol entity. It is a connect-request TPDU (transport protocol data unit). This, as we shall see in Section 11.6.3, is generated by a transport layer protocol entity to initiate the establishment of a logical connection with a peer

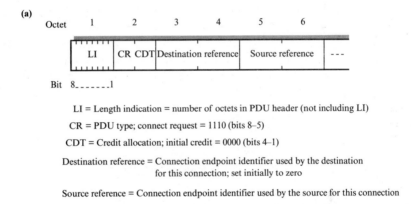

(a)

LI = Length indication = number of octets in PDU header (not including LI)

CR = PDU type; connect request = 1110 (bits 8–5)

CDT = Credit allocation; initial credit = 0000 (bits 4–1)

Destination reference = Connection endpoint identifier used by the destination for this connection; set initially to zero

Source reference = Connection endpoint identifier used by the source for this connection

(b)

```
FINITIALIZErequest ::= SEQUENCE {
        protocolId [0] INTEGER { isoFTAM (0) },
        versionNumber [1] IMPLICIT SEQUENCE {
                major INTEGER, minor INTEGER },
                -- initially { major 0, minor 0 }
        serviceType [2] INTEGER {
                reliable (0), user correctable (1) },
        serviceClass [3] INTEGER { transfer (0),
                access (1), management (2) },
        functionalUnits [4] BITSTRING {
                read (0),
                write (1),
                fileAccess (2),
                limitedFileManagement (3),
                enhancedFileManagement (4),
                grouping (5),
                recovery (6),
                restartDataTransfer (7) }
        attributeGroups [5] BITSTRING {
                storage (0),
                security (1) }
        rollbackAvailability [6] BOOLEAN DEFAULT FALSE,
        presentationContextName, [7] IMPLICIT ISO646String {"ISO8822"},
        identityOfInitiator [8] ISO646String OPTIONAL,
        currentAccount [9] ISO646String OPTIONAL,
        filestorePassword [10] OCTETSTRING OPTIONAL,
        checkpointWindow [11] INTEGER OPTIONAL}
```

Figure 11.15
Example PDU definition: (a) bit string form; (b) ASN.1 form.

transport entity as a result of a T_CONNECT.request service primitive at its user interface. The PDU in Figure 11.15(b) is associated with the application protocol entity FTAM, which we shall describe in Chapter 13.

As we can see from Figure 11.15(a), the bit string form of each PDU is made up of a number of octets and the intended use and format of each octet are precisely defined. Although this form of definition has been used for the specification of all the lower network-dependent layers, ASN.1 has been adopted for the specification of most of the application-oriented layers. Essentially, as we can see from Figure 11.15(b), ASN.1 is based on data typing as used with most high-level programming languages. Thus, a PDU defined using ASN.1 is comprised of a number of typed data elements. Both simple (primitive) types (*INTEGER* and *BOOLEAN*) and structured types (*SET* and *SEQUENCE*) are used, the latter being similar to the **record** type in Pascal.

As the name implies, ASN.1 is an abstract syntax, which means that although a data element may be of a defined type (for example, *INTEGER*), its absolute syntax in terms of the number of bits and the order of the bits used is not implied. Thus, we must use a set of encoding rules to produce the absolute or *concrete syntax* for a PDU defined in ASN.1. The resulting PDUs are simply strings of octets which are interpreted in the same (fixed) way in each system. We shall describe a more complete description of ASN.1 in Chapter 12 when we discuss the application-support protocols.

11.5.2   Protocol operation – overview

We first considered the operation of a protocol entity in Chapter 4 when discussing link-level protocols. A protocol entity is modelled in the form of a finite state machine or automaton. This means that a protocol entity can be in only one of a finite number of states at any one time. The current operational state of the automaton, together with other related protocol state information, is retained in a set of state variables maintained by the automaton.

A transition from one state to another is prompted when a valid incoming event occurs at one of the automaton interfaces. For example:

- Receipt of a service primitive from the interface with the layer above

- Receipt of a service primitive from the interface with the layer below

- Receipt of a service primitive from the interface with a **local entity** such as a **timer** or **management sublayer**

This is shown in Figure 11.16. Normally, the occurrence of a valid incoming event results in a PDU being generated by the protocol entity, which is output in the form of an outgoing event (action) at one of the layer interfaces. In addition, this change of state of the automaton may take place with, possibly, a specific internal action, such as the starting of a timer. An associated change to one or more of the automaton state variables may also occur.

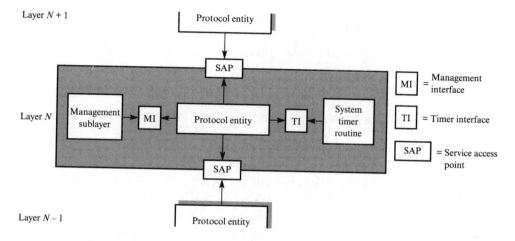

Figure 11.16
Incoming event
interfaces.

All incoming events are assumed to be **atomic**, that is, a protocol entity (automaton) carries out all the operations associated with an event (outgoing event, specific actions, change of state) before another incoming event is processed. To ensure that each incoming event is processed in an atomic way, local events such as the occurrence of timeouts are passed to the protocol entity in the same way as other incoming events. Normally, the various interfaces shown in Figure 11.16 are each implemented in the form of a pair of queues (mailboxes): one for input to the protocol entity and the other for output. The queues are then serviced by the protocol entity in a prescribed way. We shall consider this in more detail in Section 11.6.6.

In some instances, the operations performed by a protocol entity and the new state (if any) assumed by it depend on the current state of one or more **enabling conditions** or **predicates**. A predicate is a Boolean variable that depends on a combination of the values of the parameters associated with an incoming event and the current values of one or more of the automaton state variables. Normally, predicates are given the symbol P with an additional numeric qualifier. For example:

> P0: T_CONNECT.request is acceptable;
> P2: Retransmission count = Maximum.

Typical examples of their use are:

> P5& (Not P1): Outgoing event A
> New state X;
> P0: Outgoing event B
> New state Y.

If a predicate condition is not satisfied and the alternative state is not defined, a protocol error condition occurs and a predefined outgoing event and new automaton state are generated.

11.5.3 Protocol specification method

The ISO standards documents present the formal specification of a protocol entity as follows:

- A definition of all the possible incoming events at each interface

- A definition of the possible automaton states

- A definition of all the possible outgoing events generated by the protocol entity together with a list of any specific actions to be carried out

- A definition of the state variables and predicates (enabling conditions) associated with the operation of the automaton

- An extended event–state table defining, for all possible incoming event and present state combinations, the outgoing event (and any specific actions) and the new automaton state together with any alternative event and new state combinations that depend on predicates

The format of the extended event–state table used by the ISO is similar to that which we used in Chapter 4; an example is shown in Figure 11.17(a). Each entry in the table specifies the appropriate outgoing event (together with any specific actions) and the new state of the automaton for that particular (incoming) event–(present) state combination. Normally, only valid event–state combinations have an entry in the table, all other combinations are left blank. A blank entry is a protocol error and is always treated in a defined way.

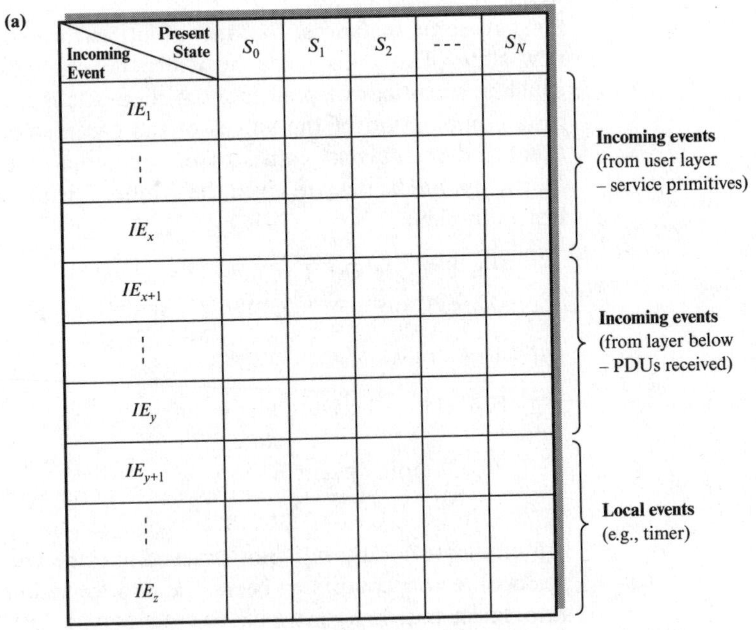

Figure 11.17
Extended event–state tables: (a) table format.

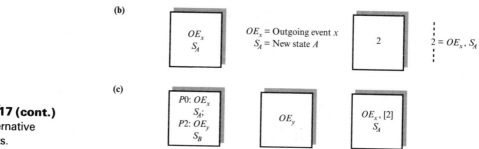

Figure 11.17 (cont.)
(b), (c) Alternative
entry formats.

Each entry in the table is specified in one of two ways, as shown in Figure 11.17(b). The entry either contains a specification of the actual outgoing event and the new state in the cell itself, or contains a reference number that refers to an entry in a separate list of outgoing event–new state specifications.

If the outgoing event and the new state are determined by predicates, these are included in the entry. An example is shown in Figure 11.17(c). Again, if none of the predicates are satisfied, a protocol error is assumed. Furthermore, if there is no state transition associated with an entry (that is, the automaton remains in the same state), only an outgoing event is specified. Similarly, if there is a specific action associated with an entry, a reference to the action in the list of actions is given. In the last example shown in Figure 11.17(c), the specific action [2] may mean, say, stop the associated timer.

11.6 Transport layer

The aims of this section are twofold: firstly, to give an example of the application of the specification methodology introduced in the previous sections and, secondly, to describe the operation and specification of the transport layer in the context of the ISO reference model.

11.6.1 Overview

In keeping with the methodology outlined, a model of the transport layer is shown in Figure 11.18. A user of the transport service (the TS_user) communicates with its underlying transport entity (or service provider) through a **transport service access point (TSAP)** using a defined set of user service primitives. The TSAP used is that associated with the initiating application entity. Service primitives cause, or are the result of, the exchange of **transport protocol data units (TPDUs)** between the two correspondent (peer) transport entities involved in a **transport connection (TC)**. The resulting TPDUs are exchanged using the services provided by the underlying network layer through an associated **network service access point (NSAP)**. Collectively, the TSAP and NSAP addresses help to identify, uniquely, the application entity (and hence the attached AP) involved in the connection.

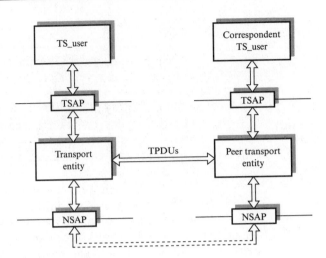

Figure 11.18
Model of transport
layer.

As already mentioned, the function of the transport layer is to provide the session layer with a reliable (error free, in sequence, with no loss or duplication) message transport facility that is independent of the QOS provided by the underlying network. To cater for the different types of network, the following five classes of service are provided to the user:

- Class 0: Simple class (normally used with a network offering a high QOS such as the telex network or a PSDN)

- Class 1: Basic error recovery class

- Class 2: Multiplexing class

- Class 3: Error recovery and multiplexing class

- Class 4: Error detection and recovery class. This contains the maximum control functions, such as error detection and retransmission and flow control. It is intended for low-quality networks such as a PSTN or a WAN or a LAN operating with a connectionless network layer.

All the classes of service assume a connection-oriented mode of operation, that is, a logical TC is established between the two correspondent transport entities before any data transfers are made. Although this is the preferred mode of working in most applications, it inevitably involves a certain level of protocol overheads in connection with the setting up and clearing of the TC. For certain selected application environments in which overheads are important, a more efficient (but less reliable) class of service based on a connectionless mode of working has been proposed. In this mode, data may be transferred between two correspondent entities without a TC first being established.

Note that the transport layer does not have to support all the different classes of service available. Normally, for a particular OSIE, the controlling authority of the environment specifies which class of service is to be used. All systems are then expected to use that class, which is chosen to best suit the QOS provided by the underlying network(s).

11.6.2   User services

We can divide the services provided by the transport layer into two categories: connection oriented and connectionless. In turn, we can divide the connection-oriented services into two subsets: those concerned with connection management and those concerned with data transfer. Connection management services allow a TS_user to establish and maintain a logical connection to a correspondent TS_user in a remote system. The data transfer services allow the exchange of data (messages) between the two correspondent users over this connection. A list of the service primitives associated with the transport layer, together with their parameters, is given in Figure 11.19 and a time sequence diagram showing the order of their use is given in Figure 11.20.

The called and calling address parameters associated with the T_CONNECT service are concatenations of the TSAP and NSAP addresses associated with the called and calling application entities involved in the connection. The QOS parameter refers to certain characteristics expected from the TC, such as throughput and error rates. Normally, these are defined for a particular network type.

The additional T_EXPEDITED_DATA service can be used only during the data transfer phase after a connection has been established and on the proviso that the two correspondent TS_users agreed on the use of this service when the TC was first established. This service is provided to allow a TS_user to send an item of data that bypasses the flow control procedure associated with the T_DATA service of class 4. We shall look at an example of its use when we consider the application-support layers in Chapter 12.

The sequence of primitives shown in Figure 11.20 assumes a successful connection establishment phase. However, if the request for a connection is unacceptable to the correspondent TS_user, then the latter issues a

Figure 11.19
User service primitives and associated parameters:
(a) connection oriented;
(b) connectionless.

(a)

Primitive	Parameters
T_CONNECT.request .indication	Calling address Called address Expedited data option Quality of service TS_user data
T_CONNECT.response .confirm	Responding address Quality of service Expedited data option TS_user data
T_DATA.request .indication	TS_user data
T_EXPEDITED_DATA.request .indication	TS_user data
T_DISCONNECT.request	TS_user data
T_DISCONNECT.indication	Disconnect reason TS_user data

(b)

Primitive	Parameters
T_UNITDATA.request .indication	Calling address Called address Quality of service TS_user data

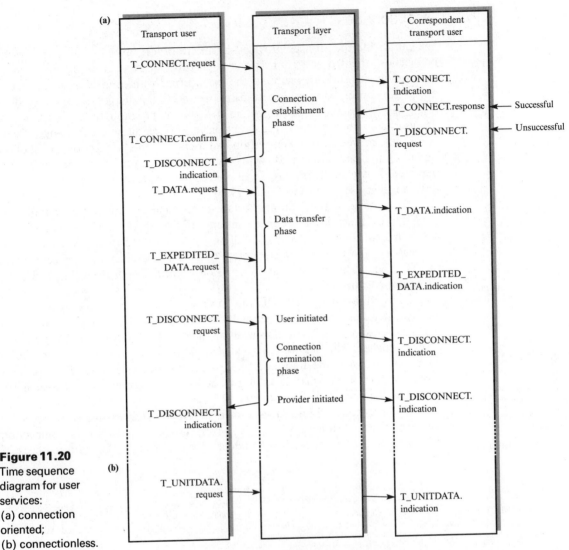

Figure 11.20
Time sequence
diagram for user
services:
(a) connection
oriented;
(b) connectionless.

T_DISCONNECT.request primitive, instead of a T_CONNECT.response primitive, with the reason for the rejection given as a parameter. Once a TC has been
established, either user can initiate its release at any time by issuing a
T_DISCONNECT.request at the user interface with the reason as a parameter.
Also, if the underlying network connection becomes disconnected, the transport
entity initiates the release of the TC using a T_DISCONNECT.indication
primitive.

The two primitives associated with the connectionless mode of working,
T_UNITDATA.request and T_UNITDATA.indication, enable a TS_user to
initiate the transfer of an item of user data without first establishing a TC.
However, with this service there is no guarantee that the transfer has been

successful and it is left to the higher application-oriented layers to recover from such eventualities. Inevitably, the protocol associated with the connection-oriented services is more complex than that associated with the connectionless mode. Hence in the remainder of this chapter we shall concentrate on the connection-oriented mode of operation.

A state transition diagram and an associated sequence table relating to the user services with the connection-oriented mode are shown in Figure 11.21. As we

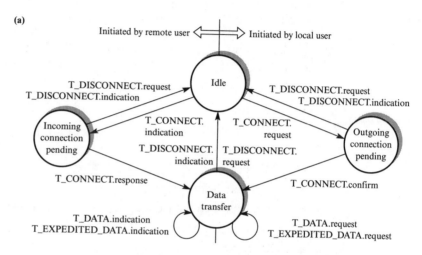

(a)

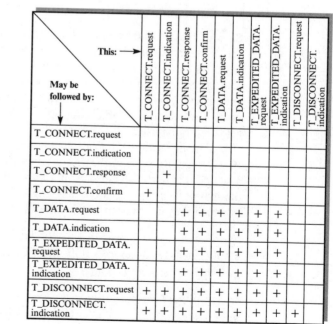

(b)

+ = Possible   Blank = Not permitted

Figure 11.21
User services: (a) state transition diagram; (b) sequence table.

can see, the sequence table gives a more complete specification of the acceptable sequence of primitives for each user.

11.6.3   Protocol operation

On receipt of a valid incoming service primitive (from either the TS_user or the network provider), the transport protocol entity generates an associated TPDU. Typically, assuming the incoming primitive is from the TS_user, the TPDU comprises the user data associated with the primitive together with additional protocol control information added by the transport entity. The generated TPDU is transferred to the correspondent transport entity using the services provided by the underlying network layer.

The TPDUs associated with the transport protocol are as follows:

- CR: connect request
- CC: connect confirm
- DR: disconnect request
- DC: disconnect confirm
- DT: data
- AK: data acknowledge
- ED: expedited data
- EA: expedited acknowledge
- RJ: reject
- ER: error

Each of these TPDU types has a number of associated fields; the precise format and contents of each field are shown in Figure 11.22. The **LI (length indicator)** field indicates the number of octets in the header, excluding the LI octet; the **class** field specifies the protocol class to be used with this connection (0–4); and the **option** field specifies whether normal (7-bit sequence number and 4-bit credit values) or extended (31-bit sequence and 16-bit credit) sequence and credit (CDT) fields are to be used.

The fields shown constitute what is known as the **fixed header** part of each PDU. In addition, most PDUs contain a **variable header** part and a **user data** part. The variable part also consists of a number of fields each represented in the form of an 8-bit field type, an 8-bit field length, and the field value. The fields and PDUs in which they are present are as follows:

- Calling TSAP address (CR and CC)
- Called TSAP address (CR and CC)
- TPDU size (CR and CC)
- Protocol version number (CR and CC)
- User security parameter (CR and CC)
- Checksum (all PDUs with class 4 – explained later in this section)

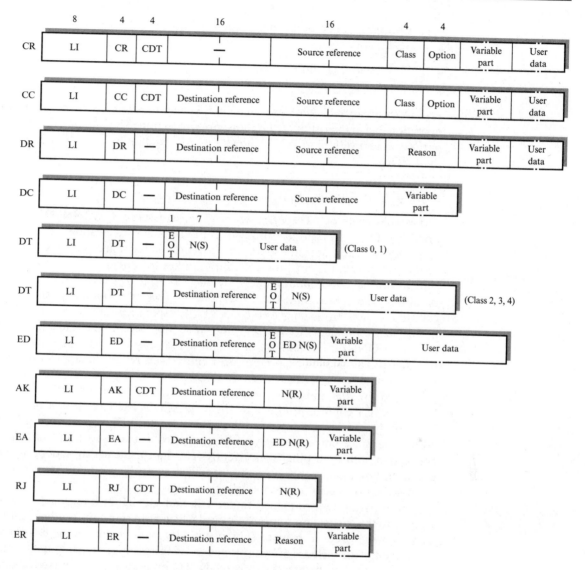

Figure 11.22
TPDU types and
header fields.

- Additional options (CR and CC)
- Alternative protocol class acceptable (CR and CC)
- Estimated acknowledgment delay time (CR and CC)
- Throughput requirement – eight values (CR and CC)
- Residual error rate (CR and CC)
- Connection priority (CR and CC)
- Transit delay requirement (CR and CC)
- Network reassignment (reconnection) attempts (CR and CC classes 1 and 3)

- User defined additional information (DR)
- AK number (AK)
- Flow control confirmation (AK)
- Invalid TPDU (ER)

As we can see, most are used in CR and CC TPDUs to negotiate the operational characteristics of the transport connection. The additional user data part associated with most PDUs allows a user to send up to 32 bytes of data with these PDUs.

Connection establishment

The establishment of a TC begins when a TS_user issues a T_CONNECT.request primitive. The local transport protocol entity responds by creating a CR TPDU and sends this to its peer transport protocol entity in the called system. On receipt of this, the peer transport protocol entity notifies the designated user in its own system of the connection request by means of a T_CONNECT.indication primitive. Then, providing the correspondent user is prepared to accept the call, it responds by issuing a T_CONNECT.response primitive. Alternatively, if the correspondent user does not wish to accept the call, it issues a T_DISCONNECT.request primitive with the reason for the rejection as a parameter. The peer transport protocol entity then relays the appropriate response in either a CC TPDU or a DR TPDU, respectively. Finally, the response is relayed by the initiating protocol entity to the user by means of the T_CONNECT.confirm primitive or the T_DISCONNECT.indication primitive, respectively, the latter containing the reason for the rejection as a parameter. Notice that since only a two-way exchange is used, if two users try to establish a connection with each other concurrently, two independent connections will be established. In practice, however, this is unlikely since all current ISO applications are based on the client–server model.

The parameters contained in the CR and CC TPDUs relay information relating to the connection being established which both transport protocol entities must know in order to manage subsequent data transfers across the established connection. This includes such information as the connection (endpoint) identifiers (references) to be associated with the TC by both the calling (source) and called (destination) transport entity, the class of service required, and the maximum length of subsequent DT TPDUs. Typically, the length is determined by the type of underlying network(s) being used and may range from 128 octets to 8192 octets increasing in powers of 2. Once the TC has been established, data can be accepted by the transport entities for transfer across the established logical connection in either direction.

Data transfer

A TS_user initiates the transfer of data to a correspondent user across a previously established connection using the T_DATA.request primitive. The local transport entity then transfers the user data (TSDU) in one or more DT TPDUs, depending on the amount of user data in the TSDU and the maximum size of the TPDU specified for the connection. Each DT TPDU contains a marker (EOT) which, when set, indicates the last TPDU in a sequence making up a single TSDU. Also, each DT TPDU contains a send sequence number N(S) which is used both to indicate the order of the TPDU in a sequence and, in conjunction with the AK TPDU, for acknowledgment and flow control. When the destination transport entity has received, and acknowledged, all the DT TPDUs making up a TSDU, it passes the reassembled block of data (that is, the TSDU) to the correspondent user using a T_DATA.indication primitive.

The acknowledgment and flow control mechanisms used vary for different classes of service. The service class selected is determined by the QOS of the underlying data network that is used to transport the TPDUs. For example, with an X.25 PSPDN the integrity and order of transmitted TPDUs are maintained by the network layer. Hence, only minimal acknowledgment and flow control mechanisms are needed in the transport protocol. However, with other types of network this is not the case, so we must use more sophisticated mechanisms, similar to those described in Chapter 4.

The acknowledgment procedure with class 4 is based on a go-back-N strategy (see Chapter 4) which works as follows. The receiver, on receipt of the next in-sequence DT TPDU or, if the TPDU completes a contiguous sequence of TPDUs, returns an AK TPDU which contains a receive sequence number, N(R), that positively acknowledges correct receipt of those DT TPDUs up to and including that with a send sequence number of $N(R) - 1$. On receipt of an out-of-sequence DT TPDU (that is, with an N(S) exceeding the next in-sequence DT TPDU expected), the receiving transport entity returns an RJ (negative acknowledgment) TPDU with an N(R) indicating the N(S) of the next in-sequence DT TPDU expected. Also, a timeout mechanism is employed for both these TPDUs to overcome the loss of an AK or RJ TPDU.

If the network layer does not ensure that DT TPDUs always arrive in sequence, the receiving transport entity uses the sequence numbers contained in each DT TPDU to reassemble them into the correct order. In such cases, it is only when a DT TPDU arrives in sequence or completes a contiguous sequence of outstanding TPDUs that the receiver returns an AK TPDU indicating their correct receipt. A typical sequence of TPDUs to implement a user data transfer request is shown in Figure 11.23.

Another factor that we must consider is that if the service provided by the network layer is of a low quality, it may lose TPDUs without notifying the sender or intended receiver. It may also pass on TPDUs containing transmission errors. Therefore, at connection establishment the user may specify a class of service which invokes a timeout and retransmission procedure, to allow for the possibility of lost TPDUs, as well as computed checksums and error-detection mechanisms, to ensure the integrity of each transmitted TPDU.

The protocol mechanism used to implement the timeout and retransmission scheme works as follows. When a transport entity sends a TPDU that requires a

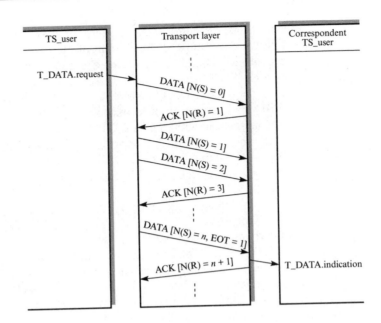

Figure 11.23
Data transfer example.

response, it sets a timer. If the timer expires before the appropriate response is received, the TPDU is retransmitted and the timer reset. This cycle is repeated a number of times. If the appropriate response is still not received, the transport entity assumes that communication with its peer has been lost. It then notifies the user with a T_DISCONNECT.indication primitive with the reason for the disconnection passed as a parameter. The use of timeouts means that duplicates may be generated, for example, TPDU received correctly but acknowledgment lost. If a DT TPDU is found to be a duplicate of a previously received TPDU, which is determined by its sequence number, an AK TPDU is returned but the duplicate is discarded.

Data integrity is accomplished by the transport protocol entity generating and including a 16-bit checksum as a parameter in the header of each TPDU transmitted. The receiver uses a similar algorithm to compute a checksum for the complete TPDU including the checksum parameter. This checksum is zero if the TPDU does not contain any errors. If the computed checksum is not zero, the TPDU is discarded, but the timeout and retransmission schemes ensure that a new copy of the TPDU is sent.

A checksum is used with all CC and CR TPDUs and also with all other TPDUs if class 4 is selected. The checksum is intended to detect any TPDUs with residual (undetected) errors after their transfer across the network. The algorithm in the standards document has been chosen to minimize the amount of processing required per TPDU. The algorithm calculates two checksum octets, X and Y, such that:

$$X = -C1 + C0; \ Y = C1 - 2C0$$

where:

$$CO = \sum_{i=1}^{L} a_i \qquad \text{(modulo 255)}$$

$$C1 = \sum_{i=1}^{L} (L+1-i)a_i \quad \text{(modulo 255)}$$

L is the number of octets in the complete TPDU, and a is the value of the ith octet in the TPDU.

An example showing the checksum generation and checking procedures is shown in Figure 11.24. The contents of the TPDU are assumed to be comprised of a string of unsigned 8-bit integers with the two checksum octets (X and Y) initially zero. The two checksum octets are then computed as follows:

(1)   Initialize $C0$ and $C1$ to zero.

(2)   Process each octet sequentially from $i = 1$ to L.

(3)   At each stage:
   (a)   add the value of the octet to $C0$
   (b)   add the new $C0$ to $C1$

(4)   Calculate X and Y such that:

$$X = -C1 + C0; \; Y = C1 - 2C0$$

Note that this procedure produces the same $C1$ as that produced by summing $(L+1-i)a_i$. Once computed, the two checksum octets (X and Y) are inserted into the TPDU prior to transmission, and a similar sequence of steps is followed at the receiver during the checking phase. Then, if *either* $C0$ or $C1$ is zero, no error is assumed. However, if $C0$ and $C1$ are *both* nonzero, an error is assumed

Assume TPDU contents are:

$i =$ 1 2 3 4 5

5	9	6	X	Y

$L = 5$

Checksum generation:

$i = 0$	$C0 = C1 = 0$	$X = Y = 0$
$i = 1$	$C0 := 0 + 5 = 5$	$C1 := 0 + 5 = 5$
$i = 2$	$C0 := 5 + 9 = 14$	$C1 := 5 + 14 = 19$
$i = 3$	$C0 := 14 + 6 = 20$	$C1 := 19 + 20 = 39$
$i = 4$	$C0 := 20 + 0 = 20$	$C1 := 39 + 20 = 59$
$i = 5$	$C0 := 20 + 0 = 20$	$C1 := 59 + 20 = 79$

$X = -79 + 1.20 = -59 \,(196)$
$Y = +79 - 2.20 = +39 \,(39)$

Checksum checking:

$i = 0$	$C0 = C1 = 0$	$X = -59 \,(196) \; Y = +39 \,(39)$
$i = 1$	$C0 := 0 + 5 = 5$	$C1 := 0 + 5 = 5$
$i = 2$	$C0 := 5 + 9 = 14$	$C1 := 5 + 14 = 19$
$i = 3$	$C0 := 14 + 6 = 20$	$C1 := 19 + 20 = 39$
$i = 4$	$C0 := 20 - 59 = -39 \,(216)$	$C1 := 39 - 39 = 0 \,(255)$
$i = 5$	$C0 := -39 + 39 = 0 \,(255)$	$C1 := 0 + 0 = 0 \,(255)$

Figure 11.24
Transport protocol checksum example.

and the TPDU is ignored. For this reason a timeout is incorporated into the protocol.

During the computation of $C0$ and $C1$, modulo 255 arithmetic is used, that is, unsigned arithmetic (no overflow and carry ignored), and the results are assumed to be in the range [0 .. 255]. To compute the two checksum octets (X and Y), 1's-complement arithmetic is used. This implies the use of an end-around-carry and a result of 255 is regarded as being zero.

The objective of a flow control mechanism is to limit the amount of data (or DT TPDUs) transmitted by the sending transport entity to a level that the receiver can accommodate. Clearly, if the transport entity is servicing only a single user, the appropriate amount of buffer storage required to process the subsequent user TSDUs may be reserved in advance. Consequently, when the TC is being established no flow control mechanism need be provided. However, if the transport entity is servicing multiple users and buffer storage is reserved on a statistical basis, then a flow control mechanism must be supported by the protocol. This again is determined by the class of service provided by the transport entity.

The flow control mechanism used with class 4 is based on a variation of the **sliding window protocol**. An initial credit value, equal to the number of outstanding (unacknowledged) DT TPDUs, for each direction of transmission is specified in the CDT field of each CR TPDU and the CC TPDU exchanged during connection establishment. The initial sequence number for each direction of transmission is set to zero when the connection is first established and this becomes the **lower window edge (LWE)**. The sender can continuously compute the **upper window edge (UWE)** by adding, modulo the size of the receive sequence field, the credit value for the connection to the LWE. The flow of DT TPDUs is stopped if N(S) becomes equal to the UWE value. The LWE is continuously incremented as AK TPDUs for outstanding DT TPDUs are received. This is shown in Figure 11.25.

The actual number of new DT TPDUs that can be transmitted by the sender may vary during the lifetime of a connection since this is completely under the control of the receiver. Each AK TPDU contains, in addition to a receive sequence number, a new credit value which specifies the number of new TPDUs that the receiver is prepared to accept after the one being acknowledged. If this value is zero, the sender must cease transmission of DT TPDUs over the connection. Normally, however, the credit value is used when the receiver allocates a fixed number of buffers for the connection. As each TPDU is received the number of new TPDUs the receiver is prepared to accept (the UWE) reduces as buffers start to be used up.

Connection termination

Connection termination (or release) is initiated when either of the TS_users issues a T_DISCONNECT.request primitive to its local transport entity with the reason for the clearing as a parameter. With class 0, termination of the TC also implies termination of the associated network connection (NC), while with the other

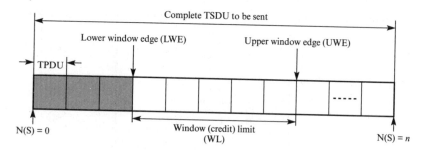

Complete TSDU to be sent

Lower window edge (LWE)

Upper window edge (UWE)

TPDU

N(S) = 0

Window (credit) limit
(WL)

N(S) = n

Note: LWE is initialized to zero and is incremented
as each AK TPDU is received.

UWE is initialized to the CDT value agreed when
the connection is established and is subsequently
incremented by the CDT value in each AK TPDU
received.

Flow is stopped if N(S) reaches UWE.

Figure 11.25
Flow control
mechanism.

classes the TC may be terminated independently of the NC. On receipt of the
T_DISCONNECT primitive, the transport entity sends a DR TPDU. It then
ignores all subsequently received TPDUs until it receives a DC TPDU. The peer
entity, on receipt of the DR TPDU, returns a DC TPDU and issues a
T_DISCONNECT.indication to the correspondent TS_user. The TC is then
assumed closed.

11.6.4 Network services

The transport layer uses the services provided by the network layer to exchange
TPDUs with a correspondent transport layer in a remote system. The network
layer can operate in either a connectionless or a connection-oriented mode. As we
saw earlier in Section 6.5.3, LANs normally operate with a connectionless
network layer while WANs normally operate with a connection-oriented network
layer. The set of service primitives associated with each mode are shown in Figure
11.26. As we can see from Figure 11.26(b), a single (unconfirmed) service primitive
(N_UNITDATA) is provided for the transfer of all information with a
connectionless mode.

To illustrate the added overheads associated with a connection-oriented
service, Figure 11.27 shows the network layer primitives necessary to establish a
TC using (a) a connection-oriented service and (b) a connectionless service. As
we can see, the CR TPDU is transferred directly using the N_UNITDATA
service in the connectionless service. In contrast, with a connection-oriented service a (network) connection must first be established before the CR TPDU
can be transferred as NS_user data. Clearly, the QOS associated with a
connectionless service is normally lower than that with a connection-oriented
service.

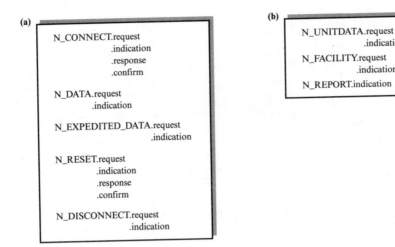

Figure 11.26
Network services:
(a) connection
oriented;
(b) connectionless.

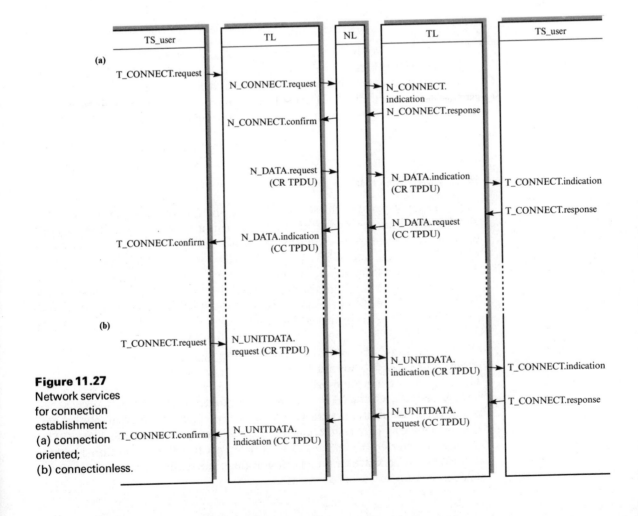

Figure 11.27
Network services
for connection
establishment:
(a) connection
oriented;
(b) connectionless.

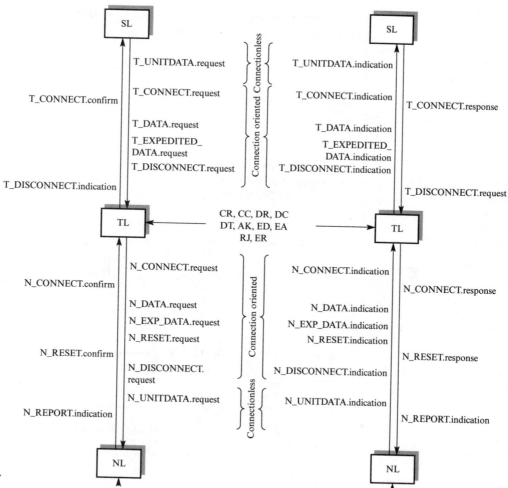

Figure 11.28
Transport layer
summary.

A summary of the various services provided and the services used by the transport layer is given in Figure 11.28 together with a list of the various TPDU types exchanged between two correspondent (peer) layers. We shall also use this style of presentation with the other protocol layers we discuss.

11.6.5 Protocol specification

As Section 11.5.3 described, in the ISO standards documents the formal specification of a protocol entity is specified in the form of an extended event–state table. This defines, for all possible incoming event–present state combinations, the appropriate outgoing event (together with any specific actions) and the new state. Furthermore, if predicates are involved, all the alternative outgoing event–new state possibilities are defined.

Normally, the event–state table(s) associated with a protocol are preceded by lists of the (abbreviated) names used for any of the following:

- Incoming events
- Automaton states
- Outgoing events
- Predicates
- Specific actions

To illustrate the protocol specification technique used by ISO, a list of these names for the connection establishment phase of the transport entity is given in Figure 11.29. Since the network service primitives used to transfer the

(a)

Name	Interface	Meaning
TCONreq	TS_user	T_CONNECT.request received
TCONresp	TS_user	T_CONNECT.response received
NCONconf	N_provider	N_CONNECT.confirm received
CR	N_provider	Connect request TPDU received
CC	N_provider	Connect confirm TPDU received

(b)

Name	Meaning
CLOSED	Transport connection is closed
WFNC	Waiting for a network connection
WFCC	Waiting for the CC TPDU
OPEN	Transport connection is open and ready for data transfer
WFTRESP	Waiting for the T_CONNECT.response from the TS_user

(c)

Name	Interface	Meaning
TCONind	TS_user	Send T_CONNECT.indication
TCONconf	TS_user	Send T_CONNECT.confirm
TDISind	TS_user	Send T_DISCONNECT.indication
NCONreq	N_provider	Send N_CONNECT.request
CR	N_provider	Send connect request TPDU
CC	N_provider	Send connect confirm TPDU
DR	N_provider	Send disconnect request TPDU
NDISreq	N_provider	Send N_DISCONNECT.request

(d)

Name	Meaning
P0	T_CONNECT.request from TS_user unacceptable
P1	Unacceptable CR TPDU received
P2	No network connection available
P3	Network connection available and open
P4	Network connection available and open and in progress
P5	Unacceptable CC TPDU received

Figure 11.29
Abbreviated names for connection establishment of the transport entity:
(a) incoming events;
(b) automaton states;
(c) outgoing events;
(d) predicates.

(a)

State \ Event	CLOSED	WFTRESP	WFNC	WFCC	OPEN	---
TCONreq	P0: TDISind CLOSED; P2: NCONreq WFNC; P3: CR WFCC; P4: WFNC					
TCONresp		CC OPEN				
NCONconf			CR WFCC			
CR	P1: DR CLOSED; NOT P1: TCONind WFTRESP					
CC	DR CLOSED			NOT P5: TCONconf OPEN; P5: TDISind NDISreq CLOSED		

(b)

State \ Event	CLOSED	WFTRESP	WFNC	WFCC	OPEN---
TCONreq	1	0	0	0	
TCONresp	0	2	0	0	
NCONconf	0	0	3	0	
CR	4	0	0	0	
CC	5	0	0	6	

0 = TDISind, NDISreq, CLOSED (Error condition)

1 = P0: TDISind, CLOSED; P2: NCONreq, WFNC; P3: CR, WFCC; P4: WFNC

2 = CC, OPEN

3 = CR, WFCC

4 = P1: DR, CLOSED; NOT P1: TCONind, WFTRESP

5 = DR, CLOSED

6 = NOT P5: TCONconf, OPEN; P5: TDISind, NDISreq, CLOSED

Figure 11.30
Event–state table
formats for
connection
establishment.

different TPDU types differ for both the type of network service and the type of TPDU being exchanged, only N_provider is normally specified in the various tables. The specific service to be used is specified as the different TPDUs are defined.

Two alternative forms of the event–state table definition associated with the connection establishment phase are shown in Figure 11.30. In Figure 11.30(a) each entry in the table specifies the actual outgoing event and the new state combination(s), whereas in Figure 11.30(b) the entry is simply an offset in a table that contains the list of event–state combinations. All blanks in the table in part (a) are error conditions and are the same as the zero entries in part (b). If none of the predicates associated with an entry are satisfied, this also constitutes an error condition. The error conditions are all treated in the defined way.

11.6.6   Protocol implementation

We introduced a basic methodology for implementing a protocol entity in Chapter 4 when we first discussed link-level protocols. The aim here is simply to illustrate how the basic methodology can be extended to allow for the fact that the transport layer is one of a number of such layers.

We stressed earlier that when we describe the operation of a communication subsystem which has been structured according to the ISO reference model, we must treat each protocol layer as an autonomous entity. This means that it provides a defined set of (user) services to the layer above it and, in turn, uses the services provided by the layer below it to transport the PDUs generated by the layer to a similar peer layer in a remote system. Similarly, when implementing the various protocol layers in the software, we must retain the same approach, otherwise the benefits gained by the adoption of a layered architecture are lost.

Normally a complete communication subsystem is implemented as a suite of task (process) modules, one per protocol layer, with additional tasks to perform local management and timer functions. Tasks communicate with each other through a set of **FIFO queues** or **mailboxes** as shown in Figure 11.31. As we shall see in Chapter 14, a communication subsystem is normally implemented using a separate processing subsystem because of the relatively high processing overheads associated with a complete communication subsystem. Intertask communication is managed by the local (real-time) **kernel** associated with the processing subsystem. The kernel also handles such functions as task scheduling and interrupt handling – for example, for the timers associated with each protocol entity.

As we have already described, a protocol layer communicates with an adjacent layer by means of the service primitives associated with that layer. Each service primitive, together with its associated parameters, is first created in the defined (local) format in a **memory buffer** known as an **event control block (ECB)**. Unlike the rigid structure (syntax) associated with PDUs, many of the parameters

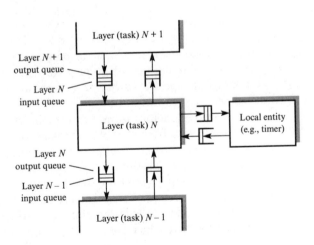

Figure 11.31
Intertask queue structure.

associated with each service primitive are in the form of a list of abstract data types. Hence, assuming a high-level language is being used for the implementation of each protocol entity (and hence task), a language-dependent typed data structure is used when passing parameters between tasks.

In general, the number and type of parameters associated with each primitive varies but, to avoid the need for a different data structure for each primitive type, there is normally just a single-typed data structure (ECB) associated with each protocol layer. At the head of the ECB is a primitive type field. This is followed by an additional (typed) field for all the possible parameters associated with the complete set of service primitives of that layer. When passing primitives between layers, the sending task indicates the type of primitive being passed at the head of the ECB. As we shall see, the receiving task uses this to determine the particular outgoing event procedure to be invoked. This procedure reads only those parameters related to it and hence those having meaningful values assigned to them.

The structure of a typical ECB is shown in Figure 11.32(a). This example relates to the transport layer and is used for all communications between the session and transport layers, that is, for all transport request, indication, response, and confirm service primitives. The complete ECB is a **record** structure and the type of the service primitive is assigned to *EventType*. We shall consider the use of the *UDBpointer* and its associated *UDBlength* shortly. The calling and called SSAP, TSAP, and NSAP fields are used with the T_CONNECT primitives while the *DestinationId* and *SourceId* are used with subsequent T_DATA primitives to relate the user data associated with the primitive to a specific TC.

To pass service primitives between layers (tasks) the initiating task simply invokes an intertask communication primitive (to the local kernel) with the address pointer of the ECB as a parameter. This causes the pointer to be inserted by the kernel at the tail of the appropriate interlayer queue. When a task is scheduled to run, it examines each of its input queues – with the layers above and below and with the timer and management tasks – to determine if an ECB is awaiting processing. If it is, the transport protocol first reads the pointer from the head of the appropriate queue and proceeds to process the incoming event. Typically, this causes a PDU to be generated and a suitably formatted message (ECB) to be created and passed to one of its output queues.

The mechanism just outlined is suitable as long as only a single application layer activity, and hence service request, is being processed at one time. However, often a number of different activities (service requests) may be processed concurrently. In such cases, either all interlayer messages are passed using a single set of queues or there is a separate set of queues associated with each active SAP (channel). The problem with the former approach is that, since conditions are often associated with the state of a protocol entity (layer) which must be met before a particular action can be carried out (for example, the send window associated with a flow control mechanism must be closed), it is sometimes necessary to suspend the processing of a message until the inhibiting condition is cleared. Normally, the latter affects only a single channel so other active channels should not be affected.

(a)

```
const octet      = 0..255;
      maxSSAP = 2;
      maxTSAP = 2;
      maxNSAP = 11;

type SSAPaddrtype = array [1..maxSSAP] of octet;
     TSAPaddrtype = array [1..maxTSAP] of octet;
     NSAPaddrtype = array [1..maxNSAP] of octet;
     TransportECBtype =

record EventType:      integer;
       UDBpointer:     ↑ UDB;
       UDBlength:      integer;
       CallingSSAP:    SSAPaddrtype;
       CallingTSAP:    TSAPaddrtype;
       CallingNSAP:    NSAPaddrtype;
       CalledSSAP:     SSAPaddrtype;
       CalledTSAP:     TSAPaddrtype;
       CalledNSAP:     NSAPaddrtype;
       DestinationId:  integer;
       SourceId:       integer;
       QOS:            integer
end;

var TransportECB : TransportECBtype;
```

(b)

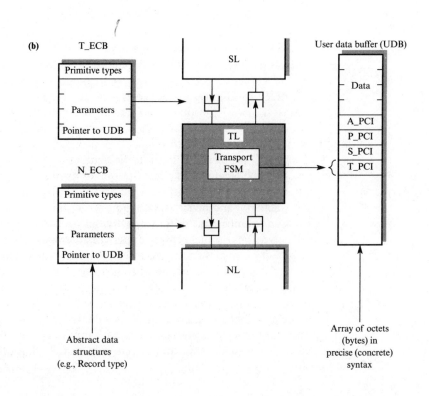

Figure 11.32
Interlayer
communication
schematic:
(a) transport ECB
structure;
(b) relationship
between ECB and
UDB.

The management of such mechanisms can become quite complicated (for example, especially when expedited data is present). To alleviate this, it is common practice to have a set of queues associated with each access point. Then, the temporary closure of a channel is readily controlled simply by suspending the processing of entries in the affected queue until the inhibiting condition is cleared. In this way, the flow of messages through the other channels (queues) is unaffected.

As we described in Section 11.4.4, each service primitive normally has user data associated with it which, in general, is a concatenation of the PCI relating to the higher protocol layers. On receipt of a service primitive (ECB), the protocol entity uses the parameters associated with the primitive, together with the current protocol state information associated with the connection, to create the PCI for the layer. This PCI is added to the user data associated with the incoming primitive to form the layer PDU which is then passed down to the next lower layer in the user data field associated with a suitable primitive. The general scheme is shown in Figure 11.13(b).

The user data associated with a primitive is held in a separate **user data buffer (UDB)**. We can deduce that the UDB contains the accumulated PCI (PDUs) for each of the higher layers. Hence, it is the contents of the UDB that are eventually transmitted by the physical layer. As Section 11.5.1 indicated, the PCI associated with each layer is defined in a rigid or concrete syntax, since it must be interpreted in the same way by two, possibly different, systems. Irrespective of the way the PDUs are defined, this takes the form of a string of octets, so each UDB is declared simply as an array of octets. The UDB pointer field in each ECB is the address pointer to the UDB containing the user data associated with the primitive. The UDB length indicates the number of octets currently in the buffer. As each layer adds its own PCI to the existing contents, it increments the UDB length by the appropriate amount. Then, when the UDB is received by the physical layer, the specified number of octets are transmitted from the UDB.

The outline structure of a single protocol layer in the context of a complete communication package is shown in Figure 11.33. Since the ECBs and associated UDBs must be accessible by each layer, they are each declared as global data structures. Normally, a pool of ECBs (for each layer) and UDBs is created when the system is first initialized and the pointers to these buffers are linked in the form of a free list. Whenever a new buffer is required, a free buffer pointer is obtained from the free list. Whenever a buffer is finished with, it is returned to the free list.

Although there is a single *EventStateTable* array associated with each layer (task), there is a separate set of state variables associated with each active channel if the layer can handle multiple service requests concurrently. For clarity, only a single set is shown in the figure. The example layer relates to the transport layer. Hence, the various event types, automaton states, outgoing event procedures, and predicates are as shown in the event–state table of Figure 11.30.

The scheduling of tasks is normally managed by the local real-time kernel. If a task is idle (waiting for an incoming event to occur) and an ECB pointer is transferred to one of its input queues, the kernel automatically schedules the task

```
program Communications_Subsystem;
global   Intertask queues (mailboxes);
         Event Control Blocks;
         User Data Buffers;
            ⋮

   task Transport_Layer;
   local type Events = (TCONreq, TCONresp, NCONconf, CR,CC, ---);
              States = (CLOSED, WFNC, WFCC, OPEN, WFTRESP, ---);
                ⋮

         var EventStateTable = array [Events, States] of 0..N;
             PresentState: States;
             EventType: Events;
             ECB: ↑ ECB Buffer;
             UDB: ↑ UDB Buffer;
                ⋮

         procedure Initialize; {Initialize EventStateTable contents and state variables}
         procedure TCONind;  ⎫
         procedure TCONconf; ⎬ List of outgoing event procedures
         procedure TDISind;  ⎭
                ⋮

         function P0: boolean; ⎫ List of predicate functions
         function P1: boolean; ⎭

         begin Initialize;
            repeat Wait for an ECB to arrive at an input interface queue;
                   EventType := type of event in ECB;
                   case EventStateTable [PresentState, EventType] of
                       0: begin TDISind, NDISreq, PresentState := CLOSED end;
                       1: begin if P0 then begin TDISind; PresentState := CLOSED end;
                          else if P2 then begin NCONreq; PresentState := WFNC end
                          else if P3 then begin CR; PresentState := WFCC end
                          else if P4 then PresentState := WFNC end
                          else begin TDISind; NDISreq; PresentState := CLOSED end
                          end;

                       2:
                        ⋮

            until Forever

         end.
            ⋮
```

Figure 11.33
Outline program
structure of a protocol
layer.

to be run. The type of event (from the ECB) is first assigned to *EventType* and this, coupled with the current *PresentState*, is used to access the *EventStateTable* array. The entry in the table defines the appropriate outgoing event procedure to be invoked and the new *PresentState*. Alternatively, if predicates are involved, the list of alternative outgoing event–new state combinations is defined. Normally, the predicates relate to a number of different conditions. Hence, they are set/reset either at the appropriate points during the processing of each event or by invoking specially written Boolean functions that compute the predicate state.

Exercises

11.1 With the aid of a sketch showing the protocols associated with the TCP/IP suite, identify in which layer PDU the following fields are present and explain their functions:
(a) IP address
(b) Protocol port address

11.2 Produce a sketch of a frame transmitted on a LAN that shows the relative position of the MAC, IP, TCP/UDP, and application protocol control information.

11.3 Explain the intended applications of the UDP.
With the aid of a sketch, identify the fields that make up a user datagram header and explain their role.

11.4 Explain the meaning of the term 'reliable stream service' and how it differs from a basic message transfer service.

11.5 With the aid of time sequence diagrams showing typical user service primitive exchanges, explain how two transport users perform the following:
(a) Client–server connection establishment
(b) Normal data transfer
(c) Forced data transfer
(d) Status interrogation
(e) Graceful connection termination
(f) Aborted termination

11.6 Produce a sketch showing the fields that make up the header of a TCP segment and explain the function of each field.

11.7 Show typical segment exchanges between two TCPs, together with descriptive text, to explain the following parts of the TCP:
(a) Client–server connection establishment
(b) Connection collision
Clearly identify the segment types being exchanged and typical sequence number values.

11.8 With the aid of a sketch showing typical segment exchanges between two TCPs, explain the normal and forced data transfer modes of the TCP.

Assuming a maximum segment size of W octets, a window of $2W$, and a round-trip delay of $3W$, sketch an example segment exchange relating to the transfer of a message of $3W$ octets. Include example sequence, acknowledgment, and window values for each segment.

11.9 With the aid of a sketch showing typical segment exchanges between two TCPs, explain the normal and abnormal (abort) connection termination alternatives of the TCP.
Include in your descriptions the use of the FIN, SEQ, and ACK flags.

11.10 Starting with the state transition diagram shown in Figure 11.9, develop a specification for a client and server TCP entity that is based on an event–state table. Clearly identify the incoming event initiating each transition and any local (specific) actions involved.

11.11 With the aid of a sketch, explain the meaning of the following terms relating to an ISO protocol layer:
(a) Service user
(b) User services
(c) Service provider
(d) Layer protocol entity
(e) Used services

11.12 In the context of the ISO reference model for open systems interconnection, explain briefly, with the aid of sketches where appropriate:
(a) The meaning and interrelationship of the terms 'network environment', 'open systems environment', and 'real systems environment'
(b) The difference between a user name (title) and a fully qualified address
(c) How the overheads associated with a user message increase as the message passes down through each protocol layer prior to transmission and decrease as it passes up through the layers on reception

11.13 Explain the aim of the ISO reference model for open systems interconnection and outline the function of each layer.

11.14 Make a sketch summarizing the structure of the ISO reference model and indicate where the following services are provided:
(a) Distributed information services
(b) Syntax-independent message interchange service
(c) Network-independent message interchange service

11.15 Sketch a model of a protocol layer, together with additional descriptions, where appropriate, to explain the meaning of the following terms:
(a) The services provided by the layer
(b) The SAPs associated with the layer
(c) The PDUs exchanged between two peer protocol entities
(d) The services used by the layer

11.16 Outline the structure of the extended event–state table used in the methodology adopted by the ISO to specify a protocol entity with particular emphasis on the meaning of each row and column. Give an example in such a table that has:
(a) A single outgoing event and new state combination
(b) A number of alternative outgoing event and new state combinations determined by predicates
(c) A specific action associated with the outgoing event

11.17 (a) Use a time sequence diagram to illustrate a typical set of user services for the transport layer and describe their functions.

(b) Define a set of TPDUs to implement these services and hence derive a time sequence diagram showing a typical sequence of TPDUs exchanged to implement the services in (a).
(c) Define a set of network service primitives and hence derive a time sequence diagram showing how the TPDUs defined in (b) are transferred using these services.

11.18 Describe the following in relation to the data transfer phase of the ISO transport protocol:
(a) The acknowledgment procedure
(b) The error-detection method used and an example of its use
(c) The flow control mechanism

11.19 The connection establishment phase of the ISO transport protocol is to be implemented.
(a) Produce a list of the incoming events, automaton states, outgoing events, and predicates associated with this phase.
(b) Derive an event–state table for the protocol entity showing clearly the outgoing event–new state possibilities for each incoming event–present state combination.

11.20 Outline a methodology for the implementation of an ISO protocol entity. Include in the description:
(a) The structure and use of an ECB
(b) The structure and use of a UDB

Chapter summary

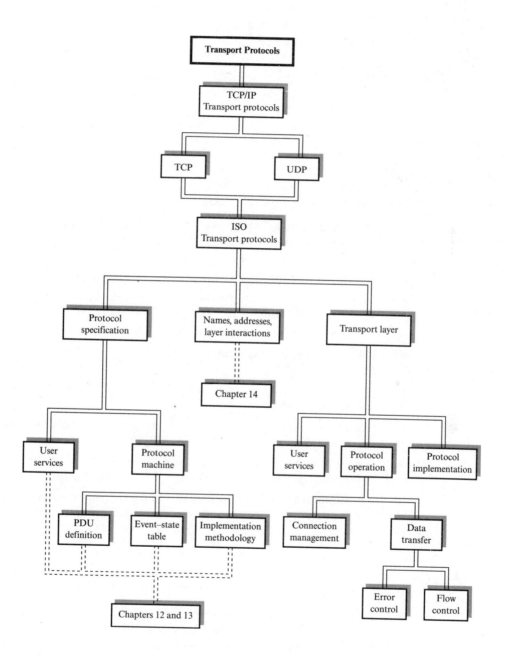

12 APPLICATION SUPPORT PROTOCOLS

Chapter objectives

When you have completed this chapter you should be able to:

- Appreciate that an OSI protocol stack has a number of intermediate application-support protocols between the application and transport layers ☞ 694
- Know the functionality of these protocols ☞ 695, 696, 697
- Describe the services and operation of the session layer and how the session protocol entity is specified in the ISO standard ☞ 697, 703
- Know the various functions associated with the presentation layer ☞ 707
- Know the roles and operation of abstract syntax notation number one (ASN.1) ☞ 709
- Know the terminology and principles involved in selected data encryption standards ☞ 718, 722, 726
- Describe the services and operation of the presentation protocol and how it is specified in the ISO standard ☞ 732, 736
- Understand the role of the association control service element (ACSE) and the remote operations service element (ROSE) ☞ 737, 740
- Appreciate the problems associated with concurrency control and multiple copy update and explain the services and operation of the commitment, concurrency, and recovery (CCR) protocol ☞ 743

Introduction

Recall from Chapter 11 that although in the TCP/IP suite application protocols (or application processes) interact directly with the transport layer protocols (UDP and TCP), in an OSI stack they interact through the protocol entities associated with the intermediate session and presentation layers. As Figure 12.1 shows, the application layer consists of two sets of protocols, each of which is known as an **application service element (ASE)**. The ASE is the combined service

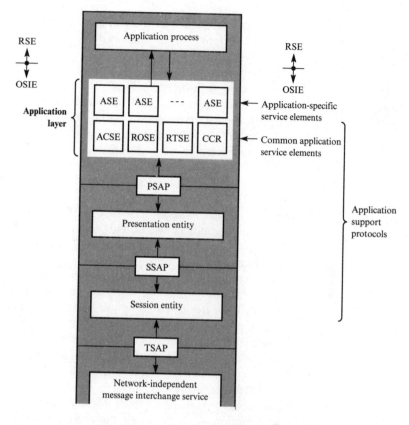

Figure 12.1
Application support
protocols in the
context of the ISO
reference model.

ASE = Application service element
ACSE = Association control service element
ROSE = Remote operations service element
RTSE = Reliable transfer service element
CCR = Concurrency control and recovery

OSIE = Open system interconnection environment
PSAP = Presentation service access point
SSAP = Session service access point
TSAP = Transport service access point
RSE = Real system environment

and protocol specification of a protocol. One set performs specific application functions while the other performs more general support functions which are also known as **common application service elements (CASEs)**. Thus in the TCP/IP suite, the functionality of the CASEs and the functionality provided by the session and presentation layers are embedded into each application protocol as appropriate.

The session layer is included in the OSI stack primarily to minimize the effects of network failures during an application transaction. In many networking applications, a transaction may occupy a considerable time and involve the transfer of a substantial amount of data. An example is a database containing a set of customer accounts or employee details which is transferred from a server application process to a client process. Clearly, if a network failure occurs toward the end of such a transfer, then the complete transfer – or multiple such transfers – may have to be repeated. The session layer provides services to reduce the effect of such failures.

If you were asked to write an application program to process records from a set of files relating to an open system application involving, say, a number of computers each belonging to a different bank or other financial institution, you would, of course, want to use a suitable high-level programming language. Each record would then be declared in the form of, say, a record structure, with the various fields in each record declared as being of suitable types. However, although the data types used may be the same as those used by the programmer who created the files, the actual machine representation of each field after compilation may be quite different in the two machines. For example, in one computer an integer type may be represented by a 16-bit value while in another it may be represented by 32 bits. Even if the two computers both use 16 bits to represent an integer type, the position of the sign bit or the order of the two bytes that make up each integer may still be different. Similarly, the character types used in different computers also differ. For example, EBCDIC may be used in one and ASCII/IA5 in another. The representation of the different types are thus said to be in an **abstract syntax** form.

The effect of this is that when we pass a block of data – for example, holding a set of records – from one computer to another, we cannot simply transfer the block of data from one computer memory to the other since the program in the receiving computer may interpret the data on the wrong byte boundaries. Consequently, when we transfer data between computers, we must ensure that the syntax of the data is known by the receiving machine and, if this is different from its local syntax, convert the data into this syntax prior to processing.

One approach to this problem is to define a **data dictionary** for the complete (distributed) application which contains an applicationwide definition of the representation of all the data types used in the application. If this representation is different from the local representation used by a machine, we must convert all data received into its local syntax prior to processing and convert it back into the standard form if it is to be sent to another machine. The form used in the data dictionary is known as the **concrete** or **transfer syntax** for the application.

This is a common requirement in many distributed applications, especially in open systems that involve interworking between computers from different manufacturers. The approach adopted by ISO is to integrate this function into the protocol stack; this is one of the main roles of the presentation layer. Others include data compression and encryption, both of which are concerned with the representation of transferred data.

A number of other functions are common to many applications. The ISO approach is to separate these from the actual application-specific functions and to implement them as a set of support protocols. If a particular support function is required in an application, then an instance of the appropriate support protocol(s) is (are) linked with the particular application-specific protocol. As we indicated earlier, all the protocols associated with the application layer are application service elements (ASEs). The ASEs that perform general support functions include the **association control service element (ACSE)**, the **remote operations service element (ROSE)**, the **reliable transfer service element (RTSE)**, and the **concurrency, control, and recovery (CCR)** service element.

Recall from Chapter 11 that two application processes/protocols can communicate in one of two ways. Either a logical connection – known as an **association** when it relates to an application – can be set up between the two processes before transferring any data (messages) associated with the application, or an application process can simply send the message directly and, if appropriate, wait for a response. The first approach is appropriate for the transfer of large volumes of data to ensure the receiver is prepared for the data before it is sent. The second may be more appropriate for a short request–response exchange. The services provided by ACSE have been defined for the first case and those associated with ROSE for the second. In addition, RTSE includes the services of both the ACSE and selected session services.

The functions provided by the CCR service element are also required in many applications. They are concerned with controlling access to a shared resource, for example, a file containing seat reservations in an airline reservation system or a file containing a customer account in a banking application. In this type of application, the files must be accessible from many sites concurrently. Consequently, steps must be taken when changing the contents of such files to ensure that the contents always reflect the operations that have been performed. Similarly, in an application that involves the availability of multiple copies of the same file at different sites, care must be taken to ensure that the contents of all copies remain consistent when changes are being made. The CCR ASE has been defined to help perform these functions.

In this chapter we shall discuss all the protocols identified and their functions and operation.

12.1 Session layer

Figure 12.2 shows the position of the session layer in relation to an OSI suite. Although the session and presentation layers are treated separately for specification purposes, they operate in close cooperation with the various protocols in the application layer to provide a particular application-support function. Hence, even if the PSAP and SSAP address selectors are used to provide additional multiplexing/demultiplexing above the transport layer, most of the service primitives associated with the application layer translate directly into equivalent presentation/session primitives. Indeed, in many instances the presentation layer passes selected service primitives directly to the session layer without modification. Alternatively, if a primitive relates to both the presentation and session layers, then the presentation entity simply adds its own protocol control information to the head of the message (PDU) it receives and passes this to the session layer in the user data parameter of a matching session service primitive.

Also, recall that connection-oriented and connectionless communication modes may be used by application entities. These two modes are supported by a connection-oriented and a connectionless presentation and session protocol. However, in practice all the OSI profiles defined to date use only the two

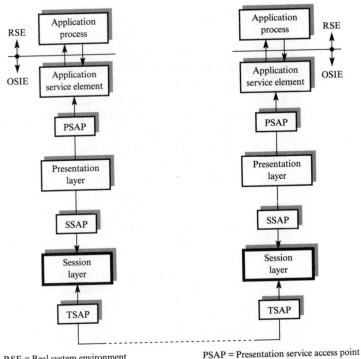

Figure 12.2
Session layer
schematic.

RSE = Real system environment PSAP = Presentation service access point
OSIE = Open system interconnection environment SSAP = Session service access point
  TSAP = Transport service access point

connection-oriented protocols. To achieve a fast response a quantity of user data – 512 octets or greater – can be transferred with the initial connect PDU and, if required, with a returned connect confirm PDU. The connection is then cleared. Alternatively, a presentation/session connection can be established and left in place. Data transfer (in both directions) is then carried out using this connection as required. Also, as we shall see in Section 12.1.2, a subset of the full session service known as the **basic combined subset (BCS)** is normally used as a way of minimizing the overheads associated with each message transfer.

We shall consider the main features of both connection-oriented protocols. The two connectionless protocols, because of their minimum functionality, are much simpler.

The session layer allows an application protocol entity, through the services offered by the presentation layer, to do the following:

- Establish a logical communication path (session connection) with another application entity, use it to exchange data (**dialog units**), and release the connection in an orderly way

- Establish synchronization points during a dialog and, in the event of errors, resume the dialog from an agreed synchronization point

- Interrupt (suspend) a dialog and resume it later at a prearranged point

- Be informed of certain exceptions that may arise from the underlying network during a session

12.1.1 Token concept

For two application entities to manage a dialog over an established (session) connection, the following set of tokens is defined:

- The data token

- The release token

- The synchronization-minor token

- The major/activity token

Each of these tokens is assigned dynamically to one session service (SS) user (that is, application entity through its related presentation entity) at a time to allow that user to carry out the corresponding service. The current owner of a token gives that user the exclusive use of the related service. For example, the **data token** is used to enforce a half-duplex data exchange between the two users and the **release token** to negotiate the release (termination) of a connection in a controlled way.

The **synchronization-minor** and **major/activity** tokens are associated with the synchronization process that may be used during a session. When two SS-users are exchanging large quantities of data, the data should be structured into a number of identifiable units so that, if a (network) fault develops during the session, only the most recently transferred data is affected. To allow a user to perform this function, a number of **synchronization points** may be inserted into sequential blocks of data before transmission. Each synchronization point is identified by a serial number which is maintained by the session protocol entity. Two types of synchronization points are provided:

- **Major**   Normally, these are associated with complete units of data (dialog units) being exchanged between two users.

- **Minor**   Normally, these are associated with parts of a dialog unit.

These allow two users to implement the associated synchronization process. Typical synchronization points established during a complete session connection are shown in Figure 12.3(a).

The concept of an **activity** allows two SS-users to distinguish between different logical pieces of work associated with a session. Although a complete session may comprise a number of activities, only one activity may be in progress at a time. In this way, an activity can be interrupted and then resumed either on the same session connection or on a different connection. Each activity is therefore made up of a number of **dialog units**. For example, an activity may relate to a number of files. A dialog unit would then relate to a single file which is in turn made up of a number of records.

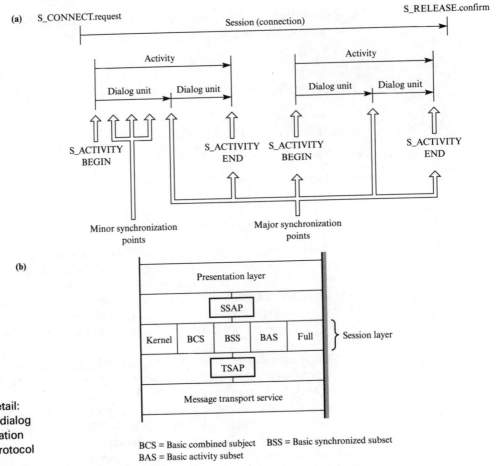

Figure 12.3
Session layer detail:
(a) activity and dialog
unit synchronization
concepts; (b) protocol
subsets.

BCS = Basic combined subject   BSS = Basic synchronized subset
BAS = Basic activity subset

12.1.2 User services

The services offered by the session layer to a user are extremely varied and hence
are grouped into a number of **functional units** to allow two SS-users to negotiate
the precise services required when the session connection is first established. The
functional units available include the following:

- **Kernel** Provides the basic (and minimal) functions of connection management and duplex data transfer.

- **Negotiated release** Provides an orderly release service.

- **Half-duplex** Provides for one-way alternate data exchange.

- **Synchronization** Provides for (re)synchronization during a session connection.

- **Activity management** Provides for identifying, starting, ending, suspending, and restarting activities.

- **Exception reporting**   Provides for reporting an exception during a session connection.

To avoid the user having to specify each required functional unit when a session connection is first established, a number of **subsets**, comprising different combinations of units, have been defined. These are summarized in Figure 12.3(b) and are as follows:

- **Basic combined subset**   Includes the kernel and half-duplex units.
- **Basic synchronized subset**   Includes the synchronization units.
- **Basic activity subset**   Includes the activity management and exception reporting units.

User service primitives are also available to implement all these functions. As an example, the services provided to implement the basic combined subset (BCS) are shown in the time sequence diagram in Figure 12.4(a).

In addition, parameters are associated with each service. For example, the parameters associated with the S_CONNECT primitives allow two SS-users to negotiate such things as the services (functional units) to be used during the session connection, initial token ownership, and (when selected) sync-point serial number settings. These are in addition to the normal calling and called addresses and a (session) connection identifier to be used during the subsequent data exchange phase. The parameters associated with the two TOKEN primitives include the type of the token – data, release, etc. The S_TOKEN_PLEASE service is used to request the specified token(s) and the S_TOKEN_GIVE service to transfer the specified token(s).

12.1.3 Session protocol

Most of the service primitives previously described result in the creation and sending of a corresponding session protocol data unit (SPDU) by the session protocol entity. For example, the SPDUs associated with the BSC service primitives are:

SPDU	*Sent in response to:*
CONNECT (CN)	S_CONNECT.request
ACCEPT (AC)	S_CONNECT.response (if successful)
REFUSE (RF)	S_CONNECT.response
DATA (DT)	S_DATA.request
GIVE TOKEN (GT)	S_GIVE_TOKEN.request
GIVE TOKEN ACK (GTA)	GT received
PLEASE TOKEN (PT)	S_PLEASE_TOKEN.request
FINISH (FN)	S_RELEASE.request
DISCONNECT (DN)	S_RELEASE.response
ABORT (AB)	S_U_ABORT.request
ABORT ACCEPT (AA)	AB received

(a)

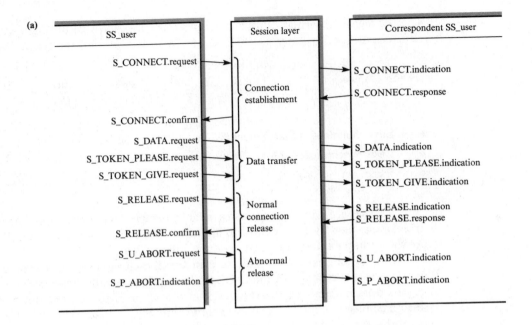

(b)

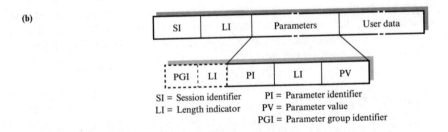

(c)

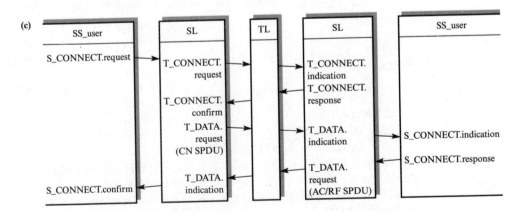

Figure 12.4 Session services: (a) user services; (b) SPDU format; (c) used services.

The general format of an SPDU is shown in Figure 12.4(b). The first two fields in all SPDUs are the **SPDU session identifier (SI)** and the **SPDU length indicator (LI)** in octets. The different SPDUs each have a number of fields – known as parameters – associated with them. Each parameter is in a standard form comprising a **parameter identifier (PI)**, a **parameter length indicator (LI)** and a **parameter value (PV)**. In some instances, parameters are grouped together; the parameter string is then preceded by a **parameter group identifier (PGI)** and a **parameter count length indicator (LI)**.

The user data associated with a service primitive can be segmented into a number of SPDUs for transfer across a transport connection. Note, however, that this is a function of the session protocol entity and is nothing to do with the segmentation procedure in the transport layer.

Before any SPDUs can be sent, a transport connection must first be established over which all SPDUs are then sent – including the CONNECT SPDU – using the T_DATA service. This is shown in Figure 12.4(c).

To illustrate the use of some of the other SPDUs, Figure 12.5 shows those that are transferred to set up a connection, to transfer data using both full duplex and half duplex, and to release the connection both normally and abnormally.

It is possible to send up to 512 bytes of data in a CONNECT (CN) SPDU. If the user data associated with the S_CONNECT.request primitive exceeds 512 bytes, the source session protocol entity can send the extra data immediately using a second SPDU known as a CONNECT DATA OVERFLOW (CDO). Similarly, if the user data associated with the resulting S_CONNECT.response primitive exceeds 512 bytes this also can be sent immediately using the additional ACCEPT DATA OVERFLOW (OA) SPDU.

With duplex data transfer, both sides of the connection can send data at any time. However, when half duplex is being used, only the current owner of the data token can send data. Hence, when the responding entity wants to return data, it must request the token from the other side before sending the data. In Figure 12.5, we assume that the submitted data in both directions requires two DATA (DT) SPDUs to send.

Finally, Figure 12.5 shows the two alternative release methods, normal and abnormal. A summary of the various SS-user services, together with the SPDUs exchanged and the used services, associated with the BCS is given in Figure 12.6.

12.1.4 Protocol specification

The formal specification of the session protocol entity is presented in the standards documents in the form outlined in Chapter 11. The aim here is to present just an introduction; refer to the relevant standards for a more complete description. We have selected the connection establishment phase for the BCS as an example.

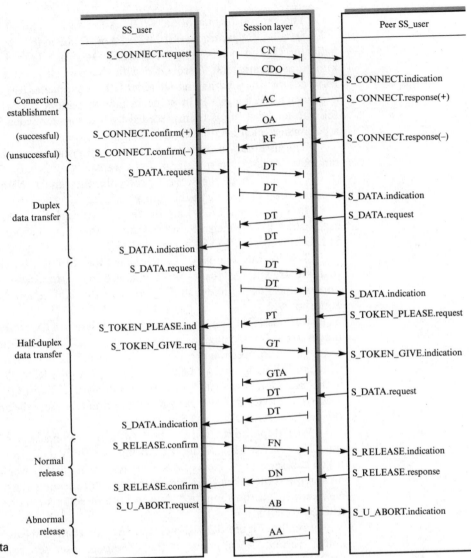

Figure 12.5
Session protocol data
units (BCS only).

Firstly, a list of the various incoming events, automaton states, outgoing events, predicates, and specific actions are given in Figure 12.7. The abbreviated names for each incoming and outgoing event, together with the layer interface to which they relate, are presented and the same names are then used in the event–state table, shown in Figure 12.8.

The underlying transport connection can be initiated by either session entity. Each session entity is normally referred to as the **session protocol machine (SPM)**. Also, a timeout mechanism is associated with the RF (REFUSE) SPDU: if the timer (STIM) expires before a T_DISCONNECT.indication is received (signaling

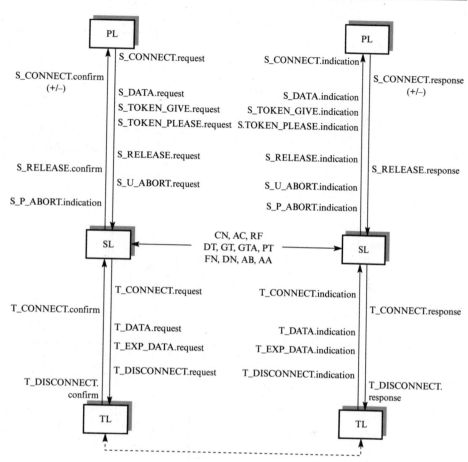

Figure 12.6
Session layer summary (BCS only).

(a)

Name	Interface	Meaning
SCONreq	SS_user	S_CONNECT.request received
SCONresp(+)	SS_user	S_CONNECT.response (accept) received
SCONresp(−)	SS_user	S_CONNECT.response (reject) received
TCONind	TS_provider	T_CONNECT.indication received
TCONconf	TS_provider	T_CONNECT.confirm received
CN	TS_provider	Connect SPDU received
AC	TS_provider	Accept SPDU received
RF	TS_provider	Refuse SPDU received
STIM	Timer	Timer STIM expires

(b)

Name	Meaning
STA 01	Idle, no transport connection
STA 01B	Wait for T_CONNECT.confirm
STA 01C	Idle, transport connection in place
STA 02	Wait for AC SPDU
STA 08	Wait for S_CONNECT.response
STA 16	Wait for T_DISCONNECT.indication
STA 713	Data transfer

Figure 12.7
Abbreviated names for session protocol specification:
(a) incoming events;
(b) automaton states.

(c)

Name	Interface	Meaning
SCONind	SS_user	S_CONNECT.indication issued
SCONconf(+)	SS_user	S_CONNECT.confirm (accept) isued
SCON conf(−)	SS_user	S_CONNECT.confirm (reject) issued
SPABTind	SS_user	S_P_ABORT.indication issued
TCONreq	TS_provider	T_CONNECT.request issued
TCONresp	TS_provider	T_CONNECT.response issued
TDISreq	TS_provider	T_DISCONNECT.request issued
CN	TS_provider	Connect SPDU sent
AC	TS_provider	Accept SPDU sent
RF	TS_provider	Refuse SPDU sent
AB	TS_provider	Abort SPDU sent

(e)

Name	Meaning
[1]	Set P1 false
[2]	Set P1 true
[3]	Stop timer STIM
[4]	Start timer STIM

Figure 12.7 (cont.)
(c) Outgoing events;
(d) predicates;
(e) specific actions.

(d)

Name	Meaning
P1	This SPM initiated TC

State / Event	STA 01	STA 01B	STA 01C	STA 02	STA 08	STA 16	---	STA 713
SCONreq	1	0	2	0	0	0		
SCONresp (+)	0	0	0	0	3	0		
SCONresp (−)	0	0	0	0	4	0		
TCONind	5	0	0	0	0	0		
TCONconf	0	6	0	0	0	0		
CN	0	0	8	0	0	7		
AC	0	0	7	9	0	12		
RF	0	0	7	10	0	12		
⋮								
STIM	0	0	0	0	0	11		

0 = SPABTind, AB, STA 01

1 = TCONreq, [2], STA 01B

2 = P1: CN, STA 02A

3 = AC, STA 713

4 = RF, [4], STA 16

5 = TCONresp, [1], STA 01C

6 = CN, STA 02A

7 = TDISreq, [3], STA 01

8 = P1: TDISreq, STA 01;
NOT P1: SCONind, STA 08

9 = SCONconf(+), STA 713

10 = SCONconf(−), TDISreq, STA 01

11 = RF, [4], STA 16

12 = STA 16

Figure 12.8
SPM event–state
table.

that the transport connection has been disconnected), the RF SPDU is retransmitted. In practice, if a different subset is used, there are a number of additional state variables associated with the SPM for retaining such information as the types of token in use with the session connection, the current assignment of tokens, the current synchronization point serial number, and so on. Nevertheless, the specification follows the same form as that discussed in Chapter 11 and hence we can use the same methodology for its implementation.

12.2 Presentation layer

The presentation layer is concerned with the representation (syntax) of the data in the messages associated with an application during its transfer between two application processes. The aim of the layer is to ensure that the messages exchanged between two application processes have a common meaning – known as **shared semantics** – to both processes. The general scheme is shown in Figure 12.9.

With any distributed application all application processes involved must know the syntax of the messages associated with the application. For example, if the application involves customer accounts, the application processes in all systems that process these must be written to interpret each field in an account in the same way. However, as Section 12.1 indicated, the representation of data types associated with a high-level programming language may differ from one computer to another. To ensure that data is interpreted in the same way, before

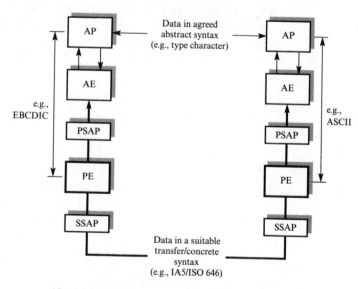

Figure 12.9
Presentation layer
schematic.

AP = Application process
AE = Application entity

PE = Presentation entity
PSAP = Presentation service access point
SSAP = Session service access point

any data is transferred between two processes it must be converted from its local (abstract) syntax into an applicationwide transfer or concrete syntax. Similarly, before any received data is processed, it must be converted into the local syntax if this is different from the transfer syntax.

Two questions arise from this: firstly, what abstract syntax should be used, and secondly, what representation should be adopted for the transfer syntax. One solution to the first question is to assume that all programming is done in the same high-level programming language and then to declare all data types relating to the application using this language. However, different programmers may prefer to use different languages. Also, the question of the transfer syntax is still unanswered.

As the representation of data in a distributed application is a common requirement, ISO (in cooperation with ITU-T) has defined a general abstract syntax that is suitable for the definition of data types associated with most distributed applications. It is known as **abstract syntax notation number one (ASN.1)**. Most new applications now use ASN.1. As the name implies, the data types associated with ASN.1 are abstract types. Hence, in addition to the abstract syntax definition, an associated transfer syntax has also been defined.

As an aid to the use of ASN.1, a number of companies now sell **ASN.1 compilers** for a range of programming languages. There is an ASN.1 compiler for Pascal and another for C. The general approach for using such compilers is shown in Figure 12.10.

Firstly, the data types associated with an application are defined using ASN.1. For example, if two application processes are to be written, one in Pascal and the other in C, the ASN.1 type definitions are first processed by each compiler. Their output is the equivalent data type definitions in the appropriate language together with a set of **encoding** and **decoding procedures/functions** for each data type. The data type definitions are linked and used with the corresponding application software, while the encoding and decoding procedures/functions are

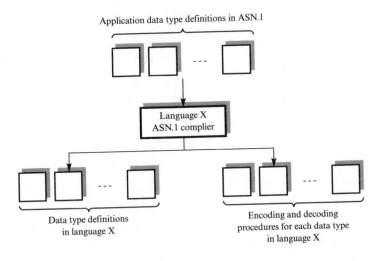

Figure 12.10
ASN.1 shared
semantics.

used by the presentation entity in each system to perform the encoding and decoding operations associated with each data type.

As we shall see in Section 12.3, each data type associated with an application has a **tag** assigned to it for identification. This tag is passed with the data type to the presentation entity which uses it to call the appropriate encoding procedure before transferring the message. The output of the encoding procedure is an octet string, the first octet of which identifies the data type. This string is used by the receiving presentation entity to invoke the corresponding decoding procedure. The output of the decoding procedure – in abstract syntax form – is then passed to the application for processing.

Although syntax conversion is the major role of the presentation layer, since it performs processing operations on all data prior to transfer and on all data that is received, it is also the best place to perform such functions as **data encryption** and, if required, **data compression**. The source presentation entity, after encoding the data in each message from its local abstract syntax into the corresponding transfer syntax, first encrypts the data – using a previously negotiated and agreed encryption algorithm/key – and then compresses the encrypted data using an appropriate (agreed) compression algorithm. The reverse functions are carried out by the receiving protocol entity prior to decoding the received data into its local abstract syntax ready for delivery to the recipient application entity. Before we discuss the operation of the presentation protocol entity, we shall consider ASN.1 and data encryption. We looked at data compression in Chapter 3.

12.3 ASN.1

ASN.1 has been defined for use both as an application syntax (for example, for defining the structure of electronic mail) and as a means of defining the structure of PDUs associated with a protocol entity. Although we cannot give a complete definition of ASN.1 in a book of this type, the following should be sufficient to enable you to interpret the meaning of a set of PDUs relating to a particular protocol entity defined in ASN.1. The principle is the same as that adopted with most high-level programming languages for defining the data types associated with the variables used in a program: as each variable is declared, the data type associated with it is also defined. Then, when a value is assigned to the variable, its syntax is of the defined type.

ASN.1 supports a number of type identifiers, which may be members of the following four classes:

- UNIVERSAL   The generalized types such as integer.

- CONTEXT-SPECIFIC   These are related to the specific context in which they are used.

- APPLICATION   These are common to a complete application entity.

- PRIVATE   These are user definable.

The data types associated with the UNIVERSAL class may be either primitive (simple) or constructed (structured). A primitive type is either a basic data type that cannot be decomposed – for example, a BOOLEAN or an INTEGER – or, in selected cases, a string of one or more basic data elements all of the same type – for example, a string of one or more bits, octets or IA5/graphical characters. The keywords used with ASN.1 are always in upper-case letters and the primitive types available include:

UNIVERSAL (primitive):	BOOLEAN
	INTEGER
	BITSTRING
	OCTETSTRING
	REAL
	ENUMERATED
	IA5String/GraphString
	NULL
	ANY

Some examples of simple types are shown in Figure 12.11(a).

As with a program listing, we may insert comments at any point in a line; the comments start with a pair of adjacent hyphens and end either with another pair of hyphens or the end of a line. The assignment symbol is ::= and the individual bit assignments associated with a BITSTRING type are given in braces with the bit position in parentheses. A similar procedure is used for the

(a)
```
          married ::= BOOLEAN -- true or false
   yrsWithCompany ::= INTEGER
      accessRights ::= BITSTRING{read(0), write(1)}
       PDUContents ::= OCTETSTRING
             name ::= IA5String
               pi ::= REAL -- mantissa;base, exponent
          workDay ::= ENUMERATED{monday(0), tuesday(1) ... friday
```

(b)
```
    personnelRecord ::= SEQUENCE{
                         empNumber INTEGER,
                         name IA5String,
                         yrsWithCompany INTEGER
                         married BOOLEAN}
```

```
    c.f. personnelRecord =  record
                         empNumber = integer;
                         name = array [1..20] of char;
                         yrsWithCompany = integer;
                         married = boolean
                     end;
```

(c)
```
    personnelRecord ::= SEQUENCE{
                         empNumber [APPLICATION1] INTEGER,
                         name [1] IA5String,
                         yrsWithCompany [2] INTEGER,
                         married [3] BOOLEAN}
```

(d)
```
    personnelRecord ::= SEQUENCE{
                         empNumber [APPLICATION1] INTEGER,
                         name [1] IMPLICIT IA5String,
                         yrsWithCompany [2] IMPLICIT INTEGER,
                         married [3] IMPLICIT BOOLEAN}
```

Figure 12.11
Some example ASN.1 type definitions:
(a) simple types;
(b) constructed type;
(c) tagging;
(d) implicit typing.

ENUMERATED type to identify the possible values of the variable. INTEGER types are signed whole numbers of, in theory, unlimited magnitude while REAL types are represented in the form $\{m, B, e\}$ where m = mantissa, B = base and e = exponent; that is, $m \times B^e$.

A NULL type relates to a single variable and is commonly used when a component variable associated with a constructed type has no type assignment. Similarly, the ANY type indicates that the type of the variable is defined elsewhere.

A constructed type is defined by reference to one or more other types, which may be primitive or constructed. The constructed types used with ASN.1 include the following:

- UNIVERSAL (constructed) SEQUENCE: a fixed (bounded), ordered list of types, some of which may be declared optional, that is, the associated typed value may be omitted by the entity constructing the sequence.

- SEQUENCEOF: a fixed or unbounded, ordered list of elements, all of the same type.

- SET: a fixed, unordered list of types, some of which may be declared optional.

- SETOF: a fixed or unbounded, unordered list of elements, all of the same type.

- CHOICE: a fixed, unordered list of types, selected from a previously specified set of types.

An example of a constructed type is shown in Figure 12.11(b), together with the equivalent type definition in Pascal for comparison purposes.

To allow the individual elements within a structured type to be referenced, ASN.1 supports the concept of **tagging**. This involves assigning a **tag** or **identifier** to each element and is analogous to the index used with the array type in most high-level languages.

The tag may be declared to be one of the following:

CONTEXT-SPECIFIC:	the tag has meaning only within the scope of the present structured type.
APPLICATION:	the tag has meaning in the context of the complete application (collection of types).
PRIVATE:	the tag has meaning only to the user.

An example of the use of tags in relation to the type definition used in Figure 12.11(b) is given in part (c). In the example, we assume that empNumber is used in other type definitions and hence is given a unique applicationwide tag. The other three variables need be referenced only within the context of this sequence type.

Another facility supported in ASN.1 is to declare a variable to be of an **implied type**, using the keyword IMPLICIT which is written immediately after the variable name and, if present, the tag number.

Normally, the type of a variable is explicitly defined, but if a variable has been declared to be of an IMPLICIT type, then the type of the variable can be implied by, say, its order in relation to other variables. It is used mainly with tagged types since the type of the variable can then be implied from the tag number. An example is shown in Figure 12.11(d), where the types of the last three variables can be implied – rather than explicitly defined – from their tag number. The benefit of this will become more apparent when we discuss the encoding and decoding rules associated with ASN.1.

To illustrate other types associated with ASN.1, let us consider the use of ASN.1 for the definitions of the protocol data units (PDUs) associated with a protocol. The PDU type definitions discussed so far are all defined in the form of an ordered bit string with the number of bits required for each field and the order of bits in the string defined unambiguously. This ensures that the fields in each PDU are interpreted in the same way in all systems.

To minimize the length of each PDU, many of the fields have only a few bits associated with them. With this type of definition, it is not easy to use a high-level programming language to implement the protocol since isolating each field in a received octet string – and subsequent encoding – can involve complex bit manipulations.

To overcome this problem, the PDU definitions of all the higher protocol layers – presentation and application – are now defined using ASN.1. By passing each PDU definition through an appropriate ASN.1 compiler, the type definitions of all the fields in each PDU are automatically produced in a suitable high-level language compatible form. The protocol can be written in the selected language using these type definitions. Again, however, since the fields are now in an abstract syntax, the corresponding encoding and decoding procedures produced by the ASN.1 compiler must be used to convert each field into/from its concrete syntax when transferring PDUs between two peer protocol entities.

The ASE that enables a file server process to be accessed and used in an open way is known as FTAM (file transfer access and management). We shall discuss its operation in Chapter 13. However, as an example of the use of ASN.1, the definition of a PDU relating to FTAM is given in Figure 12.12 – this is the same as that used for example purposes in Figure 11.15(b).

The complete set of PDUs relating to a particular protocol entity is defined as a **module**. The name of a module is known as the **module definition**. In the example of Figure 12.12, this is *ISO8571-FTAM DEFINITIONS*. It is followed by the assignment symbol (:: =); the module body is then defined between the *BEGIN* and *END* keywords.

Following *BEGIN*, the *CHOICE* type indicates that the PDUs used with FTAM belong to one of three types: *InitializePDU*, *File PDU*, or *BulkdataPDU*. A further *CHOICE* type indicates that there are six different types of PDU associated with the *InitializePDU* type: *FINITIALIZErequest*, *FINITIALIZE response*, and so on. Note that these are tagged so that they can be distinguished from one another. Also, since the tags are followed by *IMPLICIT*, the type of PDU can be implied from the tag field, that is, no further definition is needed, such as a PDU type. Note that since the *FINITIALIZErequest* PDU is always the first PDU received in relation to FTAM, it is assigned an application-specific tag number of 1. The remaining PDU types then have a context-specific tag; note that

```
ISO8571-FTAM DEFINITIONS ::=

BEGIN

PDU ::= CHOICE {
                  InitializePDU,
                  FilePDU,
                  BulkdataPDU
                  }
InitializePDU ::= CHOICE {
                  [APPLICATION 1]   IMPLICIT FINITIALIZErequest,
                  [1]               IMPLICIT FINITIALIZEresponse,
                  [2]               IMPLICIT FTERMINATErequest,
                  [3]               IMPLICIT FTERMINATEresponse,
                  [4]               IMPLICIT FUABORTrequest,
                  [5]               IMPLICIT FPABORTresponse
                  }

FINITIALIZErequest   ::= SEQUENCE {
                  protocolId [0] INTEGER { isoFTAM (0) },
                  versionNumber [1] IMPLICIT
                                  SEQUENCE { major INTEGER,
                                            minor INTEGER},
                                  -- initially { major 0, minor 0}
                  serviceType [2] INTEGER { reliable (0),
                                            user correctable (1)}
                  serviceClass [3] INTEGER { transfer (0),
                                            access (1),
                                            management (2)}
                  functionalUnits [4] BITSTRING { read (0),
                                            write (1),
                                            fileAccess (2),
                                            limitedFileManagement (3),
                                            enhancedFileManagement (4),
                                            grouping (5),
                                            recovery (6),
                                            restartDataTransfer (7) }
                  attributeGroups [5] BITSTRING { storage (0),
                                            security (1) }
                  rollbackAvailability [6] BOOLEAN DEFAULT FALSE,
                  presentationContextName [7] IMPLICIT ISO646String {"ISO8822"},
                  identifyOfInitiator [8] ISO646String OPTIONAL,
                  currentAccount [9] ISO646String OPTIONAL,
                  filestorePassword [10] OCTETSTRING OPTIONAL,
                  checkpointWindow [11] INTEGER OPTIONAL }

FINITIALIZEresponse ::= SEQUENCE {
                  ⋮

END
```

Figure 12.12
ASN.1 PDU definition
example.

the word CONTEXT is not needed as these types will have meaning in the context of FTAM. The definition of each PDU is then given and, in Figure 12.12, the *FINITIALIZErequest* PDU is defined.

The *SEQUENCE* structured type (similar to the record type in Pascal) is used in this definition to indicate that the PDU consists of a number of typed data elements, which may be primitive or constructed. Although with the *SEQUENCE* type the list of variable types is in a set order, normally the individual elements are (context specifically) tagged since, as we shall see in Section 12.3.1, this can lead to a more efficient encoded version of the PDU. The first element, protocolId, is of type *INTEGER* and is set to zero, which indicates it is ISO FTAM (*isoFTAM*).

The second element, *versionNumber*, is defined as a *SEQUENCE* of two *INTEGER* types – *major* and *minor*. As before, the use of the word *IMPLICIT* means that the type (*SEQUENCE*) can be implied from the preceding tag field and need not be encoded. A comment field is used to indicate the initial setting of the two variables. The next two elements are both of type *INTEGER*; the possible values of each are shown in the braces.

The next element, *functionalUnits*, is of type *BITSTRING*; the eight bits in the string are set to 1 or 0 depending on whether the particular unit is (1) or is not (0) required. Finally, some of the later elements in the sequence are declared *OPTIONAL*, which means that they may or may not be present in an encoded PDU. Since the individual elements in the PDU have been tagged, the receiver of the PDU can determine if the element is present or not. The keyword *DEFAULT* has a similar meaning except that if the element is not present in a PDU, it is assigned the default value.

12.3.1   Encoding

Note that ASN.1 is an abstract syntax, which means that although a data element is defined to be of a specified type, it does not necessarily have a fixed syntax. Thus even though the various data elements making up a PDU are of the same (abstract) type, their structure (syntax) may be different. Consequently, ASN.1

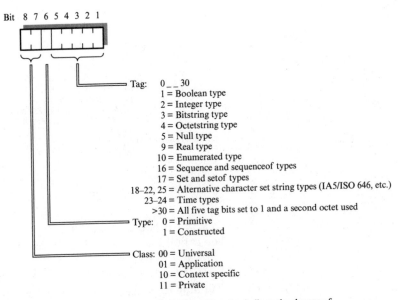

Figure 12.13
ASN.1 identifier bit definition.

has an associated encoding method which converts each field in a PDU, which has been defined in ASN.1 form, into a corresponding concrete syntax form. This concrete syntax is transferred between two application entities so that the exchanged PDU has a common meaning to both entities.

The standard representation for a value of each type is a data element comprising the following three fields:

- *Identifier*, which defines the ASN.1 type

- *Length*, which defines the number of octets in the contents field

- *Contents*, which defines the contents (which may be other data elements for a structured type)

Each field comprises one or more octets. The structure of the identifier octet is as shown in Figure 12.13. Example encodings of different typed values are given in Figure 12.14. To help readability, the content of each octet is represented as two

(a) BOOLEAN – UNIVERSAL 1

e.g., *Employed* ::= *BOOLEAN*
– – assume true

Identifier = 01 (Hex)   – – Universal 1
Length   = 01
Contents = FF

i.e., 01 01 FF

INTEGER – UNIVERSAL 2

e.g., *RetxCount* ::= *INTEGER*
– – assume = 29 (decimal)

Identifier = 02   – – Universal 2
Length   = 01
Contents = 1D   – – 29 decimal

i.e., 02 01 1D

BITSTRING – UNIVERSAL 3

e.g., *FunctionalUnits* ::= *BITSTRING* {*read* (*0*), *write* (*1*), *fileAccess* (*2*)}
– – assume read only is required

Identifier = 03
Length   = 01
Contents = 80   – – read only = 1000 0000

i.e., 03 01 80

UTCTime – UNIVERSAL 23

e.g., *UCTTime* ::= [*UNIVERSAL 23*] *IMPLICIT ISO646String*
– – assume 2.58 p.m. on 5th November 1989 = 89 11 05 14 58

Identifier = 17 (Hex)   – – Universal 23
Length   = 0A
Contents = 38 39 31 31 30 35 31 34 35 38

i.e., 17 0A 38 39 31 31 30 35 31 34 35 38

Figure 12.14
ASN.1 encoding
examples: (a) primitive.

(b) SEQUENCE/SEQUENCEOF – UNIVERSAL 16

e.g., *File ::= SEQUENCE {userName IA5String, contents OCTETSTRING}*
– – assume userName = "FRED" and contents = 0F 27 E4 Hex

Identifier = 30 (Hex)	– – Constructed, Universal 16
Length = 0B	– – Decimal 11
Contents = Identifier = 16	– – Universal 22
Length = 04	
Contents = 46 52 45 44	
Identifier = 04	– – Universal 4
Length = 03	
Contents = 0F 27 E4	

i.e., 30 0B 16 04 46 52 45 44 04 03 0F 27 E4

Tagging/IMPLICIT

e.g., *UserName ::= SET {surname [0] IMPLICIT ISO646String, password [1] ISO646String }*
– – assume surname = "BULL" and password = "KING"

Identifier = 31	– – Constructed, Universal 17
Length = 0E	– – Decimal 14
Contents = Identifier = 80	– – Context-specific 0 = surname
Length = 04	
Contents = 42 55 4C 4C	
Identifier = A1	– – Context-specific 1 = password
Length = 06	
Contents = Identifier = 16	– – Universal 22
Length = 04	
Contents = 4B 49 4E 47	

Figure 12.14 (cont.)
(b) Constructed.

i.e., 31 0E 80 04 42 55 4C 4C A1 06 16 04 4B 49 4E 47 .

hexadecimal digits and the final encoded value (as a string of octets) is given at the end of each example. If the number of octets in the contents field exceeds 127, the most significant bit of the first length octet is set to 1 and the length is defined in two (or more) octets.

In Figure 12.14(a), the identifier 01 (Hex) indicates that the class is UNIVERSAL (bits 8 and 7 = 00), it is a primitive type (bit 6 = 0), and the tag (bits 1 through 5) is 1, thus indicating it is Universal 1 and hence BOOLEAN. The length is 01 (Hex) indicating that the content is a single octet. TRUE is encoded as FF (Hex) and FALSE as 00 (Hex).

Integer values are encoded in 2's-complement form with the most significant bit used as the sign bit. Thus, a single octet can be used to represent a value in the range −128 to +127. More octets must be used for larger values. Note, however, that only sufficient octets are used to represent the actual value, irrespective of the number of bits used in the original form, that is, even if the value 29 shown in Figure 12.14(a) is represented as a 16-bit or 32-bit integer locally, only a single octet is used to represent it in its encoded form. Similarly, if the type is BITSTRING, the individual bits are assigned starting at the most significant bit with any unused bits set to zero.

With a variable of type SEQUENCE (or SEQUENCEOF), the identifier is 30 (= 0011 0000 binary). This indicates that the class is UNIVERSAL (bits 8 and 7 = 00), it is a constructed type (bit 6 = 1), and the tag equals 16 (bit 5 = 1 and bits 4 through 1 = 0). Similarly, the identifier with a SET (or SETOF) type is 31, indicating it is UNIVERSAL, constructed with tag 17.

Note also that the two fields in the type *UserName* have been context specifically tagged –[0] and [1]. The two identifiers associated with these fields are 80 (= 1000 0000 binary) and A1 (= 1010 0001 binary), respectively. The first indicates that the class is context specific (bits 8 and 7 = 10), it is a simple type (bit 6 = 0), and the tag is 0. However, the second is context specific, constructed, and the tag is 1. This is because the first context-specific tag has been declared *IMPLICIT*, in which case the type field can be implied from the tag. However, with the second, the type field must also be defined so two additional octets are required.

An example FTAM PDU encoding is given in Figure 12.15. The PDU selected is *FINITIALIZErequest*, as defined earlier in its ASN.1 form in Figure 12.12. The actual values associated with the PDU are defined in Figure 12.15(a) while Figure 12.15(b) shows how the selected values are encoded. Typically, as we shall see in more detail in Chapter 13, the various fields in the PDU are abstract data types associated with a data structure in a program. However, after encoding, the PDU is comprised of a precisely defined string of octets which, for readability, are shown in hexadecimal form. The complete octet string is then transferred to the correspondent (peer) FTAM protocol entity where it is decoded back into its (local) abstract form.

12.3.2 Decoding

On receipt of the encoded string, the correspondent entity performs an associated decoding operation. For example, the leading octet in the string is first used to determine the type of PDU received – Application-specific 1 = *FINITIALIZErequest*. Clearly, since each PDU has a unique structure, we must have a separate decoding procedure for each PDU type. Hence, on determining the type of PDU received, the corresponding decoding procedure is invoked. Once this has been done, the various fields (data elements) making up the PDU will be in their local (abstract) syntax form and processing of the PDU can start.

Figure 12.15

Example FTAM PDU encoding: (a) PDU contents.

(a)   *FINITIALIZErequest* = { *protocolId* = 0,
　　　　　　　　　　versionNumber {*major* = 0, *minor* = 0}
　　　　　　　　　　serviceType = 1,
　　　　　　　　　　serviceClass = 1,
　　　　　　　　　　functionalUnits {*read* = 0, *write* = 1, *fileAccess* = 2,
　　　　　　　　　　　　　　　limitedFileManagement = 3
　　　　　　　　　　　　　　　enhancedFileManagement = 4,
　　　　　　　　　　　　　　　grouping = 5, *recovery* = 6,
　　　　　　　　　　　　　　　restartDataTransfer = 7}
　　　　　　　　　　attributeGroups {*storage* = 0, *security* = 1}
　　　　　　　　　　rollbackAvailability = T,
　　　　　　　　　　PresentationContextName = "ISO8822"}

(b) Identifier = 61   -- Application-specific 1 = *FINITIALIZErequest*
Length   = 31   -- decimal 49
Contents = Identifier = A0   -- Context-specific 0 = *protocolId*
             Length   = 03
             Contents = Identifier = 02   -- Universal 2 – *INTEGER*
                         Length   = 01
                         Contents = 00   -- *isoFTAM*
             Identifier = A1   -- Context-specific 1 = *versionNumber*
             Length   = 06
             Contents = Identifier = 02   -- Universal 2
                         Length   = 01
                         Contents = 00   -- *major*
                         Identifier = 02   -- Universal 2
                         Length   = 01
                         Contents = 00   -- *minor*
             Identifier = A2
             Length   = 03
             Contents = Identifier = 02
                         Length   = 01
                         Contents = 01   -- *serviceType* = user correctable
             Identifier = A3
             Length   = 03
             Contents = Identifier = 02
                         Length   = 01
                         Contents = 01   -- *serviceClass* = access
             Identifier = A4   -- Context-specific 4 = *functionalUnits*
             Length   = 03
             Contents = Identifier = 03   -- Universal 3 = *BITSTRING*
                         Length   = 01
                         Contents = E0   -- *read, write, fileAccess* = 1110 000
             Identifier = A5   -- Context-specific 5 = *attributeGroups*
             Length   = 03
             Contents = Identifier = 03
                         Length   = 01
                         Contents = 40   -- *security* 0100 000
             Identifier = A6   -- Context-specific 6 = *rollbackAvailability*
             Length   = 03
             Contents = Identifier = 01   -- Universal 1 = *BOOLEAN*
                         Length   = 01
                         Contents = FF   -- *true*
             Identifier = A7   -- Context-specific 7 = *PresentationContextName*
             Length   = 07
             Contents = 49 53 4F 38 38 32 32   -- "ISO8822"

Concrete syntax of the above PDU is thus:

```
61  2F  A0  03  02  01  00  A1  06  02  01  00  02  01  00  A2
03  02  01  01  A3  03  02  01  01  A4  03  03  01  E0  A5  03
03  01  40  A6  03  01  01  FF  A7  07  49  53  32  38  38  32
32
```

Figure 12.15 (cont.)
(b) Encoded form.

12.4 Data encryption

As the knowledge of computer networking and protocols has become more widespread, so the threat of intercepting and decoding message data during its transfer across a network has increased. For example, the end systems (stations) associated with most applications are now attached to a LAN. The application may involve a single LAN or, in an internetworking environment, one or more intermediate WANs. However, with most LANs, transmissions on the shared transmission medium can readily be intercepted by any system if an intruder sets the appropriate MAC chipset into the promiscuous mode and records all transmissions on the medium. Then, with a knowledge of the LAN protocols being used, the intruder can identify and remove the protocol control information at the head of each message, leaving the message contents. The message contents, including passwords and other sensitive information, can then be interpreted.

This is known as **listening** or **eavesdropping** and its effects are all too obvious. In addition, and perhaps more sinister, an intruder can use a recorded message sequence to generate a new sequence. This is known as **masquerading** and again the effects are all too apparent. Therefore, encryption should be applied to all data transfers that involve a network. In the context of the ISO reference model, the most appropriate layer to perform such operations is the presentation layer. This section provides an introduction to the subject of data encryption.

12.4.1 Terminology

Data encryption (or **data encipherment**) involves the sending party – for example, presentation protocol entity – in processing all data prior to transmission so that if it is accidentally or deliberately intercepted while it is being transferred it will be incomprehensible to the intercepting party. Of course, the data must be readily interpreted – **decrypted** or **deciphered** – by the intended recipient. Consequently, most encryption methods involve the use of an **encryption key** which is hopefully known only by the two correspondents. The key features in both the encryption and the decryption processing. Prior to encryption, message data is normally referred to as **plaintext** and after encryption as **ciphertext**. The general scheme is thus as shown in Figure 12.16.

When deciding on a particular encryption algorithm we must always assume that a transmitted message can be intercepted and recorded, and that the intruder knows the context in which the messages are being used, that is, the type of

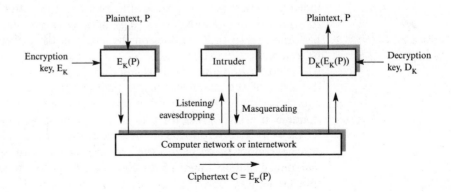

Figure 12.16
Data encryption terminology.

information being exchanged. The aim is to choose an encryption method such that an intruder, even with access to a powerful computer, cannot decipher the recorded ciphertext in a realistic time period. There are two widely used algorithms but before we discuss these, let us consider some of the more fundamental techniques on which they are based.

12.4.2   Basic techniques

The simplest encryption technique involves **substituting** the plaintext alphabet (codeword) with a new alphabet known as the **ciphertext alphabet**. For example, a ciphertext alphabet can be defined which is the plaintext alphabet simply shifted by n places where n is the key. Hence, if the key is 3, the resulting alphabet is as follows:

Plaintext alphabet:	a	b	c	d	e	f	g	...
Ciphertext alphabet:	d	e	f	g	h	i	j	...

The ciphertext is obtained by substituting each character in the plaintext message by the equivalent letter in the ciphertext alphabet.

A more powerful variation is to define a ciphertext alphabet that is a random mix of the plaintext alphabet. For example:

Plaintext alphabet:	a	b	c	d	e	f	g	...
Ciphertext alphabet:	n	z	q	a	i	y	m	...

The key is determined by the number of letters in the alphabet, for example, 26 if just lower-case alphabetic characters are to be transmitted or 128 if, say, the ASCII alphabet is being used. There are therefore $26! = 4 \times 10^{26}$ possible keys with the first alphabet or many times this with the larger alphabet. Notice that in general, the larger the key the more time it takes to break the code.

Although this may seem to be a powerful technique, there are a number of short cuts that can be used to break such codes. The intruder is likely to know the context in which the message data is being used and hence the type of data involved. For example, if the messages involve textual information, then the statistical properties of text can be exploited: the frequency of occurrence of individual letters (e, t, o, a, etc.), of two-letter combinations (th, in, er, etc.) and of three-letter combinations (the, ing, and, etc.) are all well documented. By performing statistical analyses on the letters in the ciphertext such codes can be broken relatively quickly.

Substitution involves replacing each character with a different character, so the order of the characters in the plaintext is preserved in the ciphertext. An alternative approach is to reorder (**transpose**) the characters in the plaintext. For example, if a key of 4 is used, the complete message can first be divided into a set of 4-character groups. The message is then transmitted starting with all the first characters in each group, then the second, and so on. As an example, assuming a plaintext message of 'this is a lovely day', the ciphertext is derived as follows:

```
1  2  3  4      ← key
t  h  i  s
-  i  s  -
a  -  l  o
v  e  l  y
-  d  a  y
ciphertext = t–av–hi–edisllas–oyy
```

Clearly, more sophisticated transpositions can be performed but, in general, when used alone transposition ciphers suffer from the same shortcomings as substitution ciphers. Most practical encryption algorithms tend to use a combination of the two techniques and are known as **product ciphers**.

Product ciphers

These use a combination of substitutions and transpositions. Also, instead of substituting/transposing the characters in a message, the order of individual bits in each character (codeword) is transposed. The three alternative transposition (also known as **permutation**) operations are shown in Figure 12.17(a). Each is normally referred to as a **P-box**.

The first involves transposing each 8-bit input into an 8-bit output by cross-coupling each input line to a different output line as defined by the key, and is known as a **straight permutation**. The second has a larger number of output bits than input bits; they are derived by reordering the input bits and passing selected input bits to more than one output. This is known as an **expanded permutation**.

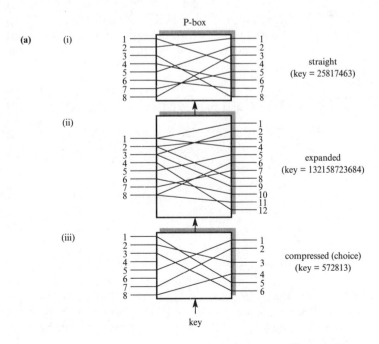

Figure 12.17
Product cipher
components:
(a) P-box examples.

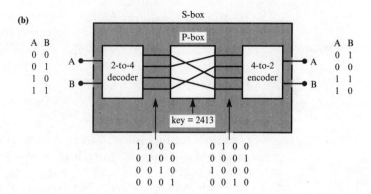

Figure 12.17 (cont.)
(b) S-box example.

The third has fewer output bits than inputs; it is formed by transposing only selected input bits. This is known as a **compressed** or **choice permutation**.

To perform a straight substitution of 8 bits requires a new set (and hence key) of 2^8 ($= 256$) 8-bit bytes to be defined. This means the key for a single substitution is 2048 bits. To reduce this, a substitution is formed by encapsulating a P-box between a decoder and a corresponding encoder, as shown in Figure 12.17(b). The resulting unit is known as an **S-box**. The example performs a 2-bit substitution operation using the key associated with the P-box. An 8-bit substitution will require four such units.

Product ciphers are formed from multiple combinations of these two basic units, as shown in Figure 12.18. Each P-box and S-box is the same as that shown in Figure 12.17. In general, the larger the number of stages the more powerful the cipher. A practical example of product ciphers is the **data encryption standard (DES)** defined by the US National Bureau of Standards. This is now widely used. Consequently, various integrated circuits are available to perform the encryption operation in hardware thereby speeding up the encryption and decryption operations.

12.4.3 The data encryption standard

The DES algorithm is a **block cipher**, which means that it works on fixed-sized blocks of data. Thus, a complete message is first split (segmented) into blocks of plaintext, each comprising 64 bits. A (hopefully) unique 56-bit key is used to

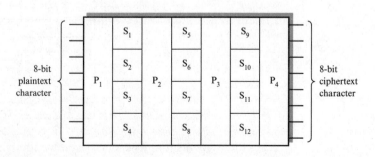

Figure 12.18
Example of a product cipher.

(a)

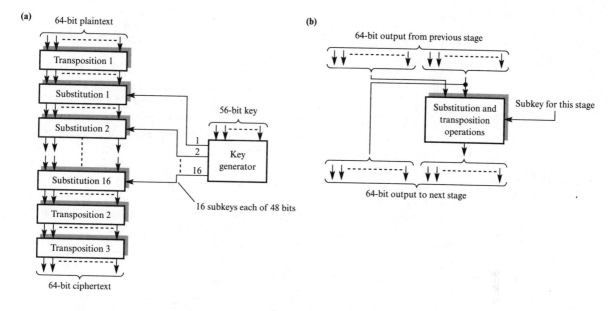

Figure 12.19
DES algorithm:
(a) overall operation;
(b) substitution
schematic.

encrypt each block of plaintext into a 64-bit block of ciphertext, which is subsequently transmitted through the network. The receiver uses the same key to perform the inverse (decryption) operation on each 64-bit data block it receives, thereby reassembling the blocks into complete messages.

The larger the number of bits used for the key, the more likely it is that the key will be unique. Also, the larger the key, the more difficult it is for someone to decipher it. The use of a 56-bit key in the DES means that there are in the order of 10^{17} possible keys from which to choose. Consequently, DES is regarded as providing sufficient security for most commercial applications.

A diagram of the DES algorithm is shown in Figure 12.19. The 56-bit key selected by the two correspondents is first used to derive 16 different subkeys, each of 48 bits, which are used in the subsequent substitution operations. The algorithm comprises 19 distinct steps. The first step is a simple transposition of the 64-bit block of plaintext using a fixed transposition rule. The resulting 64 bits of transposed text then go through 16 identical iterations of substitution processing, except that at each iteration a different subkey is used in the substitution operation. The most significant 32 bits of the 64-bit output of the last iteration are then exchanged with the least significant 32 bits. Finally, the same transposition as was performed in step 1 is repeated to produce the 64-bit block of ciphertext to be transmitted. The DES algorithm is designed so that the received block is deciphered by the receiver using the same steps as for encryption, but in the reverse order.

The 16 subkeys used at each substitution step are produced as follows. Firstly, a fixed transposition is performed on the 56-bit key. The resulting transposed key is then split into two separate 28-bit halves. Next, these two halves are rotated left independently and the combined 56 bits are transposed once again. Each subkey comprises 48 bits of transposed data. The other subkeys are produced in a similar way except that the number of rotations performed is determined by the number of the subkey.

The processing performed at each of the 16 intermediate steps in the encryption process is relatively complex as it is this that ensures the effectiveness of the DES algorithm. This processing is outlined in Figure 12.19(b). The 64-bit output from the previous iteration is first split into two 32-bit halves. However, the least significant 32-bit output is derived by performing a sequence of transposition and substitution operations on the most significant input half, the precise operations being a function of the subkey for this stage.

This mode of working of DES is known as **electronic code book (ECB)** since each block of ciphertext is independent of any other block. Thus each block of ciphertext has a unique matching block of plaintext, which is analogous to entries in a code book. The ECB mode of working is shown in Figure 12.20(a).

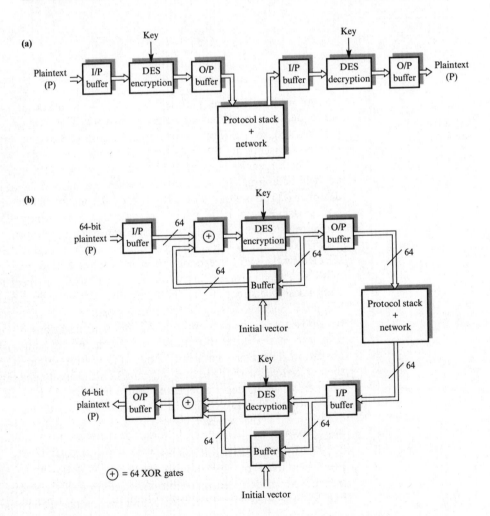

Figure 12.20
DES operational modes: (a) ECB; (b) CBC.

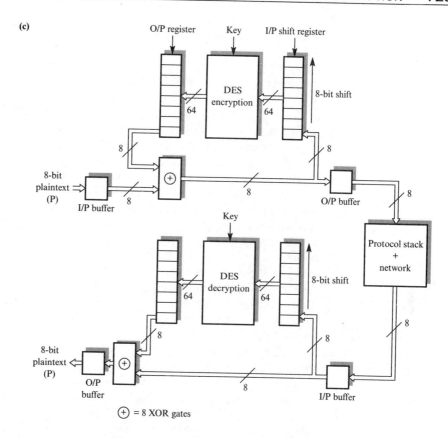

Figure 12.20 (cont.)
(c) CFM.

$\oplus$ = 8 XOR gates

Although the ECB mode of operation of DES gives good protection against errors or changes that may occur in a single block of enciphered text, it does not protect against errors arising in a stream of blocks. Since each block is treated separately in ECB mode, the insertion of a correctly enciphered block into a transmitted stream of blocks is not detected by the receiver; it simply deciphers the inserted block and treats it as a valid block. Consequently, the stream of enciphered blocks may be intercepted and altered by someone who knows the key without the recipient being aware that any modifications have occurred. Also, this mode of operation has the weakness that repetitive blocks of plaintext generate a string of identical blocks of ciphertext, a factor that can be of great benefit to someone trying to break the code (key). An alternative mode of operation is to use the notion of **chaining**. This mode of operation of DES is known as **chain block cipher (CBC)**.

Although the chaining mode uses the same block encryption method as previously described, each 64-bit block of plaintext is first exclusive-ORed with the enciphered output of the previous block before it is enciphered, as shown in Figure 12.20(b). The first 64-bit block of plaintext is exclusive-ORed with a 64-bit random number called the **initial vector**, after which subsequent blocks operate in a chained sequence as shown. Thus, since the output of a block is a function both of the block contents and the output of the previous block, any alterations to the transmitted sequence can be detected by the receiver. Also, identical blocks of plaintext yield different blocks of ciphertext. For these reasons, this is the mode of operation normally used for data communication.

Since the basic CBC mode operates with 64-bit blocks, all messages must be multiples of 64 bits. Otherwise padding bits must be added. However, as described earlier, the contents of all messages are comprised of strings of octets, so the basic unit of all messages is 8 bits rather than 64. An alternative mode of DES known as the **cipher feedback mode (CFM)** has also been defined which operates on 8-bit boundaries. A schematic of the scheme is shown in Figure 12.20(c).

With this mode, a new DES encryption operation is performed after every 8 bits of input rather than 64 with the CBC mode. A new 8-bit output is also produced which is the least significant 8 bits of the DES output exclusive-ORed with the 8 input bits. Then, after each 8-bit output has been loaded into the output buffer, the 64-bit contents of the input shift register are shifted by 8 places. The 8 most significant bits are thus lost and the new 8-bit input is loaded into the least significant 8 bits of the input shift register. The DES operation is performed on these new 64 bits and the resulting 64-bit output is loaded into the output register. The least significant 8 bits of the latter are then exclusive-ORed with the 8 input bits and the process repeats.

CFM is particularly useful when the encryption operation is being performed at the interface with the serial transmission line. This mode of operation is used with the DES integrated circuits; each new 8-bit output is loaded directly into the serial interface circuit.

Both the DES modes rely, of course, on the same key being used for both encryption and decryption. An obvious disadvantage is that some form of key notification must be used before any encrypted data is transferred between two correspondents. This is perfectly acceptable as long as the key does not change very often, but in fact it is common practice to change the key on a daily, if not more frequent, basis. Clearly, the new key cannot reliably be sent via the network, so an alternative means, such as a courier, must be used. The distribution of keys is a major problem with private key encryption systems. An alternative method, based on a public rather than a private key, is sometimes used to overcome this problem. The best known public key method is the **RSA algorithm**, named after its three inventors: Rivest, Shamir, and Adelman.

12.4.4   The RSA algorithm

The fundamental difference between a private key system and a public key system is that the latter uses a different key to decrypt the ciphertext from the key that was used to encrypt it. A public key system uses a pair of keys: one for the sender and the other for the recipient.

Although this may not seem to help, the inventors of the RSA algorithm used number theory to develop a method of generating a pair of numbers – the keys – in such a way that a message encrypted using the first number of the pair

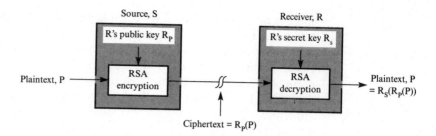

Figure 12.21
RSA schematic.

can be decrypted only by the second number. Furthermore, the second number cannot be derived from the first. This second property means that the first number of the pair can be made available to anyone who wishes to send an encrypted message to the holder of the second number since only that person can decrypt the resulting ciphertext message. The first number of the pair is known as the **public key** and the second the private or **secret key**. The principle of the method is shown in Figure 12.21.

As indicated, the derivation of the two keys is based on number theory and is therefore outside the scope of this book. However, the basic algorithm used to compute the two keys is simple and is summarized here together with a much simplified example.

To create the public key Kp: Example:

- Select two large positive prime numbers P and Q $P = 7, Q = 17$
- Compute $X = (P - 1) * (Q - 1)$ $X = 96$
- Choose an integer E which is prime relative to X, $E = 5$
  i.e., not a prime factor of X or a multiple of it, and
  which satisfies the condition indicated below for
  the computation of Ks
- Compute $N = P * Q$ $N = 119$
- Kp is then N concatenated with E $Kp = 119, 5$

To create the secret key Ks:

- Compute D such that MOD $(D * E, X) = 1$ $D * 5/96 = 1 \ D = 77$
- Ks is then N concatenated with D $Ks = 119, 77$

To compute the ciphertext C of plaintext P:

- Treat P as a numerical value $P = 19$
- $C = MOD (P^E, N)$ $C = MOD(19^5, 119)$
                                                                                       $C = 66$

To compute the plaintext P of ciphertext C:

- $P = MOD (C^D, N)$ $P = MOD(66^{77}, 119)$
                                                                                       $P = 19$

The choice of E and D in this example is best seen by considering the factors of 96. These are 1, 2, 3, 4, 6, 8, 12, 16, 24, 32, 48. The list of numbers which are prime relative to 96 are thus 5, 7, 9, 10, 11, etc. If we try the first of these, $E = 5$, then there is also a number $D = 77$ which satisfies the condition $MOD(D * E, X) = 1$ and hence these are chosen.

We can deduce from this example that the crucial numbers associated with the algorithm are the two prime numbers P and Q, which must always be kept secret. The aim is to choose a sufficiently large N so that it is impossible to factorize it in a realistic time. Some example (computer) factorizing times are:

$N = 100$ digits ≈ 1 week
$N = 150$ digits ≈ 1000 years
$N > 200$ digits ≈ 1 million years

The RSA algorithm requires considerable computation time to compute the exponentiation for both the encryption and decryption operations. However, there is a simple way of avoiding the exponentiation operation by performing instead the following algorithm which uses only repeated multiplication and division operations:

```
C := 1
begin for i = 1 to E do
        C := MOD (C * P, N)
end
```

Decryption is performed in the same way by replacing E with D and P with C in the above expression; this yields the plaintext P. For example, to compute $C = MOD (19^5, 119)$:

Step 1: $C = MOD (1 * 19, 119) = 19$
2: $C = MOD (19 * 19, 119) = 4$
3: $C = MOD (4 * 19, 119) = 76$
4: $C = MOD (76 * 19, 119) = 16$
5: $C = MOD (16 * 19, 119) = 66$

Note also that the value of N determines the maximum message that can be encoded. In the example this is 119 and is numerically equivalent to a single ASCII-encoded character. Therefore, a message comprising a string of ASCII characters would have to be encoded one character at a time.

Although a public key system offers an alternative to a private key system to overcome the threat of eavesdropping, if the public key is readily available it can be used by a masquerader to send a forged message. The question then arises as to how the recipient of a correctly ciphered message can be sure that it was sent by a legitimate source. There are a number of solutions to this problem of **message authentication**.

12.4.5 Message authentication

One solution is to exploit the dual property of public key systems, namely that not only is a receiver able to decipher all messages it receives (which have been encrypted with its own public key) using its own private key, but any receiver can

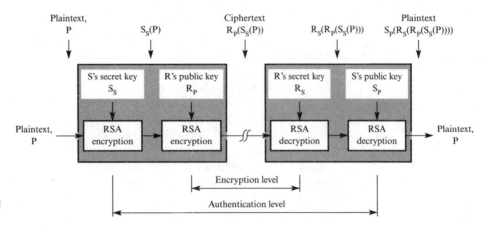

Plaintext, P $\quad$ $S_S(P)$ $\quad$ Ciphertext $R_P(S_S(P))$ $\quad$ $R_S(R_P(S_S(P)))$ $\quad$ Plaintext $S_P(R_S(R_P(S_S(P))))$

Figure 12.22
Message authentication using RSA.

also decipher a message encrypted with the sender's private key, using the sender's public key.

Figure 12.22 shows how this property may be exploited to achieve message authentication. Encryption and decryption operations are performed at two levels. The inner level of encryption and decryption is as already described. However, at the outer level, the sender uses its own private key to encrypt the original (plaintext) message. If the receiver can decrypt this message using that sender's public key, this is proof that the sender did in fact initiate the sending of the message.

Although this is an elegant solution, it has a number of limitations. Firstly, the processing overheads associated with the RSA algorithm are high. As we saw with the earlier (much simplified) example, even with a small message (value), the numbers involved can be very large. Therefore, a complete message must be divided into a number of smaller units, the size of which is a function of the computer being used. Hence, even though integrated circuits are available to help with these computations, the total message throughput with RSA is still relatively low. Secondly, the method requires two levels of encryption even though it may not be necessary to encrypt the actual message, that is, although only message authentication is required, the actual message contents must still be encrypted.

One solution is to compute a much shorter version of the message based on its contents. This is encrypted using the sender's private key and sent at the tail of the message which is sent in plaintext. The encrypted trailer to the message is analogous to a signature at the end of a letter since, when decrypted using the sender's public key, it verifies that the person did in fact send the message. The trailer is known as a **digital signature**; an example is the CRC for the message. Clearly, the generator polynomial used to compute the CRC must be secret and known only by the source and receiver.

An alternative approach, which is based on the use of private keys only, is to use a trusted third party to act as a **key distribution server**. An example is the **Kerberos system**. The basic security control mechanism employed in Kerberos is a set of encrypted **tickets** – also known as control or permission tokens – which are used to control access to the various servers that make up the system. These include a range of application servers – file servers, electronic mail servers, etc. – and the system server that issues the tickets, known as the **ticket granting server**. All messages that are exchanged between a user and the ticket granting server and between a user and an application server are encrypted using private keys which form part of the corresponding ticket. In addition, each message/ticket has a **nonce** associated with it. This comprises two date-and-time values, the first of which specifies when the nonce was first generated. A nonce is used both to verify the origin of a message and to limit the validity of a ticket to a defined lifetime. This is determined by the second date-and-time value in the nonce. This feature means an eavesdropper has only a limited time to decrypt an intercepted ticket.

The key distribution server is a networked system with which all users and application servers must be registered. It comprises two servers: an **authentication server** and a ticket granting server. The authentication server provides, firstly, management services to allow all users, together with their related passwords, to be registered. It also provides the names and secret keys of all Kerberos servers, including the ticket granting server and all application servers. This information is retained in an **authentication database**. It provides additional runtime services to enable a user to be authenticated as a registered user of the system before being allowed to access any of the Kerberos servers. A schematic diagram summarizing the various interactions between a user and the two types of server is given in Figure 12.23(a).

Running within each client workstation is a process known as the **user agent** and it is through this that all interactions between a user and the various Kerberos servers take place. Before a user (agent) can access an application server, it must first obtain from the ticket granting server an **authentication ticket** and a **session key**; the first verifies that the user has been authenticated as a registered user and the second is used to encrypt all the subsequent dialog units that are exchanged in this session between the user agent and the application server. Note that in practice more than one application server can be involved in a single session. Also, both keys have a limited lifetime associated with them to guard against a user, whose registration has expired for example, from reusing a ticket.

At the start of a session, the user is prompted by the user agent (UA) for his/her user name (1). Before the UA can communicate with the ticket granting server (TGS), the user must first be authenticated as a registered user and a (permission) ticket obtained to access the TGS. Both these functions are performed by the authentication server (AS). On receipt of the user name, the UA creates a message containing the names of the user (U) and the TGS (T) and a nonce (n_1). The UA keeps a record of the nonce used and sends the message to the AS (2).

All subsequent messages associated with the session are encrypted using various keys. These are defined in Figure 12.23(b) together with the components that make up the two tickets; the first granting permission for the UA to communicate with the TGS and the second for the UA to communicate with the application server. The contents of the messages exchanged during a successful session are listed in Figure 12.23(c).

(a)

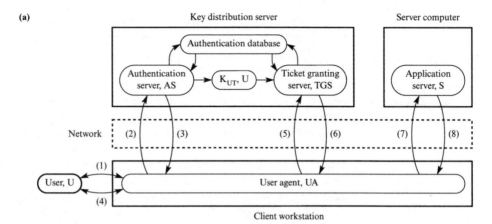

Key distribution server   Server computer

Network   (2)   (3)   (5)   (6)   (7)   (8)

(1)

User, U

(4)

User agent, UA

Client workstation

(b) K_U = The private key of the user – the user password
K_T = The private key of the TGS
K_S = The private key of the application server
K_{UT} = A session key to encrypt UA $\leftrightarrow$ TGS dialog units
K_{US} = A session key to encrypt UA $\rightarrow$ S dialog units

TGS ticket, $T_{UT} = K_T (U, T, t_1, t_2, K_{UT})$
Application server ticket, $T_{US} = K_S (U, S, t_1, t_2, K_{US})$
      t_1, t_2 = start, end of ticket lifetime

(c)

	Direction	Message
(1)	U $\leftrightarrow$ UA	User name, U
(2)	UA $\rightarrow$ AS	(U, T, n_1)
(3)	AS $\rightarrow$ UA	$K_U (K_{UT}, n_1)$; T_{UT}
(4)	U $\leftrightarrow$ UA	User password, K_U
(5)	UA $\rightarrow$ TGS	$K_{UT} (U, t)$; T_{UT}, S, n_2
(6)	TGS $\rightarrow$ UA	$K_{UT} (K_{US}, n_2)$; T_{US}
(7)	UA $\rightarrow$ S	$K_{US} (U, t)$; T_{US}, n_3
(8)	S $\rightarrow$ UA	$K_{US} (n_3)$

$K_{UT}/K_{US} (U, t)$ are both authenticators and t is a timestamp

Figure 12.23
Kerberos
authentication system:
(a) terminology and
message exchange
sequence; (b) key and
ticket definitions;
(c) message contents.

On receipt of the initial UA request message, the AS first validates the user is
registered and, if positive, proceeds to create a response message. The latter
comprises two parts. The first part comprises a newly generated session key, K_{UT} –
to be used to encrypt the subsequent UA/TGS dialog units – together with the
nonce, n_1, contained in the initial UA request message. A record is kept of K_{UT}
and this part of the response message is encrypted using the user's password, K_U –
obtained from the authentication database – as a key. The second part comprises
the permission ticket for the UA to access the TGS, T_{UT} – encrypted using the
private key of the TGS, K_T. The two-part message is then returned to the UA (3).

At this point the UA prompts the user to enter his/her password, K_U (4).
The latter is used to obtain, firstly, the nonce, n_1 – which verifies the message
relates to its earlier request – and secondly, the key K_{UT}. Clearly, a user
impersonating the registered user would not be able to decrypt this message and
hence would be foiled at this stage. The UA proceeds to use the retrieved key,

K_{UT}, to create what is referred to as an **authenticator**. This is a token which verifies the user has been authenticated and comprises the user name, U, and a timestamp, t, both encrypted using K_{UT}. To this is added the encrypted permission ticket, T_{UT}, the name of the required application server, S, and a second nonce, n_2. The complete message is then sent to the TGS (5).

The authenticator is decrypted by the TGS using the retained key K_{UT} and, since this was granted for the same user, U, it is accepted by the TGS as proof that the user has permission to be granted a session key to communicate with an application server. In response, the TGS generates a new session key, K_{US}, to be used by UA to encrypt the dialog units exchanged with the named server, S. Note that if multiple servers are accessed during the session, then multiple keys are issued at this stage, one for use with each server. The TGS then creates a message, the first part comprising K_{US} and the nonce n_2 – encrypted using K_{UT} – and the second comprising an encrypted permission ticket for the UA to access S, T_{US}. The complete message is then sent to the UA (6).

On receipt of this, the UA uses K_{UT} to decrypt the first part of the message to obtain K_{US} and the nonce n_2. The latter is used to confirm the message relates to its own earlier request message to the TGS, and K_{US} is used to create an authenticator, which verifies the user has been granted permission to access the named server. The authenticator is combined with the permission ticket granted by the TGS, T_{US}, and a third nonce n_3. The resulting message is sent by the UA to server S (7).

As Figure 12.23(b) shows, the permission ticket, T_{US}, is encrypted using the private key of S, K_S. Hence, on receipt of the message, S proceeds to use its own private key to decrypt T_{US} and obtain the name of the user, U, and the allocated session key, K_{US}. It uses the latter to decrypt the authenticator and confirm that U has been authenticated as a registered user and granted permission to access S. The server responds by returning the nonce, n_3, encrypted using K_{US} (8). This concludes the authentication procedure and the exchange of dialog units between UA and S can now commence. If required the dialog units are encrypted using K_{US}.

12.5 Presentation protocol

Although the subject of data encryption is often discussed in the context of the presentation layer, the actual presentation protocol entity is concerned only with the syntax of messages during their transfer across the network. Recall that the syntax of a message during its transfer across the network is known as the concrete (or transfer) syntax and that used by application processes, its local or abstract syntax.

The association of an abstract syntax with a compatible transfer syntax constitutes a **presentation context**. Hence, one of the functions associated with the presentation layer is to negotiate a suitable presentation context for use with this session/presentation connection. Also, since an application entity must use many of the services provided by the session layer through the services provided by the presentation layer, another function of the presentation layer is to map such services directly into the corresponding service provided by the session layer. The functions performed by the presentation layer can be summarized as follows:

- Negotiation of (an) appropriate transfer syntax(es) which is (are) suitable for conveying the type of (presentation) PS_user data messages to be exchanged
- Transformation of PS_user data from its local abstract syntax into the selected transfer syntax
- Transformation of received message data in its transfer syntax into the local abstract syntax for use by the PS_user
- Mapping application layer service requests for such functions as dialog control (token management) and synchronization control into the corresponding session service primitives

We can deduce that if the PS_user data to be exchanged during an application session consists of a variety of abstract types, then a number of different presentation contexts may be selected. The proposed presentation context(s) to be used during a session is (are) negotiated during the connection establishment phase. They are collectively referred to as the **presentation context set**. Alternatively, the two PS_users may adopt an existing **default context** for the transfer, such as IA5/ISO 646.

PS_user data, and hence application layer user data, is passed to the presentation layer in the form of **tagged data elements**, where the tag or name associated with an element identifies the presentation context associated with it. The presentation entity then applies, if necessary, the corresponding transformation on each element before forwarding it to the session layer.

12.5.1 Presentation services

A time sequence diagram showing the basic (kernel) services supported by the presentation layer is given in Figure 12.24(a). As we can see, each primitive has associated parameters. For example, the P_CONNECT parameters include the called and calling presentation (session) addresses, the session connection identifier, and other session-related parameters such as token requirements. Because the presentation and session layers form an integrated function on behalf of the application layer, most of the presentation service primitives shown result in a corresponding presentation protocol data unit (PPDU) being generated using the parameters associated with the primitives. Thus:

Service primitive	Generates PPDU
P_CONNECT.request	Connect presentation CP
P_CONNECT.response (+)	Connect presentation accept CPA
P_CONNECT.response (−)	Connect presentation reject CPR
P_DATA.request	Presentation data transfer TD
P_U_ABORT.request	Abnormal release (user) ARU
P_P_ABORT.indication	Abnormal release (provider) ARP

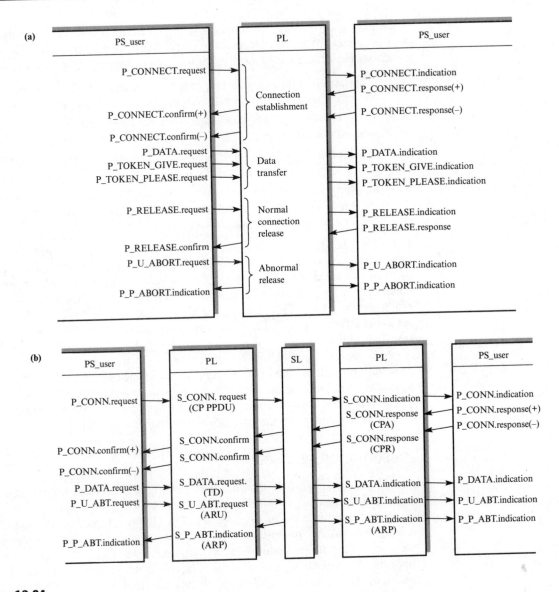

Figure 12.24
Presentation services:
(a) basic services;
(b) related session
services.

This is shown in Figure 12.24(b).

In addition, a number of presentation service primitives map directly into a corresponding SS primitive without modification, that is, without a PPDU being generated. Normally, the parameters associated with such primitives are passed in the user data field of the associated SS primitive. These include the P_RELEASE service primitives and the primitives provided for the (optional) functions of the following:

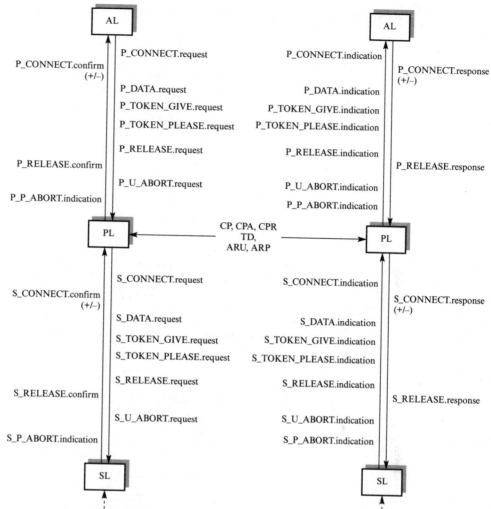

Figure 12.25
Presentation layer
summary (basic
services only).

- Synchronization control
- Token control
- Exception reporting
- Activity management

Finally, although there is always an agreed default presentation context for a connection, service primitives exist to allow two PS_users to negotiate a presentation context set for use with a connection. A summary of the various presentation services associated with the basic subset, together with the PPDUs and the session services, is given in Figure 12.25.

12.5.2   Protocol specification

To reinforce understanding of the various functions and the interrelationships between the presentation services and associated PPDUs, the connection establishment phase of the specification of the presentation protocol is summarized in Figure 12.26. As in the previous examples, the abbreviated names used in the extended event–state table for the **presentation protocol machine (PPM)** are given first. The procedure outlined in Chapter 11 can be followed for its subsequent implementation.

(a)

Name	Interface	Meaning
PCONreq	PS_user	P_CONNECT.request received
PCONresp(+)	PS_user	P_CONNECT.response (accept) received
PCONresp(−)	PS_user	P_CONNECT.response (reject) received
CP	SS_provider	CONNECT PRESENTATION PPDU received
CPA	SS_provider	CONN.PRESENT.ACCEPT PPDU received
CPR	SS_provider	CONN.PRESENT.REJECT PPDU received

(b)

Name	Meaning
STA 10	Idle, no presentation connection (PC)
STA 11	Wait for CPA PPDU
STA 12	Wait for P_CONNECT. response
STA CO	Data transfer

(c)

Name	Interface	Meaning
PCONind	PS_user	P_CONNECT.indication issued
PCONconf(+)	PS_user	P_CONNECT.confirm (accept) issued
PCONconf(−)	PS_user	P_CONNECT.confirm (reject) issued
PPABTind	PS_user	P_P_ABORT.indication issued
CP	SS_provider	CONNECT PRESENTATION PPDU sent
CPA	SS_provider	CONN.PRESENT.ACCEPT PPDU sent
CPR	SS_provider	CONN.PRESENT.REJECT PPDU sent

(d)

Name	Meaning
P1	CN PPDU acceptable
P5	Presentation contexts acceptable

(e)

Name	Meaning
[1]	Record abstract and transfer syntaxes for the defined and default context sets
[2]	Select a transfer syntax for each context set
[3]	Propose a transfer syntax for each context set

Figure 12.26
Presentation protocol specification:
(a) incoming events;
(b) automaton states;
(c) outgoing events;
(d) predicates;
(e) specific actions.

(f) State / Event	STA 10	STA 11	STA 12	----	STA CO
PCONrequest	1	0	0		
PCONresp(+)	0	0	2		
PCONresp(−)	0	0	3		
CP	4	0	0		
CPA	0	5	0		
CPR	0	6	0		
⋮					

0 = PPABTind, ARU, STA 10
1 = P5: CP, [3], STA 11
2 = CPA, [1], [2], STA CO
3 = CPR, STA 10
4 = P1: PCONDind, STA 12;
    NOT P1: CPR, STA 10
5 = PCONconf(+), [1], STA CO
6 = PCONconf(−), STA 10

Figure 12.26 (cont.)
(f) Event–state table.

12.6 Association control service element

Recall that the application layer consists of multiple protocol entities, each known as an application service element (ASE). Since a number of functions are common to many applications, the approach adopted by ISO is to implement such functions as separate ASEs (protocols) which are linked with selected application-specific ASEs when the appropriate support service is required. The combined entity, known as an **application entity**, is linked with the user application process.

To discriminate between ASEs that perform common application-support services and those that perform specific application-support services, the term **common application service (CASE)** is sometimes used to refer to the first, and the term **specific application service element (SASE)** to refer to the second. In the remainder of this chapter we describe three CASEs; various SASEs are discussed in Chapter 13.

Communication between two user application processes – and hence application entities – is carried out either using a (logical) communication channel that is set up between the two application entities before any data is exchanged, or using a simple request/response message exchange. A logical connection between two application entities is known as an association. The ASE that initiates the setting up and clearing of an association between two application-specific ASEs – SASEs – is thus known as the association control service element (ACSE).

Normally, an association is established in response to a request from a client user application process for access to a particular networked service, such as a file server. As we shall see in Chapter 13, to perform such services in an open way, a separate SASE is associated with each service present in the application layer in each networked system (computer). At one side it is known as the client ASE (SASE) and at the other as the server ASE.

Normally, on receipt of the initial service request from the client user application process, the client SASE first creates its own initialize (connection-receipt) PDU and then uses the services provided by the ACSE to establish an association with the correspondent (called) SASE. The initialize PDU and other information such as the addresses of the calling and called SASEs are passed as parameters with the ACSE associate request service primitive.

Once an association has been established, ACSE does not feature in the subsequent SASE dialog until the latter requests that the association be released (disconnected). The service primitives associated with ACSE are as follows:

- A_ASSOCIATE.request/indication/response/confirm

- A_RELEASE.request/indication/response/confirm

- A_ABORT.request/indication

- A_P_ABORT.indication

A time sequence diagram showing the interrelationship between the various application and presentation service primitives is shown in Figure 12.27. Each service primitive maps directly from one layer to the other including (but not shown) from the presentation layer to the session layer. Also, there is a single connection identifier common to all the application-oriented layers.

Figure 12.27
Interrelationship of service primitives.

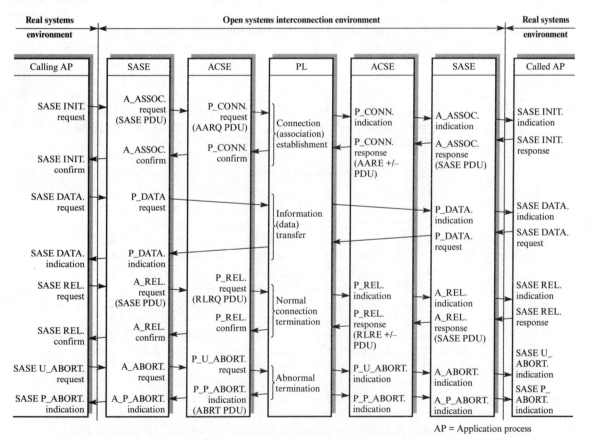

AP = Application process

The parameters associated with the A_ASSOCIATE service include the following:

- Calling and called application entity titles: these are the unique (system-wide) names used to identify each user AP (and hence the application entity (AE) to which the user AP is attached) in the OSI environment.
- Calling and called presentation addresses: these are the corresponding fully qualified addresses (P/SAP + TSAP + NSAP) associated with each AE.
- Application context name: FTAM, JTM, etc.
- Presentation context information.
- Communication quality of service (QOS).
- Connection identifier.
- Session requirements: subset, token assignment, etc.
- User data: typically, the SASE initialize PDU.

On receipt of each service primitive from the SASE, the ACSE protocol machine (entity) creates a corresponding PDU. This, together with other parameters from the service primitive, is passed to the correspondent ACSE entity in the user data parameter of the corresponding presentation service primitive. The PDUs associated with the ACSE protocol machine, together with the appropriate presentation service primitives, are also shown in Figure 12.27.

User APs communicate using names or titles. Consequently, before initiating a particular service, the user AP must obtain the corresponding fully qualified addresses of the two correspondent AEs (to which the user APs are attached). These are obtained from the local directory service agent (DSA), as we shall see in Chapter 13. Subsequent service calls to other SASEs normally have both the names and corresponding addresses of the two AEs as parameters.

Finally, to reinforce understanding of the operation of ACSE, the formal specification of the ACSE protocol machine for the association establishment phase is given in Figure 12.28. As in the previous examples, a list of the

Figure 12.28

Abbreviated names for ACSE protocol machine: (a) incoming events; (b) automaton states.

(a)

Name	Interface	Meaning
AASCreq	CS_user	A_ASSOCIATE.request received
AASCresp(+)	CS_user	A_ASSOCIATE.response (accept) received
AASCresp(–)	CS_user	A_ASSOCIATE.response (reject) received
AARQ	PS_provider	AARQ PDU received
AARE(+)	PS_provider	AARE (+) PDU received
AARE(–)	PS_provider	AARE (–) PDU received
PCONconf(–)	PS_provider	P_CONNECT.confirm (reject) received

(b)

Name	Meaning
STA 0	Idle (unassociated)
STA 1	Awaiting AARE PDU
STA 2	Awaiting A.ASSOCIATE.response
STA 5	Associated

(c)

Name	Meaning
P1	CPM can support connection

(d)

Name	Interface	Meaning
AASCind	CS_user	A_ASSOCIATE.indication issued
AASCconf(+)	CS_user	A_ASSOCIATE.confirm (accept) issued
AASCconf(–)	CS_user	A_ASSOCIATE.confirm (reject) issued
AARQ	PS_provider	AARQ PDU sent
AARE(+)	PS_provider	AARE (+) PDU sent
AARE(–)	PS_provider	AARE (–) PDU sent
AABRind	CS_user	A_ABORT.indication issued
ABRT	PS_provider	ABRT PDU sent

(e)

Event \ State	STA 0	STA 1	STA 2	---
AASCreq	1	0	0	
AASCresp(+)	0	0	2	
AASCresp(–)	0	0	3	
AARQ	4	0	0	
AARE(+)	0	5	0	
AARE(–)	0	6	0	
PCONconf(–)	0	6	0	

0 = AABRind, ABRT, STA 0
1 = P1: AARQ, STA 1
2 = AARE(+), STA 5
3 = AARE(–), STA 0
4 = P1: AASCind, STA 2;
    NOT P1: AARE(–), STA 0
5 = AASCconf(+), STA 5
6 = AASCconf(–), STA 0

Figure 12.28 (cont.)
(c) Outgoing events;
(d) predicates;
(e) event–state table.

abbreviated names and meanings of the incoming events, states, outgoing events, and predicates is given, followed by the extended event–state table. The procedure outlined in Chapter 11 can be used for its implementation.

12.7 Remote operations service element

As we shall see in Chapter 13, most application-specific ASEs operate in a connection-oriented mode: an association is set up and, after the appropriate transaction has been carried out, cleared. Considerable state information (variables) is thus retained by both ASEs for each association. In addition, a small number of ASEs operate using a short request/response message exchange with a minimum of state information being retained by each ASE. An associated support ASE, known as the **remote operations service element (ROSE)**, has been defined to support this type of application.

The semantics associated with this type of communication are clearly different from those involving a connection-oriented mode of communication. The latter is equivalent to two programs communicating with one another while the use of ROSE is equivalent to the calling process invoking a (remote) procedure

(a)

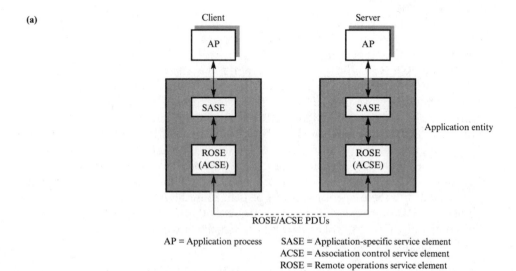

Client   Server

AP = Application process   SASE = Application-specific service element
ACSE = Association control service element
ROSE = Remote operations service element

(b)

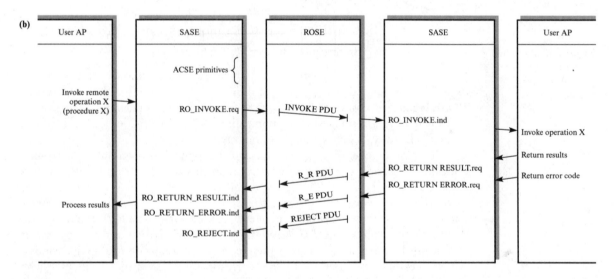

Figure 12.29
ROSE schematic and
associated service
primitives/PDUs.

to perform a specific function or operation. This mode of communication is known as a **remote procedure call** or, in the ISO terminology, a **remote operation**. Input parameters/arguments are associated with each invocation request and result parameters are possibly returned. No state information is retained after the operation has been performed, and each new request is treated as a separate entity.

The user service primitives associated with ROSE are shown in Figure 12.29 together with the PDUs that are exchanged between two ROSE protocol entities.

The RO_INVOKE service primitive is used by an AP through a related SASE to invoke a remote operation on a peer AP. It contains the arguments associated with the operation (procedure) as parameters. Although just a single

INVOKE request is shown, in practice a number of requests can be issued before a response is received. Indeed, in some instances, there may not be a result associated with an operation.

The RO_RETURN_RESULT reports the successful completion of an operation and normally has result arguments associated with it. However, not all operations return a result. If a result is expected but the operation was unsuccessful, a RO_RETURN_ERROR primitive (and associated PDU) is returned together with a defined error code number. The REJECT is returned by a ROSE protocol entity if it receives a PDU containing unrecognizable fields.

Since ROSE is a general support ASE intended for use by many ASEs, the operations to be performed and the meaning of the input and output arguments associated with these operations must be defined in the APs that use it and hence outside of ROSE. Similarly, any error messages that may be returned must have meaning only to the APs. The parameters associated with the four primitives are as follows:

- RO_INVOKE.request/indication – InvokeID, OpCode, input argument list
- RO_RETURN_RESULT.request/indication – InvokeID, output argument list
- RO_RETURN_ERROR.request/indication – InvokeID, ErrorCode
- RO_REJECT.indication – InvokeID, ProblemCode

The list of possible operations to be performed and the list of input arguments associated with each operation are defined using ASN.1. However, ROSE is concerned only with the syntax of these, and their meaning – semantics – is known only to the two communicating APs. The list of result (output) arguments, if any, is defined in the same way.

To ensure generality, each operation is assigned an **operation code number** (OpCode). OpCode and the list of input arguments together form the parameters associated with the INVOKE service primitive. In addition, since more than one invocation can be issued before a result is returned, an additional parameter known as the **invocation number** (InvokeID) is used with each INVOKE primitive. Similarly, the RO_RETURN_RESULT primitive, in addition to any result arguments, also has an invocation number as a parameter to enable the sending AP to relate any results to the corresponding invocation request. The RO_RETURN_ERROR and RO_REJECT primitives also have an invocation number parameter in addition to an **error code number** or a **problem code number**. Again the AP relates these to a specific error or problem definition.

As an example, if the AP is a (client) directory user agent AP, then OpCode 1 with, say, a single input argument, may be interpreted by the receiving (server) directory service agent AP as *perform an address resolution operation on the name in the input argument*. This, as we shall see in Chapter 13, involves consulting the directory information base to obtain the fully qualified address corresponding to the given name. Each invocation request then has a different InvokeID which is returned with either the result or the ErrorCode/ProblemCode number. The latter would be interpreted by the client in the defined way.

Normally, all ROSE PDUs are transferred using services provided by the presentation layer. To reflect the semantics associated with remote operations, the connectionless presentation and session protocols should be used. However, as indicated at the start of the chapter, currently defined OSI profiles use only connection-oriented protocols. Hence, before any invocation requests are issued, a presentation/session connection must first be in place. This is the role of ACSE. A typical application entity comprises a SASE and the ACSE and ROSE. To minimize overheads, if a connectionless network service is being used, then a connection can be set up at the start of a session and simply left open. For example, this is appropriate if the application involves many/frequent operations. Irrespective of this, all ROSE PDUs are transferred using the P_DATA service of the presentation layer.

12.8 Commitment, concurrency, and recovery

Many distributed applications involve a number of application processes that require access to a single shared resource. An example is a file system in a banking application that contains customer accounts. Typically, these are accessed concurrently by a number of client systems to perform credit and debit operations on the various accounts. To illustrate the problems that can arise in such applications, consider the sequence of operations performed by two client systems shown in Figure 12.30.

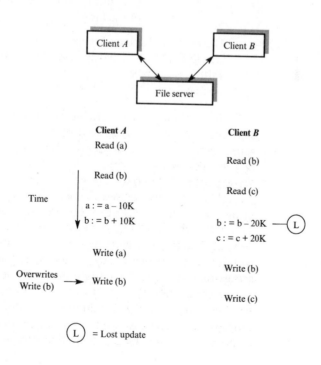

Figure 12.30
Lost update
schematic.

In the example we assume that client A is involved in transferring 10K (pounds, dollars, whatever) from account (a) to account (b) concurrently with client B transferring 20K from account (b) to account (c). Each client simply reads the appropriate two accounts from the server, performs the corresponding transfers, and returns the updated accounts to the server. As we can see, client A overwrites the update performed by client B on account (b). This is known as a **lost update**. Without an appropriate (concurrency) control mechanism, such losses can occur in all applications that involve concurrent access to a single shared resource.

A related problem can occur when multiple copies of a file are being kept in different locations. If not all copies of a file are the same (consistent), in a similar banking application a customer may be allowed to complete a withdrawal even though there is no money left as a result of an earlier withdrawal. This is known as the **multiple copy update problem**. Both problems are common to many distributed applications. The **commitment, concurrency, and recovery (CCR)** ASE has been defined to help control such operations.

CCR is a support ASE, the services of which are available to APs either directly or as pass-through services of a related SASE. For example, the user services of the ASE known as distributed transaction processing include additional primitives that are mapped directly into CCR primitives of the same name.

CCR is based on the concept of an **atomic action** with a **two-phase commit protocol** and **rollback error recovery**. Essentially, an atomic action is a sequence of operations that is performed by two or more cooperating APs such that:

- The sequence of operations is carried out without interference from an AP that is not part of the atomic action.

- The operations being carried out by each AP involved in the atomic action are either all completed successfully or are all terminated; any data modified during the preceding operations is restored to the state prior to the commencement of the atomic action.

The AP initiating an atomic action is referred to as the **master** or **superior**, since it directly or indirectly controls the entire activity associated with the atomic action. Similarly, all other APs involved in the atomic action are known as **slaves** or **subordinates**, since they are all controlled (using the CCR protocol) by the single master that initiated the atomic action.

All data affected by the operations within an atomic action is known as **bound data**. The values of all bound data at the commencement of an atomic action are known as their **initial state** and their values after the atomic action as their **final state**. On completion of an atomic action, the bound data associated with it is either committed to its final state if all operations have been carried out successfully, or is recovered to its initial state if one or more of the operations have failed. The particular action followed is accomplished using a form of **handshake procedure**: after all the operations associated with an atomic action have been carried out, the superior first asks all subordinates whether they have successfully completed their processing; hence they are said to be 'prepared to commit'. If all

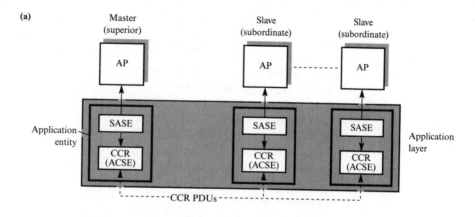

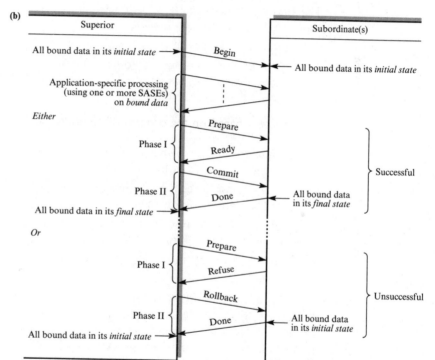

Figure 12.31
Atomic action
principles: (a) CCR
schematic; (b) two-
phase commit
sequence.

subordinates respond positively, the order to commit all bound data to its final state is given. Alternatively, if one or more of the subordinates responds negatively (or fails to respond) the order is given to recover all bound data to its initial stage. The various terms are shown in Figure 12.31.

Note that the nature of the atomic action being controlled is determined by the APs, and associated SASEs, that manipulate the bound data involved, and that the CCR protocol provides only the means whereby an AP may initiate and control the atomic action. That is, it is a purely local matter for the APs involved in the atomic action to take steps to ensure that the rules of an atomic action are adhered to. Thus, once an AP has indicated its willingness to take part in an atomic action, it is a local matter for the AP to ensure that an AP which is not involved in this atomic action is not allowed to access or manipulate any of the bound data associated with the atomic action. Normally, this is accomplished using a **locking mechanism** such as a **semaphore**. This is a form of token since, once a semaphore has been set, all other accesses to the data controlled by the semaphore are excluded until the semaphore has been reset. It is similar to the various forms of mutual exclusion mechanisms associated with concurrent programming languages such as Ada.

User service

The service primitives provided with CCR have been designed so that the atomic action that it is controlling is subjected to the following constraints:

- After the order to commit has been given by a superior, the bound data held by the superior and the subordinate(s) is in its final (permanent) state and no recovery capability is supported to allow any data to be returned to its initial (or an intermediate) state.

- A superior may order rollback to the initial state at any time prior to ordering commitment.

- A superior may not order a subordinate to commit unless it has received an offer to commit from that subordinate.

- Once a subordinate has returned an offer to commit to the superior, it may not then refuse an order to commit.

- Before returning an offer to commit, a subordinate may abort the atomic action (and hence return all bound data to its initial state) at any time.

- The superior may order rollback if any of the subordinates refuse the offer to commit.

The service primitives associated with CCR are shown in the time sequence diagram of Figure 12.32. More than one subordinate can be involved in an atomic action. Also, before an atomic action can be initiated, there must be an existing association between the superior AP (and hence SASE) and each of the subordinate APs. Normally, these are established using the ACSE. An atomic action is started when the superior AP informs each of the subordinates using the C_BEGIN service. On receipt of the C_BEGIN.indication primitive, each subordinate must create a new instance (working copy) of all bound data values to be involved – for example, to read a copy of a file from disk – and initiate the locking mechanism. In practice, the C_BEGIN primitives have the effect of establishing a session layer major synchronization point for this association.

The application-specific processing associated with the atomic action, using SASE primitives, is then carried out. Figure 12.32(b) shows the two possible termination phases. In the first, all subordinates return a positive offer to commit, using the C_READY service. In the second, one or more of the subordinates

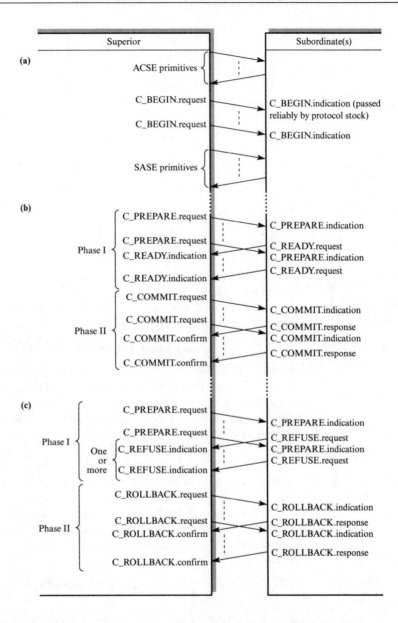

Figure 12.32
CCR service
primitives:
(a) establishment;
(b) successful;
(c) unsuccessful.

return a negative reply using the C_REFUSE service. In practice, the C_PREPARE service is optional. If it is not used, the subordinate(s) indicate(s) readiness (or otherwise) to commit with a C_READY or C_REFUSE immediately after the relevant application processing has finished. In addition, there is a confirmed service, the C_RESTART service, which may be used by either a superior or a subordinate if it becomes necessary to return all bound data involved in an atomic action to an earlier known state. It can only be used by a subordinate, however, provided it has not signaled its readiness to commit. Typically, it is used

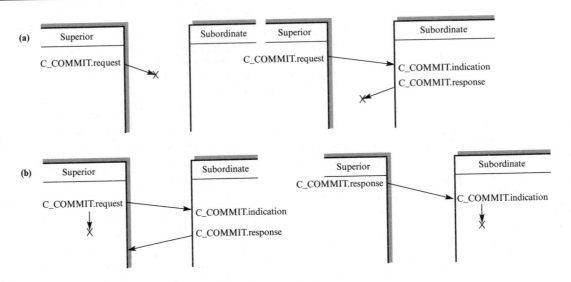

Figure 12.33
Some example
failures:
(a) communications;
(b) applications.

by a superior if a response from a subordinate times out, indicating a possible application or communication failure.

We can best illustrate some of the occasions when the RESTART service may be used by considering several possible failures that may occur during an atomic action. Some examples are shown in the time sequence diagrams in Figure 12.33. Although the failure in the examples relates to the COMMIT service, it may equally arise with a failure with the ROLLBACK service. However, we can deduce from these examples that after a failure has occurred the precise state of a subordinate may not be known. For example, in Figure 12.33(a) did the communication failure occur before the C_COMMIT request was received or after? The RESTART service is provided to allow a superior, for whatever reason, to return the state of an atomic action to an earlier known state. It is a confirmed service and may be used at any time, provided the atomic action is intact.

A superior determines the current state of a subordinate by issuing a C_RESTART.request primitive with a defined **resumption point** as a parameter. The resumption point in the request (and hence indication) primitive is one of the following:

- ACTION   Used to request the subordinate to restart the atomic action at the beginning.

- COMMIT   Used to request the subordinate to restart the atomic action after the last COMMIT point.

- ROLLBACK   Used to request the subordinate to restart the atomic action after the last ROLLBACK point.

Similarly, the resumption point in the response (and hence confirmation) primitive is one the following:

- DONE   Indicates that the subordinate has in fact done the last commit or rollback request.

- REFUSE   Indicates that the subordinate has not done the last commit request and hence the superior should issue a rollback request.

- ACTION   Indicates that the superior should restart the atomic action from the beginning.

- RETRY-LATER   Indicates that the subordinate cannot proceed with a restart at this time and therefore the superior should retry at a later time.

When an order to commit is received (C_COMMIT.indication), the subordinate(s) must update the bound data from its initial to its final state, that is, with the contents of the current working copy. Typically, this involves writing the contents to disk. A check is often carried out to ensure that the final write operation is successful before a positive C_COMMIT.response is returned by the subordinate(s). The data is then said to be **secure** or **stable**. One way of achieving this is to write two copies of the data to disk and then to read and compare them; only if the two copies are equal is the data said to be secure.

Parameters are associated with the various CCR primitives. For example, the parameters associated with the two C_BEGIN primitives include the following:

- Atomic action identifier: includes the name (title) of the master AP and a suffix to allow for the possibility of more than one atomic action being in progress concurrently.

- Atomic action timer: (if present) indicates the time interval the master waits before issuing a rollback request.

With the CCR protocol, a subordinate of one atomic action may act as a superior for another atomic action, thus creating a form of tree structure. A further parameter, branch identifier, is used to identify a specific branch in the hierarchy, and hence atomic action, in relation to the atomic action identifier assigned by the (single) master. The branch identifier is the name of the superior, for a particular (sub)atomic action in the tree, together with a branch suffix. A typical CCR tree is shown in Figure 12.34.

When we create atomic action trees of the type shown, we must take care to avoid the possibility of **deadlock**. This occurs when an AP forms an atomic action with several other APs and makes a request to one of them. If it is waiting for a response from another AP that cannot respond because it in turn is waiting for a response from an AP that itself is locked into the first atomic action, then a deadlock has occurred. A simple explanation is as follows.

Three APs (A, B, and C) are involved in a distributed information processing task. First assume that A creates an atomic action with B and C as subordinates and requests data from B. Before B can respond to a request from A, assume that B must first form an atomic action with C to request data from it. The system is now deadlocked since A is waiting on B and B is waiting on C, whose resources are locked (bound) to A. Although it will not overcome the deadlock, the timer parameter associated with an atomic action is useful in such circumstances since it ensures that an AP does not wait indefinitely for a response from another AP.

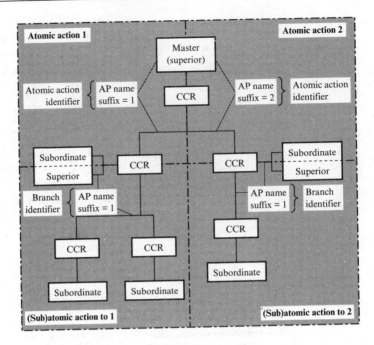

Figure 12.34
Example CCR atomic
action tree.

12.9 Reliable transfer service element

As we shall see in Chapter 13 when we consider the application service elements, some applications often use two or more of the service elements described (ACSE, ROSE, and CCR) in a single application entity. In addition, a fourth application-support service element, known as the **reliable transfer service element (RTSE)**, has been defined which is effectively a combination of two separate service elements. The aim of the RTSE is to provide the user – an application-specific service element – with a reliable means of transferring a single message (APDU), or a series of messages.

The history of the RTSE is that, at the time such a service was needed, the full set of presentation services was not complete. Thus the RTSE uses a combination of the ACSE services with a small subset of the session layer services. The latter are accessed as pass-through services of the presentation layer. The service primitives associated with the RTSE, together with the ACSE/presentation service(s) to which each is mapped, are shown in Figure 12.35.

To send each message reliably, the RTSE operates using a form of send (stop)-and-wait protocol by using a combination of the activity and data token services of the session layer. Once an association has been established, a single message (APDU) is sent by the user issuing an RT_TRANSFER.request primitive. The RTSE uses the activity service of the session layer to ensure this is transferred reliably. Thus, prior to sending the APDU the RTSE signals the start of an activity and, since the P_ACT_START is an unconfirmed service, the RTSE

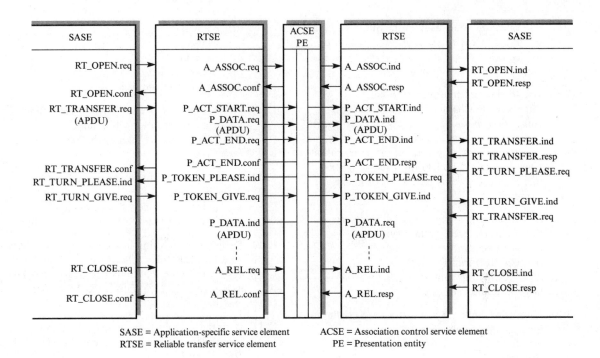

SASE	RTSE	ACSE PE	RTSE	SASE
RT_OPEN.req →	A_ASSOC.req →		→ A_ASSOC.ind	→ RT_OPEN.ind
RT_OPEN.conf ←	A_ASSOC.conf ←		← A_ASSOC.resp	← RT_OPEN.resp
RT_TRANSFER.req → (APDU)	P_ACT_START.req P_DATA.req (APDU) P_ACT_END.req	→ →	→ P_ACT_START.ind P_DATA.ind (APDU) P_ACT_END.ind	→ RT_TRANSFER.ind
				← RT_TRANSFER.resp
RT_TRANSFER.conf ←	P_ACT_END.conf ←		← P_ACT_END.resp	← RT_TURN_PLEASE.req
RT_TURN_PLEASE.ind ←	P_TOKEN_PLEASE.ind ←		← P_TOKEN_PLEASE.req	
RT_TURN_GIVE.req →	P_TOKEN_GIVE.req →		→ P_TOKEN_GIVE.ind	→ RT_TURN_GIVE.ind
				← RT_TRANSFER.req
	P_DATA.ind (APDU) ⋮		P_DATA.req (APDU) ⋮	
RT_CLOSE.req →	A_REL.req →		→ A_REL.ind	→ RT_CLOSE.ind
				← RT_CLOSE.resp
RT_CLOSE.conf ←	A_REL.conf ←		← A_REL.resp	

SASE = Application-specific service element
RTSE = Reliable transfer service element

ACSE = Association control service element
PE = Presentation entity

Figure 12.35
RTSE service primitive and mapping operations.

follows this immediately with a **P_DATA**.request with the APDU as the user data parameter. Then, to ensure this has been transferred reliably, it follows immediately by setting a synchronization point and ending the activity. Receipt of the confirm primitive indicates that the data was indeed received reliably and hence the RTSE issues an **RT_TRANSFER**.confirm to the user.

If the user wished to send a series of APDUs, instead of closing the activity each time it sends a **P_SYNC_MINOR** to checkpoint each APDU. Only when all APDUs have been transferred does it signal the end of the activity. Then, if a reply is expected, it can initiate the sending of the data token to the other side using the **RT_TURN_PLEASE/GIVE** primitive. These in turn map into the **P_TOKEN_PLEASE/GIVE** primitives. The association is then released using the **RT_CLOSE** service.

Exercises

12.1 Produce a sketch showing the relationship between the various application-support protocols discussed in this chapter and explain the functions of each protocol.

12.2 Describe the meaning of the following terms relating to the session layer:
(a) Token concept

(b) Activity
(c) Dialog unit
(d) Synchronization points
(e) Basic combined subset

12.3 With the aid of a time sequence diagram, illustrate the user service primitives in the basic combined subset of the session layer.

Show on your diagram the SPDUs that are generated by each session protocol entity to implement each of the user services shown in your diagram.

12.4 Use the implementation methodology introduced in Chapter 11 to show how the connection component of the session protocol machine can be specified in the form of structured program code. Use the specification given in Figure 12.8 and the same variable names in your program as are used in the figure.

12.5 Describe the meaning of the following terms relating to the presentation layer:
(a) Abstract syntax
(b) Concrete/transfer syntax
(c) Presentation context
Give an example of each.

12.6 Give an example ASN.1 abstract type definition for each of the following data types:
(a) Boolean
(b) Integer
(c) Bitstring
(d) Character string

12.7 Explain the meaning of the terms 'implicit', 'explicit', and 'tag' in relation to ASN.1.
Give an example sequence type definition that uses each of the types you defined in Exercise 12.6. Modify your definition to include a context-specific tag and an application-specific tag.

12.8 Define the meaning of the class, type, and tag that make up the identifier octet associated with an ASN.1 encoded type.
Use example value assignments to the data types you declared in Exercise 12.6 to illustrate how each type is encoded.

12.9 Use the two sequence type definitions derived in Exercise 12.7 to show the encoding of the sequence type and the added overheads associated with the use of tags. Clearly identify the context-specific tag in your encoding example.

12.10 With the aid of a sketch, explain the meaning of the following terms relating to data encryption:

(a) Plaintext
(b) Ciphertext
(c) Listening
(d) Masquerading
(e) Encryption and decryption keys

12.11 Use a short sentence to illustrate the difference between a substitution cipher and a transposition cipher. Define the key you use in each case.

12.12 Design an S-box that comprises a 3-to-8 decoder, a straight 8-bit permutation (P-box) and an 8-to-3 encoder. Define the key associated with your design.

12.13 Design an encryption unit for 6-bit values based on a product cipher. Use three stages in your design including the S-box design you derived in Exercise 12.12. Specify the key for your design.

12.14 With the aid of schematic logic diagrams, describe the following operational modes of the DES algorithm:
(a) ECB
(b) CBC
(c) CFM

12.15 With the aid of an example, explain the principle of operation of the RSA algorithm and how the public and secret keys are derived. Use the prime numbers 3 and 11 in your example and an E of 7.

12.16 Explain the meaning of the terms 'message authentication' and 'digital signature'.
Show how the RSA algorithm can be used to obtain message authentication.

12.17 Discriminate between the terms 'application service element' and 'application entity'.
Use a time sequence diagram to show the interrelationships between the user service primitives of the ACSE and presentation layers.

12.18 Explain the meaning of the term 'remote operation'.
List the service primitives associated with the remote operations service element (ROSE) and explain the meanings and use of the parameters associated with each primitive.

12.19 With the aid of examples, explain the meaning of the terms 'lost update' and 'multiple copy update'.

Explain the principle of operation of a two-phase commit protocol with error recovery. Include in your description the meanings of the following terms:

(a) Master (superior) and slave (subordinate)

(b) Bound and secure data

(c) Initial and final state

(d) Two-phase commit

(e) Rollback recovery

12.20 Assume an application process wishes to carry out an atomic action on a remote file. Derive a time sequence diagram showing the sequence of the CCR primitives associated with a successful and an unsuccessful atomic action.

Chapter summary

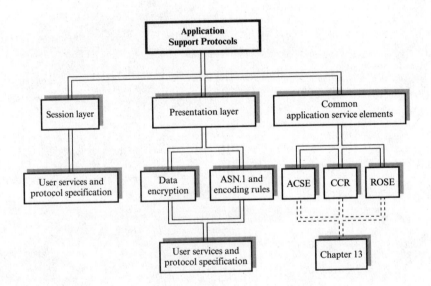

13 APPLICATION-SPECIFIC PROTOCOLS

Chapter objectives

When you have completed this chapter you should be able to:

- Know the functions of the main application-specific protocols that have been defined for use with the TCP/IP and OSI suites ☞ 757, 773

- Describe the services and operation of the following TCP/IP application protocols ☞ 759, 762, 765, 769
    - TELNET
    - FTP
    - SMTP
    - SNMP

- Describe the services and operation of the equivalent ISO application protocols ☞ 774, 779, 786, 791
    - VT
    - FTAM
    - MOTIS
    - CMISE

- Describe the services and operation of the following additional ISO application protocols ☞ 800, 801, 805
    - MMS
    - JTM
    - DTP

Introduction

Chapter 12 described a selection of the ISO protocols that provide general support services to the protocols that perform specific application functions. The latter include protocols associated with remote file access, electronic mail, and so on. As indicated, the TCP/IP suite does not have support protocols. Instead, when a particular service is needed, it is integrated directly with the application-specific protocol. Thus in a TCP/IP suite, the latter communicates directly with the transport protocols.

We use the term 'application process' to refer to the programs/software that perform the actual processing functions associated with a (distributed) application. For example, a client application process (AP) may be a program running in one computer that requires access to a file server AP that is running in another computer. The application-specific protocols provide the necessary support to enable a client to access the various server APs in an open way as if the client were running on the same machine as the server. A schematic showing the general approach with both suites is shown in Figure 13.1.

In the case of an OSI suite, the approach is to define, for each distributed application service, a **virtual device** together with a defined set of its user service primitives. There is a virtual file store/server, a virtual mail server, and so on. The application protocol associated with a particular service is implemented on the assumption that the client and server APs communicate using primitives that

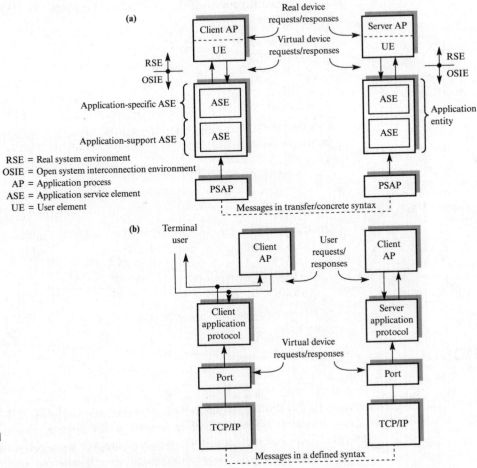

RSE = Real system environment
OSIE = Open system interconnection environment
AP = Application process
ASE = Application service element
UE = User element

Figure 13.1
Application layer schematic: (a) OSI suite; (b) TCP/IP suite.

are the same as those associated with the defined virtual device. In this way, all request and response primitives at the interface with each application protocol – and hence at the interface with the open system interconnection environment – are in a standard form. Also, each application protocol operates in a defined way that is independent of any differences that might exist in the mode of operation of the related real APs. If the services associated with the APs are different from those associated with the virtual device, an additional device-dependent software layer is used between each AP and the related application protocol to perform any mapping functions needed to convert the service primitives associated with the virtual device to and from those used with the real device. In this way, we can use existing application and server software without modification. The mapping software is known as the **user element (UE)** or **user agent (UA)**. The general scheme is shown in Figure 13.1(a).

In practice, the UE is implemented either as a separate process or in the form of a set of library procedures (or functions) that are linked to the user AP. With most services, there is an initiator AP (and hence application entity to which it is said to be attached) and a responder AP. The former acts as the initiator (or originator) of virtual device requests while the latter acts as the responder (or recipient) of virtual device requests. Also, as we described in Chapter 12, if the syntax of the data being exchanged between two user APs is different, the presentation entity performs the mapping from the agreed transfer (concrete) syntax to the local syntax as appropriate. The particular presentation context(s) to be used are negotiated when the association (connection) is first established.

In contrast, with the TCP/IP suite, in addition to implementing the protocol associated with the defined application service, each application protocol performs all the other support functions including any necessary mapping operations. Also, as we can see in Figure 13.1(b), most protocols provide a (user) terminal interface as well as a user AP interface. In general, the TCP/IP application protocols are relatively sophisticated compared with the ISO application protocols. We shall discuss selected TCP/IP application protocols first, followed by several ISO application protocols.

13.1 TCP/IP application protocols

The following selection of application protocols in the TCP/IP suite is shown in Figure 13.2:

- TELNET   Enables a user at a terminal (or a user AP) on one machine to communicate interactively with an AP, such as a text editor running on a remote machine, as if the user terminal were connected directly to it.

- FTP (file transfer protocol)   Enables a user at a terminal (or a user AP) to access and interact with a remote file system.

- SMTP (simple mail transfer protocol) Provides a networkwide mail transfer service between the mail systems associated with different machines.

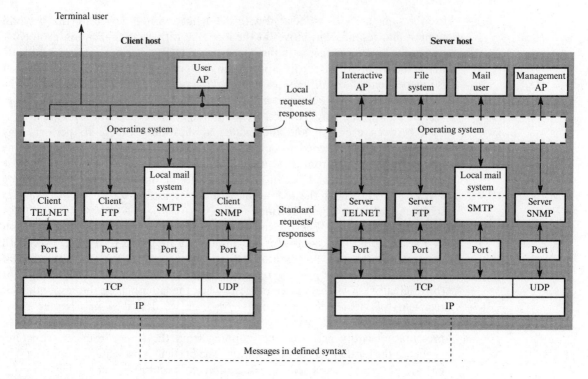

Figure 13.2
TCP/IP application
protocol summary.

• SNMP (simple network management protocol) Enables a user (for example, a network manager), to gather performance data or to control the operation of a network element (such as a bridge or gateway) via the network itself.

A common requirement with all client server interactions is that of establishing a communications path between the two application protocols/ processes involved. Therefore, before we discuss the different application protocols, let us look at how a communications path is established.

13.1.1 Establishing a transport connection

Recall from Chapter 11 that all server APs have an associated name which translates into a corresponding networkwide address. The translation procedure is carried out by a process known as the **domain name server**. (We shall discuss the operation of the server in Chapter 14, together with other system aspects.) The resulting networkwide address of a server process consists of two parts: the networkwide IP address of the host in which the process is running and a local port number. The IP address is used by the IP in each internet gateway to route datagrams across the internet to the required destination host. The port number is used by the TCP within the host – or UDP, if this is being used – to identify the specific process within that host to which a received message should be sent.

An open system includes multiple clients and servers both of different types (FTP, SMTP, etc.) and of the same type (multiple file servers, mail servers, etc.). However, all servers of the same type are assigned the same systemwide port number; a specific server is then identified by the IP address of the host in which it runs. The port numbers associated with the different server types are known as **well-known ports** and include the following:

> 21 – FTP
> 22 – TELNET
> 25 – SMTP

Hence, when a client process initiates a call to a correspondent server process, it uses as a destination address the IP address of the host in which the server is running coupled with the well-known port number of that server. As a source address it uses the IP address of its own host together with the next free (unused) port number on that host. If TCP is being used, the local TCP entity will establish a transport connection between the client and server processes – using these addresses – over which the appropriate message exchanges can take place.

13.1.2 TELNET

As we can see in Figure 13.3, the client TELNET protocol/process is accessed through the local operating system either by a user AP or, more usually, by a user at a terminal. It provides services to enable a user to log on to the operating system of a remote machine, to initiate the running of a program/process on that machine – for example, a text editor – and then to interact with it as if the user terminal/

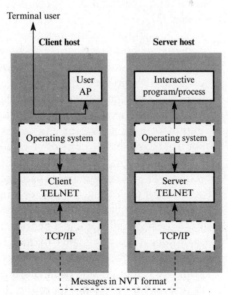

Figure 13.3
TELNET client/server
interaction schematic.

process were connected/running on the same machine. All commands (control characters) and data entered at the user terminal – or submitted by the user AP – are passed by the local operating system to the client TELNET process which then passes them, using the reliable stream service provided by TCP, to the correspondent server TELNET. The latter issues the commands on behalf of the user, through the local operating system, to the interactive process. The server TELNET is thus also known as a **pseudo terminal**. Any data output by the interactive process is returned in the same way for display on the client terminal or for interpretation by the user AP.

The two TELNET protocols communicate with each other using commands – comprising single characters or strings of characters – that are encoded in a standard format known as **network virtual terminal (NVT)**. The character set used for commands is ASCII. All input and output data relating to an interaction is transferred as ASCII strings. If this is different from the local character set being used, the corresponding TELNET will carry out any necessary mapping functions. Thus, the two TELNET protocol entities also perform the role of the presentation layer in an OSI stack.

Recall from Chapter 3 that the ASCII character set uses seven bits per character. However, all commands and data in the NVT format are encoded using 8-bit bytes. If the most significant (eighth) bit is a 0, all the characters have their normal meaning, including the ASCII control characters. Also, selected pairs of these are defined, such as CR–LF to signal a new line. In addition, an extra set of command characters is defined by setting the most significant bit to 1. Since such characters have their most significant bit set, they can be readily distinguished from the standard ASCII set. If required, they can be interspersed with a data stream that is flowing in a particular direction. A selection of the command bytes that have been defined, together with their meanings, is given in Table 13.1.

All commands are preceded by the all 1s (255) IAC byte. If a command consists of more than one byte, then the byte string must start with an SB command and terminate with an SE command. As we can see, some of the commands have the same meaning as those used with most interactive software. Others are needed because the interactive software (process) is running in a remote machine. For example, most interactive programs allow a user to control the output of long strings of characters to the terminal screen by entering defined control characters or pairs of characters. The BRK and DMARK command bytes are used to signal the same function: BRK to stop outputting and DMARK to resume. The AO command is used to request that the current output is aborted. In addition, if the output process continues outputting data after being requested to stop – for example, because the command bytes are held up by network congestion – the user normally enters a character sequence to terminate the (remote) process. If this occurs, it is signaled by the client TELNET sending an IP command byte using the TCP service primitive URGENT. Recall that data associated with this primitive is sent outside of the normal flow control window which is operating for the current connection. Hence the IP command should always be received by the server.

Table 13.1   NVT command bytes and their meaning.

Command	Decimal	Meaning
IAC	255	Interpret the following byte as a command byte
NOP	241	No operation
EC	247	Erase character
EL	248	Erase line
GA	249	Go ahead
AYT	246	Are you there
IP	244	Interrupt process
AO	245	Abort output
BRK	243	Break (stop) output
DMARK	242	Resume output
SB	250	Start option negotiation string
SE	240	End option negotiation string
WILL	251	Agreement/request option
WON'T	252	Refuse option request
DO	253	Accept request option
DON'T	254	Refuse to accept option request

As indicated, all data is normally transferred as 7-bit ASCII character strings. In addition, strings of 8-bit bytes may be sent if necessary, for example to transfer special display characters or, if an AP is the client rather than a user at a terminal, for the client and server processes to exchange blocks of binary data. To achieve this, one side enters a command known as **option negotiation**. Other operational functions can also be requested in the same way. The option codes used are listed in Table 13.2.

Option requests can be initiated by either side of a connection using the WILL, WON'T, DO, and DON'T command bytes followed by the particular code number from the table. Typical option commands are thus:

IAC, SB, WILL, '0', SE

to request the receiver to accept 8-bit binary. The receiving TELNET returns either:

IAC, SB, DO, '0', SE

Table 13.2   NVT option codes and their meaning.

Name	Code	Meaning
Transmit binary	0	Request/accept change to 8-bit binary
Echo	1	Echo characters received back to sender
Status	5	Request/reply status of receiving TELNET
Timing mark	6	Insert timing mark in returned stream
Terminal type	24	Request/response type of remote terminal
Line mode	34	Send complete lines instead of individual characters

if it is prepared to accept, or:

IAC, SB, DON'T, '0', SE

if it is not. Alternatively, the receiver can initiate the switch by sending:

IAC, SB, DO, '0', SE

The sender returns either:

IAC, SB, WILL, '0', SE

to indicate it is going to switch, or:

IAC, SB, WON'T, '0', SE

to refuse. In binary mode, any all 1s (IAC) bytes are sent twice to signal to the receiver to interpret the byte as data and not the start of a command.

The **timing mark** command performs a similar function to the synchronization function in the session layer of an OSI stack. We can deduce the use of the other commands from their meanings.

13.1.3   FTP

Access to a remote file server is a fundamental requirement in many distributed applications. In some instances a single file server may be accessed by multiple clients, while in others multiple copies of the same file may be held in a number of servers. An example application is shown in Figure 13.4.

A client FTP can be accessed either by a user at a terminal or by a user AP. Normally, a single client can support multiple such users concurrently. It provides each user with a similar set of services to those available with most file systems. Thus a user can list directories, create new files, obtain (read) the contents of existing files, perform update operations on them, delete files, and so on. Similarly, a server FTP can respond to requests from multiple clients concurrently. On receipt of each request, the server FTP interacts with its local file system to carry out the request as if it had been generated locally.

The client FTP allows a user to specify the structure of the file involved and the type of data in the file. Again these services reflect those used with most file systems. Three file structures are supported (unstructured, structured, and random access) as well as four data types (8-bit binary, text (ASCII and EBCDIC), and variable length binary). The FTP server accesses each file from its local file system and transfers it to the client FTP in an appropriate way according to its defined structure.

As an **unstructured file** can contain any type of data – binary or text – it is transferred between the two FTP protocol entities as a transparent bit stream. The user interprets the bit stream according to the data types within it.

Structured files consist of a sequence of fixed-sized records of a defined type. Hence the contents of such files are normally transferred as a string of fixed-sized blocks. Alternatively, the contents may be transferred in compressed form. This is

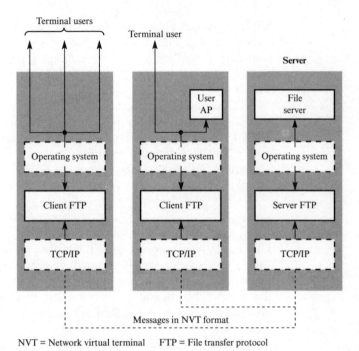

Figure 13.4
FTP client–server
interaction schematic.

appropriate with text files as they often contain long strings of the same character, such as space characters. This, and other types of redundancy, can be exploited if each FTP protocol entity applies an agreed compression algorithm to the field contents prior to transmission. In the case of an OSI stack, this is performed by the presentation layer.

Random access files are comprised of records of variable size. Normally, we refer to such records as **pages** and the file as a **paged file**. Each record/page has an associated header which includes a length and type field and positional information to indicate the position of the record/page relative to the total file contents. Each page is transferred between the two protocol entities in this same form.

In the case of compressed and block-mode transfers, the two FTP protocol entities perform checkpointing to allow large files to be transferred in a controlled way. This is similar to the synchronization services provided by the session layer in an OSI stack.

To handle multiple requests concurrently, each server FTP – and client, if it also supports multiple requests – creates (spawns) a new instance of the FTP protocol/process for each new request received. Normally, there is a single master process – with its well-known port number – to which all new requests are passed. This master process creates a new process for this connection. This **control process**, as it is known, performs the various control functions associated with the session, including the log on (with password) procedure and the definition of the structure and data types associated with the file(s) to be transferred. It also defines whether compression is to be used and, if so, the type of compression algorithm. Many implementations then create another process to handle the actual data transfers associated with the session. In such cases, a single FTP session involves two transport connections, one for exchanging control messages and the other for transferring file contents. Of course, this is all transparent to the user and server software.

The format of the messages associated with the file contents is determined by the defined structure of the file. The format of the messages exchanged between the two FTP control processes – the FTP PDUs – must also be in an agreed syntax to ensure they have the same meaning (and are interpreted in the same way) in both computers. To achieve this, we use the NVT format described in Section 13.1.2, except that option negotiation is not required with FTP.

TFTP

FTP is relatively complex since it contains all the features that are needed for a variety of file types and, if required, compression algorithms. Although we may require these in applications involving internetworks, we do not normally require this level of functionality in more local applications, such as the file transfer protocol between a networked file server and a local community of diskless workstations.

In this case, since each file transfer request issued by a client must go via the network, the server and client workstations are all connected to the same LAN segment. Also, such transfers do not require many of the functions associated with FTP. Consequently, an additional file protocol, known as the **trivial file transfer protocol (TFTP)**, is available with the TCP/IP suite.

As indicated, TFTP is intended for use primarily in LAN applications. Recall from Chapter 6 that the bit error rate probability of LANs is normally very low, so TFTP uses UDP rather than TCP for all message transfers. To overcome the possibility of corrupted messages (datagrams), a simple idle RQ (stop-and-wait) error control procedure is incorporated into the protocol. With idle RQ only a single message (block) may be sent until either an acknowledgment for the block is received or a timeout occurs. In the latter event, the waiting block is retransmitted. This is adequate because of the short transit delay associated with LANs.

TFTP uses just four message – PDU – types which are also encoded in ASCII. They are:

Read request	Sent by a client to initiate a file read operation
Write request	Sent by a client to perform a file write operation
Data block	Used to convey the file contents
Acknowledgment	Sent by either a client (read) or a server (write) to acknowledge receipt of a data block.

To initiate a file transfer operation, the client sends either a read or write message containing the file name and file type. The data associated with the file request is then transferred in fixed-sized blocks, each of which contains up to 512 bytes. Each data block has a sequence number in its header; the same number is returned in the associated acknowledgment. This is used by the receiver – client for read, server for write – to detect duplicates in the event of a lost acknowledgment. The end of a file is detected by the receipt of a data block containing less than 512 bytes.

In common with FTP, a TFTP server can support multiple client transfer requests concurrently. Hence, after the initial read or write request message has been received, the server relates subsequent data blocks or acknowledgments to the correct file transfer by means of the client port/IP addresses. This information is passed up to the TFTP by the IP/UDP on receipt of the datagram in which the data block/acknowledgment message was carried.

13.1.4   SMTP

Electronic mail – normally referred to as **e-mail** – is probably the most widely used service associated with computer networks. Local mail systems have been available with most large interactive computer systems for many years. Hence, it was a natural evolution to extend this service across the network when these were networked together.

The **simple mail transfer protocol (SMTP)** manages the transfer of mail from one host computer mail system to another. It is not responsible for accepting mail from local users or for distributing received mail to its intended recipient(s). These are the responsibility of the local mail system. The interrelationship between SMTP and the local mail system is shown in Figure 13.5.

Since SMTP interacts with the local mail system and not the user, it is masked from any mail transfers local to that machine. Only when an item of mail is to be sent to a different machine or is received from a remote machine is the SMTP scheduled to run. Normally, there is an input queue and an output queue at the interface between the local mail system – often referred to as the **native mail system** – and the client and server parts of the SMTP. The client is concerned with initiating the transfer of mail to another system while the server is concerned with receiving mail. Also, although multiple users are shown in Figure 13.5, it is possible for only a single user at, say, a personal computer to be involved.

The local mail system retains a **mailbox** for each user into which the user can deposit or retrieve mail. Each mailbox has a unique name which consists of two parts: a **local part** and a **global part**. The first is the name of the user and is unique only within that local mail system. The second, the identity of the host, must be unique within the total internet. It normally comprises a number of fields and the precise format varies for different types of establishment – education, government, military, etc. We shall look at some examples in Chapter 14 when we discuss directory services and name-to-address mapping.

There are two points to consider in the transfer of mail: the format of the mail – to ensure that it is interpreted in the same way in each system – and the SMTP used to transfer it from one machine to another. The mail format consists of a header and a body which themselves consist of a number of lines of

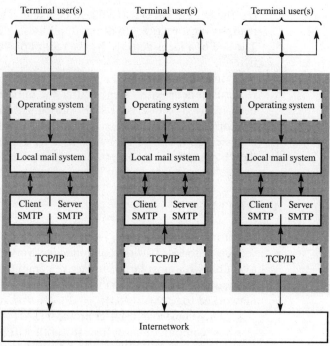

Figure 13.5
SMTP – local mail
system schematic.

SMTP = Simple mail transfer protocol

ASCII text with a blank line separating the header from the body. Only ASCII text is accepted.

Each line in the header comprises a **keyword** followed by a text string with a colon separating the two. Some keywords are compulsory while others are optional. The minimum header is:

    TO: name of recipient
    FROM: name of sender

Others include:

    TO: name of recipient
    REPLY TO: name to send reply to

and:

    TO: name of recipient
    FROM: name of sender
    CC: copies to
    SUBJECT:
    DATE:
    ENCRYPTED: encryption pointer

The ENCRYPTED keyword indicates that the body part – the contents – have been encrypted using a key which the recipient can deduce from the encryption pointer. The header, including the SUBJECT and the names of the intended recipient(s), is always in plaintext. Although in some instances the two communicating machines may be connected to the same network, if internet gateways are involved in the route, additional lines of the form:

RECEIVED FROM: identity of a gateway that forwarded the mail

may be added to the header by each gateway to provide a means of determining the route taken by the mail through the internet.

After an item of mail has been created in the standard format, the local mail system determines from the name of the recipient whether it should be deposited in a local mailbox or in the output queue ready for forwarding. To send the mail, the client SMTP first ascertains the IP address of the destination host from the directory service – known as the **domain name system** – and then uses this, together with the well-known port address of SMTP (25), to initiate the setting up of a transport connection with the server SMTP in the destination host. Once a connection has been established, the client initiates the transfer of the waiting mail to the server.

Transferring the mail involves the exchange of SMTP PDUs known as **commands**. All commands are encoded as ASCII character strings and comprise either a 3-digit number or a textual command or sometimes both. They are transferred over the established transport connection using the TCP SEND/DELIVER user primitives. The sequence of commands exchanged is shown in Figure 13.6.

Once a TCP connection has been established, the server SMTP returns command 220 back to the client to indicate it is now ready to receive the mail. The client responds by returning a HELO command together with the identity of the client machine. On receiving this, the server responds with the identity of the server machine which is used as a record of the mail transaction. The client initiates the sending of the mail header by issuing a MAIL command followed by the FROM: line from the mail header. The general acknowledgment command 250 is returned by the server. The client continues by sending a RCPT command followed by the TO: line from the mail header. This is again acknowledged by a 250 command; any further header lines are sent in the same way.

The start of the contents of the mail body are signaled when the client sends a DATA command. The server responds with a 354 command and the client then sends the mail contents as a sequence of lines terminated by a line with a single period. The server acknowledges receipt of the latter by returning a 250 command. The mail transfer phase is terminated when the client sends a QUIT command and the server returns a 221 command, following which the transport connection is cleared.

These are the basic functions associated with the SMTP, but a number of additional functions are available with some implementations. For example, if the intended recipient no longer has a mailbox at the server the server SMTP may return a forwarding address. Also, after a client SMTP has sent its mail, it may invite the server to send mail in the reverse direction – if any is waiting – before clearing the transport connection.

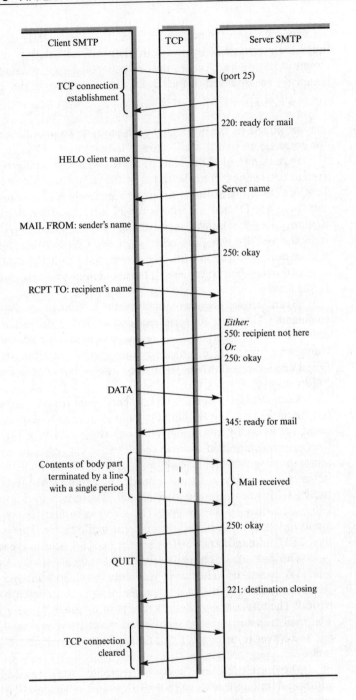

Figure 13.6   SMTP command exchange sequence.

So far we have assumed that all the intended recipient hosts use the SMTP. In practice, many other mail protocols are used in other networks. To enable mail to be exchanged with other mail systems, we must use a **mail gateway**. An example is a TCP/IP-to-OSI gateway. As the name implies, it acts as a mail transfer point between the two dissimilar mail systems/network protocols. Mail received using SMTP at one network port is forwarded using MOTIS – the ISO mail protocol – at the other network port. A number of other gateway services can be performed in the same way.

13.1.5   SNMP

The three application protocols we have discussed so far – TELNET, FTP, and SMTP – are all concerned with providing networkwide user application services. In contrast, the **simple network management protocol (SNMP)** is concerned not with user services but rather with management of all the communication protocols within each host and the various items of networking equipment that provide these services – in other words, the total networking environment.

Recall from Part 2 that a typical open system networking environment comprises a range of different items of networking equipment. These include bridges for the interconnection of similar LAN segments, routers for the interconnection of dissimilar LANs, packet switches for use in packet switching networks, various types of internetwork gateways for the interconnection of networks, the communication links that connect these, and so on.

Clearly, in any networking environment, if a fault develops and service is interrupted, users will expect the fault to be corrected and normal service to be resumed with a minimum of delay. This is often referred to as **fault management**. Similarly, if the performance of the network – for example, its response time or throughput – starts to deteriorate as a result of, say, increased levels of traffic in selected parts of the network, users will expect these to be identified and additional equipment/transmission capacity to be introduced to alleviate the problem. This is an example of **performance management**. In addition, most of the protocols associated with the TCP/IP suite have associated operational parameters, such as the time-to-live parameter associated with the IP protocol and the retransmission timer associated with TCP. As a network expands, such parameters may need to be changed while the network is still operational. This type of operation is known as **layer management**. Others include **name management**, **security management**, and **accounting management**. The SNMP has been defined to help a network manager to carry out the fault and performance management functions.

The standard approach to network management is to view all the network elements that are to be managed – protocol, bridge, gateway, etc. – as **managed objects**. Associated with each managed object is a defined set of management-related information. This includes variables – also known as attributes – that can be either read or written to by the network manager via the network. It also includes, when appropriate, a set of **fault reports** that are sent by a managed object when a related fault occurs. In the case of IP, for example, a read variable may relate to, say, the number of IP datagrams discarded when the time-to-live parameter expires, while a write variable may be the actual time-to-live timeout value. Similarly, in the case of a gateway, if a neighbor gateway ceases to respond to hello messages, in addition to modifying its routing table to reflect the loss of the link, the gateway may create and send a fault report – via the network – to alert the management system to the problem. If the management system receives a number of such reports from other neighbors, it can conclude that the gateway is probably faulty, not just a communications link.

SNMP is an application protocol so we must use a standard communication platform to enable associated messages – PDUs – to be transferred concurrently with the messages relating to user services. To achieve this, SNMP normally uses the same TCP/IPs as the other three protocols discussed. The general scheme is thus as shown in Figure 13.7.

The role of the SNMP is to allow the **manager process** in the manager station to exchange management-related messages with the management processes running in the various managed elements; hosts, gateways, etc. The management process in these elements is written to perform the defined management functions associated with that element. Examples include responding to requests for

Figure 13.7
SNMP network management software.

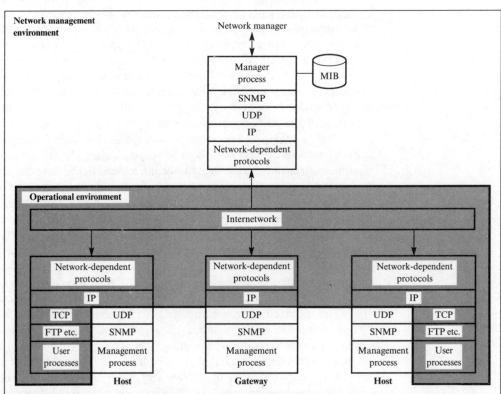

SNMP = Simple network management protocol   UDP = User datagram protocol   MIB = Management information base

specified variables (counts), receiving updated operational variables, and generating and sending fault reports.

Management information associated with a network/internet is kept at the network manager station (host) in a **management information base (MIB)**. A network manager is provided with a range of services to interrogate the information in the MIB, to initiate the entry and collection of additional information, and to initiate network configuration changes. Clearly, the manager station is the nerve center of the complete network, so strict security and authentication mechanisms are implemented. Normally, there are various levels of authority depending on the operation to be performed. In large internetworks, multiple manager stations may be used, each responsible for a particular part of the internet.

To reflect the wide range of objects to be managed, management information is often stored in a **relational database** since the information held for a single managed object is often used in several parts of the database. A simple hierarchical structure is shown in Figure 13.8.

At the top of the hierarchy is the internetwork which consists of a number of major entities, including directory services, network elements, and security services. Network elements include networks, interior and exterior gateways and, if subnets are involved, routers and bridges. At the leaves of the branches are the managed objects, each of which has a unique name. In addition, a defined set of variables/fault reports are associated with each object. Hence a major role of the

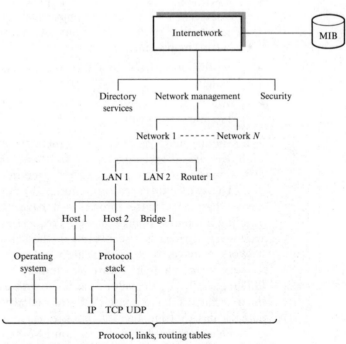

Figure 13.8
Management object hierarchy (information tree).

MIB = Management information base

authority responsible for managing and running an internet is to define the structure – known as the management information tree – and contents of the MIB. All equipment suppliers must be informed of the management information that is required for that equipment and how it is to be gathered.

The actual managed objects – and hence management information – associated with an internet may differ from one open system to another. Consequently, SNMP has been defined to gather management information in a variety of networking environments. Thus the meaning of the management information being transferred is transparent to the SNMP which simply offers a defined set of services, each with an associated set of parameters (in a defined syntax). The various management processes interpret the transferred information/commands in a defined way. This is more in line with the mode of operation of the ISO protocols than the three protocols already discussed, reflecting the fact that SNMP is a more recently introduced protocol. Recall that these three protocols integrate many application-dependent functions into their normal operation.

The user services/commands – and matching PDUs – associated with the SNMP are of the remote procedure/operation type and are thus very simple. Three primitives are available to the manager process:

- *get request*   Used to request the current value(s) associated with a declared variable (or list of variables) relating to a managed object

- *get-next-request*   Used to request the next value associated with a variable, such as a table, that comprises a list of elements

- *set-request*   Used to transfer a value to be assigned to a specified variable associated with a managed object such as an operational parameter associated with a protocol layer and two primitives which are available to the (agent) management process

- *get-response*   Used to return the value(s) associated with an earlier get-request

- *trap*   Used to report the occurrence of a fault condition, such as the loss of communication with a neighbor

The resulting messages – PDUs – generated by the SNMP in response to these primitives are all exchanged using UDP and are defined in ASN.1. A simplified definition to illustrate the approach is given in Figure 13.9.

The two SNMP protocol entities do not retain state information, which means that the manager process can have a number of outstanding requests awaiting responses. Hence, each GETrequest PDU contains a request identifier – requestID – which is also present in the subsequent response and enables the network manager process to relate it to a specific request. The varBindList is a sequence containing a variable number of object name/value pairs. In a GETrequest PDU, the value associated with each object name is NULL but in the associated GETresponse PDU the actual value is returned. Since the object name is an IA5String, its meaning is transparent to SNMP.

Finally, as we shall see in Section 13.2, an ISO management protocol known as the **common management information protocol (CMIP)** is now available. This

```
SNMP_ PDUs ::=
BEGIN
PDU ::= CHOICE {
                    GETrequest,
                    GET_NEXTrequest,
                    SETrequest,
                    GETresponse,
                    TRAP }
GETrequest ::= SEQUENCE {
                    requestID [0] INTEGER,
                    errorStatus [1] INTEGER,
                    errorIndex [2] INTEGER,
                    varBindList [3] SEQUENCE {
                                        objectID IA5String,
                                        value NULL }
                                }
GET_NEXTrequest ::=
                    |
                    |
                    |
END
```

Figure 13.9
Simplified ASN.1
definition of SNMP
PDUs.

has more sophisticated features than SNMP and may be more suitable for larger networks/internets. Because of this, it is likely to be the preferred network management protocol for some networks that nevertheless use TCP/IP rather than the equivalent ISO protocols. When used with a TCP/IP suite, the CMIP is known as **CMOT** – CMIP over TCP/IP.

13.2 ISO application protocols

In addition to the various application-support protocols described in Chapter 12, a complete suite of application-specific protocols (application service elements, ASEs) have been defined. Most are now full international standards (ISs) while others are still in draft form (DISs). Some provide similar services to the TCP/IP application protocols described in Section 13.1, while others provide additional services. The current list of ISO application protocols includes:

● *Virtual terminal (VT)* This IS provides similar services to the TELNET protocol.

● *File transfer access and management (FTAM)* This IS provides similar services to the FTP.

● *Message-oriented text interchange standard (MOTIS)* This IS provides similar services to the SMTP.

● *Common management information protocol (CMIP)* This IS provides similar services to the SNMP.

● *Job transfer and manipulation (JTM)* This IS provides a facility for a user AP to submit a job (work specification) to a remote AP for processing.

- *Manufacturing messaging service (MMS)* This IS provides a standard means whereby an AP running in a supervisory computer associated with an automated manufacturing plant can send manufacturing-related messages to a distributed community of other APs controlling a numerical machine tool, programmable controller, robot, and so on.

- *Remote database access (RDA)* This DIS provides a facility to enable an AP to access a remote database management system (DBMS).

- *Distributed transaction processing (DTP)* This DIS provides the necessary support services to enable two APs to communicate according to the rules defined in Chapter 12 for the CCR protocol.

As with the TCP/IP application protocols, the aim of the various ISO protocols is to enable two APs running in different computer systems to communicate with each other to carry out a particular distributed application function. With FTAM, for example, the aim is to enable a client process running in one computer to interact with a file server process running in a remote (and possibly different) computer, as if the client process were running in the same computer as the server.

To achieve this goal, the ISO approach is to define a virtual device model for each distributed application function – a virtual terminal, virtual file store, virtual manufacturing device, and so on. The two communicating ASEs (and hence protocols) are implemented as if the two communicating APs both operate according to this model. In this way, all (user) services associated with each ASE have a standard form and the protocol associated with the ASE can be implemented independently of any variations that might exist between the two communicating processes. Any differences that do exist are resolved outside of the open system interconnection environment by the user element that is linked with the AP. The services associated with the presentation layer then ensure that data that is exchanged between the two communicating processes has a common meaning to both processes. We shall now look at the main ISO protocols.

13.2.1 VT

The **virtual terminal (VT)** ASE enables a user at a terminal to interact with an AP running in a remote computer as if the terminal were connected directly to that computer. A wide variety of terminals exist, each with different operational characteristics. For example, there are **scroll mode terminals** that operate with single characters, **screen** or **page mode terminals** that operate with a complete screen of characters, and **form mode terminals** that are normally used in applications involving selected character/word positions to be entered against a fixed (form) template. There are many variations in each category, and a considerable amount of existing application software has been written for use with such terminals. The aim of the VT ASE is to enable such applications to be accessed in an open way using a variety of terminals.

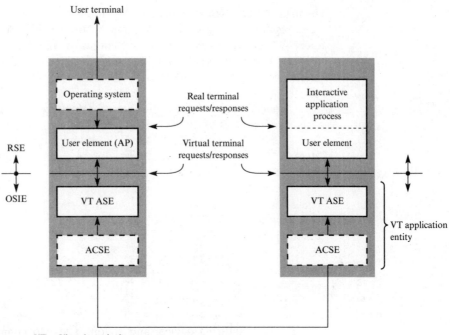

Figure 13.10
VT interaction
schematic.

VT   = Virtual terminal
ASE = Application service element
ACSE = Association control service element

Unlike the TELNET protocol, the client VT ASE (protocol) does not provide a
direct terminal interface. Instead, a local AP – user element – must always be used
to manage the interaction with the terminal. This user element interacts with the
client VT ASE according to the defined VT characteristics. If necessary, it also
performs any mapping operations between the characteristics of the two
terminals. The general scheme is shown in Figure 13.10.

Because of the wide variety of terminals, there is not just one VT. The
VT ASE allows two users to negotiate the specific VT characteristics that
are required for an application. Before any interactions can take place, both
users must agree on what is known as the **virtual terminal environment (VTE)**
that will apply for the application. In some instances only a small number of
operational parameters need to be negotiated, while others involve a much
larger number.

A number of **standard profiles** have been defined to help the two users to
negotiate the operational parameters (characteristics). The two users can adopt
the parameters relating to a specific profile or negotiate selected parameter
changes.

The two VT users communicate with one another through a shared data
structure known as the **conceptual communication area (CCA)**. A separate
copy of the CCA is maintained by each VT protocol entity. Changes to the
contents of the CCA held by each entity are initiated when the local user

element/process issues a defined VT request service primitive at the interface. The resulting changes are carried out on the local CCA and then relayed to the peer VT entity in the remote system using the VT protocol and associated PDUs. The transferred changes are then carried out and relayed to the peer user process using a matching indication primitive. The general scheme is shown in Figure 13.11(a).

Each CCA contains a number of data structures that collectively describe the characteristics of the VT being used. These are shown in Figure 13.11(b).

Associated with each terminal input and output device – keyboard, mouse, display, printer, etc. – are three objects, each comprised of a number of parameters. The objects are:

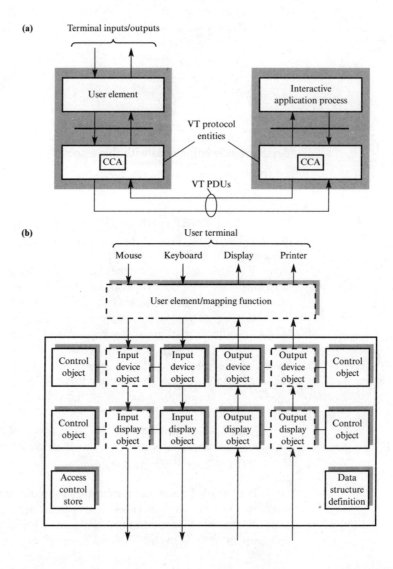

Figure 13.11
VT protocol data structures:
(a) conceptual communication area;
(b) object definitions.

- **Display objects**   These allow events relating to the associated real device to be represented by corresponding events associated with the virtual device. A display object consists of an array of elements, each holding a single character from the character set associated with the VT.

- **Control objects**   These are used to model terminal features that are not normally triggered by the user, such as a bell.

- **Device objects**   These model characteristics of the associated real device. A set of boolean variables associated with each device object indicates the state of items such as the on–off switch.

Synchronous and asynchronous modes of operation are supported. In the synchronous mode, the input and output functions at each side of a connection/association are combined. A number of tokens must be used to control the order of interaction between the user and the remote process. In the asynchronous mode, the input and output functions are separate, enabling each side to initiate an event concurrently. The **access control store (ACS)** holds the current assignment of the tokens being used when the synchronous mode has been selected. In practice, tokens are transferred using the token control service provided by the session (through presentation) layer. The **data structure definition (DSD)** contains the type definitions of the parameters associated with the display, control, and device objects being used with this association.

User services

The VT ASE is used in conjunction with the ACSE support protocol. Consequently, primitives exist to establish an association:

VT_ASSOCIATE.request/indication/response/confirm

to negotiate the terminal characteristics to be used with this association:

VT_START_NEG.request/indication/response/confirm
VT_NEG_INVITE.request/indication
VT_NEG_OFFER.request/indication
VT_NEG_ACCEPT.request/indication
VT_NEG_REJECT.request/indication
VT_END_NEG.request/indication/response/confirm

to initiate the transfer of the changes associated with the CCA:

VT_DATA.request/indication

to control any token(s) that may be in use (synchronous mode):

VT_REQUEST_TOKEN.request/indication
VT_GIVE_TOKEN.request/indication

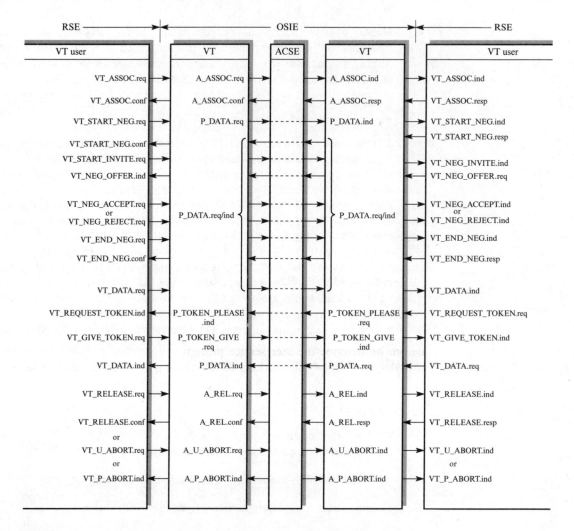

Figure 13.12
VT user services and
ACSE interaction.

and finally to terminate an association:

VT_RELEASE.request/indication/response/confirm
VT_U_ABORT.request/indication
VT_P_ABORT.indication

The VT protocol entity generates a PDU in response to each of the service primitives. These are transferred to the peer entity as shown in Figure 13.12. The PDUs generated by the **VT_ASSOCIATE, RELEASE,** and **ABORT** primitives are transferred as user data with the equivalent **A_ASSOCIATE** primitives of ACSE. The PDUs relating to the remainder are transferred using **P_DATA** except for the two token control PDUs which are sent using the **P_TOKEN_PLEASE** and **P_TOKEN_GIVE** services.

13.2.2 FTAM

Note that the various ASEs are not concerned with providing a specific application service but rather with allowing a related service provided by a user AP in the real system environment (RSE) to be accessed and used in an open way. As an example, the file transfer access and management (FTAM) ASE allows a distributed community of client processes (APs) to access and manage a remote file server implemented as a user AP running on a computer, possibly from a different manufacturer from the client system. Each client process (and hence the application entity to which it is attached) is referred to as an **initiator AP** and the server process as the **responder AP** as shown in Figure 13.13.

The primitives used by the client APs to access and manage the remote file store, as well as the primitives used to access and manage the real file store, are local (that is, machine dependent) matters. In this way, existing file systems and associated access software can be used. All the user needs to provide (assuming the OSI software is in place) is the associated user element to perform the necessary mapping functions.

Virtual file store model

Before we describe the user service primitives associated with FTAM, we must consider the (virtual) file store model to which the primitives relate. Clearly, the

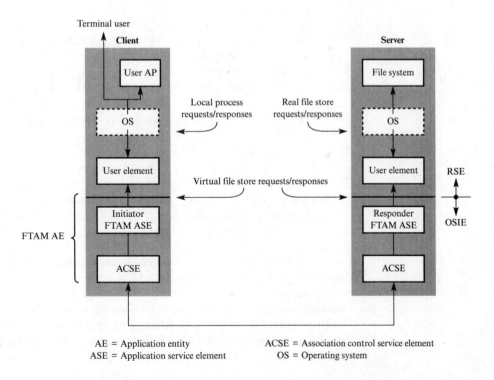

Figure 13.13
FTAM virtual device
interfaces.

AE = Application entity   ACSE = Association control service element
ASE = Application service element   OS = Operating system

aim is to adopt a model that is sufficiently flexible to allow any real file system to be readily accessed and managed with a minimum set of mapping functions.

The virtual file store is modeled as an addressable entity with which a remote user (initiator) may communicate (have an association). An arbitrary number of initiators may have an association with the (responder) file store at any one time. The file store may comprise an arbitrary number of files, each of which has a number of associated attributes, including:

- A filename: this allows the file to be referenced unambiguously.

- Permitted actions: these indicate the range of actions (read, insert, replace, etc.) that can be performed on the file.

- Access control: read-only, read-write, etc.

- File size.

- Presentation context of file contents.

- Identity of creator.

- Date and time of creation.

- Identity of last modifier/reader.

- Date and time of last access.

- Content type.

- Encryption key.

There are three commonly used file structures: unstructured, flat, and hierarchical. As the name implies, there is no apparent structure to an **unstructured file**. An example is a text file. Although this has structure to the user, it is transparent to the file system and hence only complete files can be read or written.

A **flat file** consists of an ordered sequence of records (data units), which may be of variable length and type. Normally, each record has an identifier (label) associated with it enabling individual records to be read or written. However, note that even though a record may comprise a number of (user identifiable) data elements, these are not identifiable by the file system.

A **hierarchical file**, in addition to having identifiable records, has an associated structure. This is a tree structure with a number of branch nodes. Typically, each branch node has an associated identifier and a data record. The nodes are normally identified in a known order so that a node can be identified by its position relative to other nodes. Alternatively, if it has an associated identifier, a node can be identified by giving a path name from the root. The other two structures are special cases of the hierarchical structure. The virtual file store selected by ISO is based on a hierarchical structure. The related structure and terminology are shown in Figure 13.14.

The structure of the tree consists of a **single root node** with **internal nodes** and **leaves** connected by directed **arcs**. A node can belong to only one level. Each node gives access to its **subtree**, which is known as a **file access data unit (FADU)**. The contents of a file in the file store are held in one or more **data units (DUs)**. At most, there can be only one DU assigned to a node, which means that a DU may be

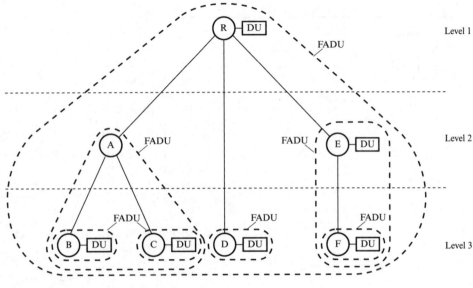

Figure 13.14
Virtual file store access
structure.

DU   = Data unit
FADU = File access data unit
R, A, B, C, D, E, F = Identifiers

accessed by the identification of the node FADU. Access to each node within the FADU is in the assumed order: R, A, B, C, D, E, F.

A DU is a typed data object (scalar, vector, set) and contains elements of atomic data called **data elements**. Associated with each data element is an abstract syntax (character, octet, integer, etc.); all the elements within a DU are related. The normal relationship of elements is in the form of a tree, although alternative relationships, such as a single data element or a vector, may be used. The tree is traversed in the order just outlined; the accessed DUs are passed to the presentation entity in the same sequence. The presentation entity treats each element as independent and uses the corresponding (negotiated) transfer syntax to transfer the elements while maintaining their relative order.

The actions relating to the file store are invoked by corresponding service primitives. These include create, open, close, and delete on complete files, and locate, read, insert, replace, extend, and erase on the DUs within a file.

Service primitives

Given this brief overview of the virtual file store model, we can now define the user service primitives associated with FTAM. These services are grouped into a nested set of **regimes**, as shown in Figure 13.15(a). A corresponding regime is entered as progressively more contextual details are established.

Associated with each regime is a defined set of service primitives, as shown in the simplified state transition diagram in Figure 13.15(b). A summary of the services associated with each regime is as follows:

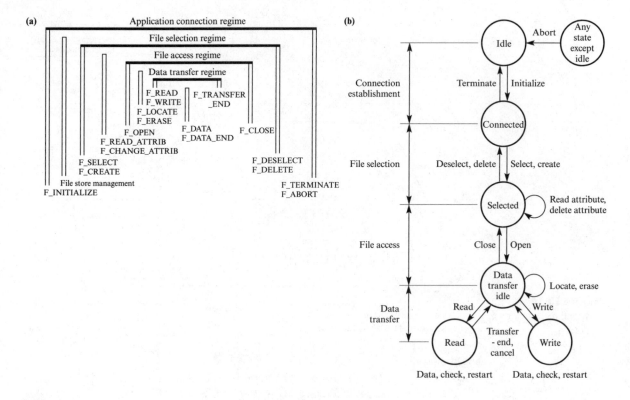

Figure 13.15
FTAM service
primitives: (a) services
regimes; (b) simplified
state transition
diagram.

- **Application connection (association)** is not specific to FTAM but rather relates to ACSE. In relation to FTAM, it establishes the authorization and accounting information necessary for the ensuing operations on the file store.

- **File selection** identifies (or creates) a unique file (FADU) to which operations in subsequent phases relate. The selection (identification) process is in terms of a file name; operations performed in subsequent phases relate to this file.

- **File access** establishes a regime in which file data transfer can take place. It includes the establishment of both the capabilities required for the transfer and a suitable access context.

- **Data transfer** includes commands (read, write, etc.) that relate to actions on the DU within the accessed (identified) FADU. Smaller data elements may be identified for presentation purposes but they cannot be accessed individually.

As with some of the other protocol layers, the service primitives associated with FTAM are grouped into a number of functional units (FUs). FUs required during a specific (dialog) session are specified during the association establishment phase. Supported FUs include:

- **Kernel** Provides facilities for application association and termination, file selection (deselection), and file opening (closing).

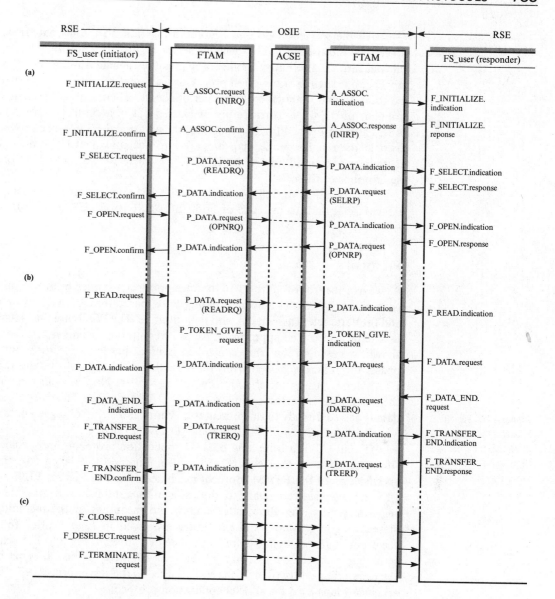

Figure 13.16
FTAM service
primitive: (a),
(c) kernel FU;
(b) read FU.

- **Read**   Provides facilities for reading files (bulk data) and individual DUs.
- **Write**   Provides facilities for writing files (bulk data) and individual DUs.
- **File access**   Provides facilities for locating and erasing FADUs.
- **Limited file management**   Provides facilities for file creation and deletion and for reading attributes.

Some of the primitives associated with each FU are shown in the time sequence diagram of Figure 13.16. Note that for brevity only the request primitives are shown in Figure 13.16(c). In practice, they are each confirmed services.

All the services shown in Figure 13.16 relate to the **normal transfer mode** since they are used primarily when a server maintains a separate set of files for each client. An alternative mode, known as the **reliable transfer mode**, is used in applications such as transaction processing, where it is common for a single file to be accessed and updated by a number of clients concurrently. All changes to the contents of the file must therefore be carried out in a controlled way. The CCR ASE has been defined for this function; the additional FTAM primitives that are used in the reliable mode map directly into an equivalent CCR primitive. The mappings are listed in Table 13.3. Refer back to Section 12.8 for further descriptions of these.

To operate in the reliable mode, the FTAM application entity consists of the FTAM ASE and an instance of both the ACSE and CCR application-support ASEs.

Protocol

As we can see from Figure 13.16, on receipt of each service primitive, the FTAM protocol entity creates a corresponding PDU based on the service primitive type and the parameters associated with the primitive. The PDUs are then passed in the user data field of the appropriate ACSE/presentation primitive. In the sequence shown, we assume that the data token is used; hence, before the data transfer phase, the token is passed from the initiating FTAM entity to the responding FTAM entity using the P_TOKEN_GIVE service. Note that in the data phase there is no PDU corresponding to the F_DATA service. This is because the file data is passed directly to the presentation entity as a string of tagged data elements – in their abstract syntax – using the P_DATA service.

Finally, to illustrate how the ISO application protocols are specified and to formalize some of the sequences shown in Figure 13.16, a part of the formal specification of the FTAM protocol machine is given in Figures 13.17 and 13.18. The parts considered relate to the association establishment and file selection regimes. Firstly, the abbreviated names and meanings of the incoming events, states, outgoing events, and predicates are given in Figure 13.17 followed by the event–state tables in Figure 13.18. The two tables in Figure 13.18 relate to the initiating protocol entity (that is, the entity linked to the client process) and the responding entity (that is, the entity linked to the server process). This mode of specification is used for all ISO application protocols.

Table 13.3   FTAM to CCR mappings for reliable file service.

FTAM	*CCR*	*Use*
F_BEGIN_GROUP	C_BEGIN	Signal the start of an atomic transaction
F_END_GROUP	C_COMMIT	Signal the end of the atomic transaction
F_RECOVER	C_ROLLBACK	Return to start of atomic transaction
F_RESTART	C_RESTART	Indicates current state of the sending side

(a)

Name	Interface	Meaning
F_INIRQ	FS_user	F_INITIALIZE.request received
F_INIRP	FS_user	F_INITIALIZE.response received
F_SELRQ	FS_user	F_SELECT.request received
F_SELRP	FS_user	F_SELECT.response received
INIRQ	CS_provider	Initialize request PDU received
INIRP	CS_provider	Initialize response PDU received
SELRQ	PS_provider	Select request PDU received
SELRP	PS_provider	Select response PDU received

(b)

Name	Meaning
STA 0	Application connection closed
STA 1	Association pending
STA 2	Application connection open
STA 3	Select pending
STA 4	Selected

(c)

Name	Interface	Meaning
F_INIIN	FS_user	F_INITIALIZE.indication issued
F_INICF	FS_user	F_INITIALIZE.confirm issued
F_SELIN	FS_user	F_SELECT.indication issued
F_SELCF	FS_user	F_SELECT.confirm issued
INIRQ	CS_provider	Initialize request PDU issued
INIRP	CS_provider	Initialize response PDU received
SELRQ	PS_provider	Select request PDU issued
SELRP	PS_provider	Select response PDU issued
F_ABTIN	FS_user	F_ABORT.indication issued
ABTRQ	CS_provider	Abort request PDU issued

(d)

Name	Meaning
P1	F_INITIALIZE.request acceptable
P2	INIRP PDU acceptable
P3	INIRQ PDU acceptable
P4	SELRP PDU acceptable
P5	F_SELECT.response acceptable

(e)

Name	Meaning
[1]	Initialize state variables
[2]	Set rejection parameter accordingly

Figure 13.17 Abbreviated names for FTAM protocol machine: (a) incoming events; (b) automaton states; (c) outgoing events; (d) predicates; (e) specific actions.

(a)

State / Event	STA 0	STA 1	STA 2	STA 3	---
F_INIRQ	1	0	0	0	
INIRP	0	2	0	0	
F_SELRQ	0	0	3	0	
SELRP	0	0	0	4	
⋮					

0 = F_ABTIN, ABTRQ, STA 0
1 = P1: INIRQ, [1], STA 1;
    NOT P1: F_INICF, [2], STA 0
2 = P2: F_INICF, STA 2;
    NOT P2: F_INICF, [2], STA 0
3 = SELRQ, STA 3
4 = P4: F_SELCF, STA 4;
    NOT P4: F_SELCF, [2], STA 2

(b)

State / Event	STA 0	STA 1	STA 2	STA 3	---
INIRQ	1	0	0	0	
F_INIRP	0	2	0	0	
SELRQ	0	0	3	0	
F_SELRP	0	0	0	4	
⋮					

0 = F_ABTIN, ABTRQ, STA 0
1 = P3: F_INIIN, [1], STA 1;
    NOT P3: INIRP, [2], STA 0
2 = INIRP, STA 2;
3 = F_SELIN, STA 3
4 = P5: SELRP, STA 4;
    NOT P5: SELRP, [2], STA 2

Figure 13.18
Event–state table for FTAM protocol machine: (a) initiating entity; (b) responder entity.

13.2.3 MOTIS

MOTIS, the ISO electronic mail system, plays a similar role to the SMTP in the TCP/IP suite. In practice, MOTIS is a complete message (mail) transfer system rather than a single protocol. It is thus also known as the ISO **message handling system (MHS)** and is based on the public X.400 message handling service which has been defined by ITU-T.

ITU-T recommendation X.400 has been defined to provide an international electronic messaging service that is similar in principle to the current (hand delivered) mail system. It consists of a suite of protocols each of which performs a specific function in relation to the complete MHS. The various entities (and their associated protocols) that make up the set of X.400 recommendations are identified in Figure 13.19.

The user interface to the system is assumed to be a terminal (such as a personal computer) that has sufficient processing and memory capabilities to enable the user interactively to create a message (mail) and to read and browse through messages that have been received. This is one of the functions of the **user agent (UA)**. Also, since the MHS should be used for a variety of message types, the UA must be able to communicate with a similar peer UA in a remote terminal so that a transferred message has the same meaning in both terminals. This is the role

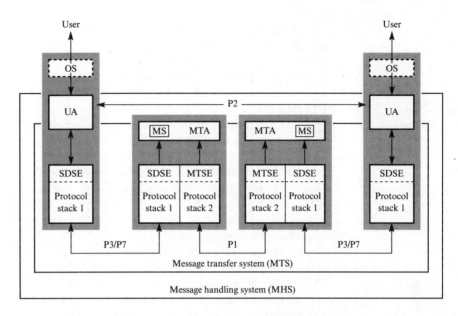

Figure 13.19
X.400 functional
model.

OS = Operating system   SDSE = Submit/deliver service element

UA = User agent   MTSE = Message transfer service element

MTA = Message transfer agent   MS = Message store

of the **P2 protocol**. Clearly, the structure and meaning of messages will differ from one application to another so a suite of protocols is defined, each protocol intended for use in a particular application domain. For example, the standard relating to simple person-to-person messaging is known as the **interpersonal messaging (IPM) protocol**.

Once a message has been prepared and the UA has added its own protocol information, it is passed to a companion service element known as the **submit/ deliver service element (SDSE)**. The role of SDSE is to control the submission and reception of messages to and from the equivalent of the local post office, known as the **message transfer agent (MTA)**. A defined protocol is used for controlling the transfer of messages between the SDSE and its local MTA. Known simply as the **P3 protocol**, it covers the submission and delivery procedures together with related functions such as charging.

UAs communicate with one another using globally unique names. However, within the MTS fully qualified addresses are used, that is, PSAP addresses. On receipt of a message, the local MTA must first perform a name-to-address translation. The structures of the names and addresses are defined in ITU-T recommendation X.500. Associated with the MTA is a directory service agent which performs this translation function (see Chapter 14). Essentially, if the two user terminals are both connected to, say, the international X.25 network, then the addresses are the X.121 addresses of the terminals and have the structure described in Chapter 8. Alternatively, if an internetwork is being used, then addresses of the type described in Chapter 9 are used.

Once the MTA has obtained the addresses, it creates the equivalent of an electronic envelope by adding the address of both the originator (sender) and recipient (receiver) – together with other information specific to the MTS – to the head of the message received from the UA. It then sends the message using the appropriate protocol stack under the control of a third protocol known as the **P1 protocol**.

On receipt of a message addressed to one of its UAs (terminals), an MTA tries to deliver it to the SDSE in the terminal using the P3 protocol. However, since the user terminal is normally located remotely from the MTA, it might be switched off or out of service. To allow for this, an MTA has a **message store (MS)** associated with it. If a UA is not available, the message is deposited into the MS for later delivery. A fourth protocol, known as the **P7 protocol**, is then used to control the interaction between a user, through its UA, and the local MS to retrieve any waiting messages.

Although this description relates to the X.400 public messaging service, the ISO MHS is based on this to ensure compatibility. A typical private system for use with a large site is shown in Figure 13.20.

A site-wide messaging system must be able to support both local messaging and intersite messaging. In the example, each user terminal (workstation, personal computer, etc.) communicates with a site-wide message server. If a received message is addressed to a user at the same site, the MTA in the server either relays it directly to the recipient or places it in the local message store for later delivery. Alternatively, if the message is addressed to a user off-site, since it is a private system, it must initiate the submission of the message to the public X.400 system. Typically, the message server has a direct connection to the same public network as is used by the X.400 MTS. Hence, in Figure 13.20 we assume that the server has an MTA associated with it. If this is not the case, an SDSE is used.

Message format

As indicated earlier, there is a range of different message types, each with its own P2 protocol. However, irrespective of the message type all messages consist of an MTS header – the envelope – and the message contents. The addresses and other fields in the header are used by the MTS to transfer the message to its intended destination. These are in a standard form for all message types. In the same way as the contents of an envelope in normal hand-delivered mail (a letter, invoice, etc.) have an additional heading for use by the recipient, so the message contents have an additional heading for use by the UA. This heading changes for different messaging applications – personal (letters, memos, etc.), business (invoices, orders, etc.), and so on. As an example, the structure and contents of a message relating to the IPM protocol are shown in Figure 13.21.

In practice, both the MTS header and the contents heading can have many more fields than are shown. Also, the MHS allows for different types of user terminal. Hence, if the recipient terminal is different from the originator's terminal, then the MTA will endeavor to perform the necessary conversion. If

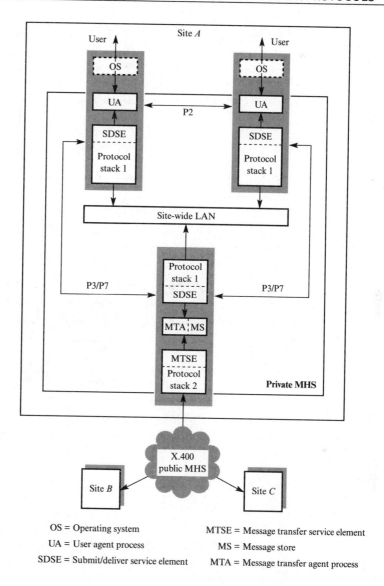

Figure 13.20
MOTIS functional
model.

OS = Operating system   MTSE = Message transfer service element
UA = User agent process   MS = Message store
SDSE = Submit/deliver service element   MTA = Message transfer agent process

it cannot do this, the message will be discarded and an appropriate reason
code returned to the originator's MTA and from there to the UA. An example
conversion might be from an X.400 terminal – and hence character set – to a
Teletex or telex terminal.

The **encryption identifier** field in the MTS header, in common with the other
fields, is just an example from a group of fields that collectively enable the initiator
MTA to specify the type of security level being used with the message contents
during their transfer across the MTS. If the message contents are being encrypted,
the encryption identifier will enable the destination MTA to select the appropriate
key for decryption. Other fields include a checksum on the contents – or encrypted

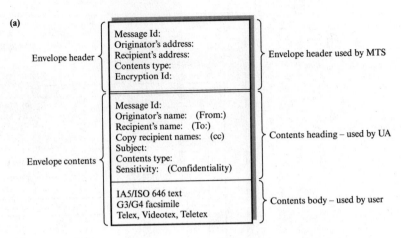

(a)

Envelope header {
```
Message Id:
Originator's address:
Recipient's address:
Contents type:
Encryption Id:
```
} Envelope header used by MTS

Envelope contents {
```
Message Id:
Originator's name:   (From:)
Recipient's name:   (To:)
Copy recipient names:   (cc)
Subject:
Contents type:
Sensitivity:   (Confidentiality)
```
} Contents heading – used by UA

```
IA5/ISO 646 text
G3/G4 facsimile
Telex, Videotex, Teletex
```
} Contents body – used by user

(b)

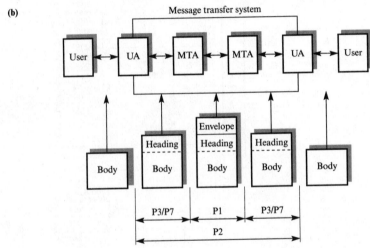

Figure 13.21
Message formats:
(a) interpersonal
message format;
(b) message
construction.

contents – or the digital signature of the originator and/or recipient. See Section 12.4 for further descriptions of these. Also, note that unlike the SMTP, the complete message contents, including the heading, are treated as a single entity for encryption purposes.

MHS protocols

As Figures 13.19 and 13.20 showed, the ASEs and associated protocol stack differ with each protocol. In practice, the SDSE is made up of three separate service elements, as we can see in Figure 13.22.

The two ASEs associated with the P3 protocol are the **message submission service element (MSSE)** and the **message delivery service element (MDSE)**, while the ASE associated with the P7 protocol is the **message retrieval service element (MRSE)**. The MSSE controls the submission of messages by the UA to its local MTA. Similarly, the MDSE controls the delivery of the received messages from

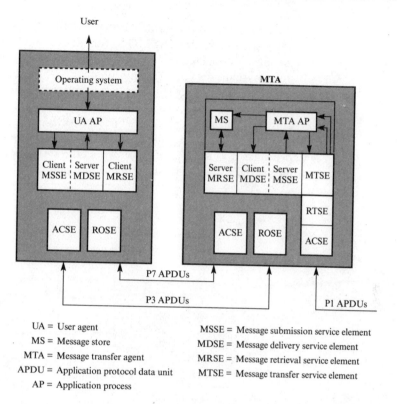

Figure 13.22
MHS protocols.

UA = User agent
MS = Message store
MTA = Message transfer agent
APDU = Application protocol data unit
AP = Application process

MSSE = Message submission service element
MDSE = Message delivery service element
MRSE = Message retrieval service element
MTSE = Message transfer service element

the MTA to the recipient UA. The MSRE is used by a UA to retrieve stored messages from the MS.

Both protocols use the ACSE and ROSE application-support protocols. Recall that ACSE allows an association to be established between the two message handling ASEs, whereas ROSE allows for a general remote invocation-request/ reply-message transfer service. In this application, the message is carried in either the request (MSSE) or the reply (MDSE/MRSE).

The **message transfer service element (MTSE)** associated with the P1 protocol is used with the RTSE and ACSE service elements. Recall that RTSE is an early protocol that uses ACSE and the session activity service. It enables a single message – or series of messages – to be transferred reliably between two (MTSE) ASEs using a basic stop-and-wait protocol. The remainder of the protocol stack used with each application entity depends on the type of network/link being used. In the case of the P3 and P7 protocols, this can be a LAN or a dial-up circuit. Similarly, for the P1 protocol it can be an X.25-based PSPDN, a frame relay ISDN, or a private internetwork.

13.2.4 SMAE

The ISO network management protocol that is equivalent to the SNMP in a TCP/IP suite is known as the **common management information service element**

(CMISE). This is only one component of the complete OSI **system management application entity (SMAE)**. One function of the SMAE is to allow a network manager to manage remotely the various (managed) objects associated with an open system networking environment – protocols, bridges, routers, packet switches, etc. It also provides a general facility for managing any networking system such as the various systems and subsystems that make up a complete telecommunications network. The CMISE provides only a basic service for sending and receiving management-related messages. Additional functionality is provided by a second ASE known as the **system management application service element (SMASE)**. The structure of the complete SMAE is shown in Figure 13.23.

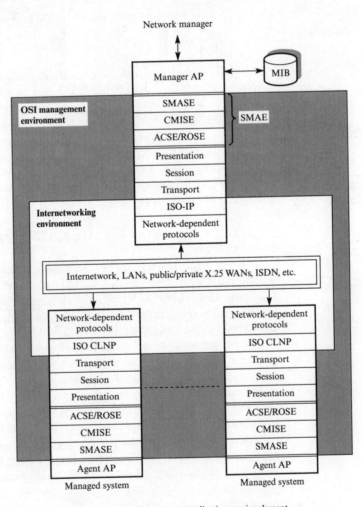

Figure 13.23
OSI system management components.

SMASE = System management application service element
CMISE = Common management information service element
SMAE = System management application entity
MIB = Management information base

All systems that contain one or more managed objects – that is, network elements that are to be managed by the network manager – must contain the complete SMAE. Also, although not shown in Figure 12.23, in some cases management processes may use the file transfer services of the FTAM/ACSE application entity, for example, to download object code after an object has been initialized. The manager, through the manager AP and the associated MIB, interacts with the agent AP associated with a particular system to manage the various (managed) objects associated with that system. As with a TCP/IP suite, the MIB at the manager station contains configuration, performance, fault, and other information relating to the complete network. The various software components associated with the manager AP provide the manager with the necessary facilities to manage the complete network.

Terminology

Before we discuss the operation of the two management service elements, let us define some of the relevant terminology.

The term **managed object (MO)** originates from the object-oriented design methodology on which the overall structure is based. It refers to any network element that is to be managed. Also, all elements to be managed must be logically represented by a managed object in the MIB. Thus, a managed object is a logical representation of a real item of hardware, software, data structure, etc. It is defined by the following:

- The **attributes** associated with it

- The **management operations** that can be applied to it

- The **behavior** it exhibits in response to applied operations

- The **notifications** (events) that it can generate

Although in practice a managed object may be the logical representation of a complicated item of equipment – a bridge, router, computer, etc. – as far as the network management system is concerned, only those attributes, operations, behaviour, and notifications that have been defined for use with it in the MIB are visible to the network management system. This style of representation is based on the object-oriented design feature of **encapsulation** (or **information hiding**) which means that all implementation and other related details are hidden from the network management system.

An attribute – normally referred to as a variable in the SNMP – is a property of a managed object that reflects its current state. An attribute can have one or more values associated with it, such as a bridge port, a retransmission counter, a timer setting, or the contents of a routing table. Any operations to be performed on an attribute are directed to the managed object to which the attribute relates rather than to the attribute directly. It is then a local matter how the managed object (procedure/program) carries out the specified operation.

Operations that can be performed on the attributes of a managed object are as follows:

- **Get attribute value** returns the attribute value(s).

- **Set attribute value** sets the specified attributes to the values supplied with the operation.

- **Derive attribute value** sets the specified attributes to their default (or other previously specified) values.

- **Add attribute value** adds additional values to an attribute comprising a set of values.

- **Remove attribute value** removes values from a set of attribute values.

In addition, the following three operations relate to a complete managed object rather than to an attribute:

- **Create** creates a new managed object.

- **Delete** deletes an existing managed object.

- **Action** performs an action relating to this type of object.

A notification is emitted by a managed object when an internal or external event occurs. An example of an external event is the loss of communication with a neighboring element. An internal notification might be a retransmission count exceeding a defined limit. Notifications are also known as **event reports**.

The behaviour of a managed object relates to the effect of operations on it. It also covers the rules under which selected operations can be performed and the consequences of performing such operations. Examples include the rules relating to the creation or deletion of a managed object and the consequences of performing these functions.

All managed objects belong to a **managed object class** which defines the type of the managed object. There can be many instances of managed objects from this class, all of which have the same attributes, operations, behaviour, and notifications associated with them. However, each instance is allocated a unique name and all operations then relate to that specific instance of the managed object class. An example of a class is the ISO-TP4 transport protocol, of which there can be many instances.

Managed object classes must be specified in a standard way so that the attribute values associated with them have the same meaning to both the manager AP and the agent AP. Typically, the manager AP may run on an advanced workstation while the agent may be running on a microprocessor-based item of equipment such as a modem or router. All classes are defined using ASN.1 and a library of all classes is maintained for the total system. All attribute values relating to a managed object are then transferred in their concrete syntax form to ensure they have the same meaning in all systems.

Managed object classes are arranged in a hierarchy known as an **inheritance tree**. Each class is a subclass of its parent in the tree. The term 'inheritance' is another feature of object-oriented design and is used to indicate that a subclass

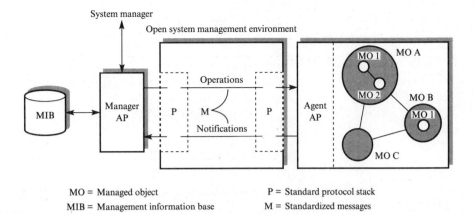

Figure 13.24
Manager–agent
interaction schematic.

MO = Managed object   P = Standard protocol stack
MIB = Management information base   M = Standardized messages

inherits all the characteristics – attributes, etc. – of its parent. When a new class is defined, only the additional characteristics that are to be associated with the new class need be defined. For example, a class **managed bridge** could be defined as a subclass of bridge. An instance of the managed bridge would have the same characteristics as an instance of bridge but, in addition, would have network management software.

Managed object classes and instances of classes have specified **relationships** with one another. For example, if two object instances are bridge 1 and LAN 2, then a relationship might be 'bridge 1 is **connected to** LAN 2'. Another relationship is that of **containment** which has the same meaning as the term *is part of*. An example might be 'port 2 **is part of** bridge 3'. Other relationships are possible, including higher-level relationships such as 'MOA is managed by NM2' or 'NM1 is managed by NM8', where MO means managed object and NM network manager. A schematic showing the use and interrelationship of some of these terms is given in Figure 13.24.

As we can see, the operations and notifications exchanged between the manager AP and an agent AP relate to a specific managed object. The intermediate SMAEs ensure that the information exchanged and the mode of interaction are carried out in an open way. It is a local matter how an agent AP carries out specified operations or generates defined notifications.

CMISE

The common management information service element (CMISE) provides the manager–agent AP above it – through the SMASE – with a generalized set of services to invoke remotely management procedures relating to operations, notifications, and other data manipulation functions. The services are of the remote operation (procedure) type; in some instances a request/reply (confirmed) message exchange is involved, while in others a unidirectional (unconfirmed) message transfer occurs. CMISE, therefore, uses the ACSE and ROSE application-support service elements. ACSE can establish an association

Table 13.4 CMIS service primitives.

Service	Type	Support ASE
M_INITIALIZE	C	ACSE
M_TERMINATE	C	ACSE
M_ABORT	U	ACSE
M_EVENT_REPORT	C/U	ROSE
M_GET	C	ROSE
M_SET	C/U	ROSE
M_ACTION	C/U	ROSE
M_CREATE	C	ROSE
M_DELETE	C	ROSE
M_CANCEL_GET	C	ROSE

C = Confirmed   U = Unconfirmed

with a peer CMISE and ROSE to relay the remote operation and notification invocation requests and, if required, responses. A list of the services provided is given in Table 13.4.

Remember that the services provided by the CMISE – known as **common management information services (CMIS)** – are general management services. Their effect is a function of the way the managed objects interpret the information associated with each service. The M_INITIALIZE, TERMINATE, and ABORT services establish an association with a specified agent AP. All the resulting APDUs map directly into the equivalent ACSE primitives. Similarly, the APDUs relating to the other services are all transferred using an appropriate ROSE primitive. The various services have a direct relationship with the operations listed earlier.

- **M_GET** is a general service that enables a manager AP to request the retrieval of management information from a specified agent AP. It is a confirmed service since there are results associated with it. An example is the retrieval of the current status of a managed object.

- **M_SET** is a general service that enables a manager AP to request the modification of some management information relating to a managed object. It can be unconfirmed or confirmed if a result is expected. An example is to set a timeout value and, if required, obtain an acknowledgment.

- **M_EVENT_REPORT** enables an agent AP to notify the manager AP of the occurrence of an event relating to a managed object. This can also be confirmed or unconfirmed.

- **M_CREATE, DELETE,** and **ACTION** all relate to a complete managed object rather than to an attribute. An example is to create a new instance of, say, a protocol entity – CREATE – and then to initialize it – ACTION.

M_CANCEL_GET is used to cancel an earlier M_GET operation. It is useful, for example, if there is a long string of result values associated with the earlier M_GET since it allows a manager to interrupt the transfer operation.

These services are general services. Each service primitive includes an **invoke identifier** that is used by the recipient to carry out a related – previously defined – management operation. The other parameters are interpreted by the recipient in relation to this. For example, the parameters associated with the M_EVENT_REPORT primitive include the following:

- *Invoke identifier*   Used to specify the notification involved and allow the recipient to relate the other parameters to this

- *Mode*   Confirmed or unconfirmed

- *Object class*   The class of the managed object

- *Object instance*   The specific managed object that has generated the notification

- *Event type*   The type of event

- *Event time*   The time it occurred

- *Event information*   Details relating to the event

The protocol associated with CMISE is known as the **common management information protocol (CMIP)**. It generates an equivalent APDU for each of the service primitives listed. Each parameter associated with a primitive has an equivalent field in the APDU. Thus, on receipt of a service primitive, a CMIP creates an equivalent APDU and sends this using the services of either ACSE or ROSE. On receipt of an APDU it performs the reverse function.

Most of the parameters associated with the CMIS that relate to the ACSE are mapped directly into the equivalent parameters of the corresponding ACSE service. However, a small number of parameters of each primitive form the APDU of CMIP and the latter is then passed in the user data parameter of the appropriate ACSE primitive. Because of the close relationship between the CMISE remote operations and notifications and the equivalent ROSE services, they are normally defined together. To illustrate this a small section of the CMIP definitions after they have been included with the ROSE operations is shown in Figure 13.25.

Remember from Section 12.7 that there are no real parameters/arguments associated with the ROSE. These are generated by the application-specific ASE to which it is linked. First, the APDU types associated with the ROSE protocol are defined and then linked with the CMIP APDU definitions. Thus the m-EventReport CMIP APDU is carried in a ROIV PDU of ROSE. The value of the **invoke identifier** parameter associated with the M_EVENT_REPORT primitive is then assigned to the invokeID field of the ROSE ROIVapdu. Each APDU associated with CMIP has a different **operation-value**; it is zero for **m-EventReport**. The argument field of the ROIVapdu is that associated with, in this case, CMIP. Hence it is that defined in Figure 13.25 relating to **EventReportArgument**. All the

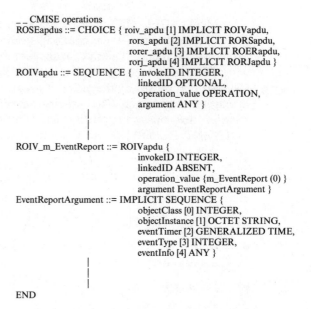

```
                          _ _ CMISE operations
                        ROSEapdus ::= CHOICE { roiv_apdu [1] IMPLICIT ROIVapdu,
                                               rors_apdu [2] IMPLICIT RORSapdu,
                                               rorer_apdu [3] IMPLICIT ROERapdu,
                                               rorj_apdu [4] IMPLICIT RORJapdu }
                        ROIVapdu ::= SEQUENCE {   invokeID INTEGER,
                                               linkedID OPTIONAL,
                                               operation_value OPERATION,
                                               argument ANY }
                                                   |
                                                   |
                                                   |
                        ROIV_m_EventReport ::= ROIVapdu {
                                               invokeID INTEGER,
                                               linkedID ABSENT,
                                               operation_value {m_EventReport (0) }
                                               argument EventReportArgument }
                        EventReportArgument ::= IMPLICIT SEQUENCE {
                                               objectClass [0] INTEGER,
                                               objectInstance [1] OCTET STRING,
                                               eventTimer [2] GENERALIZED TIME,
                                               eventType [3] INTEGER,
                                               eventInfo [4] ANY }
                                                   |
                                                   |
                                                   |
                        END
```

Figure 13.25
CMISE PDU
definition schematic in
relation to the ROSE
PDUs.

other CMIP APDUs are defined in a similar way. Other ASEs that use ROSE are all defined in a similar way.

SMASE

CMISE is now an international standard used by many of the major suppliers of telecommunications and computer networking equipment in various network management applications. However, the management services it offers are general services. Consequently, it is left to the implementer of the manager and agent APs to define the contents and structure of the MIB and the operations and notifications that can be performed on the attributes relating to each managed object. This is perfectly adequate for modest applications, such as the management of a single network. However, for the management of all aspects of a large global internetwork or telecommunications system, it means that many of the management-related functions have to be defined outside of the open system management environment. Additional issues include accounting management – charges for access or use of a managed object – and security management – access control and authentication procedures to be applied to users trying to gain access to a managed object. All these issues must be addressed by any system management facility.

Recall that the aim of the combined system management application entity (SMAE) is not just to provide services to manage the various networking elements that make up an internetwork – communication lines, packet switches, intermediate systems/gateways, routers, bridges, protocol stacks, etc. – but rather to provide the services that are necessary for a total **integrated network management system (INMS)**. To achieve this goal, as was shown earlier in Figure 13.23, the SMAE contains an additional service element on top of the CMISE known as the system management application service element (SMASE). Its function is to provide a higher level of management services on top of those provided by CMISE yet still within the open system management environment.

SMASE comprises a set of **system management functions (SMFs)**. Each SMF uses the underlying generalized services provided by CMISE to perform its own system management function. We can view the total SMAE as consisting of a set of **network management profiles**, each performing a specific management function in the context of the total integrated network management system. SMFs are also known as **management application services (MASs)**.

Each SMF provides a defined set of services that can be performed on the managed objects that relate to a particular management function. Associated with each SMF is a set of generic managed objects that relate to that function together with a definition of their attributes and the related operations and notifications. Associated with each of the managed objects in a set is the ASN.1 definition – a template – of all the parameters that are associated with each of the corresponding CMISE primitives. In this way, a management application is provided with a higher level of abstraction since it need specify only the name of a managed object, together with the list of parameters that are to be associated with the operation/ notification to be performed. SMASE then uses the corresponding ASN.1 template to create the corresponding service primitive that is compatible with those associated with CMISE.

Unlike CMISE, SMASE is still in the process of being developed. It is planned that, over a period of time, a range of SMFs/MASs will be defined as the OSI SMAE is used in various applications. Already a number of SMFs have been defined. Some are listed in Table 13.5 together with their use.

Table 13.5   A selection of system management functions and their use.

SMF	Use
Alarm reporting	Defines the syntax and semantics of events generated by managed objects
Event management reporting	Defines the mechanism for controlling and filtering the reporting of events
Log control	Defines the mechanism for establishing, controlling the operation of, and selecting the contents of the event report logs (records)
Security alarm reporting	Defines the syntax and semantics for generating alarm notifications in the event of security violations
Accounting metering	Defines the mechanism for recording and reporting the use of network resources for accounting purposes
Workload monitoring	Defines the mechanism for monitoring the use of network resources for the purpose of evaluating performance
Measurement summary	Defines the mechanism for obtaining statistical summaries of the operating characteristics of network resources
Object management	Defines the mechanism to create and delete objects and to manage the attributes associated with objects
State management	Defines object states and the mechanisms to detect and modify states
Relationship management	Defines the mechanisms for establishing and maintaining relationships between objects

MIB

The naming principles associated with the objects in an OSI environment are fully compatible with those described in Section 13.1.5 in the context of the SNMP associated with a TCP/IP suite. Thus there is a management information tree (MIT) that defines the names of all the managed objects that are present in the MIB. The tree structure reflects the containment rules associated with each instance of a managed object. The name of an instance of a managed object is a combination of the following:

- The name of the next higher-order managed object to which it is linked – its superior
- An additional name that uniquely identifies it within the scope of its superior

In this way, the name of a managed object consists of a sequence of names starting at the root and working out to that object in the tree. The total name of an object is known as its **distinguished name (DN)**, and each constituent part as its **relative distinguished name (RDN)**. The DN allows a managed object to be uniquely identified within the total management system. However, it is usually only necessary to define a name within the scope of a managed object other than the root. This is known as a **partial distinguished name (PDN)**. An example is an internetwork comprising multiple networks and a local manager referring to the names of objects within the scope of a single network.

In addition to the MIT, two other trees are defined in the MIB. One is the **inheritance tree** and the other the **registration tree**. The inheritance tree is used to show the superclass–subclass relationships between managed object classes. Thus, in the inheritance tree a particular class appears only once, whereas in the MIT multiple instances of the same class can be present at different locations within the tree. The registration tree is used to manage the assignment of identifiers to managed objects. Recall that these must be unique within the context of the total management system since they are used in CMIP APDUs.

13.2.5 MMS

The **manufacturing message service (MMS)** is an ASE that has been developed for use in fully automated manufacturing environments. Within such environments, there is often a requirement for all the computer-based equipment to exchange messages in an open way. Normally, each manufacturing cell has an associated cell controller (control computer) which, in addition to communicating on a factorywide basis with other systems using, say, FTAM, controls the computer-based equipment associated with the cell. Typically, this equipment includes robot controllers (RCs), numerical machine tool controllers (NCs), automatic guided vehicle controllers (AGVs), programmable logic controllers (PLCs), and so on. MMS has been defined to allow the cell controller to exchange messages with all this automated equipment in an open way.

A typical sequence of events might be as follows. Firstly, at a factorywide level, FTAM passes information about a part or component to a cell controller.

The controller uses MMS to send appropriate commands to the automated equipment associated with the cell to cause the part (component) to be manufactured and/or assembled. Typically, commands such as the following:

- Select and load a specific set of tools in an NC.
- Request an RC to select an item of raw material and place it on an AGV.
- Instruct the AGV to transport the material to the NC.

are issued by the cell controller (CC). Status messages are returned to the CC as tasks are completed.

Service primitives

As the specific MMS primitives associated with each device (CC, RC, NC, etc.) vary, subsets of the total service are defined for use with each type of device. For example, the services associated with a CC include the following:

- Establish an association with a specific controller (context management).
- Cause a controller to read a data file from the CC containing, say, tool data or operating instructions (obtain file).
- Download a program to a controller (program load) from the CC.
- Remotely control the operation of a controller (job control).
- Read and change (write) selected variables associated with a controller program (variable access).
- Request a controller to identify the MMS services that it supports (identity).

As with FTAM, the service primitives are grouped into a number of functional units (FUs); a list of some of the primitives associated with each FU is given in Table 13.6. Note that these are only examples and, of course, there are parameters associated with each primitive. As the table shows, MMS also supports a limited file service for local use within a cell, for example, to transfer a file containing the parts list associated with a controlled device. Of necessity, it is far less sophisticated than FTAM.

13.2.6   Job transfer and manipulation

The **job transfer and manipulation (JTM)** service is a collection of JTM SASEs located on different open systems. Collectively, the JTM elements (entities) form what is referred to as the **JTM service provider**. In the same way that FTAM does not actually implement a file service (that is, it only provides an environment for a real file system to be accessed and managed in an open way), so JTM provides an environment where documents relating to jobs, referred to as **job specifications**, may be transferred between real (open) systems and the jobs executed by them. Indeed, the type of job transferred is transparent to the JTM service provider.

The AP that submits a specification of an OSI job, through an associated UE, is known as the **initiating agency**. A job specification completely specifies the

Table 13.6   A selection of the services associated with MMS.

Functional unit	Service primitive	Confirmed
Context management	Initiate	Yes
	Release (Conclude)	Yes
	Abort	No
Obtain file	ObtainFile	Yes
File transfer	FileOpen	Yes
	FileClose	Yes
	FileRead	Yes
Program load	LoadFromFile	No
	StoreToFile	No
Job control	Start	No
	Stop	No
Variable access	Read	Yes
	Write	Yes
Device status	Status	No
	UnsolicitedStatus	No
General services	Reject	No
	Cancel	Yes
	Identify	No

job to be carried out. For example, with a simple application of JTM, the job specification may relate to the specification of a program together with the data to be run by an AP on a remote computer system, or to a document to be printed by a remote print server AP. With a more sophisticated application, it may relate to, say, an order for an item of equipment from a remote supplier's computer, or to an invoice or statement relating to an order. Clearly, the type of processing associated with a job may vary. In its simplest form it may involve the processing of the document, resulting from the job specification, while in others the initial job specification may spawn other associated job specifications (subjobs).

The AP that actually executes a job is known as the **execution agency** while the AP that receives the requests from the JTM service provider for information/ data relating to a job is known as the **source agency** – for example, a local file store. As the time between submitting a job specification and the job being completed may be long, the initiating agency may specify an AP to follow the progress of the job when it submits a job specification. This AP is known as the **job monitor**. Whenever a significant event occurs in the lifetime of the job, the JTM service provider creates a **report document** and sends this to the associated job monitor. The initiating agency may then make enquiries as to the current status of the job. Finally, after an execution agency has completed all the work associated with a job specification, the JTM service provider submits a document to a nominated AP – the **sink agency**.

We can see that JTM is concerned mainly with the movement of documents (which relate to jobs) between APs. The APs are known as agencies to the JTM service provider. The various agencies associated with JTM are

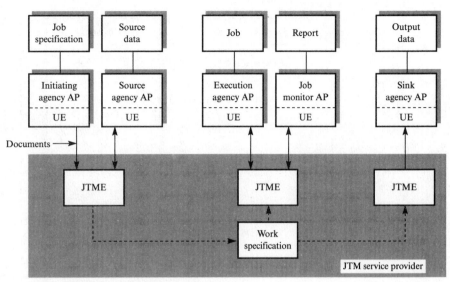

Figure 13.26
Model of JTM service.

JTME = Job transfer and manipulation entity

shown in Figure 13.26. Although each AP (agency) is shown as a separate entity, one or more of the APs may be associated with the same system. For example, the initiating and sink agencies may be in the same system, or the sink and monitor agencies, and so on.

JTM services

The full range of services associated with JTM is too extensive to describe here; we shall look at only the user services associated with what is known as the **basic class**. This class supports only a restricted form of job specification – a single job. It does not result in any subjobs being spawned. Also, as there is no secondary monitor agency, the only events reported are those related to an abnormal operation.

The user service primitives associated with the basic class are shown in the time sequence diagram of Figure 13.27. The initiating agency (AP) is known as the **JTM service requester** and the various agencies (APs) that receive requests from the JTM service provider are known as **JTM service responders.** The use of the various services are as follows:

- J_INITIATE_WORK allows an initiation agency to submit an OSI job specification document to its local JTM entity.

- J_GIVE allows a JTM entity associated with the JTM service provider to request a document from a source or an execution agency.

- J_DISPOSE allows a JTM entity to pass a document to an execution or sink agency.

- J_TASKEND allows an execution agency to signal completion of an activity associated with a job to its local JTM entity.

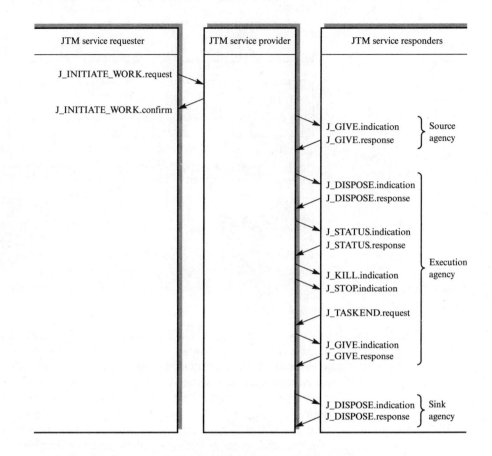

Figure 13.27
JTM basic class
service primitives.

- J_STATUS allows a JTM entity to obtain information about the progress of an activity associated with a job.

- J_KILL allows a JTM entity abruptly to terminate all activity associated with a job.

- J_STOP allows a JTM entity temporarily to stop all activity associated with a job.

Again, parameters are associated with each primitive. For example, the parameters associated with the J_INITIATE_WORK.request primitive include the following:

- Name of initiating agency AP
- Local identifier
- OSI job name
- Authorization
- Name of source agency AP
- Name of execution agency AP

- Name of sink agency AP
- Pointer to document containing job specification
- JTM action parameter

A JTM action parameter is present with all primitives and indicates the type of action associated with this primitive. This may be either document movement or work manipulation; for example, the latter would be associated with a J_DISPOSE primitive passed to an execution agency. In general, the response and confirm primitives have only the local identifier used with the corresponding indication and request primitives.

13.2.7 DTP

The **distributed transaction processing (DTP)** ASE is being developed to control the operations associated with transaction processing systems that involve multiple open systems. Recall from Chapter 12 that many distributed applications involve multiple users (clients) requiring to access a single shared resource concurrently.

An example is a database or a file system in a banking application containing customer accounts of which a distributed community of client systems require access for both reading and update operations. The CCR ASE has been defined to help control such applications to ensure the contents of the database/file store remain consistent and reflect all the operations that have been initiated. We described an application of the CCR that involves just a single resource in Section 13.2.2 in relation to the reliable service associated with the FTAM ASE.

In addition to such uses, CCR supports the control of multiple (nested) transactions that involve several operating systems. Such requirements are typical of many distributed transaction processing applications. The DTP ASE has been defined for use in such applications together with the nested services of CCR.

A transaction involves multiple operations that are performed according to the following rules:

- **Atomicity** The operations are either all performed or none of them are performed.

- **Consistency** The operations associated with a successful transaction transform any data involved from one consistent state to another consistent state.

- **Isolation** Intermediate results associated with the operations are not accessible from outside and, if several transactions are running concurrently, they are controlled as if they were performed sequentially.

- **Durability** If faults occur while the operations are being performed, then they are recovered to a consistent state.

These are often referred to as **acid rules**. The DTP ASE provides services to control the exchange of information between the APs that are involved in distributed transactions according to these rules.

Typical DTP systems involve multiple APs that are carrying out interrelated transactions between them. An example is a distributed community of client systems accessing the reservation systems of multiple airlines. Clearly, many booking operations will involve multiple interrelated transactions on several systems. These must be controlled in such a way that it is equivalent to a single client accessing each system sequentially. Also, if a client system crashes during a series of transactions, then it must be detected and each server returned to a known consistent state.

Services

A complete DTP application entity comprises the DTP ASE and the support services provided by the ACSE and CCR ASEs. A typical distributed transaction processing application is shown in Figure 13.28.

Each client AP may wish to initiate a transaction that involves multiple servers and hence multiple subtransactions. The aim of the DTP service is to provide each client with services that enable it to carry out such transactions concurrently with other clients. For each (distributed) transaction the user APs involved are organized in the form of a tree structure with the client initiating the original transaction at the root. The root AP, known as the master (superior), then initiates a transaction with multiple servers, each of which is known as a subordinate or slave. In more sophisticated applications, while the operations associated with a transaction are being performed, a subordinate may wish to initiate a subtransaction. An example is if there are multiple copies of, say, a file held by a server. Hence, before responding to a commit request the server may wish to initiate the updating of each copy thus creating what is known as a **transaction tree**.

There are various levels of complexity associated with transaction processing systems. In some instances access to just a single resource may need to be controlled while in others multiple concurrent transactions each involving transaction trees may need to be controlled. Therefore, the user services

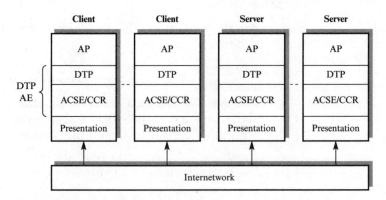

Figure 13.28
DTP application
schematic.

DTP = Distributed transaction processing
AE = Application entity

associated with the DTP are divided into a number of functional units (FUs) each of which provides a defined control function. The services associated with the various FUs are as follows:

- The **kernel** FU provides the services for a user to establish an association with a server and initiate a transaction (begin a dialog), perform any operations (data transfers) associated with this, signal an error back to the initiator, and close the transaction and association (end dialog).

- The **commit** FU provides the additional services needed to enable a client to carry out a transaction according to the acid rules and hence involves the two-phase commit with rollback error recovery services of CCR.

- The **polarized control** FU provides services to enable a single server to be accessed by only one user at a time.

- The **unchained transaction** FU allows a superior to block the creation of a transaction subtree and then to allow it at a later time.

- The **handshake** FU allows two clients to synchronize the processing function associated with a transaction.

Exercises

13.1 Produce a sketch, together with descriptive text, to explain the meaning of the following terms relating to a TCP/IP suite and an OSI stack:
(a) User requests/responses
(b) Virtual device requests/responses
(c) Real device requests/responses
Hence identify the differences in terms of implementation and structure between the two.

13.2 Explain the meaning of the following terms in relation to the TELNET protocol:
(a) Virtual terminal
(b) Network virtual terminal
(c) Pseudo terminal
Using the commands listed in Table 13.1, produce a sequence of the commands exchanged between a client and server TELNET protocol to negotiate the following options:
(d) Change from 7-bit ASCII to 8-bit binary
(b) Echo any characters you receive
Assume first the client is making the request and then the server. How are FF (hex) bytes transferred in the 8-bit binary mode?

13.3 Explain the meaning of the following terms relating to a file store:

(a) Unstructured
(b) Structured
(c) Random access
(d) Flat
(e) Hierarchical
Explain how the FTP in a TCP/IP suite handles the first three structures.

13.4 List the four message types associated with the trivial FTP and explain their meanings.
Assuming an unstructured file containing 1K characters, use a time sequence diagram to show how this could be transferred between a client and server TFTP using the message types just described.

13.5 Explain the meaning of the following terms relating to an e-mail system:
(a) Mailbox
(b) Native mail
(c) Mailbox name
(d) Mail header and keywords

13.6 Use a time sequence diagram to illustrate a typical command message exchange sequence relating to the SMTP to send an item of mail from one mail system to another with a copy to a third system.

13.7   Produce a sketch, together with descriptive text, to show the interrelationship between the terms 'operational environment' and 'network management environment'. Include in your sketch a typical protocol suite relating to a host and a gateway.

13.8   Produce a sketch of a typical – but simplified – management information tree for a campus network comprising a number of LANs interconnected by routers.

List the five user service primitives associated with the SNMP and explain their use in relation to your MIT.

Define the PDU names corresponding to each service primitive and an example definition of one such PDU in ASN.1.

13.9   In the context of an OSI stack, explain the meaning and interrelationship between the following terms:
(a)   Service element
(b)   Application-specific service element
(c)   Application-support service element
(d)   Application entity
Give an example of the last and identify the other terms in relation to this.

13.10   With the aid of a sketch, explain the meaning of the following terms relating to the ISO VT protocol:
(a)   Virtual terminal
(b)   User element
(c)   Conceptual communication area
Identify the data structures that make up the last and explain their functions.

13.11   With the aid of a sketch, describe the structure and how the elements of a file are identified in the virtual file store model used with the ISO FTAM protocol. Include the meaning of the terms:
(a)   FADU
(b)   DU
(c)   Data element

13.12   With the aid of a state transition diagram, explain the four service regimes associated with the FTAM user services. Outline a typical sequence to read a data unit from a named file.

Clearly explain the operation of the F_READ/WRITE services.

13.13   Discriminate between the terms 'normal' and 'reliable transfer' modes in relation to FTAM.

List the additional services associated with the reliable transfer mode and explain how they relate to the services of the CCR application-support protocol.

13.14   With the aid of a sketch, explain the meaning of the following terms relating to the ISO mail standard MOTIS:
(a)   UA
(b)   IPM protocol
(c)   SDSE
(d)   MTA
(e)   MS
Identify the various protocols associated with MOTIS and how they relate to your sketch. Give a brief explanation of the functions of each.

13.15   Explain the format of messages associated with the ISO MHS and how each component part is interpreted by the various protocols identified in Exercise 13.14.

13.16   Identify the protocols associated with the various elements that might be used for a campus e-mail system that is compatible with the public X.400 standard. In relation to this, explain how mail (messages) is sent
(a) internally, and (b) externally.

13.17   Produce a sketch showing the ASEs that make up an SMAE in an OSI management system and explain the function of each service element. Include in your descriptions the meaning of the term 'SMF'.

13.18   Explain how the ISO management protocol differs from the SNMP used in a TCP/IP suite.

13.19   In relation to the OSI management framework, explain the meaning of the terms:
(a)   Managed object
(b)   Attributes
(c)   Operations
(d)   Behavior
(e)   Notifications
Give examples of the operations that can be performed on the attributes of a managed object and how a managed object generates notifications.

13.20 Explain the meaning of the following terms used in relation to a managed object:
  (a) Information hiding
  (b) Managed object class
  (c) Inheritance tree
  (d) Containment
  (e) Managed object instance
  (f) Management information tree
  (g) Distinguished name
  (h) Relative and partial distinguished names

13.21 Outline the function and services associated with each of the following ISO ASEs:
  (a) MMS
  (b) JTM
  (c) DTP

Chapter summary

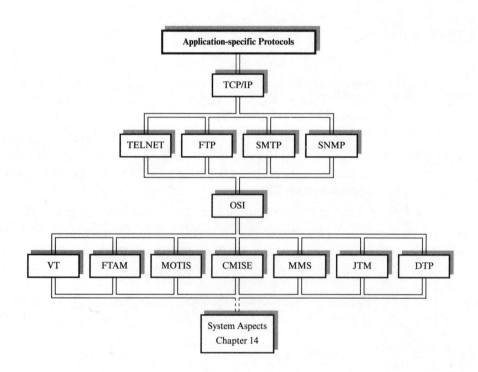

14 SYSTEM ASPECTS

Chapter objectives

When you have completed this chapter you should be able to:

- Explain the structure and operation of the domain name system used in a TCP/IP suite and how the names associated with an open system environment are managed ☞ 814

- Explain the structure and operation of the X.500 directory system and the protocols associated with it ☞ 820, 826

- Know the architecture of the MAP and TOP suites and their intended applications ☞ 828

- Understand how the various protocols that make up both a TCP/IP suite and an OSI suite interact one with another to implement a specific user application service ☞ 831, 835

- Understand how a protocol suite is structured in relation to its local operating system ☞ 847

- Explain the main issues that are involved in relation to the implementation of the various components that make up a protocol suite ☞ 851, 853, 855

Introduction

Chapters 11–13 have been concerned primarily with describing the function, operation, and specification of the different protocol entities defined to enable open systems to be established in a range of application environments. In this chapter we shall discuss some of the issues relating to the operation and implementation of a complete communication subsystem based on these open standards.

Recall that user applications use symbolic names for communication purposes whereas numerical addresses are used within the open system interconnection environment (OSIE). Thus, we must first discuss how the protocol suite associated with an open application performs the name-to-address mapping function as well as how the assignment of names to users is managed. Both these functions form part of what is known as directory services.

We shall also consider some examples of open system environments based on the TCP/IP and ISO protocols, and take a more detailed look at how the various protocols that make up an open system suite cooperate and interact with one another to perform the required communication support function. We shall then consider the implementation of the two complete protocol suites. The chapter concludes with a short discussion of the standards work that is going on in addition to the communication standards.

14.1   Directory services

As we have already mentioned, addresses are used within the OSIE to identify the source and destination application processes (APs) involved in a network session. An address consists of two parts: one for use by the network/internetwork to route messages to the required host/end system and the other for use within the host/end system to route a received message to the required AP.

The network-related part is analogous to a telephone number. If all calls involve just a single site – a PABX or a private network – then the numbers can be relatively short since they need to identify a telephone outlet only within that limited environment. In the case of a computer network this is analogous to the point-of-attachment address associated with a single network such as a LAN. If, however, the telephone is connected to a PTT or public-carrier network, the numbers must be longer to identify and route calls across many national and possibly international exchanges. International telephone numbers are analogous to the X.121 addresses used with the X.25 PSPDN or to an IP or ISO CLNP address if multiple network types are involved. In both cases, the address ensures that a host/end system address is unique within the total network/internetwork.

The second part of the address, which identifies a specific application process within a host, takes different forms with the two suites. With TCP/IP, this is the role of the port address, while in an OSI suite, because multiple intermediate layers exist between the transport and application protocols, this is the role of the interlayer address selectors/service access points: TSAP, SSAP, and PSAP. The addresses used with each protocol suite are shown in Figure 14.1.

The addresses in both suites are comprised of a significant number of digits. In a TCP/IP suite, the IP address is a 32-bit integer which, in dotted decimal, can be up to 12 decimal digits. The port number is a further three digits (eight bits). In an OSI suite, the network-related address can be as long as 40 decimal digits with additional digits for interlayer multiplexing/demultiplexing. Consequently, it is not feasible to use addresses – even in decimal form – outside of the OSIE.

Within the real system environment users – people and APs – are known by **symbolic names** rather than addresses. In the same way that users of the telephone system use directory services to find the telephone number of a called party, so the **directory services** associated with an OSIE are used to find the address of a named

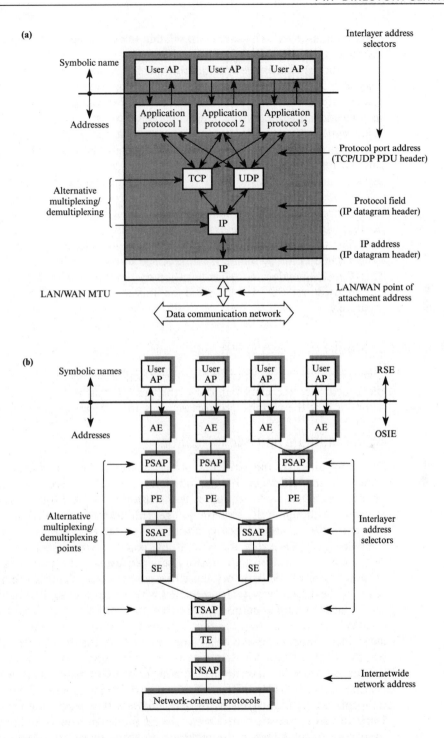

Figure 14.1 Address composition (a) TCP/IP; (b) OSI.

destination user/AP. This **address resolution service** is the most frequently used of the directory services.

Although names are essential for long addresses, they are also necessary for other reasons. Names isolate the users/APs from any knowledge of the network configuration which may, of course, change. For example, a subnetwork (LAN) may be added or removed or a different public data service used to interconnect subnetworks. Also, in some applications, a user AP should be able to migrate from one location on a network to another without, ideally, other APs being aware of this. Therefore, the directory service must provide not only an address resolution service, but also services to allow the contents of the directory, containing the list of symbolic names and their corresponding addresses, to be changed and updated in a controlled way. The **binding** between the symbolic name of an AP and its address – location – is therefore said to be dynamic.

The total directory system in a TCP/IP suite is known as the **domain name system** while in an OSI suite it is the **X.500 directory**. Although the latter is an ITU-T recommendation, it has been jointly developed with ISO. The directory system used by ISO is thus based on this standard. We shall consider each separately.

14.1.1 Domain name system

Two interrelated issues must be considered with any directory system. The first is the structure of the names and how their assignment is to be administered; the second is how the various directory services are to be implemented.

Name structure and administration

With any internet, the structure of the names is important since it strongly influences the efficiency of the directory services. There are basically two approaches. One is to adopt a **flat structure** and the other a **hierarchical structure**. Although a flat structure, in general, uses the overall name space more efficiently, the resulting directory must be administered centrally. Also, as in large internets (and hence directories) multiple copies of the directory are normally maintained to speed up the directory services, using a flat address space means that all copies of the directory must be updated when changes occur. For these reasons, the directory systems associated with all but the smallest networks use a hierarchical naming structure.

Again we can draw an analogy with the structure and assignment of subscriber numbers in the telephone system. At the highest level there is a country code, followed by an area code within that country, and so on. The assignment of numbers can be administered in a distributed rather than a centralized way. The assignment of country codes is administered at international level, the assignment of area codes within each country at national level, and so on, down to the point where the assignment of numbers within a local area can be administered within that area. This can be done knowing that as long as each higher-level number is unique within the corresponding level in the address hierarchy, the combined number will be unique within the total address space.

The adoption of a hierarchical structure also means that the various directory services can be carried out more efficiently, since it is possible to partition the directory in such a way that most address resolution operations – and other services – can be carried out locally. For example, if names are assigned according to the geographical distribution of hosts, then the directory can be partitioned in a similar way. Since most network transactions, and hence directory service requests, are between hosts situated in the same local area – for example, between a community of workstations and a local server or e-mail system – then the majority of service requests can be resolved locally. Relatively few transactions have to be referred to another site; these are known as **referrals**.

As an example we shall consider the hierarchical address structure used with the Internet. Recall from Chapter 9 that the Internet consists of a number of interconnected internets. Because these internets were interconnected relatively recently, each had its own naming hierarchy in place before the Internet was created. To accommodate this, there are a number of alternative partitioning possibilities, known as **organizations** or **domains**, at the highest level in the hierarchy (tree). The names of these domains are listed in Table 14.1.

All hosts attached to a network or subnet of the Internet must be registered with one of these organizational domains. The overall directory for the Internet is partitioned according to these domains. The choice of domain to be registered under is made to minimize the number of referrals. Hence, if a host is to be attached to a network that belongs to an educational institution, since it is likely that most network transactions will involve hosts that are attached to its own network or to those of other educational institutions, it is registered within the EDU domain. Similarly, if a host is attached to a network belonging to a military research establishment it is registered within the MIL domain, and so on.

Each domain uses an appropriate naming hierarchy. In the EDU domain the next level in the hierarchy is the names of the different educational institutions,

Table 14.1 Domain names used in the Internet.

Domain name	Meaning
COM	Commercial organizations
EDU	Educational institutions
GOV	Government institutions
MIL	Military groups
NET	(Internet) network support centers
ORG	Other organizations
INT	Internal organizations
USA	⎫
UK	⎬ Country codes for geographical assignments
⎪	⎭

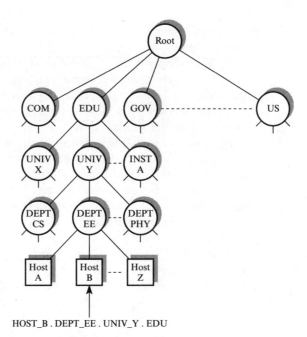

Figure 14.2
Domain name
hierarchy.

while in the COM domain it is each (registered) commercial organization. The general scheme and naming convention are as shown in Figure 14.2.

Each component of a domain name is known as a **label**. As Figure 14.2 shows, labels are written with the local label on the left and the top domain on the right, each separated by a period.

The prefixes to each label are only to illustrate a typical hierarchical breakdown. In practice, each label is simply the registered domain name for that level in the hierarchy.

As indicated earlier, the adoption of a hierarchical structure means that names can be assigned locally rather than centrally. Thus in the case of an educational institution, as long as the institution – and hence name – is registered with the EDU domain name authority, the authorized computer manager at that institution can assign names as well as IP addresses to hosts that are to be attached to that institution network.

Domain name server

Associated with each institution network is a host (computer) that runs an application protocol/process known as the **domain name server (DNS)**. Associated with this is a database known as the **directory information base (DIB)** which contains all the directory-related information for that institution. When a new host is to be registered, the manager interactively enters the name and IP address – and other information – that have been assigned to that host into the DIB of the local domain name server. A user can then initiate transactions that involve the Internet.

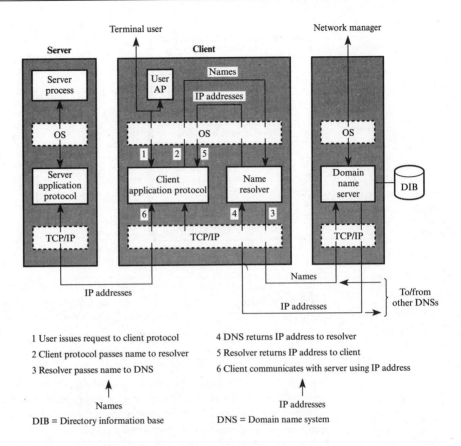

Figure 14.3
Name-to-address resolution protocols and sequence.

1 User issues request to client protocol
2 Client protocol passes name to resolver
3 Resolver passes name to DNS

4 DNS returns IP address to resolver
5 Resolver returns IP address to client
6 Client communicates with server using IP address

Names

DIB = Directory information base

IP addresses

DNS = Domain name system

When initiating a network transaction involving a particular application protocol, a terminal user or an AP will use the name of the host machine on which the server is running when communicating with its local client protocol. Before this protocol can initiate the setting up of a transport connection with the server, it must ascertain the IP address of the host in which the server runs. In a TCP/IP suite all server protocols/processes are allocated a fixed port number – the well-known port – so it is not necessary to maintain port numbers in the DIB.

To obtain the IP address of a named server, each host has a client protocol/process known as the **name resolver**. Its position is shown in Figure 14.3 together with the outlined sequence of events that the client protocol follows to carry out the name-to-address mapping.

On receipt of the name, the client application protocol passes it to the name resolver using the standard interprocess communication primitive supported by the local operating system. The resolver then creates a resolution request message in the standard message format of the domain name server protocol. This format is shown in Figure 14.4.

A resolver can have multiple requests outstanding at any time. Hence the **identification** field is used to relate a subsequent response message to an earlier request message. The type of message – request/response – and additional

(a)   1   16   (b)

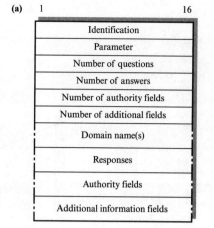

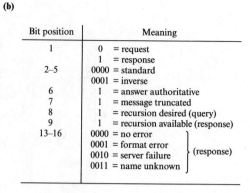

Bit position	Meaning
1	0 = request
	1 = response
2–5	0000 = standard
	0001 = inverse
6	1 = answer authoritative
7	1 = message truncated
8	1 = recursion desired (query)
9	1 = recursion available (response)
13–16	0000 = no error
	0001 = format error
	0010 = server failure } (response)
	0011 = name unknown

Figure 14.4
Domain name server protocol: (a) message format; (b) parameter bit definition.

qualifiers relating to responses – format error, server failure, etc. – are given in the **parameter** field. Responses also contain information about the server(s) – its **authority** and IP address. In addition, each request and response message can contain multiple requests/responses.

The name resolver passes the request message – using the standard TCP/IPs and messages – to its local domain name server. If the request is for a server (host) on this network, the local domain name server obtains the corresponding IP address from its DIB and returns it in a reply message. If it does not contain the required address, then it must seek help from another server by creating a request message. This is known as a referral and the aim is to minimize the number of referrals that are needed. To achieve this, the servers are organized in a hierarchical structure as shown in Figure 14.5(a).

As we can see, a higher-level server associated with each organization tree incorporates a table containing the names and IP addresses of all the name servers associated with the organizations/institutions registered with that domain hierarchy. On receipt of a request that it cannot resolve, the local domain name server creates and sends a referral request to the higher-level server. This first checks the domain name associated with the request and, assuming it is for another server within the same domain, uses the name to access the IP address from its own name table. It returns this in a response message to the local server which then makes a direct request to the indicated server for the required IP address. The sequence of the messages exchanged is shown in Figure 14.5(b).

Similarly, a further level of referral must be initiated by the higher-level server to resolve a request that involves an organization in another domain. In the scheme shown, the root server would have a table containing the names and IP addresses of all the higher-level domain servers and, on receipt of a request involving another domain, it would relay the request via the root server. The required domain server would then respond directly as before.

In practice, the amount of information associated with the intermediate domain name servers is only modest since the number of entries in its referral table

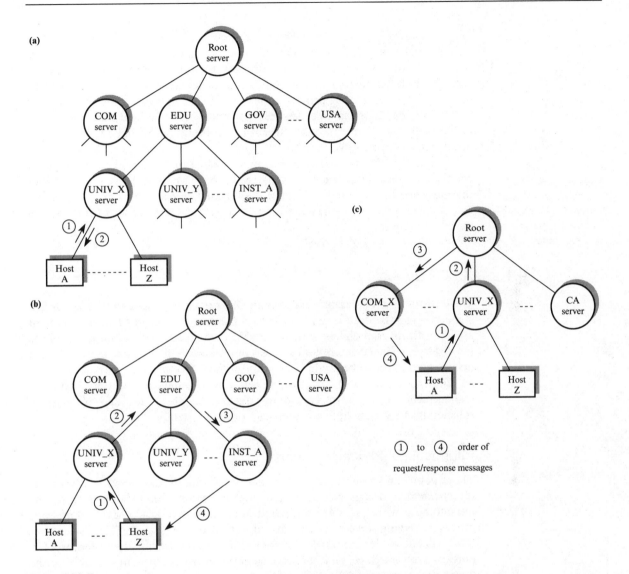

Figure 14.5
Domain name server hierarchy: (a) local request; (b) higher-level request; (c) collapsed hierarchy.

is determined by the number of institutions/organizations and not by the number of hosts at each site. To reduce the number of message exchanges, the alternative structure shown in Figure 14.5(c) is also used. With this approach, the root server contains the IP address of all the servers in all registered organizations. Each referral request can then be answered with a maximum of four message exchanges.

Although this scheme reduces the number of message exchanges, like the scheme shown in the figure it still leads to a significant load on the internet because many messages may need to be transmitted over several networks to resolve each query. To minimize this, each local server maintains a record of the most recently referred names – and their IP addresses – together with the names and IP addresses of the servers that provided the addresses. This information is retained in a table known as the **name cache**. On receipt of a request for which it does not have a local entry, the local server searches its name cache and, if an entry is present, responds with it. In the response message, it resets the authoritative flag to zero and puts the answer in the authority field together with the name and IP address of the server that provided the answer. This allows for the information being out of date, for example, as a result of a network reconfiguration. On receipt of the reply, the client can either accept the information or make a new request directly to the name server.

To ensure that the list of cached entries is reasonably up to date, a timeout period is associated with each entry. The value of this period is given by the server that provided the information. Hence the timeout for each entry may vary. Once an entry timeout expires, the entry is removed and any new requests for that entry have to be referred.

14.1.2   X.500 directory

The directory services associated with an OSI suite are those used with the X.500 standard. The standard consists of several parts, each concerned with a different aspect of the overall directory function. The complete system is known simply as the **directory**. The structure and services associated with the directory have been defined so that it can be used not only to provide directory services to the APs in an OSI suite, but also to provide services to other applications, such as management processes in system management applications, and to message transfer agents within an X.400 message transfer system.

Information and directory model

The structure and naming convention associated with the directory is based on the object-oriented design principles that were described in Section 13.2.3. The terminology, which is similar to that used with the X.400/MOTIS message message handling service, is summarized in Figure 14.6(a).

All entries in the DIB are known as **objects** which are **instances** of a particular **object class**. Objects are organized in a tree structure known as the **directory information tree (DIT)**. All objects at a particular level in a branch hierarchy belong to the same object class. Objects at the next higher level of the tree from a class of objects are members of the superclass of those objects while those at the next lower level are members of their subclass.

Associated with each object class (and hence object) is a set of **attributes** each of which has a **type** and one or more **values**. The attribute type identifies the class of the object, for example, the country code, C. At least one of the values must be the name of the object, for example, UK. The attribute structure of each object is shown relative to a leaf object although all objects in the tree have the same structure. A more formal definition of the attribute structure is given in Figure 14.6(b) together with a definition of the terminology associated with object names. Both are expressed in ASN.1.

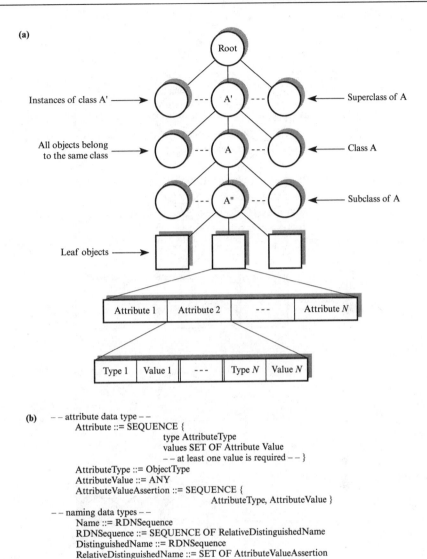

(a)

Instances of class A' ⟶

All objects belong
to the same class ⟶

Leaf objects ⟶

Root

A'

A

A"

⟵ Superclass of A

⟵ Class A

⟵ Subclass of A

| Attribute 1 | Attribute 2 | --- | Attribute N |

| Type 1 | Value 1 | --- | Type N | Value N |

(b)   – – attribute data type – –
    Attribute ::= SEQUENCE {
            type AttributeType
            values SET OF Attribute Value
                – – at least one value is required – – }
    AttributeType ::= ObjectType
    AttributeValue ::= ANY
    AttributeValueAssertion ::= SEQUENCE {
                AttributeType, AttributeValue }
  – – naming data types – –
    Name ::= RDNSequence
    RDNSequence ::= SEQUENCE OF RelativeDistinguishedName
    DistinguishedName ::= RDNSequence
    RelativeDistinguishedName ::= SET OF AttributeValueAssertion

Figure 14.6
DIT structure:
(a) terminology;
(b) attribute definition
in ASN.1.

The naming convention is similar in principle to that used in the domain name system. However, with X.500 each label is referred to as a **relative distinguished name (RDN)** – as with X.400 – and the complete list of labels associated with an entry (object) in the tree as the **distinguished name (DN)**. As with the domain name system, the RDNs used must be unique at any level in a branch hierarchy. Consequently, they are assigned by the administrative authority responsible for that level. A (simplified) portion of a DIT is shown in Figure 14.7(a). The names used may relate, for example, to an X.400 mail system.

In the example, the Country (C), Organization (O), Organizational Unit (OU) and Common Name (CN) are all class (attribute) types; UK, UNIV, SWAN, etc. are the corresponding attribute values. Note that the object class

(a)

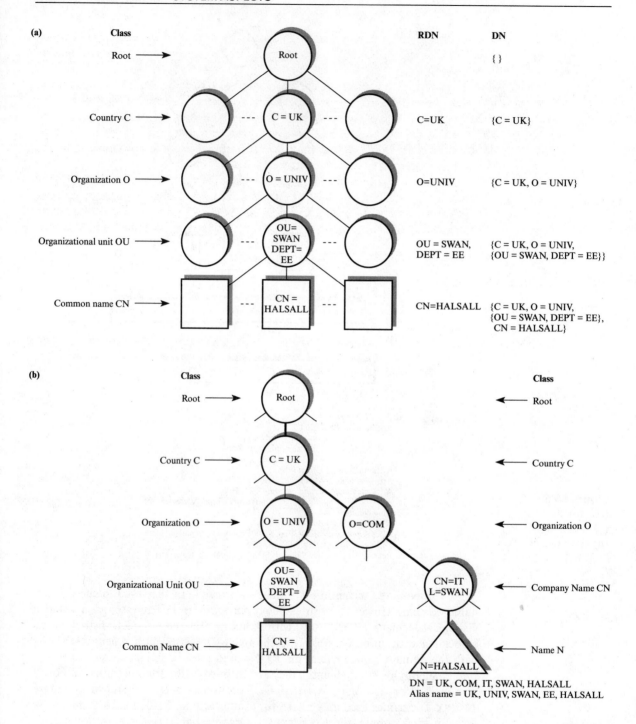

Class		RDN	DN
Root →	Root		{ }
Country C →	C = UK	C=UK	{C = UK}
Organization O →	O = UNIV	O=UNIV	{C = UK, O = UNIV}
Organizational unit OU →	OU=SWAN DEPT=EE	OU = SWAN, DEPT = EE	{C = UK, O = UNIV, {OU = SWAN, DEPT = EE}}
Common name CN →	CN = HALSALL	CN=HALSALL	{C = UK, O = UNIV, {OU = SWAN, DEPT = EE}, CN = HALSALL}

(b)

Class			Class
Root →	Root	←	Root
Country C →	C = UK	←	Country C
Organization O →	O = UNIV O=COM	←	Organization O
Organizational Unit OU →	OU=SWAN DEPT=EE	CN=IT L=SWAN	← Company Name CN
Common Name CN →	CN = HALSALL	N=HALSALL	← Name N

DN = UK, COM, IT, SWAN, HALSALL
Alias name = UK, UNIV, SWAN, EE, HALSALL

Figure 14.7   Example DIT contents: (a) e-mail names; (b) alias example.

Organizational Unit has an additional attribute of type DEPT, the value of which is EE. The RDN and DN for each object name in the tree are as given at the side of the tree.

Entries with **alias names** can be included at the leaves of the DIT, in addition to entries with object names. An alias (name) entry in the DIT, in addition to having a DN, always points to (gives the DN of) an object in a different part of the DIT. This object need not be a leaf entry. Hence an alias name allows an object to belong to more than one branch of the DIT and therefore to have more than one name. An example is shown in Figure 14.7(b).

The tree is an extension of the tree in Figure 14.7(a). An object COM – company – is defined as of class Organization (O = COM). This has a subclass Company Name (CN = IT, L = SWAN) which in turn has a subclass Name (N = HALSALL). The last one is a leaf node and is an alias name for HALSALL in the other organizational branch. It thus has an additional alias name attribute giving the DN of the other entry in the tree.

Directory services

The model of the directory service is shown in Figure 14.8. All users access the directory through an AP known as the **directory user agent (DUA)**. As we indicated earlier, the directory should meet the needs of a range of different

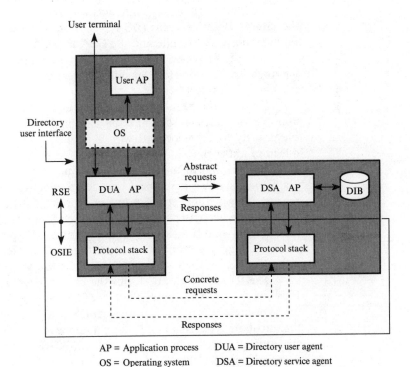

Figure 14.8
Directory services model.

AP = Application process   DUA = Directory user agent
OS = Operating system   DSA = Directory service agent
                            DIB = Directory information base

Table 14.2   Directory services: request types.

Directory interrogation requests

READ	Requests the values of some or all of the attributes associated with an object entry; the user, through the DUA, supplies the attribute types that are required.
COMPARE	Requests the directory to compare a given value – for example, a password – with that associated with a given attribute of a given entry.
LIST	Requests the list of immediate subordinates of a given entry.
SEARCH	Requests the values of all attributes within a defined portion of the DIT that satisfy a given filter.
ABANDON	Informs the directory that the user is no longer interested in the result of an earlier request.

Directory modification requests

ADD_ENTRY	Requests that a given object name or alias name – with attributes – is added to a specified location of the DIT as a real entry.
REMOVE_ENTRY	Requests that a given object name or alias name – which must be leaf entities – be removed from the DIT.
MODIFY_ENTRY	Requests a sequence of changes to be made to a given entry. Either all changes are carried out successfully or none of them are carried out. The changes include: addition, removal, or replacement of given attributes or attribute values.
MODIFY_RDN	Requests the RDN associated with an object or alias leaf entry is changed to that given.

applications. Thus the user can be either a person at a terminal or an AP. To resolve each request, a DUA interacts with the directory through an AP known as the **directory service agent (DSA)**. The DUA plays a similar role to the name resolver in a TCP/IP suite and the DSA in the domain name server.

Services provided by a DUA to a user are classified as either **directory interrogations** or **directory modifications**. These are listed, together with their meanings, in Table 14.2.

Most of the requests shown have a number of associated **qualifiers**. For example, the user can set a limit on the length of time, the scope of a search, and the priority to be associated with a request – **control qualifiers**. In addition, a directory entry may have an associated security mechanism, such as a digital signature, that has to be given before a request is initiated – **security qualifiers**. And if a request involves a number of entries, a **filter qualifier** can be included with the request. This qualifier specifies one or more conditions that an entry must satisfy before it can become part of the response. An example is a request in an X.400 messaging system for, say, all company names of a given type in a specified town or city. Similarly, a user can browse through the contents of the directory by using a combination of the LIST and SEARCH services.

The READ service performs the basic address resolution (look-up) service. It causes the DUA to supply the DN of an object together with the attribute type of the result that is required. The local DSA returns any value(s) corresponding to that attribute type. In an OSI internet application, the DN is that of a server and the attribute type the (fully qualified) PSAP address. Similarly, in an OSI messaging system, the DN(s) is (are) the originator/recipient name(s) and the attribute type their originator/recipient address(es) in the total messaging system.

Alternatively, an alias name can be provided instead of a DN. Also, the values of a number of attribute types can be requested with a single request.

The directory always reports the outcome of each request made of it. Clearly, any of the requests may fail for reasons such as violations of the security mechanism associated with an entry or problems with the parameters provided – for example, invalid name or attribute value. In such cases an error message is returned with an appropriate error type.

In applications that require user authentication before access is granted to an entry in the directory an **authentication attribute**, such as a password, can be included with the entry. The directory then only returns a positive response to a request if the correct password is submitted, otherwise an error message is returned. For example, this is necessary with a network manager station. The manager – through an appropriate interactive AP – has to provide the correct password before being allowed to add/remove/modify entries in the directory. Similarly, with a networked resource such as a file server that contains confidential information, a set of attributes can be used containing the passwords of only those users who are allowed access to the server. Any other users simply receive an error message.

These are examples of **simple authentication**. In more demanding applications, the authentication attribute may be the user's password encrypted using that user's public key. In this case an authenticated password is obtained only if the user provides the password encrypted using its private key. This is an example of **strong authentication** and requires the DSA process to perform additional security processing.

Directory structure

As we have already discussed, for all but the smallest, a directory must be structured in a distributed way. The physical distribution normally reflects the logical distribution of the DIT. The total DIB is divided into a number of partitions that relate to the structure of the DIT. A DSA is associated with each partition that provides access to it. The general scheme is shown in Figure 14.9(a).

On receipt of a request from one of its local DUAs, a DSA first searches its DIT partition for the required information. If this information is present, it responds directly to the DUA. If it is not, then it must refer the request to another, higher-level, DSA – a referral. The procedure is the same as that used in the domain name system. However, in addition to referrals the DSA supports two search procedures: chaining and multicasting.

With **chaining**, if a DSA receives a request for which it only has part of the required information, it creates a request for the remainder of the information and sends this to the DSA which it thinks has the information. This type of request is known as a **chained request** since, if the recipient DSA does not have all the required information either, then it too will create a new (chained) request, and so on. The response to a chained request must always return along the path taken by the matching request. The recipient DSA combines the received information with its own contribution and returns this to the next DSA in the chain or to the DUA

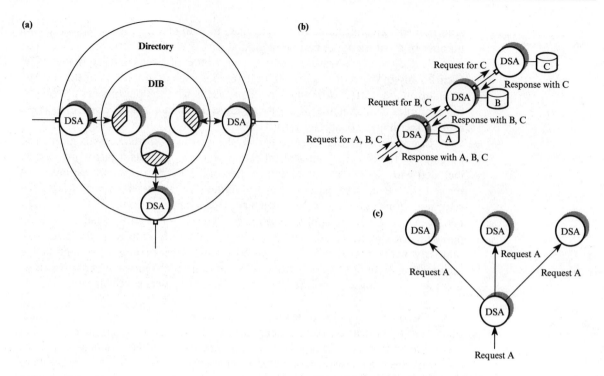

Figure 14.9
Directory operation:
(a) structure;
(b) chaining;
(c) multicasting.

if the end of the chain has been reached. The general scheme is shown in Figure 14.9(b).

Multicasting is similar to flooding. If a DSA does not have the required information relating to a request in its DIB partition, it forwards a copy of the request to all the other DSAs it has knowledge of. If one of them has the information, it returns this to the requesting DSA and from there to the user. This is shown in Figure 14.9(c).

As with the domain name system, a DSA maintains a cache of the network addresses of all the other DSAs in the system with which it communicates to minimize the number of referrals. Hence, on receipt of a request for which it has to generate a referral it can normally send the request directly to the appropriate DSA or inform the DUA of the address of the DSA that should be used to answer the request. The DUA then issues a new request directly to that DSA.

Directory protocols

Remember that the DUA and DSA are APs and not protocols. In terms of the ISO reference model they are in the real system environment and not the OSIE. All communications between a DUA and a DSA take place using standard request–response (remote operations) messages that are in an abstract syntax. Similarly, all messages that are exchanged between DSAs are in an abstract syntax and are of the same request–response type. All messages relating to both exchanges are defined using ASN.1. In addition to the definition of these messages, supporting

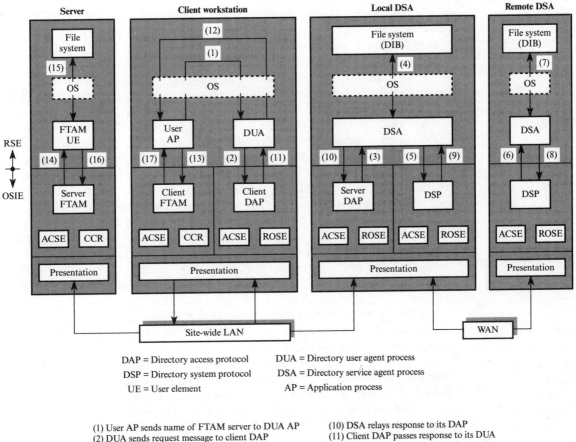

Figure 14.10
X.500 directory
protocols and example
message/APDU
exchange.

DAP = Directory access protocol   DUA = Directory user agent process
DSP = Directory system protocol   DSA = Directory service agent process
UE = User element   AP = Application process

(1) User AP sends name of FTAM server to DUA AP   (10) DSA relays response to its DAP
(2) DUA sends request message to client DAP   (11) Client DAP passes response to its DUA
(3) Server DAP passes request to local DSA   (12) Response returned to user AP
(4) Local DSA checks its DIB for object   (13) User AP issues FTAM request
(5) Local DSA sends referral request to DSP   (14) Server FTAM issues request to UE
(6) Remote DSP passes request to its DSA   (15) Local file access carried out
(7) Remote DSA obtains attribute from its DIB   (16) Data returned to server FTAM
(8) Remote DSA returns response to its DSP   (17) Data passed to user AP
(9) DSP passes response to the local DSA

protocols must be used to ensure these message exchanges are carried out in an open way, that is, the messages exchanged have the same meaning in the two communicating systems.

To achieve this, two supporting protocols have been defined, each of which uses the ACSE and ROSE application-support service elements and, of course, the services provided by the presentation layer. The protocol associated with the DUA-to-DSA message exchanges is known as the **directory access protocol (DAP)** and that associated with the DSA-to-DSA message exchanges as the **directory system protocol (DSP)**. An example arrangement is shown in Figure 14.10.

The arrangement assumes that the user AP running in the client workstation wants to obtain a file from a file server that is connected to the same site-wide LAN. Before initiating the (remote) file request to its local FTAM application entity – assumed to be comprised of the FTAM client ASE and the ACSE and CCR service elements – it must first obtain the fully qualified PSAP address of the server which it knows only by its application title (name). Numbers (1) through (12) indicate the sequence of the messages exchanged to obtain this address.

As indicated, both the DAP and DSP use remote operations – remote procedure call – for communications and hence these are supported by DAP/ ROSE. After an association has been established between the DUA and its local DSA – using the services of ACSE – all requests from the DUA are implemented by invoking a suitable remote operation/procedure in the local DSA using the services of DAP/ROSE. The server name and PSAP address attribute type are passed as arguments in an RO_INVOKE primitive and the result is returned in an argument of the RO_RESULT primitive.

In the sequence shown, we assume that the local DSA associated with the site does not have the required address in its DIB – in practice, unlikely – and must refer the request to a remote DSA. Steps (5) through (9) indicate the message exchanges that take place to obtain the address from the remote DSA. After the local DSA receives the requested attribute – PSAP address – it relays this address back to the requesting DUA and from there to the user AP – steps (10) through (12).

The remote AP can then initiate the file access request to the remote file server/system using the services provided by the local (client) FTAM application entity. The sequence of messages resulting from this are (13) through (17). In practice, more messages are exchanged than are shown since an association must first be established between the client and server APs – using the services of ACSE – and messages relating to the file selection and open procedures must be exchanged before any file data is transferred. The sequences are intended to illustrate the operation of X.500, not FTAM.

14.2   Example OSI environments

Recall from Chapter 9 that the Internet is by far the largest OSIE currently in existence. Moreover, as well as providing communications support for a wide range of internetwide applications to many thousands of users, it is still being used as a testbed for investigating many issues relating to internetworking and the associated network protocols.

In contrast, there are currently relatively few networks based on the OSI suite. Until relatively recently this has been primarily because of the lack of firm standards for the higher application-oriented layers. However, a full set of standards is now available and as a result many new open system environments are being defined based on the OSI suite.

In the public sector, a number of OSI environments are being established by the PTTs and public carriers. These include X.400 public messaging networks as well as Teletex, Videotex and facsimile networks. All of the equipment used to provide access to such networks uses a full OSI suite. Normally, the protocols used at each layer are ITU-T X-series recommendations, but these are fully compatible with the equivalent ISO standards. As Section 14.1.2 described, the X.500 directory is now also a full international standard and will further promote the use of OSI suites. Collectively, the services provided by such networks are referred to by the PTTs as **teleservices**. Those just listed were first introduced in Chapter 8 when WANs were discussed.

In the private sector, two examples of OSIEs are MAP and TOP. In the manufacturing industry, an initiative by General Motors of the United States has resulted in the selection of a set of protocols, all based on ISO standards, to achieve open systems interconnection within an automated manufacturing plant. The resulting protocols are known as **manufacturing automation protocols (MAPs)**. A typical MAP network, together with the protocols selected for use with it, is shown in Figure 14.11.

As we can see, MAP is based on a factorywide, backbone cable distribution network. The cable is coaxial and operates at 10 Mbps. Because of the wide range of communication requirements within a factory, the broadband mode of working has been selected. The MAC sublayer is ISO 8802.4, the token bus standard, selected because of its deterministic access time. Both the network layer and the LLC sublayer operate in a connectionless mode and the transport layer operates using the class 4 connection-oriented protocol known as TP 4. The distributed information services currently include FTAM and MMS, each of which operates through an ACSE application-support service element.

For communications within a manufacturing cell (that is, for exchanging messages between, say, a cell controller and a distributed set of robots and other computer-controlled machines), the simpler and less costly carrierband transmission method is used. Since most communications within a cell are local, a reduced set of protocols has been selected. The time overheads associated with the full seven-layer model are significant and, in some instances, unacceptable for communications between the cell controller and the automated equipment. The reduced set of protocols selected comprises MMS (which also includes a basic file service) interfaced directly to the LLC sublayer, which operates in a connection-oriented mode. In this way, the time overheads associated with intracell communications are much reduced. The resulting system is known as the **enhanced performance architecture (EPA)**. Normally, a cell controller supports both the full seven-layer MAP architecture and the EPA; hence, in addition to performing a local supervisory or control function, the cell controller can communicate on a factorywide basis over the backbone network.

In a similar way, an initiative by the Boeing Corporation (also from the United States) has resulted in the selection of a set of ISO standards to achieve open systems interconnection in a technical and office environment. The selected protocols are known as **technical and office protocols (TOPs)**. A typical establishmentwide TOP network, together with the protocols selected for use with it, is shown in Figure 14.12.

The transmission medium used with a TOP network is also coaxial cable operating at 10 Mbps. In general, the communication requirements in such environments are limited to voice (which is normally already provided by the

(a)

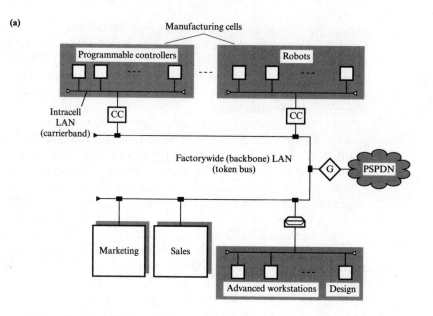

(b)

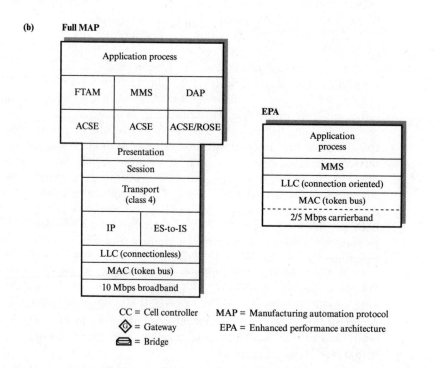

Figure 14.11 MAP network: (a) schematic; (b) protocols.

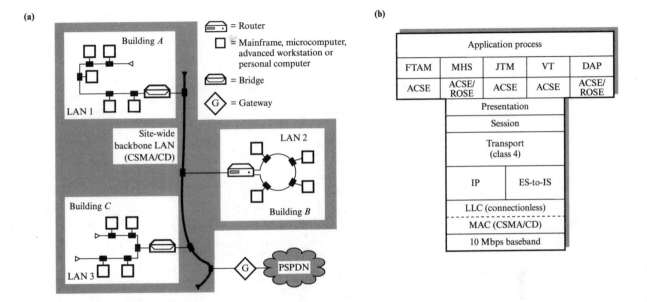

Figure 14.12
TOP network:
(a) schematic;
(b) protocols.

existing telephone system) and data, the latter being primarily concerned with communications between a distributed community of advanced workstations (for example, performing computer-aided design). The cable is operated in a baseband mode and the MAC protocol is ISO 8802.3 (CSMA/CD). As with MAP, the network layer and LLC sublayer operate in a connectionless mode while the transport layer uses the class 4 service. The distributed information services selected include FTAM, MHS, JTM, and VT.

These are just some examples of currently established OSIEs. As the administrative authorities in other application domains move toward open systems, many others will evolve.

14.3 Layer interactions

To gain an understanding of the operation of complete communication suites, we must understand how the various protocols – protocol entities – that make up each suite interact to carry out a particular network operation. Let us consider an application domain that consists of a number of client workstations that communicate with a networked file server. Assume that the network is a single LAN. First we shall look at the message (PDU) exchanges relating to a TCP/IP suite and then at those involving an OSI suite.

14.3.1 TCP/IP

A typical sequence of frame transmissions on the LAN cable between a single (client) user AP and the file server, together with the layer interactions that take

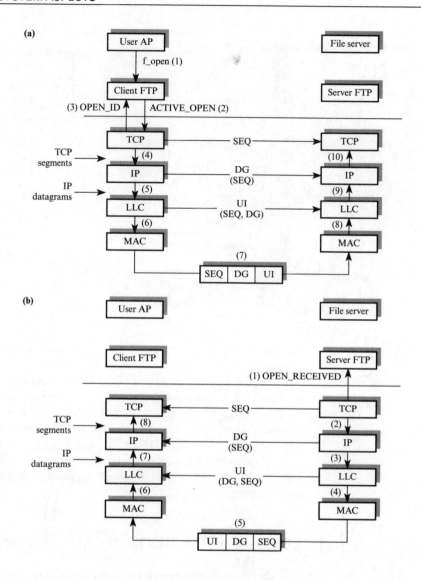

Figure 14.13
TCP/IP layer interactions to implement a remote file open.

place relating to each transmission, is given in Figure 14.13(a–f). For clarity, we assumed that the client FTP has already obtained the IP address of the server from its local name resolver and that all the messages exchanged are correctly formed and no transmission errors occur. The sequence relates only to opening a (remote) file ready for reading or writing.

The server would first have issued a PASSIVE_OPEN to its local TCP to inform it that it is active and waiting to receive new file transfer requests. The sequence starts with the client user AP – perhaps a user at a terminal – initiating a file operation by issuing an f_open request to its local client FTP. This includes all the necessary additional information such as the name of the server and the file name. The client FTP first obtains the IP address of the server – not shown – and

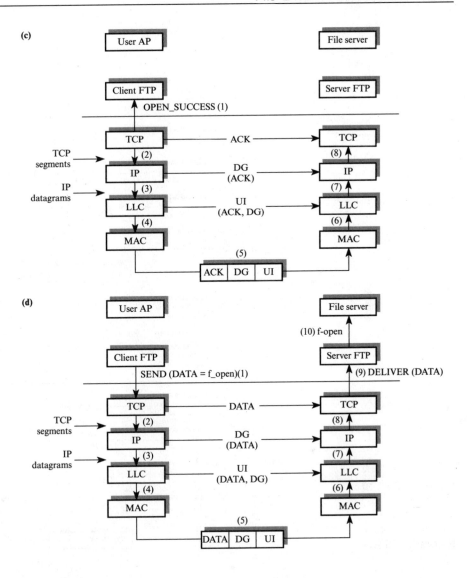

Figure 14.13 (cont.)

then initiates the setting of a transport connection (TC) between the client and server FTPs using the IP address of the server and the well-known port address of the FTP (21).

The sequence starts with the client FTP issuing an ACTIVE_OPEN request. The resulting layer interactions are shown Figure 14.13(a) where the numbers in parentheses indicate the sequence in which the interactions occur. The local TCP first responds by returning an OPEN_ID to the client FTP to enable it to relate subsequent messages to this port address and hence TC. It then creates and sends a SYN segment – as described in Chapter 11 – containing the well-known port address of the server. It passes the SYN segment to the IP for transmission together with the IP address of the server. The IP, in turn, creates an IP datagram

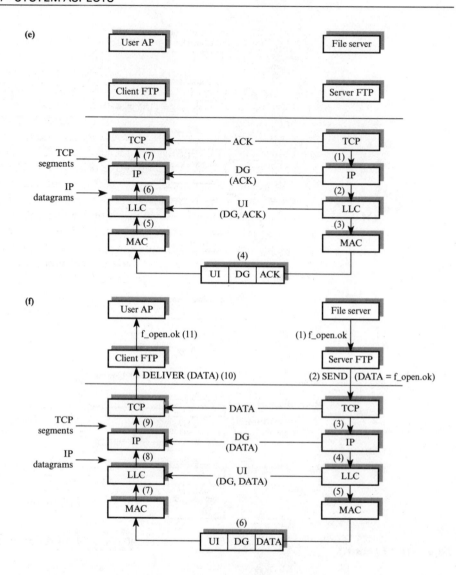

Figure 14.13 (cont.)

with this address in its header and the SYN segment in the user data area. This is sent using the LLC and MAC sublayers associated with the LAN. Each adds its own protocol control information (PCI) at the head of the IP datagram; the composition of the actual frame that is transmitted on the cable medium is shown at the bottom of the figure. On receipt of the frame, the MAC, LLC, and IP layers each interpret their own PCI at the head of the frame and pass on the remaining data to the next higher layer. Thus only the SYN segment remains when it arrives at the TCP layer.

On receipt of the SYN, the TCP responds as in Figure 14.13(b). It first informs the local FTP server that a new connection request has been received and then establishes the return path of the TC by returning its own SYN segment. This is transferred in the same way as before. The TCP at the client side then proceeds as shown in Figure 14.13(c).

The TCP first issues an OPEN_SUCCESS to the client FTP – indicating that a TC is now in place – and returns an ACK segment to the server TCP to complete the connection establishment procedure. At the same time, the client FTP responds as shown in Figure 14.13(d). It first sends an f_open request message to the server FTP over the established TC as user data. This is transferred to the server side in a DATA segment. On receipt, the TCP passes the f_open request to the server using a DELIVER primitive. The server then issues an f_open to its local file system in the normal way as if it is a local call.

Since the f_open is passed in a DATA segment, the TCP at the server returns an ACK. The sequence is shown in Figure 14.13(e). Part (f) shows the file system responding positively to the open request to its local server FTP; again this is passed back in a DATA segment. The client FTP relays the open acknowledgment to the user AP which proceeds to initiate subsequent read and write operations on the opened file.

The sequences shown have been simplified for descriptive purposes. However, they illustrate how each layer performs its own functionality within the context of the complete protocol suite.

14.3.2 OSI

Before we describe the equivalent sequence with an OSI suite, we must define the **application profile** of the suite being used. We shall assume the following:

- The selected OSIE is based on TOP.

- The application entity comprises just FTAM and the ACSE application service elements.

- The network-dependent protocol layers (network, LLC, and MAC) all operate using the connectionless mode.

- The transport layer provides a class 4 connection-oriented service.

A typical sequence of frame transmissions on the LAN cable medium between a client (initiator) AP and the server (responder) AP, together with the layer interactions that take place relating to each transmission, is given in Figure 14.14. For clarity, we assume that all service primitives and associated PDUs are of the correct structure (and hence accepted) and that no transmission errors occur.

To initiate a remote file operation, the client user AP (through its linked user element) first issues an F_INITIALIZE.request primitive. This results in the layer interactions depicted in Figure 14.14(a), where the numbers in parentheses indicate the sequence in which the interactions occur. As we can see, on receipt of the request primitive (1), the initiator FTAM entity generates an INIRQ PDU, using the parameters associated with the service request, and writes the ASN.1 encoded version of the PDU into the user data buffer (UDB). This buffer is simply

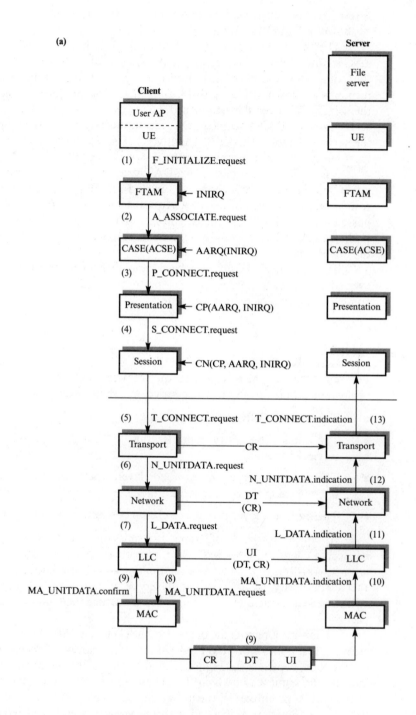

Figure 14.14   (a) OSI layer interactions.

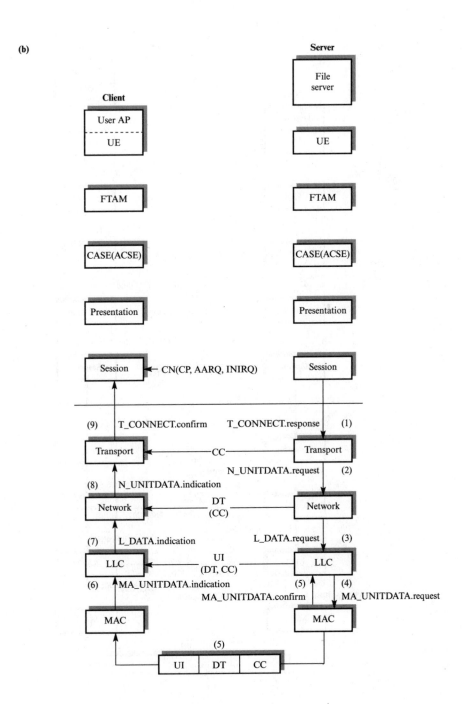

Figure 14.14 (cont.)   (b) OSI·layer interactions.

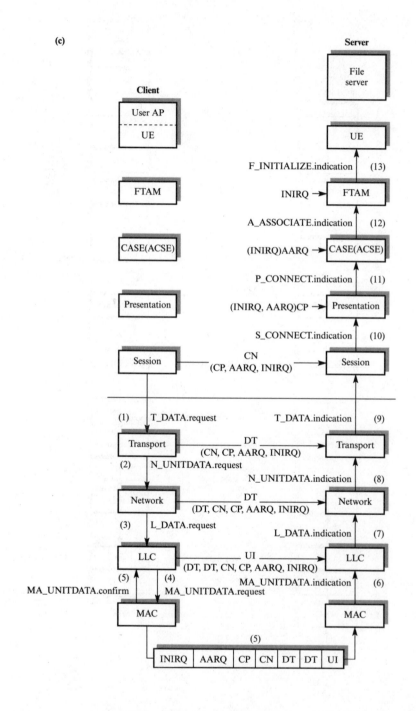

Figure 14.14 (cont.)   (c) OSI layer interactions.

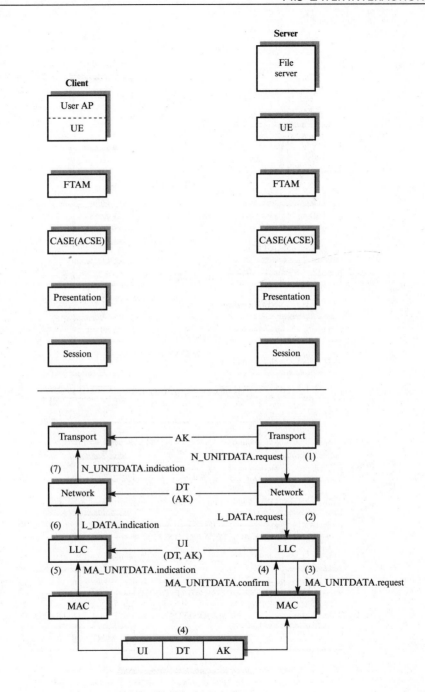

Figure 14.14 (cont.)   (d) OSI layer interactions.

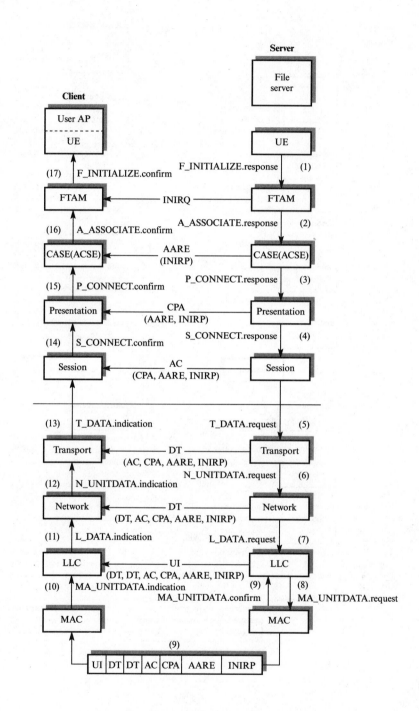

Figure 14.14 (cont.)   (e) OSI layer interactions.

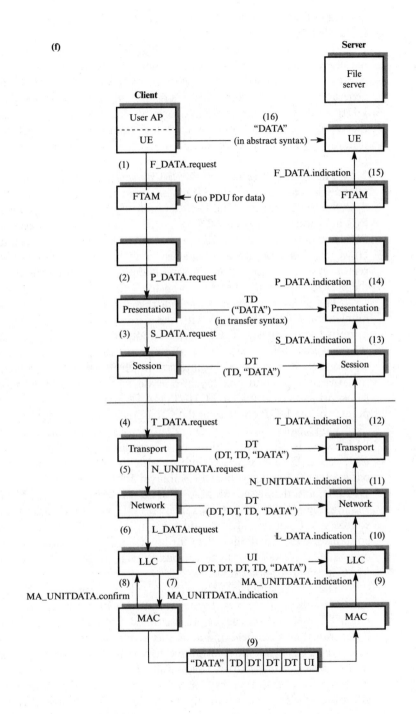

Figure 14.14 (cont.)   (f) OSI layer interactions.

an array of octets (bytes); the contents of the UDB are eventually transmitted on the cable medium.

The address pointer of the UDB is passed to the ACSE in the user data parameter of an A_ASSOCIATE.request primitive (2) together with additional parameters as defined for use with this primitive. The ACSE entity, in turn, generates its own PCI and adds this at the tail of the existing INIRQ PDU in the UDB. Collectively, the two parts form an AARQ PDU. The address pointer of the UDB is then passed in the user data parameter of a P_CONNECT.request primitive, again with additional parameters as defined for use with this primitive (3).

The same procedure is followed by the presentation entity: it generates its own PCI, adds this to the UDB (to form a CP PDU) and finally issues an S_CONNECT.request primitive (4). Similarly, the session entity generates its own PCI and adds this to the UDB to form a CN PDU. We described the various PDUs relating to the ACSE, presentation and session layers in Chapter 11. However, at this point we assume that a TC is not currently established with the remote system. Hence, before the session entity can transfer the composite PDU to the peer session entity, it must establish a TC.

The session entity uses the address information (and the specified communication QOS) associated with the parameters of the S_CONNECT.request primitive and issues a T_CONNECT.request primitive (5). On receipt of this, the transport entity creates a CR PDU, using the parameters associated with the service request, and writes this into a new UDB. As we have indicated, we assume that the network and link layers operate in a connectionless mode. Hence the transport entity issues an N_UNITDATA.request primitive with the address pointer of the UDB containing the CR PDU as a parameter (6).

On receipt of this, the network entity uses the parameters to generate its own PCI and adds this at the tail of the CR in the UDB to form a DT PDU. It then issues an L_DATA.request primitive with the address pointer of the UDB as a parameter (7). Similarly, the LLC sublayer adds its own PCI to the UDB to form a UI PDU, and then issues an MA_UNITDATA.request to the MAC sublayer (8). Finally, the MAC sublayer adds its own PCI (which includes the destination and source LAN addresses) and adds this to the UDB. At this point, the UDB contains the PCI relating to the four layers in the order transport, network, LLC, and MAC. (We described the various PDUs relating to the network, LLC, and MAC layers in Chapter 6.)

The MAC sublayer now initiates the transmission of the complete UDB contents. It first gains access to the shared cable medium (according to the CSMA/CD MAC method) and, as the preassembled frame contents are being transmitted, it generates the FCS field and adds this at the tail of the frame. It then issues an MA_UNITDATA.confirm primitive to the LLC sublayer to inform it that the frame has been transmitted successfully (9). Note that since the MAC PCI is the same for each frame transmitted – that is, the same source and destination addresses – it is not shown in any of the figures for reasons of clarity.

On receipt of the frame, the MAC sublayer in the server station stores the complete frame in a UDB so that the UDB contents are in the same order as they were transmitted. Note that, although the frame (and hence UDB contents) comprises PCIs relating to a number of protocol layers, since the PCI for each layer (and hence PDU) is in a precisely defined (fixed) format, each layer can readily access and interpret just its own PCI. Hence, on receipt of the complete frame, the MAC sublayer first interprets its own PCI and then passes the address pointer of the UDB up to the LLC sublayer using an MA_UNITDATA.indication primitive (10).

In practice, as we shall see later, the UDB also contains an address offset which indicates the start address of the next PCI to be processed. On receipt of the UDB pointer, the LLC sublayer uses the address offset to determine the start address of its own PCI. Having established the type of PDU received (UI), it then processes the remaining PCI pertaining to it according to the standard format and issues an L_DATA.indication primitive, with appropriate parameters, to the network layer (11). In turn, the network layer processes its own PCI in the UDB and issues an N_UNITDATA.indication primitive to the transport layer (12). Finally, the transport entity processes its own PCI and issues a T_CONNECT.indication primitive to the session layer (13).

Assuming it is prepared to establish a TC, the recipient session entity responds by issuing a T_CONNECT.response primitive. The resulting layer interactions are shown in Figure 14.14(b). On receipt of the T_CONNECT.response primitive (1), the transport entity first creates a CC PDU, writes this into a (new) UDB and issues an N_UNITDATA.request primitive to the network layer (2). The same procedure is then followed as in Figure 14.14(a), finishing when the transport entity issues a T_CONNECT.confirm to the originating session layer to confirm that a TC has been established (9).

The originating session entity is now able to transfer the waiting CN PDU (which includes the CP, AARQ and INIRQ PCI in its user data field) across the TC. It does this by issuing a T_DATA.request primitive with the address pointer of the UDB containing the waiting CN PDU as a parameter. The resulting interlayer interactions are as shown in Figure 14.14(c). As we can see, a similar sequence ensues as in the earlier examples except that this time the lower network-dependent layers simply add their own PCIs after the CN PDU in the UDB.

On receipt of the UDB at the server station (5), each protocol layer processes its own PCI and passes the remaining contents up to the next higher protocol layer. Finally, on receipt of the UDB, the FTAM entity (12) issues an F_INITIALIZE.indication primitive to the responder UE with parameters constructed from the INIRQ PDU (13). In addition, since the PCI relating to the application-oriented layers is passed as user data in a DT TPDU by the calling transport entity, the called transport entity, after passing the UDB to the session layer (containing the CN PDU), initiates the sending of an acknowledgment for the DT TPDU. The sequence shown in Figure 14.14(d) traces the resulting interactions. As we can see, the interactions are similar to those shown in Figure 14.14(b) except that in this case the TPDU is an acknowledge – AK.

On receipt of the F_INITIALIZE.indication primitive, the server AP (through its linked UE) responds by issuing an F_INITIALIZE.response primitive to its attached FTAM entity. The interactions that follow are outlined in

Figure 14.14(e). As we can see, since a TC has now been established, the UDB contents eventually transmitted (9) contain PCIs relating to all the protocol layers. Hence, as the received UDB is passed up through the layers in the client system, each layer reads and interprets the PCI relating to it. Finally, the initiating FTAM entity issues an F_INITIALIZE.confirm primitive to the client UE (17).

As Chapter 13 showed, the normal sequence with FTAM would have the required file selected and opened before any specific action was carried out on the file. Each of these steps would result in a sequence similar to that just followed. However, the sequence shown in Figure 14.14(f) traces the layer interactions that occur when the client AP is sending data to the server. Clearly, this is preceded by an additional F_WRITE.request primitive. The data being transferred may be in an abstract syntax but the data transferred between the two presentation entities – that is, the TD PDU – must be in an agreed transfer (concrete) syntax. Also, the ACSE entity is blanked out since it does not feature in the data transfer phase.

UDB decoding

To reinforce understanding of the layer interactions shown in Figure 14.14, the contents of a typical transmitted frame are shown in Figure 14.15(a). This frame corresponds to that shown earlier in Figure 14.14(a). The contents of the frame, and hence the UDB, are shown as a string of octets with each octet represented as two hexadecimal digits. We also assume that the frame contains a destination and a source MAC address.

To illustrate how the received frame is interpreted by the various protocol layers, the decoded version of the frame is shown in Figure 14.15(b). We assume that 16-bit MAC addresses are used; hence, the MAC protocol entity first reads and interprets the first four octets in the UDB – the destination and source addresses. The UDB pointer is then passed to the LLC sublayer as the user data parameter of an MA_UNITDATA.indication primitive with an address offset of 4.

On receipt of the UDB pointer, the LLC protocol entity reads and interprets its own PCI from the UDB; first the SAP and SSAP octets and then the control field octet. From the latter, it determines that the frame is a UI (unnumbered information) frame and hence interprets it as the end of its own PCI. It increments the address offset to 7 and passes the UDB pointer to the network layer as the user data parameter of an L_DATA.indication primitive.

A similar procedure is followed by the network and transport layers. First, the network protocol entity reads and interprets the appropriate number of octets, according to the network protocol. It passes the UDB pointer to the transport layer, with the address offset suitably incremented, as the user data parameter of an N_UNITDATA.indication primitive. Similarly, the transport protocol entity reads and interprets its own PCI. At this point, the UDB is exhausted, so the transport entity simply issues a T_CONNECT.indication primitive to the session layer using some of the fields from the received UDB to form the necessary parameters.

(a) 00 2E 36 39 FE 0E 03 81 21 01 09 1C 00 21 00 00 0B

49 00 02 02 00 00 00 00 2E FE 00 0B 49 00 03 08 00

00 00 36 39 0E 00 08 E0 00 00 70 00 40 97 B7

(b) MAC PCI

00 2E = Destination address
36 39 = Source address

LLC PCI

FE = DSAP
0E = SSAP
03 = UI (unnumbered information)

Network PCI

81   = Network protocol identifier
21   = Header length
01   = Version number
09   = PDU lifetime
1C   = 0001 1100 = no segmentation, DT PDU
00 21 = PDU segment length
00 00 = Checksum (ignored)
0B   = Destination address length
49 00 02 02 00 00 00 00 2E FE 00 = Destination address
                                       49 = AFI (local)
                                   00 02 = IDI
                                   02 00 = SI
                                   00 00 2E = PA
                                       FE = LSAP ⎫
                                       00 = NSAP ⎬ SEL
                                            ⎭
0B   = Source address length
49 00 03 08 00 00 00 36 39 0E 00 = Source address

Transport PCI

08   = Length indicator
E0   = 1110 = CR TPDU, 0000 = CDT
00 00 = Destination reference
70 00 = Source reference
40   = Class 4 service
70 00 = Checksum

Figure 14.15
Example UDB
decoding: (a) UDB
(frame) contents;
(b) decoded fields.

Address parameters

The parameters associated with each service primitive include address information. For example, the calling and called addresses associated with the F_INITIALIZE.request primitive are fully qualified addresses obtained from, say, the local directory server. They include the P/SSAP, TSAP, and NSAP, with the latter including the NSAP and LSAP extensions (or suffixes) relating to the interlayer interfaces, and also the physical network address. As the service primitives resulting from the F_INITIALIZE.request pass down through the protocol layers, each protocol entity reads and embeds its own SAP into the PCI associated with that layer. Hence, as the primitives pass down through the layers, the size of the address parameters diminishes until, at the MAC sublayer, only the physical network address remains. Similarly, as the service primitives pass up through the protocol layers at the server, the address parameters are reconstructed as each protocol entity reads its SAP from the PCI and adds this to the existing addresses. This is shown in Figure 14.16(a).

Session and transport connection identifiers are assigned to the application association and transport connections as they are established. Subsequent service primitives include only the relevant connection identifier as a parameter. When implementing each protocol entity, a record of the calling and called addresses, in addition to the protocol state information relating to each connection, must be retained. This is shown in Figure 14.16(b).

Once each TPDU associated with a connection is passed to the network layer, the network entity can access the corresponding stored NSAPs, which include the physical network address and the NSAP and LSAP extensions. In this way, the complete address information will have been inserted when the complete PDU is transmitted by the MAC layer. In the chosen example, we assume that the network-oriented layers operate in the connectionless mode. However, for connection-oriented mode, a separate network connection identifier must be used.

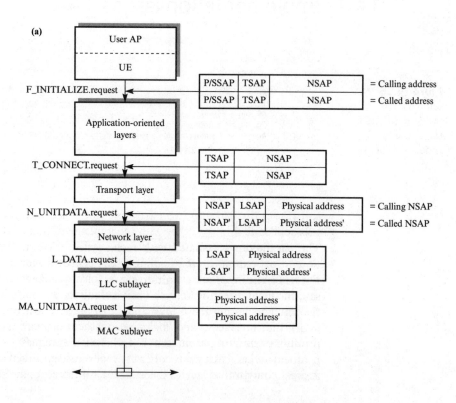

Figure 14.16
Address parameters:
(a) connection
request.

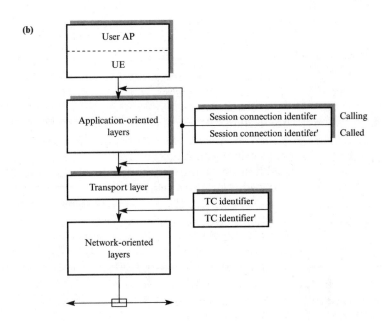

Figure 14.16 (cont.)
(b) Data transfer.

14.4 Implementation issues

Associated with any computer operating system there is a set of primitives (calls), each with a defined set of parameters, that allow a user program/process to access the various peripherals that are attached to the computer in a high-level, user-friendly way. Thus there are primitives to interact with a printer, a terminal, and so on. Primitives are also provided to interact with the local file system to create/delete/modify/read/write files. The issue here is what primitives should be provided to a user application program/process to interact with a networked resource such as a file server.

Clearly, the user must be isolated from the detailed implementation of the protocol suite and should be provided with a similar set of primitives to those used to access and use a similar facility. To achieve this, the overall communications software is divided into two parts: one concerned with the implementation of the protocol suite and the other with the implementation of the user interface.

In the case of a TCP/IP suite, the user interface at the client side is normally an integral part of the client application protocol such as the client FTP. This is normally implemented as a separate AP that can communicate with either a user at a terminal or a user AP through primitives supported by the local operating system. The remainder of the suite – TCP, IP, etc. – is implemented as a separate entity that is accessed by the client protocol/process in a standard way, again through primitives provided by the operating system.

A similar structure is used at the server side; the server application protocol/process communicates with the local file system using the standard user primitives

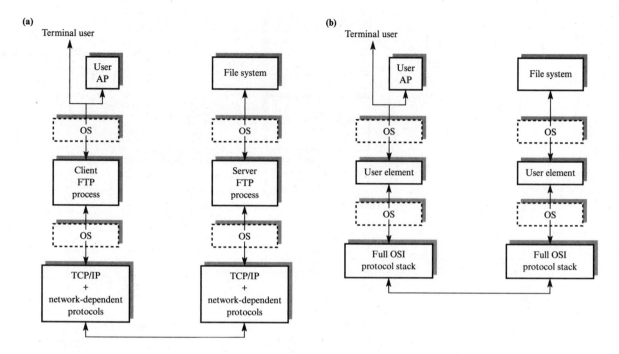

Figure 14.17
Protocol architectures:
(a) TCP/IP suite;
(b) OSI suite.

provided by the operating system. It is thus transparent to the file system whether the service requests are coming from a local AP or from a remote process. The general scheme is shown in Figure 14.17(a), where the application protocol is assumed to be FTP.

In the case of an OSI suite, the application protocol (entity) and the user interface are normally separated into two quite separate entities. The application protocol is normally linked with the remainder of the protocol stack. The general scheme is shown in Figure 14.17(b).

Normally, the interface with the protocol software is through a set of high-level primitives provided by the operating system. With TCP/IP, these are similar to those shown earlier in Figure 11.4, while with an OSI suite they are the same as those associated with the particular application entity being accessed.

The protocol software can be implemented in one of two ways. With TCP/IP, it is normally implemented as part of the basic input-output system (BIOS) of the local operating system and hence forms an integral part of the operating system. However, with an OSI suite the processing overheads associated with the full protocol stack are high, as we can deduce from Figure 14.4. To minimize the processing load on the host main processor, the protocol software is often implemented on a separate plug-in board which includes the network interface chipset, some memory, and a local processor. This scheme is shown in Figure 14.18(a).

Typically, the complete communication subsystem is implemented on a separate printed circuit board that plugs into the internal bus – interconnection mechanism – of the host system. This board contains, in addition to the local

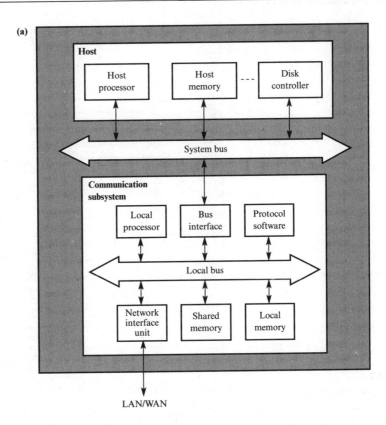

Figure 14.18
Overall architecture:
(a) hardware.

LAN/WAN

(communication) processor, memory for the protocol software, additional memory for storing protocol state information relating to each layer (local), and message buffers being passed between layers (shared), and also the circuitry that is required to perform the physical interface to the communication network. The latter may be a public WAN or a LAN, the only differences being the type of interface circuitry required and, as described in Part 2, slightly different network protocol software.

Normally, the shared memory is **multiported**, that is, it may be accessed directly by the network interface unit, the local processor and, via the system bus in the system, the host processor. In this way, all memory buffers (containing interlayer messages and user data) are directly accessible to each. When information is passed between the buffers (and between layers), only the address pointer to the buffer is utilized, thereby avoiding the added overheads associated with physically transferring blocks of data from one layer or device (and hence part of memory) to another.

An associated software structure for use with this architecture is shown in Figure 14.18(b). We have already stressed that when describing the operation of a communication subsystem structured according to the ISO reference model, we must treat each protocol layer as an autonomous entity which provides a defined

(b)

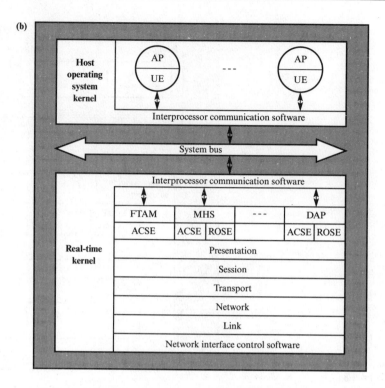

Figure 14.18 (cont.)
(b) Software.

set of user services to the layer above it and, in turn, uses the services provided by the layer below it to transport the PDUs generated by the layer to a similar peer layer in a remote system. In the same way, when implementing the various protocol layers in software, we must retain the same approach otherwise the benefits gained by the adoption of a layered architecture will be lost.

Therefore, the communication subsystem is implemented as a suite of task (process) modules (one per protocol entity) with additional tasks for management (see later) and timer functions. Tasks communicate with each other through a set of FIFO queues or mailboxes as shown in Figure 14.19. Intertask communication is managed by the local real-time kernel which is also responsible for such functions as task scheduling and interrupt handling, which are generated by the timer task, for example, and the network interface unit. Communication between the subsystem and the host is through the interprocessor communication software, a copy of which is in both systems. Typically, the software is interrupt driven to ensure a synchronized transfer of information between the two systems. Thus, whenever the host processor wishes to transfer information to the communication processor, it first writes the information into a free memory buffer associated with the application entity and then generates an interrupt to the communication processor. The interrupt service routine in the latter first reads the address pointer of the buffer, determines the SASE involved, and then places the pointer at the tail of the appropriate input queue to await processing. A similar procedure is followed for passing information in the reverse direction.

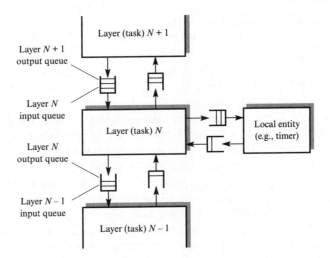

Figure 14.19
Interlayer
communication
schematic.

14.4.1   Interlayer communication

A user AP gains access to the distributed information services supported by the communications subsystem through the defined set of primitives associated with its local user element (UE). The UE can be either a separate process or a set of library procedures (or functions) that is linked to the user AP prior to running.

As described in Section 11.6.6, interlayer primitives and their associated parameters are passed between layers using a typed data structure known as an **event control block (ECB)**. Since the number and types of the parameters associated with the primitives for each layer are usually different, there is a separate ECB data structure for each layer, which is used for passing all service primitives from a higher layer to that layer, that is, for all request, indication, response, and confirm primitives received and issued by the layer from and to the higher layer. A typical ECB relating to the transport layer was shown in Figure 11.34.

Thus, to communicate with an SASE, the UE first obtains a free ECB relating to it (in practice, the address pointer to a buffer in shared memory), writes the necessary parameters associated with the primitive into the ECB, and initiates the transfer of the address pointer of the ECB to the SASE using the interprocessor communication software. Any user data associated with the primitive is written into a separate buffer, the user data buffer (UDB). The address pointer of the UDB associated with the primitive is then written into the ECB together with an indication of the amount of data it contains.

On receipt of the service primitive (ECB), the selected SASE entity uses the parameters associated with the primitive, together with any protocol state information associated with the connection (association), to create the PCI for the layer. This is added to any user data already in the UDB to form an SASE APDU. The SASE then obtains a free ECB associated with the presentation entity (task), writes the appropriate primitive type and parameter information into it (including the address pointer of the UDB containing the APDU and the updated length of its contents), and issues a send message request to the local real-time kernel. The kernel transfers the ECB address pointer to the input queue of the presentation task and, if it is idle (waiting for an incoming event), schedules the task to be run.

Each layer task performs a similar function, first adding its own PCI to the UDB and then passing an appropriate primitive and associated parameters to the next lower layer using a free ECB of that layer, as shown in Figure 14.20(a). Remember that the PCI associated with each layer is in a concrete syntax comprising a string of octets. Thus, each UDB is simply an array of octets. The contents of the UDB are eventually transmitted under the control of the network interface hardware and software.

Clearly, the amount of user data contained within a UDB, after it has passed through all the protocol layers, will vary from, say, a few hundred octets if only PCI is involved to, possibly, several thousand octets if, say, the contents of a file are being transferred. To allow for this, each UDB is of a fixed length and a linked-list strategy is used to handle composite dialog units (PDUs) exceeding this length. Thus, if a UDB becomes full, a new UDB pointer is obtained from the free list, and this is linked to the UDB that is now full. This is shown in a schematic form in Figure 14.20(b).

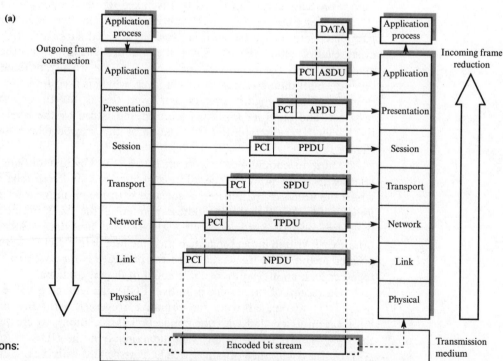

Figure 14.20
Layer interactions:
(a) schematic.

(b)

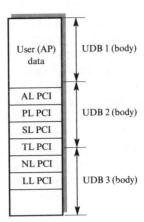

Figure 14.20 (cont.)
(b) UDB structure and
contents.

14.4.2   User element implementation

We can conclude from Section 14.4.1 that the primitives received by the UE are from two sources: those from the user AP and those from the interface with an SASE via the interprocessor communication software. Clearly, the primitives in each case may be of different types. For example, the primitives from the user AP may relate either to a confirmed service (that is, a request primitive that will subsequently generate a confirm primitive) or to an unconfirmed service (that is, a request primitive with no confirm). Similarly, the primitives from the SASE interface may also be of different types. For example, they may be either a confirm primitive returned in response to an earlier request primitive, an indication primitive that requires no response, or an indication primitive that requires a response.

Hence, for the UE to respond to each incoming primitive in the correct way, the UE must retain a record of the last received primitive relating to this SASE session. In practice, this is best accomplished by using an event–state table similar to that defined for each protocol machine. As with the implementation strategy for each protocol machine, the UE retains a state variable for each active session, which indicates the current status of the interface, that is, the previous primitive received. On receipt of an incoming primitive (event), the state variable is used to determine the processing to be carried out, from the event–state table.

As an example, assume that a user AP has a UE linked to it and is accessing a remote file server AP through an OSIE-supporting FTAM and that the set of user primitives provided is as follows:

- f_open (input_file, status)

- f_read (input_file, message_buffer, status)

- f_write (input_file, message_buffer, status)

- f_close (input_file, status)

The parameter **input_file** is the full path name (title) of the file to be manipulated; thus it includes the unique OSIE-wide name of the server system together with the name of the FTAM entity within that system and the name of the file to be operated on. The parameter **status** is an indication of the success or failure of the network request and, in the event of a failure, the reason for the failure. The **message_buffer** parameter is a pointer that indicates where the data relating to the transfer request (read or write) is to be put or found.

Each of these primitives has an associated library procedure, and the complete set of procedures – the FTAM UE – is linked to the user AP. A suitable event–state table for the UE is shown in Figure 14.21.

We can readily deduce from the short list of user primitives provided that each primitive results in multiple FTAM primitives. For example, the library procedure f_open generates a sequence of FTAM primitives associated with the services F_INITIALIZE, F_SELECT, and F_OPEN. Similarly, the f_read procedure generates a sequence related to the services F_READ, F_DATA, and F_TRANSFER_END. Thus, the f_open procedure, after first obtaining the fully qualified address of the remote (called) FTAM entity from the directory service, creates an F_INITIALIZE.request primitive and initiates its transfer, together with its associated parameters, to the local FTAM entity in an FTAM ECB. Typically, this is accomplished using an appropriate interprocess communication primitive through the interprocessor communication software (ICP). The user AP, through the linked f_open procedure, is then suspended while waiting for an F_INITIALIZE.confirm primitive (ECB). The interface thus enters the WTINICF state.

The F_INITIALIZE.confirm primitive, together with its associated parameters, is transferred by the local FTAM entity (in an FTAM ECB), again using an interprocess communication primitive and the ICP software. The user AP is rescheduled at the point of suspension in the f_open procedure. The user AP, as can be deduced from the event–state table, then issues an F_SELECT.request primitive, again with parameters deduced from the initial call, and enters the WTSELCF state. Similarly, on receipt of the F_SELECT.confirm primitive, it issues an F_OPEN.request. Finally, on receipt of the F_OPEN.confirm primitive, the interface enters the OPEN state and returns to the initiating user AP at the statement immediately following the f_open procedure call, the status parameter indicating the success or failure of the call.

A successful f_open procedure is typically followed by an f_read or f_write call, which again results in a sequence of FTAM primitives. Finally, when all transfers are complete, the user AP initiates the termination of the association – and hence FTAM transaction – using the f_close procedure.

We can deduce that, if a piece of software exists with these same user primitives, then to change to an open system we only need to change or rewrite the existing library procedures required to interface with the FTAM. Remember, however, that in addition to generating the appropriate FTAM primitives we may have to convert the file contents into or from the agreed transfer syntax. Also, the UE at the server may need to convert the incoming FTAM primitives into those used by the particular server (file system) being used.

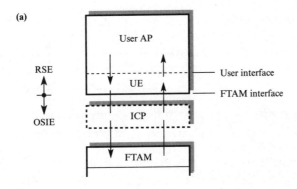

(a)

User AP

User interface

UE

FTAM interface

RSE

OSIE

ICP

FTAM

(b)

State / Primitive	CLOSED	WTINICF	WTSELCF	WTOPNCF	OPEN	---	
f_open	1						} From user interface
f_read					5		
f_write							
f_close							
F_INICF		2					} From FTAM interface
F_SELCF			3				
F_OPNCF				4			
⋮							

1: F_INIRQ, WTINICF

2: F_SELRQ, WTSELCF

3: F_OPNRQ, WTOPNCF

4: OPEN (return)

F_INIRQ/CF = F_INITIALIZE.request/confirm
F_SELRQ/CF = F_SELECT.request/confirm
F_OPNRQ/CF = F_OPEN.request/confirm
WTINICF   = Wait for F_INITIALIZE.confirm
WTSELCF   = Wait for F_SELECT.confirm
WTOPNCF   = Wait for F_OPEN.confirm

Figure 14.21
FTAM UE structure:
(a) interfaces;
(b) event–state table.

14.4.3 Layer management

In addition to the tasks (protocol entities) associated with each layer, a complete communication subsystem has two other tasks: a timer task, which performs the necessary timeout functions associated with the various protocol entities (state machines), and a system management task which, as its name implies, is responsible for both layer and system management functions. These functions include the gathering of protocol error statistics and the setting of operational

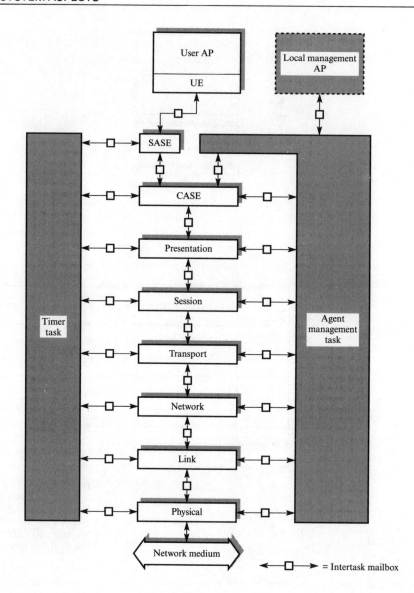

Figure 14.22
Complete
communication
subsystem schematic.

parameters associated with each protocol layer (entity). A complete communication subsystem is shown in Figure 14.22.

Timer task

As indicated in Chapter 11, to ensure that incoming events associated with each protocol machine are atomic, the interface between the timer task and each of the protocol entities (tasks) using its services is through a separate intertask mailbox or queue. Since there is a single timer task for the complete subsystem, there is normally only a single input queue associated with it. Also, as with other intertask communication, there is a single type of ECB associated with the timer task, which is used for all communications with it.

A suitable set of user service primitives associated with the timer task is as follows:

- TIMER.start (layer ID, timer ID, time)

- TIMER.cancel (layer ID, timer ID)

- TIMER.expired (timer ID)

Since there is a single input queue associated with the timer task, the two input primitives (start and cancel) each have a layer ID parameter associated with them to identify the protocol layer issuing the primitive. Also, since with each layer a number of timers may be running (active) concurrently, the timer ID parameter is used to identify with which timer the primitive is associated. Typically, the connection identifier is used for this purpose. The time parameter indicates the time interval, in terms of system clock ticks, that must elapse before the timer task informs the appropriate protocol entity that the named timer has expired.

To initiate a timeout operation (for example, to limit the time a protocol entity waits for a suitable response to an outgoing event), the protocol entity first obtains a free (timer) ECB and writes the layer and timer identities together with the required time interval as parameters within it. It then initiates the transfer of the ECB pointer to the timer task input queue (mailbox) by issuing a suitable intertask communication primitive – for example, send message – to the local real-time kernel. On receipt of the request, the timer task creates an entry in a table indicating the identity of the timer and the time duration associated with it. The latter is simply a counter variable.

Normally, the timer task is interrupt driven from a system clock. This means that a signal (the interrupt) is generated at preprogrammed time intervals, equal to the minimum clock tick time of, say, one second, and the timer task is scheduled to run. First, it determines whether there are any ECBs in its input queue awaiting processing and, if so, processes them. The outstanding time interval associated with any currently active timers are each decremented by one (tick). If any of the timers become zero, indicating that the timeout interval for the timer has expired, a TIMER.expired primitive is generated (in an ECB) and the ECB pointer is transferred to the appropriate layer (timer) input queue using an intertask communication primitive. When the layer task is next scheduled to run, it examines not only its input queues with the layers (protocol entities) above and below it, but also its input queue from the timer task. Any entries in each queue are processed in an atomic way, including any actions resulting from a timeout occurring if the entry is from the input queue with the timer task.

If, after initiating a timer for a particular outgoing event, the protocol entity receives a suitable response (incoming event), it initiates the cancellation of the timer by passing a suitable TIMER.cancel primitive (in an ECB) to the timer task input queue, again using an intertask primitive supported by the real-time kernel.

When the timer task is next scheduled to run, it removes the named timer from the timer table.

Agent management task

Each layer, in addition to maintaining state information (variables) relating to the current operational state of the protocol machine, maintains a set of variables relating to various operational statistics for layer management purposes. Some examples of the statistical information gathered by each layer task are as follows:

- ACSE   The number of negative A_ASSOCIATE.response primitives received; the number of ABORT APDUs received and sent.

- Presentation   The number of unsuccessful CPR (connect presentation response) PPDUs received and sent, with the reason codes; the number of unrecognized PPDUs received.

- Session   The number of RF (refuse) SPDUs received and sent; the number of AB (abort) SPDUs received and sent.

- Transport   The number of protocol errors that have occurred; the number of times a timeout expires on a transmitted TPDU; the number of TPDUs that have a bad checksum.

- Network   The number of NPDUs received and sent; the number of NPDUs discarded because of an unknown NSAP.

- LLC   The number of test LPDUs received and sent; the number of protocol errors.

- MAC   The number of collisions and retransmission attempts (CSMA/CD); the number of token pass failures (token bus).

Normally, most of the information is maintained by simple counters whose current contents may be requested by the **agent management task (AMT)** in response to a request from the network manager AP. However, if a particular event occurs in a layer, indicating a possible fault (for example, when a predefined threshold limit for a variable is reached), the layer (task) may inform the AMT directly.

The AMT must also have a facility for informing a layer of the specific operational parameters (characteristics) to be used, such as:

- Window limit (TL)

- Timeout interval (all layers)

- Routing table contents (NL)

- Maximum retransmission limit (CSMA/CD)

- Target token rotation time (token bus)

As with the timer task, a set of service primitives must be defined (together with an associated ECB type and intertask queue structure) to enable these functions to be carried out in an atomic way. A typical set of primitives for the AMT to interact with the various layers is as follows:

- GET_VALUE.request/confirm (parameter value) is used by the AMT to obtain a statistic from a specific layer.

- SET_VALUE.request/confirm (parameter ID, parameter value) is used by the AMT to set an operational parameter for a specific layer.

- ACTION.request/confirm (action ID, action value) is used by the AMT, say, to add one or more entries to a routing table.

- EVENT.indication (layer ID, event identifier, event value) is used by a layer entity to inform the AMT of, say, a threshold limit being reached.

14.5 Related standards

The goal of an open system protocol suite is to enable APs running in computer systems from different manufacturers to cooperate to perform a particular distributed processing function. The presentation services associated with the protocol suite ensure that the syntax of the messages exchanged have the same meanings in all systems. However, recall that the presentation services are not concerned with the structure or meaning of the information being exchanged. They simply treat the data as a stream of suitably defined data types – for example, character strings – and then use a suitable transfer syntax and, if necessary, syntax conversions, to ensure these are compatible with the syntax used in each cooperating system. The application processes interpret the structure and meaning of the transferred messages.

Clearly, if application processes are to cooperate to achieve a particular distributed processing task, they must agree on the structure and meaning of the messages associated with the application as well as on the order in which they are exchanged. One approach to the ordering is to define a virtual device for the application, such as a virtual file server. All messages exchanged must be ordered according to the order defined for the virtual device. In addition, all parties must have knowledge of the type and structure of the messages being exchanged.

In addition to the protocols that are needed within the message handling system to transfer messages to their intended destination – based on the addresses associated with the message envelope – there is a protocol above the communications stack that relates to the type and structure of the messages being exchanged, that is, relating to the body part. The interpersonal message protocol was identified in Chapter 13, but in practice there is a range of standards under development that relate to other types of information. For example, the **electronic data interchange (EDI)** standard is being defined for the exchange of trade-related documents such as purchase orders, invoices, and dispatch notes. Similarly, standards are being defined for the design, materials, and other documentation relating to products associated with the manufacturing industry, as are standards relating to the structure and contents of documents associated with office automation. Although all of these standards are of direct relevance to public (and private) X.400 messaging systems, they are also applicable when documents are being exchanged using, say, file transfer. A complete definition of these standards is outside the scope of the book, but let us look at two of them briefly.

14.5.1   EDI

The goal of the EDI standard is to enable possibly noncompatible computers to exchange trade-related documents, such as purchase orders, shipping documents, and quotations, in a standard message format. In general, these standards are being pushed by the major corporations that have a diverse range of suppliers of equipment and products. Only when all the relevant documentation is in a standard form can the whole trading cycle be automated. This is, of course, on top of an open system stack for communication purposes.

The message standard associated with EDI is a defined common format with a defined structure. The content, quantity, and position of all elements that comprise a document can all be defined using the standard. The terminology associated with the standard is given in Figure 14.23(a) in relation to the structure of a typical form used in such application environments.

Each page relating to a document is known as a **transaction set**. This is made up of a number of **data segments** each of which corresponds to a line or box on the form. A data segment is made up of one or more **data elements**. The overall format used is shown in Figure 14.23(b). The start and end of each component part is signaled by defined character strings and the individual data segments/elements have separators associated with them. The encoding rules are relatively simple and the character set is very limited.

For each application a particular set of transactions is defined and used by each communicating party. A number of message standards have been defined for use in various industries such as the motor trade, rail, and grocery.

14.5.2   ODA

The term ODA is an acronym of **open document architecture**. Office documents are items such as memoranda, letters, forms, and reports, which may include not only textual information but also other types of media such as images for company logos or institution crests.

A document contains information that relates to its **content** and its **structure**. The content of a document is any information that can be presented in a two-dimensional form, such as printed on paper or displayed on a screen. The structure is provided to do the following:

- Delimit portions within a document, such as areas of a page for images or different types of content elements – its layout structure.

- Delimit portions of a document that have a logical meaning, such as chapters and paragraphs – its **logical structure**.

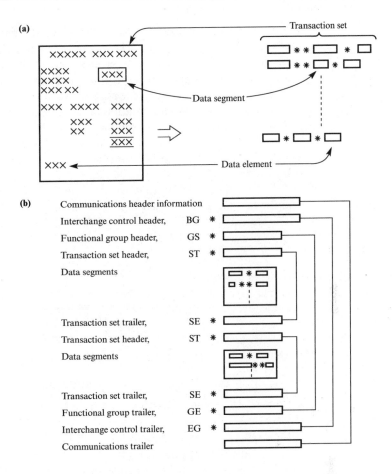

Figure 14.23
EDI terminology:
(a) form encoding;
(b) overall document
structure.

- Use different types of coding for the different content types.
- Allow documents to be processed.

The rules for representing structured documents are collectively called the **document architecture**.

For the purpose of interchange, a document is represented as a collection of constituent parts, each of which has a set of attributes. Each attribute has a name and a value and expresses a characteristic of a structural element. The types of constituent parts defined include:

- Document profile
- Logical structure
- Layout structure
- Content description
- Presentation style
- Layout style

The **document profile** consists of a set of attributes that specify characteristics of the document as a whole. The **content** description consists of the definition of a set of content elements. The **presentation** and **layout styles** are both sets of attributes which relate to the format and appearance of the document content on the presentation media. The separation of styles from the document structures allows the layout and presentation of a document to be modified without affecting its logical structure. For example, this is important in the publishing world. Typically, the author is concerned only with the content and the editor can modify the layout to fit it with other information. The relationship between the logical and layout descriptions is shown in Figure 14.24.

The layout description includes pages, frames (a rectangular area), blocks, and positioning and dimensioning data for frames and blocks relative to a page. The logical descriptions are independent of the layout (such as page) descriptions. For example, at the lowest level are text units which may be defined as paragraphs

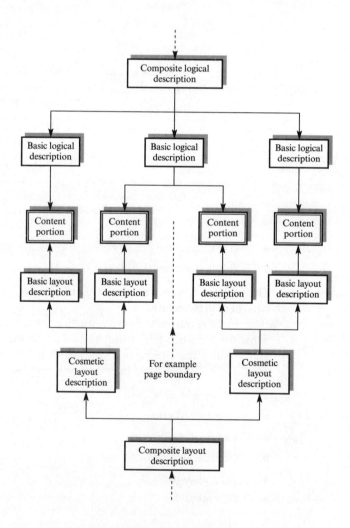

Figure 14.24
Example relationship between logical and layout descriptions.

or figures; these may then be grouped into a logical element (object). The logical structure defines the correct sequence of elements whereas the layout structure defines how they are positioned on, say, a page or pages.

Unlike EDI, ODA uses ASN.1 for defining the various structures. It is now supported by all the major vendors of office automation software and equipment and in time will remove the tedious conversion and reformatting operations that are currently necessary with most word processing software.

Exercises

14.1 Give an example of a symbolic name that might be used to refer to a networked server.
List the components of the equivalent address associated with the server in the following:
(a) The TCP/IP environment
(b) The OSI environment

14.2 Give an example of the symbolic name of a networked server assuming the following:
(a) A flat naming structure
(b) A hierarchical structure
Identify the implications of using each structure in relation to the management of names and the subsequent partitioning of the resulting directory.

14.3 Give an example of a name hierarchy in relation to the TCP/IP domain system.
Identify selected domain names (labels) in the hierarchy and explain the philosophy behind their assignment in relation to the overall management of the directory.

14.4 Identify the protocols associated with the domain name system.
Produce a sketch of a typical arrangement of these protocols in relation to a client system, a server, and a domain name server. Outline the sequence of messages that are exchanged between these protocols to obtain the TCP/IP address of the server.

14.5 With the aid of an outline domain name server hierarchy, give examples, with explanations, of how a name is resolved when the required server is:
(a) Local to the same name server
(b) At a higher layer in the hierarchy

Explain the meaning of the term 'name cache' and how such a mechanism can be used to minimize the use of referrals.

14.6 Explain, with the aid of examples, the meanings of the following terms in relation to the X.500 directory system:
(a) Directory information tree
(b) Relative distinguished name
(c) Distinguished name
(d) Alias name

14.7 Explain the functions of the directory user agent (DUA) and directory service agent (DSA) in relation to the X.500 directory system.
Explain the messages that are exchanged in order for a DUA to request the PSAP address of a named server. Clearly identify the use of the attribute type and attribute values.

14.8 With the aid of a sketch of an example name server hierarchy, explain the meaning of the following terms:
(a) Referral
(b) Chaining
(c) Multicasting

14.9 Identify the communication protocols that are associated with the DUA and DSA application processes.
With the aid of a sketch, trace the sequence of messages that are exchanged between a DUA and DSA through these protocols to determine the address of a named object – for example, a server.

14.10 Explain the meaning of the acronyms MAP and TOP and identify the application domain and protocols associated with each.

14.11 Use a template of the various protocols that make up the TCP/IP suite to trace the sequence of messages exchanged to carry out a networked request. Use for example purposes the f_open request associated with a networked file server.

14.12 Repeat Exercise 14.11 using an example OSI suite.

14.13 Discriminate between the terms 'address selector' and 'connection identifier' in relation to an OSI suite.

14.14 Describe a typical implementation structure for a TCP/IP and an OSI suite in terms of the processes that are involved and how they interact using the local operating system of the machine in which the various processes are running.

14.15 Explain the role of the user element in relation to an application process that is using an OSI stack for communication purposes. With the aid of an example, clearly describe how it harmonizes the services used by the application process and those provided at the interface with the protocol stack.

Chapter summary

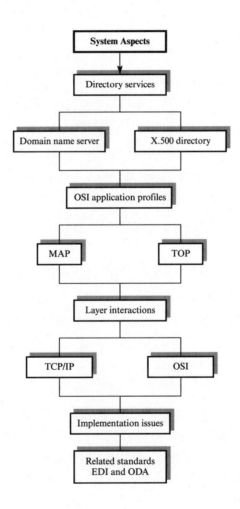

Appendix A

FORWARD ERROR CONTROL

Introduction

With an automatic repeat request (ARQ) error control scheme, additional check digits are appended to each transmitted message (frame) to enable the receiver to detect when an error is present in a received message, assuming certain types of error. If an error is detected, additional control procedures are used to request another copy of the message. With forward error control (FEC), sufficient additional check digits are added to each transmitted message to enable the receiver not only to detect the presence of one or more errors in a received message but also to locate the position of the error(s). Furthermore, since the message is in a binary form, correction is achieved simply by inverting the bit(s) that have been identified as erroneous.

In practice, the number of additional check digits required for error correction is much larger than that needed for just error detection. In most applications involving terrestrial (land-based) links, ARQ methods similar to those described in Chapter 4 are more efficient than FEC methods, and hence are the most frequently used. Such methods rely on a return path for acknowledgment purposes. However, in certain applications, a return path may simply not be available or the round-trip delay associated with it may be very long compared with the data transmission rate of the link. For example, frequently only a unidirectional link is used when transmitting information back from a space probe. Similarly, with many satellite links the propagation delay may be such that several hundred messages may be transmitted by the sending station before a message, and hence an acknowledgment, is received in the reverse direction. In such applications, FEC methods are often used, normally in conjunction with ARQ methods, to reduce the number of retransmissions. The aim of this appendix is to give an introduction to the techniques most widely used with FEC methods.

A.1 Hamming single-bit code

In practice, this FEC method is of limited use for data transmission. Nevertheless, we shall look at it briefly to introduce the subject and some of the terms associated with coding theory. Clearly, a comprehensive description of the subject of coding theory is beyond the scope of this book and hence the aim here is simply a brief introduction. If you have an interest in coding theory and would like to gain a more extensive coverage, consult the bibliography at the end of the book.

The term used in coding theory to describe the combined message unit, comprising the useful data bits and the additional check bits, is **codeword**. The minimum number of bit positions in which two valid codewords differ is known as the **Hamming distance** of the code. For example, consider a coding scheme that has seven data bits and a single parity bit per codeword. Assuming even parity is being used, consecutive codewords in this scheme are as follows:

```
0000000   0
0000001   1
0000010   1
0000011   0
```

We can see from this list that such a scheme has a Hamming distance of 2, as each valid codeword differs in at least two bit positions. This means that it does not detect 2-bit errors since the resulting (corrupted) bit pattern will be a different but valid codeword. However, it does detect all single-bit errors since, if a single bit in a codeword is corrupted, an invalid codeword will result.

In general, the error-detecting and error-correcting properties of a coding scheme are both related to its Hamming distance. It can be shown that to detect n errors, we must use a coding scheme with a Hamming distance of $n + 1$, while to correct for n errors, we must use a code with a Hamming distance of $2n + 1$.

The simplest error-correcting coding scheme is the Hamming single-bit code. Such a code detects not only when a single-bit error is present in a received codeword but also the position of the error. The corrected codeword is derived by inverting the identified erroneous bit. This type of code is known as a **block code**, since the original message to be transmitted is treated as a single block (frame) during the encoding and subsequent decoding processes. In general, with a block code, each block of k source digits is encoded to produce an n-digit block (n greater than k) of output digits. The encoder is said to produce an (n, k) code. The ratio k/n is known as the **code rate** or **code efficiency** while the difference $1 - k/n$ is known as the **redundancy**.

To illustrate this, consider a Hamming code to detect and correct for single-bit errors assuming each codeword contains a 7-bit data field – an ASCII character, for example. Such a coding scheme requires four check bits since, with this scheme, the check bits occupy all bit positions that are powers of 2. This code is known as an $(11, 7)$ block code with a rate of $7/11$ and a redundancy of $1 - 7/11$. For example, the bit positions of the value 1001101 are as follows:

```
11  10  9  8  7  6  5  4  3  2  1
 1   0  0  x  1  1  0  x  1  x  x
```

The four bit positions marked 'x' are used for the check bits, which are derived as follows. The 4-bit binary numbers corresponding to those bit positions with a binary 1 are added together using modulo-2 arithmetic and the four check bits are the following 4-bit sum:

$$
\begin{array}{l}
11 = 1\ 0\ 1\ 1 \\
\ 7 = 0\ 1\ 1\ 1 \\
\ 6 = 0\ 1\ 1\ 0 \\
\ 3 = 0\ 0\ 1\ 1 \\
\hline
\ \ \ = 1\ 0\ 0\ 1
\end{array}
$$

The transmitted codeword is thus:

$$
\begin{array}{ccccccccccc}
11 & 10 & 9 & 8 & 7 & 6 & 5 & 4 & 3 & 2 & 1 \\
1 & 0 & 0 & [1] & 1 & 1 & 0 & [0] & 1 & [0] & [1]
\end{array}
$$

Similarly, at the receiver, the 4-bit binary numbers corresponding to those bit positions with a binary 1, including the check bits, are again added together. If no errors have occurred, the modulo-2 sum is zero:

$$
\begin{array}{l}
11 = 1\ 0\ 1\ 1 \\
\ 8 = 1\ 0\ 0\ 0 \\
\ 7 = 0\ 1\ 1\ 1 \\
\ 6 = 0\ 1\ 1\ 0 \\
\ 3 = 0\ 0\ 1\ 1 \\
\ 1 = 0\ 0\ 0\ 1 \\
\hline
\ \ \ \ 0\ 0\ 0\ 0
\end{array}
$$

Now consider a single-bit error: say bit 11 is corrupted from 1 to 0. The new modulo-2 sum is now:

$$
\begin{array}{l}
8 = 1\ 0\ 0\ 0 \\
7 = 0\ 1\ 1\ 1 \\
6 = 0\ 1\ 1\ 0 \\
3 = 0\ 0\ 1\ 1 \\
1 = 0\ 0\ 0\ 1 \\
\hline
\ \ \ 1\ 0\ 1\ 1
\end{array}
$$

Firstly, the sum is nonzero, which indicates an error, and secondly, the modulo-2 sum, equivalent to decimal 11, indicates that bit 11 is the erroneous bit. The latter is inverted to obtain the corrected codeword and hence data bits.

It can also be shown that if two bit errors occur, the modulo-2 sum is nonzero, thus indicating an error, but the positions of the errors cannot be determined from the sum. The Hamming single-bit code can correct for single-bit errors and detect two-bit errors but other multiple-bit errors cannot be detected.

As we saw in Chapter 2, the main types of error in many data communication networks are error bursts rather than, say, isolated single- or double-bit errors. Hence, although the Hamming coding scheme in its basic form appears to be inappropriate for use with such networks, a simple technique is often used to extend the application of such a scheme.

Consider, for example, a requirement to transmit a block of data, comprising a string of, say, eight ASCII characters, over a simplex channel that has a high probability of an error burst (of, say, seven bits). The controlling device first converts each ASCII character into its 11-bit codeword form to give a block of eight 11-bit codewords. Then, instead of transmitting each codeword separately, the controlling device transmits the contents of the block of codewords a column at a time. Thus the eight, say, most significant bits are transmitted first, then the eight next most significant bits and so on, finishing with the eight least significant bits. The controlling device at the receiver then performs the reverse operation, reassembling the transmitted block in memory, prior to performing the detection and, if necessary, correction operation on each codeword.

The effect of this approach is, firstly, that a standard USRT device can be used as the transmission interface circuit and, secondly, and more importantly, that if an error burst of up to seven bits does occur, it affects only a single bit in each codeword rather than a string of bits in one or two codewords. This means that, assuming just a single error burst in the 88 bits transmitted, the receiver can determine a correct copy of the transmitted block of characters.

Although the approach just outlined provides a way of extending the usefulness of this type of encoding scheme, Hamming codes are used mainly in applications that have isolated single-bit errors; an example is in error-correcting semiconductor memory systems. The preferred method of achieving FEC in data communication systems is based on **convolutional codes** and we shall now briefly consider this type of encoding process.

A.2 Convolutional codes

Block codes are *memoryless* codes as each output codeword depends only on the current k-bit message block being encoded. In contrast, with a convolutional code, the continuous stream of source bits is operated upon to produce a continuous stream of output (encoded) bits. Because of the nature of the encoding process, the sequence of source bits is said to be convolved (by applying a specific binary operation on them) to produce the output bit sequence. Also, each bit in the output sequence is dependent not only on the current bit being encoded but also on the previous sequence of source bits, thus implying some form of memory. In practice, as we shall see, this takes the form of a shift register of a finite length, known as the **constraint length**, and the convolution (binary) operation is performed using one or more modulo-2 adders (exclusive-OR gates).

Encoding

An example of a convolutional encoder is shown in Figure A.1(a). With this encoder, the three-bit shift register provides the memory and the two modulo-2 adders the convolution operation. For each bit in the input sequence, two bits are

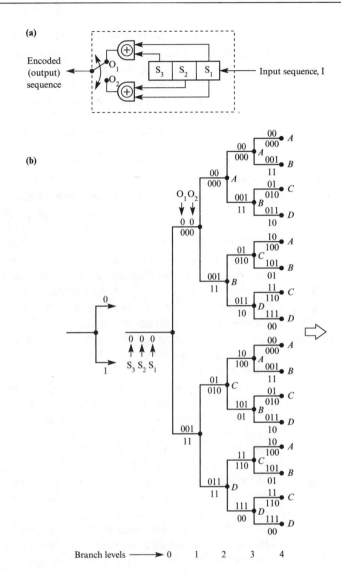

Figure A.1
Convolutional codes:
(a) example encoder
circuit; (b) tree
diagram
representation.

output, one from each of the two modulo-2 adders. The encoder shown is thus known as a rate $1/2(k/n)$ convolutional encoder with a constraint length of 3.

Because of the memory associated with a convolutional encoder, we must have a convenient means of determining the specific output bit sequence generated for a given input sequence. Three techniques can be used, each based on a form of diagrammatic representation: a tree diagram, a state diagram, and a trellis diagram. In practice, the last is the most frequently used method because it is the most useful for demonstrating the decoding operation. However, before we can draw this, we must determine the outputs for each possible input sequence using either the tree or state diagram.

As an example, Figure A.1(b) shows the **tree diagram** for the encoder in Figure A.1(a). The branching points in the tree are known as nodes and the tree shows the two possible branches at each node; the upper of the two branches corresponds to a 0 input bit and the lower branch to a 1 bit. The pair of output bits corresponding to the two possible branches at each node are shown on the outside of each branch line.

As we can see, with a tree diagram the number of branches in the tree doubles for each new input bit. However, the tree is repetitive after the second branch level since, after this level, there are only four unique branch nodes. These are known as **states** and are shown as A, B, C, and D in the figure.

As we can see, from any one of these nodes the same pair of output bits and new node state occurs, irrespective of the position of the node in the tree. For example, from any node C the same pair of branch alternatives occur: 10 output and new state A for a 0 input, or 01 output and new state B for a 1 input.

Once we have identified the states for the encoder using the tree diagram, we can draw the **trellis diagram**. As an example, the trellis diagram for the same encoder is as shown in Figure A.2(b). As we can see, after the second branch level, the repetitive nature of the tree diagram is exploited by representing all the possible encoder outputs in a more reduced form.

The trellis diagram shows the outputs that result from this encoder for all possible input bit sequences. Then, for a specific input sequence, a single path through the trellis – and hence sequence of output bits – results. As an example, Figure A.2(c) shows the path through the trellis, and hence the output sequence, corresponding to the input sequence 110101 . . . .

Initially, we assume that the shift register is cleared, that is, it is set to all 0s. After the first bit in the input sequence has been shifted (entered) into the shift register, its contents are 001. The outputs from the two modulo-2 adders are $0 + 1 = 1$ (adder 1) and $0 + 1 = 1$ (adder 2). Thus, the first two output bits are 11 and these are output before the next input bit is entered into the shift register. Since the input bit was a 1, the lower branch path on the trellis diagram is followed and the output is 11, as derived.

After the second input bit has been entered, the shift register contains 011. The two adder outputs are $0 + 1 = 1$ (adder 1) and $1 + 1 = 0$ (adder 2). Thus, the two output bits are 10 and again these are output before the next input bit is processed. Again, since the input bit was a 1, the lower branch on the trellis diagram is followed and the output is 10, as derived. Continuing, the third input bit makes the shift register contents 110 and hence the two output bits are 11; $1 + 0 = 1$ (adder 1) and $1 + 0 = 1$ (adder 2). Also, since the input bit was a 0, the upper branch path on the trellis diagram is followed. This process then continues.

Decoding

The aim of the decoder is to determine the *most likely* output sequence, given a received bit stream (which may have errors) and a knowledge of the encoder used at the source. The decoding procedure is equivalent to comparing the received

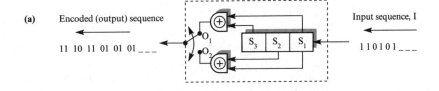

(a) Encoded (output) sequence — 11 10 11 01 01 01 _ _ _ — O_1 O_2 — S_3 S_2 S_1 — Input sequence, I — 110101 _ _ _

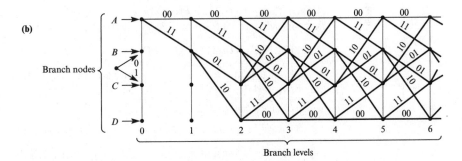

Input sequence I	Shift register contents S_1 S_2 S_3	Output sequence O_1 O_2
1	1 → 0 → 0	1 1
1	1 → 1 → 0	1 0
0	0 → 1 → 1	1 1
1	1 → 0 → 1	0 1
0	0 → 1 → 0	0 1
1	1 → 0 → 1	0 1

(b)

Branch nodes

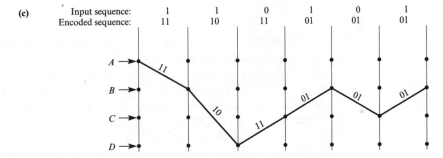

(c)

Figure A.2
Convolutional
encoder: (a) circuit;
(b) trellis diagram;
(c) example output.

sequence with all the possible sequences that may be obtained with the respective encoder and then selecting the sequence that is closest to the received sequence. As Section A.1 mentioned, the Hamming distance between two codewords is the number of bits that differ between them. Therefore, when selecting the sequence that is closest to the received sequence, the Hamming distance between the received sequence and each of the possible sequences is computed, and the one with the least distance is selected. Clearly, in the limit this necessitates comparing the complete received sequence with all the possible sequences, and hence paths through the trellis. This is impractical in most cases and hence we must compromise.

Essentially, a running count is maintained of the distance between the actual received sequence and each possible sequence but, at each node in the trellis, only a single path is retained. There are always two paths merging at each node and the path selected is the one with the minimum Hamming distance, the other is simply terminated. The retained paths are known as **survivor paths** and the final path selected is the one with a continuous path through the trellis with a minimum aggregate Hamming distance. This procedure is known as the **Viterbi algorithm**. The decoder, which aims to find the most likely path corresponding to the received sequence, is known as a **maximum-likelihood decoder**. Example A.1 describes the Viterbi algorithm.

Example A.1

Assume that a message sequence of 1001110... is to be sent using the encoder shown in Figure A.1 (a). From the trellis diagram for this encoder, we can deduce that this will yield a transmitted (output) sequence of:

11   01   10   11   10   00   11...

Now assume a burst error occurs so that two bits of this encoded sequence are corrupted during transmission. The received sequence is as follows:

11   01   00   11   11   00   11...
           ↑   ↑

Use the Viterbi algorithm to determine from this the most likely transmitted sequence.

The various steps associated with the encoding and decoding procedures are shown in Figure A.3. Part (a) shows the path through the trellis corresponding to the original output from the encoder and part (b) shows how the survivor paths are chosen. The number shown by each path merging at a node in Figure A.3(b) is the accumulated Hamming distance between the path followed to get to that node and the actual received sequence.

If the path chosen is that starting at the root node (branch level 0), the received sequence is 11 and the Hamming distances for the two paths are 2 for path 00 and 0 for path 11. These two distance values are added to the paths emanating from these nodes. Thus, at branch level 1, the received sequence is 01 and the two paths from node A have Hamming distances of 1 for path 00 and 1 for path 11. The accumulated distances are thus $2 + 1 = 3$ for each path. Similarly, the two paths emanating from node B have Hamming distances of 0 for path 01 and 2 for path 10, and hence the accumulated distances are $0 + 0 = 0$ and $0 + 2 = 2$, respectively. A similar procedure is repeated at branch level 2.

At branch level 3 and onwards, however, the selection process starts. Thus, the two paths merging at node A (at branch level 3) have accumulated distances

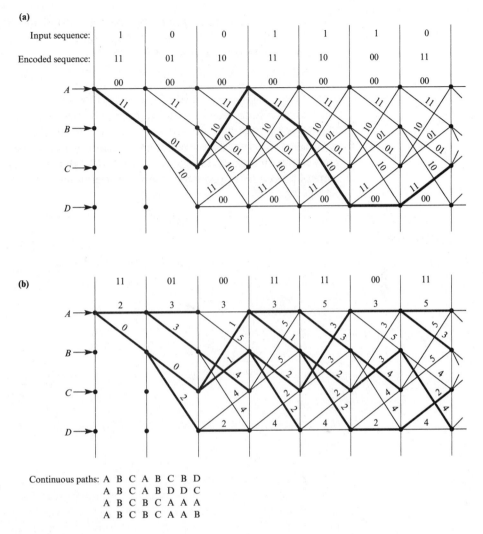

Figure A.3
Convolutional
decoder: (a) encoder
output; (b) survivor
paths.

Continuous paths:
A B C A B C B D
A B C A B D D C
A B C B C A A A
A B C B C A A B

of 3 and 1, of which the latter is selected to be the survivor path for this node – this is shown as a bold line on the trellis diagram. A similar selection process is followed at nodes *B*, *C*, and *D*. At node *C*, however, we can see that the two merging paths both have the same accumulated distance of 4. In such cases, the upper path is selected. Also, after the selection process, all subsequent distances are calculated relative to the accumulated distance associated with the selected path.

It now remains to select the most likely path and hence the output sequence. Although the decoding procedure continues, by inspection of the portion of the trellis shown, we can see that:

- Only four paths have a continuous path through the trellis.

- The distance corresponding to the path *ABCABDDC* is the minimum.

Thus, this is the path that is selected, the corresponding output sequence being 11 01 10 11 10 00 11..., which corresponds to the original encoded (and hence transmitted) sequence.

■ ■

Finally, note that no FEC methods can identify all errors. In general, codes like the convolutional code are used primarily to reduce the error probability (bit error rate) of a link to a more acceptable level. A typical reduction with a rate 1/2 convolutional code is between 10^2 and 10^3. Hence, assuming an ARQ error control procedure is also being used, the overall link efficiency is much improved.

Appendix B

TRANSMISSION CONTROL CIRCUITS

As Section 3.6 indicated, special integrated circuits are available to perform most of the functions associated with the different types of transmission control scheme. As an example, this appendix describes the circuit used to perform the various control functions associated with character-oriented data transmission. The circuit is known as a **universal synchronous asynchronous receiver transmitter (USART)**.

The term 'universal' is used since the device can be programmed to operate in both character-oriented transmission modes: asynchronous and synchronous. The specific mode and operating characteristics are selected by writing – under program control – a predefined bit pattern into one of the internal control registers of the device. When programmed to operate in the asynchronous mode, the device is normally referred to as a **universal asynchronous receiver transmitter (UART)** while in the synchronous mode it is known as a **universal synchronous receiver transmitter (USRT)**.

Essentially, a UART accepts a character in parallel form from a controlling device – for example, a microprocessor – and then transmits it out bit serially, together with a start and stop bit(s) and, if selected, a parity bit. Similarly, on input, it receives the serial bit stream, removes the start and stop bits, checks the parity, and then makes the received character available to be read by the controlling device in parallel form. It includes all the necessary circuitry to achieve bit (clock) synchronization as well as additional modem control circuitry. A schematic showing the main registers associated with a USART is given in Figure B.1(a); part (b) shows a typical interfacing arrangement to use the device as a UART.

To use the device, the **mode register** is first loaded with the required bit pattern to define the required operating characteristics; this is known as initialization. With asynchronous transmission, the user may select 5, 6, 7, or 8 bits per character, odd, even, or no parity, one or more stop bits, and a particular clock rate ratio. The last of these is also referred to as the **baud rate factor**. Depending on the required bit rate, a clock source of the appropriate frequency is applied to the transmit and receive clock inputs. The most commonly used bit rates with asynchronous transmission are 110, 300, 1200, 2400, 4800, 9600, and 19 200 bps. Hence, if say a $\times 16$ clock rate is selected, then the transmit and receive clock inputs are 1760 (110×16), 4800 (300×16), etc., respectively. For the device

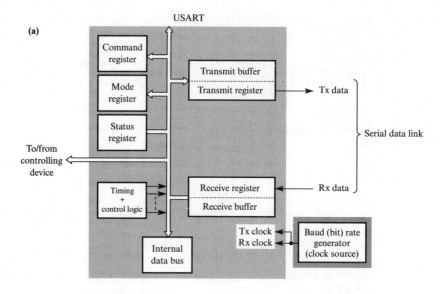

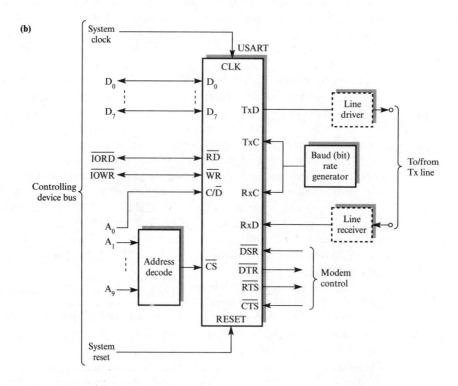

Figure B.1 USART schematic: (a) main device registers; (b) device interfacing.

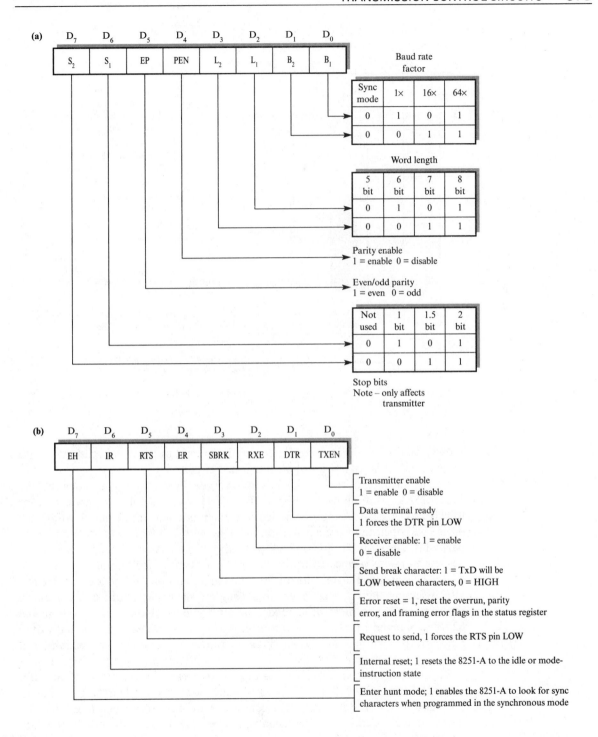

Figure B.2 Mode/command/status register bit definitions of the Intel 8251A: (a) mode; (b) command.

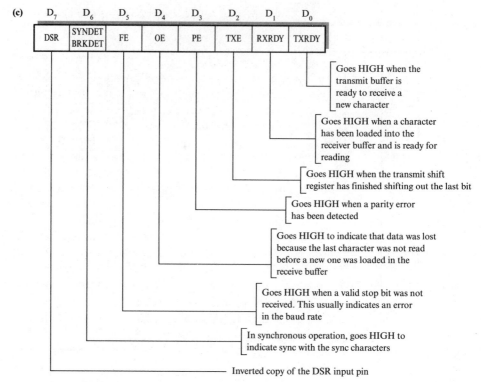

(c)

D$_7$	D$_6$	D$_5$	D$_4$	D$_3$	D$_2$	D$_1$	D$_0$
DSR	SYNDET BRKDET	FE	OE	PE	TXE	RXRDY	TXRDY

Goes HIGH when the transmit buffer is ready to receive a new character

Goes HIGH when a character has been loaded into the receiver buffer and is ready for reading

Goes HIGH when the transmit shift register has finished shifting out the last bit

Goes HIGH when a parity error has been detected

Goes HIGH to indicate that data was lost because the last character was not read before a new one was loaded in the receive buffer

Goes HIGH when a valid stop bit was not received. This usually indicates an error in the baud rate

In synchronous operation, goes HIGH to indicate sync with the sync characters

Inverted copy of the DSR input pin

Figure B.2 (cont.)
(c) Status.

shown, we assume that the clock circuitry is external to the device, although with some devices it is part of the same integrated circuit.

The meaning of the various bits in the mode register of a typical device – the Intel 8251A – are shown in Figure B.2(a). Hence, assuming a mode byte of 01111010 (7A hexadecimal) is loaded into the mode register at initialization, the device will operate in the asynchronous mode with 7 bits per character, an even parity bit, one stop bit, and a clock rate ratio of ×16. A clock source of ×16 the desired bit rate is connected to the transmit and receive clock inputs.

The **command byte** controls the actual operation of the device. Hence, after selecting the required operational mode (and prior to transmitting data), the command byte must be loaded. The assignments of the various bits in the 8251A command byte are shown in Figure B.2(b). As we can see, the individual bits perform such functions as enabling the transmitter and receiver sections, and controlling the modem interface. The three bits of general use are the error reset (ER), the receiver enable (RXE) and the transmitter enable (TXEN). Hence, if a command byte of 00010011 (13 Hex) is loaded after the mode byte and prior to the transmission of data, any error conditions are reset (described later) and the transmitter and receiver sections enabled. The UARTs at both ends of the data link must, of course, be programmed to operate in the same mode and with the same operational characteristics.

The controlling device determines the current state of a UART by reading the contents of a third register (known as the **status register**) and testing specific bits within it. These are **status** or **flag bits**; the composition of the status register in the 8251A is shown in Figure B.2(c).

To transmit a character, the controlling device first waits until the TXRDY (transmit ready) flag becomes set which indicates the transmit buffer is empty. The character is then loaded into the transmit buffer and is subsequently transferred to the PISO transmit register by the control logic within the device when the last stop bit of the previous character has been transmitted to line. At this point the TXEMPTY flag becomes set and is reset when a new character is loaded into the transmit buffer. The TXEMPTY flag is particularly useful when a line is being operated in the half-duplex mode since in this mode the controlling device must know when the last character in a message – the final stop bit(s), in practice – has been transmitted to line.

On receipt of a character, the individual bits from the line are sampled and shifted bit serially into the SIPO receive register and, on receipt of the final stop bit, the character is transferred by the control logic to the receive buffer. At this point the RXRDY (receive ready) flag becomes set which indicates to the controlling device that a character is ready to be read. The RXRDY flag is then reset by the UART when the received character is read from the receive buffer. In addition, during the reception process, the UART indicates to the controlling device the occurrence (or otherwise) of three possible error conditions:

- PE (parity error) is set if the computed parity bit for a character is different from that selected.

- OE (overrun error) is set if a received character is transferred to the receive buffer before the previous character was read, thereby losing the latter.

- FE (framing error) is set if a valid stop bit was not received and normally indicates the clock rate ratio is incorrect.

To program the USART to operate in the synchronous mode (that is, as a USRT), the two least significant bits of the mode register are both set to binary 0. The next four bits have the same meaning as for asynchronous transmission: number of bits per character and parity selection – odd, even, or no parity. The two most significant bits have a different meaning. The ESD (external sync detect) bit – S_1 – is used to indicate whether the character synchronization procedure is to be carried out externally or internally and is normally set to internal. Finally, the SCS bit (sync character select) – S_2 – is used to indicate whether one or two SYN characters are to be transmitted whenever the transmit buffer is empty, for example, prior to transmitting a frame.

Before loading the frame contents, as with asynchronous transmission, the command register must be loaded. The use of the various bits is the same as for asynchronous transmission. The additional bit of interest with synchronous transmission is the EH bit (enter hunt mode). Assuming internal sync detect has been selected, the EH bit is set to start the character synchronization procedure associated with the receive section of the device.

Table B.1

$\overline{CS}$	$C/\overline{D}$	$\overline{RD}$	$\overline{WR}$	Operation
0	1	1	0	Write to mode/command register
0	0	1	0	Write to transmit buffer
0	1	0	1	Read status register
0	0	0	1	Read receive buffer
1	X	X	X	Device disabled

X = Either 0 or 1

Once the functional definition of the 8251A has been programmed – using the mode register – two or more SYN characters are loaded (to enable the receiver to obtain character synchronization before the frame contents are received).

The controlling device determines the current state of the 8251A by reading the contents of the status register and interpreting the individual bits within it. These again are the same as those used with asynchronous transmission. The additional bit used with synchronous transmission is the SYNDET (sync detect) bit which indicates that the receiver section has achieved character synchronization when it is in the hunt mode. Normally the controlling device then reads each subsequent character as it is received and waits for the start-of-frame character that signals a new frame.

With the 8251A, the controlling device accesses the various registers – control and data – using a combination of the chip select (CS), the read (RD) and write (WR), and the control/data (C/D) lines. The bar above a signal indicates that it is active when low – binary 0 – rather than when it is a binary 1. A summary of the use of the various lines is given in Table B.1.

As we can see, the C/D line is set to 1 when the controlling device is communicating with a control register and a 0 with a data register, the actual register being determined by the state of the RD and WR lines. For example, to read the status register, the C/D line is set to 1, while to read a character from the receive buffer it is set to 0. Note that to write to the mode/command registers two successive write operations must be carried out; the first byte is loaded into the mode register and the second into the command register.

Finally, we have discussed the operation of just a single device type – the USART – all the other transmission control devices operate in a similar way.

Appendix C

SUMMARY OF STANDARDS ORGANIZATIONS

American National Standards Institute (ANSI) A national standards organization comprising members from computer manufacturers and users in the United States. It is also the US member body of ISO. Its members are involved in the development of standards at all levels in the ISO reference model.

ATM Forum A worldwide organization of companies who are involved in the manufacture of networking equipment. It develops standards relating to private ATM networks.

British Standards Institution (BSI) A national standards organization concerned with the production of standards for use by all forms of manufacturing and consumer industries. It is the British member of ISO and acts as a source for all their documents.

Electronics Industries Association (EIA) A US national standards organization comprising members from the electronics industry. In the context of data and computer communications, it has produced a range of (physical) interface standards for connecting peripherals to a computer and, more recently, through the contribution of General Motors, has been actively involved in the development of the layer 7 standard for manufacturing message service (MMS). It is a member of ANSI and, through them, ISO.

European Computer Manufacturers Association (ECMA) This comprises members from computer manufacturers in Europe including some European divisions of American companies. It produces its own standards and also contributes to ITU-T and ISO. Its members are actively involved in the development of standards at all levels of the ISO reference model.

European Telecommunications Standards Institute (ETSI) A European standards body that produces standards for regulatory purposes by the EU and EFTA countries. It produces standards relating to telecommunication services, public data networks, videotex, and digital cellular services which are issued as European Telecommunication Standards (ETSs), also known as NETs.

Institute of Electrical and Electronics Engineers (IEEE) A US professional society that also takes part in the development of standards for the computer industry. In the context of computer communications, it has been responsible for the production of standards relating to LANs and, in particular, for those concerned with the physical, MAC and LLC (sub)layers.

International Organization for Standardization (ISO) An international standards organization comprising designated standards bodies of the participating countries. It is concerned with a wide range of standards, each of which is controlled by a separate technical committee. The technical committee that produces standards for the computer industry is TC97 – Information Processing Systems. This committee has been responsible for the production of the basic ISO reference model for OSI and also for the production of the various protocol standards for each layer in the reference model.

International Telecommunications Union – Telecommunications (ITU-T) formerly **International Telegraph and Telephone Consultative Committee (CCITT)** An international standards organization consisting of the Postal, Telegraph, and Telephone (PTT) authorities of the member countries. It is concerned primarily with the development and production of standards for interfacing equipment to public telecommunications networks. These include the analog PSTN, ISDN, and PPSDN. It also produces standards for facsimile, Teletex, Videotex, and other value-added services (teleservices).

National Bureau of Standards (NBS)   A US national standards organization concerned with the production of standards relating to both ISO and ITU-T. It issues standards for equipment purchased by the US federal government in the general area of information processing. These are known as federal information processing standards (FIPS).

OSI Network Management Forum (NMF)   A worldwide organization of telecommunications and computer companies, service providers, and service users. The NMF develops standards for network management based on ISO/OSI management protocols.

Appendix D

GLOSSARY OF TERMS AND ABBREVIATIONS

Abstract syntax notation one (ASN.1) An abstract syntax used to define the structure of the protocol data units associated with a particular protocol entity.

Address resolution protocol (ARP) The protocol in the TCP/IP suite that is used to obtain the network point of attachment address of a host corresponding to its internetwide IP address.

Advanced Research Projects Agency (ARPA) The former name of the US government agency that funded the creation of the ARPANET and later the Internet – now DARPA.

American Standards Committee for Information Interchange (ASCII) In normal usage this refers to the character code defined by this committee for the interchange of information between two communicating devices. The ASCII character set is in widespread use for the transfer of information between a computer and a peripheral device such as a visual display unit or a printer.

Amplitude modulation (AM) A modulation technique to allow data to be transmitted across an analog network, such as a switched telephone network. The amplitude of a single (carrier) frequency is varied (modulated) between two levels – one for binary 0 and the other for binary 1.

Application layer This corresponds to layer 7 of the ISO reference model for open systems interconnection. It comprises a number of application-oriented protocols and forms the user interface to the various distributed information processing services supported.

ARPANET The wide area network funded by ARPA/DARPA that links many universities, research, and defense establishments throughout the United States and other countries. In addition to carrying live traffic, it has been used as a development testbed for research into internetworking – now part of the larger Internet.

Association control service element (ACSE) A protocol entity forming part of the application layer. It provides the generalized (common) function of establishing and clearing a logical association (connection) between two application entities.

Asynchronous transfer mode (ATM) The proposed mode of operation of the emerging broadband integrated services digital network. All information to be transmitted – voice, data, image, video – is first fragmented into small, fixed-sized frames known as cells. These are switched and routed using packet switching principles – also known as cell or fast-packet switching. The first networks that are based on this mode of operation are ATM LANs.

Asynchronous transmission Strictly, this implies that the receiver clock is not synchronized to the transmitted clock when data is being transmitted between two devices connected by a transmission line. More generally, it indicates that data is being transmitted as individual characters. Each character is preceded by a start signal and terminated by one or more stop signals, which are used by the receiver for synchronization purposes.

Automatic repeat request (ARQ) A technique used for error control over a transmission line. If errors in a transmitted message are detected by the receiving device, it requests the sending device to retransmit the message together with any other messages that may have been affected.

Bandwidth The difference between the highest and lowest sinusoidal frequency signals that can be transmitted across a transmission line or through a network. It is measured in hertz (Hz) and also defines the maximum information-carrying capacity of the line or network.

Baseband   A particular operating mode of a transmission line: each binary digit (bit) in a message is converted into one of two voltage (sometimes current) levels – one for binary 1 and the other for binary 0. The voltages are then applied directly to the line. The line signal varies with time between these two voltage levels as the data is transmitted.

Basic mode   An ISO international standard protocol defined to control the exchange of data between a master (primary) station and multiple slave (secondary) stations which are connected by means of a multidrop link.

Baud   The number of line signal variations per second. It also indicates the rate at which data is transmitted on a line, although this is strictly correct only when each bit is represented by a single signal level on the transmission line. Hence, the bit rate and the line signal rate are both the same.

Binary synchronous control (BSC)   The name used by IBM for the ISO basic mode protocol.

Bit stuffing (zero bit insertion)   A technique used to allow pure binary data to be transmitted on a synchronous transmission line. Each message block (frame) is encapsulated between two flags, which are special bit sequences. If the message data contains a possibly similar sequence, then an additional (zero) bit is inserted into the data stream by the sender, and is subsequently removed by the receiving device. The transmission method is said to be data transparent.

Block sum check   This is used for the detection of errors when data is being transmitted. It is comprised of a set of binary digits (bits), which are the modulo-2 sum of the individual characters/octets in a frame (block) or message.

Bridge   A device used to link two homogeneous local area subnetworks, that is, two subnetworks utilizing the same physical and medium access control method.

Broadband   A particular mode of operation of a coaxial cable. A single coaxial cable can be used to transmit a number of separate data streams simultaneously by assigning each stream a portion of the total available bandwidth. Data is transmitted by modulating a single frequency signal from the selected frequency band and is received by demodulating the received signal.

Broadcast   A means of transmitting a message to all devices connected to a network. Normally, a special address, the broadcast address, is reserved to enable all the devices to determine that the message is a broadcast message.

Bus   A network topology in widespread use for the interconnection of communities of digital devices distributed over a localized area. The transmission medium is normally a single coaxial cable to which all the devices are attached. Each transmission thus propagates the length of the medium and is received by all other devices connected to the medium.

Checksum   *See* block sum check.

Circuit switching   The mode of operation of a telephone network and also some of the newer digital data networks. A communication path is first established through the network between the source (calling) and destination (called) terminals, and this is used exclusively for the duration of the call or transaction. Both terminals must operate at the same information transfer rate.

Coaxial cable   A type of transmission medium consisting of a center conductor and a concentric outer conductor. It is used when high data transfer rates (greater than 1 Mbps) are required.

Commitment, concurrency, and recovery (CCR)   A protocol entity forming part of the application layer. It allows two or more application processes to perform mutually exclusive operations on shared data. It also provides control to ensure that the operations are performed either completely or not at all. It uses the concepts of an atomic action and a two-phase commit protocol.

Community antenna television (CATV)   A facility used in the context of local area data networks, since the principles and network components used in CATV networks can also be used to produce a flexible underlying data transmission facility over a local area. CATV networks operate using the broadband mode of working.

Common application service element (CASE)   A collection of protocol entities forming part of the application layer that are responsible for providing some common services, such as establishing a logical connection (association) between two application protocol entities.

Common management information protocol (CMIP)   The ISO application layer protocol used to retrieve and send management-related information across an OSI network.

Continuous RQ   A part of a data link protocol concerned with error control. It endeavors to ensure that, if a frame (message) is corrupted during transmission, another copy of the frame is sent. To improve the efficiency of utilization of the data link, frames are transmitted continuously; hence, retransmission requests relating to corrupted frames may be received after a number of other frames have been transmitted.

Crosstalk An unwanted signal that is picked up in a conductor as a result of some external electrical activity.

CSMA/CD Carrier sense, multiple access with collision detection. A method used to control access to a shared transmission medium, such as a coaxial cable bus to which a number of stations are connected. A station that wishes to transmit a message first senses (listens to) the medium and transmits the message only if the medium is quiet – no carrier present. Then, as the message is being transmitted, the station monitors the actual signal on the transmission medium. If this is different from the signal being transmitted, a collision is said to have occurred and been detected. The station then ceases transmission and retries again later.

Cyclic redundancy check (CRC) A method used for the detection of errors when data is being transmitted. A CRC is a numeric value computed from the bits in the message to be transmitted. It is appended to the tail of the message prior to transmission and the receiver detects the presence of errors in the received message by recomputing a new CRC.

Data circuit terminating equipment (DCE) The equipment provided by the network authority (provider) for the attachment of user devices to the network. It takes on different forms for different network types.

Data link layer This corresponds to layer 2 of the ISO reference model for open systems interconnection. It is concerned with the reliable transfer of data (no residual transmission errors) across the data link being used.

Data terminal equipment (DTE) A generic name for any user device connected to a data network. It includes such devices as visual display units, computers, and office workstations.

Datagram A type of service offered on a packet switched data network (*see also* virtual call). A datagram is a self-contained packet of information that is sent through the network with minimum protocol overheads.

Decibel A measure of the strength of a signal relative to another signal. The number of decibels is computed as ten times the log of the ratio of the power in each

signal or twenty times the log of the amplitude (voltage or current) of each signal.

Defense Advanced Research Projects Agency (DARPA) *See* ARPA.

Delay distortion Distortion of a signal caused by the frequency components making up the signal having different propagation velocities across a transmission medium.

Directory service (DS) A protocol entity forming part of the application layer in an OSI suite that is concerned with the translation of symbolic names (or titles), as used by application processes, into fully qualified network addresses, as used within the open systems interconnection environment. Also known as X.500.

Distributed queue, dual bus (DQDB) An optical fiber-based network that can be used as a high-speed LAN or MAN that is compatible with the evolving broadband ISDN. It operates in a broadcast mode by using two buses, each of which transmits small fixed-sized frames – known as cells – in opposite directions. Each bus can operate at hundreds of megabits per second.

Domain name system (DNS) The application protocol used in the TCP/IP suite to map the symbolic names used by humans into the equivalent fully qualified network address.

EIA-232D Standard laid down by the American EIA for interfacing a digital device to a PTT-supplied modem. Also used as an interface standard for connecting a peripheral device, such as a visual display unit or a printer, to a computer.

Error rate The ratio of the average number of bits that are corrupted to the total number of bits that are transmitted for a data link or system.

Ethernet The name of the LAN invented at the Xerox Corporation Palo Alto Research Center. It operates using the CSMA/CD medium access control method. The early specification was refined by a joint team from Digital Equipment Corporation, Intel Corporation, and Xerox Corporation and this in turn has now been superseded by the IEEE 802.3 – ISO 8802.3 – international standard.

Extended binary coded decimal interchange code (EBCDIC) The character set used on all IBM computers.

Exterior gateway protocol (EGP) A protocol used in relation to large internetworks that comprise multiple smaller internetworks interconnected together. The interconnection devices used are known as exterior gateways and the EGP is the protocol they use to advertise the IP addresses of the networks present in each of the smaller internetworks.

Fast Ethernet　A generic term used to describe the high-speed – 100 Mbps – LANs that are compatible with the 10 Mbps CSMA/CD (ethernet) networks.

Fast select　An optional facility with the X.25 protocol that allows user data to be sent in the call setup and call clearing packets.

Fiber distributed data interface (FDDI)　An optical fiber-based ring network that can be used as a high-speed LAN or MAN. It provides a user bit rate of 100 Mbps and uses a control token medium access control method.

Fiber optic　*See* optical fiber.

File transfer access and management (FTAM)　A protocol entity forming part of the application layer. It enables user application processes to manage and access a (distributed) file system.

File transfer protocol (FTP)　The application protocol in the TCP/IP suite that provides access to a networked file server.

Flow control　A technique to control the rate of flow of frames or messages between two communicating entities.

Frame　The unit of information transferred across a data link. Typically, there are control frames for link management and information frames for the transfer of message data.

Frame check sequence (FCS)　A general term given to the additional bits appended to a transmitted frame or message by the source to enable the receiver to detect possible transmission errors.

Frequency-division multiplexing (FDM)　A technique to derive a number of separate data channels from a single transmission medium, such as a coaxial cable. Each data channel is assigned a portion of the total available bandwidth.

Frequency-shift keying (FSK)　A modulation technique to convert binary data into an analog form comprising two sinusoidal frequencies. It is widely used in modems to allow data to be transmitted across a (analog) switched telephone network.

Full-duplex　A type of information exchange strategy between two communicating devices whereby information (data) can be exchanged in both directions simultaneously. It is also known as two-way simultaneous.

Gateway　A device that routes datagrams (packets) between one network and another. Typically, the two networks operate with different protocols, and so the gateway also performs the necessary protocol conversion functions.

Half-duplex　A type of information exchange strategy between two communicating devices whereby information (data) can be exchanged in both directions alternately. It is also known as two-way alternate.

High-level data link control (HDLC)　An internationally agreed standard protocol defined to control the exchange of data across either a point-to-point data link or a multidrop data link.

Host　Normally a computer belonging to a user that contains (hosts) the communication hardware and software necessary to connect the computer to a data communication network.

Idle RQ　A part of a data link protocol concerned with error control. It endeavors to ensure that another copy is sent if a frame (message) is corrupted during transmission. After a frame is sent by the source, it must wait until either an indication of correct (or otherwise) receipt is received from the receiver or for a specified time before sending another frame. It is also known as send (or stop) and wait.

Integrated services digital network (ISDN)　The new generation of worldwide telecommunications network that utilizes digital techniques for both transmission and switching. It supports both voice and data communications.

Interior gateway protocol (IGP)　The routing protocol used in the gateways of a TCP/IP internetwork to obtain the shortest path routes through the internet.

Intermediate system (IS)　The name used by ISO to describe the device that interconnects two networks together – also known as a router or a gateway.

International alphabet number 5 (IA5)　The standard character code defined by ITU-T and recommended by ISO. It is almost identical to the ASCII code.

Internet　The abbreviated name given to a collection of interconnected networks. Also, the name of US government funded internetwork based on the TCP/IP suite.

Internet control message protocol (ICMP)　A component part of the internet protocol in the TCP/IP suite that handles error and other control messages that are returned by internet gateways and hosts.

Internet protocol (IP)　The TCP/IP that provides connectionless network service between multiple packet switched networks interconnected by gateways.

Job transfer and manipulation (JTM)　A protocol entity forming part of the application layer. It enables user application processes to transfer and manipulate documents relating to jobs (processing tasks).

Local area network (LAN) A data communication network used to interconnect a community of digital devices distributed over a localized area of up to, say, $10\,km^2$. The devices may be office workstations, mini- and microcomputers, intelligent instrumentation equipment, etc.

Logical link control (LLC) A protocol forming part of the data link layer in LANs. It is concerned with the reliable transfer of data across the data link between two communicating systems.

Management information base (MIB) The name of the database used to hold the management information relating to a network or internetwork.

Manchester encoding A scheme used to encode clocking (timing) information into a binary data stream prior to transmission. The resulting encoded signal has a transition (positive or negative) in the middle of each bit cell period with the effect that the clocking information (required to receive the signal) is readily extracted from the received signal.

Manufacturing message service (MMS) A protocol entity forming part of the application layer. It is intended for use specifically in the manufacturing or process control industry. It enables a supervisory computer to control the operation of a distributed community of computer-based devices.

Medium access control (MAC) Many LANs use a single common transmission medium – for example, a bus or ring – to which all the interconnected devices are attached. A procedure must be followed by each device, therefore, to ensure that transmissions occur in an orderly and fair way. In general, this is known as the medium access control procedure. Two examples are CSMA/CD and (control) token.

Message handling service (MHS) A protocol entity forming part of the application layer. It provides a generalized facility for exchanging electronic messages between systems. It is also known as X.400.

Metropolitan area network (MAN) A network that links a set of LANs that are physically distributed around a town or city.

Microwave A type of communication based on electromagnetic radiation by means of a transmitting aerial and a receiving antenna or dish. It is used for both terrestrial links and satellite links.

Modem The device that converts a binary (digital) data stream into an analog (continuously varying) form, prior to transmission of the data across an analog

network (MODulator), and reconverts the received signal back into its binary form (DEModulator). Since each access port to the network normally requires a full-duplex (two way simultaneous) capability, the device must perform both the MODulation and DEModulation functions; hence the single name MODEM is used. As an example, a modem is normally required to transmit data across a telephone network.

Multidrop A network configuration that supports more than two stations on the same transmission medium.

Multiplexer A device to enable a number of lower bit rate devices, normally situated in the same location, to share a single higher bit rate transmission line. The data-carrying capacity of the latter must be in excess of the combined bit rates of the low bit rate devices.

Multipoint *See* multidrop.

Network layer This corresponds to layer 3 of the ISO reference model for open systems interconnection. It is concerned with the establishment and clearing of logical or physical connections across the network being used.

Network management A generic term embracing all the functions and entities involved in the management of a network. This includes configuration management, fault handling, and the gathering of statistics relating to usage of the network.

Noise The extraneous electrical signals that may be generated or picked up in a transmission line. Typically, it may be caused by neighboring electrical apparatus. If the noise signal is large compared with the data-carrying signal, the latter may be corrupted and result in transmission errors.

NRZ/NRZI Two similar (and related) schemes for encoding a binary data stream. The first has the property that a signal transition occurs whenever a binary 1 is present in the data stream and the second whenever a binary 0 is present. The latter is utilized with certain clocking (timing) schemes.

Open system A vendor-independent set of interconnected computers that all utilize the same standard communications protocol stack based on either the ISO/OSI protocols or TCP/IP.

Open systems interconnection (OSI) The protocol suite that is based on ISO protocols to create an open systems interconnection environment.

Optical fiber A type of transmission medium over which data is transmitted in the form of light waves or pulses. It is characterized by its potentially high bandwidth, and hence data-carrying capacity, and its high immunity to interference from other electrical sources.

Packet assembler/disassembler (PAD)   A device used with an X.25 packet switching network to allow character-mode terminals to communicate with a packet-mode device, such as a computer.

Packet switching   A mode of operation of a data communication network. Each message to be transmitted through the network is first divided into a number of smaller, self-contained message units known as packets. Each packet contains addressing information. As each packet is received at an intermediate node (exchange) within the network, it is first stored and, depending on the addressing information contained within it, forwarded along an appropriate link to the next node and so on. Packets belonging to the same message are reassembled at the destination. This mode of operation ensures that long messages do not degrade the response time of the network. Also, the source and destination devices may operate at different data rates.

Parity   A mechanism used for the detection of transmission errors when single characters are being transmitted. A single binary digit, known as the parity bit, the value (1 or 0) of which is determined by the total number of binary 1s in the character, is transmitted with the character so that the receiver can determine the presence of single-bit errors by comparing the received parity bit with the (recomputed) value it should be.

Phase-shift keying (PSK)   A modulation technique to convert binary data into an analog form comprising a single sinusoidal frequency signal with a phase that varies according to the data being transmitted.

Physical layer   This corresponds to layer 1 of the ISO reference model for open systems interconnection. It is concerned with the electrical and mechanical specification of the physical network termination equipment.

Piggyback   A technique to return acknowledgment information across a full-duplex (two-way simultaneous) data link without the use of special (acknowledgment) messages. The acknowledgment information relating to the flow of messages in one direction is embedded (piggybacked) into a normal data-carrying message flowing in the reverse direction.

Postal, Telegraph, and Telephone (PTT)   The administrative authority that controls all the postal and public telecommunications networks and services in a country.

Presentation layer   This corresponds to layer 6 of the ISO reference model for open systems interconnection. It is concerned with the negotiation of a suitable transfer (concrete) syntax for use during an application session and, if this is different from the local syntax, for the translation to and from this syntax.

Protocol   A set of rules formulated to control the exchange of data between two communicating parties.

Protocol data unit (PDU)   The message units exchanged between two protocol entities.

Protocol entity   The code that controls the operation of a protocol layer.

Public switched data network (PSDN)   A communication network set up and controlled by a public telecommunications authority for the exchange of data.

Public switched telephone network (PSTN)   The (analog) telephone network.

Remote operations service element (ROSE)   A protocol entity forming part of the application layer. It provides a general facility for initiating and controlling operations remotely.

Ring   A network topology in widespread use for the interconnection of communities of digital devices distributed over a localized area, such as a factory or block of offices. Each device is connected to its nearest neighbor until all the devices are connected in the form of a closed loop or ring. Data is transmitted in one direction only and, as each message circulates around the ring, it is read by each device connected in the ring. After circulating around the ring, the source device removes the message from the ring.

Router   A device used to interconnect two or more LANs together, each of which operates with a different medium access control method – also known as a gateway or intermediate system.

RS-422/RS-423   Standards laid down by the American EIA for interfacing a digital device to a PTT-supplied modem.

Send and wait   *See* idle RQ.

Service access point (SAP)   The subaddress used to identify uniquely a particular link between two protocol layers in a specific system.

Session layer   This corresponds to layer 5 of the ISO reference model for open systems interconnection. It is concerned with the establishment of a logical connection between two application entities and with controlling the dialog (message exchange) between them.

Shortest-path first (SPF) The algorithm used in a gateway/router/intermediate system to find the shortest path between itself and all the other gateways in an internetwork.

Signal-to-noise ratio The ratio between the power in a signal and the (unwanted) power associated with the line or system noise. It is normally expressed in decibels.

Simple mail transfer protocol (SMTP) The application protocol in a TCP/IP suite that is used to transfer mail between an interconnected set of (native) electronic mail systems.

Simple network management protocol (SNMP) The application protocol in a TCP/IP suite used to send and retrieve management-related information across a TCP/IP network.

Simplex A type of information exchange strategy between two communicating devices whereby information (data) can be passed only in one direction.

Slotted ring A type of local area (data) network. All the devices are connected in the form of a (physical) ring and an additional device known as a monitor is used to ensure that the ring contains a fixed number of message slots (binary digits) that circulate around the ring in one direction only. A device sends a message by placing it in an empty slot as it passes. This is read by all other devices on the ring and subsequently removed by the originating device.

Specific application service element (SASE) A collection of protocol entities forming part of the application layer responsible for providing various specific application services, such as file transfer and job transfer.

Star A type of network topology in which there is a central node that performs all switching (and hence routing) functions.

Statistical multiplexer (stat mux) A device used to enable a number of lower bit rate devices, normally situated in the same location, to share a single, higher bit rate transmission line. The devices usually have human operators, and hence data is transmitted on the shared line on a statistical basis rather than, as is the case with a basic multiplexer, on a preallocated basis. It endeavors to exploit the fact that each device operates at a much lower mean rate than its maximum rate.

Subnet In the ISO documents it refers to an individual network that forms part of a larger internetwork.

Synchronous transmission A technique to transmit data between two devices connected by a transmission line. The data is normally transmitted in the form of blocks, each comprising a string of binary digits. With synchronous transmission, the transmitter and receiver clocks are in synchronism; a number of techniques are used to ensure this.

TCP/IP The complete suite of protocols including IP, TCP, and the associated application protocols.

Teletex An international telecommunications service that provides the means for messages, comprising text and selected graphical characters, to be prepared, sent, and received.

TELNET The application protocol in the TCP/IP suite that enables a user at a terminal to interact with a program that is running in another computer.

Time-division multiplexing (TDM) A technique to share the bandwidth (channel capacity) of a shared transmission facility to allow a number of communications to be in progress either concurrently or one at a time.

Token bus A type of local area (data) network. Access to the shared transmission medium, which is implemented in the form of a bus to which all the communicating devices are connected, is controlled by a single control (permission) token. Only the current owner of the token is allowed to transmit a message on the medium. All devices wishing to transmit messages are connected in the form of a logical ring. After a device receives the token and transmits any waiting messages, it passes the token to the next device on the ring.

Token ring A type of local area (data) network. All the devices are connected in the form of a (physical) ring and messages are transmitted by allowing them to circulate around the ring. A device can transmit a message on the ring only when it is in possession of a control (permission) token. A single token is passed from one device to another around the ring.

TP 4 The class 4 transport protocol in an OSI suite. This contains error control and flow control functions and is used with connectionless networks/internetworks.

Transmission control protocol (TCP) The protocol in the TCP/IP suite that provides a reliable full-duplex message transfer service to application protocols.

Transmission medium The communication path linking two communicating devices. Some examples are twisted pair wire, coaxial cable, optical fiber cable, and a microwave (radio) beam.

Transport layer   This corresponds to layer 4 of the ISO reference model for open systems interconnection. It is concerned with providing a network-independent, reliable, message interchange service to the application-oriented layers (layers 5 through 7).

Twisted pair   A type of transmission medium consisting of two insulated wires twisted together to improve its immunity to interference from other (stray) electrical signals that might otherwise corrupt the signal being transmitted.

User datagram protocol (UDP)   A connectionless (best try) transport layer protocol in the TCP/IP suite.

Videotex   A telecommunications service that allows users to deposit and access information to and from a central database facility. Access is through a special terminal comprising a TV set equipped with a special decoder.

Virtual call (circuit)   A type of service offered on a packet switched data network (*see also* datagram). Using this service, prior to sending any packets of information relating to a particular call (message transfer), a virtual circuit is established through the network from source to destination. All information-carrying packets relating to this call then follow the same route and the network ensures that the packets are delivered in the same order as they were entered.

Virtual terminal   A protocol entity forming part of the application layer. It enables an application process to have a dialog with a remote terminal in a standard way, irrespective of the make of the terminal.

V.24/V.35   Standards laid down by the ITU-T for interfacing a digital device to a PTT-supplied modem. V.24 is also used as an interface standard for connecting a peripheral device, such as a visual display unit or a printer, to a computer.

Wide area network (WAN)   Any form of network – private or public – that covers a wide geographical area.

Wireless LAN   A LAN that uses either radio or infrared as the transmission medium. Requires different MAC methods from those used with wired LANs.

X.3/X.28/X.29   A set of internationally agreed standard protocols defined to allow a character-oriented device, such as a visual display terminal, to be connected to a packet switched data network.

X.25   An internationally agreed standard protocol defined for the interface of a data terminal device, such as a computer, to a packet switched data network.

X.400   *See* message handling services (MHS).

X.500   *See* directory services (DS).

Zero bit insertion   *See* bit stuffing.

BIBLIOGRAPHY AND FURTHER READING

The following books cover a similar range of material to that covered in this book:

Stallings W. (1991). *Data and Computer Communications* 3rd edn. Macmillan

Tanenbaum A.S. (1988). *Computer Networks* 2nd edn. Prentice-Hall

The first is more biased toward the electronic engineer and the second toward the computer scientist. Other selected suggestions are as follows:

Chapter 1

Cargill C. (1989). *Information Technology Standardization: Theory, Process and Organizations*. Bedford MA: Digital Press

Cerf V. and Cain E. (1983). The DOD architecture model. *Computer Networks*, (October)

Clarke D. (1988). The design philosophy of the DARPA Internet protocols. In *Proc. SIGCOM 88 Symposium*

Day J.D. and Zimmermann H. (1983). The OSI reference model. In *Proc. IEEE*, **71**, 1334–40

Folts H. (1981). Coming of age: A long awaited standard for heterogenous networks. *Data Communications*

Green P. (1980). An introduction to network architectures and protocols. *IEEE Transactions on Communications*, (April)

ISO (1984). *Basic Reference Model for Open Systems Interconnection* (ISO 7498)

Vormax M. (1980). Controlling the mushrooming communications net. *Data Communications*, (June)

Walker S. (1982). Department of Defense Data Network. *Signal*, (October)

Wood D. (1985). Computer networks: a survey. In *Computer Communications* Vol. II, Englewood Cliffs NJ: Prentice-Hall

Chapter 2

Ash J. and Richards D. (1994). Data over analog systems. In *Data Communications and Networks 3*, IEE London, pp. 6–24

Bachmann L. (1983). Statistical multiplexers gain sophistication and status. *Mini Micro Systems*, (March)

Bertine H.U. (1980). Physical level protocol. *IEEE Transactions on Communications*, **28**(4), 433–44

Bleazard G.B. (1982). *Handbook of Data Communications*. NCC Publications

Chou W. (1983). *Computer Communications* Vol. I. Englewood Cliffs NJ: Prentice-Hall

Cooper E. (1984). *Broadband Network Technology*. Mountain View CA: Sytek Press

Davies D.W. and Barber D.L.A. (1973). *Communication Networks for Computers*. Wiley

EIA (1987). *EIA-232D Standard Interface Between Data Terminal Equipment and Data Communication Equipment Employing Serial Binary Data Interchange*

Finnie G. (1989). VSATs: a technical update. *Telecommunications*, (February)

Freeman R. (1981). *Telecommunication Transmission Handbook*. Wiley

Jennings F. (1986). *Practical Data Communications*. Blackwell

McClelland F.M. (1983). Services and protocols of the physical layer. In *Proc. IEEE*, **71**, 1372–7

Mehravari N. (1984). TDMA in a random access environment: an overview. *IEEE Communications Magazine*, **22**, 54–9

Mok A.K. and Ward S.A. (1979). Distributed broadcast channel access. *Computer Networks*, **3**, 327–35

Murano K. *et al.* (1990). Echo cancellation and applications. *IEEE Communication Magazine*, (January)

Nielson D. (1985). Packet radio: an area coverage digital radio network. In *Computer Communications* Vol. II. Englewood Cliffs NJ: Prentice-Hall

Oetting J. (1979). A comparison of modulation techniques for digital radio. *IEEE Transactions on Communications*, (December)

Pearson J.E. (1992). *Basic Communication Theory*. Englewood Cliffs NJ: Prentice-Hall

Roberts L. (1973). Dynamic allocation of satellite capacity through packet reservation. In *Proceedings NCC*, pp. 711–16

Schwartz M. (1989). *Telecommunication Networks*. Reading MA: Addison-Wesley

Sklar B. (1988). *Digital Communications: Fundamentals and Applications*. Prentice-Hall

Chapter 3

Bleazard G.B. (1982). *Handbook of Data Communications*. NCC Publications

Fletcher J. (1982). An arithmetic checksum for serial transmissions. *IEEE Transactions on Communications*, (January)

Jennings F. (1986). *Practical Data Communications*. Blackwell

McNamara J.E. (1982). *Technical Aspects of Data Communication*. Digital Press

Peterson W.W. (1981). *Error Correcting Codes*. MIT Press

Ramabadroan T. and Gaitonde S. (1988). A tutorial on CRC computations. *IEEE Micro*, (August)

Spragins J.D. *et al.* (1981). *Telecommunications: Protocols and Design*. Reading MA: Addison-Wesley

Storer J.A. (1988). *Data Compression: Methods and Theory*. Computer Science Press

Vitter J.S. (1987). Design and analysis of dynamic Huffman codes. *Journal of the ACM*, (October)

Welch T.A. (1984). A technique for high performance data compression. *IEEE Computer*, (June)

Witten I.H. *et al.* (1987). Arithmetic coding for data compression. *Comm. ACM*, **30**, (June) 520–40

Chapter 4

Bleazard G.B. (1982). *Handbook of Data Communications*. NCC Publications

Budkowski S. and Dembinski P. (1988). An introduction to Estelle. *Computer Networks and ISDN Systems*, **14**, (January)

Choi T.Y. (1985). Formal techniques for the specification, verification and construction of communication protocols. *IEEE Communications Magazine*, **23**, (January) 46–52

Chou W. (1983). *Computer Communications, Vol. I: Principles*. Prentice-Hall

Conrad J. (1980). Character-oriented data link control protocols. *IEEE Transactions on Communications*, (April)

Conrad J. (1983). Services and protocols of the data link layer. *Proc. IEEE*

Danthine A.A.S. (1970). Protocol representation with finite-state models. *IEEE Transactions on Communications*. **COM28**, (April) 632–43

Davies D.W. *et al.* (1979). *Computer Networks and their Protocols*. Wiley

Pouzin L. and Zimmermann H. (1978). A tutorial on protocols. *Proc. IEEE*, (November)

Schwartz M. (1987). *Telecommunication Networks: Protocols, Modeling and Analysis*. Reading MA: Addison-Wesley

Spragins J.D. *et al.* (1991). *Telecommunications: Protocols and Design*. Reading MA: Addison-Wesley

Vissers C.A. *et al.* (1983). Formal description techniques. *Proc. IEEE*, **71**, (December) 1356–64

Chapter 5

Black U. (1982). Data link controls: the great variety calls for wise and careful choices. *Data Communications*, (June)

Black U. (1989). *Data Networks: Concepts, Theory and Practice*. Prentice-Hall

Bleazard G.B. (1982). *Handbook of Data Communications*. NCC Publications

Brodd W. (1983). HDLC, ADCCP and SDLC: what's the difference. *Data Communications*, (August)

Brodd W. and Boudrow P. (1983). Operational characteristics: BSC versus SDLC. *Data Communications*, (October)

Carlson D.E. (1980). Bit-oriented data link control procedures. *IEEE Transactions on Communications*, (April)

Field J. (1986). Logical link control. *IEEE Infocom 86*, (April)

Held G. (1983). Strategies and concepts for linking today's personal computers. *Data Communications*, (May)

IEEE (1985). *Logical Link Control* (ANSI/IEEE Std. 802.2). IEEE

Jennings F. (1986). *Practical Data Communications*. Blackwell

Schwartz M. (1987). *Telecommunication Networks: Protocols, Modeling and Analysis*. Reading MA: Addison-Wesley

Spragins J.D. *et al.* (1991). *Telecommunications: Protocols and Design*. Reading MA: Addison-Wesley

Chapter 6

Black U. (1987). *Computer Networks: Protocols, Standards and Interfaces*. Prentice-Hall

Bux W. *et al.* (1983). Architecture and design of a reliable token-ring network. *IEEE Journal on Selected Areas in Communications*, (November)

Chlamtac I. and Fanta W.R. (1980). Message-based priority access to local networks. *Computer Communications*, (April)

Chou W. (1983). *Computer Communications, Vol. I: Principles*. Prentice-Hall

Dixon R. *et al.* (1983). A token ring network for local data communications. *IBM Systems Journal*, (1 and 2)

Fine M. and Tobagi F. (1984). Demand assignment multiple-access schemes in broadcast bus local area networks. *IEEE Transactions on Computers*, (December)

Finley M. (1984). Optical fibres in local area networks. *IEEE Communications Magazine*, (August)

Golomb S.W. and Scholtz R.A. (1965). Generalized Barker sequences. *IEEE Transactions on Information Theory*, **11**(4), 533–7

Halls G.A. (1994). HiperLAN: the high performance radio local area network standard. *IEE Electronics and Communications Engineering Journal*, **6**(6), 289–96

Hammond J. (1986). *Performance Analysis of Local Computer Networks*. Reading MA: Addison-Wesley

Heyman D.P. (1982). An analysis of the carrier-sense multiple-access protocol. *Bell System Technical Journal*, (October)

Heywood P. (1981). The Cambridge ring is still making the rounds. *Data Communications*, (July)

Hopper A. *et al.* (1986). *Local Area Network Design*. Wokingham: Addison-Wesley

IEEE (1985). *802.3 CSMA/CD Access Method and Physical Layer Specifications*. IEEE

IEEE (1985). *802.4 Token-passing Bus Access Method*. IEEE

IEEE (1985). *802.5 Token Ring Access Method and Physical Layer Specifications*. IEEE

IEEE (1985). *802.2 Logical Link Control*. IEEE

Kahn J.M. *et al.* (1994). Non-directed infrared links for high capacity wireless LANs. *IEEE Personal Communications*, **1**(2), 12–25

Schwartz M. (1987). *Telecommunication Networks: Modeling and Analysis*. Reading MA: Addison-Wesley

Spragins J.D. *et al.* (1991). *Telecommunications: Protocols and Design*. Reading MA: Addison-Wesley

Stallings W. (1987). *Local Networks – an Introduction*. 3rd edn. New York NY: Macmillan

Stallings W. (1990). *Handbook of Computer Communication Standards Vol. 2: Local Area Network Standards*. Sams

Stuck B.W. (1983). Calculating the maximum throughput rate in local area networks. *IEEE Computer*, **16**, (May) 72–6

Tsui T.S. and Clarkson T.G. (1994). Spread spectrum communication techniques. *IEE Journal Electronics and Communications Engineering*, **6**(1), 3–12

Chapter 7

Backes F. (1988). Transparent bridges for interconnection of IEEE 802 LANs. *IEEE Network*, (January)

Bederman S. (1986). Source routing. *Data Communications*, (February)

Bux W. *et al.* (1987). Interconnection of local area networks. *IEEE Journal on Selected Areas in Communications*, special issue (December)

Caves K. (1994). Second generation LANs and MANs. In *Data Communications and Networks 3*, IEE London, pp. 149–83

Dixon R. and Pitt D. (1988). Addressing, bridging and source routing. *IEEE Network*, (January)

Hamner M. and Samsen G. (1988). Source routing bridge implementation. *IEE Network*, (January)

Hart J. (1988). Extending the IEEE 802.1 bridge standard to remote bridges. *IEEE Network*, (January)

Hewlett Packard (1994). *IEEE 802.12: Demand Priority Access Method and Physical Layer Specifications*. Draft standard

IEEE (1988). *802.1 D, MAC Bridges*. IEEE

IEEE (1988). *802.5 Appendix D, Multiring Networks (Source Routing)*. IEEE

Johnson M. (1987). Proof that timing requirements of the FDDI token ring protocol are satisfied. *IEEE Transactions on Communications*, (June)

Joshi S.P. (1986). High-performance networks – a focus on the FDDI standard. *IEEE Micro*, **6**, (June) 8–14

Karvelas D. and Papamichail M. (1992). DQDB: a fast converging bandwidth balancing mechanism that requires no bandwidth LAN. In *IEEE ICC 92 Conference Proceedings*, pp. 142–6

Kummerle K. (1987). *Advances in Local Area Networks*. New York: IEEE Press

Limb J.O. (1984). Performance of local area networks at high speed. *IEEE Communications*, **22**, (August) 41–5

Pitt D.A. (1988). Bridging – the double standard. *IEEE Network*, **2**, (January) 94–5

Ross F.E. (1986). FDDI – a tutorial. *IEEE Communications*, **24**, (May) 10–15

Ross F.E. (1989). An overview of FDDI – the fiber distributed data interface. *IEEE Journal on Selected Areas of Communications*, (September)

Seifert W.M. (1988). Bridges and routers. *IEEE Network Magazine*, **2**, (January) 57–64

Spragins J.D. *et al.* (1991). *Telecommunications: Protocols and Design*. Reading MA: Addison-Wesley

St Clair J. (1994). *100 Base–T Specification*. Fast Ethernet Alliance

Stallings W. (1990). *Local Networks* 3rd edn. New York NY: Macmillan

Strole N. (1983). A local communication based on interconnected token access rings: a tutorial. *IBM Journal of Research and Development*, (September)

Chapter 8

Black U. (1987). *Computer Networks: Protocols, Standards and Interfaces*. Prentice-Hall

Black U. (1989). *Data Networks: Concepts, Theory and Practice*. Prentice-Hall

Bleazard G.B. (1982). *Handbook of Data Communications*. NCC Publications

Burg F. (1983). Design considerations for using the X.25 packet layer on data terminal equipment. In *Proceedings IEEE Infocom 83*

Bush J. (1989). Frame-relay services promise WAN bandwidth on demand. *Data Communications*, (July)

Deasington R.J. (1988). *X.25 Explained: Protocols for Packet Switched Networks* 2nd edn. Ellis Horwood

Decina M. (1986). CCITT recommendations on the ISDN: a review. *IEEE Journal on Selected Areas of Communications*, **SAC.4**, (May) 320–5

Dhas C.R. and Konangu V.K. (1986). X.25: an interface to public packet networks. *IEEE Communications*, **24**, (September) 118–25

Duc N. and Chew E. (1985). ISDN protocol architecture. *IEEE Communications*, (March)

Gerla M. and Kleinrock L. (1980). Flow control: a comparative survey. *IEEE Transactions on Communications*, (April)

Irland M.I. (1978). Buffer management in a packet switch. *IEEE Transactions on Communications*, **COM.26**, (March) 328–37

Kostas D. (1984). Transition to ISDN – an overview. *IEEE Communications*, (January)

Lai W. (1989). Frame relaying service: an overview. *Proceedings IEEE Infocom 89*, (April)

Land J. (1987). *The Integrated Services Digital Network (ISDN)*. NCC Publications

Schwartz M. (1987). *Telecommunications Networks: Modeling and Analysis*. Reading MA: Addison-Wesley

Spragins J.D. *et al.* (1991). *Telecommunications: Protocols and Design*. Reading MA: Addison-Wesley

Stallings W. (1989). *ISDN: An Introduction*. New York NY: Macmillan

Chapter 9

Bell P. and Jabbour K. (1986). Review of point-to-point network routing algorithms. *IEEE Communications Magazine*, (January)

Boule R. and Moy J. (1989). Inside routers: a technology guide for network builders. *Data Communications*, (September)

Burg F. and Iorio N. (1989). Networking of networks: interworking according to OSI. *IEEE Journal on Selected Areas of Communications*, (September)

Comer D.E. (1991). *Internetworking with TCP/IP, Volume 1* 2nd edn. Prentice-Hall

DARPA (1981). *Internet Control Message Protocol* (RFC 792)

DARPA (1983). *Internet Protocol* (RFC 791)

Gopal I. (1985). Prevention of store-and-forward deadlock in computer networks. *IEEE Transactions on Communications*, (December)

ISO (1988). *Connectionless-mode Network Service (Internetwork Protocol)* (ISO 8473).

Markley R.W. (1990). *Data Communications and Interoperability*. Prentice-Hall

McConnell J. (1988). *Internetworking Computer Systems*. Prentice-Hall

McQuillan J. *et al.* (1980). The new routing algorithm for the ARPANET. *IEEE Transactions on Communications*, (May)

Moy J. (1989). *The OSPF Specification, RFC 1131 DDN Network Information Centre*. Menlo Park CA: SRI International

Moy J. and Chiappa N. (1989). OSPF: a new dynamic routing standard. *Network World*, (August)

Parulkar G. (1990). The next generation of internetworking. *Computer Communications Review*, (January)

Piscitello D. *et al.* (1986). Internetworking in an OSI environment. *Data Communications*, (May)

Sheltzer A. *et al.* (1982). Connecting different types of networks with gateways. *Data Communications*, (August)

Schoch J.F. (1978). Internetwork naming, addressing and routing. In *Proceedings COMPCON 78*

Spragins J.D. *et al.* (1991). *Telecommunications: Protocols and Design*. Reading MA: Addison-Wesley

Weissberger A.J. and Israel J.E. (1987). What the new internetworking standards provide. *Data Communications*, (February)

Chapter 10

ATM Forum (1994). *ATM User/Network Interface Specification*, (July)

Caves K. (1994). Second generation LANs and MANs. In *Data Communications and Networks 3*, IEE London, pp. 149–83

Caves K. (1994). Wide area networking. In *Data Communications and Networks 3*, IEE London, pp. 118–48

Cuthbert L.G. and Sapanel J.-C. (1993). *ATM – The Broadband Telecommunications Solution*. London: The Institution of Electrical Engineers

Gerla M. *et al.* (1993). Internetting LANs and MANs to B-ISDN for connectionless traffic support. *IEEE JSAC*, **11**(8), (October) 1145–59

Händel R., Huber M.N. and Schroder S. (1994). *ATM Networks: Concepts, Protocols, Applications* 2nd Edition. Wokingham: Addison-Wesley

Heinanen J. (1993). *Multiprotocol Encapsulation Over ATM Adaptation Layer 5*. RFC 1483

ITU-TS (1993). *B-ISDN ATM Adaptation Layer (AAL) Specificiation*. Draft recommendation I.363

ITU-TS (1993) *Support of Broadband Connectionless Data Service on B-ISDN*. Draft recommendation I.364

Karak N. (1995). Data communication in ATM networks. *IEEE Network*, (May/June) 28–37

Lanbach M. (1994). *Classical IP and ARP over ATM*. RFC 1577

Le Boudec J.-L. (1992). The asynchronous transfer mode: a tutorial. In *Computer Networks and ISDN System 24*, North Holland, pp. 279–309

McDysan D.E. and Spohn D.L. (1995). *ATM Theory and Application*. McGraw-Hill

Newman P. (1994). ATM local area networks. *IEEE Communicatons Magazine*, (March) 86–98

Sutherland S.L. and Burgin J. (1993). B-ISDN interworking. *IEEE Communications Magazine*, (August) 60–3

Truong H.L. *et al.* (1995). LAN emulation on an ATM network. *IEEE Communicatons Magazine*, (May) 70–85

Chapter 11

Black U. (1987). *Computer Networks: Protocols, Standards and Interfaces*. Prentice-Hall

Black U. (1989). *Data Networks: Concepts, Theory and Practice*. Prentice-Hall

Cockburn A. (1987). Efficient implementation of the OSI transport protocol checksum algorithm using 8/16-bit arithmetic. *Computer Communications Review*, (July)

Comer D.E. (1991). *Internetworking with TCP/IP, Volume 1* 2nd edn. Prentice-Hall

DARPA (1983). *Transmission Control Protocol* (RFC 793)

DARPA (1983). *User Datagram Protocol* (RFC 768)

Davidson J. (1988). *An Introduction to TCP/IP*. New York: Springer Verlag

Groenback I. (1986). Conversion between the TCP and ISO transport protocols as a method of achieving interoperability between data communication systems. *IEEE Journal on Selected Areas in Communications*, (March)

ISO (1985). *Connection-oriented Transport Service and Protocol* (ISO 8072/3)

Karn P. and Partridge C. (1987). Improving round-trip time estimates in reliable transport protocols. In *Proceedings ACM SIGCOMM 87*, pp. 2–7

Limmington P.F. (1983). Fundamentals of the layer service definitions and protocol specifications. *Proc. IEEE*, **71**, (December) 1341–5

Markley R.W. (1990). *Data Communications and Interoperability*. Prentice-Hall

McConnell J. (1988). *Internetworking Computer Systems*. Prentice-Hall

Neumann J. (1983). OSI transport and session layers: services and protocol. In *Proceedings INFOCOM 83*

Rose M.T. and Cass D.E. (1987). OSI transport services on top of the TCP. *Computer Networks and ISDN Systems*, **12**, 159–73

Spragins J.D. *et al.* (1991). *Telecommunications: Protocols and Design*. Reading MA: Addison-Wesley

Sunshine C.A. and Dalal Y.K. (1978). Connection management in transport protocols. *Computer Networks*, **2**, 454–73

Needham R.M. and Schroeder M.D. (1978). Using encryption for authentication in large networks of computers. *Communications ACM*, **21**, (December) 993–9

Neumann J. (1983). OSI transport and session layers: services and protocol. In *Proceedings INFOCOM 83*

Rivest R.L., Shamir A. and Adleman L. (1978). On a method for obtaining digital signatures and public key cryptosystems. *Comm. ACM*, **21**, (February) 120–6

Tardo J.J. (1985). Standardizing cryptographic services at OSI higher layers. *IEEE Communications*, **23**, (July) 25–9

Chapter 12

Abbruscato C.R. (1984). Data encryption equipment. *IEEE Communications*, **22**, (September) 15–21

Caneschi F. (1986). Hints for the interpretation of the ISO session layer. *Computer Communication Review*, (July)

Diffie W. and Hellman M.E. (1976). New directions in cryptography. *IEEE Transactions on Information Theory*, **IT-22**, (November) 644–54

Diffie W. and Hellman M.E. (1977). Exhaustive cryptoanalysis of the NBS data encryption standard. *IEEE Computer Magazine*, **10**, (June) 74–84

Emmons W.F. and Chandler A.S. (1983). OSI session layer: services and protocols. *Proceedings IEEE*, **71**, (December) 1397–1400

Hellman M.E. (1987). Commercial encryption. *IEEE Network Magazine*, **1**, (April) 6–10

Henshall J. and Shaw A. (1988). *OSI Explained – End-to-End Computer Communication Standards*. Ellis Horwood

ISO (1986). *Connection-oriented Session Service and Protocol Definitions* (IS 8326/7)

ISO (1987). *Connection-oriented Presentation Service and Protocol Definitions* (IS 8822/3)

ISO (1988). *Commitment Concurrency and Recovery* (IS 8649/50)

ISO (1988). *ASN.1 and its Encoding Rules* (IS 8824/5)

ISO (1988). *Association Control Service Element* (IS 8649/50)

Jueneman J.J. *et al.* (1985). Message authentication. *IEEE Communications*, **23**, 29–40

National Bureau of Standards (1977). *Data Encryption Standard*. Federal Information Processing Standard Publication

Chapter 13

Black U. (1987). *Computer Networks: Protocols, Standards and Interfaces*. Prentice-Hall

Black U. (1989). *Data Networks: Concepts, Theory and Practice*. Prentice-Hall

Chilton P. (1990). *X.400: The Messaging and Interconnection Medium for the Future*. NCC Publications

Comer D.E. (1991) *Internetworking with TCP/IP, Volume 1* 2nd edn. Prentice-Hall

Davidson J. (1988). *An Introduction to TCP/IP*. New York: Springer Verlag

Gilmore B. (1987). A user view of virtual terminal standardization. *Computer Networks and ISDN Systems*, **13**, 229–33

Henshall J. and Shaw A. (1988). *OSI Explained: End-to-End Computer Communication Standards*. Ellis Horwood

ISO (1987). *File Transfer Access and Management* (IS 8571/4)

ISO (1987). *Job Transfer and Manipulation* (IS 8831/2)

ISO (1988). *Virtual Terminal* (IS 9040/1)

Klerer S.M. (1988). The OSI management architecture: an overview. *IEEE Network*, **2**, (March) 20–9

Lewan D. and Long H. (1983). The OSI file service. *Proc. IEEE*, (December)

Limmington P.F. (1984). The virtual filestore concept. *Computer Networks*, **8**, 13–16

McLeod-Reisig S.E. and Huber K. (1986). ISO virtual terminal protocol and its relationship to TELNET. In *Proceedings IEEE Computer Networking Symposium*, pp. 110–19

Svoboda L. (1984). File servers for network-based distributed systems. *Computing Surveys*, **16**, (December) 353–98

Chapter 14

Baran P. (1964). On distributed communication networks. *IEEE Transactions on Communication Systems*, **CS12**, (March) 1–9

Black U. (1988). *Data Communications and Distributed Networks*. Prentice-Hall

Comer D.E. (1991). *Internetworking with TCP/IP: Volume 1* 2nd edn. Prentice-Hall

Dolan M. (1984). Minimal duplex connection capability in the top three layers of the OSI reference model. In *Proceedings SIGCOM 84*

Henshall J. and Shaw A. (1988). *OSI Explained: End-to-End Computer Communication Standards*. Ellis Horwood

Hutchison G. and Desmond C.L. (1987). Electronic data exchange. *IEEE Network Magazine*, **1**, (October) 16–20

Langsford A. (1984). The open system users programming interfaces. *Computer Networks*, **8**, 3–12

Partridge C. (1986). Mail routing using domain names: an informal tour. In *Proceedings USENIX Summer Conference*

Sloman M. and Kramer J. (1987). *Distributed Systems and Computer Networks*. Prentice-Hall

Appendix A

Hamming R.W. (1950). Error detecting and error correcting codes. *Bell System Technical Journal*, **29**, (April) 147–60

Peebles P.Z. (1987). *Digital Communication Systems*. Prentice-Hall

Petersen W.W. (1961). *Error Correcting Codes*. MIT Press

Sklar B. (1988). *Digital Communications*. Prentice-Hall

Sweeney P. (1991). *Error Control Coding*. Prentice-Hall

Viterbi A.J. (1971). Convolutional codes and their performance in communication systems. *IEEE Transactions on Communication Systems*, **19**(5)

IEEE standards can be obtained from: IEEE Press, 345 East 47th Street, New York, NY10017, USA.

ISO and ITU-T standards can be obtained from: International Telecommunications Union, Place de Nations, 1211 Geneva, Switzerland.

INDEX

ACRONYMS

(cont. from inside front cover)

MAS	Management application service		PDN	Partial distinguished name/Public data network
MCP	MAC conversion protocol			
MDSE	Message delivery service element		PDU	Protocol data unit
MHS	Message handling service		PDX	Private digital exchange
MIB	Management information base		PE	Presentation entity
MID	Message/Multiplexing identifier		PIM	Physical interface module
MII	Media-independent interface		PISO	Parallel in, serial out
MIT	Management information tree		PIXEL	Picture element
MLP	Multilink procedure		PLC	Physical layer convergence/Programmable logic controller
MMR	Modified–modified read			
MMS	Manufacturing messaging service		PLP	Packet layer protocol
MO	Managed object		PMD	Physical medium dependent
MOTIS	Message-oriented text interchange standard		PPDU	Packet PDU
MRSE	Message retrieval service element		PPDU	Presentation PDU
MS	Message store		PPM	Presentation protocol machine/Pulse position modulation
MSS	MAN switching system			
MSSE	Message submission service element		PPSDN	Public packet switched data network
MTA	Message transfer agent		PRI	Primary rate interface
MTSE	Message transfer service element		PSAP	Presentation service access point
MUX	Multiplexer		PSDN	Packet switched data network
			PSE	Packet switching exchange
NAK	Negative acknowledgment		PSK	Phase-shift keying
NBS	National Bureau of Standards		PSPDN	Packet switched PDN
NC	Network connection		PSTN	Public switched telephone network
NEXT	Near end crosstalk		PTE	Path termination equipment
NMS	Network management system		PTI	Payload type identifier
NNPP	Normal next-port pointer		PTT	Post, telephone, and telecommunications (authority)
NPA	Network point of attachment			
NPDU	Network-layer PDU		PVC	Permanent virtual connection
NRM	(Unbalanced) normal response mode			
NRZ	Non-return to zero		QA	Queued arbitrated
NRZI	Non-return to zero inverted		QOS	Quality of service
NS	Network service		QPDS	Queued packet distributed switch
NSAP	Network service access point			
NSDU	Network service data unit		RARP	Reverse ARP
NT	Network termination		RC	Request counter/Robot controller
			RCU	Remote concentrator unit
OFDM	Orthogonal frequency division multiplexing		RDA	Remote database access
OOK	On–off keying		RDN	Relative distinguished name
OSI	Open systems interconnection		RF	Radio frequency
OSIE	Open system internetworking environment		RI	Ring indication
OSPF	Open shortest path first		RIP	Routing information protocol
			ROM	Read only memory
PA	Point of attachment/Pre arbitrated		ROSE	Remote operations service element
PABX	Private automatic branch exchange		RP	Root port
PAD	Packet assembler–disassembler		RPC	Root path cost
PAM	Pulse amplitude modulated		RSE	Real system environment
PAU	Portable access unit		RTS	Request to send
PBX	Private branch exchange		RTSE	Reliable transfer service element
PCI	Protocol connection identifier		RVCI	Ring virtual channel identifier
PDH	Plesiochronous digital hierarchy			